MOULTON'S INVALUABLE REFERENCE WORK,

a standard on library shelves since the early 1900's, is now available to a new generation of readers in a completely reset new edition. The original eight volumes have been streamlined by the judicious removal of obsolete text; writers omitted by Moulton have been added and others supplemented; and helpful bibliographical and/or critical studies have been supplied for all authors. The new *Moulton* is now more useful than ever.

IN ITS NEW FORMAT

Moulton includes all important authors from Beowulf to the early 20th century—and over 1,700 critics from England, the United States, and elsewhere. Besides major literary figures, the work also includes, as did the original, writers in such fields as history, philosophy, religion, and science, as well as journalists and art and music critics. Through the fully identified excerpts, *Moulton* provides an overall view of each writer's development, his critical reputation, and his standing in the history of literature. To fill out the portraits, it offers also aspects of a writer's life other than the purely literary—such as William Morris' furniture designs and Sir John Vanbrugh's architectural designs for Blenheim Castle.

continued on back flap

D1385090

The

CHELSEA HOUSE LIBRARY
of LITERARY CRITICISM

The

CHELSEA HOUSE LIBRARY
of LITERARY CRITICISM

The

NEW MOULTON'S
LIBRARY *of* LITERARY CRITICISM

Volume 11

Bibliographical Supplement and Index

General Editor

HAROLD BLOOM

1990
CHELSEA HOUSE PUBLISHERS
NEW YORK   PHILADELPHIA

MANAGING EDITOR
S. T. Joshi

ASSOCIATE EDITORS
Janet Benton
Jack Bishop
Peter Cannon
Beth Heinsohn
Patrick Nielsen Hayden
Teresa Nielsen Hayden

EDITORIAL COORDINATOR
Karyn Gullen Browne

COPY CHIEF
Richard Fumosa

EDITORIAL STAFF
Leslie D'Acri
Anne Knepler
Susanne E. Rosenberg

DESIGN
Susan Lusk

Printed and bound in the United States of
America.

First Printing

1 3 5 7 9 8 6 4 2

Library of Congress Cataloging in Publication
Data

The New Moulton's library of literary criti-
    cism. (The Chelsea House library of literary
    criticism)
    Cover title: The New Moulton's.
    Rev. ed. of: Moulton's library of literary crit-
    icism.
    Contents: v. 1. Medieval—early Renais-
sance.—   —v. 11. Bibliographical supple-
ment and index.
    1. English literature—History and criticism
—Collected works. 2. American literature—
History and criticism—Collected works. I.
Bloom, Harold. II. Moulton's library of literary
criticism.
PR85.N39 1985   820'.9   84–27429
ISBN 0–87754–779–3 (v. 1)
        1–55546–775–X (v. 11)

CONTENTS

PREFACE

This *Bibliographical Supplement and Index* concludes our series *The New Moulton's Library of Literary Criticism*. We have included bibliographies of the 532 authors covered in the series, a complete table of contents of each chapter in the series, an alphabetical index to authors covered in the series, and an index to critics.

In the *Author Bibliographies* for this series, we have listed every separate book publication—including pamphlets, broadsides, collaborations, and works edited or translated by the author—only for works published in the author's lifetime. We have been intentionally selective in listing posthumous works, citing only those editions of collected or selected works that are textually or historically important or contain previously unpublished or uncollected material. Offprints of periodical articles and facsimile editions have not been listed. Titles are those of the first edition, although where a work was published under a now unfamiliar title we have supplied the commonly known title in carets (e.g., ⟨Rasselas⟩ for Samuel Johnson's *The Prince of Abissinia*). Where a work was published with no title we have supplied one in carets. Works of doubtful authorship have been placed in square brackets; forgeries or works known to be spurious are not listed. In selected instances we have supplied dates of revised editions where these are significant (e.g., the first and second editions of Sidney's *Arcadia*, 1590 and 1593). Pseudonymous works are listed but the pseudonyms under which these works were published are not.

For plays we have listed date of publication, rather than date of production; unpublished plays are not listed. Periodicals edited by the author are not listed except where the author has written nearly the whole of the periodical (e.g., Johnson's *The Rambler*). All works by an author, whether in English or in other languages, have been listed; English translations of foreign-language works are not listed unless the author himself has done the translation. In some instances non-literary works—e.g., the artwork of William Blake—have also been listed.

This series is arranged chronologically by the death date of the author; the bibliographies have also been so arranged, and the bibliography for William Shakespeare, who occupies Volume 2 of the series, has been placed in its proper chronological sequence (between Richard Hakluyt and Francis Beaumont). Only in the case of Shakespeare have we listed every printing or edition of his work published during and just after his lifetime. For authors writing before the invention of printing (*Beowulf* to Sir Thomas Malory, excepting William Caxton), we have listed works in order of writing (supplying conjectural dates of writing in carets), with a list of separate editions of these works and then a selective listing of collected and selected works. As the bibliographies are arranged chronologically, we have appended an alphabetical index to the bibliographies.

The *Series Contents* list every item used in each chapter of the series, in the order in which the items appear; we have not, however, listed the sections (*Personal, General, Works*, etc.) into which the chapters are sometimes divided. If an item was used more than once it is listed for each time it is used.

In the *Index to Critics* we have given the name of the chapter and the page number on which the critic's work is cited. Although our series is numbered consecutively through the ten volumes, a reader cannot be expected to know in which volume a given chapter or page appears. Hence an entry reading "John Dryden 4:2035" refers to an item in the chapter on John Dryden appearing in Volume 4, page 2035 of the series. Page citations in the *Index to Authors* are listed analogously.

S. T. Joshi

AUTHOR BIBLIOGRAPHIES

AUTHOR BIBLIOGRAPHIES

BEOWULF (c. 8th century)

De Danorum Rebus Gestis Secul. III & IV: Poema Danicum Dialecto Anglo-Saxonica: Ex Bibliotheca Cottoniana Musaei Britannici. Ed. Grim. Johnson Thorkelin. 1815.

The Anglo-Saxon Poem of Beowulf: The Travellers Son and The Battle of Finnes-burh. Ed. John M. Kemble. 1833, 1835.

Beo-wulf og Scopes Widsið, to Angelsaxiske Digte. Ed. Frederik Schaldemose. 1847.

The Anglo-Saxon Poems of Beowulf, the Scôp or Gleeman's Tale, and The Fight at Finnsburg. Ed. Benjamin Thorpe. 1855.

Beowulfes Beorh; eller, Bjovulfs-drapen, det old-angelske Heltedigt, paa Grund-sproget. Ed. N. F. S. Grundtvig. 1861.

Beowulf. Ed. Moritz Heyne (1863; 2 vols.); rev. ed. Adolf Socin (1888; rev. Levin L. Schücking, 1908).

Beovulf nebst den Fragmenten Finnsburg und Waldere. Ed. Chrn. W. M. Grein. 1867.

Carmen de Beóvulfi, Gautam Regis Rebus Praeclare Gestis atque Interitu, Quale Fuerit ante Quam in Manus Interpolatoris, Monachi Vestsaxonici, Inciderat. Ed. Chlodovico Ettmüllero. 1875.

Beowulf: A Heroic Poem of the Eighth Century. Ed. Thomas Arnold. 1876.

Das Beowulfslied nebst den kleineren epischen, lyrischen, didaktischen und geschichtlichen Stücken. Ed. R. P. Wulcker. 1881.

Beowulf: An Anglo-Saxon Poem, and The Fight at Finnsburg. Ed. James M. Garnett. 1882.

Autotypes of the Unique Cotton ms. Vitellius A XV in the British Museum, with a Transliteration. Ed. Julius Zupitza. 1882.

Beowulf: Berichtigter Text mit knappem Apparat und Wörterbuch. Ed. A. Holder. 1882–96. 2 vols.

Das altenglische Volksepos in der ursprünglichen strophischen Form. Ed. Hermann Möller. 1883.

Beowulf. Ed. A. J. Wyatt. 1894.

Das Beowulflied, als Anhang das Finn-Bruchstück und die Waldhere-Bruchstücke. Ed. Moritz Trautmann. 1904.

Beowulf, nebst dem Finnsburg-Bruchstück. Ed. F. Holthausen. 1905–06. 2 vols.

Beowulf. Ed. W. J. Sedgefield. 1910.

Beowulf, with the Finnsburg Fragment. Ed. R. W. Chambers. 1914.

Beowulf and The Fight at Finnsburg. Ed. Fr. Klaeber. 1922.

Beowulf and the Finnsburg Fragment. Ed. Clarence Griffin Child. 1932.

Beowulf. Ed. Martin Lehnert. 1939.

Heyne-Schücking's Beowulf. Ed. Else von Schaubert. 1946–49. 3 vols.

The Thorkelin Transcriptions of Beowulf in Facsimile. Ed. Kemp Malone. 1951.

Beowulf, with the Finnsburg Fragment. Ed. C. L. Wrenn. 1953.

Beowulf, and Judith. Ed. Elliott Van Kirk Dobbie. 1953.

The Poems of British Museum Ms. Cotton Vitellius A.XV: Béowulf (fol. 132a–201b) and Judith (fol. 209b). Supplement, the Fight at Finn's Stronghold. Ed. Francis Peabody Magoun. 1955.

Béowulf and Judith: Done in Normalized Orthography. Ed. Francis P. Magoun. 1959.

The Nowell Codex: British Museum Cotton Vitellius A. XV. Second Manuscript. Ed. Kemp Malone. 1963.

Béowulf and Judith: Done in Normalized Orthography. Eds. Francis P. Magoun and Jess B. Bessinger. 1966.

Beowulf: Complete Text in Old English and Modern English. Ed. E. Talbot Donaldson. 1967.

Beowulf: Reproduced in Facsimile from the Unique Manuscript, British Museum MS. Cotton Vitellius A. XV. Ed. Norman Davis. 1967.

Beowulf: An Interlinear Translation. Ed. Thomas J. McLeod. 1970.

Beowulf: An Edition with Manuscript Spacing Notation and Graphotactic Analyses. Ed. Robert D. Stevick. 1975.

Beowulf: Anglo-Saxon Text with Modern English Parallel/Modern English Parallel Text. Ed. John Porter. 1975.

Beowulf und die kleineren Denkmäler der altenglischen Heldensage Waldere und Finnsburg. Ed. Gerhard Nickel. 1976–82. 3 vols.

Beowulf: A Dual-Language Edition. Ed. Howard D. Chickering, Jr. 1977.

Beowulf. Ed. Michael Swanton. 1978.

CÆDMON (c. 680)

Hymn ⟨c. 680⟩. Ed. Humphry Wanley (1705; in "Catalogus Historico-Criticus" in *Linguarum Veterum Septentrionalium Thesaurus Grammatico-Criticus et Archeologus* by George Hickes); ed. Henry Sweet (1885; in *The Oldest English Texts*); ed. Israel Gollancz (1927; in *The Caedmon Manuscript of Anglo-Saxon Biblical Poetry, Junius XI, in the Bodleian Library*); ed. Albert Hugh Smith (1933; in *Three Northumbrian Hymns*); ed. Elliott V. K. Dobbie (1937; in *The Manuscripts of Caedmon's Hymn and Bede's Death Song*); ed. W. F. Bolton (1963; in *An Old English Anthology*); ed. John C. Pope (1964; in *Seven Old English Poems*); ed. Richard Hamer (1970; in *A Choice of Anglo-Saxon Verse*).

THE VENERABLE BEDE (c. 673–735)

De Orthographia ⟨c. 700⟩. Ed. C. W. Jones (1975; *Opera* [CCSL, Volume 123A]).

De Arte Metrica ⟨c. 701–02⟩. 1473; ed. C. B. Kendall (1975; *Opera* [CCSL, Volume 123A]).

De Schematibus et Tropis ⟨c. 701–02⟩. 1473; ed. C. B. Kendall (1975; *Opera* [CCSL, Volume 123A]).

De Natura Rerum ⟨703⟩. Ed. C. W. Jones (1975; *Opera* [CCSL, Volume 123A]).

De Locis Sanctis ⟨c. 703⟩. Ed. Jacob Gretzer (1619; in *De Situ Terrae* by Saint Adamnan); ed. P. Geyer (1898; in *Itinera Hierosolymitana*); ed. F. Fraiport (1965; in *Itineraria et Alia Geographica* [CCSL, Volume 175]).

De Temporibus ⟨c. 703⟩. Ed. John Sichardus (1529); ed. C. W. Jones (1943); ed. C. W. Jones (1980; *Opera* [CCSL, Volume 123C]).

Vita Sancti Cuthberti (verse) ⟨c. 705–16⟩. Ed. Werner Jaager (1935).

Vita Sancti Cuthberti (prose) ⟨c. 705–16⟩. Ed. Bertram Colgrave (1940; in *Two Lives of St. Cuthbert*).

Vita Felicis ⟨before 709⟩. Ed. Thomas W. Mackay (1971; Ph.D. diss., Stanford University).

In Epistolas Septem Catholicas ⟨c. 709⟩. Ed. David Hurst (1983; *Opera* [CCSL, Volume 121]).

Expositio Actuum Apostolorum ⟨c. 709⟩. Ed. M. L. W. Laistner (1939); ed. M. L. W. Laistner (1983; *Opera* [CCSL, Volume 121]).

In Lucae Evangelium Expositio ⟨c. 709–15⟩. Ed. David Hurst (1960; *Opera* [CCSL, Volume 120]).

In Primam Partem Samuhelis Libri IIII ⟨c. 716⟩. 1533; ed. David Hurst (1962; *Opera* [CCSL, Volume 119]).

De Tabernaculo ⟨c. 720–25⟩. 1533; ed. David Hurst (1979; *Opera* [CCSL, Volume 119A]).

In Proverbia Salomonis ⟨c. 720–30⟩. Ed. David Hurst (1983; *Opera* [CCSL, Volume 119B]).

In Cantica Canticorum ⟨c. 720–30⟩. Ed. David Hurst (1983; *Opera* [CCSL, Volume 119B]).

De Temporum Ratione ⟨725⟩. Ed. John Sichardus (1529); ed. C. W. Jones (1943; with *De Temporibus*); ed. C. W. Jones (1977; *Opera* [CCSL, Volume 123B]).

In Marci Evangelium Expositio ⟨c. 725–30⟩. Ed. David Hurst (1960; *Opera* [CCSL, Volume 120]).

In Ezram et Neemiam ⟨c. 725–31⟩. 1533; ed. David Hurst (1979; *Opera* [CCSL, Volume 119A]).

De Templo ⟨c. 729–31⟩. Ed. David Hurst (1979; *Opera* [CCSL, Volume 119A]).

Homilia Evangelii Libri II ⟨c. 730–35⟩. Ed. David Hurst (1965; *Opera* [CCSL, Volume 122]).

Historia Ecclesiastica Gentis Anglorum ⟨completed 731⟩. c. 1475; 1550; 1601; ed. Abraham Whelock (1643–44; 2 vols.); ed. P. F. Chiffletius (1681); ed. John Smith (1722); ed. Joseph Stevenson (1838); ed. Robert Hussey (1848); ed. Alfred Holder (1882); ed. Charles Plummer (1896; 2 vols.); ed. J. E. King (1930; 2 vols.); eds. Bertram Colgrave and R. A. B. Mynors (1969).

Libri Quatuor in Principium Genesis ⟨completed c. 731⟩. Ed. C. W. Jones (1967; *Opera* [CCSL, Volume 118A]).

Opera. Ed. Joannes Hervagius. 1563. 4 vols.

Complete Works. Ed. J. A. Giles. 1843–44. 12 vols.

Opera [Patrologia Latina]. Ed. J.-P. Migne. 1850–51. 6 vols.

Opera [Corpus Christianorum Series Latina (CCSL)]. 1960– .

CYNEWULF (c. 8th century)

The Fates of the Apostles ⟨late 8th c.⟩. Ed. George P. Krapp (1906); ed. Kenneth R. Brooks (1961).

Christ II ⟨late 8th c.⟩. Ed. Israel Gollancz (1892); ed. Albert S. Cook (1900); ed. S. K. Das (1975).

Juliana ⟨after 750⟩. Ed. William Strunk, Jr. (1904); ed. Rosemary Woolf (1975).

Elene ⟨after 750⟩. Ed. Jacob Grimm (1840); ed. Julius Zupitza (1877); ed. Charles W. Kent (1889); ed. Ferdinand Holthausen (1905 [4th ed. 1936]); ed. Albert S. Cook (1919); ed. Pamela O. E. Gradon (1958).

JOHN SCOTUS ERIGENA (fl. 850)

De Divina Praedestinatione Liber ⟨851⟩. Ed. Goulven Madec. (1978).

Annotationes in Marcianum ⟨c. 859–60⟩. Ed. Cora E. Lutz (1939).

⟨Translations of works by St. Dionysius⟩ ⟨860–62; rev. c. 865–70⟩. In *Opera*.

Ambigua by Maximus the Confessor (translator) ⟨c. 862–64⟩. 1681 (with *De Divisione Naturae*).

De Divisione Naturae ⟨Periphyson⟩ ⟨c. 864–66⟩. 1681 (with *Ambigua*); ed. C. B. Schlüter (1838); eds. I. P. Sheldon-Williams and Ludwig Bieler (1968–81; 3 vols.).

Expositiones super Ierarchiam Caelestem S. Dionysii ⟨c. 865–70⟩. Ed. J. Barbet (1975).

Homilia in Prologum Sancti Evangelii Secundum Joannem ⟨c. 870⟩. Ed. Édouard Jeaneau (1969).

Commentarius in Evangelium Johannis ⟨c. 870⟩. Ed. Édouard Jeauneau (1972).

Opera. Ed. Henricus Josephus Floss. 1853. (Patrologia Latina 122.)

ALFRED THE GREAT (849–901)

Pastoral Care by Saint Gregory (translator) ⟨c. 890–97⟩. Ed. Henry Sweet (1871–72; 2 vols.); ed. Thomas A. Carnicelli (1975–78; 2 vols.).

De Consolatione Philosophiae by Boethius (translator) ⟨c. 890–97⟩. Ed. Walter J. Sedgefield (1899).

Soliloquies by Saint Augustine (translator) ⟨c. 897–99⟩. Ed. Henry L. Hargrove (1902); ed. Wilhelm Endter (1922); ed. Thomas A. Carnicelli (1979).

Psalms ⟨Paris Psalter⟩ (translator) ⟨c. 890–99⟩. Eds. James W. Bright and Robert L. Ramsay (1907).

ÆLFRIC (c. 955–c. 1025)

Catholic Homilies: First Series ⟨989⟩. Ed. Benjamin Thorpe (1844–46; 2 vols.).

Catholic Homilies: Second Series ⟨992⟩. Ed. Malcolm Godden (1979).

De Temporibus Anni ⟨992–1002⟩. Ed. Heinrich Henel (1942).

Grammar and Glossary ⟨992–1002⟩. Ed. Julius Zupita (1880).

Colloquy ⟨992–1002⟩. Ed. G. N. Garmonsway (1939).

Interrogationes by Alcuin (translator) ⟨992–1002⟩. Ed. G. E. Maclean (1883).

Lives of the Saints ⟨992–1002⟩. Ed. Walter W. Skeat (1881–1900; 4 vols.).

Hexameron (translator) ⟨992–1002⟩. Ed. H. W. Norman (1849).

Heptateuch (translator) ⟨992–1005⟩. Ed. S. J. Crawford (1922).

Admonitio (translator) ⟨1002–05⟩. Ed. H. W. Norman (1849; with *Hexameron*).

Selected Homilies. Ed. Henry Sweet. 1885.

Die Hirtenbrief Ælfrics. Ed. Bernhard Fehr. 1914.

Homilies: A Supplementary Collection. Ed. John C. Pope. 1967–68. 2 vols.

WILLIAM OF MALMESBURY (c. 1095–1143)

De Gestis Regum Anglorum Libri Quinque ⟨completed 1120⟩. 1596; ed. Thomas Duffus Hardy (1840; 2 vols.); ed. William Stubbs (1887–89; 2 vols.).

De Gestis Pontificum Anglorum Libri Quinque ⟨completed 1125⟩. 1596; ed. N. E. S. A. Hamilton (1870).

Vita Wulfstani ⟨c. 1124–43⟩. Ed. Reginald R. Darlington (1928).

De Antiquitate Glastoniensis Ecclesiae ⟨c. 1129–39⟩. 1691 (in *Rerum Anglicarum Scriptores Veteres*, Volume 2); ed. John Scott (1981).

Vita Sancti Dunstani ⟨c. 1129–39⟩. Ed. William Stubbs (1874; in *Memorials of Saint Dunstan*).

Polyhistor ⟨c. 1140⟩. Ed. Helen Testroet Ouellette (1982).

Historiae Novellae Libri Duo ⟨c. 1140–43⟩. 1596; ed. Thomas Duffus Hardy (1840; 2 vols.); ed. William Stubbs (1887–89; 2 vols.); ed. R. A. B. Mynors (1955).

GEOFFREY OF MONMOUTH (c. 1100–1154)

Historia Regum Britanniae ⟨completed c. 1136⟩. Ed. Ivo Cavallatus (1508, 1517); ed. Jerome Commelin (1587; in *Rerum Britannicarum Scriptores Vetustiores ac Praecipui*); ed. J. A. Giles (1844); ed. Albert Schulz (1854); ed. Acton

Griscom (1929); ed. Edmond Faral (1929; in *La Légende arthurienne*, Volume 3); ed. Jacob Hammer (1951).

Vita Merlini ⟨c. 1148⟩. Ed. William Henry Black (1830); ed. Francisque Michel (1837); ed. John Jay Parry (1925); ed. Edmond Faral (1929; in *La Légende arthurienne*); ed. Basil Clarke (1973).

GIRALDUS CAMBRENSIS (c. 1147–1223)

Topographia Hibernica ⟨1187⟩. 1584 (in Richard Stanyhurst, *De Rebus in Hibernica Gestis*); *Opera*, Volume 5; ed. John M. O'Meara (1949).

Expugnatio Hibernica ⟨1187⟩. *Opera*, Volume 5; eds. A. B. Scott and F. X. Martin (1978).

Itinerarium Kambriae ⟨1191⟩. 1585 (in Ludovico da Ponte, *Britanniae Historiae Libri Sex*); *Opera*, Volume 6.

Vita Galfridi Archiepiscopi Eboracensis ⟨1193⟩. *Opera*, Volume 4.

Descriptio Kambriae ⟨1194⟩. 1585 (in Ludovico da Ponte, *Britanniae Historiae Libri Sex*); *Opera*, Volume 6.

Gemma Ecclesiastica ⟨c. 1197⟩. *Opera*, Volume 2.

Symbolum Electorum ⟨1199⟩. *Opera*, Volume 1.

Invectiones ⟨1200–16⟩. *Opera*, Volume 3; ed. W. S. Davies (1920).

De Rebus a Se Gestis ⟨c. 1208–16⟩. *Opera*, Volume 1.

Speculum Duorum ⟨c. 1208–16⟩. Eds. R. B. C. Huygens and Yves Lefevre (1974).

Speculum Ecclesiae ⟨c. 1215–20⟩. *Opera*, Volume 4.

De Principis Instructione ⟨c. 1217⟩. Ed. J. S. Brewer (1846); *Opera*, Volume 8.

De Jure et Statu Menevensis Ecclesiae Dialogus ⟨c. 1218⟩. *Opera*, Volume 3.

Opera. Eds. J. S. Brewer, James F. Dimock, and George F. Warner. 1861–91. 8 vols.

ROGER BACON (1214–1292)

Quaestiones super Libros I–VI Physicorum Aristotelis ⟨1240s⟩. Ed. F. Delorme (1928; Books I–IV).

Epistolae de Secretis Operibus Naturae et de Nullitate Magiae ⟨c. 1250⟩. 1542; ed. J. S. Brewer (1859).

Opus Majus ⟨1266–67⟩. 1733 (Parts I–VI); ed. John Henry Bridges (1897–1900; 3 vols.).

Opus Minus ⟨1266–67⟩. Ed. J. S. Brewer (1859; Parts III–VI).

De Retardatione Accidentium Senectutis ⟨before 1267⟩. 1590; eds. A. G. Little and E. Withington (1928).

Opus Tertium ⟨1267⟩. Ed. J. S. Brewer (1859); ed. Pierre Duhem (1909; selections); ed. A. G. Little (1912; selections).

Compendium Studii Philosophiae ⟨1272⟩. Ed. J. S. Brewer (1859).

Compendium Studii Theologiae ⟨1292⟩. Ed. H. Rashdall (1911).

Grammatica Graeca ⟨n.d.⟩. Eds. Edmund Nolan and S. A. Hirsch (1902).

De Arte Chymiae Scripta. 1603.

Opera Hactenus Inedita. Eds. Robert Steele et al. 1905–40. 16 vols.

Roger Bacon's Philosophy of Nature. Ed. David C. Lindberg. 1983.

THOMAS OF ERCELDOUNE (c. 1225–c. 1300)

[*Sir Tristrem: A Metrical Romance of the Thirteenth Century, by Thomas of Erceldoune Called the Rhymer* ⟨late 13th c.–early 14th c.⟩. Ed. Sir Walter Scott (1804); ed. Eugen Kölbing (1882); ed. George P. McNeill (1886).]

[*The Romance and Prophecies of Thomas of Erceldoune* ⟨late 13th c.–early 14th c.⟩. Ed. James A. H. Murray. 1875.]

[*Thomas of Erceldoune: Sammlung Englischer Denkmäler in Kritischen Ausgaben*. Ed. Alois Brandl. 1880.]

[*The Loathly Lady* in Thomas of Erceldoune, *with a Text of the Poem Printed in 1652*. Ed. William P. Albrecht. 1954.]

[*Thomas of Erceldoune*. Ed. Ingeborg Nixon. 1980–83. 2 vols.]

WILLIAM OF OCCAM (1270–1347)

Commentarius in Primum Librum Sententiarum ⟨c. 1317–19⟩. 1483; *Opera Theologica*, Volumes 1–4.

Quaestiones in Secundum, Tertium, et Quartum Libros Sententiarum ⟨c. 1318–24⟩. 1495; *Opera Theologica*, Volumes 5–7.

Summula Philosophiae Naturalis ⟨c. 1319–21⟩. 1494 (as *Summulae in Libros Physicorum*); *Opera Philosophica*, Volume 6.

Brevis Summa Libri Physicorum ⟨c. 1322–23⟩. *Opera Philosophica*, Volume 6.

Quodlibeta Septem ⟨1322–24⟩. 1487; *Opera Theologica*, Volume 9.

Expositio in Libros Physicorum Aristotelis ⟨c. 1322–24⟩. *Opera Philosophica*, Volumes 4–5.

Expositio in Librum Porphyrii de Praedicabilibus ⟨c. 1323⟩. *Opera Philosophica*, Volume 2.

Expositio in Librum Praedicamentorum Aristotelis ⟨c. 1323⟩. *Opera Philosophica*, Volume 2.

Summa Logicae ⟨c. 1323⟩. 1488; *Opera Philosophica*, Volume 1.

Quaestiones in Libros Physicorum Aristotelis ⟨c. 1323–24⟩. 1491; *Opera Philosophica*, Volume 6.

Expositio super Libros Elenchorum ⟨after 1324⟩. *Opera Philosophica*, Volume 3.

De Corpore Christi ⟨c. 1324⟩. 1490 (with *De Sacramento Altaris*); ed. T. Bruce Birch (1930; with *De Sacramento Altaris*).

De Sacramento Altaris ⟨c. 1324⟩. 1490 (with *De Corpore Christi*); ed. T. Bruce Birch (1930; with *De Corpore Christi*).

Opus Nonaginta Dierum ⟨1332⟩. 1495; *Opera Politica*, Volumes 1–2.

Epistola ad Fratres Minores ⟨1334⟩. Ed. C. Kenneth Brampton (1929); *Opera Politica*, Volume 3.

Tractatus contra Joannem ⟨1335⟩. *Opera Politica*, Volume 3.

Tractatus contra Benedictum ⟨1337–38⟩. *Opera Politica*, Volume 3.

Breviloquium de Potestate Papae ⟨c. 1339–40⟩. Ed. L. Baudry (1937).

Octo Quaestiones de Potestate Papae ⟨c. 1342⟩. 1496; *Opera Politica*, Volume 1.

Dialogus inter Magistrum et Discipulum ⟨completed 1343⟩. 1495.

De Imperatorum et Pontificum Potestate ⟨c. 1346–47⟩. Ed. C. Kenneth Brampton (1927).

Opera Politica. Eds. J. G. Sikes et al. (1940–63; 3 vols.); rev. ed. by H. S. Offler (1974–   ).

Opera Theologica. Eds. P. Iuvenalis Lalor et al. 1967–84. 9 vols.

Opera Philosophica. Eds. P. Iuvenalis Lalor et al. 1974–85. 6 vols.

RICHARD ROLLE OF HAMPOLE (c. 1295–1349)

Melos Amoris ⟨c. 1326–27⟩. Ed. E. J. F. Arnould (1957).

Explanationes Notabiles super Lectiones Job in Officium Mortuorum ⟨c. 1327–30⟩. 1483; 1510.

Super Apocalypsim ⟨c. 1330–40⟩. Ed. Nicole Marzac (1968).

English Psalter ⟨c. 1340–49⟩. Ed. H. R. Bramley (1884); ed. Hope Emily Allen (1931; *English Writings*).

Incendium Amoris ⟨1343⟩. Ed. Margaret Deanesly (1915).

Contra Amatores Mundi ⟨c. 1343⟩. Ed. P. F. Theiner (1968).

Emendatio Vitae ⟨c. 1343⟩. 1510 (with *Speculum Spiritualium*).

Meditations on the Passion ⟨after 1343⟩. Ed. Harald Lindqvist (1917); ed. Hope Emily Allen (1931; *English Writings*).

The Form of Living ⟨c. 1348–49⟩. Ed. Geraldine E. Hodgson (1910); ed. Hope Emily Allen (1931; *English Writings*).

De Emendatione Peccatoris. 1533.

De Emendatione Peccatoris Opusculum, cum Aliis Aliquot Appendicibus. 1535.

In Psalterium Davidicum atque Alia Quaedam Sacrae Scripturae Monumenta. Ed. Johann Fabri. 1536.

English Prose Treatises. Ed. George G. Perry. 1866.

Yorkshire Writers: Rolle and His Followers. Ed. C. Horstmann. 1895–96. 2 vols.

Some Minor Works. Ed. Geraldine E. Hodgson. 1923.

Selected Works. Ed. G. C. Heseltine. 1930.

English Writings. Ed. Hope Emily Allen. 1931.

SIR JOHN MANDEVILLE (c. 1300–c. 1372)

Travels.

> French version ⟨c. 1356⟩. Ed. Malcolm Letts (1953; with English text [Bodleian Rawlinson D. 99]).
>
> English versions:
>
>> Harleian ms.: c. 1496 (Richard Pynson); 1499 (Wynkyn de Worde); ed. John Ashton (1887).
>>
>> Cotton ms.: 1725; ed. A. W. Pollard (1900); ed. P. Hamelius (1919–23; 2 vols.).
>>
>> Egerton ms.: ed. Sir George F. Warner (1889); ed. Malcolm Letts (1953).
>
> Latin versions:
>
>> Vulgate: 1483.
>>
>> British Museum Royal 13 E. IX: ed. M. C. Seymour (1963; with English text [Bodleian E. Museo 116]).

DUNS SCOTUS (c. 1265–c. 1308)

Questiones Subtilissimae super Libros Metaphysicorum Aristotelis ⟨c. 1300⟩. 1497.

Quaestiones super Libros Aristotelis de Anima ⟨c. 1300⟩. c. 1485.

De Modis Significandi seu Grammatica Speculativa ⟨c. 1300⟩. 1480; ed. M. Fernández García (1902).

Opus Oxoniense ⟨Ordinatio⟩ ⟨1302–04⟩. 1472; ed. M. Fernández García (1912–14; 2 vols.).

Opus Parisiense ⟨Reportata Parisiensia⟩ ⟨1302–04⟩. 1478 (Book I); 1505.

Tractatus de Primo Principio ⟨c. 1305⟩. Ed. Evan Roche (1949); ed. Allan B. Wolter (1966); ed. Wolfgang Kluxen (1974).

Quaestiones Quodlibetales ⟨c. 1305–07⟩. 1474.

Opera. 1580. 2 vols.

Opera Omnia. Ed. Luke Wadding. 1639 (12 vols.), 1891–95 (26 vols.).

Summa Theologica. 1728–38. 5 vols.

Opera Omnia. Eds. Charles Balić et al. 1950– .

Philosophical Writings. Ed. Allan Wolter. 1962.

Duns Scotus on the Will and Morality. Ed. Allan Wolter. 1986.

JOHN WYCLIF (c. 1324–1384)

De Universalibus ⟨before 1360⟩. Ed. Michael Henry Dziewicki (1905; *Latin Works*, Volume 17, Part 2).

De Compositione Hominis ⟨c. 1360⟩. Ed. Rudolf Beer (1884; *Latin Works*, Volume 3).

Quaestiones XIII Logicae et Philosophiae ⟨c. 1360–62⟩. Ed. Rudolf Beer (1891; *Latin Works*, Volume 11).

De Actibus Anime ⟨before 1361⟩. Ed. Michael Henry Dziewicki (1902; *Latin Works*, Volume 17, Part 1).

De Logica ⟨before 1362⟩. Ed. Michael Henry Dziewicki (1893–99; 3 vols.; *Latin Works*, Volume 14, Parts 1–3).

De Ente Praedicamentali ⟨c. 1362⟩. Ed. Rudolf Beer (1891; *Latin Works*, Volume 11).

Summa de Ente ⟨c. 1365⟩. Ed. S. Harrison Thomson (1930).

De Trinitate ⟨c. 1365⟩. Ed. Allen duPont Breck (1962).

De Dominio Divino ⟨c. 1366⟩. Ed. Reginald Lane Poole (1890; *Latin Works*, Volume 10).

De Ente ⟨before 1367⟩. Ed. Michael Henry Dziewicki (1909; *Latin Works*, Volume 20).

De Benedicta Incarnatione ⟨before 1367⟩. Ed. Edward Harris (1886; *Latin Works*, Volume 6).

De Mandatis Divinis ⟨c. 1375–76⟩. Eds. Johann Loserth and F. D. Matthew (1922; *Latin Works*, Volume 22).

De Officio Pastorali (English) ⟨before 1376⟩. Ed. F. D. Matthew (1880; *English Works*).

De Civilio Dominio ⟨before 1377⟩. Eds. Reginald Lane Poole and Johann Loserth (1885–1904; 4 vols.; *Latin Works*, Volume 2, Parts 1–4).

De Officio Pastorali (Latin) ⟨before 1378⟩. Ed. Gotthard Victor Lechler (1863).

De Veritate Sacrae Scripturae ⟨1378⟩. Ed. Rudolf Buddensieg (1905–07; 3 vols.; *Latin Works*, Volume 18, Parts 1–3).

De Officio Regis ⟨c. 1378–79⟩. Eds. Alfred W. Pollard and Charles Sayle (1887; *Latin Works*, Volume 8).

De Ecclesia ⟨c. 1378–79⟩. Ed. Johann Loserth (1886; *Latin Works*, Volume 4).

Speculum Ecclesie Militantis ⟨c. 1379⟩. Ed. Alfred W. Pollard (1886; *Latin Works*, Volume 5).

De Potestate Papae ⟨c. 1379⟩. Ed. Johann Loserth (1907; *Latin Works*, Volume 19).

De Simonia ⟨c. 1379–80⟩. Eds. Dr. Herzberg-Fränkel and Michael Henry Dziewicki (1898; *Latin Works*, Volume 16).

De Papa ⟨c. 1380⟩. Ed. F. D. Matthew (1880; *English Works*).

De Eucharistia Tractatus Maior ⟨1381⟩. Ed. Johann Loserth (1892; *Latin Works*, Volume 12).

De Apostasia ⟨1383⟩. Ed. Michael Henry Dziewicki (1889; *Latin Works*, Volume 9).

De Fundatione Sectarum ⟨1383⟩. Ed. Rudolf Buddensieg (1883; *Latin Works*, Volume 1, Part 1).

The Grete Sentence of Curs ⟨1383⟩. Ed. Thomas Arnold (1871; *Select English Works*, Volume 3).

The Chirche and Hir Membris ⟨c. 1383–84⟩. Ed. James Henthorn Todd (1851; *Three Treatises*).

De Blasphemia ⟨c. 1383–84⟩. Ed. Michael Henry Dziewicki (1893; *Latin Works*, Volume 13).

Opus Evangelicum ⟨c. 1384⟩. Ed. Johann Loserth (1895–96; 2 vols.; *Latin Works*, Volume 15, Parts 1–2).

Bible (translator ⟨with others?⟩) ⟨completed c. 1384⟩. Eds. Josiah Forshall and Sir Frederic Madden (1850; 3 vols.); ed. Melvin Macye Cammack (1938).

Sermones ⟨c. 1360–84⟩. Ed. Johann Loserth (1887–90; 4 vols.; *Latin Works*, Volume 7, Parts 1–4).

English Sermons ⟨c. 1360–84⟩. Ed. Thomas Arnold (1869–71; 2 vols.; *Select English Works*, Volumes 1–2); ed. Anne Hudson (1983– ; 4 vols. [projected]).

Dialogorum Libri Quattuor. 1525.

Wicklieffes Wicket. Ed. Miles Coverdale. 1548.

Tracts and Treatises. Ed. Robert Vaughan. 1845.
Three Treatises. Ed. James Henthorn Todd. 1851.
Select English Works. Ed. Thomas Arnold. 1869–71. 3 vols.
English Works. Ed. F. D. Matthew. 1880.
Latin Works. 1883–1922. 22 vols.
Select English Writings. Ed. Herbert E. Winn. 1929.
Selections from English Wycliffite Writings. Ed. Anne Hudson. 1978.

JOHN BARBOUR (c. 1316–1395)

The Bruce ⟨1375⟩. c. 1570; ed. Andro Hart (1616); ed. Andrew Anderson (1670); ed. John Pinkerton (1790); ed. John Jamieson (1820; 2 vols.); ed. Cosmo Innes (1856); ed. Walter W. Skeat (1870–89; 4 vols.); ed. W. M. Mackenzie (1909); ed. Alexander Kinghorn (1960; selections).

WILLIAM LANGLAND (c. 1322–c. 1400)

The Vision of Piers Plowman.
  A-text ⟨1362–63⟩. Ed. Walter W. Skeat (1867); ed. R. W. Chambers (1912; selections); eds. Thomas A. Knott and David C. Fowler (1952); ed. George Kane (1960).
  B-text ⟨1377⟩. Ed. Robert Crowley (1550); ed. Owen Rogers (1561); ed. Thomas Wright (1842; 2 vols.); ed. Walter W. Skeat (1869); ed. J. F. Davis (1896; selections); ed. J. A. W. Bennett (1972; selections); eds. George Kane and E. Talbot Donaldson (1975).
  C-text ⟨c. 1393⟩. Ed. Thomas Dunham Whitaker (1813); ed. Walter W. Skeat (1873); eds. Elizabeth Salter and Derek Pearsall (1967; selections); ed. Derek Pearsall (1979).

GEOFFREY CHAUCER (c. 1340–1400)

The Book of the Duchess ⟨1369⟩. Ed. Frederick J. Furnivall (1871); ed. Helen Phillips (1982).
The Romaunt of the Rose (translator) ⟨before 1370⟩. Ed. Frederick J. Furnivall (1911); ed. Stephen G. Nichols (1967); ed. Ronald Sutherland (1968).
The Parlement of Foules ⟨1377⟩. 1477 (William Caxton); 1530 (Wynkyn de Worde); ed. C. M. Drennan (1911); ed. Derek S. Brewer (1960).
The Hous of Fame ⟨c. 1380–1381⟩. 1484 (William Caxton); ed. Walter W. Skeat (1893); ed. C. M. Drennan (1921).
Boece de Consolacione (translator) ⟨c. 1381–1385⟩. 1478 (William Caxton); ed. Richard Morris (1868); ed. Frederick J. Furnivall (1886).
Troilus and Criseyde ⟨c. 1382–1385⟩. 1483 (William Caxton); 1517 (Wynkyn de Worde); 1526; ed. Robert Kilburn Root (1926); ed. Raymond Cullis Goffin (1935); ed. Georges Bonnard (1943); ed. Robert M. Lumiansky (1952); ed. Daniel Cook (1966); ed. Derek S. Brewer (1978); ed. Barry A. Windeatt (1984).
The Legend of Good Women ⟨c. 1385–1386⟩. Ed. Frederick J. Furnivall (1871–90; 3 vols.); ed. Walter W. Skeat (1889).
The Canterbury Tales ⟨begun 1386⟩. 1478 (William Caxton); 1492; 1498 (Wynkyn de Worde); ed. Thomas Morrell (1737); ed. Thomas Tyrwhitt (1775–78; 5 vols.); ed. Frederick J. Furnivall (1868–79; 36 parts in 9); ed. Alfred W. Pollard (1894; 2 vols.); ed. Walter W. Skeat (1908); ed. John Matthews Manly (1928); eds. John Matthews Manly, Edith Rickert et al. (1940; 8 vols.); ed. Arthur C. Cawley (1958); ed. John Halverson (1971); ed. Robert A. Pratt (1974); ed. Paul G. Ruggiers (1978); ed. Norman Francis Blake (1980); eds. A. Kent Hieatt and Constance Hieatt (1981); ed. Derek Pearsall (1985).
The Treatise on the Astrolabe ⟨1391⟩. Ed. A. E. Brae (1870);

ed. Walter W. Skeat (1872); ed. Robert Theodore Gunther (1930).
Workes. 1526. 3 vols.
Workes. Ed. William Thynne. 1532.
Workes. Ed. John Stowe. 1561.
Workes. Ed. Thomas Speght. 1598.
Works. Eds. John Urry et al. 1721.
A Supplementary Parallel-Text Edition of Chaucer's Minor Poems (Containing Most of Those That Could Not Be Got into the Parallel-Text Edition). Ed. Frederick J. Furnivall. 1871–80. 2 vols.
Complete Works. Ed. Walter W. Skeat. 1894–97. 7 vols.
Works. Eds. Alfred W. Pollard, Mark Harvey Liddell, H. F. Heath, and William S. McCormick. 1898.
Collected Works. Ed. Alfred W. Pollard. 1928–29. 8 vols.
Complete Works. Ed. Fred Norris Robinson. 1933, 1957.
The Portable Chaucer. Ed. Theodore Morrison. 1949.
Complete Works. Ed. Kemp Malone. 1953.
Chaucer's Poetry: An Anthology for the Modern Reader. Ed. E. Talbot Donaldson. 1958.
Chaucer's Major Poetry. Ed. Albert C. Baugh. 1963.
Selections from the Tales of Canterbury and Short Poems. Ed. Robert A. Pratt. 1966.
Lyrics and Allegory. Ed. James Reeves. 1971.
Troilus and Criseyde and Selected Short Poems. Eds. Donald R. Howard and James Dean. 1976.
Complete Poetry and Prose. Ed. John H. Fisher. 1977.
Chaucer According to Caxton: Minor Poems and Boece, 1478. Ed. Beverly Boyd. 1978.
Poetical Works: A Facsimile of Cambridge University Library MS. Gg.4.27. Ed. Derek S. Brewer. 1979–81. 3 vols.
A Variorum Edition of the Works. Eds. Paul G. Ruggiers, Donald C. Baker et al. 1983–   .

JOHN GOWER (c. 1325–1408)

Cinkante Balades ⟨before 1374⟩. Ed. Earl Gower (1818); ed. Edmund Stengel (1886).
Speculum Meditantis ⟨*Mirour de l'omme*⟩ ⟨c. 1378⟩. Ed. G. C. Macaulay (1899; in *Complete Works*, Volume 1).
Vox Clamantis ⟨c. 1378–93⟩. Ed. H. O. Coxe (1850).
Confessio Amantis ⟨1390⟩. 1483 (William Caxton); ed. Thomas Berthelette (1532, 1554); ed. Reinhold Pauli (1857; 3 vols.); ed. Henry Morley (1889); ed. Russell A. Peck (1968).
Cronica Tripertita ⟨c. 1400⟩. Ed. H. O. Coxe (1850).
Complete Works. Ed. G. C. Macaulay. 1899–1902. 4 vols.
Selections. Ed. J. A. W. Bennett. 1968.
Selected Poetry. Ed. Carole Weinberg. 1983.

JOHN LYDGATE (c. 1370–c. 1451)

The Churl and the Birde (translator) ⟨c. 1400⟩. c. 1477 (William Caxton); c. 1493; c. 1499 (Wynkyn de Worde); ed. M. M. Sykes (1822); ed. Henry Noble MacCracken (1934; *Minor Poems*, Volume 2).
The Flour of Curtesye ⟨c. 1400–02⟩. Ed. William Thynne (1532; in *The Workes of Geffray Chaucer*); ed. Walter W. Skeat (1897; in *The Complete Works of Geoffrey Chaucer*); ed. Henry Noble MacCracken (1934; *Minor Poems*, Volume 2).
The Complaint of the Black Knight ⟨c. 1402⟩. n.d. (Wynkyn de Worde; as *The Complainte of a Lovers Lyfe*); 1508 (as *The Mayng or Disport of Chaucer* in *The Knightly Tale of Golagrus*); ed. William Thynne (1532; in *The Workes of Geffray Chaucer*); ed. Walter W. Skeat (1897; in *The Works of Geoffrey Chaucer*, Volume 7); ed. George S. Stevenson

(1918); ed. Henry Noble MacCracken (1934; *Minor Poems*, Volume 2); ed. John Norton-Smith (1966; *Poems*).
Isopis Fabules (translator) ⟨c. 1406–08⟩. Ed. Henry Noble MacCracken (1934; *Minor Poems*, Volume 2).
Reson and Sensuallite (translator) ⟨before 1412⟩. Ed. Ernst Sieper (1901–03; 2 vols.).
The Temple of Glas ⟨before 1412⟩. c. 1477 (William Caxton); c. 1500 (Wynkyn de Worde); c. 1505; c. 1530; ed. J. Schick (1891); ed. John Norton-Smith (1966; *Poems*).
The Troy Book (translator) ⟨1412–20⟩. 1513; 1555; ed. Henry Bergen (1906–35; 4 vols.).
On the Departing of Thomas Chaucer ⟨c. 1414⟩. Ed. Henry Noble MacCracken (1934; *Minor Poems*, Volume 2); ed. John Norton-Smith (1966; *Poems*).
[*The Assembly of Gods* ⟨c. 1420⟩. 1498 (Wynkyn de Worde; as *The Interpretacion of the Names of Goddis and Goddises*); 1529; 1540; ed. Oscar Lovell Triggs (1895, 1896).]
The Siege of Thebes ⟨after 1420⟩. c. 1495 (Wynkyn de Worde; as *The Storye of Thebes*); eds. Axel Erdmann and Eilert Ekwall (1911–30; 2 vols.).
The Lyf of Our Lady ⟨c. 1421–22⟩. 1484 (William Caxton); 1531; ed. Charles Edward Tame (c. 1872); eds. Joseph A. Lauritis et al. (1961).
The Serpent of Division ⟨1422⟩. n.d.; 1559; ed. Henry Noble MacCracken (1911).
On Gloucester's Approaching Marriage ⟨c. 1422–23⟩. Ed. Henry Noble MacCracken (1934; *Minor Poems*, Volume 2).
Mummings ⟨c. 1424–30⟩. Ed. Henry Noble MacCracken (1934; *Minor Poems*, Volume 2).
Guy of Warwick ⟨after 1425⟩. Ed. Henry Noble MacCracken (1934; *Minor Poems*, Volume 2).
The Pilgrimage of the Life of Man by Guillaume de Deguileville (translator) ⟨c. 1426–28⟩. Ed. Frederick J. Furnivall (1899–1904; 3 vols.).
Danse Macabre (translator) ⟨c. 1431⟩. 1554 (with *The Fall of Princes*); ed. Sir William Dugdale (1658; in *The History of St. Paul's Cathedral*); eds. Florence Warren and Beatrice White (1931).
The Fall of Princes by Boccaccio (adaptation) ⟨c. 1431–39⟩. 1494; 1527; 1554; ed. Henry Bergen (1923–27; 4 vols.).
King Henry VI's Triumphal Entry into London ⟨1432⟩. Ed. Henry Noble MacCracken (1934; *Minor Poems*, Volume 2).
The Horse the Ghoos and the Sheep ⟨c. 1436–40⟩. 1477 (William Caxton); 1500 (Wynkyn de Worde); ed. M. M. Sykes (1822); ed. M. Degenhart (1900); ed. Henry Noble MacCracken (1934; *Minor Poems*, Volume 2).
The Lyfe of Seint Albon and the Lyfe of Seint Amphabel (translator) ⟨1439⟩. 1534; ed. C. Horstmann (1882); ed. J. E. van der Westhuizen (1974); ed. George F. Reinecke (1985).
Testament ⟨c. 1445⟩. c. 1515; ed. Hans Beutner (1914); ed. Henry Noble MacCracken (1934; *Minor Poems*, Volume 2).
The Nightingale (translator) ⟨c. 1446⟩. Ed. Otto Glauning (1900; *Minor Poems*).
A Sayenge of the Nyghtyngale (translator) ⟨c. 1446⟩. Ed. Otto Glauning (1900; *Minor Poems*).
Fabula Duorum Mercatorum ⟨c. 1446⟩. Ed. Henry Noble MacCracken (1934; *Minor Poems*, Volume 2).
The Governaune of Kynges and Prynces ⟨*Secreta Secretorum*⟩ by Pseudo-Aristotle (translator) ⟨c. 1446–49⟩. 1511; ed. Robert Steele (1894); ed. Theodor Prosiegel (1903).
Puerbes ⟨proverbs⟩ (translator). c. 1515 (Wynkyn de Worde).

Minor Poems. Ed. J. O. Halliwell. 1840.
Minor Poems: The Two Nightingale Poems. Ed. Otto Glauning. 1900.
Minor Poems. Ed. Henry Noble MacCracken. 1911–34. 2 vols.
Poems. Ed. John Norton-Smith. 1966.

THOMAS OCCLEVE (c. 1370–1426)

The Letter of Cupid ⟨1402⟩. Ed. William Thynne (1532; in *The Workes of Geffray Chaucer*); ed. Walter W. Skeat (1897; in *The Complete Works of Geoffrey Chaucer*, Volume 7); ed. Frederick J. Furnivall (1892; *Works*, Volume 1); ed. W. Tod Ritchie (1930; in *The Bannatyne Manuscript*, Volume 4).
The Mother of God ⟨before 1405⟩. Ed. William Thynne (1532; in *The Workes of Geffray Chaucer*); ed. John Leyden (1801; in *The Complaynt of Scotland*); ed. Frederick J. Furnivall (1892; *Works*, Volume 1); ed. M. C. Seymour (1981; *Selections*).
The Compleynte of the Virgin by Guillaume de Deguileville (translator) ⟨before 1405⟩. Ed. Frederick J. Furnivall (1892; *Works*, Volume 1); ed. M. C. Seymour (1981; *Selections*).
La Male Regle de T. Hoccleve ⟨1406⟩. Ed. Frederick J. Furnivall (1892; *Works*, Volume 1); ed. Eleanor Prescott Hammond (1927; in *English Verse between Chaucer and Surrey*); ed. M. C. Seymour (1981; *Selections*).
De Regimine Principum (translator) ⟨c. 1411⟩. Ed. Thomas Wright (1860); ed. Frederick J. Furnivall (1897; *Works*, Volume 3); ed. M. C. Seymour (1981; *Selections*; selections).
Legend of the Virgin and Her Sleeveless Garment ⟨c. 1413⟩. Ed. Arthur Beatty (1902; as *A New Ploughman's Tale*); ed. Beverly Boyd (1964; in *The Middle English Miracles of the Virgin*).
The Remonstrance against Sir John Oldcastle ⟨1415⟩. Ed. Alexander B. Grosart (1880; in *The Poems of Richard James*); ed. Frederick J. Furnivall (1892; *Works*, Volume 1); ed. M. C. Seymour (1981; *Selections*).
Thomas Hoccleve's Complaint ⟨1421⟩. Ed. Frederick J. Furnivall (1892; *Works*, Volume 1); ed. M. C. Seymour (1981; *Selections*).
Dialog with a Friend ⟨1422⟩. Ed. Frederick J. Furnivall (1892; *Works*, Volume 1); ed. M. C. Seymour (1981; *Selections*).
Lerne to Dye ⟨c. 1422⟩. Ed. Frederick J. Furnivall (1892; *Works*, Volume 1).
The Tale of Jereslaus's Wife and Her False Brother-in-Law ⟨c. 1422⟩. Ed. Frederick J. Furnivall (1892; *Works*, Volume 1).
The Tale of Jonathas ⟨c. 1422⟩. Ed. William Browne (1614; in *The Shepherd's Pipe*); ed. Frederick J. Furnivall (1892; *Works*, Volume 1); ed. M. C. Seymour (1981; *Selections*).
Poems. Ed. George Mason. 1796.
Works. 1892 [Volume 1; ed. Frederick J. Furnivall]; 1897 [Volume 3; ed. Frederick J. Furnivall]; 1925 [Volume 2; ed. Israel Gollancz].
Selections. Ed. M. C. Seymour. 1981.

WILLIAM CAXTON (c. 1422–1492)

The Recuyell of the Historyes of Troye by Raoul Lefevre (translator). c. 1475.
The Game and Playe of the Chesse by Jacobus de Cessolis (translator). c. 1475.
The History of Jason by Raoul Lefevre (translator). c. 1477.
The Advertisement. c. 1479.

The Metamorphoses of Ovid (translator) ⟨1480⟩. Ed. George
    Hibbert (1819); eds. Stephen Gaselee and H. F. B. Brett-
    Smith (1924; selections).
[*Vocabulary in French and English* (translator). 1480.]
The Mirror of the World by Gautier de Metz (translator). 1481.
Reynard the Fox (translator). 1481.
Godfrey of Boloyne (translator). 1481.
The Curial by Alain Chartier (translator). c. 1483.
The Knight of the Tower by Geoffrey de La Tour Landry (trans-
    lator). 1484.
Fables of Aesop (translator). 1484.
The Book of the Order of Chivalry of Knighthood by Ramon
    Lull (translator). 1484.
Caton (translator). c. 1484.
The Golden Legend by Jacobus de Varagine (translator).
    c. 1484.
The Life of Charles the Great (translator). 1485.
Paris and Vienne (translator). 1485.
The Book of Good Manners by Jacques Legrand (translator).
    1487.
The Life of Saint Winifred by Prior Robert of Shrewsbury
    (translator). c. 1487.
The Royal Book by Lorens d'Orleans (translator). c. 1487.
Four Sons of Aymon (translator). c. 1488.
Blanchardin and Eglantine (translator). c. 1488.
Doctrinal of Sapience (translator). 1489.
The Book of the Feats of Arms and Chivalry by Christine de
    Pisan (translator). c. 1489.
Eneydos (translator). 1490.
The Art and Craft to Know Well to Die (translator). 1490.
[*Ars Moriendi: The Craft for to Die for the Health of a Man's
    Soul.* 1491.]
Fifteen Odes by Saint Birgitta [?] (translator). 1491.
Vitas Patrum (translator). 1495.
Prologues and Epilogues. Ed. W. J. B. Crotch. 1928.
Caxton's Own Prose. Ed. N. F. Blake. 1973.

SIR THOMAS MALORY (d. c. 1470)

Le Morte Darthur ⟨completed c. 1470⟩. 1485 (William Cax-
    ton); 1529 (Wynkyn de Worde); ed. Wyllyam Copland
    (1557); ed. Thomas East (c. 1585); 1634 (3 parts); ed.
    Joseph Haslewood (1816; 3 vols.); ed. Robert Southey
    (1817; 2 vols.); ed. Thomas Wright (1858; 3 vols.); ed. H.
    Oskar Sommer (1889–91; 3 vols.); ed. F. J. Simmons
    (1893–94); ed. A. W. Pollard (1900; 3 vols.); ed. R. M.
    Lumiansky (1982).
Works. Ed. Eugène Vinaver. 1947 (3 vols.), 1967 (3 vols.).

ROBERT HENRYSON (c. 1430–1506)

Orpheus and Eurydice. 1508.
*The Morall Fabillis of Esope the Phrygian Compylit in Elo-
    quent and Ornate Scottis Meter.* 1570.
The Testament of Cresseid. 1593.
Poems and Fables. Ed. David Laing. 1865.
Poems. Ed. G. Gregory Smith. 1906–14. 3 vols.
Poems: A Revised Text. Ed. W. M. Metcalfe. 1917.
Poems and Fables. Ed. H. Harvey Wood. 1933.
Poems. Ed. Charles Elliott. 1963.
Henryson. Ed. Hugh MacDiarmid. 1973.

GAVIN DOUGLAS (c. 1474–1522)

*The XIII. Bukes of Eneados of the Famose Poete Virgill Trans-
    latet out of Latyne Verses into Scottish Metir.* 1553.
The Palis of Honoure. c. 1553.
Select Works. 1787.
Poetical Works. Ed. John Small. 1874. 4 vols.

Virgil's Aenead (translator). Ed. D. F. C. Coldwell. 1957–64.
    4 vols.
A Selection from His Poetry. Ed. Sydney Goodsir Smith. 1959.
Selections. Ed. David F. C. Coldwell. 1964.
Shorter Poems. Ed. Priscilla J. Bawcutt. 1967.

JOHN SKELTON (c. 1460–c. 1529)

The Bowge of Courte. 1499.
A Ballade of the Scottysshe Kynge. 1513.
The Tunnyng of Elynour Rummyng. c. 1521.
A Goodly Garlande or Chapelet of Laurell. 1523.
Dyvers Balettys and Dyties Solacyous. c. 1527.
Agaynste a Comely Coystrowne. c. 1527.
A Replycacion agaynst Certayne Yong Scolers. c. 1528.
Magnyfycence. c. 1530.
Collyn Clout. c. 1531.
Certayne Bokes. 1545.
Phyllyp Sparowe. 1545.
Why Come Ye Nat to Courte? 1545.
Pithy Pleasant and Profitable Workes. Ed. John Stowe. 1568.
Poetical Works. Ed. Alexander Dyce. 1843. 2 vols.
Poems. Ed. Richard Hughes. 1924.
John Skelton. 1927.
Complete Poems. Ed. Philip Henderson. 1931.
Poems. Ed. Ronald Gant. 1949.
A Selection from His Poems. Ed. Vivian de Sola Pinto. 1950.
Poems. Ed. Robert S. Kinsman. 1969.
Complete English Poems. Ed. John Scattergood. 1983.

WILLIAM DUNBAR (c. 1460–c. 1522)

⟨*Poems.*⟩ 1508.
*The Thistle and the Rose: A Poem in Honour of Margaret,
    Queen to James IV King of Scots.* 1750.
Select Poems. 1788.
Poems. Ed. David Laing. 1834. 2 vols.
Poems. Ed. John Small. 1884–93. 3 vols.
Poems. Ed. H. Bellyse Baildon. 1907.
Poems. Ed. W. Mackay MacKenzie. 1932.
Selections from the Poems. Ed. Hugh MacDiarmid. 1952.
Poems. Ed. James Kinsley. 1958.
Selected Poems. Ed. Florence Ridley. 1969.
Poems. Ed. James Kinsley. 1979.

SIR THOMAS MORE (1478–1535)

Luciani Opuscula (translated into Latin; with Desiderius Eras-
    mus). 1506.
The Lyfe of Johan Picus Erle of Myrandula. c. 1510.
Utopia. 1516.
A Mery Jest How the Sergeant Would Lerne to Be a Frere.
    1516.
Thomas Morus Eduardo Leo. c. 1519.
Epigrammata. 1520.
Epistola ad Germanum Brixium. 1520.
Eruditissimi Viri Ferdinandi Baravelli Opus Elegans. 1523.
The Supplycacyon of Soulys. 1529.
*A Dyaloge of Syr Thomas More, Wherein Be Treated Divers
    Maters.* 1529.
The Confutacyon of Tyndales Answere. 1532–33. 2 vols.
The Debellacyon of Salem and Bizance. 1533.
The Apologye. 1533.
A Letter Impugnynge the Erronyouse Wrytyng of John Fryth.
    1533.
*The Answere to the Fyrst Parte of the Poysoned Booke Which a
    Nameless Heretyke Hath Named the* Souper of the Lorde.
    1534.
The Boke of the Fayre Gentylwoman. 1540.

A Dialoge of Comfort against Tribulacion. 1553.
Works in the Englysh Tonge. Ed. William Rastell. 1557.
Lucubrationes. 1563.
Opera Omnia. 1565.
Epistola in Qua Respondet Literis Joannis Pomerani. 1568.
Dissertatio Epistolica. 1625.
Epistola ad Acadamiam Oxon. Ed. Richard James. 1633.
Opera Omnia. 1689.
The Wisdom and Wit of Blessed Thomas More: Being Extracts from Such of His Works as Were Written in English. Ed. T. E. Brigett. 1892.
Selections from His English Works. Eds. P. S. Allen and H. M. Allen. 1924.
The Four Last Things. Ed. D. O'Connor. 1935.
Correspondence. Ed. Elizabeth Francis Rogers. 1947.
Complete Works. Eds. Richard S. Sylvester et al. 1963– .
The Essential More. Eds. James J. Greene and John P. Dolan. 1967.

WILLIAM TYNDALE (c. 1484–1536)

A Compendious Introduction unto the Pistle to the Romayns. 1520.
New Testament (translator). 1525.
The Obedience of a Christen Man. 1528.
The Parable of the Wicked Mammon. 1528.
The Examinacion of Master William Thorpe; The Examinacion of Syr J. Oldcastell (editor). 1530.
Pentateuch (translator). 1530.
The Practyse of Prelates. c. 1530.
An Answere unto Sir T. Mores Dialoge. c. 1530.
An Exposicion uppon the v. vi. vii. chapters of Mathew. c. 1533.
The Prayer and Complaint of the Plowman (editor). 1531.
The Exposition of the Fyrste Epistle of Seynt Jhon. 1531.
The Souper of the Lorde. 1533.
[*Enchiridion* by Erasmus (translator). 1533.]
A Fruitefull and Godly Treatise Expressing the Right Institution of the Sacraments. c. 1533.
The Testament of W. Tracie Esquier, Expounded (with John Frith). 1535.
A Pathway into the Holy Scripture. c. 1536.
A Briefe Declaration of the Sacraments. c. 1548.
Whole Works (with John Frith and Robert Barnes). 1572. 2 vols.
The Works of the English and Scottish Reformers (with John Frith). Ed. Thomas Russell. 1828–29. 4 vols.
Doctrinal Treatises and Introductions to Different Portions of the Holy Scriptures. Ed. Henry Walter. 1848.
Expositions and Notes, Together with The Practice of Prelates. Ed. Henry Walter. 1849.
An Answer to More's Dialogue; The Supper of the Lord; and William Tracy's Testament Expounded. Ed. Henry Walter. 1850.
Work. Ed. S. L. Greenslade. 1938.
Work. Ed. G. E. Duffield. 1964.

SIR THOMAS WYATT (1503–1542)

Plutarckes Boke of the Quyete of Mynde (translator). 1528.
Certayne Psalmes Chosen out of the Psalter of David. 1549.
Poems (with Henry Howard, Earl of Surrey). Ed. George Sewell. 1717.
Works. Ed. George Frederick Nott. 1816.
Poetical Works. Ed. Sir Nicholas Harris Nicolas. 1831.
Poetical Works. Ed. Robert Bell. 1854.
Poetical Works. Ed. George Gilfillan. 1858.

Poems. Ed. A. K. Foxwell. 1913. 2 vols.
Poetry. Ed. E. M. W. Tillyard. 1929.
Collected Poems. Ed. Kenneth Muir. 1949.
Unpublished Poems. Ed. Kenneth Muir. 1961.
Collected Poems. Eds. Kenneth Muir and Patricia Thomson. 1969.
Collected Poems. Ed. Joost Daalder. 1975.

SIR THOMAS ELYOT (c. 1499–1546)

[*Papyrii Gemini Elatis Hermathena; seu, De Eloquentia Victoria.* 1522.]
The Education or Bringinge Up of Children by Plutarch (translator). c. 1530.
The Boke Named the Governour. 1531.
[*Howe One May Take Profyte of His Enemyes* by Plutarch (translator). c. 1531.]
A Dialogue between Lucian and Diogenes of Life by Lucian (translator). c. 1532.
Pasquil the Playne. 1533.
Of the Knowledg Whiche Maketh a Wise Man. 1533.
The Doctrinall of Princis by Isocrates (translator). c. 1533.
A Swete and Devoute Sermon of Mortalitie of Man ⟨by Saint Cyprian⟩; *The Rules of a Christian Lyfe* by Pico della Mirandola (translator). 1534.
The Castell of Helthe. c. 1537.
The Dictionary of Syr Thomas Elyot ⟨*Bibliotheca Eliotae*⟩. 1538.
The Bankette of Sapience. 1539.
The Defence of Good Women. 1540.
The Image of Governance, Compiled of the Actes and Sentences Notable of Alexander Severus. 1541.
A Preservative agaynste Deth. 1545.

HENRY HOWARD, EARL OF SURREY
(c. 1516–1547)

An Excellent Epitaffe of Syr Thomas Wyat. 1542.
The Fourth Boke of Virgill (translator). 1554.
Certain Bokes of Virgiles Aenaeis (translator). 1557.
Songes and Sonettes (with others). 1557.
Poems (with Sir Thomas Wyatt). Ed. George Sewell. 1717.
Works. Ed. George Frederick Nott. 1815–16. 2 vols.
Poetical Works. Ed. Sir Nicholas Harris Nicolas. 1831.
Poetical Works. Ed. Robert Bell. 1854.
Poems. Ed. Frederick Morgan Padelford. 1920.
To a Lady. Ed. Douglas Geary. 1957.
Poems. Ed. Emrys Jones. 1964.
Selected Poems. Ed. Dennis Keene. 1985.

ALEXANDER BARCLAY (c. 1475–1552)

[*A Castell of Laboure* by Pierre Gringore (translator). c. 1503.]
The Shyp of Folys of the Worlde. 1509.
[*The Gardyners Passetaunce Touchyng the Outrage of Fraunce.* c. 1512.]
The Lyfe of the Glorious Martyr Saynt George by Baptista Spagnuoli (translator). c. 1515.
The Fyfte Eglog. c. 1518.
The Myrrour of Good Maners by Domenicus Mancinus (translator). c. 1518.
Vocabula by John Stanbridge (editor). 1519.
The Famous Cronycle of the Warre agaynst Jugurth by Sallust (translator). c. 1520.
The Introductory to Wryte and to Pronounce Frenche. 1521.
The Book of Codrus and Mynalcas: The Fourth Egloge. c. 1521.
The First Eclogue by Pius II (translator). c. 1523.
The Eglogs. c. 1530.

The Cytezen and Uplondyshman: An Eclogue. Ed. F. W. Fairholt. 1847.
Certayne Egloges. 1885.
Eclogues. Ed. Beatrice White. 1928.

THOMAS, LORD VAUX (1510–1556)

The Paradyse of Daynty Devises (with Richard Edwards). 1576.
Poems. Ed. Alexander B. Grosart. 1876.
Poems. Ed. Larry P. Vonalt. 1960.

SIR JOHN CHEKE (1514–1557)

Τoυ ἐν ἁγίοις ὁμιλίαι δύο by John Chrysostom (translated into Latin). 1543.
De Providentia Dei, ac Fato, Orationes Sex by John Chrysostom (translated into Latin). 1545.
The Hurt of Sedicion Howe Greveous It Is to a Commune Welth. 1549.
De Obitu Doctissimi et Sanctissimi Theologi Doctoris Martini Buceri, Epistolae Duae; Item, Epigrammata Varia cum Graecae tum Latinè Conscripta in Eundem Ministrum (with Nicholas Carr). 1551.
Defensio Verae et Catholicae Doctrinae de Sacramento Corporis et Sanguinis Christi by Thomas Cranmer (translated into Latin). 1553.
De Bello Apparatu Liber by Emperor Leo VI (translated into Latin). 1554.
De Pronuntiatione Graecae Potissimum Linguae Disputationes cum Stephano Wintoniensi Episcopo, Septem Contrariis Epistolis Comprehensae, Magna Quadam & Elegentia & Eruditione Refertae. 1555.
Reformation Legum Ecclesiasticarum (translated into Latin; with Walter Haddon). 1571.
The Gospel According to Saint Matthew and Part of the First Chapter of the Gospel According to Saint Mark, Translated into English from Greek; Also VII Original Letters. Ed. James Goodwin. 1843.

NICHOLAS UDALL (c. 1506–c. 1557)

Floures for Latine Spekynge. 1533.
Apophthegmes Compiled in Latin by Erasmus (translator). 1542.
The First Tome of the Paraphrase of Erasmus upon the Newe Testament (translator). 1548.
A Discourse concerning the Lordes Supper. c. 1550.
Compendiosa Totius Anatomiae Delineatio. 1553.
Ralph Roister Doister. c. 1566.
Dramatic Writings. Ed. John S. Farmer. 1906.

ROGER ASCHAM (1515–1568)

Toxophilus: The Schole of Shootinge Conteyned in Two Bookes. 1545.
A Report and Discourse on the Affaires and State of Germany. c. 1570.
The Scholemaster; or, Plaine and Perfite Way of Teachyng Children to Understand, Write, and Speake the Latin Tong. 1570.
Familiarium Epistolarum Libri Tres. 1576.
Apologia pro Caena Dominica (etc.). Ed. Edward Grant. 1577.
Epistolarum Libri Quator. Ed. W. Elstob. 1703.
English Works. Ed. James Bennet. 1761.
Whole Works. Ed. J. A. Giles. 1864–65. 4 vols.
English Works. Ed. William Aldis Wright. 1904.

MILES COVERDALE (1488–1568)

A Paraphrasis upon Al the Psalmes of David. 1534.
Bible (translator). 1535.

Goostly Psalmes and Spirituall Songes Drawen out of the Holy Scripture. c. 1536.
Proverbs, Ecclesiastes, Wisdom, Ecclesiasticus, The Story of Bel (translator). 1537.
How and Whither a Chrysten Man Ought to Flye the Horryble Plague of the Pestilence by Andreas Osiander (translator). 1537.
New Testament (translator). c. 1537.
A Very Excellent and Swete Exposition upon the XXII. Psalme by Martin Luther (translator). 1538.
An Exposicion upon the Songe of the Blessed Virgine Mary, Called Magnificat (translator). 1538.
Annotations in the Boke of Josue. c. 1538.
Bible ⟨Great Bible⟩ (translator). 1539.
The Psalter or Booke of the Psalmes; Wher unto Are Added Other Devoute Praiers. c. 1540.
The Christen State of Matrimonye by Heinrich Bullinger (translator). 1541.
A Confutacion of That Treatise, Which One John Standish Made agaynst the Protestacion of D. Barnes in the Year M.D.XL. c. 1541.
The Actes of the Disputation in the Cowncell of the Empire Holden at Regenspurg (translator). 1542.
A Christen Exhortacion unto Customable Swearers. c. 1543.
A Shorte Recapitulacion or Abrigement of Erasmus Enchiridion. 1545.
The Defence of a Certayne Poor Christen Man (translator). 1545.
The Olde Fayth by Heinrich Bullinger (translator). 1547.
[*The Christen Rule or State of All the World from the Hyghest to the Lowest.* c. 1547.]
Wicklieffes Wicket by John Wyclif (editor). 1548.
A Faythful and True Prognostication upon the Yeare M.CCCCC.LXIX. (translator). c. 1548.
The Psalter or Psalmes of David. 1549.
The Second Tome of the Paraphrase of Erasmus upon the Newe Testament (translator; with John Olde). 1549.
The Order That the Church and Congregation of Chryst in Denmark Doth Use. c. 1549.
A Faythful and Most Godly Treatyse concernynge the Most Sacred Sacrament by John Calvin (translator). c. 1549.
A Spyrytuall and Moost Precyouse Pearle by Otto Werdmüller (translator). 1550.
[*The Hope of the Faythful, Declarying the Resurrection of Our Lorde Jesus Chryst* by Otto Werdmüller [?] (translator). c. 1554.]
[*An Exhortacion to the Carienge of Chrystes Crosse.* c. 1555.]
A Most Frutefull, Piththye and Learned Treatise, How a Christen Man Ought to Behave Himself in the Danger of Death by Otto Werdmüller (translator). c. 1555.
Certain Most Godly, Fruitful, and Comfortable Letters of the True Saintes and Holy Martyrs of God (editor). 1564.
Fruitfull Lessons, upon the Passion, Buriall, Resurrection, Ascension, and of the Sending of the Holy Ghost. 1593.
Writings (with John Foxe and John Bale). 1831.
Memorials. Ed. J. J. Lowndes. 1838.
Writings and Translations. Ed. George Pearson. 1844.
Remains. Ed. George Pearson. 1846.

JOHN KNOX (c. 1513–1572)

An Admonition That the Faithful Christians in London, Newcastel, Barwycke and Others, May Avoide Gods Vengeaunce. 1554.
A Confession and Declaration of Praiers. 1554.

A *Faythfull Admonition Made unto the Professours of Gods Truthe in England.* 1554.

A *Godly Letter Sent too the Fayethfull in London, Newcastell, Barwycke, and to All Other within the Realme of Englande.* 1554.

The Copie of a Letter Sent to the Ladye Mary Dowagire, Regent of Scotland. 1556.

The Appellation of John Knoxe from the Cruell and Most Injust Sentence Pronounced against Him by the False Bishoppes and Clergie of Scotland. 1558.

The First Blast of the Trumpet against the Monstrous Regiment of Women. 1558.

The Copie of an Epistle Sent unto the Inhabitants of Newcastle and Barwike; in the End Whereof Is Added A Briefe Exhortation to England for the Spedie Imbrasing of Christes Gospel. 1559.

An Answer to a Great Nomber of Blasphemous Cavillations. 1560.

The Coppie of the Ressoning Which Was betwix the Abbote of Crossraguell and John Knox. 1563.

A Sermon Preached in the Publique Audience of Church of Edenbrough, the 19. of August 1565. 1566.

To His Loving Brethren. 1571.

An Answer to a Letter of a Jesuit Named Tyrie. 1572.

A Fort for the Afflicted. 1580.

Exposition upon the Fourth of Mathew. 1583.

The History of the Reformation of Religioun within the Realme of Scotland. 1587.

The First Booke of Discipline. 1719.

Writings. c. 1830.

The History of the Reformation in Scotland ⟨etc.⟩. Ed. William M'Gavin. 1831.

John Knox's Judgment on the True Nature of Christian Worship. 1842.

Works. Ed. David Laing. 1846–48. 6 vols.

JOHN HEYWOOD (c. 1497–c. 1575)

A Mery Play, betwene Johan Johan the Husbande, Tyb His Wife and Syr Jhän the Preest. 1533.

The Pardoner and the Frere. 1533.

The Play of the Wether. 1533.

A Play of Love. 1534.

Gentylnes and Nobylyte. 1536.

The Foure PP. c. 1545.

A Dialogue Conteinying the Number in Effect of All the Proverbes in the Englishe Tongue concerning Two Maner of Mariages. 1546.

An Hundred Epigrammes. 1550.

A Balade Specifienge Partly the Maner, Partly the Matter, in the Most Excellent Meetyng and Lyke Mariage betwene Our Soveraigne Lord and Our Soveraigne Lady, the Kynges and Queenes Highnes. 1554.

Two Hundred Epigrammes. 1555.

The Spider and the Flie. 1556.

A Breefe Balet Touching the Traytorous Takynge of Scarborow Castell. 1557.

A Fourth Hundred Epygrams. 1560.

A Ballad againsdt Sklander and Detraccion. 1562.

Woorkes. 1562.

Of a Number of Rattes. c. 1562.

A Dialogue on Wit and Folly ⟨Wytty and Witless⟩. Ed. F. W. Fairholt. 1846.

Dramatic Writings. Ed. John S. Farmer. 1905.

Proverbs, Epigrams, and Miscellanies. Ed. John S. Farmer. 1906.

Works and Miscellaneous Short Poems. Ed. Burton A. Milligan. 1956.

GEORGE GASCOIGNE (1530–1577)

A Hundreth Sundrie Flowers ⟨with *Supposes* by Ariosto (translator) and *Jocasta* (translator; with Francis Kinwelmarsh)⟩. 1573.

The Glasse of Government. 1575.

Posies. 1575.

The Whole Arte of Venerie or Hunting. 1575.

A Delicate Diet, for Daintemouthde Droonkardes. 1576.

[*The Complainte of Phylomene.* 1576.]

The Droomme of Doomes Day. 1576.

The Princelye Pleasures at the Courte of Kenelwoorth. 1576.

The Spoyle of Antwerpe. 1576.

The Steele Glas. 1576.

Whole Woorkes. Ed. A. Jeffes. 1587.

Complete Poems. Ed. W. Carew Hazlitt. 1869–70. 2 vols.

Complete Works. Ed. John W. Cunliffe. 1907–10. 2 vols.

The Steele Glas and The Complainte of Phylomene. Ed. William L. Wallace. 1975.

The Green Knight and Selected Prose. Ed. Roger Pooley. 1982.

RAPHAEL HOLINSHED (d. 1580)

The Chronicles of Englande, Scotlande and Ireland. 1577. 2 vols.

The Castrations of the Last Edition of Holinshed's Chronicle. Ed. J. Blackbourne. 1723.

Chronicles. Eds. Sir Henry Ellis et al. 1807–08. 6 vols.

GEORGE BUCHANAN (1506–1582)

Rudimenta Grammatices Thomae Linacri (translated into Latin). 1533.

Medea by Euripides (translated into Latin). 1544.

Jephthes; sive, Votum. 1554.

Alcestis by Euripides (translated into Latin). 1556.

De Caleto nuper ab Henrico II Recepta Carmen. 1558.

Psalmorum Davidis Paraphrasis Poetica. 1564–65.

Varia Poemata. 1566.

Tragoediae Selectae Aeschyli, Sophoclis, Euripidis (translated into Latin). 1567.

Elegiarum Liber I., Sylvarum Liber I., Endecasyllabon Lib. I. 1567.

Ane Admonitioun Direct to the Trew Lordis, Mantenaris of the Kingis Graces Authoritie. 1571.

De Maria Scotorum Regina. c. 1571.

Ane Detectioun of the Duinges of Marie Quene of Scottes. c. 1571.

Baptistes; sive, Calumnia. 1577.

Poemata Quae Supersunt Omnia. 1577.

De Jure Regni apud Scotos. 1579.

Rerum Scoticarum Historia. 1582.

Elegiarum Liber I., Silvarum Liber I., Hendecasyllabon Liber I., Epigrammaton Libri III, De Sphaera Fragmentum. 1584.

De Prosodia. 1595.

Vita. 1595.

Poemata Omnia. Ed. John Ray. 1615.

Poemata Quae Supersunt Omnia. 1621. 3 vols.

Ad Viros Sui Saeculi Clarissimos Eorumque ad Eundem Epistolae. Ed. James Oliphant. 1711.

Opera Omnia. Ed. Thomas Ruddiman. 1715. 2 vols.

Vernacular Writings. Ed. P. Hume Brown. 1892.

Tragedies. Eds. P. Sharratt and P. G. Walsh. 1983.

SIR PHILIP SIDNEY (1554–1586)

A Woorke concerning the Trewnesse of the Christian Religion by *Philip of Mornay Lord of Pessie Marlie* (translator; with Arthur Golding). 1587.

The Countesse of Pembrokes Arcadia. ⟨Eds. Fulke Greville, Lord Brooke, and Matthew Gwinne?⟩ 1590, 1593.

Syr P. S. His Astrophel and Stella. 1591.

The Defence of Poesie. 1595.

The Countesse of Pembrokes Arcadia: The Third Time Published with New Additions. 1598.

The Psalmes of David (translator; with others). Ed. S. W. Singer. 1823.

Miscellaneous Works. Ed. William Gray. 1829.

The Correspondence of Sir Philip Sidney and Hubert Languet. Ed. Steuart A. Pears. 1845.

Complete Poems. Ed. Alexander B. Grosart. 1873. 2 vols.

Defence of Poesie; Letter to Queen; Defence of Leicester. Ed. George E. Woodberry. 1908.

Complete Works. Ed. Albert Feuillerat. 1912–26. 4 vols.

Poems. Ed. William A. Ringler, Jr. 1962.

Selected Prose and Poetry. Ed. Robert Kimbrough. 1969.

Selected Poetry and Prose. Ed. David Kalstone. 1970.

Miscellaneous Prose. Eds. Katherine Duncan-Jones and Jan van Dorsten. 1973.

Selected Poems. Ed. Katherine Duncan-Jones. 1973.

JOHN FOXE (1517–1587)

A Fruitful Sermon Made of the Angelles by Martin Luther (translator). c. 1547.

To Young Men and Maidens by Joannes Oecolampadius (translator). c. 1548.

An Instruccyon of Christen Fayth by Urbanus Regius (translator). c. 1548.

De Non Plectendis Morte Adulteris. 1548.

De Lapsis in Ecclesiam Recipiendis. 1549.

Expostulatio Jesu Christi cum Humano Genere. c. 1550. Lost.

De Censura sive Excommunicatione Ecclesiastica. 1551.

Tables of Grammar. 1552.

Commentarii Rerum in Ecclesia Gestarum: Liber Primus. 1554.

Christus Triumphans; Panegyricon. 1556.

Locorum Communium Tituli et Ordines. 1557.

De Predicamentis Tabulae. 1557.

Ad Inclytos ac Praeponentes Algiae Proceres, Ordines et Status. 1557.

Mira ac Elegans Historia by John Philpot (translator). c. 1557. Lost.

Germaniae ad Angliam Gratulatio. 1559.

A Frendly Farewel by Nicholas Ridley (editor). 1559.

Rerum in Ecclesia Gestarum Commentarii. 1559–63. 2 vols.

Syllogiston. c. 1560.

A Brief Exhortation. 1563.

Actes and Monuments ⟨*The Book of Martyrs*⟩. 1563, 1570 (2 vols.).

Concio Funebris in Obitum Augustae Memoriae Ferdinandi Caesaris by Edmund Grindal (translated into Latin). 1564.

A Sermon of Christ Crucified. 1570.

Reformatio Legum Ecclesiasticarum (editor). 1571.

De Christo Crucifixo Concio. 1571.

The Gospels of the Fower Evangelistes (editor). 1571.

Pandectae Locorum Communium. 1572.

Contra Hieron. Osorium (with Walter Haddon). 1577.

A Commentarie upon the Fiftene Psalmes ⟨Psalms 120–134⟩ by Martin Luther, tr. Henry Bull (editor). 1577.

De Oliva Evangelica Concio. 1578.

Papa Confutatus. 1580.

De Christo Gratis Justificante. 1583.

A Godlie Exposition upon Certeine Chapters of Nehemiah by James Pilkington (editor). 1585.

Eicasmi; seu, Meditationes. 1687.

Writings (with John Bale and Miles Coverdale). 1831.

Acts and Monuments. Ed. S. R. Cattley. 1837–41 (8 vols.), 1843–49 (8 vols.).

Two Latin Comedies: Titus et Gesippus; Christus Triumphans. Ed. John Hazel Smith. 1973.

THOMAS WATSON (c. 1557–1592)

Sophoclis Antigone; huic Adduntur Pompae Quaedam, ex Singulis Tragoediae Actis Derivatae (translator). 1581.

The ΕΚΑΤΟΜΠΑΘΙΑ; or, Passionate Centurie of Love. 1582.

Amyntas. 1585.

Compendium Memoriae Localis. c. 1585.

Helenae Raptus by Coluthus (adaptation). 1586.

A Gratification unto John Case, for His Learned Booke, Lately in Praise of Musicke. 1589.

Meliboeus; sive, Ecloga in Obitum D. Francisci Walsinghami. 1590. Eng. tr. 1590.

The First Sett, of Italian Madrigalls Englished, Not to the Sense of the Originall Dittie, but after the Affection of the Noate. 1590.

Amintae Gaudia. 1592.

Poems. Ed. Edward Arber. 1870.

ROBERT GREENE (1558–1592)

Mamillia: A Mirrour or Looking-Glasse for the Ladies of England. 1583.

Arbasto: The Anatomie of Fortune. 1584.

Gwydonius: The Carde of Fancie. 1584.

The Debate between Follie and Love by Louis Labé (translator). 1584.

Morando: The Tritameron of Love. 1584–87. 2 vols.

The Myrrour of Modestie. 1584.

An Oration or Funerall Sermon Uttered at Roome, at the Buriall of Gregorie the 13 (translator). 1585.

Planetomachia. 1585.

Euphues His Censure to Philautus. 1587.

Penelopes Web. 1587.

Alcida: Greenes Metamorphosis. 1588.

Pandosto: The Triumph of Time. 1588.

Perimedes the Blacke-Smith. 1588.

Ciceronis Amor: Tullies Love. 1589.

Menaphon: Camillas Alarum to Slumbering Euphues. 1589.

The Spanish Masquerado. 1589.

Greenes Never Too Late. 1590.

Greenes Mourning Garment. 1590.

The Royal Exchange by Orazio Rinaldi (adaptation). 1590.

Greenes Farewell to Folly. 1591.

A Maydens Dreame: Upon the Death of the Right Honorable Sir Christopher Hatton. 1591.

A Notable Discovery of Coosenage. 1591.

The Second Part of Conny-Catching. 1591.

A Disputation betweene a Hee Conny-Catcher and a Shee Conny-Catcher. 1592.

The Blacke Bookes Messenger. 1592.

Philomela: The Lady Fitzwalters Nightingale. 1592.

A Quip for an Upstart Courtier. 1592.

Greenes Groats-Worth of Witte, Bought with a Million of Repentance. 1592.

The Repentance of Robert Greene, Maister of Artes. 1592.

Mamillia: The Second Part of the Triumph of Paris. 1593.

The Historie of Orlando Furioso (adaptation). 1594.

The Honorable Historie of Frier Bacon and Frier Bongay. 1594.

A Looking Glasse for London and England (with Thomas Lodge). 1594.

The Scottish Historie of James the Fourth. 1598.

The Comicall Historie of Alphonsus, King of Aragon. 1599.

Greenes Orpharion. 1599.

A Pleasant Conceyted Comedie of George à Greene. 1599.

A Paire of Turtle Doves; or, The Tragicall History of Bellora and Fidelio by Juan de Flores (translator). 1606.

Dramatic Works and Poems. Ed. Alexander Dyce. 1831. 2 vols.

Poems (with Christopher Marlowe). Ed. Robert Bell. 1856.

Life and Complete Works in Prose and Verse. Ed. Alexander B. Grosart. 1881–86. 15 vols.

Plays and Poems. Ed. J. Churton Collins. 1905. 2 vols.

Robert Greene. Ed. Thomas H. Dickinson. 1909.

Poetry. Ed. Tetsumaro Hayashi. 1977.

CHRISTOPHER MARLOWE (1564–1593)

Tamburlaine the Great. 1590.

The Troublesome Raigne and Lamentable Death of Edward the Second. 1594.

The Tragedie of Dido Queene of Carthage (with Thomas Nashe). 1594.

The Massacre at Paris. c. 1594.

Epigrammes ⟨by Sir John Davies⟩ *and Elegies* ⟨of Ovid (translator)⟩. c. 1595.

All Ovids Elegies ⟨Amores⟩ (translator). c. 1595–1600.

Hero and Leander (with George Chapman). 1598.

Lucans First Book Translated Line for Line. 1600.

The Tragicall History of D. Faustus. 1604.

The Famous Tragedy of the Rich Jew of Malta. 1633.

Works. Ed. Alexander Dyce. 1850. 3 vols.

Poems (with Robert Greene). Ed. Robert Bell. 1856.

Works. Ed. A. H. Bullen. 1885. 3 vols.

Christopher Marlowe. Ed. Havelock Ellis. 1887.

Works. Ed. C. F. Tucker Brooke. 1910.

Life and Works. Eds. Tucker Brooke et al. 1930. 6 vols.

Complete Plays. Ed. Irving Ribner. 1963.

Poems. Ed. Millar MacLure. 1968.

Complete Poems. Ed. Roma Gill. 1971.

Complete Works. Ed. Fredson T. Bowers. 1973. 2 vols.

Complete Plays and Poems. Eds. E. D. Pendry and J. C. Maxwell. 1976.

Complete Works. Ed. Roma Gill. 1987–　.

THOMAS KYD (1558–1594)

The Householders Philosophie by Torquato Tasso (translator). 1588.

The Spanish Tragedie. 1592.

The Trueth of the Most Wicked and Secret Murthering of John Brewen. 1592.

Cornelia. 1594.

Works. Ed. Frederick S. Boas. 1901.

ROBERT SOUTHWELL (c. 1561–1595)

An Epistle of Comfort. 1587.

Marie Magdalens Funerall Teares. 1591.

Saint Peters Complaint, with Other Poemes. 1595.

Moeoniae; or, Certaine Excellent Poems Omitted in the Last Impression of Peters Complaint. 1595.

The Triumphs over Death. 1595.

A Short Rule of Good Life ⟨with An Epistle of a Religious Priest unto His Father⟩. c. 1597.

An Humble Supplication to Her Majestie. c. 1600.

S. Peters Complaintt; and Saint Mary Magdalens Funerall Teares; with Sundry Other Poems. 1616.

St. Peters Complaint; Mary Magdalens Teares; with Other Works. 1620.

Prose Works. Ed. W. Joseph Walter. 1828.

Complete Poems. Ed. Alexander B. Grosart. 1872.

A Hundred Meditations on the Love of God. Ed. J. Morris. 1873.

Spiritual Exercises and Devotions. Ed. J. M. de Buck. 1931.

Poems. Eds. James H. McDonald and Nancy Pollard Brown. 1967.

Two Letters and Short Rules of a Good Life. Ed. Nancy Pollard Brown. 1973.

GEORGE PEELE (1556–1596)

The Araygnement of Paris. 1584.

The Device of the Pageant Borne before Wollstone Dixi Lord Maior of the Citie of London. 1585.

A Farewell Entituled to the Famous and Fortune Generalls of Our English Forces, Sir John Norris and Syr Frauncis Drake. 1589.

An Eglogue Gratulatorie Entituled to the Right Honourable and Renowned Shepheard of Albions Arcadia, Robert Earle of Essex and Ewe; Whereunto Is Annexed A Tale of Troy. 1589.

Polyhymnia. 1590.

Descensus Astreae. 1591.

The Hunting of Cupid. 1591.

The Honour of the Garter. 1593.

The Famous Chronicle of King Edward the First. 1593.

The Battell of Alcazar. 1594.

The Old Wives Tale. 1595.

The Love of King David and Fair Bethsabe, with the Tragedie of Absalon. 1599.

Merrie Conceited Jests of George Peele. 1607.

Works. Ed. Alexander Dyce. 1828–39. 3 vols.

Anglorum Feriae. Ed. R. Fitch. c. 1830.

Plays and Poems. Ed. Henry Morley. 1887.

Works. Ed. A. H. Bullen. 1888. 2 vols.

Life and Works. Eds. Charles Tyler Prouty et al. 1952–70. 3 vols.

George Peele. Ed. Sally Purcell. 1972.

EDMUND SPENSER (1552–1599)

The Shepheardes Calender. 1579.

Three Proper, and Wittie, Familiar Letters; Two Other, Very Commendable Letters (with Gabriel Harvey). 1580.

The Faerie Queene. 1590 [Books 1–3]; 1596 [Books 4–6]; 1609 [Books 1–12].

Muiopotmos. 1590.

Complaints. 1591.

Daphnaida: An Elegie upon the Death of the Noble and Vertuous Douglas Howard. 1591.

Prosopoia; or, Mother Hubbard's Tale. 1591.

Axiochus by Plato ⟨spurious⟩ (translator). 1592.

Colin Clouts Come Home Againe. 1595.

Amoretti and Epithalamion. 1595.

Fowre Hymnes. 1596.

Prothalamion; or, A Spousall Verse. 1596.

The Faerie Queen; The Shepheards Calendar; Together with Other Works. 1611 (First Folio).
Works. 1679.
Works. Ed. John Hughes. 1715. 6 vols.
Poetical Works. Ed. John Aikin. 1802. 6 vols.
Works. Ed. Henry John Todd. 1805. 8 vols.
Poetical Works. Ed. John Mitford. 1839. 5 vols.
Poetical Works. Ed. George S. Hillard. 1839. 5 vols.
Poetical Works. Ed. Francis J. Child. 1855. 5 vols.
Poetical Works. Ed. George Gilfillan. 1859. 5 vols.
Poetical Works. Ed. J. Payne Collier. 1862. 5 vols.
Complete Works. Eds. Richard Morris and John W. Hales. 1869.
Complete Works in Verse and Prose. Ed. Alexander B. Grosart. 1882–84. 9 vols.
Poems. Ed. W. B. Yeats. 1906.
Poetical Works. Eds. J. C. Smith and Ernest de Selincourt. 1909–10. 3 vols.
Works. Ed. W. L. Renwick. 1928–34. 4 vols.
Works: A Variorum Edition. Eds. Edwin Greenlaw, Charles Grosvenor Osgood, Frederick Morgan Padelford et al. 1932–57. 11 vols.
Selected Poetry. Ed. William Nelson. 1964.

GEORGE PUTTENHAM (c. 1530–c. 1600)

[*The Arte of English Poesie, Contrived into Three Books: The First of Poets and Poesie; the Second of Proportion; the Third of Ornament.* 1589.]
[*The Arte of English Poesie.* Ed. Edward Arber. 1869.]
[*The Arte of English Poesie.* Eds. Gladys Doidge Willcock and Alice Walker. 1936.]

RICHARD HOOKER (1553–1600)

Of the Lawes of Ecclesiastical Politie. 1593 [Books 1–4], 1617–18 [with *Certayne Divine Tractates, and Other Godly Sermons;* 6 parts]; 1597 [Book 5]; 1648 [Books 6–8].
A Learned Discourse of Justification, Workes, and How the Foundation of Faith Is Overthrowne. Ed. Henry Jackson. 1612.
The Answere to a Supplication Preferred by Mr. Walter Travers to the HH. Lordes of the Privie Counsell. Ed. Henry Jackson. 1612.
A Learned and Comfortable Sermon of the Certaintie and Perpetuitie of Faith in the Elect. Ed. Henry Jackson. 1612.
A Learned Sermon on the Nature of Pride. Ed. Henry Jackson. 1612.
A Remedie against Sorrow and Feare, Delivered in a Funerall Sermon. Ed. Henry Jackson. 1612.
Two Sermons upon Part of S. Judes Epistle. Ed. Henry Jackson. 1614.
Works. Ed. John Gauden. 1662. 2 parts.
Works. 1666.
Works. Ed. W. S. Dobson. 1825. 2 vols.
The Ecclesiastical Polity and Other Works. Ed. Benjamin Hanbury. 1830. 3 vols.
Works. Ed. John Keble. 1836. 3 vols.
Works. Ed. John Keble, rev. Richard William Church and Francis Paget. 1888. 3 vols.
Works (Folger Library Edition). Eds. W. Speed Hill et al. 1977– .

THOMAS NASHE (c. 1567–c. 1600)

The Anatomie of Absurditie. 1589.
The Returne of the Renowned Cavaliero Pasquill of England. 1589.
An Almond for a Parrat. 1590.

The First Part of Pasquils Apologie. 1590.
A Wonderfull, Strange and Miraculous, Astrologicall Prognostication. 1591.
Pierce Penilesse His Supplication to the Divell. 1592.
Strange Newes, of the Intercepting Certaine Letters. 1592.
Christs Teares over Jerusalem. 1593.
The Terrors of the Night. 1594.
The Unfortunate Traveller; or, The Life of Jacke Wilton. 1594.
The Tragedie of Dido Queene of Carthage (with Christopher Marlowe). 1594.
Have with You to Saffron-Walden. 1596.
Nashes Lenten Stuffe. 1599.
A Pleasant Comedie, Called Summers Last Will and Testament. 1600.
Complete Works. Ed. Alexander B. Grosart. 1883–85. 6 vols.
The Choise of Valentines. Ed. John S. Farmer. 1899.
Works. Ed. Ronald B. McKerrow. 1904–10. 5 vols.
Selected Works. Ed. Stanley Wells. 1964.
The Unfortunate Traveller and Other Works. Ed. J. B. Steane. 1972.

JOHN LYLY (c. 1554–1606)

Euphues: The Anatomy of Wit. 1579.
Euphues and His England. 1580.
A Moste Excellent Comedie of Alexander, Campaspe and Diogenes. 1584.
Sapho and Phao. 1584.
Pappe with an Hatchett. 1589.
A Whip for an Ape; or, Martin Displaied. 1589.
Endimion, the Man in the Moone. 1591.
Gallathea. 1592.
Midas. 1592.
Mother Bombie. 1594.
The Woman in the Moone. 1597.
Loves Metamorphosis. 1601.
Six Court Comedies. Ed. Edward Blount. 1632.
Dramatic Works. Ed. F. W. Fairholt. 1858. 2 vols.
Complete Works. Ed. R. Warwick Bond. 1902. 3 vols.

SIR EDWARD DYER (1543–1607)

[*A Sweet and Pleasant Sonet, Entituled: My Minde to Me a Kindgome Is.* c. 1624.]
Writings in Verse and Prose. Ed. Alexander B. Grosart. 1872.
At the Court of Queen Elizabeth: The Life and Lyrics of Sir Edward Dyer. Ed. Ralph M. Sargent. 1935.

THOMAS SACKVILLE, EARL OF DORSET (1536–1608)

The Tragedy of Gorboduc ⟨*Ferrex and Porrex*⟩ (with Thomas Norton). 1565.
Poetical Works. 1820.
Works. Ed. Reginald W. Sackville-West. 1859.

WILLIAM WARNER (c. 1558–1609)

Pan His Syrinx, or Pipe, Compact of Seven Reedes; Including in One, Seven Tragical and Comicall Arguments. c. 1584.
Albions England; or, Historicall Map of the Same Island. 1586 [Books 1–4], 1589 [Books 1–6], 1592 [Books 1–9], 1596 [Books 1–12], 1602 [Books 1–13; with *An Epitome of the Whole Historie of England*], 1606 [Books 14–16; as *A Continuance of Albions England*].
Menaecmi by Plautus (translator). 1595.

BARNABE BARNES (c. 1569–1609)

Parthenophil and Parthenophe: Sonnettes, Madrigals, Elegies and Odes. 1593.

A Divine Centurie of Spirituall Sonnets. 1595.

Foure Bookes of Offices: Enabling Privat Persons for the Speciall Service of All Good Princes and Policies. 1606.

The Divils Charter: A Tragedie Conteining the Life and Death of Pope Alexander the Sixt. 1607.

Poems. Ed. Alexander B. Grosart. 1875. 2 parts.

GEORGE TURBERVILLE (c. 1544–1597)

The Heroycall Epistles of the Learned Poet Publius Ovidius Naso in English Verse; with Aulus Sabinus Aunsweres to Certaine of the Same (translator). 1567.

Epitaphes, Epigrams, Songs and Sonets, with a Discourse of the Friendly Affections of Tymetes to Pyndara His Ladie. 1567.

The Eglogs of the Poet B. Mantuan Carmelitan (translator). 1567.

A Plaine Path to Perfect Vertue by Dominicus Mancinus (translator). 1568.

The Book of Faulconrie and Hauking, for the Onely Delight and Pleasure of All Nobleman and Gentleman (editor). 1575.

Tragicall Tales Translated out of Sundrie Italians, with Some Other Broken Pamphlettes and Epistles Sent to Certaine His Frends in England, at His Being in Moscovia 1569 (translator). 1587.

SIR JOHN HARINGTON (1560–1612)

Orlando Furioso in English Heroical Verse (translator). 1591, 1634 (with *Epigrams*).

A New Discourse of a Stale Subject, Called the Metamorphosis of Ajax. 1596.

An Anatomie of the Metamorpho-sed Ajax. 1596.

An Apologie, or, Rather, a Retraction. 1596.

The Englishmans Doctor; or, The School of Salerne (translator). 1607.

Epigrams Both Pleasant and Serious, Never Before Printed. 1615.

The Most Elegant and Witty Epigrams Digested in Foure Bookes, Three Whereof Never Before Published. 1618.

A Briefe View of the State of the Church of England in Q. Elizabeth's and King James His Reigne, to the Yeere 1608. Ed. John Chetwind. 1653.

Nugae Antiquae: Being a Miscellaneous Collection of Original Papers in Prose and Verse (with others). Ed. Henry Harington. 1769–75. 2 vols.

A Short View of the State of Ireland. Ed. William D. Macray. 1879.

A Tract on the Succession of the Crown. Ed. Clemens R. Markham. 1880.

Letters and Epigrams, Together with The Prayse of Private Life. Ed. Norman Egbert McClure. 1930.

The Arundel Harington Manuscript of Tudor Poetry (editor; with John Harington). Ed. Ruth Hughey. 1960. 2 vols.

A Supplie or Addicion to the Catalogue of Bishops, *to the Yeare 1608.* Ed. R. H. Miller. 1979.

HENRY CONSTABLE (1562–1613)

Examen pacifique de la doctrine des Huguenots: Prouvant que nous ne duerions pas condemner les Huguenots pour heretiques jusques à ce qu'on ait faict nouvelle preuve. 1589.

Diana: The Praises of His Mistress, in Certaine Sweete Sonnets. 1592, c. 1594.

A Discoverye of a Counterfecte Conference Helde at a Counterfecte Place, by Counterfecte Travellers, for Thadvancement of a Counterfecte Tytle, and Invented, Printed, and

Published by One (Person) That Dare Not Avowe His Name. 1600.

Spirituall Sonnettes to the Honour of God, and Hys Sayntes. Ed. Thomas Park. 1815.

Diana: The Sonnets and Other Poems. Ed. William Carew Hazlitt. 1859.

Poems and Sonnets. Ed. John Gray. 1897.

Poems. Ed. Joan Grundy. 1960.

SIR THOMAS OVERBURY (1581–1613)

A Wife, Now a Widowe. 1614, 1614 (with *Characters* and *Conceited News* [with others]), 1638 (16th ed.).

The First and Second Part of the Remedy of Love by Ovid (translator). 1620.

Observations in His Travailes upon the State of the XVII. Provinces as They Stood Anno Dom. 1609. 1626.

Miscellaneous Works in Verse and Prose. 1756.

Miscellaneous Works in Verse and Prose. Ed. Edward F. Rimbault. 1856.

The Overburian Characters; to Which Is Added A Wife. Ed. W. J. Paylor. 1936.

RICHARD HAKLUYT (c. 1552–1616)

Divers Voyages Touching the Discoverie of America, and the Ilands Adjacent to the Same, Made First of All by Our Englishmen, and Afterward by the Frenchmen and Britons. 1582.

A Notable History Containing Foure Voyages Made by Certayne French Captaynes unto Florida by René de Laudonnière (translator). 1587.

De Orbo Novo by Pietro Martire d'Anghiera (editor). 1587.

The Principall Navigations, Voiages and Discoveries of the English Nation, Made by Sea or over Land to the Most Remote and Farthest Distant Quarters of the Earth at Any Time within the Compasse of These 1500 Yeeres. 1589, 1598–1600 (3 vols.).

The Discoveries of the World from Their First Originall unto the Yeere of Our Lord 1555 by Antonio Galvano (translator). 1601.

Virginia Richly Valued, by the Description of the Maine Land of Florida, Her Next Neighbour by Hernando de Soto (translator). 1609.

Hakluyt's Collection of the Early Voyages, Travels, and Discoveries of the English Nation. Ed. R. H. Evans. 1809–12. 5 vols.

A Discourse concerning Western Planting. Eds. Leonard Wood and Charles Deane. 1877.

The Principal Navigations, Voyages, Traffiques and Discoveries of the English Nation. Ed. Edmund Goldsmid. 1884–90. 16 vols.

Early English and French Voyages, Chiefly from Hakluyt, 1534–1608. Ed. Henry S. Burrage. 1906.

The Original Writings and Correspondence of the Two Richard Hakluyts. Ed. E. G. R. Taylor. 1935. 2 vols.

Voyages and Documents. Ed. Janet Hampden. 1958.

Virginia Voyages from Hakluyt. Eds. David B. Quinn and Alison M. Quinn. 1973.

WILLIAM SHAKESPEARE (1564–1616)

Venus and Adonis. 1593, 1594, 1596, 1599, 1602, 1617, 1620, 1627, 1630, 1636.

The Rape of Lucrece. 1594, 1598, 1600, 1616, 1617, 1624, 1632.

Henry VI. 1594, 1595, 1600, 1619.

Titus Andronicus. 1594, 1600.

The Taming of the Shrew. 1594.

Romeo and Juliet. 1597, 1599, 1609.
Richard III. 1597, 1598.
Richard II. 1597, 1598, 1608.
Love's Labour's Lost. 1598.
Henry IV. 1598, 1599, 1604, 1608, 1610, 1613.
The Passionate Pilgrim. 1599, 1612.
A Midsummer Night's Dream. 1600.
The Merchant of Venice. 1600.
Much Ado about Nothing. 1600.
Henry V. 1600, 1602.
The Phoenix and the Turtle. 1601, 1611.
The Merry Wives of Windsor. 1602, 1619.
Hamlet. 1603, 1604, 1611.
King Lear. 1608.
Troilus and Cressida. 1609.
Sonnets. 1609.
Pericles. 1609.
Othello. 1622.
Mr. William Shakespeares Comedies, Histories & Tragedies. Eds. John Heminge and Henry Condell. 1623 (First Folio), 1632 (Second Folio), 1663 (Third Folio), 1685 (Fourth Folio).
Poems. 1640.
Works. Ed. Nicholas Rowe. 1709. 6 vols.
Works. Ed. Alexander Pope. 1723–25. 6 vols.
Works. Ed. Lewis Theobald. 1733. 7 vols.
Works. Ed. Thomas Hanmer. 1743–44. 6 vols.
Works. Ed. William Warburton. 1747. 8 vols.
Plays. Ed. Samuel Johnson. 1765. 8 vols.
Twenty of the Plays of Shakespeare. Ed. George Steevens. 1766. 4 vols.
Plays and Poems. Ed. Edmond Malone. 1790. 10 vols.
The Family Shakespeare. Ed. Thomas Bowdler. 1807. 4 vols.
Pictorial Edition of the Works of Shakespeare. Ed. Charles Knight. 1838–43. 8 vols.
Works. Ed. J. Payne Collier. 1842–44. 8 vols.
Works. Ed. H. N. Hudson. 1851–56. 11 vols.
Works. Ed. Alexander Dyce. 1857. 6 vols.
Works. Ed. Richard Grant White. 1857–66. 12 vols.
Works (Cambridge Edition). Eds. William George Clark, John Glover, and William Aldis Wright. 1863–66. 9 vols.
A New Variorum Edition of the Works of Shakespeare. Eds. H. H. Furness et al. 1871–   .
Works. Ed. W. J. Rolfe. 1871–96. 40 vols.
The Pitt Press Shakespeare. Ed. A. W. Verity. 1890–1905. 13 vols.
The Warwick Shakespeare. 1893–1938. 13 vols.
The Temple Shakespeare. Ed. Israel Gollancz. 1894–97. 40 vols.
The Arden Shakespeare. Eds. W. J. Craig, R. H. Case et al. 1899–1924. 37 vols.
The Shakespeare Apocrypha. Ed. C. F. Tucker Brooke. 1908.
The Yale Shakespeare. Eds. Wilbur L. Cross, Tucker Brooke, and Willard Highley Durham. 1917–27. 40 vols.
The New Shakespeare (Cambridge Edition). Eds. Arthur Quiller-Couch and John Dover Wilson. 1921–62. 38 vols.
The New Temple Shakespeare. Ed. M. R. Ridley. 1934–36. 39 vols.
Works. Ed. George Lyman Kittredge. 1936.
The Penguin Shakespeare. Ed. G. B. Harrison. 1937–59. 36 vols.
The New Clarendon Shakespeare. Ed. R. E. C. Houghton. 1938–   .
The Arden Shakespeare. Eds. Una Ellis-Fermor et al. 1951–   .

The Complete Pelican Shakespeare. Ed. Alfred Harbage. 1969.
The Complete Signet Classic Shakespeare. Ed. Sylvan Barnet. 1972.
The Oxford Shakespeare. Ed. Stanley Wells. 1982–   .
The New Cambridge Shakespeare. Ed. Philip Brockbank. 1984–   .

FRANCIS BEAUMONT (c. 1585–1616)

Salmacis and Hermaphroditus. 1602.
The Maske of the Inner Temple and Grayes Inne. 1613.
The Knight of the Burning Pestle. 1613.
Poems. 1640, 1653.

JOHN FLETCHER (1579–1625)

The Faithfull Shepheardesse. c. 1609.
The Elder Brother (with Philip Massinger). 1637.
Monsieur Thomas. 1639.
Wit with-out Money. 1639.
The Bloody Brother; or, Rollo, Duke of Normandy ⟨with George Chapman? or: and Philip Massinger?⟩. 1639.
The Night Walker; or, The Little Theife. 1640.
Rule a Wife and Have a Wife. 1640.
The Wild-Goose Chase. 1652.
[*The Widow* (with Thomas Middleton). 1652.]
The Custom of the Country (with Philip Massinger). 1717.
Sir John van Olden Barnavelt (with Philip Massinger). Ed. Wilhelmina P. Frijlinck. 1922.

BEAUMONT AND FLETCHER

The Woman Hater. 1607.
Cupids Revenge. 1615.
The Scornful Ladie. 1616.
A King and No King. 1619.
The Maides Tragedy. 1619.
Phylaster; or, Love Lyes a Bleeding. 1620.
The Tragedy of Thierry King of France and His Brother Theodoret (with Philip Massinger). 1621.
Comedies and Tragedies. 1647 (First Folio). [Contains: *The Mad Lover* by John Fletcher; *The Spanish Curate* by John Fletcher and Philip Massinger; *The Little French Lawyer* by John Fletcher and Philip Massinger; *The Noble Gentleman* by Beaumont and Fletcher; *The Captain* by Beaumont and Fletcher; *Beggar's Bush* by John Fletcher and Philip Massinger; *The Coxcomb* by Beaumont and Fletcher; *The False One* by John Fletcher and Philip Massinger; *The Chances* by John Fletcher; *The Loyal Subject* by John Fletcher; *The Laws of Candy* by John Fletcher and John Ford; *The Lovers' Progress* by John Fletcher and Philip Massinger; *The Island Princess* by John Fletcher; *The Humorous Lieutenant* by John Fletcher; *The Nice Valour* by John Fletcher ⟨with Thomas Middleton?⟩; *The Maid in the Mill* by John Fletcher and William Rowley; *The Prophetess* by John Fletcher and Philip Massinger; *The Tragedy of Bonduca* by John Fletcher; *The Sea Voyage* by John Fletcher and Philip Massinger; *The Double Marriage* by John Fletcher and Philip Massinger; *The Pilgrim* by John Fletcher; *The Knight of Malta* by John Fletcher, Philip Massinger, and Nathan Field; *The Woman's Prize* by John Fletcher; *Love's Cure* by John Fletcher and Philip Massinger; *The Honest Man's Fortune* by John Fletcher ⟨and Philip Massinger? and Nathan Field?⟩; *The Queen of Corinth* by John Fletcher, Philip Massinger, and Nathan Field; *Women Pleas'd* by John Fletcher; *A Wife for a Month* by John Fletcher; *Wit at Several Weapons* by Beaumont and Fletcher ⟨and Thomas Middleton? and William

Rowley?⟩; *The Tragedy of Valentinian* by John Fletcher;
The Fair Maid of the Inn by John Fletcher ⟨and Philip
Massinger? and William Rowley? and John Ford?⟩; *Love's
Pilgrimage* by John Fletcher ⟨and Francis Beaumont?⟩;
The Masque of the Inner Temple and Gray's Inn by
Francis Beaumont; *Four Plays or Moral Representa-
tions in One* by Beaumont and Fletcher and Nathan
Field.]
Fifty Comedies and Tragedies. 1679 (Second Folio).
Works. 1711. 7 vols.
Works. 1750. 10 vols.
Dramatick Works. Ed. George Colman the Elder. 1778.
10 vols.
Works. Ed. Henry Weber. 1812. 14 vols.
Works. Ed. Alexander Dyce. 1843–46. 11 vols.
*Beaumont and Fletcher; or, The Finest Scenes, Lyrics and
Other Beauties of Those Two Poets.* Ed. Leigh Hunt.
1855.
Lyric Poems. Ed. Ernest Rhys. 1897.
Beaumont and Fletcher. Ed. Arnold Glover and A. R. Waller.
1905–12. 10 vols.
Songs and Lyrics from the Plays. Ed. Edmund H. Fellowes.
1928.
Dramatic Works. Eds. Fredson T. Bowers et al. 1966–   .

SIR WALTER RALEGH (c. 1554–1618)

A Report of the Truth of the Fight about the Iles of the Acores.
1591. 2 parts.
*The Discoverie of the Large, Rich and Bewtiful Empire of Gui-
ana; with a Relation of the Great and Golden City of
Manoa.* 1596.
The History of the World. 1614.
The Prerogative of Parlaments in England. 1628.
Sir Walter Raleighs Instructions to His Sonne, and to Posterity.
1632. 2 parts.
[*Tubus Historicus: An Historical Perspective; Discovering the
Empires and Kingdoms of the World.* 1636.]
[*The Life and Death of Mahomat.* 1637.]
The Prince; or, Maxims of State. 1642.
*To Day a Man, Tomorrow None; or, Sir Walter Rawleigh's
Farewell to His Lady, the Night before Hee Was Beheaded.*
1644.
*A Discourse of the Originall and Fundamentall Cause of Nat-
ural Warre with the Mysery of Invasive Warre.* 1650.
Sir Walter Rawleigh His Apologie for His Voyage to Guiana.
1650.
[*Observations concerning the Royall Navy.* 1650.]
Judicious and Select Essayes and Observations. 1650.
Maxims of State. 1650. 3 parts.
*Sir Walter Raleigh's Sceptick; or, Speculations; and Observa-
tions on the Magnificency and Opulency of Cities; His
Seat of Government; and Letters to the Kings Majestie.*
1651.
[*All Is Not Gold That Glisters.* 1651.]
[*Observations, Touching Trade & Commerce with the Hol-
lander.* 1653.]
Remains. 1657. 2 parts.
[*The Cabinet-Council.* 1658.]
The Pilgrimage. 1681.
[*An Introduction to a Breviary of the History of England.*
1693.]
[*A Discourse of Sea-Ports.* 1700.]
*Three Discourses: I. Of a War with Spain, and Our Protecting
the Netherlands; II. Of the Original and Fundamental*

*Cause of Natural, Arbitrary and Civil War; III. Of Ec-
clesiastical Power.* 1702.
[*A Military Discourse.* 1734.]
*The Interest of England with Regard to Foreign Alliances, Ex-
plained in Two Discourses.* 1750.
*Works. Political, Commercial, and Philosophical; Together
with His Letters and Poems.* Ed. Thomas Birch. 1751.
2 vols.
Poems. Ed. Sir Samuel Egerton Brydges. 1813.
Works. 1829. 8 vols.
Choice Passages from the Writings and Letters. Ed. Alexander
B. Grosart. 1892.
*Sir Walter Ralegh: "The Shepherd of the Ocean": Selections
from His Poetry and Prose.* Ed. Frank Cheney Hersey.
1916.
Selections from His Historie of the World, His Letters, etc. Ed.
G. E. Hadow. 1917.
Poems. Ed. Agnes M. C. Latham. 1929.
Selected Prose and Poetry. Ed. Agnes M. C. Latham. 1965.
A Choice of Sir Walter Raleigh's Verse. Ed. Robert Nye.
1972.
Selected Writings. Ed. Gerald Hammond. 1984.

SAMUEL DANIEL (1563–1619)

*The Worthy Tract of Paulus Jovius, Contayning a Discourse of
Rare Inventions, Both Military and Amorous Called Im-
prese* (translator). 1585.
*Delia: Contayning Certain Sonnets; with The Complaint of
Rosamond.* 1592.
Delia and Rosamond Augmented; Cleopatra. 1594. 3 parts.
*The Civile Warres between the Two Houses of Lancaster and
Yorke.* 1595 [Books 1–4]; 1595 [Books 1–5]; 1609 [Books
1–8].
Poeticall Essayes. 1599.
Works. 1601.
*A Panegyrike Congratulatorie to the Kings Majestie; Also Cer-
taine Epistles.* 1603.
*A Panegyrike Congratulatorie to the Kings Majestie; Also Cer-
taine Epistles; with A Defence of Ryme.* 1603. 2 parts.
The True Description of a Royall Masque. 1604.
The Vision of the 12. Goddesses. 1604.
Certaine Small Poems; with The Tragedy of Philotas. 1605.
The Queenes Arcadia: A Pastoral Trage-comedie. 1606.
Songs for the Lute Viol and Voice. 1606.
*A Funerall Poem uppon the Death of the Late Noble Earle of
Devonshyre.* c. 1606.
Certaine Small Works. 1607 (2 parts); 1611 (4 parts).
The First Part of the Historie of England. 1612.
Hymens Triumph: A Pastorall Tragecomaedie. 1615.
The Collection of the Historie of England. c. 1618.
Whole Workes in Poetrie. Ed. John Daniel. 1623.
[*An Introduction to a Breviary of the History of England.*
1693.]
Poetical Works. 1718. 2 vols.
Complete Works in Verse and Prose. Ed. Alexander B. Grosart.
1885–96. 5 vols.
*A Selection from the Poetry of Samuel Daniel and Michael
Drayton.* Ed. H. C. Beeching. 1899.
Poems and A Defence of Ryme. Ed. Arthur Colby Sprague.
1930.
Musophilus: Containing a General Defense of All Learning.
Ed. Raymond Himelick. 1965.
*Samuel Daniel—The Brotherton Manuscript: A Study in Au-
thorship.* Ed. John Pitcher. 1981.

THOMAS CAMPION (1567–1620)

Poemata: Ad Thamesin; Fragmentum Umbrae; Liber Elegiarum; Liber Epigrammatum. 1595.

A Booke of Ayres, Set Foorth to Be Song to the Lute, Orpherian and Base Violl by Philip Rosseter (words and music; with others). 1601.

Observations in the Art of English Poesie. 1602.

The Discription of a Maske, Presented before the Kinges Majestie at White-Hall, on Twelfth Night Last, in Honour of the Lord Hayes, and His Bride, Daughter and Heire to the Honourable the Lord Dennye. 1607.

Two Bookes of Ayres: The First Containing Divine and Morall Songs; the Second, Light Conceits of Lovers. 1610.

A New Way of Making Fowre Parts in Counterpoint, by a Most Familiar, and Infallible Rule. 1610.

The First Booke of Ayres: Containing Divine and Morall Songs. c. 1613.

A Relation of the Late Royall Entertainment Given by the Right Honourable the Lord Knowles, at Cawsome-House neere Redding. 1613.

Songs of Mourning: Bewailing the Untimely Death of Prince Henry. 1613.

The Description of a Maske: Presented in the Banqueting Roome at Whitehall, on Saint Stephens Night Last, at the Mariage of the Right Honourable the Earle of Somerset: and the Right Noble the Lady Frances Howard. 1614.

The Third and Fourth Booke of Ayres. c. 1617.

[*The Ayres That Were Sung and Played, at Brougham Castle in Westmerland, in the Kings Entertainment.* 1618.]

Epigrammatum Libri II; Umbra; Elegiarum Liber Unus. 1619.

A Friends Advice, in an Excellent Ditty, concerning the Variable Changes in This Life. c. 1659.

The Art of Descant; or, Composing of Musick in Parts, by a Most Familiar and Easie Rule. 1664.

Works. Ed. A. H. Bullen. 1889.

Lyric Poems. Ed. Ernest Rhys. 1896.

Songs and Masques, with Observations in the Art of English Poesy. Ed. A. H. Bullen. 1903.

Poetical Works in English. Ed. Percival Vivian. 1907.

Works. Ed. Percival Vivian. 1909.

Selected Poems. Eds. G. D. H. Cole and M. I. Cole. 1928.

Works. Ed. Walter R. Davis. 1967.

Selected Songs. Ed. W. H. Auden. 1973.

WILLIAM CAMDEN (1551–1623)

Britannia; sive, Florentissimorum Regnorum, Angliae, Scotiae, Hiberniae, et Insularum Adiacentium ex Intima Antiquitate Chorographica Descriptio. 1586.

Institutio Graecae Grammatices Compendiaria. 1595.

Reges, Reginae, Nobiles & Alij in Ecclesia Collegiata B. Petri Westmonasterij Sepulti, usque ad Annum 1600. 1600.

Anglica, Hibernica, Normannica, Cambrica à Veteribus Scripta (editor). 1602.

Remaines of a Greater Worke, concerning Britaine. 1605. 2 parts.

Annales Rerum Anglicarum et Hibernicarum Regnante Elizabetha. 1615–25. 2 vols.

GILES FLETCHER (c. 1586–1623)

Christs Victorie and Triumph in Heaven and Earth, over and after Death. 1610.

The Reward of the Faithfull. 1623.

Poems. Ed. Alexander B. Grosart. 1868.

Complete Poems. Ed. Alexander B. Grosart. 1876.

Poetical Works (with Phineas Fletcher). Ed. Frederick S. Boas. 1908–09. 2 vols.

PHINEAS FLETCHER (1582–1650)

Locustae; vel, Pietas Jesuitica ⟨with Eng. tr.: *The Locusts; or, The Apollyonists*⟩. 1627. 2 parts.

Brittain's Ida. 1628.

Sicelides: A Piscatory. 1631.

Joy in Tribulation; or, Consolations for Afflicted Spirits. 1632.

The Way to Blessednes; or, A Treatise or Commentary on the First Psalme. 1632.

De Literis Antiquae Britanniae by Giles Fletcher the Elder (editor). 1633.

The Purple Island; or, The Isle of Man; Together with Piscatorie Eclogs and Other Poetical Miscellanies. 1633. 2 parts.

A Father's Testament. 1670.

Piscatory Eclogues, with Other Poetical Miscellanies. 1771.

Poems. Ed. Alexander B. Grosart. 1869. 4 vols.

The Spenser of His Age: Selected Poetry. Ed. Walter Jerrold. 1905.

Poetical Works (with Giles Fletcher). Ed. Frederick S. Boas. 1908–09. 2 vols.

Venus and Anchises (Brittain's Ida) and Other Poems. Ed. Ethel Seaton. 1926.

THOMAS LODGE (1558–1625)

Protagones can know Apelles by his line . . . ⟨*A Defence of Poetry, Music and Stage Plays*⟩. 1579.

The Straunge and Wonderfull Adventures of Don Simonides by Barnaby Rich (revised by Lodge). 1581.

An Alarum against Usurers; Heereunto Are Annexed the Delectable Histories of Forbonius and Prisceria; with the Lamentable Complaint of Truth over England. 1584.

Scillaes Metamorphosis: Enterlaced with the Unfortunate Love of Glaucus; Whereunto Is Annexed the Delectable Discourse of the Discontented Satyre; with Sundrie Other Poems and Sonnets. 1589.

Rosalynde: Euphues Golden Legacie. 1590.

Catharos: Diogenes in His Singularitie. 1591.

The Famous, True and Historicall Life of Robert Second Duke of Normandy. 1591.

Euphues Shadow: The Battaile of the Sences; Hereunto Is Annexed the Deafe Mans Dialogue, Contayning Philamis Athanatos. 1592.

The Life and Death of William Long Beard. 1593.

Phillis: Honoured with Pastorall Sonnets, Elegies, and Amorous Delights; Where-unto Is Annexed, The Tragicall Complaynt of Elstred. 1593.

The Wounds of Civill War: Lively Set Forth in the Tragedies of Marius and Scilla. 1594.

A Looking Glasse for London and England (with Robert Greene). 1594.

A Fig for Momus: Containing Pleasant Varietie, Included in Satyres, Eclogues, and Epistles. 1595.

The Divel Conjured. 1596.

A Margarite of America. 1596.

Wits Miserie and the Worlds Madnesse. 1596.

Prosopopeia: Containing the Teares of the Holy, Marie. 1596.

The Flowers of Lodowicke of Granado by Luis de Granada (translator). 1601.

The Famous and Memorable Workes of Josephus (translator). 1602.

A Treatise of the Plague by François Valleriola (translator). 1603.

[*A Paradise of Praiers: Containing the Puritie of Devotion, and Meditation* by Luis de Granada (translator). 1609.]

The Workes of Lucius Annaeus Seneca (translator). 1614.

A Learned Summary upon the Famous Poeme of William of Saluste Lord of Bartas (translator). 1621.

The Countesse of Lincolnes Nurserie (editor). 1622.

Glaucus and Silla, with Other Lyrical and Pastoral Poems. Ed. S. W. Singer. 1819.

Complete Works. Ed. Edmund Gosse. 1883. 4 vols.

NICHOLAS BRETON (c. 1545–c. 1626)

A Smale Handfull of Fragrant Flowers. 1575.

A Floorish upon Fancie. 1577.

The Workes of a Young Wyt, Trust Up with a Fardell of Pretie Fancies. 1577.

A Discourse in Commendation of the Valiant Gentleman, Maister Frauncis Drake. 1581.

The Historie of the Life and Fortune of Don Federigo di Terra Nuova. 1590.

Brittons Bowre of Delights: Contayning Many, Most Delectable and Fine Devises, of Rare Epitaphes, Pleasant Poems, Pastoralls and Sonnets (with others). 1591.

The Pilgrimage to Paradise, Joyned with the Countesse of Penbrooke's Love. 1592.

Marie Magdalens Love; A Solemne Passion of the Soules Love. 1595.

Auspicante Jehova: Maries Exercise. 1597.

The Arbor of Amorous Devises (with others). 1597.

The Wil of Wits, Wits Will or Wils Wit, Chuse You Whether. 1597.

Wits Trenchmour, in a Conference Had betwixt a Scholler and an Angler. 1597.

The Passions of the Spirit. 1599.

Pasquils Mad-Cap, and His Message. 1600.

The Second Part of Pasquil's Mad-Cap Intituled: The Fooles-Cap. 1600.

Pasquils Mistresse; or, The Worthie and Unworthie Woman. 1600.

Pasquils Passe, and Passeth Not. 1600.

Melancholike Humours, in Verses of Diverse Natures. 1600.

The Strange Fortunes of Two Excellent Princes. 1600.

No Whippinge, Nor Trippinge: But a Kinde Friendly Snippinge. 1601.

A Divine Poem, Divided into Two Parts: The Ravisht Soule, and the Blessed Weeper. 1601.

An Excellent Poeme, upon the Longing of a Blessed Heart. 1601.

The Soules Heavenly Exercise Set Downe in Diverse Godly Meditations, Both Prose and Verse. 1601.

[*The Passion of a Discontented Minde.* 1601.]

The Mothers Blessing. 1602.

Olde Mad-Cappes New Gally-Mawfrey. 1602.

A Poste with a Madde Packet of Letters. 1602–05. 2 parts.

The Soules Harmony. 1602.

Wonders Worth the Hearing. 1602.

A True Description of Unthankfulnesse. 1602.

A Dialogue Full of Pithe and Pleasure. 1603.

A Merrie Dialogue betwixt the Taker and the Mistaker. 1603, 1635 (as *A Mad World My Masters*).

Grimellos Fortunes, with His Entertainment in His Travaile. 1604.

The Passionate Shepheard; or, The Shepheardes Love. 1604.

[*A Piece of Friar Bacons Brazen-Heads Prophesie.* 1604.]

[*The Case Is Altered: How? Aske Dalio, and Millo.* 1604.]

An Olde Mans Lesson, and: A Young Mans Love. 1605.

Honest Counsaile: A Merrie Fitte of a Poeticall Furie. 1605.

The Honour of Valour. 1605.

I Pray You Be Not Angrie: A Pleasant and Merry Dialogue, betweene Two Travellers. 1605.

The Soules Immortal Crowne. 1605.

Choice, Chance, and Change; or, Conceites in Their Colours. 1606.

A Murmurer. 1607.

Wits Private Wealth: Stored with Choice Commodities to Content the Minde. 1607.

Divine Considerations of the Soule, concerning the Excellencie of God, and the Vilenesse of Man. 1608.

The Uncasing of Machivils Instructions to His Sonne. 1613.

I Would, and Would Not. 1614.

Characters upon Essaies Morall, and Divine. 1615.

The Good and the Badde; or, Descriptions of the Worthies, and Unworthies of This Age. 1616.

Crossing of Proverbs. 1616. 2 parts.

The Hate of Treason, with a Touch of the Late Treason. 1616.

Machiavells Dogge. 1617.

The Shepheards Delight. c. 1617.

The Court and Country; or, A Briefe Discourse betweene the Courtier and Country-man. 1618.

Conceyted Letters, Newly Layde Open. 1618.

Strange Newes out of Divers Countries. 1622.

Soothing of Proverbs, with Only True Forsooth. 1626.

Fantasticks: Serving for a Perpetuall Prognostication. 1626.

The Figure of Foure. 1626–31. 2 parts.

Works in Verse and Prose. Ed. Alexander B. Grosart. 1879. 2 vols.

A Bower of Delights: Being Interwoven Verse and Prose from the Works. Ed. Alexander B. Grosart. 1893.

A Mad World My Masters and Other Prose Works. Ed. Ursula Kentish-Wright. 1929. 2 vols.

Two Pamphlets: Grimellos Fortunes; An Ode Mans Lesson. Ed. E. G. Morice. 1936.

Poems Not Hitherto Reprinted. Ed. Jean Robertson. 1952.

LANCELOT ANDREWES (1555–1626)

The Wonderfull Combate, for Gods Glorie and Mans Salvation, betweene Christ and Satan. 1592.

Quaestionis, Numquid per Ius Divinum, Magistratui Liceat, a Reo Iusiurandum Exigere, Theologica Determinatio. 1593.

A Serom on the Pestilence. 1603.

The Copie of the Sermon Preached on Good Friday Last before the Kings Majestie. 1604.

A Sermon Preached before the Kings Majestie, at Hampton Court, concerning the Right and Power of Calling Assemblies. 1606. Latin tr. 1608 (as *Concio Habita Coram Serenissimo, Jacobo, Rege*).

Concio Latinè Habita Coram Regia Majestate, in Aula Grenuici. 1606.

Tortura Torti. 1609.

A Sermon Preached before the Kings Majestie at White-hall, on Monday the 25. of December, Being Christmas Day, Anno 1609. 1610.

Responsio ad Apologiam Cardinalis Bellarmini, Quam Nuper Edidit contra Praefationem Monitoriam Jacobi Regis. 1610.

A Sermon Preached before His Majestie on Sunday the Fifth of August Last, at Holbendie. 1610.

A Sermon Preached before His Majestie at White-hall, on Tuesday the 25. of December Last, Being Christmas Day. 1610.

Two Sermons Preached before the Kings Majestie at Whitehall. 1610.

Two Sermons Preached before the Kings Majestie. 1610.

A Sermon Preached before His Majestie at White-hall, on the 24. of March Last, Being Easter Day. 1611.

Scala Coeli: Nineteene Sermons concerning Prayer. 1611.

A Sermon Preached before His Majestie, at Whitehall on Easter Day Last. 1614.

A Sermon Preached before His Majestie, at Whitehall the Fift of November Last, 1617. 1618.

A Sermon Preached before his Majestie at Whitehall, on Easter Day Last. 1618.

Sermons. 1618–20. 4 parts.

XCVI Sermons. Eds. William Laud and John Buckeridge. 1629. 3 parts.

Opuscula Quaedam Posthuma. Eds. William Laud and John Buckeridge. 1629. 2 parts.

Stricturae; or, A Briefe Answer to the XVIII. Chapter of the First Booke of Cardinal Perron's Reply Written in French, to King James. 1629.

Institutiones Piae; or, Directions to Pray. Ed. Henry Isaacson. 1630.

A Patterne of Catechisticall Doctrine. 1630.

A Sermon of the Pestilence, Preached at Chiswick, 1603. 1636.

A Summarie View of the Government Both of the Old and New Testament. 1641.

The Morall Law Expounded. 1642.

A Learned Discourse of Ceremonies Retained and Used in Christian Churches. Ed. Edward Leigh. 1653.

Ἀποσπασματια Sacra; or, A Collection of Posthumous and Orphan Lectures. 1657.

The Form of Consecration of a Church or Chappel. 1659.

Preces Privatae Graecè & Latinè. Ed. John Lampshire. 1675. 2 parts.

Of Justification in Christ's Name: A Sermon Preached at Whitehall. 1740.

Seventeen Sermons. Ed. Charles Daubeny. 1821.

On the Pillars of Government. 1823.

Works. Eds. J. P. Wilson and James Bliss. 1841–54. 11 vols.

The Duty of a Nation and Its Members in Time of War. Ed. T. S. Polehampton. 1854.

Of Being Doers of the Word. 1858.

Selections from the Sermons. Ed. J. S. Utterton. 1865.

Εὐχαι ἰδιαι καθημεριναι. 1867.

Greek Devotions. Ed. Peter Goldsmith Medd. 1892.

Devotions. Ed. Henry Veale. 1895.

Sermons. Ed. G. M. Story. 1967.

SIR FRANCIS BACON (1561–1626)

Essayes. 1597, 1612.

A Declaration of the Practices and Treasons Attempted and Committed by Robert Late Earle of Essex. 1601.

A Briefe Discourse, Touching the Happie Union of the Kingdomes of England, and Scotland. 1603.

Apologie, in Certaine Imputations concerning the Late Earle of Essex. 1604.

Certaine Considerations Touching the Better Pacification and Edification of the Church of England. 1604.

The Two Bookes of the Proficience and Advancement of Learning, Divine and Humane. 1605.

De Sapientia Veterum Liber. 1609.

The Charge Touching Duells. 1614.

Instauratio Magna ⟨Novum Organum⟩. 1620.

Historia Naturalis ⟨Historia de Ventis⟩. 1622.

The Historie of the Raigne of King Henry the Seventh. 1622.

De Dignitate et Augmentis Scientarum. 1623.

Historia Vitae et Mortis. 1623.

Apophthegmes New and Old. 1625.

Essays, Civil and Moral. 1625.

The Translation of Certaine Psalmes into English Verse. 1625.

Sylva Sylvarum; or, A Naturall History. 1626.

Considerations Touching a Warre with Spaine. 1629.

Certaine Miscellany Works. 1629.

The Use of the Law. 1629.

The Elements of the Common Lawes of England. 1630.

Operum Moralium et Civilium Tomus. 1638.

Cases of Treason. 1641.

The Confession of Faith. 1641.

A Speech concerning the Article of Naturalization of the Scottish Nation. 1641.

The Office of Constables. 1641.

Three Speeches. 1641.

A Wise and Moderate Discourse concerning Church-Affairs. 1641.

An Essay of a King. 1642.

The Learned Reading of Sir Francis Bacon. 1642.

Ordnances. 1642.

Remaines. 1648.

The Felicity of Queen Elizabeth. 1651.

A True and Historical Relation of the Poysoning of Sir Thomas Overbury. 1651.

Scripta in Naturali et Universali Philosophia. 1653.

Resuscitatio. Ed. William Rawley. 1657–70. 2 vols.

A Letter of Advice to the Duke of Buckingham. 1661.

A Charge at a Sessions Holden for the Verge. 1662.

Opera Omnia. 1665.

Baconiana. 1679.

Opera Omnia. Ed. Henry Wetston. 1684. 6 vols.

Letters. Ed. Robert Stephens. 1702.

Philosophical Works. Ed. Peter Shaw. 1733. 3 vols.

Law Tracts. 1737.

Works. 1740. 4 vols.

Works. Eds. James Spedding, Robert Leslie Ellis, and Douglas Denon Heath. 1857–74. 14 vols.

Selected Writings. Ed. Hugh G. Dick. 1955.

SIR JOHN DAVIES (1569–1626)

Orchestra; or, A Poeme of Dauncing. 1596.

Epigrammes ⟨by Davies⟩ and Elegies ⟨of Ovid (tr. Christopher Marlowe)⟩. 1598.

Hymnes of Astraea, in Acrosticke Verse. 1599.

Nosce Teipsum: This Oracle Expounded in Two Elegies: 1. Of Humane Knowledge; 2. Of the Soule of Man, and the Immortalitie Thereof. 1599, 1619 (with *Hymnes of Astraea*), 1622 (with *Hymnes of Astraea* and *Orchestra*).

A Discoverie of the True Causes Why Ireland Was Never Entirely Subdued. 1612.

Le Primer Report des cases & matters en ley resolves & aduidges en les courts del roy en Ireland. 1615.

Poetical Works. Ed. Thomas Davies. 1773.

Historical Tracts. Ed. George Chalmers. 1786.

Works in Prose and Verse. Ed. Alexander B. Grosart. 1869–76. 3 vols.

Complete Poems. Ed. Alexander B. Grosart. 1876. 2 vols.

Poems. Ed. Robert Krueger, 1975.

CYRIL TOURNEUR (c. 1575–1626)

The Transformed Metamorphosis. 1600.

The Revengers Tragedie. 1607.

A Funerall Poeme: Upon the Death of the Most Worthie and True Souldier, Sir Francis Vere, Knight. 1609.

The Atheist's Tragedie; or, The Honest Man's Revenge. 1611.

Three Elegies on the Most Lamented Death of Prince Henrie (with John Webster and Thomas Heywood). 1613.

Plays and Poems. Ed. John Churton Collins. 1878. 2 vols.

[*Charlemagne; or, The Distracted Emperor.* Ed. Franck L. Schoell. 1920.]

Complete Works. Ed. Allardyce Nicoll. 1930.

[*The Honest Mans Fortune* (with others). Ed. Johan Gerritsen. 1952.]

WILLIAM ROWLEY (c. 1585–1626)

The Travailes of the Three English Brothers (with John Day and George Wilkins). 1607.

A Search for Money; or, The Lamentable Complaint for the Loose of the Wandring Knight, Mounsieur L'Argent. 1609.

Hymen's Holiday; or, Cupid's Vagaries. 1616. Lost.

A Faire Quarrell (with Thomas Middleton). 1617.

A Courtly Masque: The Device Called, The World Tost at Tennis (with Thomas Middleton). 1620.

A New Wonder, a Woman Never Vext. 1632.

A Match at Mid-night. 1633.

All's Lost by Lust. 1633.

A Shoo-maker a Gentleman. 1638.

Comedies and Tragedies (with Francis Beaumont, John Fletcher et al.). 1647. See under Beaumont and Fletcher.

The Changeling (with Thomas Middleton). 1653.

[*The Spanish Gipsie* (with Thomas Middleton ⟨and Thomas Dekker? or: and John Ford?⟩). 1653.]

The Fool without Book. 1653. Lost.

A Knave in Print; or, One for Another. 1653. Lost.

Fortune by Land and Sea (with Thomas Heywood). 1655.

The Old Law; or, A New Way to Please You (with Thomas Middleton and Philip Massinger). 1656.

The Witch of Edmonton (with Thomas Dekker and John Ford). 1658.

Nonesuch. 1660. Lost.

The Booke of the Four Hundred Loves. 1660. Lost.

The Parliament of Love (with Philip Massinger). 1660.

A Cure for a Cuckold (with John Webster ⟨and Thomas Heywood?⟩). 1661.

[*The Birth of Merlin* ⟨with Thomas Middleton?⟩. 1662.]

All's Lost by Lust and A Shoemaker a Gentleman. Ed. Charles Wharton Stork. 1910.

THOMAS MIDDLETON (1580–1627)

The Wisdome of Solomon Paraphrased. 1597.

Micro-Cynicon: Sixe Snarling Satyres. 1599.

The Ghost of Lucrece. 1600.

[*Blurt Master-Constable; or, The Spaniard's Night Walke* ⟨with Thomas Dekker?⟩. 1602.]

The Ant and the Nightingale; or, Father Hubburds Tales. 1604.

The Blacke Booke. 1604.

The Honest Whore; with, the Humours of the Patient Man, and the Longing Wife (with Thomas Dekker). 1604.

Michaelmas Terme. 1607.

The Phoenix. 1607.

[*The Puritan.* 1607.]

Your Five Gallants. c. 1607.

The Familie of Love. 1608.

A Mad World, My Masters. 1608.

A Trick to Catch the Old-One. 1608.

Sir R. Sherley, Sent Ambassadour in the Name of the King of Persia, to Sigismond the Third, King of Poland and Swecia, His Royall Entertainement into Cracovia. 1609.

[*The Second Maiden's Tragedy.* 1611.]

The Roaring Girle; or, Moll Cut-Purse (with Thomas Dekker). 1611.

The Manner of His Lordships Entertainment on Michaelmas-Day Last at That Most Famous and Admired Worke of the Running Stream from Amwell Head into the Cesterne neere Islintone. 1613.

The Triumphs of Truth: A Solemnity. 1613.

Civitatis Amor, the Cities Love: An Entertainment by Water, at Chelsey, and White-hall. 1616.

A Faire Quarrell (with William Rowley). 1617.

The Tryumphs of Honor and Industry: A Solemnity. 1617.

The Peace-Maker; or, Great Brittaines Blessing. 1618.

The Inner-Temple Masque; or, Masque of Heroes. 1619.

The Triumphs of Love and Antiquity: An Honourable Solemnity. 1619.

The Mariage of the Old and New Testament ⟨*Gods Parliament-House*⟩. 1620.

A Courtly Masque: The Device Called, The World Tost at Tennis (with William Rowley). 1620.

Honorable Entertainments, Compos'de for the Service of This Noble Cittie. 1621.

The Sunne in Aries: A Noble Solemnity. 1621.

The Triumphs of Honor and Virtue: A Noble Solemnity. 1622.

The Triumphs of Integrity: A Noble Solemnity. 1623.

A Game at Chaess. c. 1624.

The Triumphs of Health and Prosperity: A Noble Solemnity. 1626.

A Chast Mayd in Cheape-side. 1630.

[*The Bloody Banquet* ⟨with Thomas Dekker?⟩. c. 1639.]

Comedies and Tragedies (with Francis Beaumont, John Fletcher et al.). 1647. See under Beaumont and Fletcher.

The Widow (with John Fletcher). 1652.

The Changeling (with William Rowley). 1653.

The Spanish Gipsie (with William Rowley? and/or Thomas Dekker? and/or John Ford?). 1653.

The Old Law; or, A New Way to Please You (with Philip Massinger and William Rowley). 1656.

No Wit, No Help Like a Womans. Revised by James Shirley. 1657.

Two New Plays, viz.: More Dissemblers Besides Women; Women Beware Women. 1657.

The Mayor of Quinborough ⟨*Hengist, King of Kent*⟩. 1661.

Any Thing for a Quiet Life. 1662.

[*The Birth of Merlin* ⟨with William Rowley?⟩. 1662.]

The Witch. Ed. J. Reed. 1778.

Works. Ed. Alexander Dyce. 1840. 5 vols.

Works. Ed. A. H. Bullen. 1885–86. 8 vols.

Thomas Middleton. Ed. Havelock Ellis. 1887–90. 2 vols.

Three Plays. Ed. Kenneth Muir. 1975.

Selected Plays. Ed. David L. Frost. 1978.

FULKE GREVILLE, LORD BROOKE (1554–1628)

[*The Countesse of Pembrokes Arcadia* by Philip Sidney (editor; with Matthew Gwinne). 1590.]

The Tragedy of Mustapha. 1609.

Certaine Learned and Elegant Workes Written in His Youth and Familiar Exercise with Sir Philip Sidney. 1633.

The Life of the Renowned Sr Philip Sidney. Ed. P. B. 1652.

Remains: Being Poems of Monarchy and Religion. 1670.

Works in Verse and Prose. Ed. Alexander B. Grosart. 1870. 4 vols.

The Friend of Sir Philip Sidney: Being Selections from the Works. Ed. Alexander B. Grosart. 1894.
Caelica. Ed. Una Ellis-Fermor. 1936.
Poems and Dramas. Ed. Geoffrey Bullough. 1939. 2 vols.
Selected Poems. Ed. Thom Gunn. 1968.
Selected Writings. Ed. Joan Rees. 1973.
Prose Works. Ed. John Gouws. 1986.

GABRIEL HARVEY (c. 1550–1631)

Ode Natalitia; vel, Opus Eius Feriae Quae S. Stephani Pro-tomartyris Nomine Celebrata Est. 1575.
Ciceronianus; vel, Oratio post Reditum Habita Contabrigiae ad Suos Auditores. 1577.
Rhetor; vel, Duorum Dierum Oratio, de Natura, Arte, et Exer-citatione Rhetorica. 1577.
Valdinatis; Smithus; vel, Musarum Lachrymae: Pro Obitu Thomae Smithi. 1578.
Gratulationum Valdinensium Libri Quator. 1578. 4 parts.
Three Proper and Wittie Familiar Letters: Touching the Earth-quake in Aprill Last; Two Other, Very Commendable Let-ters (with Edmund Spenser). 1580.
Three Letters, and Certaine Sonnets: Especially Touching Rob-ert Greene and Other Parties, by Him Abused. 1592, 1592 (as *Four Letters, and Certaine Sonnets*).
Pierces Supererogation; or, A New Prayse of the Old Asse. 1593.
A New Letter, of Notable Contents with a Straunge Sonet, Intituled Gorgon; or, The Wonderfull Yeare. 1593.
[The Trimming of Thomas Nashe Gentleman, by the High-Tituled Patron Don Richardo de Medico Campo. 1597.]
Letter-Book. Ed. E. J. L. Scott. 1884.
Works. Ed. Alexander B. Grosart. 1884–85. 3 vols.
Marginalia. Ed. G. C. Moore Smith. 1913.
Lopez the Jew (the Protoype of Shylock), Executed 1594: An Opinion. Ed. Frank Marcham. 1927.

MICHAEL DRAYTON (1563–1631)

The Harmonie of the Church: Containing, the Spirituall Songes and Holy Hymnes, of Godly Men, Patriarkes and Prophetes. 1591.
Idea: The Shepheards Garland, Fashioned in Nine Eglogs; Ro-wands Sacrifice to the Nine Muses. 1593.
Peirs Gaveston Earle of Cornwall: His Life, Death, and For-tune. c. 1593.
Ideas Mirrour: Amours in Quatorzains. 1594.
Matilda: The Faire and Chaste Daughter of the Lord Robert Fitzwater. 1594.
Endimion and Phoebe; Ideas Latmus. c. 1594.
Mortimeriados: The Lamentable Civell Warres of Edward the Second and the Barrons. 1596.
The Tragicall Legend of Robert, Duke of Normandy; with the Legend of Matilda the Chast, and the Legend of Piers Gaveston. 1596.
Englands Heroicall Epistles. 1597.
The First Part of the True and Honorable Historie, of Sir John Old-castle, the Good Lord Cobham. 1600.
The Barron's Wars in the Raign of Edward the Second; with England's Heroicall Epistles. 1603.
To the Majestie of King James: A Gratulatorie Poem. 1603.
The Owle. 1604.
A Paean Triumphall: Composed for the Societie of the Gold-smiths of London: Congratulating His Highnes Magnifi-cent Entring the Citie. 1604.
Moyses in a Map of His Miracles. 1604.
Poems. 1605.

Poemes Lyrick and Pastorall: Odes, Eglogs, The Man in the Moone. c. 1606.
The Legend of Great Cromwel. 1607.
Poly-Olbion; or, A Chorographicall Description of Tracts, Riv-ers, Mountaines, Forests, and Other Parts of This Re-nowned Isle of Great Britaine. 1612 [Part 1]; 1622 [Part 2].
Poems. 1619. 7 parts.
The Battaile of Agincourt; The Miseries of Queene Margarite; Nimphidia, the Court of Fayrie; The Quest of Cinthia; The Shepheards Sirena; The Moone-Calfe; Elegies upon Sundry Occasions. 1627.
The Muses Elizium, Lately Discovered, by a New Way over Parnassus. 1630.
Works. Ed. Charles Coffey. 1748.
Works. 1753. 4 vols.
Poems. Ed. J. Payne Collier. 1856.
Complete Works. Ed. Richard Hooper. 1876. 3 vols.
Selections from the Poems. Ed. A. H. Bullen. 1883.
The Baron's Wars, Nymphidia, and Other Poems. Ed. Henry Morley. 1887.
Minor Poems. Ed. Cyril Brett. 1907.
Complete Works. Eds. J. William Hebel et al. 1931–41. 5 vols.
Poems. Ed. John Buxton. 1953. 2 vols.

JOHN DONNE (1572–1631)

Pseudo-Martyr. 1610.
Conclave Ignati. 1611. Eng. tr. 1611.
An Anatomy of the World. 1611.
The First Anniversarie. 1612.
The Second Anniversarie. 1612.
A Sermon upon the XV. Verse of the XX. Chapter of the Booke of Judges. 1622.
A Sermon upon the XX. Verse of the V. Chapter of the Booke of Judges. 1622.
A Sermon upon the VIII. Verse of the I. Chapter of the Acts of the Apostles. 1622.
Encaenia: The Feast of Dedication. 1623.
Three Sermons upon Speciall Occasions. 1623.
Devotions upon Emergent Occasions. 1624.
A Sermon upon the Eighth Verse of the First Chapter of the Acts of the Apostles. 1624.
The First Sermon Preached to King Charles. 1625.
Foure Sermons upon Speciall Occasions. 1625.
A Sermon, Preached to the Kings M^{tie.} at Whitehall, 24. Febr. 1625. 1626.
Five Sermons upon Speciall Occasions. 1626.
A Sermon of Commemoration of the Lady Danvers (with George Herbert). 1627.
Deaths Duell. 1632.
Juvenilia; or, Certain Paradoxes and Problems. 1633.
Poems. 1633.
Six Sermons upon Speciall Occasions. 1634.
Sapientia Clamitans. 1638.
LXXX Sermons. 1640.
Biathanatos. 1647.
Fifty Sermons. 1649.
Essayes in Divinity. 1651.
Letters to Severall Persons of Honour. 1651.
Cabala: Mysteries of State. 1654.
A Collection of Letters Made by Sr Tobie Mathews, K^t. 1660.
XXVI Sermons. 1660.
Poetical Works. 1779. 3 vols.
Works. Ed. Henry Alford. 1839. 6 vols.
Poetical Works. Ed. James Russell Lowell. 1855.
Complete Poems. Ed. Alexander B. Grosart. 1872. 2 vols.

Poems. Ed. E. K. Chambers. 1896. 2 vols.
Poems. Ed. Herbert J. C. Grierson. 1912. 2 vols.
Sermons: Selected Passages. Ed. Logan Pearsall Smith. 1919.
Complete Poetry and Selected Prose. Ed. John Hayward. 1929.
Poetry and Prose. Ed. H. W. Garrod. 1946.
Divine Poems. Ed. Helen Gardner. 1952.
Sermons. Eds. George R. Potter and Evelyn M. Simpson. 1953–62. 10 vols.
The Anniversaries. Ed. Frank Manley. 1963.
Elegies and Songs and Sonnets. Ed. Helen Gardner. 1965.
Satires, Epigrams and Verse Letters. Ed. W. Milgate. 1967.
Complete Poetry. Ed. John T. Shawcross. 1967.
Selected Prose. Ed. Evelyn Simpson. 1967.
Complete English Poems. Ed. A. J. Smith. 1971.
Epithalamions, Anniversaries, and Epodes. Ed. W. Milgate. 1978.
Paradoxes and Problems. Ed. Helen Peters. 1980.
Complete English Poems. Ed. C. A. Patrides. 1985.
Selected Prose. Ed. Neil Rhodes. 1987.

THOMAS DEKKER (c. 1572–1632)

The Shomakers Holiday; or, The Gentle Craft; with the Humorous Life of Simon Eyre, Shoomaker, and Lord Maior of London. 1600.
The Pleasant Comedie of Old Fortunatus. 1600.
Satiro-mastix; or, The Untrussing of the Humorous Poet ⟨with John Marston?⟩. 1602.
[*Blurt Master-Constable; or, The Spaniard's Night Walke* ⟨with Thomas Middleton?⟩. 1602.]
The Pleasant Comedie of Patient Grissil (with Henry Chettle and William Haughton). 1603.
1603: The Wonderfull Yeare: Wherein Is Shewed the Picture of London, Lying Sicke of the Plague. 1603.
Newes from Graves-end, Sent to Nobody. 1604.
The Honest Whore; with, the Humours of the Patient Man, and the Longing Wife (with Thomas Middleton). 1604.
[*The Meeting of Gallants at an Ordinarie; or, The Walkes in Powles.* 1604.]
The Magnificent Entertainment: Given to King James, Queene Anne His Wife, and Henry Frederick the Prince, upon the Day of His Majesties Tryumphant Passage (from the Tower) through His Honourable Citie (and Chamber) of London. 1604.
[*The Famous Historye of the Life and Death of Captaine Thomas Stukeley.* 1605.]
The Double PP: A Papist in Armes, Bearing Ten Severall Sheilds, Encountred by the Protestant, at Ten Severall Weapons; a Jesuite Marching before Them. 1606.
Newes from Hell: Brought by the Divells Carrier. 1606, 1607 (as *A Knight's Conjuring: Done in Earnest; Discovered in Jest*).
The Seven Deadly Sinnes of London: Drawne in Seven Severall Coaches, through the Seven Severall Gates of the Citie, Bringing the Plague with Them. 1606.
[*The London Prodigall.* 1606.]
[*Jests to Make You Merie* (with George Wilkins). 1607.]
The Famous History of Sir Thomas Wyat (with John Webster). 1607.
West-ward Hoe (with John Webster). 1607.
North-ward Hoe (with John Webster). 1607.
The Whore of Babylon. 1607.
The Dead Tearme; or, Westminsters Complaint for Long Vacations and Short Termes. 1608.
The Belman of London: Bringing to Light the Most Notorious Villanies That Are Now Practiced in the Kingdome. 1608.

Lanthorne and Candle-Light; or, The Bell-mans Second Nights Walke; in Which Hee Brings to Light, a Broode of More Strange Villanies Then Ever Were Till This Yeare Discovered. 1608.
[*The Great Frost: Cold Doings in London, Except It Be at the Lotterie.* 1608.]
[*The Merry Devill of Edmonton.* 1608.]
Foure Birds of Noahs Oarke: Viz. 1. The Dove; 2. The Eagle; 3. The Pelican; 4. The Phoenix. 1609.
The Guls Horne-Booke. 1609.
The Ravens Almanack: Foretelling of a Plague, Famine, and Civill Warre. 1609.
Worke for Armorours; or, The Peace is Broken: Open Warres Likely to Happin This Year 1609: God Helpe the Poore, the Rich Can Shift. 1609.
The Roaring Girle; or, Moll Cut-Purse (with Thomas Middleton). 1611.
If It Be Not Good the Divel Is in It. 1612.
Troia-Nova Triumphans: London Triumphing; or, The Solemne, Magnificent, and Memorable Receiving of That Worthy Gentleman, Sir John Swinerton Knight, into the Citty of London, after His Returne from Taking the Oath of Maioralty at Westminster. 1612.
A Strange Horse-Race, at the End of Which, Comes In the Catch-Pols Masque; and after That the Bankrouts Banquet: Which Done, the Divell, Falling Sicke, Makes His Last Will and Testament, This Present Yeare. 1613.
[*The Cold Yeare: 1614.* 1615.]
The Artillery Garden: A Poem Dedicated to the Honor of All Those Gentlemen, Who (There) Practize Millitary Discipline. 1616.
[*The Owles Almanacke: Prognosticating Many Strange Accidents Which Shall Happen to This Kingdome of Great Britaine This Yeare, 1618.* 1618.]
Dekker His Dreame: In Which, Beeing Rapt with a Poeticall Enthusiasme, the Great Volumes of Heaven and Hell to Him Were Opened, in Which He Read Many Wonderfull Things. 1620.
The Virgin Martir (with Philip Massinger). 1622.
A Rod for Run-awayes: Gods Tokens, of His Feareful Judgements, Sundry Wayes Pronounced upon This City, and on Severall Persons, Both Flying from It, and Staying in It. 1625.
Brittannia's Honor: Brightly Shining in Severall Magnificent Shewes or Pageants, to Celebrate the Solemnity of the Right Honourable Richard Deane, at His Inauguration into the Mayoralty of the Honourable City of London. 1628.
[*Look Up and See Wonders: A Miraculous Apparition in the Ayre, Lately Seene in Barke-shire at Bawlkin Grene neere Hatford.* 1628.]
Warres, Warre, Warres. 1628.
Londons Tempe; or, The Feild of Happines: In Which Feild Are Planted Several Trees of Magnificence, State and Bewty, to Celebrate the Solemnity of the Right Honorable James Campebell, at His Inauguration into the Honorable Office of Praetorship, or Maioralty of London. 1629.
[*London Looke Back, at That Yeare of Yeares 1625; and Looke Forward, upon This Yeare, 1630: Written Not to Terrifie, but to Comfort.* 1630.]
The Blacke Rod: and the White Rod: (Justice and Mercie) Striking, and Sparing, London. 1630.
The Second Part of the Honest Whore, with the Humors of the Patient Man, the Impatient Wife. 1630.
A Tragi-Comedy: Called, Match Mee in London. 1631.

Penny-Wise Pound Foolish; or, A Bristow Diamond, Set in Two Rings, and Both Crack'd. 1631.
The Noble Spanish Souldier; or, A Contract Broken, Justly Reveng'd (with Samuel Rowley and John Day). 1634.
The Wonder of a Kingdome. 1636.
[*The Bloodie Banquet* ⟨with Thomas Middleton?⟩. 1639.]
[*The Spanish Gipsie* (with Thomas Middleton ⟨and William Rowley? or: and John Ford?⟩). 1653.]
The Sun's-Darling: A Moral Masque (with John Ford). 1656.
Lust's Dominion; or, The Lascivious Queen ⟨with John Day and William Haughton?⟩. 1657.
The Witch of Edmonton (with William Rowley and John Ford). 1658.
Dramatic Works. Ed. R. H. Shepherd. 1873. 4 vols.
Non-Dramatic Works. Ed. Alexander B. Grosart. 1884–86. 5 vols.
Thomas Dekker. Ed. Ernest Rhys. 1887.
[*Charlemagne; or, The Distracted Emperor.* Ed. Franck L. Schoell. 1920.]
[*The Welsh Embassador.* Eds. Harold Littledale and W. W. Greg. 1920.]
Plague Pamphlets. Ed. F. P. Wilson. 1925.
Dramatic Works. Ed. Fredson T. Bowers. 1953–61. 4 vols.
Selected Writings. Ed. E. D. Pendry. 1967.

GEORGE HERBERT (1593–1633)

Oratio Habita Coram Dominis Legatis. 1623.
Oratio qua Auspicatissimum Serenissimi Principis Caroli Reditum ex Hispaniis Celebravit. 1623.
A Sermon of Commemoration of the Lady Danvers (with John Donne). 1627.
The Temple: Sacred Poems and Private Ejaculations. 1633.
Hygasticon by Leonard Lessius (translator). 1634.
A Priest to the Temple; or, The Countrey Parson His Character, and Rule of Holy Life. 1652.
Remains. 1652.
Works. 1835–36. 2 vols.
Complete Works. Ed. Alexander B. Grosart. 1874. 3 vols.
English Works. Ed. George Herbert Palmer. 1905. 3 vols.
Works. Ed. F. E. Hutchinson. 1941.
Poems. Ed. Helen Gardner. 1961.
Latin Poetry: A Bilingual Edition. Eds. and trs. Mark McCloskey and Paul R. Murphy. 1965.
A Choice of Herbert's Verse. Ed. R. S. Thomas. 1967.
Selected Poems. Ed. Gareth Reeves. 1971.
George Herbert. Ed. W. H. Auden. 1973.
English Poems. Ed. C. A. Patrides. 1974.

SIR EDWARD COKE (1552–1634)

Les Reports de Edward Coke. 1600–15. 11 parts.
The Lord Coke His Speech and Charge; with a Discoverie of the Abuses and Corruption of Officers. 1607.
A Booke of Entries: Containing Perfect and Approved Presidents of Counts, Declarations, Informations, Necessarie to Be Known. 1614.
The First Part of the Institutes of the Lawes of England; or, A Commentarie upon Littleton. 1628.
A Little Treatise of Baile and Mainprize. 1635.
The Compleat Copy-Holder: Wherein Is Contained a Learned Discourse of the Antiquity and Nature of Manors and Copy-Holds. 1641.
The Second Part of the Institutes of the Lawes of England: Containing the Exposition of Many Ancient, and Other Statutes. 1642.
The Third Part of the Institutes of the Laws of England: Con-
cerning High Treason, and Other Pleas of the Crown, and Criminall Causes. 1644.
The Fourth Part of the Institutes of the Laws of England: Concerning the Jurisdiction of the Courts. 1644.
Le Reading del Mon Seignior Coke, sur Lestatute de 27 E.1 Appelle Lestatute de Finibus Levatis. 1662.
Three Law Tracts. Ed. William Hawkins. 1764..

GEORGE CHAPMAN (c. 1559–1634)

[*Fidele and Fortunio, the Two Italian Gentlemen* by Luigi Pasqualigo (translator). 1585.]
Σκία νυκτός: *The Shadow of Night: Containing Two Poeticall Hymnes.* 1594.
Ovids Banquet of Sence: A Coronet for His Mistresse Philosophie, and His Amorous Zodiacke. 1595.
Seaven Bookes of the Iliades of Homere ⟨Books 1–2, 7–11⟩ (translator). 1598.
Achilles Shield: Translated out of His ⟨Homer's⟩ *Eighteenth Book of Iliades.* 1598.
Hero and Leander (with Christopher Marlowe). 1598.
The Blinde Begger of Alexandria, Most Pleasantly Discoursing His Variable Humours in Disguised Shapes Full of Conceite and Pleasure. 1598.
A Pleasant Comedy Entituled: An Humerous Dayes Myrth. 1599.
Al Fooles. 1605.
Eastward Hoe (with Ben Jonson and John Marston). 1605.
The Gentleman Usher. 1606.
Monsieur D'Olive. 1606.
[*Sir Gyles Goosecappe Knight.* 1606.]
Bussy D'Ambois. 1607.
The Conspiracie, and Tragedie of Charles Duke of Byron, Marshall of France. 1608.
Euthymiae Raptus; or, The Teares of Peace; with Interlocutions. 1609.
Homer, Prince of Poets: Translated According to the Greeke in Twelve Books ⟨1–12⟩ *of His Iliads.* c. 1610.
May-Day. 1611.
The Iliads of Homer (translator). 1611.
An Epicede or Funerall Song: On the Most Disastrous Death, of the High-Borne Prince of Men, Henry Prince of Wales, &c. 1612.
Petrarchs Seven Penitentiall Psalmes, Paraphrastically Translated; with Other Philosophicall Poems, and a Hymne to Christ upon the Cross. 1612.
The Widdowes Teares. 1612.
The Memorable Masque of the Two Honorable Houses or Innes of Court; the Middle Temple, and Lyncolns Inne. 1613.
The Revenge of Bussy D'Ambois. 1613.
Andromeda Liberata; or, The Nuptials of Perseus and Andromeda. 1614.
Eugenia; or, True Nobilities Trance for the Most Memorable Death of William Lord Russell. 1614.
A Free and Offenceless Justification of Andromeda Liberata. 1614.
Homer's Odysses ⟨Books 1–12⟩ (translator). c. 1614.
Twenty-four Books of Homers Odisses (translator). c. 1615.
The Divine Poem of Museus: First of All Bookes (translator). 1616.
The Whole Works of Homer (translator). c. 1616.
The Georgicks of Hesiod (translator). 1618.
[*Two Wise Men and All the Rest Fooles; or, A Comicall Morall, Censuring the Follies of This Age.* 1619.]
Pro Vere, Autumni Lachrymae: Inscribed to the Immortal Mem-

orie of the Most Pious and Incomparable Souldier, Sir Horatio Vere, Knight: Beseiged, and Distrest in Mainhem. 1622.

The Crowne of All Homers Workes: Batrachomyomachia or the Battaile of Frogs and Mise; His Hymn's and Epigrams. c. 1625.

A Justification of a Strange Action of Nero; in Burying with a Solemne Funerall, One of the Cast Hayres of His Mistresse Poppaea; Also a Just Reproofe of a Romane Smell-Feast, Being the Fifth Satyre of Juvenall (translator). 1629.

The Warres of Pompey and Caesar: Out of Whose Events Is Evicted This Proposition: Only a Just Man Is a Freeman. 1631.

The Tragedie of Chabot Admirall of France. Revised by James Shirley. 1639.

[*The Bloody Brother; or, Rollo, Duke of Normandy* (with John Fletcher ⟨and Philip Massinger?⟩). 1639.]

[*The Tragedy of Alphonsus Emperor of Germany.* 1654.]

[*The Second Maiden's Tragedy.* 1824.]

Comedies and Tragedies. Ed. R. H. Shepherd. 1873. 3 vols.

Works. Ed. R. H. Shepherd. 1874–75. 3 vols.

George Chapman. Ed. William Lyon Phelps. 1895.

Plays and Poems. Ed. Thomas Marc Parrott. 1910–14. 2 vols. (plays only).

[*Charlemagne; or, The Distracted Emperor.* Ed. Franck L. Schoell. 1920.]

Poems. Ed. Phyllis Brooks Bartlett. 1941.

Plays: The Comedies. Eds. Allan Holaday et al. 1970.

JOHN MARSTON (c. 1575–1634)

The Metamorphosis of Pigmalions Image; and Certaine Satyres. 1598.

The Scourge of Villainie: Three Bookes of Satyres. 1598.

Jacke Drums Entertainment; or, The Comedie of Pasquill and Katherine (with others). 1601.

[*Satiromastix; or, The Untrussing of the Humorous Poet* (with Thomas Dekker). 1602.]

The History of Antonio and Mellida: The First Part. 1602.

Antonios Revenge: The Second Part. 1602.

The Malcontent. 1604, 1604 (3rd ed. revised by John Webster).

The Dutch Courtezan. 1605.

Eastward Hoe (with George Chapman and Ben Jonson). 1605.

Parasitaster; or, The Fawne. 1606.

The Wonder of Women; or, The Tragedie of Sophonisba. 1606.

What You Will. 1607.

[*Histrio-Mastix; or, The Player Whipt.* 1610.]

The Insatiate Countesse. 1613.

Workes. 1633.

Works. Ed. J. O. Halliwell. 1856. 3 vols.

Poems. Ed. Alexander B. Grosart. 1879. 2 parts.

Works. Ed A. H. Bullen. 1887. 3 vols.

Plays. Ed. H. Harvey Wood. 1934–39. 3 vols.

Poems. Ed. Arnold Davenport. 1961.

Selected Plays. Eds. MacDonald P. Jackson and Michael Neill. 1986.

JOHN WEBSTER (c. 1578–c. 1634)

The Malcontent (with John Marston). 1604.

The Famous History of Sir Thomas Wyat (with Thomas Dekker). 1607.

West-ward Hoe (with Thomas Dekker). 1607.

North-ward Hoe (with Thomas Dekker). 1607.

The White Divel. 1612.

Three Elegies on the Most Lamented Death of Prince Henry (with Cyril Tourneur and Thomas Heywood). 1613.

The Tragedy of the Dutchesse of Malfy. 1623.

The Devils Law-Case. 1623.

Monuments of Honor. 1624.

Appius and Virginia ⟨with Thomas Heywood?⟩. 1654.

A Cure for a Cuckold (with William Rowley ⟨and Thomas Heywood?⟩). 1661.

Works. Ed. Alexander Dyce. 1830. 4 vols.

Webster and Tourneur. Ed. John Addington Symonds. 1888.

Works. Ed. F. L. Lucas. 1927. 4 vols.

Three Plays. Ed. D. C. Gunby. 1972.

Selected Plays. Eds. Jonathan Dollimore and Alan Sinfield. 1983.

EDWARD FAIRFAX (c. 1575–1635)

Godfrey of Bulloigne by Torquato Tasso (translator). 1600.

A Discourse of Witchcraft. 1858.

Daemonologia: A Discourse on Witchcraft; with Two Eclogues. Ed. William Grainge. 1882.

Godfrey of Bulloigne: A Critical Edition of Edward Fairfax's Translation of Tasso's Gerusalemma Liberata, Together with Fairfax's Original Poems. Eds. Kathleen M. Lea and T. M. Gang. 1981.

RICHARD CORBETT (1582–1635)

Certain Elegant Poems. Ed. John Donne the Younger. 1647.

Poëtica Stromata; or, A Collection of Sundry Pieces in Poetry. 1648.

Poems. Ed. William Crook. 1672.

Poems; to Which Is Now Added Oratio in Funus Henrici Principis. Ed. Octavius Gilchrist. 1807.

Poems. Eds. J. A. W. Bennett and H. R. Trevor-Roper. 1955.

THOMAS RANDOLPH (1605–1635)

Aristippus; or, The Joviall Philosopher; to Which Is Added, The Conceited Pedlar. 1630.

The Jealous Lovers. 1632.

[*Cornelianum Dolium* (with Richard Braithwait). 1638.]

Poems; with The Muses Looking-Glasse and Amyntas. 1638. 3 parts.

Πλουτοφθαλμια Πλουτογαμια ⟨*Hey for Honesty, Down with Knavery*⟩ by Aristophanes (adaptation; revised by F. J.). 1651.

The Prodigal Scholar. 1660. Lost. [Same as *The Drinking Academy?*]

Poetical and Dramatic Works. Ed. W. Carew Hazlitt. 1875. 2 vols.

Poems and Amyntas. Ed. John Jay Parry. 1917.

Poems. Ed. G. Thorn-Drury. 1929.

[*The Drinking Academy.* Eds. Hyder E. Rollins and Samuel A. Tannenbaum. 1930.]

BEN JONSON (c. 1572–1637)

Every Man out of His Humor. 1600.

Every Man in His Humor. 1601.

The Fountaine of Self-Love; or, Cynthias Revels. 1601.

Poetaster; or, The Arraignment. 1602.

Part of King James His Royall and Magnificent Entertainment. 1604.

Sejanus His Fall. 1605.

Eastward Hoe (with George Chapman and John Marston). 1605.

Hymenaei; or, The Solemnities of Masque, and Barriers. 1606.

Volpone; or, The Foxe. 1607.

The Characters of Two Royall Masques, the One of Blacknesse, the Other of Beautie. 1608.

The Masque of Queenes. 1609.

The Case Is Alterd. 1609.

Catiline His Conspiracy. 1611.

The Alchemist. 1612.

Workes. 1616 (First Folio).

Lovers Made Men: A Masque. 1617.

The Masque of Augures. c. 1622.

Time Vindicated to Himselfe, and to His Honors. c. 1623.

Neptunes Triumph for the Returne of Albion. c. 1624.

The Fortunate Isles and Their Union. c. 1625.

Loves Triumph through Callipolis. 1630.

The New Inne; or, The Light Heart. 1631.

Chloridia: Rites to Chloris and Her Nymphs. 1631.

The Gypsies Metamorphos'd. 1640.

Workes. 1640 (Second Folio). 2 vols.

Works. 1692 (Third Folio). 2 vols.

Works. Ed. Peter Whalley. 1756. 7 vols.

Works. Ed. William Gifford. 1816. 9 vols.

Notes on Ben Jonson's Conversations with William Drummond. Ed. David Laing. 1842.

Ben Jonson. Ed. Brinsley Nicholson. 1893–94. 3 vols.

Complete Plays. Ed. Felix E. Schelling. 1906. 2 vols.

Works. Eds. C. H. Herford, Percy Simpson, and Evelyn M. Simpson. 1925–52. 11 vols.

Poems. Ed. Bernard H. Newdigate. 1936.

Selected Works. Ed. Harry Levin. 1938.

Poems. Ed. George Burke Johnston. 1954.

Complete Poetry. Ed. William B. Hunter, Jr. 1963.

Complete Masques. Ed. Stephen Orgel. 1969.

Plays and Masques. Ed. Robert M. Adams. 1979.

Complete Plays. Ed. G. A. Wilkes. 1981. 2 vols.

Complete Poems. Ed. George Parfitt. 1982.

SIR HENRY WOTTON (1568–1639)

Ad Illustrissimum Virum Marcum Velserum Duumvirum Augustae Vindeliciae Epistola. 1612.

The Elements of Architecture, Collected from the Best Authors and Examples. 1624.

A Meditation upon the XXIIth Chapter of Genesis. 1631.

Ad Regem e Scotia Reducem Plausus et Vota. 1633.

A Parallel betweene Robert Late Earle of Essex and George Late Duke of Buckingham. 1641.

A Short View of the Life and Death of George Villiers, Duke of Buckingham. 1642.

Reliquiae Wottonianae; or, A Collection of Lives, Letters, Poems; with Characters of Sundry Personages; and Other Incomparable Pieces of Language and Art. Ed. Izaak Walton. 1651.

The State of Christendom; or, A Most Exact and Curious Discovery of Many Secret Passages and Hidden Mysteries of the Times. 1657.

Letters to Sir Edmund Bacon. 1661.

Poems. Ed. Alexander Dyce. 1843.

Letters and Dispatches to James the First and His Ministers, in the Years MCDXVII–XX. Ed. George Tomline. 1850.

Life and Letters. Ed. Logan Pearsall Smith. 1907. 2 vols.

A Philosophical Survey of Education; or, Moral Architecture; and The Aphorisms of Education. Ed. H. S. Kermode. 1938.

ROBERT BURTON (1577–1640)

The Anatomy of Melancholy: What It Is; with All the Kindes, Causes, Symptomes, Prognostickes, and Severall Cures of It. 1621.

Philosophaster, Comoedia: Nunc Primum in Lucem Producta; Poemata Adhuc Sparsim Edita, Nunc in Unum Collecta. Ed. W. E. Buckley. 1862.

The Anatomy of Melancholy. Ed. A. R. Shilleto. 1893. 3 vols.

The Anatomy of Melancholy. Eds. Floyd Dell and Paul Jordan-Smith. 1927. 2 vols.

Philosophaster; Together with His Other Minor Writings in Prose and Verse. Ed. Paul Jordan-Smith. 1931.

PHILIP MASSINGER (1583–1640)

The Tragedy of Thierry King of France and His Brother Theodoret (with Beaumont and Fletcher). 1621.

The Virgin Martir (with Thomas Dekker). 1622.

The Duke of Millaine. 1623.

The Bond-Man: An Antient Storie. 1624.

The Roman Actor. 1629.

The Picture: A Tragaecomedie. 1630.

The Renegado: A Tragaecomedie. 1630.

The Emperour of the East: A Tragae-comoedie. 1632.

The Fatall Dowry (with Nathan Field). 1632.

The Maid of Honour. 1632.

A New Way to Pay Old Debts. 1633.

The Great Duke of Florence: A Comicall Historie. 1636.

The Elder Brother (with John Fletcher). 1637.

The Unnaturall Combat. 1639.

[*The Bloody Brother; or, Rollo, Duke of Normandy* (with John Fletcher ⟨and George Chapman?⟩. 1639.]

Comedies and Tragedies (with Francis Beaumont, John Fletcher et al.). 1647. See under Beaumont and Fletcher.

Three New Plays, viz.: The Bashful Lover; The Guardian; A Very Woman. 1655.

The Old Law; or, A New Way to Please You (with Thomas Middleton and William Rowley). 1656.

The City-Madam. 1658.

The Custom of the Country (with John Fletcher). 1717.

Dramatic Works. Ed. Thomas Coxeter. 1759. 4 vols.

Dramatick Works. Ed. John Monck Mason. 1779. 4 vols.

Plays. Ed. William Gifford. 1805. 4 vols.

Dramatic Works (with John Ford). Ed. Hartley Coleridge. 1840.

Believe as You List. Ed. T. C. Croker. 1849.

Plays. Ed. Francis Cunningham. 1871.

Philip Massinger. Ed. Arthur Symons. 1887–89. 2 vols.

Philip Massinger. Ed. Lucius A. Sherman. 1912.

Sir John van Olden Barnavelt (with John Fletcher). Ed. Wilhelmina P. Frijlinck. 1922.

The Parliament of Love. Ed. Kathleen Marguerite Lea. 1929.

Poems. Ed. Donald S. Lawless. 1968.

Plays and Poems. Eds. Philip Edwards and Colin Gibson. 1976. 5 vols.

Selected Plays. Ed. Colin Gibson. 1978.

JOHN FORD (c. 1586–c. 1640)

Fames Memoriall; or, The Earle of Devonshire Deceased. 1606.

Honor Triumphant; or, The Peeres Challenge, by Armes Defensible, at Tilt, Turney, and Barriers. 1606.

The Golden Meane: Discoursing the Noblenesse of Perfect Virtue in Extreames. 1613.

A Line of Life: Pointing at the Immortalitie of a Vertuous Life. 1620.

The Lovers Melancholy. 1629.

The Broken Heart. 1633.

Loves Sacrifice. 1633.

'Tis Pity Shees a Whore. 1633.

The Chronicle Historie of Perkin Warbeck. 1634.

The Fancies, Chast and Noble. 1638.

The Ladies Triall. 1639.

Comedies and Tragedies (with Francis Beaumont, John Fletcher et al.). 1647. See under Beaumont and Fletcher.

The Queen; or, The Excellency of Her Sex. 1653.

[*The Spanish Gipsie* (with Thomas Middleton ⟨and Thomas Dekker? or: and William Rowley?⟩). 1653.]

The Sun's-Darling (with Thomas Dekker). 1656.

The Witch of Edmonton (with Thomas Dekker and William Rowley). 1658.

Dramatic Works. Ed. Henry Weber. 1811.

Dramatic Works. Ed. William Gifford. 1827. 2 vols.

Dramatic Works (with Philip Massinger). Ed. Hartley Coleridge. 1840.

John Ford. Ed. Havelock Ellis. 1888.

Three Plays. Ed. Keith Sturgess. 1970.

Selected Plays. Ed. Colin Gibson. 1986.

THOMAS CAREW (c. 1594–1640)

Coelum Britannicum: A Masque at White-hall in the Banqueting-House. 1634.

Poems. 1640.

Poems, with a Maske. 1651.

Poems, Songs and Sonnets, Together with a Masque. 1670.

A Selection from the Poetical Works. Ed. John Fry. 1810.

Works. Ed. Thomas Maitland. 1824.

Poems. Ed. William Carew Hazlitt. 1870.

Poems and Masque. Ed. Joseph Woodfall Ebsworth. 1893.

Poems. Ed. Arthur Vincent. 1898.

Poems, with His Masque Coelum Britannicum. Ed. Rhodes Dunlap. 1949.

THOMAS HEYWOOD (c. 1573–1641)

Oenone and Paris. 1594.

The First and Second Partes of King Edward the Fourth. 1599.

[*A Warning for Fair Women.* 1599.]

A Pleasant and Conceited Comedie Wherein Is Shewed How a Man May Chuse a Good Wife from a Bad. 1602.

[*The Famous Historye of the Life and Death of Captaine Thomas Stukeley.* 1605.]

If You Know Not Me, You Know No Bodie; or, The Troubles of Queen Elizabeth. 1605–06. 2 parts.

[*The Fayre Mayde of the Exchange.* 1607.]

A Woman Kilde with Kindnesse. 1607.

The Two Most Worthy and Notable Histories Which Remaine Unmained to Posterity, viz., The Conspiracie of Cateline Undertaken against the Government of the Senate of Rome, and the Warre Which Jugurth for Many Years Maintained against the Same State by Sallust (translator). 1608.

The Rape of Lucrece. 1508.

Troia Britanica; or, Great Britaines Troy. 1609.

The Golden Age. 1611.

An Apology for Actors. 1612.

The Brazen Age. 1613.

Three Elegies on the Most Lamented Death of Prince Henrie (with Cyril Tourneur and John Webster). 1613.

A Marriage Triumphe, Solemnized in an Epithalamium, in Memorie of the Happie Nuptials between the High and Mightie Prince Count Palatine and the Most Excellent Princesse the Lady Elizabeth. 1613.

The Silver Age. 1613.

Publii Ovidii Nasonis de Arte Amandi; or, The Art of Love (translator). c. 1613.

The Four Prentises of London. 1615.

Γυναίκειον; *or, Nine Bookes of Various History concerning Women.* 1624, 1657 (as *The Generall History of Women*).

A Funeral Elegie upon King James. 1625.

Englands Elizabeth: Her Life and Troubles during Her Minoritie from the Cradle to the Crowne. 1631.

The Fair Maid of the West. 1631. 2 parts.

The Felicitie of Man by Sir Richard Barckley (editor). 1631.

Londons Jus Honorarium. 1631.

The Iron Age. 1632. 2 parts.

Londini Artium & Scientiarum Scaturigo. 1632.

The English Traveller. 1633.

Londini Emporia. 1633.

The Late Lancashire Witches (with Richard Brome). 1634.

A Pleasant Comedy Called A Mayden-Head Well Lost. 1634.

The Hierarchie of the Blessed Angells. 1635.

Londini Situs Salutis. 1635.

Philocothonista; or, The Drunkard Opened, Dissected and Anatomized. 1635.

The Wonder of This Age. 1635.

A Challenge for Beautie. 1636.

Loves Maistresse; or, The Queens Masque. 1636.

The New-Yeeres Gift. 1636.

The Three Wonders of This Age. 1636.

A True Discourse of the Two Infamous Upstart Prophets, R. Farnham, Weaver, of White-Chappell, and J. Bull, Weaver, of St. Butolphs Algate. 1636.

A Curtaine Lecture. 1637.

Londini Speculum. 1637.

The Phoenix of These Late Times; or, The Life of Mr. Henry Welby, Esq. 1637.

Pleasant Dialogues and Dramma's, Selected out of Lucian, Erasmus, Textor, Ovid, &c. (translator). 1637.

The Royall King, and the Loyall Subject. 1637.

A True Description of His Majesties Royall Ship, Built This Year 1637, at Wooll-witch in Kent. 1637.

Porta Pietatis. 1638.

The Wise-Woman of Hogsdon. 1638.

The Life and Death of Queene Elizabeth. 1639.

Londini Status Pacatus. 1639.

A True Relation of the Lives and Deaths of the Two Most Famous English Pyrats, Purser and Clinton. 1639.

The Exemplary Lives and Memorable Acts of Nine the Most Worthy Women of the World. 1640.

The Black Box of Roome Opened. 1641.

Brightmans Predictions and Prophecies (adaptation). 1641.

A Dialogue or Accidental Discourse betwixt Mr. Alderman Abell and Richard Kilvert. 1641.

The Life of Merlin, Sirnamed Ambrosius: His Prophecies and Predictions Interpreted. 1641.

Machiavel's Ghost, as He Lately Appeared to His Deare Sons, the Modern Projectors. 1641.

A New Plot Discovered. 1641.

The Rat-Trap; or, The Jesuites Taken in Their Owne Net. 1641.

Reader, Here You'l Plainly See / Judgement Perverted by These Three: / A Priest, a Judge, a Patentee. 1641.

A Revelation of Mr. Brightmans Revelation. 1641.

[*Appius and Virginia* (with John Webster). 1654.]

Fortune by Land and Sea (with William Rowley). 1655.

[*The Famous and Remarkable History of Sir Richard Whittington.* 1656.]

[*A Cure for a Cuckold* (with John Webster and William Rowley). 1661.]

Dramatic Works. Eds. J. Payne Collier and Barron Field. 1841–51. 2 vols.

The Book of Sir Thomas More (with others). 1844.

Dramatic Works. Ed. R. H. Shepherd. 1874. 6 vols.

Thomas Heywood. Ed. A. W. Verity. 1888.

The Captives; or, The Lost Recovered. Ed. Alexander Corbin Judson. 1921.

⟨*Callista; or,*⟩ *The Escapes of Jupiter.* Ed. Henry D. Janzen. 1978.

Pageants. Ed. David M. Bergeron. 1986.

SIR JOHN SUCKLING (1609–1641)

Aglaura. 1638.

The Discontented Colonell. c. 1640.

A Coppy of a Letter Written to the Lower House of Parliament Touching Divers Grievances and Inconveniences of the State, &c. 1641.

A Letter from France, Deploring His Sad Estate and Flight. 1641.

A Coppy of a Letter Found in the Privy Lodgings at Whitehall. 1641.

Fragmenta Aurea. 1646 (4 parts); 1672 (5 parts).

*A Letter to M*ʳ *H. German in the Beginning of the Late Long Parliament, Anno 1640.* c. 1660.

Works. 1676. 5 parts.

Works: Containing His Poems, Letters and Plays. 1709.

Works. 1770. 2 vols.

Selections from the Works. Ed. Alfred Suckling. 1836.

Poems, Plays and Other Remains. Ed. William Carew Hazlitt. 1874. 2 vols.

Poems. Ed. John Gray. 1896.

Love Poems. 1902.

Works. Ed. A. Hamilton Thompson. 1910.

Poems and Letters from Manuscript. Ed. Herbert Berry. 1960.

Works. Eds. Thomas Clayton and L. A. Beaurline. 1971. 2 vols.

WILLIAM BROWNE (1591–c. 1643)

Two Elegies Consecrated to the Never-Dying Memorie of the Most Worthily Admyred Henry, Prince of Wales (with Christopher Brooke). 1613.

Britannia's Pastorals. 1613 [Book 1]; 1616 [Book 2].

The Shepheards Pipe. 1614.

[*The History of Polexander* by Martin Le Roy, sieur du Parc et de Gomberville (translator). 1647.]

Works. Eds. William Thompson and Thomas Davies. 1772. 3 vols.

Original Poems, Never Before Published. Ed. Sir Samuel Egerton Brydges. 1815.

Whole Works. Ed. William Carew Hazlitt. 1868–69. 2 vols.

Poems. Ed. Gordon Godwin. 1894. 2 vols.

Circe and Ulysses: The Inner Temple Masque. Ed. Gwyn Jones. 1954.

WILLIAM CARTWRIGHT (1611–1643)

The Royall Slave. 1639.

To the Right Honourable Philip, Earle of Pembroke and Mountgomery, upon His Lordships Election of Chancellor of the University of Oxford. 1641.

Comedies, Tragi-Comedies, with Other Poems. 1651. 2 parts.

An Off-Spring of Mercy, Issuing out of the Womb of Cruelty; or, A Passion Sermon Preached at Christschurch in Oxford. 1652.

November; or, Signal Days. 1671.

Life and Poems. Ed. R. Cullis Goffin. 1918.

Plays and Poems. Ed. G. Blakemore Evans. 1951.

GEORGE SANDYS (1578–1644)

A Relation of a Journey Begun An: Dom: 1610: Containing a Description of the Turkish Empire, of Ægypt, of the Holy Land, of the Remote Parts of Italy, and Lands Adjoyning. 1615.

Ovid's Metamorphosis (translator). 1621 [Books 1–5]; 1626 [Books 1–15].

[*Sacrae Heptades; or, Seaven Problems concerning Antichrist.* 1625.]

A Paraphrase upon the Psalmes of David, and upon the Hymnes Dispersed throughout the Old and New Testaments. 1636, 1638 (as *A Paraphrase upon the Divine Poems*).

Christ's Passion by Hugo Grotius (translator). 1640.

A Paraphrase upon the Song of Solomon. 1641.

Selections from the Metrical Paraphrase of the Psalms, the Book of Job and Other Portions of Holy Scripture. Ed. Henry John Todd. 1839.

Poetical Works. Ed. Richard Hooper. 1872. 2 vols.

FRANCIS QUARLES (1592–1644)

A Feast for Worms: Set Forth in a Poeme of the History of Jonah. 1620.

Hadassa; or, The History of Queene Ester. 1621.

Job Militant; with Meditations Divine and Morall. 1624.

Sions Elegie, Wept by Jeremie the Prophet, Periphras'd. 1624.

Sions Sonets: Sung by Solomon the King, Periphras'd. 1625.

Argalus and Parthenia. 1629.

Divine Poems. 1630.

The Historie of Samson. 1631.

Divine Fancies: Digested into Epigrammes, Meditations, and Observations. 1632.

Emblemes ⟨with *Lusus Poëticus Poëtis*⟩. 1635.

An Elegie upon the Truely Lamented Death of the Right Honourable Sir Julius Caesar. 1636.

*An Elegie upon My Deare Brother, the Jonathan of My Heart, M*ʳ· *John Wheeler.* 1637.

Hieroglyphikes of the Life of Man. 1638.

Memorials upon the Death of Sir Robert Quarles. 1639.

Emblemes ⟨with *Hieroglyphikes of the Life of Man*⟩. 1639.

Enchiridion. 1640.

Sighes at the Contemporary Deaths of Those Incomparable Sisters, the Countesse of Cleaveland, and Mistrisse Cicily Killegrue ⟨with *An Elegie upon the Truely Lamented Death of Sir John Wolstenholme*⟩. 1640.

Threnodes on Lady Marsham and William Cheyne. 1641.

Observations concerning Princes and States, upon Peace and Warre. 1642.

The Loyall Convert. 1644.

The Whipper Whipt: Being a Reply upon a Scandalous Pamphlet, Called The Whip. 1644.

Boanerges and Barnabas; or, Judgement and Mercy for Afflicted Soules. 1644 [Part 2; as *Barnabas and Boanerges; or, Wine and Oyle for Afflicted Soules*]; 1646 [Part 1; as *Judgement and Mercy for Afflicted Soules*].

The Shepheards Oracles. 1644, 1646.

The New Distemper. 1645.

The Profest Royalist: His Quarrell with the Times: Maintained in Three Tracts, viz. The Loyall Convert, The New Distemper, The Whipper Whipt. 1645.

Solomons Recantation, Entituled: Ecclesiastes, Paraphrased. 1645.

Hosanna; or, Divine Poems on the Passion of Christ. 1647.
The Virgin Widow. 1649.
Complete Works in Prose and Verse. Ed. Alexander B. Grosart. 1880–81. 3 vols.
Hosanna; or, Divine Poems on the Passion of Christ, and Threnodes. Ed. John Horden. 1960.
Selections. 1971.

WILLIAM CHILLINGWORTH (1602–1644)

The Religion of Protestants a Safe Way to Salvation; or, An Answer to a Booke Entitled Mercy and Truth; *or, Charity Maintain'd by Catholiques, Which Pretends to Prove the Contrary.* 1638, 1644 (with *The Apostolical Institution of Episcopacy* and *IX. Sermons*).
The Apostolicall Institution of Episcopacy. 1644.
A Sermon Preached before His Majesty at Reading. 1644.
A Sermon Preached at the Publike Fast before His Majesty at Christ-Church in Oxford. 1644.
Letter Touching Infallibility. 1662.
The Religion of Protestants; with an Addition of Some Genuine Pieces Never Before Printed. Ed. John Patrick. 1687. 3 parts.
Works. 1704.

WILLIAM LAUD (1573–1645)

A Sermon Preached before His Majesty at Wansted. 1621.
A Sermon Preached at White-Hall on the 24. of March, 1621, Beeing the Day of the Beginning of His Majestie's Most Gracious Reigne. 1622.
An Answere to Mr Fishers Relation of a Third Conference betweene a Certain B., as He Stiles Him, and Himselfe. 1624.
A Sermon Preached before His Majestie, at White-Hall. 1625.
A Sermon Preached at Westminster, at the Opening of the Parliament. 1625.
A Sermon Preached before His Majestie at White-Hall, at the Solemne Fast Then Held. 1626.
A Sermon Preached at Westminster, at the Opening of the Parliament. 1628.
XCVI Sermons by Lancelot Andrewes (editor; with John Buckeridge). 1629. 3 parts.
Opuscula Quaedam Posthuma by Lancelot Andrewes (editor; with John Buckeridge). 1629. 2 parts.
A Speech Delivered in the Starr-Chamber, at the Censure of J. Bastwick, H. Burton & W. Prinn, concerning Pretended Innovations in the Church. 1637.
A Relation of the Conference betweene William Laud and Mr. Fisher, the Jesuite. 1639.
A Letter Sent by William Laud, Archbishop of Canterbury, with Divers Manuscripts to the University of Oxford. 1641.
A True Copy of a Letter Sent to the University of Oxford, When He Resign'd His Office of Chancellour. 1641.
A Letter Sent from the Archbishop of Canterbury, Now Prisoner in the Tower, to the Vice Chancellor, Doctors, and the Rest of the Convocation at Oxford, Intimating His Humble Desires to His Majesty, for a Speedy Reconcilement between Him and His High Court of Parliament. 1642.
The Copy of the Petition Presented to the Honourable Houses of Parliament by the Lord Archbishop of Canterbury, &c., Wherein the Said Archbishop Desires That He May Not Be Transported beyond the Seas into New England with Master Peters, in Regard to His Extraordinary Age and Weaknesse. 1643.
The Archbishop of Canterbury's Speech; or, His Funerall Sermon, Preached by Himself on the Scaffold on Tower-Hill. 1644.
A Commemoration of King Charles His Inauguration. 1645.
Officium Quotidianum; or, A Manual of Private Devotions. 1650.
Seven Sermons Preached upon Severall Occasions. 1651.
A Summarie of Devotions. 1667.
The History of the Troubles and Tryal of the Most Revered Father in God, and Blessed Martyr, William Laud, Wrote by Himselfe during His Imprisonment in the Tower. Ed. Henry Wharton. 1695.
The Second Volume of the Remains of William Laud. Eds. Henry and Edmund Wharton. 1700.
Liturgy, Episcopacy, and Church Ritual: Three Speeches. 1840.
Works. Eds. William Scott and James Bliss. 1847–60. 7 vols.

EDWARD LORD HERBERT (1583–1648)

De Veritate. 1645. 2 parts.
De Causis Errorum; Una cum Tractatu de Religione Laici, et Appendice ad Sacerdotes; nec non Quibusdam Poematibus. 1645. 3 parts.
The Life and Reigne of King Henry the Eighth. 1649.
De Religione Gentilium, Eorumque apud Eos Causis. 1663.
Occasional Verses. 1665.
The Life of Edward Lord Herbert of Cherbury, Written by Himself. 1764.
The Expedition to the Isle of Rhé. Ed. the Earl of Powis. 1860.
Poems. Ed. John Churton Collins. 1881.
Poems, English and Latin. Ed. G. C. Moore Smith. 1923.
De Religione Laici. Ed. and tr. Harold R. Hutcheson. 1944.

WILLIAM DRUMMOND (1585–1649)

Teares on the Death of Meliades. 1613.
Poems. c. 1614.
Poems: Amorous, Funerall, Divine, Pastoral, in Sonnets, Songs, Sextains, Madrigals. 1616.
In Memory of Euphemia Kyninghame. 1616.
Forth Feasting: A Panegyricke to the Kings Most Excellent Majestie. 1617.
A Midnight's Trance. 1619.
Flowres of Sion; to Which Is Adjoyned His Cypresse Grove. 1623.
Auctarium Bibliothecae Edinburgenae. 1627.
The Entertainment of the High and Mighty Monarch Charles King of Great Britaine, France, and Ireland. 1633.
To the Exequies of the Honourable Sr Antonye Alexander, Knight: A Pastorall Elegie. 1638.
Polemo-Medinia inter Vitarvam et Nebernam. c. 1645.
The Drunkards Character. 1646.
The History of Scotland from the Year 1423 until the Year 1542, Containing the Lives and Reigns of James the I. the II. the III. the IV. the V. 1655.
Poems. 1656.
The Drunkard Forewarn'd. 1680.
Works. Eds. John Sage and Thomas Ruddiman. 1711. 2 parts.
Poems. 1790.
Poems. Ed. Thomas Maitland. 1832.
Poems. Ed. Peter Cunningham. 1833.
Notes on Ben Jonson's Conversations with William Drummond. Ed. David Laing. 1842.
Poetical Works. Ed. William B. Trumbull. 1856.
Poems. Ed. W. C. Ward. 1894. 2 vols.
Poetical Works, with A Cypress Grove. Ed. L. E. Kastner. 1913. 2 vols.

Poems and Prose. Ed. Robert H. MacDonald. 1976.

JOHN WINTHROP (1588–1649)

Antinomians and Familists Condemned by the Synod of Elders in New-England. 1644.

A Declaration of Former Passages and Proceedings betwixt the English and Narrowgansets, with Their Confederates. 1645.

A Journal of the Transactions and Occurrences in the Settlement of Massachusetts and the Other New-England Colonies, from the Year 1630 to 1644 ⟨*History of New England*⟩. Ed. Noah Webster. 1790.

Some Old Puritan Love-Letters: John and Margaret Winthrop 1613–1638. Ed. Joseph Hopkins Twitchell. 1893.

Conclusions for the Plantation in New England. 1896.

Wintrhop Papers 1498–1649 (with others). 1929–47. 5 vols.

RICHARD CRASHAW (c. 1613–1649)

Epigrammatum Sacrorum Liber. 1634.

Steps to the Temple. 1646.

Carmen Deo Nostro. 1652.

A Letter to the Countess of Denbigh, against Irresolution and Delay in Matters of Religion. 1653.

Poemata et Epigrammata. 1670.

Epigrammata Sacra Selecta. 1682.

Poetry. Ed. Peregrine Philips. 1785.

The Suspicion of Herod. 1834.

Poetical Works. Ed. George Gilfillan. 1857.

Complete Works. Ed. Alexander B. Grosart. 1872–73. 2 vols.

Delights of the Muses. Ed. J. R. Tutin. 1900.

Poems. Ed. A. R. Waller. 1904.

Poems English, Latin, and Greek. Ed. L. C. Martin. 1927.

Complete Poetry. Ed. George Walton Williams. 1970.

JOHN SELDEN (1584–1654)

The Duello or Single Combat. 1610.

Jani Anglorum Facies Altera. 1610.

Titles of Honor. 1614.

Analecton Anglo-Britannicon Libri Duo. 1615.

De Dis Syris Syntagmata II. 1617.

The Historie of Tithes. 1618.

Historiae Novorum sive Sui Saeculi Libri VI by Eadmer the Monk (editor). 1623.

Marmora Arundelliana (editor; with Richard James and Patrick Young). 1628.

De Successionibus in Bona Defuncti, seu Jure Haereditario, ad Leges Ebraeorum. 1631.

Mare Clausum; seu, De Dominio Maris Libri Duo. 1635.

De Jure Naturali et Gentium juxta Disciplinam Ebraeorum Libri Septem. 1640.

A Brief Discourse concerning the Power of the Peeres and Comons of Parliament, in Point of Judicature. 1640.

Ecclesiae Suae Origines by Eutychius (editor). 1642.

The Priviledges of the Baronage of England. 1642.

De Anno Civili & Calendario Veteris Ecclesiae seu Reipublicae Judaicae Dissertatio. 1644.

Uxor Ebraica; seu, De Nuptiis et Divortiis ex Jure Civili, id est Divino et Talmudico, Veterum Ebraeorum Libri Tres. 1646.

De Synedriis et Prefecturis Judicis Veterum Ebraeorum. 1650–55. 3 vols.

Vindiciae Secundum Integritatem Existimationis Suae. 1653.

Θεάνθρωπος; or, *God Made Man.* 1661.

A Brief Discourse Touching the Office of Lord Chancellor of England. Ed. William Dugdale. 1671.

Of the Judicature in Parliaments. 1681.

Tracts. 1683. 3 parts.

Table-Talk. Ed. Richard Milward. 1689.

Opera Omnia. Ed. David Wilkins. 1726. 3 vols.

Ad Fletam Dissertatio. Ed. David Ogg. 1925.

Table-Talk. Ed. Sir Frederick Pollock. 1927.

WILLIAM HABINGTON (1605–1654)

Castara. 1634. 2 parts.

The Queen of Arragon. 1640.

The Historie of Edward the Fourth, King of England. 1640.

Observations upon Historie. 1641.

Castara. Ed. Edward Arber. 1870.

Poems. Ed. Kenneth Allott. 1948.

JOSEPH HALL (1574–1656)

Virgidemiarum: Six Bookes. 1597–98.

[*The Anathomie of Sin.* 1603.]

The Kings Prophecie; or, Weeping Joy. 1603.

Meditations and Vowes, Divine and Morall. 1605.

Mundus Alter et Idem; sive, Terra Australis. c. 1605.

Heaven upon Earth; or, Of True Peace and Tranquillitie of Minde. 1606.

The Arte of Divine Meditation. 1607.

Holy Observations. 1607. 2 parts.

Characters of Vertues and Vices. 1608.

Pharisaisme and Christianity. 1608.

Epistles. 1608 [Volumes 1–2], 1610 [Volume 3, Part 2], 1611 [Volume 3, Part 1].

The Passion-Sermon. 1609.

Salomon's Divine Arts. 1609. 4 parts.

The Peace of Rome. 1609.

A Common Apologie of the Church of England. 1610.

Polemices Sacrae Pars Prior: Roma Irreconciliabilis. 1611.

Contemplations upon the Principall Passages of the Holy Storie. 1612 [Volume 1], 1614 [Volume 2], 1615 [Volume 3], 1618 [Volume 4], 1620 [Volume 5], 1622 [Volume 6], 1623 [Volume 7], 1626 [Volume 8; as *Contemplations upon the Historicall Part of the Old Testament*].

An Holy Panegyrick. 1613.

A Recollection of Such Treatises as Have Bene Heretofore Severally Published. 1615.

Quo Vadis? A Just Censure of Travell, as It Is Commonly Undertaken by the Gentlemen of Our Nation. 1617.

The Righteous Mammon: An Hospitall Sermon. 1618.

The Honor of the Married Clergie Mayntayned. 1620.

The Great Impostor Laid Open. 1623.

The Best Bargaine. 1623.

A Sermon Preached at the Restored and Reedified Chapell of the Earle of Exceter. 1624.

The True Peace-Maker. 1624.

Columba Noae Olivum Adferens Jactatissimae Christi Arcae. 1624.

Works. 1625, 1628 (2 vols.).

A Sermon of Publike Thanksgiving for the Wonderfull Mitigation of the Late Mortalitie. 1626.

The Olde Religion. 1628.

One of the Sermons Preacht at Westminster, on the Day of the Publike Fast. 1628.

One of the Sermons Preach't to the Lords of the High Court of Parliament, in Their Solemne Fast Held on Ash Wednesday. 1629.

An Answer to Pope Urban His Inurbanitie. 1629.

The Reconciler. 1629.

The Hypocrite. 1630.

Occasionall Meditations. 1630.

A Plaine and Familiar Explication—by Way of Paraphrase—of All the Hard Texts in the Whole Divine Scripture of the Old and New Testament. 1633.

Propositiones Catholicae. 1633.

The Residue of the Contemplation upon the New Testament, with Sermons. 1634.

Henochismus; sive, Tractatus de Modo Ambulandi cum Deo. 1635.

Αυτοσχεδιάσματα; *vel, Meditatiunculae Subitanae.* 1635.

The Character of Man. 1635.

The Remedy of Prophaneness; or, Of the True Sight and Feare of the Almighty. 1637.

Exeter—at the Consecration of a New Burial Place. 1637.

Certaine Irrefragable Propositions Worthy of Serious Consideration. 1639.

An Humble Remonstrance to the High Court of Parliament. 1640.

Christian Moderation. 1640. 2 parts.

Episcopacie by Divine Right. 1640. 3 parts.

A Letter Sent to an Honourable Gentleman in Way of Satisfaction. 1641.

A Defence of the Humble Remonstrance. 1641.

A Sermon Preach't to His Majesty, at the Court of White-hall. 1641.

A Short Answer to the Tedious Vindication of Smectymnuus. 1641.

A Survay of the Foolish, Seditious, Scandalous, Prophane Libell, The Protestation Protested. 1641.

Osculum Pacis. 1641.

A Letter Lately Sent by a Reverend Bishop from the Tower to a Private Friend. 1642.

A Modest Confutation of ⟨John Milton's⟩ Animadversions upon the Remonstrants Defence against Smectymnuus. 1642.

The Lawfulnes and Unlawfulnes of an Oath or Covenant. 1643.

A Modest Offer of Some Meet Considerations. 1644.

The Devout Soul; or, Rules of Heavenly Devotion. 1644.

The Peace-Maker: Laying Forth the Right Way of Peace, in the Matter of Religion. 1644.

The Remedy of Discontentment. 1645.

The Balme of Gilead; or, Comforts for the Distressed Both Morall and Divine. 1646.

Three Tractates. 1646.

Christ Mysticall; or, The Blessed Union of Christ and His Members. 1647.

Satans Fiery Darts Quenched; or, Temptations Repelled. 1647.

Bishop Hall's Hard Measure. 1647.

The Breathings of the Devout Soul. 1648.

Pax Terris. 1648.

Select Thoughts: One Century. 1648.

Resolutions and Decisions of Divers Practicall Cases of Conscience. 1649.

Χειροθεσία; *or, The Apostolique Institution of Imposition of Hands, for Confirmation, Revised.* 1649.

The Revelation Unrevealed. 1650.

Susurrium cum Deo: Soliloquies. 1651.

Holy Raptures; or, Patheticall Mediatations of the Love of Christ; Together with a Treatise of Christ Mysticall. 1652.

The Great Mysterie of Godliness. 1652.

The Holy Order or Fraternity of the Mourners of Sion. 1654.

Select Thoughts; or, Choice Helps for a Pious Spirit. 1654. 2 parts.

An Apologeticall Letter to a Person of Quality. 1655.

A Letter concerning Christmasse. 1659.

The Invisible World. 1659.

The Shaking of the Olive-Tree: Remaining Works. 1660. 2 parts.

Works. 1662. 3 vols.

Divers Treatises: Third Tome. 1662.

Psittacorum Regio: The Land of Parrots; or, She-Land. 1669.

Episcopal Admonition: Sent in a Letter to the House of Commons, April 28, 1628. 1681.

Contemplations on the History of the New Testament. Ed. W. Dodd. 1714. 2 vols.

Extracts from Various Devotional Writings. Ed. J. Riland. 1784.

Selections from Works. Ed. Basil Montagu. 1807.

Works. Ed. Josiah Pratt. 1808. 10 vols.

Sacred Aphorisms. Ed. R. B. Exton. 1823.

Select Tracts. Ed. C. Bradley. 1824.

Works. Ed. Peter Hall. 1837–39. 12 vols.

Works. Ed. Philip Wynter. 1863. 10 vols.

Devotions, Sacred Aphorisms, and Religious Table Talk. Ed. J. W. Morris. 1867.

Complete Poems. Ed. Alexander B. Grosart. 1879.

Heaven upon Earth and Characters of Vertues and Vices. Ed. Rudolf Kirk. 1948.

Collected Poems. Ed. A. Davenport. 1949.

JOHN HALES (1584–1656)

Oratio Funebris Habita in Collegio Mertonensi Quo Die T. Bodleio Funus Ducebatur. 1613.

A Sermon concerning the Abuses of Obscure and Difficult Places of Holy Scripture, and the Remedies against Them. 1617.

Dissertatio de Pace et Concordia Ecclesiae. 1630.

A Way towards the Finding of a Decision of the Chiefe Controversie Now Debated concerning Church Government. 1641.

A Tract concerning Schisme and Schismaticks. 1642.

Of the Blasphemie against the Holy-Ghost. 1646.

Golden Remains. Ed. Peter Gunning. 1659. 3 parts.

Sermons Preached at Eton. 1660.

Several Tracts. 1677.

Works. Ed. Sir David Dalrymple. 1765. 3 vols.

WILLIAM BRADFORD (1588–1657)

A Relation of Journall of the Beginning and Proceedings of the English Plantation Setled at Plimoth in New England. 1622.

A Dialogue, or the Sum of a Conference betweene Some Yonge-Men, Born in New England, and Sundry Ancient-Men, That Came out of Holand and Old England. 1648.

History of Plymouth Plantation. Ed. Charles Deane. 1856.

A Dialogue or Third Conference between Some Young Men Born in New England, and Some Ancient Men Which Came out of Holland and Old England, concerning the Church and the Government Thereof. Ed. Charles Deane. 1870.

Letter Book. 1906.

A Letter to the Reverend John Cotton. 1914.

Of Plymouth Plantation 1620–1647. Ed. Samuel Eliot Morison. 1952.

Collected Verse. Ed. Michael G. Runyan. 1974.

RICHARD LOVELACE (1618–c. 1657)

Lucasta: Epodes, Odes, Sonnets, Songs, &c.; to Which Is Added Amarantha: A Pastorall. 1649.

Lucasta: Posthume Poems. Ed. D. P. Lovelace. 1659–60. 2 parts.

Lucasta. Ed. S. W. Singer. 1817–18. 2 vols.
Lucasta. Ed. William Carew Hazlitt. 1864.
Lucasta. Ed. William Lyon Phelps. 1921. 2 vols.
Poems. Ed. C. H. Wilkinson. 1925. 2 vols.

JOHN CLEVELAND (1613–1658)

*The Character of a London-Diurnall; with Severall Select Po-
    ems* ⟨with others?⟩. 1644.
The Scots Apostacy. 1646.
*The Character of a Moderate Intelligencer; with Some Select
    Poems.* 1647.
The Kings Disguise. 1647.
*The Character of a Country Committee-Man, with the Eare-
    marke of a Sequestrator.* 1649.
Majestas Intemerata; or, The Immortality of the King. 1649.
[*Jeremias Redivivus; or, An Elegiacall Lamentation on the
    Death of Our English Josias Charles the First, King of
    Great Britaine, &c., Publiquely Murdered by His Cal-
    vino-Judaicall Subjects.* 1649.]
The Hue and Cry after Sir John Presbyter. 1649.
Poems; with Additions. 1651. 2 parts.
The Character of a Diurnal-Maker. 1654.
The Idol of the Clownes; or, The Insurrection of Wat the Tyler.
    1654.
Cleaveland's Petition to His Highness the Lord Protector. 1657.
*The Rustick Rampant; or, Rural Anarchy Affronting Monar-
    chy.* 1658.
*J. Cleaveland Revived: Poems, Orations, Epistles, and Other of
    His Genuine Incomparable Pieces, Never before Published.*
    1659.
On the Most Renowned Prince Rupert. 1660.
*Clievelandi Vindiciae; or, Clieveland's Genuine Poems, Ora-
    tions, Epistles, &c.* Eds. John Lake and Samuel Drake.
    1677.
Works. Eds. John Lake and Samuel Drake. 1687.
Poems. Ed. John M. Berdan. 1903.
Poems. Eds. Brian Morris and Eleanor Withington. 1967.

SIR THOMAS URQUHART (1611–1660)

Epigrams: Divine and Moral. 1641.
*The Trissotetras; or, A Most Exquisite Table for Resolving All
    Manner of Triangles.* 1645.
Εκσκυβαλαυρον; *or, The Discovery of a Most Exquisite Jewel.*
    1652.
Παντοχρονοχανον; *or, A Peculiar Promptuary of Time.* Ed.
    George Paton. 1652.
*Logopandecteision; or, An Introduction to the Universal Lan-
    guage.* 1653. 2 parts.
The Works of Mr. Francis Rabelais (translator). 1653 [Book 1];
    1653 [Book 2]; 1693 [Book 3]; 1694 [5 vols.; with Peter
    Anthony Motteux].
Tracts. Ed. David Herd. 1774.
Works. Ed. Thomas Maitland. 1834.
The Life and Death of the Admirable Crichtoun. Ed. Hamish
    Miles. 1927.
Selections. Ed. John Purves. 1942.
*A Challenge from Sir Thomas Urquhart to His Cousin John
    Urquhart of Craigfingtray in 1658.* Ed. C. H. Wilkinson.
    1948.
The Jewel. Eds. R. D. S. Jack and R. J. Lyall. 1983.

THOMAS FULLER (1608–1661)

*David's Hainous Sinne, Heartie Repentance, Heavie Punish-
    ment.* 1631.
The Historie of the Holy Warre. 1639.

Joseph's Partlie-Coloured Coat. 1640.
The Holy State ⟨with *The Profane State*⟩. 1642.
A Fast Sermon Preached on Innocents Day. 1642.
*A Sermon at the Collegiat Church of S. Peter in Westminster,
    on the 27. of March, Being the Day of His Majesties
    Inauguration.* 1643.
A Sermon of Reformation. 1643.
*Truth Maintained; or, Positions Delivered in a Sermon at the
    Savoy.* 1643.
*Jacob's Vow: A Sermon Preached before His Majesty, and the
    Prince His Highnesse.* 1644.
*Good Thoughts in Bad Times: Consisting of Personall Medita-
    tions, Scripture Observations, Historicall Applications,
    Mixt Contemplations.* 1645.
*Feare of Losing the Old Light; or, A Sermon Preached in
    Exeter.* 1646.
Andronicus; or, The Unfortunate Politician. 1646.
The Cause and Cure of a Wounded Conscience. 1647.
*Good Thoughts in Worse Times: Consisting of Personall Med-
    itations, Scripture Observations, Meditations on the
    Times, Meditations on All Kinds of Prayers, Occasional
    Meditations.* 1647.
A Sermon of Assurance. 1647.
A Sermon of Contentment. 1648.
*Good Thoughts in Bad Times, Together with Good Thoughts in
    Worse Times.* 1649.
The Just Mans Funeral. 1649.
*A Pisgah-Sight of Palestine and the Confines Thereof, with the
    History of the Old and New Testament Acted Thereon.*
    1650.
*A Comment on the Eleven First Verses of the Fourth Chapter of
    S. Matthew's Gospel, concerning Christs Temptations:
    Delivered in XII. Sermons.* 1652.
Perfection and Peace: Delivered in a Sermon. 1653.
*The Infants Advocate: Of Circumcision on Jewish Children and
    Baptisme on Christian Children.* 1653.
Two Sermons. 1654.
A Comment on Ruth; Together with Two Sermons. 1654.
A Triple Reconciler. 1654.
Life out of Death: A Sermon. 1655.
*The Church-History of Britain from the Birth of Jesus Christ,
    untill the Year M.DC.XLVIII; ⟨etc.⟩.* 1655. 6 parts.
Antheologia; or, The Speech of Flowers. 1655.
A Collection of Sermons. 1656.
*The Best Name on Earth, Together with Several Other Sermons
    Lately Preached at S. Brides and in Other Places.* 1657.
*A Sermon Preached at St Clemens Danes, at the Funeral of Mr.
    George Heycock.* 1657.
*The Sovereigns Prerogative, and the Subjects Priviledge: Dis-
    cussed betwixt Courtiers and Patriots in Parliament, the
    Third and Fourth Yeares of the Reign of King Charles*
    (editor). 1657.
The Appeal of Injured Innocence. 1659.
An Alarum to the Counties of England and Wales. 1660.
Mixt Contemplations in Better Times. 1660.
A Panegyrick to His Majesty, on His Happy Return. 1660.
[*Andronicus: A Tragedy.* 1661.]
The History of the Worthies of England. 1662.
Poems and Translations in Verse. Ed. Alexander B. Grosart.
    1868.
Pulpit Speaks: Being xix. Sermons. Ed. Morris Fuller. 1886.
Collected Sermons. Eds. John Eglington Bailey and William
    E. A. Axon. 1891. 2 vols.
Fuller's Thoughts. Ed. A. R. Waller. 1902.
Selections. Ed. E. K. Broadus. 1928.

KATHERINE PHILIPS (1632–1664)

Pompey by Pierre Corneille (translator). 1663.

Poems. 1664.

Poems; to Which Is Added Corneille's Pompey and Horace. 1667. 2 parts.

Familiar Letters (with others). Eds. Thomas Brown and Charles Gildon. 1697. 2 vols.

Letters from Orinda to Poliarchus 〈Sir Charles Cotterell〉. 1705.

Selected Poems. Ed. J. R. Tutin. 1904–05. 2 vols.

SIR KENELM DIGBY (1603–1665)

Articles of Agreement Made between the French King and Those of Rochell; Also a Relation of the Brave Sea-Fight Made by Sr. Kenelam Digby. 1628.

A Conference with a Lady about Choyce of Religion. 1638.

[*Sir Kenelme Digbyes Honour Maintained.* 1641.]

A Coppy of 1. The Letter Sent by the Queenes Majestie 〈Henriette Maria〉 *concerning the Collection of the Recusants Mony for the Scottish Warre; 2. The Letter Sent by Sir Kenelme Digby and Mr.* 〈Walter〉 *Montague concerning the Contribution.* 1641.

Observations upon Religio Medici. 1643.

Observations on the 22. Stanza in the 9th. Canto of the 2d. Book of Spencers Faery Queen. 1643.

Two Treatises, in the One of Which the Nature of Bodies; in the Other the Nature of Mans Soule Is Looked Into. 1644.

[*The Royall Apologie; or, An Answer to the Declaration of the House of Commons, the 11. of February, 1647.* 1648.]

Letters between the Ld George Digby and Sr Kenelm Digby K^t concerning Religion. 1651.

A Discourse concerning Infallibility in Religion. 1652.

A Treatise of Adhering to God 〈by Saint Albert, Bishop of Ratisbon (translator)〉; *Also a Conference with a Lady about Choyce of Religion.* 1654.

Discours touchant la guerison des playes par la poudre de sympathie. 1658.

A Discourse concerning the Vegetation of Plants. 1661.

Choice and Experimental Receipts in Physick and Chirurgery. 1668.

The Closet of the Eminently Learned Sir Kenelme Digbie K^t Opened. 1669.

Of Bodies, and of Man's Soul, to Discover the Immortality of Reasonable Souls; with Two Discourses of the Powder of Sympathy and of the Vegetation of Plants. 1669. 2 parts.

Private Memoirs. Ed. Sir Nicholas Harris Nicolas. 1827.

Journal of a Voyage into the Mediterranean, A.D. 1628. Ed. John Bruce. 1868.

Poems. Ed. Henry A. Bright. 1877.

JAMES SHIRLEY (1596–1666)

The Wedding. 1629.

The Gratefull Servant. 1630.

The Schoole of Complement 〈Love Tricks〉. 1631.

Changes; or, Love in a Maze. 1632.

A Contention for Honour and Riches. 1633.

The Wittie Faire One. 1633.

The Bird in a Cage. 1633.

The Triumph of Peace: A Masque. 1633.

The Traytor. 1635.

Hide Park. 1637.

The Gamester. 1637.

The Young Admirall. 1637.

The Example. 1637.

The Lady of Pleasure. 1637.

The Dukes Mistris. 1638.

The Royall Master. 1638.

The Ball. 1639.

The Maides Revenge. 1639.

The Tragedie of Chabot Admirall of France by George Chapman (revised by Shirley). 1639.

Loves Crueltie. 1640.

The Opportunitie. 1640.

The Coronation. 1640.

The Constant Maid. 1640.

St Patrick for Ireland. 1640.

The Humorous Courtier. 1640.

A Pastoral Called The Arcadia. 1640.

Poems, &c. 1646. 4 parts.

Via ad Latinam Linguam Complanata: The Way Made Plain to the Latine Tongue; the Rules Composed in English and Latine Verse, for the Greater Delight and Benefit of Learners. 1649, 1651 (as Grammatica Anglo-Latina).

Six New Playes, viz. The Brothers, The Sisters, The Doubtfull Heir, The Imposture, The Cardinall, The Court Secret. 1653. 6 parts.

Cupid and Death: A Masque. 1653.

The Gentleman of Venice. 1655.

The Politician. 1655.

Εἰσαγωγή; *sive, Introductorium Anglo-Latino-Graecum.* 1656.

The Rudiments of Grammar: The Rules Composed in English Verse for the Greater Benefit and Delight of Young Beginners. 1656, 1660 (as Manuductio).

No Wit, No Help Like a Womans by Thomas Middleton (revised by Shirley). 1657.

Honoria and Mammon; Whereunto Is Added The Contention of Ajax and Ulisses, for the Armor of Achilles. 1659.

The True Impartial History and Wars of the Kingdom of Ireland. 1692.

An Essay towards an Universal and Rational Grammar. Ed. Jenkin T. Philipps. 1726.

Dramatic Works and Poems. Eds. William Gifford and Alexander Dyce. 1833. 6 vols.

James Shirley. Ed. Edmund Gosse. 1888.

Poems. Ed. Ray Livingstone Armstrong. 1941.

GEORGE WITHER (1588–1667)

Prince Henries Obsequies; or, Mournefull Elegies upon His Death. 1612.

Epithalamia; or, Nuptiall Poems. 1612.

Abuses Stript, and Whipt; or, Satyrical Essaies; Also the Scourge: Epigrams. 1613.

A Satyre: Dedicated to His Most Excellent Maiestie. 1614.

Fidelia. 1615.

The Shepheards Hunting: Being, Certaine Eglogs Written during the Time of the Authors Imprisonment in the Marshalsey. 1615.

A Preparation to the Psalter. 1619.

Exercises upon the First Psalme. 1620.

Workes: Containing Satyrs, Epigrams, Eclogues, Sonnets, and Poems. 1620.

The Songs of the Old Testament (translator). 1621.

Wither's Motto: Nec Habeo, Nec Careo, Nec Curo. 1621.

Faire-Virtue, the Mistresse of Phil'arete. 1622.

Juvenilia. 1622.

The Hymnes and Songs of the Church (translator). 1623.

The Schollers Purgatory, Discovered in the Stationers Commonwealth, and Described in a Discorse Apologeticall. 1624.

Britain's Remembrancer: Containing a Narrative of the Plague Lately Past. 1628.

The Psalmes of David (translator). 1632.

A Collection of Emblemes, Ancient and Modern. 1634–35. 4 books.

The Nature of Man by Nemesius (translator). 1636.

A New Song of a Young Mans Opinion of the Difference between Good and Bad Women. c. 1640.

Heleluiah; or, Britains Second Remembrancer. 1641.

A Prophesie Written Long Since for This Year, 1641. 1641.

Read and Wonder: A Warre between Two Entire Friends, the Pope and the Divell. 1641.

Mercurius Rusticus; or, A Countrey Messenger. 1643.

Campo-Musae; or, The Field-Musings of Captain George Wither. 1643.

Se Defendendo: A Shield, and Shaft, against Detraction. 1643.

The Speech without Doore. 1644.

The Two Incomparable Generalissimo's of the World, with Their Armies Briefly Described and Embattailled. 1644.

The Great Assises Holden in Parnassus by Apollo and His Assessours. 1645.

Vox Pacifica: A Voice Tending to the Pacification of God's Wrath. 1645.

Justitiarius Justificatus: Justice Justified. 1646.

To the Most Honourable the Lords and Commons in Parliament Assembled: The Humble Declaration and Petition of Geo. Wither. 1646.

What Peace to the Wicked? 1646.

Opobalsamum Anglicanum: An English Balme, Lately Pressed out of a Shrub, and Spread upon These Papers. 1646.

Carmen Expostulatorium. 1647.

Amygdala Britannica: Almonds for Perrets. 1647.

The Doubtfull Almanack. 1647.

Major Wither's Disclaimer. 1647.

The Tired Petitioner, to His Noble Friends, Who Are Members of the Honourable House of Commons. c. 1647.

Prosopopoeia Britannica: Britans Genius, or, Good-Angel, Personated. 1648.

Carmen-Ternarium Semi-Cynicum. c. 1648.

Articles Presented against This Parliament. 1648.

A Si Quis; or, Queries. 1648.

A Thankful Retribution. 1649.

An Allarum from Heaven; or, A Memento to the Great Councell. 1649.

Vaticinium Votivum; or, Palaemon's Prophetick Prayer. 1649.

Carmen Eucharisticon: A Private Thank-Oblation. 1649.

Respublica Anglicana; or, The Historie of Parliament in Their Late Proceedings. 1650.

The True State of the Cause of George Wither Esq. 1650.

Three Grains of Spirituall Frankincense Infused into Three Hymnes of Praise. 1651.

British Appeals, with Gods Mercifull Replies, on Behalf of the Common-wealth of England. 1651.

A Timelie Caution. 1652.

The Modern States-man. 1653.

The Dark Lantern, Containing a Dim Discoverie (with *The Perpetuall Parliament*). 1653.

Westrow Revived: A Funerall Poem without Fiction. 1653.

To the Parliament of the Common-wealth of England: The Humble Petition of G. W. 1654.

The Protector. 1655.

Vaticinium Casuale. 1655.

Boni Ominis Votum: A Good Omen to the Next Parliament. 1656.

A Suddain Flash, Timely Discovering Some Reason Wherefore the Stile of Protector Should Not Be Deserted by These Nations. 1657.

An Address to Members of Parliament in Their Single Capacities. 1658.

A Cause Allegorically Stated. 1658.

The Petition, and Narrative of Geo. Wither, Esq. 1659.

Salt upon Salt: Made out of Certain Ingenious Verses upon the Late Storm and the Death of His Highness Ensuing. 1659.

Epistolium-Vagum-Prosa-Metricum; or, An Epistle at Randome. 1659.

A Cordial Confection to Strengthen Their Hearts Whose Courage Begins to Fail. 1659.

Furor-Poeticus (i.e.) Propheticus. 1660.

Fides-Anglicana; or, A Plea for the Publick-Faith of These Nations. 1660.

Speculum Speculativum; or, A Considerating-Glass: Being an Inspection into the Present and Late Sad Condition of These Nations. 1660.

Joco-Serio: Strange News, of a Discourse between Two Dead Giants. 1661.

A Triple Paradox: Affixed to a Counter-Mure Raised against the Furious Batteries of Restraint, Slander, and Poverty, the Three Engines of the World, the Flesh, and the Devil. 1661.

An Improvement of Imprisonment, Disgrace, Poverty, into Real Freedom, Honest Reputation, Perdurable Riches. 1661.

The Prisoners Plea. 1661.

A Declaration of Major George Withers. 1662.

Verses Intended to the King's Majesty. 1662.

Paralellogrammaton: An Epistle to the Three Nations of England, Scotland, and Ireland. 1662.

A Proclamation in the Name of the King of Kings, to All the Inhabitants of the Isles of Great Brittain. 1662.

Tuba-Pacifica: Seasonable Precautions, Whereby Is Sounded Forth a Retreat from the War Intended between England and the United-Provinces. 1664.

Meditations upon the Lords Supper. 1665.

A Memorandum to London, Occasioned by the Pestilence There Begun This Present Year. 1665.

Three Private Meditations. 1665.

Sigh for the Pitchers. 1666.

Vaticinia Poetica. 1666.

Ecchoes from the Sixth Trumpet. 1666.

Vox et Lacrimae Anglorum; or, The True English-mans Complaints, to Their Representatives in Parliament. 1668.

Divine Poems (by Way of Paraphrase) on the Ten Commandments. 1688.

[*The Grateful Acknowledgement of a Late Trimming Regulator.* 1688.]

Predictions for the Overthrow of Popery. c. 1688.

The Strange and Wonderful Prophecy, concerning the Kingdom of England. 1689.

Extracts from Juvenilia. Ed. Alexander Dalrymple. 1785.

Select Lyrical Passages, Written about 1622. Ed. Sir Samuel Egerton Brydes. 1815.

Juvenilia. Eds. J. M. Gutch and John Mott. 1820. 4 vols.

Miscellaneous Works. 1872–78. 6 vols.

Vox Vulgi: A Poem in Censure of the Parliament of 1661. Ed. W. D. Macray. 1880.

Poems. Ed. Henry Morley. 1891.

Poetry. Ed. Frank Sidgwick. 1902. 2 vols.

The History of the Pestilence 1625. Ed. J. Milton French. 1932.

JEREMY TAYLOR (1613–1667)

A Sermon Preached in Saint Maries Church in Oxford, upon the Anniversary of the Gunpowder-Treason. 1638.

Of the Sacred Order, and Offices of the Episcopacy, by Divine Institution, Apostolicall Tradition, & Catholike Practice. 1642.

The Psalter of David; with Titles and Collects According to the Manner of Each Psalme. 1644.

A Discourse concerning Prayer ex Tempore, or, by Pretence of the Spirit. 1646.

A New and Easie Institution of Grammar (with William Wyat). 1647.

ΘΕΟΛΟΓΙΑ ΕΚΛΕΚΤΙΚΗ: *A Discourse of the Liberty of Prophesying.* 1647.

Treatises of 1. The Liberty of Prophesying; 2. Prayer ex Tempore; Together with A Sermon Preached at Oxon. on the Anniversary of the 5 of November. 1648.

An Apology for Authorised and Set Forms of Liturgie. 1649.

The Great Exemplar of Sanctity and Holy Life According to the Christian Institution. 1649.

Treatises of 1. The Liberty of Prophesying; 2. Episcopacie; 3. The History of the Life & Death of the Ever Blessed Jesus Christ; 4. An Apology for Authorized and Set-Forms of Lyturgie; Together with a Sermon Preached at Oxon. on the Anniversary of the 5. of November. 1650.

The Rule and Exercises of Holy Living. 1650.

A Funerall Sermon, Preached at the Obsequies of the Right Honble and Most Vertuous Lady, the Lady Frances, Countesse of Carbery. 1650.

Clerus Domini; or, A Discourse of the Divine Institution, Necessity, Sacredness, and Separation of the Office Ministeriall. 1651.

XXVIII Sermons Preached at Golden Grove; Together with a Discourse of the Divine Institution, Necessity, Sacredness, and Separateness of the Office Ministeriall. 1651.

The Rule and Exercises of Holy Dying. 1651.

A Short Catechism for the Institution of Young Persons in the Christian Religion; to Which Is Added, An Explication of the Apostolical Creed. 1652.

A Discourse of Baptisme: Its Institution, and Efficacy upon All Believers. 1652.

Two Discourses: 1. Of Baptisme; 2. Of Prayer ex Tempore. 1652.

XXV Sermons Preached at Golden-Grove. 1653.

ΕΝΙΑΥΤΟΣ: *A Course of Sermons for All the Sundaies of the Year.* 1653.

The Real Presence and Spirituall of Christ in the Blessed Sacrament. 1654.

The Golden Grove; or, A Manuall of Daily Prayers and Letanies, Fitted to the Dayes of the Week. 1655.

Unum Necessarium; or, The Doctrine and Practice of Repentance. 1655.

A Further Explication of the Doctrine and Practice of Repentance. 1655.

A Further Explication of the Doctrine of Originall Sin. 1656.

An Answer to a Letter Written by the R.R. the Ld Bp of Rochester, concerning the Chapter of Original Sin, in the Unum Necessarium. 1656.

Deus Justificatus; or, A Vindication of the Glory of the Divine Attributes in the Question of Original Sin. 1656.

Deus Justificatus: Two Discourses of Original Sin. 1656.

ΣΥΜΒΟΛΟΝ ΗΘΙΚΟΠΟΛΕΜΙΚΟΝ; *or, A Collection of Polemical and Moral Discourses.* 1657.

A Discourse of the Nature, Offices and Measures of Friendship, with Rules of Conducting It. 1657.

A Collection of Offices or Forms of Prayer Publick and Private. 1658.

A Sermon Preached at the Funerall of That Worthy Knight Sr. George Dalston. 1658.

Ductor Dubitantium; or, The Rule of Conscience in All Her Generall Measures. 1660. 2 vols.

The Worthy Communicant; or, A Discourse of the Nature, Effects, and Blessings Consequent to the Worthy Receiving of the Lords Supper. 1660.

A Sermon Preached at the Consecration of Two Archbishops and Ten Bishops, in the Cathedral of S. Patrick in Dublin. 1661.

A Sermon Preached at the Opening of the Parliament of Ireland. 1661.

Rules and Advices to the Clergy of the Diocese of Down and Connor. 1661.

Via Intelligentiae: A Sermon Preached to the University of Dublin. 1662.

The Righteousness Evangelicall Describ'd. 1663.

A Sermon Preached in Christ-Church, Dublin, at the Funeral of the Most Reverend Father in God, John, Late Lord Arch-bishop of Armagh and Primate of All Ireland; with a Succinct Narrative of His Whole Life. 1663.

ΧΡΙΣΙΣ ΤΕΛΕΙΩΤΙΚΗ: *A Discourse of Confirmation.* 1663.

ΕΒΔΟΜΑΣ ΕΜΒΟΛΙΜΑΙΟΣ: *A Supplement to the ENI-ΑΥΤΟΣ; or, Course of Sermons for the Whole Year: Being Seven Sermons Explaining the Nature of Faith and Obedience; in Relation to God and the Ecclesiastical and Secular Powers Respectively.* 1663.

A Dissuasive from Popery to the People of Ireland. 1664.

ΔΕΚΑΣ ΕΜΒΟΛΙΜΑΙΟΣ: *A Supplement to the ENI-ΑΥΤΟΣ: Being Ten Sermons Explaining the Nature of Faith, and Obedience, in Relation to God, and the Ecclesiastical and Secular Powers Respectively.* 1667.

The Second Part of the Dissuasive from Popery: In Vindication of the First Part. 1667.

The Rule and Exercises of Holy Living ⟨with *The Rule and Exercises of Holy Dying*⟩. 1674. 2 parts.

Antiquitates Christianae. 1675.

Christ's Yoke an Easy Yoke, and Yet the Gate to Heaven a Strait Gate, in Two Excellent Sermons. 1675.

Opuscula: The Measures of Friendship, with Additional Tracts. 1678.

Whole Works. Ed. Reginald Heber. 1822. 15 vols.

Works. Ed. T. S. Hughes. 1831. 5 vols.

On the Reverence Due to the Altar. Ed. John Barrow. 1848.

Whole Works. Ed. Reginald Heber, rev. Charles Page Eden. 1854. 10 vols.

Poems and Verse Translations. Ed. Alexander B. Grosart. 1870.

The Golden Grove: Selected Passages from the Sermons and Writings. Ed. Logan Pearsall Smith. 1930.

The House of Understanding: Selections from the Writings. Ed. Margaret Gest. 1954.

The Wisdom of Jeremy Taylor: An Anthology of His Writings. Ed. Richard Tatlock. 1954.

ABRAHAM COWLEY (1618–1667)

Poeticall Blossomes. 1633.

Loves Riddle: A Pastorall Comaedie. 1638.

Naufragium Joculare. 1638.

The Prologue and Epilogue to a Comedie ⟨*The Guardian*⟩ *Pre-*

sented, at the Entertainment of the Prince His Highnesse, by the Schollers of Trinity College in Cambridge. 1642.
[A Satyre against Separatists. 1642.]
A Satyre: The Puritan and the Papist. 1643.
The Mistress; or, Severall Copies of Love-Verses. 1647.
[The Foure Ages of England; or, The Iron Age. 1648.]
The Guardian. 1650.
Poems. 1656. 5 parts.
Ode, upon the Blessed Restoration and Returne of His Sacred Majestie, Charls the Second. 1660.
A Proposition for the Advancement of Experimental Philosophy. 1661.
The Visions and Prophecies concerning England, Scotland, and Ireland, of Ebenezer Grebner. 1661.
Plantarum Libri Dio. 1662.
Verses Lately Written upon Several Occasions. 1663.
Cutter of Coleman-Street. 1663.
Works. 1668. 5 parts.
Poemata Latina. Ed. Thomas Sprat. 1668.
A Poem on the Late Civil War. 1679.
The Second Part of the Works. 1681.
The Second and Third Parts of the Works. 1689. 2 parts.
Select Works. Ed. Richard Hurd. 1772. 2 vols.
Poetical Works. 1777. 4 vols.
Works in Prose and Verse. 1809. 3 vols.
Essays. 1819.
Complete Works in Verse and Prose. Ed. Alexander B. Grosart. 1881. 2 vols.
Prose Works. Ed. J. Rawson Lumby. 1887.
English Writings. Ed. A. R. Waller. 1905–06. 2 vols.
Essays and Other Prose Writings. Ed. Alfred B. Gough. 1915.
The Mistress, with Other Select Poems. Ed. John Sparrow. 1926.
Poetry and Prose. Ed. L. C. Martin. 1949.
The Civil War. Ed. Allan Pritchard. 1973.

SIR WILLIAM D'AVENANT (1606–1668)

The Tragedy of Albovine, King of the Lombards. 1629.
The Cruell Brother. 1630.
The Just Italian. 1630.
The Temple of Love. 1634.
The Triumphs of the Prince d'Amour. 1635.
The Platonick Lovers. 1636.
The Witts. 1636.
Britannia Triumphans. 1637.
Luminalia; or, The Festivall of Light. 1637.
Madagascar, with Other Poems. 1638.
Salmacida Spolia. 1639.
To the Honourable Knights, Citizens, and Burgesses of the Houses of Commons, Assembled in Parliament. 1641.
The Unfortunate Lovers. 1643.
[London, King Charles His Augusta, or City Royal: Of the Founders, the Names, and Oldest Honours of That City. 1648.]
Love and Honour. 1649.
A Discourse upon Gondibert; with an Answer to It by Mr Hobbs. 1650.
Gondibert: An Heroick Poem. 1651.
The Siege of Rhodes. 1656.
The First Days Entertainment at Rutland-House, by Declamations and Musick: After the Manner of the Ancients. 1657.
The Cruelty of the Spaniards in Peru. 1658.

A Panegyrick to His Excellency, the Lord Generall Monk. 1659.
The History of Sr Francis Drake. 1659. Part 1 only.
Poem upon His Sacred Majesties Most Happy Return to His Dominions. 1660.
Poem to the King's Most Sacred Majesty. 1663.
The Rivals (adaptation). 1668.
The Man's the Master. 1669.
The Tempest; or, The Enchanted Island (adaptation; with John Dryden). 1670.
The Law against Lovers. 1673.
Works. 1673. 3 parts.
Macbeth (adaptation). 1674.
The Seventh and Last Canto of the Third Book of Gondibert. 1685.
Dramatic Works. Eds. James Maidment and W. H. Logan. 1872–74. 5 vols.
Selected Poems. Ed. Douglas Bush. 1943.
Shorter Poems and Songs from the Plays and Masques. Ed. A. M. Gibbs. 1972.

WILLIAM PRYNNE (1600–1669)

The Perpetuitie of a Regenerate Mans Estate. 1626.
The Unlovelinesse, of Love-Lockes. 1628.
A Briefe Survay and Censure of Mr Cozens His Couzening Devotions. 1628.
Healthes Sicknesse. 1628.
God, No Imposter Nor Deluder; or, An Answer to a Popish and Arminian Cavill, in the Defence of Free-Will. 1629.
The Church of Englands Old Antithesis to New Arminianisme. 1629, 1630 (as Anti-Arminianisme).
A Short Relation of the True Beginning, and Progresse, of Bowing at the Name of Jesus. 1630.
Lame Giles His Haultings; or, A Brief Survey of Giles Widdowes His Confutation. 1630.
Histrio-Mastix: The Players Scourge; or, Actors Tragedie. 1633.
A Breviate of the Prelates Intollerable Usurpations. 1635.
Certain Queres Propounded to the Bowers in the Name of Jesus. 1636.
[A Divine Tragedy Lately Acted. 1636.]
A Looking Glasse for All Lordly Prelates. 1636.
The Unbishoping of Timothy and Titus. 1636.
The Lords Day, the Sabbath Day. c. 1636.
Newes from Ipswich: Discovring Certaine Late Detestable Practices of Some Domineering Lordly Prelates. c. 1636.
Briefe Instructions for Church-Wardens and Others to Observe in All Episcopal or Archdiaconall Visitations and Spirituall Courts. 1637.
A Catalogue of Such Testimonies as Evidence Bishops and Presbyters to Be Both One. 1637.
A Briefe Relation of Certaine Speeches in the Starre-Chamber. 1637.
A Quench-Coale; or, A Briefe Inquirie, in What Place of the Church or Chancell the Lords-Table Ought to Be. 1637.
XVI. New Queres Proposed to Our Lord Prelates. 1637.
Woodstreet-Compters-Plea, for Its Prisoner. 1638.
Lord Bishops None of the Lords Bishops. 1640.
The Antipathie of the English Lordly Prelacie, Both to Regall Monarchy, and Civill Unity. 1641. 2 parts.
The Humble Petition of Mr. Prynne, Late Exile, and Close Prisoner in the Ile of Jersey. 1641.
An Humble Remonstrance to His Maiesty, against the Tax of Ship-Money. 1641.
Mount-Orgueil; or, Divine and Profitable Meditations; to

Which Is Prefixed a Poetical Description, of Mount-Orgueil Castle. 1641.

A New Discovery of the Prelates Tyranny. 1641.

[*A Terrible Out-cry against the Loytering Exalted Prelates.* 1641.]

The Aphorismes of the Kingdome. 1642.

A Pleasant Purge, for a Roman Catholike, to Evacuate His Evill Humours. 1642.

A Soveraigne Antidote to Prevent, Appease, and Determine Our Unnaturall and Destructive Civill Wars. 1642.

A Vindication of Psalme 105.15. 1642.

[*Vox Populi; or, The Peoples Humble Discovery, of Their Own Loyaltie, and His Maiesties Ungrounded Jealousie.* 1642.]

Articles of Impeachment. 1643.

A Catalogue of Printed Books Written by William Prynne. 1643, 1660.

The Doome of Cowardize and Treachery. 1643.

An Humble Remonstrance against the Tax of Ship-Money Lately Imposed. 1643.

A Revindication of the Anoynting and Priviledges of Faithfull Subjects. 1643. 2 parts.

The Popish Royall Favourite; or, A Full Discovery of His Majesties Extraordinary Favours to, and Protections of Notorious Papists. 1643.

Romes Master-Peece; or, The Grand Conspiracy of the Pope. 1643.

The Soveraigne Power of Parliaments and Kingdomes. 1643. 4 parts.

The Treachery and Disloyalty of Papists to Their Soveraignes. 1643.

A Breviate of the Life of William Laud. 1644.

A Checke to Britannicus for Justifying Condemned Nat: Fiennes. 1644.

Faces About; or, A Recrimination Charged upon Mr. John Goodwin, in the Point of Fighting against God. 1644.

The Falsities and Forgeries of the Anonymous Author of The Fallacies of Mr. William Prynne, Discovered and Confuted. 1644.

Four Serious Questions of Grand Importance, concerning Suspention from the Sacrament. 1644.

A Full Reply to Certaine Briefe Observations and Anti-Queries on Master Prynnes Twelve Questions. 1644.

Independency Examined, Unmasked, Refuted, by Twelve New Particular Interrogatories. 1644.

A Moderate Apology against a Pretended Calumny. 1644.

To the Honourable Knights, Citizens, and Burgesses in This Present Parliament Assembled (with Clement Walker). 1644.

A True and Full Relation of the Persecution of Nathaniel Fiennes (with Clement Walker). 1644.

Twelve Considerable Serious Questions Touching Church Government. 1644.

The Antidote Animadverted. 1645.

A Fresh Discovery of Some Prodigious New Wandring-Blasing-Stars. 1645.

Hidden Workes of Darkness Brought to Publike Light. 1645.

[*A Just Defence of John Bastwick against the Calumnies of John Lilburne.* 1645.]

The Lyar Confounded; or, A Brief Refutation of John Lilburne's Seditious Calumnies. 1645.

Truth Triumphing over Falshood, Antiquity over Novelty. 1645.

A Vindication of Foure Serious Questions of Grand Importance. 1645.

The Whole Triall of Connor Lord Macquire. 1645.

Canterburies Doome; or, The First Part of a Compleat History of the Commitment, Charge, Tryall, Condemnation, Execution of William Laud. 1646.

Diotrephes Catechised; or, Sixteen Important Questions Touching the Ecclesiastical Jurisdiction. 1646.

A Gagge for Long-Hair'd Rattle-Heads Who Revile All Civill Roundheads. 1646.

Minors No Senators. 1646.

Scotlands Ancient Obligation to England. 1646.

Scotlands Publick Acknowledgement of Gods Just Judgement. 1646.

Suspention Suspended; or, The Divines of Syon-Colledge Late Claim of the Power of Suspending Scandalous Persons, from the Lords Supper. 1646.

Twelve Questions of Publick Concernment, Touching the Regulation of Some Abuses in the Law and Legal Proceedings. 1646. Lost.

An Account of the Kings Late Revenue and Debts. 1647.

A Brief Justification of the XI. Accused Members, from a Scandalous Libel. 1647.

A Counterplea to the Cowards Apologie. 1647.

A Declaration of the Officers and Armies, Illegal, Injuries, Proceedings and Practises against the XI. Impeached Members. 1647.

VIII Queries upon the Late Declarations of, and Letters from, the Army. 1647.

A Full Vindication and Answer of the XI. Accused Members. 1647.

The Hypocrites Unmasking; or, a Clear Discovery of the Grosse Hypocrisy of the Officers. 1647.

The Levellers Levelled to the Very Ground. 1647.

The Lords & Commons First Love to, Zeale for, and Earnest Vindication of Their Members. 1647.

New Presbyterian Light Springing out of Independent Darkness. 1647.

IX Proposals by Way of Interrogation. 1647.

IX Queries upon the Printed Charge of the Army against the XI. Members. 1647.

A Plain, Short, and Probable Expedient, to Settle the Present Distractions. 1647.

The Sword of Christian Magistracy Supported. 1647.

The Totall and Finall Demands Already Made by the Agitators and Army. 1647.

Twelve Queries of Publick Concernment Humbly Submitted to the Serious Consideration of the Great Councell. 1647.

The University of Oxfords Plea Refuted. 1647.

A Vindication of Sir William Lewis from One Part of His Particular Charge. 1647.

Ardua Regni; or, XII. Arduous Doubts of Great Concernment to the Kingdome. 1648.

Articles of Impeachment. 1648.

A Breife Memento to the Present Unparliamentary Junto Touching Their Present Intentions and Proceedings to Depose and Execute, Charles Steward. 1648.

The Case of the Impeached Lords, Commons, and Citizens; Truely Stated. 1648.

The County of Somerset Divided into Severall Classes. 1648.

Mr. Prynnes Demand of His Liberty to the Generall. 1648.

Irenarchies Redivivus; or, A Brief Collection of Sundry Statutes and Petitions in Parliament concerning the Clandestine Dis-commissioning of Justices of Peace. 1648.

A Just and Solemn Protestation and Remonstrance of the Lord Mayor. 1648.

Mr. Pryn's Last and Finall Declaration to the Commons. 1648.

The Machiavilian Cromwellist, and Hypocritical Perfidious New Statist. 1648.

[*Mercurius Rusticus: Containing News from the Severall Counties.* 1648.]

Mr. Prinns Charge against the King. 1648.

A New Magna Charta: Enacted and Confirmed by the High and Mighty States, the Remainder of the Lords and Commons. 1648.

The Petition of the Right of the Free-holders and Free-men to the Lords and Commons. 1648.

A Plea for the Lords. 1648.

Practicall Law, Controlling and Countermanding the Common Law. 1648.

A Publike Declaration and Solemn Protestation of the Free-men of England. 1648.

A Remonstrance and Declaration of Severall Counties, Cities. 1648.

A True and Ful Relation of the Officers and Armies Forcible Seising of Divers Eminent Members of the Commons House. 1648.

A Declaration and Protestation against the Present Actings and Proceedings of the Generall, and Generall Councell (with Clement Walker). 1649.

A Declaration and Protestation of the Peers against the Usurpations of the Commons. 1649.

An Historical Collection of the Ancient Parliaments. 1649. Part 1 only.

Foure True and Considerable Positions for the Sitting Members, the New Court, and Other to Ruminate Upon. 1649.

A Legall Vindication of the Liberties of England, against Illegall Taxes. 1649.

Mr. Prynnes Letter to the Generall the Third of January 1648. 1649.

New-Babels Confusion; or, Severall Votes against Certain Papers, Entituled, The Agreement of the People. 1649.

A Proclamation Proclaiming Charls Prince of Wales, King of Great Brittaine, France, and Ireland. 1649.

Prynne the Member Reconciled to Prynne the Barrester. 1649.

A Publike Declaration and Protestation of the Secured and Secluded Members. 1649.

Six Propositions of Undoubted Verity, Fit to Be Considered in Our Present Exigency. 1649.

[*Six Serious Quaeries concerning the Kings Triall by the New High Court of Justice.* 1649.]

The Substance of a Speech Made in the House of Commons. 1649.

Summary Reasons against the New Oath & Engagement. 1649.

A Vindication of the Imprisoned and Secluded Members of the House of Commons, from the Aspersions Cast upon Them. 1649.

The Vindication of William Prynne Esquire. 1649.

A Brief Apologie for All Non-Subscribers. 1650.

Sad and Serious Politicall Considerations, Touching the Invasive War against Our Presbyterian Protestant Brethren in Scotland. 1650.

The Time-Serving Proteus, and Ambidexter Divine, Uncased to the World. 1650.

Christi Servus Etiam in Summa Captivitate Liber. 1653.

A Gospel Plea (Interwoven with a Rational and Legal) for the Lawfulnes & Continuance of the Ancient Setled Maintenance and Tenthes. 1653.

Jus Patronatus; or, A Briefe Legal and Rational Plea for Advowsons, or Patrons. 1654.

A Seasonable, Legall, and Historicall Vindication and Chro-nological Collection of the Good, Old, Fundamentall, Liberties, Franchises, Rights, Laws of All English Freemen. 1654.

The Works of William Prynne of Swainswick, Esquire; since His Last Imprisonment. 1655. 6 parts.

A New Discovery of Free-State Tyranny. 1655.

A Legal Resolution of Two Important Queres. 1656.

A New Discovery of Some Romish Emissaries, Quakers. 1656.

A Seasonable Vindication of Free-Admission, and Frequent Admission of the Holy Communion to All. 1656.

A Short Demurrer to the Jewes Long Discontinued Remitter into England. 1656. 2 parts.

A Summary Collection of the Principal Fundamental Rights, Liberties, Properties of All English Freemen. 1656, 1658 (as Demophilos).

An Appendix to a Seasonable Vindication of Free-Admission. 1657.

King Richard the Third Revived. 1657.

Pendennis and All Other Standing Forts Dismantled. 1657.

The Lords Supper Briefly Vindicated. 1658.

A Probable Expedient for the Present and Future Publique Settlement. 1658.

Some Popish Errors, Unadvisedly Embraced, and Pursued by Our Anti-Communion Ministers. 1658.

The Subjection of All Traytors in Ireland. 1658.

Twelve Serious Queres Proposed to All Conscientious Electors of Knights, Citizens and Burgesses, for the Assembly. 1658.

Twelve Several Heads of Public Grievances. 1658. Lost.

An Answer to a Proposition in Order to the Proposing of a Commonwealth or Democracy. 1659.

Beheaded Dr. John Hewytts Ghost Pleading. 1659.

A Brief Necessary Vindication of the Old and New Secluded Members. 1659.

Concordia Discors; or, The Dissonant Harmony of Sacred Publique Oathes. 1659.

The Curtaine Drawne; or, The Parliament Exposed to View. 1659.

A Brief Register, Kalendar and Survey of Parliamentary Writs, 1203 till 1483. 1659–64. 4 parts.

Historiarchos; or, The Exact Recorder. 1659.

Loyalty Banished; or, England in Mourning. 1659.

The New Cheaters Forgeries, Detected. 1659.

The Remainder, or Second Part of a Gospel Plea. 1659.

The Remonstrance of the Noble-Men, Burgesses and Commons of the Late Eastern, Southern, and Western Associations, Who Desire to Shew Themselves Faithfull. 1659.

The Re-publicans and Other Spurious Good Old Cause. 1659.

A Short, Legal, Medicinal, Usefull, Safe, Easie Prescription, to Recover Our Kingdom, Church, Nation from Their Present Dangerous Confusion. 1659.

Six Important Quaeres, Propounded to the Re-sitting Rump. 1659.

Ten Considerable Quaeries concerning Tithes. 1659.

Ten Quaeres, upon the Ten New Commandements of the General Council of Officers. 1659.

To the Right Honourable, the Lord Mayor. 1659.

The True Good Old Cause Rightly Stated, and the False Uncased. 1659.

Bathonia Rediviva; To the Kings Most Excellent Majesty: The Humble Address of the City of Bath. 1660.

A Brief Narrative of the Manner How Divers Members of the House of Commons Were Again Forcibly Shut Out. 1660.

The Case of the Old, Secured, Secluded, and Now Excluded Members. 1660.

Conscientious, Serious Theological and Legal Queres. 1660.

A Copy of the Presentment and Indictment Found against Colonel Matthew Alured ⟨etc.⟩. 1660.
A Full Declaration of the True State of the Secluded Members Case. 1660.
Mr. Pryns Letter and Proposals, to Our Gracious Lord and Sovereign King. 1660.
A Plea for Sr George Booth. 1660.
The Privileges of Parliament. 1660.
Seasonable and Healing Instructions. 1660.
Seven Additional Quaeres in Behalf of the Secluded Members. 1660.
The Signal Loyalty and Devotion of Gods True Saints and Pious Christians, towards Their Kings. 1660.
Three Seasonable Quaeres, Proposed to All Those Cities Whose Respective Citizens, Knights and Burgesses Have Been Forcibly Excluded. 1660.
[*The Title of Kings Proved to be Jure Divino.* 1660.]
A Short Sober Pacific Examination of Appurtenances of the Common Prayer. 1661.
Sundry Reasons Humbly Tendred to the Most Honourable House of Peers. 1661. Lost.
A Moderate, Seasonable Apology for Liberty in, Not Bowing at, or to the Name of Jesus. 1662.
An Exact Chronological Vindication and Historical Demonstration of Our Kings Supreme Ecclesiastical Jurisdiction. 1665 [Volume 2]; 1666 [Volume 1]; 1668 [Volume 3].
Aurum Reginae; or, A Compendious Tractate, and Chronological Collection of Records in the Tower concerning Queen-Gold. 1668.
Brief Animadversions on the Fourth Part of the Institutes of the Laws Compiled by Sir Edward Cooke. 1669.

SIR JOHN DENHAM (1615–1669)

The Sophy. 1642.
Coopers Hill. 1642.
Mr. Hampdens Speech Occasioned upon the Londoners Petition for Peace. 1643.
The Anatomy of a Play. 1651.
The Destruction of Troy: An Essay upon ⟨i.e. translation of⟩ *the Second Book of Virgils* Aeneis. 1656.
[*A Panegyrick on His Excellency the Lord General George Monck.* 1659.]
A Relation of a Quaker, That to the Shame of His Profession, Attempted to Bugger a Mare near Colchester. 1659.
[*The Prologue to His Majesty at the First Play Presented at the Cock-Pit in Whitehall.* 1660.]
The Second Advice to the Painter, for Drawing the History of Our Navall Business. 1667.
On Mr. Abraham Cowley His Death and Burial. 1667.
Poems and Translations, with The Sophy. 1668.
[*The Famous Battel of the Catts, in the Province of Ulster.* 1668.]
Cato Major of Old Age. 1669.
A Version of the Psalms of David. 1714.
Poetical Works. 1780.
Poetical Works (with Edmund Waller). Ed. George Gilfillan. 1857.
Poetical Works. Ed. Theodore Howard Banks, Jr. 1928.
Expans'd Hieroglyphicks: A Critical Edition of Coopers Hill. Ed. Brendan O'Hehir. 1969.

ANNE BRADSTREET (1612–1672)

The Tenth Muse Lately Sprung Up in America. Ed. John Woodbridge. 1650, 1678 (as *Several Poems Compiled with Great Variety of Wit and Learning, Full of Delight*).

Works in Prose and Verse. Ed. John Harvard Ellis. 1867.
Poems. Ed. Charles Eliot Norton. 1897.
Works. Ed. Jeannine Hensley. 1967.
Poems. Ed. Robert Hutchinson. 1969.
Complete Works. Eds. Joseph R. McElrath, Jr., and Allan P. Robb. 1981.

MARGARET CAVENDISH, DUCHESS OF NEWCASTLE (1623–1673)

Philosophicall Fancies. 1653.
Poems, and Fancies. 1653.
The World's Olio. 1655.
Philosophical and Physical Opinions. 1655, 1668.
Nature Pictures Drawn by Fancies Pencil to the Life (with William Cavendish). 1656.
Plays. 1662.
Orations of Divers Sorts, Accommodated to Divers Places. 1662.
CCXI Sociable Letters. 1664.
Philosophical Letters; or, Modest Reflections upon Some Opinions in Natural Philosophy Maintained by Several Learned Authors of This Age. 1664.
Observations upon Experimental Philosophy; to Which Is Added, The Description of a New Blazing World. 1666. 4 parts.
The Life of the Thrice Noble, High and Puissant Prince William Cavendishe, Duke, Marquess, and Earl of Newcastle. 1667.
Plays, Never Before Printed. 1668. 5 parts.
Select Poems. Ed. Sir Samuel Egerton Brydges. 1813.
A True Relation of the Birth, Breeding, and Life of Margaret Cavendish, Duchess of Newcastle. Ed. Sir Samuel Egerton Brydges. 1814.
The Cavalier and His Lady: Selections from the Works of the First Duke and Duchess of Newcastle. Ed. Edward Jenkins. 1872.
Letters to Her Husband. Ed. W. R. Goulding. 1909.
The Life of the (1st) Duke of Newcastle and Other Writings. 1916.

ROBERT HERRICK (1591–1674)

Hesperides; or, The Works Both Humane and Divine ⟨with Noble Numbers⟩. 1648.
A Song for Two Voices. c. 1700.
Select Poems from the Hesperides. Ed. John Nott. 1810.
Works. Ed. Thomas Maitland. 1823. 2 vols.
Hesperides. Ed. William Carew Hazlitt. 1869. 2 vols.
Complete Poems. Ed. Alexander B. Grosart. 1876. 3 vols.
Selections. Ed. Austin Dobson. 1882.
Hesperides and Noble Numbers. Ed. Alfred Pollard. 1891. 2 vols.
Poetical Works. Ed. George Saintsbury. 1893. 2 vols.
Lyric Poems. Ed. Ernest Rhys. 1897.
Poems. Ed. Thomas Bailey Aldrich. 1900.
Poems. Ed. John Masefield. 1906.
Poetical Works. Ed. Frederick W. Moorman. 1915. 2 vols.
Poetical Works. Ed. Humbert Wolfe. 1928. 4 vols.
Poetical Works. Ed. Leonard C. Martin. 1956.
Selected Poems. Ed. John Hayward. 1962.
Complete Poetry. Ed. J. Max Patrick. 1963.
Selected Poems. Ed. David Jesson-Dibley. 1980.

JOHN MILTON (1608–1674)

A Maske Presented at Ludlow Castle 1634 ⟨Comus⟩. 1637.
Epitaphium Damonis. c. 1640.

Of Reformation Touching Church Discipline in England, and the Causes That Hitherto Have Hindered It. 1641.

Of Prelatical Episcopacy, and Whether It May Be Deduc'd from the Apostolical Times. 1641.

Animadversions upon the Remonstrant's Defence, against Smectymnuus. 1641.

The Reason of Church-Government Urg'd against Prelaty. 1641.

An Apology against a Pamphlet Call'd A Modest Confutation of the Animadversions upon the Remonstrant against Smectymnuus. 1642.

The Doctrine and Discipline of Divorce. 1643.

Of Education. 1644.

The Judgement of Martin Bucer concerning Divorce (translator). 1644.

Areopagitica: A Speech for the Liberty of Unlicenc'd Printing. 1644.

Colasterion: A Reply to a Nameless Answer against the Doctrine and Discipline of Divorce. 1645.

Poems. 1645.

Tetrachordon. 1645.

Poems Both English and Latin. 1645.

The Tenure of Kings and Magistrates. 1649.

Observations upon the Articles of Peace with the Irish Rebels. 1649.

Eikonoklastes. 1649.

Pro Populo Anglicano Defensio. 1651.

Pro Populo Anglicano Defensio Secunda. 1654.

Pro Se Defensio contra Alexandrum Morum. 1655.

The Cabinet Council. 1658.

A Treatise of Civil Power in Ecclesiastical Causes. 1659.

Considerations Touching the Likeliest Means to Remove Hirelings out of the Church. 1659.

The Readie and Easy Way to Establish a Free Commonwealth. 1660.

Brief Notes upon a Late Sermon Titl'd The Fear of God and the King *by Matthew Griffith.* 1660.

Paradise Lost. 1667.

Accedence Commenc't Grammar. 1669.

The History of Britain. 1670.

Paradise Regain'd; to Which Is Added Samson Agonistes. 1671.

Artis Logicae Plenior Institutio. 1672.

Of True Religion, Haeresy, Schism, Toleration, and What Best Means May Be Urg'd against the Growth of Popery. 1673.

Poems upon Several Occasions. 1673.

A Declaration. 1674.

Epistolarum Familiarum Liber. 1674.

Literae Pseudo-Senatus Anglicani. 1676.

Character of the Long Parliament. 1681.

A Brief History of Moscovia. 1682.

Republican Letters. 1682.

Letters of State from the Year 1649 till the Year 1659. 1694.

A Complete Collection of the Historical, Political, and Miscellaneous Works. Ed. John Toland. 1694–98. 3 vols.

Poetical Works. Ed. Patrick Hume. 1695.

Poetical Works. 1707. 2 vols.

Original Letters and Papers of State Addressed to Oliver Cromwell. Ed. John Nickolls. 1743.

Prose Works. Ed. Charles Symmons. 1806. 7 vols.

De Doctrina Christiana Libri. Ed. Charles Richard Sumner. 1825.

Poetical Works. Ed. John Mitford. 1832. 3 vols.

Works in Verse and Prose. Ed. John Mitford. 1841. 8 vols.

Poetical Works. Ed. George Gilfillan. 1853. 2 vols.

Poetical Works. Ed. David Masson. 1874. 3 vols.

A Common-place Book. Ed. A. J. Horwood. 1876.

Sonnets. Ed. Mark Pattison. 1883.

Poetical Works. Ed. H. C. Beeching. 1900.

Poetical Works. Ed. William Aldis Wright. 1903.

Poems. Ed. Herbert J. C. Grierson. 1925. 2 vols.

Works. Eds. Frank Allen Patterson et al. 1931–38. 18 vols.

Private Correspondence and Academic Exercises. Eds. and trs. Phyllis B. Tillyard and E. M. W. Tillyard. 1932.

Poetical Works. Ed. Helen Darbishire. 1952–55. 2 vols.

Complete Prose Works. Eds. Don M. Wolfe et al. 1953– . 8 vols.

The Cambridge Milton. Eds. John Broadbent et al. 1972– .

The Macmillan Milton. Eds. C. A. Patrides et al. 1972– .

Selected Prose. Ed. C. A. Patrides. 1974.

EDWARD HYDE, EARL OF CLARENDON
(1609–1674)

Mr. Hides' Argument before the Lords in the Upper House of Parliament. 1641.

*M*ʳ *E. Hyde's Speech at a Conference betweene Both Houses, at the Transmission of the Severall Impeachments against the Lord Chiefe Barron Davenport, M*ʳ *Barron Trevor, and M*ʳ *Barron Weston.* 1641.

Two Speeches Made in the House of Peers, for, and against Accommodation. 1642.

Transcendent and Multiplied Rebellion and Treason, Discovered, by the Lawes of the Land. 1645.

An Answer to a Pamphlet, Entit'led, A Declaration of the Commons of England. 1648.

A Letter from a True and Lawfull Member of Parliament, to One of His Highness Councell upon Occasion of the Last Declaration. 1656.

His Majesties Gracious Speech, Together with the Lord Chancellors. 1660.

Second Thoughts; or, The Case of a Limited Toleration. c. 1660.

A Collection of the Orders Heretofore Used in Chancery (editor; with Sir Harbottle Grimston). 1661.

To the Right Honourable, the Lords Spiritual and Temporal, in Parliament Assembled: The Humble Petition and Address of Edward Earl of Clarendon. 1667.

Animadversions upon a Book, Intituled, Fanaticism Fanatically Imputed to the Catholick Church, *by Dr. Stillingfleet.* 1673.

A Brief View and Survey of the Dangerous and Pernicious Errors to Church and State, in Mr. Hobbes's Book, Entitled Leviathan. 1676.

Two Letters: One to His Royal Highness the Duke of York; the Other to the Dutchess, Occasioned by Her Embracing the Roman Catholick Religion. c. 1680.

The History of the Rebellion and Civil Wars in England, Begun in the Year 1641. 1702–04. 3 vols.

The Characters of Robert, Earl of Essex, Favourite to Queen Elizabeth, and George, D. of Buckingham, Favourite to K. James I. and K. Ch. I. 1706.

The History of the Rebellion and Civil Wars in Ireland. 1719–20.

An Appendix to the History of the Grand Rebellion. 1724.

A Collection of Several Tracts. 1727.

The Life of Edward Earl of Clarendon. 1759. 3 vols.

State Papers (editor). Eds. Richard Scrope and Thomas Monkhouse. 1767–86. 3 vols.

Characters of Eminent Men in the Reigns of Charles I and II. Ed. E. Turner. 1793.

Religion and Policy, and the Countenance and Assistance Each Should Give the Other. 1811. 2 vols.

Essays Moral and Entertaining. Ed. James Stenier Clarke. 1815. 2 vols.

The History of the Rebellion and Civil Wars in England. Ed. W. D. Macray. 1888. 6 vols.

Notes Which Passed at Meetings of the Privy Council between Charles II and the Earl of Clarendon 1660–1667. Ed. W. D. Macray. 1896.

Selections from the History of the Rebellion and the Life by Himself. Ed. G. Huehns. 1959.

THOMAS TRAHERNE (1637–1674)

Roman Forgeries; or, A True Account of False Records Discovering Impostures and Counterfeit Antiquities of the Church of Rome. 1673.

Christian Ethicks; or, Divine Morality, Opening the Way to Blessedness, by the Rules of Vertue and Reason. 1675.

A Serious and Patheticall Contemplation of the Mercies of God. 1699.

Poetical Works. Ed. Bertram Dobell. 1903.

Centuries of Meditations. Ed. Bertram Dobell. 1908.

Poems of Felicity. Ed. H. I. Bell. 1910.

Poetical Works. Ed. Gladys I. Wade. 1932.

Felicities. Ed. Sir Arthur Quiller-Couch. 1935.

Centuries, Poems, and Thanksgivings. Ed. H. M. Margoliouth. 1958. 2 vols.

Poems, Centuries, and Three Thanksgivings. Ed. Anne Ridler. 1966.

ANDREW MARVELL (1621–1678)

[*An Elegy upon the Death of My Lord Francis Villiers.* c. 1648.]

The First Anniversary of the Government under His Highness the Lord Protector. 1655.

The Character of Holland. 1665.

The Rehearsall Transpros'd. 1672 [Part 1]; 1673 [Part 2].

Mr. Smirke; or, The Divine in Mode. 1676.

An Account of the Growth of Popery and Arbitrary Government in England. 1677.

Remarks upon a Late Disingenuous Discourse by T. D. 1678.

A Short Historical Essay concerning General Councils. 1680.

Miscellaneous Poems. Ed. Mary Palmer ⟨Marvell⟩. 1681.

Works. Ed. Thomas Cooke. 1726. 2 vols.

Works. Ed. Captain Edward Thompson. 1776. 3 vols.

Complete Works. Ed. Alexander B. Grosart. 1872–75. 4 vols.

Poems and Satires. Ed. George A. Aitken. 1892. 2 vols.

Poems and Letters. Ed. H. M. Margoliouth. 1927. 2 vols.

Poems Printed from the Unique Copy in the British Museum, with Some Other Poems. Ed. Hugh Macdonald. 1952.

Selected Poems. Ed. Joseph H. Summers. 1961.

Latin Poetry. Eds. and trs. William A. McQueen and Kiffin A. Rockwell. 1964.

Selected Poetry. Ed. Frank Kermode. 1967.

Complete Poetry. Ed. George deForest Lord. 1968.

Poems and Letters. Ed. H. M. Margoliouth, rev. Pierre Legouis and E. E. Duncan-Jones. 1971. 2 vols.

Complete Poetry. Ed. Elizabeth Story Donno. 1972.

The Press, That Villainous Engine. 1984.

THOMAS HOBBES (1588–1679)

The Peloponnesian Warre by Thucydides (translator). 1629.

De Mirabilibus Pecci. c. 1636.

A Briefe of the Art of Rhetorick. 1637.

Elementa Philosophiae, Sectio Tertia: De Cive. 1642. Eng. tr. 1651 (as *Philosophicall Rudiments concerning Government and Society*).

Humane Nature; or, The Fundamental Elements of Policie. 1650.

De Corpore Politico; or, The Elements of Law, Moral and Politick. 1650.

A Discourse upon Gondibert ⟨by Sir William D'Avenant⟩; *with an Answer to It* ⟨by Hobbes⟩. 1650.

Leviathan; or, The Matter, Forme, and Power of a Commonwealth Ecclesiasticall and Civill. 1651. Latin tr. 1670.

Epistolica Dissertatio de Principiis Iusti et Decori. 1651.

Of Libertie and Necessitie. 1654.

Elementorum Philosophiae Sectio Prima: De Corpore. 1655. Eng. tr. 1656 (as *Elements of Philosophy: The First Section, concerning Body*).

Στιγμαί. 1657.

Elementorum Philosophiae Sectio Secunda: De Homine. 1658.

Examinatio et Emendatio Mathematicae Hodiernae. 1660.

Dialogus Physicus de Natura Aeris. 1661.

Problemata Physica. 1662.

Seven Philosophical Problems and Two Propositions of Geometry. 1662.

Mr Hobbes Considered in His Loyalty, Religion, Reputation, and Manners: By Way of Letter to Dr Wallis. 1662.

De Principiis et Ratiocinatione Geometrarum. 1666.

Opera Philosophica Quae Latine Scripsit Omnia. 1668. 2 vols.

Quadratura Circuli, Cubatio Sphaerae, Duplicatio Cubi. 1669.

Three Papers Presented to the Royal Society against Dr. Wallis. 1671.

Rosetum Geometricum. 1671.

Lux Mathematica. 1672.

The Travels of Ulysses by Homer (translator). 1673.

Epistola ad Dominum Antonium à Wood. 1674.

Principia et Problemata Aliquot Geometrica ante Desperata. 1674.

A Supplement to Mr. Hobbes His Works. 1675.

Homer's Iliads (translator). 1676.

Decameron Physiologicum; or, Ten Dialogues of Natural Philosophy. 1678.

Behemoth; or, The Long Parliament. 1679.

Vita. 1679.

The Last Sayings, or Dying Legacy of Mr. Thomas Hobbs of Malmesbury. 1680.

An Historical Narration concerning Heresie. 1680.

Tracts. 1681–82. 2 vols.

Tripos. 1684.

Historia Ecclesiastica. 1688.

Moral and Political Works. 1750.

English Works. Ed. Sir William Molesworth. 1839–45. 11 vols.

Opera Philosophica Quae Latine Scripsit. Ed. Sir William Molesworth. 1839–45. 5 vols.

The Elements of Law, Natural and Politic. Ed. Ferdinand Tönnies. 1889.

The Metaphysical System of Hobbes. Ed. Mary Whiton Calkins. 1905.

Selections. Ed. Frederick J. E. Woodbridge. 1930.

Body, Man, and Citizen: Selections. Ed. Richard S. Peters. 1962.

Critique du De Mundo de Thomas White. Eds. Jean Jacquot and Harold Whitmore Jones. 1973.

Philosophical Works (Clarendon Edition). Eds. Howard Warrender et al. 1983–   .

SAMUEL BUTLER (1613–1680)

Mola Asinaria. 1659.

The Lord Roos His Answer to the Marquesse of Dorchester's Letter. 1660.

Hudibras. 1663 [Part 1]; 1664 [Part 2]; 1678 [Part 3].

To the Memory of the Most Renowned Du-vall: A Pindarick Ode. 1671.

Two Letters. 1672.

Mercurius Menippeus: The Loyal Satirist. 1682.

The Plagiary Exposed; or, An Old Answer to a Newly Revised Calumny. 1691.

Posthumous Works in Prose and Verse. 1715–17. 3 vols.

Genuine Remains. Ed. Robert Thyer. 1759. 2 vols.

Poetical Works. Ed. John Mitford. 1853. 2 vols.

Poetical Works. Ed. George Gilfillan. 1854. 2 vols.

Poetical Works. Ed. Reginald Brimley Johnson. 1893. 3 vols.

Complete Works. Eds. A. R. Waller and Rene Lamar. 1905–28. 3 vols.

Characters. Ed. Charles W. Daves. 1970.

Hudibras, Parts I and II, and Selected Other Writings. Eds. John Wilders and Hugh de Quehen. 1973.

Prose Observations. Ed. Hugh de Quehen. 1979.

JOHN WILMOT, EARL OF ROCHESTER
(1647–1680)

To All Gentlemen, Ladies, and Others. c. 1675.

Corydon and Cloris; or, The Wanton Shepherdess. c. 1676.

A Satyr against Mankind. 1679.

A Letter from Artemiza in the Town, to Chloe in the Country. 1679.

Upon Nothing: A Poem. 1679.

A Very Heroical Epistle from My Lord All-Pride to Dol-Common. 1679.

Poems on Several Occasions. 1680.

A Letter to Dr. Burnet. 1680.

A Pastoral Dialogue between Alexis and Strephon. 1683.

Sodom; or, The Quintessence of Debauchery. 1684. Lost.

Valentinian: A Tragedy. 1685.

Poems on Several Occasions, with Valentinian. 1691.

Familiar Letters (with others). Eds. Thomas Brown and Charles Gildon. 1697. 2 vols.

Miscellaneous Works (with the Earl of Roscommon). 1707.

Collected Works. Ed. John Hayward. 1926.

Poetical Works. Ed. Quilter Johns. 1933.

The Rochester-Savile Letters 1671–1680. Ed. John Harold Wilson. 1941.

A Satire against Mankind and Other Poems. Ed. Harry Levin. 1942.

Selected Lyrics and Satires. Ed. Ronald Duncan. 1948.

Poems. Ed. Vivian de Sola Pinto. 1953.

The Famous Pathologist; or, The Noble Mountebank (with Thomas Alcock). Ed. Vivian de Sola Pinto. 1961.

The Gyldenstolpe Manuscript: Miscellany of Poems (with others). Eds. Bror Danielsson and David M. Vieth. 1967.

Complete Poems. Ed. David M. Vieth. 1968.

Lyrics and Satires. Ed. David Brooks. 1980.

Letters. Ed. Jeremy Treglown. 1980.

Selected Poems. Ed. Paul Hammond. 1982.

Poems. Ed. Keith Walker. 1984.

SIR THOMAS BROWNE (1605–1682)

Religio Medici. 1642.

Pseudodoxia Epidemica; or, Enquiries into Very Many Received Tenents, and Commonly Presumed Truths. 1646.

Hydriotaphia: Urne-Buriall; or, A Discourse of the Sepulchrall

Urns Lately Found in Norfolk; Together with The Garden of Cyrus; or, The Quincunciall, Lozenge, or Net-work Plantations of the Ancients, Artificially, Naturally, Mystically Considered. 1658.

Certain Miscellany Tracts. 1683.

Works. 1686.

A Letter to a Friend upon Occasion of the Death of His Intimate Friend. 1690.

Posthumous Works. 1712.

Christian Morals. Ed. John Jeffrey. 1716, 1756.

Works. Ed. Simon Wilkins. 1835–36. 4 vols.

Notes and Letters on the Natural History of Norfolk. Ed. Thomas Southwell. 1902.

Works. Ed. Geoffrey Keynes. 1928–31 (6 vols.), 1964 (4 vols.).

Religio Medici and Other Works. Ed. L. C. Martin. 1964.

The Prose of Sir Thomas Browne. Ed. Norman J. Endicott. 1967.

Selected Writings. Ed. Geoffrey Keynes. 1968.

IZAAK WALTON (1593–1683)

Reliquiae Wottonianae by Sir Henry Wotton (editor). 1651.

The Compleat Angler; or, The Contemplative Man's Recreation. 1653.

The Life of Mr. Rich. Hooker. 1665.

The Life of Mr. George Herbert. 1670.

The Lives of Dr. John Donne, Sir Henry Wotton, Mr. Richard Hooker, Mr. George Herbert. 1670.

The Life of Dr. Sanderson, Late Bishop of Lincoln. 1678. 2 parts.

Love and Truth: In Two Letters concerning the Distempers of the Present Times. 1680.

The Compleat Angler. Ed. Sir John Hawkins. 1760.

Waltoniana: Inedited Remains in Verse and Prose. Ed. R. H. Shepherd. 1878.

Lives. Ed. A. H. Bullen. 1884.

The Compleat Angler. Ed. Andrew Lang. 1896.

The Compleat Angler and the Lives of Donne, Wotton, Hooker, Herbert, and Sanderson. Ed. A. W. Pollard. 1901.

The Compleat Angler. Ed. George A. B. Dewar. 1902.

The Compleat Angler; The Lives of Donne, Wotton, Hooker, Herbert, and Sanderson; with Love and Truth and Miscellaneous Writings. Ed. Geoffrey Keynes. 1929.

The Lives of John Donne, Sir Henry Wotton, Richard Hooker, George Herbert, and Robert Sanderson. Ed. S. B. Carter. 1951.

The Compleat Angler. Ed. John Buxton. 1982.

The Compleat Angler. Ed. Jonquil Bevan. 1983.

ROGER WILLIAMS (c. 1604–1683)

A Key into the Language of America; or, An Help to the Language of the Natives in That Part of America, Called New-England. 1643.

The Bloudy Tenent, of Persecution, for Cause of Conscience, Discussed, in a Conference betweene Truth and Peace. 1644.

Mr. Cottons Letter Lately Printed, Examined and Answered. 1644.

Queries of Highest Consideration. 1644.

[*A Paraenetick or Humble Address to the Parliament and Assembly for (Not Loose, but) Christian Libertie.* 1644.]

The Bloody Tenent Yet More Bloody. 1652.

The Examiner Defended. 1652.

Experiments of Spiritual Life & Health. 1652.

The Fourth Paper, Presented by Maior Butler, to the Honour-

able Committee of Parliament, for the Propagating the Gospel of Christ Jesus. 1652.

The Hireling Ministry None of Christs. 1652.

George Fox Digg'd out of His Burrows. 1676.

To the King's Most Excellent Majesty. c. 1681.

Letters 1632–1682. Ed. John Russell Bartlett. 1874.

An Answer to a Letter Sent from Mr. Coddington of Rode Island, to Governour Leveret of Boston in What Concerns R. W. of Providence. 1922.

Letters and Papers 1629–1682. 1924.

An Answer to a Scandalous Paper Which Came to My Hand from the Massachusets Clamouring against the Purchase and Slandering the Purchasers of Qunnunnagut Iland, and Subscribed by John Easton. Ed. Frederick S. Peck. 1945.

Complete Writings. 1963. 7 vols.

JOHN OLDHAM (1653–1683)

Upon the Marriage of the Prince of Orange with the Lady Mary. 1677.

Garnets Ghost, Addressing to the Jesuits, Met in Private Caball, Just after the Murther of Sir Edmund-Bury Godfrey. 1679.

The Clarret Drinker's Song; or, The Good Fellows Design. 1680.

Satyrs upon the Jesuits, Written in the Year 1679, Upon Occasion of the Plot, Together with the Satyr against Vertue, and Some Other Pieces. 1681.

Some New Pieces Never Before Publisht. 1681.

Anacreon Done into English out of the Original Greek (translator; with Abraham Cowley and others). 1683.

Poems, and Translations. 1683.

Remains in Verse and Prose. 1684.

Works, Together with His Remains. 1684. 4 parts.

A Second Musical Entertainment Perform'd on St. Cecilia's Day. 1685.

Works. 1722. 2 vols.

A Character of the Reverend ———. 1725.

Compositions in Prose and Verse. Ed. Edward Thompson. 1770. 3 vols.

Poetical Works. Ed. Robert Bell. 1854.

THOMAS OTWAY (1652–1685)

Alcibiades. 1675.

Don Carlos, Prince of Spain. 1676.

Titus and Berenice; with a Farce (by Molière) *Called The Cheats of Scapin* (translator). 1677.

Friendship in Fashion. 1678.

The History and Fall of Caius Marius. 1680.

The Orphan; or, The Unhappy Marriage. 1680.

The Poet's Complaint of His Muse; or, A Satyr against Libells. 1680.

The Souldiers Fortune. 1681.

Venice Preserv'd; or, A Plot Discover'd. 1682.

Epilogue to Venice Preserv'd Spoken upon the Duke of York's Coming to the Theatre. 1682.

Prologue to The City-Heiress. 1682.

Epilogue to Her Highness on Her Return from Scotland. 1682.

Prologue (by Otway) *and Epilogue* (by John Dryden) *to Constantine the Great* (by Nathaniel Lee). 1683.

The Atheist; or, The Second Part of The Souldier's Fortune. 1684.

Windsor Castle: In a Monument to Our Late Sovereign K. Charles II. of Ever Blessed Memory. 1685.

The History of the Triumvirates (translator). 1686.

Works. 1712. 2 vols.

Plays. 1736. 2 vols.

Works. 1757. 3 vols.

Works. Ed. Thomas Thornton. 1813. 3 vols.

Thomas Otway. Ed. Roden Noel. 1888.

Complete Works. Ed. Montague Summers. 1926. 3 vols.

Works. Ed. J. C. Ghosh. 1932. 2 vols.

EDMUND WALLER (1606–1687)

An Honourable and Worthy Speech Made in Parliament, against the Prelates Innovations, False Doctrin and Discipline, &c. 1641.

Speech in Parliament at a Conference of Both Houses in the Painted Chamber. 1641.

A Worthy Speech Made in the House of Commons This Present Parliament. 1641.

A Speech Made in the Honourable House of Commons concerning Episcopacie, Whether It Should Be Committed or Rejected. 1641.

To the Kings Most Excellent Majesty. 1641.

Speech in the House of Commons. 1643.

Works. 1645.

Poems. 1645. 2 parts.

[*The Life and Death of William Laud, Late Archbishop of Canterburie.* 1645.]

A Panegyrick to My Lord Protector. 1655.

Upon the Late Storme, and of the Death of His Highnesse Ensuing the Same. 1658.

A Passion of Dido for Aeneas by Vergil (translator; with Sidney Godolphin). 1658.

Three Poems upon the Death of His Late Highnesse Oliver, Lord Protector of England, Scotland and Ireland (with John Dryden and Thomas Sprat). 1659.

To the King, upon His Majesties Happy Return. 1660.

To My Lady Morton. 1661.

A Poem on St James's Park as Lately Improved by His Majesty. 1661.

To the Queen, upon Her Majesties Birthday. 1663.

Pompey the Great by Pierre Corneille (translator; with others). 1664.

[*Upon Her Majesty's New Buildings at Somerset House.* 1665.]

Instructions to a Painter for the Drawing of the Posture & Progress of His Maties Forces at Sea, under the Command of His Highness Royal. 1666.

An Answer of Mr. Waller's Painter to His Many New Advisers. 1667.

Of the Lady Mary, &c. 1677.

A Poem on the Present Assembling of the Parliament. 1679.

Divine Poems. 1685.

A Poem upon the Present Assembly of Parliament. 1685.

The Maid's Tragedy (by Beaumont and Fletcher (adaptation)); *with Some Other Pieces.* 1690.

The Second Part of Mr. Waller's Poems. 1690.

Works in Verse and Prose. Ed. Elijah Fenton. 1729.

Works. Ed. Thomas Park. 1806. 2 vols.

Poetical Works (with Sir John Denham). Ed. George Gilfillan. 1857.

Poems. Ed. George Thorn-Drury. 1893. 2 vols.

GEORGE VILLIERS, DUKE OF BUCKINGHAM
(1628–1687)

The Declaration of the Duke of Buckingham, and the Earles of Holland, and Peterborough. 1648.

The Duke of Buckingham's Speech in a Late Conference. 1668.

An Epitaph upon Thomas Late Lord Fairfax. c. 1671.

A *Letter to Sir Thomas Osborn, One of His Majesties Privy
Council, upon the Reading of a Book, Called* The Present
Interest of England. 1672.
The Rehearsal (with Thomas Sprat). 1672.
Two Speeches (with Anthony Ashley Cooper, First Earl of
Shaftesbury). 1675.
*A Prophetic Lampoon, Made Anno 1659, Relating to What
Would Happen to the Government under Charles II.*
c. 1675.
[*Poetical Reflections on a Late Poem Entituled* Absalom and
Achitophel. 1681.]
The Chances by Beaumont and Fletcher (adaptation). 1682.
*A Short Discourse upon the Reasonableness of Men's Having a
Religion or Worship of God.* 1685.
*The Duke of Buckingham His Grace's Letter, to the Unknown
Author of a Paper, Entituled, A Short Answer to His
Grace the Duke of Buckingham's Paper, concerning Re-
ligion, Toleration, and Liberty of Conscience.* 1685.
Miscellaneous Works. Ed. Thomas Brown. 1704, 1715
(2 vols.).
*A Conference on the Doctrine of Transubstantiation between
His Grace the Duke of Buckingham and Father Fitzger-
ald.* 1714.
The Country Gentleman: A "Lost" Play and Its Background
(with Sir Robert Howard). Eds. Arthur H. Scouten and
Robert D. Hume. 1976.
*Buckingham, Public and Private Man: The Prose, Poems, and
Commonplace Book.* Ed. Christine Phipps. 1985.

CHARLES COTTON (1630–1687)

A Panegyrick to the King's Most Excellent Majesty. 1660.
The Morall Philosophy of the Stoicks by Guillaume du Vair
(translator). 1664.
*Scarronides; or, Virgile Travestie: Being the First Book of Vir-
gil's Æneis in English Burlesque.* 1664.
*Scarronides; or, Virgile Travestie, in Imitation of the Fourth
Book of Virgil's Æneis in English Burlesque.* 1665.
*Scarronides; or, Virgile Travestie: A Mock-Poem on the First
and Fourth Books of Virgil's Æneis.* 1667.
The Nicker Nicked; or, The Cheats of Gaming Discovered.
1669.
The History of the Life of the Duke of Espernon by Guillaume
Girard (translator). 1670.
Horace by Pierre Corneille (translator). 1671.
The Fair One of Tunis (translator). 1674.
Commentaries by Blaise de Lasseran-Massencombe, Seigneur
de Montluc (translator). 1674.
The Compleat Gamester. 1674.
*Burlesque upon Burlesque; or, The Scoffer Scoft: Being Some of
Lucians Dialogues* (translator). 1675.
The Planters Manual. 1675.
The Compleat Angler: Part 2. 1676.
[*The Confinement.* 1679.]
The Wonders of the Peake. 1681.
Ἐρωτοπολις: *The Present State of Betty-Land.* 1681.
Essays by Michel de Montaigne (translator). 1685–86. 3 vols.
Poems on Several Occasions. 1689.
Memoirs by Louis, Sieur de Pontis (translator). Ed. Beresford
Cotton. 1694.
Genuine Works. 1715.
[*The Valiant Knight; or, The Legend of St. Peregrine.* 1888.]
Poems. Ed. J. R. Tutin. 1903.
Poems. Ed. John Beresford. 1923.
Poems. Ed. John Buxton. 1958.
Selected Poems. Ed. Ken Robinson. 1983.

JOHN BUNYAN (1628–1688)

Some Gospel-Truths Opened According to the Scriptures.
1656.
A Vindication of the Book Called Some Gospel-Truths
Opened. 1657.
A Few Sighs from Hell; or, The Groans of a Damned Soul.
1658.
The Doctrine of the Law and Grace Unfolded. 1659.
Profitable Meditations, Fitted to Mans Different Condition.
c. 1661.
*I Will Pray with the Spirit, and I Will Pray with the Under-
standing Also.* 1663.
Christian Behaviour; or, The Fruits of True Christianity.
c. 1663.
*A Mapp Shewing the Order & Causes of Salvation & Damna-
tion.* c. 1663.
*One Thing Is Needful; or, Serious Meditations upon the Four
Last Things, Death, Judgment, Heaven and Hell; unto
Which Is Added, Ebal and Gerizzim; or, The Blessing and
the Curse; with Prison Meditations.* c. 1665.
The Holy City; or, the New Jerusalem. 1665.
Prison Meditations. 1665.
The Resurrection of the Dead, and Eternall Judgement.
c. 1665.
Grace Abounding to the Chief of Sinners. 1666.
A Confession of My Faith, and a Reason of My Practice. 1672.
A Christian Dialogue. c. 1672.
A New and Useful Confordance to the Holy Bible. c. 1672.
*A Defence of the Doctrine of Justification, by Faith in Jesus
Christ.* 1672.
*Difference in Judgment about Water-Baptism, No Bar to Com-
munion.* 1673.
*The Barren Fig-Tree; or, The Doom and Downfall of the Fruit-
less Professor.* 1673.
*Peaceable Principles and True; or, A Brief Answer to Mr. D'An-
vers and Mr. Paul's Books.* c. 1674.
Light for Them That Sit in Darkness. 1675.
Instruction for the Ignorant. 1675.
Saved by Grace; or, A Discourse of the Grace of God. c. 1676.
The Strait Gate; or, Great Difficulty of Going to Heaven.
1676.
*The Pilgrim's Progress from This World, to That Which Is to
Come.* 1678 [Part 1]; 1684 [Part 2].
Come, & Welcome, to Jesus Christ. 1678.
A Treatise of the Fear of God. 1679.
*The Life and Death of Mr. Badman, Presented to the World in
a Familiar Dialogue Between Mr. Wiseman, and Mr.
Attentive.* 1680.
*The Holy War Made by Shaddai upon Diabolus for the Re-
gaining of the Metropolis of the World; or, The Losing and
Taking Again of the Town of Mansoul.* 1682.
*The Greatness of the Soul, and Unspeakableness of the Loss
Thereof.* 1683.
A Case of Conscience Resolved. 1683.
A Holy Life, the Beauty of Christianity. 1684.
Seasonable Counsel; or, Advice to Sufferers. 1684.
A Caution to Stir Up to Watch against Sin. c. 1684.
A Discourse upon the Pharisee and the Publicane. 1685.
*Questions about the Nature and Perpetuity of the Seventh-
Day-Sabbath.* 1685.
A Book for Boys and Girls; or, Country Rhimes for Children
⟨Divine Emblems⟩. 1686.
*Good News for the Vilest of Men; or, A Help for Despairing
Souls.* 1688.

The Advocateship of Jesus Christ Clearly Explained and Largely Improved. 1688.

A Discourse of the Building, Nature, Excellency, and Government of the House of God. 1688.

The Water of Life; or, A Discourse Shewing the Richness and Glory of the Grace and Spirit of God. 1688.

Solomon's Temple Spiritualiz'd; or, Gospel-Light Fetcht out of the Temple at Jerusalem. 1688.

The Acceptable Sacrifice; or, The Excellency of a Broken Heart. 1689.

Mr John Bunyan's Last Sermon. 1689.

Works. Ed. Charles Doe. 1692.

The Heavenly Foot-Man; or, A Description of the Man That Gets to Heaven. 1698.

Works. Ed. John Wilson. 1736–37. 2 vols.

A Relation of the Imprisonment of Mr. John Bunyan, Minister of the Gospel at Bedford, in November, 1660. 1765.

Works. Ed. George Whitefield. 1767–68. 2 vols.

Works. Ed. George Offor. 1853. 3 vols.

Entire Works. Ed. Henry Stebbing. 1859–60. 4 vols.

Selections. Ed. A. T. Quiller-Couch. 1908.

The Bedside Bunyan: An Anthology of the Writings of John Bunyan. Ed. Arthur Stanley. 1947.

God's Knotty Leg: Selected Writings. Ed. Henri Talon. 1961.

Miscellaneous Works. Eds. Roger Sharrock et al. 1976– .

APHRA BEHN (1640–1689)

The Forc'd Marriage; or, The Jealous Bridegroom. 1671.

The Amorous Prince; or, The Curious Husband. 1671.

[*Covent Garden Drolery* (editor). 1671.]

The Dutch Lover. 1673.

Abdelazar; or, The Moor's Revenge. 1677.

The Town-Fopp; or, Sir Timothy Tawdrey. 1677.

The Debauchee; or, The Credulous Cuckold. 1677.

The Counterfeit Bridegroom; or, The Defeated Widow (adaptation; with Thomas Betterton). 1677.

The Rover; or, The Banish't Cavalier. 1677.

Sir Patient Fancy. 1678.

The Feign'd Curtizans; or, A Night's Intrigue. 1679.

The Revenge; or, A Match in Newgate. 1680.

The Second Part of The Rover. 1681.

The False Count; or, A New Way to Play an Old Game. 1682.

The Roundheads; or, The Good Old Cause. 1682.

A Prologue to Like Father, Like Son; or, The Mistaken Brothers. 1682.

The City-Heiress; or, Sir Timothy Treat-all. 1682.

Prologue to Romulus. 1682.

The Young King; or, The Mistake. 1683.

Prologue ⟨to Valentinian⟩. 1684.

Love Letters between a Nobleman and His Sister. 1684–87. 3 parts.

Poems upon Several Occasions, with a Voyage to the Island of Love. 1684.

Miscellany: Being a Collection of Poems by Several Hands (editor). 1685.

A Pindarick on the Death of Our Late Sovereign. 1685.

A Poem Humbly Dedicated to Catherine Queen Dowager. 1685.

A Pindarick Poem on the Happy Coronation of His Sacred Majesty James II. and His Illustrious Consort Queen Mary. 1685.

La Montre; or, The Lover's Watch by Balthazar de Bonnecourse (translator). 1686.

The Emperor of the Moon. 1687.

The Luckey Chance; or, An Alderman's Bargain. 1687.

To the Most Illustrious Prince Christopher Duke of Albemarle, on His Voyage to His Government of Jamaica: A Pindarick. 1687.

[*To the Memory of George Duke of Buckingham.* 1687.]

A Congratulatory Poem to Her Most Sacred Majesty on the Universal Hopes of All Loyal Persons for a Prince of Wales. 1688.

Two Congratulatory Poems to Their Most Sacred Majesties. 1688.

The Fair Jilt; or, The History of Prince Tarquin and Miranda. 1688.

A Poem to Sir Roger L'Estrange. 1688.

A Congratulatory Poem to the King's Most Sacred Majesty on the Happy Birth of the Prince of Wales. 1688.

Oroonoko; or, The Royal Slave. 1688.

Three Histories: Oroonoko; The Fair Jilt; Agnes de Castro. 1688.

To Poet Bavius. 1688.

Lycidus; or, The Lover in Fashion (adaptation); *Together with a Miscellany of New Poems by Several Hands.* 1688.

Agnes de Castro by Jean-Baptiste de Brilhac (translator). 1688.

The History of Oracles, and the Cheats of the Pagan Priests by Fontenelle (translator). 1688.

A Discovery of New Worlds by Fontenelle (translator). 1688.

A Congratulatory Poem to Her Most Sacred Majesty Queen Mary, upon Her Arrival in England. 1689.

A Pindaric Poem to the Reverend Doctor Burnet. 1689.

The Lucky Mistake. 1689.

The History of the Nun; or, The Fair Vow-Breaker. 1689.

The Widdow Ranter; or, The History of Bacon in Virginia. 1690.

The Younger Brother; or, The Amorous Jilt. 1696.

Histories and Novels. 1696, 1698.

The Unfortunate Bride; or, The Blind Lady a Beauty; The Unfortunate Happy Lady; The Dumb Virgin. 1698.

The Wandring Beauty. 1698.

Histories, Novels, and Translations. 1700.

Plays. 1702. 2 vols.

Plays, Histories and Novels. Ed. R. H. Shepherd. 1871. 6 vols.

Works. Ed. Montague Summers. 1915. 6 vols.

Selected Writing. Ed. Robert Phelps. 1950.

RICHARD BAXTER (1615–1691)

Aphorismes of Justification. 1649. 2 parts.

The Saints Everlasting Rest. 1650. 4 parts.

Plain Scripture Proof of Infants Church-Membership and Baptism. 1651.

The Humble Petition of Many Thousands of the County of Worcester. 1652.

The Worcester-shire Petition to the Parliament for the Ministry of England Defended. 1653.

The Right Method for a Settled Peace of Conscience, and Spiritual Comfort. 1653.

Christian Concord; or, The Agreement of the Associated Pastors and Churches of Worcestershire. 1653.

Richard Baxter's Apology against the Modest Exceptions of Mr. T. Blake, and the Digression of Mr. G. Kendall. 1654. 4 parts.

True Christianity; or, Christ's Absolute Dominion and Man's Necessary Selfe-Resignation and Subjection. 1655.

Making Light of Christ and Salvation Too Oft the Issue of Gospel Invitations. 1655.

A Sermon of Judgement. 1655.

Rich: Baxter's Confession of His Faith. 1655.

Humble Advice; or, The Heads of Those Things Which Were

Offered to Many Honourable Members of Parliament at the End of His Sermon at the Abby in Westminster. 1655.

The Unreasonableness of Infidelity. 1655. 4 parts.

The Quakers Catechism. 1655.

The Agreement of Divers Ministers of Christ in the County of Worcester and Some Adjacent Parts for Catechizing or Personal Instructing All in Their Several Parishes That Will Consent Thereunto. 1656.

Gildas Silvianus: The Reformed Pastor. 1656.

Certain Disputations of Right to Sacraments, and the True Nature of Visible Christianity. 1657.

The Safe Religion; or, Three Disputations for the Reformed Catholike Religion, against Popery. 1657.

A Treatise of Conversion. 1657.

One Sheet against the Quakers. 1657.

A Winding-Sheet for Popery. 1657.

One Sheet for the Ministry, against the Malignants of All Sorts. 1657.

A Second Sheet for the Ministry. 1657.

Directions to Justices of Peace, Especially in Corporations, for the Discharge of Their Duty to God. 1657.

Richard Baxter's Account of His Present Thoughts concerning the Controversies about the Perseverance of the Saints. 1657.

The Crucifying of the World, by the Cross of Christ. 1658.

Of Saving Faith. 1658.

Confirmation and Restauration, the Necessary Means of Reformation, and Reconciliation; for the Healing of the Corruptions and Divisions of the Church. 1658.

The Judgment and Advice of the Assembly of the Associated Ministers of Worcestershire. 1658.

Of Justification. 1658.

A Call to the Unconverted. 1658.

Directions and Perswasions to a Sound Conversion. 1658.

The Grotian Religion Discovered. 1658.

Five Disputations of Church-Government, and Worship. 1659.

A Key for Catholicks. 1659.

A Holy Commonwealth; or, Political Aphorisms, Opening the True Principles of Government. 1659.

A Treatise of Self-Denyall. 1660.

Catholick Unity; or, The Only Way to Bring Us All to Be of One Religion. 1660.

Universal Concord. 1660. Part 1 only.

The True Catholick and Catholick Church Described. 1660.

A Treatise of Death. 1660.

A Sermon of Repentance. 1660.

Right Rejoycing; or, The Nature and Order of Rational and Warrantable Joy. 1660.

The Life of Faith, as It Is the Evidence of Things Unseen. 1660.

The Successive Visibility of the Church of Which the Protestants Are the Soundest Members. 1660.

The Vain Religion of the Formal Hypocrite. 1660.

A Petition for Peace; with the Reformation of the Liturgy. 1661.

Two Papers of Proposals concerning the Discipline and Ceremonies of the Church of England. 1661.

Now or Never: The Holy, Serious, Diligent Believer Justified, Encouraged, Excited and Directed. 1662.

The Mischiefs of Self-Ignorance, and the Benefits of Self-Acquaintance. 1662.

A Saint or a Brute. 1662.

The Last Work of a Believer. c. 1662.

Fair-Warning; or, XXV. Reasons against Toleration and Indulgence of Popery. 1663.

The Divine Life, in Three Treatises: The First, Of the Knowledge of God; the Second, Of Walking with God; the Third, Of Conversing with God in Solitude. 1664.

Short Instructions for the Sick. 1665.

Two Sheets for Poor Families. 1665.

The Reasons for the Christian Religion. 1667.

Directions for Weak Distempered Christians, to Grow Up to a Confirmed State of Grace. 1669. 2 parts.

The Cure of Church-Divisions. 1670.

A Defence of the Principles of Love, Which Are Necessary to the Unity and Concord of Christians. 1671.

A Second Admonition to Mr. Edward Bagshaw. 1671.

The Divine Appointment of the Lord's Day Proved. 1671.

The Duty of Heavenly Meditation. 1671.

How Far Holinesse Is the Design of Christianity. 1671.

The Difference between the Power of Magistrates and Church-Pastors, and the Roman Kingdom & Magistracy under the Name of a Church & Church-Government Usurped by the Pope. 1671.

Gods Goodness, Vindicated for the Help of Such—Especially in Melancholy—as Are Tempted to Deny It. 1671.

The Church Told of Mr. Ed. Bagshaw's Scandals. 1672.

More Reasons for the Christian Religion and No Reason against It. 1672.

Sacrilegious Desertion of the Holy Ministry Rebuked. 1672.

Two Treatises: The First of Death, on 1 Cor. 15.26; the Second of Judgment, on 2 Cor. 5.10.11. 1672. 2 parts.

The Certainty of Christianity without Popery. 1672.

A Christian Directory; or, A Summ of Practical Theologie, and Cases of Conscience. 1673. 4 parts.

Full and Easie Satisfaction Which Is the True and Safe Religion. 1674.

The Poor Man's Family Book. 1674. 2 parts.

An Appeal to the Light; or, Richard Baxter's Account of Four Accused Passages of a Sermon on Eph. 1.3. 1674.

Richard Baxter's Catholick Theologie. 1675. 4 parts.

Two Disputations of Original Sin. 1675.

More Proofs of Infants Church-Membership and Consequently Their Right to Baptism. 1675.

Select Arguments and Reasons against Popery. 1675.

A Treatise of Justifying Righteousness. 1676. 5 parts.

Rich. Baxter's Review of the State of Christian's Infants. 1676.

The Judgment of Non-Conformists, of the Interest of Reason, in Matters of Religion. 1676.

The Judgment of Nonconformists about the Difference between Grace and Morality. 1676.

Naked Popery; or, The Naked Falsehood of a Book Called the Catholick Naked Truth. 1676–77. 2 parts.

What Is the True Church? 1679.

The Nonconformists Plea for Peace. 1679.

The Second Part of the Nonconformists Plea for Peace. 1680. 2 parts.

Richard Baxters Answer to Dr. Edward Stillingfleet's Charge of Separation. 1680.

The Defence of the Nonconformists Plea for Peace. 1680.

A Moral Prognostication. 1680.

Church-History of the Government of Bishops and Their Councils Abbreviated. 1680.

The True and Only Way of Concord of All the Christian Churches. 1680. 3 parts.

A Sermon Preached at the Funeral of That Faithful Minister of Christ Mr. John Corbet. 1680.

A True Believers Choice and Pleasure: Instanced in the Exemplary Life of Mrs. Mary Coxe. 1680.

Faithful Souls Shall Be with Christ. 1681.

Compassionate Counsel to All Young-Men. 1681.

A Breviate for the Life of Margaret, the Daughter of Francis Charlton and Wife of Richard Baxter. 1681.

Poetical Fragments. 1681.

An Apology for the Nonconformists Ministry. 1681.

A Treatise of Episcopacy. 1681. 2 parts.

A Second True Defence of the Meer Nonconformists. 1681.

A Search for the English Schismatick. 1681.

A Third Defence of the Cause of Peace. 1681. 2 parts.

Methodus Theologiae Christianae. 1681. 2 parts.

Mr. Baxter's Vindication of the Church of England. 1682.

The True History of Councils Enlarged and Defended. 1682. 2 parts.

An Answer to Mr. Dodwell and Dr. Sherlocke. 1682.

How to Do Good to Many; or, The Publick Good Is the Christian's Life. 1682.

Of the Immortality of Mans Soul, and the Nature of It, and Other Spirits, 1682. 2 parts.

Additional Notes on the Life and Death of Sir Matthew Hale. 1682.

The Ready Way of Confuting Mr. Baxter: A Specimen of the Present Mode of Controversie in England. 1682.

The Catechizing of Families. 1683.

Obedient Patience. 1683.

Richard Baxter's Dying Thoughts upon Phil. I.23. 1683.

Richard Baxter's Farewel Sermon, Prepared to Have Been Preached to His Hearers at Kidderminster at His Departure, but Forbidden. 1683.

Additions to the Poetical Fragments. 1683.

Catholick Communion Defended. 1684. 2 parts.

Schism Detected in Both Extreams. 1684. 2 parts.

Catholick Communion Defended against Both Extreams. 1684. 5 parts.

Whether Parish Congregations Be True Christian Churches. 1684. 2 parts.

Catholick Communion Doubly Defended (with John Owen). 1684.

One Thing Necessary; or, Christ's Justification of Mary's Choice. 1685.

A Paraphrase on the New Testament. 1685.

R. Baxter's Sence of the Subscribed Articles of Religion. 1689.

A Treatise of Knowledge and Love Compared. 1689.

Cain and Abel Malignity. 1689.

The English Nonconformity, as under King Charles II and King James II. 1689.

The Scripture Gospel Defended. 1690. 2 parts.

An End of Doctrinal Controversies Which Have Lately Troubled the Churches by Reconciling Explication, without Much Disputing. 1691.

The Glorious Kingdom of Christ, Described and Clearly Vindicated, against the Bold Asserters of a Future Calling and Reign of the Jews. 1691.

A Reply to Mr. Tho. Beverley's Answer to My Reasons against His Doctrine of the Thousand Years Middle Kingdom, and of the Conversion of the Jews. 1691.

Of National Churches. 1691.

Against the Revolt to a Foreign Jurisdiction. 1691.

Church Concord. 1691. 2 parts.

Richard Baxter's Penitent Confession. 1691.

The Certainty of the Worlds of Spirit. 1691.

The Protestant Religion Truely Stated and Justified. Eds. Daniel Williams and Matthew Sylvester. 1692.

The Grand Question Resolved, What We Must Do to Be Saved. 1692.

Paraphrase on the Psalms of David in Metre, with Other Hymns. Ed. Matthew Sylvester. 1692.

Universal Redemption of Mankind by the Lord Jesus Christ. Eds. Joseph Reade and Matthew Sylvester. 1694.

Two Treatises Tending to Awaken Secure Sinners. 1696.

Reliquiae Baxterianae; or, Mr. Richard Baxter's Narrative of the Most Memorable Passages of His Life and Times. Ed. Matthew Sylvester. 1696. 2 parts.

Practical Works. 1707. 4 vols.

The Signs and Causes of Melancholy: Collected out of the Works. Ed. Samuel Clifford. 1716.

Observations on Some Important Points in Divinity. Ed. Ely Bates. 1793.

Baxteriana. Ed. Arthur Young. 1815.

Richard Baxter on the Sacraments. Ed. James S. Pollock. 1880.

The Poor Husbandman's Advocate to Rich Racking Landlords. Ed. F. J. Powicke. 1926.

Some Unpublished Correspondence of the Reverend Richard Baxter and the Reverend John Eliot, the Apostle of the American Indians, 1656–1682. Ed. F. J. Powicke. 1931.

Richard Baxter and Puritan Politics. Ed. Richard Schlatter. 1957.

ROBERT BOYLE (1627–1691)

Some Motives and Incentives to the Love of God ⟨Seraphick Love⟩. 1659.

New Experiments Physio-Mechanicall, Touching the Spring of the Air. 1660.

Certain Physiological Essays. 1661.

The Sceptical Chymist. 1661.

Some Considerations Touching the Style of the H. Scriptures. 1661.

Some Considerations Touching the Usefulnesse of Experimental Naturall Philosophy. 1663 [Volume 1]; 1671 [Volume 2].

Experiments and Considerations Touching Colours. 1664.

Occasional Reflections upon Several Subjects. 1665.

New Experiments and Observations Touching Cold. 1665.

Hydrostatical Paradoxes, Made out by New Experiments, (For the Most Part Physical and Easie). 1666.

The Origine of Formes and Qualities. 1666.

A Continuation of New Experiments Physico-Mechanicall, Touching the Spring and Weight of the Air. 1669 [Part 1]; 1680 [Part 2; as *Experimentorum Novum Physico-Mechanicorum Continuatio Secunda*].

Tracts about the Cosmicall Qualities of Things; Cosmical Suspitions; the Temperature of the Subterraneall Regions; the Temperature of the Submarine Regions; the Bottom of the Sea. 1671.

Tracts of a Discovery of the Admirable Rarefaction of the Air. 1671.

An Essay about the Origine & Virtues of Gems. 1672.

Tracts Containing New Experiments, Touching the Relation betwixt Flame and Air. 1672.

Essays of the Strange Subtilty, Great Efficacy, Determinate Nature of Effluviums. 1673.

Tracts Consisting of Observations about the Saltness of the Sea. 1674.

The Excellency of Theology, Compar'd with Natural Philosophy. 1674.

Tracts Containing Suspicions about Some Hidden Qualities of the Air. 1674.

Experiments, Notes, &c. about the Mechanical Origine or Production of Divers Particular Qualities. 1675. 11 parts.

Opera Varia. 1677.

An Historical Account of a Degradation of Gold. 1678.

The Aerial Noctiluca. 1680.

New Experiments, and Observations, Made upon the Icy Noctiluca. 1681/2.
A Discourse of Things above Reason. 1681.
Memoirs for the Natural History of Humane Blood. 1683/4.
Experiments and Considerations about the Porosity of Bodies. 1684.
Short Memoirs for the Natural Experimental History of Mineral Waters. 1684/5.
Of the High Veneration Man's Intellect Owes to God. 1685.
An Essay of the Great Effects of Even Languid and Unheeded Motion. 1685.
Of the Reconcileableness of Specifick Medicines to the Corpuscular Philosophy. 1685.
A Free Enquiry into the Vulgarly Receiv'd Notion of Nature. 1685/6.
The Martyrdom of Theodora, and of Didymus. 1687.
Reasons Why a Protestant Should Not Turn Papist. 1687.
Receipts Sent to a Friend in America. 1688. Lost.
A Disquisition about the Final Causes of Natural Things. 1688.
An Advertisement of Mr. Boyle, about the Loss of Many of His Writings. 1688.
Medicina Hydrostatica; or, Hydrostaticks Applyed to the Materia Medica. 1690.
The Christian Virtuoso. 1690. 2 parts.
Experimenta & Observationes Physicae. 1691.
The General History of the Air. 1692.
General Heads for the Natural History of a Country. 1692.
Medicinal Experiments; or, A Collection of Choice Remedies, for the Most Part Simple, and Easily Prepared. 1692, 1693–94 (3 vols.).
A Free Discourse against Customary Swearing. 1695.
Opera Omnia. 1696–97. 3 vols. in 4.
Works Epitomiz'd. Ed. Richard Boulton. 1699–1700. 3 vols.
Theological Works. 1715. 3 vols.
Philosophical Works. Ed. Peter Shaw. 1725. 3 vols.
Works. 1744. 5 vols.
Works. 1772. 6 vols.
Robert Boyle on Natural Philosophy: An Essay, with Selections from His Writings. Ed. Marie Boas Hall. 1965.

SIR GEORGE ETHEREGE (c. 1634–c. 1691)

The Comical Revenge; or, Love in a Tub. 1664.
She Wou'd If She Cou'd. 1668.
The Man of Mode; or, Sr Fopling Flutter. 1676.
Works: Containing His Plays and Poems. 1704.
Works. Ed. A. W. Verity. 1888.
Dramatic Works. Ed. H. F. B. Brett-Smith. 1927. 2 vols.
Letterbook. Ed. Sybil Rosenfeld. 1928.
Poems. Ed. James Thorpe. 1963.
Letters. Ed. Frederick Bracher. 1974.
Plays. Ed. Michael Cordner. 1982.

THOMAS SHADWELL (c. 1642–1692)

The Sullen Lovers; or, The Impertinents. 1668.
The Royal Shepherdess (adaptation). 1669.
The Humorists. 1671.
The Miser by Molière (adaptation). 1672.
Epsom-Wells. 1673.
Notes and Observations on The Empress of Morocco (with John Dryden and John Crowne). 1674.
Psyche. 1675.
The Libertine. 1676.
The Virtuoso. 1676.

The History of Timon of Athens, the Man-Hater (adaptation). 1678.
A True Widow. 1679.
The Woman-Captain. 1680.
The Lancashire Witches and Ted O Divelly the Irish Priest. 1682.
The Medal of John Bayes: A Satyr against Folly and Knavery. 1682.
[*Satyr to His Muse.* 1682.]
Some Reflections upon the Pretended Parallel in the Play Called The Duke of Guise. 1683.
A Lenten Prologue Refus'd by the Players. 1683.
The Tenth Satyr of Juvenal (translator). 1687.
The Squire of Alsatia. 1688.
A Congratulatory Poem on His Highness the Prince of Orange His Coming into England. 1689.
A Congratulatory Poem to the Most Illustrious Queen Mary upon Her Arrival in England. 1689.
[*The Address of John Dryden, Laureat to His Highness the Prince of Orange.* 1689.]
Bury-Fair. 1689.
The Amorous Bigotte; with the Second Part of Tegue O Divelly. 1690.
Ode on the Anniversary of the King's Birth. 1690.
Ode to the King, on His Return to Ireland. c. 1690.
The Scowrers. 1691.
Votum Perenne: A Poem to the King on New-Years-Day. 1692.
Ode on the King's Birth-day. 1692.
The Volunteers; or, The Stock-Jobbers. 1693.
Works. 1693.
Dramatick Works. 1720. 4 vols.
Thomas Shadwell. Ed. George Saintsbury. 1903.
Complete Works. Ed. Montague Summers. 1927. 5 vols.

NATHANIEL LEE (c. 1649–1692)

The Tragedy of Nero, Emperour of Rome. 1675.
Sophonisba; or, Hannibal's Overthrow. 1676.
Gloriana; or, The Court of Augustus Caesar. 1676.
The Rival Queens; or, The Death of Alexander the Great. 1677.
To the Prince and Princess of Orange, upon Their Marriage. 1677. Lost.
Mithridates, King of Pontus. 1678.
Oedipus (with John Dryden). 1679.
Caesar Borgia, Son of Pope Alexander the Sixth. 1680.
Theodosius; or, The Force of Love. 1680.
Lucius Junius Brutus, Father of His Country. 1681.
To the Duke on His Return. 1682.
The Duke of Guise (with John Dryden). 1683.
Constantine the Great. 1684.
The Princess of Cleve. 1689.
On Their Majesties Coronation. 1689.
On the Death of Mrs. Behn. 1689.
The Massacre of Paris. 1690.
Works. 1694, 1713 (2 vols.).
Works. Eds. Thomas B. Stroup and Arthur L. Cooke. 1954–55. 2 vols.

HENRY VAUGHAN (1621–1695)

Poems, with the Tenth Satyre of Juvenal Englished. 1646.
Silex Scintillans; or, Sacred Poems and Private Ejaculations. 1650, 1655 (2 parts).
Olor Iscanus: A Collection of Some Select Poems and Translations. 1651.
The Mount of Olives; or, Solitary Devotions. 1652.

Flores Solitudinis: Certain Rare and Elegant Pieces. 1654. 2 parts.

Hermetical Physick by Heinrich Nolle (translator). 1655.

The Chymists Key to Open and to Shut; or, The True Doctrine of Corruption and Generation by Heinrich Nolle (translator). 1657.

Thalia Rediviva: The Pass-Times and Diversions of a Countrey-Muse, in Choice Poems on Several Occasions. 1678.

Works in Prose and Verse. Ed. Alexander B. Grosart. 1870–71. 4 vols.

Secular Poems. Ed. J. R. Tutin. 1893.

Poems. Ed. E. K. Chambers. 1896. 2 vols.

Poems. Ed. Edward Hutton. 1904.

Works. Ed. L. C. Martin. 1914 (2 vols.), 1957.

Poems, Essay and Two Letters. Ed. Francis Meynell. 1924.

Secular Poems. Ed. E. L. Marilla. 1958.

Poetry and Selected Prose. Ed. L. C. Martin. 1963.

Complete Poetry. Ed. French Vogle. 1964.

A Selection from Henry Vaughan. Ed. Christopher Dixon. 1967.

Complete Poems. Ed. Alan Rudrum. 1976.

GEORGE SAVILE, MARQUIS OF HALIFAX
(1633–1695)

Observations upon a Late Libel, Called A Letter from a Person of Quality to His Friend, concerning the King's Declaration. 1681.

[*A Seasonable Addresse to Both Houses of Parliament concerning the Succession, the Fears of Popery, and Arbitrary Government.* 1681.]

A Letter to a Dissenter upon Occasion of His Majesties Late Gracious Declaration of Indulgence. 1687.

The Lady's New-Years Gift; or, Advice to a Daughter. 1688.

The Character of a Trimmer. 1688.

[*A Letter from a Clergy-man in the City, to His Friend in the Country, Containing His Reasons for Not Reading the Declaration.* 1688.]

The Anatomy of an Equivalent. 1688.

The Character of the Protestants of Ireland. 1689.

Maxims Found amongst the Papers of the Great Almansor. 1693.

A Rough Draft of a New Model at Sea. 1694.

Some Cautions Offered to the Consideration of Those Who Are to Chuse Members to Serve in the Ensuing Parliament. 1695.

Miscellanies. 1700. 8 parts.

A Character of King Charles the Second, and Political, Moral and Miscellaneous Thoughts and Reflections. 1750.

Savile Correspondence (with others). Ed. W. D. Cooper. 1858.

Life and Letters, with a New Edition of His Works. Ed. H. C. Foxcroft. 1898. 2 vols.

Complete Works. Ed. Walter Raleigh. 1912.

The Rochester-Savile Letters 1671–1680. Ed. John Harold Wilson. 1941.

Complete Works. Ed. J. P. Kenyon. 1969.

SIR WILLIAM TEMPLE (1628–1699)

Upon the Death of Mrs. Catherine Philips. 1664.

Lettre d'un marchand de Londres à son amy à Amsterdam depuis la dernière bataille de mer. 1666.

Poems. c. 1670.

An Essay upon the Advancement of Trade in Ireland. 1673.

Observations upon the United Provinces of the Netherlands. 1673.

Miscellanea. 1680 [Part 1]; 1690 [Part 2]; 1701 [Part 3].

Memoirs of What Past in Christendom from the War Begun in 1672 to the Peace Concluded 1679. 1692.

An Answer to a Scurrilous Pamphlet Lately Printed, Intituled A Letter from Monsieur de Cros to the Lord ———. 1693.

An Introduction to the History of England. 1695.

The Temple of Death. 1695.

Letters Written by Sir William Temple during His Being Ambassador at the Hague, to the Earl of Arlington, and Sir John Trevor. 1699.

Letters Written by Sir W. Temple, Bart., and Other Ministers of State. 1700 [Volumes 1–2]; 1703 [Volume 3].

Select Letters to the Prince of Orange (Now King of England), King Charles the II^d and the Earl of Arlington; to Which Is Added An Essay upon the State and Settlement of Ireland. 1701.

Memoirs, Part III: From the Peace Concluded in 1679 to the Time of the Author's Retirement from Publick Business. 1709.

Works. 1720. 2 vols.

Works. 1754. 4 vols.

Miscellanies. 1761.

Essays. Ed. J. A. Nicklin. 1903.

Essays on Ancient and Modern Learning and on Poetry. Ed. J. E. Spingarn. 1909.

Early Essays and Romances. Ed. G. C. Moore Smith. 1930.

Three Essays. Ed. F. J. Fielden. 1939.

Five Miscellaneous Essays. Ed. Samuel Holt Monk. 1963.

William Temple's Analysis of Sir Philip Sidney's Apology for Poetry: *An Edition and Translation.* Ed. and tr. John Webster. 1984.

JOHN DRYDEN (1631–1700)

Three Poems upon the Death of His Late Highnesse Oliver, Lord Protector of England, Scotland and Ireland (with Edmund Waller and Thomas Sprat). 1659.

Astraea Redux. 1660.

To His Sacred Majesty. 1661.

My Lord Chancellor, Presented on New-Years-Day. 1662.

The Rival Ladies. 1664.

The Indian-Queen. 1665.

The Indian Emperour. 1667.

Annus Mirabilis. 1667.

Secret-Love; or, The Maiden Queen. 1668.

Sr Martin Mar-All. 1668.

Of Dramatic Poesy: An Essay. 1668.

The Tempest; or, The Enchanted Island (adaptation; with Sir William D'Avenant). 1670.

Tyrannick Love; or, The Royal Martyr. 1670.

An Evening's Love; or, The Mock-Astrologer. 1671.

The Conquest of Granada by the Spaniards. 1672.

Marriage-à-la-Mode. 1673.

The Assignation; or, Love in a Nunnery. 1673.

Amboyna. 1673.

Notes and Observations on The Empress of Morocco (with Thomas Shadwell and John Crowne). 1674.

Aureng-Zebe. 1676.

The State of Innocence and Fall of Man. 1677.

All for Love; or, The World Well Lost. 1678.

Oedipus (with Nathaniel Lee). 1679.

Troilus and Cressida; or, Truth Found Too Late. 1679.

The Kind Keeper; or, Mr. Limberham. 1680.

Epilogue Spoke before His Majesty at Oxford. 1680.

The Spanish Fryar; or, The Double Discovery. 1681.

His Majesties Declaration Defended. 1681.

Absalom and Achitophel. 1681.
A Prologue Spoken at Mithridates King of Pontus 〈by Nathaniel Lee〉. 1682.
Prologue to The Loyal Brother 〈by Thomas Southerne〉. 1682.
The Medall: A Satyre against Sedition. 1682.
Mac Flecknoe. 1682.
Prologue to his Royal Highness. 1682.
Prologue to the Duchess on Her Return from Scotland. 1682.
Religio Laici; or, A Layman's Faith. 1682.
The Second Part of Absalom and Achitophel (with Nahum Tate). 1682.
Prologue to the King and Queen. 1683.
The Duke of Guise (with Nathaniel Lee). 1683.
The Vindication of The Duke of Guise. 1683.
Plutarch's Lives (editor). 1683–86. 5 vols.
Prologue 〈by Thomas Otway〉 *and Epilogue* 〈by Dryden〉 *to* Constantine the Great 〈by Nathaniel Lee〉. 1684.
Prologue to The Disappointment 〈by Thomas Southerne〉. 1684.
Miscellany Poems (with others). 1685.
Sylvae (with others). 1685.
Threnodia Augustalis. 1685.
Albion and Albanius. 1685.
A Defence of the Papers Written by the Late King of Blessed Memory, and Duchess of York, against the Answer Made to Them. 1686.
The Hind and the Panther. 1687.
A Song for St. Cecilia's Day. 1687.
Britannia Rediviva. 1688.
The Life of St. Francis Xavier by Dominick Bouhours (translator). 1688.
Don Sebastian, King of Portugal. 1690.
Amphitryon; or, The Two Socia's. 1690.
King Arthur; or, The British Worthy. 1691.
Works. 1691.
Eleonora: A Panegyrical Poem Dedicated to the Memory of the Late Countess of Abingdon. 1692.
Cleomenes, the Spartan Heroe. 1692.
The Satires of Decimus Junius Juvenalis, Together with the Satires of Aulus Persius Flaccus (translator; with others). 1693.
Works. 1693. 4 vols.
Examen Poeticum (with others). 1693.
Love Triumphant; or, Nature Will Prevail. 1694.
De Arte Graphica by C. A. Du Fresnoy (translator). 1695.
An Ode on the Death of Mr. Henry Purcell. 1696.
The Works of Virgil (translator). 1697.
Alexander's Feast; or, The Power of Musique. 1697.
The Pilgrim by John Fletcher (adaptation). 1700.
Fables Ancient and Modern (with others). 1700.
Works. 1701. 4 vols.
Poems on Various Occasions and Translations from Several Authors. 1701.
Comedies, Tragedies and Operas. 1701. 2 vols.
Dramatick Works. Ed. William Congreve. 1717. 6 vols.
Original Poems and Translations. Ed. Thomas Broughton. 1743. 2 vols.
Select Essays on the Belles Lettres. 1750.
Poems and Fables. 1753.
Original Poems. 1756. 2 vols.
Miscellaneous Works. Ed. Samuel Derrick. 1760. 4 vols.
Critical and Miscellaneous Prose Works. Ed. Edmond Malone. 1800. 4 vols.
Poetical Works. Ed. Thomas Park. 1806. 3 vols.
Works. Ed. Sir Walter Scott. 1808. 18 vols.

Poetical Works. Ed. H. J. Todd. 1811. 4 vols.
Poetical Works. Ed. John Mitford. 1832–33. 5 vols.
Poetical Works. Ed. Robert Bell. 1854. 3 vols.
Poetical Works. Ed. George Gilfillan. 1854. 2 vols.
Poetical Works. Ed. W. D. Christie. 1870.
Essays. Ed. C. D. Yonge. 1882.
Works. Ed. Sir Walter Scott, rev. George Saintsbury. 1882–93. 18 vols.
Satires. Ed. John Churton Collins. 1893.
Essays. Ed. W. P. Ker. 1900. 2 vols.
Dramatic Essays. Ed. W. H. Hudson. 1912.
Poetry and Prose. Ed. David Nichol Smith. 1925.
Dramatic Works. Ed. Montague Summers. 1931–32. 6 vols.
The Best of Dryden. Ed. Louis I. Bredvold. 1933.
Poems. Ed. Bonamy Dobrée. 1934.
Letters. Ed. Charles E. Ward. 1942.
Selected Poems. Ed. Geoffrey Grigson. 1950.
Prologues and Epilogues. Ed. William Bradford Gardner. 1951.
Poems and Prose. Ed. Douglas Grant. 1955.
Works. Eds. Edward Niles Hooker, H. T. Swedenberg, Jr., et al. 1956– .
Poems. Ed. James Kinsley. 1958. 4 vols.
Of Dramatic Poesy and Other Critical Essays. Ed. George Watson. 1962. 2 vols.
Literary Criticism. Ed. Arthur C. Kirsch. 1966.
Four Comedies. Eds. L. A. Beaurline and Fredson Bowers. 1967.
Four Tragedies. Eds. L. A. Beaurline and Fredson Bowers. 1967.
A Choice of Dryden's Verse. Ed. W. H. Auden. 1973.

SIR CHARLES SEDLEY (c. 1639–1701)

Pompey the Great by Pierre Corneille (translator; with others). 1664.
The Mulberry Garden. 1668.
Antony and Cleopatra. 1677.
Bellamira; or, The Mistress. 1687.
Reflections upon Our Late and Present Proceedings in England. 1689.
Speech in the House of Commons. 1691.
The Happy Pair; or, A Poem on Matrimony. 1702.
Miscellaneous Works; to Which Is Added, The Death of Marc Antony. Ed. Captain William Ayloffe. 1702. 3 parts.
Poetical Works and Speeches in Parliament. Ed. Captain William Ayloffe. 1707. 2 parts.
Works. 1722. 2 vols.
Poetical and Dramatic Works. Ed. Vivian de Sola Pinto. 1928. 2 vols.

SAMUEL PEPYS (1633–1703)

The Portugal History. 1677.
Memoires Relating to the State of the Royal Navy of England for Ten Years. 1690.
An Account of the Preservation of King Charles II after the Battle of Worcester (editor). Ed. Sir David Dalrymple. 1766.
Memoirs: Comprising His Diary from 1659 to 1669, and a Selection from His Private Correspondence. Ed. Richard, Lord Braybrooke. 1825 (2 vols.), 1858 (6th rev. ed.; 4 vols.).
Life, Journals, and Correspondence. Ed. John Smith. 1841. 2 vols.
Diary and Correspondence. Ed. Mynors Bright. 1875–79. 6 vols.

Diary. Ed. Henry B. Wheatley. 1893–99. 10 vols.
Naval Minutes. Ed. J. R. Tanner. 1926.
Private Correspondence and Miscellaneous Papers 1679–1703. Ed. J. R. Tanner. 1929. 2 vols.
Further Correspondence 1662–1679. Ed. J. R. Tanner. 1929.
Letters and the Second Diary. Ed. R. G. Howarth. 1932.
Shorthand Letters. Ed. Edwin Chappell. 1933.
Tangier Papers. Ed. Edwin Chappell. 1933.
Mr. Pepys upon the State of Christ-Hospital. Ed. Rudolf Kirk. 1935.
The Letters of Samuel Pepys and His Family Circle. Ed. Helen Truesdell Heath. 1955.
Diary. Ed. J. P. Kenyon. 1963.
Charles II's Escape from Worcester: A Collection of Narratives Assembled by Samuel Pepys. Ed. William Matthews. 1966.
Diary. Eds. Robert Latham and William Matthews. 1970–83. 11 vols.
Samuel Pepys' Penny Merriments. Ed. Roger Thompson. 1976.
The Illustrated Pepys. Ed. Robert Latham. 1978.
The Shorter Pepys. Ed. Robert Latham. 1985.

SIR ROGER L'ESTRANGE (1616–1704)

To a Gentleman, a Member of the House of Commons. 1646.
L'Estrange His Appeale from the Court Martiall to the Parliament. 1647.
Lestrange His Vindication to Kent. 1649.
The Liberty of the Imprisoned Royalist. 1649.
An Appeal in the Case of the Late King's Party. 1660.
L'Estrange His Apology. 1660.
A Rope for Pol; or, The Hue and Cry after Marchmont Needham. 1660.
Let Me Speake Too? 1659.
The Fanatique Powder-Plot. 1660.
Peace to the Nation. 1660.
No Blinde Guides, in Answer to a Seditious Pamphlet of J. Milton's, Intituled Brief Notes upon a Late Sermon. 1660.
Physician Cure Thyself; or, An Answer to a Seditious Pamphlet, Entitled Eye-Salve for the English Army. 1660.
[A Plea for a Limited Monarchy. 1660.]
Sir Politique Uncased; or, A Sober Answer to A Letter Intercepted. c. 1660.
A Caveat to the Cavaliers; or, An Antidote against Mistaken Cordials. 1661.
A Modest Plea Both for the Caveat, and the Author of It. 1661.
The Relaps'd Apostate; or, Notes upon a Presbyterian Pamphlet Entitled, A Petition for Peace. 1661.
State-Divinity; or, A Supplement to The Relaps'd Apostate. 1661.
Interest Mistaken; or, The Holy Cheat. 1661.
To the Right Honourable Edward Earl of Clarendon, Lord High Chancellor of England. 1661.
A Whipp, a Whipp for the Schismatical Animadverter upon the Bishop of Worcester's Letter. 1662.
A Memento Directed to All Those That Truly Reverence the Memory of King Charles the Martyr. 1662, 1682 (as *A Memento Treating of the Rise, Progress and Remedies of Seditions*).
Truth and Loyalty Vindicated, from the Reproaches and Clamours of Mr. Edward Bagshaw. 1662.
The Visitation; or, The Long Look'd-for Comes at Last. 1662.
Toleration Discuss'd. 1663.

Considerations and Proposals in Order to the Regulation of the Press. 1663.
England's Interest Asserted in the Improvement of Its Native Commodities & More Especially the Manufacture of Wool. 1663.
The Intelligencer. 1663. 17 nos.
The Intelligencer ⟨with supplement, *The Newes*⟩. 1663–65. 207 nos.
Publick Intelligence. 1665. 1 no.
An Essay; or, A Narrative of the Two Great Fights at Sea between the English and the Dutch. 1666.
Dolus an Virtus? 1667.
The Visions of Quevedo (translator). 1667.
A General Note of the Prices of Binding of All Sorts of Books. 1669.
A Guide to Eternity by Giovanni Bona (translator). 1672.
A Discourse of the Fishery. 1674.
News from New-England: Being a True and Last Account of the Present Bloody Wars Carried On betwixt the Infidels, Natives, and the English Christians, and Converted Indians of New-England. 1676.
Poor Robin's Vision: Wherein Is Described, the Present Humours of the Times. 1677.
A Humble Address with Some Proposals for the Future Preventing of the Decrease of the Inhabitants of This Realm. 1677.
The Parallel; or, An Account of the Growth of Knavery, under the Pretended Fears of Arbitrary Government and Popery. 1677.
A Treatise of Wool and Cattel. 1677.
Flora's Vagaries. 1677.
A Register of the Nativity of the Present Christian Princes. 1678.
Tyranny and Popery Lording It over the Consciences, Lives, Liberties, and Estates Both of King and People. 1678.
The Gentleman 'Pothecary (translator). 1678.
Five Love Letters from a Nun to a Cavalier (translator). 1678.
Seneca's Morals, by Way of Abstract. 3 parts.
The History of the Plot; or, A Brief and Historical Account of the Charge and Defence of Edward Coleman, Esq; William Ireland, Thomas Pickering, etc. 1679.
An Answer to the Appeal from the Country to the City. 1679.
The Case Put, concerning the Succession of His Royal Highness the Duke of York. 1679.
The Reformed Catholique; or, The True Protestant. 1679.
The Free-Born Subject; or, The Englishmans Birthright Asserted against All Tyrannical Usurpations Either in Church or State. 1679.
Citt and Bumpkin: In a Dialogue over a Pot of Ale concerning Matters of Religion and Government. 1680.
Citt and Bumpkin: The Second Part. 1680.
A Seasonable Memorial in Some Historical Notes upon the Liberties of the Presse and Pulpit. 1680.
A Further Discovery of the Plot, Drawn from the Narrative and Depositions of Dr. Titus Oates. 1680.
L'Estrange's Narrative of the Plot. 1680.
The Casuist Uncas'd, in a Dialogue betwixt Richard and Baxter. 1680.
Discovery upon Discovery, in Defence of Doctor Oates against B. W.'s Libellous Vindication of Him. 1680.
A Letter to Miles Prance. 1680.
L'Estrange's Case in a Civil Dialogue betwixt 'Zekiel and Ephraim. 1680.
A Short Answer to a Whole Litter of Libels. 1680.
The Committee; or, Popery in Masquerade. 1680.

A Compendious History of the Most Remarkable Passages of the Last Fourteen Years. 1680.

Goodman Country to His Worship the City of London. 1680.

The Presbyterian Sham; or, A Commentary upon the New Old Answer of the Assembly of Divines to Dr. Stillingfleet's Sermon. 1680.

[*The State and Interest of the Nation, with Respect to His Royal Highness the Duke of York, Discours'd at Large.* 1680.]

Twenty Select Colloquies out of Erasmus (translator). 1680.

Tully's Offices (translator). 1680.

To the Reverend Dr. Thomas Ken. c. 1680.

The Character of a Papist in Masquerade: Supported by Authority and Experience, in Answer to The Character of a Popish Successor. 1681.

A Reply to the Second Part of The Character of a Popish Successor. 1681.

L'Estrange His Appeal Humbly Submitted to the Kings Most Excellent Majesty and the Three Estates Assembled in Parliament. 1681.

L'Estrange No Papist: In Answer to a Libel Entituled L'Estrange a Papist. 1681.

An Apology for the Protestants (translator). 1681.

Machivil's Advice to His Son (translator). 1681.

Seven Portuguese Letters (translator). 1681.

The Observator. 1681–87. 3 vols.

Mr. Roger Le Strange's Sayings with Brief Notes to Prevent Misapprehensions. 1681.

The Dissenter's Sayings, in Requital for L'Estrange's Sayings. 1681.

Dissenters Sayings: The Second Part. 1681.

Notes upon Stephen College. 1681.

[*A Hue and Cry after Dr. T. O.* 1681.]

The Reformation Reform'd; or, A Short History of New-Fashion'd Christians. 1681.

A Word concerning Libels and Libellers. 1681.

The Shammer Shamm'd. 1681.

A Letter out of Scotland to His Friend, H. B. in London. 1681.

A New Dialogue between Some Body and No Body. 1681.

Dialogue upon Dialogue. 1681.

The Accompt Clear'd, in Answer to a Libel Intituled A True Account from Chichester concerning the Death of Habin the Informer. 1681.

A Collection of Several Tracts in Quarto. 1682.

The Apostate Protestant. 1682.

Remarks on the Growth and Progress of Non-Conformity. 1682.

[*Reflections upon Two Scurrilous Libels, Called* Speculum Crape-gownorum. 1682.]

A Sermon Prepared to Be Preach'd. 1682.

Considerations upon a Printed Sheet, Entitled The Speech of the Late Lord Russel to the Sheriffs. 1683.

[*The Lawyer Outlaw'd.* 1683.]

[*Theosebia; or, The Churches Advocate.* 1683.]

The Whore's Rhetorick. 1683.

Five Love Letters Written by a Cavalier. 1683.

The Observator Defended. 1685.

Agiatis, Queen of Sparta by Pierre d'Ortigue, sieur de Vaumorière (translator). 1686.

An Answer to A Letter to a Dissenter, *upon Occasion of His Majesties Late Gracious Declaration of Indulgence.* 1687.

A Brief History of the Times. 1687–88. 3 parts.

A Reply to the Reasons of the Oxford-Clergy against Addressing. c. 1687.

Two Cases Submitted to Consideration. 1687.

The Spanish Decameron; or, 5 Novels by Cervantes and 5 by A. del Castillo Solorzano (translator). 1687.

Heraclitus Ridens Redivivus; or, a Dialogue between Harry ⟨Henry Care⟩ *and Roger concerning the Times.* c. 1688.

A Dialogue between Sir R. L. and T⟨itus⟩ O⟨ates⟩, D⟨octor⟩. 1689.

[*Some Queries concerning the Election of Members for the Ensuing Parliament.* 1690.]

The Fables of Æsop and Other Eminent Mythologists, with Morals and Reflexions (translator). 1692.

Terence's Comedies, tr. Laurence Eachard (revised by Eachard and L'Estrange). 1698.

Fables and Storyes Moralized: Being a Second Part of the Fables of Æsop (translator; with others). 1699.

The Works of Flavius Josephus (translator). 1702.

[*The Spanish Pole-Cat; or, The Adventures of Seniora Rufine* by A. del Castillo Solorzano ⟨translator; with others⟩. 1717.]

Selections from The Observator. Ed. Violet Jourdain. 1970.

JOHN LOCKE (1632–1704)

The Fundamental Constitutions of Carolina. 1670.

[*A Letter from a Person of Quality, to His Friend in the Country.* 1675.]

Epistola de Tolerantia. 1689.

A Second Letter concerning Toleration. 1690.

An Essay concerning Humane Understanding. 1690, 1706 (5th rev. ed.).

Two Treatises of Government. 1690.

A Third Letter for Toleration. 1692.

Some Considerations of the Consequences of the Lowering of Interest and Raising the Value of Money. 1692.

Some Thoughts concerning Education. 1692.

Short Observations on a Printed Paper, Intituled, For Encouraging the Coining Silver Money in England, and After for Keeping It Here. 1695.

The Reasonableness of Christianity, as Delivered in the Scriptures. 1695.

A Vindication of The Reasonableness of Christianity, &c., *from Mr.* ⟨John⟩ *Edwards's Reflections.* 1695.

Further Considerations concerning Raising the Value of Money. 1695.

Several Papers Relating to Money, Interest and Trade, &c. 1696.

A Letter to the Right Reverend Edward Ld Bishop of Worcester, concerning some Passages Relating to Mr. Locke's Essay concerning Humane Understanding. 1697.

Mr. Locke's Reply to the Right Reverend The Lord Bishop of Worcester's Answer to His Letter. 1697.

A Second Vindication of The Reasonableness of Christianity. 1697.

Mr. Locke's Reply to the Right Reverend the Lord Bishop of Worcester's Answer to His Second Letter. 1699.

Æsop's Fables, in English and Latin (translator). 1703.

A Paraphrase and Notes on the Epistle of St. Paul to the Galatians. 1705.

Posthumous Works. Eds. Peter King and Anthony Collins. 1706.

A Paraphrase and Notes on the First Epistle of St. Paul to the Corinthians. 1706.

A Paraphrase and Notes on the Second Epistle of St. Paul to the Corinthians. 1706.

A Paraphrase and Notes on the Epistle of St. Paul to the Romans. 1707.

A Paraphrase and Notes on the Epistle of St. Paul to the Ephesians. 1707.

An Essay for the Understanding of St. Paul's Epistles, by Consulting St. Paul Himself. 1707.

Some Familiar Letters between Mr. Locke, and Several of His Friends. 1708.

Discourses on the Being of God by Pierre Nicole (translator). 1712.

Works. 1714. 3 vols.

Remains. 1714.

A Collection of Several Pieces Never Before Printed. Eds. Pierre Desmaizeaux and Anthony Collins. 1720.

Observations upon the Growth and Culture of Vines and Olives. 1766.

Works. 1794. 9 vols.

Original Letters (with Anthony Ashley Cooper, Third Earl of Shaftesbury, and Algernon Sidney). Ed. Thomas Forster. 1830.

Philosophical Works. Ed. J. A. St. John. 1843.

Lettres inédites à ses amis Nicolas Thoynard, Philippe van Limbouch et Edward Clarke. Eds. Henry Ollion and T. J. de Beer. 1912.

The Correspondence of John Locke and Edward Clarke. Ed. Benjamin Rand. 1927.

Directions concerning Education: Being the First Draft of His Thoughts concerning Education. Ed. Frederick George Kenyon. 1933.

An Early Draft of Locke's Essay, Together with Excerpts from His Journals. Eds. R. I. Aaron and Jocelyn Gibb. 1936.

John Locke on Politics and Education. Ed. Howard R. Penniman. 1947.

Locke's Travels in France 1675–1679 as Related in His Journals, Correspondence and Other Papers. Ed. John Lough. 1953.

Essays on the Law of Nature. Ed. W. von Leyden. 1954.

Scritti editi e inediti sulla tolleranza. Ed. Carlo Augusto Viano. 1961.

Educational Writings. Ed. James L. Axtell. 1968.

Works (Clarendon Edition). Eds. P. H. Nidditch et al. 1975– . 30 vols. (projected).

The Locke Reader. Ed. John W. Yotton. 1977.

Draft A of Locke's Essay concerning Human Understanding: The Earliest Extant Autograph Version. Ed. Peter H. Nidditch. 1980.

Draft B of Locke's Essay concerning Human Understanding: The Fullest Extant Autograph Version. Ed. Peter H. Nidditch. 1982.

JOHN EVELYN (1620–1706)

Of Liberty and Servitude by Sieur de la Mothe le Vayer (translator). 1649.

The State of France, as It Stood in the IXth Yeer of This Present Monarch, Lewis XIIII. 1652.

An Essay on ⟨i.e. translation of⟩ *the First Book of T. Lucretius Carus De Rerum Natura.* 1656.

The French Gardiner by Nicolas de Bonnefons (translator). 1658.

The Golden Book of St. John Chrysostom (translator). 1659.

A Character of England. 1659.

An Apologue for the Royal Party. 1659.

The Late News or Message from Bruxels Unmasked. 1660.

[*The Manner of Ordering Fruit-Trees* by Sieur Le Gendre (translator). 1660.]

A Panegyrick to Charles the Second. 1661.

Fumifugium; or, The Inconvenience of the Aer and Smoak of London Dissipated. 1661.

Narrative of the Encounter between the French and Spanish Ambassadors at the Landing of the Swedish Ambassador. 1661. Lost.

Instructions concerning Erecting of a Library by Gabriel Naudé (translator). 1661.

Tyrannus; or, The Mode. 1661.

Sculptura; or, The History, and Art of Chalcography and Engraving in Copper. 1662.

Μυστήριον τῆς Ἀνομίας: *That Is, Another Part of the Mystery of Jesuitism; Together with the Imaginary Heresy* by Antoine Arnauld and Pierre Nicole (translator). 1664.

Sylva; or, A Discourse of Forest-Trees, and the Propagation of Timber in His Majesties Dominions; To Which Is Annexed Pomona; also Kalendarium Hortense. 1664.

A Parallel of the Antient Architecture with the Modern; with Leon Baptista Alberti's Treatise of Statues by Roland Fréart (translator). 1664.

The Pernicious Consequences of the New Heresie of the Jesuites against the King and the State by Pierre Nicole (translator). 1666.

The English Vineyard Vindicated. 1666.

Publick Employment and an Active Life Prefer'd to Solitude. 1667.

An Idea of the Perfection of Painting by Roland Fréart (translator). 1668.

The History of the Three Late Famous Impostors. 1669.

Navigation and Commerce, Their Original and Progress. 1674.

A Philosophical Discourse of Earth. 1676.

Mundus Muliebris; or, The Ladies Dressing-Room Unlock'd, and Her Toilette Spread. 1690.

The Compleat Gard'ner by de la Quintyne (translator). 1693.

Numismata: A Discourse of Medals, Antient and Modern. 1697.

Acetaria: A Discourse of Sallets. 1699.

Memoirs, Illustrative of the Life and Writings of John Evelyn. Ed. William Bray. 1818. 2 vols.

Miscellaneous Writings. Ed. William Upcott. 1825.

The Life of Mrs. Godolphin. Ed. Samuel Wilberforce. 1847.

The History of Religion. Ed. R. M. Evanson. 1850. 2 vols.

Diary and Correspondence. Ed. John Forster. 1850–52. 4 vols.

Diary. Ed. Henry B. Wheatley. 1879. 4 vols.

Diary. Ed. Austin Dobson. 1906. 3 vols.

Seven Letters. Ed. Francis Evelyn Rowley Heygate. 1914.

Memoires for My Grand-son. Ed. Geoffrey Keynes. 1926.

Directions for the Gardiner at Says-Court. Ed. Geoffrey Keynes. 1932.

A Devotionarie Book. Ed. Walter Frere. 1936.

London Revived: Consideration for Its Rebuilding in 1666. Ed. E. S. de Beer. 1938.

Diary. Ed. E. S. de Beer. 1955. 6 vols.

Manuscript on Bees from Elysium Britannicum. Ed. D. A. Smith. 1966.

Diary. Ed. John Bowle. 1983.

GEORGE FARQUHAR (1678–1707)

Love and a Bottle. 1699.

The Adventures of Covent Garden: In Imitation of Scarron's City Romance. 1699.

The Constant Couple; or, A Trip to the Jubilee. 1700.

Sir Harry Wildair: Being the Sequel of the Trip to the Jubilee. 1701.

The Inconstant; or, The Way to Win Him. 1702.

Love and Business: In a Collection of Occasionary Verse, and Epistolary Prose; A Discourse Likewise upon Comedy in Reference to the English Stage. 1702.

The Twin-Rivals. 1703.

The Stage-Coach. 1704.
The Recruiting Officer. 1706.
The Beaux' Stratagem. 1707.
Comedies. 1707.
Barcellona, a Poem; or, The Spanish Expedition under the Command of Charles Earl of Peterborough. c. 1710.
Works. c. 1711. 2 vols.
The Dramatic Works of Wycherley, Congreve, Vanbrugh, and Farquhar. Ed. Leigh Hunt. 1840.
Dramatic Works. Ed. Alexander Charles Ewald. 1892. 2 vols.
George Farquhar. Ed. William Archer. 1906.
A Discourse on Comedy, The Recruiting Officer, and The Beaux' Stratagem. Ed. Louis A. Strauss. 1914.
Complete Works. Ed. Charles Stonehill. 1930. 2 vols.

THOMAS SPRAT (1635–1713)

Three Poems upon the Death of His Late Highnesse Oliver, Lord Protector of England, Scotland and Ireland (with John Dryden and Edmund Waller). 1659.
The Plague of Athens. 1659.
Observations on Monsieur de Sorbier's Voyage into England. 1665.
The History of the Royal-Society of London, for the Improving of Natural Knowledge. 1667.
Poemata Latina by Abraham Cowley (editor). 1668.
The Rehearsal (with George Villiers, Duke of Buckingham). 1672.
A Sermon Preached before the King at White-Hall. 1677.
A Sermon Preached at the Anniversary Meeting of the Sons of Clergy-men. 1678.
A Sermon Preached before the Honourable House of Commons. 1678.
A Sermon Preached before the King at White-Hall. 1678.
A Sermon Preach'd before the Lord Mayor. 1682.
A Sermon Preached before the Artillery Company of London at St. Mary Le Bow. 1682.
A Sermon Preached before the Right Honourable Sir Henry Tulse, Lord Mayor: Being the Anniversary Day of His Majestie's Birth, and Happy Return to His Kingdoms. 1684.
A True Account and Declaration of the Horrid Conspiracy against the Late King. 1685.
A Letter to the Right Honourable the Earl of Dorset and Middlesex, concerning His Sitting in the Late Ecclesiastical Commission. 1688.
The Lord Bishop of Rochester's Letter to the Lords Commissioners of His Majestie's Ecclesiastical Court. 1688.
The Lord Bishop of Rochester's Letter to the Ecclesiastical Commissioners, before His Dismission. c. 1688.
The Bishop of Rochester's Second Letter to the Earl of Dorset and Middlesex. 1689.
A Sermon Preached before the King and Queen at Whitehal, on Good-Friday. 1690.
A Relation of the Late Wicked Contrivance of Stephen Blackhead and Robert Young, against the Lives of Several Persons, by Forging an Association under Their Hands. 1692–93. 2 parts.
A Sermon Preach'd to the Natives of the County of Dorset. 1693.
A Sermon Preached before the King and Queen, at Whitehall, on Good-Friday. 1694.
A Discourse Made by the Lord Bishop of Rochester to the Clergy of His Diocese, at His Visitation in the Year 1695. 1696.
Sermons Preached on Several Occasions. 1697.

A Sermon Preach'd at the Anniversary Meeting of the Sons of the Clergy. 1705.
A Sermon Preach'd before the Queen, at St. James's Chapel, on Good-Friday. 1712.

THOMAS RYMER (1641–1713)

Reflections on Aristotle's Treatise of Poesie by René Rapin (translator). 1674.
The Tragedies of the Last Age Consider'd and Examined by the Practice of the Ancients and by the Common Sense of All Ages. 1678.
Edgar; or, The English Monarch: An Heroick Tragedy. 1678.
A General Draught and Prospect of Government in Europe, and Civil Policy. 1681.
An Epistle to Mr. Dryden. 1688.
A Poem on the Prince of Orange His Expedition and Success in England. 1688.
A Poem on the Arrival of Queen Mary. 1689.
A Short View of Tragedy. 1692.
Letters to the Right Reverend the Ld. Bishop of Carlisle. 1702–06. 3 letters.
Foedera, Conventiones, Literae et Cujuscunque Generis Acta Publica, inter Reges Angliae (editor). 1704–17. 17 vols. (vols. 16–17 ed. Robert Sanderson).
Critical Works. Ed. Curt A. Zimansky. 1956.

ANTHONY ASHLEY COOPER, THIRD EARL OF SHAFTESBURY (1671–1713)

Select Sermons by Benjamin Whichot (editor). 1698.
An Inquiry concerning Virtue. 1699.
A Letter concerning Enthusiasm. 1708.
Sensus Communis: An Essay on the Freedom of Wit and Humour. 1709.
The Moralists: A Philosophical Rhapsody. 1709.
Soliloquy; or, Advice to an Author. 1710.
Characteristicks of Men, Manners, Opinions, Times. 1711. 3 vols.
A Notion of the Historical Draught or Tablature of the Judgment of Hercules. 1713.
Several Letters Written by a Noble Lord to a Young Man at the University. 1716.
Letters to Robert Molesworth, Esq. Ed. John Toland. 1721.
Original Letters (with John Locke and Algernon Sidney). Ed. Thomas Forster. 1830.
Life, Unpublished Letters, and Philosophical Regimen. Ed. Benjamin Rand. 1900.
Second Characters; or, The Language of Forms. Ed. Benjamin Rand. 1914.

GILBERT BURNET (1643–1715)

A Discourse on the Memory of That Rare and Truely Virtuous Person Sir Robert Fletcher of Saltoun. 1665.
A Modest and Free Conference betwixt a Conformist and a Non-Conformist, about the Present Distempers of Scotland. 1669.
A Vindication of the Authority, Constitution, and Laws of the Church and State of Scotland. 1673.
[*Rome's Glory; or, A Collection of Divers Miracles Wrought by Popish Saints.* 1673.]
The Mystery of Iniquity Unvailed. 1673.
An Account Given by J. Ken a Jesuit, of the Truth of Religion, Examined. 1674.
Subjection for Conscience-Sake Asserted (with *The Royal Martyr Lamented*). 1675.

A *Rational Method for Proving the Truth of the Christian Religion, as It Is Professed in the Church of England.* 1675.

A *Relation of a Conference Held about Religion, at London.* 1676.

A *Modest Survey of the Most Considerable Things in a Discourse Lately Published, Entituled* Naked Truth. 1676.

A *Vindication of the Ordinations of the Church of England.* 1677.

The Memoires of the Lives and Actions of James and William, Dukes of Hamilton and Castleheard. 1677.

The New Politick Lights of Modern Romes Church-Government by Sforza Pallavicino (translator). 1678, 1681 (as *The Policy of Rome*).

A *Sermon Preached at St. Dunstans in the West at the Funeral of Mrs. Anne Seile.* 1678.

A *Letter Written upon the Discovery of a Late Plot.* 1678.

The Unreasonableness and Impiety of Popery: In a Second Letter Written upon the Discovery of the Late Plot. 1678.

A *Relation of the Barbarous and Bloody Massacre of about an Hundred Thousand Protestants in the Year 1572.* 1678.

A *Decree Made at Rome the Second of March, 1679, Condemning Some Opinions of the Jesuits and Other Casuits* by Pope Innocent IX (translator). 1679.

The History of the Reformation of the Church of England. 1679 [Volume 1]; 1681 [Volume 2]; 1715 [Volume 3].

The Infallibility of the Church of Rome Examined and Confuted. 1680.

Some Passages of the Life and Death of the Right Honourable John, Earl of Rochester. 1680.

A *Sermon Preached before the Lord Mayor and Aldermen of the City of London, at Bow Church: Being the Anniversary Fast for the Burning of London.* 1680.

The Conversion & Persecutions of Eve Cohan, Now Called Elizabeth Verboon, a Person of Quality of the Jewish Religion. 1680.

The Last Words of Lewis du Moulin. 1680.

A *Sermon Preached on the Fast-Day, at St. Margarets Westminster before the Honourable House of Commons.* 1681.

A *Sermon Preached before the Aldermen of the City of London, at St. Lawrence-Church.* 1681.

An Exhortation to Peace and Union. 1681.

The Life and Death of Sir Matthew Hale. 1682.

The History of the Rights of Princes in the Disposing of Ecclesiastical Benefices and Church-Lands. 1682. 2 parts.

The Last Confession, Prayers and Meditations of Lieuten. John Stern; Together with the Last Confession of George Borowsky (with Anthony Horneck). 1682.

A *Sermon Preached at the Funeral of Mr. James Houblon.* 1682.

News from France: In a Letter Giving a Relation of the Present State of the Difference between the French King and the Court of Rome. 1682.

An Answer to the Animadversions on the History of the Rights of Princes. 1682.

The Letter Writ by the Last Assembly General of the Clergy of France to the Protestants (translator). 1683.

Utopia by Sir Thomas More (translator). 1684.

A *Sermon Preached at the Chappel of the Rolls, on the Fifth of November, 1684: Being Gun-powder Treason-Day.* 1684.

The Life of William Bedell, D.D., Bishop of Kilmore in Ireland. 1685.

An Impartial Survey and Comparison of the Protestant Religion, as by Law Established, with the Main Doctrines of Popery. 1685.

A *Letter to Mr. Simon Lowth: Occasioned, by His Late Book Of the Subject of Church-Power.* 1685.

An Answer to a Letter to Dr. Burnet Occasioned by His Letter to Mr. Lowth. 1685.

A *Letter Occasioned by the Second Letter to Dr. Burnet.* 1685.

A *Letter Written to Dr. Burnet, Giving an Account of Cardinal Pool's Secret Powers.* 1685.

A *Letter, Containing Some Remarks on the Two Papers, Writ by His Late Majesty King Charles the Second, concerning Religion.* 1686.

Reflections on Mr. Varillas's History of the Revolutions That Have Happened in Europe in Matters of Religion, and More Particularly on His Ninth Book That Relates to England. 1686.

Some Letters: Containing an Account of What Seemed Most Remarkable in Switzerland, Italy, c. 1686.

Reasons against the Repealing the Acts of Parliament concerning the Test. 1687.

Some Reflections on His Majesty's Proclamation for a Toleration in Scotland. 1687.

A *Letter, Containing Some Reflections on His Majesties Declaration for Liberty of Conscience.* 1687.

A *Relation of the Death of the Primitive Persecutors* by Lactantius (translator). 1687.

The Citation of Gilbert Burnet, D.D. 1687.

An Answer to a Paper Printed with Allowance, Entituled, A New Test of the Church of England's Loyalty. 1687.

The Earl of Melfort's Letter to the Presbyterian Ministers in Scotland; Together with Some Remarks. 1687.

An Answer to Mr Henry Payne's Letter, concerning His Majesty's Declaration of Indulgence. 1687.

A *Defence of the Reflections on the Ninth Book of the First Volume of Mr. Varillas's History of Heresies.* 1687.

A *Continuation of Reflections on Mr. Varillas's History of Heresies.* 1687.

Supplement to Dr. Burnet's Letters Relating to His Travels. 1687.

Six Papers. 1687.

Three Letters concerning the Present State of Italy. 1688.

A *Letter Writ by Mijn Heer Fagel to Mr. James Stewart, Giving an Account of the Prince and Princess of Orange's Thoughts concerning the Repeal of the Test and the Penal Laws* (translator). 1688.

Reflections on the Oxford Theses Relating to the English Reformation ⟨with *Reflections on the Relation of the English Reformation* by Obadiah Walker⟩. 1688.

An Enquiry into the Reasons for Abrogating the Test Imposed on All Members of Parliament. 1688.

Animadversions on the Reflections upon Dr. B.'s Travels. 1688.

Reflections on a Late Pamphlet, Entitled Parliamentum Pacificum. 1688.

Dr. Burnet's Vindication of Himself from the Calumnies with Which He Is Aspersed, in a Pamphlet, Entituled, Parliamentum Pacificum. 1688.

An Apology for the Church of England, with Relation to the Spirit of Persecution: For Which She Is Accused. 1688.

Some Extracts, out of Mr. James Stewart's Letters, Which Were Communicated to Myn Heer Fagel (editor). 1688.

An Edict in the Roman Law by Justinian (translator). 1688.

A *Censure of M. de Meaux's History of the Variations of the Protestant Churches.* 1688.

An Enquiry into the Measures of Submission to the Supream Authority. 1688.

A Letter to a Lord, upon His Happy Conversion from Popery to the Protestant Religion. 1688.

A Sermon Preached in the Chappel of St. James's, before His Highness the Prince of Orange. 1689.

Reflections on a Paper, Intituled, His Majesty's Reasons for Withdrawing Himself from Rochester. 1689.

An Enquiry into the Present State of Affairs, and in Particular, Whether We Owe Allegiance to the King in These Circumstances? 1689.

A Sermon Preached before the House of Commons: Being the Thanksgiving-Day for Deliverance of This Kingdom from Popery, and Arbitrary Power. 1689.

A Sermon Preached at the Coronation of William III. and Mary II. 1689.

A Pastoral Letter Writ to the Clergy of His Diocess, concerning the Oaths of Allegiance and Supremacy to K. William and Q. Mary. 1689.

A Sermon Preached before the House of Peers on the 5th. of November 1689: Being Gun-powder Treason-Day. 1689.

Tracts. 1689. 2 vols.

An Exhortation to Peace and Unity. 1689.

A Letter to Mr. Thevenot: Containing a Censure of M. Le Grand's History of King Henry the Eighth's Divorce *(with* A Censure of M. de Meaux's *History of the Variations of the Protestant Churches).* 1689.

A Collection of Eighteen Papers. 1689.

A Sermon Preached before the King & Queen, at White-Hall, on Christmas-Day, 1689. 1690.

A Sermon Preached at Bow-Church, before the Court of Aldermen. 1690.

A Sermon Preached before the Queen, at White-Hall: Being the Monthly-Fast. 1690.

[A Short Directory concerning Proper Rules How to Prepare Young Persons for Confirmation. 1690.]

A Sermon Preached before the King and Queen, at White-Hall, on the 19ᵗʰ Day of October, 1690: Being the Day of Thanksgiving, for His Majesties Preservation and Success in Ireland. 1690.

A Sermon Preached at the Funeral of the Right Honourable Anne, Lady-Dowager Brook. 1691.

A Sermon Preached at Whitehall before the King and Queen: Being the Fast Day. 1691.

A Sermon Preached at White-Hall, on the 26th of Novemb. 1691: Being the Thanksgiving-Day for the Preservation of the King, and the Reduction of Ireland. 1691.

A Sermon Preached at the Funeral of the Honourable Robert Boyle. 1692.

A Discourse of the Pastoral Care. 1692.

A Letter Writ by the Bishop of Salisbury to the Bishop of Coventry and Litchfield, concerning a Book Lately Published, Called, A Specimen of Some Errors and Defects in the History of the Reformation of the Church of England. 1693.

A Sermon Preach'd before the Queen, at White-Hall. 1694.

Four Discourses Delivered to the Clergy of the Diocese of Sarum. 1694.

A Sermon Preached before the Queen at Whitehall on the 29th of May, 1694: Being the Anniversary of King Charles II His Birth and Restauration. 1694.

A Sermon Preached at the Funeral of the Most Reverend Father in God John Tillotson, Lord Archbishop of Canterbury. 1694.

A Sermon Preach'd before the King, at St. James-Chappel. 1695.

An Essay on the Memory of the Late Queen. 1695.

Animadversions on Mr. Hill's Book, Entitled, A Vindication of the Primitive Fathers, against the Imputations of Gilbert, Lord Bishop of Sarum. 1695.

Reflections upon a Pamphlet, Entituled, Some Discourses upon Dr. Burnet and Dr. Tillotson, Occasioned by the Late Funeral-Sermon of the Former upon the Later. 1696.

A Sermon Preached before the King, at Whitehall, on Christmas-Day, 1696. 1697.

A Sermon Preached before the King, at Whitehall on the Third Sunday in Lent. 1697.

A Sermon Preach'd before the King, at Whitehall, on the Second of December, 1697: Being the Day of Thanksgiving for the Peace. 1698.

Of Charity to the Household of Faith. 1698.

An Exposition of the Thirty-nine Articles of the Church of England. 1699.

Charitable Reproof. 1700.

Reflections on a Book, Entituled, The Rights, Powers, and Privileges of an English Convocation, Stated and Vindicated. 1700.

Remarks on the Examination of the Exposition of the Second Article of Our Church. 1702.

Speech in the House of Lords, upon the Bill against Occasional Conformity. 1704.

A Sermon Preach'd at St. James's Church, upon the Reading the Brief for the Persecuted Exiles of the Principality of Orange. 1704.

On the Propagation of the Gospel in Foreign Parts. 1704.

A Charge Given at the Triennial Visitation of the Diocesse of Salisbury. 1704.

A Collection of Several Tracts and Discourses Written in the Years 1677 to 1704. 1704. 3 vols.

A Memorial Drawn by King William's Special Direction, Intended to Be Given In at the Treaty of Reswick. 1705.

A Sermon Preach'd in Lent, at the Chappel of St. James's. 1706.

Because Iniquity Shall Abound, the Love of Many Shall Wax Cold. 1706.

A Sermon Preach'd at the Cathedral Church of Salisbury on the xxviiᵗʰ Day of June MDCCVI: Being the Day of Thanksgiving for the Great Successes God Has Given to the Arms of Her Majesty and Her Allies in Flanders and Spain. 1706.

A Sermon Preach'd before the Queen, and the Two Houses of Parliament, at St. Paul's, on the 31st of December, 1706, the Day of Thanksgiving for the Wonderful Successes of This Year. 1707.

A Letter from the Bishop of Salisbury, to the Clergy of His Diocese: To Be Read at the Triennial Visitation in April and May, 1708. 1708.

Speech in the House of Lords, on the First Article of the Impeachment of Dr. Henry Sacheverell. 1710.

A Sermon Preach'd in the Cathedral-Church of Salisbury. 1710.

An Exposition of the Church Catechism, for the Use of the Diocese of Sarum. 1710.

Two Sermons, Preached in the Cathedral Church of Salisbury. 1710.

A Sermon Preach'd at St. Brides before the Lord-Mayor and the Court of Aldermen. 1711.

A Letter from the Bishop of Salisbury, to the Clergy of His Diocese: To Be Read at the Triennial Visitation in May, 1711. 1711.

Some Sermons Preach'd on Several Occasions; and An Essay towards a New Book of Homilies. 1713.

An Introduction to the Third Volume of the History of the Reformation of the Church of England. 1713.

A Collection of Speeches, Prefaces, Letters, &c., with a Description of Geneva and Holland. 1713.

Four Letters Which Pass'd between the Right Reverend the Lord Bishop of Sarum and Mr. Henry Dodwell. Ed. Robert Nelson. 1713.

A Sermon Preach'd at St. Bridget's-Church, before the Right Honourable the Lord Mayor, the Aldermen and Governours of the Several Hospitals of the City. 1714.

A Sermon Preach'd, and a Charge Given at the Triennial Visitation of the Diocese of Salisbury. 1714.

A Sermon Preach'd before His Majesty King George, at the Royal Chappel at St. James's. 1714.

History of His Own Time. 1724 [Volume 1; ed. Gilbert Burnet the Younger]; 1734 [Volume 2; ed. Thomas Burnet].

Thoughts on Education. 1761.

The Lives of Sir Matthew Hale and John Earl of Rochester. 1820. 2 parts.

History of His Own Time. Ed. Martin Joseph Routh. 1823. 6 vols.

History of His Own Time. Ed. Osmund Airy. 1897–1902. 3 vols.

A Supplement to Burnet's History of My Own Time. Ed. H. C. Foxcroft. 1902.

Some Unpublished Letters. Ed. H. C. Foxcroft. 1907.

NAHUM TATE (1652–1715)

Poems. 1677.

Brutus of Alba; or, The Enchanted Lovers. 1678.

A Poem on the Present Assembling of the Parliament. 1679.

The Loyal General. 1680.

The History of King Richard the Second ⟨*The Sicilian Usurper*⟩ (adaptation). 1681.

The History of King Lear (adaptation). 1681.

The Ingratitude of a Common-wealth; or, The Fall of Caius Martius Coriolanus (adaptation). 1682.

The Second Part of Absalom and Achitophel (with John Dryden). 1682.

A Prologue to the Last New Play A Duke and No Duke. 1684.

A Song for St. Caecilia's Day. 1685.

A Duke and No Duke (adaptation). 1685.

Cuckolds-Haven; or, An Alderman No Conjurer (adaptation). 1685.

Poems, by Several Hands, and on Several Occasions (editor). 1685.

On the Sacred Memory of Our Late Sovereign; with a Congratulation to His Present Majesty. 1685.

Syphilis; or, A Poetical History of the French Disease by Girolamo Fracastoro (translator). 1686.

A Memorial for the Learned by J. D. (editor). 1686.

The Æthiopian History of Heliodorus (translator; with others). 1686.

The Island-Princess by John Fletcher (adaptation). 1687.

A Pastoral Elegy on the Death of Mr. John Playford. 1687.

An Account of His Excellence Roger, Earl of Castlemaine's Embassy by John Michael Wright (translator). 1688.

A Pastoral in Memory of His Grace the Illustrious Duke of Ormond. 1688.

The Life of Alexander the Great by Quintus Curtius, tr. anon. (editor). 1690.

A Pastoral Dialogue. 1690.

The Prologue to King William and Queen Mary. c. 1690.

A Poem Occasioned by the Late Discontents and Disturbances in the State. 1691.

A Poem, Occasioned by His Majesty's Voyage to Holland, the Congress at the Hague, and Present Siege of Mons. 1691.

The Political Anatomy of Ireland by Sir William Petty (editor). 1691.

Characters of Vertue and Vice by Joseph Hall (adaptation). 1691.

A Present for the Ladies: Being an Historical Vindication of the Female Sex. 1692.

An Ode upon Her Majesty's Birth-day. 1693.

The Life of Louis of Bourbon Late Prince of Condé (translator). 1693.

Guzman by Roger Boyle, Earl of Orrery (editor). 1693.

A Poem on the Late Promotion of Several Eminent Persons in Church and State. 1694.

In Memory of Joseph Washington, Esq. 1694.

The Four Epistles of A. G. Busbequius concerning His Embassy into Turkey (translator). 1694.

An Ode upon the Ninth of January 1693/4, the First Secular Day since the University of Dublin's Foundation by Queen Elizabeth. 1694.

An Ode upon His Majesty's Birth-day. 1694.

Mausolaeum: A Funeral Poem on Our Late Gracious Sovereign Queen Mary. 1695.

An Elegy on the Most Reverend Father in God, His Grace, John, Late Lord Archbishop of Canterbury. 1695.

An Essay of a New Version of the Psalms of David (translator; with Nicholas Brady). 1695, 1695.

Miscellanea Sacra (editor). 1696.

The Original, Nature, and Immortality of the Soul by Sir John Davies (editor). 1697.

The Innocent Epicure by S. J. (editor). 1697.

An Essay on Poetry by John Sheffield, Duke of Buckingham (editor). 1697.

The Anniversary Ode for the Fourth of December, 1697: His Majesty's Birth-day; Another for New-Year's-Day, 1697/8. 1698.

A Consolatory Poem to the Right Honourable John Lord Cutts, upon the Death of His Most Accomplish'd Lady. 1698.

Elegies. 1699.

An Essay of a Character of the Right Honourable Sir George Treby. 1700.

Funeral Poems; Together with a Poem on the Promotion of Several Eminent Persons. 1700.

Panacea: A Poem upon Tea. 1700.

An Elegy in Memory of the Much Esteemed and Truely Worthy Ralph Marshall, Esq. 1700.

A Supplement to the New Version of Psalms (with Nicholas Brady). 1700.

A Congratulatory Poem on the New Parliament Assembled on This Great Conjuncture of Affairs. 1701.

The Kentish Worthies. 1701.

An Ode upon the Assembling of the New Parliament. 1702.

A Song on the Queen's Coronation. 1702.

A Monumental Poem in Memory of the Right Honourable Sir George Treby. 1702.

Portrait-Royal: A Poem upon Her Majesty's Picture. 1703.

The Song for New-Year's Day. 1703.

The Triumph; or, Warriours Welcome: A Poem on the Glorious Successes of the Last Year. 1705.

Britannia's Prayer for the Queen. 1706.

A Congratulatory Poem, to the Right Honourable Richard Earl Rivers, upon His Lordship's Expedition. 1706.

Majestas Imperii Britannici by Lewis Maidwell (adaptation). 1706.

The Triumph of Union; with the Muse's Address for the Consummation of It in the Parliament of Great Britain. 1707.

The Muse's Memorial of the Happy Recovery of the Right Honourable Richard Earl of Burlington, from a Dangerous Sickness. 1707.

Injur'd Love; or, The Cruel Husband (adaptation). 1707.

The Song for the New-Year. 1708.

A Congratulatory Poem to His Royal Highness Prince George of Denmark, upon the Glorious Successes at Sea. 1708.

The Celebrated Speeches of Ajax and Ulysses by Ovid (translator; with Aaron Hill). 1708.

An Essay for Promoting of Psalmody. 1710.

The Song of Her Majesty's Birthday. 1711.

An Hymn to Be Sung by the Charity-Children at Bath ("While shepherds watched their flocks by night"). 1712.

The Muse's Memorial, of the Right Honourable Earl of Oxford. 1712.

The Muse's Bower: An Epithalamium on the Auspicious Nuptials of the Right Honourable the Marquis of Caermarthen, with the Lady Elizabeth Harley. 1713.

The Triumph of Peace. 1713.

A Congratulatory Poem, on Her Majesties Happy Recovery, and Return to Meet Her Parliament. 1714.

A Poem Sacred to the Glorious Memory of Her Late Majesty Queen Anne. 1716.

The Constant Gallant; or, Truth Found Out at Last (adaptation). c. 1765.

WILLIAM WYCHERLEY (1641–1715)

Hero and Leander, in Burlesque. 1669.

Love in a Wood; or, St. James's Park. 1672.

The Gentleman Dancing-Master. 1673.

The Country-Wife. 1675.

The Plain-Dealer. 1677.

Epistles to the King and Duke. 1683.

Miscellany Poems: As Satyrs, Epistles, Love-Verses, Songs, Sonnets, etc. 1704. Vol. 1 only.

The Folly of Industry; or, The Busy Man Expos'd: A Satyr. 1704.

On His Grace the Duke of Marlborough. 1707.

Works. 1713, 1720 (2 vols.).

Posthumous Works in Prose and Verse. Eds. Lewis Theobald and Alexander Pope. 1728–29. 2 vols.

The Dramatic Works of Wycherley, Congreve, Vanbrugh, and Farquhar. Ed. Leigh Hunt. 1840.

William Wycherley. Ed. W. C. Ward. 1888.

Complete Works. Ed. Montague Summers. 1924. 4 vols.

Complete Plays. Ed. Gerald Weales. 1966.

Plays. Ed. Arthur Friedman. 1979.

Plays. Ed. Peter Holland. 1981.

NICHOLAS ROWE (1674–1718)

The Ambitious Step-Mother. 1701.

Tamerlane. 1702.

[*The Mournfull Muse: An Elegy on the Much Lamented Death of King William III.* 1702.]

The Fair Penitent. 1703.

The Biter. 1705.

Ulysses. 1706.

A Poem upon the Late Glorious Successes of Her Majesty's Arms. 1707.

The Golden Verses of Pythagoras (translator). 1707.

The Royal Convert. 1708.

The Works of Mr. William Shakespear (editor). 1709. 6 vols.

Callipaedia by Claude Quillett (translator; with others). 1712.

The Tragedy of Jane Shore. 1714.

Maecenas: Verses Occasion'd by the Honours Conferr'd on the Right Honourable Earl of Hallifax. 1714.

Poems on Several Occasions. 1714.

Tragedies. 1714. 2 vols.

The Tragedy of the Lady Jane Grey. 1715.

Poetical Works. 1715.

Ode for the New Year. 1716.

Lucan's Pharsalia (translator). 1718.

Dramatick Works. 1720. 2 vols.

Works. 1728. 3 vols.

Plays. 1735–36. 2 vols.

Works. Ed. Anne Deanes Devenish. 1747. 2 vols.

The Fair Penitent and Jane Shore. Ed. Sophie Chantal Hart. 1907.

Three Plays: Tamerlane; The Fair Penitent; Jane Shore. Ed. J. R. Sutherland. 1929.

THOMAS PARNELL (1679–1718)

An Essay on the Different Stiles of Poetry. 1713.

Homer's Battle of the Frogs and Mice, with the Remarks of Zoilus (translator). 1717.

Poems on Several Occasions. 1722.

Works in Verse and Prose. 1755.

Posthumous Works. 1758.

Poetical Works. 1786.

Poetical Works. Ed. John Mitford. 1833.

Poetical Works (with Thomas Tickell). 1854.

Poetical Works. Ed. George A. Aitken. 1894.

Poems. Ed. Lennox Robinson. 1927.

SIR SAMUEL GARTH (1661–1719)

Oratio Laudatoria in Aedibus Collegii Regalis Med. London. Habita. 1697.

A Short Account of the Proceedings of the College of Physicians, London, in Relation to the Sick Poor of the Said City and Suburbs Thereof. 1697.

The Dispensary. 1699.

A Prologue to Tamerlane. 1704.

Prologue Spoken at the First Opening of the Queen's New Theatre in the Hay-market. 1705.

A Poem to the Earl of Godolphin. 1710.

Prologue for the 4th of November, 1711: Being the Anniversary of the Birth-day of the Late K. William. 1711.

A Poem upon His Majesties Accession. 1714.

Claremont. 1715.

General Observations and Prescriptions in the Practice of Physick on Several Persons of Quality. 1715.

Ovid's Metamorphosis (editor). 1717. [Book 1 (tr. John Dryden); Book 2 (tr. Joseph Addison); Book 3 (tr. Joseph Addison); Book 4 (tr. Laurence Eusden and Joseph Addison); Book 5 (tr. Arthur Maynwaring); Book 6 (tr. Samuel Croxall); Book 7 (trs. Nahum Tate and [   ] Stonestreet); Book 8 (trs. Samuel Croxall, John Dryden, and James Vernon); Book 9 (trs. John Gay, Alexander Pope, Stephen Harvey, and John Dryden); Book 10 (trs. William Congreve, John Dryden, Samuel Croxall, John Ozell, and Laurence Eusden); Book 11 (trs. Samuel Croxall and John Dryden); Book 12 (tr. John Dryden); Book 13 (trs. John Dryden, Temple Stanyon, Samuel Croxall, [   ] Catcot, and Nicholas Rowe); Book 14 (tr. Samuel Garth);

Book 15 (trs. John Dryden, Catcott, Samuel Garth, and Leonard Welsted).]
Works. 1769.
Poetical Works. 1771.

JOSEPH ADDISON (1672–1719)

A Poem to His Majesty, Presented to the Lord Keeper. 1695.
Musarum Anglicanarum Analecta; sive, Poemata Quaedam Melioris Notae, seu Hactenus Inedita, seu Sparsim Edita, Volume 2 (editor). 1699. 2 vols.
The Campaign, a Poem, to His Grace the Duke of Marlborough. 1705.
Remarks on Several Parts of Italy, &c. in the Years 1701, 1702, 1703. 1705.
[*A Description of the Play-House in Dorset-Garden.* 1706.]
Rosamond. 1707.
The Present State of War, and the Necessity of an Augmentation, Consider'd. 1708.
The Tatler (with Sir Richard Steele and others). 1709–11. 271 nos.
The Whig-Examiner. 1710. 5 nos.
The Spectator (with Sir Richard Steele and others). 1711–12, 1714. 635 nos.
[*The Thoughts of a Tory Author concerning the Press.* 1712.]
The Guardian (with Sir Richard Steele and others). 1713. 175 nos.
Cato. 1713.
The Late Tryall and Conviction of Count Tariff. 1713.
The Free-holder. 1715–16. 55 nos.
The Drummer; or, The Haunted House. 1716.
To Her Royal Highness the Princess of Wales, with the Tragedy of Cato; To Sir Godfrey Kneller, on His Picture of the King. 1716.
[*An Answer to a Pamphlet Entituled* An Argument to Prove the Affections of the People of England to Be the Best Security of Government. 1716.]
A Dissertation upon the Most Celebrated Roman Poets (in Latin; with Eng. tr. by Christopher Hayes). 1718.
The Resurrection. 1718.
Poems on Several Occasions, with a Dissertation upon the Roman Poets. 1719. 2 parts.
The Old Whig. 1719. 2 nos.
Notes upon the Twelve Books of Paradise Lost: *Collected from* The Spectator. 1719.
Maxims, Observations, and Reflections, Moral, Political, and Divine. Ed. Charles Beckingham. 1719–20. 2 parts.
Works. Ed. Thomas Tickell. 1721. 4 vols.
Miscellanies in Verse and Prose. 1725. 4 parts.
Miscellaneous Works, in Verse and Prose. 1726. 3 vols.
The Christian Poet: A Miscellany of Divine Poems. 1728.
The Evidences of the Christian Religion. 1730.
A Discourse on Antient and Modern Learning. 1734.
Letters (with Alexander Pope, Sir William Trumbull, and Richard Steele). 1735.
Poetical Works. 1750.
Dramatic Works. 1750.
Poems on Several Occasions. 1751.
The Papers of Joseph Addison, Esq. in the Tatler, Spectator, Guardian, *and* Freeholder; *Together with His Treatise on the Christian Religion.* 1790. 4 vols.
Papers in the Tatler, Spectator, *and* Freeholder. Ed. Anna Laetitia Barbauld. 1804. 3 vols.
Works. Ed. Richard Hurd. 1811. 6 vols.
Works. Ed. G. W. Greene. 1856. 6 vols.
Some Portions of Essays Contributed to the Spectator *Now First*

Printed from His MS. Note Book. Ed. J. D. Campbell. 1864.
Essays. Ed. John Richard Green. 1880.
Selections from the Writings. Eds. Barrett Wendell and Chester N. Greenough. 1905.
Miscellaneous Works. Ed. Adolph C. Guthkelch. 1914. 2 vols.
Essays. Ed. Sir James George Frazer. 1915. 2 vols.
Letters. Ed. Walter Graham. 1941.
The Spectator (with Sir Richard Steele and others). Ed. Donald F. Bond. 1965. 5 vols.

ANNE FINCH, COUNTESS OF WINCHILSEA
(1666–1720)

The Spleen: A Pindarique Ode; Together with A Prospect of Death: A Pindarique Essay (by John Pomfret). 1709.
Miscellany Poems, on Several Occasions. 1713.
Poems. Ed. Myra Reynolds. 1903.
Poems and Extracts Chosen by William Wordsworth for an Album Presented to Lady Mary Lowther, Christmas 1819. Ed. Harold Littledale. 1905.
Poems. Ed. John Middleton Murry. 1928.
Selected Poems. Ed. Denys Thompson. 1987.

JOHN HUGHES (1677–1720)

The Triumph of Peace. 1698.
The Court of Neptune. 1699.
The House of Nassau: A Pindarick Ode. 1702.
An Ode in Praise of Musick. 1703.
A Review of the Case of Ephraim and Judah. 1705.
Advices from Parnassus by Traiano Boccalini, tr. anon. (revised by Hughes). 1706.
A Complete History of England, from the Earliest Time, to the Death of His Late Majesty King William III, Volumes 1–2 (editor). 1706.
Fontenelle's Dialogues of the Dead (translator). 1708.
An Ode before the Nobility and Gentry. 1712.
The History of the Revolutions in Portugal by Aubert de Vertot d'Aubeuf (translator). 1712.
The Letters of Abelard to Héloise (translator). 1713.
An Ode to the Creator of the World: Occasion'd by the Fragments of Orpheus. 1713.
The Lay-Monk. 1714. 40 nos.
The Works of Mr. Edmund Spenser (editor). 1715. 6 vols.
Apollo and Daphne: A Masque. 1716.
An Ode for the Birth-day of Her Royal Highness the Princess of Wales. 1716.
Orestes. 1717.
A Layman's Thoughts on the Late Treatment of the Bishop of Bangor. 1717.
Charon; or, The Ferry-Boat: A Vision. 1719.
The Ecstasy: An Ode. 1720.
The Siege of Damascus. 1720.
Poems on Several Occasions, with Some Select Essays in Prose. Ed. William Duncombe. 1735.
The Complicated Guilt of the Late Rebellion. 1745.
The Correspondence of John Hughes and Several of His Friends; to Which Are Added Several Pieces by Mr. Hughes, Never Before Published, and the Original Plan of The Siege of Damascus. 1773. 2 vols.

MATTHEW PRIOR (1664–1721)

On the Coronation of the Most August Monarch K. James II. and Queen Mary. 1685.
The Hind and the Panther Transvers'd to the Story of the Country Mouse and the City Mouse (with Charles Montagu, Earl of Halifax). 1687.

The Orange. 1688.

A Pindarique on His Majesties Birth-day. 1690.

An Ode in Imitation of the Second Ode of the Third Book of Horace. 1692.

For the New Year: To the Sun. 1694.

To the King: An Ode on His Majesty's Arrival in Holland. 1695.

An English Ballad: In Answer to Mr. Despreaux's Pindarique Ode on the Taking of Namure. 1695.

Verses Humbly Presented to the King at His Arrival in Holland. 1696.

A New Answer to an Argument against a Standing Army. 1697.

Carmen Saeculare, for the Year 1700. 1700.

To a Young Gentleman in Love: A Tale. 1702.

Prologue, Spoken at Court before the Queen, on Her Majesty's Birth-day. 1704.

A Letter to Monsieur Boileau Depreaux; Occasion'd by the Victory at Blenheim. 1704.

An English Padlock. 1705.

Pallas and Venus: An Epigram. 1706.

An Ode, Humbly Inscrib'd to the Queen, on the Late Glorious Success of Her Majesty's Arms. 1706.

Poems on Several Occasions. 1707, 1709.

Horace Lib. I. Epist. IX. (adaptation). 1711.

To the Right Honourable Mr. Harley, Wounded by Guiscard. 1711.

Earl Robert's Mice: A Tale in Imitation of Chaucer. 1712.

[A Fable of the Widow and Her Cat. 1712.]

Walter Danniston ad Amicos (adaptation). c. 1712.

A Memorial against the Fortifying the Ports and Harbours of Dunkirk and Mardike. 1715.

A Second Collection of Poems on Several Occasions. 1716.

The Dove. 1717.

Poems on Several Occasions. 1718.

[Upon Lady Katherine H–de's First Appearing at the Play-House in Drury-Lane. 1718.]

Verses Spoke to the Lady Henrietta-Cavendish Holles Harley. 1719.

The Conversation: A Tale. 1720.

Colin's Mistakes: Written in Imitation of Spenser's Style. 1721.

A Supplement to Mr. Prior's Poems. 1722.

The Turtle and the Sparrow. 1723.

Down-Hall. 1723.

Miscellaneous Works. Ed. J. Bancks. 1740. 2 vols.

Lyric Poems: Being Twenty Four Songs. 1741.

Poetical Works. 1777. 3 vols.

Poetical Works. Ed. Thomas Park. 1779. 2 vols.

Poetical Works. Ed. John Mitford. 1835. 2 vols.

Poetical Works. Ed. George Gilfillan. 1858.

Selected Poems. Ed. Austin Dobson. 1889.

Poetical Works. Ed. John Mitford, rev. Reginald Brimley Johnson. 1892.

Writings. Ed. A. R. Waller. 1905–07. 2 vols.

Shorter Poems. Ed. Francis Bickley. 1923.

Literary Works. Eds. H. Bunker Wright and Monroe K. Spears. 1959. 2 vols.

THOMAS D'URFEY (1653–1723)

Archerie Reviv'd; or, The Bow-Man's Excellence (with Robert Shotterel). 1676.

The Siege of Memphis; or, The Ambitious Queen. 1676.

Madam Fickle; or, The Witty False One. 1677.

A Fond Husband; or, The Plotting Sisters. 1677.

The Fool Turn'd Trick. 1678.

Trick for Trick; or, The Debauch'd Hypocrite by John Fletcher (adaptation). 1678.

Squire Oldsapp; or, The Night-Adventurers. 1679.

The Virtuous Wife; or, Good Luck at Last. 1680.

Love Triumphant; or, A Poem on the Numerous Loyal Addresses to His Majesty. 1681.

Sir Barnaby Whigg; or, No Wit Like a Woman's. 1681.

The Progress of Honesty; or, A View of a Court and City: A Pindarique Poem. 1681.

The Lions Elegy; or, Verses on the Death of the Three Lions in the Tower. 1681.

Butler's Ghost; or, Hudibras: The Fourth Part. 1682.

The Royalist. 1682.

The Injured Princess; or, The Fatal Wager. 1682.

Scandalum Magnatum; or, Potapski's Case: A Satyr against Polish Oppression. 1682.

A New Collection of Songs and Poems. 1683.

Choice New Songs, Never Before Printed. 1684.

Several New Songs. 1684.

The Prologue to Mr. Lacy's New Play, Sir Hercules Buffoon; or, The Poetical Esquire. 1684.

The Malcontent: A Satyr: Being the Sequel of The Progress of Honesty. 1684.

A Third Collection of New Songs, Never Printed Before. 1685.

An Elegy upon the Late Blessed Monarch King Charles II. and Two Panegyricks upon Their Present Sacred Majesties King James and Queen Mary. 1685.

A Common-wealth of Women. 1686.

The Banditti; or, A Ladies Distress. 1686.

The Compleat Collection of Mr. D'Urfey's Songs and Odes. 1687.

A Poem Congratulatory on the Birth of the Young Prince. 1688.

A Fool's Preferment; or, The Three Dukes of Dunstable. 1688. 2 parts.

An Ode on the Anniversary of the Queens Birth. 1690.

New Poems. 1690.

Collin's Walk through London and Westminster. 1690.

Momus Ridens. 1690–91. 19 nos.

Love for Money; or, The Boarding School. 1691.

Bussy d'Ambois; or, The Husband's Revenge by George Chapman (revised by D'Urfey). 1691.

A Pindarick Ode, on New-Year's-Day. 1691.

The Moralist; or, A Satyr upon the Sects. 1691.

The Triennial Mayor; or, The New Raparees. 1691.

A Pindarick Poem on the Royal Navy. 1691.

The Weesils: A Satyrical Fable. 1691.

The Weesil's Trap'd. 1691.

The Marriage-Hater Match'd. 1692.

[Zelinda by Vincent de Voiture (translator). 1692.]

The Richmond Heiress: or, A Woman Once in the Right. 1693.

The Canonical Statesman's Grand Argument Discuss'd. 1693.

The Comical History of Don Quixote. 1694 [Part 1]; 1694 [Part 2]; 1696 [Part 3].

The Songs to the New Play of Don Quixote. 1694 [Part 1]; 1694 [Part 2]; 1696 [Part 3].

Gloriana: A Funeral Pindarique Poem, Sacred to the Blessed Memory of That Ever-Admir'd and Most Excellent Princess, Our Late Gracious Soveraign Lady Queen Mary. 1695.

The Intrigues at Versailles; or, A Jilt in All Humours. 1697.

Albion's Blessing. 1698.

The Campaigners; or, The Pleasant Adventures at Brussels. 1698.

A Choice Collection of New Songs and Ballads. 1699.

The Famous History of the Rise and Fall of Massaniello. 1699 [Part 2]; 1700 [Part 1].

An Ode, for the Anniversary Feast Made in Honour of St. Caecilia. 1700.

An Essay towards the Theory of the Intelligible World. c. 1700. Part 3 only.

The Bath; or, The Western Lass. 1701.

The Old Mode and the New; or, Country Miss with Her Furbeloe. 1703.

Tales Tragical and Comical (translator). 1704.

A New Ode, or, Dialogue between Mars, the God of War, and Plutus, or Mammon, God of Riches. 1706.

Stories, Moral and Comical (translator). 1707.

The Trophies; or, Augusta's Glory. 1707.

Honour and Opes; or, The British Merchant's Glory. 1708.

The French Pride Abated; or, A Friendly Admonition to Lowly Humility. 1708.

The Modern Prophets; or, New Wit for a Husband. 1709.

Musa et Musica; or, Honour and Musick. 1710.

Songs Compleat, Pleasant and Divertive (editor). 1719. 5 vols.

Wit and Mirth; or, Pills to Purge Melancholy. 1719–20. 6 vols.

New Opera's, with Comical Stories and Poems, on Several Occasions. 1721.

The English Stage Italianiz'd, in a New Dramatic Entertainment, Called Dido and Aeneas; or, Harlequin. 1727.

Songs. Ed. Cyrus Lawrence Day. 1933.

Wit and Mirth; or, Pills to Purge Melancholy. Ed. Cyrus Lawrence Day. 1959. 3 vols.

Two Comedies: Madam Fickle and a Fond Husband. Ed. Jack A. Vaughn. 1976.

ELKENAH SETTLE (1648–1724)

Mare Clausum; or, A Ransack for the Dutch. 1666.

An Elegie on the Late Fire and Ruines of London. 1667.

Cambyses, King of Persia. 1671.

Herod and Mariamne by Samuel Pordage (editor). 1673.

The Empress of Morocco. 1673.

Love and Revenge. 1675.

A Poem to the Charming Fair One. c. 1675.

The Conquest of China, by the Tartars. 1676.

Ibrahim the Illustrious Bassa. 1677.

Pastor Fido; or, The Faithful Shepherd by Giovanni Battista Guarini (adaptation). 1677.

Londons Defiance of Rome. 1679.

The Female Prelate: Being the Life and Death of Pope Joan. 1680.

The Life and Death of Major Clancie, the Grandest Cheat of This Age. 1680.

Fatal Love; or, The Forc'd Inconstancy. 1680.

The Character of a Popish Successour, and What England May Expect from Such a One. 1681.

A Vindication of the Character of a Popish Successour. 1681.

An Heroick Poem on the Right Honourable Thomas Earl of Ossory. 1681.

The Heir of Morocco, with The Death of Gayland. 1682.

Absalom Senior; or, Achitophel Transpros'd. 1682.

A Pindarick Poem, to His Grace Christopher Duke of Albemarle, Lately Elected Chancellour of the University of Edinburgh. 1682.

A Narrative ⟨of the Popish Plot⟩. 1683.

A Supplement to the Narrative. 1683.

[*Animadversions on the Late Speech and Confession of the Late William Lord Russel.* 1683.]

A Panegyrick on the Loyal and Honourable Sir George Jefferies, Lord Chief Justice of England. 1683.

Remarks on Algernon Sidney's Paper, Delivered to the Sheriffs at His Execution. 1683.

An Heroick Poem on the Coronation of the High and Mighty Monarch James II. 1685.

Reflections on Several of Mr. Dryden's Plays. 1687.

Insignia Bataviae; or, The Dutch Trophies Display'd. 1688.

An Epilogue to the French Midwife's Tragedy. 1688.

A View of the Times; with Britain's Address to the Prince of Orange. 1689.

Uzziah and Jotham. 1690.

Distress'd Innocence; or, The Princess of Persia. 1691.

The Triumphs of London. 1691.

The Notorious Impostor; or, The History of the Life of William Morell, Alias Bowyer. 1692. 2 parts.

The Triumphs of London. 1692.

Diego Redivivus. 1692.

The Triumphs of London. 1693.

The New Athenean Comedy. 1693.

The Triumphs of London. 1694.

The Ambitious Slave; or, A Generous Revenge. 1694.

The Triumphs of London. 1695.

Philaster; or, Love Lies a Bleeding by Beaumont and Fletcher (adaptation). 1695.

Augusta Lachrymans: A Funeral Tear, to the Memory of the Worthy and Honour'd Michael Godfrey, Esq; Unfortunately Slain by a Cannon Ball, Near His Majesty's Person, in the Trenches, at the Siege of Namure. 1695.

A Funeral Tear, to the Memory of the Honourable Capt. James Killegrew. 1695.

Sacellum Apollinare: A Funeral Poem to the Memory of That Great Patriot & Statesman, George Late Marquiss of Hallifax. 1695.

Glory's Resurrection: Being the Triumphs of London Revived. 1698.

A Defence of Dramatick Poetry: Being a Review of Mr. Collier's View of the Immorality and Profaneness of the Stage. 1698.

A Farther Defence of Dramatick Poetry. 1698.

The Triumphs of London. 1699.

Augusta Lacrimans: A Funeral Poem to the Memory of the Honourable Sir Josiah Child. 1699.

A Congratulatory Poem to the Right Honourable the Earl of Albemarle. 1699.

The Triumphs of London. 1700.

Sacellum Honoris: A Congratulatory Poem to the Right Honourable the Marquis of Tavistock, on His Happy Return from Travel. 1700.

The Scaffold Lately Erected at Westminster-Hall. 1701.

Minerva Triumphans: The Muses Essay, to the Honour of That Generous Foundation the Cotton Library at Westminster. 1701.

The Virgin Prophetesse; or, The Fate of Troy. 1701.

The Triumphs of London. 1701.

Carmen Irenicum. 1702.

Eusebia Triumphans. 1702.

A Funeral Tear, to the Memory of the Right Honourable Charles, Earl of Burlington. 1704.

Fears and Dangers Fairly Display'd: Being a New Memorial of the Church of England. 1706.

The Siege of Troy. 1707.

Carmen Irenicum. 1707.

Augusta Triumphans: Ramilly and Turin; or, A Hymn to Victory. 1707.

Virtuti Sacellum: A Funeral Poem to the Pious Memory of Sir Robert Clayton. 1707.

The Triumphs of London. 1708.

Threnodium Apollinare: A Funeral Poem to the Memory of Dr. E. Tyson. 1708.

Threnodium Apollinare: A Funeral Poem to the Memory of Henry Bare, Baron of Coleraine. 1708.

Virtuti Sacellum: A Funeral Poem to the Memory of S^{r}John Buckworth. 1709.

Augusta Lacrymans: A Funeral Poem to the Memory of the Honourable Sr Charles Thorold. 1709.

Thalia Lacrimans: A Funeral Poem to the Memory of the Honoured Lytton Lytton. 1710.

A Pindarick Poem on the Propagation of the Gospel in Foreign Parts. 1711.

Augusta Triumphans: To the Lieutenancy of the Honourable City of London. 1711.

The City-Ramble; or, A Play-House Wedding. 1711.

Threnodia Hymenaea: A Funeral Poem, to the Memory of the Honoured George Carter, Esq. 1712.

Augusta Lacrimans: A Funeral Poem to the Memory of the Honoured Charles Baynton, Esq. 1712.

Honori Sacellum: A Funeral Poem to the Memory of the Honourable Thomas, Earl of Coventry. 1712.

Threnodia Apollinaris: A Funeral Poem to the Memory of Dr. M. Lister. 1712.

Threnodia Hymenaea: A Funeral Poem, to the Memory of the Right Honourable William Earl of Kingston. 1713.

Irene Triumphans. 1713.

Memoriae Fragranti: A Funeral Poem to the Memory of Lady Margaret Woolfe. 1713.

Threnodia Britannica: A Funeral Poem to the Memory of Our Late Soveraign Lady Anne, Queen of Great Britain. 1714.

Honori Sacellum: A Funeral Poem to the Memory of the Right Honourable Robert Ld. Tamworth. 1714.

Augusta Lacrimans: A Funeral Poem to the Memory of the Honoured John Seale. 1714.

Carmen Natalitium: A Congratulatory Poem to the Right Honourable Thomas Lord Pelham, on His Birth Day's Happy Anniversary. 1714.

Thalia Triumphans: To the Honoured David Mitchel Esq; on His Happy Marriage. 1715.

Thalia Triumphans: To the Worthy Mr. William Westfield, on His Happy Marriage. 1715.

Rebellion Displayed; or, Our Present Distractions Set Forth in Their True Light. 1715.

Thalia Triumphans: A Congratulatory Poem to the Right Honourable William Lord Craven, on His Happy Marriage. 1715.

Thalia Triumphans: To the Honoured Mr Joshua Ironmonger, on His Happy Marriage. 1716.

Thalia Triumphans: To the Honoured Walter Cary, Esq; on His Happy Marriage. 1717.

A Poem on the Birth-day of His Most Sacred Majesty King George. 1717.

The Eucharist; or, The Holy Sacrament of Our Lord's Supper: A Divine Poem. 1717.

Thalia Triumphans: A Congratulatory Poem, to the Honourable Sir Edw. Littleton, Bar. on His Happy Marriage. 1718.

The Lady's Triumph. 1718.

Augusta Lacrimans: A Funeral Poem to the Memory of the Honourable Sir James Bateman. 1718.

Threnodia Apollinaris: A Funeral Poem to the Memory of Joseph Addison, Esq. 1719.

Thalia Triumphans: A Congratulatory Poem to the Honoured Montague-Gerald Drake, Esq; on His Happy Marriage. 1719.

Augusta Lacrimans: A Funeral Poem to the Memory of the Honourable Sir Daniel Wray. 1719.

A Funeral Poem to the Memory of John, Earl of Dundonald. 1720.

The Right of Sovereigns, with the Popular Argument of Kings de Facto, and Kings de Jure, Set at Full Light. c. 1720.

Thalia Triumphans: A Congratulatory Poem to the Honoured John Green, Esq; on His Happy Marriage. c. 1720.

Thalia Triumphans: A Congratulatory Poem to the Honoured Edmund Morris, Esq; on His Happy Marriage. 1721.

Honori Sacellum: The Muses Congratulatory Address, to the Right Honourable William Lord North and Grey. 1721.

Thalia Triumphans: A Congratulatory Poem to the Honoured John Buissiere, Esq; on His Happy Marriage. 1722.

Threnodia Britannica: A Funeral Oblation to the Most Noble Prince John Duke of Marlborough. 1722.

Threnodia Apollinaris: A Funeral Poem, to the Memory of the Right Honourable William Earl Cowper. 1723.

Threnodia Apollinaris: A Funeral Poem to the Memory of the Honourable Sir Christopher Wren. 1723.

JEREMY COLLIER (1650–1726)

The Difference between the Present and Future State of Our Bodies. 1686.

Animadversions upon the Modern Explication of 11 Hen. 7 Cap. 1. 1689.

The Desertion Discuss'd. 1689.

Vindiciae Juris Regii; or, Remarques upon a Paper, Entituled, An Enquiry into the Measures of Submission to the Supream Authority. 1689.

Miscellanies, in Five Essays. 1694.

Miscellanies upon Moral Subjects: The Second Part. 1695.

A Perswasive to Consideration, Tender'd to the Royalists, Particularly Those of the Church of England. 1695.

A Defence of the Absolution Given to Sr William Perkins. 1696.

A Reply to The Absolution of a Penitent. 1696.

A Short View of the Immorality and Profaneness of the English Stage. 1698.

A Defence of the Short View of the Profaneness and Immorality of the English Stage. 1699.

A Second Defence of the Short View of the Profaneness and Immorality of the English Stage. 1700.

The Great Historical, Geographical, Genealogical and Poetical Dictionary by Louis Moreri (revised by Collier). 1701. 2 vols.

The Emperor Marcus Antoninus His Conversation with Himself (translator). 1701.

Tully's Five Books De Finibus, tr. S. P. (revised by Collier). 1702.

Mr. Collier's Dissuasive from the Play-House; in a Letter to a Person of Quality Occasion'd by the Late Calamity of the Tempest. 1703.

A Caution against Inconsistency; or, The Connexion between Praying and Swearing. 1703.

A Supplement to the Great Historical, Geographical, Genealogical and Poetical Dictionary. 1705.

A Letter to a Lady concerning the New Play House. 1706.

An Ecclesiastical History of Great Britain. 1708–14. 2 vols.

A Farther Vindication of the Short View of the Profaneness and Immorality of the English Stage. 1708.

An Essay upon Gaming. 1713.

An Answer to Some Exceptions in Bishop Burnet's Third Part of the History of the Reformation, &c. *against Mr. Collier's* Ecclesiastical History. 1715.

A Panegyrick upon the Maccabees by Saint Gregory ⟨with works by Saint Cyprian⟩ (translator). 1716.

Reasons for Restoring Some Prayers and Directions as They Stand in the Communion Service of the First English Reform'd Liturgy, Compiled by the Bishops in the Reign of Kind Edward VI. 1717.

Some Considerations on Doctor Kennet's Second and Third Letters. 1717.

A Defence of the Reasons for Restoring Some Prayers and Directions of King Edward the Sixth's First Liturgy. 1718.

A Communion Office. 1718.

A Vindication of the Reasons *and* Defence. 1718–19. 2 parts.

A Farther Defence, &c.: Being an Answer to a Reply to the Vindication of the Reasons *and* Defence for Restoring Some Prayers and Directions in King Edward VI's First Liturgy. 1720.

An Appendix to the Three English Volumes in Folio of Morery's Great Historical, Geographical, Genealogical and Poetical Dictionary. 1721.

Several Discourses upon Practical Subjects. 1725.

God Not the Origin of Evil. 1726.

A Short View of the Profaneness and Immorality of the English Stage, with the Several Defences of the Same. 1730.

A Collection of Tracts. 1736. 5 parts.

Pearls of Great Price; or, Maxims, Reflections, Characters and Thoughts, on Miscellaneous Subjects. Ed. James Elmes. 1838.

SIR JOHN VANBRUGH (1664–1726)

The Relapse; or, Virtue in Danger. 1697.

Æsop (adaptation). 1697. 2 parts.

The Provok'd Wife. 1697.

A Short Vindication of the Relapse *and the* Provok'd Wife, *from Immorality and Prophaneness.* 1698.

The Pilgrim by John Fletcher (adaptation). 1700.

The False Friend (adaptation). 1702.

The Confederacy (adaptation). 1705.

The Mistake (adaptation). 1706.

The Country House (adaptation). 1715.

Sir John Vanbrugh's Justification, of What He Depos'd in the Duchess of Marlborough's Late Tryal. 1718.

Plays. 1719. 2 vols.

A Journey to London. Ed. Colley Cibber. 1728.

The Provok'd Husband; or, A Journey to London (with Colley Cibber). 1728.

Comedies. 1730. 2 vols.

The Dramatic Works of Wycherley, Congreve, Vanbrugh, and Farquhar. Ed. Leigh Hunt. 1840.

Plays. Ed. W. C. Ward. 1893. 2 vols.

Sir John Vanbrugh. Ed. A. E. H. Swaen. 1896.

Complete Works. Eds. Bonamy Dobrée and Geoffrey Webb. 1927–28. 4 vols.

SIR ISAAC NEWTON (1642–1727)

Lectiones XVIII by Isaac Barrow (editor). 1669–70. 2 parts.

Geographia Generalis by Bernhard Varen (editor). 1672.

Philosophiae Naturalis Principia Mathematica. 1687.

Opticks; or, A Treatise on the Reflexions, Refractions, Inflections and Colours of Light; Also Two Treatises of the Species and Magnitude of Curvilinear Figures. 1704. 2 parts.

Arithmetica Universalis; sive, De Compositione et Resolutione Arithmetica Liber, cui Accessit Halleiana. Ed. William Whiston. 1707.

Analysis per Quantitatum Series, Fluxiones ac Differentias; cum Enumeratione Linearum Tertii Ordinis. Ed. William Jones. 1711.

The Chronology of Ancient Kingdoms Amended. Ed. John Conduitt. 1728.

Lectiones Opticae. 1729.

The Present State of Ireland: Being Sir Isaac Newton's Representation about the Gold and Silver Coins. 1729.

Observations upon the Prophecies of Daniel, and the Apocalypse of St. John. 1733. 2 parts.

Opuscula Mathematica, Philosophica et Philologica. Ed. Giovanni di Castiglione. 1744. 3 vols.

Two Letters to Mr. Le Clerc. 1754.

Four Letters to Doctor Bentley: Containing Some Arguments in Proof of a Deity. 1756.

Opera Quae Exstant Omnia. Ed. Samuel Horsley. 1779–85. 5 vols.

Thirteen Letters to John Covel. Ed. Dawson Turner. 1848.

Correspondence of Sir Isaac Newton and Professor Cotes. Ed. Joseph Edleston. 1850.

Theological Manuscripts. Ed. H. MacLachlan. 1950.

Papers and Letters on Natural Philosophy. Eds. I. Bernard Cohen and Robert E. Schofield. 1958.

Correspondence. Eds. H. W. Turnbull et al. 1959–77. 7 vols.

Unpublished Scientific Papers: A Selection from the Portsmouth Collection in the University Library, Cambridge. Eds. A. Rupert Hall and Marie Boas Hall. 1962.

Mathematical Papers. Eds. D. T. Whiteside et al. 1967–81. 8 vols.

Certain Philosophical Questions: Newton's Trinity Notebook. Eds. J. E. McGuire and Martin Tammy. 1983.

Optical Papers. Ed. Alan E. Shapiro. 1984– . 3 vols. (projected).

COTTON MATHER (1663–1728)

A Poem Dedicated to the Memory of the Reverend and Excellent Mr. Urian Oakes. 1682.

The Boston Ephemeris: An Almanack for the ⟨Dyonisian⟩ Year of the Christian Æra MDCLXXXIII. 1683.

An Elegy on the Much-to-Be-Deplored Death of That Never-to-Be-Forgotten Person, the Reverend Mr. Nathanael Collins. 1685.

The Call of the Gospel. 1686.

Military Duties, Recommended to an Artillery Company. 1687.

The Declaration, of the Gentlemen, Merchants, and Inhabitants of Boston, and the Countrey Adjacent. 1689.

Early Piety, Exemplified in the Life and Death of Mr. Nathanael Mather. 1689.

Memorable Providences, Relating to Witchcrafts and Possessions. 1689.

Right Thoughts in Sad Hours. 1689.

Small Offers towards the Service of the Tabernacle in the Wilderness. 1689.

Souldiers Counselled and Comforted. 1689.

Work upon the Ark: Meditations upon the Ark as a Type of the Church. 1689.

Addresses to Old Men, and Young Men, and Little Children. 1690.

A Companion for Communicants. 1690.

The Present State of New-England. 1690.

The Serviceable Man. 1690.

Speedy Repentance Urged. 1690.

The Way to Prosperity. 1690.

The Wonderful Works of God Commemorated. 1690.

Serious Thoughts in Dying Times. c. 1690.

Little Flocks Guarded against Grievous Wolves. 1691.

A Scriptural Catechism. 1691.

Some Considerations on the Bills of Credit Now Passing in New-England. 1691.

Things to Be Look'd For. 1691.

The Triumphs of the Reformed Religion in America: The Life of the Renowned John Eliot. 1691.

Balsamum Vulnerarium ex Scriptura: The Cause and Cure of a Wounded Spirit. 1692.

Blessed Unions: An Union with the Son of God by Faith. 1692.

Fair Weather; or, Considerations to Dispel the Clouds, & Allay the Storms, of Discontent. 1692.

A Midnight Cry. 1692.

Optanda: Good Men Described, and Good Things Propounded. 1692.

Ornaments for the Daughters of Zion; or, The Character and Happiness of a Vertuous Woman. 1692.

The Wonders of the Invisible World: Observations as Well Historical as Theological, upon the Nature, the Number, and the Operations of the Devils. 1693.

The Day, & the Work of the Day. 1693.

Rules for the Society of Negroes. 1693.

Unum Necessarium: Awakenings for the Unregenerate; or, The Nature and Necessity of Regeneration. 1693.

Warnings from the Dead. 1693.

Winter-Meditations. 1693.

Early Religion, Urged. 1694.

A Short History of New-England. 1694.

Batteries upon the Kingdom of the Devil. 1694.

Brontologia Sacra; The Voice of the Glorious God in the Thunder. 1695.

Durable Riches. 1695.

Help for Distressed Parents. 1695.

Johannes in Eremo. 1695.

Memoria Wilsoniana; or, Some Dues unto the Memory of the Reverend & Renowned Mr. John Wilson. 1695.

Observanda: The Life and Death of the Late Q. Mary. 1695.

Piscator Evangelicus; or, The Life of Mr. Thomas Hooker. 1695.

The Christian Thank-Offering. 1696.

Cry against Oppression. 1696. Lost.

A Good Master Well Served: A Brief Discourse on the Necessary Properties & Practices of a Good Servant. 1696.

Things for a Distress'd People to Think Upon. 1696.

Ecclesiastes: The Life of the Reverend & Excellent Jonathan Mitchel. 1697.

Faith at Work. 1697.

Gospel for the Poor. 1697. Lost.

Humiliations Follow'd with Deliverances. 1697.

Pietas in Patriam: The Life of His Excellency Sir William Phips, Knt. 1697.

Present from a Far Countrey to the People of New England. 1697.

Songs of the Redeemed: A Book of Hymns. 1697. Lost.

Terrabilia Dei. 1697.

The Thoughts of a Dying Man. 1697.

The Way to Excel: Meditations, Awakened by the Death of the Reverend Mr. Joshua Moodey. 1697.

The Boston Ebenezer: Some Historical Remarks, on the State of Boston. 1698.

Eleutheria; or, An Idea of the Reformation in England. 1698.

A Good Man Making a Good End: The Life and Death, of the Reverend Mr. John Baily. 1698.

Mens Sana in Corpore Sano: A Discourse upon Recovery from Sickness. 1698.

A Pastoral Letter to the English Captives, in Africa. 1698.

Decennium Luctuosum: An History of Remarkable Occurrences, in the Long War, Which New-England Hath Had with the Indian Salvages. 1699.

The Faith of the Fathers. 1699.

A Family Well-Ordained. 1699.

Pillars of Salt: An History of Some Criminals Executed in This Land. 1699.

The Serious Christian; or, Three Great Points of Practical Christianity. 1699.

Thirty Important Cases (editor). 1699.

To His Excellency, Richard, Earl of Bellomont: Address of the Ministers. 1699.

Indian Primer. c. 1699. Lost.

A Cloud of Witnesses. 1700.

The Everlasting Gospel. 1700.

Grace Triumphant; or, A Notable Example of a Great Sinner, Becoming a Great Saint. 1700.

The Great Physician. 1700.

A Letter of Advice to the Churches of the Non-conformists in the English Nation. 1700.

A Monitory, and Hortatory Letter, to Those English, Who Debauch the Indians, by Selling Strong Drink unto Them. 1700.

A Pillar of Gratitude. 1700.

Reasonable Religion; or, The Truth of the Christian Religion, Demonstrated. 1700.

The Religious Marriner. 1700.

Things That Young People Should Think Upon. 1700.

A Warning to the Flocks against Wolves in Sheeps Cloathing. 1700.

The Young Mans Monitor. 1700. Lost.

The Old Principles of New England. c. 1700.

American Tears upon the Ruines of the Greek Churches. 1701.

A Christian at His Calling. 1701.

A Collection of Some of the Many Offensive Matters, Contained in a Pamphlet, Entituled, The Order of the Gospel Revived. 1701.

A Companion for the Afflicted. 1701.

Death Made Easie & Happy. 1701.

⟨*Extract of Certain Select Passages* (editor).⟩ 1701. Lost.

The Good Linguist. 1701. Lost.

A Letter concerning the Terrible Sufferings of Our Protestant Brethren, on Board the French Kings Galleyes. 1701.

Thaumatographica Christiana: The Wonders of Christianity. 1701.

Triumphs over Troubles. 1701.

The Young Mans Preservative. 1701.

An Advice, to the Churches of the Faithful. 1702.

Cares about the Nurseries. 1702.

Christianity to the Life; or, The Example of the Lord Jesus Christ. 1702.

Christianus per Ignem; or, A Disciple Warming of Himself and Owning of His Lord. 1702.

A Letter to Ungospellized Plantations. 1702.

Magnalia Christi Americana; or, The Ecclesiastical History of New-England from Its First Planting in the Year 1620. unto the Year of Our Lord, 1698. 1702. 7 parts.

Maschil; or, The Faithful Instructor. 1702.

A Monitory Letter to Them Who Needlessly & Frequently Absent Themselves from the Publick Worship of God. 1702.

Much in a Little; or, Three Brief Essayes, to Sum Up the Whole Christian Religion. 1702.

Necessary Admonitions. 1702.

The Pourtraiture of a Good Man. 1702.

Proposals for the Preservation of Religion in the Churches. 1702.

A Seasonable Testimony to the Glorious Doctrines of Grace. 1702.

Wholesome Words. c. 1702.

Agreeable Admonitions for Old & Young. 1703.

Conversion Exemplified. 1703.

The Day Which the Lord Hath Made: A Discourse concerning the Institution and Observation of the Lords-Day. 1703.

The Duty of Children. 1703.

A Family-Sacrifice. 1703.

The Glory of Goodness. 1703.

Great Consolations; or, A Brief Essay upon the Joy of a Tempted Christian, Triumphing over His Temptations. 1703. Lost.

The High Attainment: A Brief Discourse concerning Resignation to the Will of God. 1703.

Jedediah; or, A Favourite of Heaven Described. 1703. Lost.

Meat out of the Eater; or, Funeral Discourse Occasioned by the Death of Several Relatives. 1703.

Methods and Motives for Societies to Suppress Disorders. 1703.

The Retired Christian; or, The Duty of Secret Prayer. 1703.

The Armour of Christianity. 1704.

A Comforter of the Mourners. 1704.

Εὕρηκα: The Vertuous Woman Found: A Short Essay on the Memory of Mrs. Mary Brown. 1704.

A Faithful Monitor: Offering, an Abstract of the Lawes in the Province of the Massachusett-Bay, New-England. 1704.

Faithful Warnings to Prevent Fearful Judgments. 1704.

The Nets of Salvation. 1704.

A Servant of the Lord, Not Ashamed of His Lord. 1704.

A Tree Planted by the Rivers of Water. 1704.

Le Vrai Patron des Saines Paroles. 1704.

A Weaned Christian. 1704.

Youth in Its Brightest Glory. 1704.

Baptistes; or, A Conference, about the Subject and Manner of Baptism. 1705.

A Faithful Man, Described and Rewarded. 1705.

Family-Religion, Excited and Assisted. 1705.

The Hatchets, to Hew Down the Tree of Sin, Which Bears the Fruit of Death. 1705.

A Letter; about the Present State of Christianity, among the Christianized Indians of New-England. 1705.

Lex Mercatoria; or, The Just Rules of Commerce Declared. 1705.

Mare Pacificum: A Short Essay upon Those Noble Principles of Christianity, Which May Always Compose and Rejoyce, the Mind of the Afflicted Christian. 1705.

Monica Americana: A Funeral-Sermon, Occasioned by the Death of Mrs. Sarah Leveret. 1705.

Nicetas; or, Temptations to Sin. 1705.

Parental Wishes and Charges; or, The Enjoyment of a Glorious Christ. 1705.

The Religion of the Closet. 1705.

The Rules of a Visit. 1705.

The Christian Temple; or, An Essay upon a Christian Considered as a Temple. 1706.

A Conquest over the Grand Excuse of Sinfulness and Slothfulness. 1706.

Free-Grace, Maintained & Improved. 1706.

Good Fetch'd out of Evil. 1706.

Good Lessons for Children. 1706.

The Good Old Way; or, Christianity Described, from the Glorious Lustre of It, Appearing in the Lives of the Primitive Christians. 1706.

Heavenly Considerations. 1706. Lost.

The Impenitent Sinner. 1706. Lost.

The Negro Christianized: An Essay to Excite and Assist That Good Work, the Instruction of Negro-Servants in Christianity. 1706.

Private Meetings Animated & Regulated. 1706.

Vigilantius; or, A Servant of the Lord Found Ready for the Coming of the Lord. 1706.

A Young Follower of a Great Saviour. 1706. Lost.

Another Tongue Brought In, to Confess the Great Saviour of the World. 1707.

The Best Ornaments of Youth. 1707.

The Fall of Babylon: A Short and Plain Catechism, Which Detects & Confutes the Principles of Popery. 1707.

Frontiers Well-Defended. 1707.

A Golden Curb, for the Mouth. 1707.

The Greatest Concern in the World. 1707.

A Memorial of the Present Deplorable State of New-England. 1707.

Ornamental Piety. 1707. Lost.

The Souldier Told, What He Shall Do. 1707.

The Spirit of Life Entring into the Spiritually Dead. 1707.

A Treacle Fetch'd out of a Viper: A Brief Essay upon Falls into Sins. 1707.

A Very Needful Caution. 1707.

Corderius Americanus: An Essay upon the Good Education of Children. 1708.

The Deplorable State of New-England. 1708.

A Good Evening for the Best of Dayes. 1708.

The Man of God Furnished. 1708.

Sober Considerations, on a Growing Flood of Iniquity. 1708.

Winthropi Justa: A Sermon at the Funeral of the Honourable John Winthrop Esq. 1708.

The Bonds of the Covenant. 1709. Lost.

A Christian Conversing with the Great Mystery of Christianity. 1709.

The Cure of Sorrow. 1709.

The Desires of the Repenting Believer. 1709.

Nunc Dimittis, Briefly Descanted On. 1709.

The Sailours Companion and Counsellor. 1709.

The Summ of the Matter. 1709. Lost.

The Temple Opening: A Particular Church Considered as a Temple of the Lord. 1709.

Work Within-Doors. 1709.

Youth in Its Brightest Glory. 1709.

Bonifacius: An Essay upon the Good, That Is to Be Devised and Designed, by Those Who Desire to Answer the Great End of Life, and to Do Good While They Live. 1710.

Christianity Demonstrated. 1710.

Dust and Ashes: An Essay upon Repentance to the Last. 1710.

Elizabeth in Her Holy Retirement. 1710.

The Heavenly Conversation. 1710.

To the Learned & Worthy Professors, of the Renowned University of Glasgow. 1710.

Man Eating the Food of Angels: The Gospel of the Manna, to Be Gathered in the Morning. 1710.

Nehemiah: A Brief Essay on Divine Consolations. 1710.

Proposals of Some Consequence. 1710. Lost.

Theopolis Americana: An Essay on the Golden Street of the Holy City. 1710.

Advice from Taberah. 1711.
Compassions Called For. 1711.
The Fisher-mans Calling. 1711.
Manly Christianity. 1711.
Memorials of Early Piety: Occurring in the Holy Life & Joyful Death of Mrs. Jerusha Oliver. 1711.
The Old Pathes Restored. 1711.
Orphanotrophium; or, Orphans Well-Provided For. 1711.
Perswasions from the Terror of the Lord. 1711.
The Right Way to Shake Off a Viper. 1711.
Awakening Thoughts, on the Sleep of Death. 1712.
Grace Defended. 1712.
Grata Brevitas. 1712.
Pastoral Desires. 1712.
Reason Satisfied: and Faith Established. 1712.
Repeated Warnings: Another Essay, to Warn Young People against Rebellions That Must Be Repented Of. 1712.
Seasonable Thoughts upon Mortality. 1712.
A Soul Well-Anchored. 1712.
Thoughts for the Day of Rain. 1712.
A Town in Its Truest Glory. 1712.
A True Survey & Report of the Road. 1712.
The Wayes and Joyes of Early Pietry. 1712.
Winter Piety. 1712.
The Young Man Spoken To. 1712.
The A, B, C. of Religion. 1713.
Adversus Libertinos; or, Evangelical Obedience Described and Demanded. 1713.
Advice from the Watch Tower. 1713.
The Best Way of Living. 1713.
A Christian Funeral. 1713.
A Flying Roll, Brought Forth, to Enter into the House and Hand of the Thief. 1713.
Golgotha: A Lively Description of Death. 1713.
Hezekiah: A Christian Armed with Strength from Above; to Keep Him from Fainting in a Day of Adversity. 1713.
A Letter, about a Good Management under the Distemper of the Measles. 1713.
A Man of His Word: A Very Brief Essay, on Fidelity, in Keeping of Promises and Engagements. 1713.
Nepenthes Evangelicum: A Brief Essay, upon a Soul at Ease. 1713.
A Present of Summer-Fruit. 1713.
The Sad Effects of Sin: A True Relation of the Murder Committed by David Wallis, on His Companion Benjamin Stolwood. 1713.
Tabitha Rediviva: An Essay to Describe and Commend the Good Works of a Vertuous Woman. 1713.
Things to Be More Thought Upon. 1713.
What Should Be Most of All Tho't Upon. 1713.
The Will of a Father Submitted To. 1713.
Death Approaching: A Very Brief Essay on a Life Drawing Nigh unto the Grave. 1714.
Duodecennium Luctuosum: The History of a Long War with Indian Salvages. 1714.
The Glorious Throne: A Short View of Our Great Lord-Redeemer, on His Throne. 1714.
Insanabilia: An Essay upon Incurables. 1714.
A Life of Piety Resolv'd Upon. 1714.
Maternal Considerations: An Essay on the Consolations of God. 1714.
A Monitor for Communicants. 1714.
A New Offer to the Lovers of Religion and Learning. 1714.
The Sacrificer: An Essay upon the Sacrifices, Wherewith a

Christian, Laying a Claim to an Holy Priesthood, Endeavours to Glorify God. 1714.
The Saviour with His Rainbow. 1714.
A Short Life, Yet Not a Vain One: A Short Essay on the Vanity of Mortal Man. 1714.
Verba Vivifica. 1714.
Vita Brevis: An Essay upon Withering Flowers. 1714.
Benedictus: Good Men Described, and the Glories of Their Goodness, Declared. 1715.
The Grand Point of Solicitude. 1715.
Just Commemorations: The Death of Good Men, Considered. 1715.
A Monitor for the Children of the Covenant. 1715.
Nuncia Bona a Terra Longinqua: A Brief Account of Some Good & Great Things a Doing for the Kingdom of God, in the Midst of Europe. 1715.
Parentalia: An Essay upon the Blessings and Comforts Reserved for Pious Children after the Death of Their Parents. 1715.
Shaking Dispensations: An Essay upon the Mighty Shakes, Which the Hand of Heaven, Hath Given, and Is Giving, to the World. 1715.
A Sorrowful Spectacle. 1715.
Successive Generations: Remarks upon the Changes of a Dying World. 1715.
Verba Opportuna: The Circumstances of Boston Considered. 1715.
Life Swiftly Passing and Quickly Ending. 1715–16.
The Christian Cynick. 1716.
The City of Refuge: The Gospel of the City Explained. 1716.
The Echo's of Devotion. 1716.
Fair Dealing between Debtor and Creditor. 1716.
A Good Evening Accommodated with a Good Employment. 1716. Lost.
Menachem: A Very Brief Essay, on Tokens for Good. 1716.
Piety Demanded. 1716.
The Resort of Piety: Our Saviour Considered and Exhibited, as a Tree of Life. 1716.
The Servants of Abraham. 1716. Lost.
The Stone Cut out of the Mountain. 1716.
Utilia: Real and Vital Religion Served. 1716.
Anastasius. 1717. Lost.
The Case of a Troubled Mind. 1717.
Febrifugium: An Essay for the Cure of Ungoverned Anger. 1717.
Hades Look'd Into: The Power of Our Great Saviour over the Invisible World. 1717.
Icono-clastes: An Essay upon the Idolatry, Too Often Committed under the Profession of the Most Reformed Christianity. 1717.
Instructions to the Living, from the Condition of the Dead. 1717.
Malachi; or, The Everlasting Gospel. 1717.
Piety and Equity, United. 1717.
Raphael: The Blessings of an Healed Soul Considered. 1717. Lost.
A Speech Made unto His Excellency, Samuel Shute, Esq. 1717.
The Thankful Christian. 1717.
The Tribe of Asher. 1717.
The Valley of Baca: The Divine Sov'reignty Displayed & Adored. 1717.
Victorina: A Sermon Preach'd, on the Decease and at the Desire, of Mrs. Katherin Mather. 1717.
The Voice of the Dove. 1717. Lost.

Zelotes: A Zeal for the House of God. 1717.

Brethren Dwelling Together in Unity. 1718.

Faith Encouraged. 1718.

A Man of Reason: A Brief Essay to Demonstrate, That All Men Should Hearken to Reason. 1718.

Marah Spoken To: A Brief Essay to Do Good unto the Widow. 1718.

The Obedient Sufferer. 1718.

Proposals for Printing by Subscription Psalterium Americanum. 1718.

Providence Asserted and Adored. 1718. Lost.

Psalterium Americanum: The Book of Psalms (translator). 1718.

Vanishing Things: An Essay on Dying Man. 1718.

Concium ad Populum: A Distressed People Entertained with Proposals for the Relief of Their Distresses. 1719.

Desiderius; or, A Desireable Man Describ'd. 1719.

Genethlia Pia; or, Thoughts for a Birth-day. 1719.

A Glorious Espousal: A Brief Essay, to Illustrate and Prosecute the Marriage. 1719.

An Heavenly Life. 1719.

An History of Seasonable Interpositions of Divine Providence. 1719.

A New Year Well-Begun. 1719.

The Religion of an Oath. 1719.

Sincere Piety Described and the Trial of Sincerity Assisted. 1719.

A Testimony against Evil Customs. 1719.

The Tryed Professor: A Very Brief Essay, to Detect and Prevent Hypocrisy. 1719.

Vigilius; or, The Awakener. 1719.

A Voice from Heaven: An Account of a Late Uncommon Appearance in the Heavens. 1719.

Youth Advised: An Essay on the Sins of Youth. 1719. Lost.

A Year and a Life Well Concluded. 1719–20.

A Brother's Duty: An Essay on Every Man His Brother's Keeper. 1720. Lost.

Coheleth: A Soul upon Recollection, Coming into Incontestible Sentiments of Religion. 1720.

Detur Digniori: The Righteous Man Described & Asserted as the Excellent Man. 1720.

The Quickened Soul. 1720.

The Salvation of the Soul Considered. 1720.

Undoubted Certainties; or, Piety Enlivened from the View of What the Living Do Certainly Know of Death Approaching. 1720.

The Accomplished Singer. 1721.

The Ambassadors Tears: A Minister of the Gospel, Making His Just and Sad Complaint of an Unsuccessful Ministry. 1721.

The Christian Philosopher: A Collection of the Best Discoveries in Nature, with Religious Improvements. 1721.

Genuine Christianity. 1721.

Honesta Parsimonia; or, Time Spent as It Should Be. 1721.

India Christiana: A Discourse, Delivered unto the Commissioners, for the Propagation of the Gospel among the American Indians. 1721.

A Pastoral Letter, to Families Visited with Sickness. 1721.

Silentarius: A Brief Essay on the Holy Silence and Godly Patience, That Sad Things Are to Be Entertained Withal. 1721.

Some Account of What Is Said of Inoculating or Transplanting the Small Pox (with Zabdiel Boylston). 1721.

Three Letters from New-England, Relating to the Controversy of the Present Time (with Increase Mather). 1721.

Tremenda: The Dreadful Sound with Which the Wicked Are to Be Thunderstruck. 1721.

Two Sermons (with Benjamin Wadsworth). 1721.

The World Alarm'd: A Surprizing Relation, of a New Burning-Island, Lately Raised out of the Sea. 1721.

An Account of the Method and Success of Inoculating the Small-Pox, in Boston in New-England. 1722.

The Angel of Bethesda, Visiting the Invalids of a Miserable World. 1722.

Bethiah: The Glory Which Adorns the Daughters of God. 1722.

Columbanus; or, The Doves Flying to the Windows of Their Saviour. 1722.

Divine Afflations. 1722.

A Friendly Debate, or, A Dialogue between Academicus and Sawny & Mundungus, Two Eminent Physicians (with Isaac Greenwood). 1722.

Love Triumphant. 1722.

The Minister. 1722.

Pia Desideria; or, The Smoaking Flax, Raised into a Sacred Flame. 1722.

Sober Sentiments: In an Essay upon the Vain Presumption of Living & Thriving in the World. 1722.

The Soul upon the Wing: An Essay on the State of the Dead. 1722.

A Brief Memorial, of Matters and Methods for Pastoral Visits. 1723.

Coelistinus: A Conversation in Heaven. 1723.

Euthanasia: A Sudden Death Made Happy and Easy to the Dying Believer. 1723.

A Father Departing: A Sermon on the Departure of the Venerable and Memorable Dr. Increase Mather. 1723.

A Good Character; or, A Walk with God Characterized. 1723.

The Lord-High-Admiral of All the Seas, Adored: A Brief Essay upon the Miracle of Our Saviour Walking upon the Water. 1723.

The Pure Nazarite. 1723.

Some Seasonable Enquiries Offered. 1723.

Useful Remarks: An Essay upon Remarkables in the Way of Wicked Men. 1723.

Valerius: The Prosperity of the Soul Proposed and Promoted. 1723.

The Voice of God in a Tempest. 1723.

The Converted Sinner. 1724.

Decus ac Tutamen: A Brief Essay on the Blessings Enjoy'd by a People That Have Men of a Right Character Shining upon Them. 1724.

Light in Darkness. 1724.

The Nightingale: An Essay on Songs among Thorns. 1724.

Parentator: Memoirs of Remarkables in the Life and Death of the Ever-Memorable Dr. Increase Mather. 1724.

Religious Societies. 1724.

Stimulator; or, The Case of a Soul Walking in Darkness. 1724.

Tela Praevisa: A Short Essay, on Troubles to Be Look'd For. 1724.

The True Riches: A Present of Glorious and Immense Riches. 1724.

The Words of Understanding. 1724.

Christodulus: A Good Reward of a Good Servant. 1725.

Deus Nobiscum: A Very Brief Essay, on the Enjoyment of God. 1725.

Edulcorator: A Brief Essay on the Waters of Marah Sweetened. 1725.

El-Shaddai: A Brief Essay, on All Supplied in an Alsufficient Saviour. 1725.

Une Grande Voix du ciel à la France. 1725.

The Palm-Bearers: A Brief Relation of Patient and Joyful Sufferings. 1725.

A Proposal for an Evangelical Treasury. 1725.

Renatus: A Brief Essay on a Soul Passing from Death to Life. 1725.

Virtue in It's Verdure. 1725.

Vital Christianity: A Brief Essay on the Life of God, in the Soul of Man. 1725.

Zalmonah: The Gospel of the Brasen Serpent, in the Mosaic History. 1725.

The Choice of Wisdom. 1726.

Diluvium Ignis: De Secundo ac Optando Jehovae-Jesu Adventu. 1726.

Ecclesiae Monilia: The Peculiar Treasure of the Almighty King Opened. 1726.

Fasciculus Viventium; or, All Good Wishes in One. 1726.

A Good Old Age: A Brief Essay on the Glory of Aged Piety. 1726.

Hatzar-Maveth: Comfortable Words. 1726.

The Instructor. 1726.

Lampadarius: A Very Brief Essay, to Show the Light, Which Good Men Have in Dark Hours Arising to Them. 1726.

Manuductio ad Ministerium: Directions for a Candidate of the Ministry. 1726.

Nails Fatened; or, Proposals of Piety Reasonably and Seasonably Complyed Withal. 1726.

Pietas Matutina: One Essay More, to Bespeak and Engage Early Piety; Made, on an Occasion Taken from the Early Departure of Mrs. Elizabeth Cooper. 1726.

Ratio Disciplinae Fratrum Nov Anglorum: A Faithful Account of the Discipline Professed and Practised in the Churches of New-England. 1726.

Some Seasonable Advice unto the Poor. 1726.

Suspiria Vinctorum: Some Account of the Condition to Which the Protestant Interest in the World Is at This Day Reduced. 1726.

Terra Beata: A Brief Essay, on the Blessing of Abraham. 1726.

The Vial Poured out upon the Sea: A Remarkable Relation of Certain Pirates Brought unto a Tragical and Untimely End. 1726.

Agricola; or, The Religious Husbandman. 1727.

The Balance of the Sanctuary. 1727.

Baptismal Piety. 1727.

Boanerges: A Short Essay to Preserve and Strengthen Good Impressions Produced by Earthquakes. 1727.

Christian Loyalty; or, Some Suitable Sentiments on the Withdraw of King George the First, of Glorious Memory, and the Access of King George the Second, unto the Throne of the British Empire. 1727.

Hor-Hagidgad: An Essay upon an Unhappy Departure. 1727.

Ignorantia Scientifica: A Brief Essay on Mans Not Knowing His Time. 1727.

Juga Jucuda: A Brief Essay to Obtain from Young People, an Early and Hearty Submission to the Yoke of Their Saviour, and His Religion. 1727.

The Marrow of the Gospel: A Very Brief Essay, on the Union between the Redeemer and the Beleever. 1727.

Restitutus: The End of Life Pursued, and Then, the Hope in Death Enjoyed, by the Faithful. 1727.

Signatus: The Sealed Servants of God. 1727.

The Terror of the Lord: Some Account of the Earthquake That Shook New-England, in the Night, between the 29 and 30 of October. 1727. 1727.

The Comfortable Chambers, Opened and Visited. 1728.

The Mystical Marriage: A Brief Essay, on the Grace of the Redeemer Espousing the Soul of the Believer. 1728.

The Widow of Naim: Remarks on the Illustrious Miracle Wrought by Our Almighty Redeemer, on the Behalf of a Desolate Widow. 1728.

Diary 1681–1724. Ed. C. W. Ford. 1911–12. 2 vols.

Selections. Ed. Kenneth B. Murdock. 1926.

Diary for the Year 1712. Ed. William R. Manierre III. 1964.

Selected Letters. Ed. Kenneth Silverman. 1971.

SIR RICHARD BLACKMORE (1654–1729)

Prince Arthur: An Heroick Poem. 1695.

King Arthur: An Heroic Poem. 1697.

A Short History of the Last Parliament. 1699.

A Satyr against Wit. 1700.

A Paraphrase on the Book of Job, as Likewise on the Songs of Moses, Deborah, David, on Four Select Psalms, Some Chapters of Isaiah, and the Third Chapter of Habakkuk. 1700.

The Report of the Physicians and Surgeons, Commanded to Assist at the Dissecting the Body of His Late Majesty at Kensington (with others). 1702.

A Hymn to the Light of the World. 1703.

Eliza: An Epick Poem. 1705.

Advice to the Poets: A Poem Occasion'd by the Wonderful Success of Her Majesty's Arms in Flanders. 1706.

The Kit-Cats: A Poem. 1708.

Instructions to Vander Bank: A Sequel to the Advice to the Poets. 1709.

The Nature of Man: A Poem. 1711.

Creation: A Philosophical Poem. 1712.

The Lay-Monastery: Consisting of Essays, Discourses, etc. 1714.

Essays upon Several Subjects. 1716, 1717 (2 vols.).

A Collection of Poems on Several Subjects. 1718.

Just Prejudices against the Arian Hypothesis. 1721.

Modern Arians Unmask'd. 1721.

A New Version of the Psalms of David. 1721.

A Discourse upon the Plague. 1721.

Redemption: A Divine Poem. 1722.

A True and Impartial History of the Conspiracy against the Person and Government of King William III. of Glorious Memory, in the Year 1695. 1723.

Alfred: An Epick Poem. 1723.

A Treatise upon the Small-Pox. 1723.

A Treatise of Consumptions and Other Distempers Belonging to the Breast and Lungs. 1724.

A Treatise of the Spleen and Vapours. 1725.

A Critical Dissertation upon the Spleen. 1725.

Discourses on the Gout, a Rhematism, and the King's Evil. 1726.

Dissertations on a Dropsy, a Tympany, the Jaundice, the Stone, and a Diabetes. 1727.

Natural Theology; or, Moral Duties Consider'd Apart from Positive. 1728.

The Accomplished Preacher; or, An Essay upon Divine Eloquence. Ed. Joseph White. 1731.

WILLIAM CONGREVE (1670–1729)

Incognita; or, Love and Duty Reconcil'd. 1692.
The Old Batchelour. 1693.
The Double-Dealer. 1694.
The Mourning Muse of Alexis: A Pastoral, Lamenting the Death of Our Late Gracious Mary of Ever Blessed Memory. 1695.
Love for Love. 1695.
A Pindarique Ode, Humbly Offer'd to the King on His Taking Namure. 1695.
The Mourning Bride. 1697.
The Birth of the Muse. 1698.
Amendments of Mr. Collier's False and Imperfect Citations, &c. from the Old Batchelour, Double Dealer, Love for Love, Mourning Bride. 1698.
The Way of the World. 1700.
The Judgment of Paris: A Masque. 1701.
A Hymn to Harmony, Written in Honour of St. Cecilia's Day, MDCI. 1703.
The Tears of Amaryllis for Amyntas: A Pastoral Lamenting the Death of the Late Lord Marquiss of Blanford. 1703.
A Pindarique Ode, Humbly Offer'd to the Queen, on the Victorious Progress of Her Majesty's Arms, under the Conduct of the Duke of Marlborough. 1706.
Works. 1710. 3 vols.
Five Plays. 1710. 5 parts.
The Dramatick Works of John Dryden (editor). 1717. 6 vols.
An Impossible Thing by Jean de La Fontaine (adaptation). 1720.
A Letter to the Right Honourable the Lord Viscount Cobham. 1729.
Last Will and Testament. 1729.
Dramatick Works. 1733. 5 parts.
Poems upon Several Occasions. 1752.
The Dramatic Works of Wycherley, Congreve, Vanbrugh, and Farquhar. Ed. Leigh Hunt. 1840.
William Congreve. Ed. Alexander Charles Ewald. 1887.
Comedies. Ed. G. S. Street. 1895. 2 vols.
Complete Works. Ed. Montague Summers. 1923. 4 vols.
Comedies. Ed. Bonamy Dobrée. 1925.
Comedies. Ed. Joseph Wood Krutch. 1927.
The Mourning Bride, Poems, and Miscellanies. Ed. Bonamy Dobrée. 1928.
Works. Ed. F. W. Bateson. 1930.
Comedies. Ed. Norman Marshall. 1948.
Letters and Documents. Ed. John C. Hodes. 1964.
Complete Plays. Ed. Herbert Davis. 1967.
Comedies. Ed. Anthony G. Henderson. 1982.
Comedies. Ed. Eric S. Rump. 1985.

SIR RICHARD STEELE (1672–1729)

The Procession: A Poem on Her Majesty's Funeral. 1695.
The Christian Hero: An Argument Proving That No Principles but Those of Religion Are Sufficient to Make a Great Man. 1701.
The Funeral; or, Grief a-la-Mode. 1702.
The Lying Lover; or, The Ladies Friendship. 1704.
The Tender Husband; or, The Accomplish'd Fools. 1705.
A Prologue to the University of Oxford. 1706.
The Tatler (with Joseph Addison and others). 1709–11. 271 nos.
The Funeral and The Tender Husband. 1711.
The Spectator (with Joseph Addison and others). 1711–12. 555 nos.

The Funeral, The Lying Lover, and The Tender Husband. 1712.
The Englishman's Thanks to the Duke of Marlborough. 1712.
The Guardian (with Joseph Addison and others). 1713. 175 nos.
The Englishman: Being the Sequel to The Guardian (with others). 1713–14. 56 nos.
A Letter to Sir M. W. concerning Occasional Peers. 1713.
The Importance of Dunkirk Consider'd: In Defence of the Guardian of August the 7th. 1713.
The Crisis; or, A Discourse Representing, from the Most Authentic Records, the Just Causes of the Late Happy Revolution; with Some Seasonable Remarks on the Danger of a Popish Successor. 1714.
A Defence of The Crisis, *Containing a Farther Vindication of the Late Happy Revolution.* 1714.
The Englishman: Being the Close of the Paper So Called; with an Epistle concerning the Whiggs, Tories and New Converts. 1714.
Speech upon the Proposal of Sir Thomas Hanmer for Speaker of the House of Commons. 1714.
The Ladies Library (editor). 1714. 3 vols.
The Romish Ecclesiastical History of Late Years. 1714.
A Letter to a Member of Parliament concerning the Bill for Preventing the Growth of Schism. 1714.
The French Faith Represented in the Present State of Dunkirk. 1714.
The Lover: Written in Imitation of The Tatler. 1714. 40 nos.
A Defence of Drinking to the Pious Memory of K. Charles I. 1714.
Mr. Steele's Apology for Himself and His Writings: Occasioned by His Expulsion from the House of Commons. 1714.
Poetical Miscellanies, Consisting of Original Poems and Translations (editor). 1714.
The Reader. 1714. 9 nos.
Extracts of Remarkable Passages out of Mr. Steele's Writings. c. 1714.
An Account of the State of Roman-Catholick Religion throughout the World: Written for the Use of Pope Innocent XI by Urbano Cerri (translator; with others). 1715.
The Englishman: Second Series (with others). 1715. 38 nos.
A Letter from the Earl of Mar to the King, before His Majesty's Arrival in England. 1715.
Political Writings. 1715.
Town-Talk: In a Letter to a Lady in the Country. 1715–16. 9 nos.
The British Subject's Answer to the Pretender's Declaration. 1716.
Chit-Chat: In a Letter to a Lady in the Country. 1716. 3 nos.
The Tea Table. 1716. 3 nos. Lost.
[*A Vindication of Sir Richard Steele, against a Pamphlet Intituled, A Letter to the Right Worshipful R. S. concerning His Remarks on the Pretender's Declaration.* 1716.]
A Letter to a Member, &c. concerning the Condemn'd Lords, in Vindication of Gentlemen Calumniated in the St. James's Post of Friday, March the 2d. 1716.
Sir Richard Steele's Speech, with Mr. Lydell, Mr. Hampden, and Mr. Tuffnell's Speeches for Repealing of the Triennial Act and Their Reasons for the Septennial Bill. 1716.
Sir Richard Steele's Account of Mr. Desaguliers' New-Invented Chimneys. 1716.
An Account of the Fish-Pool: Consisting of a Description of the Vessel So Call'd, Lately Invented and Built for the Importation of Fish Alive, and in Good Health, from Parts However Distant (with Joseph Gillmore). 1718.

The Plebeian. 1719. 4 nos.

The Joint and Humble Address of the Tories and Whiggs, concerning the Intended Bill of Peerage. 1719.

The Antidote: In a Letter to the Free-thinker, Occasion'd by the Management of the Present Dispute between Dr. Woodward and Certain Other Physicians. 1719.

The Antidote: Number II: In a Letter to the Free-thinker, Occasion'd by Later Actions between Dr. Woodward and Dr. Mead. 1719.

A Letter to the Earl of O⟨xfor⟩d, concerning the Bill of Peerage. 1719.

The Spinster: In Defence of the Woollen Manufacturers. 1719.

The Crisis of Property: An Argument Proving That the Annuitants for Ninety-nine Years, as Such, Are Not in the Condition of Other Subjects of Great Britain. 1720.

A Nation a Family: Being the Sequel of The Crisis of Property; *or, A Plan for the Improvement of the South Sea Proposal.* 1720.

The State of the Case between the Lord-Chamberlain of His Majesty's Household, and the Governor of the Royal Company of Comedians. 1720.

The Theatre. 1720. 28 nos.

An Answer to a Whimsical Pamphlet, Call'd, The Character of Sir John Edgar, *&c.* 1720.

The Conscious Lovers. 1723.

[*The Censor Censur'd; or,* The Conscious Lovers *Examin'd.* 1723.]

Dramatick Works. 1723, 1732 (4 parts).

Letters (with Alexander Pope, Sir William Trumbull, and Joseph Addison). 1735.

Works. 1759.

Epistolary Correspondence. Ed. John Nichols. 1787. 2 vols.

Selections from the Tatler, Spectator, *and* Guardian. Ed. Austin Dobson. 1885.

Richard Steele. Ed. George A. Aitken. 1894.

Selections from the Works. Ed. George Rice Carpenter. 1897.

Essays. Ed. L. E. Steele. 1902.

Letters. Ed. R. Brimley Johnson. 1927.

Correspondence. Ed. Rae Blanchard. 1941.

Tracts and Pamphlets. Ed. Rae Blanchard. 1944.

Occasional Verse. Ed. Rae Blanchard. 1952.

Periodical Journalism 1714–16. Ed. Rae Blanchard. 1959.

The Spectator (with Joseph Addison and others). Ed. Donald F. Bond. 1965. 5 vols.

Plays. Ed. Shirley Strum Kenny. 1971.

SAMUEL CLARKE (1675–1729)

Some Reflections on That Part of a Book Called Amyntor; *or,* The Defence of Milton's Life. 1699.

Three Practical Essays, viz. on Baptism, Confirmation, Repentance. 1699.

A Paraphrase on the Four Evangelists. 1701. 4 parts.

The Whole Duty of a Christian. 1704.

A Demonstration of the Being and Attributes of God. 1705, 1716 (3 parts).

The Great Duty of Universal Love and Charity. 1705.

A Letter to Mr. Dodwel. 1706, 1731.

Optice by Sir Isaac Newton (translated into Latin). 1706. 3 parts.

A Discourse concerning the Unchangeable Obligations of Natural Religion, and the Truth and Certainty of the Christian Religion. 1706.

A Defense of an Argument Made Use of in a Letter to Mr Dodwel, to Prove the Immateriality and Natural Immortality of the Soul. 1707.

The Second Defense of an Argument Made Use of in a Letter to Mr Dodwel, to Prove the Immateriality and Natural Immortality of the Soul. 1707.

A Third Defense of an Argument Made Use of in a Letter to Mr Dodwel, to Prove the Immateriality and Natural Immortality of the Soul. 1708.

A Fourth Defense of an Argument Made Use of in a Letter to Mr Dodwel, to Prove the Immateriality and Natural Immortality of the Soul. 1708.

A Sermon Preached at the Funeral of Dame Mary Cooke. 1709.

A Sermon Preached before the Honourable House of Commons at the Church of St. Margaret Westminster. 1709.

A Sermon Preached before the Queen at St. James's Chapel. 1710.

A Sermon Preached at the Parish-Church of St. James's Westminster, on Tuesday, Nov. 7, 1710: Being the Day of Thanksgiving for the Successes of the Fore-going Campaign. 1710.

The Government of Passion. 1711.

The Scripture-Doctrine of the Trinity. 1712.

C. Julii Caesaris Quae Extant (editor). 1712.

A Reply to the Objections of Robert Nelson, Esq; and of an Anonymous Author, against Dr Clarke's Scripture-Doctrine of the Trinity. 1714.

A Letter to the Reverend Dr. Wells, in Answer to His Remarks, &c. 1714.

Sermons on Several Subjects by John Moore (editor). 1715.

Remarks upon a Book, Entituled, A Philosophical Enquiry concerning Human Liberty. 1717.

A Collection of Papers, Which Passed between the Late Learned Mr. Leibnitz, and Dr. Clarke, in the Years 1715 and 1716, Relating to the Principles of Natural Philosophy and Religion. 1717. 2 parts.

Physica by Jacques Rohault (editor; with Latin tr.). 1718.

Six Sermons on Several Occasions. 1718. 6 parts.

The Modest Plea, &c. Continued; or, A Brief and Distinct Answer to Dr. Waterland's Queries, Relating to the Doctrine of the Trinity. 1720.

The Book of Common Prayer (adaptation). 1724.

XVII Sermons on Several Occasions. 1724.

Observations on Dr. Waterland's Second Defense of His Queries. 1724.

A Sermon upon Occasion of the Erecting of a Charity-School, as a House of Education for Women-Servants. 1725.

An Exposition of the Church-Catechism. Ed. John Clarke. 1729.

Homeri Ilias (editor; with Latin tr.). 1729–32. 2 vols.

Sermons. Ed. John Clarke. 1730–31. 10 vols.

Works. 1738. 4 vols.

Homeri Odyssea (editor; with Latin tr.). 1740. 2 vols.

Forty Sermons. 1806.

Oeuvres Philosophiques. Ed. Amédée Jacques. 1843.

The Leibniz-Clarke Correspondence. Ed. H. G. Alexander. 1956.

DANIEL DEFOE (1660–1731)

[*A Letter to a Dissenter from His Friend at The Hague.* 1688.]

[*Reflections upon the Late Great Revolution.* 1689.]

[*The Advantages of the Present Settlement, and the Great Danger of a Relapse.* 1689.]

[*An Account of the Late Horrid Conspiracy to Depose Their Present Majesties K. William and Q. Mary.* 1691.]

A Compleat History of the Late Revolution. 1691.

A New Discovery of an Old Intreague. 1691.

Reflections upon the Late Horrid Conspiracy Contrived by

Some of the French Court to Murther His Majesty in Flanders. 1692.

[*A Dialogue betwixt Whig and Tory.* 1693.]

The Englishman's Choice, and True Interest, in a Vigorous Prosecution of the War against France. 1694.

[*Some Seasonable Queries on the Third Head, viz.: A General Naturalization.* c. 1697.]

The Character of the Late Dr. Samuel Annesley. 1697.

Some Reflections on a Pamphlet Lately Publish'd. 1697.

An Essay upon Projects. 1697.

An Enquiry into the Occasional Conformity of Dissenters. 1697.

An Argument Shewing, That a Standing Army, with Consent of Parliament, Is Not Inconsistent with a Free Government. 1698.

A Brief Reply to the History of Standing Armies in England. 1698.

[*Some Queries concerning the Disbanding of the Army.* 1698.]

The Poor Man's Plea for a Reformation of Manners and Suppressing Immorality in the Nation. 1698.

The Interests of the Several Princes and States of Europe Consider'd. 1698.

Lex Talionis. 1698.

The Pacificator. 1700.

The Two Great Questions Consider'd. 1700.

The Two Great Questions Further Consider'd. 1700.

[*Reasons Humbly Offer'd for a Law to Enact the Castration of Popish Ecclesiastics.* 1700.]

The Six Distinguishing Characters of a Parliament-Man. 1700.

The Danger of the Protestant Religion Consider'd, from the Present Prospect of a Religious War in Europe. 1701.

The True-Born Englishman: A Satyr. 1701.

The Succession to the Crown of England, Considered. 1701.

The Free-Holders Plea against Stock-Jobbing Elections of Parliament Men. 1701.

A Letter to Mr. How. 1701.

The Livery Man's Reasons. 1701.

The Villainy of Stock-Jobbers Detected. 1701.

[*The Apparent Danger of an Invasion.* 1701.]

[*The Present Case of England, and the Protestant Interest.* 1701.]

Legion's Memorial. 1701.

Ye True-Born Englishmen Proceed. 1701.

The History of the Kentish Petition. 1701.

The Present State of Jacobitism Considered. 1701.

An Argument, Shewing that the Prince of Wales, Tho' a Protestant, Has No Just Pretensions to the Crown of England. 1701.

Reasons against a War with France. 1701.

Legion's New Paper. 1702.

The Original Power of the Collective Body of the People of England, Examined and Asserted. 1702.

The Mock-Mourners: A Satyr. 1702.

Reformation of Manners: A Satyr. 1702.

A New Test of the Church of England's Loyalty. 1702.

Good Advice to the Ladies. 1702.

The Spanish Descent. 1702.

An Enquiry into Occasional Conformity. 1702.

The Opinion of a Known Dissenter on the Bill for Preventing Occasional Conformity. 1702.

The Shortest-Way with the Dissenters. 1702.

A Brief Explanation of a Late Pamphlet, Entituled, The Shortest Way with the Dissenters. 1703.

A Dialogue between a Dissenter and the Observator. 1703.

King William's Affection to the Church of England Examin'd. 1703.

A Collection of the Writings of the Author of The True-Born Englishman. 1703.

More Reformation: A Satyr upon Himself. 1703.

The Shortest Way to Peace and Union. 1703.

A True Collection of the Writings of the Author of The True-Born Englishman. 1703–05. 2 vols.

A Hymn to the Pillory. 1703.

The Sincerety of the Dissenters Vindicated. 1703.

A Hymn to the Funeral Sermon. 1703.

The Case of Dissenters as Affected by the Late Bill Proposed in Parliament for Preventing Occasional Conformity. 1703.

An Enquiry into the Case of Mr. Asgil's General Translation. 1703.

A Challenge of Peace, Address'd to the Whole Nation. 1703.

Some Remarks on the First Chapter in Dr. Davenant's Essays. 1703.

Peace without Union. 1703.

The Dissenters Answer to the High-Church Challenge. 1704.

An Essay on the Regulation of the Press. 1704.

A Serious Inquiry into This Grand Question. 1704.

The Parallel. 1704.

A Review of the Affairs of France: and of All Europe. 1704–13. 9 vols.

The Lay-Man's Sermon upon the Late Storm. 1704.

Royal Religion: Being Some Enquiry after the Piety of Princes. 1704.

Moderation Mantain'd. 1704.

Legion's Humble Address to the Lords. 1704.

The Christianity of the High-Church Considered. 1704.

More Short-Ways with the Dissenters. 1704.

[*The Address.* 1704.]

The Dissenter Misrepresented and Represented. 1704.

A New Test of the Church of England's Honesty. 1704.

The Storm. 1704.

An Elegy on the Author of The True-Born English-man, *with an Essay on the Late Storm.* 1704.

[*A True State of the Difference between Sir George Rook Knt and William Colepeper, Esq.* 1704.]

A Hymn to Victory. 1704.

The Protestant Jesuite Unmask'd. 1704.

Giving Alms No Charity. 1704.

Queries upon the Bill against Occasional Conformity. 1704.

The Double Welcome: A Poem to the Duke of Marlbro. 1705.

Persecution Anatomiz'd. 1705.

The Consolidator; or, Memoirs of Sundry Transactions from the World in the Moon. 1705.

The Experiment; or, The Shortest Way with the Dissenters Exemplified. 1705.

A Hint to the Blackwell-Hall Factors. 1705.

Advice to All Parties. 1705.

The Dyet of Poland: A Satyr. 1705.

The Ballance; or, A New Test of the High-Fliers of All Sides. 1705.

The High-Church Legion; or, The Memorial Examin'd. 1705.

A Collection from Dyer's Letters. 1705.

Party-Tyranny. 1705.

An Answer to the L⟨or⟩d H⟨aver⟩sham's Speech. 1705.

Declaration without Doors. 1705.

A Hymn to Peace. 1706.

A Reply to a Pamphlet Entituled The L⟨or⟩d H⟨aver⟩sham's Vindication of His Speech. 1706.

The Case of Protestant Dissenters in Carolina. 1706.

Remarks on the Bill to Prevent Frauds Committed by Bankrupts. 1706.

Remarks on the Letter to the Author of the State-Memorial. 1706.

An Essay at Removing National Prejudices against a Union with Scotland. 1706. 4 parts.

An Essay on the Great Battle at Ramellies. 1706.

Jure Divino: A Satyr in Twelve Books. 1706.

A Sermon on the Fitting Up of Dr. Burges's Late Meeting House. c. 1706.

⟨Preface to⟩ *De Laune's Plea for the Non-Conformists.* 1706.

Daniel Defoe's Hymn for the Thanksgiving. 1706.

A True Relation of the Apparition of One Mrs. Veal. 1706.

A Letter from Mr. Reason, to the High and Mighty Prince of the Mob. 1706.

An Answer to My Lord Beilhaven's Speech. 1706.

The Vision: A Poem. 1706.

[*Observations on the Fifth Article of the Treaty of Union.* 1706.]

Considerations in Relation to Trade Considered. 1706.

A Seasonable Warning; or, The Pope and King of France Unmasked. 1706.

A Reply to the Scots Answer. 1706.

Caledonia: A Poem in Honour of Scotland, and the Scots Nation. 1706.

[*The State of the Excise after the Union.* 1706.]

[*The State of the Excise &c. Vindicated.* 1706.]

A Short Letter to the Glasgow-men. 1706.

The Rabbler Convicted. 1706.

The Advantages of Scotland by an Incorporate Union with England. 1706.

[*A Letter concerning Trade, from Several Scots-Gentlemen That Are Merchants in England, to Their Country-men That Are Merchants in Scotland.* 1706.]

An Enquiry into the Disposal of the Equivalent. 1706.

A Scots Poem. 1707.

A Fifth Essay, at Removing National Prejudices. 1707.

Two Great Questions Considered. 1707.

The Dissenters in England Vindicated. 1707.

Passion and Prejudice. 1707.

Proposals for Printing by Subscription a Compleat History of the Union. 1707.

[*A Discourse upon an Union of the Two Kingdoms of England and Scotland.* 1707.]

[*Remarks upon the Lord Haversham's Speech in the House of Peers, Feb.15, 1707.* 1707.]

A Short View of the Present State of the Protestant Religion in Britain. 1707.

[*The True-Born Britain.* 1707.]

A Voice from the South. 1707.

A Modest Vindication of the Present Ministry. 1707.

The Trade of Britain Stated. 1707.

An Historical Account of the Bitter Sufferings, and Melancholy Circumstances of the Episcopal Church in Scotland. 1707.

De Foe's Answer to Dyer's Scandalous News Letter. 1707.

Dyers News Examined as to His Swedish Memorial against the Review. 1707.

Reflections upon the Prohibition Act. 1708.

Advice to the Electors of Great Britain. 1708.

[*A Memorial to the Nobility of Scotland.* 1708.]

[*Scotland in Danger.* 1708.]

An Answer to a Paper concerning Mr. De Foe. 1708.

The Scot's Narrative Examin'd. 1709.

A Brief History of the Poor Palatine Refugees. 1709.

The History of the Union of Great Britain. 1709.

Parson Plaxton of Barwick. 1709.

A Letter to Mr. Bisset. 1709.

A Letter from Captain Tom to the Mobb. 1710.

A Reproof to Mr. Clark. 1710.

Advertisement from Daniel De Foe, to Mr. Clark. c. 1710.

A Speech without Doors. 1710.

The Age of Wonders. 1710.

Greenshields out of Prison and Toleration Settled in Scotland. 1710.

A Vindication of Dr. Henry Sacheverell. c. 1710.

Instructions from Rome, In Favour of the Pretender. c. 1710.

[*The Recorder of B⟨anbu⟩ry's Speech to Dr. Sach⟨eve⟩rell.* 1710.]

The Ban⟨bur⟩y Apes; or, The Monkeys Chattering to the Magpie. c. 1710.

A Collection of the Several Addresses in the Late King James's Time: Concerning the Conception and Birth of the Pretended Prince of Wales. c. 1710.

[*Dr. Sacheverell's Disappointment at Worcester.* 1710.]

[*A New Map of the Laborious and Painful Travels of Our Blessed High Church Apostle.* 1710.]

[*High-Church Miracles: or Modern Inconsistencies.* 1710.]

[*A Short Historical Account of the Contrivances and Conspiracies of the Men of Dr. Sacheverell's Principles, in the Late Reigns.* c. 1710.]

Four Letters to a Friend in North Britain. 1710.

[*Seldom Comes of Better; or, A Tale of a Lady and Her Servants.* 1710.]

[*A Letter from a Dissenter in the City of a Dissenter in the Country.* 1710.]

An Essay upon Publick Credit. 1710.

A New Test of the Sence of the Nation. 1710.

[*A Letter from a Gentleman at the Court of St. Germains.* 1710.]

A Condoling Letter to the Tattler. c. 1710.

[*Queries to the New Hereditary Right-Men.* 1710.]

An Essay upon Loans. 1710.

A Word against a New Election. 1710.

A Supplement to the Faults on Both Sides. 1710.

The British Visions. 1710.

Atalantis Major. 1710.

R⟨ogue⟩'s on Both Sides. 1711.

A Short Narrative of the Life and Actions of His Grace John, D. of Marlborough. 1711.

Vox Dei & Naturae. 1711.

Counter Queries. c. 1711.

[*The Quaker's Sermon.* 1711.]

[*Captain Tom's Remembrance to His Old Friends the Mob of London, Westminster, Southwark and Wapping.* 1711.]

A Seasonable Caution to the General Assembly. 1711.

[*A Spectators Address to the Whigs.* 1711.]

The Secret History of the October Club, from Its Original to This Time. 1711. 2 parts.

[*The Succession of Spain Consider'd.* 1711.]

Eleven Opinions about Mr. H⟨arle⟩y. 1711.

[*The Re-Representation; or, A Modest Search after the Great Plunderers of the Nation.* 1711.]

[*The Representation Examined: Being Remarks on the State of Religion in England.* 1711.]

Reasons for a Peace; or, The War at an End. 1711.

An Essay upon the Trade to Africa. 1711.

[*The Scotch Medal Decipher'd.* 1711.]

A Speech for Mr. D⟨und⟩asse Younger of Arnistown, If He Should Be Impeach'd. 1711.

A True Account of the Designs and Advantages of the South-Sea Trade. 1711.

An Essay on the South-Sea Trade. 1711.

The True State of the Case between the Government and the Creditors of the Navy. 1711.

Reasons Why This Nation Ought to Put a Speedy End to This Expensive War. 1711.

Reasons Why a Party among Us, and Also among the Confederates, Are Obstinately Bent against a Treaty of Peace with the French at This Time. 1711.

Armageddon; or, The Necessity of Carrying On the War. 1711.

The Ballance of Europe. 1711.

[*Worcestershire-Queries about Peace.* 1711.]

An Essay at a Plain Exposition of That Difficult Phrase, A Good Peace. 1711.

The Felonious Treaty. 1711.

An Essay on the History of Parties, and Persecution in Britain. 1711.

A Defence of the Allies and the Late Ministry. 1712.

A Justification of the Dutch from Several Late Scandalous Reflections. 1712.

No Queen; or, No General. 1712.

The Conduct of Parties in England. 1712.

Peace or Poverty. 1712.

Some Queries Humbly Propos'd upon the Bill for Toleration to the Episcopal Clergy in Scotland. c. 1712.

A Letter from a Gentleman in Scotland, to His Friend at London. 1712.

[*The Case of the Poor Skippers and Keel-Men of Newcastle.* c. 1712.]

[*A Farther Case Relating to the Poor Keel-Men of Newcastle.* 1712.]

[*The History of the Jacobite Clubs.* 1712.]

[*Imperial Gratitude.* 1712.]

The Highland Visions; or, The Scots New Prophecy. 1712.

[*Plain English, with Remarks and Advice to Some Men Who Need Not Be Nam'd.* 1712.]

Wise as Serpents: Being an Enquiry into the Present Circumstances of the Dissenters. 1712.

The Present State of the Parties in Great Britain. 1712.

Reasons against Fighting. 1712.

The Present Negotiations of Peace Vindicated from the Imputation of Trifling. 1712.

The Validity of the Renunciations of Foreign Powers Enquired Into. 1712.

An Enquiry into the Danger and Consequences of a War with the Dutch. 1712.

A Further Search into the Conduct of the Allies and the Late Ministry as to Peace and War. 1712.

The Justice and Necessity of a War with Holland. 1712.

An Enquiry into the Real Interest of Princes in the Persons of Their Ambassadors. 1712.

A Seasonable Warning and Caution against the Insinuations of Papists and Jacobites in Favour of the Pretender. 1712.

Hannibal at the Gates; or, The Progress of Jacobitism. 1712.

A Strict Enquiry into the Circumstances of a Late Duel. 1713.

Reasons against the Succession of the House of Hanover. 1713.

[*Not⟨tingh⟩am Politicks Examin'd.* 1713.]

The Second-Sighted Highlander. 1713.

And What if the Pretender Should Come? 1713.

An Answer to a Question That No Body Thinks Of, viz.: But What If the Queen Should Die? 1713.

An Essay on the Treaty of Commerce with France. 1713.

An Account of the Abolishing of Duels in France. 1713.

Union and No Union. 1713.

Mercator. 1713–14. 181 nos.

Considerations upon the Eighth and Ninth Articles of the Treaty of Commerce and Navigation. 1713.

Some Thoughts upon the Subject of Commerce with France. 1713.

The Trade of Scotland with France, Consider'd. 1713.

A General History of Trade. 1713. 4 parts.

The Honour and Prerogative of the Queen's Majesty Vindicated. 1713.

Memoirs of Count Tariff. 1713.

A Brief Account of the Present State of the African Trade. 1713.

[*Reasons concerning the Immediate Demolishing of Dunkirk.* 1713.]

[*A Letter from a Member of the House of Commons to His Friends in the Country, Relating to the Bill of Commerce.* 1713.]

Whigs Turn'd Tories, and Hanoverian-Tories, from Their Avow'd Principles, Prov'd Whigs; or, Each Side in the Other Mistaken. 1713.

A View of the Real Dangers of the Succession, from the Peace with France. 1713.

Extracts from Several Mercators. 1713.

A Letter to the Dissenters. 1713.

Proposals for Imploying the Poor in and about the City of London. 1713.

A Letter to the Whigs. 1714.

Memoirs of John, Duke of Melfort. 1714.

The Scots Nation and Union Vindicated. 1714.

Reasons for Im⟨peaching⟩ the L⟨or⟩d H⟨igh⟩ T⟨reasure⟩r, and Some Others of the P⟨resent⟩ M⟨inistry⟩. 1714.

[*A Letter to Mr. Steele.* 1714.]

The Remedy Worse Than the Disease. 1714.

The Weakest Go to the Wall; or, The Dissenters Sacrific'd by All Parties. 1714.

A Brief Survey of the Legal Liberties of the Dissenters. 1714.

The Schism Act Explain'd. 1714.

The Secret History of the White Staff. 1714–15. 3 parts.

Advice to the People of Great Britain. 1714.

A Secret History of One Year. 1714.

[*Tories and Tory Principles Ruinous to Both Prince and People.* 1714.]

[*Impeachment, or No Impeachment.* 1714.]

[*The Bristol Riot.* 1714.]

The Pernicious Consequences of the Clergy's Intermedling with Affairs of State, with Reasons Humbly Offer'd for Passing a Bill to Incapacitate Them from the Like Practice for the Future. c. 1714.

[*A Full and Impartial Account of the Late Disorders in Bristol.* 1714.]

The Secret History of the Secret History of the White Staff, Purse and Mitre. 1715.

Strike While the Iron's Hot. 1715.

Memoirs of the Conduct of Her Late Majesty and Her Last Ministry. 1715.

Treason Detected. 1715.

The Immorality of the Priesthood. 1715.

The Secret History of State Intrigues in the Management of the Scepter. 1715.

The Candidate: Being a Detection of Bribery and Corruption as It Is Just Now in Practice All over Great Britain. 1715.

A Reply to a Traiterous Libel, Entituled, English Advice to the
Freeholders of Great Britain. 1715.

The Protestant Jubilee. 1715.

[*A Letter to a Merry Young Gentleman Intituled Tho. Burnet,
Esq.* 1715.]

*Burnet and Bradbury; or, The Confederacy of the Press and
Pulpit for the Blood of the Last Ministry.* 1715.

A View of the Present Management of the Court of France.
1715.

The Fears of the Pretender Turn'd into the Fears of Debauchery.
1715.

*A Friendly Epistle by Way of Reproof from One of the People
Called Quakers.* 1715.

*An Appeal to Honour and Justice, Tho' It Be of His Worst
Enemies, by Daniel De Foe.* 1715.

[*Some Reasons Offered by the Late Ministry in Defence of Their
Administration.* 1715.]

The Family Instructor. 1715.

*A Sharp Rebuke from One of the People Called Quakers to
Henry Sacheverell.* 1715.

An Apology for the Army. 1715.

The Second-Sighted Highlander. 1715.

Some Methods to Supply the Defects of the Late Peace. 1715.

[*A Remonstrance from Some Country Whigs to a Member of a
Secret Committee.* 1715.]

[*The Happiness of the Hanover Succession.* 1715.]

An Attempt towards a Coalition of English Protestants. 1715.

*An Account of the Riots, Tumults, and Other Treasonable
Practices since His Majesty's Accession to the Throne* (editor). 1715.

*A Seasonable Expostulation with, and Friendly Reproof unto,
James Butler.* 1715.

[*His Majesty's Obligations to the Whigs Plainly Proved.* 1715.]

*A Brief History of the Pacifick Campaign in Flanders Anno
1712, and of the Fatal Cessation of Arms.* 1715.

*Some Considerations on the Danger of the Church from Her
Own Clergy.* 1715.

A Letter from a Gentleman of the Church of England.
1715.

An Humble Address to Our Soveraign Lord the People. 1715.

*The History of the Wars of His Present Majesty Charles XII
King of Sweden.* 1715.

An Account of the Conduct of Robert Earl of Oxford. 1715.

A Hymn to the Mob. 1715.

*Hanover or Rome: Shewing the Absolute Necessity of Assisting
His Majesty.* 1715.

*An Account of the Great and Generous Actions of James Butler
(Late Duke of Ormond).* 1715.

A View of the Scots Rebellion. 1715.

The Traiterous and Foolish Manifesto of the Scots Rebels.
1715.

Bold Advice; or, Proposals for the Entire Rooting Out of Jacobitism in Great Britain. 1715.

[*An Address to the People of England, Shewing the Unworthiness of Their Behavior to King George.* 1715.]

*A Trumpet Blown in the North, and Sounded in the Ears of
John Eriskine.* 1715.

[*A Letter from One Clergy-Man to Another, upon the Subject
of the Rebellion.* 1715.]

[*A Conference with a Jacobite, Wherein the Clergy of the
Church of England Are Vindicated from the Charge of
Hypocrisy and Perjury.* 1716.]

[*Proper Lessons for the Tories.* 1716.]

Some Account of the Two Nights Court at Greenwich. 1716.

[*The Case of the Protestant Dissenters in England.* 1716.]

[*The Address of the Episcopal Clergy to the Diocese of Aberdeen,
to the Pretender, with Remarks upon the Said Address.*
1716.]

[*The Address of the Magistrates and Town Council of Aberdeen,
to the Pretender, with Remarks upon the Said Address.*
1716.]

*Some Thoughts of an Honest Tory in the Country, upon the
Late Dispositions of Some People to Revolt.* 1716.

[*The Declaration of the Free-Holders of Great Britain, in Answer to That of the Pretender.* 1716.]

*The Conduct of Some People, about Pleading Guilty, with
Some Reasons Why It Was Not Thought Proper to Show
Mercy to Some Who Desir'd It.* 1716.

*An Account of the Proceedings against the Rebels, and Other
Prisoners, Tried before the Lord Chief Justice Jefferies.*
1716.

The Proceedings of the Government against the Rebels, Compared with the Persecutions of the Late Reigns. 1716.

[*Remarks upon the Speech of James late Earl of Derwentwater,
Beheaded on Tower-Hill for High-Treason.* 1716.]

An Essay upon Buying and Selling of Speeches. 1716.

Some Considerations on a Law for Triennial Parliaments.
1716.

The Triennial Act Impartially Stated. 1716.

Arguments about the Alteration of Triennial Elections of Parliament. 1716.

[*The Ill Consequences of Repealing the Triennial Act.* 1716.]

[*A Dialogue between a Whig and a Jacobite, upon the Subject
of the Late Rebellion.* 1716.]

A True Account of the Proceedings at Perth. 1716.

*Remarks on the Speeches of William Paul Clerk, and John Hall
of Otterburn, Esq., Executed at Tyburn for Rebellion, the
13th of July 1716.* 1716.

[*The Annals of King George.* 1716–17. 2 vols.]

The Layman's Vindication of the Church of England. 1716.

Secret Memoirs of the New Treaty of Alliance with France.
1716.

*Secret Memoirs of a Treasonable Conference at S⟨omerset⟩
House.* 1717.

[*Some National Grievances Considered.* 1717.]

*The Danger of Court Differences; or, The Unhappy Effects of a
Motley Ministry.* 1717.

The Quarrel of the School-Boys at Athens. 1717.

[*Faction in Power; or, The Mischiefs and Dangers of a High-
Church Magistracy.* 1717.]

An Impartial Enquiry into the Conduct of the Right Honourable Charles Lord Viscount T⟨ownshend⟩. 1717.

*An Argument Proving That the Design of Employing and
Enobling Foreigners Is a Treasonable Conspiracy.*
1717.

[*An Account of the Swedish and Jacobite Plot.* 1717.]

A Curious Little Oration Deliver'd by Father Andrew. 1717.

An Expostulatory Letter to the B⟨ishop⟩ of B⟨angor⟩. 1717.

Fair Payment No Spunge. 1717.

What If the Swedes Should Come? 1717.

*The Question Fairly Stated, Whether Now Is the Time to Do
Justice to the Friends of the Government as Well as to Its
Enemies?* 1717.

Christianity No Creature of the State. 1717.

The Danger and Consequences of Disobliging the Clergy Consider'd. 1717.

[*Reasons for a Royal Visitation.* 1717.]

Memoirs of the Church of Scotland. 1717.

A Farther Argument against Enobling Foreigners. 1717.

The Conduct of Robert Walpole, Esq. 1717.

[*The Report Reported.* 1717.]

A Short View of the Conduct of the King of Sweden. 1717.

[*A General Pardon Consider'd.* 1717.]

Observation on the Bishop's Answer to Dr. Snape, by a Lover of Truth. 1717.

[*A Vindication of Dr. Snape.* 1717.]

A Reply to the Remarks upon the Lord Bishop of Bangor's Treatment of the Clergy and Convocation. 1717.

Minutes of the Negotiations of Monsr. Mesnager at the Court of England towards the Close of the Last Reign. 1717.

Memoirs of Some Transactions during the Late Ministry of Robert E. of Oxford. 1717.

A Declaration of Truth to Benjamin Hoadly. 1717.

[*A History of the Clemency of Our English Monarchs.* 1717.]

The Conduct of Christians Made a Sport of Infidels. 1717.

[*The Old Whig and Modern Whig Revived.* 1717.]

A Letter to Andrew Snape. 1717.

The Case of the War in Italy Stated. 1717.

Considerations on the Present State of Affairs in Great-Britain. 1718.

The Defection Farther Consider'd. 1718.

Some Persons Vindicated against the Author of the Defection. 1718.

Memoirs of the Life and Eminent Conduct of That Learned and Reverend Divine Daniel Williams, D.D. 1718.

Mr. de la Pillonniere's Vindication. 1718.

The New British Inquisition; or, The Racking of Mr. Pillonniere. 1718.

[*A Brief Answer to a Long Libel.* 1718.]

A Letter from the Jesuits to Father de la Pilloniere. 1718.

[*A Golden Mine of Treasure Open'd for the Dutch.* 1718.]

Miserere Cleri; or, The Factions of the Church. 1718.

[*Some Reasons Why It Could Not Be Expected That the Government Wou'd Permit the Speech or Paper of James Shepheard.* 1718.]

[*The Jacobites Detected.* 1718.]

[*Dr. Sherlock's Vindication of the Test Act Examin'd.* 1718.]

[*A Brief Comment upon His Majesty's Speech.* 1718.]

A Vindication of the Press. 1718.

[*A Letter from Some Protestant Dissenting Laymen.* 1718.]

Memoirs of Publick Transactions in the Life and Ministry of His Grace the D. of Shrewsbury. 1718.

[*A Letter from Paris, Giving an Account of the Death of the Late Queen Dowager.* 1718.]

A History of the Last Session of the Present Parliament. 1718.

A Letter to the Author of the Flying-Post. 1718.

A Continuation of Letters Written by a Turkish Spy at Paris. 1718.

The History of the Reign of King George. 1718.

The Memoirs of Majr. Alexander Ramkins. 1718.

A Friendly Rebuke to One Parson Benjamin. 1719.

[*Observations and Remarks upon the Declaration of War against Spain.* 1719.]

[*Merry Andrew's Epistle to His Old Master Benjamin.* 1719.]

The Life and Strange Surprizing Adventures of Robinson Crusoe, of York, Mariner, Written by Himself. 1719.

A Letter to the Dissenters. 1719.

The Anatomy of Exchange-Alley. 1719.

Some Account of the Life and Most Remarkable Actions of George Henry Baron de Goertz. 1719.

The Just Complaint of the Poor Weavers Truly Represented. 1719.

The Farther Adventures of Robinson Crusoe: Being the Second and Last Part of His Life. 1719.

The Gamester. 1719. 2 nos.

A Brief State of the Question, between the Printed and Painted Callicoes and the Woollen and Silk Manufacture. 1719.

Charity Still a Christian Virtue. 1719.

The Dumb Philosopher; or, Great Britain's Wonder. 1719.

The King of Pirates: Being an Account of the Famous Enterprises of Captain Avery, the Mock King of Madagascar, with His Rambles and Piracies. 1719.

The Manufacturer. 1719–20.

The Female Manufacturers Complaint. 1720.

An Historical Account of the Voyages and Adventures of Sir Walter Raleigh, with the Discoveries and Conquests He Made for the Crown of England. 1720.

The History of the Wars, of His Present Majesty Charles XII, King of Sweden, with a Continuation to the Time of His Death. 1720.

The Chimera; or, The French Way of Paying National Debts Laid Open. 1720.

[*The Case of the Fair Traders.* 1720.]

The Trade to India Critically and Calmly Consider'd. 1720.

The Case Fairly Stated between the Turky Company and the Italian Merchants. 1720.

[*The Compleat Art of Painting* by C. A. Du Fresnoy (translator). 1720.]

[*A Letter to the Author of the* Independent Whig. 1720.]

[*The History of the Life and Adventures of Mr. Duncan Campbell, a Gentleman.* 1720.]

Memoirs of a Cavalier; or, A Military Journal of the Wars in Germany, and the Wars in England, from the Year 1632 to the Year 1648. 1720.

The Life, Adventures, and Pyracies of the Famous Captain Singleton. 1720.

Serious Reflections during the Life and Surprising Adventures of Robinson Crusoe, with His Vision of the Angelick World. 1720.

[*The South-Sea Scheme Examin'd.* 1720.]

A True State of the Contracts Relating to the Third Money-Subscription Taken by the South-Sea Company. 1721.

A Vindication of the Honour and Justice of Parliament. 1721.

Brief Observations on Trade and Manufactures. 1721.

The Case of Mr. Law, Truly Stated. 1721.

A Collection of Miscellany Letters, Selected out of Mist's Weekly Journal (editor). 1722. 4 vols.

The Fortunes and Misfortunes of the Famous Moll Flanders, Written from Her Own Memorandums. 1722.

Due Preparations for the Plague as Well for Soul as Body. 1722.

Religious Courtship: Being Historical Discourses, on the Necessity of Marrying Religious Husbands and Wives Only. 1722.

A Journal of the Plague Year: Being Observations or Memorial of the Most Remarkable Occurrences, as Well Public as Private, Which Happened in London during the Last Great Visitation in 1665. 1722.

A Brief Debate upon the Dissolving the Last Parliament. 1722.

An Impartial History of the Life and Actions of Peter Alexowitz, the Present Czar of Muscovy. 1722.

The History and Remarkable Life of the Truly Honourable Col. Jacque, Commonly Call'd Col. Jack. 1722.

[*A Memorial to the Clergy of the Church of England.* 1723.]

[*The Wickedness of a Disregard to Others.* 1723.]

[*Considerations on Publick Credit.* 1724.]

The Fortunate Mistress; or, A History of the Life and Vast Variety of Fortunes of Mademoiselle de Beleau, Afterwards

Called the Countess de Wintselsheim, in Germany, Being the Person Known by the Name of the Lady Roxana, in the Time of King Charles II. 1724.

The Great Law of Subordination Consider'd. 1724.

A General History of the Robberies and Murders of the Most Notorious Pyrates, and Also Their Policies, Discipline and Government, from Their First Rise and Settlement in the Island of Providence, in 1717, to the Present Year 1724. 1724.

A Tour thro' the Whole Island of Great Britain, Divided into Circuits or Journies. 1724–26. 3 vols.

The Royal Progress. 1724.

A Narrative of the Proceedings in France. 1724.

A Narrative of All the Robberies, Escapes Etc. of John Sheppard: Giving an Exact Description of the Manner of His Wonderful Escape from the Castle in Newgate. 1724.

Some Farther Account of the Original Disputes in Ireland. 1724.

The History of the Remarkable Life of John Sheppard. 1724.

A New Voyage round the World. 1724.

[*An Epistle from Jack Sheppard.* 1725.]

The Life of Jonathan Wild. 1725.

Every-body's Business in No-body's Business. 1725.

The True and Genuine Account of the Life and Actions of the Late Jonathan Wild. 1725.

An Account of the Conduct and Proceedings of the Late John Gow, Alias Smith, Captain of the Late Pirates. 1725.

The Complete English Tradesman, in Familiar Letters. 1725.

A General History of Discoveries and Improvements, in Useful Arts. 1725–26. 4 parts.

A Brief Case of the Distillers. 1726.

A Brief Historical Account of the Lives of the Six Notorious Street-Robbers. 1726.

An Essay upon Literature. 1726.

The Political History of the Devil. 1726.

Unparallel'd Cruelty; or, The Tryal of Captain Jeane of Bristol. 1726.

The Friendly Daemon; or, The Generous Apparition. 1726.

The Four Years Voyages of Capt. George Roberts: Being a Series of Uncommon Events, Which Befell Him in a Voyage to the Islands of the Canaries, Cape de Verde and Barbadoes, from Whence He Was Bound to the Coast of Guiney. 1726.

Mere Nature Delineated; or, A Body without a Soul. 1726.

Some Considerations upon Street-Walkers. 1726.

The Protestant Monastery. 1726.

A System of Magick; or, A History of the Black Art. 1726.

The Evident Approach of a War, and Something of the Necessity of It, in Order to Establish Peace and Preserve Trade. 1727.

Conjugal Lewdness; or, Matrimonial Whoredom. 1727.

The Evident Advantages to Great Britain and Its Allies from the Approaching War, Especially in Matters of Trade. 1727.

A Brief Deduction of the Original Progress and Immense Greatness of the British Woolen Manufacture. 1727.

An Essay on the History and Reality of Apparitions. 1727.

A New Family Instructor. 1727.

Parochial Tyranny. 1727.

Some Considerations on the Reasonableness and Necessity of Encreasing and Encouraging the Seamen. 1728.

Augusta Triumphens; or, The Way to Make London the Most Flourishing City in the Universe. 1728.

A Plan of the English Commerce. 1728.

[*The Memoirs of an English Officer.* 1728.]

Atlas Maritimus and Commercialis. 1728.

The History of the Pyrates. 1728.

An Impartial Account of the Late Famous Siege of Gibraltar. 1728.

Second Thoughts Are Best; or, A Further Improvement of a Late Scheme to Prevent Street Robberies. 1728.

Street-Robberies, Consider'd: The Reason of Their Being So Frequent, with Probable Means to Prevent 'Em, Written by a Converted Thief; to Which Is Prefixed Some Memoirs of His Life. 1728.

Reasons for a War, in Order to Establish the Tranquillity and Commerce of Europe. 1729.

The Unreasonableness and Ill Consequences of Imprisoning the Body for Debt. 1729.

An Humble Proposal to the People of England, for the Encrease of Their Trade. 1729.

An Enquiry into the Pretensions of Spain to Gibraltar. 1729.

Some Objections Humbly Offered to the Consideration of the Hon. House of Commons, Relating to the Present Intended Relief of Prisoners. 1729.

The Advantages of Peace and Commerce; with Some Remarks on the East-India Trade. 1729.

Madagascar; or, Robert Drury's Journal, during Fifteen Years Captivity on That Island, Written by Himself, Digested into Order, and Now Published at the Request of His Friends (editor). 1729.

A Brief State of the Inland or Home Trade of England. 1730.

The Perjur'd Free Mason Detected, and Yet the Honour and Antiquity of the Society of Free Masons Preserv'd and Defended, by a Free Mason. 1730.

Fortune's Fickle Distribution. 1730.

An Effectual Scheme for the Immediate Preventing of Street Robberies. 1730.

Novels. Ed. Sir Walter Scott. 1810. 12 vols.

Novels and Miscellaneous Works. 1840–41. 20 vols.

Life and Recently Discovered Writings. Ed. William Lee. 1869. 3 vols.

The Compleat English Gentleman. Ed. K. D. Bülbring. 1890.

Romances and Narratives. Ed. George A. Aitken. 1895. 16 vols.

Of Royall Education: A Fragmentary Treatise. Ed. K. D. Bülbring. 1895.

Works. Ed. G. H. Maynadier. 1903–04. 16 vols.

Novels and Selected Writings. 1927–28. 14 vols.

A Review of the Affairs of France: and of All Europe, Ed. A. W. Secord. 1938. 22 vols.

Meditations. Ed. George H. Healy. 1946.

Letters. Ed. George H. Healy. 1955.

JOHN GAY (1685–1732)

Wine. 1708.

The Present State of Wit. 1711.

The Mohocks. 1712.

An Argument Proving from History, Reason, and Scripture, That the Present Mohocks and Hawkubites Are the Gog and Magog Mention'd in the Revelations. 1712.

Rural Sports. 1713.

The Wife of Bath. 1713.

The Fan. 1714.

The Shepherd's Week. 1714.

A Letter to a Lady. 1715.

The What D'Ye Call It. 1715.

Trivia. 1716.

Court Poems (with Lady Mary Wortley Montagu). 1716.
Three Hours after Marriage (with Alexander Pope and John Arbuthnot). 1717.
Daphnis and Chloe. 1720.
Two Epistles: One to the Earl of Burlington, the Other to a Lady. 1720.
Poems on Several Occasions. 1720. 2 vols.
The Poor Shepherd. c. 1720.
A Panegyrical Epistle to Mr. Thomas Snow. 1721.
An Epistle to Her Grace Henrietta Dutchess of Marlborough. 1722.
[*A Poem Address'd to the Quidnunc's.* 1724.]
The Captives. 1724.
Blueskin's Ballad. c. 1725.
To a Lady on Her Passion for Old China. 1725.
Fables. 1727 [Vol. 1]; 1738 [Vol. 2].
The Beggar's Opera. 1728.
Polly. 1729.
Acis and Galatea. 1732.
Achilles. 1733.
The Distress'd Wife. 1743.
The Rehearsal at Goatham. 1754.
Plays. 1760.
Works. 1770. 4 vols.
Miscellaneous Works. 1773–75. 6 vols.
Poetical Works. 1777. 3 vols.
Poetical, Dramatic and Miscellaneous Works. 1795. 6 vols.
Poetical Works. 1854. 2 vols.
Poetical Works. Ed. John Underhill. 1893. 2 vols.
Plays. 1923. 2 vols.
Poetical Works, Including Polly, The Beggar's Opera, and Selections from the Other Dramatic Work. Ed. G. C. Faber. 1926.
Poems. Ed. Alan Ross. 1950.
Letters. Ed. C. F. Burgess. 1966.
Poetry and Prose. Eds. Vinton A. Dearing and Charles E. Beckwith. 1974. 2 vols.
Dramatic Works. Ed. John Fuller. 1983. 2 vols.

BERNARD MANDEVILLE (1670–1733)

De Medicina Oratio Scholastica. 1685.
Disputatio Philosophica de Brutorum Operationibus. 1689.
Disputatio Medica Inauguralis de Chylosi Vitiata. 1691.
Some Fables after the Easie and Familiar Method of Monsieur de la Fontaine (translator). 1703, 1704 (as *Aesop Dress'd; or, A Collection of Fables Writ in Familiar Verse*).
[*The Pamphleteers: A Satyr.* 1703.]
Typhon; or, The Wars between the Gods and Giants: A Burlesque Poem in Imitation of the Comical Mons. Scarron. 1704.
[*The Planter's Charity.* 1704.]
The Grumbling Hive; or, Knaves Turn'd Honest. 1705.
The Virgin Unmask'd; or, Female Dialogues betwixt an Elderly Maiden Lady, and Her Niece. 1709.
The Female Tatler (with Thomas Baker). 1709–10. 111 nos.
A Treatise of the Hypochondriack and Hysterick Passions, Vulgarly Call'd the Hypo in Men and Vapours in Women. 1711.
Wishes to a Godson, with Other Miscellany Poems. 1712.
The Fable of the Bees; or, Private Vices, Publick Benefits. 1714 [Part 1]; 1729 [Part 2].
[*The Mischiefs That Ought Justly to Be Apprehended from a Whig-Government.* 1714.]
Free Thoughts on Religion, the Church, and National Happiness. 1720.

A Modest Defence of Publick Stews; or, An Essay upon Whoring, as It Is Now Practis'd in These Kingdoms. 1724.
An Enquiry into the Causes of the Frequent Executions at Tyburn. 1725.
[*Remarks upon Two Late Presentments of the Grand-Jury of the County of Middlesex.* 1729.]
An Enquiry into the Origin of Honour, and the Usefulness of Christianity in War. 1732.
A Letter to Dion, Occasion'd by His Book Call'd Alciphron; or, The Minute Philosopher. 1732.
The Divine Instinct Recommended to Men by Béat Louis de Muralt (translator). 1751.

JOHN DENNIS (1657–1734)

Poems in Burlesque. 1692.
Poems and Letters upon Several Occasions. 1692.
The Passion of Byblis by Ovid (translator). 1692.
The Impartial Critick; or, Some Observations upon a Late Book, Entituled, A Short View of Tragedy, Written by Mr. Rymer. 1693.
Miscellanies in Verse and Prose. 1693, 1697 (as *Miscellanies*).
The Court of Death: A Pindarique Poem, Dedicated to the Memory of Her Most Sacred Majesty, Queen Mary. 1695.
Remarks on a Book Entitul'd, Prince Arthur, an Heroick Poem. 1696.
The Nuptials of Britain's Genius and Fame: A Pindarick Poem on the Peace. 1697.
A Plot and No Plot. 1697.
The Usefulness of the Stage, to the Happiness of Mankind, to Government, and to Religion: Occasion'd by a Late Book, Written by Jeremy Collier. 1698.
Rinaldo and Armida. 1699.
Iphigenia. 1700.
Familiar and Courtly Letters by Vincent de Voiture (translator; with others). 1700. 7 parts.
⟨*The Seaman's Case.*⟩ c. 1700.
The Advancement and Reformation of Modern Poetry: A Critical Discourse. 1701.
The Comical Gallant; or, The Amours of Sir John Falstaffe (adaptation). 1702.
The Danger of Priestcraft to Religion and Government; with Some Politick Reasons for Toleration. 1702.
An Essay on the Navy. 1702.
The Monument: A Poem Sacred to the Immortal Memory of the Best and Greatest of Kings, William the Third. 1702.
A Proposal for Putting a Speedy End to the War. 1703.
Britannia Triumphans; or, The Empire Sav'd, and Europe Deliver'd. 1704.
Liberty Asserted. 1704.
The Person of Quality's Answer to Mr. Collier's Letter: Being a Dissuasive from the Play-House. 1704.
The Grounds of Criticism in Poetry, Contain'd in Some New Discoveries Never Made Before, Requisite for the Writing and Judging of Poems Surely. 1704.
Gibralter; or, The Spanish Adventure. 1705.
The Battle of Ramillia; or, The Power of Union. 1706.
An Essay on the Opera's after the Italian Manner. 1706.
Orpheus and Eurydice. 1707.
Appius and Virginia. 1709.
An Essay upon Publick Spirit: Being a Satyr in Prose upon the Manners and Luxury of the Times. 1711.
Reflections Critical and Satyrical, upon a Late Rhapsody, Call'd, An Essay upon Criticism. 1711.

An Essay upon the Genius and Writings of Shakespear; with Some Letters of Criticism to the Spectator. 1712.

Remarks upon Cato: A Tragedy. 1713.

A Poem upon the Death of Her Late Sacred Majesty Queen Anne, and the Most Happy and Auspicious Accession of His Sacred Majesty King George. 1714.

John Dennis, the Sheltring Poet's Invitation to Richard Steele, the Secluded Party-Writer, and Member; to Come and Live with Him in the Mint: In Imitation of Horace's Fifth Epistle, Lib. I. 1714.

Priestcraft Distinguish'd from Christianity. 1715.

A True Character of Mr. Pope, and His Writings. 1716.

Remarks upon Mr. Pope's Translation of Homer; with Two Letters concerning Windsor Forest, *and the* Temple of Fame. 1717.

Select Works. 1718. 2 works.

The Characters and Conduct of Sir John Edgar, Call'd by Himself Sole Monarch of the Stage in Drury-Lane; and His Three Deputy Governours: In Two Letters. 1720.

The Characters and Conduct of Sir John Edgar, and His Three Deputy-Governours: In a Third and Fourth Letter. 1720.

The Invader of His Country; or, The Fatal Resentment (adaptation). 1720.

Original Letters, Familiar, Moral and Critical. 1721.

A Defence of Sir Fopling Flutter, *a Comedy Written by Sir George Etheridge.* 1722.

Julius Caesar Acquitted and His Murderers Condemn'd: In a Letter to a Friend. 1722.

Remarks on a Play, Call'd The Conscious Lovers: A Comedy. 1723.

Vice and Luxury Publick Mischiefs; or, Remarks on a Book Intitul'd The Fable of the Bees. 1724.

The Stage Defended, from Scripture, Reason, Experience, and the Common Sense of Mankind. 1726.

Miscellaneous Tracts. 1727. Vol. 1 only.

The Faith and Duties of Christians by Thomas Burnet (translator). 1728.

Remarks on Mr. Pope's Rape of the Lock: *In Several Letters to a Friend; with a Preface, Occasion'd by the Late Treatise on the Profound, and the Dunciad.* 1728.

Remarks upon Several Passages in the Preliminaries to the Dunciad, and upon Several Passages in Pope's Preface to His Translation of Homer's Iliad. 1729.

Pope Alexander's Supremacy and Infallibility Examin'd (with George Duckett). 1729. 3 parts.

A Treatise concerning the State of Departed Souls by Thomas Burnet (translator). 1730.

Critical Works. Ed. Edward Niles Hooker. 1939–43. 2 vols.

Plays. Ed. J. W. Johnson. 1980.

JOHN ARBUTHNOT (1667–1735)

Of the Laws of Chance by Christiaan Huygens (translator). 1692.

Theses Medicae de Secretione Animali. 1696.

An Examination of Dr. Woodward's Account of the Deluge, &c. 1697.

An Essay on the Usefulness of Mathematical Learning. 1701.

Tables of the Grecian, Roman and Jewish Measures, Weights and Coins: Reduc'd to the English Standard. 1705.

A Sermon Preach'd to the People at the Mercat-Cross of Edinburgh, on the Subject of the Union. 1706.

Law Is a Bottomless-Pit. 1712.

John Bull in His Senses: Being the Second Part of Law Is a Bottomless-Pit. 1712.

John Bull Still in His Senses; or, Law Is a Bottomless-Pit. 1712.

An Appendix to John Bull Still in His Senses; or, Law Is a Bottomless Pit. 1712.

Lewis Baboon Turned Honest, and John Bull Politician: Being the Fourth Part of Law Is a Bottomless-Pit. 1712.

The History of John Bull. 1712.

[*The Story of the St. Alb–ns Ghost; or, The Apparition of Mother Haggy.* 1712.]

Proposals for Printing a Very Curious Discourse, Intitled ΨΕΥΔΟΛΟΓΙΑ ΠΟΛΙΤΙΚΗ; *or, A Treatise of the Art of Political Lying.* 1712.

An Invitation to Peace; or, Toby's Preliminaries to Nestor Ironside. 1713.

[*The Longitude Examin'd.* 1714.]

[*Notes and Memorandums of the Six Days Preceding the Death of a Late Right Reverend* ———. 1715.]

[*The State Quacks; or, The Political Botchers.* 1715.]

To the Right Honourable the Mayor and Alderman of the City of London: The Humble Petition of the Colliers, Cooks, Cook-Maids, Blacksmiths, Jack-makers, Brasiers, and Others. 1716.

Three Hours after Marriage (with Alexander Pope and John Gay). 1717.

A Letter to the Reverend Mr. Dean Swift, Occasion'd by a Satire Said to Be Written by Him, Entitled, A Dedication to a Great Man. 1719.

[*An Account of the Sickness and Death of Dr. W—dw–rd.* 1719.]

[*A Letter from the Facetious Dr. Andrew Tripe at Bath, to His Loving Brother.* 1719]

[*The Life and Adventures of Don Bilioso de L'Estomac, Translated from the Original Spanish into French; Done from the French into English; with a Letter to the College of Physicians.* 1719.]

Annus Mirabilis. 1722.

[*A Supplement to Dean Sw—t's Miscellanies.* 1723.]

Reasons Humbly Offer'd by the Company Exercising the Trade and Mystery of Upholders, against Part of the Bill, for the Better Viewing, Searching, Examining Drugs, Medicines, &c. 1724.

[*A Poem Address'd to the Quidnunc's.* 1724.]

[*The Ball.* 1724.]

It Cannot Rain but It Pours; or, London Strow'd with Rarities. 1726.

[*The Most Wonderful Wonder That Ever Appeared to the Wonder of the British Nation.* 1726.]

[*The Manifesto of Lord Peter.* 1726.]

[*A Learned Dissertation on Dumpling: Its Dignity, Antiquity, and Excellence.* 1726.]

[*The Devil to Pay at St. James's.* 1727.]

Miscellanies in Prose and Verse (with Alexander Pope and Jonathan Swift). 1727 [Volumes 1–2]; 1732 [Volume 3].

Tables of Ancient Coins, Weights and Measures, Explain'd and Exemplify'd in Several Dissertations. 1727.

Oratio Anniversaria Harvaeana. 1727.

[*Kiss My A— Is No Treason; or, An Historical and Critical Dissertation upon the Art of Selling Bargains.* 1728.]

[*Gulliver Decypher'd.* 1728.]

An Account of the State of Learning in the Empire of Lilliput. 1728.

[*The Congress of the Bees; or, Political Remarks on the Bees Swarming at St. James's.* 1728.]

A Brief Account of Mr. John Ginglicutt's Treatise concerning the Altercation or Scolding of the Ancients. 1731.

An Essay concerning the Nature of Aliments, and the Choice of Them, According to the Different Constitutions of Human Bodies. 1731. 2 vols.

[*Harmony in an Uproar: A Letter to F—d—k H—d—l, Esq.* 1731.]

An Essay concerning the Effects of Air upon Human Bodies. 1733.

The Freeholder's Political Catechism. 1733.

ΓΝΩΘΙ ΣΕΑΥΤΟΝ: *Know Thyself.* 1734.

[*Critical Remarks on Capt. Gulliver's Travels.* 1735.]

Memoirs of the Extraordinary Life, Works and Discoveries, of Martinus Scriblerus (with Alexander Pope). 1741.

[*The History of John Bull: Part III.* 1744.]

Miscellanies. 1746.

Miscellaneous Works. 1751. 2 vols.

Life and Works. Ed. George A. Aitken. 1892.

GEORGE LILLO (1693–1739)

Silvia; or, The Country Burial. 1730.

The London Merchant; or, The History of George Barnwell. 1731.

The Christian Hero. 1735.

Fatal Curiosity. 1737.

Marina (adaptation). 1738.

Elmerick; or, Justice Triumphant. 1740.

Britannia and Batavia: A Masque. 1740.

Works. 1740.

Arden of Feversham (adaptation; with John Hoadly). 1762.

Works. Ed. Thomas Davies. 1775. 2 vols.

The London Merchant and Fatal Curiosity. Ed. Adolphus William Ward. 1906.

THOMAS TICKELL (1685–1740)

Oxford. 1707.

A Poem, to His Excellency the Lord Privy-Seal, on the Prospect of Peace. 1713.

The Prologue to the University of Oxford. 1713.

An Imitation of the Prophecy of Nereus: From Horace, Book I. Ode XV. 1715.

The First Book of Homer's Iliad (translator). 1715.

An Epistle from a Lady in England to a Gentleman at Avignon. 1717.

An Ode, Occasioned by His Excellency the Earl Stanhope's Voyage to France. 1718.

An Ode Inscribed to the Right Honourable the Earl of Sunderland at Windsor. 1720.

Works by Joseph Addison (editor). 1721. 4 vols.

Kensington Garden. 1722.

To Sir Godfrey Kneller, at His Country Seat. 1722.

Lucy and Colin: A Song, Written in Imitation of William and Margaret. 1725.

A Poem in Praise of the Horn-Book. 1728.

On Her Majesty's Re-building the Lodgings of the Black Prince, and Henry V, at Queen's-College, Oxford. 1733.

Poetical Works. 1796.

Poetical Works. Ed. Thomas Park. 1807.

Poetical Works (with Thomas Parnell). 1854.

RICHARD BENTLEY (1662–1742)

The Folly of Atheism, and (What Is Now Called) Deism. 1692.

Matter and Motion Cannot Think; or, A Confutation of Atheism from the Faculties of the Soul. 1692.

A Confutation of Atheism from the Structure and Origin of Humane Bodies. 1692. 3 parts.

A Confutation of Atheism from the Origin and Frame of the World. 1692–93. 3 parts.

The Folly and Unreasonableness of Atheism. 1693. 8 parts.

Of Revelation and the Messias. 1696.

Callimachi Hymni, Epigrammata, et Fragmenta (editor; with J. G. Graevius). 1697. 2 vols.

A Proposal for Building a Royal Library. 1697.

Dissertation upon the Epistles of Phalaris; with an Answer to the Objections of the Honourable Charles Boyle. 1699.

Emendationes in Menandri et Philemonis Reliquias, ex Nupera Editione Joannis Clerici. 1710.

The Present State of Trinity College in Cambridg, in a Letter from Dr. Bentley to the Right Reverend John Lord Bishop of Ely. 1710.

Q. Horatius Flaccus (editor). 1711.

Remarks upon a Late Discourse of Free-Thinking, in a Letter to F. H. D. D. 1713.

A Sermon upon Popery. 1715.

A Sermon Preached before His Majesty, King George, at His Royal Chapel of St. James's. 1717.

Ἡ Καινη ΔιαΘηκη *Graece: Proposals for Printing.* 1720.

P. Terentii Afri Comoediae; Phaedri Fabulae Aesopiae; Publii Syri et Aliorum Veterum Sententiae (editor). 1726.

The Case of Trinity College in Cambridge: Whether the Crown or the Bishop of Ely Be the General Visitor. 1729.

Paradise Lost by John Milton (editor). 1732.

M. Manilii Astronomicon (editor). 1739.

Richardi Bentleii et Doctorum Virorum Epistolae. Ed. Charles Burney. 1807.

Epistolae Bentleii, Graevii, Ruhnkenii, Wyttenbachii Selectae. Ed. Friedrich Karl Kraft. 1831.

Works. Ed. Alexander Dyce. 1836–38. 3 vols.

Correspondence. Ed. Christopher Wordsworth. 1842. 2 vols.

Critica Sacra. Ed. Arthur Ayres Ellis. 1862.

Bentley's Plautine Emendations from His Copy of Gronovius. Ed. E. A. Sonnenschein. 1883.

Some Letters of Richard Bentley. Ed. Elfriede Hulshoff Pol. 1959.

RICHARD SAVAGE (c. 1697–1743)

The Convocation; or, A Battle of Pamphlets. 1717.

Love in a Veil. 1719.

The Tragedy of Sir Thomas Overbury. 1724.

The Authors of the Town: A Satire Inscribed to the Author of The Universal Passion. 1725.

Miscellaneous Poems and Translations (editor). 1726.

A Poem Sacred to the Glorious Memory of Our Late Most Gracious Sovereign Lord, King George. 1727.

The Bastard. 1728.

[*Nature in Perfection; or, The Mother Unveil'd.* 1728.]

An Author to Be Lett. 1729. 1 no.

The Wanderer. 1729.

Verses Occasion'd by the Right Honourable the Lady Viscountess Tyrconnel's Recovery at Bath. 1730.

A Poem to the Memory of Mrs. Oldfield. 1730.

A Collection of Pieces in Verse and Prose, Which Have Been Publish'd on Occasion of the Dunciad (editor). 1732.

The Volunteer Laureat: A Poem Most Humbly Address'd to Her Majesty on Her Birth-day. 1732.

An Epistle to the Right Honourable Sir Robert Walpole. 1732.

The Volunteer-Laureat: Most Humbly Inscribed to Her Majesty, on Her Birth-day. 1733.

On the Departure of the Prince and Princess of Orange. 1734.

⟨*The Volunteer Laureat.*⟩ 1734. Lost.

The Progress of a Divine: A Satire. 1735.

A Poem on the Birth-day of the Prince of Wales. 1735.

The Volunteer-Laureat: Most Humbly Inscribed to Her Majesty, on Her Birth-day. 1735.

The Volunteer Laureat: A Poem on Her Majesty's Birthday. 1736.

Of Public Spirit in Regard to Public Works: An Epistle to His Royal Highness Frederick, Prince of Wales. 1737.

The Volunteer Laureat: An Ode on Her Majesty's Birth-day. 1737.

Volunteer Laureat, Number VII: A Poem Sacred to the Memory of the Late Queen. 1738.

London and Bristol Compar'd: A Satire. 1744.

Various Poems: The Wanderer; The Triumph of Mirth and Health; and The Bastard. 1761.

Works. 1775. 2 vols.

Poetical Works. 1791. 2 vols.

Poetical Works. Ed. Clarence Tracy. 1962.

HENRY CAREY (c. 1687–1743)

The Records of Love. 1710. 12 nos.

Poems on Several Occasions. 1713.

The Contrivances; or, More Ways Than One. 1715.

Hanging and Marriage; or, The Dead-Man's Wedding. 1722.

Namby-Pamby; or, A Panegyrick on the New Versification Addressed to A⟨mbrose⟩ P⟨hillips⟩. 1725.

A Hue and a Cry after M——k, Late Master to a Corporation in the City of Dublin. 1726.

A Learned Dissertation on Dumpling. 1726.

Mocking Is Catching; or, A Pastoral Lamentation for the Loss of a Man and No Man. 1726.

Faustina; or, The Roman Songstress: A Satyr, on the Luxury and Effeminacy of the Age. c. 1726.

Pudding and Dumpling Burnt to Pot; or, A Compleat Key to the Dissertation on Dumpling. 1727.

The Grumbletonians; or, The Dogs without-Doors: A Tale. 1727.

[The Disappointment. 1732.]

The Tragedy of Chrononhotonthologos. 1734.

Of Stage Tyrants: An Epistle to the Right Honourable Philip Earl of Chesterfield. 1735.

The Honest Yorkshire-man. 1736.

Margery; or, A Worse Plague Than the Dragon. 1738.

An Ode to Mankind: Address'd to the Prince of Wales. 1741.

Cupid and Hymen: A Voyage to the Isles of Love and Matrimony. 1742.

Dramatick Works. 1743.

Songs and Poems. Ed. Moira Gibbings. 1924.

Poems. Ed. Frederick T. Wood. 1930.

ALEXANDER POPE (1688–1744)

An Essay on Criticism. 1711.

Windsor-Forest. 1713.

Ode for Musick ⟨Ode on St. Cecilia's Day⟩. 1713.

Proposals for a Translation of Homer's Ilias. 1713.

The Narrative of Dr. Robert Norris. 1713.

The Rape of the Lock: An Heroi-comical Poem. 1714.

The Temple of Fame: A Vision. 1715.

A Key to the Lock; or, A Treatise Proving, beyond All Contradiction, the Dangerous Tendency of a Late Poem, Entituled, The Rape of the Lock, to Government and Religion. 1715.

The Dignity, Use and Abuse of Glass-Bottles. 1715.

The Iliad of Homer (translator). 1715 [Books 1–4]; 1716 [Books 5–8]; 1717 [Books 9–12]; 1718 [Books 13–16]; 1720 [Books 17–21]; 1720 [Books 22–24].

A Full and True Account of a Horrid and Barbarous Revenge by Poison on the Body of Mr. Edmund Curll, Bookseller. 1716.

To the Ingenious Mr. Moore, Author of the Celebrated Worm-Powder. 1716.

A Further Account of the Most Deplorable Condition of Mr. Edmund Curll, Bookseller. 1716.

A Roman Catholick Version of the First Psalm. 1716.

God's Revenge against Punning. 1716.

Pope's Miscellany (editor). 1717. 2 vols.

Three Hours after Marriage (with John Gay and John Arbuthnot). 1717.

The Court Ballad. 1717.

Works. 1717 [Volume 1]; 1735 [Volume 2].

A Complete Key to the Non-Juror. 1718.

Eloisa to Abelard. 1719.

Duke upon Duke. 1720.

The Works of John Sheffield, Duke of Buckingham (editor). 1723.

The Works of Shakespear (editor). 1723–25. 6 vols.

The Odyssey of Homer (translator). 1725 [Books 1–4]; 1725 [Books 5–9]; 1725 [Books 10–14]; 1726 [Books 15–19]; 1726 [Books 20–24].

The Discovery. 1727.

A Receipt to Make a Soop. 1727.

Miscellanies in Prose and Verse (with Jonathan Swift and John Arbuthnot). 1727 [Volumes 1–2]; 1732 [Volume 3].

The Dunciad. 1728.

Posthumous Works in Prose and Verse by William Wycherley (editor; with Lewis Theobald). 1728–29. 2 vols.

The Dunciad Variorum. 1729.

An Epistle to the Right Honourable Richard Earl of Burlington ⟨Moral Essays 4⟩. 1731.

Of the Use of Riches: An Epistle to the Right Honourable Allen Lord Bathurst ⟨Moral Essays 3⟩. 1733.

The First Satire of the Second Book of Horace (adaptation). 1733.

An Essay on Man. 1733 [Epistle 1]; 1733 [Epistle 2]; 1733 [Epistle 3]; 1734 [Epistle 4].

The Impertinent by John Donne (adaptation). 1733.

An Epistle to the Right Honourable Richard Lord Visc^t. Cobham ⟨Moral Essays 1⟩. 1734.

The Second Satire of the Second Book of Horace (adaptation). 1734.

Sober Advice from Horace. 1734.

An Epistle to Dr. Arbuthnot. 1735.

Of the Characters of Women: An Epistle to a Lady ⟨Moral Essays 2⟩. 1735.

Letters (with Sir William Trumbull, Richard Steele, and Joseph Addison). 1735.

A Narrative of the Method by Which the Private Letters of Mr. Pope Have Been Procured and Published by Edmund Curll. 1735.

Ethic Epistles, Satires, &c. 1735.

New Letters (with others). 1736.

Poems: A Chosen Selection. 1736.

Works. 1736. 4 vols.

Horace: His Ode to Venus (adaptation). 1737.

Works in Prose. 1737 [Volume 1]; 1741 [Volume 2].

The Second Epistle of the Second Book of Horace (adaptation). 1737.

The First Epistle of the Second Book of Horace (adaptation). 1737.

The Sixth Epistle of the First Book of Horace (adaptation). 1738.

An Imitation of the Sixth Satire of the Second Book of Horace. 1738.

The First Epistle of the First Book of Horace (adaptation). 1738.

One Thousand Seven Hundred and Thirty Eight. 1738.

The Universal Prayer. 1738.

Poems and Imitations of Horace. 1738.

Selecta Poemata Italorum Qui Latine Scripserunt (editor). 1740. 2 vols.

Memoirs of the Extraordinary Life, Works, and Discoveries of Martinus Scriblerus (with John Arbuthnot). 1741.

The New Dunciad. 1742.

A Blast upon Bays; or, A New Lick at the Laureate. 1742.

Verses on the Grotto at Twickenham. 1743.

Last Will and Testament. 1744.

The Character of Katharine, Late Duchess of Buckingham and Normanby. 1746.

Works. Ed. William Warburton. 1751. 9 vols.

Works. Ed. Joseph Warton. 1797. 9 vols.

Works. Ed. William Lisle Bowles. 1806. 10 vols.

Works. Ed. Alexander Dyce. 1831. 3 vols.

Works. Ed. Robert Carruthers. 1853. 4 vols.

Works. Eds. Whitwell Elwin and William John Courthope. 1871–89. 10 vols.

Collected Poems. Ed. Bonamy Dobrée. 1924.

The Best of Pope. Ed. George Sherburn. 1929.

Prose Works. Eds. Norman Ault and Maynard Mack. 1936. Vol. 1 only.

Works (Twickenham Edition). Eds. John Butt et al. 1939–69. 11 vols.

Selected Poetry and Prose. Ed. W. K. Wimsatt. 1951.

Correspondence. Ed. George Sherburn. 1956. 5 vols.

Poetical Works. Ed. Herbert Davis. 1966.

LEWIS THEOBALD (1688–1744)

A Pindarick Ode on the Union. 1707.

Naufragium Britannicum: A Panegyrical Poem. 1707.

The Life and Character of Marcus Portius Cato (translator). 1713.

Plato's Dialogue of the Immortality of the Soul ⟨Phaedo⟩ (translator). 1713.

The Mausoleum: A Poem Sacred to the Memory of Her Late Majesty Queen Anne. 1714.

The Cave of Poverty: A Poem Written in Imitation of Shakespeare. 1714.

A Critical Discourse upon the Iliad *of Homer by Antoine Houdart de la Motte* (translator). 1714.

Electra by Sophocles (translator). 1714.

Ajax by Sophocles (translator). 1714.

Plutus by Aristophanes (translator). 1715.

The Clouds by Aristophanes (translator). 1715.

Monsieur LeClerc's Observations upon Mr. Addison's Travels through Italy (translator). 1715.

Oedipus King of Thebes by Sophocles (translator). 1715.

The Persian Princess; or, The Royal Villain. 1715.

A Complete Key to the Last New Farce, The What D'Ye Call It (with Benjamin Griffin). 1715.

The Perfidious Brother by Henry Mestayer (revised by Theobald). 1715.

The Censor. 1715, 1717. 96 nos.

A Translation of Book I of the Odyssey (translator). 1716.

The History of the Loves of Antiochus and Stratonice: In Which Are Interspers'd Some Accounts Relating to Greece and Syria. 1717.

Memoirs of Sir Walter Raleigh. 1719.

The Tragedy of King Richard the II (adaptation). 1720.

A Dramatick Entertainment, Call'd Harlequin, a Sorcerer; with the Loves of Pluto and Proserpine. 1725.

Shakespeare Restored; or, A Specimen of the Many Errors, as Well Committed, as Unamended, by Mr. Pope in His Late Edition of This Poet. 1726.

Double Falsehood; or, The Distrest Lovers (adaptation). 1728.

The Posthumous Works of William Wycherley (editor; with Alexander Pope). 1728–29. 2 vols.

Perseus and Andromeda. 1730.

A Miscellany of Original Poems, Translations, &c. (editor). 1732.

An Epistle Humbly Addressed to the Right Honourable John, Earl of Orrery. 1732.

The Works of Shakespeare (editor). 1733. 7 vols.

The Fatal Secret. 1735.

JONATHAN SWIFT (1667–1745)

A Discourse of the Contests and Dissensions between the Nobles and the Commons in Athens and Rome. 1701.

A Tale of a Tub, Written for the Universal Improvement of Mankind; to Which Is Added an Account of a Battel between the Antient and Modern Books in St. James's Library. 1704.

Predictions for the Year 1708, by Isaac Bickerstaff Esq. 1708.

The Accomplishment of the First of Mr. Bickerstaff's Predictions: Being an Account of the Death of Mr. Partrige. 1708.

An Elegy on Mr. Patrige, the Almanack-Maker. 1708.

A Vindication of Isaac Bickerstaff Esq. 1709.

A Letter from a Member of the House of Commons in Ireland to a Member of the House of Commons in England, concerning the Sacramental Test. 1709.

Baucis and Philemon, Imitated from Ovid. 1709.

A Meditation upon a Broom-Stick. 1710.

The Virtues of Sid Hamet the Magician's Rod. 1710.

A Learned Comment upon Dr. Hare's Excellent Sermon Preach'd before the D. of Marlborough on the Surrender of Bouchain (with Mary de la Rivière Manley). 1711.

An Apology for the Tale of a Tub. 1711.

A Short Character of His Excellency T. E. of W⟨harton⟩. 1711.

Some Remarks upon a Pamphlet, Entitl'd, A Letter to the Seven Lords of the Committee Appointed to Examine Gregg. 1711.

Miscellanies in Prose and Verse. 1711.

A New Journey to Paris by Sieur de Baudrier (translator). 1711.

The Conduct of the Allies. 1711.

An Excellent New Song: Being the Intended Speech of a Famous Orator against Peace. 1711.

The W—ds—r Prophecy. 1711.

Some Advice Humbly Offer'd to the Members of the October Club, in a Letter from a Person of Honour. 1712.

The Fable of Midas. 1712.

Some Remarks on the Barrier Treaty between Her Majesty and the States-General. 1712.

A Proposal for Correcting, Improving, and Ascertaining the English Tongue. 1712.

Some Reasons to Prove, That No Person Is Obliged by His Principles, as a Whig, to Oppose Her Majesty or Her Present Ministry. 1712.

T—l—nd's Invitation to Dismal, to Dine with the Calves-Head Club. 1712.

Peace and Dunkirk. 1712.

A Hue and Cry after Dismal. 1712.

Dunkirk Still in the Hands of the French. 1712. Lost.

A Letter from the Pretender to a Whig-Lord. 1712.

A Letter of Thanks from My Lord W****n to the Lord B^p of S. Asaph. 1712.

Mr. C——n's Discourse of Free-Thinking. 1713.

Part of the Seventh Epistle of the First Book of Horace Imitated. 1713.

The Importance of the Guardian Considered. 1713.

A Preface to the B——p of S–r–m's Introduction to the Third Volume of the History of the Reformation of the Church of England. 1713.

The First Ode of the Second Book of Horace Paraphras'd. 1714.

The Publick Spirit of the Whigs. 1714.

A Rebus Written by a Lady, on the Rev. D—n S——t, with His Answer. c. 1714.

A Letter from a Lay-Patron to a Gentleman, Designing for Holy Orders. 1720.

A Proposal for the Universal Use of Irish Manufacture. 1720.

An Elegy on the Much Lamented Death of Mr. Demar. 1720.

Miscellaneous Works Comical and Diverting. 1720.

Run upon the Bankers. 1720.

The Bubble. 1721.

The Present Miserable State of Ireland. 1721.

Epilogue to Be Spoke at the Theatre-Royal This Present Saturday in the Behalf of the Distressed Weavers. 1721.

The Bank Thrown Down. 1721.

[*Subscribers to the Bank Plac'd According to Their Order and Quality.* 1721.]

[*A Letter to the K⟨ing⟩ at Arms from a Reputed Esquire, One of the Subscribers to the Bank.* 1721.]

[*The Wonderful Wonder of Wonders.* 1722.]

The Last Speech and Dying Words of Ebenezor Elliston. 1722.

The First of April. c. 1723.

Some Arguments against Enlarging the Power of Bishops in Letting of Leases. 1723.

A Letter to the Shop-Keepers, Tradesmen, Farmers, and Common People of Ireland, concerning the Brass Half-Pence Coined by Mr. Woods, by M. B. Drapier. 1724.

A Letter to Mr. Harding the Printer, by M. B. Drapier. 1724.

Some Observations upon a Paper, Call'd, The Report of the Committee of the Most Honourable the Privy-Council in England, Relating to Wood's Half-Pence, *by M. B. Drapier.* 1724.

A Serious Poem upon William Wood. 1724.

A Letter to the Whole People of Ireland, by M. B. Drapier. 1724.

To His Grace the Arch-Bishop of Dublin. 1724.

An Excellent New Song upon His Grace Our Good Lord Archbishop of Dublin. 1724.

Prometheus. 1724.

Seasonable Advice. 1724.

The Presentment of the Grand-Jury of the County of the City of Dublin. 1724.

A Letter to the Right Honourable the Lord Viscount Molesworth, by M. B. Drapier. 1724.

[*A Second Letter from a Friend to the Right Honourable —— ——.* 1725.]

His Grace's Answer to Jonathan. 1725.

Sphinx. 1725.

Fraud Detected; or, The Hibernian Patriot ⟨The Drapier's Letters⟩. 1725.

A Letter from D. S——t. to D. S⟨medle⟩y. 1725.

The Birth of Manly Virtue, from Callimachus. 1725.

A Riddle by the Revd. Doctor S——t to My Lady C⟨artere⟩t. 1725.

Cadenus and Vanessa. 1726.

Travels into Several Remote Nations of the World, in Four Parts, by Lemuel Gulliver, First a Surgeon, and Then a Captain of Several Ships ⟨Gulliver's Travels⟩. 1726. 2 vols.

[*A Letter to the Freemen and Freeholders of the City of Dublin.* 1727.]

[*Advice to the Electors of the City of Dublin.* 1727.]

Miscellanies in Prose and Verse (with Alexander Pope and John Arbuthnot). 1727 [Volumes 1–2]; 1732 [Volume 3].

A Short View of the State of Ireland. 1728.

An Answer to a Paper, Called, A Memorial of the Poor Inhabitants, Tradesmen, and Labourers of the Kingdom of Ireland. 1728.

The Intelligencer (with Thomas Sheridan). 1728. 20 nos.

The Journal of a Dublin Lady. 1729.

A Modest Proposal for Preventing the Children of Poor People from Being a Burthen to Their Parents, or the Country, and for Making Them Beneficial to the Publick. 1729.

On Paddy's Character of the Intelligencer. c. 1729.

An Epistle to His Excellency John Lord Carteret, Lord Lieutenant of Ireland. 1730.

An Epistle upon an Epistle from a Certain Doctor to a Certain Great Lord. 1730.

An Epistle to His Excellency John Lord Carteret; to Which Is Added an Epistle upon an Epistle: Being a Christmas-Box for Doctor D⟨ela⟩ny. 1730.

A Libel on D—— D—— and a Certain Great Lord. 1730.

A Panegyric on the Reverend D—n S——t. 1730.

To Doctor D–L—Y, on the Libels Writ against Him. 1730.

An Answer to Dr. D——ny's Fable of the Pheasant and the Lark. 1730.

Lady A–S–N Weary of the Dean. 1730.

An Apology to the Lady C—R—T on Her Inviting Dean S–F–T to Dinner. 1730.

A Vindication of His Excellency the Lord C——T, from the Charge of Favouring None but Tories, High-Churchmen and Jacobites. 1730.

An Excellent New Ballad; or, The True En——sh D—n to Be Hanged for a R–pe. 1730.

Horace, Book I. Ode XIV., Paraphrased and Inscribed to Ir——d. 1730.

Traulus. 1730. 2 parts.

With favour and fortune fastidiously blest. c. 1730.

Helter Skelter; or, The Hue and Cry after the Attornies, Going to Ride the Circuit. 1730.

The Place of the Damn'd. 1730.

A Proposal Humbly Offer'd to the P——t, for the More Effectual Preventing the Further Growth of Popery. 1731.

A Soldier and a Scholar; or, The Lady's Judgment upon Those Two Characters in the Persons of Captain —— and D—n S——T. 1732.

Considerations upon Two Bills Sent Down from the R—— H—— the H—— of L—to the H—ble H—— of C—— Relating to the Clergy of I*****D. 1732.

An Examination of Certain Abuses, Corruptions, and Enormities in the City of Dublin. 1732.

An Elegy on Dicky and Dolly. 1732.

The Lady's Dressing Room; to Which Is Added a Poem on Cutting Down the Old Thorn at Market Hill. 1732.

The Advantages Propos'd by Repealing the Sacramental Test, Impartially Considered. 1732.

Quaeries Wrote by Dr. J. Swift in the Year 1732, Very Proper to Be Read (at This Time) by Every Member of the Established Church. c. 1732.

An Answer to a Late Scandalous Poem, Wherein the Author Most Audaciously Presumes to Cast Indignity upon Their Highnesses the Clouds, by Comparing Them to a Woman. 1733.

The Life and Genuine Character of Doctor Swift. 1733.

A Serious and Useful Scheme to Make an Hospital for Incurables; to Which Is Added a Petition of the Footmen in and about Dublin. 1733.

Some Considerations Humbly Offered to the Right Honourable the Lord-Mayor, the Court of Aldermen, and Common Council of the Honourable City of Dublin, in the Choice of a Recorder. 1733.

The Drapier's Miscellany. 1733.

The Presbyterians Plea of Merit in Order to Take Off the Test, Impartially Examined. 1733.

Advice to the Free-Men of the City of Dublin. 1733.

An Epistle to a Lady, Who Desired the Author to Make Verses on Her, in the Heroick Stile; Also a Poem, Occasion'd by Reading Dr. Young's Satires, Called, The Universal Passion. 1733.

On Poetry: A Rhapsody. 1733.

Some Reasons against the Bill for Settling the Tyth of Hemp, Flax, &c. by a Modus. 1734.

A Beautiful Young Nymph Going to Bed, Written for the Honour of the Fair Sex; to Which Are Added Strephon and Chloe, and Cassinus and Peter. 1734.

Miscellanies in Prose and Verse: Volume the Fifth. 1735.

A Collection of Poems, &c., Omitted in the Fifth Volume of Miscellanies. 1735.

The Furniture of a Woman's Mind. c. 1735.

Works. 1735. 4 vols.

Poetical Works. 1736.

Reasons Why We Should Not Lower the Coins Now Current in This Kingdom. 1736.

A Proposal for Giving Badges to the Beggars in All the Parishes of Dublin. 1737.

Works. 1738. 6 vols.

Political Tracts. 1738. 2 vols.

An Imitation of the Sixth Satire of the Second Book of Horace. 1738.

The Beasts Confession to the Priest, on Observing How Most Men Mistake Their Own Talents. 1738.

A Complete Collection of Genteel and Ingenious Conversation, According to the Most Polite Mode and Method Now Used at Court, and in the Best Companies of England, in Three Dialogues. 1738.

Verses on the Death of Doctor Swift. 1739.

Some Free Thoughts upon the Present State of Affairs, Written in the Year 1714. 1741.

Letters to and from Dr. Jonathan Swift from the Year 1714 to 1737. 1741.

Three Sermons. 1744.

Directions to Servants. 1745.

Works. 1746. 8 vols.

The Story of the Injured Lady. 1746.

A True Copy of the Late Rev. Dr. Jonathan Swift's Will. 1746.

Works. 1751. 14 vols.

Brotherly Love: A Sermon. 1754.

Works. Ed. John Hawkesworth. 1755. 12 vols.

The History of the Four Last Years of the Queen. 1758.

Works. 1763. 11 vols.

Sermons. 1763.

Letters Written by the Late Jonathan Swift, D.D., and Several of His Friends. Eds. John Hawkesworth and Deane Swift. 1768–69. 6 vols.

Works. 1768. 13 vols.

Works. 1772. 20 vols.

Works. Eds. John Hawkesworth et al. 1774. 15 vols.

Poetical Works. 1778. 4 vols.

The Beauties of Swift. 1782.

Works. Ed. Thomas Sheridan. 1784. 17 vols.

Miscellaneous Pieces, in Prose and Verse, Not Inserted in Mr. Sheridan's Edition of the Dean's Works. 1789.

Sermons. 1790. 2 vols.

Works. 1801. 19 vols.

Works. Ed. Sir Walter Scott. 1814. 19 vols.

Poetical Works. Ed. John Mitford. 1833–34. 3 vols.

Prose Works. Ed. Temple Scott. 1898–1909. 12 vols.

Unpublished Letters. Ed. George Birkbeck Hill. 1899.

The Journal to Stella. Ed. George A. Aitken. 1901.

Poems. Ed. W. E. Browning. 1910. 2 vols.

Correspondence. Ed. F. Erlington Ball. 1910–14. 6 vols.

Vanessa and Her Correspondence with Swift. Ed. A. M. Freeman. 1921.

Satires and Personal Writings. Ed. William Alfred Eddy. 1932.

Letters to Charles Ford. Ed. David Nichol Smith. 1935.

The Drapier's Letters to the People of Ireland. Ed. Herbert Davis. 1935.

Poems. Ed. Harold Williams. 1937. 3 vols.

Prose Works. Ed. Herbert Davis. 1939–68. 14 vols.

The Journal to Stella. Ed. Harold Williams. 1948. 2 vols.

An Enquiry into the Behaviour of the Queen's Last Ministry. Ed. Irvin Ehrenpreis. 1956.

Collected Poems. Ed. Joseph Horrell. 1956. 2 vols.

Correspondence. Ed. Harold Williams. 1963–65. 5 vols.

Poetical Works. Ed. Herbert Davis. 1967.

Complete Poems. Ed. Pat Rogers. 1983.

Jonathan Swift. Eds. Angus Ross and David Woolley. 1984.

Account Books. Eds. Paul V. Thompson and Dorothy Jay Thompson. 1984.

FRANCIS HUTCHESON (1694–1746)

An Inquiry into the Original of Our Ideas of Beauty and Virtue. 1725.

Alterations and Additions Made in the Second Edition of the Inquiry into Beauty and Virtue. 1726.

An Essay on the Nature and Conduct of the Passions and Affections, with Illustrations on the Moral Sense. 1728.

De Naturali Hominum Socialitate Oratio Inauguralis. 1730.

Considerations on Patronages: Addressed to the Gentlemen of Scotland. 1735.

Letters between the Late Mr. Gilbert Burnet and Mr. Hutchinson, concerning the True Foundation of Virtue or Moral Goodness. 1735.

Metaphysicae Synopsis, Ontologiam et Pneumatologiam Complectens. 1742.

Philosophiae Moralis Institutio Compendiaria. 1742.

The Meditations of M. Aurelius Antoninus (translator). 1742.

Reflections upon Laughter, and Remarks upon the Fable of the Bees. 1750.

A System of Moral Philosophy. Ed. Francis Hutcheson the Younger. 1755. 2 vols.

Logicae Compendium. 1759.

An Inquiry concerning Beauty, Order, Harmony, Design. Ed. Peter Kivy. 1973.

ISAAC WATTS (1674–1748)

Horae Lyricae: Poems Chiefly of the Lyric Kind. 1706.

Hymns and Spiritual Songs. 1707.

A Sermon Preach'd at Salters-Hall, to the Societies for Reformation of Manners, in the Cities of London and Westminster. 1707.

An Essay against Uncharitableness. 1707.

A Guide to Prayer; or, A Free and Rational Account of the Gift, Grace, and Spirit of Prayer. 1715.

Divine Songs Attempted in Easy Language for the Use of Children. 1715.

The Psalms of David Imitated. 1719.

Sermons on Various Subjects. 1721–27. 3 vols.

The Art of Reading and Writing English. 1721.

The Christian Doctrine of the Trinity. 1722.

Death and Heaven; or, The Last Enemy Conquer'd and Separate Spirits Made Perfect. 1722.

A Hopeful Youth Falling Short of Heaven. 1723.

Three Dissertations Relating to the Christian Doctrine of the Trinity. 1724.

Logick; or, The Right Use of Reason in the Enquiry after Truth. 1725.

Dissertations Relating to the Christian Doctrine of the Trinity: The Second Part. 1725.

The Knowledge of the Heavens and Earth Made Easy. 1726.

A Defense against the Temptation to Self-Murther. 1726.

The Religious Improvement of Publick Events. 1727.

Prayers Composed for the Use and Imitation of Children. 1728.

An Essay towards the Encouragement of Charity Schools. 1728.

A Caveat against Infidelity. 1729.

Discourses of the Love of God and the Use and Abuse of the Passions in Religion. 1729.

Catechisms. 1730.

An Humble Attempt towards the Revival of Practical Religion among Christians, and Particularly the Protestant Dissenters. 1731.

The Strength and Weakness of Human Reason. 1731.

A Sermon on Occasion of the Decease of Mrs. Sarah Abney. 1732.

A Short View of the Whole Scripture History. 1732.

An Essay on the Freedom of the Will in God and in Creatures. 1732.

An Essay toward the Proof of a Separate State of Souls between Death and Resurrection. 1732.

The Doctrine of the Passions Explain'd and Improv'd. 1732.

Philosophical Essays on Various Subjects; with Some Remarks on Mr. Locke's Essay on the Human Understanding. 1733.

A Preservative from the Sins and Follies of Childhood and Youth. 1734.

Reliquiae Juveniles. 1734.

A Discourse on the Way of Instruction by Catechisms, and of the Best Manner of Composing Them. 1736.

Watt's Compleat Spelling-Book. 1737.

The Redeemer and the Sanctifier. 1737.

Humility Represented in the Character of St. Paul. 1737.

The Holiness of Times, Places, and People under the Jewish and Christian Dispensations Consider'd and Compared. 1738.

A New Essay on Civil Power in Things Sacred. 1739.

Self-Love and Vertue Reconciled Only by Religion. 1739.

The World to Come; or, Discourses on the Joys or Sorrows of Departed Souls at Death. 1739, 1945 (2 vols.).

Serious Considerations concerning the Doctrines of Election and Reprobation. Ed. John Wesley. 1740.

The Ruin and Recovery of Mankind. 1740.

The Improvement of the Mind; or, A Supplement to the Art of Logick. 1741.

The Harmony of All the Religions Which God Ever Prescribed. 1742.

A Faithful Enquiry after the Ancient and Original Doctrine of the Trinity. 1745. Part 1 only.

Orthodoxy and Charity United. 1745.

Useful and Important Questions concerning Jesus, the Son of God. 1746.

The Glory of Christ as God-Man Display'd. 1746.

Evangelical Discourses on Several Subjects. 1747.

The Rational Foundation of a Christian Church, and the Terms of Christian Communion. 1747.

Works. Eds. David Jennings and Philip Doddridge. 1753. 6 vols.

Posthumous Works. Eds. David Jennings and Philip Doddridge. 1754.

Works. Ed. Edward Parsons. 1800. 7 vols.

Some Cursory Remarks on Reading the Book of Common Prayer, the Articles of Religion, and the Ordering of Bishops, Priests and Deacons. Ed. Gabriel Watts. 1801.

Poetical Works. Ed. Thomas Park. 1807. 2 vols.

Works. Ed. George Burder. 1810–11. 9 vols.

Nine Sermons Preached in the Years 1718–19. Ed. John Pye Smith. 1812.

Four Letters. Ed. Samuel A. Green. 1898.

JAMES THOMSON (1700–1748)

Winter. 1726.

Summer. 1727.

A Poem Sacred to the Memory of Sir Isaac Newton. 1727.

Spring. 1728.

Britannia. 1729.

A Poem to the Memory of Mr. Congreve. 1729.

The Tragedy of Sophonisba. 1730.

The Seasons. 1730, 1744.

Winter; to Which Is Added His Three Following Poems, viz.: A Hymn on the Seasons, To the Memory of Sir Isaac Newton, and Britannia. 1730.

Autumn. 1730.

The Seasons, A Hymn, A Poem to the Memory of Sir Isaac Newton, and Britannia. 1730. 5 parts.

The Four Seasons and Other Poems. 1735. 4 parts.

Antient and Modern Italy Compared: Being the First Part of Liberty. 1735.

Greece: Being the Second Part of Liberty. 1735.

Rome: Being the Third Part of Liberty. 1735.

Britain: Being the Fourth Part of Liberty. 1736.

The Prospect: Being the Fifth Part of Liberty. 1736.

Works. 1736.

A Poem to the Memory of the Right Honourable the Lord Talbot, Late Chancellor of Great Britain. 1737.

Liberty. 1738.

Agamemnon. 1738.

Edward and Eleonora. 1739.

Alfred (with David Mallet). 1740.

Tancred and Sigismunda. 1745.

The Castle of Indolence: An Allegorical Poem. 1748.

Coriolanus. 1749.

Works. Ed. George, Lord Lyttelton. 1750. 4 vols.

Poems on Several Occasions. 1750.

A Collection of Letters Written to Aaron Hill, Esq. (with others). 1751.

Works. Ed. Patrick Murdoch. 1762. 2 vols.

Poetical Works. Ed. Sir Nicholas Harris Nicolas. 1830. 2 vols.

Poetical Works. Ed. George Gilfillan. 1853.

Poetical Works. Ed. William Michael Rossetti. 1873.

Poetical Works. Ed. D. C. Tovey. 1897. 2 vols.

The Seasons, The Castle of Indolence and Other Poems. Ed. Henry D. Roberts. 1906. 2 vols.

Complete Poetical Works. Ed. J. Logie Robertson. 1908.

Letters and Documents. Ed. Alan D. McKillop. 1958.

The Castle of Indolence and Other Poems. Ed. Alan D. McKillop. 1961.

The Seasons and The Castle of Indolence. Ed. James Sambrook. 1972.

The Seasons. Ed. James Sambrook. 1981.

Liberty, The Castle of Indolence, and Other Poems. Ed. James Sambrook. 1986.

AMBROSE PHILIPS (1674–1749)

Life of John Williams by John Hacket (revised by Philips). 1700.

Pastorals. 1710.

The Distrest Mother (adaptation). 1712.

An Epistle to the Right Honourable Charles Lord Halifax. 1714.

The Thousand and One Days: Persian Tales by François Petis de la Croix (translator). 1714–15. 3 vols.

The Pretender's Flight; or, A Mock Coronation. 1716.

An Epistle to the Honourable James Craggs, Esq. 1717.

The Freethinker. 1718–21. 350 nos.

The Briton. 1722.

Humfrey, Duke of Gloucester. 1723.

[*A Collection of Old Ballads* (editor). 1723–25. 3 vols.]

An Ode (in the Manner of Pindar) on the Death of the Right Honourable William, Earl of Cowper. 1723.

An Epilogue Spoke by Mr. Griffith, to Their Graces, the Duke and Dutchess of Grafton, at the Theatre-Royal in Dublin. c. 1724.

To the Honourable Miss Carteret. 1725.

Poems. 1725.

Three Tragedies, viz. The Distrest Mother; The Briton; Humfrey Duke of Gloucester. 1725.

To Miss Georgiana, Youngest Daughter of Lord Carteret. 1725.

A Supplication for Miss Carteret, in the Small-pox. 1725.

The Tea-pot; or, The Lady's Transformation. c. 1725.

To His Excellency the Lord Carteret, &c.: Departing from Dublin. 1726.

To Miss Pulteney, Daughter of Daniel Pulteney, Esq. 1727.

Pastorals, Epistles, Odes, and Other Original Poems, with Translations from Pindar, Anacreon, and Sappho. 1748.

Letters to Several Ministers of State by Hugh Boulter (editor). 1769–70. 2 vols.

Poems. Ed. Mary G. Segar. 1937.

AARON HILL (1685–1750)

Camillus. 1707.

The Invasion: A Poem to the Queen. 1708.

The Celebrated Speeches of Ajax and Ulysses by Ovid (translator; with Nahum Tate). 1708.

The Walking Statue; or, The Devil in the Wine-Cellar. 1709.

A Full and Just Account of the Present State of the Ottoman Empire in All Its Branches. 1709.

Elfrid; or, The Fair Inconstant; to Which is Added The Walking Statue. 1710.

The Dedication of the Beech-Tree. 1714.

An Impartial Account of the Nature, Benefit and Design of a New Discovery and Undertaking to Make a Pure, Sweet, and Wholesome Oil from the Fruit of the Beech Tree. 1714.

Proposals for Raising a Stock of One Hundred Thousand Pounds, for Laying Up Great Quantities of Beech-Mast for Two Years. 1714.

An Account of the Rise and Progress of the Beech-Oil Invention. 1715.

An Impartial State of the Case between the Patentee, Annuitants, and Sharers in the Beech-Oil Company. 1716.

The Fatal Vision; or, The Fall of Siam. 1716.

Four Essays. 1718.

The Northern-Star: Sacred to the Memory of the Immortal Czar of Russia. 1718.

The Creation: A Pindaric Illustration of a Poem Originally Written by Moses, on That Subject. 1720.

Gideon; or, The Resurrection of Israel. 1720, 1749 (as *Gideon; or, The Patriot*).

The Fatal Extravagance. 1720.

The Judgment-Day. 1721.

King Henry the Fifth; or, The Conquest of France by the English (adaptation). 1723.

The Plain-Dealer (with William Bond). 1724–25. 117 nos.

The Progress of Wit: A Caveat. 1730.

Advice to the Poets. 1731.

Athelwold. 1732.

[*See and Seem Blind; or, A Critical Dissertation on the Publick Diversions.* 1732.]

The Prompter (with William Popple). 1734–36. 173 nos.

The Tragedy of Zara by Voltaire (adaptation). 1736.

Alzira by Voltaire (adaptation). 1736.

The Tears of the Muses: In a Conference between Prince Germanicus, and a Male-content Party. 1737.

An Enquiry into the Merit of Assassination. 1738.

The Fanciad: An Heroic Poem. 1743.

The Impartial: An Address without Flattery. 1744.

The Art of Acting. 1746. Part 1 only.

Free Thoughts on Faith; or, The Religion of Reason. 1746.

Merope by Voltaire (adaptation). 1749.

The Roman Revenge (adaptation). 1753.

Works. 1753. 4 vols.

The Insolvent; or, Filial Piety. 1758.

Dramatic Works. 1760. 2 vols.

The Prompter (with William Popple; selections). Eds. William W. Appleton and Kalman A. Burnim. 1966.

HENRY ST. JOHN, VISCOUNT BOLINGBROKE (1678–1751)

A Letter to the Examiner. 1710.

[*Considerations upon the Secret History of the White Staff.* 1714.]

A Copy of My Lord Bolingbroke's Letter to My Lord ———. 1715.

The Representation of the Lord Viscount Bolingbroke. 1715.

The Craftsman. 1726–50. 965 nos.

The Occasional Writer. 1727. 3 nos.

[*Observations on the Publick Affairs of Great-Britain.* 1729.]

The Craftsman Extraordinary. 1729–34. 3 nos.

A Letter to Caleb D'Anvers, Esq., concerning the State of Affairs in Europe. 1730.

The Case of Dunkirk Faithfully Stated and Impartially Considered. 1730.

The Monumental Inscription on the Column at Blenheim-House. 1731.

A Final Answer to the Remarks on the Craftsman's Vindication. 1731.

The Freeholder's Political Catechism. 1733.

A Dissertation on Parties. 1735.

The Famous Dedication to the Pamphlet Entitled A Dissertation upon Parties. 1735.

Letters to a Young Nobleman on the Study and Use of History. 1738.

The Idea of a Patriot King. c. 1740.

[*A Congratulatory Letter to a Certain Right Honourable Person upon His Late Disappointment.* 1743.]

Remarks on the History of England. 1743.

A Collection of Political Tracts. 1748.

Letters on the Spirit of Patriotism; on the Idea of a Patriot King; and on the State of the Parties at the Accession of King George the First. 1749.

A Familiar Epistle to the Most Impudent Man Living. 1749.

Last Will and Testament. 1752.

Letters to Dr. Jonathan Swift. 1752.

Letters on the Study and Use of History. 1752. 2 vols.

Reflections concerning Innate Moral Principles. 1752.

A Letter to Sir William Windham; Some Reflections on the Present State of the Nation; A Letter to Mr. Pope. 1753.

Works. Ed. David Mallet. 1754. 5 vols.

Miscellaneous Works. 1768. 4 vols.

Letters and Correspondence. Ed. Gilbert Parke. 1798. 4 vols.

Extracts from the Political Writings. Ed. Stuart Erskine. 1897.

Historical Writings. Ed. Isaac Kramnick. 1972.

JOSEPH BUTLER (1692–1752)

Several Letters to the Reverend Dr. Clarke, Relating to the First Volume of the Sermons Preached at Mr. Boyle's Lecture. 1716.

Fifteen Sermons Preached at the Rolls Chapel. 1726.

The Analogy of Religion, Natural and Revealed, to the Constitution and Course of Nature. 1736.

A Sermon Preached before the Incorporated Society for the Propagation of the Gospel in Foreign Parts. 1739.

A Sermon Preached before the Right Honourable the Lord-Mayor. 1740.

A Sermon Preached before the House of Lords. 1741.

A Sermon Preached before the Parish-Church of Christ-Church, London. 1745.

A Sermon Preached before the House of Lords. 1747.

A Sermon Preached before His Grace Charles Duke of Richmond. 1748.

Fifteen Sermons Preached at the Rolls Chapel; to Which Are Added, Six Sermons Preached on Publick Occasions. 1749.

A Change Deliver'd to the Clergy, at the Primary Visitation of the Diocese of Durham. 1751.

Works. Ed. Samuel Halifax. 1804. 2 vols.

Some Remains. Ed. Edward Steere. 1853.

Sermons and Remains. Ed. Edward Steere. 1862.

Works. Ed. W. E. Gladstone. 1896. 2 vols.

Works. Ed. J. H. Bernard. 1900. 2 vols.

GEORGE BERKELEY (1685–1753)

Arithmetica absque Algebra aut Euclide Demonstrata. 1707.

An Essay towards a New Theory of Vision. 1709.

A Treatise concerning the Principles of Human Knowledge. 1710. Part 1 only.

Passive Obedience; or, The Christian Doctrine of Not Resisting the Supreme Power, Proved and Vindicated upon the Principles of the Law of Nature. 1712.

Three Dialogues between Hylas and Philonous. 1713.

Advice to the Tories Who Have Taken the Oath. 1715.

An Essay towards Preventing the Ruine of Great Britain. 1721.

De Motu; sive, De Motus Principio & Natura, et de Causa Communicationis Motuum. 1721.

A Proposal for the Better Supplying of Churches in Our Foreign Plantations, and for Converting the Savage Americans to Christianity, by a College to Be Erected in the Summer Islands, Otherwise Called the Isles of Bermudas. 1724.

A Sermon Preached before the Incorporated Society for the Propagation of the Gospel in Foreign Parts. 1732.

Alciphron; or, The Minute Philosopher: Containing an Apology for the Christian Religion, against Those Who Are Called Free-Thinkers. 1732. 2 vols.

The Theory of Vision; or, Visual Language: Shewing the Immediate Presence and Providence of a Deity, Vindicated and Explained. 1733.

The Analyst; or, A Discourse Addressed to an Infidel Mathematician. 1734.

A Defence of Free-Thinking in Mathematics. 1735.

Reasons for Not Replying to Mr. Walton's Full Answer in a Letter to P. T. P. 1735.

The Querist: Containing Several Queries, Proposed to the Consideration of the Public. 1735–37. 3 parts.

A Discourse Addressed to Magistrates and Men in Authority. 1738.

Siris: A Chain of Philosophical Reflexions and Inquiries concerning the Virtues of Tar Water. 1744.

A Letter to T—— P——, Esq; Containing Some Farther Remarks on the Virtues of Tar-Water. 1744.

A Letter to Thomas Prior, Esq; concerning the Usefulness of Tar-Water in the Plague. 1747.

Two Letters, the One to Thomas Prior, Esq; concerning the Usefulness of Tar-Water in the Plague; the Other to the Rev. Dr. Hales, on the Benefit of Tar-Water in Fevers. 1747.

A Word to the Wise; or, An Exhortation to the Roman Catholic Clergy of Ireland. 1749.

Maxims concerning Patriotism, by a Lady. 1750.

A Miscellany. 1752.

Works. Ed. Joseph Stock. 1784. 2 vols.

Works. 1820. 3 vols.

Works. Ed. G. N. Wright. 1843. 2 vols.

Works. Ed. Alexander Campbell Fraser. 1871. 4 vols.

Works. Ed. George Sampson. 1897–98. 3 vols.

Berkeley and Percival: The Correspondence of George Berkeley and Sir John Percival. Ed. Benjamin Rand. 1914.

Commonplace Book. Ed. G. A. Johnson. 1930.

Philosophical Commentaries, Generally Called the Commonplace Book. Ed. A. A. Luce. 1944.

Works. Eds. A. A. Luce and T. E. Jessop. 1948–57. 9 vols.

The Principles of Human Knowledge; Three Dialogues between Hylas and Philonous. Ed. G. J. Warnock. 1962.

Philosophical Works. Ed. M. R. Ayers. 1975.

Philosophical Commentaries. Ed. George H. Thomas. 1976.

HENRY FIELDING (1707–1754)

The Masquerade. 1728.

Love in Several Masques. 1728.

The Temple Beau. 1730.

The Author's Farce and The Pleasures of the Town. 1730.

Tom Thumb: A Tragedy. 1730.

Rape upon Rape; or, The Justice Caught in His Own Trap. 1730.

The Letter-Writers; or, A New Way to Keep a Wife at Home. 1731.

The Welsh Opera; or, The Grey Mare the Better Horse. 1731.

The Genuine Grub-Street Opera. 1731.

The Lottery. 1732.

The Modern Husband. 1732.

The Old Debauchees. 1732.

The Covent-Garden Tragedy. 1732.

The Mock Doctor; or, The Dumb Lady Cur'd. 1732.

The Miser (adaptation). 1733.

The Intriguing Chamber Maid by Jean François Regnard (adaptation). 1734.

Don Quixote in England. 1734.

An Old Man Taught Wisdom; or, The Virgin Unmask'd. 1735.

The Universal Gallant; or, The Different Husbands. 1735.

Pasquin: A Dramatic Satire on the Times. 1736.

Tumble-down Dick; or, Phaeton in the Suds. 1736.

The Historical Register for the Year 1736; to Which Is Added a Very Merry Tragedy, Called, Eurydice Hiss'd; or, A Word to the Wise. 1737.

The Military History of Charles XII, King of Sweden by Gustavus Alderfeld (translator; with others). 1740. 3 vols.

Of True Greatness: An Epistle to the Right Honourable George Dodington, Esq. 1741.

ΤΗΣ ΟΜΗΡΟΥ VEPNON-ΙΑΔΟΣ, ΡΑΨΩΔΙΑ ἡ ΓΡΑΜΜΑ Α' *(The Vernon-iad).* 1741.

An Apology for the Life of Mrs. Shamela Andrews. 1741.

[*The Crisis: A Sermon on Revel. xiv. 9, 10, 11.* 1741.]

The Opposition: A Vision. 1742.

The History of the Adventures of Joseph Andrews, and of His Friend Mr. Abraham Adams. 1742.

A Full Vindication of the Dutchess Dowager of Marlborough. 1742.

Miss Lucy in Town: A Sequel to The Virgin Unmask'd. 1742.

Plutus, the God of Riches by Aristophanes (translator; with William Young). 1742.

Some Papers Proper to Be Read before the Royal Society, concerning the Terrestrial Chrysipus. 1743.

The Wedding-Day. 1743.

Miscellanies. 1743. 3 vols.

The Adventures of David Simple by Sarah Fielding (revised by Fielding). 1744.

An Attempt towards a Natural History of the Hanover Rat. 1744.

A Serious Address to the People of Great Britain. 1745.

A Dialogue between the Devil, the Pope, and the Pretender. 1745.

The History of the Present Rebellion in Scotland. 1745. Lost.

Dramatick Works. 1745. 2 vols.

The Charge to the Jury. 1745.

The True Patriot; and the History of Our Own Times. 1745–46. 33 nos.

The Female Husband; or, The Surprising History of Mrs. Mary. 1746.

Art of Love by Ovid (translator). 1747.

Familiar Letters between the Principal Characters in David Simple (with Sarah Fielding). 1747.

[*A Compleat and Authentick History of the Rise, Progress, and Extinction of the Late Rebellion.* 1747.]

A Dialogue between a Gentleman of London, Agent for Two Court Candidates, and an Honest Alderman of the Country Party. 1747.

A Proper Answer to a Late Scurrilous Libel. 1747.

The Jacobite's Journal. 1747–48. 49 nos.

[*The Important Triflers.* 1748. Lost.]

The History of Tom Jones, a Foundling. 1749. 6 vols.

A Charge Delivered to the Grand Jury, at the Sessions of the Peace, Held for the City and Liberty of Westminster. 1749.

A True State of the Case of Bosavern Penlez. 1749.

An Enquiry into the Causes of the Late Increase of Robbers. 1751.

A Plan of the Universal Register Office (with John Fielding). 1752.

Amelia. 1752. 4 vols.

The Covent-Garden Journal. 1752. 72 nos.

Examples of the Interposition of Providence in the Detection and Punishment of Murder. 1752.

A Proposal for Making an Effectual Provision for the Poor. 1753.

A Clear State of the Case of Elizabeth Canning. 1753.

The Journal of a Voyage to Lisbon. 1755.

Works. Ed. Arthur Murphy. 1762. 4 vols.

The Fathers; or, The Good-Natur'd Man. 1778.

The Beauties of Fielding. 1782.

Works. Ed. Alexander Chalmers. 1806. 10 vols.

Works. Ed. Thomas Roscoe. 1840.

Works. Ed. James P. Browne. 1871–72. 11 vols.

Writings. Ed. David Herbert. 1872.

Works. Ed. Leslie Stephen. 1882. 10 vols.

Works. Ed. George Saintsbury. 1893. 12 vols.

Works. Ed. Edmund Gosse. 1898–99. 12 vols.

Complete Works. Ed. W. E. Henley. 1903. 16 vols.

Works. Ed. G. H. Maynadier. 1903. 12 vols.

Selected Essays. Ed. Gordon Hall Gerould. 1905.

Works. Ed. George Saintsbury. 1926. 12 vols.

Novels. 1926. 10 vols.

Works (Wesleyan Edition). Eds. Martin C. Battestin et al. 1967– .

COLLEY CIBBER (1671–1757)

A Poem, on the Death of Our Late Soveraign Lady Queen Mary. 1695.

Love's Last Shift; or, The Fool in Fashion. 1696.

Womans Wit; or, The Lady in Fashion. 1697.

Xerxes. 1699.

The Tragical History of King Richard III (adaptation). 1700.

Love Makes a Man; or, The Fop's Fortune (adaptation). 1701.

She Wou'd and She Wou'd Not; or, The Kind Impostor. 1703.

The Careless Husband. 1705.

Perolla and Izadora. 1706.

The School-Boy; or, The Comical Rival. 1707.

The Comical Lovers (adaptation). 1707.

The Double Gallant; or, The Sick Lady's Cure. 1707.

The Lady's Last Stake; or, The Wife's Resentment. 1708.

The Rival Fools (adaptation). 1709.

[*The Secret History of Arlus and Odolphus.* 1710.]

[*Cinna's Conspiracy* by Pierre Corneille (translator). 1713.]

[*Hob; or, The Country Wake* by Thomas Dogget (adaptation). 1715.]

Venus and Adonis: A Masque. 1715.

Myrtillo: A Pastoral Interlude. 1716.

The Non-Juror (adaptation). 1718.

Ximena; or, The Heroick Daughter (adaptation). 1719.

The Refusal; or, The Ladies Philosophy (adaptation). 1721.

Plays. 1721. 2 vols.

Caesar in Ægypt. 1725.

A Journey to London by Sir John Vanbrugh (editor). 1728.

The Provok'd Husband; or, A Journey to London (with Sir John Vanbrugh). 1728.

The Rival Queans, with The Humours of Alexander the Great. 1729.

Love in a Riddle: A Pastoral. 1729.

Damon and Phillida: A Pastoral Farce. 1729.

An Ode to His Majesty, for the New Year. 1731.

An Ode for His Majesty's Birth-day. 1731.

The Blind Boy. c. 1735.

Venus and Adonis and Myrtillo: A Pastoral Interlude. 1736.

An Apology for the Life of Mr. Colley Cibber, Comedian. 1740.

A Letter from Mr. Cibber to Mr. Pope, Inquiring into the Motives That Might Induce Him, in His Satyrical Works, to Be So Frequently Fond of Mr. Cibber's Name. 1742.

A Second Letter from Mr. Cibber to Mr. Pope. 1742.

The Egotist; or, Colley upon Cibber. 1743.

Another Occasional Letter from Mr. Cibber to Mr. Pope. 1744.

Papal Tyranny in the Reign of King John. 1745.

The Character and Conduct of Cicero, Considered, from the History of His Life by the Reverend Dr. Middleton. 1747.

The Lady's Lecture: A Theatrical Dialogue, between Sir Charles Easy and His Marriageable Daughter. 1748.

A Rhapsody upon the Marvellous: Arising from the First Odes of Horace and Pindar. 1751.

Verses to the Memory of Mr. Pelham, Addressed to His Grace the Duke of Newcastle. 1754.

Dramatic Works. 1760. 4 vols.

Dramatic Works. 1777. 5 vols.

Three Sentimental Comedies: Love's Last Shift; The Careless Husband; The Lady's Last Stake. Ed. Maureen Sullivan. 1973.

ALLAN RAMSAY (1686–1758)

A Poem to the Memory of the Famous Archibald Pitcairn, M.D. 1713.

The Battel; or, Morning-Interview: An Heroic-Comical Poem. 1716.

Christ's-Kirk on the Green (with James I of Scotland). 1718.

Elegies on Maggy Johnston, John Cowper, and Lucky Wood. 1718.

Scots Songs. 1718.

The Scriblers Lash'd. 1718.

Tartana; or, The Plaid. 1718.

Edinburgh's Address to the Country. c. 1718.

Lucky Spence's Last Advice. c. 1718.

Content. 1719.

Familiar Epistles between W⟨illiam⟩ H⟨amilton⟩ and A—— R———. 1719.

Richy and Sandy: A Pastoral on the Death of Mr. Joseph Addison. c. 1719.

An Epistle to W⟨illiam⟩ H⟨amilton⟩, on the Receiving the Compliment of a Barrel of Loch-fyne Herrings from Him. c. 1719.

To Mr. Law. 1720.

Patie and Roger: A Pastoral. 1720.

A Poem on the South-Sea. 1720.

Poems. 1720.

Prologue, Spoken by One of the Young Gentlemen, Who for Their Improvement and Diversion, Acted The Orphan, *and* Cheats of Scapin, *the Last Night of the Year 1719.* 1720.

The Prospect of Plenty: A Poem on the North-Sea Fishery. 1720.

Bessy Bell and Mary Gray. c. 1720.

Edinburgh's Salutation to the Most Honourable, My Lord Marquess of Carnarvon. c. 1720.

The Young Laird and Edinburgh Katy. c. 1720.

Bagpipes No Musick: A Satyre on Scots Poetry. c. 1720.

Grubstreet Nae Satyre: In Answer to Bagpipes No Musick. c. 1720.

An Ode, with a Pastoral Recitative on the Marriage ⟨of⟩ the Right Honourable James Earl of Wemyss, and Mrs. Janet Charteris. c. 1720.

An Elegy on Patie Birnie, the Famous Fiddler of Kinghorn. 1721.

Poems. 1721.

The Rise and Fall of Stocks, 1720. 1721.

Robert, Richy and Sandy: A Pastoral on the Death of Matthew Prior, Esq. 1721.

A Tale of Three Bonnets. 1722.

To the Honourable, Sr John Clerk of Pennycuik Bart., on the Death of His Most Accomplished Son, John Clerk Esqr. 1722.

The Fair Assembly. 1723.

Jenny and Meggy, a Pastoral: Being a Sequel to Patie and Roger. 1723.

The Nuptials: A Masque on the Marriage of His Grace James Duke of Hamilton, and Lady Anne Cochran. 1723.

The Tea-Table Miscellany (editor). 1723–37. 4 vols.

The Ever Green: Being a Collection of Scots Poems, Wrote by the Ingenious before 1600 (editor). 1724. 2 vols.

Health. 1724.

Miscellaneous Works. 1724.

The Monk and the Miller's Wife; or, All Parties Pleas'd. 1724.

Mouldy-Mowdiwart; or, The Last Speech of a Wretched Miser. 1724.

The Poetick Sermon: To R—— Y—— Esquire. 1724.

On Pride: An Epistle to ———. 1724.

On Seeing the Archers Diverting Themselves at the Butts and Rovers, &c. 1724.

An Ode Sacred to the Memory of Her Grace Anne Dutchess of Hamilton. c. 1724.

The Gentle Shepherd: A Scots Pastoral Comedy. 1725.

A Scots Ode, to the British Antiquarians. 1726.

An Ode to the Memory of Sir Isaac Newton. 1727.

A New Miscellany of Scots Songs (editor). 1727.

Some Few Hints in Defence of Dramatic Entertainments. c. 1727.

Poems. 1728. 2 vols.

Collection of Thirty Fables. 1730.

The Scarborough Miscellany (editor). 1732.

Poems. 1733.

An Address of Thanks from the Society of Rakes, to the Pious Author of An Essay upon Improving and Adding to the Strength of Great Britain and Ireland by Fornication. 1735.

A Collection of Scots Proverbs (editor). 1737.

To the Honourable, Duncan Forbes of Culloden. 1737.

The Caledonian Miscellany (with others). 1740.

The Vision. 1748.

Poems. 1751. 2 vols.

Poems on Several Occasions. 1776.

Poems. 1797. 2 vols.

Poems. Eds. George Chalmers and Alexander Fraser Tytler, Lord Woodhouselee. 1800. 2 vols.

Poetical Works. 1818. 3 vols.

Poetical Works. Ed. William Tennant. 1819.

Select Poetical Works. 1838.

Poems. Ed. J. Logie Robertson. 1887.

Works. Eds. Burns Martin et al. 1951–74. 6 vols.

Poems of Allan Ramsay and Robert Fergusson. Eds. Alexander M. Kinghorn and Alexander Law. 1974.

JONATHAN EDWARDS (1703–1758)

God Glorified in the Work of Redemption, by the Greatness of Man's Dependence upon Him, in the Whole of It. 1731.

A Divine and Supernatural Light. 1734.

A Faithful Narrative of the Surprizing Work of God in the

Conversion of Many Hundred Souls in Northampton, and the Neighbouring Towns and Villages of New-Hampshire in New-England. 1737.

A *Letter to the Author of the Pamphlet Called* An Answer to the Hampshire Narrative. 1737.

Discourses on Various Important Subjects, Nearly concerning the Great Affair of the Soul's Eternal Salvation. 1738.

The Distinguishing Marks of a Work of the Spirit of God. 1741.

The Resort and Remedy of Those That Are Bereaved by the Death of an Eminent Minister. 1741.

Sinners in the Hands of an Angry God. 1741.

Some Thoughts concerning the Present Revival of Religion in New-England. 1742.

The Great Concern of a Watchman for Souls. 1743.

The True Excellency of a Minister of the Gospel. 1744.

Copies of Two Letters Cited by the Rev. Mr. Clap, in His Late Printed Letter to a Friend in Boston. 1745.

An Expostulatory Letter to the Rev. Mr. Clap. 1745.

The Church's Marriage to Her Sons, and to Her God. 1746.

A Treatise concerning Religious Affections. 1746.

True Saints, When Absent from the Body, Are Present with the Lord. 1747.

An Humble Attempt to Promote Explicit Agreement and Visible Union of God's People. 1747.

A Strong Rod Broken and Withered. 1748.

An Account of the Life of the Late Reverend Mr. David Brainerd (editor). 1749.

An Humble Inquiry into the Rules of the Word of God. 1749.

Christ the Great Example of Gospel Ministers. 1750.

A Farewel-Sermon. 1751.

Misrepresentations Corrected, and Truth Vindicated, in a Reply to the Rev. Mr. Solomon Williams's Book, Intituled, The True State of the Question concerning the Qualifications Necessary to Lawful Communion in the Christian Sacraments. 1752.

True Grace, Distinguished from the Experience of Devils. 1753.

A Careful and Strict Enquiry into the Modern Prevailing Notions of That Freedom of the Will, Which Is Supposed to Be Essential to Moral Agency, Vertue and Vice, Reward and Punishment, Praise and Blame. 1754.

The Great Christian Doctrine of Original Sin Defended. 1758.

Remarks on the Essays, On the Principles of Morality, and Natural Religion. 1758.

The Life and Character of the Late Mr. Jonathan Edwards: Together with a Number of His Sermons on Various Important Subjects. Ed. Samuel Hopkins. 1765. 2 parts.

Two Dissertations. 1765.

A History of the Work of Redemption. 1774.

Sermons. 1780.

The Eternity of Hell Torments. 1788.

Practical Sermons. 1788.

Twenty Sermons on Various Subjects. 1789.

Miscellaneous Observations on Important Theological Subjects. 1793.

Remarks on Important Theological Controversies. 1796.

Works. Eds. Edward Williams and Edward Parsons. 1806–11 (8 vols.), 1847 (2 supplementary vols.).

Advice to Young Converts. 1807.

Account of Abigail Hutchinson. 1816.

Select Sermons. 1834.

Works. Ed. Edward Hickman. 1834. 2 vols.

Works. 1843. 4 vols.

Selections from the Unpublished Writings. Ed. Alexander B. Grosart. 1865.

Observations concerning the Scripture Oeconomy of the Trinity and Covenant of Redemption. Ed. Egbert C. Smyth. 1880.

An Unpublished Essay on the Trinity. Ed. George P. Fisher. 1903.

Select Sermons. Ed. H. Norman Gardiner. 1904.

Representative Selections. Ed. Clarence H. Faust. 1935.

Images or Shadows of Divine Things. Ed. Perry Miller. 1948.

Puritan Sage: Collected Writings. Ed. Vergilius Ferm. 1953.

The Philosophy of Jonathan Edwards: From His Private Notebooks. Ed. Harvey G. Townsend. 1955.

Works. Eds. Perry Miller et al. 1957– .

The Mind: A Reconstructed Text. Ed. Leon Howard. 1963.

Basic Writings. Ed. Ola Elizabeth Winslow. 1966.

Selected Writings. Ed. Harold P. Simonson. 1970.

Treatise on Grace and Other Posthumously Published Writings. Ed. Paul Helm. 1971.

WILLIAM COLLINS (1721–1759)

Persian Eclogues. 1742.

Verses Humbly Address'd to Sir Thomas Hanmer on His Edition of Shakespear's Works. 1743, 1744.

Odes on Several Descriptive and Allegorical Subjects. 1747.

Ode Occasion'd by the Death of Mr. Thomson. 1749.

The Passions: An Ode for Music. 1750.

Poetical Works. Ed. John Langhorne. 1765.

Poetical Works. 1788.

Eclogues and Miscellaneous Pieces. Ed. Benjamin Strutt. 1796.

Poetical Works. 1797.

Poetical Works. Ed. Alexander Dyce. 1827.

Poems. Ed. William Crowe. 1828.

Poetical Works. Ed. Sir Samuel Egerton Brydges. 1830.

Poetical Works (with Oliver Goldsmith and Thomas Warton). Ed. George Gilfillan. 1854.

Poetical Works. Ed. W. Moy Thomas. 1858.

Poems. Ed. W. C. Bronson. 1898.

Poetical Works. Ed. Christopher Stone. 1907.

Poems. Ed. Edmund Blunden. 1929.

Drafts and Fragments of Verse. Ed. J. S. Cunningham. 1956.

Poems (with Thomas Gray and Oliver Goldsmith). Ed. Roger Lonsdale. 1969.

Works. Eds. Richard Wendorf and Charles Ryskamp. 1979.

WILLIAM LAW (1686–1761)

A Sermon Preached at Hazelingfield, 7 July 1713: Being the Day Appointed by Her Majesty's Royal Proclamation for a Publick Thanksgiving to Her Majesty's General Peace. 1713.

The Bishop of Bangor's Late Sermon, and His Letter to Dr Snape in Defence of It, Answer'd. 1717.

A Second Letter to the Bishop of Bangor. 1717.

A Reply to the Bishop of Bangor's Answer to the Representation of the Committee of Convocation. 1719.

Three Letters to the Bishop of Bangor. 1721. 3 parts.

Remarks upon a Late Book, Entituled, The Fable of the Bees. 1724.

The Absolute Unlawfulness of the Stage-Entertainment Fully Demonstrated. 1726.

A Practical Treatise upon Christian Perfection. 1726.

A Serious Call to a Devout and Holy Life. 1729.

The Case of Reason, or Natural Religion Fairly Stated: In Answer to a Book Entitul'd, Christianity as Old as the Creation. 1731.

[*The Oxford Methodists.* 1733.]

A Demonstration of the Errors of a Late Book Called A Plain

Account of the Nature and End of the Sacrament of the Lord's Supper. 1737.

The Grounds and Reasons of Christian Regeneration; or, The New-Birth. 1739.

An Earnest and Serious Answer to Dr Trapp's Discourse, of the Folly, Sin and Danger of Being Righteous Overmuch. 1740.

An Appeal to All That Doubt, or Disbelieve the Truths of the Gospel; to Which Are Added, Some Animadversions upon Dr Trap's Late Reply. 1742.

The Spirit of Prayer; or, The Soul Rising out of the Vanity of Time into the Riches of Eternity. 1749–50. 2 parts.

Extract of a Letter in Answer to One Requesting a Conversation on the Spiritual Life. c. 1750.

An Answer to the Question, "Where Shall I Go, or What Shall I Do, to Be in the Truth?": In a Letter to a Friend. c. 1750.

The Way to Divine Knowledge. 1752.

The Spirit of Love: Being an Appendix to The Spirit of Prayer. 1752–54. 2 parts.

Works. 1753–76. 9 vols.

Reflections on a Favourite Amusement. 1756.

A Short but Sufficient Confutation of Dr. Warburton's Projected Defence (as He Calls It) of Christianity, in His Divine Legation of Moses. 1757.

Of Justification by Faith and Works: A Dialogue between a Methodist and a Churchman. 1760.

A Collection of Letters on the Most Interesting and Important Subjects. Eds. T. Law and G. W. 1760.

An Humble, Earnest, and Affectionate Address to the Clergy. 1761.

An Extract from the Rev. Mr. Law's Later Works. 1768. 2 vols.

Letters to a Lady Inclined to Enter into the Communion of the Church of Rome. 1779.

Extracts from the Letters and Writings. Ed. Maria Ashby. 1828.

Works. Ed. G. B. Morgan. 1892–93. 9 vols.

The Divine Indwelling: Selection from the Letters. Ed. A. Murray. 1897.

Liberal and Mystical Writings. Ed. William Scott Palmer and W. P. Du Bose. 1908.

The Spirit Is Life: A Selection from the Letters. Ed. M. M. Schofield. 1917.

Selected Mystical Writings. Ed. Stephen Hobhouse. 1938.

The Pocket William Law. Ed. Arthur W. Hopkinson. 1950.

The Spirit of Prayer and The Spirit of Love: The Full Text. Ed. Sidney Spencer. 1969.

SAMUEL RICHARDSON (1689–1761)

The Apprentice's Vade Mecum; or, The Young Man's Pocket-Companion. 1734.

[*A Seasonable Examination of the Pleas and Pretensions of the Proprietors of, and Subscribers to, Play-Houses, Erected in Defiance of the Royal Licence.* 1735.]

Æsop's Fables, tr. Sir Roger L'Estrange (editor). 1740.

The Negotiations of Sir Thomas Roe (editor; with others). 1740.

Pamela; or, Virtue Rewarded. 1741 [Volumes 1–2]; 1742 [Volumes 3–4].

Letters Written to and for Particular Friends ⟨*Familiar Letters*⟩. 1741.

A Tour thro' the Whole Island of Great Britain by Daniel Defoe (editor). 1742. 4 vols.

Clarissa; or, The History of a Young Lady. 1748. 7 vols.

Letters and Passages Restored from the Original Manuscripts of the History of Clarissa. 1751.

The Case of Samuel Richardson, of London, Printer; with Regard to the Invasion of His Property in The History of Sir Charles Grandison, *before Publication, by Certain Booksellers in Dublin.* 1753.

The History of Sir Charles Grandison. 1754. 7 vols.

An Address to the Public, on the Treatment Which the Editor of the History of Sir Charles Grandison *Has Met With from Certain Booksellers and Printers in Dublin.* 1754.

Copy of a Letter to a Lady, Who Was Solicitous for an Additional Volume to the History of Sir Charles Grandison. 1754.

A Collection of Moral and Instructive Sentiments, Maxims, Cautions, and Reflexions, Contained in the Histories of Pamela, Clarissa, *and* Sir Charles Grandison. 1755.

The Paths of Virtue Delineated; or, The History in Miniature of the Celebrated Pamela, Clarissa Harlowe, and Sir Charles Grandison, Familiarised and Adapted to the Capacities of Youth. 1756.

The Life and Heroic Actions of Balbe Berton, Chevalier de Grillon by Marguerite de Lussan (tr. anon.; revised by Richardson). 1760. 2 vols.

The History of Sir William Harrington by Anna Meades (revised by Richardson). 1771. 4 vols.

Correspondence. Ed. Anna Laetitia Barbauld. 1804. 6 vols.

Works. 1811. 19 vols.

Novels. 1824. 3 vols.

Works. 1883. 12 vols.

Novels. 1901–02. 19 vols.

Novels. Ed. Ethel M. M. McKenna. 1902. 20 vols.

Novels. 1929–31. 18 vols.

Selected Letters. Ed. John Carroll. 1964.

Clarissa: Preface, Hints of Prefaces, and Postscript. Ed. R. F. Brissenden. 1964.

The Richardson-Sinistra Correspondence and Sinistra's Prefaces to Clarissa. Ed. William C. Slattery. 1969.

LADY MARY WORTLEY MONTAGU (1689–1762)

Court Poems (with John Gay). 1716.

Verses Address'd to the Imitator of the First Satire of the Second Book of Horace. 1733.

An Elegy to a Young Lady, in the Manner of Ovid ⟨by James Hammond⟩; *with an Answer.* 1733.

The Dean's Provocation for Writing The Lady's Dressing-Room. 1734.

The Nonsense of Common-Sense. 1737–38. 9 nos.

Six Town Eclogues; with Some Other Poems. 1747.

Letters Written during Her Travels in Europe, Asia and Africa. 1763. 3 vols.

An Additional Volume to the Letters. 1767.

Poetical Works. 1768.

Works. Ed. James Dallaway. 1803. 5 vols.

Original Letters to Sir James and Lady Frances Steuart. Ed. John Dunlop. 1818.

Letters and Works. Ed. Lord Wharncliffe. 1837. 3 vols.

Letters. Ed. Sarah J. Hale. 1856.

Letters. Ed. R. Brimley Johnson. 1906.

Travel Letters. Ed. A. W. Lawrence. 1930.

The Nonsense of Common-Sense 1737–1738. Ed. Robert Halsband. 1947.

Complete Letters. Ed. Robert Halsband. 1965–67. 3 vols.

Selected Letters. Ed. Robert Halsband. 1970.

Essays and Poems and Simplicity: A Comedy. Eds. Robert Halsband and Isobel Grundy. 1977.

JOHN BYROM (1692–1763)

A Review of the Proceedings against Dr. Bentley, in the University of Cambridge. 1719.

Tunbridgiale: Being a Description of Tunbridge. 1726.

A Full and True Account of an Horrid and Barbarous Robbery, Committed on Epping-Forest, upon the Body of the Cambridge Coach. 1728.

Proposals for Printing, by Subscription, a New Method of Short-Hand, for General Use. 1739.

An Epistle to a Friend: Occasioned by a Sermon Intituled, The False Claims to Martyrdom Consider'd. 1747.

An Epistle to a Gentleman of the Temple. 1749.

Enthusiasm: A Poetical Essay. 1752.

The Immortality of the Soul by Isaac Hawkins Browne (translator). 1754.

The Universal English Short-Hand. 1767.

Miscellaneous Poems. 1773. 2 vols.

Seasonable Alarming and Humiliating Truths in a Metrical Version of Some Passages from the Works of William Law. Ed. F. Okely. 1774.

Miscellaneous Poems. Ed. James Nichols. 1814.

Private Journal and Literary Remains. Ed. Richard Parkinson. 1854–57. 4 vols.

Poems. Ed. Adolphus William Ward. 1894–1912. 5 vols.

Selections from the Journals and Papers. Ed. Henri Talon. 1950.

Sir Lowbred O——n; or, The Hottentot Knight. n.d.

WILLIAM SHENSTONE (1714–1763)

Poems upon Several Occasions. 1737.

The Judgment of Hercules. 1741.

The School-Mistress. 1742.

Works in Verse and Prose. Ed. Robert Dodsley. 1764 [Volumes 1–2]; 1769 [Volume 3].

Poetical Works. 1771.

Miscellaneous Poems by Joseph Giles (editor). 1771.

Poetical Works. Ed. George Gilfillan. 1854.

Poetical Works. Ed. Charles Cowden Clarke. 1880.

Essays on Men and Manners. Ed. Havelock Ellis. 1927.

Letters. Ed. Marjorie Williams. 1939.

Letters. Ed. Duncan Mallam. 1939.

Shenstone's Miscellany 1749–1763 (editor). Ed. Ian A. Gordon. 1952.

CHARLES CHURCHILL (1732–1764)

The Rosciad. 1761.

The Apology: Addressed to the Critical Reviewers. 1761.

Night: An Epistle to Robert Lloyd. 1761.

The Ghost. 1762 [Books 1–2]; 1762 [Book 3]; 1763 [Book 4].

The North Briton (with John Wilkes and others). 1762–63. 46 nos.

The Conference. 1763.

An Epistle to William Hogarth. 1763.

The Prophecy of Famine: A Scots Pastoral. 1763.

Poems. 1763.

The Duellist. 1764.

The Candidate. 1764.

Gotham. 1764 [Book 1]; 1764 [Book 2]; 1764 [Book 3].

Independence. 1764.

The Times. 1764.

The Farewell. 1764.

Poems. 1764. 2 vols.

The Journey: A Fragment. 1765.

Poems: Volume II. 1765. 11 parts.

Sermons. 1765.

Poetical Works. Ed. William Tooke. 1804. 2 vols.

Poetical Works. Ed. George Gilfillan. 1855.

Poems. Ed. James Laver. 1933. 2 vols.

The Correspondence of John Wilkes and Charles Churchill. Ed. Edward H. Weatherley. 1954.

Poetical Works. Ed. Douglas Grant. 1956.

EDWARD YOUNG (1683–1765)

An Epistle to the Right Honourable the Lord Lansdown. 1713.

A Poem on the Last Day. 1713.

An Epistle to the Lord Viscount Bolingbroke, Sent with A Poem on the Last Day. 1714.

The Force of Religion; or, Vanquish'd Love. 1714.

On the Late Queen's Death, and His Majesty's Accession to the Throne. 1714.

Orationes Duae Codringtono Sacrae (with Digby Cotes). 1716.

Busiris, King of Egypt. 1719.

A Paraphrase on Part of the Book of Job. 1719.

A Letter to Mr. Tickell: Occasioned by the Death of the Right Honourable Joseph Addison. 1719.

The Revenge. 1721.

The Universal Passion. 1725 [Parts 1–4]; 1726 [Part 7]; 1727 [Part 5]; 1728 [Parts 1–7; as *Love of Fame*].

The Instalment: To the Right Honourable Sir Robert Walpole. 1726.

Poetic Works. 1726.

Cynthio. 1727.

A Vindication of Providence; or, A True Estimate of Human Life. 1728.

Ocean: An Ode Occasion'd by His Majesty's Late Royal Encouragement of the Sea-Service; to Which Is Prefix'd An Ode to the King; and a Discourse on Ode. 1728.

An Apology for Princes; or, The Reverence Due to Government. 1729.

Imperium Pelagi: A Naval Lyrick Written in Imitation of Pindar's Spirit, Occasion'd by His Majesty's Return, Sept. 1729, and the Succeeding Peace. 1730.

Two Epistles to Mr. Pope, concerning the Authors of the Age. 1730.

A Sea-Piece Containing I. The British Sailor's Exultation; II. His Prayer before Engagement. 1733.

The Foreign Address; or, The Best Argument for Peace. 1734.

Poetical Works. 1741. 2 vols.

The Complaint; or, Night-Thoughts on Life, Death, and Immortality. 1742 [Parts 1–3]; 1743 [Parts 4–5]; 1744 [Parts 6–7]; 1745 [Part 8]; 1745 [Part 9; as *The Consolation*].

The Brothers. 1753.

An Account of the Two Brothers, Perseus and Demetrius (Very Necessary for the Readers and Spectators of the New Tragedy). 1753.

The Centaur Not Fabulous: In Five Letters to a Friend on the Life in Vogue. 1755.

Works. 1757 [Volumes 1–4]; 1767 [Volume 5].

An Argument, Drawn from the Circumstances of Christ's Death, for the Truth of His Religion. 1758.

Conjectures on Original Composition: In a Letter to the Author of Sir Charles Grandison. 1759.

Resignation. 1762.

The Beauties of Dr. Young's Night-Thoughts. 1769.

Poems on Several Occasions. 1771.

Dramatic Works. 1778.

Works. Ed. Thomas Park. 1811–13. 4 vols.

Poetical Works. Ed. John Mitford. 1834. 2 vols.

Complete Works. Ed. James Nichols. 1854. 2 vols.

Correspondence. Ed. Henry Pettit. 1971.

DAVID MALLET (c. 1705–1765)

William and Margaret: An Old Ballad. 1723.
A Poem in Imitation of Donaides. 1725.
The Excursion. 1728.
Eurydice. 1731.
Of Verbal Criticism: An Epistle to Mr. Pope, Occasioned by Theobald's Shakespear, and Bentley's Milton. 1733.
Verses Presented to His Highness the Prince of Orange on His Visiting Oxford (with Walter Harte). 1734.
Mustapha. 1739.
Alfred (with James Thomson). 1740.
The Life of Francis Bacon. 1740.
Poems on Several Occasions. 1743.
Works. 1743. 4 parts.
Amyntor and Theodor; or, The Hermit. 1747.
A Congratulatory Letter to Selim, on the Three Letters to the Whigs. 1748.
The Works of Henry St. John, Lord Viscount Bolingbroke (editor). 1754. 5 vols.
Britannia. 1755.
Observations on the Twelfth Article of War. 1757.
Works. 1759. 3 vols.
Edwin and Emma. 1760.
Verses on the Death of Lady Anson. 1760.
Truth, in Rhyme: Addressed to a Certain Noble Lord. 1761.
Poems on Several Occasions. 1762.
Elvira. 1763.
Poetical Works. 1796.
Ballads and Songs. Ed. F. Dinsdale. 1857.

LAURENCE STERNE (1713–1768)

To the Rev. Mr. James at Leeds. 1741.
Query upon Query: Being an Answer to J. S.'s Letter Printed in the York-Courant *October 20, 1741.* 1741.
An Answer to J. S.'s Letter, Address'd to a Freeholder of the County of York. 1741.
The Case of Elijah and the Widow of Zerephath. 1747.
The Abuses of Conscience. 1750.
A Political Romance, Addressed to —— ——, Esq; of York. 1759.
The Life and Opinions of Tristram Shandy, Gentleman. 1760 [Volumes 1–2]; 1761 [Volumes 3–4]; 1762 [Volumes 5–6]; 1765 [Volumes 7–8]; 1767 [Volume 9].
The Sermons of Mr. Yorick. 1760 [Volumes 1–2]; 1766 [Volumes 3–4]; 1769 [Volumes 5–7].
A Sentimental Journey through France and Italy. 1768. 2 vols.
Letters from Yorick to Eliza. 1773.
Letters to His Friends on Various Occasions. 1775.
Letters to His Most Intimate Friends. 1775. 3 vols.
Works. 1780. 10 vols.
Original Letters. 1788.
Seven Letters Written by Sterne and His Friends, Hitherto Unpublished. Ed. W. Durrant Cooper. 1844.
Works. Ed. James P. Browne. 1873. 4 vols.
Works. Ed. George Saintsbury. 1894. 6 vols.
Works and Life. Ed. Wilbur L. Cross. 1904. 12 vols.
Letter to the Rev. Mr. Blake. 1915.
Works. 1926–27. 7 vols.
Letters. Ed. Lewis Perry Curtis. 1935.
Works. Eds. Melvyn New and Joan New. 1976– .

WILLIAM FALCONER (1732–1769)

A Poem on the Death of Frederick, Prince of Wales. 1751.
The Shipwreck. 1762.

Ode on the Duke of York's Second Departure for England, as Rear Admiral. 1763.
The Demagogue. 1766.
Proposals for Printing, by Subscription, an Universal Dictionary of the Marine. c. 1768.
An Universal Dictionary of the Marine. 1769.
Poetical Works. 1796.
The Shipwreck and Other Poems. 1822.
Poems. Ed. John Mitford. 1836.
Poetical Works (with James Beattie and Robert Blair). Ed. George Gilfillan. 1854.
Poetical Works (with Thomas Campbell). 1880.

MARK AKENSIDE (1721–1770)

The Pleasures of Imagination. 1744.
An Epistle to the Rev. Mr. Warburton. 1744.
An Epistle to Curio. 1744.
Dissertatio Medica Inauguralis de Orto et Incremento Foetus Humani. 1744.
Odes on Several Subjects. 1745.
Friendship and Love; to Which Is Added A Song. 1745.
The Museum; or, Literary and Historical Register (editor). 1746–47. 3 vols.
An Ode to the Earl of Huntingdon. 1748.
An Ode to the Country Gentlemen of England. 1758.
Notes on the Postscript to a Pamphlet Intituled Observations Anatomical and Physiological, *by Alexander Monro.* 1758.
Oratio Anniversaria in Theatro Collegii Regalis. 1760.
De Dysenteria Commentarius. 1764.
An Ode to the Late Thomas Edwards. 1766.
The Works of William Harvey (editor). 1766.
Poems. Ed. Jeremiah Dyson. 1772.
Works in Prose and Verse. Ed. John Garnett. 1808. 2 vols.
Poems. Ed. Alexander Dyce. 1835.
Poetical Works (with John Dyer). Ed. Robert A. Willmott. 1855.
Poetical Works. Ed. George Gilfillan. 1857.

THOMAS CHATTERTON (1752–1770)

The Execution of Sir Charles Bawdin. 1772.
Poems, Supposed to Have Been Written at Bristol, by Thomas Rowley and Others, in the Fifteenth Century. Ed. Thomas Tyrwhitt. 1777.
Miscellanies in Prose and Verse. Ed. John Broughton. 1778.
A Supplement to Chatterton's Miscellanies. 1784.
Supplement to Chatterton's Miscellanies (Kew Gardens). c. 1785.
The Romaunte of a Knyghte. 1788.
The Revenge: A Burletta, with Additional Songs. 1795.
Works. Eds. Robert Southey and Joseph Cottle. 1803. 3 vols.
Ella and Other Pieces. Ed. James Glassford. 1837.
Poetical Works, with a Selection of His Letters. Ed. C. B. Willcox. 1842. 2 vols.
Poetical Works. Ed. Walter W. Skeat. 1871. 2 vols.
The Rowley Poems. Ed. Robert Steele. 1898. 2 vols.
Poems. Ed. Sidney Lee. 1905. 2 vols.
Complete Poetical Works. Ed. Henry D. Roberts. 1906. 2 vols.
The Letter Paraphras'd: An Unpublished Poem. Ed. M. O. Hunter. 1933.
Complete Works. Eds. Donald S. Taylor and Benjamin B. Hoover. 1971. 2 vols.

THOMAS GRAY (1716–1771)

An Ode on a Distant Prospect of Eton College. 1747.
An Elegy Wrote in a Country Church Yard. 1751.

Designs by R. Bentley for Six Poems by Mr. T. Gray. 1753.

Poems. 1756.

Odes. 1757.

The Union. 1761.

Poems. 1768.

Ode Performed in the Senate-House at Cambridge, July 1, 1769. 1769.

A Catalogue of the Antiquities, Houses, Parks, Plantations, Scenes, and Situations in England and Wales. Ed. William Mason. 1773.

The Bard (with Latin tr. by R. Williams). 1775.

Poems. Ed. William Mason. 1775.

Poetical Works. 1782.

Poems. Ed. Gilbert Wakefield. 1786.

Poetical Works. Ed. Stephen Jones. 1799.

Works. Ed. Thomas James Mathias. 1814. 2 vols.

Works. Ed. John Mitford. 1816. 2 vols.

Letters. 1819–21. 2 vols.

Poems and Letters. 1820.

Correspondence of Thomas Gray and the Rev. Norton Nichols, with Other Pieces Hitherto Unpublished. Ed. John Mitford. 1843.

Correspondence of Thomas Gray and William Mason. Ed. John Mitford. 1853.

Select Poems. Ed. William J. Rolfe. 1876.

Works in Prose and Verse. Ed. Edmund Gosse. 1884. 4 vols.

Gray and His Friends: Letters and Relics. Ed. Duncan C. Tovey. 1890.

Letters. Ed. Duncan C. Tovey. 1900. 3 vols.

Essays and Criticisms. Ed. Clark Sutherland Northup. 1911.

Poems, with a Selection of Letters and Essays. Ed. John Drinkwater. 1912.

Correspondence. Ed. Paget Toynbee. 1915. 2 vols.

Correspondence. Eds. Paget Toynbee and Leonard Whibley. 1935. 3 vols.

Poems. Ed. Leonard Whibley. 1939.

Selected Letters. Ed. Joseph Wood Krutch. 1952.

Poems (with William Collins and Oliver Goldsmith). Ed. Roger Lonsdale. 1969.

TOBIAS SMOLLETT (1721–1771)

Advice: A Satire. 1746.

Reproof: A Satire; The Sequel to Advice. 1747.

The Adventures of Roderick Random. 1748. 2 vols.

The Adventures of Gil Blas by Alain René Le Sage (translator). 1748. 4 vols.

The Regicide; or, James the First, of Scotland. 1749.

The Adventures of Peregrine Pickle. 1751. 4 vols.

A Treatise on the Theory and Practice of Midwifery by William Smellie (editor). 1751.

An Essay on the External Use of Water. 1752.

[*A Faithful Narrative of the Base and Inhuman Arts That Were Lately Practiced upon the Brain of Habbakkuk Hilding.* 1752.]

The Adventures of Ferdinand Count Fathom. 1753. 2 vols.

Select Essays on Commerce, Agriculture, Mines, Fisheries, and Other Useful Subjects (translator). 1754.

A Collection of Cases and Observations in Midwifery by William Smellie (editor). 1754.

Travels through Different Cities of Germany, Italy, Greece, and Several Parts of Asia by Alexander Drummond (editor). 1754.

The History and Adventures of the Renowned Don Quixote by Cervantes (translator). 1755. 2 vols.

A Compendium of Authentic and Entertaining Voyages (editor). 1756. 7 vols.

The Reprisal; or, The Tars of Old England. 1757.

A Complete History of England. 1757–58. 4 vols.

The Modern Part of the Universal History (editor; with others). 1759–66. 44 vols.

Continuation of the Complete History of England. 1760–61, 1765. 5 vols.

The Works of M. Voltaire (translator; with others). 1761–66. 26 vols.

The Life and Adventures of Sir Launcelot Greaves. 1762. 2 vols.

A Collection of Preternatural Cases and Observations in Midwifery by William Smellie (editor). 1764.

[*The Orientalist.* 1764.]

Travels through France and Italy. 1766. 2 vols.

The Present State of All Nations (editor). 1768–69. 8 vols.

The History and Adventures of an Atom. 1769. 2 vols.

The Expedition of Humphry Clinker. 1771. 3 vols.

An Ode to Independence. 1773.

Select Works. 1775–76. 8 vols.

The Adventures of Telemachus, Son of Ulysses by François de Salignac de la Mothe Fénelon (translator). 1776. 2 vols.

Plays and Poems. 1777.

Miscellaneous Works. 1790. 6 vols.

Works. 1793–94. 10 vols.

Miscellaneous Works. Ed. Robert Anderson. 1796. 6 vols.

Works. Ed. John Moore. 1797. 8 vols.

Miscellaneous Works. Ed. Thomas Roscoe. 1841.

Works. Ed. David Herbert. 1870.

Works. Ed. James P. Browne. 1872. 8 vols.

Works. Ed. W. E. Henley and Thomas Seccombe. 1899–1901. 12 vols.

Works. Ed. George Saintsbury. 1899–1903. 12 vols.

Works. Ed. G. H. Maynadier. 1902. 12 vols.

Works. Ed. 1925–26. 11 vols.

Letters. Ed. Edward S. Noyes. 1926.

Letters: A Supplement to the Noyes Collection. Ed. Francesco Cordasco. 1950.

Letters. Ed. Lewis M. Knapp. 1970.

CHRISTOPHER SMART (1722–1771)

Carmen Cl. Alexandri Pope in S. Caeciliam Latine Redditum. 1743, 1746.

On the Eternity of the Supreme Being: A Poetical Essay. 1750.

The Horatian Canons of Friendship: Being the Third Satire of the First Book of Horace Imitated. 1750.

An Occasional Prologue and Epilogue to Othello. 1751.

A Solemn Dirge, Sacred to the Memory of His Royal Highness Frederic Prince of Wales. 1751.

On the Immensity of the Supreme Being: A Poetical Essay. 1751.

An Index to Mankind; or, Maxims Selected from the Wits of All Nations (editor). 1751.

Poems on Several Occasions. 1752.

[*The Muses Banquet; or, A Present from Parnassus* (editor). 1752. 2 vols.]

On the Omniscience of the Supreme Being: A Poetical Essay. 1752.

[*Be Merry and Be Wise; or, The Cream of the Jests, and the Marrow of Maxims, for the Conduct of Life* (editor). 1753.]

The Hilliad: An Epic Poem. 1753.

[*Mother Midnight's Comical Pocket-Book.* 1753.]

On the Power of the Supreme Being: A Poetical Essay. 1754.

On the Goodness of the Supreme Being: A Poetical Essay. 1756.
[*A Collection of Poems for the Amusement of Children Six Foot High* (editor). 1756.]
[*A Collection of Pretty Poems for the Amusement of Children Three Feet High* (editor). 1756.]
The Works of Horace, Translated Literally into English Prose. 1756. 2 vols.
Hymn to the Supreme Being, on Recovery from a Dangerous Fit of Illness. 1756.
The Universal Visiter and Memorialist for the Year 1756 (editor; with Richard Rolt). 1756.
The Nonpareil; or, The Quintessence of Wit and Humour: Being a Choice Selection of Those Pieces That Were Most Admired in the Ever-to-Be-Remember'd Midwife; or, Old Woman's Magazine (editor). 1757.
Poems on the Attributes of the Supreme Being. 1761.
Mrs. Midnight's Orations and Other Select Pieces as They Were Spoken at the Oratory in the Hay-Market, London. 1763.
A Song to David. 1763.
Poems. 1763.
Poems on Several Occasions. c. 1763.
Ode to the Right Honourable the Earl of Northumberland, on His Being Appointed Lord Lieutenant of Ireland; with Some Other Pieces. 1764.
A Poetical Translation of the Fables of Phaedrus. 1765.
A Translation of the Psalms of David. 1765.
The Works of Horace, Translated into Verse. 1767. 4 vols.
The Parables of Our Lord and Saviour Jesus Christ, Done into Familiar Verse, with Occasional Applications, for the Use and Improvement of Younger Minds. 1768.
Hymns, for the Amusement of Children. 1771.
Poems. Ed. Francis Newbery. 1791. 2 vols.
A Song to David and Other Poems. Ed. Edmund Blunden. 1924.
Rejoice in the Lamb: A Song from Bedlam ⟨Jubilate Agno⟩. Ed. William Force Stead. 1939.
Collected Poems. Ed. Norman Callan. 1949. 2 vols.
Poems. Ed. Robert Brittain. 1950.
Jubilate Agno. Ed. W. H. Bond. 1954.
Selected Poems. Ed. Marcus Walsh. 1979.
Poetical Works. Eds. Karina Williamson and Marcus Walsh. 1980–83. 2 vols.

PHILIP DORMER STANHOPE, EARL OF CHESTERFIELD (1694–1773)

Speech of Senacherib Ragman, of St. Giles in the Fields, Esq., to His Fellow Prisoners. 1738.
The Case of the Hanover Forces (with Edmund Waller). 1743.
A Vindication of a Late Pamphlet Intitled, The Case of the Hanover Troops (with Edmund Waller). 1743.
A Farther Vindication of The Case of the Hanover Troops (with Edmund Waller). 1743.
Four Letters Publish'd in Old England; or, The Constitutional Journal. 1743.
The Interest of Hanover Steadily Pursued. 1743.
[*An Apology for a Late Resignation: In a Letter from an English Gentleman to His Friend at The Hague.* 1748.]
Speech in the H—se of L—ds against a Bill for Licencing All Dramatic Performances. 1749.
Witticisms; or, The Grand Pantheon of Genius, Sentiment, and Taste. 1773.
Letters to His Son Philip Stanhope, Together with Several Other Pieces on Various Subjects. Ed. Eugenia Stanhope. 1774. 2 vols.

Advice to His Son on Men and Manners; or, A New System of Education. 1775.
Principles of Politeness and of Knowing the World. Ed. John Trusler. 1775.
Miscellaneous Works. Ed. M. Maty. 1777–78. 3 vols.
Letters to Alderman George Faulkner, Dr. Madden, Mr. Sexton, Mr. Derrick, and the Earl of Arran. 1777.
Characters of Eminent Personages of His Own Time. 1777.
The Beauties of Chesterfield. 1778.
The Art of Pleasing; or, Instructions for Youth in the First Stage of Life, in a Series of Letters to the Present Earl of Chesterfield. 1783.
Supplement to the Letters to His Son. 1787.
Letters to Arthur Charles Stanhope, Esq., Relative to the Education of His Lordship's Godson. 1817.
Letters. Ed. Lord Mahon. 1845–53. 5 vols.
Letters, Sentences, and Maxims. 1870.
Letters to His Godson and Successor. Ed. the Earl of Carnarvon. 1890.
Chesterfield's Worldly Wisdom. Ed. George Birkbeck Hill. 1891.
Letters, with the Characters. Ed. John Bradshaw. 1892. 3 vols.
Letters to His Son. Ed. Charles Strachey. 1901. 2 vols.
Letters to Lord Huntingdon. Ed. A. Francis Steuart. 1923.
Poetical Works. 1927.
Letters to His Son. Ed. Robert K. Root. 1929.
Letters. Ed. Phyllis M. Jones. 1929.
Private Correspondence of Chesterfield and Newcastle 1744–46. Ed. Sir Richard Lodge. 1930.
Letters. Ed. Bonamy Dobrée. 1932. 6 vols.
Letters and Other Pieces. Ed. Richmond P. Bond. 1935.
Some Unpublished Letters. Ed. Sidney L. Gulick, Jr. 1937.
Letters to His Son. Ed. James Harding. 1973.

OLIVER GOLDSMITH (c. 1730–1774)

The Memoirs of a Protestant, Condemned to the Galleys of France for His Religion by Jean Marteilhe (translator). 1758. 2 vols.
An Enquiry into the Present State of Polite Learning in Europe. 1759.
The Bee. 1759. 8 nos.
The Mystery Revealed: Containing a Series of Transactions and Authentic Testimonials Respecting the Supposed Cock-Lane Ghost. 1762.
The Citizen of the World. 1762. 2 vols.
Plutarch's Lives (translator; with others). 1762. 7 vols.
The Life of Richard Nash, of Bath, Esq. 1762.
[*The Art of Poetry on a New Plan* (revised by Goldsmith). 1762. 2 vols.]
[*The Martial Review; or, A General History of the Late Wars.* 1763.]
An History of England in a Series of Letters from a Nobleman to His Son. 1764. 2 vols.
An History of the Lives, Actions, Travels, Sufferings, and Deaths of the Most Eminent Martyrs and Primitive Fathers of the Church. 1764.
The Traveller; or, A Prospect of Society. 1765.
The Geography and History of England. 1765.
Essays. 1765.
Edwin and Angelina: A Ballad. 1765.
The Vicar of Wakefield. 1766. 2 vols.
A Concise History of Philosophy and Philosophers by Jean H. S. Formey (translator). 1766.

Poems for Young Ladies in Three Parts: Devotional, Moral, and Entertaining (editor). 1767.
The Beauties of English Poesy (editor). 1767. 2 vols.
The Good Natur'd Man. 1768.
The Present State of the British Empire in Europe, America, Africa, and Asia (editor). 1768.
The Roman History from the Foundation of the City of Rome to the Destruction of the Western Empire. 1769. 2 vols.
The Deserted Village. 1770.
Life of Thomas Parnell, D.D. 1770.
Life of Henry St. John, Lord Viscount Bolingbroke. 1770.
The History of England from the Earliest Times to the Death of George II. 1771. 4 vols.
Threnodia Augustalis. 1772.
Dr. Goldsmith's Roman History, Abridged by Himself for the Use of Schools. 1772.
She Stoops to Conquer; or, The Mistakes of a Night. 1773.
Retaliation. 1774.
The Grecian History from the Earliest State to the Death of Alexander the Great. 1774. 2 vols.
An History of the Earth and Animated Nature. 1774. 8 vols.
An Abridgement of the History of England from the Invasion of Julius Caesar to the Death of George II. 1774.
The Comic Romance of Monsieur Scarron (translator). 1775. 2 vols.
Select Poems. 1775.
Poems. 1775.
Miscellaneous Works. 1775.
The Haunch of Venison: A Poetical Epistle to Lord Clare. 1776.
A Survey of Experimental Philosophy, Considered in Its Present State of Improvement. 1776. 2 vols.
Poems and Plays. 1777.
Poetical and Dramatic Works. 1780. 2 vols.
The Beauties of Goldsmith. 1782.
Poetical Works. 1784.
Poems. 1786.
Miscellaneous Works. 1791. 2 vols.
Miscellaneous Works. 1792. 7 vols.
Miscellaneous Works. Ed. Samuel Rose. 1801. 4 vols.
Miscellaneous Works. Ed. Washington Irving. 1825. 4 vols.
Poetical Works. Ed. John Mitford. 1831.
The Captivity: An Oratorio. 1836.
Works. 1848. 4 vols.
Poetical Works. Ed. Robert Aris Willmott. 1859.
Miscellaneous Works. Ed. David Masson. 1869.
Selected Poems. Ed. Austin Dobson. 1887.
Poems and Plays. Ed. Austin Dobson. 1889. 2 vols.
Plays. Ed. Austin Dobson. 1893.
The Good Natur'd Man and She Stoops to Conquer. Eds. Austin Dobson and George P. Baker. 1905.
Plays. Ed. Charles E. Doble. 1909.
Selected Essays. Ed. J. H. Lobban. 1910.
Complete Poetical Works. Ed. Austin Dobson. 1911.
The Bee and Other Essays, Together with the Life of Nash. 1914.
New Essays. Ed. Ronald S. Crane. 1927.
Collected Letters. Ed. Katharine C. Balderston. 1928.
The Grumbler: An Adaptation. Ed. Alice I. Perry Wood. 1931.
The Vicar of Wakefield and Other Writings. Ed. Frederick W. Hilles. 1955.
Collected Works. Ed. Arthur Friedman. 1966. 5 vols.
Poems (with Thomas Gray and William Collins). Ed. Roger Lonsdale. 1969.

ROBERT FERGUSSON (1750–1774)

Poems. 1773.
Auld Reekie. 1773.
A Poem to the Memory of John Cunningham. 1773.
Poems on Various Subjects. 1779.
The Ghaists: A Kail-Yard Eclogue. 1796.
The Farmer's Ingle. c. 1797.
Poetical Works. Ed. David Irving. 1800.
Works. Ed. Alexander Peterkin. 1805.
The Daft Days: The King's Birth-day in Edinburgh; and Braid Claith. 1808.
Poetical Works. Ed. Alexander B. Grosart. 1851.
Poems. Ed. Robert A. Aitken. 1895.
Scots Poems. 1898.
Poetical Works. Ed. Robert Ford. 1905.
Selected Poems. Ed. Alexander Law. 1947.
Scots Poems. Ed. John Telfer. 1948.
Poems. Ed. Matthew P. McDiarmid. 1954–56. 2 vols.
Unpublished Poems. Ed. William E. Gillis. 1955.
Poems of Allan Ramsay and Robert Fergusson. Eds. Alexander M. Kinghorn and Alexander Law. 1974.

DAVID HUME (1711–1776)

A Treatise of Human Nature. 1739–40. 2 vols.
An Abstract of A Treatise of Human Nature. 1740.
Essays Moral and Political. 1741–42. 2 vols.
A Letter from a Gentleman to His Friend Containing Some Observations on Religion and Morality. 1745.
Three Essays Moral and Political, Never Before Published. 1748.
Philosophical Essays concerning Human Understanding. 1748.
A True Account of the Behaviour and Conduct of Archibald Stewart. 1748.
An Enquiry concerning the Principles of Morals. 1751.
The Petition of the Bellmen. 1751.
Political Discourses. 1752.
Scotticisms. 1752.
Essays and Treatises on Several Subjects. 1753–56. 4 vols.
History of Great Britain. 1754–62. 6 vols.
Four Dissertations. 1757.
Two Essays. 1777.
Dialogues concerning Natural Religion. 1779.
Philosophical Works. 1825. 4 vols.
Letters. Ed. Thomas Murray. 1841.
Philosophical Works. Eds. T. H. Green and T. H. Grose. 1874–75. 4 vols.
Letters to William Strahan. Ed. George Birkbeck Hill. 1888.
Letters. Ed. J. Y. T. Greig. 1932.
Political Essays. Ed. Charles W. Hendel. 1953.
New Letters. Eds. Raymond Klibansky and Ernest C. Mossner. 1954.
Writings on Economics. Ed. Eugene Rotwein. 1955.
The Philosophy of David Hume. Ed. V. C. Chappell. 1963.
Ethical Writings. Ed. Alasdair MacIntyre. 1965.

SAMUEL FOOTE (1720–1777)

The Genuine Memoirs of the Life of Sir John Dinely Goodere. c. 1741.
A Treatise on the Passions, So Far as They Regard the Stage. 1747.
The Roman and English Comedy Consider'd and Compar'd, with Remarks on The Suspicious Husband, and an Examen into the Merits of the Present Comic Actors. 1747.
Mr. Foote's Original Address to the Public. c. 1750.
Taste. 1752.

The Englishman in Paris. 1753.
The Knights. 1754.
The Englishman Return'd from Paris. 1756.
The Author. 1757.
The Minor. 1760.
A Letter from Mr. Foote, to the Reverend Author of the Remarks, Critical and Christian, on the Minor. 1760.
Epilogue to The Minor; *or, A Methodist Sermon.* c. 1760.
The Orators. 1762.
The Comic Theatre: Being a Free Translation of All the Best French Comedies (translator; with others). 1762. 5 vols.
The Mayor of Garret ⟨Garratt⟩. 1764.
The Lyar (adaptation). 1764.
The Patron. 1764.
The Commissary. 1765.
Doctor Last in His Chariot (with Isaac Bickerstaffe). 1769.
[*Wilkes: An Oratorio.* 1769.]
The Lame Lover. 1770.
An Apology for The Minor: *In a Letter to the Rev. Mr. Baine.* 1771.
The Maid of Bath. 1771, 1778.
The Bankrupt. 1776.
Wit for the Ton! The Convivial Jester; or, Sam Foote's Last Budget Opened. c. 1777.
The Tailors: A Tragedy for Warm Weather. 1778.
The Devil upon Two Sticks. 1778.
The Nabob. 1778.
The Cozeners. 1778.
A Trip to Calais; to Which Is Annexed, The Capuchin. 1778.
Works. 1778. 3 vols.
Dramatic Works. 1797. 2 vols.
Works. 1799. 2 vols.
Dramatic Works. 1809. 2 vols.
Works. Ed. John Bee ⟨i.e. John Badcock⟩. 1830. 3 vols.
Bon-Mots of Samuel Foote and Theodore Hook. Ed. Walter Jerrold. 1894.
Plays (with Arthur Murphy). Ed. George Taylor. 1984.

WILLIAM WARBURTON (1698–1779)

Miscellaneous Translations, in Prose and Verse, from Roman Poets, Orators, and Historians. 1724.
A Critical and Philosophical Inquiry into the Causes of Prodigies and Miracles as Related by Historians. 1727.
The Legal Judicature in Chancery Stated (with Samuel Burroughs). 1727.
An Apology for Sir Robert Sutton. 1733.
The Alliance between Church and State. 1736.
The Divine Legation of Moses. 1738–41. 2 vols.
A Vindication of the Author of the Divine Legation of Moses. 1738.
Faith Working by Charity to Christian Edification. 1738.
A Vindication of Mr. Pope's Essay on Man, *from the Misrepresentations of Mr. de Crousaz.* 1740, 1742 (as *A Critical and Philosophical Commentary on Mr. Pope's* Essay on Man).
The Nature, Extent and Right Improvement of Christian Liberty. 1741.
A Sermon Preached at the Abbey-Church at Bath. 1742.
Remarks on Several Occasional Reflections, in Answer to the Rev. Dr. Middleton, Dr. Pococke, the Master of the Charter House, Dr. Richard Grey, and Others. 1744.
Remarks on Several Occasional Reflections, in Answer to the Reverend Doctors Stebbing and Sykes. 1745.
A Faithful Portrait of Popery. 1745.

A Sermon Occasioned by the Present Unnatural Rebellion. 1745.
The Nature of National Offences Truly Stated. 1746.
An Apologetical Dedication to the Reverend Dr. Henry Stebbing. 1746.
A Sermon Preach'd on the Thanksgiving Appointed to Be Observed the Ninth of October for the Suppression of the Late Unnatural Rebellion. 1746.
Two Sermons. 1746.
The Works of Shakespear (editor). 1747. 8 vols.
A Letter from an Author, to a Member of Parliament, concerning Literary Property. 1747.
A Letter to the Editor of the Letters on the Spirit of Patriotism, the Idea of a Patriot-King, *and the* State of the Parties. 1749.
A Letter to the Lord Viscount B⟨olingbrok⟩e: Occasion'd by His Treatment of a Deceased Friend. 1749.
Julian; or, A Discourse concerning the Earthquake and Fiery Eruption Which Defeated That Emperor's Attempt to Rebuild the Temple at Jerusalem. 1750.
The Works of Alexander Pope (editor). 1751. 9 vols.
The Principles of Natural and Revealed Religion Occasionally Opened and Explained. 1753–67. 3 vols.
A View of Lord Bolingbroke's Philosophy, in Four Letters to a Friend. 1754–55. 4 parts.
A Sermon Preached before His Grace Charles, Duke of Marlborough, and the R^t. R^ev. Isaac, Lord Bishop of Worcester, Presidents, the Vice-Presidents and Governors of the Hospital for the Small-pox. 1755.
Natural and Civil Events the Instruments of God's Moral Government. 1756.
Remarks on Mr. David Hume's Essay on the Natural History of Religion (with Richard Hurd). 1757.
A Sermon Preached before the Right Honourable the Lords Spiritual and Temporal in Parliament Assembled, in the Abbey Church, Westminster. 1760.
The People's Prayer for Peace. 1761.
A Rational Account of the Nature and End of the Sacrament of the Lord's Supper. 1761.
A Warning to the Presbyterians of Edinburgh. 1762.
The Doctrine of Grace; or, The Office and Operations of the Holy Spirit Vindicated from the Insults of Infidelity, and the Abuses of Fanaticism. 1763. 2 vols.
A Sermon Preached before the Incorporated Society for the Propagation of the Gospel in Foreign Parts. 1766. 2 parts.
A Sermon Preached at St. Lawrence Jewry. 1767.
Sermons and Discourses on Various Subjects and Occasions. 1767.
Works. Ed. Richard Hurd. 1788 (8 vols.), 1811 (12 vols.).
Tracts, by Warburton, and a Warburtonian ⟨Richard Hurd⟩; *Not Admitted into the Collections of Their Respective Works.* Ed. Samuel Parr. 1789.
Letters of a Late Eminent Prelate to One of His Friends. Ed. Richard Hurd. 1808.
Letters to the Hon. Charles Yorke, from 1752 to 1770. 1812.
Works. 1841. 13 vols.
A Selection from the Unpublished Papers. Ed. Francis Kilvert. 1841.

DAVID GARRICK (1717–1779)

The Lying Valet. 1741.
Mr. Garrick's Answer to Mr. Macklin's Case. 1743.
An Essay on Acting. 1744.
Lethe; or, Esop in the Shades. 1745.
Prologue ⟨by Samuel Johnson⟩ *and Epilogue* ⟨by Garrick⟩ *Spo-*

ken at the Opening of the Theatre in Drury-Lane 1747.
1747.

Miss in Her Teens; or, The Medley of Lovers. 1747.

Romeo and Juliet (adaptation). 1748.

Hamlet (adaptation). 1751.

Every Man in His Humour by Ben Jonson (adaptation). 1752.

An Ode on the Death of Mr. Pelham. 1754.

The Fairies: An Opera Taken from A Midsummer Night's
Dream. 1755.

Catherine and Petruchio (adaptation). 1756.

The Tempest (adaptation). 1756.

To Mr. Gray on His Odes. 1757.

The Male-Coquette; or, Seventeen Fifty-seven. 1757.

Lilliput: A Dramatic Entertainment. 1757.

Isabella; or, The Fatal Marriage by Thomas Southerne (adaptation). 1757.

Florizel and Perdita: A Dramatic Pastoral, Alter'd from The
Winter's Tale. 1758.

The Gamesters by James Shirley (adaptation). 1758.

Antony and Cleopatra (abridged by Garrick and Edward
Capell). 1758.

The Guardian. 1759.

[*High Life below Stairs.* 1759.]

*Reasons Why David Garrick, Esq., Should Not Appear on the
Stage.* 1759.

The Enchanter; or, Love and Magic: A Musical Drama. 1760.

The Fribbleriad. 1761.

The Provok'd Wife by Sir John Vanbrugh (adaptation). 1761.

Cymbeline (adaptation). 1762.

The Farmer's Return from London. 1762.

A Midsummer Night's Dream (adaptation). 1763.

Mahomet the Impostor by Voltaire, trs. James Miller and John
Hoadley (adaptation). 1765.

The Sick Monkey: A Fable. 1765.

The Clandestine Marriage (with George Colman the Elder).
1766.

Neck or Nothing: A Farce. 1766.

The Country Girl by William Wycherley (adaptation). 1766.

Cymon: A Dramatic Romance. 1767.

A Peep behind the Curtain; or, The New Rehearsal. 1767.

Dramatic Works. 1768. 3 vols.

*Songs, Chorusses, &c., Which Are Introduced in the New En-
tertainment of the Jubilee.* 1769.

*An Ode upon Dedicating a Building, and Erecting a Statue, to
Shakespeare, at Stratford upon Avon.* 1769.

King Arthur; or, The British Worthy by John Dryden (adaptation). 1770.

*The Institution of the Garter; or, Arthur's Round Table Re-
stored.* 1771.

The Irish Widow. 1772.

The Jubilee in Honor of Shakespeare. 1773.

The Chances by John Fletcher (adaptation). 1773.

Albumazar by Thomas Tomkis (adaptation). 1773.

Macbeth (adaptation). 1773.

King Lear (adaptation). 1773.

Alfred by James Thomson and David Mallet (adaptation).
1773.

A New Dramatic Entertainment Called A Christmas Tale.
1774.

Bon Ton; or, High Life above Stairs. 1775.

*May-Day; or, The Little Gipsy; to Which Is Added the Theat-
rical Candidates: A Musical Prelude.* 1775.

Zara by Aaron Hill (adaptation). 1776.

Rule a Wife and Have a Wife by Beaumont and Fletcher
(adaptation). 1776.

The Alchymist by Ben Jonson (adaptation). 1777.

The Roman Father by William Whitehead (adaptation). 1778.

Poetical Works. Ed. George Kearsley. 1785. 2 vols.

Dramatic Works. 1798. 3 vols.

Private Correspondence. Ed. James Boaden. 1831–32. 2 vols.

Some Unpublished Correspondence. Ed. George Pierce Baker.
1907.

*The Lying Valet; A Peep behind the Curtain; Bon Ton: Three
Farces.* Ed. Louise Brown Osborn. 1925.

*Three Plays: Harlequin's Invasion; The Jubilee; The Meeting of
the Company; or, Bayes's Art of Acting.* Ed. Elizabeth P.
Stern. 1926.

*The Diary of David Garrick: Being a Record of His Trip to Paris
in 1751.* Ed. Ryllis Clair Alexander. 1928.

*Pineapples of Finest Flavour: A Selection of Sundry Unpub-
lished Letters.* Ed. David Mason Little. 1930.

*The Journal of David Garrick, Describing His Visit to France
and Italy in 1763.* Ed. George Winchester Stone, Jr.
1939.

*Letters of David Garrick and Georgina, Countess Spencer 1759–
1769.* Eds. Earl Spencer and Christopher Dobson. 1960.

Letters. Eds. David M. Little and George M. Kahrl. 1963. 3
vols.

Plays. Eds. Harry William Pedicord and Frederick Louis Berg-
mann. 1980–82. 7 vols.

Plays (with George Colman the Elder). Ed. E. R. Wood.
1982.

SIR WILLIAM BLACKSTONE (1723–1780)

An Essay on Collateral Consanguinity. 1750.

An Analysis of the Laws of England. 1756.

*To the Reverend Doctor Randolph, Vice Chancellor of the Uni-
versity of Oxford.* 1757.

A Discourse on the Study of the Law. 1758.

*Considerations on the Question, Whether Tenants by Copy of
Court Roll Are Freeholders Qualified to Vote on Elections
for Knights of the Shire.* 1758.

The Great Charter and Charter of the Forest. 1759.

A Treatise on the Law of Descents in Fee-Simple. 1759.

Law Tracts. 1762. 2 vols.

Commentaries on the Laws of England. 1765–69. 4 vols.

*A Reply to Dr. Priestley's Remarks on the Fourth Volume of
Commentaries on the Laws of England.* 1769.

*The Case of the Late Election for the County of Middlesex
Considered on the Principles of the Constitution.* 1769.

A Letter to the Author of The Question Stated. 1769.

*Tracts, Chiefly Relating to the Antiquities and Laws of Eng-
land.* 1771.

*Reports of Cases Determined in the Several Courts of
Westminster-Hall from 1746 to 1779* (editor). 1781.
2 vols.

The American Students' Blackstone. Ed. George Chase. 1876–
77. 2 vols.

Dissertation on the Accounts of All Souls College, Oxford. Ed.
Sir William Anson. 1898.

HENRY HOME, LORD KAMES (1696–1782)

Remarkable Decisions of the Court of Session from 1716 to 1728
(editor). 1728.

Essays upon Several Subjects in Law. 1732.

*Answers for Sir William Ker of Greenhead, and Patrick Murray
of Chirry-Trees, to the Petition of Andrew Hog of Harcus.*
1733.

Unto the Right Honourable the Lords of Council and Session: The Petition of Andrew Hog of Harcus. 1738.

The Decisions of the Court of Session (editor). 1741. 2 vols.

Memorials for the Brewers of Glasgow, in Relation to the Duties of Excise Payable by Them. 1742.

Essays upon Several Subjects concerning British Antiquities. 1747.

Essays on the Principles of Morality and Natural Religion. 1751.

Statute Law of Scotland Abridged (editor). 1757.

Historical Law-Tracts. 1758. 2 vols.

Principles of Equity. 1760.

Introduction to the Art of Thinking. 1761.

Elements of Criticism. 1762. 3 vols.

Progress of Flax-Husbandry in Scotland. 1766.

Remarkable Decisions of the Court of Session from 1730 to 1752 (editor). 1766.

Sketches of the History of Man. 1774. 2 vols.

The Gentleman Farmer. 1776.

Elucidations Respecting the Common and Statute Law of Scotland. 1777.

Loose Hints upon Education, Chiefly concerning the Culture of the Heart. 1781.

An Essay on the Hereditary and Indefeasible Right of Kings: Composed in the Year 1745. 1797.

HENRY BROOKE (c. 1703–1783)

Universal Beauty. 1735.

Tasso's Jerusalem (translator). 1738.

Gustavus Vasa, the Deliverer of His Country. 1739.

Prospectus of a Work to Be Entitled Ogygian Tales; or, A Curious Collection of Irish Fables. 1743.

Fables for the Female Sex (with Edward Moore). 1744.

A History of Ireland from the Earliest Times Proposed. 1744.

The Farmer's Letters to the Protestants of Ireland. 1745. 6 parts.

The Secret History and Memoirs of the Barracks of Ireland. 1745.

The Last Speech of John the Good, Vulgarly Called Jack the Giant Queller. 1748.

New Fables (with Edward Moore). 1749.

The Songs in Jack the Gyant Queller: An Antique History. 1749.

An Occasional Letter from the Farmer to the Freeman of Dublin. 1749.

A New System of Fairery by Comte de Caylus (translator). 1750. 2 vols.

The Spirit of the Party. 1753. 3 parts.

A Description of the College-Green Club. 1753.

The Interests of Ireland Considered. 1759.

An Essay on the Ancient and Modern State of Ireland. 1760.

Liberty and Common-Sense to the People of Ireland. 1760.

The Case of the Roman Catholics of Ireland. 1760.

The Tryal of the Cause of the Roman Catholics. 1761.

The Earl of Essex. 1761.

A Proposal for the Restoration of Public Wealth and Credit. c. 1762.

The Fool of Quality; or, The History of Henry Earl of Moreland. 1765–70. 5 vols.

Redemption. 1772.

Juliet Grenville; or, The History of the Human Heart. 1774. 3 vols.

A Collection of Pieces; to Which Are Added, Several Plays and Poems. 1778. 4 vols.

Poetical Works. 1792. 4 vols.

SAMUEL JOHNSON (1709–1784)

A Voyage to Abyssinia by Father Jerome Lobo (translator). 1735.

London: A Poem in Imitation of the Third Satire of Juvenal. 1738.

Marmor Norfolciense; or, An Essay on an Ancient Prophetical Inscription, in Monkish Rhyme. 1739.

A Compleat Vindication of the Licensers of the Stage. 1739.

A Commentary on Mr. Pope's Principles of Morality by J. P. de Crousaz (translator). 1739.

The Life of Admiral Blake. 1740.

An Account of the Life of Mr. Richard Savage. 1744.

Miscellaneous Observations on the Tragedy of Macbeth. 1745.

A Sermon Preached before the Sons of the Clergy. 1745.

Prologue ⟨by Johnson⟩ *and Epilogue* ⟨by David Garrick⟩ *Spoken at the Opening of the Theatre in Drury-Lane 1747.* 1747.

The Plan of a Dictionary of the English Language. 1747.

The Vanity of Human Wishes: The Tenth Satire of Juvenal, Imitated. 1749.

Irene. 1749.

The Rambler. 1750–52. 208 nos.

A New Prologue Spoken by Mr. Garrick at the Representation of Comus. 1750.

An Essay on Milton's Use and Imitation of the Moderns, in His Paradise Lost. 1750.

A Dictionary of the English Language. 1755. 2 vols.

Proposals for Printing, by Subscription, the Dramatick Works of William Shakespeare. 1756.

The Idler. 1758–60. 104 nos.

The Prince of Abissinia ⟨Rasselas⟩. 1759.

Preface to His Edition of Shakespear's Plays. 1765.

The Plays of William Shakespeare (editor). 1765. 8 vols.

The False Alarm. 1770.

Thoughts on the Late Transactions Respecting Falkland's Islands. 1771.

Miscellaneous and Fugitive Pieces. Ed. Thomas Davies. 1773–74. 3 vols.

The Patriot. 1774.

A Journey to the Western Islands of Scotland. 1775.

Proposals for Publishing the Works of Mrs. Charlotte Lennox. 1775.

Taxation No Tyranny: An Answer to the Resolutions and Address of the American Congress. 1775.

Political Tracts. 1776.

Prefaces, Biographical and Critical, to the Works of the English Poets ⟨Lives of the English Poets⟩. 1779–81. 10 vols.

The Beauties of Johnson. 1781–82. 2 vols.

Poetical Works. Ed. George Kearsley. 1785.

Prayers and Meditations. Ed. George Strahan. 1785.

Debates in Parliament. Ed. George Chalmers. 1787. 2 vols.

Works. Ed. Sir John Hawkins. 1787. 11 vols.

Letters. Ed. Hester Lynch Piozzi. 1788. 2 vols.

A Sermon for the Funeral of His Wife. 1788.

Sermons on Different Subjects. 1788–89. 2 vols.

The Celebrated Letter to Philip Dormer Stanhope, Earl of Chesterfield. Ed. James Boswell. 1790.

Works. Ed. Arthur Murphy. 1792. 12 vols.

An Account of the Life of Dr. Samuel Johnson ⟨Annals⟩. Ed. Richard Wright. 1805.

A Diary of a Journey into North Wales, in the Year 1774. Ed. R. Duppa. 1816.

Works. Ed. Francis Pearson Walesby. 1825. 9 vols.

Poetical Works. Ed. George Gilfillan. 1855.

The Six Chief Lives from Johnson's Lives of the Poets. Ed. Matthew Arnold. 1878.

Letters. Ed. George Birkbeck Hill. 1892. 2 vols.

Lives of the English Poets. Ed. George Birkbeck Hill. 1905. 3 vols.

Johnson on Shakespeare. Ed. Walter Raleigh. 1908.

Prose and Poetry. Ed. R. W. Chapman. 1922.

Selected Letters. Ed. R. W. Chapman. 1925.

The French Journals of Mrs. Thrale and Dr. Johnson. Eds. Moses Tyson and Henry Guppy. 1932.

The Queeney Letters: Being Letters Addressed to Hester Maria Thrale by Dr. Johnson, Fanny Burney, and Mrs. Thrale-Piozzi. Ed. the Marquis of Lansdowne. 1934.

Poems. Eds. David Nichol Smith and Edward L. MacAdam. 1941, 1974.

Letters. Ed. R. W. Chapman. 1952. 3 vols.

Works (Yale Edition). Ed. A. T. Hazen et al. 1958– .

Selected Writings. Ed. R. T. Davies. 1965.

Political Writings. Ed. J. P. Hardy. 1968.

Selected Writings. Ed. Patrick Cruttwell. 1968.

Complete English Poems. Ed. J. D. Fleeman. 1971.

Early Biographical Writings. Ed. J. D. Fleeman. 1973.

Johnson as Critic. Ed. John Wain. 1973.

Samuel Johnson. Ed. Donald Greene. 1984.

WILLIAM WHITEHEAD (1715–1785)

The Danger of Writing Verse: An Epistle. 1741.

Ann Boleyn to Henry the Eighth: An Epistle. 1743.

An Essay on Ridicule. 1743.

Atys and Adrastus: A Tale in the Manner of Dryden's Fables. 1744.

*On Nobility: An Epistle to the Earl of ****** ⟨Ashburnham⟩.* 1744.

The Roman Father. 1750.

An Hymn to the Nymph of Bristol Spring. 1751.

Poems on Several Occasions, with The Roman Father. 1754.

Creusa, Queen of Athens. 1754.

Elegies, with an Ode to the Tiber. 1757.

Verses to the People of England. 1758.

A Charge to Poets. 1762.

The School for Lovers. 1762.

A Trip to Scotland. 1770.

Plays and Poems. 1774–88. 3 vols.

Variety: A Tale for Married People. 1776.

The Goat's Beard: A Fable. 1777.

CHARLES WESLEY (1707–1788)

Hymns and Sacred Poems (with John Wesley). 1739.

The Life of Faith, Exemplified in the Eleventh Chapter of St. Paul's Epistle to the Hebrews. 1740.

Hymns and Sacred Poems ⟨second collection⟩ (with John Wesley). 1740.

A Short Account of the Death of Mrs. Hannah Richardson. 1741.

A Collection of Psalms and Hymns (with John Wesley). 1741.

Hymns on God's Everlasting Love (with John Wesley). 1741.

A Sermon Preach'd before the University of Oxford. 1742.

The Whole Armour of God. 1742.

An Elegy on the Death of Robert Jones, Esq., of Fonmon Castle, in Glamorganshire, South-Wales. 1742.

Hymns and Sacred Poems ⟨third collection⟩ (with John Wesley). 1742.

A Collection of Hymns (with John Wesley). 1742.

The Nature, Design, and General Rules of the United Societies,

in London, Bristol, Kingswood, and Newcastle-upon-Tyne (with John Wesley). 1743.

Hymns for Times of Trouble and Persecution (with John Wesley). 1744.

Hymns for Times of Trouble (with John Wesley). 1744.

A Hymn at the Sacrament. 1745.

A Short View of the Difference between the Moravian Brothren, Lately in England, and the Reverend Mr. John and Charles Wesley: Extracted Chiefly from a Late Journal (with John Wesley). 1745.

Hymns on the Lord's Supper (with John Wesley). 1745.

Hymns for the Nativity of Our Lord (with John Wesley). 1745.

Hymns for Our Lord's Resurrection (with John Wesley). 1746.

Hymns for Ascension Day (with John Wesley). 1746.

Hymns of Petition and Thanksgiving for the Promise of the Father (with John Wesley). 1746.

Gloria Patri, &c.; or, Hymns to the Trinity (with John Wesley). 1746.

Hymns on the Great Festivals, and Other Occasions (with John Wesley). 1746.

Hymns for the Public Thanksgiving-Day (with John Wesley). 1746.

Hymns for the Watch-Night (with John Wesley). 1746.

Funeral Hymns. 1746.

Graces before Meat (with John Wesley). 1746.

Hymns for Children (with John Wesley). 1746.

Hymns for Those That Seek, and Those That Have, Redemption in the Blood of Jesus Christ. 1747.

Hymns and Sacred Poems (with John Wesley). 1747.

Minutes of Some Late Conversations between the Revd. M. Wesleys and Others (with John Wesley). 1749.

Minutes of Some Late Conversations between the Revd. M. Wesleys and Others (with John Wesley). 1749.

Hymns Composed for the Use of the Brethren (with John Wesley). 1749.

Hymns and Sacred Poems. 1749. 2 vols.

The Cause and Cure of Earthquakes. 1750.

Hymns for New Year's Day, 1750 (with John Wesley). 1750.

Hymns Occasioned by the Earthquake (with John Wesley). 1750. 2 parts.

Hymns for New Year's Day, 1751 (with John Wesley). 1751.

Minutes of Several Conversations between the Reverend Mr. John Wesley and Charles Wesley, and Others (with John Wesley). 1753.

Hymns and Spiritual Songs (with John Wesley). 1755.

Hymns for New Year's Day, 1755 (with John Wesley). 1755.

An Epistle to the Reverend Mr. John Wesley. 1755.

Hymns for the Year 1756 (with John Wesley). 1756.

Hymns for New Year's Day, 1758 (with John Wesley). 1758.

Hymns of Intercession for All Mankind (with John Wesley). 1758.

Funeral Hymns ⟨second series⟩. 1759.

Hymns on the Expected Invasion, 1759. 1759.

Hymns to Be Used on the Thanksgiving Day, Nov. 29, 1759, and After It. 1759.

Reasons against a Separation from the Church of England ⟨by John Wesley⟩; *with Hymns for the Preachers among the Methodists* ⟨by Charles Wesley⟩. 1760.

Hymns for Those to Whom Christ Is All in All (with John Wesley). 1761.

Select Hymns; with Tunes Annext: Designed Chiefly for the Use of the People Called Methodists (with John Wesley). 1761. 2 vols.

Cautions and Directions Given to the Greatest Professors in the Methodist Societies. 1762.

Short Hymns on Select Passages of the Holy Scriptures. 1762. 2 vols.

Minutes of Several Conversations between the Rev. Mr. John and Charles Wesley, and Others (with John Wesley). 1763.

Hymns for Children. 1763.

Minutes of Some Late Conversations, between the Rev. M. Wesleys and Others (with John Wesley). 1765.

Hymns for the Use of Families, and on Various Occasions. 1767.

Hymns on the Trinity. 1767.

Minutes of Several Conversations between the Reverend Messieurs John and Charles Wesley and Others (with John Wesley). 1770.

An Epistle to the Reverend Mr. George Whitefield: Written in the Year 1755. 1770.

An Elegy on the Late Reverend George Whitefield, M.A., Who Died September 30, 1770, in the 56th Year of His Age. 1771.

Preparation for Death, in Several Hymns (with John Wesley). 1772.

Minutes of Some Late Conversations between the Rev. M. Wesleys and Others (with John Wesley). 1777.

An Ode on the Death of Dr. Boyle. 1779.

A Hymn for the Rev. John Wesley. 1779.

Minutes of Some Late Conversations between the Rev. Mr. John and Charles Wesley and Others (with John Wesley). 1780.

Minutes of Several Conversations between the Reverend Mr. John and Charles Wesley and Others: From the Year 1744 to the Year 1780 (with John Wesley). 1780.

Hymns Written in the Time of the Tumults, June, 1780. 1780.

A Collection of Hymns for the Use of the People Called Methodists (with John Wesley). 1780.

The Protestant Association: Written in the Midst of the Tumults, June, 1780. 1781.

A Collection of Psalms and Hymns for the Lord's Day (with John Wesley). 1784.

Prayers for Condemned Malefactors. 1785.

Minutes of Some Late Conversations between the Rev. Messrs. Wesley and Others (with John Wesley). 1786.

Hymns for Children. Ed. John Wesley. 1790.

Some Account of the Life of Charles Wesley: Collected from His Private Journal. Ed. John Whitehead. 1793.

Sermons. Ed. Mrs. Samuel Wesley. 1816.

Journal; to Which Are Appended Selections from His Correspondence and Poetry. Ed. Thomas Jackson. 1849. 2 vols.

A Poetical Version of Nearly the Whole of the Psalms of David. Ed. Henry Fish. 1854.

Charles Wesley Seen in His Finer and Less Familiar Poems. Ed. F. M. Bird. 1867.

Poetical Works of John and Charles Wesley. Ed. George Osborn. 1868–72. 13 vols.

Eucharistic Manuals (with John Wesley). Ed. W. E. Dutton. 1880. 2 parts.

Early Journal 1736–1739. Ed. John Telford. 1910.

The Treasure House of Charles Wesley. Ed. John Telford. 1933.

Prayers and Praises. Ed. J. Alan Kay. 1958.

Representative Verse. Ed. Frank Baker. 1962.

A Rapture of Praise: Hymns (with John Wesley). Ed. H. A. Hodges. 1966.

The American War under the Conduct of Sir William Howe. Ed. Donald Baker. 1975.

Selected Prayers, Hymns, Journal Notes, Sermons, Letters and Treatises (with John Wesley). Ed. Frank Whiting. 1981.

BENJAMIN FRANKLIN (1706–1790)

A Dissertation on Liberty and Necessity, Pleasure and Pain. 1725.

A Modest Enquiry into the Nature and Necessity of a Paper-Currency. 1729.

Poor Richard, 1733: An Almanack for the Year of Christ 1733. 1732.

Poor Richard, 1734: An Almanack for the Year of Christ, 1734. 1733.

Poor Richard, 1735: An Almanack for the Year of Christ, 1735. 1734.

A Defense of the Rev. Mr. Hemphill's Observations; or, An Answer to the Vindication of the Reverend Commission. 1735.

A Letter to a Friend in the Country, Containing the Substance of a Sermon Preach'd at Philadelphia, in the Congregation of the Rev. Mr. Hemphill, concerning the Terms of Christian and Ministerial Communion. 1735.

Poor Richard, 1736: An Almanack for the Year of Christ 1736. 1735.

Some Observations on the Proceedings against the Rev. Mr. Hemphill; with a Vindication of His Sermons. 1735.

Poor Richard, 1737: An Almanack for the Year of Christ 1737. 1736.

Poor Richard, 1738: An Almanack for the Year of Christ 1738. 1737.

Poor Richard, 1739: An Almanack for the Year of Christ 1739. 1738.

Poor Richard, 1740: An Almanack for the Year of Christ 1740. 1739.

Poor Richard, 1741: An Almanack for the Year of Christ 1741. 1740.

Poor Richard, 1742: An Almanack for the Year of Christ 1742. 1741.

Poor Richard, 1743: An Almanack for the Year of Christ 1743. 1742.

Poor Richard, 1744: An Almanack for the Year of Christ 1744. 1743.

A Proposal for Promoting Useful Knowledge among the British Plantations in America. 1743.

An Account of the New Invented Pennsylvanian Fire-Places: Wherein Their Construction and Manner of Operation Is Particularly Explained; Their Advantages above Every Other Method of Warming Rooms Demonstrated; and All Objections That Have Been Raised against the Use of Them, Answered and Obviated. 1744.

A Catalog of Choice and Valuable Books Consisting of Near 600 Volumes in Most Faculties and Sciences, viz: Divinity, History, Law, Mathematics, Philosophy, Physic, Poetry, &c., Which Will Begin to Be Sold for Ready Money Only, by Benj. Franklin at the Post Office in Philadelphia, on Wednesday the 11th of April 1744 at Nine O Clock in the Morning: and for Despatch, the Lowest Price Is Mark'd in Each Book. 1744.

Poor Richard, 1745: An Almanack for the Year of Christ 1745. 1744.

Poor Richard, 1746: An Almanack for the Year of Christ, 1746. 1745.

Poor Richard, 1747: An Almanack for the Year of Christ 1747. 1746.

[*Reflections on Courtship and Marriage: In Two Letters to a Friend.* 1746.]

G. R.: By the Honourable the President and Council of the Province of Pennsylvania; a Proclamation for a General Fast. 1747.

⟨An Association for the General Defense of the City and Province.⟩ 1747. Lost.

Plain Truth; or, Serious Considerations on the Present State of the City of Philadelphia, and Province of Pennsylvania. 1747.

Note, This Almanack Us'd to Contain but 24 Pages, and Now has 36; yet the Price Is Very Little Advanced: Poor Richard Improved: Being an Almanack and Ephemeris of the Motions of the Sun and Moon; the True Places and Aspects of the Planets; the Rising and Setting of the Sun; and the Rising, Setting and Southing of the Moon, for the Bissextile Year, 1748. 1747.

Poor Richard Improved: Being an Almanack for the Year of Our Lord 1749. 1748.

Poor Richard Improved: Being an Almanack for the Year of Our Lord 1750. 1749.

Proposals Relating to the Education of Youth in Pensilvania. 1749.

Poor Richard Improved: Being an Almanack for the Year of Our Lord 1751. 1750.

Experiments and Observations on Electricity, Made at Philadelphia in America. 1751.

Idea of the English School, Sketch'd Out for the Consideration of the Trustees of the Philadelphia Academy. 1751.

Poor Richard Improved: Being an Almanack for the Year of Our Lord 1752. 1751.

Poor Richard Improved: Being an Almanack for the Year of Our Lord 1753. 1752.

A Letter from Benjamin Franklin to a Gentleman in New Jersey, Dated Philadelphia, June 6th, 1753. 1753.

Poor Richard Improved: Being an Almanack for the Year of Our Lord 1754. 1753.

Supplemental Experiments and Observations on Electricity. 1753.

New Experiments and Observations on Electricity. 1754.

Poor Richard Improved: Being an Almanack for the Year of Our Lord 1755. 1754.

Some Account of the Pennsylvania Hospital. 1754.

Advertisement, Lancaster, April 26, 1755. 1755.

Poor Richard Improved: Being an Almanack for the Year of Our Lord 1756. 1755.

Poor Richard Improved: Being an Almanack for the Year of Our Lord 1757. 1756.

Poor Richard Improved: Being an Almanack for the Year of Our Lord 1758. 1757.

[An Historical Review of the Constitution and Government of Pensylvania. 1759.]

Some Account of the Success of Inoculation for the Small-Pox in England and America. 1759.

1. And it came to pass after these things that Abraham sat in the door of his tent . . . ⟨Parable against Persecution⟩. c. 1759.

Father Abraham's Speech to a Great Number of People . . . ⟨The Way to Wealth⟩. 1760.

The Interest of Great Britain Considered, with Regard to Her Colonies, and the Acquisitions of Canada and Guadaloupe; to Which Are Added, Observations concerning the Increase of Mankind, Peopling of Countries, &c. 1760.

Cool Thoughts on the Present Situation of Our Public Affairs. 1764.

A Narrative of the Late Massacres, in Lancaster County, of a Number of Indians, Friends of This Province, by Persons Unknown. 1764.

Remarks on a Late Protest against the Appointment of Mr. Franklin an Agent for This Province. 1764.

Magna Britannia; Her Colonies Reduc'd. 1765.

Experiments and Observations on Electricity, Made at Philadelphia in America. 1769.

Letters to the Merchants Committee of Philadelphia (with John Neuville). 1770.

[Considerations on the Agreement of the Lords Commissioners of His Majesty's Treasury, with the Honourable Thomas Walpole and His Associates, for Lands upon the River Ohio, in North America. 1774.]

Of the Stilling of Waves by Means of Oil: Extracted from Sundry Letters between Benjamin Franklin, M.D., F.R.S., William Brownrigg, M.D., F.R.S. and the Reverend Mr. Parish. 1774.

Directions to the Deputy Post-Masters, for Keeping Their Accounts. 1775.

Tables of the Port of All Single Letters Carried by Post in the Northern District of North America, as Established by Congress. 1775.

The Following Paper Is Supposed To Have Been Written by a Celebrated American Philosopher (Doctor Benjamin Franklin) at Paris; for the Purpose of Borrowing Money for the Use of the United States of America: and It Has Had a Wonderful Effect; Large Sums Having Been Lent, in Consequence of the Sound and Irrefutable Facts and Arguments Contained in It. 1777.

Political, Miscellanous, and Political Pieces. Ed. Benjamin Vaughan. 1779. 2 vols.

Franklin's Game of Chess, with Anecdotes ⟨Morals of Chess⟩. c. 1780.

Advice to Such as Would Remove to America. 1784.

Rapport des Commissaires chargés par le Roi, de l'examen du magnétisme animal (with others). 1784.

Two Tracts. 1784.

⟨Proclamation of the President and Executive Council, Offering a Reward for the Apprehension of Daniel Shays and Others.⟩ 1787.

Philosophical and Miscellaneous Papers. Ed. Edward Bancroft. 1787.

[Avis aux faiseurs de constitutions. 1789.]

Rules for Reducing a Great Empire to a Small One. 1793.

Works. Ed. Benjamin Vaughan. 1793. 2 vols.

Advice to a Young Tradesman. c. 1800.

Necessary Hints to Those Who Would Be Rich. 1805.

Complete Works in Philosophy, Politics, and Morals. 1806. 3 vols.

Works. Ed. William Duane. 1808–18. 6 vols.

The Art of Swimming. 1816.

Memoirs of the Life and Writings of Benjamin Franklin, Written by Himself to a Late Period ⟨Autobiography, parts 1–3⟩, and Continued to the Time of His Death, by His Grandson, Now First Published from the Original MSS., Comprising the Private Correspondence and Public Negotiations of Dr. Franklin, and a Selection from his Political, Philosophical, and Miscellaneous Works. Ed. William Temple Franklin. 1818. 3 vols.

The Art of Making Money Plenty in Every Man's Pocket. c. 1830.

Works. Ed. Jared Sparks. 1836–40. 10 vols.

Autobiography ⟨parts 1–4⟩. Ed. John Bigelow. 1868.

Rules from a Club Established in Philadelphia. 1883.

Complete Works. Ed. John Bigelow. 1887–89. 10 vols.

Writings. Ed. Albert Henry Smyth. 1905. 10 vols.

"My Dear Girl": The Correspondence of Benjamin Franklin with Polly Stevenson, Georgiana and Catherine Shipley. Ed. James Madison Stifler. 1927.

Autobiographical Writings. Ed. Carl Van Doren. 1945.

A Benjamin Franklin Reader. Ed. Nathan G. Goodman. 1945.

Letters and Papers of Benjamin Franklin and Richard Jackson 1753–1785. Ed. Carl Van Doren. 1947.

Benjamin Franklin and Catharine Ray Greene: Their Correspondence 1755–1790. Ed. William Greene Roelker. 1949.

Letters of Benjamin Franklin and Jane Mecom. Ed. Carl Van Doren. 1950.

Letters to the Press 1758–1775. Ed. Verner W. Crane. 1950.

Papers. Eds. Leonard W. Labaree et al. 1959– .

The Political Thought of Benjamin Franklin. Ed. Ralph L. Ketcham. 1965.

Writings. Ed. J. A. Leo Lemay. 1987.

ADAM SMITH (1723–1790)

The Theory of Moral Sentiments. 1759, 1790 (6th rev. ed.; 2 vols.).

An Inquiry into the Nature and Causes of the Wealth of Nations. 1776 (2 vols.), 1791 (6th rev. ed.; 3 vols.).

Essays on Philosophical Subjects. 1795.

Works. 1811–12. 5 vols.

Lectures on Justice, Police, Revenue and Arms Delivered in the University of Glasgow: Reported by a Student in 1763. Ed. Edwin Cannan. 1896.

Adam Smith's Moral and Political Philosophy. Ed. Herbert W. Schneider. 1948.

Lectures on Rhetoric and Belles Lettres Delivered in the University of Glasgow: Reported by a Student in 1762–63. Ed. John M. Lothian. 1963.

Early Writings. Ed. J. Ralph Lindgren. 1967.

The Wisdom of Adam Smith. Ed. Benjamin A. Rogge. 1976.

Works and Correspondence (Glasgow Edition). 1976–83. 6 vols. in 7.

The Essential Adam Smith. Eds. Robert L. Heilbroner and Laurence J. Malone. 1986.

THOMAS WARTON (1728–1790)

Five Pastoral Eclogues. 1745.

The Pleasures of Melancholy. 1747.

The Triumph of Isis. 1749.

Verses on Miss Cotes and Miss Wilmot. 1749.

A Description of the City, College, and Cathedral of Winchester. 1750.

Newmarket: A Satire. 1751.

Ode for Music as Performed at a Theatre in Oxford. 1751.

The Union; or, Select Scots and English Poems (editor). 1753.

Observations on the Faerie Queene *of Spenser.* 1754, 1762 (2 vols.).

Inscriptionum Romanorum Metricarum Delectus (editor). 1758.

Mons Catharinae, prope Wintoniani. 1760.

A Companion to the Guide, and a Guide to the Companion: A Supplement to All Accounts of Oxford. c. 1760.

The Life and Literary Remains of Ralph Bathurst. 1761. 2 vols.

The Oxford Sausage; or, Select Poetical Pieces (editor). 1764.

Anthologiae Graecae a Constantino Cephala Conditae Libri Tres (editor). 1766.

Theocriti Syracusii Quae Supersunt (editor). 1770. 2 vols.

The Life of Sir Thomas Pope, Founder of Trinity College. 1772.

The History of English Poetry from the Close of the Eleventh to the Commencement of the Eighteenth Century. 1774 [Volume 1]; 1778 [Volume 2]; 1781 [Volume 3]; 1789 [Volume 4; fragmentary].

Poems. 1777.

Specimen of a Parochial History of Oxfordshire. 1782.

An Enquiry into the Authenticity of the Poems Attributed to Thomas Rowley. 1782.

Verses on Sir Joshua Reynolds's Painted Window at New College. 1782.

Poems upon Several Occasions by John Milton (editor). 1785.

Verses Left under a Stone. c. 1790.

Essays on Gothic Architecture (with others). 1800.

Poetical Works. Ed. Richard Mant. 1802. 2 vols.

Poetical Works. Ed. T. Park. 1805.

Poems (with others). Ed. Robert Aris Willmott. 1854.

Poetical Works (with William Collins and Oliver Goldsmith). Ed. George Gilfillan. 1854.

The Hamlet: An Ode Written in Whichword Forest. 1859.

The Three Wartons: A Choice of Their Verse. Ed. Eric Partridge. 1927.

The Correspondence of Thomas Percy and Thomas Warton. Eds. M. G. Robinson and Leah Dennis. 1951.

A History of English Poetry: An Unpublished Continuation. Ed. Rodney M. Baine. 1953.

JOHN WESLEY (1703–1791)

A Collection of Forms of Prayer for Every Day in the Week. 1733.

A Treatise on Christian Prudence by John Norris (abridged by Wesley). 1734.

Reflections upon the Conduct of Human Life by John Norris (abridged by Wesley). 1734.

The Christian Pattern; or, The Treatise of the Imitation of Christ by Thomas à Kempis (editor and translator). 1735.

A Sermon Preached at St. Mary's in Oxford. 1735.

A Collection of Psalms and Hymns. 1737.

A Collection of Psalms and Hymns. 1738.

A Sermon on Salvation by Faith. 1738.

The Doctrine of Salvation, Faith and Good Works: Extracted from the Homilies of the Church of England (editor). 1739.

An Abstract of the Life and Death of the Reverend Learned and Pious Mr. Thomas Halyburton, M.A. (editor). 1739.

Free Grace: A Sermon Preach'd at Bristol. 1739.

Nicodemus; or, A Treatise on the Fear of Man by August Herman Franck (editor). 1739.

An Extract of the Rev. Mr. John Wesley's Journal, from His Embarking for Georgia to His Return to London. 1739.

Two Treatises by Robert Barnes (editor). 1739.

Hymns and Sacred Poems (with Charles Wesley). 1739.

Serious Considerations concerning the Doctrines of Election and Reprobation by Isaac Watts (editor). 1740.

The Nature and Design of Christianity ⟨A Practical Treatise upon Christian Perfection⟩ by William Law (abridged by Wesley). 1740.

An Extract of the Rev. Mr. John Wesley's Journal, from February 1, 1737–38, to His Return from Germany. 1740.

Hymns and Sacred Poems ⟨second collection⟩ (with Charles Wesley). 1740.

An Extract from the Rev. Mr. John Wesley's Journal with Regard to the Affidavit Made by Captain Roger Williams. 1741.

An Extract of the Life of Monsieur de Renty by John Baptist S. Jure (editor). 1741.

Serious Considerations on Absolute Predestination by Robert Barclay (editor). 1741.

A Dialogue between a Predestinarian and His Friend. 1741.

The Scripture Doctrine concerning Predestination, Election, and Reprobation (editor). 1741.

The Almost Christian: A Sermon Preached at St. Mary's, Oxford, before the University. 1741.

Christian Perfection. 1741.

A Collection of Psalms and Hymns (with Charles Wesley). 1741.

Hymns on God's Everlasting Love (with Charles Wesley). 1741.

The Character of a Methodist. 1742.

The Principles of a Methodist. 1742.

An Extract from the Rev. Mr. John Wesley's Journal, from August 12, 1738, to Nov. 1, 1739. 1742.

Hymns and Sacred Poems ⟨third collection⟩ (with Charles Wesley). 1742.

A Collection of Hymns (with Charles Wesley). 1742.

Thoughts on Married and a Single Life. 1743.

The Nature, Design, and General Rules of the United Societies, in London, Bristol, Kingswood, and Newcastle-upon-Tyne (with Charles Wesley). 1743.

A Practical Treatise on Christian Perfection by William Law (editor). 1743.

An Earnest Appeal to Men of Reason and Religion. 1743.

The Pilgrim's Progress by John Bunyan (abridged by Wesley). 1743.

A Word in Season; or, Advice to a Soldier. c. 1743.

A Serious Call to a Holy Life by William Law (abridged by Wesley). 1744.

The Distinguishing Marks of a Work of the Spirit of God by Jonathan Edwards (editor). 1744.

An Extract of Count Zinzendorf's Discourses on the Redemption of Man by the Death of Christ (editor). 1744.

The Life of God in the Soul of Man by Henry Scougall (abridged by Wesley). 1744.

A Brief Account of the Occasion, Process, and Issue of a Late Tryal by George Whitefield (abridged by Wesley). 1744.

An Extract of the Reverend Mr. John Wesley's Journal, from November 1, 1739, to September 3, 1741. 1744.

A Narrative of the Late Work of God at and near Northampton, in New England by Jonathan Edwards (abridged by Wesley). 1744.

Scriptural Christianity: A Sermon Preached at St. Mary's Church in Oxford, before the University. 1744.

The Case of John Nelson by John Nelson (editor). 1744.

Rules of the Band Societies. 1744.

A Collection of Moral and Sacred Poems (editor). 1744. 3 vols.

Hymns for Times of Trouble and Persecution (with Charles Wesley). 1744.

Hymns for Times of Trouble (with Charles Wesley). 1744.

Instructions for Children by Claude Fleury and M. Poiret (translator). 1745.

A Farther Appeal to Men of Reason and Religion. 1745. 3 parts.

An Answer to the Rev. Mr. Church's Remarks on the Rev. Mr. John Wesley's Last Journal. 1745.

Thoughts concerning the Present Revival of England in New-England by Jonathan Edwards (abridged by Wesley). 1745.

An Extract of Mr. Richard Baxter's Aphorisms of Justification (editor). 1745.

A Short View of the Difference between the Moravian Brethren, Lately in England, and the Reverend Mr. John and Charles Wesley: Extracted Chiefly from a Late Journal (with Charles Wesley). 1745.

A Collection of Receits for the Use of the Poor. 1745.

A Dialogue between an Antinomian and His Friend. 1745.

A Second Dialogue between an Antinomian and His Friend. 1745.

Modern Christianity: Exemplified at Wednesbury, and Other Adjacent Places in Staffordshire. 1745.

Advice to the People Called Methodists. 1745.

A Collection of Prayers for Families (editor). 1745.

A Letter to the Author of The Craftsman *concerning Real Christianity, Disparag'd under the Name of Methodism.* 1745.

A Word in Season; or, Advice to an Englishman. 1745.

A Word to a Drunkard. 1745.

"Swear Not at All." 1745.

A Word to a Sabbath Breaker. 1745.

Remember the Sabbath Day, to Keep It Holy. 1745.

A Word to a Condemned Malefactor. 1745.

A Word to a Protestant. 1745.

Hymns on the Lord's Supper (with Charles Wesley). 1745.

Hymns for the Nativity of Our Lord (with Charles Wesley). 1745.

A Word to a Street Walker. c. 1745.

Lessons for Children and Others (editor). 1746–54. 4 parts.

A Word of Advice to Saints and Sinners by Thomas Willcocks (abridged by Wesley). 1746.

The Principles of a Methodist Farther Explain'd. 1746.

Sermons on Several Occasions. 1746–50 [Volumes 1–3]; 1760 [Volume 4]; 1788 [Volumes 5–8]; 1800 [Volume 9].

A Short Account of the Death of Samuel Hitchens by James Hitchens (editor). 1746.

Hymns for Our Lord's Resurrection (with Charles Wesley). 1746.

Hymns for Ascension Day (with Charles Wesley). 1746.

Hymns of Petition and Thanksgiving for the Promise of the Father (with Charles Wesley). 1746.

Gloria Patri, &c.; or, Hymns to the Trinity (with Charles Wesley). 1746.

Hymns on the Great Festivals, and Other Occasions (with Charles Wesley). 1746.

Hymns for the Public Thanksgiving-Day (with Charles Wesley). 1746.

Hymns for the Watch-Night (with Charles Wesley). 1746.

Graces before Meat (with Charles Wesley). 1746.

Hymns for Children (with Charles Wesley). 1746.

Primitive Physick; or, An Easy and Natural Method of Curing Most Diseases. 1747.

A Short Account of the Death of Thomas Hitchens by James Hitchens (editor). 1747.

A Letter to the Right Reverend the Lord Bishop of London. 1747.

A Word to a Freeholder, &c. 1747.

Hymns and Sacred Poems (with Charles Wesley). 1747.

A Letter to a Person Lately Join'd with the People Call'd Quakers. 1748.

A Word to a Methodist. 1748.

A Letter to a Clergyman. 1748.

A Short Latin Grammar. 1748.

A Short English Grammar. 1748.

De Christi Imitando Libri Tres by Thomas à Kempis (editor). 1748.

Mathurini Corderii Colloquia Selecta (editor). 1748.

Historiae et Praecepta Selecta (editor). 1748.

Instructiones Pueriles (editor). 1748.

A Serious Answer to Dr. Trapp's Four Sermons on the Sin,

Folly, and Danger of Being Righteous Overwell by William Law (editor). 1748.

A Letter to a Friend concerning Tea. 1748.

An Extract of the Revd. John Wesley's Journal, from Sept. 3, 1741, to October 27, 1743. 1749.

A Letter to the Reverend Dr. Conyers Middleton, Occasioned by His Late Free Enquiry. 1749.

The Manners of the Ancient Christians by Claude Fleury (editor). 1749.

A Token for Children by James Janeway (editor). 1749.

Directions concerning Pronunciation and Gesture. 1749.

A Plain Account of the People Called Methodists. 1749.

A Short Account of the School in Kingswood, near Bristol. 1749.

Bellum Catilinarum et Jugurthinum by Sallust (editor). 1749.

Excellentium Imperatorium Vitae by Nepos (editor). 1749.

Excerpta ex Ovidio, Virgilio, Horatio, Juvenali, Persio, et Martiali (editor). 1749.

A Christian Library (editor). 1749–55. 50 vols.

An Answer to a Letter Published in the Bath Journal, *April 17, 1749.* 1749.

A Short Address to the Inhabitants of Ireland: Occasioned by Some Late Occurrences. 1749.

A Letter to a Roman Catholick. 1749.

Minutes of Some Late Conversations between the Revd. M. Wesleys and Others (with Charles Wesley). 1749.

Minutes of Some Late Conversations between the Revd. M. Wesleys and Others (with Charles Wesley). 1749.

Hymns Composed for the Use of the Brethren (with Charles Wesley). 1749.

A Letter to the Author of The Enthusiasm of Methodists and Papists Compar'd. 1750.

A Compendium of Logick by Henry Aldrich (abridged by Wesley). 1750.

A Letter to the Revd. Mr. Baily, of Corke. 1750.

A Short Account of God's Dealings with Mr. Thomas Hogg by Thomas Hogg (editor). 1750.

Fabulae Selectae by Phaedrus (editor). 1750.

Colloquia Selecta by Erasmus (editor). 1750.

Hymns for New Year's Day, 1750 (with Charles Wesley). 1750.

Hymns Occasioned by the Earthquake (with Charles Wesley). 1750. 2 parts.

Hymns for New Year's Day, 1751 (with Charles Wesley). 1751.

Thoughts upon Infant-Baptism by William Wall (abridged by Wesley). 1751.

A Short Hebrew Grammar. 1751.

A Short French Grammar. 1751.

A Second Letter to the Author of The Enthusiasm of Methodists and Papists Compar'd. 1751.

Serious Thoughts upon the Perseverence of the Saints. 1751.

A Second Letter to the Lord Bishop of Exeter. 1752.

Predestination Calmly Considered. 1752.

A Short Method of Converting All the Roman Catholicks in the Kingdom of Ireland. 1752.

Serious Thoughts concerning Godfathers and Godmothers. 1752.

Some Account of the Life and Death of Matthew Lee. 1752.

An Extract of the Life and Death of Mr. John Janeway by James Wheatley (editor). 1753.

An Extract of the Reverend John Wesley's Journal, from October 27, 1743, to November 17, 1746. 1753.

The Advantages of the Members of the Church of England over Those of the Church of Rome. 1753.

The Complete English Dictionary. 1753.

Minutes of Several Conversations between the Reverend Mr. John Wesley and Charles Wesley, and Others (with Charles Wesley). 1753.

Hymns and Spiritual Songs (with Charles Wesley). 1753.

An Extract of the Reverend Mr. John Wesley's Journal, from November 25, 1746, to July 20, 1749. 1754.

An Answer to All Which the Revd. Dr. Gill Has Printed on the Final Perseverence of the Saints. 1754.

Hymns for New Year's Day, 1755 (with Charles Wesley). 1755.

Queries Humbly Proposed to the Right Reverend and Right Honourable Count Zinzendorf. 1755.

Catholick Spirit. 1755.

Serious Thoughts Occasioned by the Late Earthquake at Lisbon. 1755.

Explanatory Notes upon the New Testament. 1755.

A Letter to Reverend Mr. Law: Occasioned by Some of His Late Writings. 1756.

An Address to the Clergy. 1756.

An Extract of the Reverend John Wesley's Journal, from July 20, 1749, to October 30, 1751. 1756.

[*A Short Account of the Death of Richard Moore* (editor). 1756.]

The Good Soldier: Extracted from a Sermon Preached to a Company of Volunteers, Raised in Virginia by Samuel Davies (editor). 1756.

[*A Word to Those Freemen of the Established Church Who Make the Scriptures the One Rule of Their Faith and Practice.* 1756.]

Hymns for the Year 1756 (with Charles Wesley). 1756.

The Doctrine of Original Sin: According to Scripture, Reason, and Experience. 1757.

A Sufficient Answer to Letters to the Author of Theron and Aspasio. 1757.

Hymns for New Year's Day, 1758 (with Charles Wesley). 1758.

A Letter to Gentlemen at Bristol. 1758.

The Great Assize: A Sermon Preached at the Assizes at St. Paul's Church, Bedford. 1758.

A Letter to the Rev. Dr. Free. 1758.

A Second Letter to the Rev. Dr. Free. 1758.

A Short Account of the Life and Death of Nathaniel Otten. 1758.

A Letter to the Rev. Mr. Potter. 1758.

The Case of the Unhappy People of Custrin. 1758.

Hymns of Intercession for All Mankind (with Charles Wesley). 1758.

A Preservative against Unsettled Notions in Religion. 1758.

A Short Explanation of the Ten Commandments by Ezekiel Hopkins (abridged by Wesley). 1759.

An Extract of the Rev. Mr. John Wesley's Journal, from Nov. 2, 1750 ⟨i.e. 1751⟩, *to October 28, 1754.* 1759.

A Letter to the Reverend Mr. Downes. 1759.

A Sermon on Original Sin. 1759.

Reasons against a Separation from the Church of England ⟨by John Wesley⟩; *with Hymns for the Preachers among the Methodists* ⟨by Charles Wesley⟩. 1760.

The Desideratum; or, Electricity Made Plain and Useful. 1760.

Original Letters between the Rev. Mr. John Wesley and Mr. Richard Thompson, Respecting the Doctrine of Assurance. 1760.

An Extract of the Rev. Mr. John Wesley's Journal, from February 16, 1755, to June 16, 1758. 1761.

Hymns for Those to Whom Christ Is All in All (with Charles Wesley). 1761.

Select Hymns; with Tunes Annext: Designed Chiefly for the Use of the People Called Methodists (with Charles Wesley). 1761. 2 vols.

A Letter to the Rev. Mr. Horne: Occasioned by His Late Sermon Preached before the University of Oxford. 1762.

Thoughts on the Imputed Righteousness of Christ. 1762.

A Blow at the Root; or, Christ Stabbed in the House of His Friends. 1762.

Wandering Thoughts. 1762.

A Letter to the Right Reverend the Lord Bishop of Gloucester: Occasioned by His Tract on the Office and Operations of the Holy Spirit. 1763.

A Sermon Preached before the Society for Reformation of Manners. 1763.

A Discourse on Sin in Believers. 1763.

Farther Thoughts upon Christian Perfection. 1763.

A Survey of the Wisdom of God in the Creation; or, A Compendium of Natural Philosophy (editor). 1763 (2 vols.), 1770 (3 vols.), 1777 (5 vols.).

Minutes of Several Conversations between the Rev. Mr. John and Charles Wesley, and Others (with Charles Wesley). 1763.

An Extract from Milton's Paradise Lost, *with Notes* (editor). 1763.

An Extract of the Rev. Mr. John Wesley's Journal, from June 17, 1758, to May 5, 1760. 1764.

Letters Wrote by Jane Cooper; to Which Is Prefixt Some Account of Her Life and Death (editor). 1764.

A Treatise on Justification by John Goodwin (editor). 1765.

Thoughts on a Single Life. 1765.

A Short History of Methodism. 1765.

The Scripture-Way of Salvation: A Sermon on Ephes. ii. 8. 1765.

Minutes of Some Late Conversations, between the Rev. M. Wesleys and Others (with Charles Wesley). 1765.

A Short Greek Grammar. 1765.

Explanatory Notes upon the Old Testament. 1765. 3 vols.

The Lord Our Righteousness: A Sermon Preached at the Chapel in West-Street, Seven-Dials. 1766.

Some Remarks on a Defence of the Preface to the Edinburgh Edition of Aspasio Vindicated. 1766.

Minutes of Some Late Conversations between the Reverend Mr. Wesley and Others. 1766.

A Plain Account of Christian Perfection as Believed and Taught by the Rev. Mr. John Wesley, from the Year 1725 to the Year 1765. 1766.

Rev. Sir, near two years and a half ago . . . 1766.

A Word to a Smuggler. 1767.

An Extract of the Rev. Mr. John Wesley's Journal, from May 6, 1760, to Oct. 28, 1762. 1767.

Christian Letters by Joseph Alleine (editor). 1767.

The Witness of the Spirit: A Sermon on Romans viii. 16. 1767.

Thoughts on the Sin of Onan by Dr. Tissot (editor). 1767.

Minutes of Some Late Conversations between Rev. Mr. Wesley and Others. 1767.

An Extract of the Rev. Mr. John Wesley's Journal, from October 29, 1762, to May 25, 1765. 1768.

The Repentance of Believers: A Sermon on Mark i. 15. 1768.

A Letter to the Reverend Dr. Rutherforth. 1768.

An Extract of Miss Mary Gilbert's Journal (editor). 1768.

The Good Steward. 1768.

An Extract from the Rev. Mr. Law's Later Works (editor). 1768. 2 vols.

An Extract from the Life of the Late Mr. David Brainerd (editor). 1768.

Minutes of Some Late Conversations between the Rev. Mr. Wesley and Others. 1768.

Advices with Respect to Health by Dr. Tissot (editor). 1769.

An Extract from the Journal of Elizabeth Harper (editor). 1769.

An Extract of Letters by Mrs. L*** (editor). 1769.

Minutes of Some Late Conversations between the Rev. Mr. Wesley and Others. 1769.

My dear brother, two years ago . . . 1769.

A Short Account of the Death of Mary Langson, of Taxall, in Cheshire by Thomas Olivers (editor). 1770.

The Question, What Is an Arminian? Answered. 1770.

The Doctrine of Absolute Predestination Stated and Asserted by Augustus Toplady (abridged by Wesley). 1770.

Some Account of the Experience of E. J. (editor). 1770.

A Short Account of Ann Rogers by John Johnson (editor). 1770.

Free Thoughts on the Present State of Public Affairs. 1770.

A Sermon on the Death of the Rev. Mr. George Whitefield. 1770.

Minutes of Some Late Conversations between the Rev. Mr. Wesley and Others. 1770.

Minutes of Several Conversations between the Reverend Messieurs John and Charles Wesley and Others (with Charles Wesley). 1770.

An Extract from Dr. Young's Night-Thoughts on Life, Death, and Immortality (editor). 1770.

An Extract of the Rev. Mr. John Wesley's Journal, from May 27, 1765, to May 18, 1768. 1771.

A Letter to the Reverend Mr. Fleury. 1771.

A Defence of the Minute of Conference (1770) Relating to Calvinism. 1771.

The Consequence Proved. 1771.

Minutes of Some Late Conversations between the Rev. Mr. Wesley and Others. 1771.

Works. 1771–74. 32 vols.

A Vindication of the Rev. Mr. Wesley's Last Minutes by John Fletcher (editor). 1771.

Thoughts upon Liberty. 1772.

Thoughts concerning the Origin of Power. 1772.

Prayers for Children. 1772.

Minutes of Some Late Conversations between the Rev. Mr. Wesley and Others. 1772.

Some Remarks on Mr. Hill's Review of All the Doctrines Taught by Mr. John Wesley. 1772.

Preparation for Death, in Several Hymns (with Charles Wesley). 1772.

Thoughts on the Present Scarcity of Provisions. 1773.

Some Remarks on Mr. Hill's Farrago Double-Distilled. 1773.

Some Account of the Life and Death of Nicholas Mooney (abridged by Wesley). 1773.

A Short Roman History. 1773.

A Sermon on Romans viii. 29, 30. 1773.

Minutes of Some Late Conversations between the Rev. Mr. Wesley and Others. 1773.

A Short Account of the Life and Death of Miss Alice Gilbert (editor). 1773.

A Treatise concerning Religious Affections by Jonathan Edwards (abridged by Wesley). 1773.

Select Parts of Mr. Herbert's Sacred Poems (editor). 1773.

Thoughts upon Slavery. 1774.

A Sermon at the Opening of the New Meeting-House at Wakefield. 1774.

Thoughts upon Necessity. 1774.

An Extract of the Rev. Mr. John Wesley's Journal, from May 14, 1768, to September 1, 1770. 1774.

Minutes of Some Late Conversations between the Reverend Mr. Wesley and Others. 1774.

The First Part of an Equal Check to Pharisaism and Antinomianism by John Fletcher (abridged by Wesley). 1774.

A Calm Address to Our American Colonies. 1775.

A Sermon on 1st John v. 7. 1775.

Minutes of Some Late Conversations between the Reverend Mr. Wesley and Others. 1775.

The Important Question: A Sermon Preached in Taunton, Somersetshire. 1775.

A Sermon Preached at St. Matthew's, Bethnal Green, for the Benefit of the Widows and Orphans of the Soldiers Who Lately Fell, near Boston in New-England. 1775.

Some Observations on Liberty: Occasioned by a Late Tract. 1776.

A Seasonable Address to the More Serious Part of the Inhabitants of Great Britain, Respecting the Unhappy Contest between Us and Our American Brethren. 1776.

Minutes of Some Late Conversations between the Rev. Mr. Wesley and Others. 1776.

A Concise History of England from the Earliest Times to the Death of George II. 1776. 4 vols.

An Extract of the Life of Madame Guion (editor). 1776.

An Account of the Extraordinary Deliverance of Thomas Cross by Thomas Cross (editor). 1776.

The Saints' Everlasting Rest by Richard Baxter (abridged by Wesley). 1776.

A Calm Address to the Inhabitants of England. 1777.

A Sermon on Numbers xxiiii. 23: Preached on Laying the Foundation of the New Chappel, near the City Road, London. 1777.

An Extract of the Rev. Mr. John Wesley's Journal, from Sep. 2, 1770, to Sep. 12, 1773. 1777.

Thoughts upon God's Sovereignty. 1777.

An Answer to Mr. Rowland Hill's Tract, Entitled Imposture Detected. 1777.

Minutes of Some Late Conversations between the Rev. M. Wesleys and Others (with Charles Wesley). 1777.

A Short Account of the Death of Elizabeth Hindmarsh (editor). 1777.

A Sermon Preached in Lewisham Church, before the Humane Society. 1777.

A Letter to the Rev. Mr. Thomas Maxfield, Occasioned by a Late Publication. 1778.

A Serious Address to the People of England, with Regard to the State of the Nation. 1778.

A Compassionate Address to the Inhabitants of Ireland. 1778.

A Call to Backsliders: A Sermon on Psalm lxxxvi. 7, 8. 1778.

Some Account of the Late Work of God in North America, in a Sermon on Ezekiel i. 16. 1778.

Minutes of Some Late Conversations between the Rev. Mr. Wesley and Others. 1778.

Dublin, Tuesday, July 7, 1778: Minutes of the Irish Conference (editor). 1778.

An Answer to Several Objections against This Work ⟨The Arminian Magazine⟩: In a Letter to a Friend. 1778.

An Extract of the Rev. Mr. John Wesley's Journal, from September 13, 1773, to January 2, 1776. 1779.

Popery Calmly Considered. 1779.

Minutes of Some Late Conversations, &c., at London. 1779.

A Letter to the Printer of the Public Advertiser. 1780.

An Account of the Conduct of the War in the Middle Colonies by Joseph Galloway (editor). 1780.

Reflections on the Rise and Progress of the American Rebellion. 1780.

A Letter to Mr. John Whittingham. 1780.

Minutes of Some Late Conversations between the Rev. Mr. John and Charles Wesley and Others (with Charles Wesley). 1780.

Minutes of Several Conversations between the Reverend Mr. John and Charles Wesley and Others: From the Year 1744 to the Year 1780 (with Charles Wesley). 1780.

Directions for Renewing Our Covenant with God. 1780.

A Collection of Hymns for the Use of the People Called Methodists (with Charles Wesley). 1780.

A Letter to the Printer of The Public Advertiser, *Occasioned by the Late Act Passed in Favour of Popery.* 1781.

A Short Account of the Life of Mr. Thomas Mitchell by Thomas Mitchell (editor). 1781.

The History of Henry, Earl of Moreland ⟨The Fool of Quality⟩ by Henry Brooke (abridged by Wesley). 1781. 2 vols.

An Extract from a Reply to the Observations of Lieut. Gen. Sir William Howe, on a Pamphlet, Entitled, Letters to a Nobleman by Joseph Galloway (editor). 1781.

An Extract of a Letter to the Right Honourable Lord Viscount H**e on His Naval Conduct in the American War by Joseph Galloway (editor). 1781.

Minutes of Some Late Conversations between the Rev. Mr. John Wesley and Others. 1781.

A Concise Ecclesiastical History from the Birth of Christ to the Beginning of the Present Century. 1781. 4 vols.

An Estimate of the Manners of the Present Time. 1782.

An Extract from John Nelson's Journal: Being an Account of God's Dealing with Him from His Youth to the Forty-second Year of His Age (editor). 1782.

An Alarm to Unconverted Sinners by Joseph Alleine (editor). 1782.

A Call to the Unconverted by Richard Baxter (editor). 1782.

Minutes of Some Late Conversations between the Rev. J. Wesley and Others. 1782.

Hymns for the National Fast. 1782.

Hymns for the Nation in 1782. 1782. 2 parts.

An Extract of the Rev. Mr. John Wesley's Journal, from January 1, 1776, to August 8, 1779. 1783.

The Duty and Advantage of Early Rising. 1783.

The Case of the Bristal House. 1783.

Minutes of Some Late Conversations between the Rev. Mr. Wesley and Others. 1783.

Minutes of Some Late Conversations between the Rev. Mr. J. Wesley and Others. 1783.

Minutes of Some Late Conversations between the Rev. Mr. Wesley and Others. 1784.

The Sunday Service of the Methodists in the United States of America, with Other Occasional Services. 1784.

A Collection of Psalms and Hymns for the Lord's Day (with Charles Wesley). 1784.

A Short Account of God's Dealings with Mr. John Haime (editor). 1785.

Minutes of Some Late Conversations between the Rev. John Wesley, M.A., and Others. 1785.

Minutes of Some Late Conversations between the Rev. Mr. Wesley and Others. 1785.

A Sermon Preached on Occasion of the Death of the Rev. Mr. John Fletcher, Vicar of Madeley, Shropshire. 1785.

A Pocket Hymn-Book, for the Use of Christians of All Denominations (editor). 1785.

An Extract of the Rev. Mr. John Wesley's Journal, from August 9, 1779, to August 26, 1782. 1786.

Minutes of Some Late Conversations between the Rev. Messrs. Wesley and Others (with Charles Wesley). 1786.

A Short Account of the Life and Death of the Rev. Mr. John Fletcher. 1786.

The Sunday Service of the Methodists in His Majesty's Dominions; with Other Occasional Services. 1786.

Conjectures concerning the Nature of Future Happiness by M. Bonnet (translator). 1787.

Minutes of Some Late Conversations between the Rev. John Wesley, M.A., and Others. 1787.

Minutes of Some Late Conversations between the Rev. J. Wesley and Others. 1787.

A Pocket Hymn-Book for the Use of Christians of All Denominations (editor). 1787.

Minutes of Some Late Conversations between the Rev. J. Wesley and Others. 1788.

An Extract of the Rev. Mr. John Wesley's Journal, from September 4, 1782, to June 28, 1786. 1789.

Minutes of Some Late Conversations between the Rev. Mr. John Wesley, M.A., and Others. 1789.

Minutes of Some Late Conversations between the Rev. Mr. Wesley and Others. 1789.

The Case of Dewsbury House. 1789.

Minutes of Several Conversations between the Rev. Mr. Wesley and Others, from the Year 1744 to the Year 1789. 1789.

The Life of Mr. Silas Told (abridged by Wesley). 1790.

A Sermon Preached at Leeds before the Methodist Preachers. 1790.

Letters That Passed between the Rev. John Wesley, and Rev. John Atlay, Relative to the People and Preaching-House at Dewsbury. 1790.

A Short Account of the Life and Death of Jane Newland, of Dublin (editor). 1790.

Minutes of Some Late Conversations between the Rev. Mr. Wesley and Others. 1790.

The New Testament, with an Analysis of the Several Books and Chapters (editor and translator). 1790.

The Rules of the Strangers' Friend Society in Bristol. 1790.

Hymns for Children by Charles Wesley (editor). 1790.

An Extract of the Rev. Mr. John Wesley's Journal, from June 29, 1786, to Oct. 24, 1790. 1791.

The Beauties of John Wesley. 1802.

Works. Ed. Joseph Benson. 1809–13. 17 vols.

Journal. 1827. 4 vols.

Works. Ed. Thomas Jackson. 1829–31. 14 vols.

Select Letters, Chiefly on Personal Religion. Ed. Thomas Jackson. 1837.

Narrative of a Remarkable Transaction in the Early Life of John Wesley. Ed. Charles Hook. 1848.

Poetical Works of John and Charles Wesley. Ed. George Osborn. 1868–72. 13 vols.

Eucharistic Manuals (with Charles Wesley). Ed. W. E. Dutton. 1880. 2 parts.

The Living Thoughts of John Wesley. Ed. J. H. Potts. 1891.

Journal. 1903. 4 vols.

Journal. Ed. F. W. Macdonald. 1906. 4 vols.

Journal. Ed. Nehemiah Curnock. 1909–16. 8 vols.

Letters. Ed. George Eayrs. 1915.

Standard Sermons. Ed. Edward H. Sugden. 1921. 2 vols.

Letters. Ed. John Telford. 1931. 8 vols.

Journal. Ed. Nora Ratcliff. 1940.

Prayers. Ed. Frederick C. Gill. 1951.

Selections from the Journal. Ed. Hugh Martin. 1955.

Selected Letters. Ed. Frederick C. Gill. 1956.

John Wesley. Ed. A. C. Outler. 1964.

John Wesley: An Autobiographical Sketch of the Man and His Thought, Chiefly from His Letters. Ed. Ole E. Borgen. 1966.

A Rapture of Praise: Hymns (with Charles Wesley). Ed. H. A. Hodges. 1966.

John Wesley in Wales 1739–1790: Entries from His Journal and Diary Relating to Wales. Ed. A. H. Williams. 1971.

Works. Eds. Frank Baker et al. 1975–   . 34 vols. (projected).

Selected Prayers, Hymns, Journal Notes, Sermons, Letters and Treatises (with Charles Wesley). Ed. Frank Whiting. 1981.

Works. Ed. Albert C. Outler. 1984–   .

Journal: A Selection. Ed. Elizabeth Jay. 1987.

SIR JOSHUA REYNOLDS (1723–1792)

A Discourse, Delivered at the Opening of the Royal Academy. 1769.

A Discourse, Delivered to the Students of the Royal Academy, on the Distribution of the Prizes. 1769.

A Discourse, Delivered to the Students of the Royal Academy, on the Distribution of the Prizes. 1771.

A Discourse, Delivered to the Students of the Royal Academy, on the Distribution of the Prizes. 1772.

A Discourse, Delivered to the Students of the Royal Academy, on the Distribution of the Prizes. 1773.

A Discourse, Delivered to the Students of the Royal Academy, on the Distribution of the Prizes. 1775.

A Discourse, Delivered to the Students of the Royal Academy, on the Distribution of the Prizes. 1777.

Seven Discourses Delivered in the Royal Academy. 1778.

A Discourse, Delivered to the Students of the Royal Academy, on the Distribution of the Prizes. 1779.

Two Discourses. 1781. 2 parts.

A Discourse, Delivered to the Students of the Royal Academy, on the Distribution of the Prizes. 1783.

A Discourse, Delivered to the Students of the Royal Academy, on the Distribution of the Prizes. 1785.

A Discourse, Delivered to the Students of the Royal Academy, on the Distribution of the Prizes. 1786.

A Discourse, Delivered to the Students of the Royal Academy, on the Distribution of the Prizes. 1789.

A Discourse, Delivered to the Students of the Royal Academy, on the Distribution of the Prizes. 1791.

Works. Ed. Edmond Malone. 1797. 2 vols.

Johnson and Garrick. 1816.

Discourses Delivered at the Royal Academy. 1820. 2 vols.

Literary Works. Ed. Henry William Beechey. 1835. 2 vols.

Notes and Observations on Pictures. Ed. William Cotton. 1859.

Discourses. Ed. Roger Fry. 1905.

Letters. Ed. Frederick Whiley Hilles. 1929.

Portraits. Ed. Frederick W. Hilles. 1952.

Discourses on Art. Ed. Robert R. Wark. 1959.

GILBERT WHITE (1720–1793)

The Natural History and Antiquities of Selborne, in the County of Southampton. 1789.

A Naturalist's Calendar, with Observations in Various Branches of Natural History. Ed. John Aikin. 1795.

Works in Natural History. Ed. John Aikin. 1802. 2 vols.

Life and Letters. Ed. Rashleigh Holt-White. 1901. 2 vols.

Journals. Ed. Walter Johnson. 1931.

Writings. Ed. H. J. Massingham. 1938. 2 vols.

WILLIAM ROBERTSON (1721–1793)

The Situation of the World at the Time of Christ's Appearance, and Its Connexion with the Success of His Religion, Considered. 1755.

The History of Scotland during the Reigns of Queen Mary and of King James VI. till His Accession to the Crown of England. 1759. 2 vols.

Memorial Relating to the University of Edinburgh. 1768.

The History of the Reign of the Emperor Charles V. 1769. 3 vols.

A New Geographical and Historical Grammar by Thomas Salmon (revised by Robertson). 1772.

The History of America. 1777 (2 vols.), 1800 (4 vols.).

An Historical Disquisition concerning the Knowledge Which the Ancients Had of India. 1791.

Beauties of Dr. Robertson. 1810.

Historical Works. 1813. 6 vols.

Works. 1817. 12 vols.

Works. 1824. 11 vols.

The Beauties of Robertson: Consisting of Selections from His Works. Ed. Alfred Howard. c. 1834.

GEORGE COLMAN THE ELDER (1732–1794)

The Connoisseur (with Bonnell Thornton). 1754–56. 140 nos.

Poems by Eminent Ladies (editor; with Bonnell Thornton). 1755. 2 vols.

[*A Letter of Abuse to D——d G———k, Esq.* 1757.]

Two Odes (with Robert Lloyd). 1760.

Polly Honeycombe: A Dramatick Novel. 1760.

The Jealous Wife. 1761.

Critical Reflections on the Old English Dramatick Writers. 1761.

The Musical Lady. 1762.

Terrae-Filius. 1763. 4 nos.

Philaster by Beaumont and Fletcher (adaptation). 1763.

The Deuce Is in Him. 1763.

A Fairy Tale (adaptation). 1763.

The Comedies of Terence (translator). 1765.

The Clandestine Marriage (with David Garrick). 1766.

The English Merchant (adaptation). 1767.

The History of King Lear (adaptation). 1768.

A True State of the Differences Subsisting between the Proprietors of Covent-Garden-Theatre. 1768.

An Epistle to Dr. Kenrick. 1768.

T. Harris Dissected. 1768.

The Oxonian in Town. 1770.

Man and Wife; or, The Shakespeare Jubilee. 1770.

The Portrait: A Burletta. 1770.

The Fairy Prince by Ben Jonson (adaptation). 1771.

Comus by John Milton (adaptation). 1772.

The Man of Business. 1774.

An Occasional Prelude, Performed at the Opening of the Theatre-Royal, Covent-Garden. 1776.

New Brooms! An Occasional Prelude, Performed at the Opening of the Theatre-Royal, in Drury-Lane. 1776.

The Spleen; or, Islington Spa. 1776.

Epicoene; or, The Silent Woman by Ben Jonson (adaptation). 1776.

Polly by John Gay (adaptation). 1777.

The Sheep Shearing (adaptation). 1777.

Dramatick Works. 1777. 4 vols.

The Dramatick Works of Beaumont and Fletcher (editor). 1778. 10 vols.

Bonduca by John Fletcher (adaptation). 1778.

The Manager in Distress: A Prelude on Opening the Theatre-Royal in the Hay-Market. 1780.

Fatal Curiosity by George Lillo (adaptation). 1783.

Epistola ad Pisones, De Arte Poetica by Horace (translator). 1783.

[*A Very Plain State of the Case; or, The Royalty Theatre versus the Theatres Royal.* 1787.]

Poems on Several Occasions. 1787. 3 vols.

Tit for Tat; or, The Mutual Deception by Joseph Atkinson (adaptation). 1788.

Ut Pictura Poesis! or, The Enraged Musician: A Musical Entertainment Founded on Hogarth. 1789.

Some Particulars of the Life of the Late George Colman, Esq.: Written by Himself. 1795.

Plays (with David Garrick). Ed. E. R. Wood. 1982.

EDWARD GIBBON (1737–1794)

Essai sur l'étude de la littérature. 1761.

Mémoires littéraires de la Grande Bretagne, pour l'an 1767 (with Georges Deyverdun). 1768.

Mémoires littéraires de la Grande Bretagne, pour l'an 1768 (with Georges Deyverdun). 1769.

Critical Observations on the Sixth Book of the Aeneid. 1770.

The History of the Decline and Fall of the Roman Empire. 1776 [Volume 1]; 1781 [Volumes 2–3]; 1788 [Volumes 4–6].

A Vindication of Some Passages in the Fifteenth and Sixteenth Passages of the History of the Decline and Fall of the Roman Empire. 1779.

Mémoire justificatif pour servir de réponse à l'exposé &c. de la cour de France. 1779.

Miscellaneous Works. Ed. John, Lord Sheffield. 1796 (2 vols.), 1814 (5 vols.).

[*Speech on the Day of Election of Members to Serve in Parliament for the Borough of Petersfield.* c. 1813.]

The Antiquities of the House of Brunswick. Ed. John, Lord Sheffield. 1814.

Memoirs. Ed. John, Lord Sheffield. 1827. 2 vols.

Private Letters. Ed. Rowland E. Prothero. 1896. 2 vols.

The History of the Decline and Fall of the Roman Empire. Ed. J. B. Bury. 1909–14. 7 vols.

Gibbon's Journal to January 28th, 1763. Ed. D. M. Low. 1929.

Le Journal de Gibbon à Lausanne, 17 août 1763–19 avril 1764. Ed. Georges A. Bonnard. 1945.

Miscellanea Gibboniana. Eds. Gavin R. de Beer, Georges A. Bonnard, and Louis Junod. 1952.

Letters. Ed. J. E. Norton. 1956. 3 vols.

The Autobiography of Edward Gibbon. Ed. Dero A. Saunders. 1961.

Gibbon's Journey from Geneva to Rome: His Journal from 20 April to 2 October 1764. Ed. Georges A. Bonnard. 1961.

Memoirs of My Life. Ed. Georges A. Bonnard. 1966.

English Essays. Ed. Patricia B. Craddock. 1972.

SIR WILLIAM JONES (1746–1794)

Histoire de Nader Chach, connu sous le nom de Thahmas Kuli Khan, empereur de Perse (translator). 1770. Eng. tr. 1773.

A Grammar of the Persian Language. 1771.

Lettre à Monsieur A*** du P***, dans laquelle est compris l'examen de sa traduction des livres attribués à Zoroastre. 1771.

Dissertation sur la littérature orientale. 1771.

Poems: Consisting Chiefly of Translations from the Asiatick Languages; to Which Are Added Two Essays. 1772.

An Oration Intended to Have Been Spoken in the Theatre at Oxford. 1773.

Poeseos Asiaticae Commentariorum Libri Sex. 1774.

The Speeches of Isaeus concerning the Law of Succession to Property at Athens (translator). 1779.

An Inquiry into the Legal Mode of Suppressing Riots. 1780.

A *Speech on the Nomination of Candidates to Represent the County of Middlesex.* 1780.

Ad Libertatem. 1780.

An Essay on the Law of Bailments. 1781.

The Muse Recalled: An Ode. 1781.

The Moullakát; or, Seven Arabian Poems, Which Were Suspended on the Temple at Mecca (translator). 1782.

The Mahomedan Law of Succession to the Property of Intestates (translator). 1782.

An Ode on Imitation of Alcaeus. 1782.

The Principles of Government, in a Dialogue between a Scholar and a Peasant. 1782.

Speech to the Assembled Inhabitants of the Counties of Middlesex and Surry, the Cities of London and Westminster, and the Borough of Southwark. 1782.

A Letter to a Patriot Senator, Including the Heads of a Bill for a Constitutional Representation of the People. 1783.

A Discourse on the Institution of a Society for Enquiring into the History, Antiquities, Arts, Sciences, and Literature of Asia. 1784.

Lailá Majnún, a Persian Poem of Hátifí (translator). 1788.

Sacontalá; or, The Fatal Ring: An Indian Drama by Cálidás (translator). 1789.

Al Sirajiyyah; or, The Mohammedan Law of Inheritance (translator). 1792.

An Ode: What Constitutes a State? c. 1795.

Institutes of Hindu Law; or, The Ordinances of Menu, According to the Gloss of Culluca. 1794.

Works. Ed. Anna Maria Jones. 1799. 6 vols.

Works. 1807. 13 vols.

Poetical Works. Ed. Thomas Park. 1808.

Poetical Works. 1810. 2 vols.

Three Tracts. 1819.

Discourses Delivered before the Asiatic Society. Ed. F. Elmes. 1821. 2 vols.

Letters. 1821. 2 vols.

The Hindu Wife and the Hymns. 1881.

Poems. Ed. Jonathan Benthall. 1961.

Letters. Ed. Garland Cannon. 1970. 2 vols.

JAMES BOSWELL (1740–1795)

[*A View of the Edinburgh Theatre during the Summer Season,* 1759. 1760.]

Observations, Good or Bad, Stupid or Clever, Serious or Jocular, on Squire Foote's Dramatic Entertainment, Intituled, The Minor. 1760.

An Elegy on the Death of an Amiable Young Lady. 1761.

An Ode to Tragedy. 1761.

A Collection of Original Poems by Scotch Gentlemen, Volume 2 (editor; with others). 1762.

The Cub, at New-Market: A Tale. 1762.

Critical Strictures on the New Tragedy of Elvira, *Written by Mr. David Malloch* (with Andrew Erskine and George Dempster). 1763.

Letters between the Honourable Andrew Erskine, and James Boswell, Esq. 1763.

Disputatio Juridica ad Tit. X. Lib. XXXIII. Pand. de Supellectile Legata. 1766.

The Douglas Cause. 1767.

Dorando, a Spanish Tale. 1767.

The Essence of the Douglas Cause. 1767.

Letters of the Right Honourable Lady Jane Douglas; with Several Other Important Pieces of Private Correspondence (editor; with others). 1767.

An Account of Corsica: The Journal of a Tour to That Island; and Memoirs of Pascal Paoli. 1768.

British Essays in Favour of the Brave Corsicans (editor). 1769.

Verses, in the Character of a Corsican at Shakespeare's Jubilee, at Stratford-upon-Avon. 1769.

Reflections on the Late Alarming Bankruptcies in Scotland. 1772.

The Decision of the Court of Session upon the Question of Literary Property. 1774.

The Mournful Case of Poor Misfortunate and Unhappy John Reid. 1774.

The Patriotic Chamberlain: An Excellent New Song for Midsummer Day 1776. 1776.

A Letter to Robert Macqueen, Lord Braxfield, on His Promotion to Be One of the Judges of the High Court of Justiciary. 1780.

An Excellent New War Song. 1782.

A Letter to the People of Scotland, on the Present State of the Nation. 1783.

A Letter to the People of Scotland, on the Alarming Attempt to Infringe the Articles of the Union, and Introduce a Most Pernicious Innovation, by Diminishing the Number of the Lords of Session. 1785.

Opinion of English Counsel on the Bill Diminishing the Number of the Lords of Session in Scotland. 1785.

The Journal of a Tour to the Hebrides, with Samuel Johnson, LL.D. 1785.

Two New Songs: Houses Shut Up; or, Rowland in the Dumps; Rowland Deceived, a Carlisle Song. 1786.

December 12, 1786: To Rowland Stephenson, Esq. Banker in London and Candidate for Carlisle: The Address and Remonstrance of Independent Old Freemen. 1786.

Grand Committee, Bluebell, Carlisle, 13 Dec. 1786: Modest Proposals for Chairing Mr. Rowland Stephenson in Case He Shall Lose His Election. 1786.

[*Carlisle, Dec. 14, 1786: Attempt to Chair Mr. Stephenson.* 1786.]

[*Carlisle: Whereas chairing any candidate . . .* 1786.]

Case of Chairing: Opinion of James Boswell, Esq. of the Inner Temple, Barrister at Law. 1786.

Ring Lost. 1788.

[*Ode by Dr. Samuel Johnson to Mrs. Thrale, upon Their Supposed Approaching Nuptials.* c. 1788.]

Small Paper Book Lost. 1789.

The Celebrated Letter from Samuel Johnson, LL.D. to Philip Dormer Stanhope, Earl of Chesterfield (editor). 1790.

A Conversation between His Most Sacred Majesty George III. and Samuel Johnson, LL.D. (editor). 1790.

William Pitt, the Grocer of London: An Excellent New Ballad. 1790.

No Abolition of Slavery; or, The Universal Empire of Love. 1791.

The Life of Samuel Johnson, LL.D. 1791. 2 vols.

Song for the Glorious 26th of June. 1792.

Proposals for Publishing a New and Improved Edition of Shakespeare Illustrated by Charlotte Lennox. 1793.

It is impossible for me an enthusiastic Tory . . . 1793.

The Principal Corrections and Additions to the First Edition of Mr. Boswell's Life of Dr. Johnson. 1793.

[*For the* European Evening Post: *Too True a Prophesy, Written Some Time Ago.* c. 1794.]

Life of Johnson. Ed. Edmond Malone. 1799. 4 vols.

Life of Johnson. Ed. John Wilson Croker. 1831. 5 vols.

Boswelliana. Ed. Richard Monckton Milnes, Lord Houghton. 1856.

Boswelliana: Folium Reservatum. Ed. Richard Monckton Milnes, Lord Houghton. 1856.
Letters Addressed to the Rev. W. J. Temple. Ed. Sir Philip Francis. 1857.
Boswelliana: The Commonplace Book. Ed. Charles Rogers. 1874.
Life of Johnson. Ed. George Birkbeck Hill. 1887. 6 vols.
Letters. Ed. Chauncey Brewster Tinker. 1924. 2 vols.
Note Book 1776–1777, Recording Particulars of Johnson's Early Life Communicated by Him and Others in Those Years. Ed. R. W. Chapman. 1925.
The Hypochondriack: Being the Seventy Essays Appearing in the London Magazine *from November, 1777, to August, 1783.* Ed. Margaret Bailey. 1928.
Private Papers. Eds. Geoffrey Scott and Frederick A. Pottle. 1928–34. 18 vols.
On the Profession of a Player: Three Essays Now First Reprinted from the London Magazine *for August, September, and October, 1770.* 1929.
Life of Johnson. Ed. George Birkbeck Hill, rev. L. F. Powell. 1934–40. 6 vols.
Private Papers (Yale Edition). Eds. Frederick A. Pottle et al. 1950– .

THOMAS REID (1710–1796)

An Inquiry into the Human Mind, on the Principles of Common Sense. 1764.
Essays on the Intellectual Powers of Man. 1785.
Essays on the Active Powers of Man. 1788.
Analysis of Aristotle's Logic. 1806.
Works. 1813–15. 4 vols.
Works. Ed. G. N. Knight. 1843. 2 vols.
Works. Ed. Sir William Hamilton. 1846. 2 vols.
Philosophical Orations Delivered in Graduation Ceremonies in King's College, Aberdeen. Ed. Walter Robson Humphreys. 1937.
Lectures on the Fine Arts. Ed. Peter Kivy. 1973.
Inquiry and Essays. Eds. Keith Lehrer and Ronald E. Beaublossom. 1975.

JAMES MACPHERSON (1736–1796)

The Highlander: An Heroic Poem. 1758.
Fragments of Ancient Poetry Collected in the Highlands of Scotland. 1760.
Fingal: An Ancient Epic Poem, Together with Several Other Poems, Translated from the Galic Language. 1762.
Temora: An Ancient Epic Poem, Together with Several Other Poems, Translated from the Galic Language. 1763.
The Works of Ossian. 1765. 2 vols.
An Introduction to the History of Great Britain and Ireland. 1771.
The Iliad Translated into Prose. 1773. 2 vols.
The History of Great Britain from the Restoration to the Accession of the House of Hannover. 1775. 2 vols.
Original Papers: Containing the Secret History of Great Britain from the Restoration to the Accession of the House of Hanover. 1775. 2 vols.
The Rights of Great Britain Asserted against the Claims of America. 1776.
A Short History of the Opposition during the Last Session of Parliament. 1779.
The Poems of Ossian. Ed. Malcolm Laing. 1805. 2 vols.
The Poems of Ossian. Ed. Archibald Clerk. 1870. 2 vols.

ROBERT BURNS (1759–1796)

Poems, Chiefly in the Scottish Dialect. 1786, 1787.
The Scots Musical Museum, Volumes 2–5 (editor). 1787–1803. 6 vols.
The Ayrshire Garland. c. 1789.
The Prayer of Holy Willie. 1789.
The Whistle. c. 1791.
An Address to the Deil. 1795.
Wham will we send to London Town. c. 1795–96.
Fy, let us a' to K⟨irkcudbright⟩. c. 1795–96.
What will buy my Troggin? c. 1795–96.
An Unco' Mornfu Tale. 1796.
Elegy on the Year Eighty-eight. 1799.
The Jolly Beggars: A Cantata. 1799.
The Kirk's Alarm: A Satire. 1799.
Holy Willie's Prayer, Letter to John Goudie, and Six Favourite Songs. 1799.
Extempore Verses on Dining with Lord Daer. 1799.
The Inventory. 1799.
The Henpeck'd Husband ⟨etc.⟩. 1799.
The Merry Muses of Caledonia (editor). 1799.
Works. Ed. James Currie. 1800. 4 vols.
Poems Ascribed to Robert Burns. 1801.
Letters Addressed to Clarinda, &c. 1802.
The Beauties of Burns. 1802.
Reliques of Robert Burns. Ed. R. H. Cromek. 1808.
Prose Works. 1816.
Letters and Correspondence. 1817. 2 vols.
Letters. 1819. 2 vols.
Works, Including His Letters to Clarinda and the Whole of His Suppressed Poems. 1821. 4 vols.
Songs and Ballads. Ed. J. Barwick. 1823.
Poetical Works, Including Several Pieces Not Inserted in Dr. Currie's Edition. 1823. 2 vols.
Letters, Chronologically Arranged. 1828.
Works. Eds. James Hogg and William Motherwell. 1834–36. 5 vols.
Works. Ed. Allan Cunningham. 1834. 8 vols.
Poetical Works. 1839. 3 vols.
The Correspondence between Burns and Clarinda. Ed. W. C. M'Lehose. 1843.
Life and Works. Ed. Robert Chambers. 1851. 4 vols.
Poetical Works. Ed. George Gilfillan. 1856. 2 vols.
Poetical Works. Ed. Robert Aris Willmott. 1856.
Poems, Songs, and Letters. Ed. Alexander Smith. 1868.
Poetical Works. Ed. William Michael Rossetti. 1871.
Common Place Book. 1872.
Works. Ed. William Scott Douglas. 1877–79. 6 vols.
Poetical Works. Ed. George A. Aitken. 1893. 3 vols.
Complete Poetical Works. Ed. J. Logie Robertson. 1896. 3 vols.
Poetry. Eds. W. E. Henley and T. F. Henderson. 1896–97. 4 vols.
Burns and Mrs. Dunlop: Correspondence. Ed. William Wallace. 1898. 2 vols.
The Glenriddell Manuscripts. 1914. 2 vols.
Journal of a Tour in the Highlands Made in 1787. Ed. J. C. Ewing. 1927.
Letters. Ed. J. De Lancey Ferguson. 1931. 2 vols.
Common Place Book 1783–1785. Eds. James Cameron Ewing and Davidson Cook. 1938.
The Merry Muses of Caledonia. Eds. James Barke and Sydney Goodsir Smith. 1959.
Poems and Songs. Ed. James Kinsley. 1968. 3 vols.

CHARLES MACKLIN (c. 1699–1797)

The Case of Charles Macklin, Comedian. 1743.
Mr. Macklin's Reply to Mr. Garrick's Answer. 1743.
King Henry the VII; or, The Popish Impostor. 1746.
M–ckl–n's Answer to Tully. 1755.
An Apology for the Conduct of Mr. Charles Macklin, Comedian. 1773.
The Genuine Arguments of the Council, with the Opinion of the Court of King's Bench, on Cause Shewn, Why an Information Should Not Be Exhibited against J. S. James ⟨et al.⟩ *for a Conspiracy to Deprive Charles Macklin of His Livelihood.* 1774.
Love à-la-Mode. 1779.
The True-Born Irishman; or, The Irish Fine Lady. 1783.
The Man of the World. 1785.
The Man of the World; Love à la Mode. Ed. Arthur Murphy. 1793.
Four Comedies. Ed. J. O. Bartley. 1968.

HORACE WALPOLE (1717–1797)

The Lessons for the Day. 1742.
The Beauties: An Epistle to Mr. Eckardt, the Painter. 1746.
Epilogue to Tamerlane, *on the Suppression of the Rebellion.* 1746.
Aedes Walpolianae; or, A Description of the Collection of Pictures at Houghton-Hall in Norfolk, the Seat of the Right Honourable Sir Robert Walpole, Earl of Orford. 1747.
A Letter to the Whigs: Occasion'd by The Letter to the Tories. 1747.
A Second and Third Letter to the Whigs. 1748.
Three Letters to the Whigs. 1748.
The Original Speech of Sir W⟨illia⟩m St⟨anho⟩pe. 1748.
The Speech of Richard White-Liver Esq; in Behalf of Himself and His Brethren. 1748.
A Letter from Xo Ho, a Chinese Philosopher at London, to His Friend Lien Chi at Peking. 1757.
A Catalogue of the Royal and Noble Authors of England. 1758. 2 vols.
Fugitive Pieces in Verse and Prose. 1758.
A Dialogue between Two Great Ladies. 1760.
Catalogue of Pictures and Drawings in the Holbein-Chamber, at Strawberry-Hill. 1760.
Catalogues of the Pictures of the Duke of Devonshire, General Guise, and the Late Sir Paul Methuen. 1760.
Anecdotes of Painting in England. 1762–71. 4 vols.
The Opposition to the Late Minister Vindicated. 1763.
A Counter-Address to the Public, on the Late Dismission of a General Officer. 1764.
The Magpie and Her Brood. 1764.
The Castle of Otranto. 1765.
An Account of the Giants Lately Discovered. 1766.
Historic Doubts on the Life and Reign of King Richard the Third. 1768.
The Mysterious Mother. 1768.
Works. 1770. 2 vols.
Reply to Dean Milles. 1770.
Memoires du Comte de Grammont by Anthony Hamilton (editor). 1772.
A Description of the Villa of Horace Walpole at Strawberry-Hill, Near Twickenham. 1774, 1784.
A Letter to the Editor of the Miscellanies of Thomas Chatterton. 1779.

Essay on Modern Gardening (with French tr. by Duc de Nivernois). 1785.
Hieroglyphic Tales. 1785.
Postscript to the Royal and Noble Authors. 1786.
Works. Ed. Mary Berry. 1798. 5 vols.
Notes on the Portraits at Woburn Abbey. 1800.
A Catalogue of the Royal and Noble Authors of England, Scotland and Ireland. Ed. Thomas Park. 1806. 5 vols.
Letters to George Montagu. Ed. John Martin. 1818.
Letters to the Rev. William Cole, and Others. Ed. John Martin. 1818.
Private Correspondence. 1820. 4 vols.
Memoires of the Last Ten Years of the Reign of George the Second. Ed. Lord Holland. 1822. 2 vols.
Letters to the Earl of Hertford. Ed. John Wilson Croker. 1825.
Letters to Sir Horace Mann. Ed. Lord Dover. 1833. 3 vols.
Letters. Ed. John Wright. 1840. 6 vols.
Memoirs of the Reign of King George the Third. Ed. Sir Denis Le Marchant. 1845.
Letters Addressed to the Countess of Ossory. Ed. R. Vernon Smith. 1848. 2 vols.
Correspondence of Horace Walpole and William Mason. Ed. John Mitford. 1851. 2 vols.
Letters. Ed. Peter Cunningham. 1857–59. 9 vols.
Journal of the Reign of King George the Third from the Year 1771 to 1783. Ed. John Doran. 1859. 2 vols.
Some Unpublished Letters. Ed. Sir Spencer Walpole. 1902.
Letters. Ed. Mrs. Paget Toynbee. 1903–05. 16 vols.
Supplement to the Letters. Ed. Paget Toynbee. 1918–25. 3 vols.
The Castle of Otranto and The Mysterious Mother. Ed. Montague Summers. 1925.
A Selection of the Letters. Ed. W. S. Lewis. 1926. 2 vols.
Miscellaneous Antiquities. Ed. W. S. Lewis. 1927. 16 vols.
Correspondence (Yale Edition). Eds. W. S. Lewis et al. 1937–81. 48 vols.
Memoirs and Portraits. Ed. Matthew Hodgart. 1963.
Selected Letters. Ed. W. S. Lewis. 1973.
Horace Walpole's Miscellany 1786–1795. Ed. Lars E. Troide. 1978.

WILLIAM MASON (1725–1797)

Musaeus: A Monody to the Memory of Mr. Pope, in Imitation of Milton's "Lycidas." 1747.
Isis: An Elegy. 1747.
Ode Performed in the Senate-House at Cambridge, at the Installation of Thomas Holles, Duke of Newcastle, Chancellor of the University. 1749.
Elfrida: A Dramatic Poem, Written on the Model of the Antient Greek Tragedy. 1752.
Odes. 1756.
Caractacus: A Dramatic Poem, Written on the Model of the Ancient Greek Tragedy. 1759.
Elegies. 1763.
Poems. 1764.
A Supplement to Dr. Watts' Psalms and Hymns (editor). 1769.
The English Garden. 1772 [Book 1]; 1776 [Book 2]; 1779 [Book 3]; 1781 [Book 4].
A Catalogue of the Antiquities, House, Parks, Plantations, Scenes, and Situations in England and Wales by Thomas Gray (editor). 1773.
An Heroic Epistle to Sir W. Chambers. 1773.
An Heroic Postscript to the Public, Occasioned by Their Favourable Reception of a Late Heroic Epistle to Sir Wm. Chambers. 1774.

The Poems of Mr. Gray (editor). 1775.
Ode to Mr. Pinchbeck upon His Newly Invented Patent Candle-Snuffers. 1776.
An Epistle to Dr. Shebbeare; to Which Is Added An Ode to Sir Fletcher Norton, in Imitation of Horace, Ode VIII Book IV. 1777.
An Archaeological Epistle to the Reverend and Worshipful Jeremiah Milles, D.D., Dean of Exeter, President of the Society of Antiquaries. 1782.
A Copious Collection of Those Portions of the Psalms of David, Bible, and Liturgy, Which Have Been Set to Music (editor). 1782.
The Dean and the 'Squire: A Political Eclogue. 1782.
King Stephen's Watch: A Tale Founded on Fact. 1782.
Ode to the Hon. William Pitt. 1782.
The Art of Painting by C. A. Du Fresnoy (translator). 1783.
Epistle to the Right Hon. William Pitt, Petitioning for the Vacant Laureateship. 1785.
Animadversions on the Present Government of the York Lunatic Asylum. 1788.
An Occasional Discourse, Preached in the Cathedral of York, on the Subject of the African Slave-Trade. 1788.
Secular Ode in Commemoration of the Glorious Revolution. 1788.
Essays, Historical and Critical, on English Church Music. 1795.
Poetical Works. 1805.
Sappho: A Lyrical Drama (with Italian tr. by Thomas James Mathias). 1809.
Religio Clerici. 1810.
Works. 1811. 4 vols.
The Correspondence of Horace Walpole and the Rev. William Mason. Ed. John Mitford. 1851. 2 vols.
The Correspondence of Thomas Gray and William Mason. Ed. John Mitford. 1853.
Satirical Poems. Ed. Paget Toynbee. 1926.
The Correspondence of Richard Hurd and William Mason. Eds. Ernest Harold Pearce and Leonard Whibley. 1932.
Horace Walpole's Correspondence with William Mason. Eds. W. S. Lewis, Grover Cronin, Jr., and Charles H. Bennett. 1955. 2 vols.

EDMUND BURKE (1729–1797)

A Vindication of Natural Society. 1756.
An Account of the European Settlements in America (with William Burke and Richard Burke?). 1757. 2 vols.
A Philosophical Enquiry into the Origin of Our Ideas of the Sublime and Beautiful. 1757.
An Essay towards an Abridgment of the English History. c. 1760.
A Short Account of a Late Short Administration ⟨with others?⟩. 1766.
Observations on a Late State of the Nation. 1769.
Thoughts on the Cause of the Present Discontents. 1770.
Mr. Burke's Speech ⟨at Bristol⟩. 1774.
To the Gentlemen, Clergy, Freeholders, and Freemen, of the City of Bristol. 1774.
To the Gentlemen, Clergy, Freeholders, and Freemen, of the City of Bristol. 1774.
Speech to the Electors of Bristol. 1774.
To the Gentlemen, Clergy, Freeholders, and Freemen, of the City of Bristol. 1774.
Speeches at His Arrival in Bristol. 1774.
Speech on American Taxation. 1775.

Speech on Moving His Resolutions for Conciliation with the Colonies. 1775.
The Letters of Valens (with William Burke and Richard Burke). 1777.
Political Tracts and Speeches. 1777.
A Letter from Edmund Burke, Esq; One of the Representatives in Parliament for the City of Bristol, to John Farr, and John Harris, Esqrs. Sheriffs of That City, on the Affairs of America. 1777.
Two Letters to Gentlemen in the City of Bristol, on the Bills Depending in Parliament Relative to the Trade of Ireland. 1778.
Substances of the Speeches Made in the House of Commons, on Mr. Burke's Giving Notice of His Intention to Bring In a Bill for the Retrenchment of Public Expenses, and for the Better Securing the Independence of Parliament (with others). 1779.
The Yorkshire Question, or Petition, or Address (with William Burke and Richard Burke). 1780.
Speech on Presenting to the House of Commons a Plan for the Better Security of the Independence of Parliament, and the Oeconomical Reformation of the Civil and Other Establishments. 1780.
A Letter from a Gentleman in the English House of Commons, in Vindication of His Conduct, with Regard to the Affairs of Ireland. 1780.
To the Gentlemen Clergy, Freeholders, and Freemen of the City of Bristol. 1780.
To the Gentlemen Clergy, Freeholders, and Freemen of the City of Bristol. 1780.
Bristol, Saturday, 9th September, 1780. 1780.
To the Gentlemen, Clergy, Freeholders, and Freemen of the City of Bristol. 1780.
Speech at the Guildhall, in Bristol, upon Certain Points Relative to His Parliamentary Conduct. 1780.
Heads of Objections to Be Enquired Into Before It Will Be Adviseable to Take Paul Benfield, Esq. Again into the ⟨East India⟩ *Company's Service.* 1781.
Ninth Report from the Select Committee, Appointed to Take into Consideration the State of the Administration of Justice in the Provinces of Bengal, Bahar, and Orissa. 1783.
Eleventh Report from the Select Committee Appointed to Take into Consideration the State of the Administration of Justice in the Provinces of Bengal, Bahar, and Orissa. 1783.
A Letter to a Peer of Ireland, on the Penal Laws against Irish Catholics. 1783.
The Beauties of Fox, North, and Burke, Selected from Their Speeches (with Charles James Fox and Lord North). Ed. George Chalmers. 1784.
Speech on Mr. Fox's East India Bill. 1784.
The Deformities of Fox and Burke, Faithfully Selected from Their Speeches (with Charles James Fox). Ed. George Chalmers. 1784.
A Representation to His Majesty. 1784.
Speech on the Motion Made for Papers Relative to the Directions for Charging the Nabob of Arcot's Private Debts to Europeans, on the Revenues of the Carnatic. 1785.
Articles of Charge of High Crimes and Misdemeanors against Warren Hastings, Esquire. 1786. 22 nos.
Articles of Impeachment of High Crimes and Misdemeanors against Warren Hastings, Esquire. 1787. 3 parts.
A Letter to Philip Francis, Esq. 1788.
Substance of the Speech in the Debate on the Army Estimates. 1790.
Reflections on the Revolution in France, and on the Proceedings

in Certain Societies in London Relative to That Event. 1790.

A Letter to a Member of the National Assembly; in Answer to Some Objections to His Book on French Affairs. 1791.

Two Letters on the French Revolution. 1791.

An Appeal from the New to the Old Whigs. 1791.

A Letter to Sir Hercules Langrishe, Bart. M.P., on the Subject of Roman Catholics of Ireland. 1792.

Speech in Westminster-Hall. 1792.

Works. Eds. French Laurence and Walker King. 1792–1827. 8 vols.

Report from the Committee of the House of Commons, Appointed to Inspect the Lords Journals, in Relation to Their Proceeding on the Trial of Warren Hastings, Esquire. 1794.

Substance of the Speech to Certain Observations on the Report of the Committee of Managers. 1794.

A Letter to a Noble Lord, on the Attacks Made upon Him and His Pension. 1796.

Thoughts on the Prospect of a Regicide Peace, in a Series of Letters. 1796.

A Letter to His Grace the Duke of Portland, on the Conduct of the Minority in Parliament. 1797.

Three Memorials on French Affairs. 1797.

Two Letters on the Conduct of Our Domestick Parties, with Regard to French Politicks. 1797.

A Third Letter to a Member of the Present Parliament, on the Proposals for Peace with the Regicide Directory of France. 1797.

Posthumous Works. 1798.

The Beauties of Burke. Ed. Charles Henry Wilson. 1798. 2 vols.

Thoughts and Details on Scarcity. 1800.

Maxims and Opinions, Moral, Political, and Economical. 1804.

The Catholic Claims: Discussed in a Letter to the Hon. William Smith. 1807.

Speeches. 1816. 4 vols.

Epistolary Correspondence (with French Laurence). 1827.

Correspondence. Eds. Charles William, Earl Fitzwilliam and Sir Richard Bourke. 1844. 4 vols.

Speeches. Ed. James Burke. 1854.

Select Works. Ed. E. J. Payne. 1874–75 (2 vols.), 1876–78 (3 vols.).

Letters, Speeches and Tracts on Irish Affairs. Ed. Matthew Arnold. 1881.

Speeches on American Taxation, on Conciliation with America, and Letter to the Sheriffs of Bristol. Ed. F. G. Selby. 1895.

Works. 1906–07. 6 vols.

Correspondence of Edmund Burke and William Windham. Ed. J. G. Gilson. 1910.

Selections from His Political Writings and Speeches. 1911.

Letters: A Selection. Ed. Harold J. Laski. 1922.

Early Life, Correspondence and Writings. Ed. Arthur P. I. Samuels. 1923.

Burke's Politics: Selected Writings and Speeches on Reform, Revolution and War. Eds. Ross J. S. Hoffman and Paul Levack. 1949.

Edmund Burke, New York Agent; with His Letters to the New York Assembly, and Intimate Correspondence with Charles O'Hara 1761–1776. Ed. Ross J. S. Hoffman. 1956.

A Note-Book. Ed. W. V. F. Somerset. 1957.

Correspondence. Eds. Thomas W. Copeland et al. 1958–78. 10 vols.

The Philosophy of Edmund Burke: A Selection from His Speeches and Writings. Eds. Louis I. Bredvold and Ralph G. Ross. 1960.

Selected Works. Ed. W. J. Bate. 1960.

Selected Writings and Speeches. Ed. Peter J. Stanlis. 1963.

Edmund Burke on Indian Economy. Ed. Sunil Kumar Sen. 1969.

Edmund Burke on Government, Politics, and Society. Ed. B. W. Hill. 1975.

Writings and Speeches. Eds. Paul Langford et al. 1980– .

Selected Letters. Ed. Harvey C. Mansfield, Jr. 1984.

MARY WOLLSTONECRAFT (1759–1797)

Thoughts on the Education of Daughters; with Reflections on Female Conduct, in the More Important Duties of Life. 1787.

Mary: A Fiction. 1788.

Original Stories from Real Life; with Conversations Calculated to Regulate the Affections and Form the Mind to Truth and Goodness. 1788.

On the Importance of Religious Opinions by Jacques Necker (translator). 1788.

The Female Reader; or, Miscellaneous Pieces, in Prose and Verse, Selected from the Best Writers (editor). 1789.

Young Grandison by Maria de Cambon (translator). 1790.

A Vindication of the Rights of Man: In a Letter to the Right Honourable Edmund Burke. 1790.

Elements of Morality for the Use of Children by Christian Gotthilf Salzmann (translator). 1790–91. 2 vols.

A Vindication of the Rights of Woman; with Strictures on Political and Moral Subjects. 1792.

[*The Emigrants.* 1793.]

An Historical and Moral View of the Origin and Progress of the French Revolution; and the Effect It Has Produced in Europe. 1794.

Letters Written during a Short Residence in Sweden, Norway, and Denmark. 1796.

Posthumous Works. Ed. William Godwin. 1798. 4 vols.

Letters to Imlay. Ed. C. Kegan Paul. 1879.

Love Letters to Gilber Imlay. Ed. Roger Ingpen. 1908.

Mary Wollstonecraft. Ed. Camilla Jebb. 1912.

Four New Letters of Mary Wollstonecraft and Helen Maria Williams. Eds. Benjamin P. Kurtz and Carrie C. Antrey. 1937.

Godwin and Mary: Letters of William Godwin and Mary Wollstonecraft. Ed. Ralph M. Wardle. 1966.

A Wollstonecraft Anthology. Ed. Janet M. Todd. 1977.

Collected Letters. Ed. Ralph M. Wardle. 1979.

A Mary Wollstonecraft Reader. Eds. Barbara H. Solomon and Paula S. Berggren. 1983.

JAMES BURNETT, LORD MONBODDO (1714–1799)

Of the Origin and Progress of Language. 1773–92. 6 vols.

Antient Metaphysics; or, The Science of Universals; with an Appendix, Containing an Examination of the Principles of Sir Isaac Newton's Philosophy. 1779–99. 6 vols.

HUGH BLAIR (1718–1800)

A Poem Sacred to the Memory of the Rev. Mr. James Smith. 1736.

Dissertatio Philosophica Inauguralis, de Fundamentis & Obligatione Legis Naturae. 1739.

The Wrath of Man Praising God. 1746.

The Importance of Religious Knowledge to the Happiness of Mankind. 1750.

The Works of Shakespear (editor). 1753. 8 vols.

Observations upon a Pamphlet, Intitled, An Analysis of the
Moral and Religious Sentiments Contained in the Writ-
ings of Sapho and David Hume, Esq. 1755.
Objections against the Essays on Morality and Natural Reli-
gion *Examined* (with others). 1756.
*A Critical Dissertation on the Poems of Ossian, the Son of
Fingal.* 1763.
Heads of the Lectures on Rhetorick, and Belles Lettres. 1771.
Sermons. 1777 [Volume 1]; 1780 [Volume 2]; 1790 [Vol-
ume 3]; 1794 [Volume 4]; 1801 [Volume 5].
Lectures on Rhetoric and Belles Lettres. 1783. 2 vols.
On the Duties of the Young. 1793.
The Compassion and Beneficence of the Deity. 1796.
The Beauties of Blair. 1810.

ELIZABETH MONTAGU (1720–1800)

*An Essay on the Writings and Genius of Shakespear, Compared
with the Greek and French Dramatic Poets.* 1769, 1777.
Letters. Ed. Matthew Montagu. 1809–13. 4 vols.
*A Lady of the Last Century: Illustrated in Her Unpublished
Letters.* Ed. John Doran. 1873.
*Elizabeth Montagu, the Queen of the Blue-stockings: Her Cor-
respondence from 1720 to 1761.* Ed. Emily J. Climenson.
1906. 2 vols.
*Mrs. Montagu, "Queen of the Blues": Her Letters and Friend-
ships from 1762 to 1800.* Ed. Reginald Blunt. 1923. 2
vols.

JOSEPH WARTON (1722–1800)

Fashion: An Epistolary Satire to a Friend. 1742.
The Enthusiast; or, The Lover of Nature. 1744.
Odes on Various Subjects. 1746.
*Ranelagh House: A Satire in Prose, in the Manner of Monsieur
Le Sage.* 1747.
Poems on Several Occasions by Thomas Warton the Elder (ed-
itor). 1748.
*An Ode, Occasioned by Reading Mr. West's Translation of
Pindar.* 1749.
An Ode to Evening. 1749.
The Works of Virgil (editor and translator). 1753. 4 vols.
An Essay on the Writings and Genius of Pope. 1756 [Volume
1]; 1782 [Volume 2; as *An Essay on the Genius and Writ-
ings of Pope*].
*Sir Philip Sydney's Defence of Poetry, and Observations on
Poetry and Eloquence, from the Discoveries of Ben Jonson*
(editor). 1787.
The Works of Alexander Pope (editor). 1797. 9 vols.
The Three Wartons: A Choice of Their Verse. Ed. Eric Par-
tridge. 1927.

WILLIAM COWPER (1731–1800)

The Henriade by Voltaire (translator; with Tobias Smollett and
others). 1762.
Olney Hymns (with John Newton). 1779.
The Force of Truth by Thomas Scott (editor). 1779.
Anti-Thelyphthora: A Tale, in Verse. 1781.
Poems. 1782.
The Task. 1785.
The History of John Gilpin. 1785.
Poems. 1786. 2 vols.
Divine Hymns for Children by Rowland Hill (revised by
Cowper). 1790.
Adriano by James Hurdis (revised by Cowper). 1790.
*Proposals for Printing by Subscription, a New Translation of
the* Iliad *and* Odyssey *of Homer into Blank Verse.* 1790.
Iliad and Odyssey by Homer (translator). 1791. 2 vols.

The Power of Grace Illustrated by Helperus Ritzema van Lier
(translator). 1792.
Sir Thomas More by James Hurdis (revised by Cowper). 1792.
Original Poems, on Various Occasions by Maria Frances Ce-
cilia Cowper (revised by Cowper). 1792.
*Poems: I. On the Receipt of My Mother's Picture; II. The Dog
and the Water-Lily.* 1798.
Poems. 1798. 2 vols.
Poems by Jeanne Marie Bouvier de la Motte Guyon (trans-
lator). Ed. William Bull. 1801.
Beauties of Cowper. 1801.
*Adelphi: A Sketch of the Character, and an Account of the Last
Illness, of the Late Rev. John Cowper.* Ed. John Newton.
1802.
Life and Posthumous Writings. Ed. William Hayley. 1803–
04. 3 vols.
Latin and Italian Poems by John Milton (translator). Ed. Wil-
liam Hayley. 1808.
Cowper's Milton. Ed. William Hayley. 1810. 4 vols.
Poems. Ed. John Newton. 1813–14. 2 vols.
Posthumous Poetry. Ed. John Johnson. 1815.
Memoir of the Early Life of William Cowper. 1816.
Works. Ed. John Johnson. 1817. 10 vols.
Private Correspondence. Ed. John Johnson. 1824. 2 vols.
Poetical Works. Ed. John Mitford. 1830–31. 3 vols.
Miscellaneous Works. Ed. John S. Memes. 1834. 3 vols.
Works ⟨with *Life and Letters* by William Hayley⟩. Ed. Thomas
S. Grimshawe. 1835. 8 vols.
Life and Works. Ed. Robert Southey. 1835–37. 15 vols.
Poetical Works. Ed. George Gilfillan. 1854. 2 vols.
Poetical Works. Ed. Robert Aris Willmott. 1855.
Poetical Works. Ed. William Michael Rossetti. 1872.
Unpublished and Uncollected Poems. Ed. Thomas Wright.
1900.
Correspondence. Ed. Thomas Wright. 1904. 4 vols.
Complete Poetical Works. Ed. H. S. Milford. 1905.
Letters. Ed. E. V. Lucas. 1908.
Letters. Ed. Sir James George Frazer. 1912. 2 vols.
Unpublished and Uncollected Letters. Ed. Thomas Wright.
1925.
New Poems. 1931.
Poems. Ed. Hugh I'Anson Fausset. 1931.
Selected Poems and Letters. Ed. A. Norman Jeffares. 1963.
The Cast-Away. Ed. Charles Ryskamp. 1963.
Poetical Works. Ed. H. S. Milford, rev. Norma Russell. 1967.
Poetry and Prose. Ed. Brian Spiller. 1968.
A Choice of Cowper's Verse. Ed. Norman Nicholson. 1975.
Letters and Prose Writings. Eds. James King and Charles Rys-
kamp. 1979–86. 5 vols.
Poems. Eds. John D. Baird and Charles Ryskamp. 1980– .

ERASMUS DARWIN (1731–1802)

*Experiments Establishing a Criterion between Mucilaginous
and Purulent Matter* by Charles Darwin (editor). 1780.
Families of Plants by Linnaeus (translator). 1787. 2 vols.
*The Botanic Garden, Part II: Containing The Loves of the
Plants.* 1789.
*The Botanic Garden, Part I: Containing The Economy of Veg-
etation.* 1791.
The Botanic Garden. 1791. 2 parts.
The Golden Age: A Poetical Epistle to Thomas Beddoes. 1794.
Zoonomia; or, The Laws of Organic Life. 1794–96. 2 vols.
*A Plan for the Conduct of Female Education in Boarding
Schools.* 1797.

Phytologia; or, The Philosophy of Agriculture and Gardening. 1800.
The Temple of Nature; or, The Origin of Society. 1803.
Poetical Works. 1806. 3 vols.
Essential Writings. Ed. Desmond King-Hele. 1968.
Letters. Ed. Desmond King-Hele. 1981.

JAMES BEATTIE (1735–1803)

Original Poems and Translations. 1760.
Verses Occasioned by the Death of the Rev^d Mr. Charles Churchill. 1765.
The Judgment of Paris. 1765.
Poems on Several Subjects. 1766.
An Essay on the Nature and Immutability of Truth, in Opposition to Sophistry and Scepticism. 1770.
The Minstrel; or, The Progress of Genius. 1771 [Book 1]; 1774 [Book 2].
Essays: On Poetry and Music, as They Affect the Mind; On Laughter, and Ludicrous Composition; On the Utility of Classical Learning. 1776.
Poems on Several Occasions. 1776.
The Minstrel, with Some Other Poems. 1779.
A List of Two Hundred Scoticisms. 1779.
Dissertations Moral and Critical: On Memory and Imagination; On Dreaming; The Theory of Language; On Fable and Romance; On the Attachments of Kindred; Illustrations on Sublimity. 1783.
Evidences of the Christian Religion, Briefly and Plainly Stated. 1786. 2 vols.
Scoticisms: Arranged in Alphabetical Order, Designed to Correct Improprieties of Speech and Writing. 1787.
The Theory of Language. 1788. 2 parts.
Elements of Moral Science. 1790–93. 2 vols.
Essays and Fragments in Prose and Verse by James Hay Beattie (editor). 1794.
Poetical Works. Ed. Thomas Park. 1805.
Beauties Selected from the Writings. 1809.
A Letter to the Rev. Hugh Blair on the Improvement of Psalmody in Scotland. 1829.
Poetical Works. Ed. Alexander Dyce. 1831.
Poetical Works (with William Falconer and Robert Blair). Ed. George Gilfillan. 1854.
Some Unpublished Letters. Ed. Alexander Mackie. 1908.
London Diary 1773. Ed. Ralph S. Walker. 1946.
Day Book 1773–1798. Ed. Ralph S. Walker. 1948.

JOSEPH PRIESTLEY (1733–1804)

A Chart of Universal History. 1753.
The Scripture Doctrine of Remission. 1761.
The Rudiments of English Grammar. 1761.
A Course of Lectures on the Theory of Language, and Universal Grammar. 1762.
No Man Liveth to Himself. 1764.
A Chart of Biography. 1765.
A Description of a Chart of Biography. 1765.
An Essay on a Course of Liberal Education for Civil and Active Life. 1765.
A Syllabus of a Course of Lectures on the Study of History. c. 1765.
A Catechism for Children. 1767.
The History and Present State of Electricity, with Original Experiments. 1767.
An Essay on the First Principles of Government. 1768.
A Free Address to Protestant Dissenters, on the Subject of the Lord's Supper. 1768.

A Familiar Introduction to the Study of Electricity. 1768.
A Free Address to Protestant Dissenters, as Such. 1769.
Considerations on Differences of Opinion among Christians. 1769.
Considerations on Church-Authority. 1769.
The Present State of Liberty in Great Britain and Her Colonies. 1769.
A View of the Principles and Conduct of the Protestant Dissenters, with Respect to the Civil and Ecclesiastical Constitution of England. 1769.
Remarks on Some Paragraphs in the Fourth Volume of Dr. Blackstone's Commentaries on the Laws of England. 1769.
A New Chart of History. 1769.
A Description of a New Chart of History. 1769.
A Serious Address to the Masters of Families, with Forms of Family-Prayer. c. 1769.
Additions to the Address to Protestant Dissenters. 1770.
An Appeal to the Serious and Candid Professors of Christianity. 1770.
A Free Address to Protestant Dissenters, on the Subject of Church Discipline. 1770.
A Familiar Introduction to the Theory and Practice of Perspective. 1770.
An Answer to A Second Letter to Dr. Priestley. 1770.
Letters to the Author of Remarks on Several Late Publications Relative to the Dissenters. 1770.
An Answer to Dr. Blackstone's Reply to Remarks on the Fourth Volume of the *Commentaries on the Laws of England.* 1770.
Letters and Queries Addressed to the Anonymous Answerer of an Appeal to the Serious and Candid Professors of Christianity. 1771.
A Short Defence of Doctrine of Divinity of Christ. 1772.
The History and Present State of Discoveries Relating to Vision, Light, and Colours. 1772. 2 vols.
A Scripture Catechism. 1772.
A Familiar Illustration of Certain Passages of Scripture. 1772.
Directions for Impregnating Water with Fixed Air. 1772.
Institutes of Natural and Revealed Religion. 1772–74. 3 vols.
An Address to Protestant Dissenters, on the Subject of Giving the Lord's Supper to Children. 1773.
A Sermon Preached before the Congregation of Protestant Dissenters at Mill-Hill-Chapel in Leeds. 1773.
A Letter of Advice to Those Dissenters Who Conduct the Application to Parliament for Relief from Certain Penal Laws. 1773.
Experiments and Observations on Different Kinds of Air. 1774–77. 3 vols.
A Letter to a Layman, on the Subject of the Rev. Mr. Lindsey's Proposal for a Reformed English Church. 1774.
An Address to Protestant Dissenters of All Denominations on the Approaching Election of Members of Parliament. 1774.
An Examination of Dr. Reid's Inquiry into the Human Mind, *Dr. Beattie's* Essay on the Nature and Immutability of Truth, *and Dr. Oswald's* Appeal to Common Sense. 1774.
Hartley's Theory of the Human Mind, on the Principle of the Association of Ideas (editor). 1775.
Considerations for the Use of Young Men, and the Parents of Young Men. 1775.
Philosophical Empiricism. 1775.
Observations on Respiration, and the Use of the Blood. 1776.
Disquisitions Relating to Matter and Spirit. 1777, 1782 (2

vols.; with *The Doctrine of Philosophical Necessity Illustrated* and other works).

A Course of Lectures on Oratory and Criticism. 1777.

The Doctrine of Philosophical Necessity Illustrated. 1777.

A Harmony of the Evangelists, in Greek. 1777.

Observations on the Harmony of the Evangelists. 1777.

Miscellaneous Observations Relating to Education. 1778.

A Free Discussion of the Doctrines of Materialism, and Philosophical Necessity. 1778.

The Doctrine of Divine Influence on the Human Mind. 1779.

Experiments and Observations Relating to Various Branches of Natural Philosophy. 1779–86. 3 vols.

A Letter to the Rev. Mr. John Palmer. 1779.

A Harmony of the Evangelists, in English. 1780.

Two Letters to Dr. Newcome, Bishop of Waterford. 1780.

Letters to a Philosophical Unbeliever. 1780. 2 parts.

A Free Address to Those Who Have Petitioned for the Repeal of the Late Act of Parliament, in Favour of the Roman Catholics. 1780.

A Letter to Jacob Bryant, Esq., in Defence of Philosophical Necessity. 1780.

A Second Letter to the Rev. Mr. Palmer. 1780.

A Third Letter to Dr. Newcome, on the Duration of Our Saviour's Ministry. 1781.

A Sermon Preached at the New Meeting in Birmingham on Undertaking the Pastoral Office in That Place. 1781.

Additional Letters to a Philosophical Unbeliever. 1782.

An History of the Corruptions of Christianity. 1782. 2 vols.

The Proper Constitution of a Christian Church. 1782.

Two Discourses. 1782.

A General View of the Arguments for the Unity of God. 1783.

Letters to Dr. Horsley. 1783–86. 3 parts.

A Reply to the Animadversions on the *History of the Corruptions of Christianity.* 1783.

Forms of Prayer and Other Offices, for the Use of Unitarian Societies. 1783.

Defences of the History of the Corruptions of Christianity. 1783–86. 4 parts.

Remarks on the Monthly Review of the Letters to Dr. Horsley. 1784.

Experiments Relating to Phlogiston, and the Seeming Conversion of Water into Air. 1784.

The Importance and Extent of Free Inquiry in Matters of Religion. 1785.

An History of Early Opinions concerning Jesus Christ. 1786. 4 vols.

Letters to the Jews. 1786–87. 2 parts.

Discourses on Various Subjects, Including Several on Particular Occasions. 1787.

Letters to Dr. Horne. 1787.

An Account of a Society for Encouraging the Industrious Poor. 1787.

A Letter to the Right Honourable William Pitt. 1787.

Defences of Unitarianism for the Year 1786. 1787.

Defences of Unitarianism for the Year 1787. 1788.

A Sermon on the Subject of the Slave Trade. 1788.

Lectures on History and General Policy. 1788.

The Conduct to Be Observed by Dissenters in Order to Procure the Repeal of the Corporation and Test Acts. 1789.

Defences of Unitarianism for the Years 1788 and 1789. 1790.

Familiar Letters, Addressed to the Inhabitants of the Town of Birmingham. 1790.

Letters to the Rev. Edward Burn. 1790.

Prayer Respecting State of Christianity. 1790.

Reflections on Death: A Sermon on Occasion of the Death of the Rev. Robert Robinson, of Cambridge. 1790.

A View of Revealed Religion. 1790.

A General History of the Christian Church to the Fall of the Western Empire. 1790. 2 vols.

Letters to Candidates for Orders in Both Universities. c. 1790.

A Discourse on the Occasion of the Death of Dr. Price. 1791.

The Evidence of the Resurrection of Jesus Considered. 1791.

Letters to the Members of the New Jerusalem Church, Formed by Baron Swedenborg. 1791.

A Particular Attention to the Instruction of the Young Recommended. 1791.

Sermons (with Richard Price). 1791.

Three Tracts. 1791.

An Appeal to the Public on the Subject of the Riots in Birmingham. 1791.

The Duty of Forgiveness of Injuries. 1791.

Letters to the Right Honourable Edmund Burke. 1791.

Political Dialogues on the General Principles of Government. 1791. 1 no. only.

The Proper Objects of Education in the Present State of the World. 1791.

A Small Whole-Length of Dr. Priestley. 1792.

Letters to a Young Man. 1792–93. 2 parts.

Letters to the Philosophers and Politicians of France on the Subject of Religion. 1793.

A Sermon Preached at the Gravel Pit Meeting, in Hackney. 1793.

Experiments on the Generation of Air from Water. 1793.

Heads of Lectures on a Course of Experimental Philosophy. 1794.

A Continuation of the Letters to the Philosophers and Politicians of France ⟨An Answer to Mr. Paine's Age of Reason⟩. 1794.

Discourses on the Evidence of Revealed Religion. 1794.

The Use of Christianity, Especially in Difficult Times. 1794.

The Present State of Europe Compared with Antient Prophecies. 1794.

Two Sermons. 1794.

Observations on the Increase of Infidelity. 1795.

Unitarianism Explained and Defended. 1796.

Considerations on the Doctrine of Phlogiston. 1796.

Experiments and Observations Relating to the Analysis of Atmospherical Air. 1796.

Discourses Relating to the Evidence of Revealed Religion. 1796.

Letters to Mr. Volney. 1797.

An Address to the Unitarian Congregation at Philadelphia. 1797.

An Outline of the Evidences of Revealed Religion. 1797.

The Case of Poor Emigrants Recommended. 1797.

Letters to the Inhabitants of Northumberland and Its Neighbourhood. 1799. 2 parts.

A Comparison of the Institutions of Moses with Those of the Hindoos and Other Ancient Nations. 1799.

Works. 1799–1806. 8 vols.

The Doctrine of Phlogiston Established, and That of the Composition of Water Refuted. 1800.

An Inquiry into the Knowledge of the Antient Hebrews, concerning a Future State. 1801.

A Letter to an Antipaedobaptist. 1802.

A General History of the Christian Church from the Fall of the Western Empire to the Present Time. 1802–03. 4 vols.

Socrates and Jesus Compared. 1803.

A Letter to the Rev. John Blair Linn in Defence of the Pamphlet, Intituled, Socrates and Jesus Compared. 1803.

A Second Letter to the Rev. John Blair Linn. 1803.
Notes on All the Books of Scripture. 1803–04. 4 vols.
The Originality and Superior Excellence of the Mosaic Institution Demonstrated. 1803.
The Doctrines of Heathen Philosophy, Compared with Those of Revelation. 1804.
Index to the Bible. 1804.
Discourses, on Various Subjects, Intended to Have Been Delivered in Philadelphia. 1805.
Memoirs. Ed. Joseph Priestley the Younger. 1806–07. 2 vols.
The Importance of Religion to Enlarge the Mind of Man. 1808.
Tracts in Controversy with Bishop Horsley. 1815.
Theological and Miscellaneous Works. Ed. J. T. Rutt. 1817–31. 25 vols.
Scientific Correspondence. Ed. H. C. Bolton. 1892.
Selection from His Writings. Ed. Ira V. Brown. 1962.
Writings on Philosophy, Science, and Politics. Ed. John A. Passmore. 1965.
A Scientific Autobiography: Selected Scientific Correspondence. Ed. Robert E. Schofield. 1966.

CHARLOTTE SMITH (1749–1806)

Elegiac Sonnets and Other Essays. 1784.
Manon Lescaut by Abbé Prevost (translator). 1785. 2 vols.
The Romance of Real Life (adaptation). 1787. 3 vols.
Emmeline, the Orphan of the Castle. 1788. 4 vols.
Ethelinde; or, The Recluse of the Lake. 1789. 5 vols.
Celestina. 1791. 4 vols.
Desmond. 1792. 3 vols.
The Emigrants. 1793.
The Old Manor House. 1793. 4 vols.
D'Arcy. 1793.
The Wanderings of Warwick. 1794.
The Banished Man. 1794. 4 vols.
Rural Walks, in Dialogues Intended for the Use of Young Persons. 1795. 2 vols.
Montalbert. 1795. 3 vols.
Rambles Farther: A Continuation of Rural Walks. 1796. 2 vols.
A Narrative of the Loss of the Catharine, Venus and Piedmont Transports, and the Thomas, Golden Grove and Æolus Merchant Ships, near Weymouth. 1796.
Marchmont. 1796. 4 vols.
Minor Morals, Interspersed with Sketches of Natural History, Historical Anecdotes, and Original Stories. 1798. 2 vols.
The Young Philosopher. 1798. 2 vols.
What Is She? 1799.
The Letters of a Solitary Wanderer. 1799 (2 vols.), 1800–02 (5 vols.).
Conversations Introducing Poetry, Chiefly on Subjects of Natural History: For the Use of Children. 1804. 2 vols.
History of England from the Earliest Records to the Peace of Amiens (with others). 1806. 3 vols.
The Natural History of Birds: Intended Chiefly for Young Persons. 1807. 2 vols.
Beachy Head, with Other Poems. 1807.

HENRY KIRKE WHITE (1785–1806)

Clifton Grove: A Sketch in Verse, with Other Poems. 1803.
Remains. Ed. Robert Southey. 1807. 2 vols.
Poetical Remains. 1824.
Prose Remains. 1824.
Life and Remains. 1825.
The Beauties of Henry Kirke White. Ed. Alfred Howard. 1827.
Poetical Works. Ed. Sir Nicholas Harris Nicolas. 1830.

Memoir and Poetical Remains; also Melancholy Hours. Ed. John Todd. 1844.
Poems, Letters and Prose Fragments. Ed. John Drinkwater. 1907.

CLARA REEVE (1729–1807)

Original Poems on Several Occasions. 1769.
The Phoenix by John Barclay (translator). 1772.
The Champion of Virtue: A Gothic Story. 1777, 1778 (as *The Old English Baron: A Gothic Story*).
The Two Mentors: A Modern Story. 1783. 3 vols.
The Progress of Romance. 1785. 2 vols.
The Exiles; or, Memoirs of the Count de Cronstadt. 1788. 3 vols.
The School for Widows. 1791. 3 vols.
Plans of Education; with Remarks on the Systems of Other Writers. 1792.
Memoirs of Sir Roger de Clarendon. 1793. 3 vols.
Destination; or, Memoirs of a Private Family. 1799. 3 vols.

RICHARD HURD (1720–1808)

Remarks on a Late Book, Entitled, An Enquiry into the Rejection of the Christian Miracles by the Heathens. 1746.
Q. Horatii Flacci Ars Poetica, Epistola ad Pisones (editor). 1749.
Q. Horatii Flacci Epistola ad Augustum (editor). 1751.
The Opinion of an Eminent Lawyer (the Earl of Hardwicke), *concerning the Right of Appeal from the Vice-Chancellor of Cambridge, to the Senate.* 1751.
The Mischiefs of Enthusiasm and Bigotry. 1752.
Q. Horatii Flacci Epistolae ad Pisones et Augustum (editor). 1753.
A Sermon Preached at Trinity College in Cambridge. 1753.
On the Delicacy of Friendship. 1755.
Remarks on Mr. David Hume's Essay on the Natural History of Religion (with William Warburton). 1757.
A Letter to Mr. Mason, on the Marks of Imitation. 1757.
Moral and Political Dialogues. 1758, 1765 (with *Letters on Chivalry and Romance*; 3 vols.).
Letters on Chivalry and Romance. 1762.
Dialogues on the Uses of Foreign Travel. 1764.
*A Letter to the Rev. D*ʳ *Thomas Leland.* 1764.
A Dissertation on the Idea of Universal Poetry. 1766.
An Introduction to the Study of the Prophecies concerning the Christian Church. 1772.
Select Works of Mr. Abraham Cowley (editor). 1772. 2 vols.
Discord: A Satire. 1773.
A Moral Demonstration of the Truth of the Christian Religion by Jeremy Taylor (editor). 1776.
A Charge Delivered to the Clergy of the Diocese of Lichfield and Coventry, at the Bishop's Primary Visitation in 1775 and 1776. 1776.
Sermons Preached at Lincoln's-Inn between the Years 1765 and 1776. 1776–80. 3 vols.
A Sermon Preached before the Right Honourable the House of Lords. 1777.
A Sermon Preached before the Incorporated Society for the Propagation of the Gospel in Foreign Parts. 1781.
A Sermon Preached before the House of Lords: Being the Anniversary of King Charles's Martyrdom. 1786.
The Works of William Warburton (editor). 1788 (7 vols.), 1811 (12 vols.).
Tracts, by Warburton, and a Warburtonian ⟨Hurd⟩*; Not Admitted into the Collections of Their Respective Works.* Ed. Samuel Parr. 1789.

A Discourse, by Way of General Preface, to the Quarto Edition of Bishop Warburton's Works. 1794.

Letters of a Late Eminent Prelate to One of His Friends by William Warburton (editor). 1808.

The Works of the Right Honourable Joseph Addison (editor). 1811.

Works. 1811. 8 vols.

The Correspondence of Richard Hurd and William Mason; and Letters of Richard Hurd to Thomas Gray. Eds. Ernest Harold Pearce and Leonard Whibley. 1932.

JOHN HOME (1722–1808)

Alarm to the Households and Heritors of the City of Edinburgh. 1749.

Douglas. 1757.

Agis. 1758.

The Siege of Aquileia. 1760.

Dramatick Works. 1760.

The Fatal Discovery. 1769.

Alonzo. 1773.

Alfred. 1777.

Dramatic Works. 1798. 2 vols.

The History of the Rebellion in Scotland in 1745. 1802.

Works. 1822. 3 vols.

RICHARD PORSON (1759–1808)

Emendationes in Suidam et Hesychium et Alios Lexicographos Graecos by Jonathan Toup (editor). 1790. 4 vols.

Letters to Mr Archdeacon Travis. 1790.

Aeschyli Tragoediae Septem (editor; with Latin tr.). 1794. 2 vols.

Εὐριπιδου Ἑκαβη (editor). 1797.

Εὐριπιδου Ὀρεστες (editor). 1798.

Εὐριπιδου Φοινισσαι (editor). 1799.

Ὁμηρου Ἰλιας και Ὀδυσσεια (editor; with others). 1800–01. 4 vols.

Εὐριπιδου Μηδεια (editor). 1801.

Euripidis Tragoediae, Tom. 1: Hecuba, Orestes, Phoenissae, Medea (editor). 1802.

Adversaria. Eds. J. H. Monk and C. J. Blomfield. 1812.

Tracts and Miscellaneous Criticisms. Ed. Thomas Kidd. 1815.

Notae in Aristophanem. Ed. Peter Paul Dobree. 1820.

Φωτιου Λεξεων Συναγωγη: *E Codice Galeano Descripsit R. Porsonus.* 1822. 2 parts.

Correspondence. Ed. Henry Richard Luard. 1867.

THOMAS PAINE (1737–1809)

Common Sense: Addressed to the Inhabitants of America. 1776.

A Dialogue between the Ghost of General Montgomery Just Arrived from the Elysian Fields; and an American Delegate, in a Wood Near Philadelphia. 1776.

The American Crisis ⟨*The Crisis*⟩. 1776–83. 16 nos.

The Crisis Extraordinary. 1780.

Public Good: Being an Examination into the Claim of Virginia to the Vacant Western Territory, and of the Right of the United States to the Same. 1780.

Letter Addressed to Abbé Reynal on the Affairs of North America. 1782.

Dissertations on Government, the Affairs of the Bank, and Paper-Money. 1786.

Prospects on the Rubicon; or, An Investigation into the Causes and Consequences of the Politics to Be Agitated at the Meeting of Parliament. 1787.

Rights of Man: Being an Answer to Burke's Attack on the French Revolution. 1791–92. 2 parts.

Address and Declaration of the Friends of Universal Peace and Liberty. c. 1791.

Letter to Lord Onslow. 1792.

A Letter to Mr. Secretary Dundas, in Answer to His Speech on the Late Proclamation. 1792.

Two Letters to Lord Onslow, and One to Mr. Henry Dundas. 1792.

Paine Insulted at Dover! Letter to Mr. Secretary Dundas. 1792.

Letter Addressed to the Addressers on the Late Proclamation. 1792.

Writings. 1792.

Address to the Republic of France. c. 1792.

Opinion sur l'affaire de Louis Capet. 1793.

The Case of the Officers of Excise. 1793.

The Age of Reason: Being an Investigation of True and Fabulous Theology. 1794–95. 2 parts.

Dissertation on the First-Principles of Government. 1795.

The Decline and Fall of the English System of Finance. 1796.

Letter to George Washington, President of the United States of America, on Affairs Public and Private. 1796.

Au Conseil de cinq-cents. 1796.

Letter to George Washington, President of the United States of America. 1797.

A Letter to the Hon. Thomas Erskine, on the Prosecution of Thomas Williams, for Publishing The Age of Reason. 1797.

Letter to Camille Jordan of the Council of 500, Occasioned by Their Report on the Priests, Public Worship and on Bells. 1797.

Letter to the People of France and the French Armies on the Events of the 18th Fructidor—Sep. 4—and Its Consequences. 1797.

Agrarian Justice Opposed to Agrarian Law, and to Agrarian Monopoly. 1797.

Works. 1797. 2 vols.

A Discourse Delivered at the Society of the Theophilanthropes. 1798.

Compact Maritime. 1801.

Letters to the Citizens of America after an Absence of 15 Years in Europe. 1804.

Thomas Paine to the People of England on the Invasion of England. 1804.

Thomas Paine to the Citizens of Pennsylvania on the Proposal for Calling a Convention. 1805.

Examination of the Passages in the New Testament. 1807.

On the Causes of the Yellow Fever and the Means of Preventing It in Places Not Yet Infected with It. 1807.

On the Origin of Freemasonry. 1810.

Political Works. 1817.

Theological Works. 1818.

Miscellaneous Letters and Essays. 1819.

Writings. Ed. Moncure Daniel Conway. 1894–96. 4 vols.

Life and Writings. Ed. Daniel Edwin Wheeler. 1908. 10 vols.

Selections from the Writings. Ed. Carl Van Doren. 1922.

Six New Letters. Ed. Harry Hayden Clark. 1939.

Complete Writings. Ed. Philip S. Foner. 1945. 2 vols.

ANNA SEWARD (1742–1809)

Elegy on Captain Cook; to Which Is Added, An Ode to the Sun. 1780.

Monody on Major André. 1781.

Poem to the Memory of Lady Miller. 1782.

Louisa: A Poetical Novel in Four Epistles. 1784.

Ode on General Eliott's Return from Gibralter. 1787.

Variety: A Collection of Essays. 1788.

Llangollen Vale, with Other Poems. 1796.

Original Sonnets, on Various Subjects; and Odes Paraphrased from Horace. 1799.

Memoirs of the Life of Dr. Darwin. 1804.

Memoirs of Abelard and Eloisa. 1805.

Blindness. 1806.

Monumental Inscriptions in Ashbourn Church, Derbyshire (with Sir Brooke Boothby). 1806.

Poetical Works. Ed. Sir Walter Scott. 1810. 3 vols.

Letters. Ed. A. Constable. 1811. 6 vols.

The Beauties of Anna Seward. Ed. W. C. Oulton. 1813.

Miss Seward's Enigma. 1855.

The Swan of Lichfield: Being a Selection from the Correspondence. Ed. Hesketh Pearson. 1936.

CHARLES BROCKDEN BROWN (1771–1810)

Alcuin: A Dialogue. 1798.

Wieland; or, The Transformation: An American Tale. 1798.

Ormond; or, The Secret Witness. 1799.

Arthur Mervyn; or, Memoirs of the Year 1793. 1799–1800. 2 vols.

Edgar Huntly; or, Memoirs of a Sleep-walker. 1799. 3 vols.

Clara Howard. 1801.

Jane Talbot. 1801.

An Address to the Government of the United States, on the Cession of Louisiana to the French. 1803.

Monroe's Embassy; or, The Conduct of the Government, in Relation to Our Claims to the Navigation of the Missisippi, Considered. 1803.

A View of the Soil and Climate of the United States of America by C. F. Volney (translator). 1804.

[*The British Treaty.* 1807.]

An Address to the Congress of the United States, on the Utility and Justice of Restrictions upon Foreign Commerce. 1809.

Memoirs of Carwin, the Biloquist. 1822.

Novels. 1827. 7 vols.

Novels. 1857. 6 vols.

Complete Novels. 1887. 6 vols.

The Rhapsodist and Other Uncollected Writings. Ed. Harry R. Warfel. 1943.

Novels and Related Works. Eds. Sidney J. Krause et al. 1977–87. 6 vols.

ROBERT TANNAHILL (1774–1810)

The Soldier's Return: A Scottish Interlude in Two Acts, with Other Poems and Songs, Chiefly in the Scottish Dialect. 1807.

Poems and Songs, Chiefly in the Scottish Dialect. 1815.

The Tannahill Songster. c. 1820.

Poetical Works. 1825.

Works. Ed. Philip A. Ramsay. c. 1838.

Poetical Works. 1870.

Complete Songs and Poems. 1874.

Poems and Songs and Correspondence. Ed. David Semple. 1876.

Poems and Songs. Ed. David Semple. 1900.

Songs and Poems. 1911.

RICHARD CUMBERLAND (1732–1811)

An Elegy Written on Saint Mark's Eve. 1754.

Pharsalia by Lucan (editor). 1760.

The Banishment of Cicero. 1761.

The Summer's Tale. 1765.

A Letter to the Right Reverend Bishop of O——d, Containing Some Animadversions upon a Character of the Late Dr. Bentley. 1767.

Amelia. 1768.

The Brothers. 1770.

The West Indian. 1771.

Timon of Athens (adaptation). 1771.

The Fashionable Lover. 1772.

The Note of Hand; or, Trip to Newmarket. 1774.

The Choleric Man. 1775.

Odes. 1776.

Miscellaneous Poems: Consisting of Elegies, Odes, Pastorals, &c., Together with Calypso: A Masque. 1778.

The Battle of Hastings. 1778.

Calypso: A Masque. 1779.

Songs in The Widow of Delphi; or, The Descent of the Deities. 1780.

Anecdotes of Eminent Painters in Spain, during the Sixteenth and Seventeenth Centuries. 1782. 2 vols.

A Letter to Richard Lord Bishop of Landaff, on the Subject of His Lordship's Letter to the Late Archbishop of Canterbury. 1783.

The Mysterious Husband. 1783.

The Carmelite. 1784.

The Natural Son. 1784.

The Observer. 1785. 40 nos.

Character of the Late Lord Viscount Sackville. 1785.

The Clouds by Aristophanes (translator). c. 1786.

An Accurate Catalogue of the Several Paintings in the King of Spain's Palace at Madrid. 1787.

Arundel. 1789. 2 vols.

The Impostors. 1789.

Curtius Rescued from the Gulph; or, The Retort Courteous to the Rev. Dr. Parr, in Answer to His Learned Pamphlet, Intitled, A Sequel, etc. 1792.

Calvary; or, The Death of Christ. 1792.

Songs and Chorusses in the Comic Opera of The Armourer. 1793.

The Box-Lobby Challenge. 1794.

The Jew. 1794.

The Wheel of Fortune. 1795.

First Love. 1795.

Henry. 1795. 4 vols.

The Days of Yore. 1796.

False Impressions. 1797.

Joanna of Montfaucon: A Dramatic Romance (adaptation). 1800.

A Few Plain Reasons Why We Should Believe in Christ and Adhere to His Religion. 1801.

A Poetical Version of Certain Psalms of David. 1801.

The Sailor's Daughter. 1804.

A Melo-dramatic Piece: Being an Occasional Attempt to Commemorate the Death and Victory of Lord Viscount Nelson. 1805.

A Hint to Husbands. 1806.

Memoirs. 1806–07. 2 vols.

The Exodiad (with Sir James Bland Burgess). 1807.

The Jew of Mogodore. 1808.

John de Lancaster. 1809. 3 vols.

Retrospection: A Poem in Familiar Verse. 1811.

Posthumous Dramatick Works. 1813. 2 vols.

The British Drama (editor). 1817. 14 vols.

JOEL BARLOW (1754–1812)

The Prospect of Peace. 1778.

A Poem, Spoken at the Public Commencement at Yale College. 1781.

An Elegy on the Late Honorable Titus Hosmer, Esq. 1782.

Doctor Watts's Imitation of the Psalms of David (revised by Barlow). 1785.

A Translation of Sundry Psalms Which Were Omitted in Doctor Watts's Version. 1785.

The Vision of Columbus. 1787.

An Oration in Commemoration of the Independence of the United States. 1787.

Advice to the Privileged Orders in the Several States of Europe. 1792–93. 2 parts.

The Conspiracy of Kings. 1792.

A Letter to the National Convention of France. 1792.

New Travels in the United States of America by J. P. Brissot de Warville (translator). 1792.

Lettre adressée aux habitans du Piémont. 1793.

The Commerce of America with Europe by J. P. Brissot de Warville (translator). 1794.

[*The History of England from the Year 1765 to the Year 1794.* 1795. 5 vols.]

The Hasty-Pudding. 1796.

Political Writings. 1796.

The Second Warning; or, Strictures on the Speech Delivered by John Adams at the Opening of the Congress. 1798.

Joel Barlow to His Fellow Citizens of the United States of America. 1799. 2 parts.

A New Translation of Volney's Ruins (translator; with Thomas Jefferson). 1802. 2 vols.

Prospectus of a National Institution, to Be Established in the United States. 1806.

The Columbiad. 1807.

Oration Delivered at Washington, July Fourth, 1809. 1809.

Letter to Henry Gregoire, in Reply to His Letter on the Columbiad. 1809.

Letter Addressed to the Speaker of the H. of Representatives. 1811.

A Review of Robert Smith's Address to the People of the United States. 1811.

Message from the President of the U. States, Transmitting Copies and Extracts from the Correspondence of the Secretary of State, and the Minister Plenipotentiary of the United States at Paris (with James Madison). 1812.

The Anarchiad: A New England Poem (with others). Ed. Luther G. Riggs. 1861.

Life and Letters. Ed. Charles Burr Todd. 1886.

RICHARD BRINSLEY SHERIDAN (1751–1816)

The Love Epistles of Aristaenetus (translator; with Nathaniel Brassey Halhed). 1771.

The Ridotto of Bath: A Panegyrick. 1771.

The Rival Beauties: A Poetical Contest. 1772.

A Familiar Epistle to the Author of the Heroic Epistle to Sir William Chambers. 1774.

The Rivals. 1775.

The Duenna. 1775.

Verses to the Memory of Garrick. 1779.

The School for Scandal. 1780.

A Trip to Scarborough: Altered from Vanbrugh's Relapse. 1781.

The Critic; or, A Tragedy Rehearsed. 1781.

A Short Account of the Situations and Incidents Exhibited in the Pantomime of Robinson Crusoe. 1781.

The Legislative Independence of Ireland Vindicated in a Speech of Mr. Sheridan's. 1785.

The Genuine Speech of Mr. Sheridan Delivered in the House of Commons on a Charge &c. against Warren Hastings Esq. 1787.

Speech in Bringing Forward the Fourth Charge against Warren Hastings, Esq., Relative to the Begums of Oude. 1787.

The Celebrated Speech of Richard Brinsley Sheridan in Westminster Hall on His Summing Up the Evidence in the Begum Charge against Warren Hastings. 1788.

Speech before the High Court of Parliament on Summing Up the Evidence on the Begum Charge against Warren Hastings. 1788.

St. Patrick's Day; or, The Scheming Lieutenant. 1788.

A Comparative Statement of the Two Bills for the Better Government of India. 1788.

The Glorious First of June (with others). 1794.

Dramatic Works. 1797.

Speech in the House of Commons on the Motion to Address His Majesty on the Present Alarming State of Affairs. 1798.

Speech in the House of Commons in Reply to Mr. Pitt's Speech on the Union with Ireland. 1799.

Pizarro: A Tragedy Taken from the German Drama of Kotzebue. 1799.

Speech in the House of Commons on the Motion for the Army Establishment for the Ensuing Year. 1802.

Speech in the House of Commons on the Army Estimates. 1802.

Death of Mr. Fox. 1806.

The Forty Thieves (with Charles Ward and George Colman the Younger). 1808.

Speeches. 1816. 5 vols.

Clio's Protest; or, The Picture Varnished, with Other Poems. 1819.

Works. Ed. Thomas Moore. 1821. 2 vols.

Dramatic Works. 1828.

Dramatic Works. Ed. Leigh Hunt. 1840.

Works. Ed. James P. Browne. 1873. 2 vols.

Sheridan's Plays Now Printed as He Wrote Them. Ed. W. Fraser Rae. 1902.

Plays. Ed. Edmund Gosse. 1905. 3 vols.

Plays. Ed. Joseph Knight. 1906.

Plays and Poems. Ed. R. Crampton Rhodes. 1928. 3 vols.

Letters. Ed. Cecil Price. 1966. 3 vols.

Dramatic Works. Ed. Cecil Price. 1973. 2 vols.

JANE AUSTEN (1775–1816)

Sense and Sensibility. 1811. 3 vols.

Pride and Prejudice. 1813. 3 vols.

Mansfield Park. 1814. 3 vols.

Emma. 1816. 3 vols.

Northanger Abbey and Persuasion. 1818. 4 vols.

Novels. 1833. 5 vols.

Letters. Ed. Edward, Lord Brabourne. 1884. 2 vols.

Novels. Ed. Reginald Brimley Johnson. 1892. 10 vols.

Charades &c., Written a Hundred Years Ago by Jane Austen and Her Family. 1895.

Love and Freindship. 1922.

Novels. Ed. R. W. Chapman. 1923. 5 vols.

The Watsons. 1923.

Five Letters to Her Niece Fanny Knight. 1924.

Letters. Ed. R. Brimley Johnson. 1925.

Lady Susan. Ed. R. W. Chapman. 1925.

Fragment of a Novel Written by Jane Austen January–March 1817 ⟨*Sanditon*⟩. Ed. R. W. Chapman. 1925.

Plan of a Novel. Ed. R. W. Chapman. 1926.

Letters to Her Sister Cassandra and Others. Ed. R. W. Chapman. 1932.

⟨*Juvenilia.*⟩ 1933 [Volume 1; ed. R. W. Chapman]; 1951 [Volume 3; ed. R. W. Chapman]; 1963 [Volume 2; ed. Brian Southam].

Three Evening Prayers. 1940.

Minor Works. Ed. R. W. Chapman. 1954.

Jane Austen's "Sir Charles Grandison." Ed. Brian Southam. 1980.

The Juvenilia of Jane Austen and Charlotte Brontë. Ed. Frances Beer. 1986.

TIMOTHY DWIGHT (1752–1817)

A Dissertation on the History, Eloquence, and Poetry of the Bible. 1772.

A Valedictory Address to the Young Gentlemen, Who Commenced Bachelors of Arts, at Yale-College. 1776.

A Sermon upon the General Thanksgiving. 1778.

America; or, A Poem on the Settlement of the British Colonies. c. 1780.

A Sermon Occasioned by the Capture of the British Army, under the Command of Earl Cornwallis. 1781.

The Conquest of Canaan. 1785.

The Triumph of Infidelity. 1788.

Virtuous Rulers a National Blessing. 1791.

A Discourse, on the Genuineness and Authenticity of the New-Testament. 1794.

Greenfield Hill. 1794.

Columbia: An Ode. c. 1794.

The True Means of Establishing Public Happiness. 1795.

A Discourse Preached at the Funeral of the Reverend Elizur Goodrich. 1797.

The Duty of Americans at the Present Crisis. 1798.

The Nature, and Danger, of Infidel Philosophy. 1798.

A Discourse on the Character of George Washington, Esq. 1800.

A Discourse on Some Events of the Last Century. 1801.

The Psalms of David, tr. Isaac Watts (revised by Dwight). 1801.

A Sermon on the Death of Mr. Ebenezer Grant Marsh. 1804.

The Folly, Guilt, and Mischiefs of Duelling. 1805.

A Sermon Preached at the Opening of the Theological Institution in Andover. 1808.

A Discourse, Occasioned by the Death of His Excellency Jonathan Trumbull, Esq., Governor of the State of Connecticut. 1809.

The Charitable Blessed. 1810.

A Statistical Account of the City of New-Haven. 1811.

The Dignity and Excellence of the Gospel. 1812.

A Discourse on the Public Fast. 1812. 2 parts.

A Sermon before the American Board of Commissioners for Foreign Missions. 1813.

Remarks on the Review of Inchiquin's Letters, Published in the Quarterly Review. 1815.

Female Benevolent Society. 1815.

Theology, Explained and Defended. 1818–19. 5 vols.

Travels in New-England and New-York. 1821–22. 4 vols.

An Essay on the Stage. 1824.

Sermons. 1828. 2 vols.

President Dwight's Decisions of Questions Discussed by the Senior Class in Yale College, in 1813 and 1814. Ed. Theodore Dwight, Jr. 1833.

JUNIUS

The Political Contest: Containing a Series of Letters between Junius and Sir William Draper; Also the Whole of Junius's Letters to His Grave the D*** of G******, Brought into One Point of View. 1769.

The Political Contest: Being a Continuation of Junius's Letters, from the 8th of July Last to the Present Time. 1769.

Junius's Supposed Address to a Great Personage. 1769.

A Collection of the Letters of Atticus, Lucius, Junius, and Others. 1769.

Two Letters from Junius to the D—— of G————, on the Sale of a Patent Place in the Customs at Exeter. 1769.

The Political Contest: Containing Junius's Letters to the K——; and Modestus's Answer. 1770.

The State of the Nation, as Represented to a Certain Great Personage, by Junius and the Freeholder. 1770.

The Letters of Junius. 1770 [Volume 1]; 1774 [Volume 2].

Two Remarkable Letters of Junius and the Freeholder, Addressed to the K——. 1770.

A Complete Collection of Junius's Letters, with Those of Sir William Draper. 1770.

The Letters of Junius. 1771.

The Letters of Junius. 1771–72. 2 vols.

The Genuine Letters of Junius. 1771.

Junius: Stat Nominis Umbra. 1772. 2 vols.

The Letters of the Celebrated Junius. 1783. 2 vols.

Junius's Political Axioms, Addressed to Twelve Millions of People in Great Britain and Ireland. c. 1790.

The Letters of Junius. Ed. Robert Heron. 1802. 2 vols.

The Letters of Junius Complete. Ed. John Almon. 1806. 2 vols.

Junius: Including Letters by the Same Writer, under Other Signatures. Ed. John Mason Good. 1812. 3 vols.

The Letters of Junius. Ed. John MacDiarmid. 1822.

The Letters of Junius. Ed. J. W. Lake. 1829. 2 vols.

Junius: Including Letters by the Same Writer under Other Signatures. Ed. John Wade. 1850. 2 vols.

The Letters of Junius. Ed. C. W. Everett. 1927.

MATTHEW GREGORY LEWIS (1775–1818)

The Monk: A Romance. 1796. 3 vols.

Village Virtues: A Dramatic Satire. 1796.

The Minister by Johann Christoph Friedrich von Schiller (translator). 1797.

The Castle Spectre. 1798.

Rolla by August von Kotzebue (translator). 1799.

The Love of Gain by Juvenal (translator). 1799.

The East Indian. 1800.

Adelmorn the Outlaw: A Romantic Drama. 1801.

Alfonso, King of Castile. 1801.

Tales of Wonder. 1801. 2 vols.

The Bravo of Venice by Heinrich Zschokke (translator). 1805.

Adelgitha; or, The Fruits of a Single Error. 1806.

Feudal Tyrants; or, The Counts of Carlsheim and Sargaus: A Romance Taken from the German. 1806. 4 vols.

Romantic Tales. 1808. 4 vols.

Venoni; or, The Novice of St. Mark's. 1809.

Monody on the Death of Sir John Moore. 1809.

Timour the Tarter. 1811.

One O'Clock! or, The Knight and the Wood Daemon. 1811.

Poems. 1812.

The Harper's Daughter; or, Love and Ambition. 1813.

The Isle of Devils: An Historical Tale. 1827.

Journal of a West India Proprietor. 1834.

Life and Correspondence. Ed. Mrs. Cornwell Baron-Wilson. 1839. 2 vols.

Fairy Tales and Romances (translator; with others). 1849.

The Four Facardins by Anthony Hamilton (translator). 1899.

JOHN WOLCOT ("PETER PINDAR") (1738–1819)

Persian Love Elegies; to Which Is Added The Nymph of Tauris. 1773.

A Poetical, Supplicating, Modest and Affecting Epistle to Those Literary Colossuses, the Reviewers. 1778.

Poems on Various Subjects. 1778.

Lyric Odes to the Royal Academicians. 1782.

More Lyric Odes to the Royal Academicians. 1783.

Lyric Odes for the Year 1785. 1785.

The Lousiad: An Heroi-Comic Poem. 1785 [Canto 1]; 1787 [Canto 2]; 1791 [Canto 3]; 1792 [Canto 4]; 1795 [Canto 5].

Farewel Odes for the Year 1786. 1786.

A Poetical and Congratulatory Epistle to James Boswell, Esq., on His Journal of a Tour to the Hebrides, with the Celebrated Dr. Johnson. 1786.

Bozzy and Piozzi; or, The British Biographers: A Town Eclogue. 1786.

Ode upon Ode; or, A Peep at St. James's; or, New Year's Day; or, What You Will. 1787.

An Apologetic Postscript to Ode upon Ode. 1787.

Instructions to a Celebrated Laureat. 1787.

A Congratulatory Epistle to Peter Pindar. 1787.

Brother Peter to Brother Tom: An Expostulatory Epistle. 1788.

Peter's Pension: A Solemn Epistle to a Sublime Personage. 1788.

The King's Ode, in Answer to Peter Pindar, on the Subject of His Pension. 1788.

Peter's Prophecy; or, The President and the Poet. 1788.

Sir Joseph Banks and the Emperor of Morocco. 1788.

[*Peter Provided For, without a Pension.* 1788.]

Tales and Fables. 1788.

Poetical Works. 1788.

[*The Antagonists of Peter Pindar Cut into Atoms.* 1789.]

A Poetical Epistle to a Falling Minister. 1789.

Expostulatory Odes to a Great Duke and Little Lord. 1789.

Subjects for Painters. 1789.

[*A Letter to the Most Insolent Man Alive.* 1789.]

A Benevolent Epistle to Sylvanus Urban, alias John Nichols. 1790.

Advice to the Future Laureat: An Ode. 1790.

A Complimentary Epistle to James Bruce, Esq., the Abyssinian Traveller. 1790.

Works. c. 1790, 1792.

The Rights of Kings; or, Loyal Odes to Disloyal Academicians. 1791.

Odes to Mr. Paine, Author of The Rights of Man. 1791.

The Remonstrance; to Which Is Added, an Ode to My Ass. 1791.

A Commiserating Epistle to James Lowther, Earl of Lonsdale and Lowther. 1791.

More Money; or, Odes of Instruction to Mr. Pitt. 1792.

Odes of Importance, &c. 1792.

The Tears of St. Margaret. 1792.

A Pair of Lyric Epistles to Lord Macartney and His Ship. 1792.

Odes to Kien Long, the Present Emperor of China. 1792.

A Poetical, Serious, and Possibly Impertinent Epistle to the Pope. 1793.

The Captive King. c. 1793.

Pathetic Odes. 1794.

Celebration; or, The Academic Procession to St. James's: An Ode. 1794.

Pindariana; or, Peter's Portfolio. 1794.

Works. 1794–96 [Volumes 1–4]; 1801 [Volume 5].

Hair Powder: A Plaintive Epistle to Mr. Pitt. 1795.

The Royal Tour and Weymouth Amusements. 1795.

The Convention Bill: An Ode. 1795.

The Royal Visit to Exeter. 1795.

Liberty's Last Squeak. 1795.

The Cap: A Satiric Poem. 1795.

The Royal Sheep; to Which is Added, The Adventures of Young Whipstitch. c. 1795.

One Thousand Seven Hundred and Ninety-six. 1797.

An Ode to the Livery of London on Their Petition to His Majesty for Kicking Out His Worthy Ministers. 1797.

Tales of the Joy. c. 1798. Part 1 only.

Nil Admirari; or, A Smile at a Bishop. 1799.

Pilkington's Dictionary of Painters (editor). 1799.

Lord Auckland's Triumph; or, The Death of Crim. Con. 1800.

Poems. 1800.

Out at Last! or, The Fallen Minister. 1801.

Odes to Ins and Outs. 1801.

Tears and Smiles: A Miscellaneous Collection of Poems. 1801.

A Poetical Epistle to Benjamin Count Rumford. 1801.

The Island of Innocence: A Poetical Epistle to a Friend. 1802. Part 1 only.

Pitt and His Statue: An Epistle to the Subscribers. 1802.

The Horrors of Bribery: A Penitential Epistle. 1802.

The Middlesex Election; or, Poetical Epistles, in the Devonshire Dialect. 1802.

Great Cry and Little Wool. 1804. 2 parts.

Poems Selected from the Works. 1804.

An Instructive Epistle to John Perring, Esq., Lord Mayor of London. 1804.

The Beauties of English Poetry (editor). 1804. 2 vols.

Tristia; or, The Sorrows of Peter. 1806.

The Beauties of Pindar. Ed. Alexander Campbell. 1807.

[*The Fall of Portugal; or, The Royal Exiles.* 1808.]

One More Peep at the Royal Academy. 1808.

A Solemn, Sentimental, and Reprobating Epistle to Mrs. Clarke. 1809.

Epistle the Second to Mrs. Clarke. 1809.

Works. 1809 (4 vols.), 1812 (5 vols.).

Carlton House Fete; or, The Disappointed Bard. 1811.

An Address to Be Spoken at the Opening of the Drury Lane Theatre. 1814.

Tom Halliard: A Ballad. c. 1815.

A Most Solemn Epistle to the Emperor of China. 1817.

The Beauties of Pindar. Ed. Alfred Howard. c. 1834.

Poems. Ed. P. M. Zall. 1972.

WILLIAM HAYLEY (1745–1820)

A Poetical Epistle to an Eminent Painter. 1778.

An Elegy, on the Ancient Greek Model. 1779.

Epistle to Admiral Keppel. 1779.

Epistle to a Friend, on the Death of John Thornton, Esq. 1780.

An Essay on History, in Three Epistles to Edward Gibbon, Esq. 1780.

Ode, Inscribed to John Howard. 1780.

The Triumphs of Temper. 1781.

Poems. 1781.

An Essay on Epic Poetry, in Five Epistles to the Revd Mr Mason. 1782.

Ode to Mr. Wright of Derby. 1783.

Plays of Three Acts Written for a Private Theatre. 1784.

The Happy Prescription; or, The Lady Relieved from Her Lovers. 1785.

A Philosophical, Historical, and Moral Essay on Old Maids. 1785. 3 vols.
The Two Connoisseurs: A Comedy in Rhyme. 1785.
Poems and Plays. 1785. 6 vols.
Poetical Works. 1785. 3 vols.
Poems. 1786.
Two Dialogues: Containing a Comparative View of the Life and Writings of Philip, the Late Earl of Chesterfield, and Dr. Samuel Johnson. 1787.
Occasional Stanzas, Written at the Request of the Revolution Society. 1788.
The Young Widow; or, The History of Cornelia Sedley, in a Series of Letters. 1789. 4 vols.
The Eulogies of Howard: A Vision. 1791.
An Elegy on the Death of the Honourable Sir William Jones. 1795.
The National Advocates. 1795.
The Life of Milton; to Which Are Added, Conjectures on the Origin of Paradise Lost. 1796.
An Essay on Sculpture, in a Series of Epistles to John Flaxman. 1800.
Little Tom, the Sailor. 1800.
Designs to a Series of Ballads. 1802. 4 parts.
The Life and Posthumous Writings of William Cowper. 1803–04. 3 vols.
The Triumph of Music. 1804.
Ballads Founded on Anecdotes Relating to Animals. 1805.
Supplementary Pages to the Life of Cowper. 1806.
Latin and Italian Poems by John Milton, tr. William Cowper (editor). 1808.
Stanzas of an English Friend to the Patriots in Spain. 1808.
The Life of George Romney. 1809.
Cowper's Milton (editor). 1810. 4 vols.
Select Poems by John Dawes Worgan (editor). 1810.
Three Plays. 1811.
A Patriotic Song for the Amicable Club. 1814.
Song for the Amicable Fraternity of Felpham. 1817.
Poems on Serious and Sacred Subjects. 1818.
Memoirs of the Life and Writings of William Hayley. Ed. John Johnson. 1823. 2 vols.
Douglas D'Arcy: Some Passages in the Life of an Adventurer. 1834. 2 vols.

THOMAS BROWN (1778–1820)

Observations on the Zoonomia of Erasmus Darwin, M.D. 1798.
De Somno. 1803.
Poems. 1804. 2 vols.
Observations on the Nature and Tendency of the Doctrine of Mr. Hume, concerning the Relation of Cause and Effect. 1805.
An Examination of Some Remarks in the Reply of Dr. John Inglis to Professor Playfair. 1806.
A Short Criticism of the Terms of the Charge against Mr. Leslie, in the Protest of the Ministers of Edinburgh. 1806.
The Renovation of India; with The Prophecy of Ganges. 1808.
Two Letters on the Subject of the Present Vacancy in the Professorship of Oriental Languages. 1813.
The Paradise of Coquettes. 1814.
The War-Fiend, with Other Poems. 1816.
The Wanderer in Norway, with Other Poems. 1816.
The Bower of Spring, with Other Poems. 1817.
Agnes. 1818.
Emily, with Other Poems. 1819.
Lectures on the Philosophy of the Human Mind. 1820. 4 vols.

Poetical Works. 1820. 4 vols.
Sketch of a System of the Philosophy of the Human Mind. 1820. Part 1 only.

JOSEPH RODMAN DRAKE (1795–1820)

Poems by Croaker, Croaker & Co. and Croaker, Jun. (with Fitz-Green Halleck). 1819.
The Culprit Fay and Other Poems. 1835.
The Croakers (with Fitz-Green Halleck). 1860.
Life and Works. Ed. Frank Lester Pleadwell. 1935.

HESTER LYNCH PIOZZI (1741–1821)

The Florence Miscellany (editor). 1785.
Anecdotes of the Late Samuel Johnson, LL.D., during the Last Twenty Years of His Life. 1786.
Letters to and from Samuel Johnson; to Which Are Added Some Poems Never Before Printed (editor). 1788. 2 vols.
Observations and Reflections Made in the Course of a Journey through France, Italy, and Germany. 1789. 2 vols.
The Three Warnings: A Tale. 1792.
British Synonymy; or, An Attempt at Regulating the Choice of Words in Familiar Conversation. 1794. 2 vols.
Three Warnings to John Bull. 1798.
Retrospection; or, A Review of the Most Striking and Important Events, Characters, Situations, and Their Consequences Which the Last Eighteen Hundred Years Have Presented to the View of Mankind. 1801. 2 vols.
Love Letters of Mrs. Piozzi, Written When She Was Eighty, to W. A. Conway. 1843.
Autobiography, Letters and Literary Remains. Ed. A. Hayward. 1861. 2 vols.
The Intimate Letters of Hester Lynch Piozzi and Penelope Pennington 1788–1821. Ed. Oswald G. Knapp. 1914.
Piozzi Marginalia. Ed. Percival Merritt. 1925.
Letters. Ed. R. Brimley Johnson. 1926.
The French Journals of Mrs. Thrale and Dr. Johnson. Eds. Moses Tyson and Henry Guppy. 1932.
The Queeney Letters: Being Letters Addressed to Hester Maria Thrale by Dr. Johnson, Fanny Burney and Mrs. Thrale-Piozzi. Ed. the Marquis of Lansdowne. 1934.
Mrs. Piozzi and Isaac Watts: Being Annotations in the Autograph of Mrs. Piozzi on a Copy of the First Edition of the Philosophical Essays of Watts. Ed. James P. R. Lyell. 1934.
Thraliana: Diary 1777–1809. Ed. Katharine C. Balderston. 1942. 2 vols.
The Thrales of Streatham Park. Ed. Mary Hyde. 1977.
Dr. Johnson by Mrs. Thrale: The Anecdotes of Mrs. Piozzi in Their Original Form. Ed. Richard Ingrams. 1984.

JOHN KEATS (1795–1821)

Poems. 1817.
Endymion: A Poetic Romance. 1818.
Lamia, Isabella, The Eve of St. Agnes, and Other Poems. 1820.
Poetical Works of Coleridge, Shelley, and Keats. 1829.
Poetical Works. 1840.
Life, Letters, and Literary Remains. Ed. Richard Monckton Milnes, Lord Houghton. 1848. 2 vols.
Poetical Works. 1854.
Another Version of Keats's Hyperion ⟨*The Fall of Hyperion*⟩. Ed. Richard Monckton Milnes, Lord Houghton. 1857.
Letters to Fanny Brawne. Ed. H. Buxton Forman. 1878.
Poetical Works and Other Writings. Ed. H. Buxton Forman. 1883. 4 vols.
Letters and Poems. Ed. Jonathan Gilmer Speed. 1883. 3 vols.
Letters to His Family and Friends. Ed. Sidney Colvin. 1891.

Letters. Ed. H. Buxton Forman. 1895.

Complete Works. Ed. H. Buxton Forman. 1900–01. 5 vols.

Poems. Ed. Ernest de Selincourt. 1905.

Poetical Works. Ed. H. Buxton Forman. 1908.

The Keats Letters, Papers, and Other Relics. Ed. H. Buxton Forman. 1914.

Letters. Ed. Maurice Buxton Forman. 1931. 2 vols.

Anatomical and Physiological Note Book. Ed. Maurice Buxton Forman. 1934.

Complete Poems and Selected Letters. Ed. Clarence DeWitt Thorpe. 1935.

Poetical Works and Other Writings. Ed. H. Buxton Forman, rev. Maurice Buxton Forman. 1938–39. 8 vols.

Poetical Works. Ed. H. W. Garrod. 1939.

The Keats Circle: Letters and Papers 1816–1878. Ed. Hyder Edward Rollins. 1948. 2 vols.

Selected Letters. Ed. Lionel Trilling. 1951.

Poetical Works. Ed. H. W. Garrod, rev. John Jones. 1956.

Letters 1814–1821. Ed. Hyder Edward Rollins. 1958. 2 vols.

Selected Poems and Letters. Ed. Douglas Bush. 1959.

Poems. Ed. Miriam Allot. 1970.

Letters: A New Selection. Ed. Robert Gittings. 1970.

The Odes and Their Earliest Known Manuscripts. Ed. Robert Gittings. 1970.

Complete Poems. Ed. John Barnard. 1973.

Life and Letters. Ed. Joanna Richardson. 1981.

Complete Poems. Ed. Jack Stillinger. 1985.

PERCY BYSSHE SHELLEY (1792–1822)

Zastrozzi: A Romance. 1810.

Original Poetry by Victor and Cazire (with Elizabeth Shelley). 1810.

Posthumous Fragments of Margaret Nicholson (with Thomas Jefferson Hogg). 1810.

St Irvyne; or, The Rosicrucian: A Romance. 1811.

The Necessity of Atheism (with Thomas Jefferson Hogg). 1811.

A Poetical Essay on the Existing State of Things. c. 1811. Lost.

An Address to the Irish People. 1812.

Proposals for an Association of Those Philanthropists, Who Convinced of the Inadequacy of the Moral and Philosophical State of Ireland to Produce Benefits Which Are Nevertheless Attainable, Are Willing to Unite to Accomplish Its Regeneration. 1812.

Declaration of Rights. 1812.

The Devil's Walk: A Ballad. 1812.

A Letter to Lord Ellenborough. 1812.

Queen Mab: A Philosophical Poem, with Notes. 1813.

A Vindication of Natural Diet. 1813.

A Refutation of Deism: In a Dialogue. 1814.

Alastor; or, The Spirit of Solitude, and Other Poems. 1816.

A Proposal for Putting Reform to the Vote throughout the Kingdom. 1817.

An Address to the People on the Death of the Princess Charlotte, by the Hermit of Marlow. 1817. Lost.

History of a Six Weeks' Tour through a Part of France, Switzerland, Germany, and Holland (with Mary Shelley). 1817.

Laon and Cythna; or, The Revolution of the Golden City ⟨*The Revolt of Islam*⟩. 1818.

Rosalind and Helen: A Modern Eclogue with Other Poems. 1819.

The Cenci: A Tragedy. 1819.

Prometheus Unbound: A Lyrical Drama, with Other Poems. 1820.

Oedipus Tyrannus; or, Swellfoot the Tyrant. 1820.

Epipsychidion. 1821.

Adonais: An Elegy on the Death of John Keats. 1821.

Hellas: A Lyrical Drama. 1822.

Posthumous Poems. Ed. Mary Shelley. 1824.

Poetical Works of Coleridge, Shelley, and Keats. 1829.

The Masque of Anarchy. Ed. Leigh Hunt. 1832.

Poetical Works. Ed. Mary Shelley. 1839. 4 vols.

Essays, Letters from Abroad, Translations and Fragments. Ed. Mary Shelley. 1840. 2 vols.

Relics of Shelley. Ed. Richard Garnett. 1862.

Poetical Works. Ed. William Michael Rossetti. 1870. 2 vols.

The Daemon of the World. Ed. H. Buxton Forman. 1876.

Poetical Works. Ed. H. Buxton Forman. 1876–77. 4 vols.

Prose Works. Ed. H. Buxton Forman. 1880. 4 vols.

Select Letters. Ed. Richard Garnett. 1882.

Essays and Letters. Ed. Ernest Rhys. 1886.

The Wandering Jew (with Thomas Medwin). Ed. Bertram Dobell. 1887.

Poetical Works. Ed. George Edward Woodberry. 1892. 4 vols.

Poetical Works. Ed. F. S. Ellis. 1895. 3 vols.

Complete Poetical Works. Ed. Thomas Hutchinson. 1904.

Letters. Ed. Roger Ingpen. 1909. 2 vols.

Note Books. Ed. H. Buxton Forman. 1911. 3 vols.

A Philosophical View of Reform. Ed. T. W. Rolleston. 1920.

Complete Works. Eds. Roger Ingpen and Walter E. Peck. 1926–30. 10 vols.

The Shelley Notebook in the Harvard Library. Ed. George Edward Woodberry. 1929.

On the Vegetable System of Diet. Ed. Roger Ingpen. 1929.

Shelley and His Circle 1773–1822 (with others). Eds. Kenneth Neill Cameron, Donald H. Reiman et al. 1961– .

Letters. Ed. Frederick L. Jones. 1964. 2 vols.

The Esdaile Notebook: A Volume of Early Poems. Ed. Kenneth Neill Cameron. 1964.

Shelley's The Triumph of Life: A Critical Study Based on a Text Newly Edited from the Bodleian Manuscript. Ed. Donald H. Reiman. 1965.

Shelley's Prose; or, The Trumpet of a Prophecy. Ed. David Lee Clark. 1966.

Posthumous Poems: Mary Shelley's Fair Copy Book. Ed. Irving Massey. 1969.

Complete Poetical Works. Ed. Thomas Hutchinson, rev. G. M. Matthews. 1970.

Complete Poetical Works. Ed. Neville Rogers. 1972– . 4 vols. (projected).

Poetry and Prose. Eds. Donald H. Reiman and Sharon B. Powers. 1977.

ANN RADCLIFFE (1764–1823)

The Castles of Athlin and Dunbayne: A Highland Story. 1789.

A Sicilian Romance. 1790. 2 vols.

The Romance of the Forest. 1791. 3 vols.

The Mysteries of Udolpho: A Romance. 1794. 4 vols.

A Journey Made in the Summer of 1794, through Holland and the West Frontier of Germany, with a Return down the Rhine. 1795.

The Italian; or, The Confessional of the Black Penitents: A Romance. 1797. 3 vols.

Poems. 1815.

Novels. 1824.

Gaston de Blondeville; or, The Court of Henry III. Keeping Festival in Ardienne: A Romance; St. Alban's Abbey: A Metrical Tale; with Some Poetical Pieces. 1826. 4 vols.

Poetical Works. 1834. 2 vols.

DAVID RICARDO (1772–1823)

The High Price of Bullion, a Proof of the Depreciation of Bank Notes. 1810.

Reply to Mr. Bosanquet's Practical Observations on the Report of the Bullion Committee. 1811.

Observations on Some Passages in an Article in the Edinburgh Review *on the Depreciation of Paper Currency.* 1811.

An Essay on the Influence of a Low Price of Corn on the Profits of Stock. 1815.

Proposals for an Economical and Secure Currency. 1816.

On the Principles of Political Economy and Taxation. 1817.

Speech on Mr. Western's Motion for a Committee to Consider of the Effects Produced by the Resumption of Cash Payments. 1822.

On Protection to Agriculture. 1822.

Plan for the Establishment of a National Bank. 1824.

Works. Ed. J. R. McCulloch. 1846.

Letters to Thomas Robert Malthus 1810–1823. Ed. James Bonar. 1887.

Letters Written during a Tour on the Continent. 1891.

Letters to John Ramsay McCulloch 1816–1823. Ed. J. H. Hollander. 1895.

Letters to Hutches Trower and Others 1811–1823. Eds. James Bonar and J. H. Hollander. 1899.

Three Letters on the Price of Gold, Contributed to the Morning Chronicle *(London) in August–November 1809.* Ed. J. H. Hollander. 1903.

Economic Essays. Ed. E. C. K. Gonner. 1923.

Notes on Malthus's Principles of Political Economy. Eds. Jacob H. Hollander and T. E. Gregory. 1928.

Minor Papers on the Currency Question 1809–1823. Ed. Jacob H. Hollander. 1932.

Works and Correspondence. Eds. Piero Sraffa and M. H. Dobb. 1951–55. 10 vols.

CHARLES ROBERT MATURIN (1780–1824)

Fatal Revenge; or, The Family of Montorio: A Romance. 1807. 3 vols.

The Wild Irish Boy. 1808. 3 vols.

The Milesian Chief: A Romance. 1812. 4 vols.

Bertram; or, The Castle of Aldobrand. 1816.

Manuel. 1817.

Women; or, Pour et Contre. 1818. 3 vols.

Fredolfo. 1819.

Sermons. 1819.

Melmoth the Wanderer: A Tale. 1820. 4 vols.

The Albigenses: A Romance. 1824.

Five Sermons on the Errors of the Roman Catholic Church. 1824.

The Correspondence of Sir Walter Scott and Charles Robert Maturin. Eds. Fannie E. Ratchford and William H. McCarthy, Jr. 1937.

GEORGE GORDON, LORD BYRON (1788–1824)

Fugitive Pieces. 1806.

Poems on Various Occasions. 1807.

Hours of Idleness. 1807.

Poems Original and Translated. 1808.

English Bards and Scotch Reviewers. 1809.

Childe Harold's Pilgrimage: A Romaunt. 1812 [Cantos 1–2]; 1816 [Canto 3]; 1818 [Canto 4].

The Curse of Minerva. 1812.

The Genuine Rejected Addresses. 1812.

Waltz: An Apostrophic Hymn. 1813.

The Giaour: A Fragment of a Turkish Tale. 1813.

The Bride of Abydos: A Turkish Tale. 1813.

Poetical Works. 1813. 2 vols.

The Corsair. 1814.

Ode to Napoleon Buonaparte. 1814.

Lara; Jacqueline. 1814.

Hebrew Melodies. 1815.

The Siege of Corinth; Parisina. 1816.

A Sketch from Private Life. 1816.

Fare Thee Well! 1816.

Poems. 1816.

The Prisoner of Chillon and Other Poems. 1816.

Monody on the Death of the Right Honourable R. B. Sheridan. 1816.

The Lament of Tasso. 1817.

Manfred: A Dramatic Poem. 1817.

Beppo: A Venetian Story. 1818.

On John William Rizzo Hoppner. 1818.

My Boat Is on the Shore. 1818.

Mazeppa. 1819.

Don Juan. 1819 [Cantos 1–2]; 1821 [Cantos 3–5]; 1823 [Cantos 6–8]; 1823 [Cantos 9–11]; 1823 [Cantos 12–14]; 1824 [Cantos 15–16].

Letter to the Editor of My Grandmother's Review. 1819.

The Irish Avatar. 1821.

Marino Faliero; The Prophecy of Dante. 1821.

Sardanapalus; The Two Foscari; Cain. 1821.

Letter to **** *****, on the Rev. W. L. Bowles' Strictures on the Life and Writings of Pope. 1821.

The Vision of Judgment. 1822.

Poetical Works. 1822–24. 16 vols.

The Age of Bronze. 1823.

Heaven and Earth. 1823.

The Island; or, Christian and His Comrades. 1823.

Werner. 1823.

The Deformed Transformed. 1824.

Parliamentary Speeches. 1824.

Correspondence of Lord Byron with a Friend. Ed. R. C. Dallas. 1825. 3 vols.

Letters and Journals. Ed. Thomas Moore. 1830. 2 vols.

Dramas. 1832.

Works, with Letters and Journals. Ed. John Wright. 1832–33. 17 vols.

Tales. 1837. 2 vols.

A Selection from the Works. Ed. Algernon Charles Swinburne. 1866.

Poetical Works. Ed. William Michael Rossetti. 1870.

A Political Ode. 1880.

Works. Eds. Ernest Hartley Coleridge and Rowland E. Prothero. 1898–1904. 13 vols.

Poems. Ed. Arthur Symons. 1904.

Correspondence. Ed. John Murray. 1922. 2 vols.

Poems. Ed. Herbert J. C. Grierson. 1923.

The Ravenna Journal. 1928.

Poetry and Prose. Ed. David Nichol Smith. 1940.

Byron: A Self-Portrait: Letters and Diaries 1798–1824. Ed. Peter Quennell. 1950. 2 vols.

Selected Poetry. Ed. Leslie A. Marchand. 1951.

His Very Self and Voice: Collected Conversations. Ed. Ernest J. Lovell, Jr. 1954.

Poems. Ed. Vivian de Sola Pinto. 1963–68. 3 vols.

Selected Poetry and Prose. Ed. W. H. Auden. 1966.

Selected Prose. Ed. Peter Gunn. 1972.

Letters and Journals. Ed. Leslie A. Marchand. 1973–82. 12 vols.

Complete Poetical Works. Ed. Jerome J. McGann. 1980–   .

ANNA LAETITIA BARBAULD (1743–1825)

Corsica: An Ode. 1768.
Miscellaneous Pieces in Prose (with John Aikin). 1773.
Poems. 1773.
Devotional Pieces, Compiled from the Psalms and the Book of Job (editor). 1775.
Lessons for Children of Three Years Old. 1779. 2 parts.
Hymns in Prose for Children. 1781.
Lessons for Children from Two to Three Years Old. 1787.
Lessons for Children from Three to Four Years Old. 1788.
An Address to the Opposers of the Repeal of the Corporation and Test Acts. 1790.
Epistle to William Wilberforce, Esq., on the Rejection of the Bill for Abolishing the Slave Trade. 1791.
Civic Sermons to the People. 1792. 2 nos.
Remarks on Mr. Gilbert Wakefield's Enquiry into the Expediency and Propriety of Public or Social Worship. 1792.
Evenings at Home; or, The Juvenile Budget Opened (with John Aikin). 1792–96. 6 vols.
Sins of Government, Sins of the Nation. 1793.
[*The Religion of Nature: A Short Discourse Delivered before the National Assembly at Paris.* 1793.]
[*Reasons for National Penance, Recommended for the Fast, Appointed February XXVIII. 1794.* 1794.
Selections from the Spectator, Tatler, Guardian, *and* Freeholder *by Joseph Addison* (editor). 1804. 3 vols.
The Correspondence of Samuel Richardson (editor). 1804. 6 vols.
Lessons for Children from Two to Four Years Old. 1808. 4 parts.
The British Novelists (editor). 1810. 50 vols.
The Female Speaker; or, Miscellaneous Pieces, in Prose and Verse, Selected from the Best Writers, and Adapted to the Use of Young Women (editor). 1811.
Eighteen Hundred and Eleven. 1812.
Lessons for Children. 1812. 4 parts.
Works. 1825. 2 vols.
A Legacy for Young Ladies: Consisting of Miscellaneous Pieces, in Prose and Verse. Ed. Lucy Aikin. 1826.
A Discourse on Being Born Again. 1830.
Things by Their Right Names, and Other Stories, Fables, and Moral Pieces. Ed. Mrs. S. J. Hale. 1840.
Memoir, Letters and a Selection from the Poems and Prose Writings. Ed. Grace A. Ellis. 1874. 2 vols.
Tales, Poems and Essays. 1884.
Letters (with Maria Edgeworth). Ed. Walter Sidney Scott. 1953.

SAMUEL PARR (1747–1825)

Two Sermons Preached at Norwich. 1780.
A Discourse on the Late Fast. 1781.
A Discourse on Education and on the Plans Pursued in Charity-Schools. 1786.
De Statu Libri Tres by William Bellenden (editor). 1787.
Praefationes ad Tres Gulielmi Bellendeni Libros de Statu. 1788.
Tracts, by Warburton, and a Warburtonian ⟨Richard Hurd⟩ (editor). 1789.
A Letter from Irenopolis to the Inhabitants of Eleutheropolis; or, A Serious Address to the Dissenters of Birmingham. 1792.
A Sequel to the Printed Paper Lately Circulated in Warwickshire by the Rev. Charles Curtis. 1792.
Remarks on the Statement of Dr. Charles Combe. 1795.
A Spital Sermon. 1801.

A Sermon Preached on the Late Fast Day, at the Parish Church of Hatton, Warwickshire. 1804.
Characters of the Late Charles James Fox. 1809. 2 vols.
Four Sermons by Jeremy Taylor (editor). 1822.
A Letter to the Rev. Dr. Milner, Occasioned by Some Passages in His Book, Entitled The End of Religious Controversy. Ed. John Lynes. 1825.
Aphorisms, Opinions and Reflections. Ed. E. B. Harwood. 1826.
Works. Ed. John Johnstone. 1828. 8 vols.
Miscellaneous Writings. 1831. 2 vols.
Metaphysical Tracts by English Philosophers of the Eighteenth Century (editor). 1837.

THOMAS JEFFERSON (1743–1826)

[*A Dialogue between a Southern Delegate and His Spouse on His Return Home from the Grand Continental Congress.* 1774.]
A Summary View of the Rights of British America. 1774.
In Congress, July 4, 1776: A Declaration by the Representatives of the United States of America, in General Congress Assembled (with others). 1777.
Draught of a Fundamental Constitution for the Commonwealth of Virginia. 1783.
Notes on the Establishment of a Money Unit, and of a Coinage for the United States. 1784.
Notes on the State of Virginia. 1784, 1853 (20th ed.).
Observations on the Whale Fishery. 1788.
Report of the Secretary of State on the Subject of Establishing a Uniformity in the Weights, Measures and Coins of the United States. 1790.
Report of the Secretary of State, to Whom Was Referred, by the House of Representatives of the United States, the Petition of Joseph Isaacks of Newport in Rhode Island. 1791.
Report of the Secretary of State on the Privileges and Restriction on the Commerce of the United States in Foreign Countries. 1793.
Papers Relative to Great Britain. 1793.
Authentic Copies of the Correspondence of Thomas Jefferson, Esq., Secretary of State of the United States of America, and George Hammond, Esq., Minister Plenipotentiary of Great-Britain, on the Non-Execution of Existing Treaties, the Delivering of Frontier Posts, and on the Propriety of a Commercial Intercourse between Great-Britain and the United States. 1794.
A Manual of Parliamentary Practice, for the Use of the Senate of the United States. 1800, 1812 (4th ed.).
An Appendix to the Notes on Virginia Relative to the Murder of Logan's Family. 1800.
Speech of Thomas Jefferson, President of the United States, Delivered at His Instalment, March 4, 1801, at the City of Washington. 1801.
Correspondence of Thomas Jefferson, with His Address in the Senate Chamber, 1801, on Taking the Oath of Office as President. 1801.
Message from the President of the United States, Accompanying a Report to Him from the Secretary of War, and Sundry Documents Relative to the Establishment of Trading-Houses with Indian Tribes, and Other Regulation for Their Benefit and Accommodation. 1802.
Message from the President of the United States, Transmitting a Roll of the Persons Having Office or Employment under the United States. 1802.
Message from the President of the United States, Transmitting

Sundry Documents Respecting the French Corvette Berceau. 1802.

A New Translation of Volney's Ruins (with Joel Barlow). 1802. 2 vols.

Message from the President of the United States to the Senate and House of Representatives, Delivered at the Commencement of the First Session of the Eighth Congress. 1803.

An Account of Louisiana: Being an Abstract of Documents, in the Offices of the Departments of State and of the Treasury. 1803.

Republican Notes on Religion; and an Act Establishing Religious Freedom, Passed in the Assembly of Virginia, in the Year 1786. 1803.

Message from the President of the United States, Inclosing a Treaty and Conventions Entered Into and Ratified by the United States of America and the French Republic, Relative to the Cession of Louisiana. 1803.

Message from the President of the United States to Both Houses of Congress. 1804.

President's Speech ⟨Second Inaugural Address⟩. 1805.

Message from the President of the United States, Containing His Communication to Both Houses of Congress at the Commencement of the First Session of the Ninth Congress. 1805.

Message from the President of the United States, Respecting the Application of Hamet Caramalli, Ex-Bashaw of Tripoli. 1806.

Message from the President of the United States, Transmitting an Act of the State of South Carolina Ceding to the United States Various Forts and Fortifications, and Sites for the Erection of Forts in the Same State. 1806.

Message from the President of the United States, Communicating Discoveries Made in Exploring the Missouri, Red River, and Washita, by Captains Lewis and Clark, Doctor Sibley and Mr. Dunbar, with a Statistical Account of the Countries Adjacent. 1806.

Message from the President of the United States, Transmitting Information Touching an Illegal Combination of Private Individuals against the Peace and Safety of the Union. 1807.

Message from the President of the United States, Transmitting a Copy of the Proceedings, and of the Evidence Exhibited on the Arraignment of Aaron Burr and Others before the Circuit Court of the United States Held in Virginia in 1807. 1807.

Message from the President of the United States, Containing His Communication to Both Houses of Congress, at the Commencement of the First Session of the Tenth Congress. 1807.

The Embargo Laws, and Message from the President to the Senate and House of Representatives of the United States. 1807.

Message from the President of the United States, Communicating Documents and Information Touching the Official Conduct of Brigadier-General James Wilkinson, in Pursuance of a Resolution of the House of Representatives of the Thirteenth Instant. 1808.

Message from the President of the United States, Transmitting a Treaty of Limits between the United States of America and the Choctaw Nation of Indians. 1808.

Message from the President of the United States, Transmitting a Treaty Made at Detroit on the Seventeenth of November, 1807, between the United States and the Ottaway, Chip-peway, Wyandot and Pottawatamie Nations of Indians. 1808.

Message from the President of the United States, Transmitting a Report on the Subject of the Military Academy Established at West Point. 1808.

Message from the President of the United States, Transmitting a Letter from the Secretary of State to Mr. Monroe on the Subject of the Attack upon the Chesapeake. 1808.

Message from the President of the United States, Transmitting Correspondence—1st. On the Subject of the Attack on the Chesapeake. 2d. On the Subject of the Impressments. 3d. On the Subjects Submitted to the Joint Negotiations of Messrs. Monroe and Pinckney. 1808.

Message from the President of the United States Respecting the Execution of the Act for Fortifying the Ports and Harbours of the United States. 1808.

Message from the President of the United States to Both Houses of Congress at the Commencement of the Second Session of the Tenth Congress. 1808.

Message from the President of the United States, Communicating a Copy of His Proclamation Issued in Consequence of the Opposition in the Neighborhood of Lake Champlain to the Laws Laying an Embargo. 1808.

Correspondence between His Excellency Thomas Jefferson, President of the United States, and James Monroe, Esq., Late American Ambassador to the Court of St. James. 1808.

Message from the President of the United States, Transmitting the Annual Account of the Fund for Defraying Contingent Charges of Government during the Year 1808. 1809.

Message from the President of the United States, Communicating Certain Letters Which Passed between the British Sec. of State, Mr. Canning, and Mr. Pinckney. 1809.

The Proceedings of the Government of the United States, in Maintaining Public Right to the Beach of the Missisipi, Adjacent to New-Orleans, against the Intrusion of Edward Livingston. 1812.

A Catalog of the Extensive and Valuable Library of the Late President Jefferson, Copied from the Original MS., in His Handwriting, as Arranged by Himself. Ed. Nathaniel P. Poor. 1829.

Reports of Cases Determined in the General Court of Virginia, from 1730 to 1740; and from 1768 to 1772. 1829.

Memoir, Correspondence, and Miscellanies from the Papers. Ed. Thomas Jefferson Randolph. 1829. 4 vols.

Virginia and Kentucky Resolutions of 1798 and 1799; with Jefferson's Original Draught Thereof. 1832.

An Essay towards Facilitating Instruction in the Anglo-Saxon and Modern Dialects of the English Language. 1851.

Writings. Ed. H. A. Washington. 1853–54. 9 vols.

Early History of the University of Virginia, as Contained in the Letters of Thomas Jefferson and Joseph C. Cabell. 1856.

Cod and Whale Fisheries: Report of Hon. Thomas Jefferson, Secretary of State, on the Subject of Cod and Whale Fisheries, Made to the House of Representatives, February 1, 1791. 1872.

Writings. Ed. Paul Leicester Ford. 1892–99. 10 vols.

Writings. Eds. Andrew A. Lipscomb and Albert Ellery Bergh. 1903–04. 20 vols.

Correspondence, Printed from the Originals in the Collection of William K. Bixby. Ed. William K. Bixby. 1916.

Volney et l'Amérique, d'après des documents inédite et sa correspondance avec Jefferson. Ed. Gilbert Chinard. 1923.

Les Amitiés américaines de Madame d'Houdetot, d'après sa correspondance inédite avec Benjamin Franklin et Thomas Jefferson. Ed. Gilbert Chinard. 1924.

Jefferson et les Idéologues, d'après sa correspondance inédite avec Destutt de Tracy, Cabanis, J.-B. Say et Auguste Comte. Ed. Gilbert Chinard. 1925.

The Commonplace Book of Thomas Jefferson: A Repertory of His Ideas on Government. Ed. Gilbert Chinard. 1926.

The Literary Bible of Thomas Jefferson: His Commonplace Book of Philosophers and Poets. Ed. Gilbert Chinard. 1928.

Trois Amitiés françaises de Jefferson, d'après sa correspondance inédite avec Madame de Bréhan, Madame de Tessé et Madame de Corny. Ed. Gilbert Chinard. 1929.

The Letters of Lafayette and Jefferson. Ed. Gilbert Chinard.

Correspondence between Thomas Jefferson and Pierre Samuel Du Pont de Nemours 1798–1817. Ed. Dumas Malone. 1930.

The Correspondence of Jefferson and Du Pont de Nemours. Ed. Gilbert Chinard. 1931.

Thomas Jefferson and His Unknown Brother Randolph: Twenty-eight Letters Exchanged between Thomas and Randolph Jefferson. Ed. Bernard Mayo. 1942.

Thomas Jefferson's Garden Book 1766–1824. Ed. Edwin Morris Betts. 1944.

Basic Writings. Ed. Philip S. Foner. 1944.

Correspondence of Thomas Jefferson and Francis Walker Gilmer 1814–1826. Ed. Richard Beale Davis. 1946.

Papers. Eds. Julian Boyd et al. 1950–82. 20 vols.

Thomas Jefferson's Farm Book. Ed. Edwin Morris Betts. 1953.

The Adams-Jefferson Letters: The Complete Correspondence between Thomas Jefferson and Abigail and John Adams. Ed. Lester J. Capon. 1959. 2 vols.

Writings. Ed. Merrill D. Peterson, 1984.

WILLIAM GIFFORD (1756–1826)

The Baviad: A Paraphrastic Imitation of the First Satire of Persius. 1791.

The Maeviad. 1795.

The Baviad and Maeviad. 1797.

Epistle to Peter Pindar. 1800.

The Satires of Decimus Junius Juvenalis (translator). 1802.

An Examination of the Strictures of the Critical Reviewers on the Translation of Juvenal. 1803.

The Plays of Philip Massinger (editor). 1805.

[*An Heroic Epistle to Mr. Winsor.* 1808.]

The Works of Ben Jonson (editor). 1816. 9 vols.

The Satires of Decimus Junius Juvenalis and of Aulus Persius Flaccus (translator). 1817. 2 vols.

The Satires of A. Persius Flaccus (translator). 1821.

The Dramatic Works of John Ford (editor). 1827. 2 vols.

The Dramatic Works and Poems of James Shirley (editor; with Alexander Dyce). 1833. 6 vols.

The Beauties of Gifford: Consisting of Selections from His Poetry and Prose. Ed. Alfred Howard. c. 1834.

WILLIAM BLAKE (1757–1827)

Poetical Sketches. 1783.

There Is No Natural Religion. c. 1788.

All Religions Are One. c. 1788.

The Book of Thel. 1789.

Songs of Innocence. 1789.

The French Revolution. 1791.

The Marriage of Heaven and Hell. 1793.

For Children: The Gates of Paradise. 1793.

To the Public. 1793. Lost.

Vision of the Daughters of Albion. 1793.

America: A Prophecy. 1793.

Songs of Innocence and Experience. 1794.

Europe: A Prophecy. 1794.

The First Book of Urizen. 1794.

The Book of Ahania. 1795.

The Book of Los. 1795.

The Song of Los. 1795.

Milton. 1804.

Jerusalem: The Emanation of the Giant Albion. 1804–c. 1820.

Exhibition of Paintings in Fresco. 1809.

Blake's Chaucer: The Canterbury Pilgrims. 1809.

A Descriptive Catalogue of Pictures, Poetical and Historical Inventions, Painted by William Blake. 1809.

For the Sexes: The Gates of Paradise. c. 1818.

Laocoon. c. 1820.

On Homer's Poetry; On Virgil. c. 1821.

The Ghost of Abel. 1822.

Poems. Ed. R. H. Shepherd. 1874.

Poetical Works. Ed. William Michael Rossetti. 1874.

Works. Eds. Edwin John Ellis and W. B. Yeats. 1893. 3 vols.

Poems. Ed. W. B. Yeats. 1893.

Poetical Works. Ed. John Sampson. 1905.

Letters. Ed. Archibald G. B. Russell. 1906.

Poems. Ed. Alice Meynell. 1911.

Writings. Ed. Geoffrey Keynes. 1925. 3 vols.

Prophetic Writings. Eds. D. J. Sloss and J. P. R. Wallis. 1926. 2 vols.

Letters to Thomas Butts 1800–1803. Ed. Geoffrey Keynes. 1926.

The Poems and Prophecies. Ed. Max Plowman. 1927.

Selected Poems. Ed. Basil de Selincourt. 1927.

Note-Book. Ed. Geoffrey Keynes. 1935.

The Portable Blake. Ed. Alfred Kazin. 1946.

Selected Poetry and Prose. Ed. Northrop Frye. 1953.

Letters. Ed. Geoffrey Keynes. 1956.

Poetry and Prose. Ed. David V. Erdman. 1965.

Poems. Ed. W. H. Stevenson. 1971.

Complete Poems. Ed. Alicia Ostriker. 1977.

Writings. Ed. G. E. Bentley, Jr. 1978. 2 vols.

Paintings and Drawings. Ed. Martin Butlin. 1981. 2 vols.

DUGALD STEWART (1753–1828)

Elements of the Philosophy of the Human Mind. 1792 [Volume 1]; 1814 [Volume 2]; 1827 [Volume 3].

Outlines of Moral Philosophy. 1793.

Account of the Life and Writings of William Robertson. 1801.

Account of the Life and Writings of Thomas Reid. 1802.

A Short Statement of Some Important Facts, Relative to the Late Election of a Mathematical Professor in the University of Edinburgh. 1805.

Postscript to Mr. Stewart's Short Statement of Facts Relative to the Election of Professor Leslie. 1806.

Philosophical Essays. 1810.

Biographical Memoirs of Adam Smith, of William Robertson, and of Thomas Reid. 1811.

Some Account of a Boy Born Blind and Deaf. c. 1812.

The Philosophy of the Active and Moral Powers of Man. 1828. 2 vols.

Works. 1829. 7 vols.

Collected Works. Ed. Sir William Hamilton. 1854–60. 11 vols.

Gleanings from Dugald Stewart's Works. Ed. Ross Winans. 1872.

Analysis of Stewart's Moral Philosophy. Ed. J. Lowe. 1887.

LADY CAROLINE LAMB (1785–1828)

Glenarvon. 1816. 3 vols.
Verses from Glenarvon; *To Which Is Prefixed the Original Introduction Not Published with the Early Editions of That Work.* 1816.
A New Canto. 1819.
Gordon: A Tale: A Poetical Review of Don Juan. 1821.
Graham Hamilton. 1822. 2 vols.
Ada Reis: A Tale. 1823. 3 vols.

WILLIAM HAZLITT (1778–1830)

An Essay on the Principles of Human Action. 1805.
Free Thoughts on Public Affairs. 1806.
An Abridgment of The Light of Nature Pursued *by Abraham Tucker* (editor). 1807.
A Reply to the Essay on Population by the Rev. T. R. Malthus. 1807.
The Eloquence of the British Senate (editor). 1807. 2 vols.
A New and Improved Grammar of the English Tongue. 1810.
Memoirs of the Late Thomas Holcroft, Written by Himself and Continued ⟨by Hazlitt⟩ *to the Time of His Death.* 1816. 3 vols.
The Round Table: A Collection of Essays on Literature, Men, and Manners (with Leigh Hunt). 1817. 2 vols.
Characters of Shakespear's Plays. 1817.
A View of the English Stage. 1818.
Lectures on the English Poets. 1818.
A Letter to William Gifford, Esq. 1819.
Lectures on the English Comic Writers. 1819.
Political Essays, with Sketches of Public Characters. 1819.
Lectures Chiefly on the Dramatic Literature of the Age of Elizabeth. 1820.
Table-Talk; or, Original Essays. 1821–22. 2 vols.
Liber Amoris; or, The New Pygmalion. 1823.
Characteristics: In the Manner of Rochefoucault's Maxims. 1823.
Sketches of the Principal Picture-Galleries in England. 1824.
Select British Poets (editor). 1824.
The Spirit of the Age; or, Contemporary Portraits. 1825.
The Plain Speaker: Opinions on Books, Men, and Things. 1826. 2 vols.
Notes of a Journey through France and Italy. 1826.
The Life of Napoleon Buonaparte. 1828–30. 4 vols.
Conversations of James Northcote, Esq., R.A. 1830.
Literary Remains. Ed. Edward Bulwer-Lytton. 1836. 2 vols.
Sketches and Essays. Ed. William Hazlitt, Jr. 1839.
Winterslow: Essays and Characters Written There. Ed. William Hazlitt, Jr. 1850.
Collected Works. Eds. A. R. Waller and Arnold Glover. 1902–06. 13 vols.
New Writings. Ed. P. P. Howe. 1925–27. 2 vols.
Complete Works. Ed. P. P. Howe. 1930–34. 20 vols.
Selected Essays. Ed. Geoffrey Keynes. 1930.
Selected Writings. Ed. Ronald Blythe. 1970.
Letters. Eds. Herschel Moreland Sikes, Willard Hallam Bonner, and Gerald Lahey. 1978.

HENRY MACKENZIE (1745–1831)

The Pursuits of Happiness. 1771.
The Man of Feeling. 1771.
The Prince of Tunis. 1773.
The Man of the World. 1773. 2 vols.
Julia de Roubigné: A Tale. 1777. 2 vols.
The Mirror (with others). 1779–80. 110 nos.

The Shipwreck; or, Fatal Curiosity by George Lillo (adaptation). 1784.
The Lounger (with others). 1785–87. 101 nos.
The Letters of Brutus to Certain Celebrated Political Characters. 1791.
Dramatic Pieces from the German (translator). 1792.
Additional Letters of Brutus. 1793.
The Life of Thomas Paine by Francis Oldys (abridged by Mackenzie). 1793.
Cursory Remarks on Mr. Pitts' New Tax of Imposing a Guinea per Head on Every Person Who Wears Hairpowder. 1795.
Answer to Mr. Paine's Rights of Man. 1796.
Report of the Committee of the Highland Society of Scotland, Appointed to Inquire into the Nature and Authenticity of the Poems of Ossian (editor). 1805.
Works. 1807. 3 vols.
The Interesting Story of La Roche; Together with Louisa Venoni and The History of Sophie M———. 1808.
Works. 1808. 8 vols.
The Beauties of Mackenzie. Ed. Alfred Howard. 1813.
Works. 1815. 3 vols.
Miscellaneous Works. 1819. 3 vols.
Virginia; or, The Roman Father. c. 1820.
An Account of the Life and Writings of John Home, Esq. 1822.
Works. 1824.
Miscellaneous Works. 1836.
Anecdotes and Egotisms. Ed. Harold William Thompson. 1927.

JOHN TRUMBULL (1750–1831)

An Essay on the Use and Advantages of the Fine Arts. 1770.
An Elegy, on the Death of Mr. Buckingham St. John, Tutor of Yale College. 1771.
The Progress of Dulness. 1772 [Part 1]; 1773 [Part 2]; 1773 [Part 3].
An Elegy on the Times. 1774.
M'Fingal: A Modern Epic Poem. 1775 [Canto 1]; 1782 [Cantos 1–4].
The News-Carrier's Address to His Customers. 1783.
[*The Double Conspiracy; or, Treason Discovered but Not Published.* 1783.]
Address to the Gentlemen and Ladies That He Supplies with the Freeman's Chronicle. 1784.
Observations on the Peculiar Case of the Whig Merchant. 1785.
Biographical Sketch of the Character of Governor Trumbull. 1809.
Poetical Works. 1820. 2 vols.
Address of the Carrier of the Connecticut Courant *to His Patrons.* 1824.
The Anarchiad (with others). Ed. Luther G. Riggs. 1861.
Satiric Poems. Ed. Edwin T. Bowden. 1962.

JEREMY BENTHAM (1748–1832)

A Fragment on Government: Being an Examination of What Is Delivered on the Subject of Government in William Blackstone's Commentaries. 1776.
A View of the Hard-Labour Bill. 1778.
Defence of Usury: Shewing the Impolicy of the Present Legal Restraints on the Terms of Pecuniary Bargains. 1787.
An Introduction to the Principles of Morals and Legislation. 1789.
Panopticon; or, The Inspection House: Containing the Idea of a New Principle of Construction Applicable to Penitentiary-Houses, Prisons, and Schools. 1791. 3 vols.

Essay on Political Tactics. 1791.

Draught of a Code for the Organization of the Judicial Establishment. c. 1791. 6 parts.

Jeremy Bentham to the National Convention of France. c. 1793.

Supply without Burthen; or, Escheat Vice Taxation: Being a Proposal for Saving in Taxes by an Extension of the Law of Escheat. 1795. 2 parts.

Observations on the Poor Bill, Introduced by the Right Hon. William Pitt. 1797.

Circulating Annuities. 1801.

Letter to Lord Pelham. 1802. 2 parts.

A Plea for the Constitution. 1803.

Scotch Reform. 1808.

Pauper Management Improved. 1812.

Panopticon versus New South Wales; or, The Panopticon Penitentiary System, and the Penal Colonization System, Compared. 1812. 3 parts.

Chrestomathic Proposal: Being a Proposal for Erecting by Subscription the Chrestomathic School. c. 1814.

A Table of the Springs of Action. 1815.

Chrestomathia: Being a Collection of Papers, Explanatory of the Design of the Chrestomathic Day School. 1815. 2 parts.

Extract from the Proposed Constitutional Code. 1816.

"Swear Not at All." 1817.

Papers Relative to Codification and Public Instruction. 1817. 2 parts.

Supplement to Papers Relative to Codification and Public Instruction. 1817.

Plan of Parliamentary Reform, in the Form of a Catechism. 1817.

Jeremy Bentham, an Englishman, to the Citizens of the Several American United States. 1817.

Defence of Economy against the Late Mr. Burke. 1817.

Defence of Economy against the Right Hon. George Rose. 1817.

Church of Englandism and Its Catechism Examined. 1818. 2 parts.

The King against Sir Charles Wolseley, Baronet, and Joseph Harrison, Schoolmaster. 1820.

The Elements of the Art of Packing, as Applied to Special Juries. 1821.

Three Tracts Relative to Spanish and Portuguese Affairs. 1821.

On the Liberty of the Press, and Public Discussion. 1821.

Summary View of a Work, Entitled Not Paul, but Jesus. 1821.

Observations on the Restrictive and Prohibitory Commercial System. Ed. John Bowring. 1821.

The Analysis of the Influence of Natural Religion upon the Temporal Happiness of Mankind. Ed. George Grote. 1822.

Letter to Count Toreno on the Proposed Penal Code. 1822.

Codification Proposal Addressed to All Nations Professing Liberal Opinions. 1822.

Leading Principles of a Constitutional Code for Any State. 1823.

Not Paul, but Jesus. 1823.

Truth versus Ashhurst; or, Law as It Is, Contrasted with What It Is Said to Be. 1823.

The Book of Fallacies: From the Unfinished Papers of Jeremy Bentham. Ed. Peregrine Bingham. 1824.

Observations on Mr. Secretary Peel's House of Commons Speech Introducing His Police Magistrates' Salary Raising Bill. 1825.

Indications Respecting Lord Eldon. 1825.

Rationale of Judicial Evidence. Ed. John Stuart Mill. 1827. 5 vols.

Justice and Codification Petitions. 1829. 5 parts.

Constitutional Code: For the Use of All Nations, and All Governments Professing Liberal Opinions. 1830. Vol. 1 only.

Official Aptitude Maximised; Expense Minimised. 1830. 9 parts.

Equity Dispatch Court Proposal. 1830.

Law Reform Association Proposal. 1830.

Jeremy Bentham to His Fellow-Citizens of France, on Houses of Peers and Senate. 1830.

The Ballot: Cure for the Ballotphobia. c. 1830.

Jeremy Bentham to His Fellow Citizens of France, on Death Punishment. 1831.

Parliamentary Candidates' Proposed Declaration of Principles. 1831.

Boa Constrictor alias Helluo Curiarum: Observations on the "Resolved-on" Absorption of the Vice-Chancellor's Court. 1831.

Lord Brougham Displayed. 1832. 4 parts.

Deontology; or, The Science of Morality. Ed. John Bowring. 1834. 2 vols.

Works. Ed. John Bowring. 1838–43. 11 vols.

Anti-Icon; or, Farther Uses of the Dead to the Living. c. 1842.

Benthamiana; or, Select Extracts from the Works. Ed. John Hill Burton. 1843.

A Protest against Law Taxes. 1853.

Anti-Senatica: An Attack on the U.S. Senate, Sent by Jeremy Bentham to Andrew Jackson. Ed. Charles Warren Everett. 1926.

Jeremy Bentham's Plan for an Universal and Perpetual Peace. Ed. C. John Colombos. 1927.

Comment on the Commentaries: *A Criticism of William Blackstone's* Commentaries on the Laws of England. Ed. Charles Warren Everett. 1928.

Bentham's Theory of Fictions. Ed. C. K. Ogden. 1932.

The Limits of Jurisprudence: Being Part Two of An Introduction to the Principles of Morals and Legislation. Ed. Charles Warren Everett. 1945.

A Fragment on Government and An Introduction to the Principles of Morals and Legislation. Ed. Wilfrid Harrison. 1948.

Economic Writings. Ed. Werner Stark. 1952–54. 3 vols.

Collected Works. Eds. J. H. Burns et al. 1968– .

A Bentham Reader. Ed. Mary Peter Mack. 1969.

Bentham's Political Thought. Ed. Bhikhu Parekh. 1973.

PHILIP FRENEAU (1752–1832)

A Poem on the Rising Glory of America (with H. H. Brackenridge). 1772.

The American Village. 1772.

The New Liberty Pole—Take Care! 1775. Lost.

American Liberty. 1775.

General Gage's Soliloquy. 1775. Lost.

A Voyage to Boston. 1775.

General Gage's Confession. 1775.

On the Conqueror of America Shut Up in Boston. 1775. Lost.

The British Prison-Ship. 1781.

New Year Verses: January 1, 1783. 1783.

New Year's Verses: January 4, 1783. 1783.

New Year's Verses: January 8, 1783. 1783.

New Travels through North-America by Claude Robin (translator). 1783.

New-Year Verses. 1784.

Rivington's Confessions. c. 1784.
New Year's Verses for 1786. 1786.
Poems. 1786.
A Journey from Philadelphia to New-York. 1787.
New Year's Verses for 1788. 1788. Lost.
Miscellaneous Works. 1788.
Proposals for a Monmouth Newspaper. 1791.
The Village Merchant. 1794.
The Monmouth Almanac (with others). 1794.
Poems Written between the Years 1768 & 1794. 1795.
Megara and Altavola. 1797. Lost.
The Carrier of the Time Piece Presents the Following Address to His Patrons. 1798.
Letters on Various Interesting and Important Subjects. 1799.
Poems. 1809. 2 vols.
A Collection of Poems. 1815. 2 vols.
Poems on Various Subjects. 1861.
Poems Relating to the American Revolution. Ed. Evert A. Duyckinck. 1865.
Some Account of the Capture of the Ship Aurora. 1899.
Poems. Ed. Fred Lewis Pattee. 1902–07. 3 vols.
Unpublished Freneauana. Ed. Charles F. Heartman. 1918.
Last Poems. Ed. Lewis Leary. 1945.
Prose. Ed. Philip M. Marsh. 1955.
A Freneau Sampler. Ed. Philip M. Marsh. 1963.
Poems. Ed. Harry Hayden Clark. 1968.
Father Bombo's Pilgrimage to Mecca, 1770 (with H. H. Brackenridge). Ed. Michael Davitt Bell. 1975.
Final Poems. Ed. Judith R. Hiltner. 1979.
Newspaper Verse. Ed. Judith R. Hiltner. 1986.

GEORGE CRABBE (1754–1832)

Inebriety. 1775.
The Candidate: A Poetical Epistle to the Authors of the Monthly Review. 1780.
The Library. 1781.
The Village. 1783.
The News-Paper. 1785.
A Discourse on 2 Corinthians i.9 Read in the Chapel at Belvoir Castle after the Funeral of the Duke of Rutland. 1788.
Poems. 1807.
The Borough. 1810.
Tales. 1812.
Works. 1816. 4 vols.
The Variation of Public Opinion and Feelings Considered as It Respects Religion. 1817.
Tales of the Hall. 1819. 2 vols.
Poetical Works. 1822. 7 vols.
Lines by the Rev. George Crabbe, Ll.B. 1822.
Poetical Works. 1823. 8 vols.
Poetical Works. 1829.
Cullings from Crabbe. 1832.
Beauties of the Rev. George Crabbe. 1832.
Poetical Works. 1834. 8 vols.
Tales and Miscellaneous Poems. 1847.
Posthumous Sermons. Ed. John D. Hastings. 1850.
Poems: A Selection. Ed. Bernard Holland. 1899.
English Tales in Verse. Ed. C. H. Herford. 1902.
Selections from the Poems. Ed. Anthony Deane. 1903.
Poems. Ed. Adolphus William Ward. 1905–07. 3 vols.
Selections from the Poems. Ed. A. T. Quiller-Couch. 1908.
Poetical Works. Eds. A. J. Carlyle and R. M. Carlyle. 1908.
George Crabbe: An Anthology. Ed. F. L. Lucas. 1933.
Poems. Ed. Philip Henderson. 1946.

Poems. Ed. Geoffrey Grigson. 1950.
Selections from His Poetry. Ed. Frank Whitehead. 1955.
New Poems. Ed. Arthur Pollard. 1960.
A Selection. Ed. John Lucas.
Tales, 1812, and Miscellaneous Poems. Ed. Howard Mills. 1967.
Crabbe. Ed. C. Day Lewis. 1973.
Selected Letters and Journals. Eds. Thomas C. Faulkner and Rhonda L. Blair. 1975.

SIR JAMES MACKINTOSH (1765–1832)

Disputatio Physiologica Inauguralis, de Actione Musculari. 1787.
Arguments concerning the Constitutional Right of Parliament to Appoint a Regency. 1788.
Vindiciae Gallicae: Defence of the French Revolution, and Its English Admirers, against the Accusations of the Right Hon. Edmund Burke. 1791.
[*An Historical Sketch of the French Revolution from Its Commencement to the Year 1792.* 1792.]
A Discourse on the Study of the Law of Nature and Nations. 1799.
Plan of a Comparative Vocabulary of Indian Languages. 1806.
Substance of the Speech on Presenting a Petition from the Merchants of London, for the Recognition of the Independent States Established in the Countries of America Formerly Subject to Spain. 1824.
Speech on the Bill for Disenfranchising the Borough of East Retford, and Transferring the Elective Franchise to Birmingham. 1828.
Dissertation on the Progress of Ethical Philosophy, Chiefly during the Seventeenth and Eighteenth Centuries. 1830.
The History of England. 1830–32. 3 vols.
Speech on the Second Reading of the Bill, to Amend the Representation of the People of England and Wales. 1831.
History of the Revolution in England in 1688 (completed by William Wallace). 1834.
Memoirs. Ed. Robert James Mackintosh. 1835. 2 vols.
Tracts and Speeches 1787–1831. 1840. 5 parts.
The Life of Sir Thomas More. 1844.
Miscellaneous Works. Ed. Robert James Mackintosh. 1846. 3 vols.

SIR WALTER SCOTT (1771–1832)

The Chase and William and Helen: Two Ballads from the German of Göttfried Augustus Bürger. 1796.
Goetz of Berlichingen, with The Iron Hand: A Tragedy, Translated from the German of Goethé. 1799.
An Apology for Tales of Terror (editor). 1799.
The Eve of Saint John: A Border Ballad. 1800.
Minstrelsy of the Scottish Border (editor). 1802. 2 vols.
Sir Tristrem: A Metrical Romance by Thomas of Ercildoune (editor). 1804.
The Lay of the Last Minstrel. 1805.
A Health to My Lord Melville. 1806.
Ballads and Lyrical Pieces. 1806.
Original Memoirs Written during the Great Civil War by Sir Henry Slingsby and Captain Hodgson (editor). 1806.
Works. 1806–08. 6 vols.
Marmion: A Tale of Flodden Field. 1808.
The Works of John Dryden (editor). 1808. 18 vols.
Memoirs of Capt. George Carleton (editor). 1808.
Queenhoo-Hall: A Romance by Joseph Strutt (editor). 1808. 4 vols.

Memoirs of Robert Car⟨e⟩y, Earl of Monmouth and Fragmenta Regalia by Sir Robert Naunton (editor). 1808.

[*The Life of Edward Lord Herbert of Cherbury, Written by Himself* (editor). 1809.]

A Collection of Scarce and Valuable Tracts (editor). 1809–15. 13 vols.

English Minstrelsy (editor). 1810. 2 vols.

A Lady of the Lake. 1810.

The Poetical Works of Anna Seward (editor). 1810. 3 vols.

[*The Ancient British Drama* (editor). 1810. 3 vols.]

The Vision of Dan Roderick. 1811.

Memoirs of Count Grammont by Anthony Hamilton, tr. Abel Boyer (editor). 1811. 2 vols.

The Castle of Otranto by Horace Walpole (editor). 1811.

Secret History of the Court of King James the First (editor). 1811. 2 vols.

[*The Modern British Drama* (editor). 1811. 5 vols.]

Glenfinlas and Other Ballads, etc. with The Vision of Dan Roderick. 1812.

Works. 1812. 8 vols.

Rokeby. 1813.

The Bridal of Triermain; or, The Vale of Saint John. 1813.

[*Memoirs of the Reign of King Charles the First* by Sir Philip Warwick (editor). 1813.]

Waverley; or, 'Tis Sixty Years Since. 1814. 3 vols.

The Works of Jonathan Swift (editor). 1814. 19 vols.

The Letting of Humours Blood in the Head Vaine by Samuel Rowlands (editor). 1814.

Guy Mannering; or, The Astrologer. 1815. 3 vols.

The Lord of the Isles. 1815.

The Field of Waterloo. 1815.

Memorie of the Somervilles by James, Lord Somerville (editor). 1815. 2 vols.

The Antiquary. 1816. 3 vols.

Tales of My Landlord ⟨*The Black Dwarf; Old Mortality*⟩. 1816. 4 vols.

Harold the Dauntless. 1817.

Rob Roy. 1818. 3 vols.

Tales of My Landlord: Second Series ⟨*The Heart of Mid-Lothian*⟩. 1818. 4 vols.

My Mither is of sturdy airn. 1818.

Tales of My Landlord: Third Series ⟨*The Bride of Lammermoor; A Legend of Montrose*⟩. 1819. 4 vols.

Description of the Regalia of Scotland. 1819.

The Visionary. 1819. 3 vols.

Ivanhoe: A Romance. 1820. 3 vols.

The Monastery: A Romance. 1820. 3 vols.

The Abbot. 1820. 3 vols.

Poetical Works. 1820 (12 vols.), 1830 (11 vols.).

Miscellaneous Poems. 1820.

Trivial Poems and Triolets by Patrick Carey (editor). 1820.

Memorials of the Haliburtons (editor). 1820.

Novels and Tales. 1820. 12 vols.

Kenilworth: A Romance. 1821. 3 vols.

Northern Memoirs Writ in the Year 1658 by Richard Franck (editor). 1821.

Ballantyne's Novelist's Library (editor). 1821–24. 10 vols.

The Pirate. 1822. 3 vols.

The Poetry Contained in the Novels, Tales, and Romances, of the Author of Waverley. 1822.

The Fortunes of Nigel. 1822. 3 vols.

Halidon Hill: A Dramatic Sketch. 1822.

Carle, Now the King's Come! 1822.

Peveril of the Peak. 1822. 4 vols.

Chronological Notes of Scottish Affairs from 1680 till 1701: Being Taken Chiefly from the Diary of Lord Fountainhall (editor). 1822.

Military Memoirs of the Great Civil War: Being the Military Memoirs of John Gwynne (editor). 1822.

Historical Romances. 1822. 6 vols.

Quentin Durward. 1823. 3 vols.

A Bannatyne Garland. c. 1823.

St. Ronan's Well. 1824. 3 vols.

Redgauntlet: A Tale of the Eighteenth Century. 1824. 3 vols.

Lay of the Lindsays (editor). 1824.

Novels and Romances. 1824. 7 vols.

Tales of the Crusaders ⟨*The Betrothed; The Talisman*⟩. 1825. 4 vols.

Auld Robin Gray: A Ballad by Lady Anne Barnard (editor). 1825.

Lives of the Novelists. 1825. 2 vols.

Woodstock; or, The Cavalier. 1826. 3 vols.

Provincial Antiquities of Scotland. 1826. 2 vols.

A Letter to the Editor of the Edinburgh Weekly Journal, *from Malachi Malagrowther, on the Proposed Change of Currency.* 1826.

A Second Letter to the Editor of the Edinburgh Weekly Journal, *from Malachi Malagrowther, on the Proposed Change of Currency.* 1826.

A Third Letter to the Editor of the Edinburgh Weekly Journal, *from Malachi Malagrowther, on the Proposed Change of Currency.* 1826.

Chronicles of the Canongate ⟨*The Highland Widow; The Two Drovers; The Surgeon's Daughter*⟩. 1827. 2 vols.

The Life of Napoleon Buonaparte. 1827. 9 vols.

The Bannatyne Miscellany, Volume I (editor; with David Laing). 1827.

Memoirs of the Marchioness de la Rochejaqulein (editor). 1827.

Miscellaneous Prose Works. 1827. 6 vols.

Tales and Romances. 1827. 7 vols.

⟨*Verses to Sir Cuthbert Sharp.*⟩ 1828.

Chronicles of the Canongate, Second Series ⟨*The Fair Maid of Perth*⟩. 1828. 3 vols.

Tales of a Grandfather: Being Stories Taken from Scottish History. 1828. 3 vols.

Religious Discourses by a Layman. 1828.

Proceedings in the Court-Martial Help upon John, Master of Sinclair, 1708 (editor). 1828.

My Aunt Margaret's Mirror; The Tapestried Chamber; Death of the Laird's Jock; A Scene at Abbotsford. 1829.

Anne of Geierstein; or, The Maiden of the Mist. 1829. 3 vols.

Waverley Novels (Magnum Opus Edition). 1829–33. 48 vols.

Tales of a Grandfather: Being Stories Taken from Scottish History: Second Series. 1829. 3 vols.

Memorials of George Bannatyne 1545–1608 (editor). 1829.

Tales of a Grandfather: Being Stories Taken from the History of Scotland: Third Series. 1830. 3 vols.

The House of Aspen: A Tragedy. 1830.

The Doom of Devergoil: A Melo-Drama; Auchindrane; or, The Ayrshire Tragedy. 1830.

The History of Scotland. 1830. 2 vols.

Letters on Demonology and Witchcraft. 1830.

Tales of a Grandfather: Being Stories Taken from the History of France: Fourth Series. 1831. 3 vols.

Trial of Duncan Terig and Alexander Bane Macdonald 1754 (editor). 1831.

Tales of My Landlord: Fourth Series ⟨*Count Robert of Paris; Castle Dangerous*⟩. 1832. 4 vols.

Letters of Scott Addressed to the Rev. R. Polwhele; D. Gilbert, Esq.; Francis Douce, Esq.; &c. &c. Ed. R. Polwhele. 1832.

Tales and Romances. 1833. 7 vols.

Introductions, and Notes and Illustrations. 1833. 2 vols.

Poetical Works. Ed. John Gibson Lockhart. 1833–34. 12 vols.

Miscellaneous Prose Works. Ed. John Gibson Lockhart. 1834–36. 28 vols.

Waverley Novels (Fisher's Edition). 1836–39. 48 vols.

Waverley Novels (Abbotsford Edition). 1842–47. 12 vols.

Letters between James Ellis and Walter Scott, Esq. 1850.

Waverley Novels (Library Edition). 1852–53. 25 vols.

Poetical Works. Ed. George Gilfillan. 1857. 3 vols.

Memoirs of the Insurrection in Scotland in 1715 by John, Master of Sinclair (editor). 1858.

Poetical Works (Globe Edition). Ed. Francis Turner Palgrave. 1866.

Waverley Novels (Centenary Edition). Ed. David Laing. 1870–71. 25 vols.

Journal 1825–32. Ed. David Douglas. 1890. 2 vols.

Poetical Works (Aldine Edition). Ed. John Dennis. 1892. 5 vols.

Waverley Novels (Dryburgh Edition). 1892–94. 25 vols.

Waverley Novels (Border Edition). 1892–94. 48 vols.

Poetical Works. Ed. J. Logie Robertson. 1894.

Tales from Scott. Ed. Edward Sullivan. 1894.

Familiar Letters. Ed. David Douglas. 1894. 2 vols.

Poetical Works (Dryburgh Edition). Ed. Andrew Lang. 1895.

Waverley Novels (Edinburgh Waverley). 1901–03. 48 vols.

The Letters of Sir Walter Scott and Charles Kirkpatrick Sharpe to Robert Chambers 1821–45. 1904.

Waverley Novels (Soho Edition). 1904. 25 vols.

Waverley Novels (Oxford Scott). 1912. 24 vols.

Private Letter-Books: Selections from the Abbotsford Manuscripts. Ed. Wilfred Partington. 1930.

Sir Walter's Post-Bag: More Stories and Sidelights from the Unpublished Letter-Books. Ed. Wilfred Partington. 1932.

Waverley Novels (New Crown Edition). 1932. 25 vols.

Some Unpublished Letters of Sir Walter Scott from the Collection in the Brotherton Library. Ed. J. Alexander Symington. 1932.

Letters. Ed. Herbert J. C. Grierson. 1932–37. 12 vols.

Short Stories. Ed. David Cecil. 1934.

The Correspondence of Sir Walter Scott and Charles Robert Maturin. Eds. Fannie E. Ratchford and William H. McCarthy, Jr. 1937.

Private Letters of the Seventeenth Century. Ed. D. Grant. 1948.

Sir Walter Scott on Novelists and Fiction. Ed. Ioan Williams. 1968.

Journal. Ed. W. E. K. Anderson. 1972.

Selected Poems. Ed. Thomas Crawford. 1972.

The Prefaces to the Waverley Novels. Ed. Mark A. Weinstein. 1978.

HANNAH MORE (1745–1833)

A Search after Happiness: A Pastoral Drama. c. 1766.

The Inflexible Captive. 1774.

Sir Eldred of the Bower and The Bleeding Rock: Two Legendary Tales. 1776.

Essays on Various Subjects, Principally Designed for Young Ladies. 1777.

Ode to Dragon, Mr. Garrick's House-Dog at Hampton. 1777.

Percy. 1778.

The Fatal Falsehood. 1779.

Sacred Dramas, Chiefly Intended for Young Persons; to Which Is Added Sensibility: A Poem. 1782.

Florio: A Tale for Fine Gentlemen and Fine Ladies; and The Bas Bleu; or, Conversation: Two Poems. 1786.

Slavery. 1788.

Thoughts on the Importance of the Manners of the Great to General Society. 1788.

Bishop Bonner's Ghost. 1789.

Works in Prose and Verse. 1789. 2 vols.

An Estimate of the Religion of the Fashionable World. 1791.

Remarks on the Speech of M. Dupont, Made in the National Convention of France, on the Subjects of Religion and Education. 1793.

Village Politics. 1793.

Questions and Answers for the Mendip and Sunday Schools. 1795.

Cheap Repository Tracts (with others). 1795–96. 30 parts.

Strictures on the Modern System of Female Education. 1799. 2 vols.

Works. 1801. 8 vols.

Hints towards Forming the Character of a Young Princess. 1805. 2 vols.

Coelebs in Search of a Wife. 1808. 2 vols.

Practical Piety; or, The Influence of the Religion of the Heart on the Conduct of Life. 1811. 2 vols.

Christian Morals. 1813. 2 vols.

An Essay on the Character and Practical Writings of Saint Paul. 1815. 2 vols.

Poems. 1816.

Stories for the Middle Ranks of Society and Tales for the Common People. 1818. 2 vols.

Works. 1818–19. 19 vols.

Moral Sketches of Prevailing Opinions and Manners. 1819.

The Twelfth of August; or, The Feast of Freedom. 1819.

Bible Rhymes on the Names of All the Books of the Old and New Testament. 1821.

The Spirit of Prayer. 1825.

Works. 1830. 11 vols.

Works. 1834. 6 vols.

Letters to Zachary Macaulay, Containing Notices of Lord Macaulay's Youth. Ed. A. Roberts. 1860.

Letters. Ed. Reginald Brimley Johnson. 1925.

ARTHUR HENRY HALLAM (1811–1833)

Oration on the Influence of Italian Works of Imagination on the Same Class of Compositions in England. 1832.

Essay on the Philosophical Writings of Cicero. 1832.

Remarks on Professor Rossetti's Disquisizioni sullo spirito antipapale. 1832.

Remains in Prose and Verse. Ed. Henry Hallam. 1834.

Poems. Ed. Richard Le Gallienne. 1893.

The Love Story of In Memoriam: *Letters from Arthur Hallam to Emily Tennyson.* 1916.

Writings. Ed. T. H. Vail Motter. 1943.

Letters. Ed. Jack Kolb. 1981.

THOMAS ROBERT MALTHUS (1766–1834)

An Essay on the Principle of Population. 1798, 1826 (6th rev. ed.; 2 vols.).

An Investigation of the Cause of the Present High Price of Provisions. 1800.

A Letter to Samuel Whitbread Esqr, M.P., on His Proposed Bill for the Amendment of the Poor Laws. 1807.

A Letter to the Rt. Hon. Lord Grenville, Occasioned by Some Observations of His Lordship on the East India Company's Establishment for the Education of Their Civil Servants. 1813.

Observations on the Effects of the Corn Laws, and of a Rise or Fall in the Price of Corn on the Agriculture and General Wealth of the Country. 1814.

An Inquiry into the Nature and Progress of Rent, and the Principles by Which It Is Regulated. 1815.

The Grounds of an Opinion on the Policy of Restricting the Importation of Foreign Coin. 1815.

Statements Respecting the East India College. 1817.

Principles of Political Economy. 1820.

The Measure of Value Stated and Illustrated. 1823.

Definitions in Political Economy. 1827.

Occasional Papers on Ireland, Population and Political Economy. Ed. Bernard Semmel. 1963.

An Essay on the Principle of Population and A Summary View of the Principle of Population. Ed. Anthony Flew. 1970.

SAMUEL TAYLOR COLERIDGE (1772–1834)

The Fall of Robespierre: An Historic Drama (with Robert Southey). 1794.

A Moral and Political Lecture Delivered at Bristol. 1795.

Conciones ad Populum; or, Addresses to the People. 1795.

The Plot Discovered; or, An Address to the People, against Ministerial Treason. 1795.

An Answer to a Letter to Edward Long Fox, M.D. 1795.

Ode on the Departing Year. 1796.

Poems on Various Subjects. 1796.

The Watchman. 1796. 10 nos.

Poems (with Charles Lamb and Charles Lloyd). 1797.

Fears in Solitude; to Which Are Added France, an Ode; and Frost at Midnight. 1798.

Lyrical Ballads (with William Wordsworth). 1798, 1800 (2 vols.).

Wallenstein: A Drama Translated from the German of Frederick Schiller. 1800. 2 parts.

Poems. 1803.

The Friend. 1809–10. 28 nos.

Omniana; or, Horae Otiosiores (with Robert Southey). 1812. 2 vols.

Remorse: A Tragedy in Five Acts ⟨*Osorio*⟩. 1813.

Christabel; Kubla Khan: A Vision; The Pains of Sleep. 1816.

The Statesman's Manual; or, The Bible the Best Guide to Political Skill and Foresight ⟨*First Lay Sermon*⟩. 1816.

Biographia Literaria; or, Biographical Sketches of My Literary Life and Opinions. 1817. 2 vols.

Blessed are ye that sow beside all waters! ⟨*Second Lay Sermon*⟩. 1817.

Sibylline Leaves. 1817.

Zapolya: A Christmas Tale. 1817.

A Hebrew Dirge ⟨*Israel's Lament*⟩ by Hyman Hurwitz (translator). 1817.

General Introduction to Encyclopaedia Metropolitana ⟨*On Method*⟩. 1818.

Remarks on the Objections Which Have Been Urged against the Principle of Sir Robert Peel's Bill. 1818.

The Grounds of Sir Robert Peel's Bill Vindicated. 1818.

Prospectus of a Course of Lectures. 1818.

The Tears of a Grateful People by Hyman Hurwitz (translator). 1820.

Aids to Reflection in the Formation of a Manly Character, on the Several Grounds of Prudence, Morality and Religion. 1825.

Poetical Works. 1828. 3 vols.

Poetical Works of Coleridge, Shelley, and Keats. 1829.

On the Constitution of the Church and State According to the Idea of Each, with Aids toward a Right Judgment on the Late Catholic Bill. 1830.

The Devil's Walk: A Poem, Edited with a Biographical Memoir and Notes by Professor Porson (with Robert Southey). Ed. H. W. Montagu. 1830.

On the Prometheus *of Aeschylus.* 1834.

Poetical Works. Ed. Henry Nelson Coleridge. 1834. 3 vols.

Specimens of the Table-Talk of the Late Samuel Taylor Coleridge. Ed. Henry Nelson Coleridge. 1835. 2 vols.

Letters, Conversations, and Recollections. Ed. Thomas Allsop. 1836. 2 vols.

Literary Remains. Ed. Henry Nelson Coleridge. 1836–39. 4 vols.

Confessions of an Inquiring Spirit. Ed. Henry Nelson Coleridge. 1840.

Poems. Ed. Sara Coleridge. 1844.

Hints towards the Formation of a More Comprehensive Theory of Life. Ed. Seth B. Watson. 1848.

Notes and Lectures upon Shakespeare and Some of the Old Poets and Dramatists, with Other Literary Remains. Ed. Sara Coleridge. 1849. 2 vols.

Essays on His Own Times, Forming a Third Series of The Friend. Ed. Sara Coleridge. 1850. 3 vols.

Poems. Eds. Derwent and Sara Coleridge. 1852.

Notes Theological, Political, and Miscellaneous. Ed. Derwent Coleridge. 1853.

Complete Works. Ed. W. G. T. Shedd. 1853. 7 vols.

Seven Lectures on Shakespeare and Milton. Ed. J. Payne Collier. 1856.

Osorio: A Tragedy, as Originally Written in 1797. Ed. R. H. Shepherd. 1873.

Lectures and Notes on Shakspere and Other English Poets. Ed. T. Ashe. 1883.

The Table-Talk and Omniana of S. T. Coleridge, with Additional Table-Talk from Allsop's Recollections. Ed. T. Ashe. 1884.

Poetical Works. Ed. Thomas Ashe. 1885. 2 vols.

Critical Annotations: Being Marginal Notes Inscribed in Volumes Formerly in the Possession of Coleridge, Part I. Ed. William F. Taylor. 1889.

Poetical Works. Ed. James Dykes Campbell. 1893.

Anima Poetae. Ed. Ernest Hartley Coleridge. 1895.

Letters. Ed. Ernest Hartley Coleridge. 1895. 2 vols.

Poems: A Facsimile Reproduction. Ed. James Dykes Campbell. 1899.

Complete Poetical Works. Ed. Ernest Hartley Coleridge. 1912. 2 vols.

Letters Hitherto Uncollected. Ed. W. F. Prideaux. 1913.

Coleridge on Logic and Learning. Ed. Alice D. Snyder. 1929.

Coleridge's Shakespearean Criticism. Ed. Thomas Middleton Raysor. 1930. 2 vols.

Unpublished Letters. Ed. Earl Leslie Griggs. 1932. 2 vols.

Select Poetry and Prose. Ed. Stephen Potter. 1933.

Coleridge on Imagination. Ed. I. A. Richards. 1934.

Miscellaneous Criticism. Ed. Thomas Middleton Raysor. 1936.

The Political Thought of Samuel Taylor Coleridge. Ed. R. J. White. 1938.

The Philosophical Lectures, Hitherto Unpublished. Ed. Kathleen Coburn. 1949.

The Portable Coleridge. Ed. I. A. Richards. 1950.

Inquiring Spirit: A New Presentation of Coleridge from His Published and Unpublished Prose Writings. Ed. Kathleen Coburn. 1951.

Coleridge on the Seventeenth Century. Ed. Roberta Florence Brinkley. 1955.

Collected Letters. Ed. Earl Leslie Griggs. 1956–71. 6 vols.

Notebooks. Ed. Kathleen Coburn. 1957–73. 3 vols. in 6.

Poems. Ed. John Beer. 1963.

Collected Works. Eds. Kathleen Coburn et al. 1969–   .

Coleridge on Shakespeare: The Text of the Lectures of 1811–12. Ed. R. A. Foakes. 1971.

Verse. Eds. William Empson and David Pirie. 1973.

Imagination in Coleridge. Ed. John Spencer Hill. 1978.

Selections. Ed. H. J. Jackson. 1985.

CHARLES LAMB (1775–1834)

Poems (with Samuel Taylor Coleridge and Charles Lloyd). 1797.

Blank Verse by Charles Lloyd and Charles Lamb. 1798.

A Tale of Rosamund Gray and Old Blind Margaret. 1798.

John Woodvil: A Tragedy. 1802.

[*The Book of the Ranks and Dignities of British Society.* 1805.]

The King and Queen of Hearts, with the Rogueries of the Knave, Who Stole the Queen's Pies. 1805.

Tales from Shakespear (with Mary Lamb). 1807. 2 vols.

Adventures of Ulysses. 1808.

Specimens of English Dramatic Poets Who Lived about the Time of Shakespear. 1808.

Mrs. Leicester's School (with Mary Lamb). 1809.

Poetry for Children (with Mary Lamb). 1809. 2 vols.

[*Beauty and the Beast; or, A Rough Outside with a Gentle Heart* (with Mary Lamb). 1811.]

Prince Dorus; or, Flattery Put Out of Countenance. 1811.

Mr. H——; or, Beware a Bad Name. 1813.

Works. 1818. 2 vols.

Elia. 1823.

Elia: Second Series. 1828.

Album Verses (with others). 1830.

Satan in Search of a Wife, with the Whole Process of His Courtship and Marriage, and Who Danced at the Wedding, by an Eye Witness. 1831.

The Last Essays of Elia. 1833.

Recollections of Christ's Hospital. 1835.

Letters. Ed. Thomas Noon Talfourd. 1837. 2 vols.

Works. Ed. Thomas Noon Talfourd. 1840.

Final Memorials of Charles Lamb: Consisting Chiefly of His Letters Not Before Published. Ed. Thomas Noon Talfourd. 1848.

Eliana: Being the Hitherto Uncollected Writings. Ed. J. E. Babson. 1864.

Complete Correspondence and Works. Eds. William Carew Hazlitt and Thomas Purnell. 1870. 4 vols.

Complete Works. Ed. R. H. Shepherd. 1874.

Mary and Charles Lamb: Poems, Letters and Remains. Ed. William Carew Hazlitt. 1874.

Life, Letters, and Writings. Ed. Percy Fitzgerald. 1876. 6 vols.

Works. Ed. Alfred Ainger. 1884–88. 4 vols.

Letters. Ed. William Carew Hazlitt. 1886. 2 vols.

The Lambs: Their Lives, Their Friends, and Their Correspondence. Ed. William Carew Hazlitt. 1897.

Lamb and Hazlitt: Further Letters and Records Hitherto Unpublished. Ed. William Carew Hazlitt. 1900.

Works. Ed. William Macdonald. 1903. 12 vols.

Works of Charles and Mary Lamb. Ed. E. V. Lucas. 1903–05. 7 vols.

Letters. Ed. Henry H. Harper. 1905. 5 vols.

Works of Charles and Mary Lamb. Ed. Thomas Hutchinson. 1908. 2 vols.

Lamb's Criticism: A Selection. Ed. E. M. W. Tillyard. 1923.

Some Lamb and Browning Letters to Leigh Hunt. Ed. Luther A. Brewer. 1924.

The Letters of Charles Lamb, to Which Are Added Those of His Sister Mary Lamb. Ed. E. V. Lucas. 1935. 3 vols.

Letters of Charles and Mary Ann Lamb. Ed. Edwin W. Marrs. 1975. 2 vols.

Lamb as Critic. Ed. Roy Park. 1980.

Selected Prose. Ed. Adam Phillips. 1985.

WILLIAM COBBETT (1762–1835)

The Soldier's Friend; or, Considerations on the Late Pretended Augmentation of the Subsistence of the Private Soldiers. 1792.

Impeachment of Mr. Lafayette (translator). 1793.

Observations on the Emigration of Dr. Priestley. 1794.

A Bone to Gnaw, for the Democrats. 1795. 2 parts.

A Kick for a Bite; or, Review upon Review. 1795.

Le Tuteur anglais; ou, Grammaire régulière de la langue anglaise. 1795.

A Little Plain English, Addressed to the People of the United States, on the Treaty, Negociated with His Britannic Majesty, and on the Conduct of the President Relative Thereto. 1795.

Summary of the Law of Nations by G. F. von Martens (translator). 1795.

The Works of Peter Porcupine. 1795. 5 parts.

A Topographical and Political Description of the Spanish Port of Saint Domingo by M. L. E. Moreau de St. Méry (translator). 1796.

A New-Year's Gift to the Democrats. 1796.

A Prospect from the Congress-Gallery. 1796.

The Bloody Buoy Thrown Out as a Warning to the Political Pilots of All Nations. 1796.

The Political Censor. 1796–97. 9 nos.

The Scare-Crow. 1796.

The Life and Adventures of Peter Porcupine. 1796.

The Gros Mousqueton Diplomatique; or, Diplomatic Blunderbuss by P. A. Adet (translator). 1796.

The History of Jacobinism by William Playfair (editor). 1796. 2 vols.

A Letter to the Infamous Tom Paine, in Answer to His Letter to General Washington. 1796.

The Life of Thomas Paine. 1797.

Observations on the Debates of the American Congress, on the Addresses Presented to General Washington, on His Resignation. 1797.

Porcupine's Gazette and United States Daily Advertiser. 1797–1800. 778 nos.

A View of the Causes and Consequences of the Present War with France by Thomas Erskine (editor). 1797.

The Last Confession and Dying Speech of Peter Porcupine, with an Account of His Dissection. 1797.

Democratic Principles Illustrated by Example. 1797–98. 2 parts.

The Democratic Judge. 1798.

Observations on the Dispute between the United States and France by Robert Goodloe Harper et al. (editor). 1798.

Detection of a Conspiracy Formed by the United Irishmen with the Widest Intention of Aiding the Tyrants of France in Subverting the Government of the United States of America. 1798.

French Arrogance; or, The Cat Let out of the Bag: A Poetical Dialogue. 1798.

Remarks on the Insidious Letter of the Gallic Despots. 1798.

The Detection of Bache. 1798.

The Cannibal's Progress, tr. Anthony Aufrere (editor). 1798.

Remarks on the Explanation, Lately Published by Dr. Prestley, Respecting the Intercepted Letters of His Friend and Disciple, John H. Stone. 1799.

The Trial of Republicanism. 1799.

Proposals for Publishing, by Subscription, a New, Entire, and Neat Edition of Porcupine's Works. 1799.

The Rush-Light. 1800. 6 nos.

Cobbett's Advice. 1800.

The Porcupine. 1800-01. 365 nos.

A Collection of Facts and Observations Relative to the Peace with Bonaparte, and Including Letters to Lord Hawkesbury. 1801.

Porcupine's Works. 1801. 12 vols.

Letters to the Right Honourable Henry Addington, on the Fatal Effects of the Peace with Buonaparte. 1802.

Letters to the Right Honourable Lord Hawkesbury and the Right Hon. Henry Addington, on the Peace with Buonaparte. 1802.

Cobbett's Political Register. 1802-35. 89 vols.

Letter to Lord Auckland on the Abuses in the General Post Office. 1802.

Narrative of the Taking of the Invincible Standard. 1803.

The Empire of Germany by Jean Gabriel Peltier (translator). 1803.

Four Letters to the Chancellor of the Exchequer, on the Finances. 1803.

Important Considerations for the People of This Kingdom. 1803.

The Political Proteus: A View of the Public Character of R. B. Sheridan, Esq. 1804.

Cobbett's Parliamentary Debates (editor; with John Wright). 1804-12. 22 vols.

Cobbett's Spirit of the Public Journals. 1805.

Cobbett's Complete Collection of State Trials (editor; with John Wright and T. B. Howell). 1809-26. 33 vols.

Cobbett's Remarks on Sir F. Burdett's Letter to His Constituents. 1809.

Three Letters to the Independent Electors of the City of Bristol. 1812.

Letters to the Prince Regent. 1812. Lost.

Porcupine Revived; or, An Old Thing Made New. 1813.

Letter to the Inhabitants of Southampton on the Corn Bill. 1814.

Five Letters to Lord Sheffield on His Speech at Lewes Wool Fair. 1815.

Letters on the Late War between the United States and Great Britain. 1815.

Paper against Gold and Glory against Prosperity. 1815. 2 vols.

To the Journeymen and Labourers of England, Wales, Scotland and Ireland. 1816.

A Letter Addressed to Mr. Jabet, of Birmingham. 1816.

Our Anti-Neutral Conduct Reviewed. 1817.

Cobbett's New Year's Gift to Old George Rose. 1817.

Mr. Cobbett's Taking Leave of His Countrymen. 1817.

Cobbett's Address to the Americans. 1817.

Mr. Cobbett's Address to his Countrymen on His Future Political Works. 1817.

A Year's Residence in the United States of America. 1818-19. 3 parts.

A Grammar of the English Language, in a Series of Letters. 1818.

Correspondence between Mr. Cobbett, Mr. Tipper, and Sir Francis Burdett. 1819.

Cobbett's Evening Post. 1820. 55 nos.

Cobbett's Parliamentary Register. 1820. 2 vols.

A Letter from the Queen to the King. 1820.

An Answer to the Speech of the Attorney-General, against Her Majesty the Queen. 1820.

The Beauties of Cobbett. c. 1820. 3 parts.

The Queen's Answer to the Letter from the King to His People. 1821.

Cobbett's Monthly Religious Tracts ⟨*Cobbett's Sermons*⟩. 1821-22. 12 parts.

Preliminary Part of Paper against Gold. 1821.

The American Gardener. 1821.

Cottage Economy. 1821-22. 7 parts.

Cobbett's Too Long Petition, Nov. 1817; Letter to Tierney, July 1818; Letter to the Regent on That Wild and Visionary Project, Peel's Bill, Sept. 1819. 1822.

The Farmer's Friend. 1822.

Cobbett's Warning to Norfolk Farmers. 1822.

The Farmer's Wife's Friend. 1822.

The Horse-Hoeing Husbandry by Jethro Tull (editor). 1822.

Reduction No Robbery. 1822.

Cobbett's Collective Commentaries. 1822.

Mr. Cobbett's Publications. 1822.

Narrative. 1823. Lost.

The Norfolk Yeoman's Gazette. 1823. 13 nos.

To Lord Suffield. 1823.

A French Grammar; or, Plain Instructions for the Learning of French. 1824.

A History of the Protestant "Reformation," in England and Ireland. 1824-26. 16 parts.

Gold for Ever! Real Causes for the Fall of the Funds. 1825.

Big O. and Sir Glory; or, "Leisure to Laugh." 1825.

The Woodlands; or, A Treatise on the Preparing Ground for Planting. 1825-28. 7 parts.

Cobbett at the King's Cottage. 1826.

Cobbett's Poor Man's Friend. 1826-27. 5 nos.

Catalogue of American Trees, Shrubs, Plants, and Seeds for Sale by Mr. Cobbett. 1827.

Elements of Roman History by J. H. Sievrac (translator). 1828.

Noble Nonsense!; or, Cobbett's Exhibition of the Stupid and Insolent Pamphlet of Lord Grenville. 1828.

The English Gardener. 1828.

Facts for the Men of Kent. 1828.

A Letter to His Holiness, the Pope, on the Character, the Conduct, and the Views of the Catholic Aristocracy and Lawyers of England and Ireland. 1828.

A Treatise on Cobbett's Corn. 1828.

Letter to Mr. Huskisson, on the Subject of the American Tariff. 1828.

Englishmen, Hear Me. 1829.

The Emigrant's Guide. 1829.

Mr. Cobbett's Lecture on the Present Prospects of Merchants, Traders, and Farmers. 1829-30. 5 parts.

Advice to Young Men, and (Incidentally) to Young Women, in the Middle and Higher Ranks of Life. 1829-30. 14 parts.

An Accurate Report of Mr. Cobbett's Lecture-Speech on the Present Distresses of the Country, and Their Remedies. 1830.

Three Lectures on the State of the Country Delivered at the Music Hall, Sheffield. 1830.

Mr. Cobbett's Address to the Tax-payers of England and Scotland, on the Subject of the Seat in Parliament. 1830.

Good Friday; or, The Murder of Jesus Christ by the Jews. 1830.

Rural Rides. 1830.

Cobbett's Exposure of the Practice of the Pretended Friends of the Blacks. 1830.

French Revolution: An Address to the People of Paris Agreed to at the London Tavern. 1830.

Eleven Lectures on the French and Belgian Revolutions, and English Boroughmongering. 1830. 11 parts.

A Letter to the King. 1830.

History of the Regency and Reign of King George the Fourth. 1830–34. 2 vols.

Cobbett's Plan of Parliamentary Reform. 1830.

Cobbett's Twopenny Trash. 1830–32. 24 parts.

A Spelling Book. 1831.

Surplus Population and Poor-Law Bill. c. 1831.

Cobbett's Letter on the Abolition of Tithes. c. 1831.

Cobbett's Manchester Lectures, in Support of His Fourteen Reform Proposals. 1832.

A Geographical Dictionary of England and Wales. 1832.

Extracts from Cobbett's Register, and Mr. Cobbett's Remarks. 1832.

Mr. Cobbett's Answer to Mr. Stanley's Manifesto. 1833.

Cobbett's Tour in Scotland and in the Four Northern Counties of England in the Autumn of the Year 1832. 1833.

Cobbett's Poor Man's Friend. 1833.

Speeches. 1833. 2 parts.

The Flash in the Pan; or, Peel in a Passion. 1833.

Disgraceful Squandering of the Public Money, the Great Cause of Oppressive Taxation. 1833.

The Curse of Paper Money by William M. Gouge (editor). 1833.

A New French and English Dictionary. 1833. 2 parts.

Popay, the Police Spy. 1833.

The Rights of Industry (with John Fielden). 1833.

Four Letters to the Hon. John Stuart Wortley. 1834.

Mr. Cobbett's Speech and Other Speeches on His Motion for an Abolition of the Malt Tax. 1834.

Life of Andrew Jackson, President of the United States. 1834.

Get Gold! Get Gold! 1834.

To the Earl of Radnor, on His Reported Speech, in the House of Lords, on the Poor-Law Scheme. 1834. 5 letters.

Three Lectures on the Political State of Ireland. 1834.

Cobbett's Legacy to Labourers. 1834.

The Malt Tax Kept upon the Backs of the People by the Whigs. 1835.

Cobbett's Legacy to Parsons. 1835.

Selections from Cobbett's Political Works. Eds. J. M. Cobbett and J. P. Cobbett. 1835–37. 6 vols.

Cobbett's Legacy to Peel. 1836.

Cobbett's Reasons for War against Russia in Defence of Turkey. 1854.

The Last of the Saxons: Light and Fire from the Writings. Ed. Edwin Paxton Hood. 1854.

Mr. Cobbett's Remarks on Our Indian Empire and Company of Trading Sovereigns. 1857.

Life and Letters. Ed. Lewis Melville. 1913. 2 vols.

A History of the Last Hundred Days of English Freedom. Ed. J. L. Hammond. 1921.

Selections. Ed. A. M. D. Hughes. 1923.

The Life and Adventures of Peter Porcupine. Ed. G. D. H. Cole. 1927.

The Progress of a Ploughboy to a Seat in Parliament. Ed. William Reitzel. 1933.

Letters to Edward Thornton Written in the Years 1797 to 1800. Ed. G. D. H. Cole. 1937.

The Opinions of William Cobbett. Ed. G. D. H. Cole and Margaret Cole. 1944.

Cobbett's England. Ed. John Derry. 1968.

Letters. Ed. Gerald Duff. 1974.

Cobbett's Country Book. Ed. Richard Ingrams. 1974.

JAMES HOGG (1770–1835)

Scottish Pastorals, Poems, Songs, etc., Mostly Written in the Dialect of the South. 1801.

The Mountain Bard: Consisting of Ballads and Songs, Founded on Facts and Legendary Tales. 1807.

The Shepherd's Guide: Being a Practical Treatise on the Diseases of Sheep. 1807.

The Forest Minstrel: A Selection of Songs, Adapted to the Most Favourite Scottish Airs (with others). 1810.

The Spy. 1810–11. 52 nos.

The Queen's Wake: A Legendary Poem. 1813.

The Hunting of Badlewe: A Dramatic Tale. 1814.

Mador of the Moor. 1814.

The Pilgrims of the Sun. 1814.

A Selection of German Hebrew Melodies. c. 1815.

The Poetic Mirror; or, The Living Bards of Britain (editor). 1816.

Dramatic Tales. 1817. 2 vols.

The Long Pack: A Northumbrian Tale. 1817.

The Brownie of Bodsbeck and Other Tales. 1818. 2 vols.

A Border Garland. c. 1819.

The Jacobite Relics of Scotland: Being the Songs, Airs, and Legends of the Adherents of the House of Stuart. 1819–21. 2 vols.

Winter Evening Tales, Collected among the Cottagers in the South of Scotland. 1820. 2 vols.

The Three Perils of Man; or, War, Women, and Witchcraft: A Border Romance. 1822. 3 vols.

Poetical Works. 1822. 4 vols.

The Royal Jubilee. 1822.

The Three Perils of Woman; or, Love, Leasing and Jealousy: Domestic Scottish Tales. 1823. 3 vols.

The Private Memoirs and Confessions of a Justified Sinner. 1824.

Queen Hynde. 1825.

Select and Rare Scottish Melodies. 1829.

The Shepherd's Calendar. 1829. 2 vols.

Critical Remarks on the Psalms of David (with William Tennant). 1830.

Songs. 1831.

Altrive Tales: Collected among the Peasantry of Scotland, and from Foreign Adventurers. 1832. Vol. 1 only.

A Queer Book. 1832.

The Domestic Manners and Private Life of Sir Walter Scott. 1834.

A Series of Lay Sermons on Good Principles and Good Breeding. 1834.

The Works of Robert Burns (editor; with William Motherwell). 1834–36. 5 vols.

Tales of the Wars of Montrose. 1835. 3 vols.

Tales and Sketches. 1837. 6 vols.

Poetical Works. 1838–40. 5 vols.

Works. Ed. Thomas Thomason. 1865–66. 2 vols.

Tales. 1880. 2 vols.

A *Tour of the Highlands in 1803: A Series of Letters.* 1888.

Poems. Ed. William Wallace. 1903.

Selected Poems. Ed. John W. Oliver. 1940.

Selected Poems. Ed. Douglas S. Mack. 1970.

Memoirs of the Author's Life and Familiar Anecdotes of Sir Walter Scott. Ed. Douglas S. Mack. 1972.

Tales of Love and Mystery. Ed. David Groves. 1985.

Selected Poems and Songs. Ed. David Groves. 1986.

FELICIA DOROTHEA HEMANS (1793–1835)

Poems. 1808.

England and Spain; or, Valour and Patriotism. 1808.

The Domestic Affections and Other Poems. 1812.

The Restoration of the Works of Art to Italy. 1816.

Modern Greece. 1817.

Translations from Camoens and Other Poets, with Original Poetry. 1818.

Tales, and Historic Scenes, in Verse. 1819.

Wallace's Invocation to Bruce. 1819.

The Sceptic. 1820.

Stanzas to the Memory of the King. 1820.

Dartmoor. 1821.

Welsh Melodies. 1822.

The Vespers of Palermo. 1823.

The Siege of Valencia: A Dramatic Poem; The Last Constantine, with Other Poems. 1823.

The Forest Sanctuary and Other Poems. 1825.

The League of the Alps, The Siege of Valencia, The Vespers of Palermo, and Other Poems. Ed. Andrews Norton. 1826–27. 2 vols.

Hymns on the Works of Nature: For the Use of Children. 1827.

Poems. 1827.

Records of Woman, with Other Poems. 1828.

Poetical Works. 1828. 2 vols.

Songs of the Affections, with Other Poems. 1830.

National Lyrics and Songs for Music. 1834.

Scenes and Hymns of Life, with Other Religious Poems. 1834.

Poetical Works. 1836.

Poetical Remains. 1836.

Works. Ed. Harriet Hughes. 1839. 7 vols.

Early Blossoms: A Collection of Poems Written between Eight and Fifteen Years of Age. 1840.

Poems. Ed. Rufus W. Griswold. 1845.

Poems. 1849.

Dramatic Works. 1850.

Poems. 1865.

Poetical Works. Ed. William Michael Rossetti. 1873.

Favorite Poems. 1877.

Poems. 1896.

Poetical Works. 1914.

WILLIAM GODWIN (1756–1836)

The History of the Life of William Pitt. 1783.

A Defence of the Rockingham Party, in Their Late Coalition with Lord North. 1783.

An Account of the Seminary That Will Be Opened at Epsom, in Surrey, for the Instruction of Twelve Pupils. 1783.

Italian Letters; or, The History of the Count de St. Julian. 1783.

The Herald of Literature; or, A Review of the Most Considerable Publications That Will Be Made in the Course of the Ensuing Winter. 1784.

Sketches of History, in Six Sermons. 1784.

Damon and Delia: A Tale. 1784.

Imogen: A Pastoral Romance. 1784. 2 vols.

Instructions to a Statesman. 1784.

[*History of the Internal Affairs of the United Provinces.* 1787.]

An Enquiry concerning Political Justice and Its Influence on General Virtue and Happiness. 1793. 2 vols.

Cursory Strictures on the Charge Delivered by Lord Chief Justice Eyre to the Grand Jury. 1794.

[*A Reply to* An Answer to *Cursory Strictures.* 1794.]

Things as They Are; or, The Adventures of Caleb Williams. 1794. 3 vols.

Considerations on Lord Grenville's and Mr. Pitt's Bills, concerning Treasonable and Seditious Practices, and Unlawful Assemblies. 1795.

The Enquirer: Reflections on Education, Manners, and Literature. 1797.

Memoirs of the Life of Simon, Lord Lovat (translator). 1797.

Memoirs of the Author of A Vindication of the Rights of Woman. 1798.

Posthumous Works by Mary Wollstonecraft (editor). 1798. 4 vols.

St. Leon: A Tale of the Sixteenth Century. 1799. 4 vols.

Antonio. 1800.

Thoughts Occasioned by Dr. Parr's Spital Sermon. 1801.

Life of Geoffrey Chaucer. 1803 (2 vols.), 1804 (4 vols.).

Fables Ancient and Modern: Adapted for the Use of Children. 1805.

Fleetwood; or, The New Man of Feeling. 1805. 3 vols.

The Looking-Glass: A True History of the Early Years of an Artist. 1805.

The History of England: For the Use of Schools and Young Persons. 1806.

The Pantheon; or, Ancient History of the Gods of Greece and Rome: For the Use of Schools and Young Persons of Both Sexes. 1806.

Life of Lady Jane Grey and of Guildford Dudley, Her Husband. 1806.

Faulkener. 1807.

Essay on Sepulchres. 1809.

Dramas for Children by L. F. Jauffret (adaptation). 1809.

History of Rome. 1809.

Lives of Edward and John Philips, Nephews and Pupils of Milton. 1815.

Letters of Verax, to the Editors of The Morning Chronicle, *on the Question of a War to Be Commenced for the Purpose of Putting an End to the Possession of the Supreme Power in France by Napoleon Buonaparte.* 1815.

Maundeville: A Tale of the Seventeenth Century in England. 1817. 3 vols.

Letter of Advice to a Young American: On the Course of Studies It Might Be More Advantageous for Him to Pursue. 1818.

Of Population: Being an Answer to Mr. Malthus's Essay on That Subject. 1820.

History of the Commonwealth of England from Its Commencement to the Restoration of Charles the Second. 1824–28. 4 vols.

History of Greece. 1828.

Cloudesley: A Tale. 1830. 3 vols.

Thoughts on Man, His Nature, Productions and Discoveries. 1831.

Deloraine. 1833. 3 vols.

Lives of the Necromancers. 1834.

Essays Never Before Published. Ed. C. Kegan Paul. 1873.

The Elopement of Percy Bysshe Shelley and Mary Wollstone-

craft Godwin: As Narrated by William Godwin. Ed. H. Buxton Forman. 1911.

Tragical Consequences; or, A Disaster at Deal: Being an Unpublished Letter of William Godwin. Ed. Edmund Blunden. 1931.

Godwin and Mary: Letters of William Godwin and Mary Wollstonecraft. Ed. Ralph M. Wardle. 1966.

Uncollected Writings 1795–1822. Eds. Jack W. Marken and Burton R. Pollin. 1968.

GEORGE COLMAN THE YOUNGER (1762–1836)

Prose on Several Occasions: Accompanied with Some Pieces in Verse. 1787. 3 vols.

Ways and Means; or, A Trip to Dover. 1788.

The Battle of Hexham. 1790.

The Surrender of Calais. 1792.

Poor Old Haymarket; or, Two Sides of the Gutter: A Prelude. 1792.

The Mountaineers. 1794.

New Hay at the Old Market. 1795.

The Iron Chest (adaptation). 1796.

My Night-Gown and Slippers; or, Tales in Verse. 1797.

The Heir at Law. 1798.

Blue-Beard; or, Female Curiosity! 1798.

Feudal Times; or, The Banquet-Gallery. 1799.

The Review; or, The Wags of Windsor. 1801.

The Poor Gentleman. 1801.

Broad Grins: Comprising, with New Additional Tales in Verse, Those Formerly Published under the Title of My Night-Gown and Slippers. 1802.

John Bull; or, The Englishman's Fireside. 1803.

Epilogue to the New Play of The Maid of Bristol (by James Boaden). 1803.

Who Wants a Guinea? 1805.

Blue Devils. 1808.

The Africans; or, Love, War and Duty. 1808.

The Forty Thieves (with Richard Brinsley Sheridan and Charles Ward). 1808.

Poetical Vagaries. 1812.

Vagaries Vindicated; or, Hypocritick Hypercriticks. 1813.

Poetical Vagaries and Vagaries Vindicated. 1814.

[*The Maskers of Moorfields: A Vision.* 1815.]

Eccentricities for Edinburgh. c. 1816.

X.Y.Z. 1820.

Posthumous Letters, from Various Men; Addressed to Francis Colman, and George Colman the Elder (editor). 1820.

Posthumous Papers Relative to the Proportionate Shares of Authorship of The Clandestine Marriage *to be Attributed to the Elder Colman and Garrick.* 1820.

The Actor of All Work; or, The First and Second Floor. 1822.

The Law of Java. 1822.

Dramatic Works. 1823–24. 4 vols.

Random Records. 1830. 2 vols.

Poetical Works. 1834. 3 parts.

Poetical Works. 1840.

Broad Brins, My Nightgown and Slippers, and Other Humorous Works, Prose and Poetical. Ed. George B. Buckstone. 1872.

Plays (with Thomas Morton). Ed. Barry Sutcliffe. 1983.

JAMES MILL (1773–1836)

An Essay on the Impolicy of a Bounty on the Exportation of Grain. 1804.

Commerce Defended: An Answer to the Arguments by Which Mr. Spence, Mr. Cobbett, and Others Have Attempted to Prove That Commerce Is Not a Source of National Wealth. 1807.

Proposals for Establishing in the Metropolis a Day School for the Application of the Methods of Bell, Lancaster and Others to the Higher Branches of Education (with Francis Place). 1815.

The History of British India. 1817 (3 vols.), 1826 (6 vols.).

An Account of the Maison de Force at Ghent. 1817.

Elements of Political Economy. 1821.

Statement of the Question of Parliamentary Reform. 1821.

Essays on Government, Jurisprudence, Liberty of the Press, and Law of Nations. 1825. 4 parts.

Essays in I. Government; II. Jurisprudence; III. Liberty of the Press; IV. Prisons and Prison Discipline; V. Colonies; VI. Law of Nations; VII. Education. 1828. 7 parts.

Analysis of the Phenomena of the Human Mind. 1829. 2 vols.

On the Ballot. 1830.

A Fragment on Mackintosh. 1835.

The Principles of Toleration. 1837.

James and John Stuart Mill on Education. Ed. F. A. Cavenagh. 1931.

Selected Economic Writings. Ed. Donald Winch. 1966.

James Mill on Education. Ed. W. H. Burston. 1969.

LETITIA ELIZABETH LANDON (1802–1838)

The Fate of Adelaide, a Swiss Romantic Tale; and Other Poems. 1821.

The Improvisatrice and Other Poems. 1824.

The Troubadour; Catalogue of Pictures, and Historical Sketches. 1825.

The Golden Violet, with Its Tales of Romance and Chivalry, and Other Poems. 1827.

Poetical Works. 1827. 3 vols.

The Venetian Bracelet, The Lost Pleiad, A History of the Lyre, and Other Poems. 1828.

Poetical Works. c. 1830.

Romance and Reality. 1831. 3 vols.

The Easter Gift: A Religious Offering. 1832.

Heath's Book of Beauty (editor). 1833.

Corinne; or, Italy by Madame de Staël (translator; with Isabel Hill). 1833.

Francesca Carrara. 1834. 3 vols.

The Vow of the Peacock and Other Poems. 1835.

Traits and Trials of Early Life. 1836.

Ethel Churchill; or, The Two Brides. 1837. 3 vols.

A Birthday Tribute, Addressed to the Princess Alexandrina Victoria, on Attaining Her Eighteenth Year. 1837.

Duty and Inclination (editor). 1838. 3 vols.

Flowers of Loveliness (with Thomas Haynes Bayley and Marguerite, Countess of Blessington). 1838.

Works. 1838. 2 vols.

The Zenana, and Minor Poems. 1839.

Poetical Works. 1839. 4 vols.

Life and Literary Remains. Ed. Laman Blanchard. 1841. 2 vols.

Lady Anne Granard; or, Keeping Up Appearances. 1842. 3 vols.

Poetical Works. 1850. 2 vols.

Poetical Works. 1856. 2 vols.

Poetical Works. Ed. William B. Scott. 1873.

JOHN GALT (1779–1839)

The Battle of Largs: A Gothic Poem, with Several Miscellaneous Pieces. 1804.

Cursory Reflections on Political and Commercial Topics, as

Connected with the Regent's Accession to Royal Authority. 1812.

Voyages and Travels in the Years 1809, 1810, and 1811: Containing Statistical, Commercial and Miscellaneous Observations on Gibraltar, Sardinia, Sicily, Malta, Serigo and Turkey. 1812.

The Life and Administration of Cardinal Wolsey. 1812.

The Tragedie of Maddelen, Agamemnon, Lady Macbeth, Antonia and Clytemnestra. 1812.

Letters from the Levant: Containing Views of the State of Society, Manners, Opinions, and Commerce in Greece and Several of the Principal Islands of the Archipelago. 1813.

The New British Theatre (editor). 1814–15. 4 vols.

The Majolo: A Tale. 1816. 2 vols.

The Crusade. 1816.

The Life and Studies of Benjamin West. 1816–20. 2 vols.

The Appeal. 1818.

The Earthquake: A Tale. 1820. 3 vols.

The Wandering Jew; or, Travels and Observations of Hareach the Prolonged. 1820.

All the Voyages round the World. 1820.

A Tour of Europe and Asia. 1820. 2 vols.

George the Third: His Court and Family. 1820. 2 vols.

Glenfell; or, Macdonalds and Campbells. 1820.

The National Spelling Book by Benjamin Tabart (revised by Galt). c. 1820.

Pictures, Historical and Biographical, Drawn from English, Scottish and Irish History. 1821. 2 vols.

The Ayrshire Legatees; or, The Pringle Family. 1821.

Annals of the Parish; or, The Chronicle of Dalmailing, during the Ministry of the Rev. Micah Balwhidder. 1821.

The History of Gog and Magog. c. 1821.

The Rocking Horse. c. 1821.

A New General School Atlas. 1822.

The English Mother's First Catechism for Her Children. 1822.

Sir Andrew Wylie, of The Ilk. 1822. 3 vols.

The Provost. 1822.

Memoirs by Alexander Graydon (editor). 1822.

The Steam-Boat. 1822.

The National Reader. c. 1822.

The Entail; or, The Lairds of Grippy. 1823. 3 vols.

The Gathering of the West; or, We've Come to See the King. 1823.

Ringan Gilhaize; or, The Covenanters. 1823. 3 vols.

Modern Geography and History. 1823.

The Spaewife: A Tale of the Scottish Chronicles. 1823. 3 vols.

The Universal Traveller. 1824.

Rothelan: A Romance of the English Histories. 1824. 3 vols.

The Bachelor's Wife: A Collection of Curious and Interesting Extracts, with Cursory Observations. 1824.

The Omen. 1825.

The Last of the Lairds; or, The Life and Opinions of Malachi Mailings, Esq. of Auldbiggings. 1826.

Lawrie Todd; or, The Settlers in the Woods. 1830. 3 vols.

Southennan. 1830. 3 vols.

The Life of Lord Byron. 1830.

The Lives of the Players. 1831. 2 vols.

Bogle Corbet; or, The Emigrants. 1831. 3 vols.

The Member: An Autobiography. 1832.

The Radical: An Autobiography. 1832.

The Canadas (with Andrew Picken). 1832.

Stanley Buxton; or, The Schoolfellows. 1832. 3 vols.

Poems. 1833.

Eben Erskine; or, The Traveller. 1833. 3 vols.

The Stolen Child: A Tale of the Town. 1833.

Stories of the Study. 1833. 3 vols.

The Ouranoulogos; or, The Celestial Volume. 1833.

Autobiography. 1833. 2 vols.

Literary Life and Miscellanies. 1834. 3 vols.

Efforts. 1835.

A Contribution to the Greenock Calamity Fund. 1835.

Diary Illustrative of the Times of George IV, Volumes 3–4 by Lady Charlotte Bury (editor). 1838–39. 4 vols.

The Demon of Destiny and Other Poems. 1839.

Records of a Real Life in the Palace and the Cottage by Harriet Pigott (revised by Galt). 1839. 3 vols.

Novels. Ed. David Macbeth Moir. 1841–43. 4 vols.

Works. Ed. D. Storrar Meldrum. 1895. 8 vols.

The Howdie and Other Tales. Ed. William Roughhead. 1923.

A Rich Man and Other Stories. Ed. William Roughhead. 1925.

Works. Eds. D. Storrar Meldrum and William Roughhead. 1936. 10 vols.

Poems. Ed. G. H. Needler. 1954.

Collected Poems. Ed. Hamilton Baird Timothy. 1969– .

Selected Short Stories. Ed. Ian A. Gordon. 1978.

WINTHROP MACKWORTH PRAED (1802–1839)

Carmen Graecum Numismate Annuo Dignatum 1822. 1822.

Epigrammata Numismate Annuo Dignata 1822. 1822.

Carmen Graecum Numismate Annuo Dignatum 1823. 1823.

Lillian: A Fairy Tale. 1823.

Australasia: A Poem Which Obtained the Chancellor's Medal 1823. 1823.

Athens: A Poem Which Obtained the Chancellor's Medal 1824. 1824.

Epigrammata Numismate Annuo Dignata 1824. 1824.

The Ascent of Elijah. 1831.

Speech in Committee on the Reform Bill, on Moving an Amendment "That Freeholds Situate within Boroughs Should Confer Votes for the Borough and Not for the County." 1832.

Trash: Dedicated without Respect to J. Halse, Esq., M.P. 1833.

Political Poems. 1835.

Intercepted Letters about the Infirmary Bazaar. c. 1836.

I Remember, I Remember. c. 1840.

Poetical Works. Ed. Rufus W. Griswold. 1844.

Lillian and Other Poems. Ed. Rufus W. Griswold. 1852.

Charades. 1852.

Poetical Works. Ed. W. A. Whitmore. 1859–60. 2 vols.

Poems. 1864.

A Selection from the Works. Ed. Sir George Young. 1866.

Poems. Ed. Frederick Cooper. 1886.

Essays. Ed. Sir George Young. 1887.

Political and Occasional Poems. Ed. Sir George Young. 1888.

Every-day Characters. 1896.

Select Poems. Ed. A. D. Godley. 1909.

Poems. Ed. Ferris Greenslet. 1909.

Selected Poems. Ed. Kenneth Allott. 1953.

FANNY BURNEY (1752–1840)

Evelina; or, The History of a Young Lady's Entrance into the World. 1778. 3 vols.

Cecilia; or, Memoirs of an Heiress. 1782. 5 vols.

Brief Recollections Relative to the Emigrant French Clergy. 1793.

Camilla; or, A Picture of Youth. 1796. 5 vols.

The Wanderer; or, Female Difficulties. 1814. 5 vols.
Memoirs of Dr. Burney. 1832. 3 vols.
Diary and Letters. Ed. Charlotte Barrett. 1842–46. 7 vols.
Early Diary. Ed. Annie Raine Ellis. 1889. 2 vols.
The Queeney Letters: Being Letters Addressed to Hester Maria Thrale by Dr. Johnson, Fanny Burney and Mrs. Thrale-Piozzi. Ed. the Marquis of Lansdowne. 1934.
Edwy and Elgiva. Ed. Miriam J. Benkovitz. 1957.
Journals and Letters. Eds. Joyce Hemlow et al. 1972–84. 12 vols.
Selected Letters and Journals. Ed. Joyce Hemlow. 1986.

THEODORE EDWARD HOOK (1788–1841)

The Soldier's Return; or, What Can Beauty Do? 1805.
Catch Him Who Can! 1806.
The Invisible Girl. 1806.
Tekeli; or, The Siege of Montgatz: A Melo-drama. 1806.
The Fortress: A Melo-drama (adaptation). 1807.
Music-Mad: A Dramatic Sketch. 1808.
The Man of Sorrow. 1808 (3 vols.), 1854 (as *Ned Musgrove, the Most Unfortunate Man in the World*).
Killing No Murder. 1809.
Safe and Sound. 1809.
Darkness Visible. 1811.
The Trial by Jury. 1811.
Facts Illustrative of the Treatment of Napoleon Bonaparte in Saint Helena. 1819.
Exchange No Robbery; or, The Diamond Ring. 1820.
Tentamen; or, An Essay towards the History of Whittington. 1820.
The Radical Harmonist; or, A Collection of Songs and Toasts Given at the Crown and Anchor Dinner (editor). 1820.
Sayings and Doings: A Series of Sketches from Life. 1824. 3 vols.
Sayings and Doings: Second Series. 1825. 3 vols.
Reminiscences of Michael Kelly (editor). 1826. 2 vols.
Sayings and Doings: Third Series. 1828. 3 vols.
Maxwell. 1830. 3 vols.
Life of General, the Right Honourable Sir David Baird. 1832. 2 vols.
Love and Pride. 1833. 3 vols.
The Parson's Daughter. 1833. 3 vols.
Gilbert Gurney. 1836. 3 vols.
Jack Brag. 1837. 3 vols.
Pascal Bruno by Alexandre Dumas, tr. anon. (editor). 1837.
Gurney Married: A Sequel to Gilbert Gurney. 1838. 3 vols.
Births, Deaths, and Marriages. 1839. 3 vols.
A Day at an Inn. 183–.
Precepts and Practice. 1840. 3 vols.
Cousin Geoffrey, the Old Bachelor by Harriet Maria Gordon Smythies (editor). 1840. 3 vols.
Peter Priggins, the College Scout by James J. Hewlett (editor). 1840. 3 vols.
The French Stage and the French People by Jean Baptiste Pierre Lafitte, tr. J. A. Bernard (editor). 1841. 3 vols.
The Parish Clerk by James J. Hewlett (editor). 1841. 3 vols.
Fathers and Sons. 1842. 3 vols.
Peregrine Bunce; or, Settled at Last. 1842. 3 vols.
Life and Remains. Ed. R. H. Dalton Barham. 1849. 2 vols.
The Ramsbottom Letters. 1872.
Novels. 1872–77. 15 vols.
Choice Humorous Works. 1873.
Bon-Mots of Samuel Foote and Theodore Hook. Ed. Walter Jerrold. 1894.

WILLIAM ELLERY CHANNING (1780–1842)

The Duties of Children. 1807.
A Sermon, Delivered at the Ordination of the Rev. John Codman. 1808.
A Sermon Preached in Boston, April 5, 1810, the Day of the Public Fast. 1810.
A Sermon Preached in Boston, July 23, 1812, the Day of the Publick Fast. 1812.
A Sermon Preached in Boston, August 20, 1812, the Day of Humiliation and Prayer. 1812.
Elements of Religion and Morality, in the Form of a Catechism (with Samuel C. Thacher). 1813.
Two Sermons on Infidelity. 1813.
A Discourse, Delivered in Boston, at the Solemn Festival in Commemoration of the Goodness of God in Delivering the Christian World from Military Despotism. 1814.
A Sermon, Delivered in Boston. 1814.
A Sermon, Delivered at the Ordination of the Rev. John Emery Abbot. 1815.
Remarks on the Rev. Dr. Worcester's Letter to Mr. Channing on the "Review of American Unitarianism" in a Late Panoplist. 1815.
Remarks on the Rev. Dr. Worcester's Second Letter to Mr. Channing, on American Unitarianism. 1815.
A Letter to the Rev. Samuel C. Thacher, on the Aspersions Contained in a Late Number of the Panoplist. 1815.
Observations on the Proposition for Increasing the Means of Theological Education at the University in Cambridge. 1816.
A Sermon on War. 1816.
A Discourse on Some of the Distinguishing Opinions of Unitarians. 1819.
A Letter to Professor Stuart. 1819.
A Sermon Delivered at the Ordination of the Rev. Jared Sparks. 1819.
Note for the Second Baltimore Edition of the Rev. Mr. Channing's Sermon, Delivered at the Ordination of the Rev. Mr. Jared Sparks. 1819.
Religion a Social Principle. 1820.
A Discourse on the Evidences of Revealed Religion. 1821.
A Sermon Delivered at the Ordination of the Rev. Ezra Stiles Gannett. 1824.
Remarks on the Character and Writings of John Milton. 1826.
A Discourse, Preached at the Dedication of the Second Congregational Unitarian Church, New York. 1826.
Remarks on the Character of Napoleon Bonaparte: Occasioned by the Publication of Scott's Life of Napoleon. 1827.
A Discourse Delivered at the Installation of the Rev. Mellish Irving Motte, as Pastor of the South Congregational Society in Providence, Rhode Island. 1828.
Christian Biography: A Memoir of John Gallison, Esq. 1828.
A Continuation of the Remarks on the Character of Napoleon Bonaparte. 1828.
Sermons and Tracts. 1828.
A Sermon, Preached at the Annual Election. 1830.
Remarks on the Disposition Which Now Prevails to Form Associations. 1830.
The Importance and Means of a National Literature. 1830.
Discourses, Reviews, and Miscellanies. 1830.
Remarks on Physical Education. c. 1830.
Discourses. 1832.
The Future Life. 1834.
A Sermon Preached at the Ordination of Charles F. Barnard and Frederick T. Gray. 1834.

The Ministry of the Poor. 1835.
A Sermon on War. 1835.
Slavery. 1835.
Political Writings. 1835.
Works. 1835. 2 vols.
A Discourse Delivered at the Dedication of the Unitarian Congregational Church, in Newport, Rhode Island. 1836.
Letter to James G. Birney. 1836.
Letter on Catholicism, &c. 1836.
The Sunday School. 1837.
Letter on Creeds, &c. 1837.
Address on Temperance. 1837.
A Letter to the Abolitionists. 1837.
Remarks on Creeds, Intolerance, and Exclusion. 1837.
A Letter to the Hon. Henry Clay, on the Annexation of Texas to the United States. 1837.
A Tribute to the Memory of the Rev. Noah Worcester. 1837.
Remarks on the Character and Writings of Fenelon, Archbishop of Cambral. 1837.
Essays, Literary and Political. 1837.
Character of Napoleon and Other Essays, Literary and Philosophical. 1837. 2 vols.
Self-Culture. 1838.
The Worship of the Father, a Service of Gratitude and Joy. 1838.
A Discourse Delivered in Boston: Being a Tribute to the Memory of the Reverend Noah Webster. 1838.
Lecture on War. 1839.
Remarks on the Slavery Question, in a Letter to Jonathan Phillips, Esq. 1839.
Lectures on the Elevation of the Labouring Portion of the Community. 1840.
Christian Views of Human Suffering. 1840.
Letter to the Standing Committee of the Proprietors of the Meeting-House on Federal Street in the Town of Boston. 1840.
The Power of Unitarian Christianity to Produce an Enlightened and Fervent Piety. 1840.
A Discourse Occasioned by the Death of the Rev. Dr. Follen. 1840.
Emancipation. 1840.
Works. 1840.
The Obligation of a City to Care For and Watch Over the Moral Health of Its Members. 1841.
An Address Delivered before the Mercantile Library Company, of Philadelphia. 1841.
The Church: A Discourse Delivered in the First Congregational Unitarian Church of Philadelphia. 1841.
A Discourse on the Life and Character of the Rev. Joseph Tuckerman, D.D. 1841.
Works. 1841–43. 6 vols.
An Address Delivered at Lenox, on the First of August, 1842, the Anniversary of Emancipation in the British West Indies. 1842.
The Duty of the Free States; or, Remarks Suggested by the Case of the Creole. 1842. 2 parts.
A Discourse on the Church. 1843.
Thoughts, Selected from the Writings. Ed. Henry A. Miles. 1846.
Memoir; with Extracts from His Correspondence and Manuscripts. Ed. William Henry Channing. 1848. 3 vols.
Beauties of Channing. 1849.
A Selection from the Works. 1855.
The Perfect Life: In Twelve Discourses. Ed. William Henry Channing. 1873.

Complete Works. 1873.
Correspondence of William Ellery Channing and Lucy Aikin, from 1826 to 1874. Ed. Anna Letitia Le Breton. 1874.
Complete Works. 1880.
Note-Book. Ed. Grace Ellery Channing. 1887.
Discourses on War. Ed. Edwin D. Mead. 1903.
The Liberal Gospel. Ed. Charles H. Lyttle. 1925.
Channing Day by Day: Thoughts for Each Day Selected from the Writings. Ed. José Chapiro. 1948.
Unitarian Christianity and Other Essays. Ed. Irving H. Bartlett. 1957.
Selected Writings. Ed. David Robinson. 1985.

THOMAS ARNOLD (1795–1842)

The Effects of Distant Colonization on the Parent-State. 1815.
Quam Vim Habeat ad Informandos Juvenum Animos Poetarum Lectio? 1817.
The Christian Duty of Granting the Claims of the Roman Catholics. 1829.
Sermons. 1829–34. 3 vols.
The History of the Peloponnesian War by Thucydides (editor). 1830–35. 3 vols.
Address to the Inhabitants of Rugby about the Cholera Morbus. 1831.
Thirteen Letters on Our Social Condition, Addressed to the Editor of the Sheffield Courant. 1832.
Principles of Church Reform. 1833.
Postscript to Principles of Church Reform. 1833.
Psalms and Hymns, Selected for the Use of the Rugby Chapel (editor). 1835.
History of Rome. 1838–43. 3 vols.
Two Sermons on the Interpretation of Prophecy, Preached in the Chapel of Rugby School. 1839.
On the Divisions and Mutual Relations of Knowledge. 1839.
An Inaugural Lecture on the Study of Modern History. 1841.
Christian Life: Its Hopes, Its Hindrances, and Its Helps: Sermons, Preached Mostly in the Chapel of Rugby School. 1841.
Introductory Lectures on Modern History. 1842.
Fragment on the Church. 1844.
Life and Correspondence. Ed. Arthur Penrhyn Stanley. 1844. 2 vols.
Sermons Chiefly on the Interpretation of Scripture. Ed. Mary Arnold. 1845.
History of the Later Roman Commonwealth. 1845. 2 vols.
Miscellaneous Works. Ed. Arthur Penrhyn Stanley. 1845.
Arnold's Travelling Journals, with Extracts from the Life and Letters. Ed. Arthur Penrhyn Stanley. 1852.
Passages from the Sermons. 1857.
Sermons. Ed. Jane Arnold Forster. 1878. 6 vols.
Thomas Arnold on Education: A Selection from His Writings. Ed. T. W. Bamford. 1970.

NOAH WEBSTER (1758–1843)

A Grammatical Institute of the English Language. 1783–85. 3 parts.
Sketches of American Policy. 1785.
The New England Primer, Amended and Improved (editor). 1787.
An American Selection of Lessons in Reading and Speaking. 1787, 1804.
An Examination into the Leading Principles of the Federal Constitution Proposed by the Late Convention Held at Philadelphia. 1787.

The American Spelling Book. 1787, 1804.

Attention! or, New Thoughts on a Serious Subject: Being an Enquiry into the Excise Laws of Connecticut. 1789.

Dissertations on the English Language. 1789.

The carrier of the American Mercury, *presents . . .* 1790.

A Collection of Essays and Fugitiv Writings: On Moral, Historical, Political and Literary Subjects. 1790.

Connecticut Courant: The News-Boy's Address to His Customers. 1790.

The Little Reader's Assistant. 1790.

A Journal of the Transactions and Occurrences in the Settlement of Massachusetts and Other New-England Colonies, from the Year 1630 to 1644 by John Winthrop (editor). 1790.

The Prompter; or, A Commentary on Common Sayings and Subjects. 1791, 1803.

Effects of Slavery, on Morals and Industry. 1793.

The Revolution in France, Considered in Respect to Its Progress and Effects. 1794.

A Collection of Papers on the Subject of Bilious Fevers, Prevalent in the United States for a Few Years Past (editor). 1795.

Circular: To the Clergymen and Other Well Informed Gentlemen in the Several Towns of Connecticut. 1798.

A Letter to the Governors, Instructors and Trustees of the Universities, and Other Seminaries of Learning, in the United States, on the Errors of English Grammars. 1798.

An Oration Pronounced before the Citizens of New-Haven on the Anniversary of the Declaration of Independence of the United States. 1798.

A Brief History of Epidemic and Pestilential Diseases. 1799. 2 vols.

Ten Letters to Dr. Joseph Priestly, in Answer to His Letters *to the Inhabitants of Northumberland.* 1800.

A Rod for the Fool's Back. 1800.

A Letter to General Hamilton, Occasioned by His Letter to President Adams. 1800.

New-Haven, 1801: Sir, With a view to collect authentic facts . . . 1801.

Miscellaneous Papers, on Political and Commercial Subjects. 1802.

An Oration Pronounced before the Citizens of New Haven, on the Anniversary of the Declaration of Independence. 1802.

Elements of Useful Knowledge. 1802 [Volume 1]; 1804 [Volume 2]; 1806 [Volume 3]; 1812 [Volume 4; as *History of Animals*].

An Address to the Citizens of Connecticut. 1803.

A Compendious Dictionary of the English Language. 1806.

A Philosophical and Practical Grammar of the English Language. 1807.

A Dictionary of the English Language: For the Use of Common Schools in the United States. 1807.

A Letter to Dr. David Ramsay, of Charleston, (S.C.) Respecting the Errors in Johnson's Dictionary, and Other Lexicons. 1807.

Education of Youth in the United States. 1807.

The Peculiar Doctrines of the Gospel, Explained and Defended. 1809.

An Oration, Pronounced before the Knox and Warren Branches of the Washington Benevolent Society, at Amherst, on the Celebration of the Declaration of Independence. 1814.

A Letter to the Honourable John Pickering, on the Subject of His Vocabulary. 1817.

An Address, Delivered before the Hampshire, Franklin and Hampden Agricultural Society. 1818.

Letters to a Young Gentleman Commencing His Education. 1823.

An American Dictionary of the English Language. 1828 (2 vols.), 1841 (2 vols.).

The Elementary Spelling Book: Being an Improvement on the American Spelling Book. 1829.

Biography for the Use of Schools. 1830.

Series of Books for Systematic Instruction in the English Language. 1830.

The Elementary Primer; or, First Lessons for Children: Being an Introduction to The Elementary Spelling Book. 1831.

An Improved Grammar of the English Language. 1831.

To the Public: Lyman Cobb has lately published . . . 1831.

To the Friends of American Literature. c. 1831.

History of the United States. 1832.

A Dictionary for Primary Schools. 1833.

The New American Spelling Book. 1833.

The Holy Bible (editor). 1833.

Value of the Bible, and Excellence of the Christian Religion. 1834.

A Brief View. c. 1834.

Instructive and Entertaining Lessons for Youth. 1835.

The Teacher: A Supplement to The Elementary Spelling Book. 1836.

Genealogy. 1836.

The Little Franklin: Teaching Children to Read What They Daily Speak, and to Learn What They Ought to Know. 1836.

To the Friends of Literature. 1836.

Mistakes and Corrections. 1837.

A Letter to the Hon. Daniel Webster, on the Political Affairs of the United States. 1837.

Appeal to Americans. c. 1838.

A Manual of Useful Studies, for the Instruction of Young Persons of Both Sexes, in Families and Schools. 1839.

Observations on Language, and on the Errors of Class-Books. 1839.

A Collection of Papers on Political, Literary and Moral Subjects. 1843.

Notes on the Life of Noah Webster. Ed. Emily Ellsworth Fowler Ford. 1912. 2 vols.

Poems. Eds. Ruth Farquhar Warfel and Harry Redcay Warfel. 1936.

Letters on Yellow Fever Addressed to Dr. William Currie. Ed. Benjamin Spector. 1947.

Letters. Ed. Harry R. Warfel. 1953.

Noah Webster on Youth and Old Age. 1954.

On Being American: Selected Writings 1783–1828. Ed. Homer D. Babbidge, Jr. 1967.

ROBERT SOUTHEY (1774–1843)

The Fall of Robespierre: An Historic Drama (with Samuel Taylor Coleridge). 1794.

Poems (with Robert Lovell). 1795.

Joan of Arc. 1796.

Poems. 1797.

Letters Written during a Short Residence in Spain and Portugal, with Some Account of Spanish and Portugueze Poetry. 1797.

On the French Revolution by Jacques Necker (translator; with others). 1797.

The Annual Anthology (editor). 1799–1800. 2 vols.

Thalaba the Destroyer. 1801. 2 vols.

Amadis of Gaul by Vasco Lobeira (translator). 1803. 4 vols.

The Works of Thomas Chatterton (editor; with Joseph Cottle). 1803. 3 vols.

Madoc. 1805.

Metrical Tales and Other Poems. 1805.

Letters from England. 1807. 3 vols.

Palmerin of England by Francisco de Moraes, tr. Anthony Munday (editor). 1807. 4 vols.

The Remains of Henry Kirke White (editor). 1807. 2 vols.

Specimens of the Later English Poets (editor). 1807. 3 vols.

Chronicle of the Cid (translator; with John Hookham Frere). 1808.

The Curse of Kehama. 1810.

History of Brazil. 1810 [Volume 1]; 1817 [Volume 2]; 1819 [Volume 3].

Omniana; or, Horae Otiosiores (with Samuel Taylor Coleridge). 1812. 2 vols.

The Origin, Nature, and Object of the New System of Education. 1812.

An Exposure of the Misrepresentations and Calumnies in Mr. Marsh's Review of Sir George Barlow's Administration at Madras. 1813.

The Life of Nelson. 1813. 2 vols.

Roderick, the Last of the Goths. 1814.

Odes to His Royal Highness the Prince Regent, His Imperial Majesty the Emperor of Russia, and His Majesty the King of Prussia. 1814.

Minor Poems. 1815. 3 vols.

A Summary of the Life of Arthur, Duke of Wellington. 1816.

The Poet's Pilgrimage to Waterloo. 1816.

The Lay of the Laureate: Carmen Nuptiale. 1816.

Wat Tyler: A Dramatic Poem. 1817.

A Letter to William Smith, Esq., M.P. 1817.

The Byrth, Lyf, and Actes of King Arthur by Sir Thomas Malory (editor). 1817. 2 vols.

The Life of Wesley, and the Rise and the Progress of Methodism. 1820. 2 vols.

A Vision of Judgement. 1821.

The Expedition of Orsua and the Crimes of Aguirre. 1821.

Life of John, Duke of Marlborough. 1822.

History of the Peninsular War. 1823 [Volume 1]; 1827 [Volume 2]; 1832 [Volume 3].

The Book of the Church. 1824. 2 vols.

A Tale of Paraguay. 1825.

Vindiciae Ecclesiae Anglicanae: Letters to Charles Butler, Esq., Comprising Essays on the Romish Religion and Vindicating The Book of the Church. 1826.

All for Love and The Pilgrim to Compostella. 1829.

Sir Thomas More; or, Colloquies on the Progress and Prospects of Society. 1829. 2 vols.

Poetical Works. 1829.

The Pilgrim's Progress by John Bunyan (editor). 1830.

The Devil's Walk: A Poem by Professor Porson (with Samuel Taylor Coleridge). Ed. H. W. Montagu. 1830.

Select Works of the British Poets, from Chaucer to Jonson (editor). 1831.

Selections from the Poems. Ed. I. Moxon. 1831.

Essays Moral and Political. 1832. 2 vols.

Selections from the Prose Works. Ed. I. Moxon. 1832.

Lives of the British Admirals. 1833 [Volumes 1–2]; 1834 [Volume 3]; 1837 [Volume 4]; 1840 [Volume 5; with Robert Bell].

Letter to John Murray, Esq., "Touching" Lord Nugent. 1833.

The Doctor. 1834 [Volumes 1–2]; 1835 [Volume 3]; 1837 [Volume 4]; 1838 [Volume 5]; 1847 [Volumes 6–7; ed. J. W. Warter].

Horae Lyricae: Poems by Isaac Watts (editor). 1834.

The Works of William Cowper (editor). 1835–37. 15 vols.

Lives of Uneducated Poets. 1836.

Poetical Works. 1837–38. 10 vols.

The Life of the Rev. Andrew Bell (with C. C. Southey). 1844. 3 vols.

Select Biographies: Cromwell and Bunyan. 1844.

Oliver Newman: A New-England Tale (Unfinished), with Other Poetical Remains. Ed. H. Hill. 1845.

Robin Hood: A Fragment, with Other Fragments and Poems (with Caroline Southey). 1847.

Common-Place Book. Ed. J. W. Warter. 1849–50. 4 vols.

Life and Correspondence. Ed. C. C. Southey. 1849–50. 6 vols.

Review of Churchill's Poems. Ed. William Tooke. 1852.

Selections from the Letters. Ed. J. W. Warter. 1856. 4 vols.

Poetical Works. Ed. H. T. Tuckerman. 1860. 10 vols.

Correspondence with Caroline Bowles. Ed. Edward Dowden. 1881.

Poems. Ed. Edward Dowden. 1895.

Journal of a Tour in the Netherlands in the Autumn of 1815. 1902.

Poems. Ed. Maurice H. Fitzgerald. 1909.

Letters: A Selection. Ed. Maurice H. Fitzgerald. 1912.

Select Prose. Ed. Jacob Zeitlin. 1916.

Journal of a Tour in Scotland in 1819. Ed. C. H. Herford. 1929.

Journals of a Residence in Portugal 1800–1801, and a Visit to France 1838. Ed. Adolfo Cabral. 1960.

New Letters. Ed. Kenneth Curry. 1965. 2 vols.

A Choice of Southey's Verse. Ed. Geoffrey Grigson. 1970.

Letters to John May 1797 to 1838. Ed. Charles Ramos. 1976.

Contributions to the Morning Post. Ed. Kenneth Curry. 1984.

WASHINGTON ALLSTON (1779–1843)

The Sylphs of the Seasons, with Other Poems. 1813.

On Greenough's Group of the Angel and Child. c. 1837.

Monaldi: A Tale. 1841.

Lectures on Art, and Poems. Ed. Richard Henry Dana, Jr. 1850.

Outlines and Sketches. 1850.

Life and Letters. Ed. Jared B. Flagg. 1892.

WILLIAM BECKFORD (1760–1844)

Biographical Memoirs of Extraordinary Painters. 1780.

Dreams, Waking Thoughts, and Incidents: In a Series of Letters, from Various Parts of Europe. 1783.

Vathek. 1786 (as *An Arabian Tale*; tr. Samuel Henley), 1787 (French original).

Modern Novel Writing; or, The Elegant Enthusiast; and Interesting Emotions of Arabella Bloomville: A Rhapsodical Romance. 1796. 2 vols.

Azemia: A Descriptive and Sentimental Novel. 1797. 2 vols.

The Story of Al Raoui: A Tale from the Arabic. 1799.

A Dialogue in the Shades. 1819.

Epitaphs: Some of Which Have Appeared in the Literary Gazette *of March & April, 1823.* 1825.

Italy; with Sketches of Spain and Portugal. 1834. 2 vols.

Recollections of an Excursion to the Monasteries of Alcobaça and Batalha. 1835.

Life and Letters. Ed. Lewis Melville. 1910.

The Episodes of Vathek (tr. Frank T. Marzials). Ed. Lewis Melville. 1912.

Travel-Diaries. Ed. Guy Chapman. 1928. 2 vols.

The Vision; Liber Veritatis. Ed. Guy Chapman. 1930.

Journal in Portugal and Spain 1787–1788. Ed. Boyd Alexander. 1954.

Life at Fonthill 1807–1822, with Interludes in Paris and London: From the Correspondence of William Beckford. Ed. Boyd Alexander. 1957.

THOMAS CAMPBELL (1777–1844)

The Wounded Hussar. 1799.

The Pleasures of Hope, with Other Poems. 1799.

Poems. 1803.

Annals of Great Britain from the Ascension of George III to the Peace of Amiens. 1807. 3 vols.

Gertrude of Wyoming: A Pennsylvanian Tale, and Other Poems. 1809.

Poetical Works. Ed. Washington Irving. 1810. 2 vols.

Specimens of the British Poets, with Biographical and Critical Notes, and An Essay on English Poetry. 1819. 7 vols.

Poetical Works. 1822.

Miscellaneous Poems. 1824.

Theodric: A Domestic Tale, with Other Poems. 1824.

Inaugural Discourse on Being Installed Lord Rector of the University of Glasgow. 1827.

Poetical Works. 1828. 2 vols.

Poland: A Poem; to Which Are Added, Lines on the View from St. Leonard's. 1831.

Address of the Literary Polish Association to the People of Great Britain. 1832.

Life of Mrs. Siddons. 1834. 2 vols.

Lord Ullin's Daughter and Songs. c. 1835.

Letters from the South. 1837. 2 vols.

The Dramatic Works of William Shakespeare (editor). 1838.

Life of Petrarch. 1841. 2 vols.

The Pilgrim of Glencoe and Other Poems. 1842.

Poetical Works. 1845.

Poetical Works. Ed. W. Alfred Hill. 1851.

Complete Poetical Works. Ed. George Gilfillan. 1852.

Poetical Works. Ed. William Michael Rossetti. 1871.

Favorite Poems. 1877.

Poetical Works (with William Falconer). 1880.

The Pleasures of Hope and Gertrude of Wyoming. Ed. Henry Morley. 1891.

Selections from Campbell. Ed. W. T. Webb. 1902.

Poems. Ed. Lewis Campbell. 1904.

Complete Poetical Works. Ed. J. Logie Robertson. 1907.

JOHN STERLING (1806–1844)

Thoughts on the Foreign Policy of England. 1827.

FitzGeorge. 1832. 3 vols.

Arthur Coningsby. 1833. 3 vols.

Poems. 1839.

The Election. 1841.

Poetical Works. Ed. Rufus W. Griswold. 1842.

Strafford. 1843.

Essays and Tales. Ed. Julius Charles Hare. 1848. 2 vols.

Letters to a Friend. Ed. William Coningham. 1848.

A Correspondence between John Sterling and Ralph Waldo Emerson. Ed. Edward Waldo Emerson. 1897.

Letters to George Webbe Dasent 1838–1844. 1914.

CAROLINA OLIPHANT, BARONESS NAIRNE
(1766–1845)

Wha'll Be King But Charlie? c. 1835.

Life and Songs. Ed. Charles Rogers. 1869, 1872.

Songs. 1902.

Songs. 1911.

SYDNEY SMITH (1771–1845)

Six Sermons, Preached in Charlotte Chapel, Edinburgh. 1800.

A Sermon Preached at the Temple, upon the Conduct to Be Observed by the Established Church towards Catholics and Other Dissenters. 1807.

Two Letters on the Subject of the Catholics, to My Brother Abraham, Who Lives in the Country. 1807.

Three More Letters on the Subject of the Catholics, to My Brother Abraham, Who Lives in the Country. 1807.

Two More Letters (Being the 6th and 7th) on the Subject of the Catholics, to My Brother Abraham, Who Lives in the Country. 1808.

The Eighth, Ninth, and Last Letter on the Subject of the Catholics, to My Brother Abraham, Who Lives in the Country. 1808.

A Sermon Preached before His Grace the Archbishop of York, and the Clergy, at Malton. 1809.

Extracts from the Edinburgh Review. c. 1810.

The Lawyer That Tempted Christ. 1824.

Character of an English Judge. 1824.

The Judge That Smites Contrary to the Law. 1824.

Catholic Claims: Substance of a Speech Delivered at the Meeting of the Clergy of the Archdeaconry of Yorkshire. 1825.

A Sermon on Religious Charity. 1825.

A Letter to the Electors, upon the Catholic Question. 1826.

Mr. Dyson's Speech to the Freeholders on Reform. 1831.

Taunton Reform Meeting: Speech of Mr. Sydney Smith. 1831.

The New Reign: The Duties of Queen Victoria. 1837.

A Letter to the Archdeacon Singleton on the Ecclesiastical Commission. 1837.

A Letter to Lord John Russell on the Church Bills. 1838.

Second Letter to Archdeacon Singleton: Being the Third of the Cathedral Letters. 1838.

Third Letter to Archdeacon Singleton. 1839.

Ballot. 1839.

Works. 1839–40. 4 vols.

Letters on American Debts. 1843.

A Fragment on the Irish Roman Catholic Church. 1845.

Sermons Preached at St. Paul's Cathedral, the Foundling Hospital, and Several Churches in London, Together with Others Addressed to a County Congregation. 1846.

Elementary Sketches of Moral Philosophy, Delivered at the Royal Institution, in the Years 1804, 1805, and 1806. 1849.

The Letters of Peter Plymley, Essays, and Speeches. 1852. 3 vols.

Selections from the Writings. 1854. 2 vols.

Works. 1854. 3 vols.

Wit and Wisdom of the Rev. Sydney Smith. Ed. Evert A. Duyckinck. 1856.

Essays. 1874, 1880.

Essays Social and Political. 1874.

Selections. Ed. Ernest Rhys. 1892.

Bon-Mots of Sydney Smith and R. Brinsley Sheridan. Ed. Walter Jerrold. 1893.

The Letters of Peter Plymley, with Other Selected Writings, Sermons and Speeches. Ed. G. C. Heseltine. 1929.

Letters. Ed. Nowell C. Smith. 1953. 2 vols.

Selected Writings. Ed. W. H. Auden. 1956.

Selected Letters. Ed. Nowell C. Smith. 1956.

THOMAS HOOD (1799–1845)

Odes and Addresses to Great People (with J. H. Reynolds). 1825.

Whims and Oddities, in Prose and Verse. 1826.
National Tales. 1827. 2 vols.
Whims and Oddities, in Prose and Verse: Second Series. 1827.
The Plea of the Midsummer Fairies, Hero and Leander, Lycus the Centaur, and Other Poems. 1827.
The Epping Hunt. 1829.
The Dream of Eugene Aram. 1831.
Tylney Hall. 1834. 3 vols.
Hood's Own; or, Laughter from Year to Year. 1835.
Up the Rhine. 1840.
The Loves of Sally Brown and Ben the Carpenter. c. 1840.
Whimsicalities: A Periodical Gathering. 1844. 2 vols.
Poems. 1846. 2 vols.
Poems of Wit and Humour. 1847.
Poetical Works. 1856 (4 vols.), c. 1880 (5 vols.).
Humorous Poems. Ed. Epes Sargent. 1856.
The Headlong Career and Woful Ending of Precocious Piggy. Ed. Frances Freeling Broderip. 1859.
Fairy Land; or, Recreation for the Rising Generation (with Jane Hood). Ed. Frances Freeling Broderip. 1861.
Hood's Own: Second Series. Ed. Thomas Hood, Jr. 1861.
Works Comic and Serious, in Prose and Verse. Ed. Thomas Hood, Jr. 1862–63. 7 vols.
Serious Poems. Ed. Samuel Lucas. 1867.
Comic Poems. Ed. Samuel Lucas. 1867.
Works. Eds. Thomas Hood, Jr., and Frances Freeling Broderip. 1869–73. 10 vols.
Early Poems and Sketches. Ed. Frances Freeling Broderip. 1869.
Poetical Works. Ed. William Michael Rossetti. 1871–75. 2 vols.
Humorous Poems. Ed. Alfred Ainger. 1893.
Poems. Ed. Alfred Ainger. 1897. 2 vols.
Complete Poetical Works. Ed. Walter Jerrold. 1906.
Poems. Ed. A. T. Quiller-Couch. 1908.
Selections from Thomas Hood. 1928.
Thomas Hood and Charles Lamb: The Story of a Friendship: Being the Literary Reminiscences of Thomas Hood. Ed. Walter Jerrold. 1930.
Letters of Thomas Hood from the Dilke Papers in the British Museum. Ed. Leslie A. Marchand. 1945.
Poems. Ed. Clifford Dyment. 1948.
Selected Poems. Ed. John Clubbe. 1970.
Whimsicalities and Warnings. Ed. Julian Ennis. 1970.
Letters. Ed. Peter F. Morgan. 1973.

JOHN HOOKHAM FRERE (1769–1846)

Chronicle of the Cid (translator; with Robert Southey). 1808.
Prospectus and Specimen of an Intended National Work, Intended to Comprise the Most Interesting Particulars Relating to King Arthur and His Round Table. 1817–18. 2 vols.
Fables for Five Years Old. 1820.
The Frogs by Aristophanes (translator). 1839.
Psalms, &c. (translator). c. 1839.
Aristophanes: A Metrical Version of the Acharnians, the Knights, and the Birds (translator). 1839–40. 3 parts.
Theognis Restitutus: The Personal History of the Poet Theognis, Deduced from an Analysis of His Existing Fragments; a Hundred of These Fragments Translated, or Paraphrased in English Metre. 1842.
National Poems: I. King Arthur and His Round Table; or, The Monks and the Giants; II. Athelstan's Victory and Other Miscellaneous Writings. Ed. Richard Herne Shepherd. 1867.

Works in Verse and Prose. 1872. 2 vols.
Parodies and Other Burlesque Pieces (with George Canning and George Ellis). Ed. Henry Morley. 1890.
Aristophanes: Four Plays (translator). Ed. W. W. Merry. 1907.

MARY LAMB (1764–1847)

Tales from Shakespear (with Charles Lamb). 1807. 2 vols.
Mrs. Leicester's School (with Charles Lamb). 1809.
Poetry for Children (with Charles Lamb). 1809.
[*Beauty and the Beast; or, A Rough Outside with a Gentle Heart* (with Charles Lamb). 1811.]
Mary and Charles Lamb: Poems, Letters and Remains. Ed. William Carew Hazlitt. 1874.
The Lambs: Their Lives, Their Friends, and Their Correspondence. Ed. William Carew Hazlitt. 1897.
Works of Charles and Mary Lamb. Ed. E. V. Lucas. 1903–05. 7 vols.
Works of Charles and Mary Lamb. Ed. Thomas Hutchinson. 1908. 2 vols.
The Letters of Charles Lamb; to Which Are Added Those of His Sister Mary Lamb. Ed. E. V. Lucas. 1935. 3 vols.
Letters of Charles and Mary Ann Lamb. Ed. Edwin W. Marrs. 1975. 2 vols.

THOMAS CHALMERS (1780–1847)

Observations on a Passage in Mr Playfair's Letter to the Lord Provost of Edinburgh Relative to the Mathematical Pretensions of the Scottish Clergy. 1805.
An Enquiry into the Extent and Stability of National Resources. 1808.
The Substance of a Speech, Delivered in the General Assembly, Respecting the Merits of the Late Bill for the Augmentation of Stipends to the Clergy of Scotland. 1809.
The Two Great Instruments Appointed for the Propagation of the Gospel, and the Duty of the Christian Public to Keep Them Both in Vigorous Operation. 1813.
A Sermon, Preached before the Society for Relief of the Destitute Sick. 1813.
The Utility of Missions Ascertained by Experience. 1814.
The Influence of Bible Societies on the Temporal Necessities of the Poor. 1814.
The Evidence and Authority of the Christian Revelation. 1814.
A Sermon Preached before the Society in Scotland for Propagating Christian Knowledge. 1814.
The Duty of Giving an Immediate Diligence to the Business of the Christian Life. 1815.
Thoughts on Universal Peace. 1816.
Scripture References, Designed for the Use of Parents, Teachers, and Private Christians. 1817.
A Sermon Delivered in the Tron Church, Glasgow, on Wednesday, Nov. 19, 1817, the Day of the Funeral of Her Royal Highness the Princess Charlotte of Wales. 1817.
A Series of Discourses on the Christian Revelation, Viewed in Connection with the Modern Astronomy. 1817.
The Doctrine of Christian Charity Applied to the Case of Religious Differences. 1818.
Discourses and Sermons. 1818. 2 vols.
Considerations on the System of Parochial Schools in Scotland, and on the Advantage of Establishing Them in Large Towns. 1819.
Sermons Preached in the Tron Church, Glasgow. 1819.
The Application of Christianity to the Commercial and Ordinary Affairs of Life. 1820.
The Importance of Civil Government to Society, and the Duty of Christians in Regard to It. 1820.

The Christian and Civic Economy of Large Towns. 1821–26. 3 vols.

A Speech Delivered at the General Assembly of the Presbytery at Edinburgh. 1821.

A Speech, Delivered before the General Assembly of the Church of Scotland, Explanatory of the Measures Which Have Been Successively Pursued in St. John's Parish, Glasgow, for the Extinction of Its Compulsory Pauperism. 1822.

Works. 1822. 3 vols.

Sermons Preached in St. John's Church, Glasgow. 1823.

Statement in Regard to the Pauperism of Glasgow, from the Experience of the Last Eight Years. 1823.

A Speech, Delivered before the Synod of Glasgow and Ayr, in the Case of Principal M'Farlane, on the Subject of Pluralities. 1823.

Sermons Preached on Public Occasions. 1823. 7 parts.

On the Parliamentary Means for the Abolition of Pauperism in England. 1824.

Speeches and Tracts. 1824. 6 parts.

A Few Thoughts on the Abolition of Colonial Slavery. 1826.

On the Cruelty to Animals. 1826.

On the Respect Due to Antiquity. 1827.

On the Use and Abuse of Literary and Ecclesiastical Endowments. 1827.

The Effect of Man's Wrath in the Agitation of Religious Controversies. 1827.

Speech on the Catholic Question, at the Pro-Catholic Meeting, Edinburgh. 1829.

Second Speech on the Catholic Question. 1829.

Sermons on the Depravity of Human Nature. 1829.

Works. 1830.

A Sermon, Preached in St. George's Church, Edinburgh, on the Occasion of the Death of the Rev. Dr. Andrew Thomson. 1831.

The Efficacy of Prayer. 1832.

Evidence Given by the Rev. T. Chalmers and the Right Rev. J. Doyle, before a Select Committee of the House of Commons on the State of Ireland. 1832.

Letter to the Royal Commissioners for the Visitation of Colleges in Scotland. 1832.

On Political Economy, in Connexion with the Moral State and Moral Prospects of Society. 1832.

The Supreme Importance of a Right Moral to a Right Economical State of the Community. 1832.

Survey of the State of Education. 1833.

A Sermon Preached in the National Scotch Church, Regent Square. 1833.

On the Power, Wisdom and Goodness of God as Manifested in the Adaptation of External Nature to the Moral and Intellectual Constitution of Man. 1833. 2 vols.

Churches and Chapels; or, The Necessity and Proper Object of an Endowment. 1834.

Specimens of the Ecclesiastical Destitution of Scotland, in Various Parts of the Country. 1835.

The Cause of Church Extension, and the Question Shortly Stated between Churchmen and Dissenters in Regard to It. 1835.

On the Evils Which the Established Church in Edinburgh Has Already Suffered, and Suffers Still in Virtue of the Seat-Letting Being in the Hands of the Magistrates. 1835.

The Right Ecclesiastical Economy of a Large Town. 1835.

Reply to the Attempt to Connect the Cause of Church Accommodation with Party Politics. 1835.

Speech on the Proceedings of the Church Deputation in London. 1835.

Report of the Committee of the General Assembly of the Church of Scotland on Church Extension. 1835.

An Attempt to Point Out the Duty Which the Church Owes the People of Scotland. 1836.

On Preaching to the Common People. 1836.

Works. 1836–42. 25 vols.

Five Lectures on Predestination. 1837.

A Conference with Certain Ministers and Elders of the Church of Scotland, on the Subject of the Moderatorship of the Next General Assembly. 1837.

Church Establishments Defended. 1837.

Supplement to His Late Pamphlet on the Subject of the Moderatorship of the Next General Assembly. 1837.

The Messiah's Deity Considered (with James Orr). 1837.

Lectures on the Epistle of Paul the Apostle to the Romans. 1837–42. 4 vols.

Lectures on the Establishment and Extension of National Churches. 1838.

Substance of a Speech Delivered in the General Assembly, Respecting the Decision of the House of Lords in the Case of Auchterarder. 1839.

Remarks on the Present Position of the Church of Scotland: Occasioned by the Publication of a Letter from the Dean of Faculty to the Lord Chancellor. 1839.

A Course of Lectures on Butler's Analogy of Religion. 1839.

Paley's Evidences of Christianity. 1839.

What Ought the Church and the People of Scotland to Do Now? Being a Pamphlet on the Principles of the Church Question. 1840.

Speech on the Non-Intrusion Question. 1840.

Congregational Sermons. c. 1840.

On the Sufficiency of a Parochial System, without a Poor Rate, for the Right Management of the Poor. 1841.

A Sermon Preached before the Convocation of Ministers in St. George's Church, Edinburgh. 1842.

The Addresses Delivered at the Commencement and Conclusion of the First General Assembly of the Free Church of Scotland. 1843.

Considerations on the Economics of the Free Church for 1844. 1844.

Sermons and Discourses. 1844. 2 vols.

On the Economics of the Free Church of Scotland. 1845.

On the Evangelical Alliance: Its Design, Its Difficulties, Its Proceedings, and Its Prospects; with Practical Suggestions. 1846.

Letter on American Slave-Holding. 1846.

Churches and Schools for the Working Class. 1846.

An Earnest Appeal to the Free Church of Scotland on the Subject of Its Economics. 1846.

Miscellanies. 1847.

Refusal of Sites: Evidence of the Rev. Dr. Chalmers, Extracted from the Third Report of the Parliamentary Committee. 1847.

Posthumous Works. Ed. William Hanna. 1847–49. 9 vols.

Horae Biblicae Quotidianae: Daily Scripture Readings. 1853. 2 vols.

A Selection from the Correspondence. Ed. William Hanna. 1853.

Select Works. Ed. William Hanna. 1854–79. 12 vols.

Select Sermons. 1859.

The Correspondence between Dr. Chalmers and the Earl of Aberdeen in the Years 1839 and 1840. Ed. Grace Chalmers Wood. 1893.

Chalmers on Charity. Ed. N. Masterman. 1900.

Dr. Chalmers on the Poor Laws. Ed. Grace Chalmers Wood. 1911.

The Opinions of Dr. Chalmers concerning Political Economy and Social Reform. Ed. Grace Chalmers Wood. 1912.

Problems of Poverty: Selections from the Economic and Social Writings. Ed. Henry Hunter. 1912.

ISAAC D'ISRAELI (1766–1848)

A Defence of Poetry. 1790.

Curiosities of Literature. 1791, 1793–1817 (3 vols.).

A Dissertation on Anecdotes. 1793.

Domestic Anecdotes of the French Nation during the Last Thirty Years. 1794.

An Essay on the Manners and Genius of the Literary Character. 1795.

Miscellanies; or, Literary Recreations. 1796.

Vaurien; or, Sketches of the Times. 1797. 2 vols.

Mejnoun and Leila: The Arabian Petrarch and Laura. 1797.

Romances. 1799.

Narrative Poems. 1803.

Flim-Flams!; or, The Life and Errors of My Uncle, and the Amours of My Aunt! 1805. 3 vols.

Despotism; or, The Fall of the Jesuits: A Political Romance. 1811. 2 vols.

Calamities of Authors. 1812. 2 vols.

Quarrels of Authors; or, Some Memoirs for Our Literary History. 1814. 3 vols.

An Inquiry into the Literary and Political Character of James the First. 1816.

The Literary Character Illustrated by the History of Men of Genius. 1818, 1822 (2 vols.).

A Second Series of Curiosities of Literature. 1823. 3 vols.

Psyche. c. 1823.

Commentaries on the Life and Reign of Charles the First, King of England. 1828–31. 5 vols.

Eliot, Hampden, and Pym. 1832.

The Genius of Judaism. 1833.

Curiosities of Literature (First and Second Series). 1834. 6 vols.

The Illustrator Illustrated. 1838.

Miscellanies of Literature. 1840.

Amenities of Literature. 1841. 2 vols.

A Letter to C. P. Cooper, Esq., 26th April 1829. 1857.

Works. Ed. Benjamin Disraeli. 1858–59. 7 vols.

FREDERICK MARRYAT (1792–1848)

A Code of Signals for the Use of Vessels Employed in the Merchant Service. 1817.

Suggestions for the Abolition of the Present System of Impressment in the Naval Service. 1822.

The Naval Officer; or, Scenes and Adventures in the Life of Frank Mildmay. 1829. 3 vols.

The King's Own. 1830. 3 vols.

Newton Forster; or, The Merchant Service. 1832. 3 vols.

Peter Simple. 1834. 4 vols.

Jacob Faithful. 1834. 3 vols.

The Pacha of Many Tales. 1835. 3 vols.

Japhet in Search of a Father. 1836. 3 vols.

The Pirate and The Three Cutters. 1836.

Mr. Midshipman Easy. 1836. 3 vols.

The Diary of a Blase. 1836.

The Floral Telegraph: A New Mode of Communication by Floral Signals. 1836.

Rattlin the Reefer by Edward Howard (editor). 1836. 3 vols.

Works. 1836. 2 vols.

Snarleyyow; or, The Dog Fiend. 1837. 3 vols.

The Phantom Ship. 1839. 3 vols.

A Diary in America, with Remarks on Its Institutions. 1839. 3 vols.

Poor Jack. 1840. 12 parts.

Olla Podrida. 1840. 3 vols.

Joseph Rushbrook; or, The Poacher. 1841. 3 vols.

Masterman Ready; or, The Wreck of the Pacific. 1841–42. 3 vols.

Percival Keene. 1842. 3 vols.

Narrative of the Travels and Adventures of Monsieur Violet in California, Sonora, and Western Texas. 1843. 3 vols.

The Settlers in Canada. 1844. 2 vols.

The Mission; or, Scenes in Africa. 1845. 2 vols.

The Privateer's-man, One Hundred Years Ago. 1846. 2 vols.

The Children of the New Forest. 1847. 2 vols.

The Little Savage. Ed. Frank S. Marryat. 1848–49. 2 vols.

Valerie: An Autobiography. 1849. 2 vols.

Novels and Tales. c. 1850.

Life and Letters. Ed. Florence Marryat. 1872. 2 vols.

Novels. Ed. W. L. Courtney. 1896–98. 24 vols.

Novels. Ed. R. Brimley Johnson. 1896–98. 24 vols.

Works. 1905. 12 vols.

Readings from Marryat. Ed. Herbert Hayens. 1924.

The Marryat Book: Scenes from the Works of Captain Marryat. Ed. Harrison Dale. 1930.

EMILY BRONTË (1818–1848)

Poems by Currer, Ellis, and Acton Bell (with Charlotte and Anne Brontë). 1846.

Wuthering Heights. 1847. 2 vols.

Wuthering Heights and Agnes Grey (by Anne Brontë), *with a Biographical Notice of the Authors, a Selection from Their Literary Remains, and a Preface by Currer Bell.* 1850.

The Life and Works of Charlotte Brontë and Her Sisters. 1872–73. 7 vols.

The Works of Charlotte, Emily, and Anne Brontë. Ed. F. J. S. 1893. 12 vols.

The Life and Works of the Sisters Brontë. Eds. Mrs. Humphry Ward and Clement K. Shorter. 1899–1903. 7 vols.

The Novels and Poems of Charlotte, Emily, and Anne Brontë. 1901–07. 7 vols.

The Works of Charlotte, Emily, and Anne Brontë. Ed. Temple Scott. 1901. 12 vols.

Poems by Charlotte, Emily, and Anne Brontë. 1902.

Poems. Ed. Arthur Symons. 1906.

The Brontës: Life and Letters. Ed. Clement K. Shorter. 1908. 2 vols.

Complete Works. Eds. Clement K. Shorter and W. Robertson Nicoll. 1910–11. 2 vols.

Complete Poems. Eds. Clement K. Shorter and C. W. Hatfield. 1923.

The Shakespeare Head Brontë (with Charlotte and Anne Brontë). Eds. Thomas J. Wise and John Alexander Symington. 1931–38. 19 vols.

The Brontës: Their Lives, Friendships, and Correspondence. Eds. Thomas J. Wise and John Alexander Symington. 1932. 4 vols.

Two Poems: Love's Rebuke, Remembrance. Ed. Fanny E. Ratchford. 1934.

Gondal Poems: Now First Published from the MS. in the British Museum. Eds. Helen Brown and Joan Mott. 1938.

Complete Poems. Ed. C. W. Hatfield. 1941.

Five Essays Written in French by Emily Jane Brontë. Tr. Lorine W. Nagel. Ed. Fanny E. Ratchford. 1948.

Complete Poems. Ed. Philip Henderson. 1951.

A Selection of Poems. Ed. Muriel Spark. 1952.

Gondal's Queen: A Novel in Verse. Ed. Fanny E. Ratchford. 1955.

Poems. Ed. Rosemary Harthill. 1973.

The Novels of Charlotte, Emily, and Anne Brontë. Eds. Hilda Marsden, Ian Jack et al. 1976– .

Selected Poems (with Anne and Charlotte Brontë). Eds. Tom Winnifrith and Edward Chitham. 1985.

The Brontës: Selected Poems. Ed. Juliet R. Barker. 1985.

MARIA EDGEWORTH (1768–1849)

Adelaide and Theodore by Stéphanie, Marquise de Genlis (translator). 1783.

Letters for Literary Ladies, to Which Is Added An Essay on the Noble Science of Self-Justification. 1795.

The Parent's Assistant; or, Stories for Children. 1795 (3 vols.), 1800 (6 vols.).

Practical Education. 1798. 2 vols.

A Rational Primer (with Richard Lovell Edgeworth). 1799.

Castle Rackrent, an Hibernian Tale: Taken from Facts, and from the Manners of the Irish Squires, before the Year 1782. 1800.

Early Lessons. 1801. 10 vols.

Moral Tales for Young People. 1801. 5 vols.

Belinda. 1801. 3 vols.

Essay on Irish Bulls (with Richard Lovell Edgeworth). 1802.

Popular Tales. 1804. 3 vols.

The Modern Griselda. 1805.

Leonora. 1806. 2 vols.

Essays on Professional Education (with Richard Lovell Edgeworth). 1809.

Tales of Fashionable Life. 1809 [Vols. 1–3]; 1812 [Vols. 4–6].

Cottage Dialogues among the Irish Peasantry by Mary Leadbeater (editor). 1811.

Continuation of Early Lessons. 1814. 2 vols.

Patronage. 1814. 4 vols.

Readings on Poetry (with Richard Lovell Edgeworth). 1816.

Harrington and Ormond: Tales. 1817. 3 vols.

Comic Dramas. 1817.

Memoirs of Richard Lovell Edgeworth, Esq. (with Richard Lovell Edgeworth). 1820. 2 vols.

Rosamond: A Sequel to Early Lessons. 1821. 2 vols.

Frank: A Sequel to Frank in Early Lessons. 1822. 3 vols.

Works. 1822–25. 13 vols.

Tales and Miscellaneous Pieces. 1825. 14 vols.

Harry and Lucy Concluded: Being the Last Part of Early Lessons. 1825. 4 vols.

Little Plays for Children. 1827.

Garry Owen; or, The Snow-Woman, and Poor Bob, the Chimney-Sweeper. 1832.

Tales and Novels. 1832–33. 18 vols.

Helen. 1834. 3 vols.

Orlandino. 1848.

A Memoir of Maria Edgeworth, with a Selection from Her Letters. Ed. Frances Anne Edgeworth. 1867. 3 vols.

Classic Tales. 1883.

Life and Letters. Ed. Augustus J. C. Hare. 1894. 2 vols.

Tales from Maria Edgeworth. Ed. Austin Dobson. 1903.

Tales That Never Die. Ed. Charles Walsh. 1908.

Selections from Her Works. Ed. Sir Malcolm Cotter Seton. 1915.

The Most Unfortunate Day of My Life: Being a Hitherto Unpublished Story, Together with The Purple Jar and Other Stories. 1931.

Chosen Letters. Ed. F. V. Barry. 1931.

Letters (with Anna Laetitia Barbauld). Ed. Walter Sidney Scott. 1953.

Letters from England 1813–1844. Ed. Christina Colvin. 1971.

Maria Edgeworth in France and Switzerland: Selections from the Edgeworth Family Letters. Ed. Christina Colvin. 1979.

EBENEZER ELLIOTT (1781–1849)

The Vernal Walk. 1801.

The Soldier and Other Poems. 1810.

Night: A Descriptive Poem. 1818.

Peter Faultless to His Brother Simon; Tales of Night, in Rhyme, and Other Poems. 1820.

Love; to Which Is Added, The Giaour: A Satirical Poem. 1823.

Scotch Nationality: A Vision. 1824.

The Village Patriarch. 1829.

Corn-Law Rhymes: The Ranter. 1830.

The Splendid Village, Corn-Law Rhymes, and Other Poems. 1833.

An Address to the People of England. 1834.

The Village Patriarch, Love, and Other Poems. 1834.

Kerhonah, The Vernal Walk, and Other Poems. 1835.

Poetical Works. 1840.

Poems. Ed. Rufus W. Griswold. 1844.

Poetical Works. 1844. 3 vols.

More Verse and Prose. 1850. 3 vols.

Poetical Works. Ed. Edwin Elliott. 1876. 2 vols.

Corn-Law Rhymes and Other Verses. 1904.

MARGUERITE, COUNTESS OF BLESSINGTON (1789–1849)

Sketches and Fragments. 1822.

The Magic Lantern; or, Sketches and Scenes in the Metropolis. 1822.

Journal of a Tour through the Netherlands to Paris in 1821. 1822.

Rambles in Waltham Forest: A Stranger's Contribution to the Triennial Sale for the Benefit of the Wanstead Lying-in Charity. 1827.

Ella Stratford; or, The Orphan Child. c. 1830.

The Repealers. 1833. 3 vols.

Heath's Book of Beauty (editor). 1834–47. 14 vols.

Conversations of Lord Byron with the Countess of Blessington. 1834.

The Two Friends. 1835. 2 vols.

The Confessions of an Elderly Gentleman. 1836.

Gems of Beauty. 1836–40. 4 vols.

The Honey-moon and Other Tales. 1837.

The Victims of Society. 1837. 3 vols.

Flowers of Loveliness (with Letitia Elizabeth Landon and Thomas Haynes Bayley). 1838.

Works. 1838. 2 vols.

The Confessions of an Elderly Lady. 1838.

The Governess. 1839. 2 vols.

The Idler in Italy. 1839. 3 vols.

Desultory Thoughts and Reflections. 1839.

The Belle of a Season. 1840.

The Idler in France. 1841. 2 vols.

The Lottery of Life. 1842. 3 vols.

Meredith. 1843. 3 vols.

Etiquette of Courtship and Marriage. 1844.

Strathern; or, Life at Home and Abroad: A Story of the Present Day. 1845. 4 vols.

The Memoirs of a Femme de Chambre. 1846. 3 vols.

Lionel Deerhurst; or, Fashionable Life under the Regency by Barbara Hemphill (editor). 1846. 3 vols.
Marmaduke Herbert; or, The Fatal Error. 1847. 3 vols.
Country Quarters. 1850. 3 vols.
Literary Life and Correspondence. Ed. R. R. Madden. 1855. 2 vols.
Conversations of Lord Byron. Ed. Ernest J. Lovell, Jr. 1969.

HARTLEY COLERIDGE (1796–1849)

Poems. 1833. Vol. 1 only.
Biographia Borealis; or, Lives of Distinguished Northerns. 1833, 1852 (as *Lives of Northern Worthies*; ed. Derwent Coleridge; 3 vols.).
The Dramatic Works of Massinger and Ford (editor). 1840.
Essays and Marginalia. Ed. Derwent Coleridge. 1851. 2 vols.
Poems. Ed. Derwent Coleridge. 1851. 2 vols.
Poetical Works of Bowles, Lamb, and Hartley Coleridge. Ed. William Tirebuck. 1887.
Poems. Ed. William Bailey-Kempling. 1903.
Poems. 1907.
Complete Poetical Works. Ed. Ramsay Colles. 1908.
Essays on Parties in Poetry and on the Character of Hamlet. Ed. John Drinkwater. 1925.
Poems. 1927.
Letters. Eds. Grace Evelyn Griggs and Earl Leslie Griggs. 1936.
New Poems, Including a Selection from His Published Poetry. Ed. Earl Leslie Griggs. 1942.

THOMAS LOVELL BEDDOES (1803–1849)

The Improvisatore, with Other Poems. 1821.
The Bride's Tragedy. 1822.
Death's Jest-Book; or, The Fool's Tragedy. 1850.
Poems Posthumous and Collected. Ed. T. F. Kelsall. 1851. 2 vols.
Poetical Works. Ed. Edmund Gosse. 1890. 2 vols.
Letters. Ed. Edmund Gosse. 1894.
Poems. Ed. Ramsay Colles. 1907.
Complete Works. Ed. Edmund Gosse. 1928. 2 vols.
Thomas Lovell Beddoes: An Anthology. Ed. F. L. Lucas. 1932.
Works. Ed. H. W. Donner. 1935.
Plays and Poems. Ed. H. W. Donner. 1950.

JAMES CLARENCE MANGAN (1803–1849)

Anthologia Germanica (translator). 1845. 2 vols.
The Poets and Poetry of Munster, ed. J. O'Daly (translator). 1849.
The Tribes of Ireland: A Satire by Aenghus O'Daly (translator). 1852.
Poems. Ed. John Mitchel. 1859.
Essays in Prose and Verse. Ed. C. P. Meehan. 1884.
Irish and Other Poems. 1886.
Selected Poems. Ed. Louise Imogen Guiney. 1897.
Poems. Ed. D. J. O'Donoghue. 1903.
Prose Writings. Ed. D. J. O'Donoghue. 1904.
Autobiography. Ed. James Kilroy. 1968.

EDGAR ALLAN POE (1809–1849)

Tamerlane and Other Poems. 1827.
Al Aaraaf, Tamerlane, and Minor Poems. 1829.
Poems. 1831.
The Narrative of Arthur Gordon Pym of Nantucket. 1838.
The Conchologist's First Book. 1839.
Tales of the Grotesque and Arabesque. 1840. 2 vols.

Prospectus of The Penn Magazine. 1840.
The Murders in the Rue Morgue; The Man That Was Used Up. 1843.
Tales. 1845.
The Raven and Other Poems. 1845.
Mesmerism "in Articulo Mortis." 1846.
Prospectus of The Stylus. 1848.
Eureka: A Prose Poem. 1848.
Works. Ed. Rufus W. Griswold. 1850–56. 4 vols.
Tales of Mystery and Imagination. 1855.
Works. Ed. John H. Ingram. 1874–75. 4 vols.
Works. Ed. Richard Henry Stoddard. 1884. 8 vols.
Works. Eds. Edmund Clarence Stedman and George Edward Woodberry. 1894–95. 10 vols.
Complete Works. Ed. James A. Harrison. 1902. 17 vols.
Last Letters to Sarah Helen Whitman. Ed. James A. Harrison. 1909.
Complete Poems. Ed. J. H. Whitty. 1911.
Poems. Ed. Killis Campbell. 1917.
Letters. Ed. Mary Newton Stanard. 1925.
Best Known Works. Ed. Hervey Allen. 1931.
Complete Poems and Stories. Ed. Arthur Hobson Quinn. 1946. 2 vols.
Letters. Ed. John Ward Ostrom. 1948. 2 vols.
Selected Prose, Poetry, and Eureka. Ed. W. H. Auden. 1950.
Literary Criticism. Ed. Robert L. Hough. 1965.
Poems. Ed. Floyd Stovall. 1965.
Collected Works. Eds. Thomas Ollive Mabbott et al. 1969– .
The Science Fiction of Edgar Allan Poe. Ed. Harold Beaver. 1976.

ANNE BRONTË (1820–1849)

Poems by Currer, Ellis, and Acton Bell (with Emily and Charlotte Brontë). 1846.
Agnes Grey. 1847.
The Tenant of Wildfell Hall. 1848. 3 vols.
Wuthering Heights (by Emily Brontë) *and Agnes Grey, with a Biographical Notice of the Authors, a Selection from Their Literary Remains, and a Preface by Currer Bell.* 1850.
The Life and Works of Charlotte Brontë and Her Sisters. 1872–73. 7 vols.
The Works of Charlotte, Emily, and Anne Brontë. Ed. F. J. S. 1893. 12 vols.
The Life and Works of the Sisters Brontë. Eds. Mrs. Humphry Ward and Clement K. Shorter. 1899–1903. 7 vols.
Self-Communion. 1900.
The Works of Charlotte, Emily, and Anne Brontë. Ed. Temple Scott. 1901. 12 vols.
The Novels and Poems of Charlotte, Emily, and Anne Brontë. 1901–07. 7 vols.
Poems by Charlotte, Emily, and Anne Brontë. 1902.
The Brontës: Life and Letters. Ed. Clement K. Shorter. 1908. 2 vols.
Dreams and Other Poems. 1917.
Complete Poems. Ed. Clement K. Shorter. 1920.
The Shakespeare Head Brontë (with Emily and Charlotte Brontë). Eds. Thomas J. Wise and John Alexander Symington. 1931–38. 19 vols.
The Brontës: Their Lives, Friendships, and Correspondence. Eds. Thomas J. Wise and John Alexander Symington. 1932. 4 vols.
The Novels of Charlotte, Emily, and Anne Brontë. Eds. Hilda Marsden, Ian Jack et al. 1976–
Poems. Ed. Edward Chitham. 1979.

Selected Poems (with Emily and Charlotte Brontë). Eds. Tom Winnifrith and Edward Chitham. 1985.

The Brontës: Selected Poems. Ed. Juliet R. Barker. 1985.

WILLIAM LISLE BOWLES (1762–1850)

Fourteen Sonnets, Elegiac and Descriptive, Written during a Tour. 1789, 1789, 1798 (as *Sonnets, and Other Poems*).

Verses to John Howard, F.R.S., on His State of Prisons and Lazarettos. 1789.

The Grave of Howard. 1790.

Verses on the Benevolent Institution of the Philanthropic Society, for Protecting the Children of Vagrants and Criminals. 1790.

A Poetical Address to the Right Honourable Edmund Burke. 1791.

Elegy Written at the Hot-Wells, Bristol. 1791.

Monody, Written at Matlock, October 1791. 1791.

A Sermon Preached at the Cathedral Church of Sarum. 1795.

Elegiac Stanzas, Written during Sickness at Bath. 1796.

Hope: An Allegorical Sketch, on Recovering Slowly from Sickness. 1796.

St. Michael's Mount. 1798.

Commbe Ellen. 1798.

Song of the Battle of the Nile. 1799.

A Discourse Delivered to the Military Associations for the Town and District of Shaftesbury. 1799.

Poems. 1801.

A Sermon Preached at the Anniversary Meeting of the Sons of the Clergy. 1801.

The Sorrows of Switzerland. 1801.

The Picture: Verses Suggested by a Magnificent Landscape of Rubens. 1803.

The Spirit of Discovery; or, The Conquest of the Ocean. 1804.

Bowden Hill: The Banks of the Wye. 1806.

The Works of Alexander Pope (editor). 1806. 10 vols.

The Little Villager's Verse Book. c. 1806.

Poems, Never Before Published, Written Chiefly at Bremhill. 1809.

The Missionary. 1813, 1815, 1835 (as *The Ancient Missionary of Chili*).

Sermons on Some Important Points Respecting the Faith, the Feelings, the Spirit, and the Dispositions of Christians. 1815.

Vindiciae Wykehamicae; or, A Vindication of Winchester College. 1818.

The Plain Bible, and the Protestant Church in England. 1818.

Thoughts on the Increase of Crimes, the Education of the Poor, and the National Schools. c. 1818.

The Invariable Principles of Poetry. 1819.

A Reply to an "Unsentimental Sort of Critic," The Reviewer of Spence's Anecdotes in the Quarterly Review for October 1820. 1820.

A Vindication of the Late Editor of Pope's Works, from Some Charges Brought against Him, by a Writer in the Quarterly Review. 1821.

Two Letters to the Right Honourable Lord Byron. 1821.

The Grave of the Last Saxon; or, The Legend of the Curfew. 1822.

A Voice from St. Peter's and St. Paul's. 1823.

The Church and Parochial School. 1823.

Ellen Gray; or, The Dead Maiden's Curse. 1823.

Charity. 1823.

A Final Appeal to the Literary Public, Relative to Pope. 1825.

Lessons in Criticism to William Roscoe, Esq. 1826.

Paulus Parochialis; or, A Plain and Practical View of the Objects, Arguments, and Connection of St. Paul's Epistle to the Romans. 1826.

Days Departed; or, Banwell Hill: A Lay of the Severn Sea. 1828.

The Parochial History of Bremhull, in the Country of Wilts. 1828.

Hermes Britannicus: A Dissertation on the Celtic Deity Teutates. 1828.

St. Paul, the First Christian Missionary at Athens. 1828.

The Poetical Works of Milman, Bowles, Wilson and Barry Cornwall. 1829. 4 parts.

A Word on Cathedral-Oratorios, and Clergy-Magistrates. 1830.

The Life of Thomas Ken, D.D., Deprived Bishop of Bath and Wells. 1830. 2 vols.

A Few Words, Most Respectfully Addressed to the Lord Chancellor Brougham, on the Misrepresentations Respecting the Property and Character of the Cathedral Clergy of the Church of England. 1831.

St. John in Patmos. 1832.

The Grave of Anna; in the Island of Madeira. 1833.

A Last and Summary Answer to the Question "Of What Use Have Been, and Are, the English Cathedral Establishments?" 1833.

Inscription for a Seat in the Grounds of Sylvanus Urban, Gent. 1834.

Annals and Antiquities of Lacock Abbey, in the County of Wilts (with John Gough Nichols). 1835.

Scenes and Shadows of Days Departed. 1835.

Some Account of the Last Days of William Chillingworth. 1836.

A Discourse, Preached in Salisbury Cathedral, on King Charles's Martyrdom. 1836.

The Patronage of the English Bishops. 1836.

Further Observations on the Last Report of the Church Commissioners. c. 1837.

The English Village Church. c. 1837.

Pudens and Claudia of St. Paul. c. 1837.

The Cartoons of Raphael: A Series of Discourses. 1838.

A Final Defence of the Rights of Patronage in Deans and Chapters. 1838.

Poetical Works. Ed. George Gilfillan. 1855. 2 vols.

Poetical Works of Bowles, Lamb, and Hartley Coleridge. Ed. William Tirebuck. 1887.

A Wiltshire Parson and His Friends: The Correspondence of William Lisle Bowles. Ed. Garland Greener. 1926.

WILLIAM WORDSWORTH (1770–1850)

An Evening Walk: An Epistle in Verse. 1793.

Descriptive Sketches in Verse Taken during a Pedestrian Tour in the Italian, Grison, Swiss, and Savoyard Alps. 1793.

Lyrical Ballads (with Samuel Taylor Coleridge). 1798, 1800 (2 vols.).

Poems. 1807. 2 vols.

Concerning the Relations of Great Britain, Spain, and Portugal, to Each Other, and to the Common Enemy, at This Crisis; and Specifically as Affected by the Convention of Cintra. Ed. Thomas De Quincey. 1809.

The Excursion: Being a Portion of The Recluse. 1814.

Poems. 1815. 2 vols.

The White Doe of Rylstone; or, The Fate of the Nortons. 1815.

A Letter to a Friend of Robert Burns. 1816.

Thanksgiving Ode, with Other Short Pieces, Chiefly Referring to Recent Public Events. 1816.

Two Addresses to the Freeholders of Westmorland. 1818.

Peter Bell: A Tale in Verse. 1819.

The Waggoner: A Poem; to Which Are Added Sonnets. 1819.

The River Duddon: A Series of Sonnets; Vaudracour and Julia; and Other Poems; to Which Is Annexed A Topographical Description of the Country of the Lakes in the North of England. 1820.

Miscellaneous Poems. 1820. 4 vols.

The Little Maid and the Gentleman; or, We Are Seven. c. 1820.

Memorials of a Tour on the Continent 1820. 1822.

Ecclesiastical Sketches. 1822.

A Description of the Scenery of the Lakes in the North of England: Third Edition (Now First Published Separately) with Additions, and Illustrative Remarks upon the Scenery of the Alps. 1822.

Poetical Works. 1824. 4 vols.

Poetical Works. 1827. 5 vols.

Epitaph ⟨Ode to the Memory of Charles Lamb⟩. 1835.

Yarrow Revisited and Other Poems. 1835.

Poetical Works. 1836–37. 6 vols.

Complete Poetical Works; Together with A Description of the Country of the Lakes in the North of England. Ed. Henry Reed. 1837.

Sonnets. 1838.

Poems, Chiefly of Early and Late Years; Including The Borderers: A Tragedy. 1842.

Poems on the Loss and Re-building of St. Mary's Church, Cardiff (with others). 1842.

Verses Composed at the Request of Jane Wallas Penfold. 1843.

Grace Darling. 1843.

Kendal and Windermere Railway: Two Letters Reprinted from the Morning Post. 1845.

Poems. 1845.

Ode Performed in the Senate-House, Cambridge, at the First Commencement after the Installation of His Royal Highness the Prince Albert, Chancellor of the University. 1847.

The Prelude; or, Growth of a Poet's Mind. 1850.

Poetical Works (Centenary Edition). 1870. 6 vols.

Prose Works. Ed. Alexander B. Grosart. 1876. 3 vols.

Poems. Ed. Matthew Arnold. 1879.

Poetical Works. Ed. William Knight. 1882–86. 8 vols.

Complete Poetical Works. Ed. John Morley. 1888.

The Recluse. 1888.

Poetical Works (Aldine Edition). Ed. Edward Dowden. 1892–93. 7 vols.

Poetical Works. Ed. Thomas Hutchinson. 1895.

Prose Works. Ed. William Knight. 1896. 2 vols.

Poetical Works. Ed. Andrew J. Gorge. 1904.

Literary Criticism. Ed. Newell C. Smith. 1905.

Poems and Extracts Chosen for an Album Presented to Lady Mary Lowther, Christmas 1819 by Anne Finch, Countess of Winchilsea (editor). Ed. Harold Littledale. 1905.

Letters of the Wordsworth Family from 1787 to 1855. Ed. William Knight. 1907. 3 vols.

Poems. Ed. Newell Charles Smith. 1908. 3 vols.

The Law of Copyright. 1916.

Wordsworth and Reed: The Poet's Correspondence with His American Editor 1836–1850. Ed. Leslie Nathan Broughton. 1933.

The Early Letters of William and Dorothy Wordsworth. Ed. Ernest de Selincourt. 1935.

The Letters of William and Dorothy Wordsworth: The Middle Years. Ed. Ernest de Selincourt. 1937. 2 vols.

The Letters of William and Dorothy Wordsworth: The Later Years. Ed. Ernest de Selincourt. 1939. 3 vols.

Poetical Works. Eds. Ernest de Selincourt and Helen Darbishire. 1940–49. 5 vols.

Some Letters of the Wordsworth Family, Now First Published, with a Few Unpublished Letters of Coleridge and Southey and Others. Ed. Leslie Nathan Broughton. 1941.

Pocket Notebook. Ed. George Harris Healey. 1942.

The Critical Opinions of William Wordsworth. Ed. Markham L. Peacock, Jr. 1950.

Letters. Ed. Philip Wayne. 1954.

Selected Poetry and Prose. Ed. John Butt. 1964.

Literary Criticism. Ed. Paul M. Zall. 1966.

The Early Letters of William and Dorothy Wordsworth. Ed. Ernest de Selincourt, rev. Chester L. Shaver. 1967.

The Letters of William and Dorothy Wordsworth: The Middle Years. Ed. Ernest de Selincourt, rev. Mary Moorman and Alan G. Hill. 1969–70. 2 vols.

Prose Works. Eds. W. J. B. Owen and Jane Worthington Smyser. 1974. 3 vols.

Literary Criticism. Ed. W. J. B. Owen. 1974.

The Cornell Wordsworth. Eds. Stephen Parrish et al. 1975–   .

Poems. Ed. John O. Hayden. 1977. 2 vols.

The Letters of William and Dorothy Wordsworth: The Later Years. Ed. Ernest de Selincourt, rev. Alan G. Hill. 1978–83. 4 vols.

Selected Poetry and Prose. Ed. Geoffrey H. Hartman. 1980.

Letters: A New Selection. Ed. Alan G. Hill. 1984.

William Wordsworth. Ed. Stephen Gill. 1984.

FRANCIS, LORD JEFFREY (1773–1850)

Observations on Mr. Thewall's Letter to the Editor of the Edinburgh Review. 1804.

A Summary View of the Rights and Claims of the Roman Catholics in Ireland. 1808.

The Craniad (with John Gordon). 1817.

Speech Delivered at the Anniversary of the Fox Club in Edinburgh. 1824.

Combinations of Workmen: Substance of a Speech upon Introducing the Toast, "Freedom of Labour—but Let the Labourer Recollect That in Exercising His Own Right, He Cannot Be Permitted to Violate the Rights of Others." 1825.

Corrected Report of the Speech of the Lord Advocate of Scotland, upon the Motion of Lord John Russell, in the House of Commons, for Reform of Parliament. 1831.

To the Electors of the City of Edinburgh. 1832.

Contributions to the Edinburgh Review. 1844. 4 vols.

Samuel Richardson. 1852.

Jonathan Swift. 1853.

Peter and His Enemies. 1859.

Selections from the Essays. Ed. Lewis E. Gates. 1894.

Jeffrey's Literary Criticism. Ed. D. Nichol Smith. 1910.

Essays on English Poets and Poetry. 1913.

Letters to Ugo Foscolo. Ed. J. Purves. 1934.

Jeffrey's Criticism: A Selection. Ed. Peter F. Morgan. 1983.

MARGARET FULLER (1810–1850)

⟨*Prospectus for Language Classes.*⟩ 1836.

Conversations with Goethe by Johann Peter Eckermann (translator). 1839.

Günderode (translator). 1842.

Summer on the Lakes in 1843. 1844.

Woman in the Nineteenth Century. 1845.

Papers on Literature and Art. 1846. 2 vols.

Memoirs. Eds. Ralph Waldo Emerson, W. H. Channing, and James Freeman Clarke. 1852. 2 vols.

Woman in the Nineteenth Century and Kindred Papers. Ed. Arthur B. Fuller. 1855.

At Home and Abroad; or, Things and Thoughts in America and Europe. Ed. Arthur B. Fuller. 1856.

Life Without and Life Within; or, Reviews, Narratives, Essays, and Poems. Ed. Arthur B. Fuller. 1860.

Summer on the Lakes, with Autobiography. 1861.

Margaret Fuller and Her Friends; or, Ten Conversations. Ed. Caroline W. Healey. 1895.

Love-Letters 1845–1846. 1903.

Writings. Ed. Mason Wade. 1941.

Margaret Fuller, American Romantic: A Selection from Her Writings and Correspondence. Ed. Perry Miller. 1963.

Essays on American Life and Letters. Ed. Joel Myerson. 1978.

JOANNA BAILLIE (1762–1851)

Fugitive Verses. c. 1790.

A Series of Plays: In Which It Is Attempted to Delineate the Stronger Passions of the Mind. 1798–1812. 3 vols.

Epilogue to the Theatrical Representation at Strawberry-Hill. 1800.

Miscellaneous Plays. 1804.

The Family Legend. 1810.

The Beacon. 1812.

Metrical Legends of Exalted Characters. 1821.

A Collection of Poems, Chiefly Manuscript, and from Living Authors (editor). 1823.

The Martyr. 1826.

The Bride. 1828.

A View of the General Tenour of the New Testament Regarding the Nature and Dignity of Jesus Christ. 1831.

Complete Poetical Works. 1832.

Dramas. 1836. 3 vols.

Fugitive Verses. 1840.

Ahalya Baee. 1849.

Dramatic and Poetical Works. 1851.

JOHN JAMES AUDUBON (1785–1851)

The Birds of America. 1827–38 (4 vols.), 1840–44 (7 vols.).

Ornithological Biography; or, An Account of the Habits of the Birds of the United States of America; Accompanied by Descriptions of the Objects Represented in the Work Birds of America, *and Interspersed with Delineations of American Scenery and Manners.* 1831–39. 5 vols.

A Synopsis of The Birds of America. 1839.

The Viviparous Quadrupeds of North America (pictures). 1845–46. 2 vols.

The Viviparous Quadrupeds of North America (text; with John Bachman). 1846–54. 3 vols.

The Life and Adventures of John James Audubon, the Naturalist. Ed. Robert Buchanan. 1868.

The Life of John James Audubon, the Naturalist. Ed. Lucy Green Audubon. 1869.

Audubon and His Journals. Ed. Maria R. Audubon. 1897. 2 vols.

Delineations of American Scenery and Character. 1926.

Journal Made during His Trip to New Orleans in 1820–1821. Ed. Howard Corning. 1929.

Journal Made While Obtaining Subscriptions to His Birds of America 1840–1843. Ed. Howard Corning. 1929.

Letters 1826–1840. Ed. Howard Corning. 1930. 2 vols.

Audubon's America: The Narratives and Experiences of John James Audubon. Ed. Donald Culross Peattie. 1940.

Three Letters to John Stevens Henslowe. 1943.

Audubon's Animals: The Quadrupeds of North America. Ed. Alice Ford. 1951.

Audubon in the West. Ed. John Francis McDermott. 1965.

The 1826 Journal. Ed. Alice Ford. 1967.

Audubon by Himself: A Profile of John James Audubon from Writings. Ed. Alice Ford. 1969.

The Art of Audubon: The Complete Birds and Mammals. Ed. Roger Tory Peterson. 1979.

Audubon Reader: Best Writings. Ed. Scott Russell Sanders. 1986.

JAMES FENIMORE COOPER (1789–1851)

Precaution. 1820. 2 vols.

The Spy: A Tale of the Neutral Ground. 1821. 2 vols.

The Pioneers; or, The Sources of the Susquehanna: A Descriptive Tale. 1823. 2 vols.

Tales for Fifteen; or, Imagination and Heart. 1823.

The Pilot: A Tale of the Sea. 1823. 2 vols.

Lionel Lincoln; or, The Leaguer of Boston. 1825. 2 vols.

The Last of the Mohicans: A Narrative of 1757. 1826. 2 vols.

The Prairie. 1827. 3 vols.

The Red Rover. 1827. 3 vols.

Notions of the Americans: Picked Up by a Travelling Bachelor. 1828. 2 vols.

The Wept of Wish Ton-Wish. 1829. 2 vols.

The Water-Witch; or, The Skimmer of the Seas. 1830. 3 vols.

Works. 1831–48. 18 vols.

The Bravo: A Venetian Story. 1831. 2 vols.

Letter to Gen. Lafayette, on the Expenditure of the United States of America. 1831.

The Heidenmauer; or, The Benedictines. 1832. 2 vols.

Novels and Tales. 1833–36. 10 vols.

The Headsman; or, The Abbaye des Vignerons. 1833.

A Letter to His Countrymen. 1834.

The Monikins. 1835. 2 vols.

Hints on Manning the Navy. 1836.

Sketches of Switzerland. 1836. 4 vols.

Gleanings in Europe (France). 1837. 2 vols.

Gleanings in Europe: England. 1837. 2 vols.

The American Democrat; or, Hints on the Social and Civil Relations of the United States. 1838.

Gleanings in Europe: Italy. 1838. 2 vols.

Homeward Bound; or, The Case. 1838. 2 vols.

Home as Found. 1838.

The Chronicles of Cooperstown. 1838.

The History of the Navy of the United States of America. 1839. 2 vols.

The Pathfinder; or, The Inland Sea. 1840. 2 vols.

Mercedes of Castile; or, The Voyage to Cathay. 1840. 2 vols.

The Deerslayer; or, The First War-Path. 1841. 2 vols.

The Two Admirals. 1842. 2 vols.

The Wing-and-Wing; or, Le Feu-Follet. 1842. 2 vols.

Le Mouchoir: An Autobiographical Romance. 1843.

The Battle of Lake Erie; or, Answers to Messrs. Burges, Duer, and Mackenzie. 1843.

Wyandotté; or, The Hutted Knoll. 1843. 2 vols.

Ned Myers; or, A Life before the Mast. 1843.

Afloat and Ashore; or, The Adventures of Miles Wallingford. 1844. 4 vols.

Satanstoe; or, The Littlepage Manuscripts. 1845. 2 vols.

The Chainbearer; or, The Littlepage Manuscripts. 1845. 2 vols.

Lives of Distinguished American Naval Officers. 1846. 2 vols.

The Redskins; or, Indian and Injin: Being the Conclusion of the Littlepage Manuscripts. 1846. 2 vols.

The Crater; or, Vulcan's Peak: A Tale of the Pacific. 1847.
2 vols.
Jack Tier; or, The Florida Reef. 1848. 2 vols.
Oak Openings; or, The Bee-Hunter. 1848. 2 vols.
The Sea Lions; or, The Lost Sealers. 1849. 2 vols.
The Ways of the Hour. 1850.
Works. 1855. 33 vols.
Novels. 1867–69. 32 vols.
Correspondence. Ed. James Fenimore Cooper. 1922. 2 vols.
New York: Being an Introduction to an Unpublished Manuscript Entitled The Tours of Manhattan. Ed. Dixon Ryan Fox. 1930.
The Lake Gun. 1932.
Representative Selections. Ed. Robert E. Spiller. 1936.
Letters and Journals. Ed. James Franklin Beard. 1960–68.
6 vols.
Writings. Eds. James Franklin Beard et al. 1980– .

MARY SHELLEY (1797–1851)

History of a Six Weeks' Tour through a Part of France, Switzerland, Germany and Holland (with Percy Bysshe Shelley). 1817.
Frankenstein; or, The Modern Prometheus. 1818. 3 vols.
Valperga; or, The Life and Adventures of Castruccio, Prince of Lucca. 1823. 3 vols.
Posthumous Poems by Percy Bysshe Shelley (editor). 1824.
The Last Man. 1826. 3 vols.
The Fortunes of Perkin Warbeck: A Romance. 1830. 3 vols.
Lodore. 1835. 3 vols.
Falkner. 1837. 3 vols.
Poetical Works by Percy Bysshe Shelley (editor). 1839. 4 vols.
Essays, Letters from Abroad, Translations and Fragments by Percy Bysshe Shelley (editor). 1840. 2 vols.
Rambles in Germany and Italy in 1840, 1842 and 1843. 1844.
2 vols.
The Choice: A Poem on Shelley's Death. Ed. H. Buxton Forman. 1876.
Letters, Mostly Unpublished. Ed. Henry H. Harper. 1918.
Proserpine and Midas: Mythological Dramas. Ed. André Henri Koszul. 1922.
Harriet and Mary: Being the Relations between P. B., Harriet and Mary Shelley and T. J. Hogg as Shown in Letters between Them (with others). Ed. Walter Sidney Scott. 1944.
Letters. Ed. Frederick L. Jones. 1944. 2 vols.
Journal. Ed. Frederick L. Jones. 1947.
My Best Mary: Selected Letters. Eds. Muriel Spark and Derek Stanford. 1953.
Mathilda. Ed. Elizabeth Nitchie. 1959.
Shelley's Posthumous Poems: Mary Shelley's Fair Copy Book (editor). Ed. Irving Massey. 1969.
Collected Tales and Stories. Ed. Charles E. Robinson. 1976.
Letters. Ed. Betty T. Bennett. 1980– .
Journals. Eds. Paula R. Feldman and Diana Scott-Kilvert. 1987. 2 vols.

THOMAS MOORE (1779–1852)

Odes of Anacreon (translator). 1800.
The Poetical Works of the Late Thomas Little, Esq. 1801.
Epistles, Odes, and Other Poems. 1806.
Corruption and Intolerance. 1808.
Irish Melodies. 1808–34. 10 parts.
The Sceptic: A Philosophical Satire. 1809.
A Melologue upon National Music. 1810.
A Letter to the Roman Catholics of Dublin. 1810.

M.P.; or, The Blue-Stocking. 1811.
[*Spirit of Boccaccio's Decameron* (translator). 1812.]
Intercepted Letters; or, The Twopenny Post-Bag. 1813.
Lines on the Death of ——— (Richard Brinsley Sheridan).
1816.
Sacred Songs. 1816 [Part 1]; 1824 [Part 2].
Lalla Rookh: An Oriental Romance. 1817.
The Fudge Family in Paris. 1818.
National Airs. 1818–27. 6 parts.
Tom Crib's Memorial to Congress. 1819.
Works. 1819. 6 vols.
The Works of Richard Brinsley Sheridan (editor). 1821. 2 vols.
The Loves of the Angels. 1823.
Fables for the Holy Alliance, Rhymes for the Road, etc. 1823.
Memoirs of Captain Rock. 1824.
Memoirs of the Life of the Right Honourable Richard Brinsley Sheridan. 1825.
Evenings in Greece. c. 1825. 2 parts.
The Epicurean: A Tale. 1827.
Odes upon Cash, Corn, Catholics, and Other Matters. 1828.
Legendary Ballads. 1828.
Letters and Journals of Lord Byron (editor). 1830. 2 vols.
The Life and Death of Lord Edward Fitzgerald. 1831. 2 vols.
The Summer Fête. 1831.
Travels of an Irish Gentleman in Search of a Religion. 1833.
The Fudge Family in England: Being a Sequel to the Fudge Family in Paris. 1835.
The History of Ireland. 1835–46. 4 vols.
Poetical Works. 1840–41. 10 vols.
Songs, Ballads, and Sacred Songs. 1849.
Memoirs, Journal, and Correspondence. Ed. Lord John Russell. 1853–56. 8 vols.
Notes from the Letters of Thomas Moore to His Music Publisher, James Power. Ed. Thomas Crofton Croker. 1854.
Poetical Works. Ed. William Michael Rossetti. 1870.
Prose and Verse, Humorous, Satirical, and Sentimental. Ed. R. H. Shepherd. 1878.
Poetical Works. Ed. A. D. Godley. 1910.
Diary: A Selection. Ed. J. B. Priestley. 1925.
Lyrics and Satires. Ed. Seán O'Faoláin. 1929.
Journal 1818–1841. Ed. Peter Quennell. 1964.
Letters. Ed. Wilfred S. Dowden. 1964. 2 vols.
Journal. Eds. Wilfred S. Dowden et al. 1983– .

SARA COLERIDGE (1802–1852)

An Account of the Abipones by Martinus Dobrizhoffer (translator). 1822. 3 vols.
The Right Joyous and Pleasant History of the Feats, Gests, and Prowesses of the Chevalier Bayard by Jacques de Mailles (translator). 1825. 2 vols.
Pretty Lessons in Verse, for Good Children. 1834.
Phantasmion. 1837.
Poems by Samuel Taylor Coleridge (editor). 1844.
Biographia Literaria by Samuel Taylor Coleridge (editor; with Henry Nelson Coleridge). 1847.
Notes and Lectures upon Shakespeare by Samuel Taylor Coleridge (editor). 1849. 2 vols.
Essays on His Own Times by Samuel Taylor Coleridge (editor). 1850. 3 vols.
Poems by Samuel Taylor Coleridge (editor; with Derwent Coleridge). 1852.
Memoir and Letters. Ed. Edith Coleridge. 1873. 2 vols.
Sara Coleridge and Henry Reed. Ed. Leslie Nathan Broughton. 1937.

AMELIA OPIE (1769–1853)

The Dangers of Coquetry. 1790. 2 vols.
The Father and Daughter: A Tale in Prose, with an Epistle from the Maid of Corinth to Her Lover, and Other Poetical Pieces. 1801.
Adeline Mowbray; or, The Mother and Daughter. 1801. 3 vols.
Poems. 1802.
Elegy to the Memory of the Late Duke of Bedford: Written on the Evening of His Interment. 1802.
Simple Tales. 1806. 4 vols.
The Warrior's Return and Other Poems. 1808.
Temper; or, Domestic Scenes: A Tale. 1812. 3 vols.
Tales of Real Life. 1813. 3 vols.
Valentine's Eve. 1816. 3 vols.
New Tales. 1818. 4 vols.
Tales of the Heart. 1820. 4 vols.
Madeline. 1822. 2 vols.
White Lies: A Moral Tale. 1823.
The Negro Boy's Tale: A Poem Addressed to Children. 1824.
Illustrations of Lying, in All Its Branches. 1825. 2 vols.
Tales of the Pemberton Family, for the Use of Children. 1825.
The Black Man's Lament; or, How to Make Sugar. 1826.
Works. 1827. 12 vols.
Detraction Displayed. 1828, 1839 (as *A Cure for Scandal*).
A Wife's Duty: A Tale. 1828.
Happy Faces; or, Benevolence and Selfishness; and The Revenge. c. 1830.
Lays for the Dead. 1834.
Works. 1835. 2 vols.
Works. 1841. 3 vols.
False or True; or, The Journey to London. 1845.
Miscellaneous Tales. 1845–47. 12 vols.
The Ruffian Boy; and After the Ball; or, The Two Sir Williams. 1846.
Memorials of the Life of Amelia Opie: Selected and Arranged from Her Letters, Diaries, and Other Manuscripts. Ed. Cecilia Lucy Brightwell. 1854.
The Mysterious Stranger and Other Tales. 1870.

JAMES MONTGOMERY (1771–1854)

Franklin, the Printer, Philosopher and Patriot. c. 1790.
The History of a Church and a Warming-Pan. 1793.
Prison Amusements and Other Trifles. 1797.
The Whisperer; or, Tales and Speculations. 1798.
The Loss of Locks: A Siberian Tale. 1800.
The Ocean. 1805. Lost.
The Wanderer of Switzerland and Other Poems. 1806.
Poems on the Abolition of the Slave Trade (with James Grahame and Elizabeth Benger). 1809.
The West Indies and Other Poems. 1810.
The World before the Flood, with Other Occasional Pieces. 1813.
Verses to the Memory of the Late Richard Reynolds, of Bristol. 1816.
The State Lottery: A Dream ⟨by Samuel Roberts⟩; *also, Thoughts on Wheels* ⟨by Montgomery⟩. 1817. 2 parts.
Works. 1817. 2 vols.
Greenland and Other Poems. 1819.
Poetical Works. 1820. 3 vols.
Songs of Zion: Being Imitations of Psalms. 1822.
The Chimney-Sweeper's Friend and Climbing-Boy's Album (editor). 1824.
Prose by a Poet. 1824. 2 vols.

The Christian Psalmist; or, Hymns Selected and Original. 1825.
Poetical Works. 1826–27. 4 vols.
The Christian Poet; or, Selections in Verse, on Sacred Subjects (editor). 1827.
The Pelican Island and Other Poems. 1827.
The African Valley; or, What Christianity Can Do for the Heathen. 1828.
An Essay on the Phrenology of the Hindoos and Negroes. 1829.
Life of the Rev. David Brainerd by Jonathan Edwards (editor). 1829.
Journal of Voyages and Travels of the Rev. Daniel Tyerman and George Bennet, Esq. (editor). 1831. 2 vols.
On Man: His Motives, Their Rise, Operations, Opposition, and Results by William Bagshaw (editor). 1833. 2 vols.
Lectures on Poetry and General Literature Delivered at the Royal Institution in 1830 and 1831. 1833.
Verses in Commemoration of J. Hervey. 1833.
A Poet's Portfolio; or, Minor Poems. 1835.
Eminent Literary and Scientific Men of Italy, Spain, and Portugal. 1835–37. 3 vols.
Poetical Works. 1836. 3 vols.
Hymns for the Opening of Christ Church, Newark on Trent, 1837. 1837.
The Christian Correspondent: Letters, Private and Confidential, by Eminent Persons of Both Sexes, Exemplifying the Fruits of Holy Living, and the Blessedness of Holy Dying (editor). 1837.
A Hymn for the Wesleyan Centenary. 1839.
Our Saviour's Miracles. 1840.
Poetical Works. 1841. 4 vols.
Poems on the Loss and Re-building of St. Mary's Church, Cardiff (with William Wordsworth and others). 1842.
Poems. 1843.
The Poetical Works of John Milton (editor). 1843.
Poetical Works. Ed. Rufus W. Griswold. 1845. 2 vols.
Liturgy and Hymns for the Use of the Protestant Church of the United Brethren (editor). 1849.
Poems. 1850.
Doncaster Church, as It Was, as It Is, and as It Shall Be. 1853.
Original Hymns. 1853.
Select Poetical Works. 1853.
Sacred Poems and Hymns. Ed. John Holland. 1854.
Memoirs of the Life and Writings. Ed. John Holland and James Everett. 1854–56. 7 vols.
Poetical Works. Ed. Robert Carruthers. 1858. 5 vols.
Poems. Ed. Robert Aris Willmott. 1860.

JOHN WILSON ("CHRISTOPHER NORTH") (1785–1854)

A Recommendation of the Study of the Remains of Ancient Grecian and Roman Architecture, Sculpture, and Painting. 1807.
Lines Sacred to the Memory of the Rev. James Grahame. 1811.
The Isle of Palms and Other Poems. 1812.
The Magic Mirror: Addressed to Walter Scott, Esq. 1812.
The City of the Plague and Other Poems. 1816.
Translation from an Ancient Chaldee Manuscript. 1817.
Lights and Shadows of Scottish Life: A Selection from the Papers of the Late Arthur Austin. 1822.
Little Hannah Lee: A Winter's Story. 1823.
The Trials of Margaret Lyndsay. 1823.
The Foresters. 1825.
Poems. 1825. 2 vols.

Janus; or, The Edinburgh Literary Almanack (with John Gibson Lockhart). 1826.
Some Illustrations of Mr. M'Culloch's Principles of Political Economy. 1826.
The Poetical Works of Milman, Bowles, Wilson and Barry Cornwall. 1829. 4 parts.
Speech at the Conservative Meeting Held in Edinburgh. 1831.
The Land of Burns: A Series of Landscapes and Portraits, Illustrative of the Life and Writings of the Scottish Poet (with Robert Chambers). 1840. 2 vols.
Blind Allan: A Tale. c. 1840.
The Recreations of Christopher North. 1842. 3 vols.
Critical and Miscellaneous Essays. 1842. 3 vols.
Noctes Ambrosianae (with others). 1843. 4 vols.
The Genius and Character of Burns. 1845.
Specimens of the British Critics. 1846.
Dies Borealis; or, Christopher under Canvas. 1850.
Noctes Ambrosianae. Ed. R. Shelton Mackenzie. 1854. 5 vols.
Works. Ed. James Frederick Ferrier. 1855–58. 12 vols.
Letters from the Lakes. 1889.
Lakeland Poems. Ed. W. Bailey-Kempling. 1902.

JOHN GIBSON LOCKHART (1794–1854)

Lectures on the History of Literature, Ancient and Modern by Friedrich Schlegel (translator). 1818. 2 vols.
Peter's Letters to His Kinsfolk. 1819. 3 vols.
Statement. 1821.
Valerius: A Roman Story. 1821. 3 vols.
Letter to the Right Hon. Lord Byron. 1821.
Some Passages in the Life of Mr. Adam Blair, Minister of the Gospel at Cross-Meikle. 1822.
The History of the Ingenious Gentleman, Don Quixote of La Mancha by Cervantes, tr. Peter Anthony Motteux (editor). 1822. 5 vols.
Reginald Dalton. 1823. 3 vols.
Ancient Spanish Ballads, Historical and Romantic (translator). 1823.
The History of Matthew Wald. 1824.
Janus; or, The Edinburgh Literary Almanack (with John Wilson). 1826.
Life of Robert Burns. 1828.
The History of Napoleon Buonaparte. 1829. 2 vols.
Answers to the Edinburgh Reviewer of Croker's Boswell. c. 1831.
Letter to T. G. Lockhart, Esq. in Answer to a Late Article in the Quarterly Review. 1832.
History of the Late War. 1832.
Poetical Works of Sir Walter Scott (editor). 1833–34. 12 vols.
Miscellaneous Prose Works of Sir Walter Scott (editor). 1834–36. 28 vols.
The Complete Works of Lord Byron (editor). 1835.
Memoirs of the Life of Sir Walter Scott, Bart. 1837–38. 7 vols.
The Ballantyne-Humbug Handled, in a Letter to Sir Adam Fergusson. 1839.
Noctes Ambrosianae (with John Wilson and others). 1843. 4 vols.
Notice on the Savoy Chapel, Built by King Henry VII. and Recently Restored by Queen Victoria. 1844.
Theodore Hook: A Sketch. 1852.
Life and Letters. Ed. Andrew Lang. 1897. 2 vols.
Literary Criticism. Ed. M. Clive Hildyard. 1931.

SAMUEL ROGERS (1763–1855)

An Ode to Superstition, with Some Other Poems. 1786.
The Pleasures of Memory. 1792.

An Epistle to a Friend, with Other Poems. 1798.
The Pleasures of Memory, with Other Poems. 1799.
Verses Written in Westminster Abbey, after the Funeral of the Right Hon. Charles James Fox. 1806.
The Voyage of Columbus. 1810.
Poems. 1812.
Jacqueline. 1814.
Human Life. 1819.
Italy. 1822 [Part 1]; 1828 [Part 2].
Poems. 1834. 2 vols.
Poetical Works. 1848.
Recollections of the Table-Talk. Ed. Alexander Dyce. 1856.
Reminiscences and Table-Talk. Ed. G. H. Powell. 1903.
Recollections of the Table-Talk. Ed. Morchard Bishop. 1952.
Italian Journal. Ed. J. R. Hale. 1956.
Samuel Rogers and William Gilpin: Their Friendship and Correspondence. Ed. Carl Paul Barbier. 1959.

MARY RUSSELL MITFORD (1787–1855)

Poems. 1810.
Christina, the Maid of the South Seas. 1811.
Blanche of Castile. 1812.
Watlington Hill. 1812.
Narrative Poems on the Female Character, in the Various Relations of Life. 1813. Vol. 1 only.
Julian. 1823.
Our Village: Sketches of Rural Character and Scenery. 1824–32. 5 vols.
Foscari. 1826.
Foscari and Julian. 1827.
Dramatic Scenes, Sonnets and Other Poems. 1827.
Rienzi. 1828.
Stories of American Life (editor). 1830. 3 vols.
Mary, Queen of Scots: A Scene in English Verse. 1831.
American Stories for Little Boys and Girls (editor). 1831. 3 vols.
Lights and Shadows of American Life (editor). 1832. 2 vols.
Charles the First: An Historical Tragedy. 1834.
Belford Regis; or, Sketches of a Country Town. 1835. 3 vols.
Sadak and Kalasrade; or, The Waters of Oblivion: A Romantic Opera. 1836.
Country Stories. 1837.
Works, Prose and Verse. 1841.
Fragments des oeuvres d'Alexandre Dumas (editor). 1846.
Recollections of a Literary Life; or, Books, Places and People. 1852. 3 vols.
Atherton and Other Tales. 1854. 3 vols.
Dramatic Works. 1854. 2 vols.
The Life of Mary Russell Mitford, Related in a Selection from Her Letters to Her Friends. Ed. A. G. L'Estrange. 1870. 3 vols.
Letters: Second Series. Ed. Henry F. Chorley. 1872. 2 vols.
The Friendships of Mary Russell Mitford as Recorded in Letters from Her Literary Correspondents. Ed. A. G. L'Estrange. 1882. 2 vols.
Correspondence with Charles Boner and John Ruskin. Ed. Elizabeth Lee. 1914.
Letters. Ed. R. Brimley Johnson. 1925.

CHARLOTTE BRONTË (1816–1855)

Poems by Currer, Ellis, and Acton Bell (with Emily and Anne Brontë). 1846.
Jane Eyre: An Autobiography. 1848. 3 vols.
Shirley: A Tale. 1849. 3 vols.
Villette. 1853. 3 vols.

The Professor: A Tale. 1857. 2 vols.

The Life and Works of Charlotte Brontë and Her Sisters. 1872–73. 7 vols.

The Works of Charlotte, Emily, and Anne Brontë. Ed. F. J. S. 1893. 12 vols.

The Adventures of Ernest Alembert: A Fairy Tale. Ed. Thomas J. Wise. 1896.

The Life and Works of Charlotte Brontë and Her Sisters. Eds. Mrs. Humphry Ward and Clement K. Shorter. 1899–1903. 7 vols.

The Works of Charlotte, Emily, and Anne Brontë. Ed. Temple Scott. 1901. 12 vols.

Poems by Charlotte, Emily, and Anne Brontë. 1902.

The Brontës: Life and Letters. Ed. Clement K. Shorter. 1908. 2 vols.

Richard Cœur de Lion and Blondel: A Poem. Ed. Clement K. Shorter. 1912.

Saul and Other Poems. 1913.

Letters Recounting the Deaths of Emily, Anne and Branwell Brontë by Charlotte Brontë; to Which Are Added Letters Signed "Currer Bell" and "C. B. Nicholls." Ed. Thomas J. Wise. 1913.

The Love Letters of Charlotte Brontë to Constantin Heger. Ed. M. H. Spielmann. 1914.

The Violet: A Poem Written at the Age of Fourteen. Ed. Clement K. Shorter. 1916.

The Red Cross Knight and Other Poems. 1917.

The Swiss Emigrant's Return and Other Poems. 1917.

The Orphans and Other Poems (with Emily and Branwell Brontë). 1917.

The Four Wishes: A Fairy Tale. Ed. Clement K. Shorter. 1918.

Latest Gleanings: Being a Series of Unpublished Poems from Her Early Manuscripts. Ed. Clement K. Shorter. 1918.

Thackeray and Charlotte Brontë: Being Some Hitherto Unpublished Letters. Ed. Clement K. Shorter. 1918.

Napoleon and the Spectre: A Ghost Story. Ed. Clement K. Shorter. 1919.

Darius Codomannus: A Poem Written at the Age of Eighteen Years. 1920.

Complete Poems. Eds. Clement K. Shorter and C. W. Hatfield. 1923.

An Early Essay. Ed. M. H. Spielmann. 1924.

The Twelve Adventurers and Other Stories. Ed. C. W. Hatfield. 1925.

An Account of Her Honeymoon: In a Letter to Miss Catharine Winkworth. Ed. Thomas J. Wise. 1930.

The Spell: An Extravaganza. Ed. George Edwin MacLean. 1931.

The Shakespeare Head Brontë (with Anne and Emily Brontë). Eds. Thomas J. Wise and John Alexander Symington. 1931–38. 19 vols.

The Brontës: Their Lives, Friendships, and Correspondence. Eds. Thomas J. Wise and John Alexander Symington. 1932. 4 vols.

Legends of Angria: Compiled from the Early Writings. Eds. Fanny E. Ratchford and William Clyde DeVane. 1933.

The Miscellaneous and Unpublished Writings of Charlotte and Patrick Branwell Brontë. Eds. Thomas J. Wise and John Alexander Symington. 1936. 2 vols.

Tales from Angria. Ed. Phillis Bentley. 1954.

The Search after Hapiness. Ed. T. A. J. Burnett. 1969.

Five Novelettes. Ed. Winifred Gérin. 1971.

The Novels of Charlotte, Emily, and Anne Brontë. Eds. Hilda Marsden, Ian Jack et al. 1976–   .

Two Tales. Ed. William Holtz. 1978.

Poems. Ed. Tom Winnifrith. 1984.

Poems: A New Text and Commentary. Ed. Victor A. Neufeldt. 1985.

Selected Poems (with Anne and Emily Brontë). Eds. Tom Winnifrith and Edward Chitham. 1985.

The Brontës: Selected Poems. Ed. Juliet R. Barker. 1985.

The Juvenilia of Jane Austen and Charlotte Brontë. Ed. Frances Beer. 1986.

SIR WILLIAM HAMILTON (1788–1856)

Correspondence Relative to Phrenology between Sir William Hamilton, Bart., Dr. Spurzheim, and Mr. George Combe. 1828.

To the Right Honourable the Lord Provost, Magistrates, and Town Council, Patrons of the University of Edinburgh. 1836.

Letter to the Lord Provost of Edinburgh on the Election of a Professor of Mathematics. 1838.

Be Not Schismatics, Be Not Martyrs by Mistake. 1843.

The Works of Thomas Reid (editor). 1846. 2 vols.

A Letter to Augustus De Morgan, Esq. on His Claim to an Independent Re-discovery of a New Principle in the Theory of Syllogism. 1847.

Discussions on Philosophy and Literature, Education and University Reform. 1852.

Philosophy of Sir William Hamilton. Ed. O. W. Wright. 1853.

The Collected Works of Dugald Stewart (editor). 1854–58. 11 vols.

Lectures on Metaphysics and Logic. Eds. Henry Longueville Mansel and John Veitch. 1859–60. 4 vols.

The Metaphysics of Sir William Hamilton. Ed. Francis Bowen. 1861.

The Logic of Sir William Hamilton. Ed. Henry N. Day. 1863.

Chapters in Logic. Ed. S. S. Nelles. 1870.

JOHN WILSON CROKER (1780–1857)

The Opinion of an Impartial Observer concerning the Late Transactions in Ireland. 1803.

Familiar Epistles to Frederick J(one)s, Esq., on the Present State of the Irish Stage. 1804.

An Intercepted Letter from J—— T——, Esq., Writer at Canton, to His Friend in Dublin, Ireland. 1804.

The History of Cutchacutchoo. 1805.

The Amazoniad; or, Figure and Fashion: A Scuffle in High Life. 1806. 2 parts.

Histrionic Epistles. 1807.

A Sketch of the State of Ireland, Past and Present. 1808.

The Battles of Talavera. 1809.

Projet d'une convention pour l'échange des prisonniers de guerre de toutes les nations belligérentes. 1810.

A Sketch of the Campaign in Portugal (with Frederick Robinson). 1810.

A Key to the Orders in Council. 1812.

Letters on the Subject of the Naval War with America. 1813.

A Letter on the Fittest Style and Situation for the Wellington Testimonial About to Be Erected in Dublin. 1815.

Stories Selected from the History of England from the Conquest to the Revolution. 1817.

The New Whig Guide (with Lord Palmerston and Sir Robert Peel). 1819.

Substance of the Speech in the House of Commons, on the Roman Catholic Question. 1819.

Memoirs of the Embassy of the Marshal de Bassompierre to the Court of England in 1626 (translator). 1819.

A Letter from the King to His People. 1820.
Letters of Mary Lepel, Lady Hervey (editor). 1821.
Royal Memoirs on the French Revolution (translator). 1823.
An Answer to O'Meara's Napoleon in Exile; or, A Voice from St. Helena. 1823.
[*A Letter to the Earl of Liverpool on the Proposed Annexation of the King's Library to That of the British Museum.* 1824.]
Letters to and from Henrietta, Countess of Suffolk, and Her Second Husband, the Hon. George Berkeley, from 1712 to 1767 (editor). 1824. 2 vols.
Letters from the Honble. Horace Walpole to the Earl of Hertford (editor). 1825.
Two Letters on Scottish Affairs from E. Bradwardine Waverley Esq. to Malachi Malagrowther Esq. 1826.
Progressive Geography for Children. 1828.
Military Events of the French Revolution of 1830. 1831.
The Life of Samuel Johnson, LL.D. by James Boswell (editor). 1831. 5 vols.
Answers to the Edinburgh Reviewer of Croker's Boswell. 1831.
Speech on the Reform Question. 1831.
Speech on the Question That "The Reform Bill Do Pass." 1831.
A Letter to a Noble Lord Who Voted for the Second Reading of the Reform Bill. 1832.
Resolutions Moved by Mr. Croker, on the Report of the Reform Bill. 1832.
The Reform Ministry and the Reformed Parliament. 1833.
Johnsoniana; or, Supplement to Boswell (editor). 1835. 2 vols.
Memoirs of the Reign of George the Second by John, Lord Hervey (editor). 1848. 2 vols.
History of the Guillotine. 1853.
Correspondence between the Right Hon. J. W. Croker and the Right Hon. Lord John Russell, on Some Passages of Moore's Diary. 1854.
Essays on the Early Period of the French Revolution. 1857.
An Essay towards a New Edition of Pope's Works. 1871.
The Croker Papers. Ed. Louis J. Jennings. 1884 (3 vols.), 1885 (3 vols.).
The Croker Papers 1808–1857. Ed. Bernard Pool. 1967.

DOUGLAS JERROLD (1803–1857)

More Frightened Than Hurt: A Farce. 1821.
The Smoked Miser; or, The Benefit of Hanging: An Interlude. c. 1823.
Paul Pry: A Farcical Comedy. 1827.
Facts and Fancies. 1826.
Wives by Advertisement; or, Courting in the Newspapers: A Dramatic Satire. 1828.
John Overy, the Miser of Southwark Ferry. 1828.
Fifteen Years of a Drunkard's Life: A Melodrama. 1828.
Ambrose Gwinnett; or, A Sea-side Story. c. 1828.
The Statue Lover; or, Music in Marble: A Vaudeville. c. 1828.
Thomas á Becket: A Historical Play. 1829.
Black-Ey'd Susan; or, All in the Downs. 1829.
Vidocq, the French Police Spy: A Melodrama. 1829.
The Flying Dutchman; or, The Spectral Ship. 1829.
Law and Lions: A Farce. c. 1829.
Sally in Our Alley. c. 1829.
Bampfylde Moore Carwe; or, The Gypsey of the Glen: A Romantic Melo-drama. c. 1829.
Descart, the French Buccaneer: A Melodrama. c. 1830.
The Mutiny at the Nore: A Nautical Drama. c. 1830.
The Devil's Ducat. 1831.
Martha Willis, the Servant Maid. c. 1831.
The Bride of Ludgate. 1832.
The Golden Calf. 1832.

The Rent Day: A Domestic Drama. 1832.
The Housekeeper; or, The White Rose. 1833.
Nell Gwynne. 1833.
The Wedding Gown. 1834.
Beau Nash, the King of Bath. 1834.
The Hazard of the Die. 1835.
The Schoolfellows. 1835.
Doves in a Cage. c. 1835.
The Perils of Pippins; or, The Man Who "Couldn't Help It." 1836.
The Painter of Ghent. c. 1836.
The Man for the Ladies: A Farcical Comedy. c. 1836.
Men of Character. 1838. 3 vols.
The Hand-book of Swindling. 1839.
The White Milliner. 1841.
Bubbles of the Day. 1842.
Gertrude's Cherries; or, Waterloo in 1835. 1842.
The Prisoner of War. 1842.
Punch's Letters to His Son. 1843.
The Story of a Feather. 1844.
Time Works Wonders. 1845.
Punch's Complete Letter Writer. 1845.
The Chronicles of Clovernook, with Some Account of the Hermit of Bellyfulle. 1846.
Mrs. Caudle's Curtain Lectures. 1846.
The History of St. Giles and St. James. 1847.
The Dreamer and the Worker. 1847.
A Man Made of Money. 1849.
The Catspaw. 1850.
Retired from Business. 1851.
Writings. 1851–54. 8 vols.
Blondelle: A Story of the Day. 1852.
Cakes and Ale. 1852.
St. Cupid; or, Dorothy's Fortune. 1853.
A Heart of Gold. 1854.
The Wit and Opinions of Douglas Jerrold. Ed. Blanchard Jerrold. 1859.
The Brownrigg Papers. Ed. Blanchard Jerrold. 1860.
Works. 1863–64. 4 vols.
Other Times: Being Liberal Leaders Contributed to Lloyd's Weekly Newspaper (with Blanchard Jerrold). 1868.
Mrs. Caudle's Curtain Lectures; Mrs. Bib's Baby. 1873.
The Barber's Chair and The Hedgehog Letters. Ed. Blanchard Jerrold. 1874.
Tales. Ed. J. Logie Robertson. 1891.
The Handbook of Windling and Other Papers. Ed. Walter Jerrold. 1891.
Essays. Ed. Walter Jerrold. 1903.
Mrs. Caudle's Curtain Lectures and Other Stories and Essays. Ed. Walter Jerrold. 1907.
Whimsical Tales. 1948.
The Best of Mr. Punch: The Humorous Writings of Douglas Jerrold. Ed. Richard M. Kelly. 1970.

RUFUS WILMOT GRISWOLD (1815–1857)

The Biographical Annual: Containing Memoirs of Eminent Persons, Recently Deceased (editor). 1841.
Gems from American Female Poets (editor). 1842.
The Poets and Poetry of America (editor). 1842.
The Poetical Works of John Sterling (editor). 1842.
Readings in American Poetry (editor). 1843.
The Opal: A Pure Gift for the Holy Days (editor; with N. P. Willis). 1844.
The Songs of Béranger, in English (editor). 1844.

The Cypress Wreath: A Book of Consolation for Those Who Mourn (editor). 1844.

The Poetry of Love (editor). 1844, 1853 (as *Gift of Love: A Token of Friendship* for 1853).

Curiosities of Literature and The Literary Character Illustrated ⟨by Isaac D'Israeli⟩; *with Curiosities of American Literature* ⟨by Griswold⟩. 1844.

The Poetical Works of Winthrop Mackworth Praed (editor). 1844.

The Poetry of Flowers (editor). 1844, 1853 (as *Gift of Flowers: Love's Wreath* for 1853).

The Illustrated Book of Christian Ballads and Other Poems (editor). 1844.

Gems from the American Poets (editor). 1844.

The Poems of Ebenezer Elliott (editor). 1844.

The Poets and Poetry of England, in the Nineteenth Century (editor). 1845.

Poems by Felicia Dorothea Hemans (editor). 1845.

The Prose Works of John Milton (editor). 1845. 2 vols.

Poetical Works of James Montgomery (editor). 1845. 2 vols.

The Poetry of the Passions (editor). 1845.

The Poetry of the Sentiments (editor). 1845, 1853 (as *Gift of Sentiment: A Souvenir* for 1853).

Scenes in the Life of the Saviour: By the Poets and Painters (editor). 1846.

The Christian's Annual: A Miscellany for MDCCCXLVI (editor). 1846.

The Poetry of the Affections (editor). 1846, 1852 (as *Gift of Affection: A Souvenir* for 1852).

The Prose Writers of America (editor). 1847.

Washington and the Generals of the American Revolution. 1847. 2 vols.

Napoleon and the Marshals of the Empire by Horace Binney Wallace (editor). 1848. 2 vols.

The Sacred Poets of England and America, for Three Centuries (editor). 1849.

The Female Poets of America (editor). 1849.

Gift-Leaves of American Poetry (editor). 1849.

Poems by Frances Sargent Osgood (editor). 1850.

The Works of the Late Edgar Allan Poe (editor). 1850–56. 4 vols.

The Parthenon: Containing Original Characteristic Papers by Living American Authors (editor). 1851.

Lillian and Other Poems by Winthrop Mackworth Praed (editor). 1852.

The Republican Court; or, American Society in the Days of Washington. 1855.

The Cyclopedia of American Literature by Evert A. Duyckinck and George L. Duyckinck: *A Review.* 1856.

Washington: A Biography. 1856–60. 45 parts [Parts 1–4 by Griswold; Parts 5–45 by Benson J. Lossing].

Passages from the Correspondence and Other Papers. Ed. William M. Griswold. 1898.

SYDNEY OWENSON, LADY MORGAN (1776–1859)

Poems. 1801.

St. Clair; or, The Heiress of Desmond. 1803.

A Few Reflections Occasioned by the Perusal of a Work, Entitled Familiar Epistles to Frederick J⟨one⟩s, Esq. on the Present State of the Irish Stage. 1804.

The Novice of St. Dominick. 1806. 4 vols.

The Wild Irish Girl: A National Tale. 1806. 3 vols.

The Lay of an Irish Harp; or, Metrical Fragments. 1807.

Patriotic Sketches of Ireland, Written in Connaught. 1807. 2 vols.

Woman; or Ida of Athens. 1809. 4 vols.

The Missionary: An Indian Tale. 1811. 3 vols.

O'Donnel: A National Tale. 1814. 3 vols.

France. 1817. 2 vols.

Florence Macarthy: An Irish Tale. 1818. 4 vols.

Italy. 1821. 2 vols.

Letters to the Reviewers of Italy. 1821.

The Mohawks: A Satirical Poem. 1822.

The Life and Times of Salvator Rosa. 1824. 2 vols.

Absenteeism. 1825.

The O'Briens and the O'Flahertys: A National Tale. 1827. 4 vols.

The Book of the Boudoir. 1829. 2 vols.

France in 1829–30. 1830. 2 vols.

Dramatic Scenes from Real Life. 1833. 2 vols.

The Princess; or, The Beguine. 1835. 3 vols.

Woman and Her Master. 1840. 2 vols.

The Book without a Name (with Sir Thomas Charles Morgan). 1841. 2 vols.

Letter to Cardinal Wiseman in Answer to His Remarks on Lady Morgan's Statements Regarding St. Peter's Chair. 1851.

Passages in My Autobiography. 1859.

Memoirs: Autobiography, Diaries and Correspondence. Eds. William Hepworth Dixon and Geraldine Jewsbury. 1862. 2 vols.

Lady Morgan in France. Eds. Elizabeth Suddaby and P. J. Yarrow. 1971.

HENRY HALLAM (1777–1859)

View of the State of Europe during the Middle Ages. 1818 (2 vols.), 1855 (11th ed.; 3 vols.).

The Constitutional History of England from the Accession of Henry VII. to the Death of George II. 1827 (2 vols.), 1866 (11th ed.; 3 vols.).

Survey of the Principal Repositories of the Public Records (with R. H. Inglis). 1833.

The Remains in Prose and Verse of Arthur Henry Hallam (editor). 1834.

Introduction to the Literature of Europe in the Fifteenth, Sixteenth, and Seventeenth Centuries. 1837–39 (4 vols.), 1864 (7th ed.; 4 vols.).

Letters Addressed to Lord Ashley on the Importance of a Slavonic Chair at Oxford (with Baron Bunsen). 1844.

Supplemental Notes to the View of the State of Europe during the Middle Ages. 1848.

WASHINGTON IRVING (1783–1859)

A Voyage to the Eastern Part of Terra Firma by François Depons (translator). 1806. 3 vols.

Salmagundi (with others). 1807–08. 20 nos.

A History of New York from the Beginning of the World to the End of the Dutch Dynasty. 1809. 2 vols.

Poetical Works of Thomas Campbell (editor). 1810. 2 vols.

The Sketch Book of Geoffrey Crayon, Gent. 1819–20. 7 parts.

Bracebridge Hall; or, The Humourists: A Medley. 1822. 2 vols.

Letters of Jonathan Old-Style, Gent. 1824.

Tales of a Traveller. 1824. 4 parts.

The Miscellaneous Works of Oliver Goldsmith (editor). 1825. 4 vols.

A History of the Life and Voyages of Christopher Columbus. 1828. 3 vols.

A Chronicle of the Conquest of Granada. 1829. 2 vols.

Voyages and Discoveries of the Companions of Columbus. 1831.

Poems by William Cullen Bryant (editor). 1832.

The Alhambra: A Series of Tales and Sketches of the Moors and Spaniards. 1832. 2 vols.

Complete Works. 1834.

The Crayon Miscellany 〈*A Tour of the Prairies; Abbotsford and Newstead Abbey; Legends of the Conquest of Spain*〉. 1835. 3 vols.

The Beauties of Washington Irving. 1835.

Astoria; or, Anecdotes of an Enterprise beyond the Rocky Mountains. 1836. 2 vols.

The Rocky Mountains; or, Scenes, Incidents, and Adventures in the Far West by Captain B. L. E. Bonneville (editor). 1837. 2 vols.

The Life of Oliver Goldsmith. 1840 (2 vols.), 1849.

Works. 1840. 2 vols.

Biography and Poetical Remains of the Late Margaret Miller Davidson. 1841.

Works (Author's Revised Edition). 1848–51. 15 vols.

A Book of the Hudson. 1849.

Mahomet and His Successors. 1850. 2 vols.

Wolfert's Roost and Other Papers. 1855.

The Life of George Washington. 1855–59. 5 vols.

Life and Letters. Ed. Pierre M. Irving. 1862–64. 4 vols.

Spanish Papers and Other Miscellanies. Ed. Pierre M. Irving. 1866. 2 vols.

Works. 1872. 28 vols.

Works (Hudson Edition). 1882. 27 vols.

Letters to Mrs. William Renwick, and to Her Son, James Renwick. 1915.

Letters to Henry Brevoort. Ed. George S. Hellman. 1915. 2 vols.

Journals. Eds. William P. Trent and George S. Hellman. 1919. 3 vols.

Notes and Journal of Travel in Europe 1804–1805. Ed. William P. Trent. 1921. 3 vols.

Abu Hassan. Ed. George S. Hellman. 1924.

The Wild Huntsman (adaptation). Ed. George S. Hellman. 1924.

An Unwritten Drama of Lord Byron. Ed. Thomas Ollive Mabbott. 1925.

Diary Spain 1828–1829. Ed. Clara Louisa Penney. 1926.

Notes While Preparing Sketch Book 1817. Ed. Stanley T. Williams. 1927.

Tour in Scotland 1817 and Other Manuscript Notes. Ed. Stanley T. Williams. 1927.

Letters from Sunnyside and Spain. Ed. Stanley T. Williams. 1928.

Journal (1823–1824). Ed. Stanley T. Williams. 1931.

Washington Irving and the Storrows: Letters from England and the Continent 1821–1828. Ed. Stanley T. Williams. 1933.

Journal 1803. Ed. Stanley T. Williams. 1934.

Journal 1828 and Miscellaneous Notes on Moorish Legend and History. Ed. Stanley T. Williams. 1937.

Contributions to The Corrector. Ed. Martin Roth. 1968.

Complete Works. Eds. Henry A. Pochmann, Herbert L. Kleinfeld, Richard Dilworth Rust et al. 1969– .

LEIGH HUNT (1784–1859)

Juvenilia; or, A Collection of Poems, Written between the Ages of Twelve and Sixteen. 1801.

Classic Tales, Serious and Lively; with Critical Essays on the Merits and Reputations of the Authors (editor). 1806–07. 5 vols.

Critical Essays on the Performers of the London Theatres, In-cluding General Observations on the Practise and Genius of the Stage. 1807.

An Attempt to Shew the Folly and Danger of Methodism. 1809.

The Reformist's Answer to the Article, Entitled "State of Parties," in the Last Edinburgh Review. 1810.

The Feast of the Poets, with Notes, and Other Pieces in Verse. 1814.

The Descent of Liberty: A Mask. 1815.

The Story of Rimini. 1816.

The Round Table: A Collection of Essays on Literature, Men, and Manners (with William Hazlitt). 1817. 2 vols.

Foliage; or, Poems Original and Translated. 1818.

Hero and Leander, and Bacchus and Ariadne. 1819.

Poetical Works. 1819. 3 vols.

The Indicator. 1819–21. 76 nos.

The Literary Pocket-Book (editor). 1819–23. 5 vols.

Amyntas: A Tale of the Woods by Torquato Tasso (translator). 1820.

The Months: Descriptive of the Successive Beauties of the Year. 1821.

Ultra-Crepidarius: A Satire on William Gifford. 1823.

Flora Domestica by Bessie Kent (editor). 1823.

Sylvan Sketches by Bessie Kent (editor). 1825.

Bacchus in Tuscany: A Dithyrambic Poem by Francesco Redi (translator). 1825.

The Companion. 1828. 29 nos.

Lord Byron and Some of His Contemporaries; with Recollections of the Author's Life, and of His Visit to Italy. 1828.

The Chat of the Week. 1830. 13 nos.

The Tatler. 1830–32. 457 nos.

Christianism; or, Belief and Unbelief Reconciled. 1832.

Sir Ralph Esher; or, Adventures of a Gentleman of the Court of Charles II. 1832. 3 vols.

The Masque of Anarchy by Percy Bysshe Shelley (editor). 1832.

Poetical Works. 1832.

The Indicator and The Companion. 1834. 2 vols.

Leigh Hunt's London Journal. 1834–35. 2 vols.

Captain Sword and Captain Pen. 1835.

The Monthly Repository (with others). 1837–38. 10 nos.

A Legend of Florence. 1840.

The Dramatic Works of Richard Brinsley Sheridan (editor). 1840.

The Dramatic Works of Wycherley, Congreve, Vanbrugh, and Farquhar (editor). 1840.

The Seer; or, Common-Places Refreshed. 1840–41. 2 parts.

Notice of the Late Mr. Egerton Webbe. 1840.

The Poems of Geoffrey Chaucer, Modernized (editor; with R. H. Horne, Elizabeth Barrett Browning, and others). 1841.

The Palfrey: A Love-Story of Old Times. 1842.

One Hundred Romances of Real Life (editor). 1843.

Poetical Works. 1844.

Imagination and Fancy. 1844.

The Foster Brother: A Tale of the Wars of Chiozza by Thornton Hunt (editor). 1845. 3 vols.

Wit and Humour, Selected from the English Poets (editor). 1846.

Stories from the Italian Poets (editor). 1846. 2 vols.

Men, Women, and Books: A Selection of Sketches, Essays, and Critical Memoirs, from His Uncollected Prose Writings. 1847. 2 vols.

A Jar of Honey from Mount Hybla. 1848.

The Town: Its Memorable Characters and Events. 1848. 2 vols.

A Book for a Corner; or, Selections in Prose from Authors the Best Suited to That Mode of Enjoyment (editor). 1849. 2 vols.

Readings for the Railways; or, Anecdotes and Other Short Stories, Reflections, Maxims, Characteristics, Passages of Wit, Humour, and Poetry, etc. (editor). 1849.

Autobiography. 1850. 3 vols.

Leigh Hunt's Journal. 1850–51. 16 nos.

Table Talk; to Which Are Added Imaginary Conversations of Pope and Swift. 1851.

The Religion of the Heart: A Manual of Faith and Duty. 1853.

Works. 1854. 4 vols.

The Old Court Suburb; or, Memorials of Kensington, Regal, Critical, and Anecdotal. 1855. 2 vols.

Beaumont and Fletcher; or, The Finest Scenes, Lyrics, and Other Beauties of Those Two Poets (editor). 1855.

Stories in Verse. 1855.

Poetical Works. Ed. S. Adams Lee. 1857. 2 vols.

Poetical Works. Ed. Thornton Hunt. 1860.

A Saunter through the West End. Ed. Thornton Hunt. 1861.

Correspondence. Ed. Thornton Hunt. 1862. 2 vols.

The Book of the Sonnet (editor; with S. Adams Lee). 1867. 2 vols.

A Tale for the Chimney Corner and Other Essays. Ed. Edmund Ollier. 1869.

A Day by the Fire and Other Papers, Hitherto Uncollected. Ed. J. E. Babson. 1870.

The Wishing-Cap Papers. Ed. J. E. Babson. 1873.

Favorite Poems. 1877.

Works. 1878.

Essays. Ed. Arthur Symons. 1887.

Leigh Hunt as Poet and Essayist. Ed. Charles Kent. 1889.

Tales. Ed. William Knight. 1891.

Essays. Ed. Reginald Brimley Johnson. 1891.

Poems. Ed. Reginald Brimley Johnson. 1891.

Dramatic Essays. Eds. William Archer and Robert W. Lowe. 1894.

Essays and Sketches. Ed. R. Brimley Johnson. 1906.

Selections in Prose and Verse. Ed. J. H. Lobban. 1909.

Ballads of Robin Hood. Ed. Luther A. Brewer. 1922.

Poetical Works. Ed. H. S. Milford. 1923.

Marginalia. Ed. Luther A. Brewer. 1926.

Prefaces, Mainly to His Periodicals. Ed. R. Brimley Johnson. 1927.

Letter on Hogg's Life of Shelley. Ed. Luther A. Brewer. 1927.

Some Letters from My Leigh Hunt Portfolio. Ed. Luther A. Brewer. 1929.

Selected Essays. Ed. J. B. Priestley. 1929.

Shelley-Leigh Hunt: How Friendship Made History, Extending the Bounds of Human Freedom and Thought. Ed. R. Brimley Johnson. 1929.

My Hunt Library: The Holograph Letters. Ed. Luther A. Brewer. 1938.

Dramatic Criticism 1808–1831. Eds. Lawrence Huston Houtchens and Carolyn Washburn Houtchens. 1949.

Literary Criticism. Eds. Lawrence Huston Houtchens and Carolyn Washburn Houtchens. 1956.

Autobiography: The Earliest Sketches. Ed. Stephen F. Fogle. 1959.

Political and Occasional Essays. Eds. Lawrence Huston Houtchens and Carolyn Washburn Houtchens. 1962.

Musical Evenings; or, Selections, Vocal and Instrumental. Ed. David R. Cheney. 1964.

On Eight Sonnets by Dante. Ed. Rhodes Dunlap. 1965.

THOMAS DE QUINCEY (1785–1859)

Concerning the Relations of Great Britain, Spain, and Portugal by William Wordsworth (editor). 1809.

Close Comments upon a Straggling Speech. 1818.

Confessions of an English Opium-Eater. 1822.

Walladmor by G. W. H. Häring (adaptation). 1825. 2 vols.

Klosterheim; or, The Masque. 1832.

Letters to a Young Man Whose Education Has Been Neglected. 1843.

The Logic of Political Economy. 1844.

Writings. Ed. James T. Fields. 1851–59. 22 vols.

Selections Grave and Gay. 1853–60. 14 vols.

China: A Revised Reprint of Articles from Titan. 1857.

Works. 1862–71. 17 vols.

Works (Riverside Edition). 1877. 11 vols.

Select Essays. Ed. David Masson. 1888. 2 vols.

Collected Writings. Ed. David Masson. 1889–90. 14 vols.

The Wider Hope: Essays on Future Punishment. 1890.

Uncollected Writings. Ed. James Hogg. 1890. 2 vols.

Posthumous Works. Ed. Alexander H. Japp. 1891–93. 2 vols.

Literary Criticism. Ed. Helen Darbishire. 1909.

Selections. Ed. M. R. Ridley. 1927.

Diary 1803. Ed. Horace A. Eaton. 1927.

De Quincey at Work. Ed. Willard Hallam Bonner. 1936.

Selected Writings. Ed. Philip Van Doren Stern. 1937.

Dr. Johnson and Lord Chesterfield. 1945.

Recollections of the Lake Poets. Ed. Edward Sackville-West. 1948.

Unpublished Letters (with Elizabeth Barrett Browning). 1954.

Thomas De Quincey. Ed. Bonamy Dobrée. 1965.

New Essays: His Contributions to the Edinburgh Saturday Evening Post *and the* Edinburgh Evening Post *1827–1828.* Ed. Stuart M. Tave. 1966.

Selected Essays on Rhetoric. Ed. Frederick Burwick. 1967.

De Quincey as Critic. Ed. John E. Jordan. 1973.

WILLIAM H. PRESCOTT (1796–1859)

History of the Reign of Ferdinand and Isabella, the Catholic. 1838. 3 vols.

History of the Conquest of Mexico, with a Preliminary View of the Ancient Mexican Civilization, and the Life of the Conqueror, Hernando Cortés. 1843. 3 vols.

Biographical and Critical Miscellanies. 1845.

The History of the Conquest of Peru, with a Preliminary View of the Civilization of the Incas. 1847. 2 vols.

Memoir of Hon. John Pickering, LL.D. 1848.

History of the Reign of Philip the Second, King of Spain. 1855 [Volumes 1–2]; 1858 [Volume 3].

Memoir of the Honorable Abbott Laurence. 1856.

Complete Works. Ed. John Foster Kirk. 1873–75. 15 vols.

Works. Ed. W. H. Munro. 1904. 22 vols.

Correspondence 1833–1847. Ed. Roger Wolcott. 1925.

Unpublished Letters to Gayangos. Ed. Clara Louise Penney. 1927.

Representative Selections. Ed. William Charvat. 1943.

Literary Memoranda. Ed. C. Harvey Gardiner. 1961. 2 vols.

Papers. Ed. C. Harvey Gardiner. 1964.

THOMAS BABINGTON MACAULAY (1800–1859)

Pompeii: A Poem Which Obtained the Chancellor's Medal at the Cambridge Commencement, July 1819. 1819.

Evening: A Poem Which Obtained the Chancellor's Medal at the Cambridge Commencement, July 1821. 1821.

A Speech Delivered in the House of Commons on Lord John

Russell's Motion for Leave to Bring In a Bill to Emend the Representation of the People in England and Wales. 1831.

Speech on the Second Reading of the Third Reform Bill. 1831.

Speech on the Anatomy Bill. 1832.

A Speech on the Second Reading of the East-India Bill. 1833.

A Penal Code Prepared by the Indian Law Commissioners (with others). 1837.

Speech at a Meeting of the Electors of Edinburgh. 1839.

Critical and Miscellaneous Essays. 1840–41. 3 vols.

A Speech Delivered in the House of Commons. 1841.

Lays of Ancient Rome. 1842.

Critical and Historical Essays. 1843. 3 vols.

Speech in the House of Commons on the Proposed Discriminating Duties on Sugar. 1845.

Speech Delivered in the House of Commons on the Bill for the Abolition of Scottish University Tests. 1845.

The History of England from the Accession of James II. 1849 [Volumes 1–2]; 1855 [Volumes 3–4]; 1861 [Volume 5].

Inaugural Address Delivered on His Installation as Lord Rector of the University of Glasgow. 1849.

Speeches. 1853. 2 vols.

Speeches Corrected by Himself. 1854.

The Indian Civil Service (with others). 1855.

Were Human Sacrifices in Use among the Romans? (with Sir Robert Peel and Lord Mahon). 1860.

Correspondence between the Bishop of Exeter and Thomas Babington Macaulay in January 1849 on Certain Statements Respecting the Church of England. 1860.

Critical, Historical, and Miscellaneous Essays. 1860. 6 vols.

Miscellaneous Writings. Ed. Thomas Flower Ellis. 1860. 2 vols.

Biographies Contributed to the Encyclopaedia Britannica. 1860.

Indian Education Minutes. Ed. H. Woodrow. 1862.

Works. Ed. Lady Trevelyan. 1866. 8 vols.

Works (Albany Edition). 1898. 12 vols.

Hymn: An Effort of His Early Childhood. Ed. Lionel Horton-Smith. 1902.

Works. 1905–07. 9 vols.

Marginal Notes. Ed. G. Otto Trevelyan. 1907.

Essay and Speech on Jewish Disabilities. Eds. Israel Abrahams and S. Levy. 1910.

What Did Macaulay Say about America? Ed. Harry Miller Lydenberg. 1925.

Lays of Ancient Rome and Other Historical Poems. Ed. George Macaulay Trevelyan. 1928.

Legislative Minutes. Ed. C. D. Dharker. 1946.

Prose and Poetry. Ed. G. M. Young. 1952.

Selected Writings. Eds. John Clive and Thomas Pinney. 1972.

Letters. Ed. Thomas Pinney. 1974–81. 6 vols.

G. P. R. JAMES (1799–1860)

The Ruined City. 1828.

Adra; or, The Peruvians; The Ruined City, etc. 1829.

Richelieu: A Tale of France. 1829. 3 vols.

Darnley; or, The Field of the Cloth of Gold. 1830. 3 vols.

De L'Orme. 1830. 3 vols.

The History of Chivalry. 1830.

Philip Augustus; or, The Brothers in Arms. 1831. 3 vols.

Lives of the Most Eminent Foreign Statesmen (with Eyre Evans Crowe). 1832–38. 5 vols.

Memoirs of Great Commanders. 1832. 3 vols.

Henry Masterton; or, The Adventures of a Young Cavalier. 1832. 3 vols.

The String of Pearls. 1832. 2 vols.

France in the Lives of Her Great Men. 1832. Vol. 1 only (Charlemagne).

Delaware; or, The Ruined Family: A Tale. 1833. 3 vols.

Mary of Burgundy; or, The Revolt of Ghent. 1833. 3 vols.

The Life and Adventures of John Marston Hall. 1834. 3 vols.

The Gipsey: A Tale. 1835. 3 vols.

On the Educational Institutions of Germany. 1835.

My Aunt Pontypool. 1835. 3 vols.

One in a Thousand; or, The Days of Henry Quatre. 1835. 3 vols.

The Desultory Man. 1836. 3 vols.

A History of the Life of Edward the Black Prince, and of Various Events Connected Therewith. 1836. 2 vols.

Attila: A Romance. 1837. 3 vols.

Memoirs of Celebrated Women. 1837. 2 vols.

The Life and Times of Louis the Fourteenth. 1838. 4 vols.

The Robber: A Tale. 1838. 3 vols.

Henry of Guise; or, The States of Blois. 1839. 3 vols.

A Brief History of the United States Boundary Question: Drawn Up from Official Papers. 1839.

The Huguenot: A Tale of the French Protestants. 1839. 3 vols.

A Book of the Passions. 1839.

Charles Tyrell; or, The Bitter Blood. 1839. 2 vols.

Blanche of Navarre. 1839.

The Gentleman of the Old School: A Tale. 1839. 3 vols.

The King's Highway. 1840. 3 vols.

The Man at Harms; or, Henri de Cerons: A Romance. 1840.

Corse de Léon; or, The Brigand: A Romance. 1841. 3 vols.

Letters Illustrative of the Reign of William III from 1696 to 1708 by James Vernon (editor). 1841. 3 vols.

Bertrand de la Croix; or, The Siege of Rhodes. 1841.

The Ancient Régime: A Tale. 1841. 3 vols.

The Jacquerie; or, The Lady and the Page: An Historical Romance. 1841. 3 vols.

Some Remarks on the Corn Laws, with Suggestions for an Alteration in the Sliding Scale. 1841.

Morley Ernstein; or, The Tenants of the Heart. 1842. 3 vols.

A History of the Life of Richard Coeur-de-Lion, King of England. 1842–49. 4 vols.

The Commissioner; or, De Lunatico Inquirendo. 1843.

Forest Days: A Romance of Old Times. 1843. 3 vols.

The False Heir. 1843. 3 vols.

Eva St. Clair, and Other Collected Tales. 1843. 2 vols.

Agincourt: A Romance. 1844. 3 vols.

Arabella Stuart: A Romance from English History. 1844. 3 vols.

Rose d'Albret; or, Troublous Times: A Romance. 1844. 3 vols.

Works. 1844–49. 21 vols.

Arrah Neil; or, Times of Old. 1845. 3 vols.

The Smuggler: A Tale. 1845. 3 vols.

The Stepmother; or, Evil Doings. 1845, 1846 (3 vols.).

Heidelberg: A Romance. 1846. 3 vols.

The Life of King Henry IV., King of France and Navarre. 1847. 3 vols.

The Castle of Ehrenstein: Its Lords, Spiritual and Temporal; Its Inhabitants, Earthly and Unearthly. 1847. 3 vols.

A Whim and Its Consequences. 1847. 3 vols.

The Convict: A Tale. 1847. 3 vols.

Russell: A Tale of the Reign of Charles II. 1847. 3 vols.

Margaret Graham: A Tale Founded on Facts. 1848. 2 vols.

Beauchamp; or, The Error. 1848. 3 vols.

The Last of the Fairies. 1848.

Sir Theodore Broughton; or, Laurel Water. 1848. 3 vols.

Camaralzaman: A Fairy Drama. 1848.

An Investigation of the Circumstances Attending the Murder of

John, Earl of Gowrie and Alexander Ruthven, by Order of King James the Sixth of Scotland. 1849.

Rizzio; or, Scenes in Europe during the Sixteenth Century by William Henry Ireland (editor). 1849. 3 vols.

Dark Scenes of History. 1849. 3 vols.

The Forgery; or, Best Intentions. 1849. 3 vols.

John Jones's Tales for Little John Jones's. 1849. 2 vols.

The Flight of the Fiddlers: A Serio-Comic Verity. 1849.

The Woodman: A Romance of the Times of Richard III. 1849. 3 vols.

The Old Oak Chest: A Tale of Domestic Life. 1850. 3 vols.

Henry Smeaton: A Jacobite Story of the Reign of George I. 1851. 3 vols.

Gowrie; or, The King's Plot. 1851.

The Fate: A Tale of Stirring Times. 1851. 3 vols.

Remorse and Other Tales. 1852.

Revenge. 1852. 3 vols.

Adrian; or, The Clouds of the Mind: A Romance (with Maunsell B. Field). 1852. 2 vols.

Pequinillo: A Tale. 1852. 3 vols.

Agnes Sorel: An Historical Romance. 1853. 3 vols.

A Life of Vicissitudes: A Story of Revolutionary Times. 1852.

An Oration on the Character and Services of the Late Duke of Wellington. 1853.

Ticonderoga; or, The Black Eagle: A Tale of Times Not Long Past. 1854. 3 vols.

Prince Life: A Story for My Boy. 1856.

The Old Dominion; or, The Southampton Massacre. 1856. 3 vols.

Leonora d'Orco: A Historical Romance. 1857. 3 vols.

Lord Montagu's Page: A Historical Romance. 1858. 3 vols.

The Cavalier: An Historical Novel. 1859.

The Man in Black: An Historical Novel of the Days of Queen Anne. 1860.

Novels and Tales. c. 1860. 43 vols.

The Bride of Landeck. 1878.

ELIZABETH BARRETT BROWNING (1806–1861)

The Battle of Marathon. 1820.

Essay on Mind with Other Poems. 1826.

Prometheus Bound, Translated from the Greek of Aeschylus, and Miscellaneous Poems. 1833.

The Seraphim and Other Poems. 1838.

The Poems of Geoffrey Chaucer, Modernized (editor; with R. H. Horne, Leigh Hunt, and others). 1841.

A New Spirit of the Age (with R. H. Horne). 1844. 2 vols.

Poems. 1844. 2 vols.

Poems. 1850. 2 vols.

Casa Guidi Windows. 1851.

Two Poems (with Robert Browning). 1854.

Aurora Leigh. 1857.

Poems before Congress. 1860.

Last Poems. 1862.

The Greek Christian Poets and the English Poets. 1863.

Poetical Works. 1866. 5 vols.

A Selection from the Poetry of Elizabeth Barrett Browning. 1866–80. 2 vols.

Psyche Apocalypte: A Lyrical Drama (with R. H. Horne). 1876.

Life, Letters and Essays. 1877. 2 vols.

Letters Addressed to Richard Hengist Horne. Ed. S. R. Townshend Mayer. 1877. 2 vols.

Earlier Poems. Ed. R. H. Shepherd. 1878.

Poetical Works from 1826 to 1844. Ed. John H. Ingram. 1887.

Poetical Works. 1889–90. 6 vols.

Poetical Works. Ed. Frederick G. Kenyon. 1897.

Letters. Ed. Frederick G. Kenyon. 1897. 2 vols.

Letters (with Robert Browning). Ed. Robert Wiedemann Barrett-Browning. 1899. 2 vols.

Complete Poetical Works. Ed. Harriet Waters Preston. 1900.

Complete Works. Eds. Charlotte Porter and Helen A. Clarke. 1900. 6 vols.

Poems. Ed. Alice Meynell. 1903.

Complete Poems. 1904. 2 vols.

Epistle to a Canary. Ed. Edmund Gosse. 1913.

The Enchantress and Other Poems. 1913.

Leila: A Tale. Ed. Thomas J. Wise. 1913.

New Poems (with Robert Browning). Ed. Frederick G. Kenyon. 1914.

The Poet's Enchiridion. Ed. H. Buxton Forman. 1914.

Hitherto Unpublished Poems and Stories, with an Inedited Autobiography. Ed. H. Buxton Forman. 1914. 2 vols.

The Art of Scansion: A Letter to Uvedale Price. Ed. Alice Meynell. 1916.

Letters to Robert Browning and Other Correspondents. Ed. Thomas J. Wise. 1916.

Complete Poetical Works. Ed. Lilian Whiting. 1918. 2 vols.

Letters to Her Sister 1846–1859. Ed. Leonard Huxley. 1929.

Poetical Works, with Two Prose Essays. 1932.

Twenty-two Unpublished Letters (with Robert Browning). 1935.

Letters to B. R. Haydon. Ed. Martha Hale Shackleford. 1939.

Love Poems (with Robert Browning). Ed. Louis Untermeyer. 1946.

The Poetry of the Brownings. Ed. Clifford Bax. 1947.

Elizabeth Barrett to Miss Mitford: Unpublished Letters. Ed. Betty Miller. 1954.

Unpublished Letters (with Thomas De Quincey). 1954.

Elizabeth Barrett to Mr. Boyd: Unpublished Letters. Ed. Barbara P. McCarthy. 1955.

Letters to George Barrett (with Robert Browning). Eds. Paul Landis and Ronald E. Freeman. 1958.

Diary by E. B. B.: The Unpublished Diary of Elizabeth Barrett Browning 1831–1832. Eds. Philip Kelley and Ronald Hudson. 1969.

Letters 1845–1846 (with Robert Browning). Ed. Elvan Kintner. 1969. 2 vols.

The Barretts at Hope End: The Early Diary of Elizabeth Barrett Browning. Ed. Elizabeth Berridge. 1974.

Letters to Mrs. David Ogilvy. Eds. Peter N. Heydon and Philip Kelley. 1974.

A Variorum Edition of Sonnets from the Portuguese. Ed. Miroslava Dein Dow. 1980.

Letters to Mary Russell Mitford. Eds. Meredith B. Raymond and Mary Rose Sullivan. 1983. 3 vols.

ARTHUR HUGH CLOUGH (1819–1861)

The Close of the Eighteenth Century: A Prize Poem. 1835.

The Longest Day. c. 1840.

A Consideration of Objections against the Retrenchment Association. 1847.

The Bothie of Toper-na-fuosich: A Long-Vacation Pastoral. 1848.

Ambarvalia: Poems (with Thomas Burbidge). 1849.

Specimen Pages of Plutarch's Lives: The Translation Called Dryden's (editor). 1855.

Plutarch's Lives: The Translation Called Dryden's (editor). 1859. 5 vols.

Greek History from Themistocles to Alexander. 1860.

Poems. 1862.

Letters and Remains. 1865.
Poems and Prose Remains; with a Selection from His Letters. Ed. Blanche M. S. Clough. 1869. 2 vols.
The Bothie and Other Poems. Ed. Ernest Rhys. 1884.
Poems. 1888.
Selections from the Poems. 1894.
Poems. Ed. H. S. Milford. 1910.
Emerson-Clough Letters. Eds. Howard F. Lowry and Ralph Leslie Rusk. 1934.
Poems. Eds. H. F. Lowry, A. L. P. Norrington, and F. L. Mulhauser. 1951.
Correspondence. Ed. Frederick L. Mulhauser. 1957. 2 vols.
Selected Prose Works. Ed. Buckner B. Trawick. 1964.
A Choice of Cough's Verse. Ed. Michael Thorpe. 1969.
Poems. Ed. F. L. Mulhauser. 1974.

JAMES SHERIDAN KNOWLES (1784–1862)

The Welch Harper: A Ballad. 1796.
A Collection of Poems on Various Subjects. 1810.
The Senate; or, Social Villagers of a Kentish Town. 1817.
Virginius; or, The Liberation of Rome. 1820.
Caius Gracchus. 1823.
William Tell. 1825.
The Beggar's Daughter of Bethnal Green. 1828.
Brian Boroihme; or, The Maid of Erin. 1828.
The Elocutionist: A Collection of Pieces in Prose and Verse, Peculiarly Adapted to Display the Art of Reading (editor). 1831.
Alfred the Great; or, The Patriot King: An Historical Play. 1831.
A Masque. 1832.
The Hunchback. 1832.
The Magdalen and Other Stories. 1832.
The Wife: A Tale of Mantua. 1833.
Select Works. 1833. 2 vols.
Select Dramatic Works. 1835.
The Love-Chase. 1837.
The Daughter. 1837.
Woman's Wit; or, Love's Disguises. 1838.
The Maid of Mariendorpt. 1838.
Plays. 1838.
Love. 1839.
John of Procida; or, The Bridals of Messina. 1840.
Old Maids. 1841.
Dramatic Works. 1841–43. 3 vols.
The Rose of Arragon. 1842.
The Secretary. 1843.
Fortescue. 1846.
George Lovell. 1847. 3 vols.
The Rock of Rome; or, The Arch Heresy. 1849.
A Treatise on the Climate and Meteorology of Madeira by J. A. Mason (editor). 1850.
The Idol Demolished by Its Own Priest: An Answer to Cardinal Wiseman's Lectures on Transubstantiation. 1851.
The Gospel Attributed to Matthew Is the Record of the Whole Original Apostlehood. 1855.
Dramatic Works. 1856. 2 vols.
Alexina; or, True unto Death. 1866.
Lectures on Dramatic Literature. Eds. S. W. Abbott and Francis Harvey. 1873.
Lectures on Oratory, Gesture, and Poetry. Eds. S. W. Abbott and Francis Harvey. 1873.
Tales and Novelettes. Ed. Francis Harvey. 1874.
Various Dramatic Works. Ed. S. W. Abbott. 1874. 2 vols.

HENRY DAVID THOREAU (1817–1862)

A Week on the Concord and Merrimack Rivers. 1849.
Walden; or, Life in the Woods. 1854.
Excursions. Ed. Ralph Waldo Emerson. 1863.
The Maine Woods. 1864.
Cape Cod. 1864.
Letters to Various Persons. Ed. Ralph Waldo Emerson. 1865.
A Yankee in Canada, with Anti-Slavery and Reform Papers. 1866.
Early Spring in Massachusetts: From the Journals. Ed. H. G. O. Blake. 1881.
Summer: From the Journal. Ed. H. G. O. Blake. 1884.
Winter: From the Journal. Ed. H. G. O. Blake. 1888.
Autumn: From the Journal. Ed. H. G. O. Blake. 1892.
Writings (Riverside Edition). Eds. Horace E. Scudder et al. 1893–94. 11 vols.
Poems of Nature. Eds. Henry S. Salt and Frank B. Sanborn. 1895.
Some Unpublished Letters of Henry D. and Sophia E. Thoreau. Ed. Samuel Arthur Jones. 1899.
Writings (Manuscript Edition). Eds. Bradford Torrey and Francis H. Allen. 1906. 20 vols.
The Transmigrations of the Seven Brahmas: A Translation from the Harivansa *of Langlois* (translator). Ed. Arthur Christy. 1931.
Collected Poems. Ed. Carl Bode. 1943, 1964.
Correspondence. Eds. Walter Harding and Carl Bode. 1958.
Consciousness in Concord: The Text of Thoreau's Hitherto "Lost Journal" (1840–1841). Ed. Perry Miller. 1958.
Huckleberries. Ed. Leo Stoller. 1970.
Writings. Eds. Walter Harding et al. 1971– .
Selected Works. Ed. Walter Harding. 1975.

HENRY THOMAS BUCKLE (1821–1862)

History of Civilization in England. 1857 [Volume 1]; 1861 [Volume 2].
A Letter to a Gentleman Respecting Pooley's Case. 1859.
Essays. 1863.
Miscellaneous and Posthumous Works. Ed. Helen Taylor. 1872. 3 vols.
Introduction to the History of Civilization in England. Ed. John M. Robertson. 1904.
On Scotland and the Scottish Intellect. Ed. H. J. Hanham. 1970.

FRANCES TROLLOPE (1780–1863)

Domestic Manners of the Americans. 1832. 2 vols.
The Refugee in America. 1832. 3 vols.
The Mother's Manual; or, Illustrations of Matrimonial Economy: An Essay in Verse. 1833.
The Abbess: A Romance. 1833. 3 vols.
Belgium and Western Germany in 1833; Including Visits to Baden-Baden, Wiesbaden, Cassel, Hanover, the Harz Mountains, &c. &c. 1834. 2 vols.
Tremordyn Cliff. 1835. 3 vols.
Paris and the Parisians in 1835. 1836. 2 vols.
The Life and Adventures of Jonathan Jefferson Whitelaw; or, Scenes on the Mississippi. 1836. 3 vols.
The Vicar of Wrexhill. 1837. 3 vols.
Vienna and the Austrians, with Some Account of a Journey through Swabia, Bavaria, the Tyrol, and the Salzbourg. 1838. 2 vols.
A Romance of Vienna. 1838. 3 vols.
The Widow Barnaby. 1839. 3 vols.

The Widow Married: A Sequel to The Widow Barnaby. 1839. 3 vols.
The Life and Adventures of Michael Armstrong, the Factory Boy. 1840. 3 vols.
One Fault. 1840. 3 vols.
A Summer in Brittany by Thomas Adolphus Trollope (editor). 1840. 2 vols.
Charles Chesterfield; or, The Adventures of a Youth of Genius. 1841. 3 vols.
A Summer in Western France by Thomas Adolphus Trollope (editor). 1841. 2 vols.
The Ward of Thorpe-Combe. 1842. 3 vols.
The Blue Belles of England. 1842. 3 vols.
A Visit to Italy. 1842. 2 vols.
The Barnabys in America; or, Adventures of the Widow Wedded. 1843. 3 vols.
Hargrave; or, The Adventures of a Man of Fashion. 1843. 3 vols.
Jessie Phillips: A Tale of the Present Day. 1843. 3 vols.
The Laurringtons; or, Superior People. 1844. 3 vols.
Young Love. 1844. 3 vols.
The Attractive Man. 1846. 3 vols.
The Robertses on Their Travels. 1846. 3 vols.
Travels and Travellers: A Series of Sketches. 1846. 2 vols.
Father Eustace: A Tale of the Jesuits. 1847. 3 vols.
The Three Cousins. 1847. 3 vols.
Town and Country. 1848. 3 vols.
The Young Countess; or, Love and Jealousy. 1848. 3 vols.
The Lottery of Marriage. 1849. 3 vols.
The Old World and the New. 1849. 3 vols.
Petticoat Government. 1850. 3 vols.
Mrs. Matthews; or, Family Mysteries. 1851. 3 vols.
Second Love; or, Beauty and Intellect. 1851. 3 vols.
Uncle Walter. 1852. 3 vols.
The Young Heiress. 1853. 3 vols.
The Life and Adventures of a Clever Woman: Illustrated with Occasional Extracts from Her Diary. 1854. 3 vols.
Gertrude; or, Family Pride. 1855. 3 vols.
Fashionable Life; or, Paris and London. 1856. 3 vols.

WILLIAM MAKEPEACE THACKERAY (1811–1863)

Flore et Zéphyr. 1836.
The Yellowplush Correspondence. 1838.
Reminiscences of Major Gahagan. 1839.
The Loving Ballad of Lord Bateman (with Charles Dickens). 1839.
An Essay on the Genius of George Cruikshank. 1840.
The Paris Sketch Book. 1840. 2 vols.
Comic Tales and Sketches. 1841. 2 vols.
The Second Funeral of Napoleon: In Three Letters to Miss Smith of London; and The Chronicle of the Drum. 1841.
The Irish Sketch-Book. 1843. 2 vols.
Jeames's Diary; or, Sudden Riches. 1846.
Notes of a Journey from Cornhill to Grand Cairo, by Way of Lisbon, Athens, Constantinople, and Jerusalem. 1846.
Mrs. Perkins's Ball. 1847.
Vanity Fair: A Novel without a Hero. 1847–48. 20 parts.
The Book of Snobs. 1848.
Our Street. 1848.
The History of Pendennis. 1848–50. 24 parts.
Doctor Birch and His Young Friends. 1849.
The History of Samuel Titmarsh and The Great Hoggarty Diamond. 1849.
Miscellanies: Prose and Verse. 1849–51. 2 vols.

The Kickleburys on the Rhine. 1850.
Stubbs's Calendar; or, The Fatal Boots. 1850.
Rebecca and Rowena: A Romance upon Romance. 1850.
The History of Henry Esmond, Esq. 1852. 3 vols.
The Confessions of Fitz-Boodle and Some Passage in the Life of Major Gahagan. 1852.
A Shabby Genteel Story and Other Tales. 1852.
Men's Wives. 1852.
The Luck of Barry Lyndon: A Romance of the Last Century. 1852–53. 2 vols.
Mr. Brown's Letters to a Young Man about Town. 1853.
The English Humourists of the Eighteenth Century. 1853.
The Newcomes: Memoirs of a Most Respectable Family. 1853–55. 24 parts.
The Rose and the Ring. 1855.
Miscellanies: Prose and Verse. 1855–57. 4 vols.
Ballads. 1856.
Christmas Books. 1857.
The Virginians: A Tale of the Last Century. 1857–59. 24 parts.
Mr. Thackeray, Mr. Yates, and the Garrick Club (with Edmund Yates). 1859.
The Four Georges: Sketches of Manners, Morals, Court, and Town Life. 1860.
Lovel the Widower. 1860.
The Adventures of Philip on His Way through the World; Shewing Who Robbed Him, Who Helped Him, and Who Passed Him By. 1862. 3 vols.
Roundabout Papers. 1863.
Miscellanies. 1864. 6 vols.
Denis Duval. 1864.
Works (Library Edition). 1867–69, 1885–86. 24 vols.
Early and Late Papers Hitherto Uncollected. Ed. James T. Fields. 1867.
The Orphan of Pimlico and Other Sketches, Fragments, and Drawings. Ed. Anne Thackeray (Ritchie). 1876.
Works (De Luxe Edition). 1878–86. 26 vols.
Etchings. 1878.
Works (Standard Edition). 1883–86. 26 vols.
Sultan Stork and Other Stories and Sketches (1829–1844). Ed. R. H. Shepherd. 1887.
A Collection of Letters 1847–1855. Ed. J. O. Brookfield. 1887.
Early Writings. Ed. Charles Plumptre Johnson. 1888.
Works. Ed. Horace E. Scudder. 1889. 22 vols.
Reading a Poem. 1891.
Works (New Century Library). 1899–1900. 14 vols.
The Hitherto Unidentified Contributions of W. M. Thackeray to Punch. Ed. M. H. Spielmann. 1899.
Writings in the National Standard *and* Constitutional. Ed. W. T. Spencer. 1899.
Stray Papers: Being Stories, Reviews, Verses, and Sketches (1821–1847). Ed. Lewis Melville. 1901.
Prose Works. Ed. Walter Jerrold. 1901–03. 30 vols.
Works. Ed. Lewis Melville. 1901–07. 20 vols.
Letters to an American Family. Ed. Lucy W. Baxter. 1904.
The New Sketch Book: Being Essays Now First Collected from the Foreign Quarterly Review. Ed. Robert S. Garnett. 1906.
Works (Oxford Edition). Ed. George Saintsbury. 1908. 18 vols.
Works (Centenary Biographical Edition). Ed. Anne Thackeray Ritchie. 1910–11. 26 vols.
Some Family Letters. 1911.
Unpublished Letters. Ed. Clement K. Shorter. 1916.
W. M. Thackeray and Edward FitzGerald, a Literary Friendship: Unpublished Letters and Verses. Ed. Clement K. Shorter. 1916.

Letters of Anne Thackeray Ritchie, with Forty-two Additional Letters from Her Father. Ed. Hester Ritchie. 1924.

Letters and Private Papers. Ed. Gordon N. Ray. 1945–46. 6 vols.

Contributions to the Morning Chronicle. Ed. Gordon N. Ray. 1955.

Illustrations. Ed. John Buchanan-Brown. 1979.

The Heroic Adventures of M. Boudin. Ed. Gordon N. Ray. 1984.

WALTER SAVAGE LANDOR (1775–1864)

Poems. 1795.

Moral Epistle: Respectfully Dedicated to Earl Stanhope. 1795.

To the Burgesses of Warwick. 1797.

Gebir. 1798.

Poems from the Arabic and Persian. 1800.

Poetry. 1800.

Iambi Incerto Auctore. c. 1802.

Gebirus Poema. 1803.

Simonidea. 1806.

Three Letters, Written in Spain, to D. Francisco Riguelme. 1809.

Ode ad Gustavum Regem; Ode ad Gustavum Exulem. 1810.

Count Julian. 1812.

Letters Addressed to Lord Liverpool, and the Parliament, on the Preliminaries of Peace. 1814.

Letter to Mr. Jervis. 1814.

Idyllia Nova Quinque Heroum atque Heroidum. 1815.

Sponsalia Polyxenae. 1819.

Idyllia Heroica. 1820.

Poche osservazioni sullo stato attuale di que' popoli, che vogliono governarsi per mezzo delle rappresentanze. 1821.

Imaginary Conversations of Literary Men and Statesmen: First Series. 1824 [Volumes 1–2]; 1828 [Volume 3].

Imaginary Conversations of Literary Men and Statesmen: Second Series. 1829. 2 vols.

Gebir, Count Julian and Other Poems. 1831.

Citation and Examination of William Shakspeare. 1834.

Pericles and Aspasia. 1836. 2 vols.

The Letters of a Conservative: In Which Are Shown the Only Means of Saving What Is Left of the English Church. 1836.

Terry Hogan: An Eclogue. 1836.

A Satire on Satirists and Admonition to Detractors. 1836.

The Pentameron and Pentalogia. 1837.

Andrea of Hungary, and Giovanna of Naples. 1839.

Fra Rupert. 1840.

Works. 1846. 2 vols.

Poemata et Inscriptiones. 1847.

The Hellenics. 1847.

Italics. 1848.

Savagius Landor Lamartino. 1848.

Imaginary Conversation of King Carlo-Alberto and the Dutchess Belgioioso, on the Affairs and Prospects of Italy. 1848.

Carmen ad Heroinam. c. 1848.

Epistola ad Romanos. c. 1848.

Epistola ad Pium IX. Pontificem. 1849.

Ad Cossuthem et Bemum. 1849.

Statement of Occurrences at Llanbedr. 1849.

Popery: British and Foreign. 1851.

On Kossuth's Voyage to America. 1851.

Tyrannicide: Published for the Benefit of the Hungarians in America. 1851.

Imaginary Conversations of Greeks and Romans. 1853.

The Last Fruit off an Old Tree. 1853.

Letters of an American, Mainly on Russia and Revolution. 1854.

Antony and Octavius: Scenes for the Study. 1856.

Letter to R. W. Emerson. 1856.

Selections from the Writings. Ed. George Stillman Hillard. 1856.

Walter Savage Landor and the Honorable Mrs. Yescombe. 1857.

Mr. Landor Threatened. 1857.

Dry Sticks Fagoted by Walter Savage Landor. 1858.

Mr. Landor's Remarks on a Suit Preferred against Him, at the Summer Assizes at Taunton, Illustrating the Appendix to His Hellenics. 1858.

Savonarola e il priore di San Marco. 1860.

Heroic Idyls, with Additional Poems. 1863.

Cameos Selected from the Works. Eds. Edmund Clarence Stedman and Thomas Bailey Aldrich. 1874.

Works and Life. Ed. John Forster. 1876. 8 vols.

Selections from the Writings. Ed. Sidney Colvin. 1882.

Poems. Ed. Ernest Radford. 1889.

The Pentameron and Other Imaginary Conversations. Ed. Havelock Ellis. 1889.

Imaginary Conversations. Ed. Charles G. Crump. 1891. 6 vols.

Poems, Dialogues in Verse, and Epigrams. Ed. Charles G. Crump. 1892. 2 vols.

Longer Prose Works. Ed. Charles G. Crump. 1892–93. 2 vols.

Aphorisms. Ed. R. Brimley Johnson. 1897.

Letters and Other Unpublished Writings. Ed. Stephen Wheeler. 1897.

Letters Public and Private. Ed. Stephen Wheeler. 1899.

Shorter Works. 1904.

The Hellenics and Gebir. Ed. Arthur Symons. 1907.

Charles James Fox: A Commentary on His Life and Character. Ed. Stephen Wheeler. 1907.

An Address to the Fellows of Trinity College, Oxford, on the Alarm of Invasion (1798). 1917.

Garibaldi and the President of the Sicilian Senate: An Imaginary Conversation. 1917.

A Modern Greek Idyl. 1917.

To Elizabeth Barrett Browning and Other Verses. 1917.

A Day-Book. Ed. John Bailey. 1919.

Complete Works. Eds. T. Earle Welby and Stephen Wheeler. 1927–36. 16 vols.

A Poet's Dream. 1928.

Imaginary Conversations and Poems. Ed. Havelock Ellis. 1933.

Last Days, Letters and Conversations. Ed. H. C. Minchin. 1934.

Poetry and Prose. Ed. E. K. Chambers. 1946.

Shorter Poems. Ed. J. B. Sidgwick. 1946.

Poems. Ed. Geoffrey Grigson. 1964.

Landor: A Biographical Anthology. Ed. Herbert Van Thal. 1973.

Landor as Critic. Ed. Charles L. Proudfit. 1979.

Selected Poetry and Prose. Ed. Keith Hanley. 1981.

JOHN CLARE (1793–1864)

Proposals for Publishing a Collection of Trifles in Verse. 1817.

Poems Descriptive of Rural Life and Scenery. 1820.

The Village Minstrel and Other Poems. 1821. 2 vols.

The Shepherd's Calendar; with Village Stories and Other Poems. 1827.

The Rural Muse. 1835.

*Life and Remains: Including Letters from His Friends and Con-
    temporaries, Extracts from His Diary, Prose Fragments,
    Old Ballads (Collected by Clare).* Ed. J. L. Cherry. 1873.

Poems. Ed. Norman Gale. 1901.

Poems. Ed. Arthur Symons. 1908.

Poems Chiefly from Manuscript. Eds. Edmund Blunden and
    Alan Porter. 1920.

Madrigals and Chronicles: Being Newly Found Poems. Ed.
    Edmund Blunden. 1924.

Sketches in the Life of John Clare. Ed. Edmund Blunden.
    1931.

Poems. Ed. J. W. Tibble. 1935. 2 vols.

Poems of John Clare's Madness. Ed. Geoffrey Grigson. 1949.

Selected Poems. Ed. Geoffrey Grigson. 1950.

Letters. Eds. J. W. Tibble and Anne Tibble. 1951.

Prose. Eds. J. W. Tibble and Anne Tibble. 1951.

Later Poems. Eds. Eric Robinson and Geoffrey Summerfield.
    1964.

Selected Poems and Prose. Eds. Eric Robinson and Geoffrey
    Summerfield. 1966.

The Midsummer Cushion. Ed. Anne Tibble. 1979.

The Journal; Essays; The Journey from Essex. Ed. Anne Tibble.
    1980.

John Clare's Birds. Eds. Eric Robinson and Richard Fitter.
    1982.

Autobiographical Writings. Ed. Eric Robinson. 1983.

Natural History Prose Writings. Ed. Margaret Grainger. 1983.

John Clare. Eds. Eric Robinson and David Powell. 1984.

Later Poems 1837–1864. Eds. Eric Robinson and David Pow-
    ell. 1984. 2 vols.

Letters. Ed. Mark Storey. 1985.

NATHANIEL HAWTHORNE (1804–1864)

Fanshawe. 1828.

Twice-Told Tales. 1837, 1842 (2 vols.).

Peter Pauley's Universal History (editor; with Elizabeth Haw-
    thorne). 1837. 2 vols.

*Time's Portraiture: Being the Carrier's Address to the Patrons of
    the Salem Gazette for the First of January, 1838.* 1838.

*The Sister Years: Being the Carrier's Address to the Patrons of
    the Salem Gazette for the First of January, 1839.* 1839.

Grandfather's Chair: A History for Youth. 1841.

*Famous Old People: Being the Second Epoch of Grandfather's
    Chair.* 1841.

The Liberty Tree, with the Last Words of Grandfather's Chair.
    1841.

Biographical Stories for Children. 1842.

The Celestial Rail-Road. 1843.

Mosses from an Old Manse. 1846. 2 vols.

The Scarlet Letter: A Romance. 1850.

The House of the Seven Gables: A Romance. 1851.

A Wonder-Book for Girls and Boys. 1852.

The Snow-Image and Other Twice-Told Tales. 1852.

The Blithedale Romance. 1852.

Life of Franklin Pierce. 1852.

*Tanglewood Tales for Girls and Boys: Being a Second Wonder-
    Book.* 1853.

The Marble Faun; or, The Romance of Monte Beni. 1860.

Our Old Home: A Series of English Sketches. 1863.

*Pansie: A Fragment: The Last Literary Effort of Nathaniel
    Hawthorne.* 1864.

Works. 1865–76. 23 vols.

Passages from the American Note-Books. Ed. Sophia Haw-
    thorne. 1868. 2 vols.

Passages from the English Note-Books. Ed. Sophia Hawthorne.
    1870. 2 vols.

Passages from the French and Italian Note-Books. Ed. Una
    Hawthorne. 1871. 2 vols.

Septimius Felton; or, The Elixir of Life. Eds. Una Hawthorne
    and Robert Browning. 1872.

Writings. Ed. George Parsons Lathrop. 1875–83. 25 vols.

The Dolliver Romance and Other Pieces. Ed. Sophia Haw-
    thorne. 1876.

Doctor Grimshawe's Secret: A Romance. Ed. Julian Haw-
    thorne. 1883.

Works (Riverside Edition). Ed. George Parsons Lathrop. 1883.
    12 vols.

Complete Writings (Autograph Edition). 1900. 22 vols.

Twenty Days with Julian and Little Bunny: A Diary. 1904.

Love Letters. 1907. 2 vols.

Letters to William D. Ticknor. 1910. 2 vols.

Works. Ed. Charles Curtis Bigelow. 1923. 10 vols.

The Heart of Hawthorne's Journals. Ed. Newton Arvin. 1929.

*Hawthorne as Editor: Selections from His Writings in the
    American Magazine of Useful and Entertaining Knowl-
    edge.* Ed. Arlin Turner. 1941.

Works. Eds. William Charvat et al. 1963–   .

Hawthorne's Lost Notebook 1835–1841. Ed. Barbara S.
    Mouffe. 1978.

RICHARD COBDEN (1804–1865)

England, France, Russia and Turkey. 1834.

England, Ireland, and America. 1835.

The Sultan Manhoud, and Mehemet Ali Pasha. 1835.

Address to the Independent Electors of the Borough of Stockport.
    1836.

*National Education: A Reply to the Rev. Hugh Stowell's Let-
    ter.* 1837.

*Incorporate Your Borough! A Letter to the Inhabitants of Man-
    chester.* 1838.

*Report to the Directors to a Special Meeting of the Chamber of
    Commerce and Manufactures at Manchester on the Ef-
    fects of the Administration of the Bank of England upon
    the Commercial and Manufacturing Interests of the
    County.* 1839.

*Speech at the Town Council on Proposing a Resolution to Pe-
    tition Both Houses of Parliament for the Total and Imme-
    diate Repeal of the Corn Laws.* 1841.

*Speech in the House of Commons in Support of the Free Address
    to the Queen.* 1841.

*To the Manufacturers, Millowners, and Other Capitalists, of
    Every Shade of Political Opinion, Engaged in the Various
    Branches of the Cotton Trade, in the District of Which
    Manchester Is the Centre.* 1841.

*Corn Laws: Extracts from the Works of Thomas Perronet
    Thompson* (editor). 1842.

The Corn Laws: Speech in the House of Commons. 1842.

The Land-Tax Fraud: Speech in the House of Commons. 1842.

The Tariff. 1842.

Our Colonies: Speech in the House of Commons. 1842.

Alarming Distress: Speech in the House of Commons. 1842.

Speech in Reply to Sir Robert Peel, in the House of Commons.
    1842.

Speech at a Meeting of Members of the Anti-Corn-Law League.
    1842.

*Speech to the Anti-Corn-Law League in Reference to the Dis-
    turbances in the Manufacturing Districts.* c. 1842.

*Speech at Sheffield, Showing the True Character of the Oppo-
    nents of the League.* 1842.

Distress of the Country: Speech in the House of Commons. 1843.

Speech in the Theatre Royal, Drury Lane, London. 1843.

The New Emigration Scheme: Speech in the Theatre Royal, Drury Lane, London. 1843.

Total Repeal: Speech in the House of Commons. 1843.

Speech at a Meeting of the Anti-Corn-Law League. 1843.

Tenant Farmers and Farm Labourers: Speech on Moving for a Select Committee "to Inquire into the Effectives of Protective Duties on Imports upon the Interests of Tenant-Farmers and Farm-Labourers." 1844.

Speech in the House of Commons on Mr. Villiers' Motion for the Total Repeal of the Corn Laws. 1844.

Agricultural Distress: Speech in the House of Commons on Moving for a Select Committee to Inquire into the Extent and Causes of the Alleged Existing Agricultural Distress, and into the Interests of Landowners, Farmers, and Farm Labourers. 1845.

Letter to the Tenant Farmers of England. 1846.

Speech in the House of Commons on Sir Peel's Motion for a Committee of the Whole House on the Corn Laws. 1846.

Speech in the House of Commons. 1848.

Speech on the Income Tax. 1848.

Eloquent and Powerful Speech in the House of Commons on Mr. Hume's Motion for Parliamentary Reform and Retrenchment. 1848.

National Defences. 1848.

The National Budget for 1849. 1848.

Reform and Retrenchment: The Speeches of Richard Cobden, T. M. Gibson, and John Bright, Esq., in the Free Trade Hall. 1849.

Speeches on Peace, Financial Reform, Colonial Reform, and Other Subjects, Delivered during 1849. 1849.

Speech on the Russian Loan, Delivered at the London Tavern. 1850.

Speech at the Fourth Monthly Soirée of the National Parliamentary and Financial Reform Association. 1851.

International Reduction of Armaments: Speech in the House of Commons. 1851.

1793 and 1853, in Three Letters. 1853.

How Wars Are Got Up in India: The Origin of the Burmese War. 1853.

What Next and Next? 1856.

Remarks on the Law of Partnership and Limited Liability (with W. S. Lindsay). 1856.

On the Probable Fall of the Value of Gold by Michael Chevalier (translator). 1859.

The Three Panics: An Historical Episode. 1862.

Maritime Law and Belligerent Rights: Speech Advocating a Reform of International Maritime Law, Delivered to the Manchester Chamber of Commerce. 1862.

Letter to Henry Ashworth, Esq., upon the Present State of International Maritime Law, as Affecting the Rights of Belligerents and Neutrals. 1862.

Speech on the "Foreign Enlistment Act," in the House of Commons. 1863.

Mr. Cobden and The Times: *Correspondence between Mr. Cobden and Mr. Delane, Editor of* The Times; *with a Supplementary Correspondence between Mr. Cobden, and the Editor of the* Daily Telegraph. 1864.

Political Writings. 1867. 2 vols.

Government Manufacturing Establishments: Speech in the House of Commons. 1869.

Speeches on Questions of Public Policy. Eds. John Bright and James E. Thorold Rogers. 1870. 2 vols.

Mr. Cobden on the Land Question. 1873.

Speeches on Free Trade. 1903.

American Diaries. Ed. Elizabeth Hoon Cawley. 1952.

ELIZABETH GASKELL (1810–1865)

Life in Manchester. 1848.

Mary Barton: A Tale of Manchester Life. 1848. 2 vols.

The Moorland Cottage. 1850.

Lizzie Leigh. 1850.

Ruth. 1853. 3 vols.

Cranford. 1853.

Lizzie Leigh and Other Tales. 1855.

The Sexton's Hero and Christmas Storms and Sunshine. 1855.

North and South. 1855. 2 vols.

The Life of Charlotte Brontë. 1857. 2 vols.

Mabel Vaughan by Maria S. Cummins (editor). 1857.

My Lady Ludlow. 1858.

Round the Sofa. 1859. 2 vols.

Right at Last and Other Tales. 1860.

Lois the Witch and Other Tales. 1861.

A Dark Night's Work. 1863.

Sylvia's Lovers. 1863. 3 vols.

Cousin Phillis. 1864.

The Grey Woman and Other Tales. 1865.

Cousin Phillis and Other Tales. 1865.

Wives and Daughters: An Every-Day Story. 1866. 2 vols.

Novels and Tales. 1872–73. 8 vols.

Works. 1897. 8 vols.

Works (Knutsford Edition). Ed. Adolphus William Ward. 1906. 8 vols.

Novels and Tales. Ed. Clement K. Shorter. 1906–19. 11 vols.

Mrs. Gaskell. Ed. Esther A. Chadwick. 1911.

Letters on Charlotte Brontë. c. 1915.

"My Diary": The Early Years of My Daughter Marianne. 1923.

Letters of Mrs. Gaskell and Charles Eliot Norton 1855–1865. Ed. Jane Whitehill. 1932.

The Cage at Cranford and Other Stories. Ed. Paul Beard. 1937.

Letters. Eds. J. A. V. Chappie and Arthur Pollard. 1966.

THOMAS LOVE PEACOCK (1785–1866)

The Monks of St. Mark. 1804.

Palmyra and Other Poems. 1806.

The Genius of the Thames: A Lyrical Poem. 1810.

The Genius of the Thames, Palmyra, and Other Poems. 1812.

The Philosophy of Melancholy, with a Mythological Ode. 1812.

Sir Hornbook; or, Childe Launcelot's Expedition: A Grammatico-Allegorical Ballad. 1813.

Sir Proteus: A Satirical Ballad. 1814.

Headlong Hall. 1816.

Melincourt. 1817. 3 vols.

The Round Table; or, King Arthur's Feast. c. 1817.

Rhododaphne; or, The Thessalian Spell. 1818.

Nightmare Abbey. 1818.

Maid Marian. 1822.

The Misfortunes of Elphin. 1829.

Crochet Castle. 1831.

Paper Money Lyrics and Other Poems. 1837.

Headlong Hall; Nightmare Abbey; Maid Marian; Crochet Castle. 1837.

A Whitebait Dinner at Lovegrove's at Blackwall. 1851.

Gryll Grange. 1861.

Gl'Ingannati: The Deceived (translator). 1862.

Works. Ed. Henry Cole. 1875. 3 vols.

Works. Ed. Richard Garnett. 1891. 10 vols.

Works. Ed. R. Brimley Johnson. 1905–06. 3 vols.

Memoirs of Shelley. Ed. H. F. B. Brett-Smith. 1909.

Letters to Edward Hookham and Percy B. Shelley, with Fragments of Unpublished Mss. Eds. Richard Garnett and F. E. Sanborn. 1910.

Plays. Ed. A. B. Young. 1910.

Works (Halliford Edition). Eds. H. F. B. Brett-Smith and C. E. Jones. 1924–34. 10 vols.

A Bill for the Better Promotion of Oppression on the Sabbath Day. 1926.

Novels. Ed. David Garnett. 1948.

A Peacock Selection. Ed. H. L. B. Moody. 1966.

Memoirs of Shelley and Other Essays and Reviews. Ed. Howard Mills. 1970.

JOHN KEBLE (1792–1866)

On Translation from Dead Languages: A Prize Essay Recited in the Theatre at Oxford. 1812.

The Christian Year: Thoughts in Verse for the Sundays and Holydays throughout the Year. 1827. 2 vols.

Six Queries Tending to Oppose Mr. Peel's Candidature to Represent the University of Oxford. 1829.

A Hint from Bristol: A Plea against Reform. 1831.

National Apostasy, Considered in a Sermon Preached at St. Mary's, Oxford, before His Majesty's Judges of Assize. 1833.

Ode for the Encaenia at Oxford, in Honour of His Grace, Arthur, Duke of Wellington, Chancellor of the University of Oxford. 1834.

Lyra Apostolica (with others). 1834.

Adherence to the Apostolical Succession the Safest Course. 1834.

Richard Nelson (with Thomas Keble). 1834. 4 parts.

Sunday Lessons: The Principle of Selection. 1834.

Sermons for Saints' Days and Holidays. 1835. 4 parts.

The Works of Richard Hooker (editor). 1836. 3 vols.

Primitive Tradition Recognized in Holy Scripture. 1836.

A Postscript to the Third Edition of the Sermon Entitled Primitive Tradition Recognized in Holy Scripture. 1837.

Memorials and Communications, Addressed to His Late Majesty's Commissioners of Inquiry into the State of the Established Church (editor). 1838.

A Library of Fathers of the Holy Catholic Church (editor; with E. B. Pusey, Charles Marriott, and John Henry Newman). 1838–85. 46 vols.

Remains of the Late Reverend Richard Hurrell Froude (editor; with John Henry Newman). 1838–39. 4 vols.

The Psalter or Psalms of David (translator). 1839.

The Case of Catholic Subscription to the Thirty-nine Articles Considered. 1841.

The Child's Christian Year: Hymns for Every Sunday and Holy-day. 1841.

On the Mysticism Attributed to the Early Fathers of the Church. 1841.

Protest against the Bishop of Winchester's Refusal to Ordain the Rev. P. Young. 1842.

An Horology; or, Dial of Prayer: Dedicated to His Godchildren. 1842.

De Poeticae Vi Medica: Praelectiones Academicae Oxonii Habitae, Annis 1832–1841. 1844. 2 vols.

Heads of Consideration on the Case of Mr. Ward. 1845.

Mutual Intercession (editor; with others). 1845.

The Duty of Hoping against Hope. 1846.

Lyra Innocentium: Thoughts in Verse on Christian Children. 1846.

Sermons, Academical and Occasional. 1847.

The Strength of Christ's Little Ones: A Sermon Preached at Coggeshall for the School. 1849.

Against Profane Dealing with Holy Matrimony in Regard of a Man and His Wife's Sister. 1849.

Church Matters in MDCCCL. 1850. 2 parts.

A Selection from the Sermons and Poetical Remains of the Rev. George James Cornish (editor). 1850.

A Pastoral Letter to the Parishioners of Hursley, Occasioned by the Proposed Synodical Meeting in the Diocese of Exeter. 1851.

On the Representation of the University of Oxford: A Letter to Sir Brook W. Bridges. 1852.

A Few Very Plain Thoughts on the Proposed Addition of Dissenters to the University of Oxford. 1854.

An Argument for Not Proceeding Immediately to Repeal the Laws Which Treat the Nuptial Bond as Indissoluble. 1857.

A Sequel to the Argument against Immediately Repealing the Laws Which Treat the Nuptial Bond as Indissoluble. 1857.

On Eucharistical Adoration. 1857.

Hymns for Little Children (editor). 1857.

Easter Joy and Easter Work: A Sermon Preached on the Day of Thanksgiving for the Suppression of the Rebellion in India. 1857.

Considerations Suggested by a Late Pastoral Letter on the Doctrine of the Most Holy Eucharist. 1858.

A Sermon Preached at St. Paul's Church, Brighton, on St. Luke's Day, 1858. 1858.

The Rich and the Poor One in Christ: A Sermon Preached in St. Peter's Church, Sudbury. 1858.

Women Labouring in the Lord: A Sermon Preached at Wantage. 1863.

The Life of the Right Reverend Father in God, Thomas Wilson, D.D. 1863. 2 vols.

A Litany of Our Lord's Warnings (for the Present Distress). 1864.

Pentecostal Fear: A Sermon Preached in the Parish Church of Cuddeson. 1864.

Letter to a Member of Convocation. 1867.

Sermons, Occasional and Parochial. 1867.

"The State in Its Relations with the Church": A Paper Reprinted from the British Critic, *October, 1839.* 1869.

Miscellaneous Poems. Ed. George Moberly. 1869.

Village Sermons on the Baptismal Service. Ed. E. B. Pusey. 1869.

Letters of Spiritual Counsel and Guidance. Ed. R. F. Wilson. 1870.

Sermons for the Christian Year. 1875–80. 11 vols.

Occasional Papers and Reviews. Ed. E. B. Pusey. 1877.

Studia Sacra. Ed. J. P. Norris. 1877.

Outlines of Instructions; or, Meditations for the Church's Seasons. Ed. R. F. Wilson. 1880.

Selections from the Writings. 1883.

Maxims and Gleanings from the Writings. Ed. Caroline M. Smith. 1883.

The Christian Year, Lyra Innocentium, and Other Poems. 1914.

Correspondence of John Henry Newman with John Keble and Others 1839–1845. 1917.

CATHARINE MARIA SEDGWICK (1789–1867)

A New-England Tale; or, Sketches of New-England Character and Manners. 1822.
Mary Hollis: An Original Tale. 1822.
Redwood: A Tale. 1824. 2 vols.
The Travellers: A Tale Designed for Young People. 1825.
The Deformed Boy. 1826.
Hope Leslie; or, Early Times in the Massachusetts. 1827. 2 vols.
A Short Essay to Do Good. 1828.
Clarence; or, A Tale of Our Own Times. 1830. 2 vols.
Home: Scenes and Characters Illustrating Christian Truth. 1835.
The Linwoods; or, "Sixty Years Since" in America. 1835. 2 vols.
Tales and Sketches. 1835.
The Poor Rich Man, and the Rich Poor Man. 1836.
Live and Let Live; or, Domestic Service. 1837.
The Love Token for Children: Designed for Sunday-School Libraries. 1838.
Means and Ends; or, Self-Training. 1839.
Stories for Young Persons. 1840.
Letters from Abroad to Kindred at Home. 1841. 2 vols.
Tales and Sketches: Second Series. 1844.
The Morals of Manners; or, Hints for Our Young People. 1846.
Facts and Fancies for School-Day Readings: A Sequel to Morals of Manners. 1848.
The Boy of Mount Rhigi. 1848.
Works. 1849. 3 vols.
Tales of City Life. 1850.
A New England Tale and Miscellanies. 1852.
Married or Single? 1857. 2 vols.
Memoir of Joseph Curtis, a Model Man. 1858.
Facts and Fancies and Other Stories. 1864.
Letters from Charles Sedgwick to His Family and Friends (editor; with Katharine Sedgwick Minot). 1870.
Life and Letters. Ed. Mary E. Dewey. 1871.

FITZ-GREENE HALLECK (1790–1867)

Poems by Croaker, Croaker & Co. and Croaker, Jun. (with Joseph Rodman Drake). 1819.
Fanny. 1819.
Alnwick Castle, with other Poems. 1827.
Fanny, with Other Poems. 1839.
Poetical Works. 1847.
The Croakers (with Joseph Rodman Drake). 1860.
Young America. 1865.
Poetical Writings. Ed. James Grant Wilson. 1869.
Life and Letters. Ed. James Grant Wilson. 1869. 2 vols.
A Letter to Joel Lewis Griffing in Guilford, Connecticut in 1814. 1921.

N. P. WILLIS (1806–1867)

Sketches. 1827.
The Legendary: Consisting of Original Pieces, Principally Illustrative of American History, Scenery, and Manners (editor). 1828. 2 vols.
Fugitive Poetry. 1829.
Poem Delivered before the Society of United Brothers, at Brown University, on the Day Preceding Commencement; with Other Poems. 1831.
Melanie and Other Poems. Ed. Barry Cornwall. 1835.
Pencillings by the Way. 1835 (3 vols.), 1844.
Inklings of Adventure. 1836. 2 vols.
Bianca Visconti; or, The Heart Overtasked. 1839.

Tortesa the Usurer. 1839.
A l'Abri; or, The Tent Pitch'd. 1839, 1840 (as *Letters from under a Bridge*).
Loiterings of Travel. 1840. 3 vols.
American Scenery; or, Land, Lake, and River Illustrations of Transatlantic Nature. 1840. 2 vols.
Canadian Scenery Illustrated. 1842. 2 vols.
The Scenery and Antiquities of Ireland (with J. Stirling Coyne). 1842. 2 vols.
Sacred Poems. 1843.
Poems of Passion. 1843.
The Gipsy's Ride: An Eastern Tale. 1843.
Poems, Sacred, Passionate, and Humorous. 1844, 1868.
The Lady Jane and Other Humorous Poems. 1844.
Lecture on Fashion Delivered before the New York Lyceum. 1844.
The Opal: A Pure Gift for the Holy Days (editor; with Rufus W. Griswold). 1844.
Dashes at Life with a Free Pencil. 1845.
Complete Works. 1846.
Miscellaneous Works. 1847. 4 parts.
Poems of Early and After Years. 1848.
Prose Works. 1849.
Rural Letters and Other Records of Thought at Leisure, Written in the Intervals of More Hurried Literary Labor. 1849.
People I Have Met; or, Pictures of Society and People of Mark, Drawn under a Thin Veil of Fiction. 1849.
Life, Here and There; or, Sketches of Society and Adventure at Far-Apart Times and Places. 1850.
Trenton Falls, Picturesque and Descriptive (editor). 1851.
Memoranda of the Life of Jenny Lind. 1851.
Hurry-graphs; or, Sketches of Scenery, Celebrities and Society, Taken from Life. 1851.
The Winter Wreath (editor). 1853.
Summer Cruise in the Mediterranean on Board an American Frigate. 1853.
Fun-Jottings; or, Laughs I Have Taken a Pen To. 1853.
Health Trip to the Tropics. 1853.
Famous Persons and Places. 1854.
Out-Doors at Idlewild; or, The Shaping of a Home on the Banks of the Hudson. 1855.
The Thought-Blossom: A Memento (editor). 1855.
The Rag-Bag: A Collection of Ephemera. 1855.
Paul Fane; or, Parts of a Life Else Untold. 1857.
The Prose and Poetry of America (editor; with George P. Morris). 1857.
The Convalescent. 1859.
Poems. 1882.
Prose Writings. Ed. Henry A. Beers. 1885.

ARTEMUS WARD (CHARLES FARRAR BROWNE) (1834–1867)

Artemus Ward: His Book. 1862.
Artemus Ward: His Travels. 1865.
Artemus Ward among the Fenians; with the Showman's Observations upon Life in Washington, and Military Ardour in Baldinsville. 1866.
Artemus Ward in London and Other Papers. 1867.
Artemus Ward's Panorama (as Delivered at the Egyptian Hall, London). Eds. T. W. Robertson and E. P. Hingston. 1869.
Complete Works. 1870.
Complete Works. 1875.
Complete Works. 1898.
Letters to Charles E. Wilson 1858–1861. 1900.

Best Stories. Ed. Clifton Johnson. 1912.
Selected Works. Ed. Albert Jay Nock. 1924.

HENRY, LORD BROUGHAM (1778–1868)

Disputatio Juridica ad Tit. V. Lib. III. Digest. de Negotiis Gestis. 1800.
An Inquiry into the Colonial Policy of the European Powers. 1803. 2 vols.
A Concise Statement of the Question Regarding the Abolition of the Slave Trade. 1804.
Thoughts Suggested by Lord Lauderdale's Observations upon the Edinburgh Review. 1805.
An Inquiry into the State of the Nation at the Commencement of the Present Administration. 1806.
Speech before the House of Commons in Support of the Petitions from London, Liverpool, and Manchester, against the Orders in Council. 1808.
Speech before a Committee of the House of Commons in Opposition to a Bill for Incorporating Certain Persons by the Name of the Gas Light and Coke Company. 1809.
Speech in the House of Commons upon the Present State of Commerce and Manufactures. 1812.
Speeches Delivered during the Election at Liverpool. 1813.
An Appeal to the Allies, and the English Nation, in Behalf of Poland (with others). 1814.
Speech in the Committee of the Whole House, upon the State of the Agricultural Distresses. 1816.
Speech in the House of Commons on the State of the Nation. 1817.
Speech in the House of Commons on the Education of the Poor, and Charitable Abuses. 1818.
A Letter to Sir Samuel Romilly upon the Abuse of Charities. 1818.
[*Forman: A Tale.* 1819. 3 vols.]
Speech in the House of Lords. 1820.
Speech in the House of Lords. 1820.
Critique from the Edinburgh Review *on Lord Byron's Poems, Which Occasioned* English Bards and Scotch Reviewers. 1820.
Speech in the Case of the King v. Williams for a Libel on the Clergy. 1822.
Substance of Mr. Brougham's Speech, in the House of Commons, upon the War with Spain. 1823.
Practical Observations upon the Education of the People. 1825.
Inaugural Discourse on Being Installed Lord Rector of the University of Glasgow. 1825.
A Discourse of the Objects, Advantages, and Pleasures of Science. 1827.
Hydrostatics. 1827.
Present State of Law: Speech in the House of Commons. 1828.
The Country without a Government; or, Plain Questions upon the Unhappy State of the Present Administration. 1830.
Corrected Report of the Speech in the House of Commons on Colonial Slavery. 1830.
Reform: Speech Delivered in the House of Peers upon the Introduction of His Bill to Reform the Existing Legal Abuses of the Country. 1830.
The Result of the General Election; or, What Has the Duke of Wellington Gained by the Dissolution? 1830.
Speech on Reform in Chancery, Delivered in the House of Lords. 1831.
Speech on Parliamentary Reform, in the House of Lords. 1831.
Friendly Advice, Most Respectfully Submitted to the Lords, on the Reform Bill. 1831.
Selections from the Speeches and Writings. 1832.

Corrected Report of the Speech of the Lord Chancellor in the House of Lords, on Moving the Second Reading of the Bill to Amend the Poor Laws. 1834.
Speech in the House of Lords on the Education of the People. 1835.
Thoughts upon the Aristocracy of England. 1835.
"We Can't Afford It!" Being Thoughts upon the Aristocracy of England: Part the Second. 1835.
A Letter to Isaac Tomkins, Gent., Author of the Thoughts upon the Aristocracy, *from Mr. Peter Jenkins.* 1835.
A Discourse of Natural Theology, Showing the Nature of the Evidence and the Advantages of the Study. 1835.
Select Cases Decided by Lord Brougham in the Court of Chancery, in the Years 1833 & 1834. Ed. Charles Purton Cooper. 1835. Vol. 1 only.
Address to the Members of the Manchester Mechanics' Institution. 1835.
Speech in the House of Lords upon the Business of Parliament. 1837.
Opinions of Lord Brougham on Politics, Theology, Law, Science, Education, &c. &c. 1837.
Speech in the House of Lords on Imprisonment for Debt. 1837.
Slavery: Resolutions to Be Passed by the Lord Brougham and Vaux. 1838.
Speech in the House of Lords upon Canada. 1838.
Speech in the House of Lords upon the Slave Trade. 1838.
Speeches upon Questions Relating to Public Rights, Duties, & Interests. 1838. 4 vols.
Immediate Emancipation: Speech in the House of Lords on Slavery and the Slave Trade. 1838.
Letter to the Queen on the State of the Monarchy. 1838.
Speech in the House of Lords on Moving for a Committee of the Whole House on the Corn Laws. 1839.
The Ministry in Its Past and Present State: Being the Substance of a Speech Delivered in the House of Lords. 1839.
Answer to Lord Londonderry's Letter. 1839.
Dissertations on Subjects of Science Connected with Natural Theology. 1839. 2 vols.
Historical Sketches of Statesmen Who Flourished in the Time of George III. 1839. 2 vols.
Historical Sketches of Statesmen Who Flourished in the Time of George III: Second Series. 1839. 2 vols.
Sketches of Public Characters, Discourses and Essays. 1839. 2 vols.
A Letter on Natural Education, to the Duke of Bedford. 1839.
Lord Brougham's Reply to Lord John Russell's Letter to the Electors of Stroud, on the Principles of the Reform Act. 1839.
Speech on the "Bed-chamber Plot," Delivered in the House of Lords. 1839.
Speeches on the Administration of Justice in Ireland. 1839.
Speech at the Dover Festival on Proposing the Health of the Duke of Wellington. 1839.
The Oration of Demosthenes on the Crown (translator). 1840.
Critical and Miscellaneous Writings. 1841. 2 vols.
Speech on the Income Tax, in the House of Lords. 1842.
Political Philosophy. 1842–43. 3 vols.
Speech upon the Ashburton Treaty, Delivered in the House of Lords. 1843.
Historical Sketches of Statesmen Who Flourished in the Time of George III: Third Series. 1843. 2 vols.
Letters on Law Reform, to the Right Hon. Sir J. R. G. Graham. 1843.
Speech upon the Criminal Code, in the House of Lords. 1844.
British Constitution. 1844.

Albert Lunel; or, The Chateau of Languedoc. 1844. 3 vols.
Speech on Law Reform. 1845.
Lives of Men of Letters and Science Who Flourished in the Time of George III. 1845–46. 2 vols.
Two Discourses on the Objects, Pleasures, and Advantages, I. of Science; II. of Political Science. 1846.
Letter to Lord Lyndhurst on Criminal Police and National Education. 1847.
Speech on the Close of the Session of Parliament. 1847.
Letter to the Marquess of Lansdowne on the Late Revolution in France. 1848.
Speech in the House of Lords on Italian and French Affairs. 1848.
Speech in the House of Lords on Legislation and the Law. 1848.
Speech in the House of Lords on the Affairs of Austria and Italy. 1848.
Speech in the House of Lords on the Navigation Laws. 1849.
Speech on Foreign Affairs, in the House of Lords. 1849.
Inaugural Address on the Establishment of a Law School. 1850.
A Letter to Lord Denman upon the Legislation of 1850, as Regards the Amendment of the Law. 1850.
Parties' Witnesses: Speech in the House of Lords on Law of Evidence Bill. 1851.
[*Masters and Workmen: A Tale Illustrative of the Social and Moral Condition of the People.* 1851. 3 vols.]
History of England and France under the House of Lancaster. 1852.
Wellington Orations. 1852.
Speeches in the House of Lords on County Courts and Law Amendment. 1853.
Speeches upon National Education, House of Lords. 1854.
Speech on Criminal Law Procedure, House of Lords. 1855.
Speech upon the Slave Trade, House of Lords. 1855.
Religious Liberty Bill: Speech in the House of Lords, with the Bill, Schedules, and Notes. 1855.
Analytical View of Sir Isaac Newton's Principia (with E. J. Routh). 1855.
Works. 1855–61. 11 vols.
Contributions to the Edinburgh Review. 1856. 3 vols.
Substance of the Speech on Life Peerages. 1856.
Speech on the Property of Married Women, in the House of Lords. 1857.
Speech on Parliamentary Reform, in the House of Lords. 1857.
Lord Brougham's Acts and Bills from 1811 to the Present Time. Ed. John E. Eardley-Wilmot. 1857.
Cheap Literature for the People. 1858.
Addresses on Popular Literature and on the Monument to Sir Isaac Newton. 1858.
Installation Address of the Right Honourable Henry Lord Brougham, Chancellor of the University of Edinburgh. 1860.
Tracts, Mathematical and Physical. 1860.
Address in Opening the Congress of the National Association for Promoting Social Science. 1860.
Address at the Opening of the National Association of Social Science at Dublin. 1861.
The Case of Mr. Blundell, as Detailed to the House of Peers. 1863.
The Life and Times of Lord Brougham: Written by Himself. 1871. 3 vols.
Letters to William Forsyth. Ed. William Forsyth. 1872.
Works. 1872–73. 3 vols.
Brougham and His Early Friends: Letters to James Loch 1798–

1809. Ed. R. H. M. Buddle-Atkinson and G. A. Jackson. 1908. 3 vols.

H. H. MILMAN (1791–1868)

The Belvidere Apollo. 1812.
Alexander Tumulum Achillis Invisens. 1813.
Ode on the Arrival of the Potentates in Oxford; and Judicium Regale: An Ode. 1814.
Fazio. 1815.
A Comparative Estimate of Sculpture and Painting. 1816.
In Historia Scribenda Quaenam Praecipua inter Auctores Veteres et Novos Sit Differentia? 1816.
A Sermon Preached on the Occasion of the Melancholy Death of Her R. H. Princess Charlotte of Wales. 1817.
Samor, Lord of the Bright City: An Heroic Poem. 1818.
The Fall of Jerusalem: A Dramatic Poem. 1820.
The Belvidere Apollo, Fazio, and Other Poems. 1821.
The Martyr of Antioch: A Dramatic Poem. 1822.
Belshazzar: A Dramatic Poem. 1822.
Anne Boleyn: A Dramatic Poem. 1826.
The Office of the Christian Teacher Considered. 1826.
The Character and Conduct of the Apostles Considered as an Evidence of Christianity. 1827.
The History of the Jews. 1829. 3 vols.
The Poetical Works of Milman, Bowles, Wilson and Barry Cornwall. 1829. 4 parts.
Nala and Damayanti and Other Poems (translator). 1835.
Address Delivered at the Opening of the City of Westminster Literary, Scientific and Mechanics' Institute. 1837.
The History of the Decline and Fall of the Roman Empire by Edward Gibbon (editor). 1838–39. 12 vols.
The Life of Edward Gibbon, with Selections from His Correspondence. 1839.
A Selection of Psalms and Hymns, Adapted to the Use of the Church of St. Margaret, Westminster (editor). 1839.
Poetical Works. 1839. 3 vols.
The History of Christianity from the Birth of Christ to the Abolition of Paganism in the Roman Empire. 1840. 3 vols.
Life of Quintus Horatius Flaccus. 1854.
History of Latin Christianity; Including That of the Popes to the Pontificate of Nicholas V. 1854–55. 6 vols.
War and Peace. 1856.
Church Extension in the British Colonies and Dependencies. 1860.
Life of Thomas à Becket. 1860.
A Memoir of Lord Macaulay. 1862.
The Agamemnon and Aeschylus and the Bacchanals of Euripides (translator). 1865.
Hebrew Prophecy. 1865.
Annals of St. Paul's Cathedral. Ed. Arthur Milman. 1868.
Savonarola, Erasmus, and Other Essays Reprinted from the Quarterly Review. Ed. Arthur Milman. 1870.

SAMUEL LOVER (1797–1868)

The Parson's Horn-Book (with others). 1831.
Legends and Stories of Ireland. 1831–34. 2 vols.
Popular Tales and Legends of the Irish Peasantry (editor). 1834.
Rory O'More: A National Romance. 1837. 3 vols.
The Angel's Whisper. c. 1837.
Rory O'More (drama). c. 1837.
The White Horse of the Peppers. 1838.
Songs and Ballads. 1839.
The Happy Man. 1839.
The Hall Porter. c. 1839.

The Greek Boy. c. 1840.

Handy Andy: A Tale of Irish Life. 1842.

Treasure Trove: The First Series of Accounts of Irish Heirs: A Romantic Tale of the Last Century. 1844.

Mr. Lover's Irish Evenings: The Irish Brigade. 1844.

Characteristic Sketches of Ireland and the Irish (with William Carleton and Mrs. S. C. Hall). 1845.

The Low Back Car. c. 1846.

Land of the West. c. 1850.

Selected Writings. 1854. 10 vols.

Tom Crosbie and His Friends. 1855.

The Lyrics of Ireland (editor). 1858.

Rival Rhymes, in Honour of Burns (editor). 1859.

Metrical Tales and Other Poems. 1860.

McCarthy More; or, Possession Nine Points of the Law. c. 1861.

Original Songs for the Rifle Volunteers (with Charles Mackay and Thomas Miller). 1861.

Poetical Works. 1868.

The Life of Samuel Lover, with Selections from His Unpublished Papers and Correspondence. Ed. William Bayle Bernard. 1874. 2 vols.

Barney the Baron and The Happy Man. c. 1880.

Further Stories of Ireland. Ed. D. J. O'Donoghue. 1899.

Works. Ed. D. J. O'Donoghue. 1900. 6 vols.

Works (New Library Edition). Ed. James Jeffrey Roche. 1901. 6 vols.

Collected Writings (Treasure Trove Edition). Ed. James Jeffrey Roche. 1901–03. 10 vols.

WILLIAM CARLETON (1794–1869)

Father Butler; The Lough Dearg Pilgrim: Being Sketches of Irish Manners. 1829.

Traits and Stories of the Irish Peasantry. 1830. 2 vols.

Traits and Stories of the Irish Peasantry: Second Series. 1833. 3 vols.

Tales of Ireland. 1834.

Fardorougha the Miser; or, The Convicts of Lisnamona. 1839.

The Fawn of Spring-Vale, The Clarionet, and Other Tales. 1841. 3 vols.

Parra Sastha; or, The History of Paddy Go-Easy and His Wife Nancy. 1845.

Rody the Rover; or, The Ribbonman. 1845.

Valentine M'Clutchy, the Irish Agent; or, The Chronicles of the Castle Cumber Property. 1845. 3 vols.

The Battle of the Factions and Other Tales of Ireland. 1845.

Tales and Sketches, Illustrating the Character, Usages, etc., of the Irish Peasantry. 1845.

Denis O'Shaughnessy Going to Maynooth. 1845.

Characteristic Sketches of Ireland and the Irish (with Samuel Lover and Mrs. S. C. Hall). 1845.

Art Maguire; or, The Broken Pledge. 1845.

The Black Prophet: A Tale of Irish Famine. 1847.

The Emigrants of Ahadarra: A Tale of Irish Life. 1848.

The Irishman at Home: Characteristic Sketches of the Irish Peasantry. 1849.

The Tithe Proctor: Being a Tale of the Tithe Rebellion in Ireland. 1849.

Red Hall; or, The Baronet's Daughter. 1852. 3 vols.

Jane Sinclair, Neal Malone, &c. &c. 1852.

The Squanders of Castle Squander. 1852. 2 vols.

The Poor Scholar and Other Tales of Irish Life. 1854.

Willy Reilly and His Dear Cooleen Bawn: A Tale Founded upon Fact. 1855. 3 vols.

Alley Sheridan and Other Stories. 1858.

The Evil Eye; or, The Black Spectre. 1860.

Redmond Count O'Hanlon, the Irish Rapparee: An Historical Tale. 1862.

The Double Prophecy; or, Trials of the Heart. 1862. 2 vols.

The Silver Acre and Other Tales. 1862.

Barney Brady's Goose; The Hedge School; The Tree Tasks; and Other Irish Tales. 1869.

The Poor Scholar, Frank Martin and the Fairies, The Country Dancing Master, and Other Irish Tales. 1869.

Tubber Derg; or, The Red Well; Party Fight and Funeral; Dandy Kehoe's Christening; and Other Irish Tales. 1869.

The Fair of Emyvale and The Master and Scholar. 1870.

Works. 1872.

Works. 1881. 3 vols.

Amusing Irish Tales. 1889. 2 vols.

Stories from Carleton. Ed. W. B. Yeats. 1889.

The Red-Haired Man's Wife. 1889.

The Life of William Carleton: Being His Autobiography and Letters. Ed. David J. O'Donoghue. 1896. 2 vols.

Stories. Ed. Tighe Hopkins. 1905.

Stories of Irish Life. Ed. Darrell Figgis. 1919.

WILLIAM GILMORE SIMMS (1806–1870)

Monody, on the Death of Gen. Charles Cotesworth Pinckney. 1825.

Lyrical and Other Poems. 1827.

Early Lays. 1827.

The Vision of Cortes, Cain, and Other Poems. 1829.

The Tri-Color; or, The Three Days of Blood, in Paris; with Some Other Pieces. 1830.

Atalantis: A Story of the Sea. 1832.

Martin Faber: The Story of a Criminal. 1833.

The Book of My Lady: A Melange. 1833.

The Remains of Maynard Davis Richardson (editor). 1833.

Guy Rivers: A Tale of Georgia. 1834. 2 vols.

The Yemassee: A Romance of Carolina. 1835. 2 vols.

The Partisan: A Tale of the Revolution. 1835. 2 vols.

Mellichampe: A Legend of the Santee. 1836. 2 vols.

Martin Farber: The Story of a Crimina; and Other Tales. 1837. 2 vols.

Slavery in America: Being a Brief Review of Miss Martineau on That Subject. 1838.

Richard Huridis, or, The Avenger of Blood. 1838. 2 vols.

Carl Werner, and Imaginative Story; with Other Tales of the Imagination. 1838. 2 vols.

Pelayo: A Story of the Goth. 1838. 2 vols.

Southern Passages and Pictures. 1839.

The Damsel of Darien. 1839. 2 vols.

Border Beagles: A Tale of Mississippi. 1840. 2 vols.

The History of South Carolina from Its First European Discovery to Its Erection into a Republic. 1840.

The Kinsmen; or, The Black Riders of Congaree. 1841. 2 vols.

Confession; or, The Blind Heart: A Domestic Story. 1841. 2 vols.

Beauchampe; or, The Kentucky Tragedy: A Tale of Passion. 1842. 2 vols.

The Social Principle: The True Source of National Permanence. 1842.

Donna Florida: A Tale. 1843.

The Geography of South Carolina: Being a Companion to the History of That State. 1843.

The Prima Donna: A Passage from City Life. 1844.

The Life of Francis Marion. 1844.

Castle Dismal; or, The Bachelor's Christmas: A Domestic Legend. 1844.

The Sources of American Independence. 1844.

Helen Halsey; or, The Swamp State of Conelachita: A Tale of the Borders. 1845.

The Charleston Book (editor). 1845.

The Wigwam and the Cabin: First Series. 1845.

The Wigwam and the Cabin: Second Series. 1845.

Views and Reviews in American Literature, History and Fiction: First Series. 1845.

Count Julian; or, The Last Days of the Goth: A Historical Romance. 1845.

Grouped Thoughts and Scattered Fancies: A Collection of Sonnets. 1845.

Areytos; or, Songs of the South. 1846.

The Life of Captain John Smith, the Founder of Virginia. 1846.

Views and Reviews in American Literature, History and Fiction: Second Series. 1847.

Self-Development. 1847.

The Life of the Chevalier Bayard, "the Good Knight." 1847.

A Supplement to the Plays of William Shakspeare (editor). 1848.

Charleston, and Her Satirists. 1848. 2 parts.

Lays of the Palmetto: A Tribute to the South Carolina Regiment, in the War with Mexico. 1848.

The Cassique of Accabee: A Tale of Ashley River; with Other Pieces. 1849.

Father Abbot; or, The Home Tourist: Medley. 1849.

The Life of Nathaniel Greene, Major-General in the Army of the Revolution (editor). 1849.

Sabbath Lyrics; or, Songs from Scripture: A Christmas Gift of Love. 1849.

The Lily and the Totem; or, The Huguenots in Florida. 1850.

The City of the Silent. 1850.

[*Flirtation at the Moultrie House.* 1850.]

Katharine Walton; or, The Rebel of Dorchester. 1851.

Norman Maurice; or, The Man of the People: An American Drama. 1851.

The Golden Christmas: A Chronicle of St. John's, Berkeley. 1852.

As Good as a Comedy; or, The Tennesseean's Story. 1852.

The Sword and the Distaff; or, "Fair, Fat and Forty": A Story of the South, at the Close of the Revolution. 1852.

Michael Bonham; or, The Fall of Bexar: A Tale of Texas. 1853.

Marie de Berniere: A Tale of the Crescent City. 1853.

Egeria; or, Voices of Thought and Counsel, for the Woods and Wayside. 1853.

Works. 1853–57. 20 vols.

South-Carolina in the Revolutionary War. 1853.

Vasconselos: A Romance of the New World. 1853.

Poems Descriptive, Dramatic, Legendary and Contemplative. 1853. 2 vols.

Southward Ho! A Spell of Sunshine. 1854.

The Forayers; or, The Raid of the Dog-Days. 1855.

The Spartanburg Female College. 1855.

Eutaw: A Sequel to The Forayers. 1856.

The Power of Cotton. 1856. Lost.

The Cassique of Kiawah: A Colonial Romance. 1859.

Simms's Poems: Areytos or Songs and Ballads of the South, with Other Poems. 1860.

Works. 1860–66. 17 vols.

Sack and Destruction of the City of Columbia, S.C. 1865.

War Poetry of the South (editor). 1866.

The Army Correspondence of Colonel John Laurens (editor). 1867.

The Sense of the Beautiful. 1870.

Letters. Eds. Mary C. Simms Oliphant, Alfred Taylor Odell, and T. C. Duncan Eaves. 1952–82. 6 vols.

Writings (Centennial Edition). Eds. John Caldwell Guilds, James B. Meriwether et al. 1969–   .

CHARLES DICKENS (1812–1870)

Sketches by "Boz" Illustrative of Every-day Life and Every-day People. 1836. 2 vols.

Sunday under Three Heads. 1836.

The Village Coquettes: A Comic Opera. 1836.

The Posthumous Papers of the Pickwick Club. 1836–37. 20 parts.

The Strange Gentleman: A Comic Burletta. 1837.

Memoirs of Joseph Grimaldi (editor). 1838. 2 vols.

Sketches of Young Gentlemen. 1838.

Oliver Twist; or, The Parish Boy's Progress. 1838. 3 vols.

The Life and Adventures of Nicholas Nickleby. 1838–39. 20 parts.

The Loving Ballad of Lord Bateman (with William Makepeace Thackeray). 1839.

Sketches of Young Couples. 1840.

Master Humphrey's Clock (Old Curiosity Shop; Barnaby Rudge). 1840–41. 88 parts.

The Pic Nic Papers (editor). 1841. 3 vols.

American Notes. 1842. 2 vols.

A Christmas Carol in Prose: Being a Ghost-Story of Christmas. 1843.

The Life and Adventures of Martin Chuzzlewit, His Relatives, Friends and Enemies. 1843–44. 20 parts.

The Chimes: A Goblin Story of Some Bells That Rang an Old Year Out and a New Year In. 1845.

The Cricket on the Hearth: A Fairy Tale of Home. 1846.

Pictures from Italy. 1846.

The Battle of Life: A Love Story. 1846.

Dealings with the Firm of Dombey and Son Wholesale, Retail and for Exportation. 1846–48. 20 parts.

An Appeal to Fallen Women. 1847.

Works. 1847–67. 17 vols.

The Haunted Man and the Ghost's Bargain: A Fancy for Christmas Time. 1848.

Elegy Written in a Country Churchyard. c. 1849.

The Personal History, Adventures, Experiences and Observations of David Copperfield the Younger. 1849–50. 20 parts.

Mr. Nightingale's Diary: A Farce (with Mark Lemon). 1851.

Bleak House. 1852–53. 20 parts.

A Child's History of England. 1852–54. 3 vols.

Hard Times, for These Times. 1854.

Speech Delivered at the Meeting of the Administrative Reform Association. 1855.

Little Dorrit. 1855–57. 20 parts.

Novels and Tales Reprinted from Household Words (editor). 1856–59. 11 vols.

The Case of the Reformers in the Literary Fund (with others). 1858.

Speech at the Anniversary Festival of the Hospital for Sick Children. 1858.

Speech at the First Festival Dinner of the Playground and Recreation Society. 1858.

Works (Library Edition). 1858–59 (22 vols.), 1861–74 (30 vols.).

A Tale of Two Cities. 1859. 8 parts.

Christmas Stories from Household Words. 1859. 9 parts.

Great Expectations. 1861. 3 vols.

Great Expectations: A Drama. 1861.

The Uncommercial Traveler. 1861.

An Address on Behalf of the Printer's Pension Society. c. 1864.

⟨Speech at the⟩ *North London or University College Hospital: Anniversary Dinner in Aid of the Funds.* 1864.

Our Mutual Friend. 1864–65. 20 parts.

The Frozen Deep (with Wilkie Collins). 1866.

No Thoroughfare (with Wilkie Collins). 1867.

⟨Speech at the⟩ *Railway Benevolent Institution: Ninth Annual Dinner.* 1867.

Works (Charles Dickens Edition). 1867–75. 21 vols.

Christmas Stories from All the Year Round. c. 1868. 9 parts.

The Readings of Mr. Charles Dickens, as Condensed by Himself. 1868.

Address Delivered at the Birmingham and Midland Institute. 1869.

A Curious Dance round a Curious Tree (with W. H. Wills). 1870.

Speech as Chairman of the Anniversary Festival Dinner of the Royal Free Hospital. 1870.

The Mystery of Edwin Drood. 1870. 6 parts.

Speeches Literary and Social. Ed. R. H. Shepherd. 1870.

The Newsvendors' Benevolent and Provident Institution: Speeches in Behalf of the Institution. 1871.

Is She His Wife? or Something Singular: A Comic Burletta. c. 1872.

The Lamplighter: A Farce. 1879.

The Mudfog Papers, etc. 1880.

Letters. Eds. Georgina Hogarth and Mary Dickens. 1880–82. 3 vols.

Plays and Poems, with a Few Miscellanies in Prose Now First Collected. Ed. R. H. Shepherd. 1885. 2 vols.

The Lazy Tour of Two Idle Apprentices; No Thoroughfare; The Perils of Certain English Prisoners (with Wilkie Collins). 1890.

Works (Macmillan Edition). 1892–1925. 21 vols.

Letters to Wilkie Collins 1851–1870. Ed. Lawrence Hutton. 1892.

Works (Gadshill Edition). Ed. Andrew Lang. 1897–1908. 36 vols.

To Be Read at Dusk and Other Stories, Sketches and Essays. Ed. F. G. Kitton. 1898.

Christmas Stories from Household Stories *and* All the Year Round. 1898. 5 vols.

Works (Biographical Edition). Ed. Arthur Waugh. 1902–03. 19 vols.

Poems and Verses. Ed. F. G. Kitton. 1903.

Works (National Edition). Ed. Bertram W. Matz. 1906–08. 40 vols.

Dickens and Maria Beadnell: Private Correspondence. Ed. G. P. Baker. 1908.

The Dickens-Kolle Letters. Ed. Harry B. Smith. 1910.

Works (Centenary Edition). 1910–11. 36 vols.

Dickens as Editor: Letters Written by Him to William Henry Wills, His Sub-Editor. Ed. R. C. Lehmann. 1912.

Works (Waverley Edition). 1913–18. 30 vols.

Unpublished Letters to Mark Lemon. Ed. Walter Dexter. 1927.

Letters to the Baroness Burdett-Coutts. Ed. Charles C. Osborne. 1931.

Dickens to His Oldest Friend: The Letters of a Lifetime to Thomas Beard. Ed. Walter Dexter. 1932.

Letters to Charles Lever. Ed. Flora V. Livingston. 1933.

Mr. and Mrs. Charles Dickens: His Letters to Her. Ed. Walter Dexter. 1935.

The Love Romance of Dickens, Told in His Letters to Maria Beadnell (Mrs. Winter). Ed. Walter Dexter. 1936.

The Nonesuch Dickens. Eds. Arthur Waugh, Hugh Walpole, Walter Dexter, and Thomas Hatton. 1937–38. 23 vols.

Letters. Ed. Walter Dexter. 1938. 3 vols.

The New Oxford Illustrated Dickens. 1947–58. 21 vols.

The Heart of Dickens. Ed. Edgar Johnson. 1952.

Best Stories. Ed. Morton D. Zabel. 1959.

Speeches. Ed. K. J. Fielding. 1960.

Selected Letters. Ed. F. W. Dupee. 1960.

Letters (Pilgrim Edition). Eds. Madeline House, Graham Storey, Kathleen Tillotson et al. 1965– .

The Clarendon Dickens. Eds. John Butt, Kathleen Tillotson, and James Kinsley. 1966– .

Uncollected Writings from Household Words *1850–1859.* Ed. Harry Stone. 1968.

Complete Plays and Selected Poems. 1970.

Short Stories. Ed. Walter Allen. 1971.

Dickens in Europe: Essays. Ed. Rosalind Vallance. 1975.

The Public Readings. Ed. Phillip Collins. 1975.

Selected Short Fiction. Ed. Deborah A. Thomas. 1976.

Supernatural Short Stories. Ed. Michael Hayes. 1978.

Selected Letters. Ed. David Paroissien. 1985.

Dickens' Working Notes for His Novels. Ed. Harry Stone. 1987.

GEORGE GROTE (1794–1871)

Statement of the Question of Parliamentary Reform. 1821.

Analysis of the Influence of Natural Religion on the Temporal Happiness of Mankind. 1822.

Essentials of Parliamentary Reform. 1831.

Speech Delivered in the House of Commons, on Moving for the Introduction of the Vote by Ballot at Elections. 1833.

Vote by Ballot: Speech in the House of Commons. 1836.

Vote by Ballot: Speech in the House of Commons. 1837.

Vote by Ballot: Speech in the House of Commons. 1838.

Address of George Grote, President of the City of London Literary and Scientific Institution, at a Festival Held at the London Tavern, in Commemoration of the Twenty-first Anniversary of the Institution. 1846.

A History of Greece. 1846–56. 12 vols.

Seven Letters on the Recent Politics of Switzerland. 1847.

Plato's Doctrine Respecting the Rotation of the Earth and Aristotle's Comment upon That Doctrine. 1860.

Plato, and the Other Companions of Sokrates. 1865. 3 vols.

Review of the Work of Mr. J. S. Mill, Entitled, Examination of Sir William Hamilton's Philosophy. 1868.

Aristotle. Eds. Alexander Bain and G. Croom Robertson. 1872. 2 vols.

Poems 1815–1823. 1872.

Minor Works. Ed. Alexander Bain. 1873.

Posthumous Papers. Ed. Harriet Grote. 1874.

Fragments on Ethical Subjects. Ed. Alexander Bain. 1876.

ROBERT CHAMBERS (1802–1871)

Illustrations of the Author of Waverley: *Being Notices and Anecdotes of Real Characters, Scenes, and Incidents Supposed to Be Described in His Works.* 1822.

Notices of the Most Remarkable Fires in Edinburgh from 1385 to 1824. 1824.

Traditions of Edinburgh. 1825. 2 vols.

Walks in Edinburgh. 1825.

The Popular Rhymes of Scotland (editor). 1826.

History of the Rebellion in Scotland in 1745, 1746. 1827. 2 vols.

The Picture of Scotland. 1827. 2 vols.

History of the Rebellions in Scotland under the Marquis of Montrose, and Others, from 1638 till 1669. 1828. 2 vols.

History of the Rebellions in Scotland, under the Viscount of Dundee, and the Earl of Mar, in 1689 and 1715. 1829.

The Scottish Ballads (editor). 1829.

The Scottish Songs (editor). 1829. 2 vols.

The Life of King James the First. 1830. 2 vols.

Life of Sir Walter Scott. 1832.

Scottish Jests and Anecdotes; to Which Are Added a Selection of Choice English and Irish Jests. 1832.

A Biographical Dictionary of Eminent Scotsmen. 1832–35. 4 vols.

The Gazeteer of Scotland (with William Chambers). 1832. 2 vols.

The History of Scotland from the Earliest Period to the Present Time. 1832. 2 vols.

Minor Antiquities of Edinburgh. 1833.

Jacobite Memoirs of the Rebellion of 1745 by Robert Forbes (editor). 1834.

Poems. 1835.

History of the English Language and Literature. 1836.

The Life of Robert Burns by James Currie (expanded by Chambers). 1838.

The Poetical Works of Robert Burns (editor). 1838.

The Prose Works of Robert Burns (editor). 1839.

The Land of Burns: A Series of Landscapes and Portraits, Illustrative of the Life and Writings of the Scottish Poet (with John Wilson). 1840. 2 vols.

Popular Rhymes, Fireside Stories, and Amusements, of Scotland (editor). 1842.

Vestiges of the Natural History of Creation. 1844.

Cyclopaedia of English Literature. 1844. 2 vols.

Explanations: A Sequel to Vestiges of the Natural History of Creation. 1845.

Select Writings. 1847. 7 vols.

Ancient Sea-Margins, as Memorials of Charges in the Relative Level of Sea and Land. 1848.

Tracings of the North of Europe. 1850.

The Life and Works of Robert Burns. 1851. 4 vols.

Tracings of Iceland and the Faröe Islands. 1856.

Domestic Annals of Scotland from the Reformation to the Revolution. 1858. 2 vols.

Edinburgh Papers. 1859–61. 5 parts.

Sketch of the History of the Edinburgh Theatre-Royal. 1859.

Domestic Annals of Scotland from the Revolution to the Rebellion of 1745. 1861.

The Songs of Scotland Prior to Burns (editor). 1862.

The Book of Days: A Miscellany of Popular Antiquities, in Connection with the Calendar. 1862–64. 2 vols.

Smollett: His Life and a Selection from His Writings. 1867.

Life of Sir Walter Scott. Ed. William Chambers. 1871.

The Threiplands of Fingask: A Family Memoir. 1880.

ALICE CARY (1820–1871)

Poems (with Phoebe Cary). 1850.

Clovernook; or, Recollections of Our Neighborhood in the West. 1852.

Lyra and Other Poems. 1852.

Hagar: A Story of To-day. 1852.

Clovernook; or, Recollections of Our Neighborhood in the West: Second Series. 1853.

Clovernook Children. 1855.

Poems. 1855.

Married, Not Mated; or, How They Lived at Woodside and Throckmorton Hall. 1856.

The Josephine Gallery (editor; with Phoebe Cary). 1859.

Pictures of Country Life. 1859.

Ballads, Lyrics, and Hymns. 1866.

The Bishop's Son. 1867.

Snow-Berries: A Book for Young Folks. 1867.

A Lover's Diary. 1868.

Letter-Carrier's Fifth Annual Greeting. 1868.

From Year to Year! A Token of Remembrance (editor; with Phoebe Cary). 1869.

Last Poems (with Phoebe Cary). Ed. Mary Clemmer Ames. 1873.

Ballads for Little Folk (with Phoebe Cary). Ed. Mary Clemmer Ames. 1874.

Poetical Works (with Phoebe Cary). 1876.

Early and Late Poems (with Phoebe Cary). 1887.

Poems (with Phoebe Cary). Ed. Katharine Lee Bates. 1903.

PHOEBE CARY (1824–1871)

Poems (with Alice Cary). 1850.

Poems and Parodies. 1854.

The Josephine Gallery (editor; with Alice Cary). 1859.

Poems of Faith, Hope, and Love. 1868.

From Year to Year! A Token of Remembrance (editor; with Alice Cary). 1869.

Last Poems (with Alice Cary). Ed. Mary Clemmer Ames. 1873.

Ballads for Little Folk (with Alice Cary). Ed. Mary Clemmer Ames. 1874.

Poetical Works (with Alice Cary). 1876.

Early and Late Poems (with Alice Cary). 1887.

Poems (with Alice Cary). Ed. Katharine Lee Bates. 1903.

FREDERICK DENISON MAURICE (1805–1872)

Eustace Conway; or, The Brother and Sister. 1834. 3 vols.

Subscription No Bondage. 1835.

Letters to a Member of the Society of Friends. 1837–38. 12 parts.

The Kingdom of Christ; or, Hints on the Principles, Ordinances, and Constitution of the Catholic Church. 1837–38. 3 vols.

The Responsibilities of Medical Students. 1838.

Has the Church, or the State, the Power to Educate the Nation? A Course of Lectures. 1839.

Reasons for Not Joining a Party in the Church. 1841.

Three Letters to the Rev. W. Palmer, on the Name "Protestant"; on the Seemingly Ambiguous Character of the English Church; and on the Bishopric at Jerusalem. 1842.

Christmas Day and Other Sermons. 1843.

On Right and Wrong Methods of Supporting Protestantism. 1843.

The New Statute and Mr. Ward. 1845.

Thoughts on the Rule of Conscientious Subscription, on the Purpose of the Thirty-nine Articles, and on Our Present Perils from the Roman System. 1845.

A Few Words on the New Irish Colleges. 1845.

The Epistle to the Hebrews. 1846.

The Education Question in 1847. 1846.

The Religions of the World; and Their Relations to Christianity. 1847.

Thoughts on the Duty of a Protestant in the Present Oxford Election. 1847.

A Letter on the Attempt to Defeat the Nomination of Dr. Hampden. 1847.
Moral and Metaphysical Philosophy. 1847 [Part 1]; 1854 [Part 2]; 1857 [Part 3]; 1862 [Part 4]; 1872–73 (2 vols.).
The Lord's Prayer: Nine Sermons Preached in the Chapel of Lincoln's Inn. 1848.
Queen's College, London: Its Objects and Method. 1848.
A Sermon Preached on Easter Monday 1848. 1848.
The Prayer Book Considered Especially in Preference to the Romish System. 1849.
Christian Socialism. 1849.
Is a Decision of the Privy Council a Reason for Secession, or for Retiring into Lay Communion? 1849.
Introductory Lecture Delivered at the Opening of the Metropolitan Evening Classes for Young Men. 1849.
Queen's College, London: A Letter to the Right Hon. and Rev. the Lord Bishop of London, in Reply to the Article CLXXII. of the Quarterly Review, *Entitled "Queen's College, London."* 1850.
The Church a Family. 1850.
Reasons for Co-operation: A Lecture Delivered at the Office for Promoting Working Men's Associations. 1851.
On the Reformation of Society, and How All Classes May Contribute to It. 1851.
The Old Testament. 1851.
The Prophets and Kings of the Old Testament. 1853.
Sermons on the Sabbath Day; On the Character of the Warrior; On the Interpretation of History. 1853.
Lying and Truth: The Old Man and the New. 1853.
National Education. 1853.
Theological Essays. 1853.
The Word "Eternal" and the Punishment of the Wicked. 1853.
⟨*Scheme of a College for Working Men.*⟩ 1854.
Lectures on the Ecclesiastical History of the First and Second Centuries. 1854.
The Unity of the New Testament. 1854.
The Doctrine of Sacrifice Deduced from the Scriptures. 1854.
Death and Life. 1855.
Plan of a Female College for the Help of the Rich and of the Poor. 1855.
Administrative Reform, and Its Connexion with Working Men's Colleges. 1855.
The Patriarchs and Lawgivers of the Old Testament. 1855.
Learning and Working; The Religion of Rome, and Its Influence on Modern Civilisation. 1855.
The Gospel of St. John. 1856.
The Sabbath Day. 1856.
Sermons in the Chapel of Lincoln's Inn. Ed. J. M. Ludlow. 1856–59. 6 vols.
The Eucharist. 1857.
Milton Considered as a Schoolmaster. 1857.
The Worship of the Church a Witness for the Redemption of the World. 1857.
The Epistles of St. John. 1857.
The Gospel of Hope. 1857.
What Is Revelation? 1859.
War: How to Prepare Ourselves for It. 1859.
Sequel to the Inquiry, What Is Revelation? 1860.
A Lecture Delivered at the Opening of the Lower Norwood Working Men's Institute. 1860.
A Sermon Preached to the 19th Middlesex Volunteer Rifle Corps at Christ Church, Marylebone. 1860.
The Faith of the Liturgy; Doctrine of the Thirty-nine Articles. 1860.
Lectures on the Apocalypse. 1861.

Dialogues between a Clergyman and a Layman on Family Worship. 1862.
The Sacrifices Which We Owe to God and His Church. 1862.
The Claims of the Bible and of Science. 1863.
The Clergyman's Self-Examination concerning the Apostles' Creed. 1864.
The Gospel of the Kingdom of Heaven. 1864.
What Message Have the Clergy for the People of England? 1864.
The Conflict of Good and Evil in Our Day. 1865.
The Commandments Considered as Instruments of National Reformation. 1866.
Casuistry, Moral Philosophy, and Moral Theology: An Inaugural Lecture Delivered in the Senate House, Cambridge. 1866.
The Workman and the Franchise. 1866.
The Light of Men. 1868.
The Ground and Object of Hope for Mankind. 1868.
The Conscience. 1868.
Social Morality. 1869.
The Warrior's Prayer. 1869.
Christian Education. 1870.
A Few Words on Secular and Denominational Education. 1870.
The Lord's Prayer, the Creed, and the Commandments: A Manual for Parents and Schoolmasters. 1870.
Sermons Preached in Country Churches. 1872.
The Friendship of Books and Other Lectures. Ed. Thomas Hughes. 1874.
The Prayer Book; The Lord's Prayer. 1880.
Life of Frederick Denison Maurice, Chiefly Told in His Own Letters. Ed. Frederick Maurice. 1884.
Faith and Action: From the Writings. Ed. M. G. D. 1886.
Lessons of Hope: Readings from the Works. Ed. J. L. Davies. 1889.
The Acts of the Apostles. 1894.
Toward the Recovery of Unity: The Thought of Frederick Denison Maurice Edited from His Letters. Eds. John F. Porter and William J. Wolf. 1964.

CHARLES LEVER (1806–1872)

The Confessions of Harry Lorrequer. 1839. 11 parts.
Charles O'Malley, the Irish Dragoon. 1840–41. 20 parts.
Our Mess ⟨*Jack Hinton, the Guardsman; Tom Burke of "Ours"*⟩. 1842–44. 35 parts.
Arthur O'Leary: His Wanderings and Ponderings in Many Lands. 1844. 3 vols.
Nuts and Nutcrackers. 1845.
Tales of the Trains: Being Some Chapters of Railroad Romance. 1845.
The O'Donoghue: A Tale of Ireland Fifty Years Ago. 1845. 13 parts.
St. Patrick's Eve. 1845.
The Knight of Gwynne: A Tale of the Time of the Union. 1846–47. 20 parts.
Diary and Notes of Horace Templeton, Late Secretary of Legation at ——. 1848. 2 vols.
Roland Cashel. 1848–49. 20 parts.
Confessions of Con Cregan, the Irish Gil Blas. 1849–50. 14 parts.
Maurice Tiernay: The Soldiers of Fortune. 1850–51. 21 parts.
The Daltons; or, Three Roads in Life. 1851–52. 13 parts.
The Dodd Family Abroad. 1852–54. 20 parts.
Sir Jasper Carew: His Life and Experiences. 1854.
The Martins of Cro' Martin. 1854–56. 20 parts.

The Fortunes of Glencore. 1857. 3 vols.
Davenport Dunn: A Man of the Day. 1857–59. 22 parts.
Gerald Fitzgerald, "the Chevalier." 1859.
One of Them. 1859–61. 15 parts.
Barrington. 1862–63. 13 parts.
A Day's Ride: A Life's Romance. 1863. 2 vols.
Luttrell of Arran. 1863–65. 16 parts.
Cornelius O'Dowd upon Men, Women and Other Things in General. 1864–65. 3 vols.
A Rent in a Cloud. c. 1865.
Tony Butler. 1865. 3 vols.
Sir Brook Fossbrooke. 1866. 3 vols.
The Bramleighs of Bishop's Folly. 1868. 3 vols.
Paul Gosslett's Confessions in Love, Law, and the Civil Service. 1868.
That Boy of Norcott's. 1869.
Lord Kilgobbin: A Tale of Ireland in Our Own Time. 1872. 3 vols.
Works. 1872–73. 17 vols.
Works. 1876–78. 34 vols.
Military Novels. 1891–92. 9 vols.
Novels. 1894–95. 40 vols.
Novels. Ed. Julia Kate Neville. 1897–99. 37 vols.
Charles Lever: His Life in His Letters. Ed. Edmund Downey. 1906. 2 vols.

HORACE GREELEY (1811–1872)

The Log Cabin. 1840–41. 82 nos.
Brief Statement of the Pleadings and Argument in the Case of J. Fenimore Cooper vs. Horace Greeley and Thomas McElrath, in an Action for Libel. 1843.
Whig Songs for 1844. 1844.
An Address before the Literary Societies of Hamilton College. 1844.
The Tariff as It Is, Compared with the Substitute Proposed by Its Adversaries. 1844.
Protection and Free Trade: The Question Stated and Considered. 1844.
The Formation of Character. 1844.
Association Discussed; or, The Socialism of the Tribune *Examined: Being a Controversy between the* New York Tribune *and the* Courier and Enquirer *(with Henry J. Raymond).* 1847.
The Writings of Cassius Marcellus Clay (editor). 1848.
Alcoholic Liquors: Their Essential Nature and Necessary Effects on the Human Constitution. 1849.
Hints toward Reforms, in Lectures, Addresses, and Other Writings. 1850.
Glances at Europe: In a Series of Letters from Great Britain, France, Italy, Switzerland, &c., during the Summer of 1851. 1851.
The Tariff Question: Protection and Free Trade Considered. 1852.
The Life and Public Services of Henry Clay, Down to 1848 by Epes Sargent (editor). 1852.
The Crystal Palace and Its Lessons. 1852.
Why I Am a Whig. 1852.
What the Sister Arts Teach as to Farming. 1853.
Love, Marriage and Divorce, and the Sovereignty of the Individual: A Discourse between Henry James, Horace Greeley and Stephen P. Andrews. Ed. Stephen P. Andrews. 1853.
Art and Industry as Represented in the Exhibition at the Crystal Palace, New York—1853–4. 1853.
A History of the Struggle for Slavery Extension or Restriction in the United States from the Declaration of Independence to the Present Day. 1856.
Aunt Sally Come Up! or, The Nigger Sale. 1859.
The Kansas Gold Mines (with A. D. Richardson and Henry Villard). 1859.
An Overland Journey, from New York to San Francisco, in the Summer of 1859. 1860.
A Political Text-Book for 1860: Comprising a Brief View of Presidential Nominations and Elections (with John F. Cleveland). 1860.
Divorce: Being a Correspondence between Horace Greeley and Robert Dale Owen. 1860.
The American Conflict: A History of the Great Rebellion in the United States of America 1860–65. 1864–66. 2 vols.
The Amendment to the Constitution: Beecher's Letter and Greeley's Reply. 1866.
Letter to Messrs. Geo. W. Blunt, John A. Kennedy, John O. Stone, Stephen Hyatt, and 30 Others, Members of the Union League Club. 1867.
An Address on Success in Business, Delivered before the Students of Packard's Bryant & Stratton New York Business College. 1867.
Recollections of a Busy Life. 1868.
The Tribune Almanac for the Years 1838 to 1869 Inclusive (editor). 1868.
Essays Designed to Elucidate the Science of Political Economy. 1869.
Letters from Texas and the Lower Mississippi; to Which Are Added His Address to the Farmers of Texas, and His Speech on His Return to New York. 1871.
What I Know of Farming. 1871.
The True Issues of the Presidential Campaign: Speeches during His Western Trip and at Portland, Maine. 1872.
Greeley Illustrated. 1872.
The Greeley Record: Showing the Opinions and Sentiments of Horace Greeley on Office Seeking—the Presidency—the Democratic Party—Prominent Democrats, North and South—Secession and Secessionists. 1872.
Horace Greeley's Jokes. 1872.
Mr. Greeley's Record on the Question of Amnesty and Reconstruction, from the Hour of Gen. Lee's Surrender. 1872.
Horace Greeley's Views on Virginia, and What He Knows about the South. 1872.
Horace Greeley upon Tilden. 1874.
Greeley on Lincoln, with Letters to Charles A. Dana and a Lady Friend. Ed. Joel Benton. 1893.

EDWARD BULWER-LYTTON (1803–1873)

Ismael: An Oriental Tale, with Other Poems. 1820.
Delmour; or, A Tale of a Sylphid. 1823.
Sculpture: A Poem Which Obtained the Chancellor's Medal at the Cambridge Commencement, July 1825. 1825.
Weeds and Wildflowers. 1826.
O'Neill; or, The Rebel. 1827.
Falkland. 1827.
Pelham; or, The Adventures of a Gentleman. 1828. 3 vols.
The Disowned. 1829. 3 vols.
Devereux: A Tale. 1829. 3 vols.
Paul Clifford. 1830. 3 vols.
The Siamese Twins: A Satirical Tale of the Times. 1831.
Eugene Aram: A Tale. 1832. 3 vols.
England and the English. 1833. 2 vols.
Asmodeus at Large. 1833.
Godolphin. 1833. 3 vols.
The Pilgrims of the Rhine. 1834.

The Last Days of Pompeii. 1834. 3 vols.

A Letter to a Late Cabinet Minister on the Present Crisis. 1834.

The Student: A Series of Papers. 1835. 2 vols.

Rienzi, the Last of the Tribunes. 1835. 3 vols.

Literary Remains of William Hazlitt (editor). 1836. 2 vols.

The Duchess de la Valliere. 1836.

Athens: Its Rise and Fall; with Views of the Literature, Philosophy and Social Life of the Athenian People. 1837. 2 vols.

Ernest Maltravers. 1837. 3 vols.

Alice; or, The Mysteries: A Sequel to Ernest Maltravers. 1838. 3 vols.

Leila; or, The Siege of Granada, and Calderon the Courtier. 1838.

The Lady of Lyons; or, Love and Pride. 1838.

Richelieu; or, The Conspiracy. 1839.

The Sea-Captain; or, The Birthright. 1839.

Money. 1840.

Works. 1840. 10 vols.

Night and Morning. 1841. 3 vols.

Critical and Miscellaneous Writings. 1841. 2 vols.

Dramatic Works. 1841.

Eva: A True Story of Light and Darkness; The Ill-Omened Marriage, and Other Tales and Poems. 1842.

Zanoni. 1842. 3 vols.

The Last of the Barons. 1843. 3 vols.

The Poems and Ballads of Schiller (translator). 1844. 2 vols.

The Crisis: A Satire of the Day. 1845.

Poems. Ed. C. Donald Macleod. 1845.

The New Timon: A Romance of London. 1846.

Confessions of a Water-Patient: In a Letter to William Harrison Ainsworth. 1846.

Lucretia; or, The Children of the Night. 1847. 3 vols.

A Word to the Public. 1847.

To the Independent Freemen and Electors of the City of Lincoln. 1848.

King Arthur. 1848–49. 3 parts.

Harold, the Last of the Saxon Kings. 1848. 3 vols.

The Caxtons: A Family Picture. 1849. 3 vols.

Not So Bad as We Seem; or, Many Sides to a Character. 1851.

Letters to John Bull, Esq., on Affairs Connected with His Landed Property, and the Persons Who Live Thereon. 1851.

Outlines of the Early History of the East. 1852.

Poetical and Dramatic Works. 1852–54. 5 vols.

My Novel; or, Varieties in English Life. 1853. 4 vols.

Address to the Associated Societies of the University of Edinburgh. 1854.

Speech, Delivered at the Leeds Mechanics' Institution. 1854.

Inaugural Address on His Installation as Lord Rector of the University of Glasgow. 1857.

What Will He Do with It? 1859. 4 vols.

Novels. 1859–74. 47 vols.

The Representation of the People Bill: Speech Delivered in the House of Commons. 1859.

Dramatic Works. 1860.

St. Stephen's. 1860.

The New Reform Bill: Speech Delivered in the House of Commons. 1860.

A Strange Story. 1862. 2 vols.

Caxtoniana: A Series of Essays on Life, Literature, and Manners. 1863. 2 vols.

The Boatmen. 1864.

Novels and Romances. 1864. 43 vols.

Poems. 1865.

A Strange Story and The Haunted and the Haunters. 1865.

The Lost Tales of Miletus. 1866.

The Rightful Heir. 1868.

Novels and Romances. 1868. 11 vols.

Miscellaneous Prose Works. 1868. 3 vols.

The Odes and Epodes of Horace (translator). 1869.

Walpole; or, Every Man Has His Price. 1869.

The Coming Race. 1871.

The Parisians. 1873. 4 vols.

Kenelm Chillingly: His Adventures and Opinions. 1873. 3 vols.

Works (Knebworth Edition). 1873–77. 37 vols.

Speeches. 1874. 2 vols.

Pausanias the Spartan: An Unfinished Historical Romance. Ed. Edward Robert Bulwer Lytton. 1876.

British Archaeological Association: Inaugural Address Delivered at the Congress of the British Archaeological Association 1869. Ed. Thomas Wright. 1880.

Life, Letters and Literary Remains. Ed. Edward Robert Bulwer Lytton. 1883. 2 vols.

The Wit and Wisdom of Edward Bulwer-Lytton. Ed. Charles Kent. 1883.

Letters to His Wife. Ed. Louisa Devey. 1884.

The Lady of Lyons and Other Plays. Ed. R. Farquharson Sharp. 1890.

Novels (New Knebworth Edition). 1895–98. 29 vols.

Letters to Macready 1836–1866. 1911.

Bulwer and Macready: A Chronicle of the Early Victorian Theatre. Ed. Charles H. Shattuck. 1958.

SAMUEL WILBERFORCE (1805–1873)

A Selection of Psalms and Hymns for Public Worship (editor). 1832.

The Note Book of a Country Clergyman. 1833.

The Apostolical Ministry: Its Difficulties, Strengths, and Duties. 1833.

Journals and Letters of the Rev. Henry Martyn (editor). 1837.

The Power of God's Word Needful for National Education. 1838.

The Life of William Wilberforce (with Robert Isaac Wilberforce). 1838.

Eucharistica: Meditations and Prayers on the Most Holy Eucharist (editor). 1839.

Sermons Preached before the University of Oxford. 1839.

The Ministry of Reconciliation. 1840.

The Correspondence of William Wilberforce (editor; with Robert Isaac Wilberforce). 1840.

Agathos and Other Sunday Stories. 1840.

The Rocky Island and Other Parables. 1840.

A Charge Delivered to the Clergy of the Archdeaconry of Surrey. 1840.

A History of the Protestant Episcopal Church in America. 1840.

A Letter to Henry, Lord Brougham, on the Government-Plan of Education. 1840.

A Charge Delivered to the Clergy of the Archdeaconry of Surrey, June, 1841. 1841.

Concio ad Clerum Provinciae Cantuariensis, in Aede Paulina Habita. 1841.

The Unity of the Church. 1841.

The False Prophet. 1841.

Four Sermons Preached before Her Majesty Queen Victoria in 1841 and 1842. 1842.

Newfoundland and British North America School Society: The Nineteenth Anniversary Sermon. 1842.

A Sermon Preached in the Cathedral Church of St. Paul, at the Festival of the Sons of the Clergy. 1842.
A Charge Delivered at the Ordinary Visitation of the Archdeaconry of Surrey, November, 1842. 1842.
A Charge Delivered at the Ordinary Visitation of the Archdeaconry of Surrey, November, 1843. 1843.
St. Paul the Type of the Faithful Pastor. 1844.
Sermons. 1844.
A Charge Delivered at the Ordinary Visitation of the Archdeaconry of Surrey, November, 1844. 1844.
A Charge Delivered at the Ordinary Visitation of the Archdeaconry of Surrey, April, 1845. 1845.
The Right Mind. 1845.
A Charge Delivered to the Candidates for Ordination; and a Sermon. 1846.
A Sermon Preached at the Consecration of St. Catherine's Church, Bearwood. 1846.
The Life of Mrs. Godolphin by John Evelyn (editor). 1847.
An Address Delivered at the Confirmation at Eton College. 1847.
Pride a Hindrance to True Knowledge. 1847.
The Revelation of the Personal God, the Strength of His People. 1847.
A Sermon Preached at St. Aldate's Church, Oxford, on Behalf of a Proposed Church and Parsonage Home at Headington Quarry. 1847.
Two Sermons (with Charles Wordsworth). 1847.
Address to the Churchwardens of the Diocese (of Oxford). 1848.
Strength out of Weakness: A Sermon on the Occasion of the Jubilee of the Church Missionary Society. 1848.
A Charge Delivered to the Clergy of the Diocese of Oxford at His Primary Visitation. 1848.
Union with Christ the Condition of Communion with Angels and Saints. 1848.
Cheap Sugar Means Cheap Slaves. 1848.
The Substance of a Correspondence between the Bishop of Oxford and the Rector of Lincoln ⟨John Radford⟩, *Touching His Lordship's Claim to License the Chaplains of Lincoln College.* 1848.
Correspondence between the Lord Bishop of Oxford and Mr. Alderman Sadler. 1850.
Prayers and Rules for District Visitors. 1850.
A Charge Delivered to the Clergy of the Diocese of Oxford, at His Second Visitation. 1851.
An Address Delivered at the Confirmation at Eton College. 1851.
The Planting of Nations a Great Responsibility. 1852.
The Shouts and Weeping of a Day of Jubilee. 1852.
An Address Delivered at a Confirmation. 1853.
The Deceitfulness of Sin. 1853.
The Doom of the Unfaithful Instrument; or, Great Britain's Mission. 1853.
"I Have Much People in the City": A Sermon Preached at the Consecration of Christ Church, Denton, Manchester. 1853.
Christ Our Example in Seeking the Lost. 1853.
"Separate Me Barnabas and Saul": A Sermon Preached at the Consecration of the First Bishop of Graham's Town and Natal. 1853.
A Charge to the Diocese of Oxford, at His Third Visitation, November, 1854. 1854.
Prayers to Be Used during Our Present Troubles. 1854.
Sermons Preached and Published on Several Occasions. 1854.
Letters to Dr. Giles for Suspending the Publication of Christian Records; *with Dr. Giles's Letters in Reply.* c. 1854.

The Principles of the English Reformation. 1855.
Rome: Her New Dogma and Our Duties. 1855.
Our Reception of the Truth of Christ's Message, a Part of Our Moral Probation. 1856.
Christ the Healer: A Sermon Preached on the Opening of the New Buildings of the House of Mercy, Clewer. 1856.
National Life. 1857.
The Rebuilding of the Temple a Time of Revival. 1857.
A Charge Delivered at the Triennial Visitation of the Diocese, November, 1857. 1857.
The Gathering of Long-Parted Christian Men. 1859.
The Poor Man's Church. 1859.
Christ's Love for Man. 1860.
Addresses to the Candidates for Ordination, on the Questions in the Ordination Service. 1860.
The Word of the Lord to Ebed-melech the Ethiopian. 1860.
A Charge Delivered at the Triennial Visitation of the Diocese, November, MDCCCLX. 1860.
Gatherings for Religious Worship, a Means of Promoting Unity and Quickening. 1861.
Sketch of the Life of the Rev. John Sargent. 1861.
The Revelation of God the Probation of Man: Two Sermons. 1861.
On Penitentiary Work: Two Sermons (with H. P. Liddon). 1861.
"Cast in Meal"; or, The Poison Rendered Harmless. 1861.
The Teacher's Office as Administration of the Spirit. 1862.
Times of Success in Times of Revival. 1863.
Commemorations of the Departed. 1863.
Fellowship in Joy and Sorrow. 1863.
The Unjust Steward; and The Great High Priest: Two Sermons Preached in Maidstone. 1863.
A Charge, Delivered to the Diocese of Oxford, at His Sixth Visitation, November, 1863. 1863.
Sermons Preached before the University of Oxford: Second Series. 1863.
The Flower of Praise. 1864.
Prayers Suggested for Use in the Schools, Households, and Families, within His Diocese, under Our Present Trials. 1865.
The Voice of the Lord. 1865.
The Enduring Conflict of Christ with the Sin That Is in the World (with others). 1865.
A Sermon Preached at the Consecration of All Saints' Church, Reading. 1866.
The Conflict of Christ in His Church with Spiritual Wickedness in High Places (with others). 1866.
A Charge, Delivered to the Diocese of Oxford, at His Seventh Visitation, December, 1866. 1867.
The Victor in the Conflict (with others). 1868.
The Resurrections of the Truth. 1868.
The Giant of Voluntaryism; or, Mr. Spurgeon in the House of Lord. 1868.
A Charge, Delivered to the Diocese of Oxford, at His Eighth Visitation. 1869.
Personal Responsibility of Man (with others). 1869.
The Prophets of the Lord: Their Message to Their Own Age and to Ours (with others). 1870.
Heroes of Hebrew History. 1870.
Prayers by the Bishop of Winchester for Use in Families during the Continuance of the Present War between France and Prussia. 1870.
Sermons Delivered before the University of Oxford: Third Series. 1871.
The Voice of God in the Church. 1872.

He, Being Departed, Yet Speaketh. c. 1873.

Essays Contributed to the Quarterly Review. 1874. 2 vols.

Speeches on Missions. Ed. Henry Rowley. 1874.

Words of Counsel on Some of the Chief Difficulties of the Day. Ed. T. V. Fosbery. 1875.

Sermons Preached on Various Occasions. 1877.

Maxims and Sayings. Ed. Caroline M. Smith. 1882.

Poems. Ed. R. G. Wilberforce. 1884.

Letter-Books 1843–68. Eds. R. K. Pugh and J. F. A. Mason. 1970.

JOHN STUART MILL (1806–1873)

Rationale of Judicial Evidence by Jeremy Bentham (editor). 1827. 5 vols.

A System of Logic, Ratiocinative and Inductive. 1843 (2 vols.), 1873 (8th rev. ed.).

Essays on Some Unsettled Questions of Political Economy. 1844.

Principles of Political Economy. 1848 (2 vols.), 1871 (7th rev. ed.).

Remarks on Mr. Fitzroy's Bill. 1853.

On Liberty. 1859.

Thoughts on Parliamentary Reform. 1859. 2 vols.

Dissertations and Discussions. 1859 (2 vols.), 1867 (3 vols.), 1875 (4 vols.).

Considerations on Representative Government. 1861.

Utilitarianism. 1863, 1871 (4th rev. ed.).

Auguste Comte and Positivism. 1865.

An Examination of Sir William Hamilton's Philosophy. 1865, 1872 (4th rev. ed.).

Inaugural Address Delivered to the University of St. Andrew's. 1867.

Speech on the Admission of Women to the Electoral Franchise. 1867.

Personal Representation: Speech Delivered at the House of Commons. 1867.

England and Ireland. 1868.

Analysis of the Phenomena of the Human Mind by James Mill (editor). 1869. 2 vols.

The Subjection of Women. 1869.

Speech at the National Education League Meeting. 1870.

Speech in Favour of Women's Suffrage. 1873.

Autobiography. Ed. Helen Taylor. 1873.

Nature, The Utility of Religion, and Theism. Ed. Helen Taylor. 1874.

Socialism. Ed. W. D. P. Bliss. 1891.

Early Essays. Ed. J. W. M. Gibbs. 1897.

Correspondance inédite avec Gustave d'Eichthal. Ed. E. d'Eichthal. 1898.

Lettres inédites à Auguste Comte. Ed. L. Lévy-Brühl. 1899.

James and John Stuart Mill on Education. Ed. F. A. Cavenagh. 1931.

On Social Freedom. Ed. Dorothy Fosdick. 1941.

The Spirit of the Age. Ed. F. A. von Hayek. 1942.

Four Dialogues of Plato (translator). Ed. Ruth Borchardt. 1946.

John Stuart Mill and Harriet Taylor: Their Correspondence and Subsequent Marriage. Ed. F. A. von Hayek. 1951.

John Mill's Boyhood Visit to France: Being a Journal and Notebook Written by John Stuart Mill in France in 1820–21. Ed. Anna Jean Mill. 1960.

The Early Draft of John Stuart Mill's Autobiography. Ed. Jack Stillinger. 1961.

The Philosophy of John Stuart Mill. Ed. Marshall Cohen. 1961.

Collected Works. Eds. J. A. Robson et al. 1963–86. 25 vols.

Essays on Sex Equality (with Harriet Taylor). Ed. Alice S. Rossi. 1970.

BRYAN WALLER PROCTER ("BARRY CORNWALL") (1787–1874)

Dramatic Scenes and Other Poems. 1819.

A Sicilian Story, with Diego de Montilla, and Other Poems. 1820.

Marcian Colonna: An Italian Tale; with Three Dramatic Scenes, and Other Poems. 1820.

Mirandola. 1821.

Poetical Works. 1822. 3 vols.

The Flood of Thessaly, The Girl of Provence, and Other Poems. 1823.

Effigies Poeticae; or, Portraits of the British Poets. 1824.

The Gin: An Out-and-Out Parody on "The Sea." c. 1825.

The Poetical Works of Milman, Bowles, Wilson and Barry Cornwall. 1829. 4 parts.

English Songs and Other Small Poems. 1832.

A New Song, Called The Sea, the Sea. 1834.

The Life of Edmund Kean. 1835. 2 vols.

Melanie and Other Poems by N. P. Willis (editor). 1835.

Essays and Tales in Prose. 1853. 2 vols.

Dramatic Scenes; with Other Poems, Now First Printed. 1857.

Selections from the Poetical Works of Robert Browning (editor; with John Forster). 1863.

Charles Lamb: A Memoir. 1866.

An Autobiographical Fragment and Biographical Notes, with Personal Sketches of Contemporaries, Unpublished Lyrics, and Letters of Literary Friends. Ed. Coventry Patmore. 1877.

King of the Night. c. 1888.

The Literary Recollections of Barry Cornwall. Ed. Richard Willard Armour. 1936.

SYDNEY DOBELL (1824–1874)

The Roman: A Dramatic Poem. 1850.

Balder. 1854.

Sonnets on the War (with Alexander Smith). 1855.

England in Time of War. 1856.

Poems. 1860.

Love: To a Little Girl. 1863.

Of Parliamentary Reform: A Letter to a Politician. 1865.

England's Day: A War-Saga Commended to Gortschakoff, Grant, and Bismarck, and Dedicated to the British Navy. 1871.

Poetical Works. Ed. John Nichol. 1875. 2 vols.

Thoughts on Art, Philosophy, and Religion: Selected from the Unpublished Papers. Ed. John Nichol. 1876.

Life and Letters. Ed. Emily Jolly. 1878. 2 vols.

Poems. Ed. Emily Dobell. 1887.

America: Two Sonnets Written during the Crimean War in 1855. 1896.

Home in War Time: Poems. Ed. William G. Hutchinson. 1900.

CHARLES KINGSLEY (1819–1875)

A Sermon Preached at Eversley, Hants. 1847.

A Sermon Preached at Hawley Church, in Behalf of the New Church at York Town. 1848.

The Saint's Tragedy; or, The True Story of Elizabeth of Hungary, Landgravine of Thuringia, Saint of the Romish Church. 1848.

Twenty-five Village Sermons. 1849.

Alton Locke, Tailor and Poet: An Autobiography. 1850. 2 vols.

Cheap Clothes and Nasty. 1850.

The Application of Associative Principles and Methods to Agriculture. 1851.

The Message of the Church to Labouring Men. 1851.

Yeast: A Problem. 1851.

Who Are the Friends of Order? 1852.

Phaethon; or, Loose Thoughts for Loose Thinkers. 1852.

Sermons on National Subjects. 1852.

Hypatia; or, New Foes with an Old Face. 1853. 2 vols.

Alexandria and Her Schools. 1854.

Sermons on National Subjects: Second Series. 1854.

Who Causes Pestilence? Four Sermons, with Preface. 1854.

Glaucus; or, The Wonders of the Shore. 1855.

Sermons for the Times. 1855.

Sermons for Sailors. 1855.

Brave Words for Brave Soldiers. 1855.

Westward Ho!; or, The Voyages and Adventures of Sir Amyas Leigh, Knight, of Burrough, in the County of Devon, in the Reign of Her Most Glorious Majesty, Queen Elizabeth. 1855. 3 vols.

The Heroes; or, Greek Fairy Tales for My Children. 1856.

Two Years Ago. 1857. 3 vols.

Andromeda and Other Poems. 1858.

Esau and Jacob. c. 1858.

Miscellanies. 1859. 2 vols.

The Two Breaths. 1859.

The Good News of God: Sermons. 1859.

Why Should We Pray for Fair Weather? A Sermon. 1860.

The Limits of Exact Science as Applied to History: An Inaugural Lecture. 1860.

Town and Country Sermons. 1861.

Ode Performed in the Senate-House, Cambridge, Composed for the Installation of His Grace the Duke of Devonshire, Chancellor of the University. 1862.

Speech of Lord Dundreary, in Section D, on Friday Last, on the Great Hippocampus Question. 1862.

A Sermon on the Death of His Royal Highness, the Prince Consort. 1862.

The Gospel of the Pentateuch: A Set of Parish Sermons. 1863.

The Water-Babies: A Fairy Tale for a Land-Baby. 1863.

Hints to Stammerers. 1864.

The Roman and the Teuton: A Series of Lectures Delivered before the University of Cambridge. 1864.

Mr. Kingsley and Dr. Newman: A Correspondence on the Question Whether Dr. Newman Teaches That Truth Is No Virtue? (with John Henry Newman). 1864.

"What, Then, Does Dr. Newman Mean?": A Reply to a Pamphlet Lately Published by Dr. Newman. 1864.

David: Four Sermons Preached before the University of Cambridge. 1865.

Hereward the Wake, "Last of the English." 1866. 2 vols.

The Temple of Wisdom: A Sermon. 1866.

A Game-Law Ballad: A Rough Rhyme on a Rough Matter. c. 1866.

Three Lectures Delivered at the Royal Institution, on the Ancien Regime as It Existed on the Continent before the French Revolution. 1867.

The Water of Life and Other Sermons. 1867.

A Sermon Preached at the Volunteer Camp, Wimbledon. 1867.

Discipline and Other Sermons. 1868.

The Hermits. 1868.

An Address on Education. 1869.

God's Feast: A Sermon. 1869.

Madam How and Lady Why; or, First Lessons in Earth Lore for Children. 1870.

At Last: A Christmas in the West Indies. 1871. 2 vols.

Songs and Etchings. 1871.

Poems. 1872.

Town Geology. 1872.

Plays and Puritans and Other Historical Essays. 1873.

Prose Idylls, New and Old. 1873.

Frederick Denison Maurice. 1873.

Selections from Some of the Writings. 1873.

Westminster Sermons. 1874.

Health and Education. 1874.

South by West; or, Winter in the Rocky Mountains, and Spring in Mexico by Rose Kingsley (editor). 1874.

Lectures Delivered in America in 1874. 1875.

Letters to Young Men on Betting and Gambling. 1877.

Charles Kingsley: His Letters and Memories of His Life. Ed. Frances E. Kingsley. 1877. 2 vols.

True Words for Brave Men: A Book for Soldiers' and Sailors' Libraries. 1878.

All Saints' Day and Other Sermons. Ed. W. Harrison. 1878.

Out of the Deep: Words for the Sorrowful, from the Writings of Charles Kingsley. Ed. Frances E. Kingsley. 1880.

Works. 1880–85. 28 vols.

Living Truths from the Writings of Charles Kingsley. Ed. E. E. Brown. 1882.

From Death to Life: Fragments of Teaching to a Village Congregation, with Letters on the Life after Death. Ed. Frances E. Kingsley. 1887.

Works. 1898–99. 7 vols.

Novels and Poems. 1898–1900. 14 vols.

Life and Works. 1901–03. 19 vols.

Words of Advice to School-boys: Collected from Hitherto Unpublished Notes and Lectures. Ed. E. F. Johns. 1912.

Poems. 1913.

The Tutor's Story: An Unfinished Novel. 1916.

The Water Babies and Selected Poems. 1954.

American Notes: Letters from a Lecture Tour 1874. Ed. Robert Bernard Martin. 1958.

The Kingsleys: A Biographical Anthology (with George Kingsley and Henry Kingsley). Ed. Elspeth Huxley. 1973.

<u>HARRIET MARTINEAU</u> (1802–1876)

Devotional Exercises: Consisting of Reflections and Prayers, for the Use of Young Persons. 1823.

Christmas-Day; or, The Friends. 1825.

The Friends: A Continuation of Christmas-Day. 1826.

Addresses; with Prayers and Original Hymns, for the Use of Families and Schools. 1826.

Principle and Practice; or, The Orphan Family. 1827.

Mary Campbell; or, The Affectionate Granddaughter. 1828.

Traditions of Palestine (editor). 1830.

The Essential Faith of the Universal Church: Deduced from the Sacred Records. 1831.

Five Years of Youth; or, Sense and Sentiment. 1831.

Sequel to Principle and Practice; or, The Orphan Family. 1831.

Illustrations of Political Economy. 1832–34. 25 parts.

The Faith as Unfolded by Many Prophets. 1832.

Providence as Manifested through Israel. 1832.

Poor Laws and Paupers. 1833 [Part 1: *The Parish*]; 1833 [Part 2: *The Hamlets*]; 1833 [Part 3: *The Town*]; 1834 [Part 4: *The Land's End*].

Illustrations of Taxation. 1834. 5 parts.

The Children Who Lived by the Jordan. 1835.

Miscellanies. 1836. 2 vols.

Society in America. 1837. 3 vols.

A Retrospect of Western Travel. 1838. 3 vols.

The Guide to Trade (with others). 1838–44. 10 parts.

How to Observe: Morals and Manners. 1838.

Deerbrook. 1839. 3 vols.

The Guide to Service. 1839.

The Hour and the Man: An Historical Romance. 1841. 3 vols.

The Playfellow: A Series of Tales. 1841 [Volume 1: *The Settlers at Home*]; 1841 [Volume 2: *The Peasant and the Prince*]; 1841 [Volume 3: *Feats on the Fiord*]; 1841 [Volume 4: *The Crofton Boys*].

The Rioters: A Tale. 1842.

Life in the Sick-Room; or, Essays by an Invalid. 1844.

Dawn Island: A Tale. 1845.

Forest and Game-Law Tales. 1845–46. 3 vols.

Letters on Mesmerism. 1845.

The Billow and the Rock: A Tale. 1846.

Eastern Life, Past and Present. 1848. 3 vols.

Household Education. 1849.

The History of England during the Thirty Years' Peace 1816–1846. 1849–50 (2 vols.), 1864–66 (4 vols.), 1877–78 (4 vols.).

Two Letters on Cow-Keeping. c. 1850.

Letters on the Laws of Man's Nature and Development (with Henry George Atkinson). 1851.

Introduction to the History of the Peace, *from 1800 to 1815.* 1851.

Half a Century of the British Empire: A History of the Kingdom and the People from 1800 to 1850. 1851. Part 1 only.

Letters from Ireland. 1853.

The Positive Philosophy of Auguste Comte (editor and translator). 1853. 2 vols.

The Sickness and Health of the People of Bleaburn. 1853.

A Complete Guide to the English Lakes. 1854.

Guide to Windermere, with Tours to the Neighbouring Lakes and Other Interesting Places. 1854.

The Factory Controversy: A Warning against Meddling Legislation. 1855.

A History of the American Compromises. 1856.

Sketches from Life. 1856.

Corporate Traditions and National Rights: Local Dues on Shipping. 1857.

Guide to Keswick and Its Environs. 1857.

British Rule in India: A Historical Sketch. 1857.

Suggestions towards the Future Government of India. 1858.

Endowed Schools of Ireland. 1859.

England and Her Soldiers. 1859.

Health, Husbandry, and Handicraft. 1861.

Biographical Sketches. 1869.

Autobiography. Ed. Maria Weston Chapman. 1877. 2 vols.

The Hampdens: An Historiette. 1880.

Letters to Fanny Wedgwood. Ed. Elizabeth Sanders Arbuckle. 1983.

Harriet Martineau on Women. Ed. Gayle Graham Yeats. 1985.

JOHN FORSTER (1812–1876)

Eminent British Statesmen (with others). 1836 [Volume 2: *Sir John Eliot; Thomas Wentworth, Earl of Strafford*]; 1837 [Volume 3: *John Pym; John Hampden*]; 1838 [Volume 4: *Sir Henry Vane; Henry Marten*]; 1839 [Volumes 6–7: *Oliver Cromwell*]; 1840 (as *The Statesmen of the Commonwealth of England*; 5 vols.).

A Treatise on the Popular Progress in English History. 1840.

The Life and Adventures of Oliver Goldsmith. 1848, 1854 (as *The Life and Times of Oliver Goldsmith*; 2 vols.).

Diary and Correspondence of John Evelyn (editor). 1850–52. 4 vols.

Daniel De Foe and Charles Churchill. 1855. 2 parts.

Historical and Biographical Essays. 1858. 2 vols.

Arrest of the Five Members by Charles the First: A Chapter of History Rewritten. 1860.

The Debates on the Grand Remonstrance, November and December, 1641; with an Introductory Essay on English Freedom under the Plantagenet and Tudor Sovereigns. 1860.

Selections from the Poetical Works of Robert Browning (editor; with Bryan Waller Procter). 1863.

Sir John Eliot: A Biography 1590–1632. 1864. 2 vols.

Walter Savage Landor: A Biography. 1869. 2 vols.

The Life of Charles Dickens. 1872–74. 3 vols.

The Life of Jonathan Swift. 1875. Vol. 1 only.

Dramatic Essays (with George Henry Lewes). Eds. William Archer and Robert W. Lowe. 1896.

CAROLINE NORTON (1808–1877)

The Sorrows of Rosalie: A Tale; with Other Poems. 1829.

The Undying One and Other Poems. 1830.

Poems. 1833.

The English Annual (editor). 1834–38. 5 vols.

The Wife and Woman's Reward. 1835. 3 vols.

The Coquette and Other Tales and Sketches, in Prose and Verse. 1835. 2 vols.

A Voice from the Factories. 1836.

Observations on the Natural Claim of the Mother to the Custody of Her Infant Children, as Affected by the Common Law Right of the Father. 1837.

The Separation of Mother and Child by the Law of "Custody of Infants," Considered. 1838.

A Plain Letter to the Lord Chancellor on the Infant Custody Bill. 1839.

The Dream and Other Poems. 1840.

Lines ⟨on the young Queen Victoria⟩. 1840.

Letters, &c.: Dated from June, 1836, to July, 1841. c. 1841.

The Child of the Islands. 1845.

Poems. 1846.

Aunt Carry's Ballads for Children; Adventures of a Wood Sprite; The Story of Blanche and Brutikin. 1847.

Letters to the Mob. 1848.

A Residence at Sierra Leone by Elizabeth Melville (editor). 1849.

Love Not. c. 1850.

Stuart of Dunleath: A Story of Modern Times. 1851. 3 vols.

Altamut; or, The Charity Sister. 1852.

English Laws for Women in the Nineteenth Century. 1854.

A Letter to the Queen on Lord Chancellor Cranworth's Marriage and Divorce Bill. 1855.

The Centenary Festival ⟨of Robert Burns⟩. 1859.

The Lady of La Garaye. 1862.

Lost and Saved. 1863. 3 vols.

Old Sir Douglas. 1868. 3 vols.

The Rose of Jericho (editor). 1870.

Taxation. 187–.

Bingen on the Rhine. 1883.

Some Unrecorded Letters in the Altschul Collection of the Yale University Library. Ed. Bertha Coolidge. 1934.

Letters to Lord Melbourne. Eds. James O. Hoge and Clarke Olney. 1974.

JOHN LOTHROP MOTLEY (1814–1877)

Morton of Morton's Hope: An Autobiography. 1839. 2 vols.
Merry-Mount: A Romance of the Massachusetts Colony. 1849. 2 vols.
The Rise of the Dutch Republic: A History. 1855. 3 vols.
History of the United Netherlands from the Death of William the Silent to the Twelve Years' Truce—1609. 1860–67. 4 vols.
Causes of the American Civil War. 1861.
Letters of John Lothrop Motley and Joseph Holt. 1861.
Four Questions for the People at the Presidential Election. 1868.
Historic Progress and American Democracy: An Address Delivered before the New-York Historical Society, at Their Sixty-fourth Anniversary. 1869.
The Life and Death of John Barneveld, Advocate of Holland; with a View of the Primary Causes and Movements of the Thirty Years' War. 1874. 2 vols.
Peter the Great. 1877.
Prose Passages from the Works. Ed. Josephine E. Hodgdon. 1883.
Correspondence. Ed. George William Curtis. 1889. 2 vols.
Writings. 1900. 17 vols.
John Lothrop Motley and His Family: Further Letters and Records. Eds. Susan Motley Mildmay and Herbert St. John Mildmay. 1910.
Representative Selections. Eds. Chester Penn Higby and B. T. Schantz. 1939.

WALTER BAGEHOT (1826–1877)

Estimates of Some Englishmen and Scotchmen. 1858.
Parliamentary Reform. 1859.
The History of the Unreformed Parliament and Its Lessons. 1860.
Memoir of the Right Hon. James Wilson. 1861.
Count Your Enemies and Economise Your Expenditure. 1862.
The English Constitution. 1867.
A Practical Plan for Assimilating the English and American Money. 1869.
Physics and Politics; or, Thoughts on the Application of the Principles of "Natural Selection" and "Inheritance" to Political Society. 1872.
Lombard Street: A Description of the Money Market. 1873.
Some Articles on the Depreciation of Silver and on Topics Connected with It. 1877.
Literary Studies. Ed. Richard Holt Hutton. 1879 (2 vols.), 1895 (3 vols.).
Economic Studies. Ed. Richard Holt Hutton. 1880.
Biographical Studies. Ed. Richard Holt Hutton. 1881.
Essays on Parliamentary Reform. 1883.
Works. Ed. Forrest Morgan. 1889. 5 vols.
Works and Life. Ed. Mrs. Russell Barrington. 1915. 10 vols.
Selected Essays. 1927.
The Love Letters of Walter Bagehot and Eliza Wilson. Ed. Mrs. Russell Barrington. 1933.
Collected Works. Ed. Norman St. John-Stevas. 1965–86. 15 vols.

WILLIAM CULLEN BRYANT (1794–1878)

The Embargo; or, Sketches of the Times: A Satire. 1808.
An Oration, Delivered at Stockbridge. 1820.
Poems. Eds. Richard Henry Dana and E. T. Channing. 1821.
Poems. 1832.
Poems. Ed. Washington Irving. 1832.
Tales of the Glauber-Spa (editor). 1832. 2 vols.

Semi-Centennial Celebration of the Inauguration of Washington: Ode. 1839.
Selections from the American Poets (editor). 1840.
The Fountain and Other Poems. 1842.
An Address to the People of the United States in Behalf of the American Copyright Club (with Francis L. Hawks and Cornelius Mathews). 1843.
The White-Footed Deer and Other Poems. 1844.
A Funeral Oration, Occasioned by the Death of Thomas Cole. 1848.
Letters of a Traveller; or, Notes of Things Seen in Europe and America. 1850.
Poetical Works. Ed. F. W. N. Bayley. 1850.
Reminiscences of The Evening Post. 1851.
Complete Poetical Works. 1854.
Poems. 1855. 2 vols.
Letters of a Traveller: Second Series. 1859.
A Discourse on the Life, Character and Genius of Washington Irving. 1860.
Fifty Years: For the Fiftieth Anniversary of the Class of Williams College Which Was Graduated in 1813. 1863.
Thirty Poems. 1864.
Hymns. 1864.
Letters from the East. 1869.
Some Notices of the Life and Writings of Fitz-Greene Halleck. 1869.
The Iliad of Homer (translator). 1870. 2 vols.
A Discourse on the Life, Character and Writings of Gulian Crommelin Verplanck. 1870.
A Library of Poetry and Song (editor). 1871, 1876–78 (21 parts; as A New Library of Poetry and Song).
The Odyssey of Homer (translator). 1871–72. 2 vols.
Picturesque America; or, The Land We Live In (editor). 1872–74. 48 parts.
Orations and Addresses. 1873.
A Popular History of the United States by Sydney Howard Gay (editor). 1876–80. 4 vols.
Poetical Works. Ed. Parke Godwin. 1883. 2 vols.
Prose Writings. Ed. Parke Godwin. 1884. 2 vols.
The Complete Works of Shakespeare (editor; with Evert A. Duyckinck). 1888. 25 parts.
Unpublished Poems by Bryant and Thoreau. 1907.
Representative Selections. Ed. Tremaine McDowell. 1935.
Letters. Eds. William Cullen Bryant II and Thomas G. Voss. 1975– .

GEORGE HENRY LEWES (1817–1878)

A Biographical History of Philosophy. 1845–46 (4 vols.), 1857, 1867 (as History of Philosophy; 2 vols.).
The Spanish Drama: Lope de Vega and Calderón. 1846.
Ranthorpe. 1847.
Rose, Blanche, and Violet. 1848. 3 vols.
The Life of Maximilien Robespierre. 1849.
The Noble Heart. 1850.
A Cozy Couple (with Charles Mathews). 1850.
A Strange History (with Charles Mathews). 1850.
The Game of Speculation. 1851.
A Chain of Events (with Charles Mathews). 1852.
Taking by Storm! 1852.
Comte's Philosophy of the Sciences. 1853.
The Lawyers. 1853.
Give a Dog a Bad Name. 1854.
Sunshine through the Clouds (adaptation). 1854.
Buckstone's Adventure with a Polish Princess. 1855.
The Life and Works of Goethe, with Sketches of His Age and

Contemporaries from Published and Unpublished Sources. 1855 (2 vols.), 1875 (3rd ed.; 2 vols.).

Sea-side Studies at Ilfracombe, Tenby, the Scilly Isles, and Jersey. 1858.

The Chemistry of Common Life by J. F. W. Johnston (revised by Lewes). 1859.

The Physiology of Common Life. 1859–60. 2 vols.

Selections from the Modern British Dramatists (editor). 1861, 1867 (2 vols.).

Studies in Animal Life. 1862.

Aristotle: A Chapter from the History of Science; Including Analyses of Aristotle's Scientific Writings. 1864.

The Female Characters of Goethe. c. 1868.

Problems of Life and Mind, First Series: The Foundations of a Creed. 1874. 2 vols.

On Actors and the Art of Acting. 1875.

Problems of Life and Mind, Second Series: The Physical Basis of Mind. 1877.

Problems of Life and Mind, Third Series: The Study of Psychology (etc.). 1879. 2 vols.

The Principles of Success in Literature. Ed. Fred N. Scott. 1891.

Dramatic Essays (with John Forster). Eds. William Archer and Robert W. Lowe. 1896.

Literary Criticism. Ed. Alice R. Kaminsky. 1964.

BAYARD TAYLOR (1825–1878)

Ximena; or, The Battle of the Sierra Morena, and Other Poems. 1844.

Views A-foot; or, Europe Seen with Knapsack and Staff. 1846. 2 parts.

Rhymes of Travel, Ballads and Poems. 1849.

The American Legend. 1850.

Eldorado; or, Adventures in the Path of Empire. 1850. 2 vols.

Prize Song. 1850.

A Book of Romances, Lyrics, and Songs. 1851.

Hand-book of Literature and the Fine Arts (with George Ripley). 1852.

A Journey to Central Africa; or, Life and Landscapes from Egypt to the Negro Kingdoms of the White Nile. 1854.

Poems of the Orient. 1854.

The Lands of the Saracen; or, Pictures of Palestine, Asia Minor, Sicily, and Spain. 1855.

A Visit to India, China, and Japan in the Year 1853. 1855.

Poems of Home and Travel. 1855.

Cyclopaedia of Modern Travel: A Record of Adventure, Exploration and Discovery for the Past Fifty Years (editor). 1856, 1860 (2 vols.).

Northern Travel: Summer and Winter Pictures of Sweden, Denmark, and Lapland. 1857.

Travels in Greece and Russia, with an Excursion to Crete. 1859.

At Home and Abroad: A Sketch-Book of Life, Scenery, and Men. 1860.

Humboldt: Lecture Delivered before the Young Men's Christian Association, Schenectady. 1860.

At Home and Abroad: Second Series. 1862.

The Poet's Journal. 1862.

Hannah Thurston: A Story of American Life. 1863.

Poems. 1864.

John Godfrey's Fortunes, Related by Himself: A Story of American Life. 1864.

Poems. 1865.

The Story of Kennett. 1866.

The Picture of St. John. 1866.

Colorado: A Summer Trip. 1867.

The Golden Wedding: Joseph Taylor, Rebecca W. Taylor. 1868.

By-Ways of Europe. 1869.

Joseph and His Friend: A Story of Pennsylvania. 1870.

The Ballad of Abraham Lincoln. 1870.

Faust by Johann Wolfgang von Goethe (translator). 1870 [Book 1]; 1871 [Book 2].

Travels in Arabia (editor). 1871.

Japan in Our Day (editor). 1872.

Travels in South Africa (editor). 1872.

Beauty and the Beast and Tales of Home. 1872.

The Masque of the Gods. 1872.

Diversions of the Echo Club. 1872.

Lars: A Pastoral of Norway. 1873.

The Lake Regions of Central Africa (editor). 1873.

The Prophet. 1874.

Egypt and Iceland in the Year 1874. 1874.

America to Iceland. 1874.

Central Asia: Travels in Cashmere, Little Tibet and Central Asia (editor). 1874.

A School History of Germany from the Earliest Period to the Establishment of the German Empire in 1871. 1874.

Home Pastorals, Ballads and Lyrics. 1875.

Picturesque Europe (editor). 1875–79. 3 vols.

Boys of Other Countries: Stories for American Boys. 1876.

The National Ode: July 4, 1876. 1876.

Prince Deukalion: A Lyrical Drama. 1878.

Studies in German Literature. 1879.

Works. 1879. 15 vols.

Critical Essays and Literary Notes. Ed. Marie Hansen Taylor. 1880.

Poetical Works. 1880.

Dramatic Works. Ed. Marie Hansen Taylor. 1880.

Life and Letters. Eds. Marie Hansen Taylor and Horace E. Scudder. 1884. 2 vols.

Unpublished Letters in the Huntington Library. Ed. John Richie Schultz. 1937.

The Correspondence of Bayard Taylor and Paul Hamilton Hayne. Ed. Charles Duffy. 1945.

RICHARD HENRY DANA (1787–1879)

An Oration, Delivered before the Washington Benevolent Society at Cambridge. 1814.

Poems by William Cullen Bryant (editor); with E. T. Channing). 1821.

The Idle Man. 1821–22. 6 nos.

Poems. 1827.

A Poem Delivered before the Porter Rhetorical Society, in the Theological Seminary, Andover. 1829.

Poems and Prose Writings. 1833.

The Buccaneer and Other Poems. 1844.

Poems and Prose Writings. 1850. 2 vols.

Poetical Works (with Edgar Allan Poe). 1857.

WILLIAM LLOYD GARRISON (1805–1879)

An Address Delivered before the Free People of Color, in Philadelphia, New-York, and Other Cities, during the Month of June, 1831. 1831.

Thoughts on African Colonization; or, An Impartial Exhibition of the Doctrines, Principles and Purposes of the American Colonization Society. 1832.

An Address on the Progress of the Abolition Cause, Delivered before the African Abolition Freehold Society of Boston. 1832.

Address Delivered in Boston, New-York and Philadelphia before the Free People of Color, in April, 1833. 1833.

Slavery in the United States of America: An Appeal to the Friends of Negro Emancipation throughout Great Britain, &c. 1833.

A Selection of Anti-Slavery Hymns, for the Use of the Friends of Emancipation (editor). 1834.

Shall the Liberator Die? 1834.

The Maryland Scheme of Emancipation Examined. 1834.

Juvenile Poems, for the Use of Free American Children, of Every Complexion (editor). 1835.

An Address in Marlboro' Chapel, Boston. 1838.

An Address Delivered at the Broadway Tabernacle, New York, by Request of the People of Color of That City, in Commemoration of the Complete Emancipation of 600,000 Slaves in the British West Indies. 1838.

An Address Delivered before the Old Colony Anti-Slavery Society, at South Scituate, Mass. 1839.

[*Address in Commemoration of the Great Jubilee.* 1842.]

Sonnets and Other Poems. 1843.

Speeches at Paisley, Scotland (with Frederick Douglass). 1846.

Letter to the Secretaries of the Glasgow Emancipation Society. 1846.

American Slavery: Address on the Subject of American Slavery, and the Progress of Freedom throughout the World, Delivered in the National Hall, Holborn. 1846.

Letter Read at the Annual Meeting of the Pennsylvania Anti-Slavery Society. 1851.

Selections from the Writings and Speeches. 1852.

Letter to Louis Kossuth. 1852.

Principles and Mode of Action of the American Anti-Slavery Society. 1853.

No Compromise with Slavery: An Address Delivered in the Broadway Tabernacle, New York. 1854.

West India Emancipation: A Speech Delivered at Abington, Mass. 1854.

"No Fetters in the Bay State!" Speech before the Committee on Federal Relations, in Support of the Petitions Asking for a Law to Prevent the Recapture of Fugitive Slaves. 1859.

The "Infidelity" of Abolitionism. 1860.

The New "Reign of Terror" in the Slaveholding States, for 1859–60. 1860.

A Fresh Catalogue of Southern Outrages upon Northern Citizens. 1860.

The Loyalty and Devotion of the Colored Americans in the Revolution and War of 1812. 1861.

The Spirit of the South towards Northern Freemen and Soldiers Defending the American Flag against Traitors of the Deepest Dye. 1861.

The Abolition of Slavery the Right of the Government under the War Power. 1861.

The Abolitionists, and Their Relations to the War: A Lecture Delivered at the Cooper Institute, New York. 1862.

Southern Hatred of the American Government, the People of the North, and Free Institutions. 1862.

Letters of William Lloyd Garrison, Wendell Phillips, and James G. Blaine, and Other Valuable Reading Matter for All Who Are Interested in the Approaching Presidential Election. 1872.

Fillmore and Sumner: A Letter from William Lloyd Garrison. 1874.

Helen Eliza Garrison: A Memorial. 1876.

William Lloyd Garrison on State Regulation of Vice. c. 1879.

The Philosophy of the Single Tax Movement. 1895.

The Words of Garrison: A Centennial Selection. Eds. Wendell Phillips Garrison and Francis Jackson Garrison. 1905.

Garrison's First Anti-Slavery Address in Boston: Address at Park Street Church, Boston, July 4, 1829. 1907.

William Lloyd Garrison on Non-Resistance. Ed. Fanny Garrison Villard. 1924.

Documents of Upheaval: Selections from William Lloyd Garrison's The Liberator *1831–1865.* Ed. Truman Nelson. 1966.

Letters. Eds. Walter M. Merrill and Louis Ruchames. 1971–81. 6 vols.

CHARLES TENNYSON TURNER (1808–1879)

Poems by Two Brothers (with Alfred, Lord Tennyson). 1827.

Sonnets and Fugitive Pieces. 1830.

Sonnets. 1864.

Small Tableaux. 1868.

Sonnets, Lyrics, and Translations. 1873.

Collected Sonnets, Old and New. 1880.

Charles Tennyson. 1931.

A Hundred Sonnets. Eds. John Betjeman and Sir Charles Tennyson. 1960.

GEORGE ELIOT (MARY ANN EVANS)
(1819–1880)

The Life of Jesus Critically Examined by David Friedrich Strauss (translator). 1846. 3 vols.

The Essence of Christianity by Ludwig Feuerbach (translator). 1854.

Scenes of Clerical Life. 1858. 3 vols.

Adam Bede. 1859. 3 vols.

The Mill on the Floss. 1860. 3 vols.

Silas Marner: The Weaver of Raveloe. 1861.

Romola. 1863. 3 vols.

Felix Holt, the Radical. 1866. 3 vols.

Novels. 1867–78. 6 vols.

The Spanish Gypsy. 1868.

Agatha. 1869.

How Lisa Loved the King. 1869.

Middlemarch: A Study of Provincial Life. 1872. 4 vols.

A Legend of Jubal and Other Poems. 1874.

Daniel Deronda. 1876. 4 vols.

Novels. 1876. 9 vols.

Works (Cabinet Edition). 1878–85. 24 vols.

Impressions of Theophrastus Such. 1879.

Essays and Leaves from a Note-Book. Ed. Charles Lee Lewes. 1885.

George Eliot's Life as Related in Her Letters and Journals. Ed. J. W. Cross. 1885. 3 vols.

Complete Poems. 1888.

Letters to Elma Stuart 1872–1880. Ed. Roland Stuart. 1909.

Early Essays. Ed. George W. Redway. 1919.

Letters. Ed. R. Brimley Johnson. 1926.

Letters. Ed. Gordon S. Haight. 1954–78. 9 vols.

Essays. Ed. Thomas Pinney. 1963.

Works. Ed. Gordon S. Haight. 1980– .

A Writer's Notebook 1854–1879, and Uncollected Writings. Ed. Joseph Wiesenfarth. 1981.

Ethics by Benedict Spinoza (translator). 1981.

THOMAS CARLYLE (1795–1881)

Elements of Geometry and Trigonometry by A. M. Legendre (translator). 1824.

Wilhelm Meister's Apprenticeship: A Novel from the German of Goethe (translator). 1824. 3 vols.

The Life of Friedrich Schiller: Comprehending an Examination of His Life and Writings. 1825.

German Romance: Specimens of Its Chief Authors, with Biographical and Critical Notices (editor and translator). 1827. 4 vols.

Sartor Resartus: The Life and Opinions of Herr Teufelsdröckh. 1836.

The French Revolution: A History. 1837. 3 vols.

Critical and Miscellaneous Essays. Eds. Ralph Waldo Emerson et al. 1838. 4 vols.

Chartism. 1840.

On Heroes, Hero-Worship, and the Heroic in History. 1841.

Past and Present. 1843.

Oliver Cromwell's Letters and Speeches, with Elucidations. 1845. 2 vols.

Latter-Day Pamphlets. 1850. 8 parts.

The Life of John Sterling. 1851.

Occasional Discourse on the Nigger Question. 1853.

Collected Works. 1857–58. 16 vols.

History of Friedrich II. of Prussia, Called Frederick the Great. 1858–65. 6 vols.

Inaugural Address at Edinburgh, on Being Installed as Rector of the University There ⟨On the Choice of Books⟩. 1866.

Critical and Miscellaneous Essays. 1869. 6 vols.

Collected Works (Library Edition). 1869–71. 34 vols.

Collected Works (People's Edition). 1871–74. 37 vols.

Letters to Mrs. Basil Montagu and B. W. Procter. 1881.

Reminiscences. Ed. James Anthony Froude. 1881. 2 vols.

Last Words on Trades-Unions, Promoterism and the Signs of the Times. Ed. Jane Carlyle Aitken. 1882.

Reminiscences of My Irish Journey in 1849. Ed. James Anthony Froude. 1882.

The Correspondence of Thomas Carlyle and Ralph Waldo Emerson 1834–1872. Ed. Charles Eliot Norton. 1883. 2 vols.

The Correspondence of Thomas Carlyle and Ralph Waldo Emerson 1834–1872: Supplementary Letters. Ed. Charles Eliot Norton. 1886.

Early Letters 1814–1826. Ed. Charles Eliot Norton. 1886. 2 vols.

Correspondence between Goethe and Carlyle. Ed. Charles Eliot Norton. 1887.

Early Letters 1826–1836. Ed. Charles Eliot Norton. 1888. 2 vols.

Rescued Essays. Ed. Percy Newberry. 1892.

Last Words of Thomas Carlyle: Wotton Reinfred, a Romance; Excursion (Futile Enough) to Paris; Letters. 1892.

Lectures on the History of Literature; or, The Successive Periods of European Culture. Ed. J. Reay Greene. 1892.

Works (Centenary Edition). Ed. H. D. Traill. 1896–99. 30 vols.

Two Note Books from 23d March 1822 to 16th May 1832. Ed. Charles Eliot Norton. 1898.

Historical Sketches of Notable Persons and Events in the Reigns of James I. and Charles I. Ed. Alexander Carlyle. 1898.

Letters to His Youngest Sister. Ed. Charles Townsend Copeland. 1899.

Collectanea 1821–1855. Ed. Samuel Arthur Jones. 1903.

New Letters. Ed. Alexander Carlyle. 1904. 2 vols.

Carlyle and the London Library: Account of Its Foundation; Together with the Unpublished Letters to W. D. Christie. Ed. Frederic Harrison. 1907.

Love Letters of Thomas Carlyle and Jane Welsh Carlyle. Ed. Alexander Carlyle. 1909. 2 vols.

Letters of Thomas Carlyle to John Stuart Mill, John Sterling and Robert Browning. Ed. Alexander Carlyle. 1923.

Journey to Germany, Autumn, 1858. Ed. Richard Albert Edward Brooks. 1940.

Letters to William Graham. Ed. John Graham, Jr. 1950.

Carlyle's Unfinished History of German Literature. Ed. Hill Shine. 1951.

Carlyle: An Anthology. Ed. G. M. Trevelyan. 1953.

Letters to His Wife. Ed. Trudy Bliss. 1953.

Selected Works, Reminiscences and Letters. Ed. Julian Symons. 1955.

The Correspondence of Emerson and Carlyle. Ed. Joseph Slater. 1964.

Letters to His Brother Alexander, with Related Family Letters. Ed. Edwin W. Marrs, Jr. 1968.

Collected Letters of Thomas and Jane Welsh Carlyle. Eds. Charles Richard Sanders, Kenneth J. Fielding, Claude de L. Ryals et al. 1978– .

The Correspondence of Thomas Carlyle and John Ruskin. Ed. George Allen Cate. 1982.

A Carlyle Reader. Ed. G. B. Tennyson. 1984.

Collected Poems of Thomas and Jane Welsh Carlyle. Eds. Rodger L. Tarr and Fleming McClelland. 1986.

GEORGE BORROW (1803–1881)

Celebrated Trials, and Remarkable Cases of Criminal Jurisprudence, from the Earliest Records to the Year 1825 (editor). 1825. 6 vols.

Tales of the Wild and the Wonderful. 1825.

Faustus: His Life, Death, and Descent into Hell by F. M. von Klinger (translator). 1825.

Romantic Ballads, Translated from the Danish; and Miscellaneous Pieces. 1826.

Mousei echen Isus Gheristos i tuta puha itche ghese (editor). 1835.

Targum; or, Metrical Translations from Thirty Languages and Dialects. 1835.

The Talisman ⟨by Alexander Pushkin (translator)⟩ with Other Pieces. 1835.

El Nuevo Testamento (editor). 1837.

Embéo e Majaró Lucas (translator). 1837.

Evangelioa San Lucasen Guissan (editor). 1838.

The Zincali; or, An Account of the Gypsies in Spain. 1841. 2 vols.

The Bible in Spain; or, The Journeys, Adventures, and Imprisonments of an Englishman, in an Attempt to Circulate the Scriptures in the Peninsula. 1843. 3 vols.

Lavengro: The Scholar, the Gypsy, the Priest. 1851. 3 vols.

The Romany Rye: A Sequel to Lavengro. 1857. 2 vols.

The Sleeping Bard; or, Visions of the World, Death and Hell by Elis Wyn (translator). 1860.

Wild Wales: Its People, Language, and Scenery. 1862. 3 vols.

Romano Lavo-Lil: Word-Book of the Romany, or English Gypsy Language. 1874.

The Turkish Jester; or, The Pleasantries of Cogia Nasr Eddin Effendi (translator). 1884.

The Death of Balder by Johannes Ewald (translator). 1889.

Russian Popular Tales (translator). 1904.

Works. 1904. 4 vols.

Works. 1906. 5 vols.

Letters to the British and Foreign Bible Society. Ed. T. H. Darlow. 1911.

The Pocket Borrow. Ed. Edward Thomas. 1912.

Letters to His Wife Mary Borrow. 1913.

Letters to His Mother Ann Borrow and Other Correspondents. 1913.

A Supplementary Chapter to the Bible in Spain *Inspired by Ford's* Handbook for Travellers in Spain. 1913.

Marsk Stig: A Ballad (translator). 1913.

The Serpent Knight and Other Ballads (translator). 1913.

The King's Wake and Other Ballads (translator). 1913.

The Dalby Bear and Other Ballads (translator). 1913.

The Mermaid's Prophecy and Other Songs Relating to Queen Dagmar (translator). 1913.

Hafbur and Signe: A Ballad (translator). 1913.

The Story of Yvahka and the Bear's Ear (translator). 1913.

The Verner Raven, The Count of Vendel's Daughter, and Other Ballads (translator). 1913.

The Return of the Dead and Other Ballads (translator). 1913.

Axel Thordson and Fair Valborg: A Ballad (translator). 1913.

King Hacon's Death and Bran and the Black Dog: Two Ballads (translator). 1913.

Marsk Stig's Daughters and Other Songs and Ballads (translator). 1913.

The Tale of Brynild and King Valdemar and His Sister: Two Ballads (translator). 1913.

Proud Signild and Other Ballads (translator). 1913.

Ulf Van Yern and Other Ballads (translator). 1913.

Ellen of Villenskov and Other Ballads (translator). 1913.

The Songs of Ranild (translator). 1913.

Niels Ebbesen and Germand Gladenswayne: Two Ballads (translator). 1913.

Child Maidelvold and Other Ballads (translator). 1913.

Ermeline: A Ballad (translator). 1913.

The Giant of Bern and Orm Ungerswayne: A Ballad (translator). 1913.

Little Engel: A Ballad; with a Series of Epigrams from the Persian (translator). 1913.

Alf the Freebooter, Little Danneved and Swayne Trost, and Other Ballads (translator). 1913.

King Diderik and the Fight between the Lion and Dragon and Other Ballads (translator). 1913.

Grimmer and Kamper, The End of Sivard Snarenswayne, and Other Ballads (translator). 1913.

The Fountain of Maribo and Other Ballads (translator). 1913.

Queen Berngerd, The Bard and the Dreams, and Other Ballads (translator). 1913.

Finnish Arts; or, Sir Thor and Damsel Thure: A Ballad (translator). 1913.

Brown William, The Power of the Harp, and Other Ballads (translator). 1913.

The Song of Deirdra, King Byrge and His Brothers, and Other Ballads (translator). 1913.

Signelil: A Tale from the Cornish, and Other Ballads (translator). 1913.

Young Swaigder; or, The Force of Runes, and Other Ballads (translator). 1913.

Emelian the Fool: A Tale (translator). 1913.

The Story of Tim (translator). 1913.

Mollie Charane and Other Ballads (translator). 1913.

Grimhild's Vengeance: Three Ballads (translator). Ed. Edmund Gosse. 1913.

The Brother Avenged and Other Ballads (translator). 1913.

The Gold Horns by Adam Gottlob Oehlenschlager (translator). Ed. Edmund Gosse. 1913.

Tord of Halfsborough and Other Ballads (translator). 1914.

The Expedition to Birting's Land and Other Ballads (translator). 1914.

Ode to Lewis Morris by Goronwy Owen (translator). 1915.

Borrow in Vienna: An Unpublished Letter. 1915.

An Expedition to the Isle of Man in 1855: A Hitherto Unpublished Diary. 1915.

Welsh Poems and Ballads. Ed. Ernest Rhys. 1915.

Readings from George Borrow. Ed. S. A. Richards. 1921.

Works (Norwich Edition). Ed. Clement K. Shorter. 1923–24. 16 vols.

Selections. Ed. Humphry S. Milford. 1924.

Ballads of All Nations: A Selection (translator). Ed. R. Brimley Johnson. 1927.

Selections from George Borrow. Ed. W. E. Williams. 1927.

Celtic Bards, Chiefs and Kings. Ed. Herbert G. Wright. 1928.

BENJAMIN DISRAELI (1804–1881)

Rumpal Stilts Kin (with W. G. Meredith). 1823.

An Inquiry into the Plans, Progress, and Policy of American Mining Companies. 1825.

Lawyers and Legislators; or, Notes on the American Mining Companies. 1825.

The Present Stage of Mexico. 1825.

Vivian Grey. 1826–27. 5 vols.

The Voyage of Captain Popanilla. 1828.

The Young Duke. 1831. 3 vols.

England and France; or, A Cure for the Ministerial Gallomania. 1832.

Contarini Fleming: A Psychological Auto-biography. 1832. 4 vols.

The Wondrous Tale of Alroy; The Rise of Iskander. 1833. 3 vols.

Velvet Lawn: A Sketch. 1833.

"What Is He?" 1833.

The Crisis Examined. 1834.

The Revolutionary Epick. 1834. 2 vols.

To the Electors and Inhabitants of the Borough of Taunton. 1835.

Vindication of the English Constitution, in a Letter to a Noble and Learned Lord. 1835.

The Letters of Runnymede (with *The Spirit of Whiggism*). 1836.

Henrietta Temple: A Love Story. 1837. 3 vols.

Venetia. 1837. 3 vols.

The Tragedy of Count Alarcos. 1839.

Coningsby; or, The New Generation. 1844. 3 vols.

Sybil; or, The Two Nations. 1845. 3 vols.

Alroy; Ixion in Heaven; The Infernal Marriage; Popanilla. 1845.

Speech in the House of Commons. 1846.

Tancred; or, The New Crusade. 1847. 3 vols.

England and Denmark: Speech in the House of Commons. 1848.

The New Parliamentary Reform: Speech in the House of Commons. 1848.

The Parliament and the Government: Speech on the Labours of the Session. 1848.

Financial Policy: Speech Made in the House of Commons. 1851.

The Value of Literature to Men of Business: Address Delivered to the Members of the Manchester Athenaeum. 1852.

Lord George Bentinck: A Political Biography. 1852.

Parliamentary Reform: Speech in the House of Commons. 1852.

Mr. Disraeli to Colonel Rathbone. 1858.

The Works of Isaac Disraeli (editor). 1858–59. 7 vols.

Parliamentary Reform: Speech Delivered in the House of Commons. 1859.

Public Expenditure: A Speech Delivered in the House of Commons. 1862.

Mr. Gladstone's Finance from His Accession to Office in 1853 to His Budget of 1862. 1862.

Speech Delivered at a Public Meeting in Aid of the Oxford Diocesan Society for the Augmentation of Small Benefices. 1862.

Church Policy: Speech Delivered at a Meeting of the Oxford Diocesan Society for the Augmentation of Small Livings. 1862.

Speech at a Public Meeting of the Oxford Diocesan Society for the Augmentation of Small Livings. 1864.

"Church and Queen": Five Speeches 1860–1864. Ed. Frederick Lygon. 1865.

The Chancellor of the Exchequer in Scotland: Being Two Speeches in the City of Edinburgh. 1867.

Parliamentary Reform: A Series of Speeches on That Subject Delivered in the House of Commons 1848–1866. Ed. Montagu Corry. 1867.

The Prime Minister on Church and State: Speech at the Banquet of Her Majesty's Ministers, in the Hall of the Merchant Taylors' Company. 1868.

Mr. Disraeli v. Mr. Disraeli. 1868.

Mr. Disraeli on "The Irish Question." c. 1868.

Speeches on the Conservative Policy of the Last Thirty Years. Ed. John F. Bulley. 1870.

Lothair. 1870. 3 vols.

Novels and Tales. 1870–71. 10 vols.

Speech at Free Trade Hall, Manchester. 1872.

Speech at the Banquet of the National Union of Conservative and Constitutional Associations, at the Crystal Palace. 1872.

Mr. Osborne Morgan's Burials Bill: Speech in the House of Commons, on Moving the Rejection of the Bill in Its Second Reading. 1873.

The Ministerial Crisis: Speeches (with William Ewart Gladstone). 1873.

Address as Lord Rector of the University of Glasgow. 1873.

Speech to the Working Men's Conservative Association at Glasgow. 1873.

The Eastern Question: Speeches (with Lord Derby). 1876.

Lord Beaconsfield Interviewed: Remarkable Statements concerning the Game of Politics, the Origin and Character of Political Parties. Eds. A. C. Yates and A. G. Symonds. 1879.

Endymion. 1880.

A Warning Voice: Lord Beaconsfield's Appeal to the People of Great Britain and Ireland. 1880.

Novels and Tales (Hughenden Edition). 1881. 11 vols.

Wit and Wisdom of Benjamin Disraeli, Earl of Beaconsfield. 1881.

Selected Speeches. Ed. T. E. Kebbel. 1882. 2 vols.

Lord Beaconsfield on the Constitution. Ed. Francis Hitchman. 1884.

Home Letters Written in 1830 and 1831. Ed. Ralph Disraeli. 1885.

Correspondence with His Sister 1832–1852. Ed. Ralph Disraeli. 1886.

Tales and Sketches. Ed. J. Logie Robertson. 1891.

Works (Empire Edition). 1904–05. 20 vols.

Young England: Being Vivian Grey, Coningsby, Sybil, Tancred. Ed. Bernard N. Langdon-Davies. 1904. 4 vols.

The Revolutionary Epick and Other Poems. Ed. W. Davenport Adams. 1904.

The Pocket Disraeli. Ed. J. B. Lindenbaum. 1912.

Whigs and Whiggism: Political Writings. Ed. William Hutcheon. 1913.

Novels and Tales (Bradenham Edition). Ed. Philip Guedalla. 1926–27. 12 vols.

The Dunciad of To-day: A Satire; and The Modern Æsop. Ed. Michael Sadleir. 1928.

Letters to Lady Bradford and Lady Chesterfield. Ed. the Marquis of Zetland. 1929.

The Radical Tory: Disraeli's Political Development Illustrated from His Original Writings and Speeches. Ed. H. W. Edwards. 1937.

Letters to Frances Anne, Marchioness of Londonderry 1837–1861. Ed. the Marchioness of Londonderry. 1938.

Selections from the Novels. Ed. Eric Forbes-Boyd. 1948.

Reminiscences. Eds. Helen M. Swartz and Marvin Swartz. 1975.

JOSIAH GILBERT HOLLAND
("TIMOTHY TITCOMB") (1819–1881)

Cut-Flowers: A Collection of Poems by D. Ellen Goodman (editor). 1854.

History of Western Massachusetts. 1855. 2 vols.

Exercises at the Dedication of the New City Hall, Springfield, Mass. 1856.

The Bay-Path: A Tale of New England Colonial Life. 1857.

Timothy Titcomb's Letters to Young People, Single and Married. 1858.

Bitter-Sweet. 1858.

Gold-Foil, Hammered from Popular Proverbs. 1859.

Miss Gilbert's Career: An American Story. 1860.

Lessons in Life: A Series of Familiar Essays. 1861.

Letters to the Joneses. 1863.

Eulogy on Abraham Lincoln, Late President of the United States, Pronounced at the City Hall, Springfield, Mass. 1865.

The Life of Abraham Lincoln. 1866.

Plain Talks on Familiar Subjects: A Series of Popular Lectures. 1866.

Christ and the Twelve; or, Scenes and Events in the Life of Our Saviour and His Apostles, as Painted by the Poets (editor). 1867.

Kathrina: Her Life and Mine. 1867.

Timothy Titcomb's Testimony against Wine. c. 1867.

The Marble Prophecy and Other Poems. 1872.

Works (Brightwood Edition). 1872. 6 vols.

Garnered Sheaves: Complete Poetical Works. 1873.

Remarks on Assuming the Presidency of the Board of Public Instruction. 1873.

Arthur Bonnicastle: An American Novel. 1873.

Illustrated Library of Favorite Song (editor). 1873.

The Mistress of the Manse. 1874.

Sevenoaks: A Story of To-day. 1875.

Little Graves: Choice Selections of Poetry and Prose (editor). 1876.

Every-day Topics: A Book of Briefs. 1876.

Nicholas Minturn: A Study in a Story. 1877.

Complete Poetical Writings. 1879.

Every-day Topics: A Book of Briefs: Second Series. 1882.

Complete Works. 1897–1911. 16 vols.

SIDNEY LANIER (1842–1881)

Tiger-Lilies. 1867.

For the Golden Wedding of Sterling and Sarah Lanier. 1868.

Florida: Its Scenery, Climate, and History. 1876.

Poems. 1877.

Syllabus: Shakspere Course: Lectures I, II, III. 1878.
The Boy's Froissart (editor). 1879.
The Science of English Verse. 1880.
The Boy's King Arthur by Sir Thomas Malory (editor). 1880.
Sunrise. 1880.
The Boy's Mabinogion (editor). 1881.
The Boy's Percy by Thomas Percy (editor). 1882.
The English Novel and the Principle of Its Development. 1883.
Poems. Ed. Mary Day Lanier. 1884.
Water Lilies: A Fairy Song. 1890.
Music and Poetry: Essays upon Some Aspects and Inter-relations of the Two Arts. Ed. Henry Wysham Lanier. 1898.
Retrospects and Prospects: Descriptive and Historical Essays. Ed. Henry Wysham Lanier. 1899.
Letters 1866–1881. Ed. Henry Wysham Lanier. 1899.
Bob: The Story of Our Mocking-Bird. 1899.
Shakspere and His Forerunners: Studies in Elizabethan Poetry and Its Development from Early English. Ed. Henry Wysham Lanier. 1902. 2 vols.
The Lanier Book: Selections in Prose and Verse. Ed. Mary E. Burt. 1904.
Poem Outlines. 1908.
Letters to Col. John G. James. Ed. Margaret Lee Wiley. 1942.
Works (Centennial Edition). Eds. Charles R. Anderson et al. 1945. 10 vols.
Selected Poems. Ed. Stark Young. 1947.

ARTHUR O'SHAUGHNESSY (1844–1881)

An Epic of Women and Other Poems. 1870.
Lays of France: Founded on the Lays of Marie. 1872.
Music and Moonlight: Poems and Songs. 1874.
Toyland (with Eleanor O'Shaughnessy). 1875.
Songs of a Worker. Ed. A. W. N. Deacon. 1881.
Arthur O'Shaughnessy: His Life and His Work, with Selections from His Poems. Ed. Louise Chandler Moulton. 1894.
Poems. Ed. William Alexander Percy. 1923.

RALPH WALDO EMERSON (1803–1882)

Letter to the Second Church and Society. 1832.
A Historical Discourse, Delivered before the Citizens of Concord, on the Second Centennial Anniversary of the Town. 1835.
Nature. 1836.
Original Hymn ⟨Concord Hymn⟩. 1837.
An Oration, Delivered before the Phi Beta Kappa Society ⟨American Scholar Address⟩. 1837.
⟨*Prospectus for Carlyle's* French Revolution.⟩ 1837.
An Address Delivered before the Literary Societies of Dartmouth College. 1838.
⟨*Prospectus for Carlyle's Essays.*⟩ 1838.
Critical and Miscellaneous Essays by Thomas Carlyle (editor; with others). 1838. 4 vols.
Essays and Poems by Jones Very (editor). 1839.
Essays. 1841.
The Method of Nature: An Oration, Delivered before the Society of the Adelphi. 1841.
Man the Reformer: A Lecture on Some of the Prominent Features of the Present Age. 1842.
Nature: An Essay, and Lectures on the Times. 1844.
Orations, Lectures, and Addresses. 1844.
The Young American: A Lecture Read before the Mercantile Library Association. 1844.

Essays: Second Series. 1844.
An Address on the Anniversary of the Emancipation of the Negroes in the British West Indies. 1844.
Poems. 1847.
⟨*Prospectus to the Town and Country Club.*⟩ 1849.
Town and Country Club Constitution. 1849.
Nature; Addresses, and Lectures. 1849.
Representative Men: Seven Lectures. 1850.
Memoirs of Margaret Fuller Ossoli (editor; with James Freeman Clarke and William Henry Channing). 1852.
English Traits. 1856.
Fourth of July Breakfast and Floral Exhibition, at the Town Hall, Concord: Ode. 1857.
Boston, Nov. 2, 1859. Dear Sir:—You are invited and urged to contribute and obtain contributions to aid the defense of Capt. ⟨*John*⟩ *Brown and his companions, on trial for their lives in Virginia* (with others). 1859.
The Conduct of Life. 1860.
Excursions by Henry David Thoreau (editor). 1863.
Letters to Various Persons by Henry David Thoreau (editor). 1865.
Complete Works. 1866–83. 3 vols.
Additional Testimonial in Favour of James Hutchison Stirling. c. 1866.
May-Day and Other Pieces. 1867.
Mrs. Sarah A. Ripley. 1867.
Address ⟨at the Dedication of the Soldier's Monument⟩. 1867.
Society and Solitude. 1870.
Prose Works. 1870–79. 3 vols.
Remarks on the Character of George L. Stearns. 1872.
Parnassus (editor). 1875.
Letters and Social Aims (with Ellen and James Eliot Cabot). 1876.
Remarks at the Centennial Celebration of the Latin School. 1876.
Works (Little Classic Edition). 1876–93. 12 vols.
Fortune of the Republic: Lecture Delivered at the Old South Church. 1878.
The Preacher. 1880.
Hymns for the Free Religious Association. 1882.
The Correspondence of Thomas Carlyle and Ralph Waldo Emerson. Ed. Charles Eliot Norton. 1883. 2 vols.
Works. 1883. 3 vols.
Complete Works (Riverside Edition). Ed. James Eliot Cabot. 1883–93. 12 vols.
The Senses and the Soul and Moral Sentiment in Religion. Ed. Walter Lewin. 1885.
The Correspondence of Thomas Carlyle and Ralph Waldo Emerson 1834–1872: Supplementary Letters. Ed. Charles Eliot Norton. 1886.
Two Unpublished Essays: The Character of Socrates; The Present State of Ethical Philosophy. 1896.
A Correspondence between John Sterling and Ralph Waldo Emerson. Ed. Edward Waldo Emerson. 1897.
Letters to a Friend 1838–1853. Ed. Charles Eliot Norton. 1899.
Correspondence between Ralph Waldo Emerson and Herman Grimm. Ed. Frederick William Holls. 1903.
Complete Works (Centenary Edition). Ed. Edward Waldo Emerson. 1903–04. 12 vols.
Journals. Eds. Edward Waldo Emerson and Waldo Emerson Forbes. 1909–14. 10 vols.
Records of a Lifelong Friendship 1807–1882: Ralph Waldo Emerson and William Henry Furness. Ed. Horace Howard Furness. 1910.

Uncollected Writings: Essays, Addresses, Poems, Reviews, and Letters. Ed. Charles C. Bigelow. 1912.

Uncollected Lectures. Ed. Clarence Gohdes. 1932.

Emerson-Clough Letters. Eds. Howard F. Lowry and Ralph Leslie Rusk. 1934.

Young Emerson Speaks: Unpublished Discourses on Many Subjects. Ed. Arthur Cushman McGiffert, Jr. 1938.

Letters. Ed. Ralph L. Rusk. 1939. 6 vols.

Early Lectures. Eds. Stephen E. Whicher, Robert E. Spiller, and Wallace E. Williams. 1959–72. 3 vols.

Dante's Vita Nuova (translator). Ed. J. Christy Mathews. 1960.

Journals and Miscellaneous Notebooks. Eds. William E. Gilman, Alfred R. Ferguson et al. 1960–82. 16 vols.

The Correspondence of Emerson and Carlyle. Ed. Joseph Slater. 1964.

Collected Works. Eds. Alfred R. Ferguson et al. 1971–   .

Literary Criticism. Ed. Eric W. Carlson. 1979.

Emerson in His Journals. Ed. Joel Porte. 1982.

Essays and Lectures. Ed. Joel Porte. 1983.

Poetry Notebooks. Eds. Ralph H. Orth, Albert J. Von Franke, Linda Allardt, and David W. Hill. 1986.

WILLIAM HARRISON AINSWORTH (1805–1882)

Poems by Cheviot Tichburn. 1822.

Monody on the Death of John Philip Kemble. 1823.

The Maid's Revenge and A Summer Evening's Tale, with Other Poems. 1823.

December Tales. 1823.

The Boeotian. 1824.

The Works of Cheviot Tichburn. 1825.

Considerations on the Best Means of Affording Immediate Relief to the Operative Classes in the Manufacturing Districts. 1826.

Letters from Cockney Lands. 1826.

Sir John Chiverton: A Romance (with John Partington Aston). 1826.

Rookwood: A Romance. 1834. 3 vols.

Crichton. 1837. 3 vols.

Nick of the Woods by Robert Montgomery Bird (editor). 1837. 3 vols.

Jack Sheppard: A Romance. 1839. 3 vols.

The Tower of London: An Historical Romance. 1840.

Guy Fawkes; or, The Gunpowder Treason: An Historical Romance. 1841. 3 vols.

Old Saint Paul's: A Tale of the Plague and the Fire. 1841. 3 vols.

The Miser's Daughter. 1842. 3 vols.

Modern Chivalry; or, A New Orlando Furioso (with Catherine F. Gore). 1843. 2 vols.

Windsor Castle: An Historical Romance. 1843. 3 vols.

Saint James's; or, The Court of Queen Anne: An Historical Romance. 1844. 3 vols.

James the Second; or, The Revolution of 1688: An Historical Romance. 1848. 3 vols.

The Lancashire Witches. 1849. 3 vols.

Works. 1850–51. 14 vols.

The Star-Chamber: An Historical Romance. 1854. 2 vols.

The Flitch of Bacon; or, The Custom of Dunmow. 1854.

Ballads: Romantic, Fantastical and Humorous. 1855.

The Spendthrift. 1856.

Mervyn Clitheroe. 1857–58. 12 parts.

The Combat of the Thirty: From a Breton Lay of the Fourteenth Century. 1859.

Ovingdean Grange: A Tale of the South Downs. 1860.

The Constable of the Tower: An Historical Romance. 1861. 3 vols.

The Lord Mayor of London; or, City Life in the Last Century. 1862. 3 vols.

Cardinal Pole; or, The Days of Philip and Mary: An Historical Romance. 1863. 3 vols.

John Law the Projector. 1864. 3 vols.

The Spanish Match; or, Charles Stuart at Madrid. 1865. 3 vols.

Auriol; or, The Elixir of Life. 1865.

The Constable de Bourbon. 1866. 3 vols.

Old Court. 1867. 3 vols.

Myddleton Pomfret. 1868. 3 vols.

The South Sea Bubble: A Tale of the Year 1720. 1868.

Hilary St. Ives. 1870. 3 vols.

Talbot Harland. 1870.

Tower Hill. 1871.

Boscobel; or, The Royal Oak: A Tale of the Year 1651. 1872. 3 vols.

The Good Old Times: The Story of the Manchester Rebels of '45. 1873. 3 vols.

Merry England; or, Nobles and Serfs. 1874. 3 vols.

The Goldsmith's Wife. 1875. 3 vols.

Preston Fight; or, The Insurrection of 1715. 1875. 3 vols.

Chetwynd Calverley. 1876. 3 vols.

Works. 1876–82. 16 vols.

The Leaguer of Lathom: A Tale of the Civil War in Lancashire. 1876. 3 vols.

The Fall of Somerset. 1877. 3 vols.

Beatrice Tyldesley. 1878. 3 vols.

Collected Works. 1878–80. 31 vols.

Beau Nash; or, Bath in the Eighteenth Century. 1879. 3 vols.

Stanley Brereton. 1881. 3 vols.

Historical Romances. 1898–1901. 20 vols.

Collected Works. 1923. 12 vols.

HENRY WADSWORTH LONGFELLOW (1807–1882)

Manual de proverbes dramatiques (editor). 1830.

Elements of French Grammar by Charles Lhomond (translator). 1830.

Novelas españolas (editor). 1830.

Le Ministre de Wakefield by Oliver Goldsmith, tr. T. F. G. Hennequin (editor). 1831.

Syllabus de la grammaire italienne. 1832.

Saggi de' novellieri italiani d'ogni secolo (editor). 1832.

Outre-Mer: A Pilgrimage beyond the Sea. 1833–34. 2 nos.

Coplas de Don Jorge Manrique (translator). 1833.

Hyperion: A Romance. 1839. 2 vols.

Voices of the Night. 1839.

Poems on Slavery. 1842.

Ballads and Other Poems. 1842.

The Spanish Student. 1843.

The Waif: A Collection of Poems (editor). 1845.

The Poets and Poetry of Europe (editor). 1845.

Poems. 1845.

The Belfry of Bruges and Other Poems. 1846.

The Estray: A Collection of Poems (editor). 1847.

Evangeline: A Tale of Acadie. 1847.

Poems Lyrical and Dramatic. 1848.

Kavanagh: A Tale. 1849.

The Seaside and the Fireside. 1850.

Poems. 1850. 6 vols.

The Golden Legend. 1851.

The Song of Hiawatha. 1855.

Prose Works. 1857. 2 vols.

The Voices of the Night, Ballads, and Other Poems. 1857.
Poetical Works. 1858.
The Courtship of Miles Standish and Other Poems. 1858.
Tales of a Wayside Inn. 1863.
Noël. 1864.
Household Poems. 1865.
Complete Works. 1866. 7 vols.
The Divine Comedy of Dante (translator). 1867. 3 vols.
Flower-de-Luce. 1867.
Poetical Works. 1868.
The New-England Tragedies: I. John Endicott; II. Giles Corey of the Salem Farms. 1868.
The Building of the Ship. 1870.
Poetical Works. Ed. William Michael Rossetti. 1870.
The Alarm-Bell of Atri. 1871.
The Divine Tragedy. 1871.
Three Books of Song. 1872.
Christus: A Mystery. 1872. 3 vols.
Aftermath. 1873.
The Hanging of the Crane. 1875.
Morituri Salutamus: Poem for the Fiftieth Anniversary of the Class of 1825 in Bowdoin College. 1875.
The Masque of Pandora and Other Poems. 1875.
Poems of Places (editor). 1876–79. 26 vols.
Kéramos. 1877.
A Ballad of the French Fleet, October 1746. 1877.
Kéramos and Other Poems. 1878.
Poetical Works. 1878. 11 vols.
Early Poems. Ed. R. H. Shepherd. 1878.
Bayard Taylor. 1879.
From My Arm-Chair. 1879.
Ultima Thule. 1880.
In the Harbor: Ultima Thule, Part II. 1882.
Works. 1886. 11 vols.
Works. Ed. Samuel Longfellow. 1886–91. 14 vols.
Complete Poetical Works. Ed. Horace E. Scudder. 1893.
Poetical Works. 1904.
Poems. Ed. George Saintsbury. 1907.
Origin and Growth of the Languages of Southern Europe and of Their Literature: An Inaugural Address Delivered September 2, 1830. 1907.
Boyhood Poems. Ed. Ray W. Pettengill. 1925.
Poems. Ed. Louis Untermeyer. 1943.
Letters. Ed. Andrew Hilen. 1966–82. 6 vols.
The Shaping of Longfellow's John Endicott: A Textual History, Including Two Early Versions. Ed. Edward L. Tucker. 1985.

CHARLES DARWIN (1809–1882)

⟨*Letters on Geology.*⟩ 1835.
The Zoology of the Voyage of H.M.S. Beagle, under the Command of Captain Fitzroy, R.N., during the Years 1832 to 1836 (editor). 1838–43. 5 parts.
Journal of Researches into the Geology and Natural History of the Various Countries Visited by H.M.S. Beagle. 1839.
Questions about the Breeding of Animals. c. 1839.
The Structure and Distribution of Coral Reefs: Being the First Part of the Geology of the Voyage of the Beagle. 1842.
Geological Observations on the Volcanic Islands: Being the Second Part of the Geology of the Voyage of the Beagle. 1844.
Geological Observations on South America: Being the Third Part of the Geology of the Voyage of the Beagle. 1846.
Geology. 1849.
A Monograph of the Sub-Class Cirripedia. 1851–54. 2 parts.
A Monograph of the Fossil Lepadidae. 1851–54. 2 parts.

On the Origin of Species by Means of Natural Selection; or, The Preservation of Favoured Races in the Struggle for Life. 1859.
On the Various Contrivances by Which British and Foreign Orchids Are Fertilised by Insects, and on the Good Effects of Intercrossing. 1862.
Queries about Expression for Anthropological Inquiry. c. 1867.
The Variation of Animals and Plants under Domestication. 1868. 2 vols.
The Descent of Man, and Selection in Relation to Sex. 1871. 2 vols.
The Expression of the Emotions in Man and Animals. 1872.
Insectivorous Plants. 1875.
On the Movements and Habits of Climbing Plants. 1875.
The Effects of Cross and Self Fertilisation in the Vegetable Kingdom. 1876.
The Different Forms of Flowers on Plants of the Same Species. 1877.
The Power of Movement in Plants (with Francis Darwin). 1880.
The Formation of Vegetable Mould, through the Action of Worms, with Observations on Their Habits. 1881.
Life and Letters. Ed. Francis Darwin. 1887. 3 vols.
More Letters. Eds. Francis Darwin and A. C. Steward. 1903.
The Foundations of The Origin of Species: *Two Essays Written in 1842 and 1844.* Ed. Francis Darwin. 1909.
Diary of the Voyage of H.M.S. Beagle. Ed. Nora Barlow. 1933.
The Living Thoughts of Darwin. Eds. Julian Huxley and James Fisher. 1939.
Charles Darwin and the Voyage of the Beagle. Ed. Nora Barlow. 1945.
The Darwin Reader. Eds. Marston Bates and Philip S. Humphrey. 1957.
Evolution by Natural Selection (with Alfred Russel Wallace). Ed. Sir Gavin de Beer. 1958.
Autobiography. Ed. Nora Barlow. 1958.
Evolution and Natural Selection. Ed. Bert James Loewenberg. 1959.
Darwin for Today: The Essence of His Works. Ed. Stanley Edgar Hyman. 1963.
Darwin and Henslow: The Growth of an Idea: Letters 1831–1860. Ed. Nora Barlow. 1967.
Correspondance entre Charles Darwin et Gaston de Saporta. 1972.
Charles Darwin's Natural Selection: Being the Second Part of His Big Species Book Written from 1856 to 1858. Ed. R. C. Stauffer. 1975.
Collected Papers. Ed. Paul H. Barrett. 1977. 2 vols.
Metaphysics, Materialism, and the Evolution of Mind: Early Writings. Ed. Paul H. Barrett. 1980.
Red Notebook. Ed. Sandra Herbert. 1980.
The Essential Darwin. Eds. Robert Jastrow and Kenneth Korey. 1984.
Correspondence. Eds. Frederick Burckhardt and Sydney Smith. 1985– .
Human Nature: Darwin's View. Ed. Alexander Alland, Jr. 1985.
Works. Eds. Paul H. Barrett and R. B. Freeman. 1986. 10 vols.

RICHARD HENRY DANA, JR. (1815–1882)

Two Years before the Mast: A Personal Narrative of Life at Sea. 1840.
The Seaman's Friend: Containing a Treatise on Practical Seamanship. 1841.

Petition to Congress for More Speedy Trial of Seamen. 1847.

Niphon's Crew: Argument for the Seamen. 1849.

Lectures on Art, and Poems by Washington Allston (editor). 1850.

Improvement of Mystic River. 1851.

Speech on the Judiciary, in the Constitutional Convention. 1853.

Fugitive Slave Rescue Trials. 1854.

The Bible in Schools. 1855.

Remarks before the Committee on Federal Relations, on the Proposed Removal of Edward G. Loring, Esq., from the Office of Judge of Probate. 1855.

Opening Address and Closing Argument in the Dalton Divorce Case. 1857.

Argument against the Petition for Incorporating a New Town, to Be Called Belmont. 1857.

Full Report of R. H. Dana's Argument for Defense, in the Case of Rev. I. S. Kalloch. 1857.

To Cuba and Back: A Vacation Voyage. 1859.

Speech at Manchester, N.H. 1861.

An Argument for the Plaintiffs in the Case of the Golden Rocket *before the Supreme Court of Maine* (with Horace Gray). 1862.

The Amy Warwick: Brief before the U.S. Supreme Court. 1863.

Enemy's Territory and Alien Enemies: What the Supreme Court Decided in the Prize Causes. 1864.

Remarks on the Death of Chief Justice Taney on October 17, 1864. 1864.

A Tribute to Judge Sprague: Remarks at a Dinner Given to the Officers of the Kearsage. 1864.

An Address upon the Life and Services of Edward Everett. 1865.

Speech at a Meeting of Citizens Held at Faneuil Hall, to Consider the Subject of the Re-organization of the Rebel States. 1865.

Elements of International Law by Henry Wheaton (editor). 1866.

Speech on the Repeal of the Usury Laws. 1867.

Speech at Middleton, in the Fifth District. 1868.

Argument for the Holders of Bonds in the Boston, Hartford and Erie Railroad. 1870.

Unity of Italy: Letter to the Committee for the Meeting at the Academy of Music, New York. 1871.

The Old South: Argument before the Committee of Parishes and Religious Societies. 1872.

Oration at Lexington. 1875.

Francis Dana. 1877.

Halifax Fisheries Commission: Argument on Behalf of the United States. 1877.

Memoir of Major John R. Vinton. 1878.

Speeches in Stirring Times and Letters to a Son. Ed. Richard Henry Dana III. 1910.

Cruelty to Seamen: Being the Case of Nichols & Couch. 1937.

An Autobiographical Sketch (1815–1842). Ed. Robert F. Metzdorf. 1953.

Journal. Ed. Robert F. Lucid. 1968. 3 vols.

ANTHONY TROLLOPE (1815–1882)

The Macdermots of Ballycloran. 1847. 3 vols.

The Kellys and the O'Kellys; or, Landlords and Tenants: A Tale of Irish Life. 1848. 3 vols.

La Vendée: An Historical Romance. 1850. 3 vols.

The Warden. 1855.

Barchester Towers. 1857. 3 vols.

The Three Clerks. 1858. 3 vols.

Doctor Thorne. 1858. 3 vols.

The Bertrams. 1859. 3 vols.

The West Indies and the Spanish Main. 1859.

Castle Richmond. 1860. 3 vols.

Framley Parsonage. 1861. 3 vols.

The Civil Service as a Profession. 1861.

Tales of All Countries: First Series. 1861.

Orley Farm. 1861–62. 20 parts.

North America. 1862. 2 vols.

The Struggles of Brown, Jones and Robinson. 1862.

The Present Condition of the Northern States of the American Union. c. 1862.

Tales of All Countries: Second Series. 1863.

Rachel Ray. 1863. 2 vols.

The Small House at Allington. 1864. 2 vols.

Can You Forgive Her? 1864–65. 20 parts.

Miss Mackenzie. 1865. 2 vols.

Hunting Sketches. 1865.

The Belton Estate. 1866. 3 vols.

Travelling Sketches. 1866.

Clergymen of the Church of England. 1866.

The Last Chronicle of Barset. 1866–67. 32 parts.

Nina Balatha: The Story of a Maiden of Prague. 1867. 2 vols.

The Claverings. 1867. 2 vols.

Lotta Schmidt and Other Stories. 1867.

Linda Tressel. 1868. 2 vols.

Higher Education for Women. 1868.

British Sports and Pastimes (editor). 1868.

He Knew He Was Right. 1868–69. 32 parts.

Phineas Finn: The Irish Member. 1869. 2 vols.

Did He Steal It? 1869.

The Vicar of Bullhampton. 1869–70. 11 parts.

An Editor's Tales. 1870.

On English Prose Fiction as a Rational Amusement. 1870.

The Commentaries of Caesar. 1870.

Ralph the Heir. 1870–71. 19 parts.

Sir Harry Hotspur of Humblethwaite. 1871.

The Golden Lion of Granpere. 1872.

The Eustace Diamonds. 1873. 2 vols.

Australia and New Zealand. 1873. 2 vols.

Phineas Redux. 1874. 2 vols.

Lady Anna. 1874.

Harry Heathcote of Gangoil: A Tale of Australian Bush Life. 1874.

The Way We Live Now. 1874–75. 20 parts.

The Prime Minister. 1875–76. 8 parts.

The American Senator. 1877. 3 vols.

Christmas at Thompson Hall. 1877.

Chronicles of Barsetshire. 1878. 8 vols.

South Africa. 1878. 2 vols.

Is He Popenjoy? 1878. 3 vols.

Iceland. 1878.

How the "Mastiffs" Went to Iceland. 1878.

The Lady of Launay. 1878.

An Eye for an Eye. 1879. 2 vols.

Thackeray. 1879.

John Caldigate. 1879. 3 vols.

Cousin Henry. 1879. 2 vols.

The Duke's Children. 1880. 3 vols.

The Life of Cicero. 1880. 2 vols.

Dr. Wortle's School. 1881. 2 vols.

Ayala's Angel. 1881. 3 vols.

Why Frau Frohmann Raised Her Prices and Other Stories. 1882.

Lord Palmerston. 1882.
Marion Fay. 1882. 2 vols.
The Fixed Period. 1882. 2 vols.
The Two Heroines of Plumplington. 1882.
Kept in the Dark. 1882. 2 vols.
Not if I Know It. 1883.
Mr. Scarborough's Family. 1883. 3 vols.
The Landleaguers. 1883. 3 vols.
An Autobiography. 1883. 2 vols.
Alice Dugdale and Other Stories. 1883.
La Mere Bauche and Other Stories. 1883.
The Mistletoe Bough and Other Stories. 1883.
An Old Man's Love. 1884. 2 vols.
The Barsetshire Novels. Ed. Frederic Harrison. 1906. 8 vols.
The Noble Jilt. Ed. Michael Sadleir. 1923.
London Tradesmen. Ed. Michael Sadleir. 1927.
The Barchester Novels. Ed. Michael Sadleir. 1929. 14 vols.
Four Lectures. Ed. Morris L. Parrish. 1938.
The Tireless Traveller: Twenty Letters to the Liverpool Mercury *1875.* Ed. Bradford A. Booth. 1941.
Novels and Stories. Ed. John Hampden. 1946.
The Oxford Illustrated Trollope. Eds. Michael Sadleir and Frederick Page. 1948–54. 15 vols.
The Parson's Daughter and Other Stories. Ed. John Hampden. 1949.
The Spotted Dog and Other Stories. Ed. John Hampden. 1950.
Mary Gresley and Other Stories. Ed. John Hampden. 1951.
Letters. Ed. Bradford Allen Booth. 1951.
Letters to the Examiner. Ed. H. Garlinghouse King. 1965.
The Palliser Novels. 1973. 6 vols.
Complete Short Stories. Ed. Betty Jane Breyer. 1979–83. 5 vols.
Selected Works. Ed. N. John Hall. 1981. 62 vols.
Letters. Eds. N. John Hall and Nina Burgis. 1983. 2 vols.

DANTE GABRIEL ROSSETTI (1828–1882)

Sir Hugh the Heron: A Legendary Tale. 1843.
The Early Italian Poets from Cuillo d'Alcamo to Dante Alighieri (1100—1200—1300) in the Original Metres, Together with Dante's Vita Nuova (translator). 1861.
Notes on the Royal Academy Exhibition, 1868 (with Algernon Charles Swinburne). 1868.
Poems. 1870.
Poems. 1881.
Ballads and Sonnets. 1881.
Collected Works. Ed. William Michael Rossetti. 1886. 2 vols.
Ballads and Narrative Poems. 1893.
Sonnets and Lyrical Poems. 1894.
The House of Life. 1894.
Family-Letters. Ed. William Michael Rossetti. 1895. 2 vols.
Letters to William Allingham 1854–1870. Ed. George Birkbeck Hill. 1897.
Poems (Siddal Edition). Ed. William Michael Rossetti. 1898–1901. 7 vols.
Lenore by Gottfried Bürger (translator). Ed. William Michael Rossetti. 1900.
Poems. Ed. William Michael Rossetti. 1904. 2 vols.
Henry the Leper by Hartmann von Aue (adaptation). Ed. William P. Trent. 1905. 2 vols.
Works. Ed. William Michael Rossetti. 1911.
The Ballad of Jan Van Hunks. Ed. Theodore Watts-Dunton. 1912.
Poems and Translations 1850–1870. 1913.

A Romance of Literature (with Algernon Charles Swinburne). 1919.
John Keats: Criticism and Comments (in Five Letters to Harry Buxton Forman). 1919.
Letters to Algernon Charles Swinburne, Regarding the Attacks Made upon the Latter by Mortimer Collins and upon Both by Robert Buchanan. Ed. Thomas J. Wise. 1921.
Letters to His Publisher, F. S. Ellis. Ed. Oswald Doughty. 1928.
Dante Gabriel Rossetti: An Anthology. Ed. F. L. Lucas. 1933.
The Blessed Damozel: The Unpublished Manuscript, Text and Collations. Ed. Paull Franklin Baum. 1937.
Poems, Ballads and Sonnets. Ed. Paull Franklin Baum. 1937.
Three Rossettis: Unpublished Letters to and from Dante Gabriel, Christina, William. Ed. Janet Crump Troxell. 1937.
Sister Helen. Ed. Janet Crump Troxell. 1939.
Letters to Fanny Cornforth. Ed. Paull Franklin Baum. 1940.
Jan Van Hunks. Ed. John Robert Wahl. 1952.
The Kelmscott Love Sonnets. Ed. John Robert Wahl. 1954.
Poems. Ed. Oswald Doughty. 1957.
The Rossetti-Macmillan Letters (with Christina Rossetti and William Michael Rossetti). Ed. Lona M. Packer. 1963.
Letters. Eds. Oswald Doughty and John Robert Wahl. 1965–67. 4 vols.
Dante Gabriel Rossetti and Jane Morris: Their Correspondence. Eds. John Bryson and Janet Crump Troxell. 1976.
The Rossetti-Layland Letters. Ed. Francis L. Fennell, Jr. 1978.

JAMES THOMSON ("B.V.") (1834–1882)

A Commission of Inquiry on Royalty, etc. 1876.
The Story of a Famous Old Jewish Firm. 1876.
The Devil in the Church of England and The One Thing Needful. 1876.
The Pilgrimage to Saint Nicotine. 1878.
The City of Dreadful Night and Other Poems. 1880.
Vane's Story, Weddah and Om-el-Bonain, and Other Poems. 1881.
Address on the Opening of the New Hall of the Leicester Secular Society. 1881.
Essays and Phantasies. 1881.
The Story of the Famous Old Jewish Firm and Other Pieces in Prose and Rime. 1883.
Satires and Profanities. 1884.
A Voice from the Nile and Other Poems. 1884.
Shelley: A Poem; with Other Writings Related to Shelley; to Which Is Added an Essay on the Poems of William Blake. 1884.
Selections from Original Contributions to Cope's Tobacco Plant. Ed. Walter Lewin. 1889.
Poems, Essays and Fragments. Ed. John M. Robertson. 1892.
Poetical Works. Ed. Bertram Dobell. 1895. 2 vols.
Biographical and Critical Studies. Ed. Bertram Dobell. 1896.
Essays, Dialogues and Thoughts of Giacomo Leopardi (translator). Ed. Bertram Dobell. 1905.
James Thomson ("B.V.") on George Meredith. 1909.
Walt Whitman: The Man and the Poet. Ed. Bertram Dobell. 1910.
Poems. Ed. Gordon Hall Gerould. 1927.
Poems and Some Letters. Ed. Anne Ridler. 1963.
The Speedy Extinction of Evil and Misery: Selected Prose. Ed. William David Schaefer. 1967.

EDWARD FITZGERALD (1809–1883)

Euphranor: A Dialogue on Youth. 1851.

Polonius: A Collection of Wise Saws and Modern Instances. 1852.

Six Dramas of Calderón (translator). 1853.

Salámán and Absál: An Allegory Translated from the Persian of Jámí. 1856.

Rubáiyát of Omar Khayyám, the Astronomer-Poet of Persia (translator). 1859.

The Mighty Magician and Such Stuff as Dreams Are Made Of by Calderón (translator). 1865.

Agamemnon by Aeschylus (translator). 1865.

The Two Generals. 1868.

Readings in Crabbe: Tales of the Hall (editor). 1879.

The Downfall and Death of King Oedipus: A Drama in Two Parts, Chiefly Taken from the Oedipus Tyrannus *and* Colonaeus *of Sophocles.* 1880–81. 2 parts.

Works. 1887. 2 vols.

Letters and Literary Remains. Ed. W. Aldis Wright. 1889 (3 vols.), 1902–03 (7 vols.).

Occasional Verses. 1891.

Letters. Ed. W. Aldis Wright. 1894. 2 vols.

Letters to Fanny Kemble 1871–1883. Ed. W. Aldis Wright. 1895.

Miscellanies. Ed. W. Aldis Wright. 1900.

More Letters. Ed. W. Aldis Wright. 1901.

The Variorum and Definitive Edition of the Poetical and Prose Writings. Ed. George Bentham. 1902. 7 vols.

Minor and Apocryphal Poems. 1904.

Miscellanies. Ed. Henry Morley. 1904.

Eight Dramas of Calderón (translator). 1906.

Dictionary of Madame de Sévigné. Ed. Mary Eleanor FitzGerald Kerrich. 1914. 2 vols.

Some New Letters. Ed. F. R. Barton. 1923.

Letters to Bernard Quaritch 1853–1883. Ed. C. Quaritch Wrentmore. 1926.

A FitzGerald Friendship: Being Hitherto Unpublished Letters from Edward FitzGerald to William Bodham Donne. Eds. Nielson Campbell Hannay and Catharine Bodham Johnson. 1932.

A FitzGerald Miscellany. Ed. Charles Ganz. 1933.

White Sauce. 1956.

Letters. Ed. J. M. Cohen. 1960.

Selected Works. Ed. Joanna Richardson. 1962.

FitzGerald to His Friends: Selected Letters. Ed. Alethea Hayter. 1979.

Letters. Eds. Alfred McKinley Terhune and Annabelle Burdick Terhune. 1980. 4 vols.

JOHN RICHARD GREEN (1837–1883)

Oxford during the Last Century: Being Two Series of Papers Published in the Oxford Chronicle *and* Bucks and Berks Gazette (with George Robertson). 1859–60. 34 parts.

A Short History of the English People. 1874.

Stray Studies from England and Italy. 1876.

History of the English People. 1877–80. 4 vols.

Readings from English History (editor). 1879. 3 parts.

A Short Geography of the British Isles (with Alice Stopford Green). 1879.

Essays of Joseph Addison (editor). 1880.

The Making of England. 1881.

The Conquest of England. 1883.

Letters. Ed. Sir Leslie Stephen. 1901.

Oxford Studies. Eds. Alice Stopford Green and Kate Norgate. 1901.

Historical Studies. Ed. Alice Stopford Green. 1903.

Stray Studies: Second Series. Ed. Alice Stopford Green. 1903.

RICHARD HENRY HORNE (1803–1884)

Exposition of the False Medium and Barriers Excluding Men of Genius from the Public. 1832.

Spirit of Peers and People: A National Tragi-Comedy. 1834.

The Russian Catechism, with Explanatory Notes. 1837.

Cosmo de' Medici: An Historical Tragedy. 1837.

The Death of Marlowe. 1837.

The Life of Van Amburgh the Brute Tamer, with Anecdotes of His Pupils. c. 1838.

Gregory VII. 1840.

The History of Napoleon (editor). 1841. 2 vols.

The Poems of Geoffrey Chaucer, Modernized (editor; with Leigh Hunt, Elizabeth Barrett Browning, and others). 1841.

Orion: An Epic Poem. 1843.

A New Spirit of the Age (with Elizabeth Barrett Browning). 1844. 2 vols.

The Good-Natured Bear: A Story for Children of All Ages. 1846.

Ballad Romances. 1846.

Memoirs of a London Doll. 1846.

Judas Iscariot: A Miracle Play, with Other Poems. 1848.

The Poor Artist; or, Seven Eye-Sights and One Object. 1850.

The Duchess of Malfi by John Webster (adaptation). 1850.

Memoir of the Emperor Napoleon. c. 1850.

The Dreamer and the Worker: A Story of the Present Time. 1851. 2 vols.

The Complete Works of Shakespeare (editor). 1857.

Australian Facts and Prospects; to Which Is Prefixed the Author's Australian Autobiography. 1859.

Notes and Comments on the Two Prize Essays on the Vine by Ludovic Marie (editor). 1860.

Prometheus the Fire-Bringer. 1864.

The Two Georges: A Dialogue of the Dead. c. 1865.

The South-Sea Sisters: A Lyric Masque. 1866.

Galatea Secunda: An Odiac Cantata, Addressed to H.R.H. Prince Albert, Duke of Edinburgh, on His Arrival in the Colony of Victoria. 1867.

Parting Legacy to Australia (with John Ferncliff: An Australian Narrative Poem). 1868.

Was Hamlet Mad? Being a Series of Critiques on the Acting of the Late W. Montgomery (editor). 1871.

The Great Peace-Maker: A Submarine Dialogue. 1872.

Ode to the Mikado of Japan. 1873.

Cosmo de' Medici and Other Poems. 1875.

Psyche Apocalypte: A Lyrical Drama (with Elizabeth Barrett Browning). 1876.

Laura Dibalzo; or, The Patriot Martyrs. 1880.

King Nihil's Round Table; or, The Regicide Symposium. 1881.

Bible Tragedies: John the Baptist; or, The Valour of the Soul; Rahman: The Apocryphal Book of Job's Wife; Judas Iscariot: A Mystery. 1881.

Sithron the Star-Stricken. 1883.

King Penguin: A Legend of the South Sea Isles. Ed. F. M. Fox. 1925.

CHARLES READE (1814–1884)

Peregrine Pickle: A Biographical Play. 1851.

The Ladies' Battle; or, Un Duel en Amour! by A. E. Scribe and Gabriel Legouve (translator). 1851.

Angelo (adaptation). 1852.

The Lost Husband (adaptation). 1852.

Gold! 1853.

Peg Woffington. 1853.

Christie Johnstone. 1853.

The Courier of Lyons; or, The Attack upon the Mail by Eugene Moreau et al. (translator). 1854.

Masks and Faces; or, Before and behind the Curtain (with Tom Taylor). 1854.

Two Loves and a Life (with Tom Taylor). 1854.

The King's Rival (with Tom Taylor). 1854.

Clouds and Sunshine and Art: A Dramatic Tale. 1855.

"It Is Never Too Late to Mend": A Matter-of-Fact Romance. 1856. 3 vols.

Poverty and Pride. 1856.

The Course of True Love Never Did Run Smooth. 1857.

The Hypochondriac (adaptation). 1857.

Propria Quae Maribus: A Jeu d'Esprit; and The Box Tunnel: A Fact. 1857.

White Lies. 1857. 3 vols.

Cream: Contains Jack of All Trades: A Matter-of-Fact Romance; and The Autobiography of a Thief. 1858.

A Good Fight and Other Tales. 1859.

"It Is Never Too Late to Mend": Proofs of Its Prison Revelations. 1859.

Le Faubourg Saint-Germain. 1859.

"Love Me Little, Love Me Long." 1859. 2 vols.

The Eighth Commandment. 1860.

Monopoly versus Property. 1860.

The Cloister and the Hearth: A Tale of the Middle Ages. 1861. 4 vols.

Hard Cash: A Matter-of-Fact Romance. 1863. 3 vols.

It's Never Too Late to Mend (drama). 1865.

The Prurient Prude. 1866.

Griffith Gaunt; or, Jealousy. 1866. 3 vols.

The Double Marriage (with August Maquet). 1867.

Dora: A Pastoral Drama. c. 1867.

Foul Play (with Dion Boucicault). 1868. 3 vols.

Put Yourself in His Place. 1870. 3 vols.

Foul Play (drama; with Dion Boucicault). c. 1870.

Rachel the Reaper: A Rustic Drama. 1871.

A Terrible Temptation: A Story of the Day. 1871. 3 vols.

To the Editor of the Daily Globe, *Toronto: A Reply to Criticisms.* 1871.

Kate Peyton; or, Jealousy. 1872.

The Legal Vocabulary. 1872.

The Wandering Heir. 1873.

Cremona Violins: Four Letters Reprinted from the Pall Mall Gazette. 1873.

A Simpleton: A Story of the Day. 1873. 3 vols.

A Hero and a Martyr: A True and Accurate Account of the Heroic Feats and Sad Calamity of James Lambert. 1874.

Trade Malice: A Personal Narrative; and The Wandering Heir: A Matter-of-Fact Romance. 1875.

The Jilt. 1877.

A Woman-Hater. 1877. 3 vols.

Golden Crowns: Sunday Stories. 1877.

Dora; or, The History of a Play. 1877.

The Coming Man: Letters Contributed to Harper's Weekly. 1878.

The Well-Born Workman; or, A Man of the Day. 1878.

The Countess and the Dancer; or, High Life in Vienna. 1883.

Love and Money (with Henry Pettitt). 1883.

Readiana: Comments on Current Events. 1883.

Singleheart and Doubleface: A Matter-of-Fact Romance. 1884.

Good Stories of Man and Other Animals. 1884.

The Jilt and Other Stories. 1884.

A Perilous Secret. 1884. 2 vols.

The Picture. 1884.

Bible Characters. 1888.

Works (Uniform Library Edition). 1895. 17 vols.

Plays. Ed. Michael Hammet. 1986.

RICHARD MONCKTON MILNES,
LORD HOUGHTON (1809–1885)

The Influence of Homer. 1829.

Memorials of a Tour in Some Parts of Greece, Chiefly Poetical. 1834.

Poems of Many Years. 1838.

Memorials of a Residence on the Continent, and Historical Poems. 1838.

A Speech on the Ballot, Delivered in the House of Commons. 1839.

Poetry for the People, and Other Poems. 1840.

One Tract More; or, The System Illustrated by The Tracts of the Times, *Externally Considered.* 1841.

Palm Leaves. 1844.

Memorials of Many Scenes. 1844.

Poems, Legendary and Historical. 1844.

The Real Union of England and Ireland. 1845.

[*A Knock at the Door; or, Worsted Works Wonders.* 1846.]

Speech in the House of Commons, on Mr. Hume's Motion Respecting the Suppression of the Free State of Cracow and the Payment of the Russian-Dutch Loan. 1847.

The Life, Letters, and Literary Remains of John Keats. 1848. 2 vols.

The Events of 1848, Especially in Their Relation to Great Britain. 1849.

Answer to R. Baxter on the South Yorkshire Isle of Axholme Bill. 1852.

Speech in the House of Commons. 1852.

Private Letters from the Earl of Strafford to His Third Wife (editor). 1854.

Boswelliana by James Boswell (editor). 1856.

Boswelliana: Folium Reservatum by James Boswell (editor). 1856.

An Ode, Composed for the Opening of Their First Public Pleasure-Ground. 1856.

Another Version of Keats's Hyperion ⟨*The Fall of Hyperion*⟩ (editor). 1857.

Good Night and Good Morning. 1859.

Secret Letter from the Comte de Provence to the Marquis de Favras; Intercepted Letter from Queen Marie Antoinette to the Emperor of Austria (editor). 1862–63. 2 parts.

Introductory Address to the Members of the Philosophical Institution, Edinburgh. 1863.

Selections from the Poetical Works. 1863.

A Selection from the Works. 1867.

Official Reports of the Various Sections of the ⟨International⟩ *Exhibition* (editor). c. 1872.

Monographs, Personal and Social. 1873.

Poetical Works. 1876. 2 vols.

Recantacyons by Thomas Cranmer (editor). 1877–84. 2 parts.

Some Writings and Speeches in the Last Years of His Life. 1888.

Life, Letters, and Friendships. Ed. T. Wemyss Reid. 1890. 2 vols.

Briefe an Varnhagen von Ense (1844–1854). Ed. Walther Fischer. 1922.

HELEN HUNT JACKSON (1830–1885)

Bathmendi: A Persian Tale by Jean de Florian (translator). 1867.
Verses. 1870, 1874.
Bits of Travel. 1872.
Bits of Talk about Home Matters. 1873.
Saxe Holm's Stories. 1874.
The Story of Boon. 1874.
Mercy Philbrick's Choice. 1876.
Bits of Talk, in Verse and Prose, for Young Folks. 1876.
Hetty's Strange History. 1877.
Bits of Travel at Home. 1878.
Saxe Holm's Stories: Second Series. 1878.
Nelly Silver's Mine: A Story of Colorado Life. 1878.
Letters from a Cat: Published by Her Mistress for the Benefit of All Cats and the Amusement of Little Children by Deborah Waterman Vinal Fiske (editor). 1879.
A Century of Dishonor: A Sketch of the United States Government's Dealing with Some of the Indian Tribes. 1881.
Mammy Tittleback and Her Family: A True History of Seventeen Cats. 1881.
The Training of Children. 1882.
Report on the Condition and Needs of the Mission Indians of California (with Abbot Kinney). 1883.
The Hunter Cats of Connorloa. 1884.
Ramona: A Story. 1884.
Easter Bells. 1884.
Zeph: A Posthumous Story. 1885.
Glimpses of Three Coasts. 1886.
Sonnets and Lyrics. 1886.
Between Whiles. 1887.
Poems. 1892.
The Helen Jackson Year-Book. Ed. Harriet T. Perry. 1895.
Patsy Billings and Popsy: Two Stories of Girl Life. 1898.
Ah-wah-ne Days: A Visit to the Yosemite Valley in 1872. 1971.

SIR HENRY TAYLOR (1800–1886)

Isaac Commenus. 1827.
Philip Van Artevelde: A Dramatic Romance. 1834. 2 parts.
The Statesman. 1836.
Edwin the Fair: An Historical Drama. 1842.
Edwin the Fair and Isaac Commenus. 1845.
The Eve of the Conquest and Other Poems. 1847.
Notes from Life, in Six Essays. 1847.
Notes from Books, in Four Essays. 1849.
The Virgin Widow ⟨*A Sicilian Summer*⟩. 1850.
St. Clement's Eve. 1862.
Poetical Works. 1864. 3 vols.
Crime Considered in a Letter to the Right Hon. W. E. Gladstone. 1868.
Autobiography. 1874–77. 2 vols.
A Sicilian Summer; St. Clement's Eve; with The Eve of the Conquest and Minor Poems. 1875.
Works. 1877–78. 5 vols.
Correspondence. Ed. Edward Dowden. 1888.

WILLIAM BARNES (1801–1886)

Poetical Pieces. 1820.
Orra: A Lapland Tale. 1822.
The Etymological Glossary; or, Easy Expositor. 1829.
The Solution of the Problem to Tri-sect the Arc of a Circle. c. 1832. Lost.
A Catechism of Government in General and of England in Particular. 1833.
The Mnemonical Manual. 1833.

A Few Words on the Advantages of a More Common Adoption of the Mathematics as a Branch of Education, or Subject of Study. 1834.
A Mathematical Investigation of the Principle of Hanging Doors, Gates, Swing Bridges, and Other Heavy Bodies Swinging on Vertical Axes. 1835.
A Corrective Concordance; or, Imposition Book. 1839.
An Investigation of the Laws of Case in Language, Exhibited in a System of Natural Cases. 1840.
An Arithmetical and Commercial Dictionary. 1840.
A Pronouncing Dictionary of Geographical Names. 1841.
The Elements of Linear Perspective and the Projection of Shadows. 1842.
The Elements of English Grammar, with a Set of Questions and Exercises. 1842.
Exercises in Practical Science. 1844.
Sabbath Lays: Six Sacred Songs. 1844.
Poems of Rural Life, in the Dorset Dialect; with a Dissertation and Glossary. 1844.
Poems, Partly of Rural Life (in National English). 1846.
Outline of Geography and Ethnography for Youth. 1847.
Humilis Domus: Some Thoughts on the Abodes, Life and Social Conditions of the Poor, Especially in Dorsetshire. 1848.
Se Gefylsta (The Helper): An Anglo-Saxon Delectus: Serving as a First Class-Book of the Language. 1849.
A Philological Grammar, Grounded upon English, and Formed from a Comparison of More Than Sixty Languages. 1854.
Notes on Ancient Britain and the Britons. 1858.
Views of Labour and Gold. 1859.
The Song of Solomon in the Dorset Dialect. 1859.
Hwomely Rhymes: A Second Collection of Poems in the Dorset Dialect. 1859.
TIW: or, A View of the Roots and Stems of the English as a Teutonic Tongue. 1861.
Poems of Rural Life in the Dorset Dialect: Third Collection. 1862.
A Grammar and Glossary of the Dorset Dialect, with the History, Outspreading, and Bearings of South-western English. 1863.
A Guide to Dorchester and Its Neighbourhood. c. 1864.
Additions from Various Sources and Notes to a Glossary, with Some Pieces of Verse, of the Old Dialect of the English Colony in the Baronies of Forth and Bargy by Jacob Poole (editor). 1867.
Poems of Rural Life in Common English. 1868.
Early England and the Saxon English; with Some Notes on the Father-Stock of the Saxon-English, the Frisians. 1869.
A Selection from Unpublished Poems. 1870.
An Outline of English Speech-craft. 1878.
Poems of Rural Life in the Dorset Dialect: First-Third Collection. 1879.
An Outline of Rede-craft—Logic, with English Wording. 1880.
Ruth: A Short Drama from the Bible; with a Dissertation on the Law of the Goel-ha-dom. 1881.
A Glossary of the Dorset Dialect, with a Grammar of Its Word Shapening and Wording. 1886.
Select Poems. Ed. Thomas Hardy. 1908.
A Selection of Poems of Rural Life in the Dorset Dialect. Ed. W. M. Barnes. 1909.
Twenty Poems in Common English. Ed. John Drinkwater. 1925.
Poems Grave and Gay. Ed. Giles Dugdale. 1949.
Selected Poems. Ed. Geoffrey Grigson. 1950.
A Fadge of Barnes: Being the Pieces in Prose and Verse Contributed to The Hawk, 1867. Ed. J. Stevens Cox. 1956.

Poems. Ed. Bernard Jones. 1962. 2 vols.
Some Dorset Folklore. 1969.
One Hundred Poems. 1971.
A Selection of His Poems. Ed. Robert Nye. 1972.

EDWIN P. WHIPPLE (1819–1886)

Essays and Reviews. 1848–49. 2 vols.
Washington and the Principles of the Revolution. 1850.
Lectures on Subjects Connected with Literature and Life. 1850, 1871 (as *Literature and Life*).
Character and Characteristic Men. 1866.
Eulogy on John Albion Andrew. 1867.
The Literature of the Age of Elizabeth. 1869.
Success and Its Conditions. 1871.
Men of Mark. 1877.
Christianity and Humanity by Thomas Starr King (editor). 1877.
Some Recollections of Rufus Choate. 1879.
Recollections of Eminent Men, with Other Papers. 1886.
Memorial of Dr. and Mrs. Charles Russell of Princeton, Mass. 1886.
American Literature and Other Papers. 1887.
Outlooks on Society, Literature and Politics. 1888.
Charles Dickens: The Man and His Work. 1912. 2 vols.

EMILY DICKINSON (1830–1886)

Poems. Eds. Mabel Loomis Todd and T. W. Higginson. 1890.
Poems: Second Series. Eds. Mabel Loomis Todd and T. W. Higginson. 1891.
Letters. Ed. Mabel Loomis Todd. 1894 (2 vols.), 1931.
Poems: Third Series. Ed. Mabel Loomis Todd. 1896.
The Single Hound: Poems of a Lifetime. Ed. Martha Dickinson Bianchi. 1914.
Life and Letters. Ed. Martha Dickinson Bianchi. 1924.
Complete Poems. Ed. Martha Dickinson Bianchi. 1924.
Selected Poems. Ed. Conrad Aiken. 1924.
Further Poems Withheld from Publication by Her Sister Lavinia. Eds. Martha Dickinson Bianchi and Alfred Leete Hampson. 1929.
Poems (Centenary Edition). Eds. Martha Dickinson Bianchi and Alfred Leete Hampson. 1930.
Poems for Youth. Ed. Alfred Leete Hampson. 1934.
Unpublished Poems. Eds. Martha Dickinson Bianchi and Alfred Leete Hampson. 1935.
Bolts of Melody: New Poems. Eds. Mabel Loomis Todd and Millicent Todd Bingham. 1945.
Letters to Dr. and Mrs. Josiah Gilbert Holland. Ed. Theodora Van Wagenen Ward. 1951.
Poems. Ed. Louis Untermeyer. 1952.
Poems. Ed. Thomas H. Johnson. 1955 (3 vols.), 1960.
Letters. Eds. Thomas H. Johnson and Theodora Ward. 1958. 3 vols.
Selected Poems. Ed. James Reeves. 1959.
Selected Poems and Letters. Ed. Robert N. Linscott. 1959.
A Choice of Emily Dickinson's Verse. Ed. Ted Hughes. 1968.
Selected Letters. Ed. Thomas H. Johnson. 1971.
Manuscript Books. Ed. R. W. Franklin. 1981. 2 vols.
The Master Letters. Ed. R. W. Franklin. 1986.

HENRY WARD BEECHER (1813–1887)

An Address Delivered before the Platonean Society of the Indiana Asbury University. 1840.
The Means of Securing Good Rulers: A Sermon Delivered on the Occasion of the Death of Noah Noble, Late Governor of Indiana. 1844.

Lectures to Young Men, on Various Important Subjects. 1844, 1879.
A Dissuasive from Moral Intolerance, Delivered at Bloomington, Ind., before the Philomathean Society of the Indiana University. 1845.
A Discourse Delivered at the Plymouth Church, Brooklyn, N.Y., upon Thanksgiving Day. 1848.
Plymouth Church Manual. 1848.
Industry and Idleness, with Causes of Dishonesty; to Which Are Appended Six Warnings. 1850.
Sermon for Thanksgiving Day. 1851.
Two Papers on Politics and the Pulpit. 1851.
On the Choice of a Profession. 1851.
Star Papers; or, Experiences of Art and Nature. 1855.
Plymouth Collection of Hymns and Tunes; for the Use of Christian Congregations (editor). 1855.
Man and His Institutions: An Address to the Society for the Promotion of Collegiate and Theological Education in the West. 1856.
Defence of Kansas. 1856.
Life Thoughts, Gathered from Extemporaneous Discourses. Ed. Edna Dean Proctor. 1858.
God's Seal and Testimony. 1858.
Letter to Messrs. Brown & Co., Boston, Recommending the Torches Manufactured by Them. 1858.
The Power of the Spirit. 1858.
Men's Excuses for Not Becoming Christians and Discourses of the Christian Life: Two Sermons. 1858.
How to Become a Christian. 1858.
Selected Sermons. 1858.
Henry Ward Beecher and Theodore Parker: Mr. Beecher's Reasons for Lecturing the "Fraternity Course": Being a Reply to Certain Criticisms Made upon Him for Doing So; Including His Opinion of Total Depravity. 1859.
Notes from Plymouth Pulpit: A Collection of Memorable Passages for the Discourses. Ed. Augusta Moore. 1859.
Plain and Pleasant Talk about Fruits, Flowers, and Farming. 1859.
New Star Papers; or, Views and Experiences of Religious Subjects. 1859.
Address on Mental Culture for Women (with James T. Brady). 1859.
Woman's Influence in Politics: An Address Delivered at the Cooper Institute, New York. 1860.
Civil War: Its Causes, Its Crimes, and Its Compromises (with Archbishop Hughes). 1861.
Remarks at the Funeral of Edward Corning. 1861.
War and Emancipation: A Thanksgiving Sermon Preached in the Plymouth Church. 1861.
The Love Element in the Gospel. c. 1861.
Crime and Its Remedy. c. 1861.
Eyes and Ears. 1862.
A Sermon Delivered before the Foreign Missionary Society of New-York and Brooklyn. 1862.
Royal Truths. 1862.
Freedom and War: Discourses on Topics Suggested by the Times. 1863.
The American Cause in England! An Address on "The American War," Delivered at the Free Trade Hall, at Manchester, England. 1863.
American Rebellion: Report of the Speeches Delivered in England at Public Meetings in Manchester, Glasgow, Edinburgh, Liverpool, and London; and at the Farewell Breakfasts in London, Manchester, and Liverpool. 1864.
Sermons. 1864.

Aids to Prayer. 1864.

Oration at the Re-Raising of the Old Flag over the Ruins of Fort Sumter. 1865.

The National Bereavement. 1865.

Universal Suffrage. 1865.

Letter to the Soldiers and Sailors. 1866.

Woman's Duty to Vote: Speech at the Eleventh National Woman's Rights Convention. 1866.

The Amendment to the Constitution: Beecher's Letter and Greeley's Reply. 1866.

Letters of Henry Ward Beecher and Dr. Tyng. c. 1866.

Norwood; or, Village Life in New England. 1867.

Address on the Occasion of the Laying of the Corner Stone of the New Adelphi Academy. 1867.

On Health: An Address Delivered before the New York Medical Students' Union, Brooklyn. 1867.

Prayers from Plymouth Pulpit. 1867.

Sermons. 1868. 2 vols.

Prayers in the Congregation. 1868.

A Meeting in Anticipation of Washington's Birthday (with Roswell D. Hitchcock). 1868.

The God of Comfort. 1868.

Plymouth Pulpit: A Weekly Publication of Sermons Preached in Plymouth Church, Brooklyn. 1868–84. 484 nos.

Address on Mission Sunday Schools, Delivered before the National Sunday School Convention at Newark, N.J. 1869.

The Overture of Angels. 1870.

Familiar Talks on Themes of General Christian Experience. 1870.

One Thousand Gems from the Rev. Henry Ward Beecher. Ed. G. D. Evans. 1870.

Common Sense for Young Men on the Subject of Temperance. 1871.

Forty-eight Sermons Preached Previous to 1867. 1871. 2 vols.

Morning and Evening Exercises: Selected from the Published and Unpublished Writings. Ed. Lyman Abbott. 1871.

The Heavenly State and Future Punishment: Two Sermons. 1871.

The Life of Jesus, the Christ. 1871.

Lecture-Room Talks. Ed. T. J. Ellinwood. 1872.

A Day in Plymouth Church. 1872.

The Past and Future. 1872.

Liberty and Love: An Appeal to the Conscience to Banish the Wine-Cup. 1872.

Should the Public Libraries Be Open on Sunday? 1872.

Yale Lectures on Preaching. 1872–74. 3 vols.

The Present Fearful Commercial Pressure. 1872.

On Labor: Popular Errors in the Education of American Youth. 1872.

The Discipline of Trouble. 1873.

Account of the Services of the Silver Wedding Week in Plymouth Church, Brooklyn. Ed. Horatio C. King. 1873.

The Discipline of Sorrow. 1874.

Truth Stranger Than Fiction. 1874.

A Summer Parish: Sabbath Discourses, and Morning Service of Prayer, at the "Twin Mountain House," White Mountains, New Hampshire, during the Summer of 1874. Ed. T. J. Ellinwood. 1875.

Oratory: An Oration Delivered before the National School of Elocution and Oratory. 1876.

The Background of Mystery. 1877.

Jew and Gentile: A Sermon, Plymouth Church, Brooklyn. 1877.

The Army of the Republic, Its Services and Destiny: An Oration

Delivered at the Reunion of the Army of the Potomac at Springfield, Mass. 1878.

Past Perils and the Peril of To-day. 1878.

The Strike and Its Lessons. 1878.

Fruits of the Spirit. 1878.

In the West. 1878.

Christianity Unchanged by the Changes: Two Addresses on the "Signs of the Times." 1878.

Why the Republican Party Should Be Trusted. 1880.

Statement before the Congregational Association of New York and Brooklyn. 1882.

The Moral Uses of Luxury and Beauty. 1882.

On Free Trade and Congressional Elections. 1883.

A Circuit of the Continent: Account of a Tour through the West and South. 1884.

Address at the Brooklyn Rink. 1884.

Advice and Message to Young Men: Reply to a Letter Supporting Grover Cleveland for President. 1884.

Wendell Phillips: A Commemorative Discourse. 1884.

Beecher's "Cleveland Letters": The Two Letters on the Reconstruction of the Southern States, Written in 1866. 1884.

Comforting Thoughts. Ed. Irene Ovington. 1884.

Great Speech, Delivered in New York City, on the Conflict of Northern and Southern Theories of Man and Society. 1885.

Golden Gleams from Henry Ward Beecher's Words and Works. 1885.

Evolution and Religion. 1885.

H. B. Claflin Memorial Address. 1885.

Eulogy on General Grant. 1885.

The Beecher Book of Days. Eds. Eleanor Kirk and Caroline B. Le Row. 1886.

Henry Ward Beecher in England, 1886: Addresses, Lectures, Sermons, Prayers. c. 1886.

Last Sermons, Preached in Plymouth Church, Brooklyn. 1887.

I Am Resolved What to Do: Last Sermon Preached at Plymouth Church. 1887.

The Beecher Calendar for 1887. 1887.

Beecher as a Humorist: Selections from the Published Works. Ed. Eleanor Kirk. 1887.

Beecher: Christian Philosopher, Pulpit Orator, Patriot and Philanthropist: A Volume of Representative Selections from the Sermons, Lectures, Prayers, and Letters. 1887.

Speeches on the American Rebellion. Ed. John Alexander, Jr. 1887.

Religion and Duty: Sunday Readings. Ed. J. Reeves Brown. 1887.

Proverbs from Plymouth Pulpit. Ed. William Drysdale. 1887.

Patriotic Addresses in America and England, from 1850 to 1885. Ed. John R. Howard. 1887.

A String of Pearls: Selections. 1888.

The Crown of Life, from the Writings. Ed. Mary Storrs Haynes. 1890.

A Book of Prayer, from His Public Ministrations. Ed. T. J. Ellinwood. 1890.

"Faith": Last Morning Sermon Preached in Plymouth Church, Brooklyn. 1891.

The Hidden Manna and the White Stone: A Sermon Preached in Plymouth Church. 1892.

Bible Studies: Readings in the Early Books of the Old Testament, with Familiar Comment, Given in 1878–9. Ed. John R. Howard. 1892.

Best Thoughts. Ed. Lyman Abbott. 1893.

Metaphors, Similes, and Other Characteristic Sayings. Ed. T. J. Ellinwood. 1895.

Autobiographical Reminiscences. Ed. Truman J. Ellinwood. 1898.

Selections from the Sermons, Lectures and Essays. 1902.

A Treasury of Illustration from His Published Works and Unpublished Reports of His Spoken Words. Eds. John R. Howard and Truman J. Ellinwood. 1904.

Sermon Briefs. Eds. John R. Howard and Truman J. Ellinwood. 1905.

Lectures and Orations. Ed. Newell Dwight Hillis. 1913.

DINAH MARIA CRAIK (1826–1887)

The Ogilvies. 1849. 3 vols.

Cola Monti; or, The Story of a Genius. 1849, c. 1864 (as *Bright Schemes and Bold Strokes*).

Olive. 1850. 3 vols.

The Head of the Family. 1851. 3 vols.

Alice Learmont: A Fairy Tale. 1852.

Bread upon the Waters; A Governess's Life. 1852.

Avillion and Other Tales. 1853. 3 vols.

Agatha's Husband. 1853. 3 vols.

A Hero: Philip's Book. 1853.

The Little Luchetts: A Piece of Autobiography. 1855.

John Halifax, Gentleman. 1856. 3 vols.

Nothing New: Tales. 1857.

A Woman's Thoughts about Women. 1858.

A Life for a Life. 1859. 3 vols.

Poems. 1859.

Romantic Tales. 1859.

Domestic Stories. 1860.

Our Year: A Child's Book. 1860.

Studies from Life. 1861.

Mistress and Maid. 1863. 2 vols.

The Fairy Book: The Best Popular Fairy Stories Selected and Rendered Anew. 1863.

Christian's Mistake. 1865.

A New Year's Gift to Sick Children. 1865.

A Noble Life. 1866. 2 vols.

How to Win Love; or, Rhoda's Lesson: A Story for the Young. c. 1866.

M. de Barante: A Memoir by F. P. G. Guizot (translator). 1867.

Two Marriages. 1867. 2 vols.

A French Country Family by Henriette de Witt (translator). 1867.

The Woman's Kingdom. 1869. 3 vols.

A Brave Lady. 1870. 3 vols.

The Unkind Word and Other Stories. 1870. 2 vols.

Fair France; Impressions of a Traveller. 1871.

Little Sunshine's Holiday. 1871.

A Parisian Family by Henriette de Witt (translator). 1871.

Twenty Years Ago: From the Journal of a Girl in Her Teens (editor). 1871.

Hannah. 1872. 2 vols.

Is It True? Tales Curious and Wonderful. 1872.

The Adventures of a Brownie, as Told to My Child. 1872.

My Mother and I. 1874.

Sermons out of Church. 1875.

The Little Lame Prince. 1875.

Will Denbigh, Nobleman. 1877.

The Laurel Bush. 1877.

A Legacy: Being the Life and Remains of John Martin, Schoolmaster and Poet. 1878. 2 vols.

Young Mrs. Jardine. 1879. 3 vols.

Children's Poetry. 1881.

His Little Mother and Other Tales and Sketches. 1881.

Thirty Years: Poems New and Old. 1881.

Plain Speaking. 1882.

An Unsentimental Journey through Cornwall. 1884.

Miss Tommy. 1884.

About Money and Other Things. 1886.

King Arthur: Not a Love Story. 1886.

Work for the Idle Hands. 1886.

An Unknown Country. 1887.

Fifty Golden Years: Incidents in the Queen's Reign. 1887.

Concerning Men and Other Papers. 1888.

RICHARD JEFFERIES (1848–1887)

Jack Brass, Emperor of England. 1873.

Reporting, Editing and Authorship: Practical Hints for Beginners in Literature. 1873.

A Memoir of the Goddards of North Wilts. 1873.

The Scarlet Shawl. 1874.

Restless Human Hearts. 1875. 3 vols.

Suez-cide!!; or, How Miss Britannia Brought a Dirty Puddle and Lost Her Sugar-Plums. 1876.

World's End: A Story. 1877. 3 vols.

The Gamekeeper at Home: Sketches of Natural History and Rural Life. 1878.

Wild Life in a Southern Country. 1879.

The Amateur Poacher. 1879.

Green Ferne Farm. 1880.

Hodge and His Masters. 1880. 2 vols.

Round about a Great Estate. 1880.

Wood Magic: A Fable. 1881. 2 vols.

Bevis: The Story of a Boy. 1882. 3 vols.

Nature Near London. 1883.

The Story of My Heart: An Autobiography. 1883.

The Dewy Morn. 1884. 2 vols.

The Life of the Fields. 1884.

Red Deer. 1884.

After London; or, Wild England. 1885.

The Open Air. 1885.

Amaryllis at the Fair. 1887.

Field and Hedgerow: Being the Last Essays of Richard Jefferies. Ed. Mrs. J. Baden Jefferies. 1889.

The Toilers of the Field. 1892.

Thoughts from the Writings. Ed. H. S. H. Waylen. 1895.

Early Fiction. Ed. G. Toplis. 1896.

Jefferies' Land: A History of Swindon and Its Environs. Ed. G. Toplis. 1896.

T. T. T. 1896.

Nature and Eternity, with Other Uncollected Papers. 1907.

The Hills and the Vale. Ed. Edward Thomas. 1909.

Out-of-Doors with Richard Jefferies. Ed. Eric Fitch Daglish. 1935.

Richard Jefferies: Selections of His Work. Ed. Henry Williamson. 1937.

Jefferies' England: Nature Essays. Ed. Samuel J. Looker. 1937.

Readings from Richard Jefferies. Ed. Ronald Hook. 1940.

Nature Diaries and Note-Books. Ed. Samuel J. Looker. 1941.

Jefferies' Countryside: Nature Essays. Ed. Samuel J. Looker. 1944.

Richard Jefferies' London. Ed. Samuel J. Looker. 1944.

A Richard Jefferies Anthology. Ed. George Pratt Insh. 1945.

The Spring of the Year and Other Nature Essays. Ed. Samuel J. Looker. 1946.

The Essential Richard Jefferies. Ed. Malcolm Elwin. 1948.

Chronicles of the Hedges and Other Essays. Ed. Samuel J. Looker. 1948.

Beauty Is Immortal (Felise of The Dewy Morn), *with Some Hitherto Uncollected Essays and Manuscripts.* Ed. Samuel J. Looker. 1948.

The Old House at Coate and Hitherto Unpublished Essays. Ed. Samuel J. Looker. 1948.

The Jefferies Companion. Ed. Samuel J. Looker. 1948.

Works (Uniform Edition). Ed. C. Henry Warren. 1948–49. 6 vols.

Field and Farm: Essays Now First Collected, with Some from MSS. Ed. Samuel J. Looker. 1957.

EMMA LAZARUS (1849–1887)

Poems and Translations Written between the Ages of Fourteen and Sixteen. 1866.

Admetus and Other Poems. 1871.

Alide: An Episode of Goethe's Life. 1874.

The Spagnoletto. 1876.

Poems and Ballads of Heinrich Heine (translator). 1881.

Songs of a Semite: The Dance to Death and Other Poems. 1882.

Poems. 1889. 2 vols.

An Epistle to the Hebrews. 1900.

Selections from Her Poetry and Prose. Ed. Morris U. Schappes. 1944.

Letters 1868–1885. Ed. Morris U. Schappes. 1949.

AMOS BRONSON ALCOTT (1799–1888)

Observations on the Principles and Methods of Infant Instruction. 1830.

On the Nature and Means of Early Intellectual Education, as Deduced from Experience. 1830.

The Doctrine and Discipline of Human Culture. 1836.

Story without an End by Friedrich Wilhelm Carove, tr. Sarah Austin (editor). 1836.

Conversations with Children on the Gospels (editor). 1836–37. 2 vols.

Emerson. 1865, 1888 (as *Ralph Waldo Emerson: Philosopher and Seer*).

Tablets. 1868.

Concord Days. 1872.

Table-Talk. 1877.

Love's Morrow. 1880.

Bright visions of my sprightlier youthful days . . . 1881.

New Connecticut: An Autobiographical Poem. 1881.

Sonnets and Canzonets. 1882.

The Forester (Henry David Thoreau). 1937.

Journals. Ed. Odell Shepard. 1938.

Orphic Sayings. Ed. William Peirce Randel. 1939.

Letters. Ed. Richard L. Herrnstadt. 1969.

MATTHEW ARNOLD (1822–1888)

Alaric at Rome. 1840.

Cromwell. 1843.

The Strayed Reveller and Other Poems. 1849.

Empedocles on Etna and Other Poems. 1852.

Poems. 1853.

Poems: Second Series. 1855.

Merope. 1858.

Oratio Anniversaria in Memoriam Publicorum Benefactorum Academiae Oxoniensis ex Instituto N. Domini Crewe. 1858.

England and the Italian Question. 1859.

Popular Education in France, with Notices of That of Holland and Switzerland. 1861.

On Translating Homer. 1861.

On Translating Homer: Last Words. 1862.

Oratio Anniversaria in Memoriam Publicorum Benefactorum Academiae Oxoniensis ex Instituto N. Domini Crewe. 1862.

A French Eton; or, Middle Class Education and the State. 1864.

Essays in Criticism. 1865.

On the Study of Celtic Literature. 1867.

Saint Brandon. 1867.

New Poems. 1867.

Schools and Universities on the Continent. 1868.

Poems. 1869. 2 vols.

Culture and Anarchy: An Essay in Political and Social Criticism. 1869.

St. Paul and Protestantism. 1870.

Friendship's Garland: Being the Conversations, Letters, and Opinions of the Late Arminius, Baron von Thunder-ten-Tronckh. 1871.

A Bible-Reading for Schools (editor). 1872.

Literature and Dogma: An Essay towards a Better Apprehension of the Bible. 1873.

Higher Schools and Universities in Germany. 1874.

God and the Bible: A Review of Objections to Literature and Dogma. 1875.

Isaiah XL–LXVI with the Shorter Prophecies Allied to It (editor). 1875.

Poems. 1877. 2 vols.

Last Essays on Church and Religion. 1877.

Selected Poems. 1878.

The Six Chief Lives from Johnson's Lives of the Poets (editor). 1878.

Mixed Essays. 1879.

Poems of Wordsworth (editor). 1879.

Geist's Grave. 1881.

Poetry of Byron (editor). 1881.

Letters, Speeches and Tracts on Irish Affairs by Edmund Burke (editor). 1881.

Irish Essays and Others. 1882.

Isaiah of Jerusalem in the Authorized Version (editor). 1883.

Discourses in America. 1885.

Poems. 1885. 3 vols.

Education Department: Special Report on Certain Points Connected with Elementary Education in Germany, Switzerland, and France. 1886.

Essays in Criticism: Second Series. 1888.

Civilization in the United States: First and Last Impressions of America. 1888.

Reports on Elementary Schools 1852–1882. Ed. Francis Sandford. 1889.

On Home Rule for Ireland. 1891.

Letters. Ed. George W. E. Russell. 1895. 2 vols.

Notebooks. 1902.

Works. 1903–04. 15 vols.

Letters to John Churton Collins. 1910.

Poetry and Prose. Ed. E. K. Chambers. 1930.

Letters to Arthur Hugh Clough. Ed. Howard Foster Lowry. 1932.

The Portable Arnold. Ed. Lionel Trilling. 1949.

Poetical Works. Eds. C. B. Tinker and H. F. Lowry. 1950.

Note-Books. Eds. Howard Foster Lowry, Karl Young, and Waldo Hilary Dunn. 1952.

Five Uncollected Essays. Ed. Kenneth Allott. 1953.

Poetry and Prose. Ed. John Bryson. 1954.

Complete Prose Works. Ed. R. H. Super. 1960–77. 11 vols.

Selected Essays. Ed. Noel Annan. 1964.

Poems. Ed. Kenneth Allott. 1965.

Selected Prose. Ed. P. J. Keating. 1970.
Matthew Arnold. Eds. Miriam Allott and Robert H. Super. 1986.

LOUISA MAY ALCOTT (1832–1888)

Flower Fables. 1855.
Hospital Sketches. 1863.
The Rose Family: A Fairy Tale. 1864.
On Picket Duty and Other Tales. 1864.
Moods. 1865.
The Mysterious Key and What It Opened. 1867.
Morning-Glories and Other Stories. 1868.
Kitty's Class Day. 1868.
Aunt Kipp. 1868.
Psyche's Art. 1868.
Little Women; or, Meg, Jo, Beth, and Amy. 1868–69. 2 parts.
Hospital Sketches and Camp and Fireside Stories. 1869.
An Old-Fashioned Girl. 1870.
Will's Wonder Book. 1870.
V.V.; or, Plots and Counterparts. c. 1870.
Little Men: Life at Plumfield with Jo's Boys. 1871.
Aunt Jo's Scrap-Bag. 1872–82. 6 vols.
Work: A Story of Experience. 1873.
Eight Cousins; or, The Aunt-Hill. 1875.
Silver Pitchers and Independence: A Centennial Love Story. 1876.
Rose in Bloom: A Sequel to Eight Cousins. 1876.
A Modern Mephistopheles. 1877.
Under the Lilacs. 1878.
Jack and Jill: A Village Story. 1880.
Proverb Stories. 1882.
Spinning-Wheel Stories. 1884.
Jo's Boys and How They Turned Out: A Sequel to Little Men. 1886.
Lulu's Library. 1886–89. 3 vols.
A Glorious Fourth. c. 1887.
Jimmy's Lecture. c. 1887.
A Garland for Girls. 1888.
A Modern Mephistopheles and A Whisper in the Dark. 1889.
Life, Letters, and Journals. Ed. Ednah D. Cheney. 1889.
Comic Tragedies. 1893.
The Louisa Alcott Reader. 1908.
The Louisa Alcott Story Book. Ed. Fanny E. Coe. 1910.
Three Unpublished Poems. 1919.
Louisa Alcott's People. Ed. May Lamberton Becker. 1936.
A Round Dozen. Ed. Anne Thaxter Eaton. 1963.
Glimpses of Louisa: A Centennial Sampling of the Best Short Stories. Ed. Cornelia Meigs. 1968.
Behind a Mask: The Unknown Thrillers of Louisa May Alcott. Ed. Madeleine Stern. 1975.
Transcendental Wild Oats and Excerpts from the Fruitlands Diary. c. 1975.
Plots and Counterplots: More Unknown Thrillers of Louisa May Alcott. Ed. Madeleine Stern. 1976.
Selected Letters. Eds. Joel Myerson, Daniel Shealy, and Madeleine B. Stern. 1987.

ROBERT BROWNING (1812–1889)

Pauline: A Fragment of a Confession. 1833.
Paracelsus. 1835.
Strafford: An Historical Tragedy. 1837.
Sordello. 1840.
Bells and Pomegranates. 1841 [*Pippa Passes*]; 1842 [*King Victor and King Charles*]; 1842 [*Dramatic Lyrics*]; 1843 [*The Return of the Druses*]; 1843 [*A Blot in the 'Scutcheon*];

1844 [*Colombe's Birthday*]; 1845 [*Dramatic Romances and Lyrics*]; 1846 [*Luria and A Soul's Tragedy*].
Poems. 1849. 2 vols.
Christmas-Eve and Easter-Day. 1850.
Two Poems (with Elizabeth Barrett Browning). 1854.
Men and Women. 1855. 2 vols.
Selections from the Poetical Works. Eds. John Forster and Bryan Waller Procter. 1863.
Dramatis Personae. 1864.
Poetical Works. 1868. 6 vols.
The Ring and the Book. 1868–69. 4 vols.
Balaustion's Adventure. 1871.
Prince Hohenstiel-Schwangau, Saviour of Society. 1871.
Fifine at the Fair. 1872.
Red Cotton Night-Cap Country; or, Turf and Towers. 1873.
Aristophanes' Apology. 1875.
The Inn Album. 1875.
Pacchiarotto and How He Worked in Distemper, with Other Poems. 1876.
The Agamemnon of Aeschylus (adaptation). 1877.
La Saisiaz; The Two Poets of Croisic. 1878.
Dramatic Idyls. 1879–80. 2 vols.
Jocoseria. 1883.
Dramas. 1883. 2 vols.
Ferishtah's Fancies. 1884.
Parleyings with Certain People of Importance in Their Day. 1887.
Poetical and Dramatic Works. Ed. George Willis Cooke. 1887. 6 vols.
Poetical Works. 1888–94. 17 vols.
Asolando: Fancies and Facts. 1890.
Complete Poetic and Dramatic Works. Ed. Horace E. Scudder. 1895.
Poetical Works. Ed. Augustine Birrell. 1896. 2 vols.
Complete Works. Eds. Charlotte Porter and Helen A. Clarke. 1898. 14 vols.
Letters (with Elizabeth Barrett Browning). Ed. Robert Wiedemann Barrett Browning. 1899. 2 vols.
Works (Centenary Edition). Ed. Frederick G. Kenyon. 1912. 10 vols.
New Poems. Ed. Frederick G. Kenyon. 1914.
Complete Works. Ed. J. H. Finley. 1926. 6 vols.
Letters. Ed. Thurman L. Hood. 1933.
New Letters. Eds. William Clyde de Vane and Kenneth Leslie Knickerbocker. 1950.
Dearest Isa: Letters to Isa Blagden. Ed. Edward C. McAleer. 1951.
Letters to George Barrett (with Elizabeth Barrett Browning). Eds. Paul Landis and Ronald E. Freeman. 1958.
Browning to His American Friends: Letters between the Brownings, the Storys and James Russell Lowell. Ed. Gertrude Reese Hudson. 1965.
Learned Lady: Letters to Mrs. Thomas FitzGerald. Ed. Edward C. McAleer. 1966.
Complete Works. Eds. Roma A. King et al. 1969– . 13 vols. (projected).
Letters (with Elizabeth Barrett Browning). Ed. Elvan Kintner. 1969. 2 vols.
Poetical Works 1833–1864. Ed. Ian Jack. 1970.
Browning's Trumpeter: The Correspondence of Robert Browning and Frederick J. Furnivall. Ed. William S. Peterson. 1979.
Poems. Ed. John Pettigrew. 1981. 2 vols.
Poetical Works. Eds. Ian Jack and Margaret Smith. 1983– .

Correspondence (with Elizabeth Barrett Browning). Eds. Philip Kelley and Ronald Hudson. 1984– .

WILLIAM ALLINGHAM (1824–1889)

Poems. 1850.
Day and Night Songs. 1854.
Peace and War: An Ode. 1854.
The Music Master: A Love Story; and Two Series of Day and Night Songs. 1855.
Nightingale Valley: A Collection, Including a Great Number of the Choicest Lyrics and Short Poems in the English Language (editor). 1860.
The Ballad Book (editor). 1864.
Laurence Bloomfield in Ireland: A Modern Poem. 1864.
Fifty Modern Poems. 1865.
In Fairy Land. 1870.
Rambles. 1873.
Songs, Ballads and Stories. 1877.
Evil May-day &c. 1883.
Ashby Manor. 1883.
The Fairies: A Child's Song. 1883.
Blackberries, Picked off Many Bushes. 1884.
Irish Songs and Poems. 1887.
Rhymes for the Young Folk. 1887.
Flower Pieces and Other Poems. 1888.
Life and Phantasy. 1889.
Thought and Word and Ashby Manor. 1890.
Varieties in Prose. 1893. 3 vols.
Sixteen Poems. Ed. W. B. Yeats. 1905.
A Diary. Eds. Helen Allingham and Dollie Radford. 1907.
Poems. Ed. Helen Allingham. 1912.
By the Way: Verses, Fragments, and Notes. Ed. Helen Allingham. 1912.
Letters from William Allingham ⟨to Robert and Elizabeth Barrett Browning⟩. 1914.
Robin Redbreast and Other Verses. 1930.
Poems. Ed. John Hewitt. 1967.

WILKIE COLLINS (1824–1889)

Memoirs of the Life of William Collins. 1848. 2 vols.
Antonina; or, The Fall of Rome: A Romance of the Fifth Century. 1850. 3 vols.
Rambles beyond Railways; or, Notes in Cornwall Taken A-Foot. 1851.
Mr. Wray's Cash Box; or, The Mask and the Mystery: A Christmas Sketch. 1852.
Basil: A Story of Modern Life. 1852. 3 vols.
Hide and Seek. 1854. 3 vols.
After Dark. 1856. 2 vols.
The Dead Secret. 1857. 2 vols.
The Queen of Hearts. 1859. 3 vols.
The Woman in White. 1860. 3 vols.
No Name. 1862. 3 vols.
My Miscellanies. 1863. 2 vols.
Armadale. 1866. 2 vols.
The Frozen Deep (with Charles Dickens). 1866.
Armadale (drama). 1866.
No Thoroughfare (with Charles Dickens). 1867.
The Moonstone: A Romance. 1868. 3 vols.
Black and White: A Love Story (with Charles Fechter). 1869.
Man and Wife. 1870. 3 vols.
No Name (drama). 1870.
The Woman in White (drama). 1871.
Works. 1872. 10 vols.
Poor Miss Finch. 1872. 3 vols.

The New Magdalen. 1873. 2 vols.
The New Magdalen (drama). 1873.
Miss or Mrs.? and Other Stories in Outline. 1873.
Works. 1873–1904. 17 vols.
The Frozen Deep and Other Stories. 1874.
The Law and the Lady. 1875. 3 vols.
The Two Destinies. 1876. 2 vols.
The Haunted Hotel: A Mystery of Modern Venice; to Which Is Added, My Lady's Money. 1879. 2 vols.
A Rogue's Life: From His Birth to His Marriage. 1879.
The Fallen Leaves. 1879. 3 vols.
Considerations on the Copyright Question Addressed to an American Friend. 1880.
Jezebel's Daughter. 1880. 3 vols.
The Black Robe. 1881. 3 vols.
Heart and Science: A Story of the Present Time. 1883. 3 vols.
"I Say No." 1884. 3 vols.
The Evil Genius: A Domestic Story. 1886. 3 vols.
The Guilty River. 1886.
Little Novels. 1887. 3 vols.
The Legacy of Cain. 1889. 3 vols.
Blind Love (with Walter Besant). 1890. 3 vols.
The Lazy Tour of Two Idle Apprentices; No Thoroughfare; The Perils of Certain English Prisoners (with Charles Dickens). 1890.
Works. 1900. 30 vols.
Tales of Suspense. Eds. Robert Ashley and Herbert Van Thal. 1954.
Tales of Terror and the Supernatural. Ed. Herbert Van Thal. 1972.

GERARD MANLEY HOPKINS (1844–1889)

Poems. Ed. Robert Bridges. 1918.
A Vision of the Mermaids: A Prize Poem Dated Christmas, 1862. 1929.
Letters to Robert Bridges. Ed. Claude Colleer Abbott. 1935.
The Correspondence of Gerard Manley Hopkins and Richard Watson Dixon. Ed. Claude Colleer Abbott. 1935.
Note-Books and Papers. Ed. Humphry House. 1937.
Further Letters, Including His Correspondence with Coventry Patmore. Ed. Claude Colleer Abbott. 1938, 1956.
Some Poems. 1945.
Poems. Ed. Robert Bridges, rev. W. H. Gardner. 1948, 1967.
Selected Poems. Ed. James Reeves. 1953.
Poems and Prose. Ed. W. H. Gardner. 1953.
A Hopkins Reader. Ed. John Pick. 1953.
Journals and Papers. Ed. Humphry House. 1959.
Sermons and Devotional Writings. Ed. Christopher Devlin. 1959.
Hopkins Selections. Ed. Graham Storey. 1967.
The Windover. Ed. John Pick. 1969.
Poetry and Prose. Ed. K. E. Smith. 1976.
Selected Prose. Ed. Gerald Roberts. 1980.
Gerard Manley Hopkins. Ed. Catherine Phillips. 1986.

JOHN HENRY NEWMAN (1801–1890)

St. Bartholomew's Eve: A Tale of the Sixteenth Century (with John William Bowden). 1821.
Parish of St. Clement, Oxon.: December 1, 1824. 1824.
Elements of Logic (with Richard Whately). 1826.
Suggestions Respectfully Offered to Certain Resident Clergymen of the University, in Behalf of the Church Missionary Society. 1830.
Memorials of the Past. 1832.
The Arians of the Fourth Century. 1833.

The Restoration of Suffragan Bishops Recommended. 1833.

Tracts for the Times (editor). 1833–41. 90 nos.

Parochial Sermons. 1834–42. 6 vols.

To My Parishioners, on Occasion of Laying of the First Stone of the Church at Littlemore. 1835.

Elucidations of Dr. Hampden's Theological Statements. 1836.

Make Ventures for Christ's Sake. 1836.

Lyra Apostolica (with others). 1836.

Lectures on the Prophetical Office of the Church. 1837.

A Letter to the Rev. Godfrey Faussett, D.D., on Certain Points of Faith and Practice. 1838.

A Library of Fathers of the Holy Catholic Church (editor; with John Keble, E. B. Pusy, and Charles Marriott). 1838–85. 46 vols.

Lectures on Justification. 1838.

Hymni Ecclesiae, Excerpti e Breviariis Romano, Sarisburiensi, Eboracensi, et Aliunde (editor). 1838.

Hymni Ecclesiae, e Breviario Parisiensi (editor). 1838.

Remains of the Late Reverend Richard Hurrell Froude (editor; with John Keble). 1838–39. 4 vols.

The Church of the Fathers. 1840.

The Tamworth Reading Room. 1841.

A Letter Addressed to the Rev. R. W. Jelf, D.D., in Explanation of No. 90, in the Series Called the Tracts for the Times. 1841.

A Letter to the Right Reverend Father in God, Richard, Lord Bishop of Oxford, on Occasion of No. 90, in the Series Called the Tracts for the Times. 1841.

Mr. Vice-Chancellor, I write this respectfully to inform you . . . 1841.

The Devotions of Bishop Andrewes (editor and translator; with J. M. Neale). 1842–44. 2 parts.

Select Treatises of S. Athanasius (editor and translator). 1842–44. 2 vols.

An Essay on the Miracles Recorded in the Ecclesiastical History of the Early Ages. 1843.

Sermons, Bearing on Subjects of the Day. 1843.

Sermons, Chiefly on the Theory of Religious Belief. 1843.

⟨*Lives of the English Saints*⟩, Volumes 1–2 (editor). 1844–45.

An Essay on the Development of Christian Doctrine. 1845.

Thoughts on the Work of the Six Days of Creation by John William Bowden (editor). 1845.

Dissertatiunculae Quaedam Critico-Theologicae. 1847.

Loss and Gain. 1848.

Discourses Addressed to Mixed Congregations. 1849.

Lectures on Certain Difficulties Felt by Anglicans in Submitting to the Catholic Church. 1850.

Christ upon the Waters. 1850.

Lectures on the Present Position of Catholics in England. 1851.

Discourses on the Scope and Nature of University Education. 1852.

The Second Spring. 1852.

Verses on Religious Subjects. 1853.

Lectures on the History of the Turks in Its Relation to Christianity. 1854.

Callista: A Sketch of the Third Century. 1856.

The Office and Work of Universities. 1856.

Sermons Preached on Various Occasions. 1857.

Lectures and Essays on University Subjects. 1859.

The Tree beside the Waters. 1859.

Mr. Kingsley and Dr. Newman: A Correspondence on the Question Whether Dr. Newman Teaches That Truth Is No Virtue? (with Charles Kingsley). 1864.

Apologia pro Vita Sua: Being a Reply to a Pamphlet Entitled, What, Then, Does Dr. Newman Mean? 1864. 7 parts.

Phormio by Terence (editor). 1864.

The Dream of Gerontius. 1866.

Pincerna ⟨*Eunuchus*⟩ by Terence (editor). 1866.

A Letter to the Rev. E. B. Pusey, D.D., on His Recent Eirenicon. 1866.

The Pope and the Revolution. 1866.

Aulularia by Plautus (editor). 1866.

Verses on Various Occasions. 1868.

Parochial and Plain Sermons. 1868. 8 vols.

Dr. Newman on Anglican Orders, in a Letter Addressed to Father Coleridge. 1868.

Works (Uniform Edition). 1868–81 (36 vols.), 1908–18 (41 vols.).

An Essay in Aid of a Grammar of Assent. 1870.

Two Essays on Scripture Miracles and on Ecclesiastical. 1870.

Miscellanies from the Oxford Sermons and Other Writings. 1870.

Andria by Terence (editor). 1870.

Essays Critical and Historical. 1872. 2 vols.

Historical Sketches. 1872–73. 3 vols.

Discussions and Arguments on Various Subjects. 1872.

Orate pro Anima Jacobi Roberti Hope Scott. 1873.

The Idea of a University Defined and Illustrated. 1873.

Tracts, Theological and Ecclesiastical. 1874.

A Letter Addressed to His Grace the Duke of Norfolk on Occasion of Mr. Gladstone's Recent Expostulation. 1875.

Characteristics from the Writings. Ed. William Samuel Lilly. 1875.

The Via Media of the Anglican Church: Illustrated in Lectures, Letters and Tracts Written between 1830 and 1841. 1877. 2 vols.

Two Sermons Preached in the Church of S. Aloysius, Oxford. 1880.

Notes of a Visit to the Russian Church in the Years 1840, 184i by William Palmer (editor). 1882.

What Is of Obligation for a Catholic to Believe concerning the Inspiration of the Canonical Scriptures. 1884.

Echoes from the Oratory: Selections from the Poems. 1884.

Stray Essays on Controversial Points, Variously Illustrated. 1890.

Sayings. 1890.

Letters and Correspondence; with a Brief Autobiography. Ed. Anne Mozley. 1891. 2 vols.

Meditations and Devotions. Ed. William P. Neville. 1893.

My Campaign in Ireland, Part I: Catholic University Reports and Other Papers. Ed. William P. Neville. 1896.

Select Essays. Ed. George Sampson. 1903.

John Henry Newman. Ed. Wilfrid Meynell. 1907.

Literary Selections. 1913.

Sermon Notes 1849–1878. 1913.

The Spirit of Cardinal Newman. Ed. C. C. Martindale. 1914.

Correspondence with John Keble and Others 1839–1845. 1917.

Favorite Newman Sermons. Ed. Daniel M. O'Connell. 1932.

Cardinal Newman and William Froude, F.R.S.: A Correspondence. Ed. George Huntington Harper. 1933.

A Newman Treasury: Selections from the Prose Works. Ed. Charles Frederick Harrold. 1943.

Letters and Poems from Malta 1832–33. Ed. Joseph Galea. 1945.

Essays and Sketches. Ed. Charles Frederick Harrold. 1948. 3 vols.

The Living Thoughts of Cardinal Newman. Ed. Henry Tristram. 1948.

Sermons and Discourses 1825–39. Ed. Charles Frederick Harrold. 1949.

Sermons and Discourses 1839–57. Ed. Charles Frederick Harrold. 1949.

The Idea of a Liberal Education: A Selection from the Works. Ed. Henry Tristram. 1952.

Newman 1845–1952, the Honeymoon Years: An Anthology. Ed. James Bradley. 1953.

Autobiographical Writings. Ed. Henry Tristram. 1956.

Faith and Prejudice and Other Unpublished Sermons. 1956.

Prose and Poetry. Ed. Geoffrey Tillotson. 1957.

Letters: A Selection. Eds. Derek Stanford and Muriel Spark. 1957.

Catholic Sermons. 1957.

On Consulting the Faithful in Matters of Doctrine. Ed. John Coulson. 1961.

Philosophical Readings in Cardinal Newman. Ed. James Collins. 1961.

Letters and Diaries. Ed. Charles Stephen Dessain. 1961– .

The Newman Family Letters. Ed. Dorothea Mozley. 1962.

The Essential Newman. Ed. Vincent Ferrer Blehl. 1963.

A Newman Reader. Ed. Francis X. Connolly. 1964.

A Newman Companion to the Gospels. Ed. Armel J. Coupet. 1966.

On the Inspiration of Scripture. Eds. J. Derek Holmes and Robert Murray. 1967.

Newman the Oratorian: His Unpublished Oratory Papers. Ed. Placid Murray. 1969.

Philosophical Notebook. Ed. Edward Sillem. 1969–70. 2 vols.

Theological Papers on Faith and Certainty. Ed. J. Derek Holmes. 1976.

Theological Papers on Biblical Inspiration and Infallibility. Ed. J. Derek Holmes. 1979.

A Packet of Letters. Ed. Joyce Sugg. 1983.

RICHARD WILLIAM CHURCH (1815–1890)

The Catechetical Lectures of S. Cyril (translator). 1838.

Essays and Reviews. 1854.

Sermons Preached before the University of Oxford. 1868.

Times of Refreshment. 1868.

Hooker: Book I: Of the Laws of Ecclesiastical Polity (editor). 1868.

A Sermon Preached at the Consecration of the Right Rev. George Moberly, Lord Bishop of Salisbury. 1869.

The Twofold Debt of the Clergy. 1869.

Saint Anselm. 1870.

Civilization Before and After Christianity: Two Lectures. 1872.

The Purpose of the Christian Ministry. 1872.

On Some Influences of Christianity upon National Character: Three Lectures. 1873.

The Sacred Poetry of Early Religions: Two Lectures. 1874.

The Beginning of the Middle Ages. 1877.

Human Life and Its Conditions: Sermons Preached before the University of Oxford in 1876–1878, with Three Ordination Sermons. 1878.

Spenser. 1880.

Temper; Self-Discipline: Two Addresses to the Clergy. 1880.

The Gifts of Civilisation and Other Sermons and Lectures Delivered at Oxford and at St. Paul's. 1880.

Bacon. 1884.

The Discipline of the Christian Character. 1885.

The Disclosure of Secrets. 1885.

Advent Sermons 1885. 1886.

The Christian Church. 1887.

The Works of Richard Hooker, ed. John Keble (revised by Church and Francis Paget). 1888. 3 vols.

Miscellaneous Writings. 1888–97. 10 vols.

The Oxford Movement: Twelve Years 1833–1845. 1891.

Cathedral and University Sermons. 1892.

Village Sermons Preached at Whatley: First Series. 1892.

Village Sermons Preached at Whatley: Second Series. 1894.

Life and Letters. Ed. Mary C. Church. 1894.

Pascal and Other Sermons. 1895.

The Message of Peace and Other Christmas Sermons. 1895.

Village Sermons Preached at Whatley: Third Series. 1897.

SIR RICHARD BURTON (1821–1890)

Goa, and the Blue Mountains; or, Six Months of Sick Leave. 1851.

Scinde; or, The Unhappy Valley. 1851. 2 vols.

Sindh, and the Races That Inhabit the Valley of the Indus; with Notices of the Topography and History of the Province. 1851.

Falconry in the Valley of the Indus. 1852.

A Complete System of Bayonet Exercise. 1853.

Personal Narrative of a Pilgrimage to El-Medinah and Meccah. 1855–56. 3 vols.

First Footsteps in East Africa; or, An Exploration of Harar. 1856.

The Lake Regions of Central Africa: A Picture of Exploration. 1860. 2 vols.

The City of the Saints, and Across the Rocky Mountains to California. 1861.

The Prairie Traveller: A Hand-Book for Overland Expeditions by Randolph B. Marcy (editor). 1863.

Abeokuta and the Camaroons Mountains: An Exploration. 1863. 2 vols.

Wanderings in West Africa, from Liverpool to Fernando Po. 1863. 2 vols.

A Mission to Gelele, King of Dahome, with Notices of the So-Called "Amazons," the Grand Customs, the Yearly Customs, the Human Sacrifices, the Present State of the Slave Trade, and the Negro's Place in Nature. 1864. 2 vols.

The Nile Basin (with James M'Queen). 1864.

Wit and Wisdom from West Africa; or, A Book of Proverbial Philosophy, Idioms, Enigmas, and Laconisms (editor). 1865.

The Guide-Book: A Pictorial Pilgrimage to Mecca and Medina. 1865.

Stone Talk (Λιθοφώνημα): *Being Some of the Marvellous Sayings of a Petral Portion of Fleet Street, London, to One Doctor Polyglott, Ph.D.* 1865.

Explorations of the Highlands of the Brazil. 1869. 2 vols.

Vikram and the Vampire; or, Tales of Hindu Devilry (adaptation). 1870.

Letters from the Battle-fields of Paraguay. 1870.

Unexplored Syria: Visits to the Libanus, the Tulúl el Safá, the Anti-Libanus, the Northern Libanus, and the 'Aláh (with Charles F. Tyrwhitt-Drake). 1872. 2 vols.

Zanzibar: City, Island, and Coast. 1872. 2 vols.

The Lands of Cazembe: Lacerda's Journey to Cazembe in 1798 (editor and translator). 1873.

Kāmā Shāstra; or, The Hindoo Art of Love (translator; with F. F. Arbuthnot). 1873.

The Captivity of Hans Stade of Hesse, in A.D. 1547–1555, among the Wild Tribes of Eastern Brazil, tr. Albert Tootal (editor). 1874.

Ultima Thule; or, A Summer in Iceland. 1875. 2 vols.

Etruscan Bologna: A Study. 1876.

A New System of Sword Exercise for Infantry. 1876.

Two Trips to Gorilla Land and the Cataracts of the Congo. 1876. 2 vols.

Sind Revisited; with Notices of the Anglo-Indian Army; Railroads; Past, Present, and Future, etc. 1877. 2 vols.

The Gold-Mines of Midian and the Ruined Midianite Cities: A Fortnight's Tour in North-western Arabia. 1878.

The Land of Midian, Revisited. 1879. 2 vols.

The Kasîdah (Couplets) of Hâjî Aboû El-Yezdî: A Lay of Higher Law. 1880.

Os Lusiadas (The Lusiads) by Camões (translator). 1880. 2 vols.

Report on Two Expeditions to Midian. 1880.

Correspondence with His Excellency Riaz Pasha upon the Mines of Midian. 1880.

Report upon the Minerals of Midian. 1880.

Camoens: His Life and His Lusiads*: A Commentary.* 1881. 2 vols.

How to Deal with the Slave Scandal in Egypt. 1881.

The Partition of Turkey. 1881.

The Thermae of Monfalcone. 1881.

A Glance at the "Passion-Play." 1881.

Lord Beaconsfield: A Sketch. c. 1882.

To the Gold Coast for Gold: A Personal Narrative (with Verney Lovett Cameron). 1883. 2 vols.

The Kāmā Sutra of Vatsyayana (translator; with F. F. Arbuthnot). 1883.

Lyricks, Sonnets, Canzons, Odes, and Sextines by Camões (translator). 1884. 2 vols.

The Book of the Sword. 1884.

A Plain and Literal Translation of the Arabian Nights' Entertainments, Now Entitled The Book of the Thousand Nights and a Night; with Introduction, Explanatory Notes on the Manners and Customs of Moslem Men and a Terminal Essay upon the History of the Nights (translator). 1885–88. 16 vols.

Manuel De Moraes: A Chronicle of the Seventeenth Century by J. M. Pereira da Silva (translator; with Isabel Burton). 1886.

The Perfumed Garden of the Cheikh Nefzaoui: A Manual of Arabian Erotology (XVI. Century) (translator). 1886.

Priapeia; or, The Sportive Epigrams of Divers Poets on Priapus (translator; with Leonard C. Smithers). 1890.

Marocco and the Moors by Arthur Leared (editor). 1891.

Il Petamerone; or, Tale of Tales by Giovanni Battista Basile (translator). 1893. 2 vols.

Works (Memorial Edition). Eds. Lady Isabel Burton and Leonard C. Smithers. 1893–94. 7 vols. (incomplete).

Carmina by Catullus (translator; with Leonard C. Smithers). 1894.

The Jew, the Gypsy and El Islam. Ed. W. H. Wilkins. 1898.

Wanderings in Three Continents. Ed. W. H. Wilkins. 1901.

The Sentiment of the Sword: A Country-House Dialogue. Ed. A. Forbes Sieveking. 1911.

Selected Papers on Anthropology, Travel and Exploration. Ed. Norman M. Penzer. 1924.

Love, War and Fancy: The Customs and Manners of the East from Writings on the Arabian Nights. Ed. Kenneth Walker. 1964.

GEORGE BANCROFT (1800–1891)

Prospectus of a School to Be Established at Round Hill, Northampton, Massachusetts. 1823.

Poems. 1823.

Reflections on the Politics of Ancient Greece by Arnold H. L. Heeren (translator). 1824.

Greek Grammar (editor). 1824.

The Latin Reader (editor). 1825. 2 vols.

De Vita Excellentium Imperatorum by Nepos (editor). 1826.

Some Account of the School for the Liberal Education of Boys, Established on Round Hill, Northampton, Massachusetts. 1826.

Round Hill School. 1826.

History of the States of Antiquity by A. H. L. Heeren (translator). 1828.

History of the Political System of Europe by A. H. L. Heeren (translator). 1828–29. 2 vols.

A Grammar of the Latin Language (editor). 1829.

A Complete Course of Exercises in Latin Syntax (editor). 1830.

A History of the United States from the Discovery of the American Continent to the Present Time. 1834–74. 10 vols.

Literary and Historical Miscellanies. 1855.

On the Progress of Mankind and Reform. 1858.

Abraham Lincoln: An Address. 1866.

Joseph Reed: An Historical Essay. 1867.

History of the Formation of the Constitution of the United States. 1882. 2 vols.

A Plea for the Constitution of the U.S. 1886.

Martin Van Buren to the End of His Public Career. 1889.

History of the Battle of Lake Erie and Miscellaneous Papers. Ed. Oliver Dyer. 1891.

Life and Letters. Ed. M. A. DeWolfe Howe. 1908.

ALEXANDER WILLIAM KINGLAKE (1809–1891)

Eōthen; or, Traces of Travel Brought Home from the East. 1844.

The Invasion of the Crimea: Its Origin, and an Account of Its Progress Down to the Death of Lord Raglan. 1863–87 (8 vols.), 1877–88 (6th ed.; 9 vols.).

Selections. 1905.

JAMES RUSSELL LOWELL (1819–1891)

To the Class of '38. 1838.

Class Poem. 1838.

A Year's Life. 1841.

Poems. 1844.

Conversations on Some of the Old Poets. 1845.

On the Capture of Certain Fugitive Slaves Near Washington. c. 1845.

A Fable for Critics. 1848.

Poems: Second Series. 1848.

The Biglow Papers. 1848.

The Vision of Sir Launfal. 1848.

Poems. 1850. 2 vols.

The Poems of Maria Lowell (editor). 1855.

The Poetical Works of Mr. John Donne (editor). 1855.

The Poetical Works of Andrew Marvell (editor). 1857.

An Autograph. 1858.

All Saints: Written for Harriet Ryan's Fair. 1859.

The Biglow Papers: Second Series. 1862. 3 parts.

Fireside Travels. 1864.

Ode Recited at the Commemoration of the Living and Dead Soldiers of Harvard University. 1865.

A Christmas Carol. 1866.

To Mr. John Bartlett: On Sending Me a Seven-Pound Trout. c. 1866.

Under the Willows and Other Poems. 1869.

Poetical Works. 1869.

The Cathedral. 1870.

Among My Books. 1870.

My Study Windows. 1871.

Joseph Winlock: Died June 11, 1875. 1875.

Among My Books: Second Series. 1876.

Three Memorial Poems. 1877.

Death of President Garfield (editor). 1881.

Address Delivered before the Birmingham and Midland Institute ⟨*On Democracy*⟩. 1884.

On Religion. c. 1886.

Democracy and Other Addresses. 1887.

Early Poems. 1887.

Heartsease and Rue. 1888.

Political Essays. 1888.

The Independent in Politics. 1888.

The Compleat Angler by Izaak Walton and Charles Cotton (editor). 1889. 2 vols.

Writings (Riverside Edition). 1890. 10 vols.

Latest Literary Essays and Addresses. Ed. Charles Eliot Norton. 1892.

American Ideas for English Readers. Ed. Henry Stone. 1892.

The Old English Dramatists. Ed. Charles Eliot Norton. 1892.

Letters. Ed. Charles Eliot Norton. 1894. 2 vols.

Last Poems. Ed. Charles Eliot Norton. 1895.

The Power of Sound: A Rhymed Lecture. Ed. Charles Eliot Norton. 1896.

Lectures on English Poets. Ed. S. A. Jones. 1897.

Impressions of Spain. Ed. Joseph B. Gilder. 1899.

Early Prose Writings. 1902.

Anti-Slavery Papers. Ed. William Belmont Parker. 1902. 2 vols.

Complete Writings. 1904. 16 vols.

Four Poems. 1906.

The Round Table. 1913.

Poems. 1917.

The Function of the Poet and Other Essays. Ed. Albert Mordell. 1920.

New Letters. Ed. M. A. DeWolfe Howe. 1932.

Essays, Poems, and Letters. Ed. William Smith Clark II. 1948.

Uncollected Poems. Ed. Thelma M. Smith. 1950.

The Scholar-Friends: Letters of Francis James Child and James Russell Lowell. Eds. M. A. DeWolfe Howe and G. W. Cottrell. 1952.

Undergraduate Verses. Ed. Kenneth Walter Cameron. 1956.

Browning to His American Friends: Letters between the Brownings, the Storys and James Russell Lowell. Ed. Gertrude Reese Hudson. 1965.

HERMAN MELVILLE (1819–1891)

Typee: A Peep at Polynesian Life. 1846. 2 vols.

Omoo: A Narrative of Adventures in the South Seas. 1847.

Mardi: And a Voyage Thither. 1849. 2 vols.

Redburn: His First Voyage: Being the Sailor-Boy Confessions and Reminiscences of the Son-of-a-Gentleman, in the Merchant Service. 1849.

White-Jacket; or, The World in a Man-of-War. 1850.

Moby-Dick; or, The Whale. 1851.

Pierre; or, The Ambiguities. 1852.

Israel Potter: His Fifty Years of Exile. 1855.

The Piazza Tales. 1856.

The Confidence-Man: His Masquerade. 1857.

Battle-Pieces, and Aspects of the War. 1866.

Clarel: A Poem and Pilgrimage in the Holy Land. 1876. 2 vols.

John Marr and Other Sailors with Some Sea-Pieces. 1888.

Timoleon, etc. 1891.

Works (Standard Edition). 1922–24. 16 vols.

The Apple-Tree and Other Sketches. Ed. Henry Chapin. 1922.

Some Personal Letters and a Bibliography. Ed. Meade Minnigerode. 1922.

Journal up the Straits: October 11, 1856–May 5, 1857. Ed. Raymond Weaver. 1935.

Selected Poems. Ed. F. O. Matthiesen. 1944.

Complete Works. Ed. Howard P. Vincent. 1947–61. 6 vols.

Journal of a Visit to London and the Continent 1849–1850. Ed. Eleanor Melville Metcalf. 1948.

The Portable Melville. Ed. Jay Leyda. 1952.

Letters. Eds. Merrell R. Davis and William H. Gilman. 1960.

Writings. Eds. Harrison Hayford et al. 1968– .

EDWARD ROBERT BULWER LYTTON (1831–1891)

Clytemnestra, The Earl's Return, The Artist, and Other Poems. 1855.

The Wanderer. 1857.

Lucile. 1860.

Tannhauser; or, The Battle of the Bards (with Julian Fane). 1861.

Serbski Pesme; or, National Songs of Servia (translator). 1861.

The Ring of Amasis: From the Papers of a German Physician. 1863. 2 vols.

Poetical Works. 1867. 2 vols.

Chronicles and Characters. 1868. 2 vols.

Orval; or, The Fool of Time, and Other Imitations and Paraphrases. 1869.

Poems. 1869. 2 vols.

Julian Fane: A Memoir. 1871.

Fables in Song. 1874. 2 vols.

King Poppy: A Story without End. 1875.

Pausanias the Spartan by Edward Bulwer-Lytton (editor). 1876.

Favorite Poems. 1877.

The Imperial Bouquet of Pretty Flowers. Ed. N. A. Chick. 1877.

The Life, Letters, and Literary Remains of Edward Bulwer, Lord Lytton. 1883. 2 vols.

Glenaveril; or, The Metamorphoses. 1885. 2 vols.

Baldine and Other Tales by Karl Erdmann Edler (translator). 1886. 2 vols.

After Paradise; or, Legends of Exile, with Other Poems. 1887.

Poems. Ed. M. Bethem-Edwards. 1890.

Marah. 1892.

The Poem of the Queen Victoria by Alexandre Saint-Yves d'Alveydre (translator). 1892.

Selected Poems. 1894.

Personal and Literary Letters. Ed. Lady Betty Balfour. 1906. 2 vols.

Letters of Owen Meredith to Robert and Elizabeth Barrett Browning. Eds. Aurelia Brooks Harlan and J. Lee Harlan. 1937.

The Birth of Rowland: An Exchange of Letters in 1865 between Robert Lytton and His Wife. Ed. Lady Emily Lutyens. 1956.

JOHN GREENLEAF WHITTIER (1807–1892)

Legends of New-England. 1831.

Moll Pitcher. 1832.

The Literary Remains of John G. C. Brainard (editor). 1832.

Justice and Expediency; or, Slavery Considered with a View to Its Rightful and Effectual Remedy, Abolition. 1833.

Hymn Written for the Celebration of the 4th July, 1834. 1834.

Our Countrymen in Chains! 1834.

Mogg Megone. 1836.

Letters from John Quincy Adams to His Constituents (editor). 1837.
Poems Written during the Progress of the Abolition Question in the United States, between the Years 1830 and 1838. 1838.
Narrative of James Williams, an American Slave (with others). 1838.
Address Read at the Opening of the Pennsylvania Hall. 1838.
Poems. 1838.
New Year's Address to the Patrons of the Pennsylvania Freeman. 1839.
The North Star: The Poetry of Freedom (editor). 1840.
Moll Pitcher and The Minstrel Girl. 1840.
To the Memory of Daniel Wheeler. 1840.
New England. c. 1840.
Follen. 1842.
Lays of My Home and Other Poems. 1843.
Song of the Vermonters 1779. 1843.
Ballads and Other Poems. 1844.
To George M'Duffie, Governor of South Carolina. c. 1844.
The Stranger in Lowell. 1845.
The Branded Hand. 1845.
Voices of Freedom. 1846.
The Supernaturalism of New England. 1847.
Sketch of Daniel O'Connell. c. 1847.
Poems. 1848.
Leaves from Margaret Smith's Journal in the Province of Massachusetts Bay. 1849.
Old Portraits and Modern Sketches. 1850.
A Tract for the Times!: A Sabbath Scene. 1850.
Songs of Labor and Other Poems. 1850.
Cassandra Southwick. c. 1850.
The Chapel of the Hermits and Other Poems. 1853.
Literary Recreations and Miscellanies. 1854.
Western Emigrants. c. 1854.
Maud Muller. c. 1854.
The Panorama and Other Poems. 1856.
Poetical Works. 1857. 2 vols.
The Sycamores. 1857.
My Psalm. c. 1859.
Home Ballads and Poems. 1860.
The Quakers Are Out! 1860.
Naples—1860. 1860.
In War Time. 1863.
Song of the Negro Boatman. c. 1863.
In War Time and Other Poems. 1864.
Hymn Written for the Patriotic Dedication of the Unitarian Church in San Francisco. 1864.
National Lyrics. 1865.
Song of the Shoemakers. c. 1865.
Snow-Bound: A Winter Idyl. 1866.
Prose Works. 1866. 2 vols.
The Tent on the Beach and Other Poems. 1867.
Among the Hills and Other Poems. 1869.
From Mr. John G. Whittier, Amesbury, 9th mo. 6th, 1869: To R. C. Waterson, Jeffries Wyman, N. B. Shurtleff, &c. 1869.
Ballads of New England. 1870.
Our Master. c. 1870.
Miriam and Other Poems. 1871.
Disarmament. 1871.
Child Life: A Collection of Poems (editor). 1872.
—— *to* ——: *Edward and Elizabeth Gove, on the Fifty-fifth Anniversary of Their Marriage*. 1872.
The Pennsylvania Pilgrim and Other Poems. 1872.

Complete Poetical Works. 1873.
Child Life in Prose (editor). 1874.
Sumner. 1874.
Hazel-Blossoms (with Elizabeth H. Whittier). 1875.
Mabel Martin: A Harvest Idyl. 1876.
Songs of Three Centuries (editor). 1876.
Centennial Hymn. 1876.
Fitz-Greene Halleck. 1877.
Favorite Poems. 1877.
The River Path. 1878.
The Vision of Echard and Other Poems. 1878.
Copy of Lines Written, on His Seventy Second Birthday. 1879.
Poetical Works. 1880. 3 vols.
Poetical Works. Ed. William Michael Rossetti. 1880.
The Lost Occasion. c. 1880.
Barbara Frietchie. c. 1880.
The King's Missive and Other Poems. 1881.
In Memory. 1881.
1781 1881: Siege of Yorktown. 1881.
The Whittier Birthday Book. Ed. Elizabeth S. Owen. 1881.
Copy of a Letter. 1882.
Poems and Prose Passages. 1882.
In Memoriam: Rebecca Chase Grinnell of New Bedford. 1882.
The Bay of Seven Islands and Other Poems. 1883.
Jack in the Pulpit by Carrie Smith (revised by Whittier). 1883.
Text and Verse for Every Day of the Year: Scripture Passages and Parallel Sections from the Writings of John Greenleaf Whittier. Ed. Gertrude W. Cartland. 1884.
Early Poems. 1885.
The Reunion. 1885.
Poetical Works. Ed. Eva Hope. 1885.
Poems of Nature. 1886.
To a Cape Ann Schooner. 1886.
Saint Gregory's Guest and Recent Poems. 1886.
Norembega. 1886.
Nauhaught the Deacon. 1886.
The Worship of Nature. 1887.
Selections from the Writings. 1888.
One of the Signers. 1888.
Writings (Riverside Edition). 1888–89. 7 vols.
Dedication of the Library Building, Gammon Theological Seminary. 1889.
The Captain's Well. 1890.
Haverhill 1640–1890. 1890.
At Sundown. 1890.
Legends and Lyrics from the Poetic Works. 1890.
Life and Letters. Ed. Samuel T. Pickard. 1894. 2 vols.
Complete Poetical Works. Ed. Horace E. Scudder. 1894.
Whittier as Politician: Illustrated in His Letters to Professor Elizur Wright, Jr. Ed. Samuel T. Pickard. 1900.
Poems. Ed. Arthur Christopher Benson. 1906.
Earliest Poems. 1906.
Whittier Correspondence from the Oak Knoll Collections 1830–1892. Ed. John Albee. 1911.
Whittier's Unknown Romance: Letters to Elizabeth Lloyd. Ed. Marie V. Denervaud. 1922.
Representative Selections. Ed. Harry Hayden Clark. 1935.
Poems. Ed. Louis Untermeyer. 1945.
Whittier on Writers and Writing: Uncollected Critical Writings. Eds. Edwin Harrison Cady and Harry Hayden Clark. 1950.
Whittier and the Cartlands: Letters and Comments. Ed. Martha Hale Shackford. 1950.
Whittier. Ed. Donald Hall. 1960.

John Greenleaf Whittier's Poetry: An Appraisal and a Selection.
Ed. Robert Penn Warren. 1971.
Letters. Ed. John B. Pickard. 1975. 3 vols.

ALFRED, LORD TENNYSON (1809–1892)

Poems by Two Brothers (with Charles Tennyson). 1827.
Timbuctoo: A Poem Which Obtained the Chancellor's Medal at the Cambridge Commencement 1829. 1829.
Poems, Chiefly Lyrical. 1830.
Poems. 1833.
The Lover's Tale. 1833.
Poems. 1842. 2 vols.
The Princess: A Medley. 1847.
In Memoriam. 1850.
Ode on the Death of the Duke of Wellington. 1852.
The Charge of the Light Brigade. 1855.
Maud and Other Poems. 1855.
Stanzas on the Marriage of the Princess Royal. 1858.
Idylls of the King. 1859.
Ode for the Opening of the International Exhibition. 1862.
A Welcome. 1863.
Enoch Arden, etc. 1864.
A Selection from the Works of Alfred Tennyson. 1865.
The Holy Grail and Other Poems. 1870.
Works. 1870–77. 13 vols.
The Window; or, The Songs of the Wrens. 1871.
Gareth and Lynette, etc. 1872.
Works. 1872–73. 6 vols.
A Welcome to Her Royal Highness Marie Alexandrovna, Duchess of Edinburgh. 1874.
Works. 1874–81. 13 vols.
Queen Mary. 1875.
Harold. 1877.
Works. 1878–82. 12 vols.
Ballads and Other Poems. 1880.
Hands All Round: A National Song. 1882.
The Cup and The Falcon. 1884.
Becket. 1884.
Works. 1884–93. 10 vols.
Tiresias and Other Poems. 1885.
Gordon Boys' Morning and Evening Hymns (editor; with others). 1885.
Ode to the Opening of the Colonial and Indian Exhibition. 1886.
Locksley Hall Sixty Years After, etc. 1886.
Poetical Works. 1886–97. 17 vols.
Carmen Saeculare: An Ode in Honour of the Jubilee of Queen Victoria. 1887.
Demeter and Other Poems. 1889.
The Foresters: Robin Hood and Maid Marian. 1892.
The Death of Œnone, Akbar's Dream, and Other Poems. 1892.
Poetical Works. 1895–96. 23 vols.
Works (Farringford Edition). Ed. Eugene Parsons. 1902. 10 vols.
Works (Eversley Edition). Ed. Hallam Tennyson. 1907–08. 9 vols.
Patriotic Poems. 1914.
Alfred, Lord Tennyson and William Kirby: Unpublished Correspondence. Ed. Lorne Pierce. 1929.
The Devil and the Lady. Ed. Charles Tennyson. 1930.
Unpublished Early Poems. Ed. Charles Tennyson. 1931.
A Selection from the Poems. Ed. W. H. Auden. 1944.
Selected Poetry. Ed. Douglas Bush. 1951.
Poetical Works, Including the Plays. 1953.

Poems. Ed. Christopher Ricks. 1969.
Letters. Eds. Cecil Y. Lang and Edgar F. Shannon. 1981– .

WALT WHITMAN (1819–1892)

Leaves of Grass. 1855, 1856, 1860–61, 1867, 1871, 1876, 1881–82, 1891–92, 1897.
Walt Whitman's Drum-Taps. 1865.
Sequel to Drum-Taps. 1865.
Poems. Ed. William Michael Rossetti. 1868.
After All, Not to Create Only. 1871.
Democratic Vistas. 1871.
Memoranda during the War. 1875–76.
Two Rivulets, Including Democratic Vistas, Centennial Songs, and Passage to India. 1876.
Specimen Days and Collect. 1882–83.
November Boughs. 1888.
Complete Poems and Prose—1855–1888. 1888.
Good-Bye My Fancy. 1891.
Complete Prose Works. 1892.
Calamus: A Series of Letters Written during the Years 1868–1880. Ed. Richard Maurice Burke. 1897.
Complete Writings. Eds. Richard Maurice Burke, Thomas B. Harned, and Horace L. Traubel. 1902. 10 vols.
Criticism: An Essay. 1913.
The Gathering of the Forces: Editorials, Essays, Literary and Dramatic Reviews and Other Material Written by Walt Whitman as Editor of the Brooklyn Daily Eagle *in 1846 and 1847.* Eds. Cleveland Rodgers and John Black. 1920. 2 vols.
Uncollected Poetry and Prose. Ed. Emory Holloway. 1921. 2 vols.
The Half-Breed and Other Stories. Ed. Thomas Ollive Mabbott. 1927.
Rivulets of Prose: Critical Essays. Eds. Carolyn Wells and Alfred F. Goldsmith. 1928.
I Sit and Look Out: Editorials from the Brooklyn Daily Times. Eds. Emory Holloway and Henry S. Saunders. 1932.
New York Dissected: A Sheaf of Recently Discovered Newspaper Articles. Eds. Emory Holloway and Ralph Adimari. 1936.
Correspondence. Ed. Edwin Haviland Miller. 1961–77. 6 vols.
The Early Poems and the Fiction. Ed. Thomas L. Brasher. 1963.
Prose Works 1892. Ed. Floyd Stovall. 1963. 2 vols.
Leaves of Grass: Comprehensive Reader's Edition. Eds. Harold W. Blodgett and Sculley Bradley. 1965.
Daybooks and Notebooks. Ed. William White. 1978. 3 vols.
Leaves of Grass: A Textual Variorum of the Printed Poems. Eds. Sculley Bradley, Harold W. Blodgett, Arthur Golden, and William White. 1980. 3 vols.
Complete Poetry and Collected Prose. Ed. Justin Kaplan. 1982.
Notebooks and Unpublished Prose Manuscripts. Ed. Edward F. Grier. 1984. 6 vols.

EDWARD AUGUSTUS FREEMAN (1823–1892)

On the Architecture of the Church and Hospital of the Holy Cross, near Winchester. 1846.
Principles of Church Restoration. 1846.
Thoughts on the Study of History with Reference to the Proposed Changes in the Public Examinations. 1849.
Remarks on the Nomenclature of Gothic Architecture. 1849.
A History of Architecture. 1849.
Poems, Legendary and Historical (with G. W. Cox). 1850.
Remarks on the Architecture of Llandaff Cathedral; with an Essay towards the History of the Fabric. 1850.

An Essay on the Origin and Development of Window Tracery in England. 1850.

Notes on the Architectural Antiquities of the District of Gower, Glamorganshire. 1850.

Thoughts on the Third Form of the New Examination Statute. 1850.

The Preservation and Restoration of Ancient Monuments. 1852.

Suggestions with Regard to Certain Proposed Alterations in the University and Colleges of Oxford (with F. H. Dickinson). 1854.

Oratio in Theatro Sheldoniano Habita. 1854.

The History and Antiquities of St. David's (with William Basil Jones). 1856.

The History and Conquests of the Saracens: Six Lectures Delivered before the Edinburgh Philosophical Institution. 1856.

Parliamentary Reform: A Letter to a Member of the Late Reform Conference. 1859.

History of the Federal Government from the Foundation of the Achaean League to the Disruption of the United States. 1863. Vol. 1 only.

The Regius Professorship of Greek. 1864.

The History of the Norman Conquest of England: Its Causes and Its Results. 1867–79. 6 vols.

Old English History for Children. 1869.

Speech Made at a General Meeting of Subscribers to Extension Fund of Owens College, Manchester. 1870.

History of the Cathedral Church of Wells, as Illustrating the History of Cathedral Churches of the Old Foundation. 1870.

Historical Essays: First Series. 1871.

The Growth of the English Constitution from the Earliest Times. 1872.

General Sketch of European History. 1872.

The Unity of History: The Rede Lecture Delivered in the Senate House before the University of Cambridge. 1872.

Historical Course for Schools (editor). 1872–79. 8 vols.

Comparative Politics; with The Unity of History. 1873.

Historical Essays: Second Series. 1873.

History of Europe. 1875.

Historical and Architectural Sketches, Chiefly Italian. 1876.

The Eastern Question in Its Historical Bearings. 1876.

The Ottoman Power in Europe: Its Nature, Its Growth, and Its Decline. 1877.

The Turks in Europe. 1877.

Historical Essays: Third Series. 1879.

How the Study of History Is Let and Hindered: An Address Delivered at the Liverpool Institute. 1879.

A Short History of the Norman Conquest of England. 1880.

France: Its Growth and Consolidation. 1881.

Sketches from the Subject and Neighbour Lands of Venice. 1881.

The Historical Geography of Europe. 1881. 2 vols.

Lectures to American Audiences. 1882.

The Reign of William Rufus and the Accession of Henry the First. 1882. 2 vols.

An Introduction to American Institutional History. 1882.

Some Points in the Later History of the Greek Language. c. 1882.

Some Impressions of the United States. 1883.

English Towns and Districts: A Series of Addresses and Sketches. 1883.

A Speech Made in the Theatre, Oxford, on the Vote for the Proposed Physiological Laboratory, 1884.

The Nature and Origin of the House of Lords. 1884.

The Office of the Historical Professor: An Inaugural Lecture Read in the Museum at Oxford. 1884.

Gloucester and Its Abbey. c. 1884.

Mr. Edward A. Freeman on Surgery and Vivisection. 1885.

The Methods of Historical Study: Eight Lectures Read in the University of Oxford. 1886.

The Chief Periods of European History; with an Essay on Greek Cities under Roman Rule. 1886.

Greater Greece and Greater Britain; and George Washington the Expander of England. 1886.

Exeter. 1887.

The Proposed Degree of Doctor in Letters and in Natural Science. 1887.

Four Oxford Lectures, 1887; Fifty Years of European History; Teutonic Conquest in Gaul and Britain. 1888.

William the Conqueror. 1888.

Birmingham, Borough and City: Her Origin and Her Fellows. 1890.

Select Historical Essays. 1890.

Sketches from French Travel. 1891.

The History of Sicily from the Earliest Times. 1891–94. 4 vols.

Historical Essays: Fourth Series. 1892.

Sicily: Phoenician, Greek, and Roman. 1892.

Studies of Travel: Greece, Italy. Ed. Florence Freeman. 1893. 2 vols.

Life and Letters. Ed. W. R. W. Stephens. 1895. 2 vols.

Sketches of Travel in Normandy and Maine. Ed. Florence Freeman. 1897.

Western Europe in the Fifth Century: An Aftermath. Ed. T. Scott Holmes. 1904.

Western Europe in the Eighth Century and Onward: An Aftermath. Ed. T. Scott Holmes. 1904.

GEORGE WILLIAM CURTIS (1824–1892)

Nile Notes of a Howadji. 1851.

The Howadji in Syria. 1852.

Lotus-Eating: A Summer Book. 1852.

Rural Essays by A. J. Downing (editor). 1853.

The Potiphar Papers. 1853.

Prue and I. 1856.

Works. 1856. 5 vols.

The Duty of the American Scholar to Politics and the Times. 1856.

A Letter to the Young Men of Maine. 1856.

Patriotism. 1857.

An Address, Vindicating the Right of Woman to Elective Franchise: Delivered at the Woman's Rights Convention. 1858.

Trumps. 1861.

Life in the Open Air and Other Papers by Theodore Winthrop (editor). 1863.

The President: Why He Should Be Re-elected. 1864.

Equal Rights for Women: A Speech in the Constitutional Convention of New York, at Albany. 1867.

Fair Play for Women: An Address Delivered before the American Women Suffrage Association, Steinway Hall, New York. 1871.

American Social Science Association: Opening Address at the New York Meeting. 1874.

Charles Sumner: A Eulogy. 1874.

Burgoyne's Surrender: An Oration Delivered on the One Hundredth Anniversary of the Event, at Schuylerville, N.Y. 1877.

The Public Duty of Educated Men: Oration Delivered at the Commencement of Union College. 1877.

Civil Service Reform. c. 1878.

The Life, Character and Writings of William Cullen Bryant. 1879.

Machine Politics and the Remedy: A Lecture Delivered in the Checkering Hall, New York. 1880.

Robert Burns: An Address at the Unveiling of the Statue of the Poet, in Central Park, New-York. 1880.

Address Delivered before the Alumni of Brown University. 1882.

The Progress of Reform: An Address Delivered at the Annual Meeting of the National Civil-Service Reform League. 1883.

An Address at the Unveiling of the Statue of Washington, upon the Spot Where He Took the Oath as First President of the United States. 1883.

Wendell Phillips: A Eulogy Delivered before the Municipal Authorities of Boston, Mass. 1884.

The Year's Work in Civil-Service Reform: An Address Delivered at the Annual Meeting of the National Civil-Service Reform League. 1884.

Civil-Service Reform under the Present National Administration: An Address Delivered at the Annual Meeting of the National Civil-Service Reform League. 1885.

The Situation: An Address Delivered at the Annual Meeting of the National Civil-Service Reform League. 1886.

The Reason and the Result of Civil Service Reform: An Address Delivered before the National Civil-Service Reform League at Its Annual Meeting. 1888.

The Correspondence of John Lothrop Motley (editor). 1889. 2 vols.

Address Prepared for the Annual Meeting of the New York Civil-Service Reform Association. 1889.

George William Curtis in Harper's Weekly, May 3, 1890: Editorial. c. 1890.

The University of the State of New York: An Address Delivered at the University Convocation, Albany, N.Y. 1890.

Address: National Civil-Service Reform League, Tenth Annual Meeting, Boston. 1890.

Washington Irving: A Sketch. 1891.

From the Easy Chair. 1892.

"Party and Patronage": An Address Prepared for the Annual Meeting of the National Civil-Service Reform League. 1892.

James Russell Lowell: An Address. 1892.

The Last Public Utterances of George William Curtis. 1892.

Other Essays from the Easy Chair. 1893.

Orations and Addresses. Ed. Charles Eliot Norton. 1894. 3 vols.

From the Easy Chair: Third Series. 1894.

Literary and Social Essays. 1895.

Ars Recte Vivendi: Being Essays Contributed to "The Easy Chair." 1898.

Early Letters to John S. Dwight. Ed. George Willis Cooke. 1898.

AMELIA B. EDWARDS (1831–1892)

My Brother's Wife: A Life-History. 1855.

A Summary of English History from the Roman Conquest to the Present Time. 1856.

The Ladder of Life: A Heart-History. 1857.

The Young Marquis; or, A Story from a Reign. 1857.

The History of France from the Conquest of Gaul by the Romans to the Peace of 1856. 1858.

A Lady's Captivity among the Chinese Pirates on the Chinese Seas by Fanny Loviot (translator). 1858.

Hand and Glove. 1858.

Sights and Stories: Being Some Account of a Holiday Tour through the North of Belgium. 1862.

The Story of Cervantes. 1863.

Barbara's History. 1864. 3 vols.

Ballads. 1865.

Miss Carew. 1865. 3 vols.

Half a Million of Money. 1866. 3 vols.

Debenham's Vow. 1870, 3 vols.

In the Days of My Youth. 1873. 3 vols.

Monsieur Maurice: A New Novelette, and Other Tales. 1873. 3 vols.

Untrodden Peaks and Unfrequented Valleys: A Mid-Summer Ramble in the Dolomites. 1873.

A Night on the Borders of the Black Forest. 1874.

A Thousand Miles Up the Nile. 1877.

A Poetry-Book of Elder Poets (editor). 1878.

Lord Brackenbury. 1880. 3 vols.

Egyptian Archaeology by Sir Gaston Camille Maspero (translator). 1887.

Egypt of the Past by Sir Erasmus Wilson (editor). 1887.

Pharaohs, Fellahs and Explorers. 1891.

FANNY KEMBLE (1809–1893)

Francis the First: An Historical Drama. 1832.

Journal. 1835. 2 vols.

The Star of Seville. 1837.

Poems. 1844.

A Year of Consolation. 1847.

Answer of Frances Anne Butler to the Libel of Pierce Butler Praying a Divorce. 1848.

The Christmas Tree and Other Tales: Adapted from the German. 1856.

Journal of a Residence on a Georgian Plantation in 1838–1839. 1863.

Plays: An English Tragedy; Mary Stuart (Translated from the German of Schiller); Mademoiselle de Belle Isle (Translated from the French of Dumas). 1863.

Poems. 1866.

Record of a Girlhood. 1878. 3 vols.

Notes upon Some of Shakespeare's Plays. 1882.

Records of Later Life. 1882. 3 vols.

Poems. 1883.

The Adventures of Mr. John Timothy Homespun in Switzerland: Stolen from the French of Tartarin de Tareason aux Alpes. 1889.

Far Away and Long Ago. 1889.

Further Records 1848–1883. 1890. 2 vols.

On the Stage. Ed. George Arliss. 1926.

Fanny, the American Kemble: Her Journals and Unpublished Letters. Ed. Fanny Kemble Wister. 1972.

BENJAMIN JOWETT (1817–1893)

De Etruscorum Cultu, Moribus, et Legibus, Eorumque apud Romanos Vestigiis Oratio. 1841.

The University Censure on Dr. Hampden. 1847.

Suggestions for an Improvement of the Examination Statute (with A. P. Stanley). 1848.

The Epistles of St. Paul to the Thessalonians, Galatians, Romans (translator). 1855.

Statements of Christian Doctrine and Practice. 1861.

The Dialogues of Plato (translator). 1868–71 (4 vols.), 1892 (3rd rev. ed.; 5 vols.).

Lord Lytton: The Man and the Author. 1873.

Thucydides (translator). 1881.

Politics by Aristotle (translator). 1885.

The Republic by Plato (translator). 1888.

Essays on Men and Manners. Ed. Philip Lyttleton Gell. 1895.

College Sermons. Ed. W. H. Fremantle. 1895.

Life and Letters. Eds. Evelyn Abbott and Lewis Campbell. 1897. 2 vols.

Sermons, Biographical and Miscellaneous. Ed. W. H. Fremantle. 1899.

Letters. Eds. Evelyn Abbott and Lewis Campbell. 1899.

Sermons on Faith and Doctrine. Ed. W. H. Fremantle. 1901.

Select Passages from the Introductions to Plato. Ed. Lewis Campbell. 1902.

Select Passages from the Theological Writings. Ed. Lewis Campbell. 1902.

Theological Essays. Ed. Lewis Campbell. 1906.

The Interpretation of Scripture and Other Essays. 1906.

Scripture and Truth: Dissertations. Ed. Lewis Campbell. 1907.

Success and Failure. 1911.

Correspondence on Education with Earl Russell in 1867. Ed. J. M. Prest. 1965.

Robert Scott and Benjamin Jowett. Ed. J. M. Prest. 1966.

Dear Miss Nightingale: A Selection of Benjamin Jowett's Letters to Florence Nightingale 1860–1893. Eds. Colin Prest and Vincent Quinn. 1987.

FRANCIS PARKMAN (1823–1893)

The California and Oregon Trail: Being Sketches of Prairie and Rocky Mountain Life. 1849.

History of the Conspiracy of Pontiac, and the War of the North American Tribes against the English Colonies after the Conquest of Canada. 1851. 2 vols.

Vassall Morton. 1856.

Pioneers of France in the New World. 1865.

The Book of Roses. 1866.

The Jesuits in North America in the Seventeenth Century. 1867.

The Discovery of the Great West. 1869.

The Old Régime in Canada. 1874.

Count Frontenac and New France under Louis XIV. 1877.

Some Reasons against Woman Suffrage. 1877.

Montcalm and Wolfe. 1884. 2 vols.

Our Common Schools. 1890.

A Half-Century of Conflict. 1892. 2 vols.

Works. 1897–98. 18 vols.

Letters to E. G. Squier. Ed. Don C. Seitz. 1911.

Mr. Parkman and His Canadian Critics. 1923.

Representative Selections. Ed. Wilbur L. Schramm. 1938.

Journals. Ed. Mason Wade. 1947. 2 vols.

The Parkman Reader. Ed. Samuel Eliot Morison. 1955.

Letters. Ed. Wilbur R. Jacobs. 1960. 2 vols.

Correspondence of Francis Parkman and Henry Stevens 1845–1885. Ed. John Buechler. 1967.

JOHN ADDINGTON SYMONDS (1840–1893)

The Escorial. 1860.

The Renaissance. 1863.

Verses by John Addington Symonds the Elder (editor). 1871.

Miscellanies by John Addington Symonds the Elder (editor). 1871.

An Introduction to the Study of Dante. 1872.

The Renaissance of Modern Europe. 1872.

Miscellaneous Writings of John Conington (editor). 1872. 2 vols.

Studies of the Greek Poets. 1873–76. 2 vols.

Sketches in Italy and Greece. 1874.

The Renaissance in Italy. 1875 [Volume 1: *The Age of the Despots*]; 1877 [Volume 2: *The Revival of Learning*]; 1877 [Volume 3: *The Fine Arts*]; 1881 [Volumes 4–5: *Italian Literature*]; 1886 [Volumes 6–7: *The Catholic Reaction*].

Lyra Viginti Chordarum. c. 1875.

Genius Amoris Amari Visio. c. 1875.

The Lotos Garland of Antinous. c. 1875.

The Love Tale of Odatis and Prince Zariadres. c. 1875.

Studies in Terza Rima, etc. c. 1875.

Callicrates; Bianca; Imelda; Passio Amoris Secunda: A Rhapsody; Liber Temporis Perditi. c. 1875.

Pantarkes. c. 1875.

The Sonnets of Michelangelo Buonarroti and Tommaso Campanella (translator). 1878.

Many Moods: A Volume of Verse. 1878.

Shelley. 1878.

Rhaetica. 1878.

Tales of Ancient Greece: No. 1. Euliades and A Cretan Idyll. c. 1878.

Tales of Ancient Greece: No. 2. c. 1878.

Sketches and Studies in Italy. 1879.

Crocuses and Soldanellas. c. 1879.

Old and New. c. 1879.

New and Old: A Volume of Verse. 1880.

Sketches and Studies in Southern Europe. 1880. 2 vols.

Animi Figura. 1882.

Italian Byways. 1883.

A Problem in Greek Ethics. 1883.

Fragilia Labilia: Written Mostly between 1860 and 1862. 1884.

Wine, Women, and Song: Mediaeval Latin Students' Songs (translator). 1884.

Shakspere's Predecessors in the English Drama. 1884.

Vagabunduli Libellus. 1884.

Sir Philip Sidney. 1886.

Ben Jonson. 1886.

Religio Medici, Urn Burial, Christian Morals, and Other Essays by Sir Thomas Browne (editor). 1886.

The Dramatic Works and Lyrics of Ben Jonson (editor). 1886.

The Life of Benvenuto Cellini (translator). 1888. 2 vols.

Webster and Tourneur (editor). 1888.

The Memoirs of Count Carlo Gozzi (translator). 1890. 2 vols.

Essays, Speculative and Suggestive. 1890. 2 vols.

A Problem in Modern Ethics: Being an Enquiry into the Phenomenon of Sexual Inversion, Addressed Especially to Medical Psychologists and Jurists. 1891.

Our Life in the Swiss Highlands (with Margaret Symonds). 1892.

The Life of Michelangelo Buonarroti. 1893. 2 vols.

In the Key of Blue and Other Prose Essays. 1893.

Walt Whitman: A Study. 1893.

Midnight at Baiae: A Dream Fragment of Imperial Rome. 1893.

On the English Family of Symonds. 1894.

Giovanni Boccaccio as Man and Author. 1895.

Sketches and Studies in Italy and Greece. Ed. Horatio F. Brown. 1898. 3 vols.

The Poetry of the Hon. Roden Noel (with Emily Hickey). 1901.

Last and First: Being Two Essays: The New Spirit and Arthur Hugh Clough. 1919.

Letters and Papers. Ed. Horatio F. Brown. 1923.

Letters. Eds. Herbert M. Schueller and Robert L. Peters. 1967–69. 3 vols.

Gabriel. Eds. Robert L. Peters and Timothy D'Arch Smith. 1974.

Memoirs. Ed. Phyllis Grosskurth. 1984.

OLIVER WENDELL HOLMES (1809–1894)

Poems. 1836.

Principles of the Theory and Practice of Medicine by Marshall Hall (editor; with Jacob Bigelow). 1839.

Homœopathy, and Its Kindred Delusions. 1842.

The Position and Prospects of the Medical Student. 1844.

Urania: A Rhymed Lesson. 1846.

An Introductory Lecture. 1847.

A Scintilla; The Task. 1849.

Astræa: The Balance of Illusions. 1850.

The Benefactors of the Medical School of Harvard University. 1850.

A Song of '29. 1851.

Response to the Following Toast. 1853.

The New Eden. 1854.

Songs of the Class of MDCCCXXIX. 1854.

A triple health to friendship, science, art. 1855.

Oration Delivered before the New England Society. 1856.

Harvard College: Festival of the Association of the Alumni: The Parting Song. 1857.

Valedictory Address, Delivered to the Medical Graduates of Harvard University. 1858.

The Autocrat of the Breakfast-Table. 1858.

The Promise. 1859.

Boston Common: Three Pictures. 1859.

The Professor at the Breakfast-Table; with the Story of Iris. 1860.

Currents and Counter-Currents in Medical Science. 1860.

Elsie Venner: A Romance of Destiny. 1861.

Currents and Counter-Currents in Medical Science, with Other Addresses and Essays. 1861.

Army Hymn. 1861.

Additional Verse to the Star-Spangled Banner. 1861.

Associate Members of the United States Sanitary Commission Meeting in Boston: Address to the Public. 1861.

Holmes' Parting Hymn. c. 1861.

Songs in Many Keys. 1862.

Border Lines of Knowledge in Some Provinces of Medical Science. 1862.

Now or Never. c. 1862.

Thus Saith the Lord, "I Offer Thee Three Things." c. 1862.

Oration Delivered before the City Authorities of Boston. 1863.

Soundings from the Atlantic. 1864.

Hymn Written Expressly for the Great Central Fair. 1864.

New England's Master-Key. 1864.

Hymn. 1865.

A Memorial of Abraham Lincoln. 1865.

Humorous Poems. 1865.

The Guardian Angel. 1867.

The Atlantic Almanac 1868 (editor; with Donald G. Mitchell). 1867.

Teaching from the Chair and at the Bedside. 1867.

Thou gracious power, whose mercy lends. 1869.

A Hymn of Peace. 1869.

In Memory of Fitz-Greene Halleck. 1869.

Mechanism in Thought and Morals. 1871.

The Poet at the Breakfast-Table: His Talks with His Fellow-Boarders and the Reader. 1872.

The Claims of Dentistry. 1872.

Songs of Many Seasons 1862–1874. 1875.

Turner Sargent. 1877.

A Family Record. 1877.

Poetical Works. 1877.

Favorite Poems. 1877.

The School-Boy. 1879.

John Lothrop Motley: A Memoir. 1879.

The Iron Gate and Other Poems. 1880.

Poetical Works. 1881. 2 vols.

Poems and Prose Passages from the Works. Ed. Josephine E. Hodgdon. 1881.

Medical Highways and By-ways. 1882.

Farewell Address to the Medical School of Harvard University. 1882.

Our Dead Singer. c. 1882.

Medical Essays 1842–1882. 1883.

Pages from an Old Volume of Life: A Collection of Essays 1857–1881. 1883.

Ralph Waldo Emerson. 1885.

A Welcome to Dr. Benjamin Apthorp Gould. 1885.

A Mortal Antipathy: First Opening of the New Portfolio. 1885.

Hymn: The Word of Promise. 1886.

Hail, Columbia! 1887.

Our Hundred Days in Europe. 1887.

Poem for the Dedication of the Fountain at Stratford-on-Avon. 1887.

Before the Curfew and Other Poems, Chiefly Occasional. 1888.

Selections from the Writings. 1888.

To the Eleven Ladies Who Presented a Loving Cup to Me. 1889.

Over the Teacups. 1891.

Writings. 1891–92. 14 vols.

Complete Poetical Works. Ed. Horace E. Scudder. 1895.

Life and Letters. Ed. John T. Morse, Jr. 1896. 2 vols.

Early Poems. Ed. Nathan Haskell Dole. 1899.

A Dissertation on Acute Pericarditis. 1937.

Poem Read at the Dartmouth Commencement Exercises, July 24, 1839. 1940.

Psychiatric Offices. Ed. Clarence P. Oberndorf. 1946.

The Autocrat's Miscellanies. Ed. Alfred Mordell. 1959.

JAMES ANTHONY FROUDE (1818–1894)

The Influence of the Science of Political Economy on the Moral and Social Welfare of a Nation. 1842.

Shadows of the Clouds. 1847.

A Sermon Preached at St. Mary's Church, on the Death of the Rev. George May Coleridge. 1847.

The Nemesis of Faith. 1849.

Novels and Tales by Johann Wolfgang von Goethe (translator; with R. D. Boylan). 1854.

History of England from the Fall of Wolsey to the Defeat of the Spanish Armada. 1856–70. 12 vols.

The Pilgrim: A Dialogue on the Life and Actions of King Henry the Eighth by William Thomas (editor). 1861.

Inaugural Address Delivered to the University of St. Andrews. 1863.

The Influence of the Reformation on the Scottish Character. 1865.

Short Studies on Great Subjects. 1867. 2 vols.

Inaugural Address Delivered to the Unviersity of St. Andrews. 1869.

Calvinism: An Address Delivered at St. Andrews. 1871.

Short Studies on Great Subjects: Second Series. 1871.

Gems from Froude. 1872.

The English in Ireland in the Eighteenth Century. 1872–74. 3 vols.

Short Studies on Great Subjects: Third Series. 1877.
Life and Times of Thomas Becket. 1878.
Caesar: A Sketch. 1879.
Prayer, as It Affects the Immutability of Nature's God and Nature's Laws: A Correspondence between S. G. Potter and J. A. Froude. 1879.
Bunyan. 1880.
Two Lectures on South Africa Delivered before the Philosophical Institute, Edinburgh. 1880.
Reminiscences by Thomas Carlyle (editor). 1881. 2 vols.
Reminiscences of My Irish Journey in 1849 by Thomas Carlyle (editor). 1882.
A Lesson in Democracy: An Address Delivered in the Town Hall, Birmingham. 1882.
Thomas Carlyle: A History of the First Forty Years of His Life 1795–1835. 1882. 2 vols.
Luther: A Short Biography. 1883.
Short Studies on Great Subjects: Fourth Series. 1883.
Letters and Memorials of Jane Welsh Carlyle (editor). 1883. 3 vols.
Historical and Other Sketches. Ed. David H. Wheeler. 1883.
Thomas Carlyle: A History of His Life in London 1834–1881. 1884. 2 vols.
Oceana; or, England and Her Colonies. 1886.
The Knights Templars. 1886.
The English in the West Indies; or, The Bow of Ulysses. 1888.
Liberty and Property: An Address to the Liberty and Property Defence. 1888.
The Two Chiefs of Dunboy; or, An Irish Romance of the Last Century. 1889.
Lord Beaconsfield. 1890.
The Divorce of Catherine of Aragon: Being a Supplementary Volume to the History of England. 1891.
The Spanish Story of the Armada and Other Essays. 1892.
Life and Letters of Erasmus. 1893.
English Seamen in the Sixteenth Century. 1895.
Lectures on the Council of Trent. 1896.
Selections from the Writings. Ed. P. S. Allen. 1901.
My Relations with Carlyle. Eds. Ashley A. Froude and Margaret Froude. 1903.
Essays in Literature and History. 1906.
Essays. Ed. H. Bennett. 1907.
Selected Essays. Ed. H. G. Rawlinson. 1915.
The Froude-Ruskin Relationship, as Represented through Letters. Ed. Helen Gill Viljoen. 1966.

CHRISTINA ROSSETTI (1830–1894)

To My Mother on the Anniversary of Her Birth. 1842.
Verses. 1847.
Goblin Market and Other Poems. 1862.
Poems. 1866.
The Prince's Progress and Other Poems. 1866.
Outlines for Illuminating: Consider. 1866.
Commonplace and Other Short Stories. 1870.
Sing-Song: A Nursery Rhyme Book. 1872.
Annus Domini: A Prayer for Each Day of the Year, Founded on a Text of Holy Scripture. 1874.
Speaking Likenesses. 1874.
Goblin Market, The Prince's Progress, and Other Poems. 1875.
Seek and Find: A Double Series of Short Studies of the Benedicite. 1879.
A Pageant and Other Poems. 1881.
Called to Be Saints: The Minor Festivals Devotionally Studied. 1881.
Letter and Spirit: Notes on the Commandments. 1883.

Time Flies: A Reading Diary. 1885.
Poems. 1890.
The Face of the Deep: A Devotional Commentary on the Apocalypse. 1892.
Verses Reprinted from Called to Be Saints, Time Flies, The Face of the Deep. 1893.
New Poems. Ed. William Michael Rossetti. 1896.
Maude: A Story for Girls. Ed. William Michael Rossetti. 1897.
Redeeming the Time: Daily Musings for Lent. 1903.
Selected Poems. Ed. Alexander Smellie. 1903.
Poetical Works. Ed. William Michael Rossetti. 1904.
Family Letters. Ed. William Michael Rossetti. 1908.
Selected Poems. Ed. Charles Bell Burke. 1913.
Poems. Ed. Walter de la Mare. 1930.
Three Rossettis: Unpublished Letters to and from Dante Gabriel, Christina, William. Ed. Janet Crump Troxell. 1937.
Poems. Ed. Kathleen Jarvis. 1955.
The Rossetti-Macmillan Letters (with Dante Gabriel Rossetti and William Michael Rossetti). Ed. Lona M. Packer. 1963.
A Choice of Christina Rossetti's Verse. Ed. Elizabeth Jennings. 1970.
Complete Poems. Ed. R. W. Crump. 1979–86. 2 vols.

WALTER PATER (1839–1894)

Studies in the History of the Renaissance. 1873.
Marius the Epicurean: His Sensations and Ideas. 1885. 2 vols.
Imaginary Portraits. 1887.
Appreciations; with an Essay on Style. 1889.
Plato and Platonism. 1893.
An Imaginary Portrait (The Child in the House). 1894.
Greek Studies. Ed. Charles L. Shadwell. 1895.
Miscellaneous Studies. Ed. Charles L. Shadwell. 1895.
Gaston de Latour: An Unfinished Romance. Ed. Charles L. Shadwell. 1896.
Essays from The Guardian. Ed. Thomas Bird Mosher. 1896.
Works. 1900–01. 9 vols.
Selections. Ed. Edward Everett Hale, Jr. 1901.
Uncollected Essays. Ed. Thomas Bird Mosher. 1903.
Sketches and Reviews. 1919.
Selected Essays. Ed. H. G. Rawlinson. 1927.
The Chant of the Celestial Sailors: An Unpublished Poem. 1928.
Selected Works. Ed. Richard Aldington. 1948.
Selected Prose. Ed. Derek Patmore. 1949.
Letters. Ed. Lawrence Evans. 1970.
Selected Writings. Ed. Harold Bloom. 1974.
Three Major Texts. Ed. William F. Buckler. 1986.

ROBERT LOUIS STEVENSON (1850–1894)

The Pentland Rising: A Page of History, 1666. 1866.
The Charity Bazaar: An Allegorical Dialogue. 1868.
An Appeal to the Clergy of the Church of Scotland, with a Note for the Laity. 1875.
An Inland Voyage. 1878.
Edinburgh: Picturesque Notes. 1879.
Travels with a Donkey in the Cévennes. 1879.
Deacon Brodie; or, The Double Life (with W. E. Henley). 1880.
The Surprise. 1880. 1 no.
To F. J. S. 1881.
Virginibus Puerisque and Other Papers. 1881.
Familiar Studies of Men and Books. 1882.
New Arabian Nights. 1882. 2 vols.

Not I and Other Poems. 1882.
Moral Emblems: A Collection of Cuts and Verses. 1882.
Moral Emblems: A Second Collection of Cuts and Verses. 1882.
A Martial Elegy for Some Lead Soldiers. 1882.
The Graver & the Pen; or, Scenes from Nature, with Appropriate Verses. 1882.
Robin and Ben; or, The Pirate and the Apothecary. 1882.
The Silverado Squatters: Sketches from a Californian Mountain. 1883.
Treasure Island. 1883.
We found him first as in the dells of day. 1883.
To the Thompson Class Club, "from Their Stammering Laureate." 1883.
Admiral Guinea (with W. E. Henley). 1884.
Beau Austin (with W. E. Henley). 1884.
A Child's Garden of Verses. 1885.
More New Arabian Nights: The Dynamiter (with Fanny Van de Grift Stevenson). 1885.
Prince Otto: A Romance. 1885.
Macaire (with W. E. Henley). 1885.
The Laureat Ste'enson to the Thamson Class. 1885.
The Strange Case of Dr. Jekyll and Mr. Hyde. 1886.
Kidnapped: Being Memoirs of the Adventures of David Balfour in the Year 1751. 1886.
Some College Memories. 1886.
The Merry Men and Other Tales and Fables. 1887.
Thomas Stevenson, Civil Engineer. 1887.
Memories and Portraits. 1887.
Underwoods. 1887.
Ticonderoga. 1887.
The Hanging Judge (with Fanny Van de Grift Stevenson). 1887.
Memoir of Fleeming Jenkin. 1887.
The Black Arrow: A Tale of the Two Roses. 1888.
The Misadventures of John Nicholson: A Christmas Story. 1888.
The Master of Ballantrae: A Winter's Tale. 1889.
The Wrong Box (with Lloyd Osbourne). 1889.
On Board the Old "Equator." 1889.
The South Seas: A Record of Three Cruises ⟨*In the South Seas*⟩. 1890.
Father Damien: An Open Letter to the Reverend Dr. Hyde of Honolulu. 1890.
Ballads. 1890.
Across the Plains, with Other Memories and Essays. 1892.
The Wrecker (with Lloyd Osbourne). 1892.
A Footnote to History: Eight Years of Trouble in Samoa. 1892.
Three Plays (with W. E. Henley). 1892.
The Beach of Falesá. 1892.
Island Nights' Entertainments. 1893.
Catriona: A Sequel to Kidnapped, *Being Memoirs of the Further Adventures of David Balfour at Home and Abroad.* 1893.
The Ebb-Tide: A Trio and Quartette (with Lloyd Osbourne). 1894.
Works. Ed. Sidney Colvin. 1894–98. 28 vols.
The Amateur Emigrant from the Clyde to Sandy Hook. 1895.
Vailima Letters: Being Correspondence Addressed to Sidney Colvin, November 1890–October 1894. 1895.
The Body-Snatcher. 1895.
Fables. 1896.
Weir of Hermiston: An Unfinished Romance. 1896.
Songs of Travel and Other Verses. 1896.
Familiar Epistle in Verse and Prose. 1896.
A Mountain Town in France: A Fragment. 1896.

Plays (with W. E. Henley). 1896.
St Ives: Being the Adventures of a French Prisoner in England (with A. T. Quiller-Couch). 1897.
Three Short Poems. 1898.
A Lowden Sabbath Morn. 1898.
Letters to His Family and Friends. Ed. Sidney Colvin. 1899. 2 vols.
R.L.S. Teuila. 1899.
The Morality of the Profession of Letters. 1899.
A Stevenson Medley. Ed. Sidney Colvin. 1899.
A Christmas Sermon. 1900.
Three Letters. 1902.
Some Letters. Ed. Horace Townsend. 1902.
Essays and Criticisms. 1903.
Prayers Written at Vailima. 1905.
Tales and Fantasies. 1905.
Essays of Travel. 1905.
Essays in the Art of Writing. 1905.
Essays. Ed. William Lyon Phelps. 1906.
Works. Ed. Edmund Gosse. 1906–07. 20 vols.
Collected Works. Ed. Charles Scribner and Sons. 1908–12. 31 vols.
Pan's Pipes. 1910.
Letters. Ed. Sidney Colvin. 1911. 4 vols.
Lay Morals and Other Papers. 1911.
Works. 1911–12. 25 vols.
Records of a Family of Engineers. 1912.
Memoirs of Himself. 1912.
The Flight of the Princess and Other Pieces. 1912.
Verses by R.L.S. Ed. L. S. Livingston. 1912.
Poems and Ballads. 1913.
Desiderata: 1895. 1914.
Letters to Charles Baxter. 1914.
Letters to an Editor. Ed. Clement K. Shorter. 1914.
Poetical Fragments. 1915.
An Ode of Horace: Book II, Ode III: Experiments in Three Metres (translator). 1916.
One the Choice of a Profession. 1916.
The Waif Woman. 1916.
Poems Hitherto Unpublished. Ed. George S. Hellman. 1916. 2 vols.
New Poems and Variant Readings. 1918.
Poems Hitherto Unpublished. Eds. George S. Hellman and William P. Trent. 1921.
Hitherto Unpublished Prose Writings. Ed. Henry H. Harper. 1921.
Confessions of a Unionist. Ed. Flora V. Livingston. 1921.
Works. Eds. Lloyd Osbourne and Fanny Van de Grift Stevenson. 1922–23. 26 vols.
The Manuscripts of Stevenson's Records of a Family of Engineers: The Unfinished Chapters. Ed. J. Christian Bay. 1929.
Henry James and Robert Louis Stevenson: A Record of Friendship and Criticism. Ed. Janet Adam Smith. 1948.
Collected Poems. Ed. Janet Adam Smith. 1950, 1971.
Silverado Journal. Ed. John E. Jordan. 1954.
RLS: Stevenson's Letters to Charles Baxter. Eds. De Lancey Ferguson and Marshall Waingrow. 1956.
From Scotland to Silverado. Ed. James D. Hart. 1966.
Complete Short Stories, with a Selection of the Best Short Novels. Ed. Charles Neider. 1969. 3 vols.
Travels to Hawaii. Ed. A. Grove Day. 1973.
Selected Short Stories. Ed. Ian Campbell. 1980.
An Old Song and Edifying Letters of the Rutherford Family. Ed. Roger C. Swearingen. 1982.

From the Clyde to California: Robert Louis Stevenson's Emigrant Journey. Ed. Andrew Noble. 1985.

FREDERICK LOCKER-LAMPSON (1821–1895)

London Lyrics. 1857, 1882 (as *London Rhymes*), 1893 (12th ed.).

A Selection from the Works. 1865.

Lyra Elegantiarum: A Collection of Some of the Best Specimens of Vers de Société and Vers d'Occasion in the English Language by Deceased Authors (editor). 1867, 1891 (with Coulson Kernahan).

Patchwork. 1879.

The Rowfant Library (editor). 1886.

Memories of Men, Places, and Things, Belonging to Past Times. c. 1894.

Rowfant Rhymes. 1895.

My Confidences: An Autobiographical Sketch Addressed to My Descendants. Ed. Augustine Birrell. 1896.

Patchwork: Second Series. 1927.

THOMAS HENRY HUXLEY (1825–1895)

Manual of Human Histology by Albert von Kölliker (translator; with George Busk). 1853–54. 2 vols.

On the Educational Value of the Natural Sciences. 1854.

On Tape and Cystic Worms by Carl Theodor von Siebold (translator). 1857.

The Oceanic Hydrozoa: A Description of the Calycophoridae *and* Physophoridae *Observed during the Voyage of H.M.S. Rattlesnake in the Years 1846–1850.* 1859.

On the Genus Pterygotus (with J. W. Salter). 1859.

Address Delivered at the Anniversary Meeting of the Geological Society of London. 1862.

On Our Knowledge of the Causes of the Phenomena of Organic Nature. 1862.

Evidence as to Man's Place in Nature. 1863.

Lectures on the Elements of Comparative Anatomy. 1864.

An Elementary Atlas of Comparative Osteology. 1864.

On the Structure of the Belemnitidae. 1864.

On the Methods and Results of Ethnology. 1865.

A Catalogue of the Collections of Fossils in the Museum of Practical Geology (with Robert Etheridge). 1865.

Lessons in Elementary Physiology. 1866.

The Elements of Physiology and Hygiene (with William Jay Youmans). 1868.

Address to the Geological Society of London. 1869.

An Introduction to the Classification of Animals. 1869.

Strong Drink and Tobacco Smoke by H. P. Prescott (editor). 1869.

On the Physical Basis of Life. 1869.

Lay Sermons, Addresses and Reviews. 1870.

Address Delivered at the Anniversary Meeting of the Geological Society of London. 1870.

Address to the British Association for the Advancement of Science. 1870.

A Manual of the Anatomy of Vertebrated Animals. 1871.

More Criticisms on Darwin, and Administrative Nihilism. 1872.

Critiques and Addresses. 1873.

A Course of Practical Instruction in Elementary Biology (with H. N. Martin). 1875.

The Evidence of the Miracle of the Resurrection. 1876.

American Addresses, with a Lecture on the Study of Biology. 1877.

The Crocodilian Remains Found in the Elgin Sandstones. 1877.

A Manual of the Anatomy of Invertebrated Animals. 1877.

Physiography: An Introduction to the Study of Nature. 1877.

A Catalogue of the Cambrian and Silurian Fossils in the Museum of Practical Geology. 1878.

Hume. 1878.

A Catalogue of the Cretaceous Fossils in the Museum of Practical Geology. 1878.

Report on the Promotion of Technical Education. 1878.

A Catalogue of the Tertiary and Post Tertiary Fossils in the Museum of Practical Geology. 1878,

The Crayfish. 1880.

Introduction (to Science Primers). 1880.

Address. 1880.

Science and Culture and Other Essays. 1881.

Address Delivered at the Anniversary Meeting of the Royal Society. 1883.

Fish Diseases. 1883.

Inaugural Meeting of the Fishery Congress: Address. 1883.

Address Delivered at the Anniversary Meeting of the Royal Society. 1885.

The Advance of Science in the Last Half-Century. 1887.

Address Delivered at a Meeting Held in the Town Hall, Manchester. 1887.

A Half-Century of Science (with Grant Allen). 1888.

Social Diseases and Worse Remedies: Letters to the Times *on Mr. Booth's Scheme.* 1891.

Essays on Some Controverted Questions. 1892.

Evolution and Ethics. 1893.

Collected Essays. 1893–94. 9 vols.

Report on the Specimen of the Genus Spirula *Collected by H.M.S.* Challenger (with Paul Pelseneer). 1895.

Suggestions for a Proposed Natural History Museum in Manchester. 1896.

Scientific Memoirs. Eds. Sir Michael Foster and E. Ray Lankester. 1898–1903. 5 vols.

Life and Letters. Ed. Leonard Huxley. 1900 (2 vols.), 1903 (3 vols.).

Aphorisms and Reflections. Ed. Henrietta A. Huxley. 1907.

Autobiography and Selected Essays. Ed. Ada L. F. Snell. 1909.

Readings from Huxley. Ed. Clarissa Rinaker. 1920.

Essays. Ed. Frederick Barry. 1929.

Diary of the Voyage of H.M.S. Rattlesnake. Ed. Julian Huxley. 1935.

The Essence of T. H. Huxley: Selections from His Writings. Ed. Cyril Bibby. 1967.

T. H. Huxley on Education: A Selection from His Writings. Ed. Cyril Bibby. 1971.

EUGENE FIELD (1850–1895)

"Slug 14": A Doggerel Rhyme. 1876.

Tribune Primer. 1881.

The Symbol and the Saint: A Christmas Tale. 1886.

Culture's Garland: Being Memoranda of the Gradual Rise of Literature, Art, Music and Society in Chicago and Other Western Ganglia. 1887.

A Little Book of Profitable Tales. 1889.

A Little Book of Western Verse. 1889.

Echoes from the Sabine Farm: Being Certain Horatian Lyrics Now for the First Time Discreetly and Delectably Done into English Verse (translator; with Roswell M. Field). 1891.

With Trumpet and Drum. 1892.

Second Book of Verse. 1892.

The Holy-Cross and Other Tales. 1893.
⟨*Autobiographical Sketch.*⟩ 1894.
Love-Songs of Childhood. 1894.
Little Willie. c. 1895.
The Love Affairs of a Bibliomaniac. 1896.
The House: An Episode in the Lives of Reuben Baker, Astronomer, and of His Wife Alice. 1896.
Songs and Other Verse. 1896.
Second Book of Tales. 1896.
Eugene Field to Francis Wilson: Some Attentions. 1896.
Writings in Prose and Verse. 1896–1901. 12 vols.
The Fellowship Drinking Song Written for the Club. c. 1896.
Florence Beardsley's Story: The Life and Death of a Remarkable Woman. 1897.
Lullaby Land: Songs of Childhood. Ed. Kenneth Graham. 1897.
The Eugene Field Book: Verses, Stories, and Letters for School Reading. Eds. Mary E. Burt and Mary B. Cable. 1898.
How One Friar Met the Devil and Two Pursued Him. 1900.
The Temptation of the Friar Gonsol. 1900.
Sharps and Flats. Ed. Slason Thompson. 1900. 2 vols.
The Complete Tribune Primer. 1901.
A Little Book of Tribune Verse: A Number of Hitherto Uncollected Poems, Grave and Gay. Ed. Joseph G. Brown. 1901.
The Stars: A Slumber Story. 1901.
The Clink of the Ice and Other Poems Worth Reading. c. 1902.
Poems of Childhood. 1904.
Hoosier Lyrics. Ed. Charles Walter Brown. 1905.
John Smith U.S.A. Ed. Charles Walter Brown. 1905.
Eugene Field Reader. Ed. Alice L. Harris. 1905.
In Wink-Away Land. 1905.
Flowers from Eugene Field. 1906.
Clippings from the Denver Tribune *1881–1883.* Ed. Willard S. Morse. 1909.
Poems. 1910.
Christmas Tales and Christmas Verse. 1912.
Verse and Prose from the George H. Yenowine Collection of Books and Manuscripts. Ed. Henry H. Harper. 1917.
Some Love Letters. Ed. Thomas B. Lockwood. 1927.
Fiddle-dee-dee and Other Verses. 1929.
Some Poems of Childhood. Ed. Bertha E. Mahony. 1931.
Favorite Poems. 1940.

HARRIET BEECHER STOWE (1811–1896)

A New England Sketch. 1834.
An Elementary Geography. 1835.
The Mayflower; or, Sketches of Scenes and Characters among the Descendants of the Pilgrims. 1843.
Earthly Care, a Heavenly Discipline. c. 1845.
Uncle Tom's Cabin; or, Life among the Lowly. 1852. 2 vols.
The Two Altars; or, Two Pictures in One. 1852.
Let Every Man Mind His Own Business. 1852.
Four Ways of Observing the Sabbath. 1852.
A Key to Uncle Tom's Cabin. 1853.
Uncle Sam's Emancipation; Earthly Care, a Heavenly Discipline; and Other Sketches. 1853.
The Coral King. 1853.
Augusta Howard. 1853.
Letter to the Ladies' New Anti-Slavery Society of Glasgow. c. 1853.
The Bible the Sure Source of Comfort. 1854.
Sunny Memories of Foreign Lands. 1854. 2 vols.
Notice of the Boston Anti-Slavery Bazaar. c. 1854.
First Geography for Children. 1855.

The Christian Slave. 1855.
The May Flower and Miscellaneous Writings. 1855.
What Should We Do without the Bible? c. 1855.
Dred: A Tale of the Great Dismal Swamp. 1856. 2 vols.
Our Charley, and What to Do with Him. 1858.
Mrs. H. B. Stowe on Dr. Monod and the American Tract Society; Considered in Relation to American Slavery. 1858.
My Expectation. 1858.
Things That Cannot Be Shaken. 1858.
My Strength. 1858.
A Word to the Sorrowful. 1858.
Harriet Beecher Stowe on the American Board of Commissioners for Foreign Missions. c. 1858.
The Minister's Wooing. 1859.
The Pearl of Orr's Island. 1862.
Agnes of Sorrento. 1862.
A Reply to The Affectionate and Christian Address of Many Thousands of Women of Great Britain and Ireland, to Their Sisters, the Women of the United States, *in Behalf of Many Thousands of American Women.* 1863.
The Ravages of a Carpet. 1865.
House and Home Papers. 1865.
Stories about Our Dogs. 1865.
Little Foxes. 1866.
Religious Poems. 1867.
Queer Little People. 1867.
The Daisy's First Winter and Other Stories. 1867.
The Chimney-Corner. 1868.
Men of Our Times; or, Leading Patriots of the Day. 1868.
Oldtown Folks. 1869.
The American Woman's Home (with Catherine E. Beecher). 1869.
Lady Byron Vindicated: A History of the Byron Controversy from Its Beginning in 1816 to the Present Time. 1870.
Little Pussy Willow. 1870.
Principles of Domestic Science (with Catherine E. Beecher). 1870.
My Wife and I; or, Harry Henderson's History. 1871.
Pink and White Tyranny: A Society Novel. 1871.
Have You Seen It? Letter from Mrs. Stowe to Miss Kate Reignolds. c. 1871.
Sam Lawson's Oldtown Fireside Stories. 1872.
Palmetto-Leaves. 1873.
Woman in Sacred History. 1873.
The New Housekeeper's Manual (with Catherine E. Beecher). 1874.
We and Our Neighbors; or, The Records of an Unfashionable Street. 1875.
Betty Bright Idea. 1876.
Footsteps of the Master. 1876.
Poganuc People: Their Loves and Lives. 1878.
A Dog's Mission; or, The Story of the Old Avery House, and Other Stories. 1881.
Flowers and Fruit from the Writings of Harriet Beecher Stowe. Ed. Abbie H. Fairfield. 1888.
Dialogues and Scenes from the Writings of Harriet Beecher Stowe. Ed. Emily Weaver. 1889.
Life Compiled from Her Letters and Journals. Ed. Charles Edward Stowe. 1889.
Writings. 1896. 16 vols.
Life and Letters. Ed. Annie Fields. 1897.
Collected Poems. Ed. John Michael Moran, Jr. 1967.
Regional Sketches: New England and Florida. Ed. John R. Adams. 1972.

Uncle Tom's Cabin; The Minister's Wooing; Oldtown Folks.
1982.

COVENTRY PATMORE (1823–1896)

Poems. 1844.

Tamerton Church-Tower and Other Poems. 1853.

The Angel in the House. 1854 [Book 1: *The Betrothal*]; 1856
[Book 2: *The Espousals*]; 1863 (2 vols.).

Faithful for Ever. 1860.

The Children's Garland from the Best Poets (editor). 1862.

The Victories of Love. 1862.

Odes: Not Published. 1868.

The Unknown Eros and Other Odes. 1877, 1878.

*An Autobiographical Fragment and Biographical Notes, with
Personal Sketches of Contemporaries, Unpublished Lyrics
and Letters of Literary Friends* by Bryan Waller Procter
("Barry Cornwall") (editor). 1877.

Amelia. 1878.

*Amelia, Tamerton Church-Tower, etc.; with a Prefatory Study
on English Metrical Law.* 1878.

Poems. 1879. 4 vols.

Florilegium Amantis. Ed. Richard Garnett. 1879.

Saint Bernard on the Love of God (translator; with Marianne
Caroline Patmore). 1881.

How I Managed and Improved My Estate. 1886.

Poems: Collective Edition. 1886. 2 vols.

Hastings, Lewes, Rye and the Sussex Marshes. 1887.

Principle in Art, etc. 1889.

Religio Poetae, etc. 1893.

The Rod, the Root, and the Flower. 1895.

The Poetry of Pathos and Delight. Ed. Alice Meynell. 1896.

Works (New Uniform Edition). 1897. 5 vols.

The Angel in the House; Together with The Victories of Love.
1905.

Poems. Ed. Basil Champneys. 1906.

The Wedding Sermon. 1911.

Principle in Art, Religio Poetae and Other Essays. 1913.

Courage in Politics and Other Essays 1885–1896. Ed. Frederick Page. 1921.

Seven Unpublished Poems to Alice Meynell. 1922.

Selected Poems. Ed. Derek Patmore. 1931.

Selected Verse. 1934.

Mystical Poems of Nuptial Love. Ed. Terence L. Connolly.
1938.

A Selection of Poems. Ed. Derek Patmore. 1948.

Poems. Ed. Frederick Page. 1949.

*Essay on English Metrical Law: A Critical Edition with a
Commentary.* Ed. Mary Augustine Roth. 1961.

GEORGE DU MAURIER (1834–1896)

English Society at Home. 1880.

Peter Ibbetson. 1892. 2 vols.

Trilby. 1894. 3 vols.

The Martian. 1897.

Social Pictorial Satire: Reminiscences and Appreciations of English Illustrators of the Past Generation. 1898.

A Legend of Camelot: Pictures and Poems, etc. 1898.

Novels. 1947.

The Young du Maurier: A Selection from His Letters 1860–67.
Ed. Daphne du Maurier. 1951.

WILLIAM MORRIS (1834–1896)

The Defence of Guenevere and Other Poems. 1858.

The Life and Death of Jason. 1867.

The Earthly Paradise. 1868–70. 3 vols.

Grettis Saga: The Story of Grettir the Strong (translator; with
Eiríkr Magnússon). 1869.

*Volsunga Saga: The Story of the Volsungs & Niblungs with
Certain Songs from the Elder Edda* (translator; with Eiríkr
Magnússon). 1870.

Love Is Enough; or, The Freeing of Pharamond: A Morality.
1873.

Three Northern Love Stories, and Other Tales (translator; with
Eiríkr Magnússon). 1875.

The Aeneids of Virgil Done into English Verse. 1875.

*The Two Sides of the River, Hapless Love, and The First Foray
of Aristomenes.* 1876 ⟨or perhaps 1894?⟩.

The Story of Sigurd the Volsung and the Fall of the Niblungs.
1877.

Wake, London Lads! 1878.

*The Decorative Arts: Their Relation to Modern Life and
Progress: An Address Delivered before the Trades' Guild of
Learning.* 1878.

Address Delivered in the Town Hall, Birmingham. 1879.

Labour and Pleasure versus *Labour and Sorrow: An Address.*
1880.

Hopes and Fears for Art: Five Lectures Delivered in Birmingham, London, and Nottingham 1878–1881. 1882.

*A Summary of the Principles of Socialism Written for the
Democratic Federation* (with Henry Mayers Hyndman).
1884.

*Textile Fabrics: A Lecture Delivered in the Lecture Room of the
International Health Exhibition.* 1884.

*Art and Socialism: A Lecture; and Watchman: What of the
Night?* 1884.

Chants for Socialists: No. 1. The Day Is Coming. 1884.

The Voice of Toil, All for the Cause: Two Chants for Socialists.
1884.

The God of the Poor. 1884.

Chants for Socialists. 1885.

*Socialists at Play: Prologue Spoken at the Entertainment of the
Socialist League.* 1885.

*The Socialist League: Constitution and Rules Adopted at the
General Conference.* 1885.

Address to Trades' Unions (editor; with E. Belfort Bax). 1885.

Useful Work v. *Useless Toil.* 1885.

The Manifesto of the Socialist League. 1885.

For Whom Shall We Vote? Addressed to the Working-men Electors of Great Britain. 1885.

What Socialists Want. 1885.

A Short Account of the Commune of Paris (with E. Belfort Bax
and Victor Dave). 1886.

Socialism. 1886.

The Labour Question from the Socialist Standpoint. 1886,
1888 (as *True and False Society*).

The Pilgrims of Hope. 1886.

The Aims of Art. 1887.

The Tables Turned; or, Nupkins Awakened: A Socialist Interlude. 1887.

On the External Coverings of Roofs. 1887.

The Odyssey of Homer Done into English Verse. 1887. 2 vols.

*Alfred Linnell, Killed at Trafalgar Square, November 20, 1887:
A Death Song.* 1887.

Signs of Change: Seven Lectures Delivered on Various Occasions. 1888.

A Dream of John Ball and A King's Lesson. 1888.

Atalanta's Race and Other Tales from The Earthly Paradise.
Ed. Oscar Fay Adams. 1888.

*A Tale of the House of the Wolfings and All the Kindreds of the
Mark, Written in Prose and Verse.* 1889.

The Roots of the Mountains Wherein Is Told Somewhat of the Lives of the Men of Burgdale, Their Friends, Their Neighbours, Their Foemen, and Their Fellows in Arms. 1890.

Monopoly; or, How Labour Is Robbed. 1890.

News from Nowhere; or, An Epoch of Rest: Being Some Chapters from a Utopian Romance. 1890, 1891.

Statement of Principles of the Hammersmith Socialist Society. 1890.

The Socialist Ideal of Art. 1891.

The Story of the Glittering Plain Which Has Been Also Called the Land of Living Men or the Acre of the Undying. 1891.

Address on the Collection of Paintings of the English Pre-Raphaelite School. 1891.

Poems by the Way. 1891.

Under an Elm-Tree; or, Thoughts in the Country-Side. 1891.

William Morris: Poet, Artist, Socialist: A Selection from His Writings. Ed. Francis Watts Lee. 1891.

The Saga Library (translator; with Eiríkr Magnússon). 1891–95. 5 vols.

Manifesto of English Socialists (with Henry Mayers Hyndman and George Bernard Shaw). 1893.

The Reward of Labour: A Dialogue. 1893.

The Tale of King Florus and the Fair Jehane (translator). 1893.

Concerning Westminster Abbey. 1893.

Socialism: Its Growth and Outcome (with E. Belfort Bax). 1893.

Help for the Miners: The Deeper Meaning of the Struggle. 1893.

Gothic Architecture: A Lecture for the Arts and Crafts Exhibition Society. 1893.

Of the Friendship of Amis and Amile (translator). 1894.

An Address Delivered at the Distribution of Prizes to Students of the Birmingham Municipal School of Art. 1894.

The Wood beyond the World. 1894.

Letters on Socialism. 1894.

The Tale of the Emperor Constans, and of Over Sea (translator). 1894.

The Whys I Ams: Why I Am a Communist (with *Why I Am an Expropriationist* by Louisa Sara Bevington). 1894.

The Tale of Beowulf, Sometime King of the Folk of the Weder Geats (translator; with A. J. Wyatt). 1895.

Child Christopher and Goldilind the Fair. 1895. 2 vols.

Gossip about an Old House on the Upper Thames. 1895.

The Well at the World's End: A Tale. 1896. 2 vols.

Society for the Protection of Ancient Buildings. 1896.

Old French Romances (translator). 1896.

How I Became a Socialist. 1896.

Poetical Works. 1896. 10 vols.

The Water of the Wondrous Isles. 1897.

The Sundering Flood. Ed. May Morris. 1897.

A Note by William Morris on His Aims in Founding the Kelmscott Press. 1898.

Art and the Beauty of the Earth. 1898.

Some Hints on Pattern Designing. 1899.

The Ideal Book: An Address. 1899.

Architecture and History, and Westminster Abbey. 1900.

Art and Its Producers, and The Arts & Crafts of Today: Two Lectures. 1901.

Architecture, Industry and Wealth: Collected Papers. 1902.

Communism: A Lecture. 1903.

The Hollow Land and Other Contributions to the Oxford and Cambridge Magazine *(1856).* 1903.

Collected Works. Ed. May Morris. 1910–15. 24 vols.

The Revolt of Ghent. 1911.

Prose and Poetry (1856–1870). 1913.

Selections from the Prose Works. Ed. A. H. R. Ball. 1931.

Stories in Prose, Stories in Verse, Shorter Poems, Lectures and Essays. Ed. G. D. H. Cole. 1934.

On Art and Socialism: Essays and Lectures. Ed. Holbrook Jackson. 1947.

Letters to His Family and Friends. Ed. Philip Henderson. 1950.

Unpublished Letters. Ed. R. Page Arnot. 1951.

Mr. Morris on Art Matters. 1961.

Selected Writings and Designs. Ed. Asa Briggs. 1962.

Icelandic Journals. Ed. James Morris. 1969.

A Choice of William Morris's Verse. Ed. Geoffrey Grigson. 1969.

Unpublished Lectures. Ed. Eugene D. LeMire. 1969.

Early Romances in Prose and Verse. Ed. Peter Faulkner. 1973.

Political Writings. Ed. A. L. Morton. 1973.

The Ideal Book: Essays and Lectures on the Arts of the Book. Ed. William S. Peterson. 1982.

Collected Letters. Ed. Norman Kelvin. 1984– .

FRANCIS TURNER PALGRAVE (1824–1897)

The History of Normandy and of England by Sir Francis Palgrave, Volumes 3–4 (editor). 1851–64. 4 vols.

Preciosa: A Tale. 1852.

Idyls and Songs. 1854.

Essay on the First Century of Italian Engraving. 1855.

The Passionate Pilgrim; or, Eros and Anteros. 1858.

The Golden Treasury of Best Songs and Lyrical Poems in the English Language (editor). 1861.

Handbook to the Fine Art Collection in the International Exhibition of 1862. 1862.

A Selection from the Works of William Wordsworth (editor). 1865.

Songs and Sonnets by William Shakespeare (editor). 1865.

Essays on Art. 1866.

Hymns. 1867.

The Five Days' Entertainments at Wentworth Grange. 1868.

Gems of English Art of This Century. 1869.

A Short Sketch of European Painting. c. 1870.

Lyrical Poems. 1871.

A Lyme Garland: Being Verses, Mainly Written at Lyme Regis, or upon the Scenery of the Neighbourhood. 1874.

The Children's Treasury of English Song (editor). 1875. 2 parts.

Chrysomela: A Selection of Lyrical Poems of Robert Herrick (editor). 1877.

The Visions of England. 1880–81. 2 parts.

The Captive Child. c. 1880.

Essays on the Minor Poems of Spenser. c. 1882.

The Lay of the Last Minstrel and The Lady of the Lake by Sir Walter Scott (editor). 1883.

Marmion and The Lord of the Isles by Sir Walter Scott (editor). 1883.

The Poetical Works of John Keats (editor). 1884.

The Life of Jesus Christ Illustrated from the Italian Painters of the Fourteenth, Fifteenth, and Sixteenth Centuries. 1885.

Lyrical Poems by Alfred, Lord Tennyson (editor). 1885.

Ode for the Twentieth of June, 1887. 1887.

Glen Desseray and Other Poems Lyrical and Elegiac by John Campbell Shairp (editor). 1888.

Address to the Students, Delivered on the Prize-Day of the Salisbury School of Science & Art. 1889.

The Treasury of Sacred Song: Selected from the English Lyrical Poetry of Four Centuries (editor). 1889.

Amenophis and Other Poems. 1892.
Prothalamion, 6th July, 1893. 1893.
Landscape in Poetry from Homer to Tennyson. 1897.
Address on "The Genealogy of an University for Eight Hundred Years." 1897.
Francis Turner Palgrave: His Journals and Memories of His Life. Ed. Gwenllian F. Palgrave. 1899.

MARGARET OLIPHANT (1828–1897)

Passages in the Life of Mrs. Margaret Maitland. 1849. 3 vols.
Caleb Field: A Tale of the Puritans. 1851.
Merkland: A Story of Scottish Life. 1851. 3 vols.
Memoirs and Resolutions of Adam Graeme of Mossgray. 1852. 3 vols.
Katie Stewart. 1853.
Harry Muir: A Story of Scottish Life. 1853. 3 vols.
The Quiet Heart. 1854.
Magdalen Hepburn: A Story of the Scottish Reformation. 1854.
Lillieslief: Being a Concluding Series of Passages in the Life of Margaret Maitland. 1855. 3 vols.
Zaidee: A Romance. 1856. 3 vols.
The Athelings; or, The Three Gifts. 1857. 3 vols.
The Days of My Life. 1857.
Sundays. 1858.
The Laird of Nordlaw. 1858. 3 vols.
Orphans: A Chapter in Life. 1858.
Agnes Hopetoun's Schools and Holidays. 1859.
Lucy Crofton. 1860.
The House on the Moor. 1861.
The Last of the Mortimers. 1862.
The Life of Edward Irving. 1862. 3 vols.
Salem Chapel. 1863. 2 vols.
The Rector and The Doctor's Family. 1863. 3 vols.
Heart and Cross. 1863.
The Perpetual Curate. 1864. 3 vols.
Agnes. 1866. 3 vols.
Miss Marjoribanks. 1866. 3 vols.
A Son of the Soil. 1866.
Madonna Mary. 1867. 3 vols.
Francis of Assisi. 1868.
The Brownlows. 1868. 3 vols.
Historical Sketches of the Reign of George II. 1869. 2 vols.
The Minister's Wife. 1869. 3 vols.
John: A Love Story. 1870. 2 vols.
The Three Brothers. 1870. 3 vols.
Squire Arden. 1871. 3 vols.
At His Gates. 1872. 3 vols.
Memoir of Count de Montalembert: A Chapter of Recent French History. 1872. 2 vols.
Ombra. 1872. 3 vols.
May. 1873. 3 vols.
Innocent: A Tale of Modern Life. 1873. 3 vols.
A Rose in June. 1874. 2 vols.
For Love and Life. 1874. 3 vols.
The Story of Valentine and His Brother. 1875. 3 vols.
Whiteladies. 1875. 3 vols.
Dress. 1876.
Phebe Junior: A Last Chronicle of Carlingford. 1876. 3 vols.
The Curate in Charge. 1876. 2 vols.
The Makers of Florence: Dante, Giotto, Savonarola, and Their City. 1876.
Carità. 1877. 3 vols.
Dante. 1877.
Mrs. Arthur. 1877. 3 vols.

Young Musgrave. 1877. 3 vols.
The Primrose Path: A Chapter in the Annals of the Kingdom of Fife. 1878. 3 vols.
Molière (with Francis Tarver). 1879.
Within the Precincts. 1879. 3 vols.
The Two Mrs. Scudamores. 1879.
The Greatest Heiress in England. 1880. 3 vols.
A Beleaguered City. 1880.
Cervantes. 1880.
He That Will Not When He May. 1880. 3 vols.
Harry Joscelyn. 1881. 3 vols.
A Little Pilgrim in the Unseen. 1882.
In Trust: A Story of a Lady and Her Lover. 1882. 3 vols.
The Literary History of England in the End of the Eighteenth Century and Beginning of the Nineteenth Century. 1882. 3 vols.
Hester: A Story of a Contemporary Life. 1883. 3 vols.
It Was a Lover and His Lass. 1883. 3 vols.
Sheridan. 1883.
The Ladies Lindores. 1883. 3 vols.
Sir Tom. 1884. 3 vols.
The Wizard's Son. 1884. 3 vols.
Two Stories of the Seen and Unseen. 1885.
Madam. 1885. 3 vols.
Oliver's Bride: A True Story. 1886.
A Country Gentleman and His Family. 1886. 3 vols.
Effie Ogilvie: The Story of a Young Life. 1886. 2 vols.
A House Divided against Itself. 1887. 3 vols.
The Son of His Father. 1887. 3 vols.
The Makers of Venice: Doges, Conquerors, Painters, and Men of Letters. 1887.
A Memoir of the Life of John Tulloch. 1888.
The Land of Darkness, Along with Some Further Chapters in the Experience of the Little Pilgrim. 1888.
Joyce. 1888. 3 vols.
The Second Son. 1888. 3 vols.
Cousin Mary. 1888. 3 vols.
Neighbours on the Green: A Collection of Stories. 1889. 3 vols.
A Poor Gentleman. 1889. 3 vols.
Lady Car: The Sequel of a Life. 1889.
Kirsteen: A Story of a Scotch Family Seventy Years Ago. 1890.
Royal Edinburgh: Her Saints, Kings, Prophets and Poets. 1890.
The Duke's Daughter and The Fugitives. 1890. 3 vols.
Sons and Daughters. 1890.
The Mystery of Mrs. Blencarrow. 1890.
Janet. 1891. 3 vols.
Jerusalem: Its History and Hope. 1891.
Memoir of the Life of Laurence Oliphant and Alice Oliphant, His Wife. 1891.
The Railway Man and His Children. 1891. 3 vols.
Diana Trelawny: The Story of a Great Mistake. 1892. 2 vols.
The Cuckoo in the Nest. 1892. 3 vols.
The Heir Presumptive and the Heir Apparent. 1892. 3 vols.
The Marriage of Elinor. 1892. 3 vols.
The Victorian Age of English Literature (with F. R. Oliphant). 1892. 2 vols.
Lady William. 1893. 3 vols.
The Sorceress. 1893. 3 vols.
Thomas Chalmers, Preacher, Philosopher and Statesman. 1893.
A House in Bloomsbury. 1894. 2 vols.
Historical Sketches of the Reign of Queen Anne. 1894.
The Prodigals and Their Inheritance. 1894. 2 vols.

Who Was Lost and Is Found. 1894.
A Child's History of Scotland. 1895.
Sir Robert's Fortune: The Story of a Scotch Moor. 1895.
"Dies Irae": The Story of a Spirit in Prison. 1895.
The Makers of Modern Rome. 1895.
Two Strangers. 1895.
Jeanne D'Arc: Her Life and Death. 1896.
Old Mr. Tredgold. 1896.
The Two Marys. 1896.
The Unjust Steward; or, The Minister's Debt. 1896.
Annals of a Publishing House: William Blackwood and His Sons. 1897. 2 vols.
The Lady's Walk. 1897.
The Sisters Brontë. 1897.
The Ways of Life: Two Stories. 1897.
A Widow's Tale and Other Stories. 1898.
That Little Cutty; Dr. Barrère; Isabel Dysart. 1898.
Autobiography and Letters. Ed. Mrs. Harry Coghill. 1899.
Queen Victoria: A Personal Sketch. 1900.
Stories of the Seen and the Unseen. 1902.

HENRY GEORGE (1839–1897)

The Press: Should It Be Impersonal? 1871.
The Subsidy Question and the Democratic Party. 1871.
Our Land and Land Policy, National and State. 1871.
The Question before the People: What Is the Real Issue in the Presidential Campaign? 1876.
The American Republic: Its Dangers and Its Possibilities. 1877.
To the Voters of San Francisco. 1878.
Progress and Poverty: An Inquiry into the Cause of Industrial Depressions, and of Increase of Want with Increase of Wealth; the Remedy. 1879.
The Irish Land Question. 1881.
An American Opinion of the English Government in Ireland. c. 1882.
Social Problems. 1883.
Scotland and Scotsmen. 1884.
Moses. c. 1884.
Henry George in Canada. 1884.
Why Work Is Scarce, Wages Low, and Labor Restless. 1885.
The Crime of Poverty. 1885.
Letter to James P. Archibald concerning the Proposed Nomination of Henry George for Mayor of New York. 1886.
Protection or Free Trade: An Examination of the Tariff Question with Especial Regard to the Interests of Labor. 1886.
Justice the Object; Taxation the Means. 1887.
"Thou Shalt Not Steal." 1887.
We Want the Earth!! Why We Think We Ought to Have It and How We Propose to Get It. 1887.
The Democratic Principle. 1889.
First Principles. 1889.
The Functions of Government. 1889.
Henry George in London and Liverpool. 1889.
The Single Tax v. Social Democracy: Which Will Most Benefit the People? (with H. M. Hyndman). 1889.
"Thy Kingdom Come." 1889.
The Land for the People. c. 1889.
The "Single Tax" Faith. c. 1889.
An Address before the Ministers of San Francisco at Hall of Young Men's Christian Association. 1890.
Land and People. c. 1890.
Taxing Land Values. c. 1890.
The Condition of Labor: An Open Letter to Pope Leo XIII. 1891.
Incidence of the Single Tax. 1891.

A Perplexed Philosopher: Being an Examination of Mr. Herbert Spencer's Various Utterances on the Land Question, with Some Incidental Reference to His Synthetic Philosophy. 1892.
The Canons of Taxation. 1893.
Address before the New England Tariff Reform League. 1893.
Speech at the Labor Meeting, Cooper Union, New York. 1894.
Unemployed Labor. 1894.
Beneath the Silver Question. 1894.
Causes of the Business Depression. 1894.
The Heart of the Social Problem. 1894.
Peace by Standing Army. 1896.
The Science of Political Economy. 1897.
Speech Accepting the Nomination of the Democracy of Thomas Jefferson. 1897.
Writings (Memorial Edition). Ed. Henry George, Jr. 1898–1901. 10 vols.
Our Land and Land Policy: Speeches, Lectures, and Miscellaneous Writings. Ed. Henry George, Jr. 1901.
Complete Works (Fels Fund Library Edition). 1906–11. 10 vols.
Gems from Henry George. Ed. A. C. Auchmuty. 1908.

WILLIAM EWART GLADSTONE (1809–1898)

Speech in the House of Commons on Colonial Slavery. 1833.
The State in Its Relation with the Church. 1838, 1841 (2 vols.).
Speech Delivered in the House of Commons on the Motion of Sir George Strickland, for the Abolition of the Negro Apprenticeship. 1838.
Ecclesiastical Duties and Revenues. 1840.
Church Principles Considered in Their Results. 1840.
Inaugural Address, Delivered at the Opening of the Collegiate Institution, Liverpool. 1843.
Speech on the Second Reading of the Dissenters' Chapels Bill. 1844.
Substance of a Speech for the Second Reading of the Maynooth College Bill. 1845.
A Manual of Prayers from the Liturgy, Arranged for Family Use (editor). 1845.
Remarks upon Recent Commercial Legislation. 1845.
Substance of a Speech on the Motion of Lord John Russell for a Committee of the Whole House, with a View to the Removal of the Remaining Jewish Disabilities. 1848.
Substance of a Speech on the Affairs of Greece, and the Foreign Policy of the Administration. 1850.
Speech on the Commission of Inquiry into the State of the Universities of Oxford and Cambridge. 1850.
Report of the Special Committee Appointed by the National Assembly of France (translator). 1850.
Remarks on the Royal Supremacy, as It Is Defined by Reason, History, and the Constitution. 1850.
Ecclesiastical Titles Assumption Bill: Speech in the House of Commons on the Motion That the Bill Be Read a Second Time. 1851.
A Letter to the Earl of Aberdeen on the State Prosecutions of the Neapolitan Government. 1851.
A Second Letter to the Earl of Aberdeen, on the State Prosecutions of the Neapolitan Government. 1851.
The Roman State from 1815 to 1850 by Luigi Carlo Farini, Volumes 1–3 (translator). 1851–54.
A Letter to W. Skinner, D.D., Bishop of Aberdeen, on the Functions of Laymen in the Church. 1852.
Speech on the Second Reading of the New Zealand Constitution Bill. 1852.

Speech of the Chancellor of the Exchequer on the Financial State and Prospects of the Country. 1853.

The Advantages of Education. 1853.

The Financial Budget for 1854. 1854.

"Our Colonies." 1855.

Speech on the War and the Negotiations, in the House of Commons. 1855.

War in China. 1857.

Studies on Homer and the Homeric Age. 1858. 3 vols.

Speech of the Chancellor of the Exchequer on the Finance of the Year and the Treaty of Commerce with France, Delivered in the House of Commons. 1860.

Inaugural Address Delivered before the University of Edinburgh. 1860.

Copy of a Letter from the Chancellor of the Exchequer Addressed to the Governor and Deputy-Governor of the Bank of England. 1861.

Translations (with George William, Lord Lyttelton). 1861.

In Morte di Napoleone: Ode by Alessandro Manzoni (with Eng. tr. by Gladstone). 1861.

Mechanics' Institutes: Their Advantages, and How to Improve Them. 1862.

Address and Speeches Delivered at Manchester (before the Mechanics' Institutes). 1862.

Speech in Committee on the Customs and Inland Revenue Bill, Clause 3, Relating to the Exemption of Charities from Income-Tax. 1863.

Wedgwood: An Address. 1863.

The Financial Statements of 1853, 1860–1863; to Which Are Added, a Speech on Tax-Bills, 1861, and on Charities, 1863. 1863.

The Financial Statement of 1864. 1864.

Speech on the Bill for the Extension of the Suffrage in Towns. 1864.

Correspondence between Captain R. Sprye and W. E. Gladstone on the Commercial Opening of the Shan States, and Western Inland China, by Railway Direct from Rangoon. 1865.

Address on the Place of Ancient Greece in the Providential Order of the World, Delivered before the University of Edinburgh. 1865.

The Financial Statement of 1865. 1865.

Speeches and Address Delivered at the Election of 1865. 1865.

Speeches on Parliamentary Reform in 1866. 1866.

A Chapter of Autobiography. 1868.

Speeches Delivered at Warrington, Ormskirk, Liverpool, Southport, Newton, Leigh, and Wigan, in October, 1868. 1868.

"Ecce Homo." 1868.

Juventus Mundi: The Gods and Men of the Heroic Age. 1869.

The Irish Church: A Speech Delivered in the House of Commons. 1869.

Marriage with a Deceased Wife's Sister: Speech in the House of Commons in Support of Mr. Thomas Chambers' Marriage Bill. 1870.

A Correct Report of the Speech on Proposing the Irish Land Bill. 1870.

A Speech Delivered in the House of Commons on the Second Reading of the Irish Land Bill. 1870.

Defence of the Church in Wales. 1870.

Speeches on Great Questions of the Day. 1870.

A Corrected Report of the Speech at Greenwich. 1871.

Speech on Moving for Leave to Bring in a Bill Relating to University Education in Ireland. 1873.

The Ministerial Crisis: Speeches (with Benjamin Disraeli). 1873.

Speech in the House of Commons on Mr. Miall's Motion for the Disestablishment and Disendowment of the Church. 1873.

Address Delivered at the Distribution of Prizes in the Liverpool Collegiate Institution. 1873.

Homer's Place in History. 1874.

Speech on the Second Reading of the Church Patronage (Scotland) Bill, in the House of Commons. 1874.

The Vatican Decrees in Their Bearing on Civil Allegiance: A Political Expostulation. 1874.

Speeches of Pope Pius IX. 1875.

Vaticanism: An Answer to Replies and Reproofs. 1875.

Rome and the Newest Fashions in Religion: Three Tracts—The Vatican Decrees; Vaticanism; Speeches of the Pope. 1875.

Italy and Her Church. 1875.

Homeric Synchronism: An Enquiry into the Time and Place of Homer. 1876.

Bulgarian Horrors and the Question of the East. 1876.

A Speech Delivered at Blackheath, Together with Letters, on the Question of the East. 1876.

The Church of England and Ritualism. 1876.

Gladstone on Macleod and Macaulay. 1876.

Lessons in Massacre; or, The Conduct of the Turkish Government in and about Bulgaria since May, 1876. 1877.

The Eastern Question Association: Mr. Gladstone's Resolutions and Speech on the Eastern Question in the House of Commons. 1877.

The Sclavonic Provinces of the Ottoman Empire. 1877.

Homer. 1878.

The Paths of Honour and of Shame. 1878.

England's Mission. 1878.

Advice to Operatives. 1878.

Speech at the Complimentary Dinner Given to George Smith, Esq., LL.D., Author of The Life of Alexander Duff. 1879.

Speech at Wellington College. 1879.

The Approaching Election: Speeches Delivered in Midlothian, during November 1879. 1879.

On Epithets of Movement in Homer. 1879.

Dean Hook: An Address Delivered at Hawarden. 1879.

Inaugural Address to the Students of the University of Glasgow. 1879.

The Country and the Government. 1879.

Political Speeches in Scotland, November and December, 1879. 1879.

Gleanings of Past Years 1843–1878. 1879. 7 vols.

Political Speeches in Scotland, March and April 1880. 1880.

The Might of Right: From the Writings. Ed. E. E. Brown. 1880.

Liberal and Tory Finance: A Speech Delivered in the Corn Exchange, Edinburgh. 1880.

The Irish Land Bill. 1881.

The Irish Land Bill (Second Reading). 1881.

Speeches Delivered at Leeds on 1. Land and "Fair Trade"; 2. Ireland; 3. Free Trade; 4. Foreign and Colonial Policy. 1881.

The Conservative Legacy, 1880, Liberal Work, 1880–1883: Speech at the Inaugural Banquet, National Liberal Club. 1883.

National Expenditure: Speech in the House of Commons. 1883.

Parliamentary Oaths: Speech on the Second Reading of the Parliamentary Oaths Act Amendment Bill. 1883.

Egypt and the Soudan: Speech Delivered in the House of Commons. 1884.

Speech in the Corn Exchange, Edinburgh. 1884.

Political Speeches Delivered in August and September, 1884. 1884.

Aggression on Egypt and Freedom in the East. 1884.

Address to the Electors of Midlothian. 1885.

Soudan and Afghanistan: The Vote of Credit: Speech in the House of Commons. 1885.

Political Speeches Delivered in November, 1885. 1885.

Speeches. Ed. Henry W. Lucy. 1885.

The Irish Question: I. History of an Idea; II. Lessons of the Election. 1886.

The Government of Ireland Bill: Speech Delivered in the House of Commons. 1886.

The Government of Ireland Bill: Reply Delivered in the House of Commons. 1886.

Sale and Purchase of Land (Ireland) Bill: Speech Delivered in the House of Commons. 1886.

Home Rule Manifesto: Address to the Electors of Midlothian. 1886.

The Government of Ireland Bill: Speech Delivered on Moving the Second Reading of the Bill. 1886.

The Government of Ireland: Mr. Gladstone's Appeal to the Country: Address to the Electors of Midlothian. 1886.

Speech on the Political Situation (in Ireland) in Edinburgh. 1886.

Speeches on the Irish Question in 1886. Ed. P. W. Clayton. 1886.

The Political Situation at the Close of the Session, 1887: Speech Delivered at the Memorial Hall, Farringdon Street, London. 1887.

Gladstone on the New "Locksley Hall." 1887.

The Liberal Programme for Great Britain and Ireland. 1887.

Coercion in Ireland: Speech in the House of Commons. 1888.

Robert Elsmere and the Battle of Belief. 1888.

Channel Tunnel: Great Speech in the House of Commons. 1888.

The Treatment of the Irish Members and the Irish Political Prisoners: A Speech at Hawarden Castle, Supplemented by a Part of the Speech at Wrexham on the Same Subject. 1888.

The Workman and His Opportunities. 1889.

The Right Hon. W. E. Gladstone, M.P., on Cottage Gardens and Fruit Culture. 1889.

The Parnell Commission and the Vote of Censure upon the Irish Members: A Speech Delivered at the National Liberal Club. 1890.

Landmarks of Homeric Study, Together with an Essay on the Points of Contact between the Assyrian Tablets and the Homeric Text. 1890.

On Books and the Housing of Them. 1890.

The Impregnable Rock of Holy Scripture. 1890.

Mr. Gladstone's Sudden Reversal of Polarity (with John Tyndall). 1890.

The Duel: Free Trade—The Right Hon. W. E. Gladstone; Protection—The Hon. J. G. Blaine. 1890.

The Religious Disabilities Bill: A Speech Delivered in Moving the Second Reading of the Bill. 1891.

The Tory Small Holdings Bill: Two Speeches in the House of Commons. 1892.

Mr. Gladstone on Ulster: A Reply to the Belfast Convention: Speech at the House of the Rev. J. Guinness Rogers. 1892.

Female Suffrage: A Letter to Samuel Smith, M.P. 1892.

Archaic Greece and the East. 1892.

Special Aspects of the Irish Question: A Series of Reflections in and since 1886. 1892.

Speeches and Public Addresses. Eds. A. W. Hutton and H. J. Cohen. 1892–94. 2 vols. only.

An Academic Sketch Delivered in the Sheldonian Theatre. 1892.

The Home Rule Bill: Speech in the House of Commons. 1893.

The Life of Mr. Gladstone Told by Himself in Speeches and Public Letters. Ed. H. J. Leech. 1893.

The Odes of Horace (translator). 1894.

Thoughts from the Writings and Speeches. Ed. G. Barnett Smith. 1894.

The Psalter, with a Concordance and Other Auxiliary Matter (translator). 1895.

An Introduction to the People's Bible History. 1895.

The Armenian Question. 1895.

On the Condition of Man in a Future Life. 1896. 3 parts.

Works of Bishop Butler (editor). 1896. 2 vols.

Studies Subsidiary to the Works of Bishop Butler. 1896.

Later Gleanings: A New Series of Gleanings of Past Years, Theological and Ecclesiastical. 1897.

The Eastern Crisis: A Letter to the Duke of Westminster. 1897.

The Gladstone Birthday Book. 1897.

Arthur Henry Hallam. 1898.

Correspondence on Church and Religion. Ed. D. C. Lathbury. 1910. 2 vols.

Speeches. 1916.

Course of Commercial Policy at Home and Abroad. 1919.

Gladstone and Palmerston: Being the Correspondence of Lord Palmerston with Mr. Gladstone 1851–1865. Ed. Philip Guedalla. 1928.

The Queen and Mr. Gladstone. Ed. Philip Guedalla. 1933. 2 vols.

Gladstone to His Wife. Ed. A. Tilney Bassett. 1936.

Two Hymns by Augustus M. Toplady and J. M. Neale (translated into Latin). 1951.

The Political Correspondence of Mr. Gladstone and Lord Granville 1868–1886. Ed. Agatha Ramm. 1952–62. 4 vols.

Gladstone-Gordon Correspondence 1851–1896: Selections from the Private Correspondence of a British Prime Minister and a Colonial Governor. Ed. Paul Knaplund. 1961.

The Gladstone Diaries. Eds. M. R. D. Foot and H. C. G. Matthew. 1968– .

The Prime Ministers' Papers: W. E. Gladstone. Eds. John Brooke and Mary Sorensen. 1971–81. 4 vols.

LEWIS CARROLL (C. L. DODGSON) (1832–1898)

[*The Fifth Book of Euclid Treated Algebraically.* 1858.]

Rules for Court Circular: (A New Game of Cards for Two or More Players). 1860.

A Syllabus of Plane Algebraical Geometry: Part I. 1860.

Notes on the First Two Books of Euclid. 1860.

The Formulae of Plane Trigonometry. 1861.

Notes on the First Part of Algebra. 1861.

Endowment of the Greek Professorship. 1861.

An Index to In Memoriam. 1862.

General List of (Mathematical) Subjects and Cycle for Working Examples. 1863.

The Enunciations of the Propositions and Corollaries, Together with Questions on the Definitions, Postulates, Axioms, &c. in Euclid, Books I. and II. 1863.

Croquet Castles: For Five Players. 1863.

Examination Statute. 1864.

The New Examination Statute. 1864.

A Guide to the Mathematical Student in Reading, Reviewing, and Working Examples: Part I. 1864.

American Telegrams. 1865.
The New Method of Evaluation, as Applied to π. 1865.
The Dynamics of a Particle. 1865.
Alice's Adventures in Wonderland. 1865.
⟨*Symbols and Abbreviations for Euclid.*⟩ 1866. Lost.
Castle-Croquet: For Four Players. 1866.
The Elections to the Hebdomadal Council. 1866.
Condensation of Determinants. 1866.
Enigma. 1866.
Explication of the Enigma. 1866.
The Deserted Parks. 1867.
An Elementary Treatise on Determinants. 1867.
The Offer of the Clarendon Trustees. 1868.
The Fifth Book of Euclid Treated Algebraically. 1868.
Algebraical Formulae for Responsions. 1868.
Woodstock Election. 1868.
Phantasmagoria and Other Poems. 1869.
The Guildford Gazette Extraordinary. 1869.
Algebraical Formulae and Rules. 1870.
Arithmetical Formulae and Rules. 1870. Lost.
The Songs from Alice's Adventures in Wonderland. 1870.
Suggestions for Committee to Consider the Expediency of Reconstituting Senior Studentships at Christ Church. 1871.
To All Child-Readers of Alice's Adventures in Wonderland. 1871.
Through the Looking-Glass, and What Alice Found There. 1871.
The New Belfry of Christ Church, Oxford. 1872.
Number of Propositions in Euclid. 1872. Lost.
The Enunciations of Euclid I–VI. 1873.
The Vision of the Three T's. 1873.
Objections, Submitted to the Governing Body of Christ Church, Oxford, against Certain Proposed Alterations in the Great Quadrangle. 1873.
A Discussion of the Various Methods of Procedure in Conducting Elections. 1873.
The Blank Cheque: A Fable. 1874.
Notes by an Oxford Chiel. 1874.
Suggestions as to the Best Method of Taking Votes, Where More Than Two Issues Are to Be Voted On. 1874.
Euclid, Book V: Proved Algebraically. 1874.
Some Popular Fallacies about Vivisection. 1875.
Euclid: Books I, II (editor). 1875.
⟨*Song for Puss in Boots.*⟩ 1876. Lost.
Professorship of Comparative Philology. 1876.
A Method of Taking Votes on More Than Two Issues. 1876.
The Hunting of the Snark: An Agony in Eight Fits. 1876.
An Easter Greeting to Every Child Who Loves Alice. 1876.
Letter and Questions to Hospitals. 1876. Lost.
Fame's Penny-Trumpet. 1876.
Responsions: Hilary Term, 1877. 1877.
A Charade. 1878.
Word-Links: A Game for Two Players, or a Round Game. 1878.
Euclid and His Modern Rivals. 1879.
Doublets: A Word-Puzzle. 1879.
A Game for Two Players. 1879.
Lanrick: A Game for Two Players. 1881.
On Catching Cold. 1881.
Dreamland. 1882.
A Letter to Friends and to Members of the Dramatic Profession. 1882.
An Analysis of the Responsions Lists. 1882.
Mischmasch. 1882.

Lawn Tennis Tournaments: The True Method of Assigning Prizes. 1883.
Rules for Reckoning Postage. 1883. Lost.
Rhyme? and Reason? 1883.
Christmas Greetings: From a Fairy to a Child. 1884.
Twelve Months in a Curatorship. 1884.
Supplement to Twelve Months in a Curatorship. 1884.
Postscript ⟨*to* Twelve Months in a Curatorship⟩. 1884.
The Principles of Parliamentary Representation. 1884.
The Profits of Authorship. 1884.
The Principles of Parliamentary Representation: Supplement. 1885.
The Principles of Parliamentary Representation: Postscript to Supplement. 1885.
Letter and Prospectus. 1885.
The Proposed Procuratorial Cycle. 1885.
Postscript: Addressed to Mathematicians Only. 1885.
Suggestions as to the Election of Proctors. 1885.
A Tangled Tale. 1885.
Three Years in a Curatorship. 1886.
Remarks on the Report of the Finance Committee. 1886. Lost.
Remarks on Mr. Sampson's Proposal. 1886.
Observations on Mr. Sampson's New Proposal. 1886.
Suggestions as to the Election of Proctors. 1886.
The Game of Logic. 1886.
Alice's Adventures under Ground. 1886.
Questions in Logic. 1887.
To My Child-Friend. 1888.
Memoria Technica. 1888.
Curiosa Mathematica, Part I: A New Theory of Parallels. 1888.
The Nursery Alice. 1889.
Sylvie and Bruno. 1889.
Circular Billiards, for Two Players. 1890.
The Strange Circular. 1890.
Eight or Nine Wise Words about Letter-Writing. 1890.
A Postal Problem. 1891.
A Postal Problem: Supplement. 1891.
⟨*A Circular Addressed to the Governing Body of Christ Church, Oxford.*⟩ 1891. Lost.
⟨*A Circular about Resignation of Curatorship.*⟩ 1892. Lost.
Curiosissima Curatoria. 1892.
Syzygies and Lanrick: A Word-Puzzle and a Game for Two Players. 1893.
Curiosa Mathematica, Part II: Pillow-Problems. 1893.
Sylvie and Bruno Concluded. 1893.
A Disputed Point in Logic. 1894.
A Theorem in Logic. 1894.
A Logical Puzzle. 1894.
Logical Nomenclature: Desiderata. 1895.
Symbolic Logic, Part I: Elementary. 1896.
Resident Women-Students. 1896.
Three Sunsets and Other Poems. 1898.
The Lewis Carroll Picture Book. Ed. Stuart Dodgson Collingwood. 1899.
Freeding the Mind. Ed. William H. Draper. 1907.
Six Letters. Ed. Wilfred Partington. 1924.
Some Rare Carrolliana. Ed. Sidney Herbert Williams. 1924.
Bruno's Revenge. Ed. John Drinkwater. 1924.
Novelty and Romancement. 1925.
Further Nonsense Verse and Prose. Ed. Langford Reed. 1926.
A Tour in 1867 ⟨The Russian Journal⟩. 1928.
Collected Verse. Ed. John Francis McDermott. 1929.
A Christmas Carroll. 1930.
To M. A. B. 1931.

The Rectory Umbrella and Mischmasch. Ed. Florence Milner. 1932.
Collected Verse. 1932.
For the Train: Five Poems and a Letter. Ed. Hugh J. Schoenfield. 1932.
A Selection from the Letters of Lewis Carroll to His Child-Friends, Together with Eight or Nine Wise Words about Letter-Writing. Ed. Evelyn M. Hatch. 1933.
The Russian Journal and Other Selections. Ed. John Francis McDermott. 1935.
Complete Works. 1936.
How the Boots Got Left Behind. 1943.
Diaries. Ed. Roger Lancelyn Green. 1953. 2 vols.
Useful and Instructive Poetry. Ed. Derek Hudson. 1954.
Mathematical Recreations of Lewis Carroll: Symbolic Logic and The Game of Logic. 1958. 2 vols.
Humorous Verse. 1960.
The Annotated Alice. Ed. Martin Gardner. 1960.
The Annotated Snark. Ed. Martin Gardner. 1962.
Works. Ed. Roger Lancelyn Green. 1965.
Lewis Carroll on Education. Eds. John Fleming and Joan Fleming. 1972.
Photos and Letters to His Child Friends. Ed. Guido Almansi. 1975.
The Wasp in a Wig: A "Suppressed" Episode of Through the Looking-Glass and What Alice Found There. Ed. Edward Guiliano. 1977.
Lewis Carroll's Photographs of Nude Children. Ed. Morton N. Cohen. 1978.
Letters. Eds. Martin N. Cohen and Roger Lancelyn Green. 1979. 2 vols.
Lewis Carroll: Victorian Photographer. Ed. Helmut Gernsheim. 1980.
Complete Illustrated Works. Ed. Edward Guiliano. 1982.
Lewis Carroll. Eds. Cornel Capa et al. 1984.
Logic and Tea: The Letters of Charles L. Dodgson to Mrs. Emily Rowell and Her Daughters Ethel and Hattie. Eds. Jan Susine and F. Brewer. 1984.

WILLIAM BLACK (1841–1898)

James Merle: An Autobiography. 1864.
Love or Marriage? 1868. 3 vols.
In Silk Attire. 1869. 3 vols.
Kilmeny. 1870. 3 vols.
The Monarch of Mincing-Lane. 1871. 3 vols.
A Daughter of Heth. 1871. 3 vols.
Mr. Pisistratus Brown, M.P., in the Highlands. 1871.
The Strange Adventures of a Phaeton. 1872. 2 vols.
A Princess of Thule. 1874. 3 vols.
The Maid of Killeena and Other Stories. 1874.
Three Feathers. 1875. 3 vols.
Madcap Violet. 1876. 3 vols.
Lady Silverdale's Sweetheart and Other Stories. 1876.
Green Pastures and Piccadilly. 1877. 3 vols.
Macleod of Dare. 1878. 3 vols.
Goldsmith. 1878.
White Wings: A Yachting Romance. 1880. 3 vols.
Sunrise: A Story of These Times. 1880–81. 15 parts.
The Beautiful Wretch; The Four Macnicols; The Pupil of Aurelius. 1881. 3 vols.
Yolande: The Story of a Daughter. 1883. 3 vols.
Adventures in Thule: Three Stories of Boys. 1883.
Shandon Bells. 1883. 3 vols.
Judith Shakespeare: A Romance. 1884. 3 vols.
Works. 1884. 15 vols.

White Heather. 1885. 3 vols.
The Wise Woman of Inverness and Other Miscellanies. 1885.
Sabine Zembra. 1887. 3 vols.
In Far Lochaber. 1888. 3 vols.
The Strange Adventures of a House-Boat. 1888. 3 vols.
The Penance of John Logan and Two Other Tales. 1889.
Nanciebel: A Tale of Stratford-on-Avon. 1889.
The New Prince Fortunatus. 1890. 3 vols.
Stand Fast, Craig-Royston! 1890. 3 vols.
Donald Ross of Heimra. 1891. 3 vols.
Wolfenburg. 1892. 3 vols.
The Magic Ink and Other Tales. 1892.
Novels. 1892–98. 28 vols.
The Handsome Humes. 1893. 3 vols.
Highland Cousins. 1894. 3 vols.
Briseis. 1896.
Wild Eelin: Her Escapades, Adventures, and Bitter Sorrows. 1898.
With the Eyes of Youth and Other Sketches. 1903.

EDWARD BELLAMY (1850–1898)

Six to One: A Nantucket Idyl. 1878.
Dr. Heidenhoff's Process. 1880.
Miss Ludington's Sister: A Romance of Immortality. 1884.
Looking Backward 2000–1887. 1888.
Plutocracy or Nationalism: Which? c. 1889.
Principles and Purposes of Nationalism: Address at Trement Temple, Boston. c. 1889.
State Management of the Liquor Traffic. c. 1892.
How to Employ the Unemployed in Mutual Maintenance. c. 1893.
Equality. 1897.
The Blindman's World and Other Stories. 1898.
The Duke of Stockbridge: A Romance of Shay's Rebellion. 1900.
Edward Bellamy Speaks Again! Articles, Public Addresses, Letters. 1937.
Talks on Nationalism. 1938.
The Religion of Solidarity. 1940.
Selected Writings on Religion and Society. Ed. Joseph Schiffman. 1955.

HAROLD FREDERIC (1856–1898)

Seth's Brother's Wife: A Study of Life in the Greater New York. 1887.
The Lawton Girl. 1890.
In the Valley. 1890.
The Young Emperor William II of Germany: A Study in Character Development on a Throne. 1891.
The Return of the O'Mahony. 1892.
The New Exodus: A Study of Israel in Russia. 1892.
The Copperhead. 1893.
Marsena and Other Stories of the Wartime. 1894.
The Damnation of Theron Ware. 1896.
Mrs. Albert Grundy: Observations in Philistia. 1896.
March Hares. 1896.
In the Sixties. 1897.
The Deserter and Other Stories: A Book of Two Wars. 1898.
Gloria Mundi. 1898.
The Market-Place. 1899.
Stories of York State. Ed. Thomas F. O'Donnell. 1966.
The Harold Frederic Edition. Eds. Stanton Garner et al. 1977– .

ROBERT G. INGERSOLL (1833–1899)

An Oration at the Unveiling of a Statue of Humboldt. 1869.
Why Col. Ingersoll Opposes the Democrats. c. 1870.
An Oration on the Life and Services of Thomas Paine. 1871.
An Oration on the Gods. 1872.
Heretics and Heresies. 1874.
The Gods and Other Lectures. 1874.
The Meaning of the Declaration. 1876.
Arraignment of the Church ⟨Individuality⟩. 1876.
A Vindication of Thomas Paine. 1877.
Liberty of Man, Woman and Child. 1877.
"Hell." 1878.
Hard Times and the Way Out. 1878.
The Ghosts. 1878.
The Old and the New. 1878.
The Ghosts and Other Lectures. 1878.
Response to the Toast: Our Volunteer Soldiers. 1879.
Some Mistakes of Moses. 1879.
Ingersoll's Review of His Reviewers. 1879.
"Skulls." 1880.
What Must We Do to Be Saved? 1880.
Free Speech and an Honest Ballot. 1880.
Complete Lectures. 1880.
Farm Life in America. c. 1880.
The Christian Religion: An Enquiry. 1881.
Examination of Paymaster John H. Stevenson. 1881.
Three Great Speeches. Ed. J.B. McClure. 1881.
The Great Infidels. c. 1881.
American Secular Lectures. 1882. 12 parts.
Ingersollia: Gems of Thought from the Lectures, Speeches, and Conversations. 1882.
Six Interviews on Six Sermons by the Rev. T. De Witt Talmadge. 1882.
Memorial Oration. 1882.
Civil Rights Speech. 1883.
Lectures. 1883.
Ingersoll Catechised: His Answers to a Number of Vital Questions Propounded by the Editor of the San Franciscan. 1884.
Orthodoxy ⟨The Dying Creed⟩. 1884.
Col. Ingersoll on the Oath Question. 1884.
Prose-Poems and Selections from the Writings and Sayings. 1884.
Real Blasphemy. 1885.
Wit, Wisdom, and Eloquence of Col. R.G. Ingersoll. 1885.
Great Speeches. 1885.
The Clergy and Common Sense ⟨To the Brooklyn Divines⟩. c. 1885.
Myth and Miracle. 1886.
Opening Speech to the Jury. 1886.
Live Topics. 1886.
A Lay Sermon Delivered before the Tenth Annual Congress of the American Secular Union. 1886.
The Stage and the Pulpit: An Interview. 1887.
Faith and Fact: A Letter to the Rev. Henry M. Field. 1887.
Ingersoll and McGlynn. 1887.
God and Man: Second Letter to the Rev. Henry M. Field. 1888.
The Field-Ingersoll Discussion: Faith or Agnosticism? (with Henry Martyn Field). 1888.
Defence of Free Thought: Being His Five Hours' Speech to the Jury at the Trial for Blasphemy of C. B. Reynolds. 1888.
The Household of Faith. 1888.
Tribute to Richard H. Whiting. 1888.

A Tribute to Roscoe Conkling. 1888.
Rome or Reason (with Cardinal Manning). 1888.
Repairing the Idols: Col. Ingersoll on Mrs. Humphry Ward's Famous Novel Robert Elsmere. 1888.
Reply to Gladstone. 1888.
The Limitations of Toleration (with Frederic R. Coudert and Stewart L. Woodford). 1889.
A Wooden God. 1889.
Do I Blaspheme? 1889.
Flight of the Shadows. c. 188-.
Personal Deism Denied. c. 188-.
A Review of the Sugar Question. c. 188-.
Liberty in Literature: Testimonial to Walt Whitman. 1890.
Crimes against Criminals. 1890.
Love the Redeemer, with Reference to Count Tolstoï's Kreutzer Sonata, *and His Views on Christianity, Love, the Family, and Civilisation.* 1890.
Why Am I an Agnostic? 1890.
Art and Morality. 1890.
Advice to Parents: Keep Children out of Church and Sunday School. 1890.
Bible Idolatry. c. 1890.
Christ and Miracles ⟨Professor Huxley and Agnosticism⟩. 1891.
Creeds and Spirituality. 1891.
Shakespeare. 1891.
Difficulties of Belief. 1892.
Oration on Voltaire. 1892.
The Three Philanthropists. 1892.
The Great Ingersoll Controversy. 1892.
Ernest Renan and Jesus Christ. 1892.
Preface to a Speech Delivered to Philip G. Peabody at the Annual Meeting of the Victoria Street Antivivisection Society. 1893.
Abraham Lincoln. 1893.
An Open Letter to Indianapolis Clergymen. 1893.
About the Holy Bible. 1894.
Is Suicide a Sin? 1894.
Superstition. 1894.
Declaration of Independence and A Vision of War. 1895.
Patriotic Addresses. 1895.
Man and Machine ⟨Some Interrogation Points⟩. 1895.
Which Way? 1895.
Some Reasons Why. 1895.
What Is Religion? 1895.
The Foundations of Faith. 1896.
Lectures. 1896. 2 vols.
A Thanksgiving Sermon. 1897.
The Truth. 1897.
Why I Am an Agnostic. 1897.
Essays and Criticisms. 1897.
The House of Death: Being Funeral Orations and Addresses. 1897.
A Look Backward and a Prophecy. 1898.
A Few Reasons for Doubting the Inspiration of the Bible. 1899.
The Devil: If the Devil Should Die, Would God Make Another? 1899.
Faith That Surely Wanes: Vanishing Belief and Influence of Christianity. 1899.
Progress and What Is Religion? 1899.
The Declaration of the Free. 1899.
Lectures. 1899.
Address before the Unitarian Club of New York. c. 1899.
God in the Constitution. c. 1899.
Inaugural Address. c. 1899.
The Creed of Science. c. 1899.

Robert Burns. c. 1899.

What Would You Substitute for the Bible as a Moral Guide?
　c. 1899.

Tribute to His Brother. c. 1899.

*The Religion of Abraham Lincoln: Correspondence between
　General Charles H. T. Collis and Colonel Robert G.
　Ingersoll.* 1900.

Works (Dresden Edition). 1900. 12 vols.

Gold Speech. c. 1903.

Life. c. 1903.

Love. c. 1903.

Famous Speeches Complete. 1906.

The Philosophy of Ingersoll. Ed. Vere Goldthwaite. 1906.

Toward Humanity. Ed. Anne Montgomerie Traubel. 1908.

Lectures and Essays. 1911–12. 3 vols.

*Fifty Great Selections, Lectures, Tributes, After-Dinner
　Speeches, and Essays.* 1920.

44 Complete Lectures. 1924.

Selections from Ingersoll. Ed. Ram Gopal. 1931.

The Liberty of Man and Other Essays. 1941.

Greatest Lectures. 1944.

Letters. Ed. Eva Ingersoll Wakefield. 1951.

JOHN RUSKIN (1819–1900)

Salsette and Elephanta. 1839.

Modern Painters. 1843 [Volume 1]; 1846 [Volume 2]; 1856
　[Volumes 3–4]; 1860 [Volume 5].

The Seven Lamps of Architecture. 1849.

Poems. 1850.

*The King of the Golden River; or, The Black Brothers: A Legend
　of Stiria.* 1851.

The Stones of Venice. 1851–53. 3 vols.

Notes on the Construction of Sheepfolds. 1851.

Pre-Raphaelitism. 1851.

Giotto and His Works in Padua. 1853–60. 3 parts.

Lectures on Architecture and Painting. 1854.

*The Opening of the Crystal Palace Considered in Some of Its
　Relations to the Prospects of Art.* 1854.

*Notes on Some of the Principal Pictures Exhibited in the Rooms
　of the Royal Academy.* 1855–75. 6 nos.

The Harbours of England. 1856.

Notes on the Turner Gallery at Marlborough House. 1856.

Catalogue of the Turner Sketches in the National Gallery. 1857.

The Elements of Drawing. 1857.

The Political Economy of Art. 1857.

Cambridge School of Art: Mr. Ruskin's Inaugural Address.
　1858.

The Oxford Museum (with Henry Acland). 1859.

The Unity of Art. 1859.

The Two Paths. 1859.

The Elements of Perspective. 1859.

Collected Works. 1861–63. 15 vols.

*"Unto This Last": Four Essays on the First Principles of Polit-
　ical Economy.* 1862.

Sesame and Lilies. 1865.

*An Inquiry into Some of the Conditions at Present Affecting the
　Study of Architecture in Our Schools.* 1865.

The Ethics of the Dust. 1866.

The Crown of Wild Olive. 1866.

Time and Tide, by Weare and Tyne. 1867.

*First Notes on the General Principles of Employment for the
　Destitute and Criminal Classes.* 1868.

*The Queen of the Air: Being a Study of the Greek Myths of
　Cloud and Storm.* 1869.

Samuel Prout. 1870.

Lectures on Art. 1870.

A Paper Read at the Royal Artillery Institution, Woolwich ⟨*The
　Future of England*⟩. 1870.

*Catalogue of Examples Arranged for Elementary Study in the
　University Galleries.* 1870.

Collected Works. 1871–80. 11 vols.

*Fors Clavigera: Letters to the Workmen and Labourers of Great
　Britain.* January 1871–December 1877 [Sections 1–84;
　monthly]; 1878–84 [Sections 85–96; intermittently].

Instructions in Elementary Drawing. 1872.

*Munera Pulveris: Six Essays on the Elements of Political Econ-
　omy.* 1872.

Aratra Pentelici: Six Lectures on the Elements of Sculpture.
　1872.

*The Relation between Michael Angelo and Tintoret: Seventh of
　the Course of Lectures on Sculpture Delivered at Oxford
　1870–71.* 1872.

*The Eagle's Nest: Ten Lectures on the Relation of Natural
　Science to Art.* 1872.

The Sepulchral Monuments of Italy. 1872.

Love's Meinie: Lectures on Greek and English Birds. 1873–81.
　3 parts.

The Poetry of Architecture. 1873, 1893.

Remarks Addressed to the Mansfield Art Night Class. 1873.

*Ariadne Florentina: Six Lectures on Wood and Metal Engrav-
　ing.* 1873–76. 7 parts.

*Val D'Arno: Ten Lectures on the Tuscan Art Directly Anteced-
　ent to the Florentine Year of Victories.* 1874.

*Social Policy Must be Based on the Scientific Principle of Nat-
　ural Selection.* 1875.

Mornings in Florence. 1875–77. 6 parts.

Proserpina: Studies of Wayside Flowers. 1875–79 [Parts 1–6];
　1882–86 [Parts 7–10].

*Deucalion: Collected Studies of the Lapse of Waves, and Life of
　Stones.* 1875–79 [Parts 1–6]; 1880–83 [Parts 7–8].

Letters to The Times *on the Principal Pre-Raphaelite Pictures
　in the Exhibition of 1854.* 1876.

The Art Schools of Mediaeval Christendom by A. C. Owen
　(editor). 1876.

Bibliotheca Pastorum (editor). 1876–85. 4 vols.

*Guide to the Principal Pictures in the Academy of Fine Arts at
　Venice.* 1877. 2 parts.

St. Mark's Rest: The History of Venice. 1877–79. 6 parts.

The Laws of Fiesole. 1877–78. 4 parts.

*Notes by Mr. Ruskin on His Drawings by the Late J. M. W.
　Turner.* 1878.

Notes on Samuel Prout and William Hunt. 1879.

*Circular Respecting Memorial Studies of St. Mark's, Venice,
　Now in Progress under Mr. Ruskin's Direction.* 1879.

*Letters Addressed to the Clergy on the Lord's Prayer and the
　Church.* Ed. F. A. Malleson. 1879.

Elements of English Prosody. 1880.

*"Our Fathers Have Told Us": Sketches of the History of
　Christendom for Boys and Girls Who Have Been Held at
　Its Fonts* ⟨*The Bible of Amiens*⟩. 1880–83. 5 parts.

*Arrows of the Chase: Being a Collection of Scattered Letters
　Published Chiefly in the Daily Newspapers 1840–1880.*
　Ed. Alexander Wedderburn. 1880. 2 vols.

Poems. Ed. J. O. Wright. 1882.

Catalogue of the Collection of Siliceous Minerals. 1883.

The Story of an Idea: Epitaph on an Etrurian Tomb by Fran-
　cesca Alexander (editor). 1883.

The Art of England. 1883–84. 7 parts.

Catalogue of a Series of Specimens in the British Museum (Nat-

ural History) Illustrative of the More Common Forms of Native Silica. 1884.

Roadside Songs of Tuscany, tr. Francesca Alexander (editor). 1884–85. 10 parts.

The Pleasures of England. 1884–85. 4 parts.

The Storm Cloud of the Nineteenth Century. 1884. 2 parts.

Dame Wiggins of Lee and Her Seven Wonderful Cats (editor). 1885.

On the Old Road: A Collection of Miscellaneous Essays, Pamphlets, etc., etc., Published 1834–1885. Ed. Alexander Wedderburn. 1885. 2 vols.

Praeterita: Outlines of Scenes and Thoughts Perhaps Worthy of Memory in My Past Life. 1885–88. 28 parts.

Ulric the Farm Servant by Jeremias Gotthelf, tr. Julia Frith (editor). 1886–88. 9 parts.

Dilecta: Correspondence, Diary Notes, and Extracts from Books, Illustrating Praeterita. 1886 [Part 1]; 1887 [Part 2]; 1900 [Part 3].

Christ's Folk in the Apennine: Reminiscences of Her Friends among the Tuscan Peasantry by Francesca Alexander (editor). 1887–89. 2 vols.

Hortus Inclusus: Messages from the Wood to the Garden, Sent in Happy Days to the Sister Ladies of the Thwaite, Coniston ⟨Mary and Susie Beever⟩. Ed. Albert Fleming. 1887.

Two Letters concerning Notes on the Construction of Sheepfolds *Addressed to the Rev. F. D. Maurice.* 1889.

Ruskiniana. Ed. Alexander Wedderburn. 1890–92. 2 vols.

Poems. Ed. W. G. Collingwood. 1891. 2 vols.

Letters upon Subjects of General Interest. Ed. T. J. Wise. 1892.

Stray Letters to a London Bibliophile ⟨F. S. Ellis⟩. Ed. T. J. Wise. 1892.

Letters to William Ward. Ed. T. J. Wise. 1892. 2 vols.

Letters on Art and Literature. Ed. T. J. Wise. 1894.

Letters to Ernest Chesneau. Ed. T. J. Wise. 1894.

Letters Addressed to a College Friend ⟨Edward Clayton⟩ *1840–1845.* 1894.

Letters to the Rev. F. J. Faunthorpe. Ed. T. J. Wise. 1894.

Verona and Other Lectures. Ed. W. G. Collingwood. 1894.

Letters to the Rev. F. A. Malleson. Ed. T. J. Wise. 1896.

Letters to Frederick J. Furnivall and Other Correspondents. Ed. T. J. Wise. 1897.

Works. Eds. E. T. Cook and Alexander Wedderburn. 1903–12. 39 vols.

Comments on the Divina Commedia. Ed. G. P. Huntington. 1903.

Letters to M. G. & H. G. ⟨Mary and Hellen Gladstone⟩. 1903.

Letters to Charles Eliot Norton. Ed. Charles Eliot Norton. 1904. 2 vols.

Poems. 1908.

An Ill-Assorted Marriage: An Unpublished Letter. Ed. Clement Shorter. 1915.

Letters to William Ward. Ed. Alfred Mansfield Brooks. 1922.

The Solitary Warrior: New Letters. Ed. J. Howard Whitehouse. 1929.

Letters to Francesca and Memoirs of the Alexanders. Ed. Lucia Gray Swett. 1931.

Letters to Bernard Quaritch 1867–1888. Ed. Charlotte Quaritch Wrentmore. 1938.

The Order of Release: The Story of John Ruskin, Effie Gray and John Everett Millais Told for the First Time in Their Unpublished Letters. Ed. Admiral Sir William James. 1948.

Selected Writings. Ed. Peter Quennell. 1952.

The Gulf of Years: Letters to Kathleen Olander. Ed. Rayner Unwin. 1953.

Letters from Venice 1851–1852. Ed. John Lewis Bradley. 1955.

Diaries. Eds. Joan Evans and John Howard Whitehouse. 1956–59. 3 vols.

The Lamp of Beauty: Writings on Art. Ed. Joan Evans. 1959.

Pigwiggian Chaunts. Ed. James S. Dearden. 1960.

The Contemptible Horse: The Text of John Ruskin's Letter to "My Dear Tinie" Written from the Bridge of Allan on 31 August 1857. Ed. Norman H. Strouse. 1962.

Letters to Lord and Lady Mount-Temple. Ed. John Lewis Bradley. 1964.

Ruskin Today. Ed. Kenneth Clark. 1964.

Literary Criticism. Ed. Harold Bloom. 1965.

Dearest Mama Talbot: A Selection of Letters Written to Mrs. Fanny Talbot. Ed. Margaret Spence. 1966.

The Froude-Ruskin Friendship as Represented through Letters. Ed. Helen Gill Viljoen. 1966.

The Winnington Letters: John Ruskin's Correspondence with Margaret Alexis Bell and the Children at Winnington Hall. Ed. Van Akin Burd. 1969.

Brantwood Diary. Ed. Helen Gill Viljoen. 1971.

Sublime and Instructive: Letters to Louisa, Marchioness of Waterford, Anna Blunden and Ellen Heeton. Ed. Virginia Surtees. 1972.

Ruskin in Italy: Letters to His Parents 1845. Ed. Harold I. Shapiro. 1972.

The Ruskin Family Letters: The Correspondence of John James Ruskin, His Wife, and Their Son, John, 1801–1843. Ed. Van Akin Burd. 1973. 2 vols.

Reflections of a Friendship: John Ruskin's Letters to Pauline Trevelyan 1848–1866. Ed. Virginia Surtees. 1979.

The Correspondence of Thomas Carlyle and John Ruskin. Ed. George Allen Cate. 1982.

Letters from the Continent 1858. Ed. John Hayman. 1982.

My Dearest Dora: Letters to Dorothy Livesey, Her Family and Friends 1860–1900. Ed. Olive Wilson. 1984.

The Correspondence of John Ruskin and Charles Eliot Norton. Eds. John Lewis Bradley and Ian Onsby. 1987.

R. D. BLACKMORE (1825–1900)

Poems. 1854.

Epullia. 1854.

The Bugle of the Black Sea; or, The British in the East. 1855.

The Fate of Franklin. 1860.

The Farm and Fruit of Old: A Translation in Verse of the First and Second Georgics of Virgil. 1862.

Clara Vaughan. 1864. 3 vols.

Cradock Nowell: A Tale of the New Forest. 1866. 3 vols.

Lorna Doone: A Romance of Exmoor. 1869. 3 vols.

The Georgics of Vergil (translator). 1871.

The Maid of Sker. 1872. 3 vols.

Alice Lorraine: A Tale of the South Downs. 1875. 3 vols.

Cripps, the Carrier: A Woodland Tale. 1876. 3 vols.

Erema; or, My Father's Sin. 1877. 3 vols.

Figaro at Hastings, St. Leonards. 1877.

Mary Anerley: A Yorkshire Tale. 1880. 3 vols.

Christowell: A Dartmoore Tale. 1882. 3 vols.

The Remarkable History of Sir Thomas Upmore, Bart., M.P., Formerly Known as "Tommy Upmore." 1884. 2 vols.

Springhaven: A Tale of the Great War. 1887. 3 vols.

Kit and Kitty: A Story of West Middlesex. 1890. 3 vols.

Perlycross: A Tale of the Western Hills. 1894. 3 vols.

Fringilla: Some Tales in Verse. 1895.

Tales from the Telling-House. 1896.
Dariel: A Romance of Surrey. 1897.

CHARLES DUDLEY WARNER (1829–1900)

The Book of Eloquence: A Collection of Extracts in Prose and Verse, from the Most Eloquent Orators and Poets of Other Days and the Present Time (editor). 1853.
My Summer in a Garden. 1870.
Saunterings. 1872.
Backlog Studies. 1873.
The Gilded Age (with Mark Twain). 1873.
Baddeck, and That Sort of Thing. 1874.
In the Levant. 1877.
In the Wilderness. 1878.
Being a Boy. 1878.
Captain John Smith (1579–1631) Sometime Governor of Virginia, and Admiral of New England: A Study of His Life and Writings. 1881.
Washington Irving. 1881.
The American Newspaper: An Essay Read before the Social Science Association at Saratoga Springs. 1881.
The Work Laid upon the Southern College: An Address before the Literary Societies of Roanoke College, Salem, Virginia. 1883.
A Roundabout Journey. 1884.
Their Pilgrimage. 1887.
A-Hunting of the Deer and Other Essays. 1888.
On Horseback: A Tour in Virginia, North Carolina and Tennessee, with Notes of Travel in Mexico and California. 1888.
A Little Journey in the World. 1889.
Studies in the South and West, with Comments on Canada. 1889.
As We Were Saying. 1891.
Our Italy. 1891.
The Work of Washington Irving. 1893.
As We Go. 1894.
The Golden House. 1894.
Library of the World's Best Literature, Ancient and Modern (editor; with others). 1896. 45 vols.
The Relation of Literature to Life. 1897.
The People for Whom Shakespeare Wrote. 1897.
That Fortune. 1899.
The Education of the Negro: President's Address Delivered before the American Social Science Association at Washington. 1900.
Fashions in Literature and Other Literary and Social Essays and Addresses. 1902.
Complete Writings. 1904. 15 vols.
Charles Dickens: An Appreciation. 1913.

OSCAR WILDE (1854–1900)

Ravenna. 1878.
Vera; or, The Nihilists. 1880.
Poems. 1881.
The Duchess of Padua: A Tragedy of the XVI Century. 1883.
The Happy Prince and Other Tales. 1888.
The Picture of Dorian Gray. 1891.
Intentions. 1891.
Lord Arthur Savile's Crime and Other Stories. 1891.
A House of Pomegranates. 1891.
Salomé. 1893.
Lady Windermere's Fan: A Play about a Good Woman. 1893.
The Sphinx. 1894.
A Woman of No Importance. 1894.

Oscariana: Epigrams. 1895.
The Soul of Man ⟨under Socialism⟩. 1895.
The Ballad of Reading Gaol. 1898.
The Importance of Being Earnest: A Trivial Comedy for Serious People. 1899.
An Ideal Husband. 1899.
Sebastian Melmoth. 1904.
De Profundis. 1905.
The Rise of Historical Criticism. 1905.
Wilde v. Whistler: Being an Acrimonious Correspondence on Art between Oscar Wilde and James A. McNeill Whistler. 1906.
Works. Ed. Robert Ross. 1908. 15 vols.
The Suppressed Portion of De Profundis. Ed. Robert Ross. 1913.
Resurgam: Unpublished Letters. Ed. Clement K. Shorter. 1917.
For Love of the King: A Burmese Masque. 1922.
Selected Works with Twelve Unpublished Letters. Ed. Richard Aldington. 1946.
Complete Works. Ed. Vyvyan Holland. 1948.
Essays. Ed. Hesketh Pearson. 1950.
Five Famous Plays. Ed. Alan Harris. 1952.
Selected Writings. Ed. Richard Ellmann. 1961.
Letters. Ed. Rupert Hart-Davis. 1962.
The Artist as Critic: Critical Writings. Ed. Richard Ellmann. 1969.
Complete Shorter Fiction. Ed. Isobel Murray. 1979.
More Letters. Ed. Rupert Hart-Davis. 1985.

ERNEST DOWSON (1867–1900)

A Comedy of Masks (with Arthur Moore). 1893. 3 vols.
Majesty by Louis Couperus (translator; with Alexander Texeira de Mattos). 1894.
La Terre by Émile Zola (translator). 1894. 2 vols.
Dilemmas: Stories and Studies in Sentiment. 1895.
The History of Modern Painting by Richard Muther (translator; with G. A. Greene and A. C. Hillier). 1895–96. 3 vols.
The Girl with the Golden Eyes by Honoré de Balzac (translator). 1896.
Verses. 1896.
The Pierrot of the Minute: A Dramatic Phantasy. 1897.
Les Liaisons dangereuses by Pierre Choderlos de Laclos (translator). 1898. 2 vols.
Memoirs of Cardinal Dubois by Paul Lacroix (translator). 1899. 2 vols.
La Pucelle, the Maid of Orleans by Voltaire (translator). 1899. 2 vols.
Adrian Rome (with Arthur Moore). 1899.
Decorations in Verse and Prose. 1899.
Poems. Ed. Thomas Bird Mosher. 1902.
Poems. 1905.
Cynara: A Little Book of Verse. Ed. Thomas Bird Mosher. 1907.
The Confidantes of a King: The Mistresses of Louis XV by Edmond and Jules de Goncourt (translator). 1907. 2 vols.
The Story of Beauty and the Beast (translator). 1908.
Poems and Prose. 1919.
Complete Poems. 1928.
Poetical Works. Ed. Desmond Flower. 1934.
Poems. 1946.
Stories. Ed. Mark Longaker. 1947.
Poems. Ed. Mark Longaker. 1962.
Letters. Eds. Desmond Flower and Henry Maas. 1967.

STEPHEN CRANE (1871–1900)

Maggie: A Girl of the Streets. 1893.

The Black Riders and Other Lines. 1895.

The Red Badge of Courage: An Episode of the American Civil War. 1895.

George's Mother. 1896.

The Little Regiment and Other Episodes of the American Civil War. 1896.

The Third Violet. 1897.

The Open Boat and Other Tales of Adventure. 1898.

War Is Kind. 1899.

Active Service. 1899.

The Monster and Other Stories. 1899.

Whilomville Stories. 1900.

Wounds in the Rain: War Stories. 1900.

Great Battles of the World. 1901.

Last Words. 1902.

The O'Ruddy: A Romance (with Robert Barr). 1903.

Men, Women and Boats. Ed. Vincent Starrett. 1921.

Work. Ed. Wilson Follett. 1925–26. 12 vols.

Two Letters to Joseph Conrad. 1926.

Collected Poems. Ed. Wilson Follett. 1930.

A Battle in Greece. 1936.

Sullivan County Sketches. Ed. Melvin Schoberlin. 1949.

Love Letters to Nellie Crouse. Eds. Edwin H. Cady and Lester G. Wells. 1954.

Letters. Eds. R. W. Stallman and Lillian Gilkes. 1960.

Uncollected Writings. Ed. Olov W. Fryckstedt. 1963.

Complete Short Stories and Sketches. 1963.

War Dispatches. Eds. R. W. Stallman and E. R. Hagemann. 1964.

New York City Sketches. Eds. R. W. Stallman and E. R. Hagemann. 1966.

Poems. Ed. Joseph Katz. 1966.

Complete Novels. Ed. Thomas A. Gullason. 1967.

Notebook. Eds. Donald J. Greiner and Ellen B. Greiner. 1969.

The Portable Stephen Crane. Ed. Joseph Katz. 1969.

Works. Ed. Fredson Bowers. 1969–76. 10 vols.

Prose and Poetry. Ed. J. C. Levenson. 1984.

CHARLOTTE MARY YONGE (1823–1901)

Le Chateau de Melville; ou, Recréations du cabinet d'étude. 1838.

Abbey Church; or, Self-Control and Self-Conceit. 1844.

Scenes and Characters; or, Eighteen Months at Beechcroft. 1847.

Kings of England: A History for Young Children. 1848.

Henrietta's Wish; or, Domineering. 1850.

Kenneth; or, The Rearguard of the Grand Army. 1850.

Langley School. 1850.

Landmarks of History. 1852–57. 3 vols.

The Two Guardians; or, Home in This World. 1852.

The Heir of Redclyffe. 1853.

The Herb of the Field. 1853.

The Little Duke; or, Richard the Fearless. 1854.

The Castle Builders; or, The Deferred Confirmation. 1854.

Heartsease; or, The Brother's Wife. 1854.

The Lances of Lynwood. 1855.

The History of the Life and Death of the Good Knight Sir Thomas Thumb. 1855.

The Railroad Children. 1855.

Ben Sylvester's Word. 1856.

The Daisy Chain; or, Aspirations: A Family Chronicle. 1856. 2 vols.

Harriet and Her Sister. c. 1856.

Leonard the Lionheart. 1856.

Dynevor Terrace; or, The Clue of Life. 1857. 2 vols.

The Instructive Picture Book: Lessons from the Vegetable World. 1857.

The Christmas Mummers. 1858.

Conversations on the Catechism. 1859–62. 3 vols.

Friarswood Post Office. 1860.

Hopes and Fears; or, Scenes from the Life of a Spinster. 1860. 2 vols.

The Mice at Play. 1860.

The Strayed Falcon. 1860.

Pigeon Pie. 1860.

The Young Stepmother; or, A Chronicle of Mistakes. 1861.

The Stokesley Secret. 1861.

Countess Kate. 1862.

The Wars of Wapsburgh. 1862.

The Chosen People: A Compendium of Sacred and Church History for School-Children. 1862.

Biographies of Good Women (editor). 1863–65. 2 vols.

A History of Christian Names. 1863. 2 vols.

Sea Spleenwort and Other Stories. 1863.

The Trial: More Links of the Daisy Chain. 1864.

A Book of Golden Deeds of All Times and All Lands. 1864.

Readings from Standard Authors. 1864.

The Apple of Discord. 1864.

Historical Dramas. 1864.

The Clever Woman of the Family. 1865. 2 vols.

The Price and the Page: A Tale of the Crusade. 1865.

The Dove in the Eagle's Nest. 1866. 2 vols.

The Danvers Papers: An Invention. 1867.

A Shilling's Book of Golden Deeds. 1867.

The Six Cushions. 1867.

Cameos from English History. 1868–69. 9 vols.

The Chaplet of Pearls; or, The White and Black Ribaumont. 1868. 2 vols.

New Ground: Kaffirland. 1868.

The Pupils of St. John the Divine. 1868.

Historical Selections: A Series of Readings in English and European History (with E. M. Sewell). 1868–70. 2 vols.

A Book of Worthies, Gathered from the Old Histories and Now Written Out Anew. 1869.

Keynotes of the First Lessons for Every Day in the Year. 1869.

The Seal; or, The Inward Spiritual Grace of Confirmation. 1869.

Two Years of School Life by Elise de Pressensé (editor). 1869.

The Caged Lion. 1870.

A Storehouse of Stories (editor). 1870–72. 2 vols.

The Population of an Old Pear Tree by E. Van Bruyssel (editor). 1871.

Pioneers and Founders; or, Recent Works in the Mission Field. 1871.

A Parallel History of France and England. 1871.

Musings over the Christian Year and Lyra Innocentium. 1871.

Scripture Readings for Schools, with Comments. 1871–79. 5 vols.

P's and Q's: The Question of Putting Upon. 1872.

Questions on the Prayer-Book. 1872.

In Memoriam Bishop Patteson. 1872.

Dames of High Estate by Mme. H. de Witt (editor). 1872.

Beneath the Cross by Florence Wilford (editor). 1872.

The Pillars of the House: Under Wode under Rode. 1873. 4 vols.

Aunt Charlotte's Stories of English History for the Little Ones. 1873.

Life of John Coleridge Patteson, Missionary Bishop of the Melanesian Islands. 1873. 2 vols.

Recollections of a Page at the Court of Louis XVI by Count d'Hézecques (editor). 1873.

Questions on the Collects. 1874.

Questions on the Epistles. 1874.

Aunt Charlotte's Stories of French History for the Little Ones. 1875.

Questions on the Gospels. 1875.

My Young Alcides: A Faded Photograph. 1875.

The Recollections of Colonel de Gonneville (editor). 1875.

The Three Brides. 1876.

Aunt Charlotte's Stories of Bible History for the Little Ones. 1876.

Aunt Charlotte's Stories of Greek History for the Little Ones. 1876.

Eighteen Centuries of Beginnings of Church History. 1876. 2 vols.

Womankind. 1877.

Aunt Charlotte's Stories of Roman History for the Little Ones. 1877.

Aunt Charlotte's Stories of German History for the Little Ones. 1877.

A Man of Other Days: Recollections of the Marquis Henry Joseph Costa de Beauregard (editor). 1877. 2 vols.

The Story of the Christians and Moors of Spain. 1878.

The Disturbing Element; or, Chronicles of the Bluebell Society. 1878.

Burnt Out: A Story for Mothers' Meetings. 1879.

Magnum Bonum; or, Mother Carey's Brood. 1879.

Novels and Tales. 1879–99. 40 vols.

The Youth of Elizabeth by L. Wiesener (editor). 1879.

Short English Grammar for Use in Schools. 1879.

Love and Life: An Old Story in Eighteenth-Century Costume. 1880.

Bye-Words: A Collection of Tales New and Old. 1880.

Verses on the Gospels for Sundays and Holy Days. 1880.

Cheap Jack. 1880.

Nelly and Margaret; or, Good for Evil. c. 1880.

Lads and Lasses of Langley. 1881.

Aunt Charlotte's Evenings at Home with the Poets. 1881.

How to Teach the New Testament. 1881.

Practical Work in Sunday Schools. 1881.

Frank's Debt. 1881.

Wolf. 1881.

English History Reading-Books. 1881–85. 3 vols.

Questions on the Psalms. 1881.

Catherine of Aragon and the Sources of the English Reformation by A. du Boys (editor). 1881.

Given to Hospitality. 1882.

Sowing and Sewing: A Sexagesima Story. 1882.

Talks about the Laws We Live Under; or, At Langley Night-School. 1882.

Unknown to History: A Story of the Captivity of Mary of Scotland. 1882. 2 vols.

Langley Little Ones: Six Stories. 1882.

Pickle and His Page Boy; or, Unlooked For. 1882.

Historical Ballads (editor). 1882.

Behind the Hedges by H. de Witt (editor). 1882.

Sparks of Light by H. de Witt (editor). 1882.

Landmarks of Recent History 1770–1883. 1883.

Aunt Charlotte's Stories of American History (with J. H. Hastings Weld). 1883.

Langley Adventures. 1883.

Stray Pearls: Memoirs of Margaret de Ribaumont, Viscountess of Bellaise. 1883. 2 vols.

English Church History, Adapted for Use in Day and Sunday Schools. 1883.

Shakespeare's Plays for Schools, Abridged and Annotated. 1883.

The Miz-Maze; or, The Winkworth Puzzle (with others). 1883.

The Armourer's 'Prentices. 1884.

Memoirs of Marshall Bugeaud by Count H. d'Ideville (editor). 1884.

The Daisy Chain Birthday Book. 1885.

Higher Reading-Book for Schools, Colleges and General Use (editor). 1885.

Nuttie's Father. 1885. 2 vols.

The Two Sides of the Shield. 1885. 2 vols.

Astray: A Tale of a Country Town (with others). 1886.

Chantry House. 1886. 2 vols.

Little Rickburners. 1886.

A Modern Telemachus. 1886.

Teachings on the Catechism for the Little Ones. 1886.

Just One Tale More (with others). 1886.

Victorian Half-Century: A Jubilee Book. 1887.

What Books to Lend and What to Give. 1887.

Under the Storm; or, Steadfast's Charge. 1887.

Chips from the Royal Image by E. A. M. A. Morshead (editor). 1887.

Deacon's Book of Dates. 1888.

Beechcroft at Rochstone. 1888. 2 vols.

Conversations on the Prayer Book. 1888.

Hannah More. 1888.

Nurse's Memories. 1888.

Our New Mistress; or, Changes at Brookfield Earl. 1888.

Preparation of Prayer-Book Lessons. 1888.

A Reputed Changeling; or, Three Seventh Years Two Centuries Ago. 1889. 2 vols.

The Parent's Power: Address to the Conference of the Mothers Union. 1889.

Neighbour's Fare. 1889.

The Cunning Woman's Grandson: A Tale of Cheddar a Hundred Years Ago. 1889.

Life of H.R.H. the Prince Consort. 1890.

More Bye-words. 1890.

The Slaves of Sabinns: Jew and Gentile. 1890.

The Constable's Tower; or, The Times of Magna Charta. 1891.

Westminster Historical Reading Books. 1891–92. 2 vols.

Old Times at Otterbourne. 1891.

Seven Heroines of Christendom. 1891.

Simple Stories Relating to English History. 1891.

Twelve Stories from Early English History. 1891.

Twenty Stories and Biographies from 1066 to 1485. 1891.

Two Penniless Princesses. 1891.

The Cross Roads; or, A Choice in Life. 1892.

An Old Woman's Outlook in a Hampshire Village. 1892.

That Stack. 1892.

The Hanoverian Period, with Biographies of Leading Persons. 1892.

The Stuart Period, with Biographies of Leading Persons. 1892.

The Tudor Period, with Biographies of Leading Persons. 1892.

Chimes for the Mothers: A Reading for Each Week in the Year. 1893.

The Girl's Little Book. 1893.

Grisly Grisell; or, The Laidly Lady of Whitburn: A Tale of the Wars of the Roses, 1893. 2 vols.

The Strolling Players: A Harmony of Contrasts (with Christabel Coleridge). 1893.
The Treasure in the Marshes. 1893.
The Rubies of St. Lo. 1894.
The Story of Easter. 1894.
The Cook and the Captive; or, Attalus the Hostage. 1894.
The Long Vacation. 1895.
The Carbonels. 1895.
The Wardship of Steepcombe. 1896.
The Release; or, Caroline's French Kindred. 1896.
The Pilgrimage of Ben Beriah. 1897.
Founded on Paper; or, Uphill and Downhill between the Two Jubilees. 1898.
John Keble's Parishes: A History of Hursley and Otterbourne. 1898.
The Patriots of Palestine: A Story of the Maccabees. 1898.
Scenes from Kenneth, etc. 1899.
The Making of a Missionary; or, Day Dreams in Earnest. 1900.
The Herd Boy and His Hermit. 1900.
Modern Broods; or, Developments Unlooked For. 1900.
Reasons Why I Am a Catholic, and Not a Roman Catholic. 1901.

JOHN FISKE (1842–1901)

Ode. 1863.
Tobacco and Alcohol: I. It Does Pay to Smoke; II. The Coming Man Will Drink Wine. 1869.
The Class Room Taine: History of English Literature by Hippolyte Taine, tr. H. Van Laun (abridged by Fiske). 1872.
Myths and Myth-Makers: Old Tales and Superstitions Interpreted by Comparative Mythology. 1873.
Outlines of Cosmic Philosophy, Based on the Doctrine of Evolution, with Criticisms on the Positive Philosophy. 1875. 2 vols.
The Unseen World and Other Essays. 1876.
Darwinism and Other Essays. 1879, 1885.
The Presidents of America. 1879.
The Rev. Joseph Cook. 1881.
Evolution and Religion. 1883.
Excursions of an Evolutionist. 1884.
The Destiny of Man Viewed in the Light of His Origin. 1884.
American Political Ideas Viewed from the Standpoint of Universal History: Three Lectures Delivered at the Royal Institution of Great Britain in May 1880. 1885.
The Idea of God as Affected by Modern Knowledge. 1885.
Washington and His Country: Being Irving's Life of Washington (abridged by Fiske). 1887.
Appleton's Cyclopaedia of American Biography (editor; with James Grant Wilson). 1887–89. 6 vols.
The Critical Period of American History 1783–1789. 1888.
The Beginnings of New England; or, Puritan Theocracy in Its Relations to Civil and Religious Liberty. 1889.
The War of Independence. 1889.
Civil Government in the United States Considered with Some Reference to Its Origins. 1890.
The American Revolution. 1891. 2 vols.
The Discovery of America, with Some Account of Ancient America and the Spanish Conquest. 1892. 2 vols.
Edward Livingston Youmans, Interpreter of Science to the People. 1894.
A History of the United States for Schools. 1894.
Old Virginia and Her Neighbors. 1897. 2 vols.

Through Nature to God. 1899.
The Dutch and Quaker Colonies in America. 1899. 2 vols.
A Century of Science and Other Essays. 1899.
The Mississippi Valley in the Civil War. 1900.
Life Everlasting. 1901.
Connecticut's Part in the Federal Constitution. 1901.
Colonization of the New World. 1902.
Independence of the New World. 1902.
Modern Development of the New World. 1902.
New France and New England. 1902.
Essays Historical and Literary. 1902. 2 vols.
Writings. 1902. 12 vols.
Unpublished Orations. 1909.
Life and Letters. Ed. John Spencer Clark. 1917.
Personal Letters. Ed. H. H. Harper. 1939.
Letters. Ed. Ethel F. Fiske. 1940.

AUBREY DE VERE (1814–1902)

The Waldenses; or, The Fall of Rora: A Lyrical Sketch, with Other Poems. 1842.
The Search after Proserpine, Recollections of Greece, and Other Poems. 1843.
English Misrule and Irish Misdeeds: Four Letters from Ireland, Addressed to an English Member of Parliament. 1848.
Picturesque Sketches of Greece and Turkey. 1850. 2 vols.
Heroines of Charity. 1854.
Poems. 1855.
May Carols. 1857, 1881 (3rd rev. ed.).
Select Specimens of the English Poets (editor). 1858.
The Sisters, Inisfail, and Other Poems. 1861.
Inisfail: A Lyrical Chronicle of Ireland. 1863.
The Infant Bridal and Other Poems. 1864.
The Month of Mary. 1864.
The Church Settlement of Ireland; or, Hibernia Pacanda. 1866.
The Church Establishment in Ireland, Illustrated Exclusively by Protestant Authorities. 1867.
Ireland's Church Property and the Right Use of It. 1867.
Pleas for Secularization. 1867.
Reply to Certain Strictures by Miles O'Reilly, Esq.: Being a Postscript to Pleas for Secularization. 1868.
Ireland's Church Question: Five Essays. 1868. 5 parts.
Irish Odes and Other Poems. 1869.
The Legends of St. Patrick. 1872.
Alexander the Great: A Dramatic Poem. 1874.
St. Thomas of Canterbury: A Dramatic Poem. 1876.
The Fall of Rora, The Search after Proserpine, and Other Poems, Meditative and Lyrical. 1877.
Antar and Zara: An Eastern Romance; Inisfail, and Other Poems, Meditative and Lyrical. 1877.
Proteus and Amadeus: A Correspondence by Wilfrid S. Blunt and Charles Meynell (editor). 1878.
Legends of the Saxon Saints. 1879.
The Foray of Queen Maeve and Other Legends of Ireland's Heroic Age. 1882.
Poetical Works. 1884–98. 6 vols.
Ireland and Proportional Representation. 1885.
Legends and Records of the Church and the Empire. 1887.
Essays, Chiefly on Poetry. 1887. 2 vols.
St. Peter's Chains; or, Rome and the Italian Revolution: A Series of Sonnets. 1888.
Essays, Chiefly Literary and Ethical. 1889.
Poems: A Selection. Ed. John Dennis. 1890.
The Household Poetry Book: An Anthology of English-Speaking Poets from Chaucer to Faber (editor). 1893.

Religious Problems of the Nineteenth Century. Ed. J. G. Wenham. 1893.

Medieval Records and Sonnets. 1893.

Selections from the Poems. Ed. George Edward Woodberry. 1894.

Recollections. 1897.

Poems. Ed. Lady Margaret Domvile. 1904.

SAMUEL R. GARDINER (1829–1902)

Parliamentary Debates in 1610 (editor). 1862.

History of England from the Accession of James I. to the Disgrace of Chief Justice Coke 1603–1616. 1863. 2 vols.

Letters and Other Documents Illustrating the Relations between England and Germany at the Commencement of the Thirty Years' War (editor). 1865–68. 2 vols.

Prince Charles and the Spanish Marriage 1617–1623: A Chapter of English History, Founded Principally upon Unpublished Documents in This Country, and in the Archives of Simancas, Venice, and Brussels. 1869. 2 vols.

El Hecho de los tratados del matrimonio pretendido por el principe de Gales con la serenissima infante de Espana Maria by Francisco de Jesus (editor and translator). 1869.

Notes of the Debates in the House of Lords 1621 (editor). 1870.

The Earl of Bristol's Defence of His Negotiations in Spain (editor). 1870.

The Fortescue Papers (editor). 1871.

Debates in the House of Commons 1625 (editor). 1873.

The Thirty Years' War 1618–1648. 1874.

Speech of Sir Robert Heath (editor). 1875.

Notes of the Judgment Delivered by Sir George Croke in the Case of the Ship-Money (editor). 1875.

Letters Relating to the Mission of Sir Thomas Roe to Gustavus Adolphus 1629–30 (editor). 1875.

A History of England under the Duke of Buckingham and Charles I. 1624–1628. 1875. 2 vols.

The First Two Stuarts and the Puritan Revolution 1603–1660. 1876.

Documents Relating to the Proceedings against William Prynne in 1634 and 1637 (editor). 1877.

The Personal Government of Charles I.: A History of England from the Assassination of the Duke of Buckingham to the Declaration of the Judges on Ship-Money 1628–1637. 1877. 2 vols.

Notes of the Debates in the House of Lords (1624 and 1626) (editor). 1879.

The Hamilton Papers (editor). 1880.

Introduction to the Study of English History (with J. B. Mullinger). 1881.

Outline of English History. 1881 (2 parts), 1883 (as *Illustrated English History*; 3 parts).

The Fall of the Monarchy of Charles I. 1637–1642. 1882. 2 vols.

Four Letters of Lord Wentworth, Afterwards Earl of Strafford (editor). 1883.

A Letter from the Earl of Manchester to the House of Lords, Giving an Opinion on the Conduct of Oliver Cromwell (editor). 1883.

History of England from the Accession of James I. to the Outbreak of Civil War 1603–1642. 1883–84. 10 vols.

Historical Biographies. 1884.

Reports of Cases in the Courts of Star Chamber and High Commission (editor). 1886.

History of the Great Civil War 1642–1649. 1886–91. 3 vols.

*An Easy History of England: First Course Dealing More Es-*pecially with Social History; Second Course Dealing More Especially with Political History*. 1887–88. 2 vols.

The Constitutional Documents of the Puritan Revolution 1628–1660 (editor). 1889, 1899.

Documents Illustrating the Impeachment of the Duke of Buckingham in 1626 (editor). 1889.

A Student's History of England from the Earliest Times to 1885. 1890–91. 3 vols.

A School Atlas of English History: A Companion Atlas to the Student's History of England. 1892.

Hamilton Papers Addenda (editor). 1893.

The Tudor Period. 1893.

The Stuart Period. 1894.

Letters and Papers Illustrating the Relations between Charles the Second and Scotland in 1650 (editor). 1894.

History of the Commonwealth and Protectorate 1649–1660. 1894–1903. 3 vols.

What Gunpowder Plot Was. 1897.

Cromwell's Place in History: Founded on Six Lectures Delivered in the University of Oxford. 1897.

Oliver Cromwell. 1899.

Letters and Papers Relating to the First Dutch War 1652–1654, Volumes 1–3 (editor; with C. T. Atkinson). 1899–1930. 6 vols.

English Literature: The Civil War and the Commonwealth. 1901.

Prince Rupert at Lisbon (editor). 1902.

FRANK R. STOCKTON (1834–1902)

A Northern Voice for the Dissolution of the Union of the United States of America. 1861.

Ting-a-ling. 1870.

Round-about Rambles in Lands of Fact and Fancy. 1872.

The Home: Where It Should Be and What to Put in It (with Marian Stockton). 1873.

What Might Have Been Expected. 1874.

Tales out of School. 1876.

Rudder Grange. 1879.

A Jolly Fellowship. 1880.

The Floating Prince and Other Fairy Tales. 1881.

The Lady, or the Tiger? and Other Stories. 1884.

The Story of Viteau. 1884.

The Late Mrs. Null. 1886.

The Christmas Wreck and Other Stories. 1886.

The Casting Away of Mrs. Lecks and Mrs. Aleshine. 1886.

The Bee-Man of Orn and Other Fanciful Tales. 1887.

The Hundredth Man. 1887.

The Dusantes: A Sequel to The Casting Away of Mrs. Lecks and Mrs. Aleshine. 1888.

Amos Killbright: His Adscititious Experiences, with Other Stories. 1888.

The Great War Syndicate. 1889.

Personally Conducted. 1889.

The Stories of the Three Burglars. 1889.

The Merry Chanter. 1890.

Ardis Claverden. 1890.

The Cosmic Bean; or, The Great Show in Kobol-Land. 1891.

The Rudder Grangers Abroad and Other Stories. 1891.

The Squirrel Inn. 1891.

The House of Martha. 1891.

My Terminal Moraine. 1892.

The Clocks of Rondaine and Other Stories. 1892.

The Watchmaker's Wife and Other Stories. 1893.

Pomona's Travels: A Series of Letters to the Mistress of Rudder Grange from Her Former Handmaiden. 1894.

Fanciful Tales. Ed. Julia Elizabeth Langworthy. 1894.

The Spirit of Washington: A Paper Prepared and Read before the Washington Association of New Jersey at Their Meeting. 1895.

The Adventures of Captain Horn. 1895.

A Chosen Few. 1895.

Stories of New Jersey. 1896.

Mrs. Cliff's Yacht. 1896.

Captain Chap; or, The Rolling Stones. 1897.

A Story-Teller's Pack. 1897.

The Great Stone of Sardis. 1898.

The Girl at Cobhurst. 1898.

Buccaneers and Pirates of Our Coast. 1898.

Masterpieces of the World's Literature (editor; with Harry Thurston Peck and Julian Hawthorne). 1898–99. 20 vols.

The Associate Hermits. 1899.

The Vizier of the Two-Horned Alexander. 1899.

The Young Master of Hyson Hall. 1899.

Novels and Stories. 1899–1904. 23 vols.

Afield and Afloat. 1900.

A Bicycle of Cathay. 1900.

American Vacations in Europe: Course IV. Booklovers Reading Club (editor). 1901.

Kate Bonnet: The Romance of a Pirate's Daughter. 1902.

John Gayther's Garden and the Stories Told Therein. 1902.

The Captain's Toll-Gate. 1903.

The Magic Egg and Other Stories. 1907.

The Lost Dryad. 1912.

The Poor Count's Christmas. 1927.

Fable and Fiction. Ed. J. I. Rodale. 1949.

Best Short Stories. 1957.

The Science Fiction of Frank R. Stockton. Ed. Richard Gid Powers. 1976.

SAMUEL BUTLER (1835–1902)

Beware! Beware! Beware! 1855.

A First Year in Canterbury Settlement. 1863.

The Evidence for the Resurrection of Jesus Christ as Given by the Four Evangelists, Critically Examined. 1865.

Erewhon; or, Over the Range. 1872.

The Fair Haven: A Work in Defence of the Miraculous Element in Our Lord's Ministry upon Earth. 1873.

Life and Habit. 1878.

Evolution, Old and New; or, The Theories of Buffon, Dr. Erasmus Darwin, and Lamarck, as Compared with That of Mr. Charles Darwin. 1879.

Unconscious Memory. 1880.

Alps and Sanctuaries of Piedmont and the Canton Ticino. 1882.

Selections from Previous Works. 1884.

To the Electors of the Slade Professor of Fine Art. 1886.

Luck or Cunning, as the Main Means of Organic Modification? 1887.

Ex Voto: An Account of the Sacro Monte or New Jerusalem at Varallo-Sesia. 1888.

A Lecture on the Humour of Homer. 1892.

On the Trapanese Origin of the Odyssey. 1893.

Sample Passages from a New Prose Translation of the Odyssey. 1894.

The Life and Letters of Dr. Samuel Butler, Headmaster of Shrewsbury School, 1798–1836. 1896. 2 vols.

The Authoress of the Odyssey. 1897.

The Iliad of Homer (translator). 1898.

Shakespeare's Sonnets Reconsidered. 1899.

The Odyssey by Homer (translator). 1900.

Erewhon Revisited Twenty Years Later. 1901.

The Way of All Flesh. Ed. R. A. Streatfeild. 1903.

The Humour of Homer and Other Essays. Ed. R. A. Streatfeild. 1903.

Essays on Life, Art and Science. Ed. R. A. Streatfeild. 1904.

Seven Sonnets and A Psalm of Montreal. 1904.

God the Known and God the Unknown. 1909.

Note-Books. Ed. Henry Festing Jones. 1912.

A First Year in Canterbury Settlement, with Other Early Essays. Ed. R. A. Streatfeild. 1914.

Works and Days by Hesiod (translator). 1923.

Collected Works. Eds. Henry Festing Jones and A. T. Bartholomew. 1923–26. 20 vols.

Selections from the Note-Books. Ed. A. T. Bartholomew. 1930.

Butleriana. Ed. A. T. Bartholomew. 1932.

Further Extracts from the Note-Books. Ed. A. T. Bartholomew. 1934.

Letters between Samuel Butler and Miss E. M. A. Savage. Eds. Geoffrey Keynes and Brian Hill. 1935.

The Essential Samuel Butler. Ed. G. D. H. Cole. 1950.

Notebooks: Selections. Eds. Geoffrey Keynes and Brian Hill. 1951.

The Correspondence of Samuel Butler with His Sister May. Ed. Daniel F. Howard. 1962.

The Family Letters of Samuel Butler 1841–1886. Ed. Arnold Silver. 1962.

Note-Books. Ed. Hans-Peter Breuer. 1984–   .

BRET HARTE (1836–1902)

Outcroppings: Being Selections of California Verse (editor). 1866.

Poems by Charles Warren Stoddard (editor). 1867.

Condensed Novels and Other Papers. 1867.

The Lost Galleon and Other Tales. 1867.

The Luck of Roaring Camp and Other Sketches. 1870.

The Heathen Chinee. 1870.

Poems. 1871.

East and West Poems. 1871.

The Little Drummer; or, The Christmas Gift That Came to Rupert: A Story for Children. 1872.

Mrs. Skaggs's Husbands and Other Sketches. 1873.

An Episode of Fiddletown and Other Sketches. 1873.

Mliss: An Idyl of Red Mountain: A Story of California in 1863. 1873.

Deacon Jones' Experience. 1874.

Echoes of the Foot-Hills. 1875.

Tales of the Argonauts and Other Sketches. 1875.

Gabriel Conroy. 1875.

Two Men of Sandy Bar. 1876.

Thankful Blossom: A Romance of the Jerseys 1779. 1877.

The Story of a Mine. 1877.

"Excelsior." 1877.

The Man on the Beach. 1878.

"Jinny." 1878.

Drift from Two Stories. 1878.

The Twins of Table Mountain and Other Stories. 1879.

Complete Works. 1880–1900. 10 vols.

Works (Riverside Edition). 1882. 5 vols.

Poetical Works. 1882.

Flip and Found at Blazing Star. 1882.

In the Carquinez Woods. 1883.

On the Frontier. 1884.

By Shore and Sedge. 1885.

Maruja. 1885.

Snow-Bound at Eagle's. 1886.

Artemis in Sierra; Jack of the Tules. 1886.
The Queen of the Pirate Isle. 1887.
A Millionaire of Rough-and-Ready and Devil's Ford. 1887.
The Crusade of the Excelsior. 1887.
A Phyllis of the Sierras and A Drift from Redwood Camp. 1888.
The Argonauts of North Liberty. 1888.
Cressy. 1889.
The Heritage of Dedlow Marsh and Other Tales. 1889.
A Waif of the Plains. 1890.
A Ward of the Golden Gate. 1890.
A Sappho of Green Springs and Other Stories. 1891.
A First Family of Tasajara. 1891. 2 vols.
Colonel Starbottle's Client and Some Other People. 1892.
Susy: A Story of the Plains. 1893.
Sally Dows and Other Stories. 1893.
A Protegee of Jack Hamlin's and Other Stories. 1894.
The Bell-Ringer of Angel's and Other Stories. 1894.
Clarence. 1895.
In a Hollow of the Hills. 1895.
A Mother of Five. 1896.
Barker's Luck and Other Stories. 1896.
Poetical Works. 1896.
Writings. 1896–1914. 20 vols.
Three Partners; or, The Big Strike on Heavy Tree Hill. 1897.
Tales of Trail and Town. 1898.
Stories in Light and Shadow. 1898.
What Happened at the Fonda. 1899.
Mr. Jack Hamlin's Mediation and Other Stories. 1899.
From Sand Hill to Pine. 1900.
Under the Redwoods. 1901.
Openings in the Old Trail. 1902.
Condensed Novels: Second Series. 1902.
Sue (adaptation; with T. Edgar Pemberton). 1902.
Trent's Trust and Other Stories. 1903.
Fair the terrace that o'erlooks . . . c. 1907.
Lectures. 1909.
Poems and Stories. Ed. Charles Swain Thomas. 1912.
Stories and Poems and Other Uncollected Writings. Ed. Charles Mecker Kozlay. 1914.
Stories and Poems. Ed. William Macdonald. 1915.
Letters. Ed. Geoffrey Bret Harte. 1926.
Sketches of the Sixties (with Mark Twain). 1926.
Unpublished Limericks & Cartoons. 1933.
Selected Stories. 1946.
Best Short Stories. Ed. Robert N. Linscott. 1947.
San Francisco in 1866: Being Letters to the Springfield Republican. Eds. George R. Stewart and Edwin S. Fussell. 1951.
Berkeley: Xanadu of the San Francisco Bay. 1951.
Ah Sin: A Dramatic Work (with Mark Twain). Ed. Frederick Anderson. 1961.

LIONEL JOHNSON (1867–1902)

Sir Walter Raleigh in the Tower. 1885.
The Gordon Riots. 1893.
Bits of Old Chelsea (with Richard Le Gallienne). 1894.
The Art of Thomas Hardy. 1894.
Poems. 1895.
A Carol. 1896.
Ireland, with Other Poems. 1897.
Twenty-one Poems. Ed. W. B. Yeats. 1904.
Poetry and Ireland (with W. B. Yeats). 1908.
Selections from the Poems. Ed. Clement K. Shorter. 1908.
Post Liminium: Essays and Critical Papers. Ed. Thomas Whittemore. 1911.

Some Poems. Ed. Louise Imogen Guiney. 1912.
Poetical Works. 1915.
Religious Poems. Ed. George F. Engelbach. 1916.
Some Winchester Letters. Ed. Francis, Earl Russell. 1919.
Reviews and Critical Papers. Ed. Robert Shafer. 1921.
A New Selection from the Poems. Ed. H. V. Marrott. 1927.
Three Poems. Ed. Vincent Starrett. 1928.
Two Poems. Eds. Vincent Starrett and Edwin B. Hill. 1929.
Select Poems. 1931.
Complete Poems. Ed. Iain Fletcher. 1953, 1982.
A Letter to Edgar Jepson. 1979.
Some Letters to Richard Le Gallienne. 1979.

FRANK NORRIS (1870–1902)

Yvernelle: A Legend of Feudal France. 1892.
Moran of the Lady Letty: A Story of Adventure off the California Coast. 1898.
McTeague: A Story of San Francisco. 1899.
Blix. 1899.
A Man's Woman. 1900.
The Octopus: A Story of California. 1901.
The Pit: A Story of Chicago. 1903.
A Deal in Wheat and Other Stories of the New and Old West. 1903.
The Responsibilities of the Novelist and Other Literary Essays. 1903.
Complete Works (Golden Gate Edition). 1903. 7 vols.
Complete Works. 1905. 4 vols.
The Joyous Miracle. 1906.
The Third Circle. 1909.
Vandover and the Brute. Ed. Charles G. Norris. 1914.
The Surrender of Santiago: An Account of the Historic Surrender of Santiago to General Shafter, July 17, 1898. 1917.
Complete Works (Argonaut Manuscript Limited Edition). 1928. 10 vols.
Two Poems and Kim Reviewed. Ed. Harvey Taylor. 1930.
Frank Norris of The Wave: *Stories & Sketches from the San Francisco Weekly, 1893 to 1897.* 1931.
Letters. Ed. Franklin Walker. 1956.
Literary Criticism. Ed. Donald Pizer. 1964.
Frank Norris Petitions the President and Faculty of the University of California. 1970.
A Novelist in the Making: A Collection of Student Themes and the Novels Blix and Vandover and the Brute. Ed. James D. Hart. 1970.
Novels and Essays. Ed. Donald Pizer. 1986.

HERBERT SPENCER (1820–1903)

The Proper Sphere of Government. 1843.
Social Statics; or, The Conditions Essential to Human Happiness Specified, and the First of Them Developed. 1851.
A Theory of Population Deduced from the General Law of Animal Fertility. 1852.
Over-Legislation. 1854.
The Principles of Psychology. 1855.
Railway Morals and Railway Policy. 1855.
Essays Scientific, Political, and Speculative. 1858–63 (2 vols.), 1868–74 (3 vols.)
A System of Synthetic Philosophy. 1860–62 [*First Principles;* 6 parts]; 1864–67 [*The Principles of Biology;* 2 vols.]; 1870–72 [*The Principles of Psychology;* 2 vols.]; 1876–96 [*The Principles of Sociology;* 3 vols.]; 1892–93 [*The Principles of Ethics* ⟨*The Data of Ethics; Justice; Negative and Positive Beneficence*⟩; 2 vols.].
Education: Intellectual, Moral, and Physical. 1861.

The Classification of the Sciences; to Which Are Added Reasons for Dissenting from the Philosophy of M. Comte. 1864.

Spontaneous Generation and the Hypothesis of Physiological Units: A Reply to the North American Review. 1870.

Recent Discussions in Science, Philosophy, and Morals. 1871.

The Study of Sociology. 1873.

Descriptive Sociology; or, Groups of Sociological Facts. 1873–81. 8 parts.

Philosophy of Style. 1873.

Sins of Trade: A Sermon ⟨by William Henry Lyttelton⟩ *and The Morals of Trade.* 1874.

The Data of Ethics. 1879.

The Man versus the State. 1884.

The Nature and Reality of Religion (with Frederic Harrison). 1885.

The Factors of Organic Evolution. 1887.

Justice. 1891.

The Inadequacy of Natural Selection. 1893.

A Rejoinder to Professor Weismann. 1893.

Weismannism Once More. 1894.

Against the Metric System. 1896.

Various Fragments. 1897.

Facts and Comments. 1902.

An Autobiography. 1904. 2 vols.

Essays on Education and Kindred Subjects. 1911.

Herbert Spencer on Education. Ed. F. A. Cavenagh. 1932.

Herbert Spencer. Ed. Ann Low-Beer. 1969.

Herbert Spencer: Structure, Function and Evolution. Ed. Stanislav Andreski. 1971.

Herbert Spencer on Social Evolution: Selected Writings. Ed. J. D. Y. Peel. 1972.

RICHARD HENRY STODDARD (1825–1903)

Foot-Prints. 1849.

Poems. 1852.

Adventures in Fairy-Land. 1853.

Songs of Summer. 1857.

Town and Country and The Voices in the Shells. 1857.

The Life, Travels and Books of Alexander von Humboldt. 1859.

The Loves and Heroines of the Poets (editor). 1861.

The Last Political Writings of Gen. Nathaniel Lyon (editor). 1861.

The King's Bell. 1863.

Vates Patriae. 1864.

The Story of Little Red Riding Hood, Told in Verse. c. 1864.

The Late English Poets (editor). 1865.

Abraham Lincoln: An Horatian Ode. 1865.

"Under Green Leaves": A Book of Rural Poems (editor). 1865.

The Children in the Wood, Told in Verse. 1866.

Melodies and Madrigals: Mostly from the Old English Poets (editor). 1866.

Remember: A Keepsake (editor; with Elizabeth Stoddard). 1869.

The Story of Putnam the Brave. 1870.

The Book of the East and Other Poems. 1871.

The Female Poets of America by Rufus W. Griswold (revised by Stoddard). 1873.

Anecdote Biographies of Thackeray and Dickens (editor). 1874.

The Poets and Poetry of America by Rufus W. Griswold (revised by Stoddard). 1874.

Personal Reminiscences by Chorley, Planche, and Young (editor). 1874.

Prosper Merimee's Letters to an Incognita; with Recollections by Lamartine and George Sand (editor). 1874.

The Greville Memoirs: A Journal of the Reigns of King George

IV and King William IV by Charles Cavendish Fulke Greville (editor). 1875.

Personal Reminiscences of Lamb, Hazlitt, and Others (editor). 1875.

Personal Reminiscences by Barham, Harness, and Hodder (editor). 1875.

Personal Reminiscences by Moore and Jerdan (editor). 1875.

Personal Reminiscences by O'Keefe, Kelley, and Taylor (editor). 1875.

Personal Reminiscences by Cornelia Knight and Thomas Raikes (editor). 1875.

The Treasure-Trove Series (editor). 1875. 3 vols.

The Poets and Poetry of England, in the Nineteenth Century by Rufus W. Griswold (revised by Stoddard). 1875.

A Century After: Picturesque Glimpses of Philadelphia and Pennsylvania. 1876.

Personal Reminiscences by Constable and Gillies (editor). 1876.

The Life, Letters and Table Talk of Benjamin Robert Haydon (editor). 1876.

Anecdote Biography of Percy Bysshe Shelley (editor). 1877.

Poets' Homes: Pen and Pencil Sketches of American Poets and Their Homes. 1877.

Nathaniel Hawthorne. 1879.

Poems. 1880.

Poems of William Wordsworth (editor). 1881.

Mrs. Browning's Birthday Book (editor). 1882.

Henry Wadsworth Longfellow: A Medley in Prose and Verse (editor). 1882.

Henry W. Longfellow: A Memoir. c. 1882.

English Verse (editor; with William James Linton). 1883.

The Life of Washington Irving. 1883.

Readings and Recitations from Modern Authors: Being Pearls Gathered from the Fields of Poetry and Romance (editor; with Elizabeth Stoddard). 1884.

Selections from the Poetical Works of A. C. Swinburne (editor). 1884.

The Works of Edgar Allan Poe (editor). 1884. 8 vols.

The Lion's Cub, with Other Verse. 1890.

Under the Evening Lamp. 1892.

The Complete Poems of William Cullen Bryant (editor). 1894.

The Works of Lord Byron, with His Letters and Journals, and His Life by Thomas Moore (editor). 1900.

Recollections, Personal and Literary. Ed. Ripley Hitchcock. 1903.

W. E. H. LECKY (1838–1903)

Friendship and Other Poems. 1859.

The Religious Tendencies of the Age. 1860.

The Leaders of Public Opinion in Ireland. 1861, 1903 (2 vols.).

On the Declining Sense of the Miraculous. 1863.

History of the Rise and Influence of the Spirit of Rationalism in Europe. 1865. 2 vols.

History of European Morals from Augustus to Charlemagne. 1869. 2 vols.

A History of England in the Eighteenth Century. 1878–90 (8 vols.), 1892 (as *A History of England in the Eighteenth Century* [7 vols.] and *A History of Ireland in the Eighteenth Century* [5 vols.]).

Poems. 1891.

William Pitt. 1891.

The Political Value of History. 1892.

The Empire, Its Value and Its Growth: An Inaugural Address, Delivered at the Imperial Institute. 1893.

Democracy and Liberty. 1896. 2 vols.

The Map of Life: Conduct and Character. 1899.
Moral Aspects of the South African War. 1900.
Old-Age Pensions. 1908.
Historical and Political Essays. Ed. Elisabeth van Dedem Lecky. 1908.
Clerical Influences: An Essay on Irish Sectarianism and English Government. Eds. W. E. G. Lloyd and F. Cruise O'Brien. 1911.
A Victorian Historian: Private Letters 1859–1878. Ed. H. Montgomery Hyde. 1947.

W. E. HENLEY (1849–1903)

Deacon Brodie; or, The Double Life (with Robert Louis Stevenson). 1880.
Admiral Guinea (with Robert Louis Stevenson). 1884.
Beau Austin (with Robert Louis Stevenson). 1884.
Macaire (with Robert Louis Stevenson). 1885.
A Book of Verses. 1888.
The Graphic Gallery of Shakespeare's Heroines (editor). 1888.
Memorial Catalogue of the French and Dutch Loan Collection (editor). 1888.
Pictures at Play; or, Dialogues of the Galleries (with Andrew Lang). 1888.
A Century of Artists (editor). 1889.
Sir Henry Raeburn (editor). 1889.
Slang and Its Analogues (editor; with John S. Farmer). 1890–1904. 7 vols.
Views and Reviews: Essays in Appreciation. 1890.
Lyra Heroica (editor). 1892.
The Song of the Sword and Other Verses. 1892.
Three Plays (with Robert Louis Stevenson). 1892.
The Tudor Translations (editor). 1892–1903. 32 vols.
London Voluntaries, The Song of the Sword, and Other Verses. 1893.
A Book of English Prose (editor; with Charles Whibley). 1894.
English Classics (editor). 1894–95. 6 vols.
A London Garland (editor). 1895.
Plays (with Robert Louis Stevenson). 1895.
The Poetry of Robert Burns (editor; with T. F. Henderson). 1896–97. 4 vols.
English Lyrics, Chaucer to Poe (editor). 1897.
The Works of Lord Byron: Volume I, Letters 1804–1813 (editor). 1897.
The Poetry of Wilfred Blunt (editor; with George Wyndham). 1898.
London Types. 1898.
Poems. 1898.
The Works of Tobias Smollett (editor; with Thomas Seccombe). 1899–1901. 12 vols.
Hawthorn and Lavender: Songs and Madrigals. 1899.
The Collected Poems of T. E. Brown (editor; with H. F. Brown and H. G. Dakyns). 1900.
For England's Sake: Verses and Songs in Time of War. 1900.
I.M. Reginae Dilectissimae Victoriae. 1901.
Hawthorn and Lavender, with Other Verses. 1901.
The Works of Shakespeare (editor). 1901–04. 10 vols.
Views and Reviews: Essays in Appreciation: II. Art. 1902.
In Hospital: Rhymes and Rhythms. 1903.
A Song of Speed. 1903.
The Complete Works of Henry Fielding (editor). 1903. 16 vols.
Works. 1908. 7 vols.
Works. 1921. 5 vols.
Some Letters. Ed. de V. Payen-Payne. 1933.

GEORGE GISSING (1857–1903)

Workers in the Dawn. 1880. 3 vols.
The Unclassed. 1884. 3 vols.
Isabel Clarendon. 1886. 2 vols.
Demos: A Story of English Socialism. 1886. 3 vols.
Thyrza: A Tale. 1887. 3 vols.
A Life's Morning. 1888. 3 vols.
The Nether World. 1889. 3 vols.
The Emancipated. 1890. 3 vols.
New Grub Street. 1891. 3 vols.
Denzil Quarrier. 1892.
Born in Exile. 1892. 3 vols.
The Odd Women. 1893. 3 vols.
In the Year of the Jubilee. 1894. 3 vols.
Eve's Ransom. 1895.
The Paying Guest. 1895.
Sleeping Fires. 1895.
The Whirlpool. 1897.
Human Odds and Ends: Stories and Sketches. 1898.
Charles Dickens: A Critical Study. 1898.
The Town Traveller. 1898.
The Crown of Life. 1899.
Our Friend the Charlatan. 1901.
By the Ionian Sea. 1901.
The Private Papers of Henry Ryecroft. 1903.
Veranilda: A Romance. 1904.
Will Warburton: A Romance of Real Life. 1905.
The House of Cobwebs and Other Stories. Ed. Thomas Seccombe. 1906.
Letters to Edward Clodd. 1914.
Letters to an Editor. 1915.
Sins of the Fathers and Other Tales. 1924.
Critical Studies of the Works of Charles Dickens. Ed. Temple Scott. 1924.
Two Letters to Joseph Conrad. 1926.
A Victim of Circumstances and Other Stories. 1927.
Letters to Members of His Family. Eds. Algernon Gissing and Ellen Gissing. 1927.
Hope in Vain. 1930.
Autobiographical Notes. 1930.
Brownie. 1931.
George Gissing and H. G. Wells: Their Friendship and Correspondence. Ed. Royal A. Gettmann. 1961.
Letters to Eduard Bertz 1887–1903. Ed. Arthur C. Young. 1961.
Commonplace Book. Ed. Jacob Korg. 1962.
Letters to Gabrielle Fleury. Ed. Pierre Coustillas. 1964.
Notes on Social Democracy. 1968.
My First Rehearsal and My Clerical Rival. Ed. Pierre Coustillas. 1970.
Essays and Fiction. Ed. Pierre Coustillas. 1970.
Letters to Edward Clodd. Ed. Pierre Coustillas. 1973.
London and the Life of Literature in Late Victorian England: The Diary of George Gissing, Novelist. Ed. Pierre Coustillas. 1978.
Six Sonnets on Shakespearean Heroines. Ed. Pierre Coustillas. 1982.

SIR EDWIN ARNOLD (1832–1904)

The Feast of Belshazzar. 1852.
Poems, Narrative and Lyrical. 1853.
Griselda: A Tragedy, and Other Poems. 1856.
The Wreck of the Northern Belle. 1857.
Education in India: A Letter from the Ex-Principal of an In-

dian Government College to His Appointed Successor. 1860.

The Book of Good Counsels: From the Sanskrit of the Hitopadésa (translator). 1861.

The Marquis of Dalhousie's Administration of British India. 1862–65. 2 vols.

Political Poems by Victor Hugo and Garibaldi (translator). 1868.

The Poets of Greece. 1869.

Hero and Leander by Musaeus (translator). 1873.

The Indian Song of Songs: From the Sanskrit of the Gîta Govinda of Jayadeva (translator). 1875.

A Simple Transliteral Grammar of the Turkish Language. 1877.

The Light of Asia; or, The Great Renunciation—Mahâbhinishkrāmana: Being the Life and Teaching of Gautama, Prince of India and Founder of Buddhism, as Told in Verse by an Indian Buddhist. 1879.

Poems. 1880.

Indian Poetry: Containing a New Edition of "The Indian Song of Songs," from the Sanskrit of the Gita Govinda of Jayadeva; Two Books from "The Iliad of India" (Mahâbhârata);"Proverbial Wisdom" from the Shlokes of the Hitopadésa, and Other Oriental Poems. 1881.

Pearls of Faith; or, Islam's Rosary: Being the Ninety-nine Beautiful Names of Allah—Asmâ-el-Husnâ—with Comments in Verse from Various Oriental Sources, as Made by an Indian Mussulman. 1883.

Indian Idylls, from the Sanskrit of the Mahâbhârata (translator). 1883.

The Secret of Death, from the Sanskrit, with Some Collected Poems. 1885.

The Arnold Birthday Book. Eds. Katherine Lilian Arnold and Constance Arnold. 1885.

The Song Celestial; or, Bhagavad-Gita (translator). 1885.

India Revisited. 1886.

Death—and Afterwards. 1887.

Lotus and Jewel: Containing "In an Indian Temple," "A Casket of Gems," "A Queen's Revenge," with Other Poems. 1887.

With Sa'di in the Garden; or, The Book of Love. 1888.

Poems National and Non-Oriental, with Some New Pieces. 1888.

In My Lady's Praise: Being Poems, Old and New, Written in the Honour of Fanny, Lady Arnold, and Now Collected in Her Memory. 1889.

Poetical Works. 1889. 2 vols.

Pictures of Ancient Japanese History by T. H. Asso (revised by Arnold). 1890.

The Light of the World; or, The Great Consummation. 1891.

Seas and Lands. 1891.

Japonica. 1892.

Potiphar's Wife and Other Poems. 1892.

Selected Poems. 1892.

Adzuma; or, The Japanese Wife. 1893.

Aspects of Life. 1893.

Wandering Words. 1894.

The Tenth Muse and Other Poems. 1895.

East and West: Being Papers Reprinted from the Daily Telegraph *and Other Sources.* 1896.

Victoria, Queen and Empress: The Sixty Years. 1896.

The Chaurapanchâsika (translator). 1896.

The Queen's Justice: A True Story of Indian Village Life. 1899.

The Gulistan: The First Four Babs, or "Gateways" (translator). 1899.

The Voyage of Ithobal. 1901.

Oriental Poems. Ed. J. M. Watkins. 1904.

Indian Poetry and Indian Idylls. 1915. 2 parts.

The Arnold Poetry Reader. Ed. Edwin L. Arnold. 1920.

SIR LESLIE STEPHEN (1832–1904)

The Poll Degree from a Third Point of View. 1863.

Sketches from Cambridge. 1865.

The Times on the American War: An Historical Study. 1865.

The Playground of Europe. 1871.

Essays on Freethinking and Plainspeaking. 1873.

Hours in a Library. 1874–79 (3 vols.), 1904 (4 vols.).

History of English Thought in the Eighteenth Century. 1876. 2 vols.

Belief and Evidence. 1877.

Samuel Johnson. 1878.

Lectures and Essays by W. K. Clifford (editor; with Frederick Pollock). 1879.

The Uniformity of Nature. 1879.

Alexander Pope. 1880.

The Science of Ethics. 1882.

The Works of Henry Fielding (editor). 1882. 10 vols.

Swift. 1882.

Dictionary of National Biography (editor; with Sidney Lee). 1885–1901. 66 vols.

Life of Henry Fawcett. 1885.

What Is Materialism? 1886.

An Agnostic's Apology and Other Essays. 1893.

The Life of Sir James Fitzjames Stephen. 1895.

Social Rights and Duties: Addresses to Ethical Societies. 1896. 2 vols.

Studies of a Biographer. 1898–1902. 4 vols.

The English Utilitarians. 1900. 3 vols.

Letters of John Richard Green (editor). 1901.

George Eliot. 1902.

Robert Louis Stevenson: An Essay. 1902.

English Literature and Society in the Eighteenth Century. 1904.

Hobbes. 1904.

Life and Letters. Ed. Frederic William Maitland. 1906.

Some Early Impressions. 1924.

Men, Books, and Mountains: Essays. Ed. S. O. A. Ullmann. 1956.

Mausoleum Book. Ed. Alan Bell. 1977.

Selected Writings in British Intellectual History. Ed. Noël Annan. 1979.

KATE CHOPIN (1850–1904)

At Fault. 1890.

Bayou Folk. 1894.

A Night in Acadie. 1897.

The Awakening. 1899.

Kate Chopin and Her Creole Stories. Ed. Daniel S. Rankin. 1932.

Complete Works. Ed. Per Seyersted. 1969. 2 vols.

The Awakening and Other Stories. Ed. Lewis Leary. 1970.

The Storm and Other Stories, with The Awakening. Ed. Per Seyersted. 1974.

The Awakening and Selected Short Stories. Ed. Barbara Solomon. 1976.

A Kate Chopin Miscellany. Eds. Per Seyersted and Emily Toth. 1979.

Portraits: Short Stories. Ed. Helen Taylor. 1979.

The Awakening and Selected Stories. 1981.

LAFCADIO HEARN (1850–1904)

Ye Giglampz. 1874. 9 nos.

One of Cleopatra's Nights and Other Fantastic Romances by Théophile Gautier (translator). 1882.

Stray Leaves from Strange Literature. 1884.

La Cuisine Créole (editor). 1885.

"Gombo Zhèbes": Little Dictionary of Creole Proverbs (translator). 1885.

Some Chinese Ghosts. 1887.

Chita: A Memory of Last Island. 1889.

The Crime of Sylvestre Bonnard by Anatole France (translator). 1890.

Two Years in the French West Indies. 1890.

Youma: The Story of a West-Indian Slave. 1890.

Glimpses of Unfamiliar Japan. 1894. 2 vols.

"Out of the East": Reveries and Studies in New Japan. 1895.

Kokoro: Hints and Echoes of Japanese Inner Life. 1896.

Gleanings in Buddha-Fields: Studies of Hand and Soul in the Far East. 1897.

The Boy Who Drew Cats (translator). 1898.

Exotics and Retrospectives. 1898.

The Goblin Spider (translator). 1899.

In Ghostly Japan. 1899.

Shadowings. 1900.

A Japanese Miscellany. 1901.

The Old Woman Who Lost Her Dumpling (translator). 1902.

Kottō: Being Japanese Curios, with Sundry Cobwebs. 1902.

Chin Chin Kobakama (translator). 1903.

Kwaidan: Stories and Studies of Strange Things. 1904.

Japan: An Attempt at Interpretation. 1904.

The Romance of the Milky Way and Other Studies and Stories. 1905.

Life and Letters. Ed. Elizabeth Bisland. 1906. 2 vols.

Letters from the Raven: Being the Correspondence with Henry Watkin. Ed. Milton Bronner. 1907.

The Temptation of St. Anthony by Gustave Flaubert (translator). 1910.

Japanese Letters. Ed. Elizabeth Bisland. 1910.

Leaves from the Diary of an Impressionist: Early Writings. Ed. Ferris Greenslet. 1911.

Editorials from the Kobe Chronicle. 1913.

Fantastics and Other Fancies. Ed. Charles Woodward Hutson. 1914.

Japanese Lyrics. 1915.

Interpretations of Literature. Ed. John Erskine. 1915. 2 vols.

Appreciations of Poetry. Ed. John Erskine. 1916.

Life and Literature. Ed. John Erskine. 1917.

Japanese Fairy Tales (translator; with others). 1918.

Karma. Ed. Albert Mordell. 1918.

Talks to Writers. Ed. John Erskine. 1920.

Books and Habits from the Lectures. Ed. John Erskine. 1921.

Pre-Raphaelite and Other Poets. Ed. John Erskine. 1922.

The Fountain of Youth (translator). 1922.

Writings. 1922. 16 vols.

Essays in European and Oriental Literature. Ed. Albert Mordell. 1923.

Creole Sketches. Ed. Charles Woodward Hutson. 1924.

An American Miscellany. Ed. Albert Mordell. 1924. 2 vols.

Saint Anthony and Other Stories by Guy de Maupassant (translator). Ed. Albert Mordell. 1924.

Occidental Gleanings: Sketches and Essays. Ed. Albert Mordell. 1925. 2 vols.

Some New Letters and Writings. Ed. Sanki Ichikawa. 1925.

Editorials. Ed. Charles Woodward Hutson. 1926.

Insects and Greek Poetry. 1926.

A History of English Literature in a Series of Lectures. 1927. 2 vols.

Some Strange English Literary Figures of the Eighteenth and Nineteenth Centuries. Ed. R. Tanabé. 1927.

Supplement to A History of English Literature. 1927.

Lectures on Shakespeare. Ed. Iwao Inagaki. 1928.

Essays on American Literature. Ed. Sanki Ichikawa. 1929.

Lectures on Prosody. Ed. Teisaburo Ochiai. 1929.

Victorian Philosophy. 1930.

The Adventures of Walter Schnaffs by Guy de Maupassant (translator). 1931.

Complete Lectures. Eds. Ryuki Tanabé, Teisaburo Ochiai, and Ichiro Nishizaki. 1932–34. 3 vols.

Stories from Pierre Loti (translator). 1933.

Gibbeted. Ed. P. D. Perkins. 1933.

Spirit Photography. Ed. P. D. Perkins. 1933.

Letters from Shimane and Kyūshū. 1934.

Sketches and Tales from the French (translator). Ed. Albert Mordell. 1935.

Stories from Emile Zola (translator). Ed. Albert Mordell. 1935.

Barbarous Barbers and Other Stories. Ed. Ichiro Nishizaki. 1939.

Buying Christmas Toys and Other Essays. Ed. Ichiro Nishizaki. 1939.

Literary Essays. Ed. Ichiro Nishizaki. 1939.

The New Radiance and Other Scientific Sketches. Ed. Ichiro Nishizaki. 1939.

Oriental Articles. Ed. Ichiro Nishizaki. 1939.

Père Antoine's Date Palm. 1940.

Lectures on Tennyson. Ed. Shigetsugu Kishi. 1941.

An Orange Christmas. 1941.

Selected Writings. Ed. Henry Goodman. 1949.

Articles on Literature and Other Writings from the Cincinnati Enquirer 1873. Eds. Hojin Yano, Tadanobu Kawai, and Hiroyoshi Kishimoto. 1975.

INDEX TO BIBLIOGRAPHIES

SERIES CONTENTS

SERIES CONTENTS

Volume 1

gion and Church (1825–52), tr. Joseph Torrey, Volume 7, p. 97.
7. Henry Hallam, *Introduction to the Literature of Europe,* 1837–39, Pt. 1, Ch. 1, Par. 87; Ch. 2, Par. 33.
8. W. E. H. Lecky, *History of European Morals,* 1869, Ch. 4.
9. George S. Morris, *British Thought and Thinkers,* 1880, pp. 40–42.
10. R. Adamson, *Dictionary of National Biography,* 1885, Volume 2, p. 378.
11. W. Denton, *England in the Fifteenth Century,* 1888, p. 59.
12. W. L. Courtney, "Roger Bacon," *Fortnightly Review,* August 1889, p. 262.
13. Alfred Weber, *History of Philosophy* (1892), tr. Frank Thilly, 1896, p. 258.
14. Herbert Maxwell, "Roger Bacon," *Blackwood's Edinburgh Magazine,* November 1894, p. 610.
15. George Burton Adams, *Civilization during the Middle Ages,* 1894, p. 369.
16. R. L. Poole, *Social England,* ed. H. D. Traill, 1894, Volume 1, p. 438.

THOMAS OF ERCELDOUNE
(THOMAS THE RHYMER)

1. Thomas of Erceldoune, "Fytte First," *Sir Tristrem,* c. 1299.
2. Robert de Brunne, "Prolog," *Annals,* c. 1338.
3. John Spottiswood, *History of the Church and State of Scotland* (1639), 1851, Volume 1, p. 93.
4. Lord Hailes, *Remarks on the History of Scotland,* 1773.
5. John Finlay, *Wallace; or, The Vale of Ellerslie,* 1802.
6. Sir Walter Scott, "Essay on Romance" (1824), *Miscellaneous Works,* 1861, Volume 6, p. 207.
7. David Irving, *History of Scotish Poetry,* ed. John Aitken Carlyle, 1861, p. 60.
8. John Hill Burton, *The History of Scotland,* 1867, Volume 4, p. 119.
9. John Merry Ross, *Scottish History and Literature,* ed. James Brown, 1884, p. 107.
10. G. P. M'Neill, *Sir Tristrem,* 1886.
11. George Eyre-Todd, *Early Scottish Poetry,* 1891, p. 17.
12. W. J. Courthope, *A History of English Poetry,* 1895, Volume 1, p. 458.

DUNS SCOTUS

1. Thomas Fuller, *The History of the Worthies of England,* 1662.
2. Victor Cousin, "Lecture IX," *Course of the History of Modern Philosophy,* 1841, tr. O. W. Wight.
3. H. H. Milman, *History of Latin Christianity,* 1855, Volume 6, Bk. 14, Ch. 3, pp. 467–68.
4. J. A. Dorner, *History of the Doctrine of the Person of Christ,* 1861, Volume 1, Div. 2, p. 346.
5. Frederich Überweg, *A History of Philosophy,* tr. George S. Morris, 1871, Volume 1, p. 452.
6. W. J. Townsend, *The Great Schoolmen of the Middle Ages,* 1881, p. 263.
7. R. L. Poole, *Social England,* ed. H. D. Traill, 1894, Volume 1, p. 439.
8. George Park Fisher, *History of Christian Doctrine,* 1896, p. 232.

WILLIAM OF OCCAM

1. Thomas Fuller, *The History of the Worthies of England,* 1662.

2. Wilhelm Gottlieb Tennemann, *A Manual of the History of Philosophy* (1812), tr. A. Johnson, ed. J. R. Morell, 1852, p. 244.
3. H. H. Milman, *History of Latin Christianity,* 1855, Volume 6, Bk. 14, Ch. 3, pp. 451–72.
4. Frederick Denison Maurice, *Moral and Metaphysical Philosophy,* 1862.
5. Arthur Tilley, *The Literature of the French Renaissance,* 1885, p. 105.
6. George Park Fisher, *History of the Christian Church,* 1887, p. 271.
7. R. L. Poole, *Dictionary of National Biography,* 1895, Volume 41, p. 361.

RICHARD ROLLE OF HAMPOLE

1. Thomas Fuller, *The History of the Worthies of England,* 1662.
2. Thomas Warton, *The History of English Poetry,* 1774–81, Sec. 7.
3. Thomas Campbell, *An Essay on English Poetry,* 1819.
4. Bernhard ten Brink, *History of English Literature (To Wiclif)* (1877), tr. H. M. Kennedy, 1883, p. 296.
5. J. J. Jusserand, *A Literary History of the English People,* 1895, pp. 216–18.
6. Carl Horstmann, "Introduction" to *Richard Rolle of Hampole,* 1896.
7. T. E. Bridgett, "Richard Rolle, the Hermit," *Dublin Review,* October 1897, p. 292.
8. George Saintsbury, *A Short History of English Literature,* 1898, p. 76.

SIR JOHN MANDEVILLE

1. Sir John Mandeville, "The Prologue" to *Voiage and Travaile,* c. 1356.
2. Wynkyn de Worde, "Title," *Mandeville,* 1499.
3. John Bale, *Scriptores Illustres Majoris Britanniae,* 1548.
4. Joseph Addison, Richard Steele, *The Tatler,* No. 254 (November 23, 1710).
5. Washington Irving, "Appendix" to *The Life and Voyages of Columbus,* 1828–55, Volume 3, p. 399.
6. J. O. Halliwell-Phillips, "Introduction" to *The Voiage and Travaile of Sir John Mandeville, Kt.,* 1839, p. xii.
7. Isaac Disraeli, "Mandeville: Our First Traveller," *Amenities of Literature,* 1841, pp. 246–49.
8. George P. Marsh, *The Origin and History of the English Language,* 1862, p. 271.
9. Hippolyte Taine, *The History of English Literature,* tr. H. Van Laun, 1871, Bk. 1, pp. 85–86.
10. Bernhard Henry Becker, *Adventurous Lives,* 1878, Volume 2, p. 98.
11. Alfred H. Welsh, *Development of English Literature and Language,* 1882, Volume 1, p. 198.
12. E. B. Nicholson, H. Yule, *Encyclopaedia Britannica,* 1883 (9th ed.), Volume 15, p. 475.
13. Andrew Lang, *Letters to Dead Authors,* 1886, p. 110.
14. Henry Morley, *English Writers,* 1888, Volume 4, p. 282.
15. Donald G. Mitchell, *English Lands, Letters, and Kings: From Celt to Tudor,* 1889, p. 60.
16. J. J. Jusserand, *A Literary History of the English People,* 1895, p. 403.
17. H. G. Keene, "Sir John Mandeville," *Westminster Review,* July 1896, pp. 52–54.
18. George Saintsbury, *A Short History of English Literature,* 1898, p. 148.
19. Richard Garnett, Edmund Gosse, *English Literature: An Illustrated Record,* 1903, Volume 1, pp. 196–203.

JOHN GOWER

26. Edmund Gosse, *A Short History of Modern English Literature*, 1897, p. 24.
27. Thomas Berthelette, "Dedication" to *Confessio Amantis*, 1532.
28. Isaac Disraeli, "Gower," *Amenities of Literature*, 1841, pp. 285–91.
29. Reinhold Pauli, "Introduction" to *Confessio Amantis*, 1856, Volume 1, pp. xxxv–xxxvi.
30. Donald G. Mitchell, *English Lands, Letters, and Kings: From Celt to Tudor*, 1889, p. 128.
31. Thomas R. Lounsbury, *Studies in Chaucer*, 1891, Volume 3, p. 70.
32. F. J. Snell, "The Fourteenth Century," *Periods of European Literature*, 1899, pp. 323–24.
33. Richard Garnett, Edmund Gosse, *English Literature: An Illustrated Record*, 1903, Volume 1, pp. 175–85.

JOHN LYDGATE

1. Stephen Hawes, *The Pastime of Pleasure*, 1506, Ch. 14, Sec. 12.
2. John Skelton, *Phillyp Sparrowe*, 1508, ll. 804–12.
3. William Bullein, *A Dialogue Both Pleasaunt and Pietifull, Wherein Is a Godlie Regiment against the Fever Pestilence, with a Consolation and Comforte against Death*, 1564–73.
4. William Webbe, *A Discourse of English Poetrie*, 1586.
5. George Puttenham, *The Arte of English Poesie*, 1589.
6. Theophilus Cibber, *Lives of the Poets*, 1753, Volume 1, pp. 23–24.
7. Thomas Gray, "On the Poems of Lydgate" (1761), *Works*, ed. Edmund Gosse, 1884, Volume 1, pp. 397–99.
8. Thomas Warton, *The History of English Poetry*, 1774–81, Sec. 21.
9. Joseph Ritson, *Biographia Poetica*, 1802, pp. 87–88.
10. Sharon Turner, *The History of England during the Middle Ages*, 1814–23, Volume 5, p. 340.
11. Samuel Knapp, *Advice in the Pursuits of Literature*, 1832, p. 21.
12. Henry Hallam, *Introduction to the Literature of Europe*, 1837–39, Pt. 1, Ch. 2, Par. 48.
13. Elizabeth Barrett Browning, *The Book of the Poets* (1842), *Life, Letters and Essays of Elizabeth Barrett Browning*, 1863.
14. George Gilfillan, *Specimens with Memoirs of the Less-Known British Poets*, 1860, Volume 1, p. 47.
15. George L. Craik, *A Compendious History of English Literature and of the English Language*, 1861, Volume 1, p. 403.
16. Hippolyte Taine, *The History of English Literature*, tr. H. Van Laun, 1871, Bk. 1, pp. 137–39.
17. Henry Morley, *First Sketch of English Literature*, 1873, p. 179.
18. Thomas R. Lounsbury, *Studies in Chaucer*, 1891, Volume 3, pp. 25–27.
19. Edmund Gosse, *A Short History of Modern English Literature*, 1897, p. 36.
20. W. J. Courthope, *A History of English Poetry*, 1895, Volume 1, p. 326.
21. Isaac Disraeli, "Lydgate; the Monk of Bury," *Amenities of Literature*, 1841, pp. 312–22.
22. Bernhard ten Brink, *History of English Literature (Wyclif, Chaucer, Earliest Drama, Renaissance)*, tr. W. C. Robinson, 1892, pp. 221–34.

THOMAS OCCLEVE

1. William Browne, "Eclogue 1," *The Shepard's Pipe*, 1614–20.
2. Edward Phillips, *Theatrum Poetarum Anglicanorum*, 1675.
3. Thomas Warton, *The History of English Poetry*, 1774–81, Sec. 20.
4. George Ellis, *Specimens of the Early English Poets*, 1790–1845, Volume 1, p. 213.
5. Thomas Campbell, *An Essay on English Poetry*, 1819.
6. Isaac Disraeli, "Occleve; the Scholar of Chaucer," *Amenities of Literature*, 1841, pp. 305–11.
7. William Francis Collier, *A History of English Literature*, 1861, p. 69.
8. George P. Marsh, *The Origin and History of the English Language*, 1861, p. 455.
9. Sir Edward Creasy, *History of England*, 1870, Volume 2, p. 543.
10. William Minto, *Characteristics of English Poets*, 1874, p. 71.
11. Emelyn W. Washburn, *Studies in Early English Literature*, 1884, p. 91.
12. Bernhard ten Brink, *History of English Literature (Wyclif, Chaucer, Earliest Drama, Renaissance)*, tr. W. C. Robinson, 1892, p. 215.
13. Edmund Gosse, *A Short History of Modern English Literature*, 1897, p. 35.

WILLIAM CAXTON

1. Inscription on Tomb, St. Margaret's, Westminster, 1830.
2. John Lewis, *Life of Mayster Wyllyam Caxton*, 1737.
3. Charles Knight, *William Caxton, the First English Printer*, 1844, p. 195.
4. William Francis Collier, *A History of English Literature*, 1861, pp. 72–74.
5. Bernard Henry Becker, *Adventurous Lives*, 1878, Volume 1, p. 286.
6. William Nicolson, *English Historical Library*, 1696–1714, Pt. 1.
7. Conyers Middleton, *A Dissertation concerning the Origin of Printing in England*, 1735.
8. Edward Gibbon, "An Address" (1794), *Miscellaneous Works*, ed. John, Lord Sheffield, 1796, p. 836.
9. Thomas Frognall Dibdin, *Typographical Antiquities of Great Britain*, 1810–20.
10. William Blades, *The Biography and Typography of William Caxton*, 1877, pp. 88–90.
11. Alfred, Lord Tennyson, Epitaph on Caxton, St. Margaret's, Westminster, 1885.
12. Edmund Gosse, *A Short History of Modern English Literature*, 1897, p. 53.
13. George Saintsbury, *A Short History of English Literature*, 1898, p. 209.
14. Richard Garnett, Edmund Gosse, *English Literature: An Illustrated Record*, 1903, Volume 1, pp. 260–62.

SIR THOMAS MALORY

1. Sir Thomas Malory, *Le Morte d'Arthur*, c. 1485, Bk. 21, Ch. 13.
2. William Caxton, Colophon to first edition of *Le Morte d'Arthur*, 1485.
3. Roger Ascham, *The Scholemaster*, 1570.
4. William Nicolson, *English Historical Library*, 1696–1714, Volume 1, p. 98.
5. Sir Walter Scott, "Essay on Romance" (1824), *Miscellaneous Works*, 1861, Volume 6, p. 267.
6. David Masson, *British Novelists and Their Styles*, 1859, pp. 51–62.
7. William Minto, *Characteristics of English Poets*, 1874, p. 81.

and Profitable Works of Maister Skelton, Poete Laureate, 1568.

29. Thomas Warton, *The History of English Poetry,* 1774–81, Volume 2, pp. 336–63.
30. Isaac Disraeli, "John Skelton," *Amenities of Literature,* 1841, pp. 69–82.

WILLIAM DUNBAR

1. John Langhorne, *Genius and Valour,* 1763, ll. 61–64.
2. Thomas Warton, *The History of English Poetry,* 1774–81, Sec. 30.
3. George Dyer, "Ode 16," *Poems,* 1801, p. 89.
4. David Irving, *Lives of the Scotish Poets,* 1804.
5. Nathan Drake, *Mornings in Spring,* 1828, Volume 2, p. 4.
6. Thomas Wright, *Essays on the Middle Ages,* 1846, Volume 2, p. 292.
7. George Gilfillan, *Specimens with Memoirs of the Less-Known British Poets,* 1860, Volume 1, p. 59.
8. George L. Craik, *A Compendious History of the English Literature and of the English Language,* 1861, Volume 1, p. 456.
9. Alexander Smith, *Dreamthorp,* 1863, p. 92.
10. William Minto, *Characteristics of English Poets,* 1874, p. 99.
11. James Russell Lowell, "Spenser" (1875), *Works,* Riverside ed., Volume 4, pp. 269–71.
12. John Nichol, "William Dunbar," *The English Poets,* ed. Thomas Humphry Ward, 1880, Volume 1, pp. 149–50.
13. Thomas Bayne, *Dictionary of National Biography,* 1888, Volume 16, p. 155.
14. H. Macaulay Fitzgibbon, "Introduction" to *Early English and Scottish Poetry,* 1888, p. lix.
15. Francis Turner Palgrave, "Notes" to *The Treasury of Sacred Song,* 1889, p. 331.
16. Margaret Oliphant, *Royal Edinburgh,* 1890, p. 188.
17. Bernhard ten Brink, *History of English Literature (Fourteenth Century to Surrey),* tr. Dora L. Schmitz, 1892, p. 78.
18. F. R. Oliphant, "William Dunbar," *Blackwood's Edinburgh Magazine,* September 1893, p. 416.
19. W. J. Courthope, *A History of English Poetry,* 1895, Volume 1, pp. 370–71.
20. J. J. Jusserand, *A Literary History of the English People,* 1895, p. 511.
21. Edmund Gosse, *A Short History of Modern English Literature,* 1897, pp. 48–51.
22. Henry Morley, *A History of English Literature,* 1891, Volume 7, pp. 115–39.
23. George Eyre-Todd, *Mediaeval Scottish Poetry,* 1892, pp. 149–58.

SIR THOMAS MORE

1. Sir Thomas More, Letter to Peter Giles (1516).
2. Desiderius Erasmus, Letter to Ulrich von Hutten (1519).
3. Charles V, *Memoirs of Charles V,* 1530.
4. William Shakespeare, *King Henry VIII,* c. 1613, Act 3, Sc. 2.
5. Cresacre More, *Life of Sir Thomas More,* c. 1627.
6. Jeremy Collier, *An Ecclesiastical History of Great Britain* (1708–14), ed. Francis Barham, 1840–41, Volume 4, p. 281.
7. Joseph Addison, *The Spectator,* No. 349 (April 10, 1712).
8. Jonathan Swift, "Concerning That Universal Hatred Which Prevails against the Clergy" (1736), *Works,* ed. Sir Walter Scott, Volume 8, p. 232.

9. David Hume, *History of England,* 1754–62.
10. John Macdiarmid, *Lives of the British Statesmen,* 1807–20, Volume 1, p. 153.
11. Sir James Mackintosh, "Life of More" (1807), *Miscellaneous Essays,* 1846.
12. Sharon Turner, *The History of the Reign of Henry the Eighth,* 1826, Volume 2, p. 395.
13. Henry, Lord Brougham, *History of England and France under the House of Lancaster,* 1861, p. 361.
14. James Anthony Froude, *History of England,* 1856–70, Volume 2, Ch. 6.
15. W. R. W. Stephens, "John Colet, Dean of St. Paul's," *Good Words,* 1878, p. 405.
16. William John Loftie, "The Western Suburbs," *A History of London,* 1883, Volume 2, p. 263.
17. Henry Morley, *English Writers,* 1891, Volume 7, p. 232.
18. William Tyndale, *Answer to More,* 1531, p. 168.
19. Thomas Drant, *Sermons,* 1569–70.
20. Gilbert Burnet, *The History of the Reformation of the Church of England,* 1695–1715, Volume 1, Pt. 1, Bk. 3.
21. Isaac Disraeli, "The Psychological Character of Sir Thomas More," *Amenities of Literature,* 1841.
22. Frederick Denison Maurice, "On Books" (1865), *The Friendship of Books and Other Lectures,* ed. Thomas Hughes, 1874.
23. C. R. L. Fletcher, *The Development of English Prose Style,* 1881, p. 7.
24. Charles H. Herford, *Studies in the Literary Relations of England and Germany in the Sixteenth Century,* 1886, p. 47.
25. Donald G. Mitchell, *English Lands, Letters, and Kings: From Celt to Tudor,* 1889, p. 175.
26. Edmund Gosse, *A Short History of Modern English Literature,* 1897, p. 62.
27. Ralph Robinson, "The Epistle," translation of *Utopia,* 1551.
28. Thomas Fuller, *The History of the Worthies of England,* 1662.
29. Edward Phillips, *Theatrum Poetarum Anglicanorum,* 1675.
30. Arthur Cayley, *Memoirs of Sir Thomas More,* 1808.
31. Henry Hallam, *Introduction to the Literature of Europe,* 1837–39, Pt. 1, Ch. 4, Sec. 34–35.
32. John, Lord Campbell, "Life of Sir Thomas More," *Lives of the Lord Chancellors,* 1854–56, Volume 2, p. 72.
33. Edward Arber, "Introduction" to *Utopia,* 1869, p. 3.
34. J. M. Cowper, "Preface" to *Starkey's England in the Reign of King Henry the Eighth,* 1871, p. ciii.
35. John Sherren Brewer, *The Reign of Henry VIII,* ed. James Gairdner, 1884, Volume 1, p. 288.
36. Hannis Taylor, *Origin and Growth of the English Constitution,* 1889, Volume 2, p. 46.
37. J. J. Jusserand, *The English Novel in the Time of Shakespeare,* 1890, p. 50.
38. Bernhard ten Brink, *History of English Literature (Fourteenth Century to Surrey),* tr. Dora L. Schmitz, 1892, p. 164.
39. B. O. Flower, *The Century of Sir Thomas More,* 1896, p. 211.
40. Vida D. Scudder, *Social Ideals in English Letters,* 1898, p. 49.
41. George Saintsbury, *The Earlier Renaissance,* 1901, pp. 86–89, 238–39.
42. John, Lord Campbell, "Life of Sir Thomas More," *Lives of the Lord Chancellors,* 1854–56, Volume 2, p. 70.
43. H. R. Reichel, "Sir Thomas More," *English Prose,* ed. Henry Craik, 1893, Volume 1, p. 156.
44. William Holden Hutton, *Sir Thomas More,* 1895, p. 98.

3. Sidney Lee, *Dictionary of National Biography*, 1889, Volume 17, p. 348.
4. Bernhard ten Brink, *History of English Literature (Fourteenth Century to Surrey)*, tr. Dora Schmitz, 1892, p. 194.
5. George Saintsbury, *A Short History of English Literature*, 1898, pp. 234–35.
6. George Saintsbury, *The Earlier Renaissance*, 1901, pp. 239–40.
7. Alfred Ainger, "Sir Thomas Elyot," *English Prose*, ed. Henry Craik, 1893, Volume 1, pp. 191–92.

HENRY HOWARD, EARL OF SURREY

1. Sir Walter Scott, *The Lay of the Last Minstrel*, 1806, Canto 6, Stanza 13.
2. Anna Brownell Jameson, *The Loves of the Poets*, 1829, Volume 1, p. 187.
3. William Francis Collier, *History of English Literature*, 1861, p. 92.
4. S. Hubert Burke, *Historical Portraits of the Tudor Dynasty and the Reformation Period*, 1882, Volume 3, p. 125.
5. Sir Philip Sidney, *An Apologie for Poetrie* (1581), 1595.
6. Edward Phillips, *Theatrum Poetarum Anglicanorum*, 1675.
7. Alexander Pope, *Windsor Forest*, 1713, ll. 291–98.
8. Thomas Warton, *The History of English Poetry*, 1774–81, Sec. 37.
9. Nathan Drake, *Literary Hours*, 1798–1820, No. 6.
10. Thomas Frognall Dibdin, *The Library Companion*, 1824, p. 682.
11. Elizabeth Barrett Browning, *The Book of the Poets* (1842), *Life, Letters and Essays of Elizabeth Barrett Browning*, 1863.
12. George L. Craik, *Spenser and His Poetry*, 1845, Volume 1, p. 93.
13. Robert Bell, *Poetical Works of Surrey and Minor Contemporaneous Poets*, 1854, p. 35.
14. George Gilfillan, *Poetical Works of the Earl of Surrey*, 1856, p. 227.
15. George L. Craik, *A Compendious History of English Literature and of the English Language*, 1861, Volume 1, p. 458.
16. Thomas Arnold, *A Manual of English Literature*, 1862.
17. Hippolyte Taine, *The History of English Literature*, tr. H. Van Laun, 1871, Bk. 2, Ch. 1.
18. William Minto, *Characteristics of English Poets*, 1874, pp. 123–25.
19. James Russell Lowell, "Spenser" (1875), *Works*, Riverside ed., Volume 4, p. 274.
20. John Churton Collins, "The Earl of Surrey," *The English Poets*, ed. Thomas Humphry Ward, 1880, Volume 1, p. 255.
21. George Saintsbury, *A History of Elizabethan Literature*, 1887, p. 6.
22. W. J. Courthope, *A History of English Poetry*, 1897, Volume 2, p. 68.
23. Edmund Bolton, *Hypercritica*, 1624.
24. Edwin Guest, *A History of English Rhythms*, 1838, Volume 2, p. 239.
25. George McDonald, "St. George's Day, 1564" (1864), *The Imagination and Other Essays*, 1883, pp. 94–96.
26. Isaac Disraeli, "The Earl of Surrey and Sir Thomas Wyatt," *Amenities of Literature*, 1841, pp. 112–26.

ALEXANDER BARCLAY

1. William Bullein, *A Dialogue both Pleasaunt and Pietifull, Wherein Is a Godlie Regiment against the Feber Pestilence,*

with a Consolation and Comforte against Death, 1564–73.
2. Elizabeth Cooper, *The Muses' Library*, 1737, p. 33.
3. Thomas Warton, *The History of English Poetry*, 1774–81, Sec. 29.
4. Thomas Campbell, *An Essay on English Poetry*, 1819.
5. Isaac Disraeli, "The Ship of Fools," *Amenities of Literature*, 1841.
6. David Irving, *History of Scotish Poetry*, ed. John Aitken Carlyle, 1861, p. 327.
7. Henry Green, *Shakespeare and the Emblem Writers*, 1870, p. 65.
8. A. W. Ward, *Dictionary of National Biography*, 1885, Volume 3, p. 160.
9. Bernhard ten Brink, *History of English Literature (Fourteenth Century to Surrey)*, tr. Dora L. Schmitz, 1892, p. 99.
10. George Saintsbury, *A Short History of English Literature*, 1898, p. 167.
11. Henry Morley, "Alexander Barclay and *The Ship of Fools*," *A History of English Literature*, 1891, pp. 90–113.

THOMAS, LORD VAUX

1. George Puttenham, *The Arte of English Poesie*, 1589.
2. Thomas Warton, *The History of English Poetry*, 1774–81, Sec. 39.
3. Nathan Drake, *Shakspeare and His Times*, 1817, Volume 1, p. 713.
4. Sidney Lee, *Dictionary of National Biography*, 1899, Volume 58, p. 195.

SIR JOHN CHEKE

1. Thomas Nashe, *To the Gentlemen Students of Both Universities*, 1589.
2. Gabriel Harvey, "A New Letter of Notable Contents," 1593.
3. John Milton, *Sonnets*, 1645–46.
4. Gilbert Burnet, *The History of the Reformation of the Church of England*, 1679–1715, Volume 2, Pt. 2, Bk. 1, p. 192.
5. Edward Nares, *Memoirs of Lord Burghley*, 1828, Volume 1, p. 251.
6. Isaac Disraeli, "Vicissitudes of the English Language," *Amenities of Literature*, 1841.
7. George P. Marsh, *The Origin and History of the English Language*, 1862, p. 521.
8. Thompson Cooper, *Dictionary of National Biography*, 1887, Volume 10, p. 181.
9. Richard Garnett, Edmund Gosse, *English Literature: An Illustrated Record*, 1903, Volume 1, p. 329.
10. Henry Craik, "Sir John Cheke," *English Prose*, ed. Henry Craik, 1893, Volume 1, pp. 255–58.

NICHOLAS UDALL

1. Thomas Tusser, "The Author's Life," *Five Hundredth Points of Good Husbandrie*, 1573.
2. John Payne Collier, *History of English Dramatic Poetry*, 1831, Volume 2, pp. 448–60.
3. Hermann Ulrici, *Shakspeare's Dramatic Art*, 1839, p. 18.
4. William Durrant Cooper, "Introductory Memoirs," *Ralph Roister Doister*, 1847, p. xi.
5. William Minto, *Characteristics of English Poets*, 1874, p. 141.
6. John Addington Symons, *Shakspere's Predecessors in the English Drama*, 1884, pp. 203–4.
7. George Saintsbury, *Social England*, ed. H. D. Traill, 1895, Volume 3, p. 339.

GEORGE GASCOIGNE

1. Sir Walter Ralegh, "Upon Gascoigne's Poem, *The Steele Glasse*," 1576.
2. George Whetstone, *A Remembrance of the wel imployed life, and godly end of George Gascoigne Esquire*, 1577.
3. Edward Kirk, "Glosse to November" (1579), *Spenser's The Shepherd's Calendar*, ed. John Payne Collier, Volume 1, p. 133.
4. William Webbe, *A Discourse of English Poesie*, 1586.
5. Thomas Nashe, *Letter to the Gentlemen Students of Both Universities*, 1589.
6. George Puttenham, *The Arte of English Poesie*, 1589.
7. Edmund Bolton, *Hypercritica*, 1624.
8. Michael Drayton, "To My Most Dearely-Loved Friend Henery Reynolds, Esquire of Poets and Poesie," *Elegies*, 1627.
9. Thomas Warton, *Observations on the* Faerie Queene *of* Spenser, 1754, Volume 2, p. 168.
10. Henry Hallam, *Introduction to the Literature of Europe*, 1837–39, Pt. 2, Ch. 5, Par. 60.
11. William Carew Hazlitt, "Preface" to *Complete Poems of George Gascoigne*, 1869, Volume 1, p. xxvii.
12. John W. Hales, "George Gascoigne," *The English Poets*, ed. Thomas Humphry Ward, 1880, Volume 1, p. 264.
13. Charles H. Herford, *Studies in the Literary Relations of England and Germany in the Sixteenth Century*, 1886, p. 163.
14. George C. S. Southworth, *Introduction to the Study of English Literature*, 1888, p. 49.
15. Henry Morley, *English Writers*, 1892, Volume 8, p. 283.
16. Felix E. Schelling, *The Life and Writings of George Gascoigne*, 1894, p. 30.
17. George Saintsbury, *Social England*, ed. H. D. Traill, 1895, Volume 3, pp. 343–44.
18. W. J. Courthope, *A History of English Poetry*, 1897, Volume 2, p. 177.
19. George Saintsbury, *The Earlier Renaissance*, 1901, pp. 162–65.

RAPHAEL HOLINSHED

1. Thomas Hearne, *Reliquiae Hearnianae*, 1723.
2. Thomas Frognall Dibdin, *The Library Companion*, 1824, p. 185.
3. George P. Marsh, *Lectures on the English Language*, 1859, p. 112.
4. Thomas Arnold, *A Manual of English Literature*, 1862.
5. Donald G. Mitchell, *English Lands, Letters, and Kings: From Celt to Tudor*, 1889, p. 212.
6. Sidney Lee, *Dictionary of National Biography*, 1891, Volume 27, p. 132.
7. Mary Darmesteter, "Raphael Holinshed," *English Prose*, ed. Henry Craik, 1893, Volume 1, pp. 317–19.

GEORGE BUCHANAN

1. James Melville, *Diary*, 1601.
2. Henry Peacham, *The Compleat Gentleman*, 1622.
3. Henry Morley, *First Sketch of English Literature*, 1873, p. 404.
4. Aeneas Mackay, *Dictionary of National Biography*, 1886, Volume 7, p. 193.
5. John Knox, *History of the Reformation*, 1566.
6. James I, *Basilikon Doron*, 1616.
7. John Whitaker, *Mary Queen of Scots Vindicated*, 1787.
8. James Boswell, *Life of Johnson*, 1791.
9. Patrick Fraser Tytler, *The History of Scotland*, 1843–64, Volume 4, p. 53.
10. James Hannay, *Satire and Satirists*, 1854, p. 91.

11. Margaret Oliphant, *Royal Edinburgh*, 1890, p. 378.
12. Richard Hurd, *Commonplace Book* (c. 1808), cited in Francis Kilvert, *Memoirs of the Life and Writings of the Right Rev. Richard Hurd*, 1860, p. 225.
13. Dugald Stewart, "First Preliminary Dissertation," *Encyclopaedia Britannica*, 1815–21.
14. W. E. H. Lecky, *Spirit of Rationalism in Europe*, 1865, Volume 2, p. 175.
15. Charles Kingsley, "George Buchanan, Scholar," *Good Words*, 1868, p. 735.
16. David G. Ritchie, "George Buchanan," *Westminster Review*, November 1860, p. 522.
17. John Spottiswoode, *History of the Church and State of Scotland*, c. 1639.
18. Gilbert Burnet, *History of the Reformation of the Church of England*, 1679–1715, Pt. 1, Bk. 3.
19. Thomas Birch, *Heads of Illustrious Persons with Their Lives and Characters*, 1743–52.
20. William Robertson, *History of Scotland*, 1758–59, Volume 1, Bk. 1.
21. David Irving, *Memoirs of the Life and Writings of George Buchanan*, 1807, p. 130.
22. Henry Hallam, *Introduction to the Literature of Europe*, 1837–39, Pt. 2, Ch. 5, Par. 97.
23. Henry Morley, *English Writers*, 1892, Volume 8, p. 349.
24. George Saintsbury, *The Earlier Renaissance*, 1901, pp. 49–58.

SIR PHILIP SIDNEY

1. Edmund Spenser, Title page of *The Shepheardes Calender*, 1579.
2. Stephan Gosson, Dedication to *The Schoole of Abuse*, 1579.
3. Sir Francis Walsingham, Letter to Sir Henry Sidney (1586).
4. Fulke Greville (Lord Brooke), *On Sir Philip Sidney*, 1586.
5. Thomas Nashe, *Pierce Penilesse His Supplication to the Divell*, 1592.
6. Richard Barnfield, *The Affectionate Shepherd*, 1594.
7. Sir William Harbert, *A Prophesie of Cadwallader*, 1604.
8. Samuel Daniel, "A Funerall Poeme upon the Earle of Devonshire" (1606), *Works*, ed. Alexander B. Grosart, Volume 1, p. 176.
9. Anthony Stafford, *Niobe*, 1611, p. 112.
10. William Browne, *Britannia's Pastorals*, 1613, Volume 1, Bk. 2, Song 2.
11. Fulke Greville (Lord Brooke), *Life of Sir Philip Sidney*, c. 1628–52.
12. Sir Robert Naunton, *Fragmenta Regalia*, c. 1630.
13. John Aubrey, "Sir Philip Sidney," *Brief Lives*, 1669–96.
14. Horace Walpole, *A Catalogue of the Royal and Noble Authors of England, Scotland, and Ireland*, 1758, Volume 2, p. 230.
15. Robert Southey, *For a Tablet at Penshurst*, 1799.
16. Thomas Campbell, *An Essay on English Poetry*, 1819.
17. Percy Bysshe Shelley, *Adonais*, 1821, Stanza 45.
18. Charles Lamb, "Some Sonnets of Sir Philip Sidney," *London Magazine*, September 1823.
19. John Richard Green, *A Short History of the English People*, 1874, Ch. 7.
20. Edmund Gosse, "Sir Philip Sidney," *Contemporary Review*, November 1886, p. 638.
21. John Addington Symonds, *Sir Philip Sidney*, 1886, pp. 1, 199.
22. Donald G. Mitchell, *English Lands, Letters, and Kings: From Celt to Tudor*, 1889, p. 239.
23. Sir John Harington, "Notes on the Book XVI," *Translation of Ariosto*, 1591, p. 239.

93. John Dunlop, "Pastoral Romance," *The History of Fiction* (1814), 1842, Volume 2, pp. 262–70.
94. Henry Morley, *A First Sketch of English Literature*, 1873, pp. 391–426.
95. Walter Raleigh, *The English Novel*, 1894, pp. 49–64.
96. Duncan C. Tovey, "England's Helicon: More Lyrics from Elizabethan Songbooks," *Reviews and Essays in English Literature*, 1897, pp. 177–81.
97. Joel E. Spingarn, "The General Theory of Poetry," *A History of Literary Criticism in the Renaissance*, 1889, pp. 34–274.
98. Algernon Charles Swinburne, "Astrophel" (1894), *Works*, 1900, pp. 589–91.
99. Adolphus William Ward, "Sir Philip Sidney," *English Prose*, ed. Henry Craik, 1894, Volume 1, pp. 401–8.

JOHN FOXE

1. Philip Stubbes, *The Anatomie of Abuses*, 1583.
2. Thomas Fuller, *The History of the Worthies of England*, 1662.
3. Gilbert Burnet, "Preface" to *The History of the Reformation of the Church of England*, 1679–1715.
4. John Strype, *Memorials of Archbishop Cranmer*, 1694, Volume 3, p. 174.
5. Christopher Wordsworth, "Preface" to *Ecclesiastical Biography*, 1810.
6. Benjamin Brook, *Lives of the Puritans*, 1813.
7. Thomas Frognall Dibdin, *The Library Companion*, 1824, pp. 105–6.
8. Frederick George Lee, *The Life of Cardinal Pole*, 1888, p. 189.
9. Henry Morley, *English Writers*, 1892, Volume 8, pp. 203–4.
10. Douglas Campbell, *The Puritan in Holland, England, and America*, 1892, Volume 1, p. 442.
11. James Miller Dodds, "John Foxe," *English Prose*, ed. Henry Craik, 1893, Volume 1, pp. 327–28.
12. Allen B. Hinds, *The Making of the England of Elizabeth*, 1895, p. 43.

THOMAS WATSON

1. George Peele, "Ad Maecanatem Prologus," *The Honour of the Garter*, 1593.
2. Richard Barnfield, *The Affectionate Shepard*, 1594.
3. Edmund Spenser, *Colin Clouts Come Home Againe*, 1595, ll. 439–43.
4. Thomas Nashe, *Have with You to Saffron-Walden*, 1596.
5. Thomas Heywood, *The Hierarchy of the Blessed Angels*, 1635.
6. Sir Samuel Egerton Brydges, *British Bibliographer*, 1811, p. 4.
7. Nathan Drake, *Shakspeare and His Times*, 1817, Volume 2, p. 54.
8. Francis Turner Palgrave, "Thomas Watson the Poet," *North American Review*, January 1872, pp. 91–109.
9. William Minto, *Characteristics of English Poets*, 1874, p. 203.
10. Thomas Humphry Ward, "Thomas Watson," *The English Poets*, ed. Thomas Humphry Ward, 1880, Volume 1, p. 389.
11. Felix E. Schelling, *A Book of Elizabethan Lyrics*, 1895, p. 224.
12. George Saintsbury, *A Short History of English Literature*, 1898, p. 273.
13. Sidney Lee, *Dictionary of National Biography*, 1899, Volume 60, p. 37.

ROBERT GREENE

1. Henry Chettle, *Kind-Hart's Dreame*, 1592.
2. Gabriel Harvey, *Four Letters*, 1592.
3. Thomas Nashe, *Strange News of the Intercepting Certaine Letters*, 1592.
4. Francis Meres, *Palladis Tamia*, 1598, p. 103.
5. John Addington Symonds, *Shakspere's Predecessors in the English Drama*, 1884, pp. 544–45.
6. George Saintsbury, *A History of Elizabethan Literature*, 1887, p. 65.
7. A. H. Bullen, *Dictionary of National Biography*, 1890, Volume 23, p. 67.
8. J. J. Jusserand, *The English Novel in the Time of Shakespeare*, 1890, p. 151.
9. Thomas Nashe, *Pierce Penilesse His Supplication to the Divell*, 1592.
10. Barnabe Riche (?), *Greenes Newes both from Heaven and Hell*, 1593.
11. Anthony à Wood, *Athenae Oxonienses*, 1691–1721.
12. William Beloe, *Anecdotes of Literature and Scarce Books*, 1807, Volume 2, p. 190.
13. Nathan Drake, *Shakspeare and His Times*, 1817, Volume 1, pp. 494, 627.
14. Thomas Campbell, *Specimens of the British Poets*, 1819.
15. Hippolyte Taine, *The History of English Literature*, tr. H. Van Laun, 1871, Bk. 2, Ch. 2.
16. Edmund Gosse, "Robert Greene," *The English Poets*, ed. Thomas Humphry Ward, 1880, Volume 1, p. 402.
17. George F. Underhill, *Literary Epochs*, 1887, p. 84.
18. Frederic Ives Carpenter, "Introduction" to *English Lyric Poetry, 1500–1700*, 1897, p. xliii.
19. John Payne Collier, "Introduction to Greene's *Pandosto*," *Shakespeare's Library*, 1843, Volume 1, p. 1.
20. Charles Knight, *Studies of Shakspere*, 1849, Bk. 1, Ch. 5.
21. J. Ross Murray, *The Influence of Italian upon English Literature*, 1885, p. 24.
22. Adolphus William Ward, "Robert Greene," *English Prose*, ed. Henry Craik, 1893, Volume 1, p. 553.
23. Alexander Dyce, *Dramatic and Poetical Works of Robert Greene*, 1831, p. 34.
24. Henry Hallam, *Introduction to the Literature of Europe*, 1837–39, Pt. 2, Ch. 6, Par. 32.
25. Hermann Ulrici, *Shakspere's Dramatic Art*, 1839, pp. 39–40.
26. William Minto, *Characteristics of English Poets*, 1874, p. 243.
27. J. M. Brown, "An Early Rival of Shakespere," *New Zealand Magazine*, April 1877, p. 101.
28. Nicholas Storojenko, *Robert Greene: His Life and Works: A Critical Investigation*, tr. E. A. Brayley Hodgetts, 1878, p. 223.
29. John Addington Symonds, *Shakspere's Predecessors in the English Drama*, 1884, p. 557.
30. George Saintsbury, *A History of Elizabethan Literature*, 1887, p. 73.
31. Frederick S. Boas, *Shakspere and His Predecessors*, 1896, p. 87.
32. Edmund Gosse, *A Short History of Modern English Literature*, 1897, p. 98.
33. John Churton Collins, "General Introduction" to *The Plays and Poems of Robert Greene*, 1905, pp. 54–60.

CHRISTOPHER MARLOWE

1. Robert Greene, "To the Gentlemen Readers, *Health*," *Permedes the Blacksmith*, 1588.
2. Robert Greene, *Groatsworth of Wit*, 1592.

THOMAS KYD

ROBERT SOUTHWELL

GEORGE PEELE

EDMUND SPENSER

Volume 2
William Shakespeare

Volume 3

90. Samuel Pufendorf, *Spicilegium Controversiarum*, 1680.
91. Robert Boyle, *New Experiments and Observations Touching Cold*, 1683.
92. John Evelyn, *Numismata*, 1697.
93. Jean le Rond d'Alembert, *Preliminary Discourse to the Encyclopedia*, 1751, trs. Richard N. Schwab, Walter E. Rex.
94. Etienne Bonnot de Condillac, *An Essay on the Origin of Human Knowledge*, 1756, tr. Thomas Nugent, Pt. 2, Sec. 2, Ch. 3.
95. Jean Sylvain Bailly, *Histoire de l'astronomie moderne*, 1775–85, Volume 2, Bk. 4.
96. Dugald Stewart, *Account of the Life and Writings of Thomas Reid*, 1802–3, Sec. 2.
97. Friedrich Schlegel, *Lectures on the History of Literature*, 1815, p. 286.
98. Macvey Napier, "Lord Bacon" (1818), *Lord Bacon and Sir Walter Raleigh*, 1853, p. 14.
99. Sir David Brewster, Letter (April 26, 1824), cited in Margaret Brewster, *The Home Life of Sir David Brewster*, 1869, pp. 128–30.
100. Robert Leslie Ellis, "General Preface" to *Bacon's Philosophical Works*, 1857, Volume 1, pp. 63–64.
101. John William Draper, *History of the Intellectual Development of Europe*, 1864, Volume 2, pp. 258–60.
102. Johann Edward Erdmann, *A History of Philosophy*, tr. Williston S. Hough, 1865–76, Volume 1, pp. 682–83.
103. W. E. H. Lecky, *Spirit of Rationalism in Europe*, 1865, Volume 1, Ch. 4, Pt. 1.
104. Edward Dowden, *Shakespere: A Critical Study of His Mind and Art*, 1875, p. 16.
105. Oscar Browning, *An Introduction to the History of Educational Theories*, 1881.
106. Richard William Church, Letter to Asa Gray (1883), *Life and Letters of Dean Church*, ed. Mary C. Church, 1894, p. 376.
107. George Croom Robertson, *Hobbes*, 1886, p. 18.
108. Thomas Humphry Ward, *The Reign of Queen Victoria*, 1887, Volume 2, p. 325.
109. John Nicol, *Francis Bacon: His Life and Philosophy*, 1889, p. 242.
110. George Chapman, Dedication to *The Georgicks of Hesiod*, 1618.
111. William Rawley, "The Life of Bacon," *Resuscitatio*, 1657–61.
112. François Marie Arouet de Voltaire, "Letter 12: On Chancellor Bacon," *Letters on England (Lettres Philosophiques)*, 1734, tr. Leonard Tancock.
113. Thomas Babington Macaulay, "Lord Bacon" (1837), *Critical, Historical, and Miscellaneous Essays*, 1860, Volume 3, pp. 436–95.
114. Richard William Church, "Bacon as a Writer," *Bacon*, 1884, pp. 209–27.

SIR JOHN DAVIES

1. Edward Phillips, *Theatrum Poetarum Anglicanorum*, 1675.
2. Elizabeth Cooper, *The Muses' Library*, 1737, pp. 331–33.
3. Unsigned, *The Return from Pernassus*, 1606, Act 1, Sc. 2.
4. William Browne, *Britannia's Pastorals*, 1613, Bk. 2, Song 2.
5. Edwin P. Whipple, *The Literature of the Age of Elizabeth*, 1869, pp. 238–40.
6. John W. Hales, "Sir John Davies's Poems" (1876), *Folia Litteraria*, 1893, pp. 162–64.
7. Mary A. Ward, "Sir John Davies," *The English Poets*, ed. Thomas Humphry Ward, 1880, Volume 1, pp. 548–50.

8. George Saintsbury, *A History of Elizabethan Literature*, 1887, p. 294.
9. Edmund Gosse, *The Jacobean Poets*, 1894, pp. 8–9.
10. Richard Baxter, "Prefatory Address" to *Poetical Fragments*, 1681.
11. Thomas Campbell, *An Essay on English Poetry*, 1819.
12. Henry Hallam, *Introduction to the Literature of Europe*, 1837–39, Pt. 2, Ch. 5, Par. 70.
13. George MacDonald, "Lord Bacon and His Coevals," *England's Antiphon*, 1868, pp. 105–7.
14. Friedrich Überweg, *History of Philosophy*, tr. George S. Morris, 1871, Volume 2, p. 352.
15. George S. Morris, *British Thought and Thinkers*, 1880, pp. 67–68.
16. Alexander B. Grosart, "Memorial-Introduction" to *The Complete Poems of Sir John Davies*, 1876, pp. lix–lxxxix.
17. E. Hershey Sneath, "Biographical Sketch," *Philosophy in Poetry: A Study of Sir John Davies's Poem* Nosce Teipsum, 1903, pp. 34–48.

CYRIL TOURNEUR

1. Adolphus William Ward, *A History of English Dramatic Poetry* (1875), 1899, Volume 2, pp. 66–71.
2. George Saintsbury, *A History of Elizabethan Literature*, 1887, p. 285.
3. W. E. Henley, "Tourneur," *Views and Reviews*, 1890.
4. John Churton Collins, "Introduction" to *The Plays and Poems of Cyril Tourneur*, 1878, Volume 1, pp. xl–lvi.
5. Algernon Charles Swinburne, "Cyril Tourneur," *Nineteenth Century*, March 1887, pp. 415–27.

WILLIAM ROWLEY

1. Gerard Langbaine, *An Account of the English Dramatick Poets*, 1691.
2. Nathan Drake, *Shakspeare and His Times*, 1817, Volume 2, p. 570.
3. Thomas Campbell, *Specimens of the British Poets*, 1819.
4. Adolphus William Ward, *A History of English Dramatic Literature* (1875), 1899, Volume 2, pp. 540–45.
5. Algernon Charles Swinburne, "Thomas Middleton," *Nineteenth Century*, January 1886, pp. 145–52.
6. Edmund Gosse, *The Jacobean Poets*, 1894, pp. 130–31.
7. Thomas Seccombe, *Dictionary of National Biography*, 1897, Volume 49, p. 363.

THOMAS MIDDLETON

1. John Weever, "Ad Ro: Allot, & Chr. Middleton," *Epigrammes in the Oldest Cut and Newest Fashion*, 1599.
2. Gerard Langbaine, *An Account of the English Dramatick Poets*, 1691.
3. William Hazlitt, *Lectures on the Dramatic Literature of the Age of Elizabeth*, 1820.
4. Leigh Hunt, *Imagination and Fancy*, 1844.
5. Aldolphus William Ward, *A History of English Dramatic Literature* (1875), 1899, Volume 2, pp. 538–40.
6. Algernon Charles Swinburne, "Thomas Middleton," *Sonnets on English Dramatic Poets*, 1882.
7. A. H. Bullen, "Introduction" to *The Works of Thomas Middleton*, 1885, Volume 1, pp. xcii–xciii.
8. George Saintsbury, *A History of Elizabethan Literature*, 1887, pp. 266–73.
9. Edmund Gosse, *The Jacobean Poets*, 1894, pp. 126–29.
10. Algernon Charles Swinburne, "Thomas Middleton," *Nineteenth Century*, January 1886, pp. 138–53.

FULKE GREVILLE (LORD BROOKE)

1. Sir Robert Naunton, *Fragmenta Regalia*, c. 1630.
2. Thomas Fuller, *The History of the Worthies of England*, 1662.

SIR EDWARD COKE

GEORGE CHAPMAN

JOHN WEBSTER

8. Thomas B. Shaw, *Outlines of English Literature*, 1847, p. 130.
9. James Russell Lowell, "Library of Old Authors" (1858–64), *Works*, Riverside ed., Volume 1, pp. 279–81.
10. Edwin P. Whipple, *The Literature of the Age of Elizabeth*, 1869, pp. 139–41.
11. Adolphus William Ward, A *History of English Dramatic Literature* (1875), 1899, Volume 3, pp. 51–65.
12. Algernon Charles Swinburne, "John Webster," *Sonnets on English Dramatic Poets*, 1882.
13. James Baldwin, "English Poetry," *English Literature and Literary Criticism*, 1882, p. 238.
14. George Saintsbury, A *History of Elizabethan Literature*, 1887, p. 274.
15. John Addington Symonds, "Introduction" to *Webster and Tourneur*, 1888, pp. xi–xxii.
16. Donald G. Mitchell, *English Lands, Letters, and Kings: From Elizabeth to Anne*, 1890, p. 90.
17. Edmund Gosse, *The Jacobean Poets*, 1894, pp. 168–70.
18. Frederic Ives Carpenter, *Metaphor and Simile in the Minor Elizabethan Drama*, 1895, pp. 75–77.
19. John Webster, "Preface" to *The White Devil*, 1612.
20. John Wilson (as "H.M."), *Blackwood's Edinburgh Magazine*, August 1818, pp. 556–62.
21. Adolphus William Ward, A *History of English Dramatic Literature* (1875), 1899, Volume 3, pp. 56–59.
22. George Saintsbury, A *History of Elizabethan Literature*, 1887, p. 275.
23. Algernon Charles Swinburne, *Studies in Prose and Poetry*, 1894, p. 50.
24. John Ford, "To the Reader of the Author, and His *Dutchess of Malfi*," 1623.
25. William Rowley, "To His Friend, Mr. John Webster, upon His *Dutchess of Malfi*," 1623.
26. Charles Lamb, *Specimens of English Dramatic Poets*, 1808.
27. William Hazlitt, *Lectures on the Dramatic Literature of the Age of Elizabeth*, 1820.
28. Abraham Mills, *The Literature and the Literary Men of Great Britain and Ireland*, 1851, Volume 1, p. 345.
29. Adolphus William Ward, A *History of English Dramatic Literature* (1875), 1899, Volume 3, p. 62.
30. John Addington Symonds, "Introduction" to *Webster and Tourneur*, 1888, pp. xvii–xix.
31. Frederic Ives Carpenter, *Metaphor and Simile in the Minor Elizabethan Drama*, 1895, p. 80.
32. Charles Kingsley, "Plays and Puritans" (1859), *Plays and Puritans and Other Historical Essays*, 1873, pp. 50–56.
33. Algernon Charles Swinburne, "John Webster" (1886), *The Age of Shakespeare*, 1908, pp. 15–59.

JOHN MARSTON

1. Ben Jonson, *Conversations with William Drummond*, 1619.
2. Edward Phillips, *Theatrum Poetarum Anglicanorum*, 1675.
3. Anthony à Wood, *Athenae Oxonienses*, 1691–1721.
4. Everard Guilpin, "Of Fuscus," *Skialetheia*, 1598.
5. John Weever, "Ad I.: Marston, & Ben: Iohnson," *Epigrammes in the Oldest Cut and Newest Fashion*, 1599.
6. Unsigned, *The Return from Pernassus*, 1606, Act 1, Sc. 2.
7. Thomas Warton, *The History of English Poetry*, 1774–81, Sec. 65.
8. Charles Dibdin, A *Complete History of the Stage*, 1795, Volume 3, pp. 260–63.
9. Thomas Campbell, *An Essay on English Poetry*, 1819.
10. Edwin P. Whipple, *The Literature of the Age of Elizabeth*, 1869, pp. 125–29.

11. Adolphus William Ward, A *History of English Dramatic Literature* (1875), 1899, Volume 2, pp. 491–93.
12. William Hazlitt, *Lectures on the Dramatic Literature of the Age of Elizabeth*, 1820.
13. George Saintsbury, A *History of Elizabethan Literature*, 1887, pp. 153–55, 195–99.
14. Algernon Charles Swinburne, "John Marston," *Nineteenth Century*, October 1888, pp. 531–47.

EDWARD FAIRFAX

1. Edward Phillips, *Theatrum Poetarum Anglicanorum*, 1675.
2. John Dryden, "Preface" to *Fables*, 1700.
3. Elizabeth Cooper, *The Muses' Library*, 1737, pp. 342–44.
4. David Hume, *History of England*, 1754–62.
5. Nathan Drake, *Literary Hours*, 1798–1820, No. 28.
6. Thomas Campbell, *Specimens of the British Poets*, 1819.
7. Henry Hallam, *Introduction to the Literature of Europe*, 1837–39, Pt. 2, Ch. 5, Par. 74.
8. Henry Morley, *English Writers*, 1893, Volume 10, pp. 458–63.

RICHARD CORBETT

1. John Aubrey, "Richard Corbet," *Brief Lives*, 1669–96.
2. Anthony à Wood, *Athenae Oxonienses*, 1691–1721.
3. Thomas Campbell, *Specimens of the British Poets*, 1819.
4. David Masson, *The Life of John Milton*, 1859, Volume 1, Ch. 6.
5. George L. Craik, A *Compendious History of English Literature and of the English Language*, 1861, Volume 2, p. 21.
6. George Saintsbury, A *History of Elizabethan Literature*, 1887, p. 383.

THOMAS RANDOLPH

1. Edward Phillips, *Theatrum Poetarum Anglicanorum*, 1675.
2. Anthony à Wood, *Athenae Oxonienses*, 1691–1721.
3. Gerard Langbaine, *An Account of the English Dramatick Poets*, 1691.
4. Thomas Campbell, *Specimens of the British Poets*, 1819.
5. George L. Craik, A *Compendious History of English Literature and of the English Language*, 1861, Volume 2, p. 20.
6. Edmund Gosse, "Thomas Randolph," *The English Poets*, ed. Thomas Humphry Ward, 1890, Volume 2, pp. 219–20.
7. Algernon Charles Swinburne, "The Tribe of Benjamin," *Sonnets on English Dramatic Poets*, 1882.
8. George Saintsbury, A *History of Elizabethan Literature*, 1887, pp. 413–15.

BEN JONSON

1. Ben Jonson, *Conversations with William Drummond*, 1619.
2. Sir John Suckling, "The Wits," 1637.
3. Thomas Fuller, *The History of the Worthies of England*, 1662.
4. John Aubrey, "Ben Jonson," *Brief Lives*, 1669–96.
5. Peter Whalley, "Life of Jonson," *Jonson's Works*, 1756, p. lv.
6. George Walter Thornbury, *Shakspere's England*, 1856, Volume 2, p. 13.
7. Edwin P. Whipple, *The Literature of the Age of Elizabeth*, 1869, p. 85.
8. William Minto, *Characteristics of English Poets*, 1874, p. 338.
9. Adolphus William Ward, A *History of English Dramatic Literature* (1875), 1899, Volume 2, pp. 297–314.

20. Frederic Ives Carpenter, "Introduction" to *English Lyric Poetry, 1500–1700*, 1897, p. lix.
21. Francis Thompson, "Excursions in Criticism: VI.—Richard Crashaw," *Academy*, November 20, 1897, p. 427.
22. Herbert J. C. Grierson, "English Poetry," *The First Half of the Seventeenth Century*, 1906, pp. 169–71.
23. George Gilfillan, "The Life and Poetry of Richard Crashaw," *Poetical Works of Richard Crashaw*, 1857, pp. vii–xviii.
24. George MacDonald, "Crashaw and Marvell," *England's Antiphon*, 1868, pp. 238–46.
25. Alexander B. Grosart, "Essay on the Life and Poetry of Crashaw," *Complete Works of Richard Crashaw*, 1873, Volume 2, pp. lxii–lxxv.
26. Edmund Gosse, "Richard Crashaw" (1882/1913), *Seventeenth Century Studies*, 1913, Volume 1, pp. 157–82.
27. George Saintsbury, "Caroline Poetry," *A History of Elizabethan Literature*, 1887, pp. 364–69.
28. Francis Thompson, "Excursions in Criticism: VI.—Crashaw," *Academy*, November 20, 1897, pp. 427–28.
29. Felix E. Schelling, "Introduction" to *A Book of Seventeenth Century Lyrics*, 1899, pp. xxx–xxxiii, li–liii.
30. H. C. Beeching, "Introduction" to *Poems of Richard Crashaw*, ed. J. R. Tutin, 1905, pp. xxxvi–lv.

THOMAS HEYWOOD

1. Gerard Langbaine, *An Account of the English Dramatick Poets*, 1691.
2. Charles Dibdin, *A Complete History of the Stage*, 1795, Volume 3, pp. 105–6.
3. Charles Lamb, *Specimens of English Dramatic Poets*, 1808.
4. Thomas Campbell, *Specimens of the British Poets*, 1819.
5. William Hazlitt, *Lectures on the Dramatic Literature of the Age of Elizabeth*, 1820.
6. Edwin P. Whipple, *The Literature of the Age of Elizabeth*, 1869, pp. 122–23.
7. Algernon Charles Swinburne, "Thomas Heywood," *Sonnets on English Dramatic Poets*, 1882.
8. George Saintsbury, *A History of Elizabethan Literature*, 1887, pp. 280–84.
9. Edmund Gosse, *The Jacobean Poets*, 1894, pp. 119–22.
10. Felix E. Schelling, "The Biographical Chronicle Play," *The English Chronicle Play*, 1902, pp. 234–38.
11. Adolphus William Ward, "The Later Elisabethans," *A History of English Dramatic Literature* (1875), 1899, Volume 2, pp. 585–89.
12. Algernon Charles Swinburne, "The Romantic and Contemporary Plays of Thomas Heywood," *Nineteenth Century*, September 1895, pp. 397–410.

JOHN SELDEN

1. Edward Hyde, Earl of Clarendon, *The Life of Edward Earl of Clarendon*, c. 1668.
2. John Aubrey, "John Selden," *Brief Lives*, 1669–96.
3. Richard Bathurst, "On the Death of the Learned Mr. John Selden," *Examen Poeticum*, ed. John Dryden, 1693.
4. George Saintsbury, *Social England*, ed. H. D. Traill, 1895, Volume 4, p. 98.
5. Ben Jonson, "An Epistle to Master John Selden" (1614), *Under-Wood*, 1640.
6. John Milton, *Areopagitica*, 1644.
7. Thomas Hearne, *Reliquiae Hearnianae*, January 24, 1727.
8. W. S. M'Cormick, "John Selden," *English Prose*, ed. Henry Craik, 1893, Volume 2, pp. 165–68.

9. Unsigned, "Selden's *Table-Talk*," *Spectator*, October 14, 1893, p. 489.
10. Ben Jonson, *Conversations with William Drummond*, 1619.
11. William Nicolson, *The English Historical Library*, 1696–99.
12. John Locke, "Some Thoughts concerning Reading and Study for a Gentleman," c. 1704.
13. Edward Gibbon, *The History of the Decline and Fall of the Roman Empire*, 1776–88, Ch. 15, Note.
14. John Aikin, *The Lives of John Selden, Esq., and Archbishop Usher*, 1812.
15. Richard Milward, Dedication to Sir Matthew Hale et al., *Table Talk*, 1689.
16. Samuel Taylor Coleridge, "Notes on Selden's *Table Talk*," *Literary Remains*, ed. Henry Nelson Coleridge, 1836, Volume 2, pp. 361–62.
17. Henry Hallam, *Introduction to the Literature of Europe*, 1837–39, Pt. 3, Ch. 4, Par. 37.
18. A. Bronson Alcott, *Concord Days*, 1869, p. 249.
19. Herbert Paul, "The Autocrat of the Dinner Table," *Nineteenth Century*, April 1900, pp. 624–36.

WILLIAM HABINGTON

1. Anthony à Wood, *Athenae Oxonienses*, 1691–1721.
2. D. A. Casserly, "A Catholic Poet of the Seventeenth Century," *American Catholic Quarterly Review*, October 1877, p. 614.
3. Edward Phillips, *Theatrum Poetarum Anglicanorum*, 1675.
4. Thomas Campbell, *Specimens of the British Poets*, 1819.
5. David Masson, *The Life of John Milton*, 1859, Volume 1, Ch. 6.
6. D. A. Casserly, "A Catholic Poet of the Seventeenth Century," *American Catholic Quarterly Review*, October 1877, p. 618.
7. William Habington, "The Author," *Castara*, 1634.
8. George Talbot, "To His Best Friend and Kinsman *William Habington*, Esquire," *Castara*, 1635.
9. Samuel Egerton Brydges, *Censura Literaria*, 1805–09.
10. Henry Hallam, *Introduction to the Literature of Europe*, 1837–39, Pt. 2, Ch. 5, Par. 55.
11. George Saintsbury, *A History of Elizabethan Literature*, 1887, pp. 380–82.
12. Agnes Repplier, "English Love-Songs," *Points of View*, 1891, pp. 50–51.
13. W. T. Arnold, "William Habington," *The English Poets*, ed. Thomas Humphry Ward, 1880, Volume 2, pp. 158–62.
14. Maurice Francis Egan, "Three Catholic Poets," *Catholic World*, October 1880, pp. 132–38.

JOSEPH HALL

1. Thomas Fuller, *The History of the Worthies of England*, 1662.
2. Samuel R. Gardiner, *Academy*, April 17, 1886, p. 267.
3. Francis Meres, *Palladis Tamia*, 1598.
4. John Aubrey, "Joseph Hall," *Brief Lives*, 1669–96.
5. George G. Perry, *History of the Church of England*, 1861, Volume 1, p. 629.
6. John W. Hales, "Bishop Hall," *Antiquary*, November 1881, p. 190.
7. H. Craik, "Bishop Hall," *English Prose*, ed. Henry Craik, 1893, Volume 2, pp. 133–36.
8. John Milton, *An Apology for Smectymnuus*, 1641.
9. Peter Whalley, *An Enquiry into the Learning of Shakespeare*, 1748, pp. 41–42.

ABRAHAM COWLEY

SIR WILLIAM D'AVENANT

13. Henry Vaughan, "To Sir *William D'avenant*, upon His *Gondibert*," *Olor Iscanus*, 1651.
14. Thomas Rymer, *Preface to Rapin's Reflections on Aristotle's Treatise of Poesie*, 1694.
15. Alexander Pope (1734–36), cited in Joseph Spence, *Anecdotes, Observations and Characters of Books and Men*, ed. S. W. Singer, 1820.
16. Sir Walter Scott, *The Life of John Dryden*, 1808.
17. Isaac Disraeli, "D'Avenant and a Club of Wits," *Quarrels of Authors*, 1812–13.
18. William Hazlitt, *Lectures on the English Comic Writers*, 1819.
19. Thomas Babington Macaulay, "John Dryden" (1828), *Critical, Historical, and Miscellaneous Essays*, 1860, Volume 1, p. 350.
20. Karl Elze, "Sir William Davenant" (1869), *Essays on Shakespeare*, tr. L. Dora Schmitz, 1874, pp. 346–55.

WILLIAM PRYNNE

1. Samuel Pepys, *Diary*, July 3, 1666.
2. John Aubrey, "William Prynne," *Brief Lives*, 1669–96.
3. Thomas Hearne, *Reliquiae Hearnianae*, August 25, 1719.
4. Isaac Disraeli, "A Voluminous Author without Judgment," *Calamities of Authors*, 1812–13.
5. Adolphus William Ward, *A History of English Dramatic Literature* (1875), 1899, Volume 3, pp. 240–43.
6. Samuel R. Gardiner, *History of England*, 1883, Volume 7, pp. 13–14.
7. Anthony à Wood, *Athenae Oxonienses*, 1691–1721.

SIR JOHN DENHAM

1. John Aubrey, "Sir John Denham," *Brief Lives*, 1669–96.
2. Anthony à Wood, *Athenae Oxonienses*, 1691–1721.
3. Robert Herrick, "To M. Denham, on His Prospective Poem" (c. 1642), *Hesperides*, 1648.
4. Gerard Langbaine, *An Account of the English Dramatick Poets*, 1691.
5. Edmund Gosse, "Sir John Denham," *The English Poets*, ed. Thomas Humphry Ward, 1880, Volume 2, p. 279.
6. Adolphus William Ward, *A History of English Dramatic Literature* (1875), 1899, Volume 3, pp. 148–49.
7. John Dryden, Dedication to *The Rival Ladies*, 1664.
8. Sir John Oldham, "Bion: A Pastoral in Imitation of the *Greek of Moschus*, Bewailing the Death of the Earl of Rochester," c. 1684.
9. Joseph Addison, "An Account of the Greatest English Poets," 1694.
10. Alexander Pope, *Windsor-Forest*, 1713.
11. David Hume, *History of England*, 1754–62.
12. Oliver Goldsmith, *The Beauties of English Poesy*, 1767.
13. Henry Hallam, *Introduction to the Literature of Europe*, 1837–39, Pt. 3, Ch. 5, Pars. 36–37.
14. George L. Craik, *A Compendious History of English Literature and of the English Language*, 1861, Volume 2, p. 33.

15. Hippolyte Taine, *History of English Literature*, tr. H. Van Laun, 1871, Volume 1, Bk. 3, Ch. 1.
16. Theophilus Cibber, "Sir John Denham," *The Lives of the Poets*, 1753, Volume 3, pp. 1–6.
17. Samuel Johnson, "Denham," *Lives of the English Poets*, 1779–81.

ANNE BRADSTREET

1. Nathaniel Ward, Untitled poem, *The Tenth Muse Lately Sprung Up in America*, 1650.
2. Bathsua Makin, "An Essay to Revive the Antient Education of Gentlewomen," 1673.
3. Edward Phillips, "Women," *Theatrum Poetarum Anglicanorum*, 1675.
4. John Norton, "A Funeral Elogy, Upon That Pattern and Patron of Virtue, the Truely Pious, Peerless & Matchless Gentlewoman Mrs. Anne Bradstreet, Right Panaretes, Mirror of Her Age, Glory of Her Sex, Whose Heaven-Born-Soul Leaving Its Earthly Shrine, Chose Its Native Home, and Was Taken to Its Rest, upon 16th Sept. 1672," *Several Poems Compiled with Great Variety of Wit and Learning*, 1678.
5. Cotton Mather, "Successors," *Magnalia Christi Americana*, 1702, Bk. 2.
6. Jacob Bailey Moore, "Simon Bradstreet," *Lives of the Governors of New Plymouth, and Massachusetts Bay*, 1851, p. 388.
7. Unsigned, *North American Review*, January 1868, pp. 330–33.
8. Richard Henry Stoddard, "Richard Henry Dana," *Harper's New Monthly Magazine*, April 1879, p. 769.
9. George W. Childs, *Critical Dictionary of English Literature and British and American Authors*, 1886, p. 236.
10. Helen Campbell, *Anne Bradstreet and Her Time*, 1891, pp. 224–25.
11. John Woodbridge, "Introduction" to *The Tenth Muse Lately Sprung Up in America*, 1650.
12. Anne Bradstreet, "The Author to Her Book," *Several Poems Compiled with Great Variety of Wit and Learning*, 1678.
13. Unsigned, "Early American Poetry," *American Quarterly Review*, December 1827, pp. 494–95.
14. Helen Campbell, *Anne Bradstreet and Her Time*, 1891, p. 288.
15. Evert A. Duyckinck and George L. Duyckinck, "Anne Bradstreet," *The Cyclopædia of American Literature*, 1855, Volume 1, pp. 48–49.
16. James Anderson, "Anne Dudley, Wife of Simon Bradstreet," *Memorable Women of the Puritan Times*, 1862, pp. 265–84.
17. John Harvard Ellis, "Introduction" to *The Works of Anne Bradstreet in Prose and Verse*, 1867, pp. xi–lxxi.
18. Moses Coit Tyler, "New England: The Verse-Writers," *A History of American Literature*, 1878, Volume 1, pp. 280–88.

Volume 4

MARGARET CAVENDISH, DUCHESS OF NEWCASTLE

1. John Evelyn, *Diary*, 1667.
2. Samuel Pepys, *Diary*, May 30, 1667.
3. Leigh Hunt, "Specimens of British Poetesses," *Men, Women, and Books*, 1847.
4. William Cavendish, Duke of Newcastle, "To the Lady Newcastle, on Her Booke of Poems," *Poems, and Fancies*, 1653.

5. Margaret Cavendish, Duchess of Newcastle, "The Poetesses Hasty Resolution," *Poems, and Fancies*, 1653.
6. Margaret Cavendish, Duchess of Newcastle, "To All Noble, and Worthy Ladies," *Poems, and Fancies*, 1653.
7. Gerard Langbaine, *An Account of the English Dramatick Poets*, 1691.
8. Horace Walpole, *A Catalogue of the Royal and Noble Authors of England, Scotland, and Ireland*, 1758.
9. James Granger, *Biographical History of England*, 1769–1824.

172. Mark Pattison, *Milton*, 1879, p. 55.
173. Augustine Birrell, "John Milton," *Obiter Dicta, Second Series*, 1887, pp. 22–23.
174. Henry Van Dyke, "Milton and Tennyson," *The Poetry of Tennyson*, 1889–98, p. 80.
175. William Godwin, *History of the Commonwealth of England*, 1824, Volume 1, p. 352.
176. W. E. H. Lecky, *Spirit of Rationalism in Europe*, 1865.
177. Stopford A. Brooke, *Milton*, 1879, p. 45.
178. Leslie Stephen, *Dictionary of National Biography*, 1894, Volume 38, p. 29.
179. Order-Book of the Council of State, January 8, 1649/50.
180. Andrew Marvell, Letter to John Milton (June 2, 1654).
181. Thomas Hobbes, *Behemoth*, 1660, Pt. 4.
182. John Hackett, *The Life of Archbishop Williams*, 1693.
183. John Toland, *The Life of John Milton*, 1698.
184. Samuel Johnson, "John Milton," *Lives of the English Poets*, 1779–81.
185. William Francis Collier, A *History of English Literature*, 1861, p. 201.
186. Augustine Birrell, "John Milton," *Obiter Dicta: Second Series*, 1887, p. 34.
187. John Aubrey, "John Milton," *Brief Lives*, 1669–96.
188. Anthony à Wood, *Fasti Oxonienses*, 1691.
189. Joseph Addison, *The Spectator*, No. 267 (January 5, 1712); No. 273 (January 12, 1712); No. 279 (January 19, 1712); No. 285 (January 26, 1712).
190. François Marie Arouet de Voltaire, *An Essay upon Epick Poetry*, 1727.
191. Samuel Johnson, "John Milton," *Lives of the English Poets*, 1779–81.
192. Samuel Taylor Coleridge, "Milton" (1818), *Literary Remains*, ed. Henry Nelson Coleridge, 1836, Volume 1, pp. 166–78.
193. William Hazlitt, "On Shakspeare and Milton," *Lectures on the English Poets*, 1818.
194. Thomas Babington Macaulay, "Milton" (1825), *Critical, Historical and Miscellaneous Essays*, 1860, Volume 1, pp. 204–66.
195. Ralph Waldo Emerson, "Milton" (1838), *Complete Works*, 1904, Volume 12, pp. 247–79.
196. Walter Bagehot, "John Milton" (1859), *Collected Works*, ed. Norman St. John-Stevas, 1965, Volume 2, pp. 134–48.
197. Matthew Arnold, "Milton," *Essays in Criticism: Second Series*, 1888.

EDWARD HYDE, EARL OF CLARENDON

1. Edward Hyde, Earl of Clarendon, *The Life of Edward Earl of Clarendon*, c. 1668.
2. John Aubrey, "Edward Hyde, Earl of Clarendon," *Brief Lives*, 1669–96.
3. Gilbert Burnet, *History of His Own Time*, 1724.
4. Horace Walpole, A *Catalogue of the Royal and Noble Authors of England, Scotland, and Ireland*, 1758.
5. Thomas Babington Macaulay, "Hallam's Constitutional History" (1828), *Critical, Historical, and Miscellaneous Essays*, 1860, Volume 1, pp. 521–22.
6. Thomas Carlyle, *Historical Sketches of Noble Persons and Events in the Reigns of James I. and Charles I.*, 1844.
7. Henry Felton, *Dissertation on Reading the Classics*, 1711.
8. Horace Walpole, A *Catalogue of the Royal and Noble Authors of England, Scotland, and Ireland*, 1758.
9. David Hume, "The Commonwealth," *History of England*, 1754–62.

10. James Granger, *Biographical History of England*, 1769–1824.
11. Hugh Blair, *Lectures on Rhetoric and Belles Lettres*, 1783, Lecture 36.
12. William Godwin, "Milton and Clarendon," *The Enquirer*, 1797, pp. 415–16.
13. T. H. Lister, *Life and Administration of Edward, First Earl of Clarendon*, 1838, Volume 2, pp. 576–80.
14. Edmund Gosse, A *Short History of Modern English Literature*, 1897, pp. 150–51.
15. John Evelyn, Letter to Samuel Pepys (January 20, 1702/3).
16. Thomas Frognall Dibdin, *The Library Companion*, 1824, p. 209.
17. Robert Southey, Letter to Henry Taylor (December 31, 1825).
18. Thomas Babington Macaulay, "History" (1828), *Critical, Historical, and Miscellaneous Essays*, 1860, Volume 1, pp. 424–25.
19. François René, Vicomte de Chateaubriand, *Sketches of English Literature*, 1837, Volume 2, pp. 196–97.
20. Henry Hallam, *Introduction to the Literature of Europe*, 1837–39, Pt. 3, Ch. 7, Par. 36.
21. Isaac Disraeli, "Difficulties of Publishers of Contemporary Memoirs," *Amenities of Literature*, 1841.
22. John, Lord Campbell, *The Lives of the Lord Chancellors and Keepers of the Great Seal of England*, 1845–47.
23. George Saintsbury, A *History of Elizabethan Literature*, 1887, pp. 344–48.
24. Henry Craik, "Lord Clarendon," *English Prose*, ed. Henry Craik, 1893, Volume 2, pp. 391–93.
25. Sir James Fitzjames Stephen, "Lord Clarendon's Life," *Horae Sabbaticae: First Series*, 1892, pp. 329–44.
26. Leopold von Ranke, *History of England*, 1875, Volume 6, pp. 8–20.
27. Peter Bayne, "Clarendon," *The Chief Actors in the Puritan Revolution*, 1878, pp. 474–80.

THOMAS TRAHERNE

1. Herbert J. C. Grierson, "English Poetry," *The First Half of the Seventeenth Century*, 1906, pp. 171–74.
2. Harold Idris Bell, "Introduction" to *Traherne's Poems of Felicity*, 1910, pp. xxviii–xxxi.
3. Bertram Dobell, "An Unknown Seventeenth-Century Poet," *Athenaeum*, April 7, 1900, pp. 433–35.
4. Unsigned, *Athenaeum*, August 29, 1903, p. 276.
5. Unsigned, "'A Student of Felicity,'" *Spectator*, August 4, 1906, pp. 157–58.
6. Bertram Dobell, "Introduction" to *The Poetical Works of Thomas Traherne*, 1906, pp. xiii–xiv, lxiii–lxxxvii.
7. Bertram Dobell, "Introduction" to *Centuries of Meditation*, 1908, pp. ix–xxix.
8. Paul Elmer More, "Thomas Traherne," *Nation*, February 18, 1909, pp. 160–62.
9. Louise Collier Willcox, "A Joyous Mystic," *North American Review*, June 1911, pp. 892–904.

ANDREW MARVELL

1. John Norton, Letter to Reverend Marvell (c. January 1640).
2. John Milton, Letter to Lord Bradshaw (February 21, 1652/3).
3. John Aubrey, "Andrew Marvell," *Brief Lives*, 1669–96.
4. Richard Morton, *Pyretologia*, 1692.
5. Samuel Parker, *History of His Own Time*, 1727.
6. Charles Churchill, "The Author," 1763.
7. James Granger, *Biographical History of England*, 1769–1824.

THOMAS HOBBES

SAMUEL BUTLER

22. Hippolyte Taine, *History of English Literature*, tr. H. Van Laun, 1871, Volume 1, pp. 463–66.
23. John Richard Green, *A Short History of the English People*, 1874, Ch. 9.
24. William Michael Rossetti, "Samuel Butler," *Lives of Famous Poets*, 1878, pp. 88–89.
25. W. E. Henley, "Samuel Butler," *The English Poets*, ed. Thomas Humphry Ward, 1880, Volume 2, pp. 396–99.
26. Henry Morley, "Introduction" to *Hudibras*, 1885, p. viii.
27. Samuel Johnson, "Butler," *Lives of the English Poets*, 1779–81.
28. William Hazlitt, *Lectures on the English Comic Writers*, 1819.
29. George Gilfillan, "The Life and Works of Samuel Butler," *The Poetical Works of Samuel Butler*, 1854, Volume 1, pp. xii–xx.
30. Charles Cowden Clarke, "On the Comic Writers of England: IV. Butler," *Gentleman's Magazine*, July 1871, pp. 179–90.

JOHN WILMOT, EARL OF ROCHESTER

1. Samuel Pepys, *Diary*, February 17, 1668/9.
2. John Aubrey, "John Wilmot: Earl of Rochester," *Brief Lives*, 1669–96.
3. John Evelyn, *Diary*, November 24, 1760.
4. Francis Fane, Dedication to *Love in the Dark*, 1675.
5. Robert Parsons, *A Sermon Preached at the Earl of Rochester's Funeral*, 1680.
6. Thomas Flatman, "On the Death of My Lord Rochester: Pastoral," *Poems and Songs*, 1682.
7. Anthony à Wood, *Athenae Oxonienses*, 1691–1721.
8. Stephen Collet, *Relics of Literature*, 1823, p. 44.
9. John Sheffield, Duke of Buckingham, *An Essay on Satire*, 1675.
10. Gilbert Burnet, *Some Passages of the Life and Death of Rochester*, 1680.
11. Robert Wolseley, "Preface" to *Valentinian*, 1685.
12. Thomas Rymer, "Preface to the Reader," *Poems on Several Occasions* by the Earl of Rochester, 1691.
13. Unsigned, "The Memoirs of the Life and Character of the Late Earl of Rochester," *The Miscellaneous Works of the Right Hon. the Late Earls of Rochester and Roscommon*, 1707.
14. David Hume, *History of England*, 1754–62.
15. Horace Walpole, *A Catalogue of the Royal and Noble Authors of England, Scotland, and Ireland*, 1758.
16. William Hazlitt, *Lectures on the English Poets*, 1818.
17. Charles Cowden Clarke, "On the Comic Writers of England: VIII. English Satirists," *Gentleman's Magazine*, November 1971, pp. 694–95.
18. Hippolyte Taine, *History of English Literature*, tr. H. Van Laun, Volume 1, pp. 469–70.
19. Edmund Gosse, "Rochester," *The English Poets*, ed. Thomas Humphry Ward, 1880, Volume 2, pp. 424–25.
20. Algernon Charles Swinburne, "Social Verse" (1891), *Studies in Prose and Poetry*, 1894.
21. John Oldham, "Bion: A Pastoral in Imitation of the *Greek of Moschus*, Bewailing the Death of the Earl of Rochester" (1680), *The Works of Mr. John Oldham*, 1686, Bk. 2, pp. 73–87.
22. Samuel Johnson, "Rochester," *Lives of the English Poets*, 1779–81.

SIR THOMAS BROWNE

1. John Evelyn, *Diary*, October 17, 1671.
2. Anthony à Wood, *Athenae Oxonienses*, 1691–1721.
3. John Whitefoot, "Minutes for the Life of Sir Thomas Browne," *Posthumous Works of Sir Thomas Browne*, 1712.

4. Samuel Taylor Coleridge, "Notes on Sir Thomas Browne's *Religio Medici*" (1802), *Literary Remains*, ed. Henry Nelson Coleridge, 1836, Volume 1, pp. 241–42.
5. Samuel Taylor Coleridge, "Notes on Sir Thomas Browne's *Vulgar Errors*" (1804), *Literary Remains*, ed. Henry Nelson Coleridge, 1836, Volume 2, pp. 413–15.
6. William Hazlitt, *Lectures on the Dramatic Literature of the Age of Elizabeth*, 1820.
7. Thomas De Quincey, "Rhetoric" (1828), *Collected Writings*, ed. David Masson, Volume 10, p. 105.
8. John Tulloch, *Rational Theology and Christian Philosophy in England in the Seventeenth Century*, 1872, Volume 2, pp. 454–55.
9. George Saintsbury, *A History of Elizabethan Literature*, 1887, pp. 338–43.
10. James Russell Lowell, "In a Volume of Sir Thomas Browne," *Atlantic*, July 1890, p. 63.
11. George Saintsbury, "Sir Thomas Browne," *English Prose*, ed. Henry Craik, 1893, Volume 2, pp. 314–17.
12. Edmund Gosse, *A Short History of Modern English Literature*, 1897, pp. 153–54.
13. Thomas Browne, "To the Reader," *Religio Medici*, 1642.
14. Guy Patin, Letter (April 7, 1645).
15. John Collop, "On Doctor *Brown*: His *Religio Medici* and *Vulgar Errors*," *Poesis Rediviva*, 1656.
16. Henry Hallam, *Introduction to the Literature of Europe*, 1837–39, Pt. 3, Ch. 4, Par. 36.
17. George Daniel, "To the Reader, of Doctor Brown's Booke Entituled *Pseudodoxia Epidemika*," 1648.
18. Simon Wilkin, "Editor's Preface to *Pseudodoxia Epidemica*," *The Works of Sir Thomas Browne*, 1836, Volume 1.
19. Samuel Johnson, "The Life of Sir Thomas Browne," *Christian Morals* by Sir Thomas Browne, 1756.
20. Edward Bulwer-Lytton, "Sir Thomas Browne's *Works*," *Edinburgh Review*, October 1836, pp. 5–8.
21. Sir Leslie Stephen, "Sir Thomas Browne," *Hours in a Library* (1874–79), 1904, Volume 2, pp. 4–16, 34–41.
22. Walter Pater, "Sir Thomas Browne" (1886), *Appreciations*, 1889.

IZAAK WALTON

1. George Saintsbury, *A History of Elizabethan Literature*, 1887, p. 441.
2. W. E. Henley, "Walton," *Views and Reviews*, 1890.
3. Edmund Gosse, "Izaak Walton," *English Prose*, ed. Henry Craik, 1893, Volume 2, pp. 339–42.
4. Louise Imogen Guiney, "For Izaak Walton" (1893), *Collected Lyrics*, 1927, pp. 89–90.
5. Izaak Walton, "To all Readers of This Discourse; but Especially to the Honest Angler," *The Compleat Angler*, 1653.
6. Richard Franck, *Northern Memoirs*, 1658.
7. Charles Lamb, Letter to Samuel Taylor Coleridge (June 10, 1796).
8. Thomas Zouch, *The Life of Izaak Walton*, 1796.
9. William Hazlitt, "On John Buncle" (1815), *The Round Table*, 1817.
10. William Hazlitt, *Characteristics*, 1823.
11. Henry Hallam, *Introduction to the Literature of Europe*, 1837–39, Pt. 4, Ch. 7, Par. 45.
12. John Greenleaf Whittier, *The Bridal of Pennacook*, 1848.
13. Henry Reed, *Lectures on English Literature*, 1855, p. 31.
14. Alexander Cargill, "Izaak Walton," *Scribner's Magazine*, September 1893, pp. 272–76.
15. Eugene Field, "The Delights of Fender-Fishing," *The Love Affairs of a Bibliomaniac*, 1895, pp. 79–85.
16. James Boswell, *Life of Johnson*, 1791.

86. Thomas Babington Macaulay, *History of England*, 1848–59.
87. John Dryden, Letter to His Sons (September 3, 1697).
88. Oliver Goldsmith, *The Beauties of English Poesy*, 1767.
89. John Pinkerton (as "Robert Heron"), "Letter V: On the Spirit of Lyric Poetry," *Letters of Literature*, 1785, p. 34.
90. John Henry Newman, "Poetry with Reference to Aristotle's *Poetics*" (1828), *Essays Critical and Historical*, 1871.
91. Jonathan Swift, *The Battel of the Books*, 1704.
92. Alexander Pope, "Preface" to *The Iliad of Homer*, 1715.
93. Robert Burns, Letter to Mrs. Dunlop (May 4, 1788).
94. Henry Hallam, *Introduction to the Literature of Europe*, 1837–39, Pt. 4, Ch. 5, Par. 46.
95. John Conington, "Preface" to *The Aeneid of Virgil*, 1867.
96. Thomas James Mathias, *Pursuits of Literature* (1794), 1798.
97. James Russell Lowell, "Dryden" (1868), *Among My Books*, 1870, pp. 67–71.
98. John Dryden, "To the Reader," *Absalom and Achitophel*, 1681.
99. Joseph Addison, *The Spectator*, No. 512 (October 17, 1712).
100. Samuel Taylor Coleridge, *Table Talk*, August 6, 1832.
101. Thomas Babington Macaulay, *History of England*, 1848–59.
102. John Richard Green, *History of the English People*, 1877–80.
103. Oliver Goldsmith, *The Beauties of English Poesy*, 1767.
104. Sir Walter Scott, *The Works of John Dryden*, 1808.
105. Henry Hallam, *Introduction to the Literature of Europe*, 1837–39, Pt. 4, Ch. 5, Par. 40.
106. Jonathan Swift, "On Poetry: A Rhapsody," 1733.
107. Hugh Blair, *Lectures on Rhetoric and Belles Lettres*, 1783, Lecture 18.
108. Henry Hallam "Scott's Edition of Dryden," *Edinburgh Review*, October 1808, pp. 133–34.
109. Edmund Gosse, *A History of Eighteenth Century Literature*, 1888, pp. 90–94.
110. Stopford A. Brooke, *English Literature*, 1896, pp. 177–78.
111. W. P. Ker, "Introduction" to *Essays of John Dryden*, 1900, pp. xxvii–xxx.
112. Thomas Shadwell, *The Medal of John Bayes: A Satyr against Folly and Knavery*, 1682.
113. Samuel Johnson, "Dryden," *Lives of the English Poets*, 1779–81.
114. Thomas Babington Macaulay, "John Dryden" (1828), *Critical, Historical and Miscellaneous Essays*, 1860, Volume 1, pp. 351–75.
115. James Russell Lowell, "Dryden" (1868), *Among My Books*, 1870, pp. 4–24, 79–80.
116. George Saintsbury, "Later Dramas and Prose Works," *Dryden*, 1881, pp. 121–31.

SIR CHARLES SEDLEY

1. Samuel Pepys, *Diary*, July 1, 1663.
2. Samuel Pepys, *Diary*, October 23, 1668.
3. Gilbert Burnet, *History of His Own Time*, 1724.
4. Thomas Babington Macaulay, *History of England*, 1848–59.
5. John Richard Green, *A Short History of the English People*, 1877–80.
6. John Wilmot, Earl of Rochester, "An Allusion to Horace: The 10th Satyr of the 1st Book," 1678.
7. Thomas Shadwell, Dedication to *A True Widow*, 1679.
8. Gerard Langbaine, *An Account of the English Dramatick Poets*, 1691.

9. Alexander Pope (1734–36), cited in Joseph Spence, *Anecdotes, Observations and Characters of Books and Men*, ed. S. W. Singer, 1820.
10. Theophilus Cibber, *Lives of the Poets*, 1753.
11. Edwin P. Whipple, "Words," *American Review*, February 1845, p. 181.
12. Hippolyte Taine, *History of English Literature*, tr. H. Van Laun, 1871, Volume 1, p. 497.
13. Adolphus William Ward, *A History of English Dramatic Literature* (1875), 1899, Volume 3, pp. 447–48.
14. Edmund Gosse, "Sir Charles Sedley," *The English Poets*, ed. Thomas Humphry Ward, 1880, p. 415.
15. Agnes Repplier, "English Love-Songs," *Points of View*, 1891, pp. 41–42.
16. John Dryden, "Dedication: To My Most Honour'd Friend Sir Charles Sedley, Baronet," *The Assignation*, 1672.

SAMUEL PEPYS

1. George Hickes, Letter to Dr. Charlett (1703).
2. John Evelyn, *Diary*, May 26, 1703.
3. James Granger, *Biographical History of England*, 1769–1824.
4. Francis Lord Jeffrey, "Pepys's *Memoirs*," *Edinburgh Review*, November 1825, pp. 26–28.
5. Leigh Hunt, "Life and African Visit of Pepys," *Men, Women, and Books*, 1847.
6. James Russell Lowell, "A Great Public Character," *My Study Windows*, 1871.
7. Edmund Gosse, *A History of Eighteenth Century Literature*, 1888.
8. W. P. Ker, "Samuel Pepys," *English Prose*, ed. Henry Craik, 1894, Volume 3, pp. 219–20.
9. Sir Walter Scott, "Pepys's Memoirs," *Quarterly Review*, March 1826, pp. 288–98.
10. Robert Louis Stevenson, "Samuel Pepys" (1881), *Familiar Studies of Men and Books*, 1882.
11. Andrew Lang, "To Samuel Pepys, Esq.," *Letters to Dead Authors* (1886), 1893, pp. 245–53.

SIR ROGER L'ESTRANGE

1. Samuel Pepys, *Diary*, September 4, 1663.
2. Samuel Pepys, *Diary*, December 17, 1664.
3. Edward Hyde, Earl of Clarendon, *History of the Rebellion*, c. 1674.
4. Nahum Tate, *The Second Part of Absalom and Achitophel* by Nahum Tate and John Dryden, 1682, ll. 1025–36.
5. John Evelyn, *Diary*, May 7, 1685.
6. William Winstanley, *The Lives of the Most Famous English Poets*, 1687.
7. John Hughes, "Of Style," 1698.
8. Gilbert Burnet, *History of His Own Time*, 1724.
9. Theophilus Cibber, *The Lives of the Poets*, 1753.
10. Oliver Goldsmith, "An Account of the Augustan Age of England," *The Bee*, No. 8 (November 24, 1759).
11. James Granger, *Biographical History of England*, 1769–1824.
12. Henry Hallam, *Introduction to the Literature of Europe*, 1837–39, Pt. 4, Ch. 7, Par. 32.
13. Thomas Babington Macaulay, *History of England*, 1848–59.
14. J. H. Millar, "Sir Roger L'Estrange," *English Prose*, ed. Henry Craik, 1894, Volume 3, pp. 589–90.
15. Richard Garnett, *The Age of Dryden*, 1895, pp. 174–76.
16. George Saintsbury, *A Short History of English Literature*, 1898, pp. 525–26.
17. Oliver Elton, *The Augustan Ages*, 1899, p. 204.

JOHN LOCKE

JOHN EVELYN

8. William Smyth, *Lectures on Modern History*, 1840, Lecture 20.
9. Thomas Babington Macaulay, *History of England*, 1848–59.
10. Eugene Lawrence, *The Lives of the British Historians*, 1855, Volume 1, pp. 304–11.
11. W. E. H. Lecky, *A History of England in the Eighteenth Century*, 1877.
12. John Mackintosh, *The History of Civilisation in Scotland* (1878), 1895, Volume 3, pp. 364–65.
13. George Saintsbury, *A Short History of English Literature*, 1898, p. 523.
14. François René, Vicomte de Chateaubriand, *Sketches of English Literature*, 1837, Volume 2, p. 196.
15. Henry Hallam, *Introduction to the Literature of Europe*, 1837–39, Pt. 4, Ch. 8, Par. 49.
16. Jonathan Swift, "Short Remarks on Bishop Burnet's *History*," 1724–34.
17. Thomas Salmon, "Preface" to *An Impartial Examination of Bishop Burnet's* History of His Own Times, 1724.
18. Bevil Higgons, "Preface" to *Historical and Critical Remarks on Bishop Burnet's* History of His Own Time, 1725.
19. Thomas Hearne, *Reliquiae Hearnianae*, March 19, 1734.
20. Thomas Hearne, *Reliquiae Hearnianae*, April 9, 1734.
21. James Boswell, *Life of Johnson*, 1791.
22. Charles Lamb, Letter to Thomas Manning (March 1, 1800).
23. Richard Hurd, *Commonplace Book* (c. 1808), cited in Francis Kilvert, *Memoirs of the Life and Writings of the Right Rev. Richard Hurd*, 1860, p. 243.
24. Robert Southey, "Burnet—*History of His Own Time*," *Quarterly Review*, April 1823, p. 170.
25. Samuel Taylor Coleridge, *Table Talk*, June 15, 1830.
26. Edmund Gosse, *A History of Eighteenth Century Literature*, 1889, pp. 102–3.
27. Oliver Elton, *The Augustan Ages*, 1899, p. 192.
28. Unsigned, "Bishop Burnet's *History of His Own Time*," *Retrospective Review*, 1822, pp. 349–54.

NAHUM TATE

1. Jonathan Swift, "Dedication to Prince Posterity," *A Tale of a Tub*, 1704.
2. Joseph Addison, *The Spectator*, No. 40 (April 16, 1711).
3. Alexander Pope, *An Epistle to Dr. Arbuthnot*, 1735, ll. 175–92.
4. Samuel Richardson, *Clarissa*, 1748.
5. Thomas Davies, "*King Lear*," *Dramatic Miscellanies*, 1783, Volume 2, p. 326.
6. Charles Dibdin, *A Complete History of the Stage*, 1795, Volume 4, p. 204.
7. Leigh Hunt, "*King Lear* Revived," 1808.
8. Sir Walter Scott, *The Life of John Dryden*, 1808.
9. Charles Lamb, "On the Tragedies of Shakspeare, Considered with Reference to Their Fitness for Stage Presentation," 1812.
10. Thomas De Quincey, "Shakspeare" (1838), *Collected Writings*, ed. David Masson, Volume 4, p. 22.
11. Charles Knight, "*King Lear*," *Studies of Shakspere*, 1849.
12. Victor Hugo, *William Shakespeare*, tr. Melville B. Anderson, 1864.
13. Adolphus William Ward, *A History of English Dramatic Literature* (1875), 1899, Volume 3, pp. 427–28.
14. Kenyon West, *The Laureates of England*, 1895, pp. 62–63.
15. J. C. Wright, *The Poets Laureate*, 1896, pp. 24–25.
16. Walter Hamilton, "Nahum Tate," *The Poets Laureate of England*, 1879, pp. 124–30.

WILLIAM WYCHERLEY

1. Alexander Pope (1728–30), cited in Joseph Spence, *Anecdotes, Observations and Characters of Books and Men*, ed. S. W. Singer, 1820.
2. John Dennis (1728–30), cited in Joseph Spence, *Anecdotes, Observations and Characters of Books and Men*, ed. S. W. Singer, 1820.
3. John Dryden, "The Author's Apology for Heroic Poetry and Poetic Licence," *The State of Innocence*, 1677.
4. John Wilmot, Earl of Rochester, "An Allusion to Horace: The 10th Satyr of the 1st Book," 1678.
5. John Wilmot, Earl of Rochester, "A Session of the Poets," c. 1680.
6. Gerard Langbaine, *An Account of the English Dramatick Poets*, 1691.
7. John Dryden, "To My Dear Friend Mr. Congreve, on His Comedy, Call'd, *The Double-Dealer*," 1693.
8. Sir Samuel Garth, *The Dispensary*, 1699, Canto 4.
9. Sir Richard Steele, *The Tatler*, No. 3 (April 14, 1709).
10. François Marie Arouet de Voltaire, "On Comedy," *Letters on England (Lettres Philosophiques)*, tr. Leonard Tancock, 1734.
11. Alexander Pope (1734–36), cited in Joseph Spence, *Anecdotes, Observations and Characters of Books and Men*, ed. S. W. Singer, 1820.
12. David Hume, *History of England*, 1754–62.
13. William Hazlitt, *Lectures on the English Comic Writers*, 1819.
14. Charles Lamb, "On the Artificial Comedy of the Last Century" (1822), *The Essays of Elia*, 1823.
15. Leigh Hunt, "Biographical and Critical Notices of Wycherley, Congreve, Vanbrugh, and Farquhar," *The Dramatic Works of Wycherley, Congreve, Vanbrugh, and Farquhar*, 1840.
16. Thomas Babington Macaulay, "Leigh Hunt" (1841), *Critical, Historical and Miscellaneous Essays*, 1860, Volume 4, pp. 384–87.
17. Charles Cowden Clarke, "On the Comic Writers of England: IX. Wycherley and Congreve," *Gentleman's Magazine*, November 1871, pp. 831–34.
18. Adolphus William Ward, *A History of English Dramatic Literature* (1875), 1899, Volume 3, pp. 461–63.
19. George Meredith, "On the Idea of Comedy and of the Uses of the Comic Spirit," 1877.
20. John Richard Green, *History of the English People*, 1877–80.
21. Hippolyte Taine, *The History of English Literature*, tr. H. Van Laun, 1871, Bk. 3, Chapter 1.
22. W. C. Ward, "Introduction" to *William Wycherley*, 1888, pp. vii–xvi.

NICHOLAS ROWE

1. Thomas Hearne, *Reliquiae Hearnianae*, August 26, 1715.
2. Alexander Pope, Letter to Edward Blount (February 10, 1715/6).
3. Alexander Pope, "Epitaph Intended for Mr. Rowe," 1720.
4. William Congreve, "Of Pleasing," c. 1724.
5. William Congreve, Letter to Joseph Keally (December 9, 1704).
6. Henry Cromwell, Letter to Alexander Pope (November 5, 1710).
7. Alexander Pope, Letter to Henry Cromwell (November 11, 1710).
8. James Welwood, "Preface" to Lucan's *Pharsalia*, 1718.
9. George Sewell, "Memoirs of the Life and Writings of Nicholas Rowe," *The Miscellaneous Works of Nicholas Rowe*, 1733.

18. Henry G. Hewlett, "Poets of Society: Prior; Praed; Locker," *Contemporary Review*, July 1872, p. 244.
19. George Barnett Smith, "English Fugitive Poets," *Poets and Novelists*, 1875, pp. 393–94.
20. Edmund Gosse, *A History of Eighteenth Century Literature*, 1888, p. 134.
21. Andrew Lang, "On *Vers de Société*," *Letters on Literature*, 1889, pp. 152–53.
22. George Saintsbury, *A Short History of English Literature*, 1898, pp. 557–58.
23. Harvey Waterman Thayer, "Matthew Prior: His Relation to English *Vers de Société*," *Sewanee Review*, April 1902, pp. 182–83.
24. Samuel Johnson, "Prior," *Lives of the English Poets*, 1779–81.
25. Austin Dobson, "Introduction" to *Selected Poems of Matthew Prior*, 1889, pp. xi–lxx.

THOMAS D'URFEY

1. Joseph Addison, *The Guardian*, No. 67 (May 28, 1713).
2. John Arbuthnot, Letter to Jonathan Swift (December 11, 1718).
3. Edward F. Rimbault, *Notes and Queries*, December 8, 1866, p. 465.
4. William G. Hutchinson, "Tom D'Urfey," *MacMillan's Magazine*, November 1901, pp. 62–64.
5. Gerard Langbaine, *An Account of the English Dramatick Poets*, 1691.
6. Alexander Pope, Letter to Henry Cromwell (April 10, 1710).
7. Richard Steele, *The Guardian*, No. 20 (April 14, 1713).
8. Sir John Hawkins, *A General History of the Science and Practice of Music*, 1776, Volume 2, Ch. 173.
9. Thomas Babington Macaulay, *History of England*, 1848–59.
10. Adolphus William Ward, *A History of English Dramatic Literature* (1875), 1899, Volume 3, pp. 454–55.
11. Edmund Gosse, *Life of Congreve*, 1888, p. 110.
12. William Chappell, *Popular Music of the Olden Time*, 1859, Volume 2, pp. 621–23.
13. Walter Besant, "Tom D'Urfey," *Belgravia*, September 1872, pp. 427–36.

ELKANAH SETTLE

1. John Dryden, *The Second Part of Absalom and Achitophel* by Nahum Tate and John Dryden, 1682, ll. 412–35.
2. Gerard Langbaine, *An Account of the English Dramatick Poets*, 1691.
3. Dr. Lockier, Dean of Peterborough (1730–32), cited in Joseph Spence, *Anecdotes, Observations and Characters of Books and Men*, ed. S. W. Singer, 1820.
4. Samuel Johnson, "Dryden," *Lives of the English Poets*, 1779–81.
5. John Doran, *Their Majesties' Servants—Annals of the English Stage*, 1863, Volume 2, p. 152.
6. Adolphus William Ward, *A History of English Dramatic Literature* (1875), 1899, Volume 3, pp. 396–98.
7. John Churton Collins, "John Dryden" (1878), *Essay and Studies*, 1895, p. 46.
8. Edmund Gosse, *A History of Eighteenth Century Literature*, 1888, p. 59.
9. Richard Garnett, *The Age of Dryden*, 1895, pp. 118–19.
10. Sir Walter Scott, *The Life of John Dryden*, 1808.

JEREMY COLLIER

1. John Dryden, "Preface" to *Fables*, 1700.
2. Thomas Babington Macaulay, *History of England*, 1848–59.

3. George Saintsbury, *A Short History of English Literature*, 1898, p. 526.
4. Jeremy Collier, "Introduction" to A *Short View of the Immorality and Profaneness of the English Stage*, 1698.
5. William Congreve, *Amendments of Mr. Collier's False and Imperfect Citations*, 1698.
6. Edward Filmer, *A Defence of Plays*, 1707.
7. Colley Cibber, *An Apology for the Life of Mr. Colley Cibber*, 1740.
8. Samuel Johnson, "Congreve," *Lives of the English Poets*, 1779–81.
9. William Hazlitt, *Lectures on the English Comic Writers*, 1819.
10. Sir Walter Scott, "An Essay on the Drama," 1819.
11. Thomas Babington Macaulay, "Leigh Hunt" (1841), *Critical, Historical, and Miscellaneous Essays*, 1860, Volume 4, pp. 396–99.
12. Adolphus William Ward, *A History of English Dramatic Literature* (1875), 1899, Volume 3, pp. 511–12.
13. Richard Garnett, *The Age of Dryden*, 1895, p. 153.
14. Edmund Gosse, *Life of William Congreve*, 1888, pp. 101–12.

SIR JOHN VANBRUGH

1. Thomas Hearne, *Reliquiae Hearnianae*, September 25, 1714.
2. Abel Evans, "On Sir John Vanbrugh," 1726.
3. François Marie Arouet de Voltaire, "On Comedy," *Letters on England (Lettres Philosophiques)*, tr. Leonard Tancock, 1734.
4. Alexander Pope, *Imitations of Horace*, 1737, *Ep.* II.i.289.
5. Colley Cibber, *An Apology for the Life of Mr. Colley Cibber*, 1740.
6. Hugh Blair, *Lectures on Rhetoric and Belles Lettres*, 1783, Lecture 47.
7. William Hazlitt, *Lectures on the English Comic Writers*, 1819.
8. Henry Neele, *Lecture on the English Poets*, 1829, Lecture 4.
9. Allan Cunningham, *The Lives of the Most Eminent British Painters, Sculptors, and Architects*, 1831.
10. Samuel Astley Dunham, *Lives of the Most Eminent Scientific Men of Great Britain*, 1838.
11. Leigh Hunt, "Biographical and Critical Notices of Wycherley, Congreve, Vanbrugh, and Farquhar," *The Dramatic Works of Wycherley, Congreve, Vanbrugh, and Farquhar*, 1840.
12. Oswald Crawfurd, *English Comic Dramatists*, 1883, p. 84.
13. Edmund Gosse, *A History of Eighteenth Century Literature*, 1888, pp. 67–68.
14. Jonathan Swift, "The History of Vanbrug's House," 1706.
15. Thomas Hearne, *Reliquiae Hearnianae*, May 29, 1717.
16. Sarah Jennings Churchill, Duchess of Marlborough, "Case of the Duke of Marlborough and Sir John Vanbrugh," 1718.
17. Horace Walpole, *Anecdotes of Painting in England*, 1762.
18. Isaac Disraeli, "Secret History of the Building of Blenheim," *Curiosities of Literature*, 1791–1824.
19. Colley Cibber, *An Apology for the Life of Mr. Colley Cibber*, 1740.
20. William Hazlitt, *Lectures on the English Comic Writers*, 1819.
21. Henry Hallam, *Introduction to the Literature of Europe*, 1837–39, Pt. 4, Ch. 6, Par. 53.
22. Adolphus William Ward, *A History of English Dramatic Literature* (1875), 1899, Volume 3, pp. 477–81.

7. Joseph Addison, *The Spectator*, No. 339 (March 29, 1712).
8. Thomas Hearne, *Reliquiae Hearnianae*, July 25, 1723.
9. Thomas Hearne, *Reliquiae Hearnianae*, November 22, 1734.
10. James Beattie, "An Essay on Laughter and Ludicrous Composition," 1776.
11. Robert Southey, *Life of Cowper*, 1836.
12. George Saintsbury, A *Short History of English Literature*, 1898, p. 555.
13. Samuel Johnson, "Blackmore," *Lives of the English Poets*, 1779–81.

WILLIAM CONGREVE

1. John Dryden, Letter to Jacob Tonson (August 30, 1693).
2. William Congreve, Letter to Joseph Keally (October 14, 1704).
3. Mary de la Rivière Manley, *The New Atalantis*, 1709.
4. Jonathan Swift, *Journal to Stella*, October 26, 1710.
5. John Sheffield, Duke of Buckingham, "The Election of a Poet Laureat in 1719," 1719.
6. Alexander Pope, Postscript (1720) to *The Iliad of Homer*, 1715–20.
7. Lady Mary Wortley Montagu (1740–41), cited in Joseph Spence, *Anecdotes, Observations and Characters of Books and Men*, ed. S. W. Singer, 1820.
8. Edward Young (1757), cited in Joseph Spence, *Anecdotes, Observations and Characters of Books and Men*, ed. S. W. Singer, 1820.
9. Edward Wortley Montagu (?), *An Autobiography*, c. 1776.
10. John Dryden, "To My Dear Friend Mr. Congreve, on His Comedy, Call'd, *The Double-Dealer*," 1693.
11. Joseph Addison, "An Account of the Greatest English Poets," 1694.
12. Sir Samuel Garth, *The Dispensary*, 1699, Canto 4.
13. John Gay, "On a Miscellany of Poems," 1711.
14. François Marie Arouet de Voltaire, "On Comedy," *Letters on England (Lettres Philosophiques)*, tr. Leonard Tancock, 1734.
15. Samuel Johnson, "Congreve," *Lives of the English Poets*, 1779–81.
16. Charles Dibdin, A *Complete History of the Stage*, 1795, Volume 4, p. 274.
17. William Hazlitt, *Lectures on the English Comic Writers*, 1819.
18. Sir Walter Scott, "An Essay on the Drama," 1819.
19. Henry Neele, *Lectures on English Poetry*, 1829, p. 146.
20. Henry Hallam, *Introduction to the Literature of Europe*, 1837–39, Pt. 4, Ch. 6, Par. 50.
21. Leigh Hunt, "Biographical and Critical Notices of Wycherley, Congreve, Vanbrugh, and Farquhar," *The Dramatic Works of Wycherley, Congreve, Vanbrugh, and Farquhar*, 1840.
22. Thomas Babington Macaulay, "Leigh Hunt" (1841), *Critical, Historical and Miscellaneous Essays*, 1860, Volume 4, p. 410.
23. Adolphus William Ward, A *History of English Dramatic Literature* (1875), 1899, Volume 3, pp. 468–71.
24. Algernon Charles Swinburne, "Congreve" (1877), *Miscellanies*, 1866, pp. 53–55.
25. Austin Dobson, "William Congreve," *The English Poets*, ed. Thomas Humphry Ward, 1880, Volume 3, pp. 10–11.
26. Algernon Charles Swinburne, A *Study of Shakespeare*, 1880, p. 42, Note.
27. Oswald Crawfurd, *English Comic Dramatists*, 1883, p. 130.

28. George E. Woodberry, "Gosse's Life of Congreve," *Nation*, September 27, 1888, p. 255.
29. W. E. Henley, "Congreve," *Views and Reviews*, 1890.
30. Edmund Gosse, A *Short History of Modern English Literature*, 1897, pp. 191–92.
31. George Saintsbury, A *Short History of English Literature*, 1898, pp. 492–93.
32. William Congreve, Dedication to *The Double-Dealer*, 1694.
33. John Dryden, Letter to William Walsh (December 12, 1693).
34. Henry Hallam, *Introduction to the Literature of Europe*, 1837–39, Pt. 4, Ch. 6, Par. 52.
35. Adolphus William Ward, A *History of English Dramatic Literature* (1815), 1899, Volume 3, pp. 472–73.
36. Colley Cibber, *An Apology for the Life of Mr. Colley Cibber*, 1740.
37. Henry Hallam, *Introduction to the Literature of Europe*, 1837–39, Pt. 4, Ch. 6, Par. 51.
38. Adolphus William Ward, A *History of English Dramatic Literature* (1875), 1899, Volume 3, pp. 473–74.
39. Edmund Gosse, *Life of William Congreve*, 1888, pp. 69–70.
40. William Congreve, Dedication to *The Way of the World*, 1700.
41. Sir Richard Steele, "To Mr. Congreve, Occasion'd by His Comedy, Call'd, *The Way of the World*" (c. 1700), *Poetical Miscellanies*, 1714.
42. Charles Lamb, "On the Artificial Comedy of the Last Century" (1822), *The Essays of Elia*, 1823.
43. Henry Hallam, *Introduction to the Literature of Europe*, 1837–39, Pt. 4, Ch. 6, Par. 52.
44. Aldolphus William Ward, A *History of English Dramatic Literature* (1875), 1899, Volume 3, pp. 475–76.
45. George Meredith, "On the Idea of Comedy and of the Uses of the Comic Spirit," 1877.
46. Jonathan Swift, "To Mr. Congreve," 1693.
47. David Mallet (?), "A Poem to the Memory of Mr. Congreve," 1729.
48. William Makepeace Thackeray, "Congreve and Addison," *The English Humourists of the Eighteenth Century*, 1853, pp. 57–62.
49. Charles Cowden Clarke, "On the Comic Writers of England: IX. Wycherley and Congreve," *Gentleman's Magazine*, November 1871, pp. 834–45.

SIR RICHARD STEELE

1. Thomas Hearne, *Reliquiae Hearnianae*, March 23, 1713/4.
2. John Dennis, *The Characters and Conduct of Sir John Edgar*, 1720, Letter 4.
3. Samuel Johnson, *Life of Savage*, 1744.
4. Lady Mary Wortley Montagu, Letter to the Countess of Bute (September 22, 1755).
5. Victor Benjamin, *Original Letters, Dramatic Pieces, and Poems*, 1776.
6. Thomas Babington Macaulay, "The Life and Writings of Addison" (1843), *Critical, Historical and Miscellaneous Essays*, 1860, p. 369.
7. Leigh Hunt, A *Book for a Corner*, 1849.
8. Charles Woodward Hutson, "Sir Richard Steele," *Bookman* (New York), August 1899, p. 511.
9. Jonathan Swift, *The Importance of the* Guardian *Considered*, 1713.
10. Oliver Goldsmith, "An Account of the Augustan Age of England," *The Bee*, No. 8 (November 24, 1759).
11. Thomas De Quincey, "Schlosser's Literary History of the

Volume 5

SAMUEL CLARKE

DANIEL DEFOE

31. Samuel Taylor Coleridge, A *Course of Lectures* (1818), *Literary Remains*, ed. Henry Nelson Coleridge, 1836, Volume 1, p. 189.
32. Thomas Babington Macaulay, "John Dryden" (1828), *Critical, Historical, and Miscellaneous Essays*, 1860, Volume 1, pp. 331–32.
33. Samuel Taylor Coleridge, "Notes on *Robinson Crusoe*" (1830), *Literary Remains*, ed. Henry Nelson Coleridge, 1836, Volume 1, pp. 196–97.
34. George Borrow, *Lavengro*, 1851, Ch. 3.
35. Karl Marx, *Das Kapital*, 1867, Volume 1, Pt. 1, Ch. 1, Sec. 4.
36. H. Rider Haggard, *Books Which Have Influenced Me*, 1887, p. 66.
37. Julian Hawthorne, "Literature for Children," *Confessions and Criticisms*, 1887, pp. 122–24.
38. Frank R. Stockton, "My Favorite Novelist and His Best Book," *Munsey's Magazine*, June 1897, pp. 352–53.
39. Sir Walter Scott, "Daniel De Foe" (c. 1821), *Miscellaneous Works*, 1861, Volume 4, pp. 247–81.
40. Sir Leslie Stephen, "De Foe's Novels" (1868), *Hours in a Library* (1874–79), 1904, Volume 1, pp. 1–63.

JOHN GAY

1. Jonathan Swift, "A Libel on D—— D—— and a Certain Great Lord," 1730.
2. Jonathan Swift, "To Mr. Gay on His Being Steward to the Duke of Queenberry," 1731.
3. Jonathan Swift, *Verses on the Death of Dr. Swift*, 1731, ll. 53–54.
4. John Gay, "My Own Epitaph," 1732.
5. Alexander Pope, "Epitaph on Mr. Gay in Westminster Abbey," 1733.
6. Catherine Hyde, Duchess of Queensberry, Letter to Charles Howland (September 28, 1734).
7. Alexander Pope (1737–39), cited in Joseph Spence, *Anecdotes, Observations and Characters of Books and Men*, ed. S. W. Singer, 1820.
8. Lady Mary Wortley Montagu (1740–41), cited in Joseph Spence, *Anecdotes, Observations and Characters of Books and Men*, ed. S. W. Singer, 1820.
9. Joseph Baller, "Memoir Written by Gay's Nephew," *Gay's Chair*, ed. Henry Lee, 1820.
10. Thomas Babington Macaulay, "The Life and Writings of Addison" (1843), *Critical, Historical, and Miscellaneous Essays*, 1860, Volume 5, pp. 418–19.
11. Sir Leslie Stephen, *Alexander Pope*, 1880, pp. 112–13.
12. John Churton Collins, *Jonathan Swift*, 1893, pp. 96–97.
13. Sir Samuel Garth, "To Mr. Gay on His Poems," c. 1719.
14. Joseph Warton, *An Essay on the Genius and Writings of Pope*, 1756, Volume 1.
15. Oliver Goldsmith, *The Beauties of English Poesy*, 1767.
16. William Hazlitt, *Lectures on the English Poets*, 1818.
17. Thomas Campbell, *Specimens of the British Poets*, 1819.
18. John Wilson, "Spenser," *Blackwood's Edinburgh Magazine*, November 1833, p. 833.
19. William Makepeace Thackeray, *The English Humourists of the Eighteenth Century*, 1853.
20. Austin Dobson, "John Gay," *The English Poets*, ed. Thomas Humphry Ward, 1880, Volume 3, pp. 145–47.
21. St. Loe Strachey, *Academy*, January 6, 1883, pp. 3–4.
22. W. E. Henley, "Gay," *Views and Reviews*, 1890, pp. 183–85.
23. Edmund K. Chambers, "Introduction" to *English Pastorals*, 1895, pp. 46–47.
24. Duncan C. Tovey, "John Gay," *Reviews and Essays in English Literature*, 1897, pp. 115–17.

25. George Saintsbury, A *Short History of English Literature*, 1898, pp. 559–60.
26. John Gay, Letter to Jonathan Swift (February 15, 1727/8).
27. Catherine Hyde, Duchess of Queensberry, Letter to James Stanhope (February 27, 1728/9).
28. Mary Pendarves, Letter to Anne Granville (March 4, 1728/9).
29. John Arbuthnot, Letter to Jonathan Swift (March 19, 1728/9).
30. John, Lord Hervey, *Memoirs of the Reign of George the Second* (1729), ed. John Wilson Croker, 1848.
31. Alexander Pope (1734–36), cited in Joseph Spence, *Anecdotes, Observations and Characters of Books and Men*, ed. S. W. Singer, 1820.
32. Colley Cibber, *An Apology for the Life of Mr. Colley Cibber*, 1740.
33. Sir John Hawkins, A *General History of the Science and Practice of Music*, 1776, Ch. 190.
34. Samuel Taylor Coleridge, "Sir George Etherege, etc." (1812), *Literary Remains*, ed. Henry Nelson Coleridge, 1836, Volume 1, pp. 330–31.
35. George Hogarth, *Memoirs of the Opera in Italy, France, Germany, and England*, 1851.
36. William Bodham Donne, "The Drama" (1854), *Essays on the Drama*, 1858, p. 139.
37. Katherine Thomson, *The Literature of Society*, 1862, Volume 2, p. 217.
38. Hippolyte Taine, *History of English Literature*, tr. H. Van Laun, 1871, Bk. 3, Ch. 3.
39. Oswald Crawfurd, *English Comic Dramatist*, 1883, p. 204.
40. Augustine Birrell, *Essays about Men, Women, and Books*, 1894, pp. 112–15.
41. Samuel Johnson, "Gay," *Lives of the English Poets*, 1779–81.
42. John Underhill, "Introductory Memoir," *The Poetical Works of John Gay*, 1893, Volume 1, pp. xi–xii, lxiii–lxix.
43. George A. Aitken, "John Gay," *Westminster Review*, October 1893, pp. 395–403.

BERNARD MANDEVILLE

1. Sir John Hawkins, *The Life of Dr. Samuel Johnson*, 1787, p. 263.
2. Robert Browning, "With Bernard Mandeville," *Parleyings with Certain People of Importance in Their Day*, 1887.
3. James Boswell, *Life of Johnson*, 1791.
4. Henry Crabb Robinson, *Diary*, July 12, 1812.
5. Friedrich, Christoph Schlosser, *History of the Eighteenth Century*, tr. D. Davison, 1823.
6. Thomas Babington Macaulay, "Milton" (1825), *Critical, Historical, and Miscellaneous Essays*, 1860, Volume 1, p. 208.
7. Alexander Bain, *Moral Science*, 1869, pp. 179–80.
8. Friedrich Überweg, *History of Philosophy*, tr. George S. Morris, 1871, Volume 2, p. 378.
9. Henry Morley, *Shorter Works in English Prose*, 1880, p. 253.
10. Henry Sidgwick, *Outlines of the History of Ethics*, 1886.
11. J. Clark Murray, "The Revived Study of Berkeley," *Macmillan's Magazine*, July 1887, p. 171.
12. John Dennis, *The Age of Pope*, 1894, pp. 214–16.
13. George Saintsbury, "Bernard de Mandeville," *English Prose*, ed. Henry Craik, 1894, Volume 3, pp. 438–39.
14. Edmund Gosse, A *Short History of Modern English Literature*, 1897, pp. 225–26.
15. L. A. Selby-Bigge, "Introduction" to *British Moralists*, 1897, Volume 1, pp. 15–16.

69. Matthew Arnold, *On Translating Homer*, 1861.
70. Richard Savage, *An Account of* The Dunciad, 1732.
71. Colley Cibber, *A Letter from Mr. Cibber to Mr. Pope*, 1742.
72. John, Lord Hervey, *The Difference between Verbal and Practical Virtue*, 742.
73. Mrs. Racket (1742–43), cited in Joseph Spence, *Anecdotes, Observations and Characters of Books and Men*, ed. S. W. Singer, 1820.
74. Henry Fielding, *The Covent-Garden Journal*, No. 23 (March 21, 1752).
75. Adam Smith, *The Theory of Moral Sentiments*, 1759, Pt. 3, Ch. 2.
76. Horace Walpole, Letter to John Pinkerton (June 26, 1785).
77. William Somerville, "To the Author of the *Essay on Man*," c. 1732.
78. W. Belsham, "Remarks on Pope's *Essay on Man*," *Essays Philosophical and Moral, Historical and Literary*, 1799, Volume 1, p. 361.
79. Frederick Denison Maurice, *Moral and Metaphysical Philosophy*, 1862.
80. Sir Leslie Stephen, *History of English Thought in the Eighteenth Century*, 1876.
81. Augustine Birrell, "Pope," *Obiter Dicta: Second Series*, 1887.
82. Elijah Fenton, Letter to William Broome (September 1726).
83. Lady Mary Wortley Montagu, Letter to the Countess of Bute (June 23, 1754).
84. Oliver Goldsmith, *The Life of Richard Nash*, 1762.
85. Horace Walpole, Letter to William Mason (March 13, 1777).
86. William Cowper, Letter to William Unwin (June 8, 1780).
87. Hugh Blair, *Lectures on Rhetoric and Belles Lettres*, 1783, Lecture 37.
88. John Dennis, *A True Character of Mr. Pope, and His Writings*, 1716.
89. Alexander Pope, "Preface" to *The Works of Mr. Alexander Pope*, 1717.
90. Samuel Johnson, "Pope," *Lives of the English Poets*, 1779–81.
91. William Hazlitt, *Lectures on the English Poets*, 1818.
92. Sir Leslie Stephen, "Pope as a Moralist" (1873), *Hours in a Library* (1874–79), 1904, Volume 1, pp. 128–85.
93. G. K. Chesterton, "Pope and the Art of Satire" (1902), *Varied Types*, 1908, pp. 43–55.

LEWIS THEOBALD

1. John Dennis, *Remarks upon Mr. Pope's Translation of Homer*, 1717.
2. Thomas Hearne, *Reliquiae Hearnianae*, May 17, 1734.
3. Thomas Hearne, *Reliquiae Hearnianae*, June 13, 1734.
4. Alexander Pope, *The Dunciad*, 1743, Bk. 1, l. 133, Note.
5. William Warburton, "Preface" to *The Works of Shakespear*, 1747.
6. Samuel Johnson, *Preface to Shakespeare*, 1765.
7. Henry Hallam, *Introduction to the Literature of Europe*, 1837–39, Pt. 3, Ch. 6, Par. 54.
8. Isaac Disraeli, "Shakespeare," *Amenities of Literature*, 1841.
9. Thomas B. Shaw, *Outlines of English Literature*, 1847.
10. Charles Knight, *Studies of Shakspere*, 1849.
11. Richard Grant White, *Shakespeare's Scholar*, 1854, p. 9.
12. E. S. Dallas, *The Gay Science*, 1866, Volume 1, p. 16.
13. William John Courthope, "Preface" to *The Dunciad*, *The*

Works of Alexander Pope, eds. William John Courthope, Whitwell Elwin, 1882, Volume 4, pp. 27–28.
14. Sidney Lee, *Shakespeare's Life and Work*, 1900, pp. 175–76.
15. Alexander Pope et al., *The Dunciad, in Three Books with Notes Variorum*, 1729, Book 1, ll. 97–260.
16. John Churton Collins, "The Porson of Shakespearian Criticism," *Quarterly Review*, July 1892, pp. 109–13.

JONATHAN SWIFT

1. Sir William Temple, Letter to Sir Robert Southwell (May 29, 1690).
2. White Kennett, *Diary*, 1713.
3. Jonathan Swift, "Family of Swift," c. 1727.
4. Alexander Pope (1728–30), cited in Joseph Spence, *Anecdotes, Observations and Characters of Books and Men*, ed. S. W. Singer, 1820.
5. Alexander Pope (1742–43), cited in Joseph Spence, *Anecdotes, Observations and Characters of Books and Men*, ed. S. W. Singer, 1820.
6. John Boyle, Earl of Orrery, *Remarks on the Life and Writings of Dr. Jonathan Swift*, 1752, pp. 4–6.
7. Samuel Richardson, Letter to Lady Bradslaigh (April 22, 1752).
8. Patrick Delany, *Observations upon Lord Orrery's Remarks on the Life and Writings of Dr. Jonathan Swift*, 1754, pp. 288–91.
9. Thomas Amory, "The History of These Memoirs," *Memoirs of Several Ladies of Great Britain*, 1755, pp. xxviii–xxix.
10. Deane Swift, *An Essay upon the Life, Writings and Character, of Dr. Jonathan Swift*, 1755, pp. 365–67.
11. Horace Walpole, Letter to Sir Thomas Mann (January 13, 1780).
12. Thomas Parnell, "To Dr. Swift, On His Birthday, November 30th, 1713," 1713.
13. François Marie Arouet de Voltaire, "Letter 22: on Mr Pope and Some Other Famous Poets," *Letters on England (Lettres Philosophiques)*, tr. Leonard Tancock, 1734.
14. Alexander Pope (1734–36), cited in Joseph Spence, *Anecdotes, Observations and Characters of Books and Men*, ed. S. W. Singer, 1820.
15. Lady Mary Wortley Montagu (1740–41), cited in Joseph Spence, *Anecdotes, Observations and Characters of Books and Men*, ed. S. W. Singer, 1820.
16. William Hayley, *The Triumphs of Temper*, 1781, Canto 3, ll. 587–648.
17. William Cowper, *Table Talk*, 1782, ll. 656–61.
18. Hugh Blair, *Lectures on Rhetoric and Belles Lettres*, 1783, Lecture 17.
19. James Boswell, *Life of Johnson*, 1791.
20. George Gordon, Lord Byron, *Hints from Horace*, 1811.
21. Samuel Taylor Coleridge, *A Course of Lectures* (1818), *Literary Remains*, ed. Henry Nelson Coleridge, 1836, Volume 1, p. 140.
22. William Hazlitt, *Lectures on the English Poets*, 1818.
23. Samuel Taylor Coleridge, *Table Talk*, June 15, 1830.
24. Thomas Carlyle, *Lectures on the History of Literature*, 1838.
25. Thomas Babington Macaulay, "Sir William Temple" (1838), *Critical, Historical, and Miscellaneous Essays*, 1860, Volume 4, pp. 102–3.
26. Thomas Babington Macaulay, "The Life and Writings of Addison" (1843), *Critical, Historical, and Miscellaneous Essays*, 1860, Volume 5, pp. 376–77.
27. Thomas De Quincey, "Schlosser's Literary History of the Eighteenth Century" (1847), *Collected Writings*, ed. David Masson, Volume 11, pp. 17–18.

AMBROSE PHILIPS

AARON HILL

COLLEY CIBBER

ALLAN RAMSAY

1. William Hamilton, "Epistle to Allan Ramsay," 1719.
2. James Boswell, *Life of Johnson*, 1791.
3. Robert Burns (?), "Poem on Pastoral Poetry," c. 1794.
4. Leigh Hunt, *Autobiography*, 1850, Ch. 10.
5. William Somerville, "To Allan Ramsay upon His Publishing a Second Volume of Poems," c. 1718.
6. Joseph Ritson, "A Historical Essay on Scottish Song," *Scottish Songs*, 1794, Volume 1, pp. 63–66.
7. George Chalmers, "The Life of Allan Ramsay," *The Poems of Allan Ramsay*, 1800, Volume 1, pp. 150–53.
8. Alexander Fraser Tytler, Lord Woodhouslee, "Remarks on the Genius and Writings of Allan Ramsay," *The Poems of Allan Ramsay*, 1800, Volume 1, pp. 60–61.
9. Sir Walter Scott, "Introductory Remarks" (1830), *Minstrelsy of the Scottish Border* (1802–03), 1830, Volume 1, p. 25, Note.
10. James Grant Wilson, *The Poets and Poetry of Scotland*, 1875, Volume 1, p. 104.
11. William Minto, "Allan Ramsay," *The English Poets*, ed. Thomas Humphry Ward, 1880, Volume 3, pp. 159–62.
12. J. Logie Robertson, "Biographical Introduction" to *Poems of Allan Ramsay*, 1886, pp. 46–51.
13. Edmund Gosse, *A History of Eighteenth Century Literature* 1888, p. 139.
14. Francis T. Palgrave, *Landscape in Poetry*, 1896, p. 169.
15. Oliphant Smeaton, *Allan Ramsay*, 1896, pp. 159–60.
16. Sir Henry Craik, *A Century of Scottish History*, 1901, pp. 339–40.
17. James Beattie, "An Essay on Laughter and Ludicrous Composition," *Essays*, 1776–79, Volume 3, pp. 382–83.
18. Hugh Blair, *Lectures on Rhetoric and Belles Lettres*, 1783, Lecture 39.
19. Thomas Campbell, *Specimens of the British Poets*, 1819.
20. John Wilson (as "Christopher North"), *Noctes Ambrosianae* (March 1825), 1854.
21. Charles Ollier, Letter to Leight Hunt (January 10, 1844).
22. Leight Hunt, *A Jar of Honey from Mount Hybla*, 1848, Ch. 8.
23. William Black, "A Poetical Barber," *Once a Week*, November 26, 1864, p. 615.
24. W. W. Tulloch, "Allan Ramsay and *The Gentle Shepherd*," *Good Words*, 1886, p. 678.
25. J. C. Shairp, *On Poetic Interpretation of Nature*, 1877, pp. 194–95.
26. William Lyon Phelps, *The Beginnings of the English Romantic Movement*, 1893, p. 31.
27. Hugh Walker, *Three Centuries of Scottish Literature*, 1893, Volume 2, pp. 9–11.
28. John Dennis, *The Age of Pope*, 1894, p. 121.
29. George Eyre-Todd, *Scottish Poetry of the Eighteenth Century*, 1896, Volume 1, pp. 38–39.

JONATHAN EDWARDS

1. George Whitefield, *Diary*, October 19, 1740.
2. Jonathan Edwards, Letter to the Trustees of the College of New Jersey (October 19, 1757).
3. Unsigned, *Boston Gazette*, April 10, 1758.
4. Timothy Dwight, *The Triumph of Infidelity*, 1788.
5. James Parton, *The Life and Times of Aaron Burr*, 1858, p. 27.
6. N. H. Eggleston, "A New England Village," *Harper's New Monthly Magazine*, November 1871, p. 823.
7. George P. Fisher, "The Philosophy of Jonathan Edwards," *North American Review*, March 1879, p. 303.
8. Benjamin Franklin, Letter to Jane Mecom (July 28, 1743).

9. Ezra Stiles, *Diary*, August 10, 1787.
10. Dugald Stewart, "First Preliminary Dissertation," *Encyclopaedia Britannica*, 1815–21, Pt. 2, Sec. 7.
11. S. E. Dwight, *The Life of President Edwards*, 1829.
12. Sir James Mackintosh, *Dissertation on the Progress of Ethical Philosophy*, 1830, Sec. 5.
13. George Bancroft, *History of the United States of America*, 1834–74, Ch. 16.
14. Rufus Wilmot Griswold, *The Prose Writers of America*, 1845.
15. Friedrich Überweg, *History of Philosophy*, tr. George S. Morris, 1871, Volume 2, pp. 443–44.
16. Harriet Beecher Stowe, Letter to Charles Edward Stowe (May 1874).
17. James Russell Lowell, Letter to Sir Leslie Stephen (May 15, 1876).
18. Oliver Wendell Holmes, "Jonathan Edwards," *International Review*, July 1880, pp. 24–28.
19. F. B. Sanborn, "The Puritanic Philosophy of Jonathan Edwards," *Journal of Speculative Philosophy*, October 1883, pp. 420–21.
20. I. N. Tarbox, "Jonathan Edwards as a Man," *New Englander*, September 1884, pp. 617–18.
21. Barrett Wendell, "American Literature," *Stelligeri and Other Essays concerning America*, 1893, pp. 121–22.
22. Henry A. Beers, *Initial Studies in American Letters*, 1895, pp. 34–36.
23. F. V. N. Painter, *Introduction to American Literature*, 1897, pp. 51–56.
24. Adam Leroy Jones, *Early American Philosophers*, 1898, pp. 48–49.
25. Edward Everett Hale, Jr., "Jonathan Edwards," *American Prose*, ed. George Rice Carpenter, 1898, pp. 13–15.
26. Mark Twain, Letter to Joseph H. Twichell (February 1902).
27. Frederick Denison Maurice, *Moral and Metaphysical Philosophy*, 1862, Volume 2, pp. 469–71.
28. Austin Phelps, *English Style in Public Discourse*, 1883, pp. 31–32.
29. Charles F. Richardson, *American Literature 1607–1885*, 1887, Volume 1, pp. 141–45.
30. Alexander V. G. Allen, *Jonathan Edwards*, 1889, pp. 286–87.
31. Brander Matthews, *An Introduction to the Study of American Literature*, 1896, p. 20.
32. Williston Walker, "Jonathan Edwards," *Ten New England Leaders*, 1901, pp. 252–54.
33. W. E. H. Lecky, *Spirit of Rationalism in Europe*, 1865, Volume 1, Ch. 4, Note.
34. Alexander V. G. Allen, *Jonathan Edwards*, 1887, pp. 311–13.
35. Williston Walker, "Jonathan Edwards," *Ten New England Leaders*, 1901, pp. 257–59.
36. Samuel Hopkins, "The Life of President Edwards," *Memoirs of the Rev. Jonathan Edwards*, 1764.
37. Sir Leslie Stephen, "Jonathan Edwards," *Hours in a Library* (1874–79), 1904, Volume 2, pp. 43–45, 73–80.
38. Moses Coit Tyler, *A History of American Literature*, 1878, Volume 2, pp. 187–91.

WILLIAM COLLINS

1. Samuel Johnson, Letter to Joseph Warton (March 8, 1754).
2. Oliver Goldsmith, *An Enquiry into the Present Stage of Polite Learning*, 1759, Ch. 10.
3. William Hayley, John Sargent, Inscription on Collins's Monument, c. 1759.

WILLIAM LAW

SAMUEL RICHARDSON

31. Austin Dobson, "Richardson at Home," *Scribner's Magazine*, September 1893, p. 383.
32. J. H. Millar, "Samuel Richardson," *English Prose*, ed. Henry Craik, 1895, Volume 4, pp. 57–58.
33. Joseph Texte, *Jean-Jacques Rousseau and the Cosmopolitan Spirit in Literature* (1895), tr. J. W. Matthews, 1899, pp. 206–7.
34. Edmund Gosse, A *Short History of English Literature*, 1897, p. 242.
35. Agnes Repplier, *Varia*, 1897, pp. 202–6.
36. George Saintsbury, A *Short History of English Literature*, 1898, p. 600.
37. Wilbur L. Cross, *The Development of the English Novel*, 1899, pp. 34–37.
38. Aaron Hill, "To the Unknown Author of the Beautiful New Piece, Called *Pamela*," 1740.
39. Horace Walpole, Letter to Unknown (c. 1740).
40. Anna Laetitia Barbauld, "Life of Samuel Richardson," *The Correspondence of Samuel Richardson*, 1804, Volume 1, pp. 60–66.
41. George Gordon, Lord Byron, *Journal*, January 4, 1821.
42. Charles Lamb, "Detached Thoughts on Books and Reading" (1822), *The Essays of Elia*, 1823.
43. Austin Dobson, *Fielding*, 1883, pp. 71–72.
44. Sir John Lubbock, "A Song of Books," *The Pleasures of Life*, 1887.
45. Edmund Gosse, A *History of Eighteenth Century Literature*, 1888, p. 246.
46. H. D. Traill, "Samuel Richardson," *The New Fiction*, 1897, pp. 116–18.
47. Henry Fielding, *Jacobite's Journal*, No. 5 (January 2, 1747/8).
48. Abbé Prévost, "Preface" to *Clarissa Harlowe*, 1751.
49. Lady Mary Wortley Montagu, Letter to the Countess of Bute (March 1, 1752).
50. François Marie Arouet de Voltaire, Letter to Marie de Vichy de Chamrond, Marquise Du Deffand (April 12, 1760).
51. Samuel Johnson, "Rowe," *Lives of the English Poets*, 1779–81.
52. Charles Lamb, "Characters of Dramatic Writers, Contemporary with Shakespeare—Christopher Marlowe," 1808.
53. Benjamin Robert Hayden, *Journal*, March 3, 1813.
54. John Dunlop, *The History of Fiction* (1814), 1842, Volume 2, p. 404.
55. William Hazlitt, *Conversations with James Northcote*, 1830, Conversation 19.
56. Thomas Babington Macaulay (April 15, 1850), cited in G. Otto Trevelyan, *The Life and Letters of Lord Macaulay*, 1876, Volume 2, p. 237.
57. William Makepeace Thackeray, "Nil Nisi Bonum" (1860), *Roundabout Papers*, 1863.
58. Edward FitzGerald, Letter to John Allen (April 10, 1865).
59. John Addington Symonds (1868), cited in Horatio F. Brown, *John Addington Symonds*, 1894, p. 253.
60. Margaret Oliphant, "Historical Sketches of the Reign of George II—The Novelists," *Blackwood's Edinburgh Magazine*, March 1869, pp. 267–68.
61. H. Baxton Forman, "Samuel Richardson, as Artist and Moralist," *Fortnightly Review*, October 1869, p. 435.
62. William Forsyth, *The Novels and Novelists of the Eighteenth Century*, 1871, pp. 215–16.
63. Edmund Gosse, A *History of Eighteenth Century Literature*, 1888, pp. 248–49.
64. W. E. Henley, "Richardson," *Views and Reviews*, 1890, pp. 220–22.
65. Walter Raleigh, *The English Novel.*, 1894, pp. 158–60.

66. Lady Mary Wortley Montagu, Letter to the Countess of Bute (October 20, 1755).
67. Edward Gibbon, Letter to Catherine Porten (November 15, 1756).
68. William Hazlitt, "Why the Heroes of Romances are Insipid," 1827.
69. Robert Dale Owen, "A Chapter of Autobiography," *Atlantic*, April 1873, p. 450.
70. William C. Ward, "Samuel Richardson," *Gentleman's Magazine*, January 1890, pp. 85–86.
71. L. B. Lang, "Morals and Manners in Richardson," *National Review*, November 1899, pp. 339–40.
72. William Hazlitt, *Lectures on the English Comic Writers*, 1819.
73. Sir Walter Scott, "Samuel Richardson," *Lives of the Novelists*, 1825.
74. David Masson, "Richardson's Method," *British Novelists and Their Styles*, 1859, pp. 110–21.
75. Sir Leslie Stephen, "Richardson's Novels," *Hours in a Library* (1874–79), 1904, Volume 2, pp. 82–97, 122–27.
76. Clara Linklater Thomson, "The Art of Richardson," *Samuel Richardson*, 1900, pp. 242–48.

LADY MARY WORTLEY MONTAGU

1. Alexander Pope, "On Lady Mary Wortley Montagu's Portrait," 1719.
2. John Gay, "Mr. Pope's Welcome from Greece," 1720, ll. 57–60.
3. Richard Savage, *The Wanderer*, 1729, Canto 5.
4. François Marie Arouet de Voltaire, "On Inoculation with Smallpox," *Letters on England* (*Lettres Philosophiques*), tr. Leonard Tancock, 1734.
5. Horace Walpole, Letter to Henry Seymour Conway (September 25, 1740).
6. Frances Thynne Hertford, Duchess of Somerset (1741), cited in Emily M. Symonds, *Memoirs of the Eighteenth Century*, 1901, pp. 33–34.
7. Thomas Gray, Letter to Thomas Warton (January 31, 1761).
8. Horace Walpole, Letter to George Montagu (February 2, 1762).
9. Elizabeth Montagu, Letter to Lady Mary Wortley Montagu (February 16, 1762).
10. Edward Wortley Montagu (?), *An Autobiography*, c. 1776.
11. Edmond Malone (1879), cited in Sir James Prior, *Life of Edmond Malone*, 1860, pp. 149–50.
12. Leigh Hunt, *Men, Women, and Books*, 1847.
13. Charles Wentworth Dilke, "Lady Mary Wortley Montagu" (1861), *The Papers of a Critic*, 1875, Volume 1, p. 354.
14. Algernon Charles Swinburne, "A Century of English Poetry" (1880), *Miscellanies*, 1886, p. 42.
15. William John Courthope, "The Life of Alexander Pope," *The Works of Alexander Pope*, 1889, Volume 5, pp. 140–41.
16. Arthur R. Ropes, "Introduction" to *Lady Mary Wortley Montagu: Select Passages from Her Letters*, 1892, p. 30.
17. James Dallaway, "Memoirs of Lady Mary Wortley Montagu," *The Works of Lady Mary Wortley Montagu*, 1803.
18. Francis, Lord Jeffrey, "Lady Mary Wortley Montagu" (1803), *Contributions to the* Edinburgh Review, 1844, Volume 4, pp. 427–29.
19. George Gordon, Lord Byron, "Second Letter to John Murray on Bowles's Strictures on Pope," 1821, Note.
20. Margaret Oliphant, "Historical Sketches of the Reign of

16. John Forster, "Charles Churchill," *Edinburgh Review*, January 1845, pp. 66–67.
17. Leigh Hunt, *The Town*, 1848, pp. 294–95.
18. Hartley Coleridge, "Young and His Contemporaries," *Sketches of English Poets*, 1849.
19. James Hannay, "Memoir of Churchill," *The Poetical Works of Charles Churchill*, 1866, pp. 28–32.
20. James Russell Lowell, "Carlyle" (1866), *Works*, Riverside ed., Volume 2, p. 80.
21. George Otto Trevelyan, *The Early History of Charles James Fox*, 1880, p. 171.
22. Edmund Gosse, *A History of Eighteenth Century Literature*, 1888, pp. 324–25.
23. Tobias Smollett (?), *Critical Review*, March 1761, pp. 209–10.
24. David Garrick, Letter to Robert Lloyd (c. May 1761).
25. Thomas Davies, *Memoirs of the Life of David Garrick, Esq.*, 1780, Volume 1, pp. 305–7.
26. William Cowper, Letter to William Unwin (August 1786).
27. William Hazlitt, *Lectures on the English Poets*, 1818.
28. E. J. Payne, "Charles Churchill," *The English Poets*, ed. Thomas Humphry Ward, 1880, Volume 3, pp. 389–91.
29. George Saintsbury, *A Short History of English Literature*, 1898, pp. 584–85.
30. James Beattie, "On a Report of a Monument to Be Erected in Westminster Abbey to the Memory of a Late Author" (1765), *The Poetical Works of James Beattie*, 1831, pp. 145–52.
31. George Gilfillan, "Churchill—His Life and Writings," *The Poetical Works of Charles Churchill*, 1855, pp. iii, xv–xix.

EDWARD YOUNG

1. Jonathan Swift, *On Poetry: A Rhapsody*, 1733, ll. 305–10.
2. Elizabeth Montagu, Letter (1745).
3. Bishop Hildesley, Letter to Samuel Richardson (November 11, 1760).
4. Owen Ruffhead, *The Life of Alexander Pope, Esq.*, 1769, p. 291, Note.
5. James Boswell, *Life of Johnson*, 1791.
6. Horace Walpole, Letter to the Earl of Strafford (July 4, 1757).
7. William Warburton, Letter to Richard Hurd (May 17, 1759), *Letters from a Late Eminent Prelate*, 1808.
8. James Beattie, "On the Report of a Monument to Be Erected in Westminster Abbey to the Memory of a Late Author," 1765.
9. Samuel Johnson, "Young," *Lives of the English Poets*, 1779–81.
10. Madame de Staël, *The Influence of Literature upon Society*, 1800, Ch. 15.
11. William Hazlitt, *Lectures on the English Poets*, 1818.
12. Walter Savage Landor, "Southey and Porson," *Imaginary Conversations: Third Series*, 1828.
13. François René, Vicomte de Chateaubriand, *Sketches of English Literature*, 1837, Volume 2, pp. 251–52.
14. Elizabeth Barrett Browning, *The Book of the Poets* (1842), *Life, Letters and Essays of Elizabeth Barrett Browning*, 1863.
15. George Gilfillan, "Edward Young," *Eclectic Magazine*, January 1853, p. 136.
16. Walter Savage Landor, "Young," *Last Fruit*, 1853.
17. Hippolyte Taine, *History of English Literature*, tr. H. Van Laun, 1871, Bk. 3, Ch. 7.
18. George Saintsbury, "Edward Young," *The English Poets*,

ed. Thomas Humphry Ward, 1880, Volume 3, pp. 222–24.
19. Stopford A. Brooke, *Naturalism in English Poetry* (1902), 1920, pp. 30–34.
20. Sir Leslie Stephen, "Young's *Night Thoughts*," *Critic*, October 1902, pp. 352–53.
21. Catherine Talbot, Letter to Elizabeth Carter (September 7, 1744).
22. Edward Young (1758), cited in Joseph Spence, *Anecdotes, Observations and Characters of Books and Men*, ed. S. W. Singer, 1820.
23. François Marie Arouet de Voltaire, Letter to Pierre Le Tourneur (June 7, 1769).
24. Friedrich Melchior Grimm, Letter to the Duke of Saxe-Gotha (c. 1770), *Historical and Literary Memoirs and Anecdotes*, 1814, Volume 1, pp. 26–27.
25. Hugh Blair, *Lectures on Rhetoric and Belles Lettres*, 1783, Lecture 15.
26. James Boswell, *Life of Johnson*, 1791.
27. Unsigned, "Advertisement" to *The Complaint, and The Consolation; or, Night Thoughts*, 1797, pp. iv–vii.
28. Thomas Green, *Extracts from the Diary of a Lover of Literature* (entry for March 10, 1799), 1810, p. 67.
29. John Doran, "The Life of Edward Young, LL.D.," *The Complete Works of the Rev. Edward Young, LL.D.*, 1854, pp. lvii–lxi.
30. Walter Savage Landor, "Apology for *Gebir*," 1854.
31. Sir Leslie Stephen, *History of English Thought in the Eighteenth Century*, 1876.
32. Edmund Gosse, *A History of Eighteenth Century Literature*, 1888, pp. 212–13.
33. Thomas Campbell, "Edward Young," *Specimens of the British Poets*, 1819.
34. Evert A. Duyckinck, "Edward Young," *North American Review*, October 1854, pp. 273–78, 295–96.
35. George Eliot, "Wordliness and Other Worldliness: The Poet Young" (1857), *Essays and Leaves from a Note-Book*, 1883, pp. 41–64.

DAVID MALLET

1. William Warburton, *A Letter to the Lord Viscount B———ke, Occasioned by His Treatment of a Deceased Friend*, 1749.
2. Alexander Wedderburn, Earl of Rosslyn, Letter to David Hume (October 28, 1764).
3. Thomas Davies, *Memoirs of the Life of David Garrick, Esq.*, 1780, Volume 2, p. 47.
4. John Churton Collins, "Literary Life of Bolingbroke," *Bolingbroke: A Historical Study, and Voltaire in England*, 1886, p. 179.
5. Aaron Hill, *The Plain Dealer*, July 24, 1724.
6. David Mallet, Letter to the Editor, *The Plain Dealer*, August 24, 1724.
7. Joseph Warton, *An Essay on the Genius and Writings of Pope*, 1756, Volume 1, pp. 147–48.
8. Cuthbert Shaw, *The Race*, 1766.
9. Edward Gibbon, Letter to Dorothea Gibbon (May 24, 1776).
10. James Boswell, *Life of Johnson*, 1791.
11. William Lyon Phelps, *The Beginnings of the English Romantic Movement*, 1893, pp. 177, 180.
12. Hugh Walker, *Three Centuries of Scottish Literature*, 1893, Volume 2, pp. 82–86.
13. George Saintsbury, *A Short History of English Literature*, 1898, p. 578.
14. Samuel Johnson, "Mallet," *Lives of the English Poets*, 1779–81.

MARK AKENSIDE

1. Joseph Warton, *An Essay on the Genius and Writings of Pope,* 1782, Volume 2, p. 386, Note.
2. Sir John Hawkins, *The Life of Samuel Johnson, LL.D.,* 1787.
3. Dugald Stewart, *Elements of the Philosophy of the Human Mind,* 1827, Volume 3, p. 501.
4. Robert Aris Willmott, "Mark Akenside," *The Poetical Works of Mark Akenside and John Dyer,* 1855, pp. 26–27.
5. Hugh Miller, "The Poetry of Intellect and Fancy" (1856), *Essays,* 1862, p. 451.
6. James Beattie, "On the Report of a Monument to Be Erected in Westminster Abbey to the Memory of a Late Author," 1765, ll. 39–40.
7. James Hurdis, *The Village Curate,* 1788.
8. Thomas Carlyle, Letter to Robert Mitchell (June 14, 1815).
9. Francis, Lord Jeffrey, "Scott's Edition of Swift," *Edinburgh Review,* September 1816, p. 7.
10. Thomas Campbell, *Specimens of the British Poets,* 1819.
11. Charles Bucke, *On the Life, Writings and Genius of Akenside,* 1832, p. 28.
12. Henry T. Tuckerman, "The Scholar: Mark Akenside," *Characteristics of Literature,* 1849, pp. 250–54.
13. James Russell Lowell, "A Good Word for Winter" (1870), *My Study Windows,* 1871, p. 33.
14. John Bascom, *Philosophy of English Literature,* 1874, p. 213.
15. Sir Leslie Stephen, *History of English Thought in the Eighteenth Century,* 1876.
16. Alfred H. Welsh, *Development of English Literature and Language,* 1882, Volume 2, pp. 134–35.
17. Samuel Johnson, "Akenside," *Lives of the English Poets,* 1779–81.
18. Hugh Blair, *Lectures on Rhetoric and Belles Lettres,* 1783, Lecture 40.
19. James Boswell, *Life of Johnson,* 1791.
20. James Boswell, *Life of Johnson,* 1791.
21. William Hazlitt, *Lectures on the English Poets,* 1818.
22. Thomas Babington Macaulay, "Walpole's Letter to Sir Horace Mann" (1833), *Critical, Historical, and Miscellaneous Essays,* 1860, Volume 3, pp. 182–83.
23. Alexander Dyce, "The Life of Akenside," *The Poetical Works of Mark Akenside,* 1834, pp. 80–82.
24. William Spalding, *The History of English Literature,* 1853, p. 338.
25. George Gilfillan, "The Life of Akenside," *The Poetical Works of Akenside,* 1857, pp. 20–23.
26. Edmund Gosse, *A History of Eighteenth Century Literature,* 1888, pp. 311–12.
27. William Lyon Phelps, *The Beginnings of the English Romantic Movements,* 1893, p. 39.
28. John Dennis, *The Age of Pope,* 1894, pp. 117–18.
29. Henry A. Beers, *A History of English Romanticism in the Eighteenth Century,* 1898, pp. 140–41.
30. George Saintsbury, *A Short History of English Literature,* 1898, pp. 579–80.
31. Edward Dowden, "Mark Akenside," *The English Poets,* ed. Thomas Humphry Ward, 1880, Volume 3, pp. 341–44.

THOMAS CHATTERTON

1. Thomas Chatterton, Letter to William Barrett (1770).
2. Edwin Cross, Testimony at Inquest (August 27, 1770).
3. Horace Walpole, Letter to William Cole (May 21, 1778).
4. William Hayley, *An Essay on Epic Poetry,* 1782, Epistle 4, ll. 221–48.
5. Samuel Taylor Coleridge, "Monody on the Death of Chatterton," 1790.
6. James Montgomery, "Chatterton," 1802.
7. William Wordsworth, "Resolution and Independence," 1802.
8. William Henry Ireland, *The Confessions of William Henry Ireland,* 1805, pp. 15–17.
9. John Keats, "Dedication" to *Endymion,* 1818.
10. Thomas Brown, *Lectures on the Philosophy of the Human Mind,* 1820, Lecture 44.
11. John Keats, "To Chatterton," c. 1821.
12. Robert Southey, *A Vision of Judgment,* 1821, Sec. 11.
13. John Foster, "Chatterton" (1838), *Critical Essays,* 1856, Volume 2, p. 520.
14. Samuel Roffey Maitland, *Chatterton: An Essay,* 1857.
15. Richard Edgcumbe, "Thomas Chatterton," *Gentleman's Magazine,* December 1878, p. 579.
16. Dante Gabriel Rossetti, "Thomas Chatterton," *Five English Poets,* 1880–81.
17. Ernest Rhys, "Chatterton in Holborn," *Century Magazine,* July 1891, p. 35.
18. Charles E. Russell, "The Marvelous Boy," *Munsey's Magazine,* February 1901, p. 675.
19. Thomas Tyrwhitt, *Poems Supposed to Have Been Written at Bristol, by Thomas Rowley, in the Fifteenth Century,* 1777, Appendix.
20. Horace Walpole, Letter to William Cole (June 19, 1717).
21. Thomas Warton, *The History of English Poetry,* 1774–81, Sec. 26.
22. George Gregory, "The Life of Thomas Chatterton" (1779), *The Works of Thomas Chatterton,* 1803, Volume 1, pp. 71–73.
23. Sir Herbert Croft, *Love and Madness,* 1780, Letter 51.
24. Edmond Malone, *Cursory Observations on the Poems Attributed to Thomas Rowley,* 1782.
25. Horace Walpole, Letter to the Countess of Upper Ossory (July 4, 1785).
26. James Boswell, *Life of Johnson,* 1791.
27. Robert Southey, "Preface" to *The Works of Thomas Chatterton,* 1803.
28. John Davis, *The Life of Thomas Chatterton,* 1806, p. 2.
29. William Hazlitt, *Lectures on the English Poets,* 1818.
30. William Hazlitt, *Lectures on the English Poets,* 1818.
31. Jane Porter, Letter to John Keats (December 4, 1818).
32. John Keats, Letter to J. H. Reynolds (September 21, 1819).
33. John Keats, Letter to George and Georgiana Keats (September 22, 1819).
34. John Dix, *The Life of Thomas Chatterton,* 1837, pp. 295–97.
35. Robert Browning, "Tasso and Chatterton," *Foreign Quarterly Review,* July 1842, p. 483.
36. James Russell Lowell, "Edgar Allan Poe," *Graham's Magazine,* February 1845, p. 50.
37. Henry Giles, "Chatterton," *Lectures and Essays,* 1850, Volume 2, pp. 288–89.
38. Richard Chevenix Trench, *English Past and Present,* 1855, p. 101.
39. David Masson, *Chatterton: A Biography* (1856), 1899, pp. 319–20.
40. Daniel Wilson, *Chatterton: A Biographical Study,* 1869, pp. 316–18.
41. Thomas Carlyle, Letter to Daniel Wilson (January 10, 1870).
42. Walter W. Skeat, "Essay on the Rowley Poems," *The Poetical Works of Thomas Chatterton,* 1871, Volume 2, pp. 26–27.
43. Sir Leslie Stephen, *History of English Thought in the Eighteenth Century,* 1876.

Volume 6

WILLIAM WHITEHEAD

CHARLES WESLEY

21. John Richard Green, _History of the English People_, 1877–80, Bk. 8, Ch. 4.
22. W. E. H. Lecky, _History of England in the Eighteenth Century_, 1878–90, Ch. 9.
23. Augustine Birrell, "John Wesley," _Scribner's Magazine_, December 1899, p. 756.
24. F. J. Snell, _Wesley and Methodism_, 1900, p. 242.
25. Robert Southey, _The Life of Wesley_, 1820, Ch. 30.
26. Reginald Heber, "Southey's _Life of Wesley_," _Quarterly Review_, October 1820, p. 53.
27. Richard Watson, _Observations on Southey's_ Life of Wesley, 1820.
28. Walter Savage Landor, "Alfieri and Metastasio," _Imaginary Conversations: Third Series_, 1828.
29. Richard Watson, _The Life of the Rev. John Wesley_, 1831, Ch. 15.
30. Edward FitzGerald, Letter to John Allen (October 8, 1864).
31. Edward FitzGerald, Letter to E. B. Lowell (May 28, 1868).
32. Eugene Lawrence, "John Wesley and His Times," _Harper's Magazine_, June 1872, pp. 105, 119.
33. Alfred H. Guernsey, "John Wesley," _Galaxy Magazine_, February 1874, pp. 211–12.
34. Sir Leslie Stephen, _History of English Thought in the Eighteenth Century_, 1876.
35. A. P. Stanley, "John and Charles Wesley," _The English Poets_, ed. Thomas Humphry Ward, 1880, Volume 3, p. 258.
36. Luke Tyerman, _The Life and Times of the Rev. John Wesley_, 1890, Volume 3, pp. 656–60.
37. Hugh Price Hughes, "John Wesley," _Nineteenth Century_, March 1891, pp. 486–90.
38. J. H. Overton, _John Wesley_, 1891, pp. 169–71.
39. Henry Craik, "Introduction" to _English Prose_, ed. Henry Craik, 1895, Volume 4, pp. 5–6.
40. Frank Banfield, "Preface" to _John Wesley_, 1900, pp. 7–11.
41. John Whitehead, "A Short View of Mr. Wesley's Writings and Controversies," _The Life of the Rev. John Wesley_, 1793–96.

SIR JOSHUA REYNOLDS

1. Hester Lynch Piozzi, "The Streatham Portraits" (1773), _Autobiography, Letters and Literary Remains_, ed. A. Hayward, 1861, Volume 2, p. 14.
2. Oliver Goldsmith, _Retaliation_, 1774, ll. 137–45.
3. Samuel Johnson, Letter to Sir Joshua Reynolds (November 14, 1782).
4. Edmund Burke, _Gentleman's Magazine_, February 1792, pp. 190–91.
5. Earl of Charlemont, Letter to Edmond Malone (March 1, 1792), cited in Sir James Prior, _Life of Edmond Malone_, 1860, p. 189.
6. Edmond Malone (1792), cited in Sir James Prior, _Life of Edmond Malone_, 1860, pp. 190–91.
7. William Blake, Marginalia in Reynolds's _Works_, c. 1801–09.
8. James Northcote, _Memoirs of Sir Joshua Reynolds_, 1813.
9. James Boswell, _Life of Johnson_, 1791.
10. William Blake, Marginalia in Reynolds's _Works_, c. 1801–9.
11. William Hazlitt, "Introduction to an Account of Sir Joshua Reynolds's _Discourses_," 1814–15.
12. John Wilson (as "Christopher North"), _Noctes Ambrosianae_ (April 1829), 1854.
13. Henry William Beechey, "Memoir of Sir Joshua Reynolds," _The Literary Works of Sir Joshua Reynolds_, 1835.

14. Edmund Gosse, A _History of Eighteenth Century Literature_, 1888, p. 308.
15. Claude Phillips, _Sir Joshua Reynolds_, 1894, pp. 389–91.
16. Reginald Brimley Johnson, "Sir Joshua Reynolds," _English Prose_, ed. Henry Craik, 1895, Volume 4, pp. 299–302.
17. Allan Cunningham, "Sir Joshua Reynolds," _The Lives of the Most Eminent British Painters and Sculptors_, 1831, Volume 1, pp. 274–79.
18. Nathaniel Hawthorne, "Oxford," _The English Note-Books_, August 31, 1856.
19. John Ruskin, "The Unity of Art," _The Two Paths_, 1859.
20. James Smetham, "Sir Joshua Reynolds" (1866), _Literary Works_, ed. William Davies, 1893, pp. 17–18.
21. Frederick Keppel, "Sir Joshua Reynolds," _Scribner's Magazine_, January 1894, p. 107.
22. Sir Walter Armstrong, "Sir Joshua as a Writer and Theorist," _Sir Joshua Reynolds: First President of the Royal Academy_, 1900, pp. 175–85.

GILBERT WHITE

1. James Russell Lowell, Untitled poem (1880), cited in Rashleigh Holt-White, _The Life and Letters of Gilbert White of Selbourne_, 1901, Volume 2, p. 275.
2. Victor Plarr, "In the Country of Gilbert White," _Speaker_, June 17, 1893, p. 690.
3. James Russell Lowell, "My Garden Acquaintance" (1869), _Works_, Riverside ed., Volume 3, pp. 192–97.
4. W. Warde Fowler, "Gilbert White of Selborne," _Macmillan's Magazine_, July 1893, p. 188.
5. George H. Ellwanger, "Gilbert White's Pastoral," _Idyllists of the Country Side_, 1896, pp. 49–52.
6. Norman Moore, "Gilbert White," _English Prose_, ed. Henry Craik, 1895, Volume 4, pp. 247–48.
7. Sara A. Hubbard, "Gilbert White of Selborne," _Dial_, May 1, 1901, p. 304.
8. H. W. Tompkins, "_The Natural History of Selborne_," _Selborne_, 1905, pp. 59–63.
9. John Burroughs, "Gilbert White's Book," _Indoor Studies_, 1889.

WILLIAM ROBERTSON

1. Dugald Stewart, "Account of the Life and Writings of William Robertson" (1796), _The Collected Works of Dugald Stewart_, 1858, Volume 10, pp. 194–200.
2. Henry, Lord Cockburn, _Memorials of His Time_, 1821–30, Ch. 1.
3. W. B. O. Peabody, "Brougham's _Lives of Men of Letters and Science_," _North American Review_, October 1845, p. 410.
4. Henry Grey Graham, _Scottish Men of Letters in the Eighteenth Century_, 1901, p. 92.
5. James Boswell, _Life of Johnson_, 1791.
6. Horace Walpole, Letter to the Countess of Upper Ossory (November 23, 1791).
7. Edward Gibbon, _Memoirs of My Time_, 1792-93.
8. Thomas Brown, "Stewart's Account of Dr. Robertson," _Edinburgh Review_, April 1803, pp. 242–45.
9. Friedrich Schlegel, _Lectures on the History of Literature_, 1815.
10. Thomas Carlyle, Letter to Jane Welsh (March 7, 1824).
11. R. A. Davenport, "A Sketch of the Life of Dr. Robertson," _The Works of William Robertson_, 1826, Volume 1, p. 80.
12. Thomas Carlyle, _Lectures on the History of Literature_, 1838, pp. 184–85.
13. George Saintsbury, A _Short History of English Literature_, 1898, p. 624.

1838), cited in G. Otto Trevelyan, *The Life and Letters of Lord Macaulay*, 1876, Volume 2, p. 40.

35. Edgar Allan Poe, *Marginalia* (1844), *Essays and Reviews*, ed. G. R. Thompson, 1984, pp. 1320–21.
36. C. A. Sainte-Beuve, "Gibbon," 1853.
37. Samuel Rogers, *Table Talk*, c. 1855.
38. Henry Thomas Buckle, *History of Civilization in England*, 1857–61.
39. Frederick Denison Maurice, *Moral and Metaphysical Philosophy*, 1862.
40. John Burroughs, "Ruskin's Judgment of Gibbon and Darwin," *Critic*, May 1, 1886, p. 213.
41. Edward A. Freeman, Letter to Goldwin Smith (April 25, 1888), cited in W. R. W. Stephens, *The Life and Letters of Edward A. Freeman*, 1895, Volume 2, p. 380.
42. Woodrow Wilson, "Mere Literature," *Mere Literature and Other Essays*, 1896, p. 22.
43. Edmund Gosse, *A Short History of Modern English Literature*, 1897, pp. 258–60.
44. Maria Josepha Holroyd, Letter (1793), *The Girlhood of Maria Josepha Holroyd*, ed. J. H. Adeane, 1896, p. 273.
45. John, Lord Sheffield, "Preface" to *Miscellaneous Works of Edward Gibbon, Esquire*, 1796, Volume 1, pp. iii–vii.
46. Arthur Young, *Autobiography* (entry for May 1, 1796), ed. M. Bentham-Edwards, 1898, pp. 258–59.
47. Earl of Sheffield, "Introduction" to *The Autobiographies of Edward Gibbon*, ed. John Murray, 1896, pp. v–ix.
48. Frederic Harrison, "The New Memoirs of Edward Gibbon," *Forum*, February 1897, pp. 754–55.
49. H. H. Milman, "Guizot's Edition of Gibbon," *Quarterly Review*, January 1834, pp. 286–307.
50. Walter Bagehot, "Edward Gibbon" (1856), *Collected Works*, ed. Norman St. John-Stevas, 1965, Volume 1, pp. 378–91.
51. Sir Leslie Stephen, "Gibbon's Autobiography," *Studies of a Biographer*, 1898, Volume 1, pp. 172–87.

SIR WILLIAM JONES

1. Thomas James Mathias, *The Pursuits of Literature* (1794), 1798, p. 424.
2. William Bennet, Letter to the Dean of St. Asaph (November 1795).
3. Lord Teignmouth, *Account of the Life, Writings, and Correspondence of Sir William Jones*, *The Works of Sir William Jones*, 1804, Volume 2, pp. 268–81, 306–7.
4. Joseph Story, "Hoffman's Course of Legal Study," *North American Review*, January 1817, p. 46.
5. Thomas Campbell, *Specimens of the British Poets*, 1819.
6. Edmund Henry Barker, *Parriana*, 1828, Volume 1, pp. 322–23.
7. Sir Samuel Egerton Brydges, *Autobiography*, 1834, Volume 1, p. 190.
8. Henry Welsford, *On the Origin and Ramifications of the English Language*, 1845, pp. 308–9.
9. Francis, Lord Jeffrey, "Lord Teignmouth's *Life of Sir W. Jones*," *Edinburgh Review*, January 1805, pp. 329–32.
10. Henry Roscoe, "Sir William Jones," *Lives of Eminent British Lawyers*, 1830, pp. 325–28.

JAMES BOSWELL

1. David Hume, Letter to the Comtesse de Boufflers (January 12, 1766).
2. Fanny Burney, Letter to Samuel Crisp (October 15, 1782).
3. Horace Walpole, Letter to Sir Horace Mann (March 16, 1786).
4. James Boswell, *Life of Johnson*, 1791.
5. Sir William Forbes, *An Account of the Life and Writings*

of James Beattie, LL.D. (1806), 1824, Volume 2, pp. 166–67, Note.
6. Richard Cumberland, *Memoirs of Richard Cumberland*, 1807, Volume 2, pp. 227–28.
7. Thomas Gray, Letter to Horace Walpole (February 25, 1768).
8. William Hazlitt, "Spence's *Anecdotes*," *Edinburgh Review*, May 1820, p. 306.
9. Sir Walter Scott, Letter to John Wilson Croker (January 30, 1829).
10. F. W. Shelton, "Boswell: The Biographer," *Knickerbocker Magazine*, February 1851, pp. 153–54.
11. Arthur Clive, "Boswell and His Enemies," *Gentleman's Magazine*, July 1874, pp. 68–77.
12. Edmund Gosse, *A History of Eighteenth Century Literature*, 1888, pp. 358–60.
13. W. E. Henley, "Boswell," *Views and Reviews*, 1890, pp. 194–96.
14. Henry Craik, "James Boswell," *English Prose*, ed. Henry Craik, 1895, Volume 4, pp. 477–80.
15. P. A. Sillard, "The Prince of Biographers," *Atlantic*, August 1901, p. 214.
16. G. K. Chesterton, "Boswell's *Johnson*," *Good Words*, November 1903, pp. 775–76.
17. Joshua W. Caldwell, "A Brief for Boswell," *Sewanee Review*, July 1905, pp. 346–51.
18. James Beattie, Letter to Robert Arbuthnot (November 26, 1785), cited in Sir William Forbes, *An Account of the Life and Writings of James Beattie, LL.D.* (1806), 1824, Volume 2, pp. 161–62.
19. John Wolcot (as "Peter Pindar"), *A Poetical and Congratulatory Epistle to James Boswell, Esq. on His Journal of a Tour to the Hebrides with the Celebrated Doctor Johnson*, 1787.
20. William Cowper, Letter to Samuel Rose (June 5, 1789).
21. Hannah More, Letter to Her Sister (1785), *Memoirs of the Life and Correspondence of Mrs. Hannah More*, ed. William Roberts, 1835, Volume 1, p. 228.
22. James Boswell, Dedication to Sir Joshua Reynolds, *Life of Johnson*, 1791.
23. James Boswell, Advertisement to the First Edition of *Life of Johnson*, 1791.
24. James Boswell, *Life of Johnson*, 1791.
25. Edward Gibbon, Letter to Thomas Cadell (April 27, 1791).
26. Horace Walpole, Letter to Mary Berry (May 19, 1791).
27. Edmond Malone, Advertisement to the Fourth Editon of Boswell's *Life of Johnson*, 1804.
28. John Wilson Croker, "Preface" to *Life of Johnson*, 1831, pp. 3–13.
29. Thomas Carlyle, Letter to Johann Peter Eckermann (May 6, 1834), *Correspondence between Goethe and Carlyle*, ed. Charles Eliot Norton, 1887, p. 342.
30. John Forster, *The Life and Times of Oliver Goldsmith*, 1848, Bk. 4, Ch. 13.
31. Washington Irving, *Oliver Goldsmith: A Biography*, 1849, pp. 154–58.
32. Sir James Prior, *Life of Edmond Malone*, 1860, pp. 123–24.
33. Alexander Smith, "A Shelf in My Bookcase," *Dreamthorp*, 1863, pp. 204–6.
34. Sir Leslie Stephen, *Samuel Johnson*, 1879, pp. 91–92.
35. George Birbeck Hill, "Preface" to *Life of Johnson*, 1887, Volume 1, pp. 12–13.
36. W. Keith Leask, *James Boswell*, 1897, pp. 157–60.
37. Henry Grey Graham, *Scottish Men of Letters in the Eighteenth Century*, 1901, pp. 221–22.
38. Thomas Babington Macaulay, "Boswell's *Life of Johnson*"

(1831), *Critical, Historical, and Miscellaneous Essays*, 1860, Volume 2, pp. 390–97.
39. Thomas Carlyle, "Boswell's *Life of Johnson*" (1832), *Critical and Miscellaneous Essays*, 1839–69.
40. George Henry Lewes, "Preface" to *Life and Conversations of Dr. Samuel Johnson* by Alexander Main, 1873, pp. vii–xii.

THOMAS REID

1. James Beattie, Letter to Sir William Forbes (March 5, 1788), cited in Sir William Forbes, *An Account of the Life and Writings of James Beattie, LL.D.* (1806), 1824, Volume 2, pp. 210–11.
2. Adam Ferguson, *Principles of Moral and Political Science*, 1792, Pt. 1, Ch. 2, Sec. 2.
3. Dugald Stewart, *Account of the Life and Writings of Thomas Reid*, 1803.
4. Sir James Mackintosh, *Dissertation on the Progress of Ethical Philosophy*, 1830.
5. Henry Hallam, *Introduction to the Literature of Europe*, 1837–39, Pt. 4, Ch. 3, Par. 43.
6. James Frederick Ferrier, "Reid and the Philosophy of Common Sense" (1847), *Lectures on Greek Philosophy and Other Philosophical Remains*, eds. Sir Alexander Grant, E. L. Lushington, 1866, Volume 2, pp. 417–19.
7. Henry Thomas Buckle, *History of Civilization in England*, 1857–61.
8. Sir William Hamilton, *Lectures on Metaphysics and Logic*, 1859, Lecture 13.
9. Sir Leslie Stephen, *History of English Thought in the Eighteenth Century*, 1876.
10. George Henry Lewes, "Reid," *The Biographical History of Philosophy*, 1845–46.

JAMES MACPHERSON

1. Samuel Johnson, Letter to James Macpherson (January 20, 1775).
2. Anne Grant, Letter to Mrs. Macintosh (February 20, 1796), *Letters from the Mountains*, 1806.
3. David Hume, Letter (August 16, 1760).
4. James Macpherson, "Preface" to *Fingal*, 1762.
5. Charles Churchill, *The Prophecy of Famine*, 1763, ll. 129–30.
6. David Hume, Letter to Hugh Blair (September 19, 1763).
7. Henry Home, Lord Kames, Letter to Elizabeth Montagu (May 22, 1771), cited in Alexander Fraser Tytler, Lord Woodhouselee, *Memoirs of the Life and Writings of the Honourable Henry Home of Kames*, 1807.
8. Johann Wolfgang von Goethe, *The Sufferings of Young Werther* (1774), tr. Bayard Quincy Morgan, 1957, pp. 107–8.
9. David Hume, Letter to Edward Gibbon (March 18, 1776).
10. James Boswell, *Journal of a Tour to the Hebrides*, 1785.
11. Malcolm Laing, "Dissertation on the Supposed Authenticity of Ossian's Poems," *The History of Scotland*, 1800–04.
12. Alexander Carlyle, Letter to William M'Donald (January 9, 1802), *Report of the Committee of the Highland Society of Scotland, Appointed to Inquire into the Nature and Authenticity of the Poems of Ossian*, ed. Henry Mackenzie, 1805, Appendix, pp. 66–68.
13. Sir Walter Scott, Letter to Anna Seward (c. September 1806).
14. Friedrich Schlegel, "On the Poetry of the North" (1812), *Aesthetic and Miscellaneous Works*, tr. E. J. Millington, 1849, pp. 256–57.

15. William Wordsworth, "Essay, Supplementary to the Preface" (1815), *Lyrical Ballads* (1798), 1815.
16. William Wordsworth, "Written in a Blank Leaf of Macpherson's Ossian," 1824.
17. Thomas Babington Macaulay, "Criticisms on the Principal Italian Writers: I. Dante" (1824), *Critical, Historical, and Miscellaneous Essays*, 1860, Volume 1, p. 77.
18. Elizabeth Barrett Browning, Letter to H. S. Boyd (January 5, 1843).
19. Robert Browning, Letter to Elizabeth Barrett Browning (August 25, 1846).
20. Matthew Arnold, *On the Study of Celtic Literature*, 1867.
21. Archibald Clerk, "Dissertation on the Authenticity of the Poems of Ossian," *The Poems of Ossian*, 1870, Volume 1, pp. lxv–lxvi.
22. Hippolyte Taine, *History of English Literature*, tr. H. Van Laun, 1871, Bk. 3, Ch. 7.
23. Sir Leslie Stephen, *History of English Thought in the Eighteenth Century*, 1876.
24. John Veitch, *The Feeling for Nature in Scottish Poetry*, 1887, Volume 2, pp. 117–18.
25. William Lyon Phelps, *The Beginnings of the English Romantic Movement*, 1893, pp. 153–54.
26. Bailey Saunders, *The Life and Letters of James Macpherson*, 1894, pp. 25–26.
27. Sir Archibald Geikie, *Types of Scenery and Their Influence on Literature*, 1898, pp. 44–48.
28. Henry Grey Graham, *Scottish Men of Letters in the Eighteenth Century*, 1901, p. 241.
29. Hugh Blair, *A Critical Dissertation on the Poems of Ossian*, 1763.
30. Hugh Walker, "The Later Anglo-Scottish School of the Eighteenth Century," *Three Centuries of Scottish Literature*, 1893, Volume 2, pp. 123–30.

ROBERT BURNS

1. Robert Burns, Letter to Frances Dunlop (July 10, 1796).
2. Robert Burns, Letter to George Thomson (July 12, 1796).
3. Maria Riddell, Letter to *Dumfries Journal* (August 7, 1796), cited in James Currie, *The Life of Robert Burns*, 1800.
4. Dugald Stewart, Letter to James Currie (c. 1800), cited in James Currie, *The Life of Robert Burns*, 1800.
5. Dorothy Wordsworth, *Journal*, August 18, 1803.
6. William Wordsworth, "At the Grave of Burns," 1803.
7. John Keats, "On Visiting the Tomb of Burns," 1818.
8. Sir Walter Scott, Letter to John Gibson Lockhart (1827), cited in John Gibson Lockhart, *Memoirs of the Life of Sir Walter Scott*, 1837–38, Volume 1, pp. 1660–68.
9. Thomas De Quincey, "A Liverpool Literary Coterie" (1837), *Collected Writings*, ed. David Masson, Volume 2, p. 134.
10. George Gilfillan, "Life of Robert Burns," *The Poetical Works of Robert Burns*, 1856, Volume 1, pp. 29–30.
11. Nathaniel Hawthorne, "Some of the Haunts of Burns" (1860), *Old Our Home*, 1863.
12. Dante Gabriel Rossetti, Letter to William Bell Scott (August 25, 1871).
13. L. M. Roberts, "The Burns and Dunlop Correspondence," *Fortnightly Review*, November 1895, p. 669.
14. Henry Mackenzie, *The Lounger*, No. 97 (December 9, 1786).
15. William Cowper, Letter to Samuel Rose (July 24, 1787).
16. William Cowper, Letter to Samuel Rose (August 27, 1787).
17. Joseph Ritson, "A Historical Essay on Scotish Song," *Scotish Song*, 1794, Volume 1, pp. 74–75.
18. James Currie, *The Life of Robert Burns*, 1800.

Works, ed. Norman St. John-Stevas, 1965, Volume 1, pp. 416–17.

17. Matthew Arnold, "The Function of Criticism at the Present Time" (1864), *Essays in Criticism*, 1865.
18. John, Lord Russell, *The Life and Times of Charles James Fox*, 1866, Volume 3, pp. 122–25.
19. Edward FitzGerald, Letter to W. B. Donne (December 7, 1868).
20. E. J. Payne, "Introduction" to Burke's *Select Works*, 1874, pp. xlviii–xlix.
21. Sir Leslie Stephen, *History of English Thought in the Eighteenth Century*, 1876.
22. John Morley, *Burke*, 1879, pp. 209–12.
23. A. V. Dicey, "Morley's Burke," *Nation*, October 9, 1879, pp. 244–45.
24. Augustine Birrell, "Edmund Burke," *Obiter Dicta: Second Series*, 1887, pp. 188–95.
25. Edmund Gosse, *A History of Eighteenth Century Literature*, 1888, pp. 365–74.
26. W. Macneile Dixon, "Edmund Burke," *English Prose*, ed. Henry Craik, 1895, Volume 4, pp. 374–78.
27. Woodrow Wilson, "The Interpreter of English Liberty," *Mere Literature*, 1896, pp. 157–60.
28. Edward Gibbon, *Journal*, November 1 and 4, 1762.
29. Edmond Malone (July 28, 1789) cited in Sir James Prior, *Life of Edmond Malone*, 1860, p. 154.
30. Thomas Green, *Extracts from the Diary of a Lover of Literature* (entry for October 8, 1798), 1810.
31. Samuel Taylor Coleridge, *Table Talk*, July 8, 1827.
32. Gilbert Elliot, First Earl of Minto, Letter (June 7, 1788), cited in the Countess of Minto, *Life and Letters of Sir Gilbert Elliot*, 1874, Volume 1, p. 215.
33. Henry Flood, Letter to the Earl of Charlemont (March 1775), *The Manuscripts and Correspondence of James, First Earl of Charlemont*, 1894, Volume 2, p. 391.
34. James Russell Lowell, "Carlyle" (1868), *My Study Windows*, 1871, p. 118.
35. Lorenzo Sears, *The History of Oratory*, 1895, pp. 288–89.
36. Sir Philip Francis, Letter to Edmund Burke (February 19, 1790), *The Francis Letters*, eds. Beata Francis, Eliza Kearny, 1901, Volume 2, pp. 278–80.
37. James Beattie, Letter to Robert Arbuthnot (April 25, 1790), cited in William Forbes, *An Account of the Life and Writings of James Beattie, LL.D.* (1806), 1824, Volume 2, p. 244.
38. Horace Walpole, Letter to Mary Berry (November 8, 1790).
39. Edward Gibbon, Letter to Lord Sheffield (February 5, 1791).
40. Thomas Jefferson, Letter to Benjamin Vaughan (May 11, 1791).
41. Robert Hall, *An Apology for the Freedom of the Press*, 1793.
42. Samuel Taylor Coleridge, *Table Talk*, January 4, 1823.
43. William Hazlitt, "Arguing in a Circle," 1823.
44. William Hazlitt, "Character of Mr. Burke" (1807), *Political Essays*, 1819.
45. Edward Dowden, "Anti-Revolution: Edmund Burke," *The French Revolution and English Literature*, 1897, pp. 93–104, 132–38.

MARY WOLLSTONECRAFT

1. Mary Wollstonecraft, Letter to Gilbert Imlay (November 1795).
2. Robert Southey, Letter to Joseph Cottle (March 13, 1797).
3. John Knowles, *The Life and Writings of Henry Fuseli*, 1831, pp. 164–66.
4. Mary Shelley (c. 1851), cited in C. Kegan Paul, *William*

Godwin: His Friends and Contemporaries, 1876, Volume 1, pp. 231–32.
5. Horace Walpole, Letter to Hannah More (January 24, 1795).
6. Unsigned, *Monthly Magazine*, September 1797, pp. 232–33.
7. Percy Bysshe Shelley, Dedication ("To Mary") to *The Revolt of Islam*, 1817.
8. Thomas Carlyle, *Journal* (October 10, 1831), cited in James Anthony Froude, *Thomas Carlyle*, 1882, Volume 2, Ch. 9.
9. C. Kegan Paul, "Memoir," *Mary Wollstonecraft: Letters to Imlay*, 1879, pp. v–vi.
10. James Ashcroft Noble, *Academy*, June 25, 1855, p. 55.
11. Emma Rauschenbusch-Clough, *A Study of Mary Wollstonecraft and the Rights of Woman*, 1896, pp. 24–27.
12. George Saintsbury, *A History of Nineteenth Century Literature*, 1896, pp. 37–38.
13. Hannah More, Letter to Horace Walpole (August 18, 1792).
14. Horace Walpole, Letter to Hannah More (August 21, 1792).
15. Anne Grant, Letter to Miss Ourry (January 2, 1794), *Letters from the Mountains*, 1806.
16. C. Kegan Paul, "Memoir," *Mary Wollstonecraft: Letters to Imlay*, 1879, pp. xxiv–xxix.
17. W. E. H. Lecky, *Democracy and Liberty*, 1896, Volume 2, pp. 507–9.
18. Emma Rauschenbusch-Clough, *A Study of Mary Wollstonecraft and the Rights of Woman*, 1896, pp. 38–39.
19. Mary Wollstonecraft, "Introduction" to *A Vindication of the Rights of Woman*, 1792.
20. William Godwin, *Memoirs of the Author of a Vindication of the Rights of Woman*, 1798, pp. 78–85, 194–99.
21. Margaret Oliphant, "Mary Wollstonecraft," *The Literary History of England, 1790–1825*, 1882, Volume 2, pp. 248–53.
22. Elizabeth Robins Pennell, "The Rights of Women," *Life of Mary Wollstonecraft*, 1884, pp. 162–70.
23. John Cordy Jeaffreson, "Mary Wollstonecraft," *The Real Shelley*, 1885, Volume 2, pp. 24–27.

JAMES BURNETT, LORD MONBODDO

1. Hannah More, Letter to Her Sister (1782), *Memoirs and Correspondence of Mrs. Hannah More*, ed. William Roberts, 1835, Volume 1, pp. 146–47.
2. Thomas James Matthias, *The Pursuits of Literature* (1794), 1798, p. 331, Note.
3. Alexander Fraser Tytler, Lord Woodhouselee, *Memoirs of the Life and Writings of the Honourable Henry Home of Kames*, 1807, Volume 1, pp. 248–50, Note.
4. James McCosh, *The Scottish Philosophy*, 1874, p. 248.
5. Sir Leslie Stephen, *History of English Thought in the Eighteenth Century*, 1876.
6. William Knight, *Lord Monboddo and Some of His Contemporaries*, 1900, pp. 30–34.
7. Henry Grey Graham, "Lord Monboddo," *Scottish Men of Letters in the Eighteenth Century*, 1901, pp. 191–93.

HUGH BLAIR

1. Robert Burns, *Commonplace Book*, April 19, 1787.
2. Alexander Carlyle, *Anecdotes and Characters of the Times*, 1800–05.
3. John Hill, *An Account of the Life and Writings of Hugh Blair, D.D.*, 1808, pp. 199–203.
4. Thomas Babington Macaulay, *Journal* (November 5, 1850), cited in G. Otto Trevelyan, *The Life and Letters of Lord Macaulay*, 1876, Volume 2, p. 245.

25. William Michael Rossetti, "William Cowper," *Lives of Famous Poets*, 1878, pp. 185–87.
26. Margaret Oliphant, *The Literary History of England, 1790-1825*, 1882, Volume 1, pp. 59–60.
27. Aubrey De Vere, "Two Schools of English Poetry," *Essays Chiefly on Poetry*, 1887, Volume 2, p. 120.
28. J. C. Bailey, "William Cowper," *Macmillan's Magazine*, August 1889, pp. 263–64.
29. W. Fraser Rae, "The Bard of Olney," *Temple Bar*, April 1891, pp. 503–4.
30. Augustine Birrell, "William Cowper," *Res Judicatae*, 1892, pp. 90–91.
31. John Vance Cheney, "A Study of Cowper," *Chautauquan*, July 1892, pp. 405–6.
32. T. E. Brown, Letter to S. T. Irwin (July 16, 1895).
33. Sir Archibald Geikie, *Types of Scenery and Their Influence on Literature*, 1898, pp. 13–14.
34. George Saintsbury, *A Short History of English Literature*, 1898, pp. 588–90.
35. George A. B. Dewar, "William Cowper," *Saturday Review*, April 28, 1900, p. 521.
36. Alice Law, "William Cowper," *Fortnightly Review*, May 1900, pp. 777–79.
37. A. Edmund Spender, "The Centenary of Cowper," *Westminster Review*, May 1900, pp. 532–33, 545.
38. J. C. Tarver, "Cowper's Ouse," *Macmillan's Magazine*, June 1900, p. 144.
39. Robert Burns, Letter to Frances Dunlop (December 25, 1793).
40. Connop Thirlwall, Letter to John Candler (October 24, 1810).
41. Samuel Taylor Coleridge, *Biographia Literaria*, 1817, Ch. 1, Note.
42. Thomas Campbell, *Specimens of the British Poets*, 1819.
43. W. B. O. Peabody, "Life of Cowper," *North American Review*, January 1834, pp. 29–30.
44. Robert Southey, *Life of Cowper*, 1836, Ch. 10.
45. Thomas Babington Macaulay, "William Pitt" (1859), *Critical, Historical, and Miscellaneous Essays*, 1860, Volume 6, p. 260.
46. William Benham, "Introduction" to *The Poetical Works of William Cowper*, 1870, pp. lvii–lviii.
47. J. C. Shairp, *On Poetic Interpretation of Nature*, 1877, pp. 214–16.
48. Eva Hope, "Introduction" to *The Poetical Works of William Cowper*, 1886, pp. 24–25.
49. John Newton, Letter to Hannah More (July 17, 1791), *Memoirs and Correspondence of Mrs. Hannah More*, ed. William Roberts, 1835, Volume 1, p. 370.
50. Hannah More, Letter to John Newton (1791), *Memoirs and Correspondence of Mrs. Hannah More*, ed. William Roberts, 1835, p. 383.
51. George Gordon, Lord Byron, "Letter to —— ——, Esqre, on the Rev. W. L. Bowles's Strictures on the Life and Writings of Pope," 1821.
52. Sara Coleridge, Letter to Samuel Taylor Coleridge (October 1834), *Memoirs and Letters of Sara Coleridge*, ed. Edith Coleridge, 1873, Volume 1, pp. 100–101.
53. Reginald Heber, "Private Correspondence of Cowper," *Quarterly Review*, October 1823, p. 185.
54. John Bruce, "Memoir of William Cowper," *The Poetical Works of William Cowper*, 1865, pp. clxvii–clxviii.
55. George Edward Woodberry, "Cowper," *Studies in Letters and Life*, 1890, pp. 219–20.
56. Agnes Repplier, "Letters," *Essays in Idleness*, 1893, pp. 219–20.
57. W. P. Ker, "William Cowper," *English Prose*, ed. Henry Craik, 1895, Volume 4, pp. 424–25.
58. Walter Bagehot, "William Cowper" (1855), *Collected Works*, ed. Norman St. John-Stevas, 1965, Volume 1, pp. 291–99.
59. George Eliot, "Worldliness and Other-Worldliness: The Poet Young" (1857), *Essays and Letters from a Note-book*, 1883, pp. 62–67.

ERASMUS DARWIN

1. Samuel Taylor Coleridge, Letter to John Edwards (January 29, 1796).
2. James Keir, Letter to Robert Darwin (May 12, 1802), cited in Charles Darwin, "Preliminary Notice" to *Erasmus Darwin* by Ernst Krause, 1879, pp. 35–36.
3. Anna Seward, *Memoirs of the Life of Dr. Darwin*, 1804, pp. 1–3.
4. William Hayley, "To Dr. Darwin," 1792.
5. William Cowper, "To Dr. Darwin," 1793.
6. Samuel Taylor Coleridge, Letter to Josiah Wade (January 27, 1796).
7. Samuel Taylor Coleridge, *Biographia Literaria*, 1817, Ch. 1.
8. George L. Craik, *A Compendious History of English Literature and of the English Language*, 1861, Volume 2, pp. 393–94.
9. Thomas Hill, "Erasmus Darwin," *Bibliotheca Sacra*, July 1878, pp. 472–74.
10. Charles Darwin, "Preliminary Notice" to *Erasmus Darwin* by Ernst Krause, 1879, pp. 95–96.
11. Ernst Krause, *Erasmus Darwin*, tr. W. S. Dallas, 1879, pp. 210–16.
12. A. G. Sidgwick, "Erasmus Darwin," *Nation*, April 1, 1880, p. 254.
13. Edmund Gosse, *A History of Eighteenth Century Literature*, 1888, pp. 328–30.
14. Johann Wolfgang von Goethe, Letter to Friedrich Schiller (January 26, 1798).
15. Friedrich Schiller, Letter to Johann Wolfgang von Goethe (January 30, 1798).
16. Samuel Rogers, *Table Talk*, c. 1855.
17. Sidney Lanier, *The English Novel*, 1883.
18. William Bayne, *James Thomson*, 1898, p. 62.
19. Samuel Butler, "Philosophy of Dr. Erasmus Darwin," *Evolution, Old and New*, 1879.

JAMES BEATTIE

1. Fanny Burney, *Diary*, July 13, 1787.
2. Dugald Stewart, Letter to Sir William Forbes (c. 1806), cited in Sir William Forbes, *An Account of the Life and Writings of James Beattie, LL.D.* (1806), 1824, Volume 2, p. 376.
3. Thomas Carlyle, *Diary* (February 9, 1834), cited in James Anthony Froude, *Thomas Carlyle*, 1882, Volume 2, p. 327.
4. Richard Hurd, *Commonplace Book* (1808), cited in Francis Kilvert, *Memoirs of the Life and Writings of the Right Rev. Richard Hurd*, 1860, p. 244.
5. Alexander Chalmers, "The Life of Dr. James Beattie," *The Works of the English Poets*, 1810, Volume 18, pp. 550–51.
6. Katherine Thomson, "Mrs. Montagu and Her Friends," *Fraser's Magazine*, January 1848, p. 80.
7. George Gilfillan, "The Life and Poetry of James Beattie," *The Poetical Works of Beattie, Blair, and Falconer*, 1854, p. xxiv.
8. Hippolyte Taine, *History of English Literature*, tr. H. Van Laun, 1871, Bk. 3, Ch. 7.
9. George Saintsbury, "James Beattie," *The English Poets*, ed. Thomas Humphry Ward, 1880, Volume 3, p. 396.

4. George Gordon, Lord Byron, Letter to Robert Charles Dallas (August 27, 1811).
5. Sir Nicholas Harris Nicolas, "Memoir of Henry Kirke White," *The Poetical Works of Henry Kirke White*, 1837, pp. xlvi, li.
6. Rufus W. Griswold, "Henry Kirke White," *The Poets and Poetry of England in the Nineteenth Century*, 1844, p. 214.
7. James Russell Lowell, "Edgar Allan Poe," *Graham's Magazine*, February 1845, p. 50.
8. David Macbeth Moir, *Sketches of the Poetical Literature of the Post Half-Century*, 1851, pp. 22–24.
9. Alice Law, "A Forerunner of Keats," *Westminster Review*, September 1894, pp. 291–92.
10. Arthur Christopher Benson, "The Poetry of Keble," *Essays* (1896), 1907, pp. 180–81.
11. George Saintsbury, *A History of Nineteenth Century Literature*, 1896, p. 108.
12. Alfred H. Miles, "Henry Kirke White," *The Poets and the Poetry of the Century: Sacred, Moral and Religious Verse*, 1897, pp. 81–82.
13. George Gilfillan, "The Life and Writings of Henry Kirke White," *The Poetical Works of Henry Kirke White and James Grahame*, 1856, pp. xix–xxii.

CLARA REEVE

1. Anna Seward, Letter to the Editor, *Gentleman's Magazine*, January 1786, p. 16.
2. Henry A. Beers, *A History of English Romanticism in the Eighteenth Century*, 1898, pp. 241–45.
3. Clara Reeve, "Preface" to *The Old English Baron*, 1777.
4. Horace Walpole, Letter to William Mason (April 8, 1778).
5. Horace Walpole, Letter to William Cole (August 22, 1778).
6. John Dunlop, *The History of Fiction* (1814), 1842, p. 411.
7. John Cordy Jeaffreson, "Clara Reeve," *Novels and Novelists*, 1878, Volume 1, pp. 273–75.
8. Sir Walter Scott, "Clara Reeve" (1823), *Lives of The Novelists*, 1825.

RICHARD HURD

1. Thomas Gray, Letter to William Mason (November 8, 1765).
2. Horace Walpole, *The Last Journal of Horace Walpole during the Reign of George III*, May 28, 1776.
3. Fanny Burney, *Diary*, December 23, 1786.
4. Fanny Burney, *Diary*, January 2, 1787.
5. Edmund Gibbon, *Memoirs of My Life*, 1792–93.
6. Joseph Cradock, *Literary and Miscellaneous Memoirs*, 1828, Volume 4, p. 195.
7. Mark Pattison, "Life of Bishop Warburton" (1863), *Essays*, ed. Henry Nettleship, 1889, Volume 2, pp. 145–46.
8. Sir Leslie Stephen, *History of English Thought in the Eighteenth Century*, 1876.
9. Austin Dobson, *Fielding*, 1883, pp. 141–42, Note.
10. Horace Walpole, Letter to Henry Zouch (February 4, 1760).
11. David Hume, "My Own Life," 1776.
12. Samuel Parr, "Dedication of the Two Tracts of a Warburtonian," *Tracts by Warburton and a Warburtonian*, 1789.
13. James Boswell, *Life of Johnson*, 1791.
14. Thomas James Mathias, *The Pursuits of Literature* (1794), 1798, p. 204.
15. T. D. Whitaker, "Hurds Edition of Bishop Warburton's Works," *Quarterly Review*, June 1812, pp. 385–86.
16. Henry Hallam, *Introduction to the Literature of Europe*, 1837–39, Pt. 4, Ch. 5, Par. 26, Note.

17. Edmund Gosse, *A History of Eighteenth Century Literature*, 1888, pp. 281–82.
18. William Lyon Phelps, *The Beginnings of the English Romantic Movement*, 1893, p. 115.
19. Francis Kilvert, *Memoirs of the Life and Writings of the Right Rev. Richard Hurd*, 1860, pp. 195–206.

JOHN HOME

1. Alexander Carlyle, *Anecdotes and Characters of the Times*, 1800-05.
2. Henry Mackenzie, "Account of the Life of Mr. John Home" (1812), *The Works of John Home*, 1822, Volume 1, pp. 6–7.
3. David Hume, Letter to John Home (c. December 1754).
4. David Hume, Letter to Adam Smith (c. February 1757).
5. Charles Churchill, "The Journey," 1765, ll. 123–24.
6. Joseph Ritson, "A Historical Essay on Scotish Song," Scotish Song, 1794.
7. Sir Walter Scott, "An Essay on the Drama," 1819.
8. John Wilson (as "Christopher North"), *Noctes Ambrosianae* (April 1822), 1854.
9. William Smyth, *Lectures on Modern History*, 1840, Lecture 28.
10. John Doran, *Their Majesties' Servants—Annals of the English Stage*, 1863, Volume 1, p. 414.
11. George Saintsbury, *A Short History of English Literature*, 1898, p. 637.
12. Sir Walter Scott, "Works of John Home, Esq.," *Quarterly Review*, June 1826, pp. 201–4.
13. Hugh Walker, "Later School of XVIIIth Century," *Three Centuries of Scottish Literature*, 1893, Volume 2, pp. 107–14.

RICHARD PORSON

1. Gilbert Wakefield, Letter to Charles James Fox (October 23, 1799), *Correspondence of the Late Gilbert Wakefield with the Late Right Honourable Charles James Fox*, 1813, pp. 99–101.
2. William Beloe, *The Sexagenarian*, 1817, Volume 1, p. 217.
3. George Gordon, Lord Byron, Letter to John Murray (February 20, 1818).
4. Thomas Moore, *Journal*, September 12, 1827.
5. Pryse Lockhart Gordon, *Personal Memoirs*, 1830, Volume 1, pp. 283–87.
6. Sir Samuel Egerton Brydges, *Autobiography*, 1834, Volume 1, pp. 58–59.
7. Samuel Rogers, *Table Talk*, c. 1855.
8. William Maltby, "Porsoniana," *Recollections of the Table-Talk of Samuel Rogers*, 1856, pp. 322–24.
9. Edward Gibbon, *Memoirs of My Life*, 1792–93, Note.
10. Samuel Parr, "Extracts from a Pamphlet Published in 1795, Intituled, *Remarks on the Statement of Dr. Charles Combe*" (1795), *Works*, 1828, Volume 3, pp. 518–19.
11. Thomas De Quincey, "Notes on Walter Savage Landor" (1847), *Collected Writings*, ed. David Masson, Volume 11, pp. 421–22.
12. Thomas Babington Macaulay, *Journal* (December 25, 1850), cited in G. Otto Trevelyan, *The Life and Letters of Lord Macaulay*, 1876, Volume 2, pp. 245–46.
13. E. S. Dallas, *The Gay Science*, 1866, pp. 17–18.
14. John Churton Collins, "The Porson of Shakespearian Criticism" (1892), *Essays and Studies*, 1895, p. 282.
15. George Saintsbury, *A History of Nineteenth Century Literature*, 1896, p. 406.
16. R. C. Jebb, *Dictionary of National Biography*, 1896, Volume 46, pp. 162–63.

ROBERT TANNAHILL

1. Hugh Miller, "The Poesy of Intellect and Fancy" (1856), *Essays*, 1862, p. 449.
2. James J. Lamb, "Biographical Sketch," *The Soldier's Return*, 1873, pp. xxii–xxiii.
3. C. H. Herford, *The Age of Wordsworth*, 1897, p. 197.
4. Sir George Douglas, "Robert Tannahill," *James Hogg*, 1899, pp. 122–28.
5. James Muir, "Notice Representing the Life and Writings of Robert Tannahill," *Poems and Songs*, 1815, pp. 27–33.
6. Philip A. Ramsay, "Memoir of Tannahill," *The Works of Robert Tannahill*, 1838, pp. xxxvi–xli.

RICHARD CUMBERLAND

1. Oliver Goldsmith, *Retaliation*, 1774, ll. 61–78.
2. Thomas Davies, *Memoirs of the Life of David Garrick, Esq.*, 1780, Volume 2, pp. 275–76.
3. Richard Brinsley Sheridan, *The Critic*, 1781, Act 1, Scene 1.
4. William Beloe, *The Sexagenerian*, 1817, Volume 2, pp. 222–23.
5. Sir Samuel Egerton Brydges, *Autobiography*, 1834, Volume 1, p. 189.
6. Samuel Rogers, *Table Talk*, c. 1855.
7. Augustine Birrell, "Richard Cumberland," *Essays about Men, Women, and Books*, 1894.
8. George Barnett Smith, "The English Terence," *Fortnightly Review*, February 1900, pp. 256–57.
9. Emily Morse Symonds (as "George Paston"), "Richard Cumberland," *Little Memoirs of the Eighteenth Century*, 1901, p. 57.
10. Elizabeth Inchbald, "Remarks on *The Brothers*," *The British Theater*, 1806, Volume 18.
11. Oswald Crawfurd, *English Comic Dramatists*, 1883, p. 256.
12. George Saintsbury, *A Short History of English Literature*, 1898, p. 639.
13. Richard Cumberland, *Memoirs*, 1807, Volume 2, p. 405.
14. Francis, Lord Jeffrey, "Cumberland's *Memoirs*," *Edinburgh Review*, April 1806, pp. 107–9.
15. Nathan Drake, *Essays Illustrative of the* Rambler, Adventurer, *and* Idler, 1810, Volume 2, pp. 393–94.
16. Bayard Tuckerman, *A History of English Prose Fiction*, 1882, pp. 247–48.
17. Sir Walter Scott, "*John de Lancaster*," *Quarterly Review*, May 1809, pp. 296–305.

JOEL BARLOW

1. Unsigned, "Observations on the *Columbiad*," *Monthly Magazine*, December 1808, pp. 403–7.
2. William Cullen Bryant, "Early American Verse" (1818), *Prose Writings*, ed. Parke Godwin, 1884, Volume 1, pp. 50–52.
3. Rufus W. Griswold, "Joel Barlow," *The Poets and Poetry of America*, 1842, pp. 25–26.
4. Charles W. Everest, "Joel Barlow," *The Poets of Connecticut*, 1843, pp. 78–80.
5. A. C. Baldwin, "Joel Barlow," *New Englander*, July 1873, pp. 424–30.
6. John Bach McMaster, *A History of the People in the United States*, 1885, Volume 2, p. 399.
7. Charles Burr Todd, *Life and Letters of Joel Barlow*, 1886, p. 289.
8. Edwin P. Whipple, "American Literature" (1886), *American Literature and Other Papers*, 1887, pp. 24–25.
9. Ernest Whitney, "Joel Barlow," *New Englander*, October 1886, pp. 825–26.

10. Moses Coit Tyler, "Joel Barlow," *Three Men of Letters*, 1895, pp. 165–70.
11. Fred Lewis Pattee, *A History of American Literature*, 1896, pp. 96–97.
12. Walter C. Bronson, *A Short History of American Literature*, 1900, pp. 62–63.
13. Barrett Wendell, *A Literary History of America*, 1900, pp. 127–28.
14. Francis, Lord Jeffrey, "Barlow's *Columbiad*," *Edinburgh Review*, October 1809, pp. 24–28, 39–40.

RICHARD BRINSLEY SHERIDAN

1. Fanny Burney, *Diary*, 1779.
2. Samuel Taylor Coleridge, "To Richard Brinsley Sheridan, Esq.," 1795.
3. Francis Horner, *Journal* (January 29, 1806), *Memoirs and Correspondence of Francis Horner*, ed. Leonard Horner, 1843, Volume 1, p. 357.
4. Richard Brinsley Sheridan, Letter to Samuel Rogers (May 15, 1816).
5. George Gordon, Lord Byron, "Monody on the Death of the Right Hon. R. B. Sheridan," 1816, ll. 47–118.
6. Thomas Moore, "Lines on the Death of Sheridan," 1816.
7. Caroline Norton, "Books of Gossip: Sheridan and His Biographers," *Macmillan's Magazine*, January 1861, p. 177.
8. Marquess of Dufferin and Ava, "Introduction" to *Sheridan: A Biography* by W. Fraser Rae, 1896, Volume 1, pp. viii–ix.
9. W. Fraser Rae, *Sheridan: A Biography*, 1896, Volume 1, pp. 346–47.
10. William Ewart Gladstone, "Sheridan," *The Nineteenth Century*, June 1896, p. 1037.
11. Sir Nathaniel Wraxall (1784), *Posthumous Memoirs of His Own Time*, 1836, Volume 1, pp. 39–41.
12. Sir James Mackintosh, *Journal* (February 7, 1812), cited in Robert James Mackintosh, *Memoirs of the Life of Sir James Mackintosh*, 1853, Volume 2, pp. 203–4.
13. George Gordon, Lord Byron, *Journal*, December 17–18, 1813.
14. William Hazlitt, *Lectures on the English Comic Writers*, 1819.
15. Sir Walter Scott, "An Essay on the Drama," 1819.
16. Benjamin Robert Haydon, Letter to Mary Russell Mitford (December 10, 1825).
17. John Wilson Croker, "Memoirs of Sheridan by Dr. Watkins and Mr. Moore," *Quarterly Review*, March 1826, pp. 592–93.
18. Francis, Lord Jeffrey, "Moore's Life of Sheridan," *Edinburgh Review*, December 1826, pp. 7–8.
19. Thomas Babington Macaulay, "Machiavelli" (1827), *Critical, Historical, and Miscellaneous Essays*, 1860, Volume 1, p. 295.
20. Oswald Crawfurd, *English Comic Dramatists*, 1883, p. 262.
21. Edmund Gosse, *A History of Eighteenth Century Literature*, 1888, pp. 337–38.
22. William Winter, "Sheridan and *The School for Scandal*," *Old Shrines and Ivy*, 1892, pp. 225–30.
23. F. Marion Crawford, *The Novel: What It Is*, 1893, p. 100.
24. Sir Henry Irving, cited in W. Fraser Rae, *Sheridan: A Biography*, 1896, Volume 2, p. 322.
25. George Saintsbury, *A Short History of English Literature*, 1898, p. 641.
26. John Watkins, *Memoirs of Richard Brinsley Sheridan*, 1817, Volume 1, pp. 145–46.
27. Samuel Rogers, *Table Talk*, c. 1855.

TIMOTHY DWIGHT

JANE AUSTEN

16. Eric S. Robertson, *English Poetesses*, 1883, p. 60.
17. M. S. Stillman, "Mrs. Piozzi in Italy," *Nation*, May 5, 1892, p. 343.

JOHN KEATS

1. William Wordsworth, Letter to Benjamin Robert Haydon (January 16, 1820).
2. Joseph Severn, *Journal*, February 27, 1821.
3. William Maginn, Letter to William Blackwood (April 10, 1821), cited in Margaret Oliphant, *William Blackwood and His Sons*, 1897, Volume 1, p. 375.
4. Benjamin Robert Haydon, Letter to Mary Russell Mitford (April 21, 1821), *The Life, Letters and Table Talk of Benjamin Robert Haydon*, ed. Richard Henry Stoddard, 1876, pp. 207–9.
5. Percy Bysshe Shelley, "Fragment on Keats," 1821.
6. James Russell Lowell, "To the Spirit of Keats," 1841.
7. Aubrey De Vere, "To Keats," c. 1842.
8. Elizabeth Barrett Browning, *A Vision of Poets*, 1844, ll. 407–11.
9. Christina Rossetti, "On Keats," 1849.
10. Henry Wadsworth Longfellow, "Keats," *A Book of Sonnets*, 1873.
11. Charles Cowden Clarke, "Recollections of John Keats," *Recollections of Writers*, 1878, pp. 144, 155–56.
12. Dante Gabriel Rossetti, "John Keats," *Five English Poets*, 1880–81.
13. Andrew Lang, *Letters on Literature*, 1889, pp. 197–98.
14. David Masson, "The Story of Gifford and Keats," *Nineteenth Century*, April 1892, pp. 603–5.
15. C. and J. Ollier, Letter to George Keats (April 29, 1817).
16. George Gordon, Lord Byron, Letter to John Murray (October 12, 1820).
17. George Gordon, Lord Byron, "A Second Letter to John Murray, Esq., On the Rev. W. L. Bowles's Strictures on the Life and Writings of Pope," 1821.
18. George Gordon, Lord Byron, Letter to Percy Bysshe Shelley (April 26, 1821).
19. George Gordon, Lord Byron, "Reply to Blackwood's *Edinburgh Magazine*," 1821, Note.
20. William Hazlitt, "On Effeminancy of Character," *Table Talk*, 1821–22.
21. George Gordon, Lord Byron, *Don Juan*, 1823, Canto 11, Stanza 60.
22. William Hazlitt, "A Critical List of Authors Contained in This Volume," *Select British Poets*, 1824.
23. Edwin P. Whipple, "English Poets of the Nineteenth Century" (1845), *Essays and Reviews*, 1849, Volume 1, pp. 350–54.
24. Thomas De Quincey, "Gilfillan's Literary Portraits" (1845–46), *Collected Writings*, ed. David Masson, Volume 11, pp. 388–93.
25. Aubrey De Vere, *Edinburgh Review*, October 1849, pp. 424–26.
26. Walter Savage Landor, Letter to John Forster (March 24, 1850).
27. Walter Savage Landor, "English Hexameters" (1850), 1853.
28. George Meredith, "The Poetry of Keats," 1851.
29. Elizabeth Barrett Browning, *Aurora Leigh*, 1856, Bk. 1, ll. 1003–15.
30. John Ruskin, *Modern Painters*, 1856, Pt. 4, Ch. 16.
31. Matthew Arnold, *On Translating Homer*, 1861.
32. Matthew Arnold, "John Keats," *The English Poets*, ed. Thomas Humphry Ward, 1880, Volume 4, pp. 435–37.
33. Edmond Scherer, "Wordsworth and Modern Poetry" (1880), *Essays on English Literature*, tr. George Saintsbury, 1891, pp. 191–93.

34. John Campbell Shairp, "Poetic Style in Modern English Poetry," *Aspects of Poetry* (1881), 1882, pp. 126–28.
35. H. Buxton Forman, "Preface" to *The Poetical Works and Other Writings of John Keats*, 1883, Volume 1, pp. xviii–xxi.
36. Richard Henry Stoddard, "Introduction" to *The Poems of Algernon Charles Swinburne*, 1884, p. xi.
37. James Ashcroft Noble, "Leigh Hunt: The Man and the Writer" (1886), *The Sonnet in England and Other Essays*, 1893, p. 107.
38. Sidney Colvin, *Keats*, 1887, pp. 214–18.
39. William Michael Rossetti, *Life of Keats*, 1887, pp. 205–9.
40. John Addington Symonds, "A Comparison of Elizabethan with Victorian Poetry," *Essays Speculative and Suggestive*, 1890.
41. John Davidson, *Sentences and Paragraphs*, 1893, p. 12.
42. Hallam Tennyson, *Alfred Lord Tennyson: A Memoir*, 1897, Volume 2, p. 286.
43. John Keats, "Preface" to *Endymion*, 1818.
44. John Gibson Lockhart, "Cockney School of Poetry," *Blackwood's Magazine*, August 1818, pp. 419–22.
45. Percy Bysshe Shelley, Letter to John Keats (July 27, 1820).
46. Richard Monckton Milnes, Lord Houghton, *Life, Letters, and Literary Remains of John Keats*, 1848, Volume 2, pp. 103–8.
47. Hall Caine, "Keats," *Cobwebs of Criticism*, 1883, pp. 175–76.
48. Percy Bysshe Shelley, Letter to Marianne Hunt (November 11, 1820).
49. Percy Bysshe Shelley, Letter to Lord Byron (May 4, 1821).
50. George H. Calvert, *Brief Essays and Brevities*, 1874, p. 217.
51. Leigh Hunt, "On Belle Dame sans Mercy," *Indicator*, May 10, 1820.
52. Rufus W. Griswold, "John Keats," *The Poets and Poetry of England in the Nineteenth Century*, 1844, p. 302.
53. Hugh Miller, "The Poesy of Intellect and Fancy" (1856), *Essays*, 1862, p. 452.
54. John Ruskin, *Modern Painters*, 1860, Pt. 6, Ch. 9.
55. Sidney Lanier, *The English Novel*, 1883, p. 95.
56. Margaret J. Preston, "Keats's Greek Urn," *Century Magazine*, February 1887, p. 586.
57. Joseph Severn, Letter to Harry Buxton Forman (February 5, 1878).
58. John Addington Symonds, Letter to Edmund Gosse (February 16, 1878).
59. Richard Henry Stoddard, "John Keats and Fanny Brawne," *Appleton's Journal*, April 1878, pp. 381–82.
60. John Wilson Croker, "Keats's *Endymion*," *Quarterly Review*, April 1818, pp. 204–8.
61. John Hamilton Reynolds, "Keats and the *Quarterly Review*," *Alfred, West of English Journal and General Advertiser*, October 6, 1818.
62. Peter George Patmore, "*Endymion*, a Poetic Romance," *London Magazine*, April 1820, pp. 381–89.
63. Leigh Hunt, *The Indicator*, No. 43 (August 2, 1820); No. 44 (August 9, 1820).
64. Francis, Lord Jeffrey, "Keats's *Poems*," *Edinburgh Review*, August 1820, pp. 203–7.
65. Percy Bysshe Shelley, *Adonais: An Elegy on the Death of John Keats*, 1821.
66. James Russell Lowell, "Keats" (1854), *Works*, Riverside ed., Volume 1, pp. 241–46.
67. Algernon Charles Swinburne, "Keats" (1882), *Miscellanies*, 1886, pp. 210–18.
68. William John Courthope, "Keats' Place in English Poetry," *National Review*, September 1887, pp. 19–24.
69. Robert Bridges, "Critical Introduction" to *Poems of John*

Volume 7

5. A. P. Peabody, "American Poetry," *North American Review,* January 1856, p. 240.
6. S. G. Goodrich, *Recollections of a Lifetime,* 1856, Volume 2, pp. 111–12.
7. John Nichol, *American Literature,* 1882, pp. 88–91.
8. Edmund Clarence Stedman, *Poets of America,* 1885, p. 35.
9. Edwin P. Whipple, "American Literature" (1886), *American Literature and Other Papers,* 1887, pp. 22–23.
10. Moses Coit Tyler, *The Literary History of the American Revolution, 1763–1783,* 1897, Volume 1, pp. 220–21.
11. Barrett Wendell, *The Literary History of America,* 1900, p. 126.
12. Unsigned, "McFingal," *Southern Literary Messenger,* April 1841, pp. 321–23.

JEREMY BENTHAM

1. Sir Samuel Romilly, *Diary* (September 1817), *Memoirs of the Life of Sir Samuel Romilly,* 1840, Volume 3, pp. 315–16.
2. Edward Bulwer-Lytton (?), "The Illustrious Dead: Jeremy Bentham," *New Monthly Magazine,* July 1832, pp. 49–52.
3. Robert Dale Owen, *Threading My Way: An Autobiography,* 1874, pp. 202–5.
4. Henry Crabb Robinson, *Diary,* July 31, 1814.
5. Thomas Babington Macaulay, "Westminster Reviewer's Defence of Mill" (1829), *Critical, Historical, and Miscellaneous Essays,* 1860, Volume 2, pp. 87–91.
6. Thomas Carlyle, *Journal* (September 9, 1830), cited in James Anthony Froude, *Thomas Carlyle,* 1882, Volume 2, pp. 72–73.
7. Sir James Mackintosh, *Dissertation on the Progress of Ethical Philosophy,* 1830.
8. Frederick Denison Maurice, *Moral and Metaphysical Philosophy,* 1862.
9. Sir Leslie Stephen, *History of English Thought in the Eighteenth Century,* 1876.
10. A. V. Dicey, "Bentham," *Nation,* December 5, 1878, p. 352.
11. Margaret Oliphant, *The Literary History of England, 1790–1825,* 1882, Volume 3, pp. 302–3.
12. F. C. Montague, "Jeremy Bentham," *English Prose,* ed. Henry Craik, 1895, Volume 4, pp. 525–27.
13. George Saintsbury, *A History of Nineteenth Century Literature,* 1896, p. 344.
14. J. Holland Rose, *The Rise of Democracy,* 1897, pp. 33–34.
15. William Hazlitt, "Jeremy Bentham," *The Spirit of the Age,* 1825.
16. John Stuart Mill, "Bentham" (1838), *Dissertations and Discussions,* 1867, Volume 1, pp. 332–92.
17. Henry Sidgwick, "Bentham and Benthamism in Politics and Ethics" (1877), *Miscellaneous Essays and Addresses,* 1904, pp. 145–51, 164–69.

PHILIP FRENEAU

1. Rufus W. Griswold, "Philip Freneau," *The Poets and Poetry of America,* 1842, p. 1.
2. John Nichol, *American Literature,* 1882, pp. 93–95.
3. Edwin P. Whipple, "American Literature" (1886), *American Literature and Other Papers,* 1887, p. 22.
4. Charles F. Richardson, *American Literature, 1607–1885,* 1887, Volume 2, pp. 13–16.
5. Henry A. Beers, *Initial Studies in American Letters,* 1895, pp. 62–63.
6. Katharine Lee Bates, *American Literature,* 1897, pp. 84–85.

7. Moses Coit Tyler, *The Literary History of the American Revolution, 1763–1783,* 1897, Volume 1, p. 176.
8. Henry S. Pancoast, *An Introduction to American Literature,* 1898, p. 107.
9. Walter C. Bronson, *A Short History of American Literature,* 1900, pp. 63–65.
10. Barrett Wendell, *A Literary History of America,* 1900, pp. 133–34.
11. Mary S. Austin, *Philip Freneau: The Poet of the Revolution,* 1901, pp. 202–3.
12. Fred Lewis Pattee, "Life of Philip Freneau," *The Poems of Philip Freneau,* 1902, Volume 1, pp. xcviii–cxii.

GEORGE CRABBE

1. George Crabbe, Letter to Edmund Burke (c. February 1781).
2. George Crabbe, *The Life of George Crabbe,* 1834, Ch. 4.
3. Thomas Campbell, Letter to His Sister (July 15, 1817).
4. Thomas Moore, "Verses to the Poet Crabbe's Inkstand," 1832.
5. Samuel Rogers, *Table Talk,* c. 1855.
6. Augustine Birrell, "Edmund Burke," *Obiter Dicta: Second Series,* 1887, p. 184.
7. Samuel Johnson, Letter to Sir Joshua Reynolds (March 4, 1783).
8. Francis, Lord Jeffrey, "Crabbe's Poems," *Edinburgh Review,* April 1808, pp. 132–33.
9. George Gordon, Lord Byron, *English Bards and Scotch Reviewers,* 1809, ll. 849–53.
10. William Gifford, "Crabbe's *Borough,*" *Quarterly Review,* November 1810, p. 291.
11. John Wilson (as "Christopher North"), *Noctes Ambrosianae* (September 1825), 1854.
12. Thomas Babington Macaulay, "Mr. Robert Montgomery's Poems" (1830), *Critical, Historical, and Miscellaneous Essays,* 1860, Volume 2, p. 205.
13. John Gibson Lockhart, "Life of Crabbe, by His Son," *Quarterly Review,* January 1834, pp. 468–70.
14. Samuel Taylor Coleridge, *Table Talk,* March 5, 1834.
15. Sir Samuel Egerton Brydges, *Autobiography,* 1834, Volume 1, p. 307.
16. Henry Crabb Robinson, *Diary,* December 28, 1835.
17. John Gibson Lockhart, *Memoirs of the Life of Sir Walter Scott,* 1837–38, Ch. 83.
18. Margaret Fuller, "Modern British Poets," *Papers on Literature and Art,* 1846.
19. George Gilfillan, "George Crabbe" (1847), *A Second Gallery of Literary Portraits,* 1850.
20. David Macbeth Moir, *Sketches of the Poetical Literature of the Past Half-Century,* 1851, pp. 46–47.
21. Dante Gabriel Rossetti, Letter to William Allingham (January 23, 1855).
22. James Russell Lowell, "Chaucer" (1870), *My Study Windows,* 1871, p. 284.
23. Edward FitzGerald, Letter to Fanny Kemble (November 17, 1874).
24. Coventry Patmore, "Crabbe and Shelley" (1887), *Principle in Art,* 1889, pp. 136–40.
25. W. Fraser Rae, "Crabbe," *Temple Bar,* July 1887, p. 331.
26. George Edward Woodberry, "Crabbe," *Studies in Letters and Life,* 1890, pp. 36–37.
27. Alfred H. Miles, "George Crabbe," *The Poets and the Poetry of the Century,* 1891, Volume 1, pp. 14–16.
28. T. E. Brown, Letter to S. T. Irwin (February 26, 1893).
29. George Saintsbury, *A History of Nineteenth Century Literature,* 1896, pp. 7–9.
30. Hallam Tennyson, *Alfred Lord Tennyson: A Memoir,* 1897, Volume 2, p. 287.

35. Margaret Fuller, "Modern British Poets," *Papers on Literature and Art*, 1846.
36. Ralph Waldo Emerson, "Literature," *English Traits*, 1856.
37. Matthew Arnold, *On Translating Homer*, 1861.
38. Francis Turner Palgrave, "Sir Walter Scott," *Poetical Works of Sir Walter Scott*, 1866, p. xxvii.
39. M. D. Conway, "The Scott Centenary at Edinburgh," *Harper's New Monthly Magazine*, February 1872, p. 337.
40. William Michael Rossetti, "Walter Scott," *Lives of Famous Poets*, 1878, pp. 233–34.
41. John Tulloch, *Movements of Religious Thought in Britain during the Nineteenth Century*, 1885, p. 82.
42. William Dean Howells, "Scott," *My Literary Passions*, 1895.
43. J. Gale Pedrick, "The Heraldic Aspect of Scott's Poetical Works," *Gentleman's Magazine*, November 1898, pp. 470–71.
44. Joanna Baillie, Letter to George Thomson (February 18, 1805), cited in James Cuthbert Hadden, *George Thomson: The Friend of Burns*, 1898, p. 153.
45. Francis, Lord Jeffrey, "Scott's *Lay of the Last Minstrel*," *Edinburgh Review*, April 1805, p. 20.
46. Sir James Mackintosh, Letter to George Philips (September 25, 1805), cited in Robert James Mackintosh, *Memoirs of the Life of Sir James Mackintosh*, 1853, Volume 1, p. 254.
47. R. P. Gillies, *Memoirs of a Literary Veteran*, 1851, Ch. 19.
48. William John Courthope, "The Revival of Romance: Scott, Byron, Shelley," *The Liberal Movement in English Literature*, 1885, p. 130.
49. George Gordon, Lord Byron, Letter to Francis Hodgson (October 3, 1810).
50. Samuel Taylor Coleridge, Letter to William Wordsworth (October 1810).
51. Stendhal (Henri Beyle), *Le National*, February 19, 1830.
52. William H. Prescott, "English Literature of the Nineteenth Century," *North American Review*, July 1832, pp. 187–90.
53. Samuel Taylor Coleridge, *Table Talk*, November 1, 1833.
54. Honoré de Balzac, Letter to Mme Hanska (January 20, 1825).
55. William H. Prescott, "Sir Walter Scott" (1838), *Biographical and Critical Miscellanies*, 1845.
56. John W. Hales, *Notes and Essays on Shakespeare*, 1873, pp. 72–73.
57. James Freeman Clarke, "Culture by Reading Books," *Self-Culture*, 1880, p. 316.
58. Sidney Lanier, *The English Novel*, 1883, p. 193.
59. Andrew D. White, "Walter Scott at Work," *Scribner's Magazine*, February 1889, p. 132.
60. William Dean Howells, *Criticism and Fiction*, 1891, pp. 21–22.
61. Edmund Gosse, *A Short History of Modern English Literature*, 1897, pp. 299–302.
62. Brander Matthews, "The Historical Novel," *Forum*, September 1897, p. 84.
63. Francis Hovey Stoddard, *The Evolution of the English Novel*, 1900, pp. 104–5.
64. Jane Austen, Letter to Anna Austen (September 28, 1814).
65. Thomas Carlyle, Letter to Robert Mitchell (October 18, 1814).
66. Maria Edgeworth, Letter to James Ballantyne (October 23, 1814).
67. Mary Russell Mitford, Letter to Sir William Elford (October 31, 1814).
68. Johann Wolfgang von Goethe (1828), cited in Johann Peter Eckermann, *Conversations with Goethe*, 1830, tr. John Oxenford.
69. R. H. Barham, *Journal* (February 11, 1833), *The Life and Letters of the Rev. Richard Harris Barham*, ed. R. H. Dalton Barham, 1870, Volume 1, p. 214.
70. William C. Macready, Letter to Mrs. Pollock (March 26, 1855).
71. Alfred, Lord Tennyson (1890), cited in Hallam Tennyson, *Alfred Lord Tennyson: A Memoir*, 1897, Volume 2, p. 372.
72. John Wilson, "Ivanhoe," *Blackwood's Edinburgh Magazine*, December 1819, pp. 262–63.
73. Johann Peter Eckermann, *Conversations with Goethe*, 1830, tr. John Oxenford.
74. Sir Leslie Stephen, "Sir Walter Scott" (1871), *Hours in a Library* (1874–79), 1904, Volume 1, p. 215.
75. Fanny Kemble, Letter (May 1827), *Record of a Girlhood*, 1878.
76. Charlotte Brontë, Letter to Ellen Nussey (January 1, 1833).
77. Edward FitzGerald, Letter to Fanny Kemble (April 25, 1879).
78. William Wilberforce, Letter to J. Stephen (August 13, 1822), cited in Robert Isaac Wilberforce, Samuel Wilberforce, *The Life of William Wilberforce*, 1838, Volume 5, p. 133.
79. Edward FitzGerald, Letter to Fanny Kemble (December 1881).
80. Anne Grant, Letter to Mrs. Smith (February 6, 1824), *Memoirs and Correspondence of Mrs. Grant of Laggan*, ed. J. P. Grant, 1844, Volume 3, pp. 20–21.
81. John Ruskin, "Fiction—Fair and Foul," *Nineteenth Century*, June 1880, p. 955.
82. Sydney Smith, Letter to Lord Holland (July 1828).
83. William Francis Collier, *A History of English Literature*, 1861, pp. 411–12.
84. Johann Peter Eckermann, *Conversations with Goethe*, 1830, tr. John Oxenford.
85. William Wetmore Story, *Conversations in a Studio*, 1890, Volume 1, pp. 273–74.
86. William Hazlitt, "Sir Walter Scott," *The Spirit of the Age*, 1825.
87. Thomas Carlyle, "Sir Walter Scott" (1837), *Critical and Miscellaneous Essays*, 1839–69.
88. Walter Bagehot, "The Waverley Novels" (1858), *Collected Works*, ed. Norman St. John-Stevas, 1965, Volume 2, pp. 47–48, 62–75.
89. Sir Leslie Stephen, "Sir Walter Scott" (1871), *Hours in a Library* (1874–79), 1904, Volume 1, pp. 186–93, 200–210.
90. George Saintsbury, "Conclusion," *Sir Walter Scott*, 1897, pp. 147–56.

HANNAH MORE

1. Robert Southey, Letter to Grosvenor C. Bedford (October 10, 1795).
2. Thomas Babington Macaulay, Letter to Macvey Napier (June 15, 1837), cited in G. Otto Trevelyan, *The Life and Letters of Lord Macaulay*, 1876, Volume 1, pp. 405–6.
3. Charlotte M. Yonge, *Hannah More*, 1888, pp. 226–27.
4. W. R. W. Stephens, *The Life and Letters of Edward A. Freeman*, 1895, Volume 1, p. 6.
5. Hannah More, Letter to Mrs. Gwatkin (March 5, 1778), *Memoirs of the Life and Correspondence of Mrs. Hannah More*, ed. William Roberts, 1835, Volume 1, pp. 86–87.
6. Samuel Johnson, Letter to Hester Lynch Piozzi (April 19, 1784).

28. Matthew Arnold, "Joubert" (1864), *Essays in Criticism*, 1865.
29. Dante Gabriel Rossetti, "Samuel Taylor Coleridge," *Five English Poets*, 1880–81.
30. W. P. Ker, "Samuel Taylor Coleridge," *English Prose*, ed. Henry Craik, 1896, Volume 5, pp. 76–80.
31. Francis Thompson, "Academy Portraits: XIII. S. T. Coleridge," *Academy*, February 6, 1897, pp. 179–80.
32. Richard Garnett, "The Poetry of Coleridge" (1898), *Essays of an Ex-Librarian*, 1901, pp. 88–91.
33. Thomas B. Shaw, *Outlines of English Literature*, 1847.
34. Peter Bayne, "Samuel Taylor Coleridge," *Essays in Biography and Criticism: Second Series*, 1858, p. 142.
35. Hall Caine, *Cobwebs of Criticism*, 1883, p. 59.
36. H. D. Traill, *Coleridge*, 1884, pp. 46–53.
37. William Watson, "Coleridge's Supernaturalism," *Excursions in Criticism*, 1893, pp. 98–101.
38. Thomas Love Peacock, *Nightmare Abbey*, 1818, Ch. 8.
39. George H. Calvert, *Coleridge, Shelley, Goethe: Biographic Aesthetic Studies*, 1880, pp. 12–16.
40. George Gordon, Lord Byron, Letter to John Murray (September 30, 1816).
41. John Gibson Lockhart, "On the Lake School of Poetry: III. Coleridge," *Blackwood's Edinburgh Magazine*, October 1819, pp. 8–9.
42. John Sterling, "On Coleridge's *Christabel*" (1828), *Essays and Tales*, ed. Julius Charles Hare, 1848, Volume 1, pp. 101–2.
43. Edgar Allan Poe, "The Rationale of Verse," 1848.
44. William Watson, "Lines in a Flyleaf of *Christabel*," 1893.
45. Charles Knight, *Studies of Shakspere*, 1849, p. 560.
46. George Gilfillan, "Jeffrey and Coleridge," *A Third Gallery of Portraits*, 1854, pp. 223–26.
47. Laura Johnson Wylie, *Studies in the Evolution of English Criticism*, 1894, pp. 199–200.
48. William Hazlitt, "Mr. Coleridge," *The Spirit of the Age*, 1825.
49. Walter Pater, "Coleridge" (1865), *Appreciations*, 1889.
50. Algernon Charles Swinburne, "Coleridge" (1869), *Essays and Studies*, 1875, pp. 259–75.
51. James Russell Lowell, "Coleridge" (1885), *Works*, Riverside ed., 1890, Volume 6, pp. 69–77.
52. Edward Dowden, "Coleridge as a Poet" (1889), *New Studies in Literature*, 1895, pp. 313–54.

CHARLES LAMB (1774–1834)

1. Samuel Taylor Coleridge, "To a Friend Who Had Declared His Intention of Writing No More Poetry," 1796.
2. Samuel Taylor Coleridge, Letter to William Godwin (May 21, 1800).
3. Henry Crabb Robinson, *Diary*, July 3, 1814.
4. John Keats, Letter to George and Thomas Keats (January 5, 1818).
5. William Hazlitt, "On the Conversation of Authors: Part II" (1820), *The Plain Speaker*, 1826.
6. Charles Lamb, "An Autobiographical Sketch" (1827), *Works*, ed. E. V. Lucas, 1903, Volume 1, pp. 320–21.
7. Thomas Carlyle, *Journal* (1831), cited in James Anthony Froude, *Thomas Carlyle*, 1882, Volume 2, p. 170.
8. William Maginn, "Charles Lamb, Esq.," *Fraser's Magazine*, February 1835, p. 136.
9. William Wordsworth, "Written after the Death of Charles Lamb," 1835.
10. George Daniel, *Recollections of Charles Lamb* (c. 1835), 1927, pp. 48–51.
11. Robert Southey, Letter to Edward Moxon (February 2, 1836).
12. Edward Moxon, *Sonnets*, 1837, Pt. 2, Sonnet 12.

13. Benjamin Robert Haydon, Letter to William Wordsworth (October 16, 1842), *Life, Letters and Table Talk of Benjamin Robert Haydon*, ed. Richard Henry Stoddard, 1876, p. 201.
14. Thomas De Quincey, "Charles Lamb" (1848), *Collected Writings*, ed. David Masson, Volume 5, pp. 257–58.
15. Leigh Hunt, *Autobiography*, 1850, Ch. 16.
16. Peter George Patmore, *My Friends and Acquaintance*, 1854, Volume 1, pp. 21–28.
17. William Watson, "At the Grave of Charles Lamb, in Edmonton," *Lachrymae Musarum and Other Poems*, 1893, pp. 44–45.
18. John Wilson, "The Works of Charles Lamb," *Blackwood's Edinburgh Magazine*, August 1818, p. 599.
19. Robert Southey, Letter to C. W. W. Wynn (January 25, 1823).
20. Henry Nelson Coleridge, "The Last Essays of Elia," *Quarterly Review*, July 1835, pp. 58–64.
21. Henry F. Chorley, "Charles Lamb," *The Authors of England*, 1838, pp. 75–76.
22. Henry T. Tuckerman, "The Humorist: Charles Lamb," *Characteristics of Literature*, 1849.
23. Edward Dowden, "Charles Lamb," *The English Poets*, ed. Thomas Humphry Ward, 1880, Volume 4, pp. 326–27.
24. John Dennis, "Charles Lamb and His Friends," *Fraser's Magazine*, May 1882, pp. 613–14.
25. Margaret Oliphant, *The Literary History of England, 1790–1825*, 1892, Volume 2, pp. 11–13.
26. Algernon Charles Swinburne, "On Lamb's *Specimens of Dramatic Poets*," 1882.
27. Algernon Charles Swinburne, "Charles Lamb and George Wither" (1885), *Miscellanies*, 1886, pp. 194–200.
28. Augustine Birrell, "Charles Lamb," *Obiter Dicta: Second Series*, 1887, pp. 226–31.
29. William Tirebuck, "Introduction" to *The Poetical Works of Bowles, Lamb, and Hartley Coleridge*, 1887, pp. xx–xxiii.
30. William Hazlitt, "Elia, and Geoffrey Crayon," *The Spirit of the Age*, 1825.
31. John Forster, "Charles Lamb," *New Monthly Magazine*, February 1835, pp. 200–206.
32. Walter Pater, "Charles Lamb" (1878), *Appreciations*, 1889.
33. Brander Matthews, "Charles Lamb's Dramatic Attempts," *Lippincott's Magazine*, May 1883, pp. 493–99.
34. Paul Elmer More, "Charles Lamb," *Shelburne Essays: Second Series*, 1905, pp. 90–99.

WILLIAM COBBETT

1. Ebenezer Elliott, "Elegy on William Cobbett," 1835.
2. James Grant, *Recollections of the House of Commons*, 1835, pp. 198–99.
3. George Stovin Venables, "Cobbett; or, A Rural Ride," *Macmillan's Magazine*, November 1859, pp. 40–41.
4. Sir Henry Lytton Bulwer, "Cobbett: The Contentious Man," *Historical Characters*, 1867, Volume 2, pp. 188–90.
5. James E. Thorold Rogers, "William Cobbett," *Historical Gleanings*, 1869, Volume 1, pp. 184–85.
6. Edward Smith, *William Cobbett: A Biography*, 1878, Volume 2, pp. 297–98.
7. Margaret Oliphant, *The Literary History of England, 1790–1825*, 1882, Volume 2, pp. 360–63.
8. S. C. Hall, *Retrospect of a Long Life*, 1883, p. 135.
9. Henry Cabot Lodge, "William Cobbett," *Studies in History*, 1884, pp. 126–29.
10. Hugh E. Egerton, "A Scarce Book," *National Review*, May 1885, p. 413.

6. Robert Dale Owen, *Threading My Way: An Autobiography*, 1874, pp. 207–8.
7. S. C. Hall, *Retrospect of a Long Life*, 1883, p. 313.
8. Samuel Taylor Coleridge, "To William Godwin, Author of *Political Justice*," *Sonnets on Eminent Characters*, 1794–95.
9. William Hazlitt, *Lectures on the English Comic Writers*, 1819.
10. Percy Bysshe Shelley, *Letter to Maria Gisborne*, 1820, ll. 193–202.
11. Sir Walter Scott, Letter to Benjamin Robert Haydon (c. October 1822).
12. William Hazlitt, "William Godwin," *The Spirit of the Age*, 1825.
13. Sir Walter Scott, "*The Omen*," *Blackwood's Edinburgh Magazine*, July 1826, pp. 52–53.
14. Harriet Martineau, *A History of the Thirty Years' Peace, 1816–1846*, 1849–50, Volume 4, pp. 79–80.
15. Mark Twain, "In Defense of Harriet Shelley" (1894), *How to Tell a Story and Other Essays*, 1897, p. 97.
16. Walter Raleigh, *The English Novel*, 1894, pp. 244–48.
17. Edward Dowden, *The French Revolution and English Literature*, 1897, pp. 47–49.
18. George Saintsbury, *A Short History of English Literature*, 1898, pp. 634–35.
19. Robert Southey, Letter to Grosvenor C. Bedford (November 21–22, 1795).
20. William Godwin, "Supplement to Journal" (March 23, 1793), cited in C. Kegan Paul, *William Godwin: His Friends and Contemporaries*, 1876, Volume 1, p. 116.
21. Robert Hall, Letter to Henry Crabb Robinson (October 13, 1798), cited in *Diary, Reminiscences, and Correspondence of Henry Crabb Robinson*, ed. Thomas Sadler, 1869, Volume 1, pp. 47–48.
22. Sir James Mackintosh, "Godwin's *Lives of Milton's Nephews*," *Edinburgh Review*, October 1815, pp. 488–89.
23. John Dunlop, *The History of Fiction* (1814), 1842, Volume 2, p. 405.
24. Sir James Mackintosh, "Godwin's *Lives of Milton's Nephews*," *Edinburgh Review*, October 1815, pp. 487–88.
25. Sir Leslie Stephen, "William Godwin," *Fortnightly Review*, October 1876, p. 459.
26. Barrett Wendell, *A Literary History of America*, 1900, p. 161.
27. Mary Berry, Letter to Mrs. Cholmeley (January 2, 1800), *Extracts from the Journals and Correspondence of Miss Berry*, ed. Lady Theresa Lewis, 1866, Volume 2, p. 111.
28. Thomas Holcroft, Letter to William Godwin (September 9, 1800), cited in C. Kegan Paul, *William Godwin: His Friends and Contemporaries*, 1876, Volume 2, pp. 25–26.
29. John Dunlop, *The History of Fiction* (1814), 1842, Volume 2, p. 406.
30. Sir Leslie Stephen, "William Godwin," *Fortnightly Review*, October 1876, pp. 460–61.
31. C. H. Herford, *The Age of Wordsworth*, 1897, p. 99.
32. Charles Lamb, Letter to William Godwin (c. 1803).
33. Thomas R. Lounsbury, *Studies in Chaucer*, 1891, Volume 1, pp. 191–94.
34. Thomas De Quincey, "Notes on Gilfillan's Literary Portraits" (1845–46), *Collected Writings*, ed. David Masson, Volume 11, pp. 326–33.
35. Sir Leslie Stephen, *History of English Thought in the Eighteenth Century*, 1876.

GEORGE COLMAN THE YOUNGER

1. George Gordon, Lord Byron, *Detached Thoughts*, 1813.
2. Dr. H. S. Chinnock, Letter to R. B. Peake (January 18,

1841), cited in Richard Brinsley Peake, *Memoirs of the Colman Family*, 1841, Volume 2, pp. 452–53.
3. Richard Brinsley Peake, *Memoirs of the Colman Family*, 1841, Volume 2, pp. 415–19.
4. Leigh Hunt, Note to *The Feast of the Poets* (1811), 1814, ll. 42–43.
5. James Smith, "Colman's Epitaph," 1836.
6. Alfred H. Miles, "George Colman," *The Poets and the Poetry of the Century*, 1894, Volume 10, pp. 10–12.
7. C. H. Herford, *The Age of Wordsworth*, 1897, pp. 136–37.
8. H. Barton Baker, "George Colman, Elder and Younger," *Belgravia*, December 1881, pp. 196–201.

JAMES MILL

1. Henry, Lord Brougham, "Introduction" to "Speech on the Present State of the Law," *Speeches*, 1838, Volume 2, pp. 304–6.
2. George Grote, "Review of John Stuart Mill on the Philosophy of Sir William Hamilton" (1866), *Minor Works*, 1873, pp. 283–84.
3. Alexander Bain, *James Mill: A Biography*, 1882, pp. 425–27.
4. A. V. Dicey, "James Mill," *Nation*, September 7, 1882, pp. 204–5.
5. Thomas Moore, *Journal*, March 17, 1819.
6. Thomas Babington Macaulay, "Sir James Mackintosh" (1835), *Critical, Historical, and Miscellaneous Essays*, 1860, Volume 3, pp. 278–79.
7. Sir George Cornewall Lewis, Letter to Thomas Frankland Lewis (January 10, 1837), *Letters*, ed. Sir Gilbert Frankland Lewis, 1870, pp. 72–73.
8. Harriet Martineau, *A History of the Thirty Years' Peace, 1816–1846*, 1849–50, Volume 4, p. 77.
9. Thomas Babington Macaulay, "Mill on Government" (1820), *Critical, Historical, and Miscellaneous Essays*, 1860, Volume 2, pp. 7–8.
10. Andrew Bisset, "James Mill," *Essays on Historical Truth*, 1871, pp. 105–6.
11. G. S. Bower, *David Hartley and James Mill*, 1881, pp. 227–30.
12. John Tulloch, *Movements of Religious Thought in Britain during the Nineteenth Century*, 1885, pp. 211–16.
13. John Stuart Mill, *Autobiography*, 1873.
14. Sir Leslie Stephen, "James Mill's *Analysis*," *The English Utilitarians*, 1900, Volume 2, pp. 287–93, 311–12.

LETITIA ELIZABETH LANDON

1. Mary Howitt, Letter to Anna Howitt (October 28, 1824), *An Autobiography*, ed. Margaret Howitt, 1889, Volume 1, pp. 187–88.
2. Benjamin Disraeli, Letter to Sarah Disraeli (March 26, 1832).
3. Edward Bulwer-Lytton, Letter to Lady Blessington (1838), cited in R. R. Madden, *The Literary Life and Correspondence of the Countess of Blessington*, 1855, Volume 2, p. 183.
4. Walter Savage Landor (?), "A Lament for L. E. L." (1838), cited in R. R. Madden, *The Literary Life and Correspondence of the Countess of Blessington*, 1855, Volume 2, pp. 68–69.
5. Laman Blanchard, *The Life and Remains of L. E. L.*, 1841.
6. Harriet Martineau, *A History of the Thirty Years' Peace, 1816–1846*, 1849–50, Volume 4, pp. 75–76.
7. Dr. Anthony Todd Thomson, *Autobiographical Reminiscences of the Medical Profession*, 1874, p. 308.
8. S. C. Hall, *Retrospect of a Long Life*, 1883, pp. 395–96.

26. Sarah Austin, "Preface" to *Letters of the Rev. Sydney Smith*, 1855, pp. vii–xii.
27. Walter Bagehot, "The First Edinburgh Reviewers" (1855), *Collected Works*, ed. Norman St. John-Stevas, 1965, Volume 1, 333–38.

THOMAS HOOD

1. James Russell Lowell, "To the Memory of Hood," 1845.
2. Charles Dickens, Letter to John Watkins (October 18, 1852).
3. William Makepeace Thackeray, "On a Joke I Once Heard from the Late Thomas Hood," *Roundabout Papers*, 1863.
4. J. R. Planché, *Recollections and Reflections*, 1872, Volume 1, p. 100.
5. Henry F. Chorley, *Autobiography, Memoir, and Letters*, ed. Henry G. Hewlett, 1873, Volume 1, p. 99.
6. John Wilson (as "Christopher North"), *Noctes Ambrosianae* (November 1828), 1854.
7. R. H. Horne, "Thomas Hood and the Late Theodore Hook," *A New Spirit of the Age*, 1844, pp. 221–23.
8. Edgar Allan Poe, "The Poetic Principle" (1850), *Complete Works*, ed. James A. Harrison, 1902, Volume 14, p. 287.
9. David Macbeth Moir, *Sketches of the Poetical Literature of the Past Half-Century*, 1851, pp. 251–52.
10. William Makepeace Thackeray, *The English Humourists of the Eighteenth Century*, 1853.
11. Leigh Hunt, "Postscript" to *The Feast of the Poets* (1811), 1860.
12. David Masson, "Thomas Hood," *Macmillan's Magazine*, August 1860, pp. 319–20.
13. J. Fraser, "Thomas Hood," *Westminster Review*, April 1871, p. 354.
14. Charles Cowden Clarke, "On the Comic Writers of England: XV. Thomas Hood," *Gentleman's Magazine*, June 1872, pp. 660–61.
15. Edmund Clarence Stedman, *Victorian Poets*, 1875, pp. 73–74, 86–88.
16. William Michael Rossetti, "Thomas Hood," *Lives of Famous Poets*, 1878, pp. 380–81.
17. Austin Dobson, "Thomas Hood," *The English Poets*, ed. Thomas Humphry Ward, 1880, Volume 4, pp. 531–33.
18. S. C. Hall, *Retrospect of a Long Life*, 1883, pp. 340–42.
19. Margaret Oliphant, *The Victorian Age of English Literature*, 1892, Volume 1, pp. 235–38.
20. Richard Garnett, "Thomas Hood," *The Poets and the Poetry of the Century*, ed. Alfred H. Miles, 1894, Volume 3, pp. 216–18.
21. Hugh Walker, *The Age of Tennyson*, 1897, pp. 55–56.
22. George Gilfillan, "Thomas Hood" (1847), *A Second Gallery of Literary Portraits*, 1850, pp. 103–17.
23. Henry Giles, "Thomas Hood," *Atlantic*, November 1860, pp. 521–23.

JOHN HOOKHAM FRERE

1. Robert Southey, Letter to Charles Danvers (January 20, 1801).
2. George Ticknor, *Journal* (1819), *Life, Letters, and Journals of George Ticknor*, ed. Anna Ticknor, 1876, Volume 1, p. 267.
3. Bartle Frere, "Memoir," *The Works of John Hookham Frere*, 1872, Volume 1, pp. ccxciii–ccxcv.
4. Robert Southey, Letter to Sir Walter Scott (April 22, 1808).
5. John Wilson (as "Christopher North"), *Noctes Ambrosianae* (June 1824), 1854.
6. Sir Walter Scott, "Essay on Imitations of the Ancient Ballad," 1830.

7. James Davies, "John Hookham Frere," *Contemporary Review*, March 1872, pp. 512–13, 532–33.
8. Austin Dobson, "John Hookham Frere," *The English Poets*, ed. Thomas Humphry Ward, 1880, Volume 4, p. 240.
9. G. Barnett Smith, "John Hookham Frere," *Gentleman's Magazine*, January 1888, pp. 44–49.
10. Charles Eliot Norton, "John Hookham Frere," *North American Review*, July 1868, pp. 136–37, 160–66.

MARY LAMB

1. Charles Lamb, "Mackery End, in Hertfordshire" (1811), *The Essays of Elia*, 1823.
2. N. P. Willis, *Pencilings by the Way*, 1835, Volume 3, pp. 117–18.
3. T. Noon Talfourd, *Memoirs of Charles Lamb* (1838), ed. Percy Fitzgerald, 1892, pp. 222–25.
4. Henry Crabb Robinson, Letter (May 29, 1847).
5. Sara Coleridge, Letter to Miss Fenwick (July 6, 1847), *Memoir and Letters of Sara Coleridge*, ed. Edith Coleridge, 1873, Volume 2, pp. 120–21.
6. Gerald Massey, "Charles Lamb," *Fraser's Magazine*, May 1867, pp. 660–62.
7. Mary Cowden Clarke, "Mary Lamb," *Recollections of Writers*, 1878, pp. 177–79.
8. Mary Lamb, Letter to Sarah Stoddart (June 2, 1806).
9. Charles Lamb, Letter to William Wordsworth (June 26, 1806).
10. Mary Lamb, Letter to Sarah Stoddart (July 4, 1806).
11. Walter Savage Landor, Letter to Henry Crabb Robinson (April 1831), cited in *Diary, Reminiscences and Correspondence of Henry Crabb Robinson*, ed. Thomas Sadler, 1869, Volume 2, p. 110.
12. Anne Gilchrist, *Mary Lamb*, 1883, pp. 207–14.
13. Eric S. Robertson, *English Poetesses*, 1883, p. 130.

THOMAS CHALMERS

1. John Gibson Lockhart, *Peter's Letters to His Kinsfolk*, 1819, Letter 73.
2. Anne Grant, Letter to Mrs. Hook (September 12, 1827), *Memoir and Correspondence of Mrs. Grant of Laggan*, ed. J. P. Grant, 1844, pp. 101–2.
3. Robert Turnbull, *The Genius of Scotland*, 1847, pp. 111–12.
4. Isaac Taylor, "Memoirs of Dr. Chalmers," *North British Review*, July 1852, p. 206.
5. Thomas Carlyle, "Edward Irving" (1866), *Reminiscences*, ed. James Anthony Froude, 1881, Volume 1, pp. 159–60.
6. William Mathews, *Oratory and Orators*, 1878, pp. 400–401.
7. William M. Taylor, *The Scottish Pulpit*, 1887, p. 223.
8. Margaret Oliphant, *Thomas Chalmers*, 1893, pp. 140–42.
9. John Griscom, *A Year in Europe in 1818 and 1819*, 1823.
10. William Hazlitt, "Rev. Mr. Irving," *The Spirit of the Age*, 1825.
11. George Gilfillan, "Dr. Chalmers," *A Third Gallery of Portraits*, 1854.
12. John Brown, "Dr. Chalmers," *Horae Subsecivae: Second Series*, 1861.
13. Francis Jacox, "A Run upon a Book," *Aspects of Authorship*, 1872, p. 330.
14. James McCosh, *The Scottish Philosophy*, 1874, pp. 401–2.
15. John Tulloch, *Movements of Religious Thoughts in Britain during the Nineteenth Century*, 1885, p. 161.

6. John Gibson Lockhart, *Memoirs of the Life of Sir Walter Scott*, 1837–38, Ch. 59.
7. Edward FitzGerald, Letter to Bernard Barton (September 2, 1841).
8. Lydia Huntley Sigourney, *Pleasant Memories of Pleasant Lands*, 1842, pp. 281–82.
9. Sydney Smith, cited in Lady Holland, A *Memoir of the Rev. Sydney Smith*, 1844, Ch. 12.
10. Augustus J. C. Hare, *The Life and Letters of Maria Edgeworth*, 1894, Volume 2, p. 691.
11. Anne Grant, Letter to Mrs. Fletcher (July 6, 1809), *Memoir and Correspondence of Mrs. Grant of Laggan*, ed. J. P. Grant, 1844, Volume 1, pp. 213–14.
12. Francis, Lord Jeffrey, "Miss Edgeworth's *Fashionable Tales*," *Edinburgh Review*, July 1809, p. 388.
13. Henry Crabb Robinson, *Diary*, September 21, 1812.
14. Sir Walter Scott, "General Preface to the Waverley Novels," 1829.
15. Sir Jonah Barrington, *Personal Sketches of His Own Times*, 1830, p. 375.
16. William H. Prescott, "English Literature of the Nineteenth Century," *North American Review*, July 1832, p. 187.
17. W. B. O. Peabody, "*Helen*," *North American Review*, July 1834, pp. 180–82.
18. Sir Archibald Alison, *History of Europe from 1815 to 1852*, 1852–59, Ch. 5.
19. Abraham Hayward, "Miss Edgeworth—Her Life and Writings," *Edinburgh Review*, October 1867, p. 498.
20. Sir Spencer Walpole, A *History of England from the Conclusion of the Great War in 1815*, 1878.
21. Margaret Oliphant, *The Literary History of England, 1790–1825*, 1882, Volume 3, pp. 215–19.
22. Grace A. Oliver, A *Study of Maria Edgeworth*, 1882, p. 448.
23. Goldwin Smith, "Miss Edgeworth," *Nation*, April 12, 1883, p. 332.
24. S. C. Hall, *Retrospect of a Long Life*, 1883, p. 361.
25. Catharine J. Hamilton, *Women Writers: First Series*, 1892, p. 174.
26. Henry Craik, "Maria Edgeworth," *English Prose*, ed. Henry Craik, 1895, Volume 4, pp. 619–21.
27. George Saintsbury, A *History of Nineteenth Century Literature*, 1896, pp. 127–28.
28. Wilbur L. Cross, *The Development of the English Novel*, 1899, pp. 95–98.
29. Emily Lawless, *Maria Edgeworth*, 1904, p. 211.
30. Earl of Dudley (?), "Miss Edgeworth's *Patronage*," *Quarterly Review*, January 1814, pp. 303–8.
31. Helen Zimmern, *Maria Edgeworth*, 1883, pp. 179–92.

EBENEZER ELLIOTT

1. Thomas Carlyle, "Corn-Law Rhymes," *Edinburgh Review*, July 1832, p. 345.
2. John Wilson, "Poetry of Ebenezer Elliott," *Blackwood's Edinburgh Magazine*, May 1834, pp. 819–20.
3. W. J. Fox, "Poetry of the Poor: Ebenezer Elliott," *Westminster Review*, April 1835, p. 191.
4. Rufus W. Griswold, "Ebenezer Elliott," *The Poets and Poetry of England in the Nineteenth Century*, 1844, p. 174.
5. Edwin P. Whipple, "English Poets of the Nineteenth Century" (1845), *Essays and Reviews*, 1850, Volume 1, pp. 338–40.
6. John Watkins, *Life, Poetry, and Letters of Ebenezer Elliott*, 1850, p. 268.
7. John Greenleaf Whittier, "Elliott," 1850.

8. David Macbeth Moir, *Sketches of the Poetical Literature of the Past Half-Century*, 1851, pp. 244–46.
9. Walter Savage Landor, "On the Statue of Ebenezer Elliott by Neville Burnard," 1853.
10. Alexander Smith, "A Shelf in My Bookcase," *Dreamthorp*, 1863, pp. 210–13.
11. Edward Dowden, "Ebenezer Elliott," *The English Poets*, ed. Thomas Humphry Ward, 1880, Volume 4, pp. 495–96.
12. William Sharp, *Sonnets of This Century*, 1886, p. 287, Note.
13. Margaret Oliphant, *The Victorian Age of English Literature*, 1892, Volume 1, p. 240.
14. Richard Henry Stoddard, "Ebenezer Elliott," *Under the Evening Lamp*, 1892, pp. 146–48.
15. Francis T. Palgrave, *Landscape in Poetry*, 1896, pp. 209–11.
16. George Saintsbury, A *History of Nineteenth Century Literature*, 1896, pp. 110–11.
17. Alfred H. Miles, "Ebenezer Elliott," *The Poets and the Poetry of the Century*, ed. Alfred H. Miles, 1892, Volume 2, pp. 231–34.

MARGUERITE, COUNTESS OF BLESSINGTON

1. Thomas Moore, *Journal*, May 5, 1822.
2. Henry Crabb Robinson, *Diary*, September 28, 1832.
3. N. P. Willis, *Pencillings by the Way*, 1835, Volume 3, pp. 82–83.
4. Leigh Hunt, *Blue-Stocking Revels; or, The Feast of the Violets*, 1837, Canto 2, ll. 45–56.
5. Peter George Patmore, *My Friends and Acquaintance*, 1854, Volume 1, p. 176.
6. Miss Power, "A Memoir of the Countess of Blessington," *Life and Correspondence of the Countess of Blessington*, ed. R. R. Madden, 1855, Volume 1, pp. 16–17.
7. R. R. Madden, *The Literary Life and Correspondence of the Countess of Blessington*, 1855, Volume 1, pp. 59–60.
8. Walter Savage Landor, "The Landor-Blessington Papers" (1855), *Literary Anecdotes of the Nineteenth Century*, eds. W. Robertson Nicoll, Thomas J. Wise, 1895, Volume 1, p. 233.
9. Henry F. Chorley, *Autobiography, Memoir, and Letters*, ed. Henry G. Hewlett, 1873, Volume 1, pp. 174–75.
10. Mary Cowden Clarke, "Mrs. Shelley," *Recollections of Writers*, 1878, p. 42.
11. T. P. O'Connor, *Lord Beaconsfield: A Biography*, 1879, p. 11.
12. Henry F. Chorley, *Authors of England*, 1838, p. 30.
13. Charles Cavendish Fulke Greville, *Journal*, February 17, 1839.
14. C. C. Felton, "Literary Life of Lady Blessington," *North American Review*, July 1855, pp. 258–59.
15. S. C. Hall, *Retrospect of a Long Life*, 1883, p. 367.
16. Margaret Oliphant, *The Victorian Age of English Literature*, 1892, Volume 1, p. 13.

HARTLEY COLERIDGE

1. Samuel Taylor Coleridge, Letter to Thomas Poole (September 24, 1796).
2. William Wordsworth, "To H. C., Six Years Old," 1802.
3. Robert Southey, Letter to Charles Danvers (January 15, 1805).
4. Henry Crabb Robinson, *Diary*, September 9, 1816.
5. Caroline Fox, *Journal* (January 12, 1849), *Memories of Old Friends*, ed. Horace N. Pym, 1882, p. 254.
6. George S. Hillard, "Hartley Coleridge," *Living Age*, April 28, 1849, p. 161.

Volume 8

22. Walt Whitman, "Edgar Poe's Significance," *Critic*, June 3, 1882, p. 147.
23. Edmund Gosse, "Has America Produced a Poet?" (1889), *Questions at Issue*, 1893, pp. 88–90.
24. John Burroughs, "Mr. Gosse's Puzzle over Poe," *Dial*, October 16, 1893, pp. 214–15.
25. Joel Benton, "Poe's Opinion of 'The Raven'" (1897), *In the Poe Circle*, 1899, pp. 57–60.
26. Henry Wadsworth Longfellow, Letter to Edgar Allan Poe (May 19, 1841).
27. Margaret Fuller, "Poe's Tales," *New York Daily Tribune*, July 11, 1845.
28. Robert Louis Stevenson, *Academy*, January 2, 1875, pp. 1–2.
29. Brander Matthews, *The Philosophy of the Short-Story* (1885), 1901, pp. 44–48.
30. Francis Thompson, "A Dreamer of Things Impossible" (1901), *Literary Criticisms*, ed. Terence L. Connolly, 1948, pp. 317–22.
31. Nathaniel Hawthorne, Letter to Edgar Allan Poe (June 17, 1846), cited in George E. Woodberry, "Poe in New York," *Century Magazine*, October 1894, p. 860.
32. Eugene Benson, "Poe and Hawthorne," *Galaxy*, December 1868, pp. 747–48.
33. Henry James, *Hawthorne*, 1879, p. 62.
34. Barrett Wendell, *A Literary History of America*, 1900, pp. 208–9.
35. James Russell Lowell, "Edgar Allan Poe," *Graham's Magazine*, February 1845, pp. 49–53.
36. Charles Baudelaire, "Edgar Allan Poe: His Life and Works" (tr. Jean Alexander), *Revue de Paris*, March–April 1852, pp. 90–110.
37. George Gilfillan, "Edgar Poe," A *Third Gallery of Portraits*, 1854, pp. 380–88.
38. Edmund Clarence Stedman, "Edgar Allan Poe," *Poets of America*, 1885, pp. 225–28, 248–64.
39. George E. Woodberry, "The End of the Play," *Edgar Allan Poe*, 1885, pp. 286–301.
40. Charles Whibley, "Edgar Allan Poe," *New Review*, January 1896, pp. 617–25.
41. Lewis E. Gates, "Edgar Allan Poe," *Studies and Appreciations*, 1900, pp. 110–28.

ANNE BRONTË

1. Anne Brontë, "Last Lines," 1849.
2. Charlotte Brontë, "Preface" (c. 1850) to *The Complete Poems of Anne Brontë*, ed. Clement K. Shorter, 1920.
3. Charlotte Brontë, "Biographical Notice of Ellis and Acton Bell," *Wuthering Heights and Agnes Grey*, 1850.
4. Augustine Birrell, *Life of Charlotte Brontë*, 1887, p. 92.
5. Clement K. Shorter, *Charlotte Brontë and Her Circle*, 1896, pp. 181–84.
6. Angus M. MacKay, *The Brontës: Fact and Fiction*, 1897, pp. 20–21.
7. Hugh Walker, *The Age of Tennyson*, 1897, p. 102.
8. Anne Brontë, "Preface" to *The Tenant of Wildfell Hall*, 1848.
9. Henry F. Chorley, *Athenaeum*, July 8, 1848, pp. 670–71.
10. Edwin P. Whipple, "Novels of the Season," *North American Review*, October 1848, pp. 359–60.
11. Margaret Sweat, "Charlotte Brontë and the Brontë Novels," *North American Review*, October 1857, pp. 328–29.
12. Algernon Charles Swinburne, "Emily Brontë" (1883), *Miscellanies*, 1886, p. 264.
13. Charles Kingsley, "Recent Novels," *Fraser's Magazine*, April 1849, pp. 423–26.

14. Mary A. Ward, "Introduction" to *The Tenant of Wildfell Hall*, 1900, pp. ix–xix.

WILLIAM LISLE BOWLES

1. Thomas Moore, *Journal*, September 1, 1818.
2. Maria Edgeworth, Letter to Mrs. Edgeworth (c. September 1818).
3. George Gordon, Lord Byron, "Letter to —— ——, Esqre, on the Rev. W. L. Bowles's Strictures on the Life and Writings of Pope," 1821.
4. S. C. Hall, *Retrospect of a Long Life*, 1883, pp. 314–15.
5. Samuel Taylor Coleridge, "To the Rev. W. L. Bowles" (1894), *Sonnets on Eminent Characters*, 1794–95.
6. George Gordon, Lord Byron, *English Bards and Scotch Reviewers*, 1809, ll. 327–84.
7. Samuel Taylor Coleridge, *Biographia Literaria*, 1817, Ch. 1.
8. John Wilson, "An Hour's Talk about Poetry," *Blackwood's Edinburgh Magazine*, September 1831, pp. 475–76.
9. Robert Southey, Letter to William Lisle Bowles (July 30, 1832).
10. David Macbeth Moir, *Sketches of the Poetical Literature of the Past Half-Century*, 1851, pp. 54–57.
11. John A. Heraud, "William Lisle Bowles," *Temple Bar*, June 1863, p. 446.
12. Austin Dobson, "William Lisle Bowles," *The English Poets*, ed. Thomas Humphry Ward, 1880, Volume 4, p. 99.
13. William Tirebuck, "Introduction" to *The Poetical Works of Bowles, Lamb, and Hartley Coleridge*, 1887, pp. vii–xiv.

WILLIAM WORDSWORTH

1. Dorothy Wordsworth, *Journal*, January 29, 1802.
2. Henry Crabb Robinson, *Diary*, May 8, 1812.
3. Robert Southey, Letter to Bernard Barton (December 19, 1814).
4. John Gibson Lockhart, "Letters from the Lakes," *Blackwood's Edinburgh Magazine*, March 1819, pp. 739–40.
5. George Ticknor, *Journal* (March 21, 1819), *Life, Letters, and Journals of George Ticknor*, ed. Anna Ticknor, 1876, Volume 1, p. 287.
6. Charles Mayne Young, *Journal* (July 6, 1828), cited in Julian Charles Young, A *Memoir of Charles Mayne Young*, 1871, pp. 112–15.
7. John Wilson (as "Christopher North"), *Noctes Ambrosianae* (November 1832), 1854.
8. Thomas De Quincey, "The Lake Poets: William Wordsworth" (1839), *Collected Writings*, ed. David Masson, Volume 2, pp. 242–43.
9. Robert Browning, "The Lost Leader," *Dramatic Romances and Lyrics*, 1845.
10. Leigh Hunt, *Autobiography*, 1850, Ch. 15.
11. Ralph Waldo Emerson, "First Visit to England," *English Traits*, 1856.
12. Thomas Carlyle, "Appendix" (1867), *Reminiscences*, ed. James Anthony Froude, 1881, Volume 2, pp. 338–41.
13. Charles Burney, *Monthly Review*, June 1799, p. 210.
14. Robert Southey, Letter to John Rickman (March 30, 1804).
15. George Gordon, Lord Byron, *English Bards and Scotch Reviewers*, 1809, ll. 235–54.
16. Charles Lamb, William Gifford, "Wordsworth's *Excursion*," *Quarterly Review*, October 1814, pp. 110–11.
17. Sydney Smith, Letter to Francis, Lord Jeffrey (December 30, 1814).
18. John Keats, "Addressed to Haydon," 1816.
19. William Hazlitt, *Lectures on the English Poets*, 1818.

6. Nathaniel Hawthorne, *The French and Italian Note-Books*, April 3, 1858.
7. C. P. Cranch, "Ode," *Atlantic*, August 1870, pp. 232–33.
8. Harriet Martineau, *Autobiography*, ed. Maria Weston Chapman, 1877, Volume 1, p. 381.
9. A. Bronson Alcott, *Sonnets and Canzonets*, 1882, p. 113.
10. George William Curtis, "Editor's Easy Chair," *Harper's New Monthly Magazine*, March 1882, p. 627.
11. M. E. W. Sherwood, *An Epistle to Posterity*, 1897, pp. 37–38.
12. Edgar Allan Poe, "Sarah Margaret Fuller" (1846), *Essays and Reviews*, ed. G. R. Thompson, 1984, pp. 1172–77.
13. Thomas Carlyle, Letter to Ralph Waldo Emerson (March 2, 1847).
14. Rufus W. Griswold, "S. Margaret Fuller," *The Female Poets of America*, 1848, p. 251.
15. Thomas Powell, "S. Margaret Fuller," *The Living Authors of America*, 1850, p. 318.
16. Matthew Arnold, Letter to Arthur Hugh Clough (March 21, 1853).
17. Frederick Henry Hedge, "Madame Ossoli's *At Home and Abroad*," *North American Review*, July 1856, pp. 261–62.
18. Caroline H. Dall, "Margaret Fuller Ossoli," *North American Review*, July 1860, pp. 126–28.
19. Julia Ward Howe, *Margaret Fuller*, 1883, pp. 219–21.
20. Thomas Westworth Higginson, *Margaret Fuller Ossoli*, 1884, pp. 286–91.
21. Charles F. Richardson, *American Literature, 1607–1885*, 1887, Volume 1, pp. 431–34.
22. Helen Grey Cone, "Woman in American Literature," *Century Magazine*, October 1890, pp. 924–25.
23. Fred Lewis Pattee, *A History of American Literature*, 1896, pp. 231–34.
24. Katharine Lee Bates, *American Literature*, 1897, pp. 221–24.
25. Horace Greeley, *Memoirs of Margaret Fuller Ossoli*, 1852, Volume 2, pp. 155–57.
26. Edward Everett Hale, "Woman in the Nineteenth Century," *North American Review*, October 1855, pp. 557–59.
27. Horace Greeley, "Introduction" to *Woman in the Nineteenth Century*, 1874, p. x.

JOANNA BAILLIE

1. Henry Crabb Robinson, *Diary*, May 24, 1812.
2. Sara Coleridge, Letter to Samuel Taylor Coleridge (September 4, 1834), *Memoir and Letters of Sara Coleridge*, ed. Edith Coleridge, 1873, Volume 1, pp. 92–93.
3. George Ticknor, *Journal* (April 17, 1838), *Life, Letters, and Journals of George Ticknor*, ed. Anna Ticknor, 1876, Volume 2, p. 153.
4. Eliza Farrar, *Recollections of Seventy Years*, 1866, pp. 74–75.
5. Sir Henry Holland, *Recollections of Past Life*, 1871, p. 246.
6. Harriet Martineau, *Autobiography*, ed. Maria Weston Chapman, 1877, Volume 1, pp. 270–71.
7. Mary Berry, *Journal* (March 12, 1799).
8. Francis, Lord Jeffrey, "Miss Baillie's *Plays on the Passions*," *Edinburgh Review*, July 1803, pp. 272–86.
9. Sir Walter Scott, *Marmion*, 1808, Canto 3, Introduction.
10. William Hazlitt, *Lectures on the English Poets*, 1818.
11. Hester Lynch Piozzi, Letter to Sir James Fellowes (March 28, 1819).
12. Ebenezer Elliott, *Love*, 1823, Bk. 1.
13. John Wilson, "An Hour's Talk about Poetry" (1831), *The Recreations of Christopher North*, 1842, p. 79.

14. William H. Prescott, "English Literature of the Nineteenth Century," *North American Review*, July 1832, p. 179.
15. Thomas Campbell, *Life of Mrs. Siddons*, 1834, Ch. 17.
16. William C. Macready, *Diary*, February 17, 1836.
17. Rufus W. Griswold, "Joanna Baillie," *The Poets and Poetry of England in the Nineteenth Century*, 1844, p. 40.
18. Hartley Coleridge, "To Joanna Baillie," c. 1849.
19. Mary Russell Mitford, *Recollections of a Literary Life*, 1851, p. 152.
20. Charles D. Cleveland, *English Literature of the Nineteenth Century*, 1853, pp. 545–47.
21. Richard Holt Hutton, *Sir Walter Scott*, 1879, p. 91.
22. A. Mary F. Robinson, "Joanna Baillie," *The English Poets*, ed. Thomas Humphry Ward, 1880, Volume 4, pp. 221–22.
23. Eric S. Robertson, *English Poetesses*, 1883, p. 174.
24. C. H. Herford, *The Age of Wordsworth*, 1897, pp. 141–42.
25. Margaret Oliphant, *The Literary History of England, 1790–1825*, 1882, Volume 2, pp. 324–34.

JOHN JAMES AUDUBON

1. John Keats, Letter to George and Georgiana Keats (September 17, 1819).
2. James Grant Wilson, "Introduction" to *The Life of John James Audubon* by Lucy Green Audubon, 1869, p. v.
3. Thomas M. Brewer, "Reminiscences of John James Audubon," *Harper's New Monthly Magazine*, October 1880, pp. 667–68.
4. John Wilson (as "Christopher North"), *Noctes Ambrosianae* (January 1827), 1854.
5. John Wilson, "Audubon's *Ornithological Biography*," *Blackwood's Edinburgh Magazine*, July 1831, pp. 14–16.
6. Washington Irving, Letter to Martin Van Buren (October 19, 1836), cited in Lucy Green Audubon, *The Life of John James Audubon*, 1869, pp. 394–95.
7. John Seely Hart, *A Manual of American Literature*, 1872, pp. 120–21.
8. Francis H. Underwood, *A Hand-Book of English Literature*, 1872, p. 68.
9. John Burroughs, "The Birds of the Poets," *Scribner's Monthly*, September 1873, p. 565.
10. Frederick Saunders, *The Story of Some Famous Books*, 1887, pp. 141–44.
11. Louise Manly, *Southern Literature*, 1895, p. 155.
12. C. H. Merriam, "Audubon," *Nation*, February 24, 1898, pp. 151–52.
13. Parke Godwin, "John James Audubon" (1853), *Commemorative Addresses*, 1895, pp. 149–51, 182–87.

JAMES FENIMORE COOPER

1. Sir Walter Scott, *Journal*, November 3, 1826.
2. Edgar Allan Poe, "A Chapter on Autography" (1841), *Complete Works*, ed. James A. Harrison, 1902, Volume 15, p. 205.
3. Samuel Griswold Goodrich, *Recollections of a Lifetime*, 1856, Letter 36.
4. Horace Greeley, *Recollections of a Busy Life*, 1868, p. 261.
5. Maunsell B. Field, *Memories of Many Men and Some Women*, 1873, p. 178.
6. S. C. Hall, *Retrospect of a Long Life*, 1883, pp. 227–28.
7. William Hazlitt, "American Literature—Dr. Channing," *Edinburgh Review*, October 1829, pp. 128–29.
8. John Gibson Lockhart, "Cooper's *England*," *Quarterly Review*, October 1837, p. 330.

5. Caroline Fox, *Journal* (July 9, 1857), *Memories of Old Friends*, ed. Horace N. Pym, 1881, p. 336.
6. Harriet Martineau, *Autobiography*, ed. Maria Weston Chapman, 1877, Volume 2, p. 24.
7. Millicent Garrett Fawcett, *Some Eminent Women of Our Times*, 1889, p. 109.
8. Anne Thackeray Ritchie, "My Witches' Caldron," *Macmillan's Magazine*, February 1891, pp. 251–52.
9. William Wright, *The Brontës in Ireland*, 1893, pp. 15–16.
10. Clement K. Shorter, *The Brontës and Their Circle*, 1896, p. 21.
11. Peter Bayne, "Currer Bell," *Essays in Biography*, 1857, pp. 409–15.
12. Celia Thaxter, Letter to Elizabeth Hoxie (March 28, 1857).
13. A. Mary F. Robinson, *Emily Brontë*, 1883, pp. 5–6.
14. Anthony Trollope, *An Autobiography*, 1883, Ch. 13.
15. Andrew Lang, "Charlotte Brontë," *Good Words*, 1889, p. 239.
16. Frederic Harrison, "Charlotte Brontë's Place in Literature," *Forum*, March 1895, pp. 30–40.
17. George Saintsbury, "Three Mid-Century Novelists," *Corrected Impressions*, 1895, pp. 157–62.
18. Angus M. MacKay, *The Brontës: Fact and Fiction*, 1897, pp. 40–42.
19. Hugh Walker, *The Age of Tennyson*, 1897, pp. 103–6.
20. Francis Hovey Stoddard, *The Evolution of the English Novel*, 1900, pp. 62–65.
21. Charlotte Brontë (as "Currer Bell"), Letter to Messrs. Smith, Elder & Co. (August 24, 1847).
22. Sir George Murray Smith, "In the Early Forties," *Critic*, January 1901, p. 52.
23. Henry F. Chorley, *Athenaeum*, October 23, 1847, pp. 1100–1101.
24. John Gibson Lockhart, Letter to Mrs. Hope (December 29, 1847), cited in Andrew Lang, *The Life and Letters of John Gibson Lockhart*, 1897, Volume 2, p. 310.
25. George Eliot, Letter to Charles Bray (June 11, 1848).
26. Edwin P. Whipple, "Novels of the Season," *North American Review*, October 1848, pp. 355–57.
27. William Makepeace Thackeray, "The Last Sketch," *Cornhill Magazine*, April 1860, p. 487.
28. James Russell Lowell, Letter to Charles Eliot Norton (July 8, 1867).
29. Algernon Charles Swinburne, *A Note on Charlotte Brontë*, 1877, pp. 26–28.
30. Queen Victoria, *Journal*, November 23, 1880.
31. Augustine Birrell, *Life of Charlotte Brontë*, 1887, pp. 105–8.
32. Elizabeth Barrett Browning, Letter to Mrs. Jameson (April 2, 1850).
33. Charles Kingsley, Letter to Elizabeth Gaskell (May 14, 1857).
34. Wilbur L. Cross, *The Development of the English Novel*, 1899, pp. 231–32.
35. Harriet Martineau, *Daily News*, February 3, 1853, p. 2.
36. George Eliot, Letter to Mrs. Charles Bray (February 15, 1853).
37. Bryan Waller Procter, Letter to James T. Fields (February 1853), cited in James T. Fields, "'Barry Cornwall' and Some of His Friends," *Harper's New Monthly Magazine*, December 1875, p. 60.
38. Matthew Arnold, Letter to Mrs. Forster (April 14, 1853).
39. George Henry Lewes, "*Ruth* and *Villette*," *Westminster Review*, April 1853, pp. 485–90.
40. Catharine M. Sedgwick, Letter to Dr. Dewey (April 1853), cited in Mary E. Dewey, *Life and Letters of Catharine M. Sedgwick*, 1871, p. 349.

41. Margaret Oliphant, *The Victorian Age of English Literature*, 1892, Volume 1, pp. 307–8.
42. Elizabeth Rigby, "*Vanity Fair* and *Jane Eyre*," *Quarterly Review*, December 1848, pp. 165–76.
43. George Henry Lewes, "Currer Bell's *Shirley*," *Edinburgh Review*, January 1850, pp. 158–61.
44. John Skelton, "Charlotte Brontë," *Fraser's Magazine*, May 1857, pp. 579–82.
45. T. Wemyss Reid, *Charlotte Brontë: A Monograph*, 1877, pp. 7–13, 219–25.
46. James Oliphant, *Victorian Novelists*, 1899, pp. 72–77.
47. Lewis E. Gates, "Charlotte Brontë," *Studies and Appreciations*, 1900, pp. 129–62.

SIR WILLIAM HAMILTON

1. Anne Grant, Letter to Her Sister (July 26, 1820), *Memoir and Correspondence of Mrs. Grant and Laggan*, ed. J. P. Grant, 1844, Volume 2, pp. 267–68.
2. Thomas De Quincey, "Sir William Hamilton" (1852), *Collected Writings*, ed. David Masson, Volume 5, pp. 314–15.
3. Thomas Carlyle, Letter to John Veitch (February 19, 1868), cited in John Veitch, *Memoir of Sir William Hamilton*, 1869, pp. 121–25.
4. W. H. S. Monck, *Sir William Hamilton*, 1881, pp. 12–13.
5. Francis, Lord Jeffrey, Letter to Macvey Napier (November 23, 1829), *Selection from the Correspondence of Macvey Napier*, ed. Macvey Napier, 1879, p. 70.
6. Edwin P. Whipple, "British Critics" (1845), *Essays and Reviews*, 1850, Volume 2, pp. 117–19.
7. James Martineau, "Sir W. Hamilton's Philosophy" (1853), *Essays, Philosophical and Theological*, 1868, Volume 2, pp. 233–34.
8. William MacCall, *The New Materialism*, 1873.
9. James McCosh, *The Scottish Philosophy*, 1874, p. 417.
10. J. H. Millar, "Sir William Hamilton," *English Prose*, ed. Henry Craik, 1896, Volume 5, pp. 331–33.
11. John Stuart Mill, "Concluding Remarks," *An Examination of Sir William Hamilton's Philosophy*, 1865, Volume 2, pp. 337–54.

JOHN WILSON CROKER

1. Charles Cavendish Fulke Greville, *Diary*, September 6, 1857.
2. Louis J. Jennings, *The Croker Papers*, 1884, Volume 1, pp. 1–4.
3. John Wilson (as "Christopher North"), *Noctes Ambrosianae* (March 1823), 1854.
4. T. E. Kebbel, "John Wilson Croker," *Fortnightly Review*, November 1884, pp. 688–89.
5. Algernon Charles Swinburne, "Social Verse" (1891), *Studies in Prose and Poetry*, 1894, p. 108.
6. P. A. Sillard, "John Wilson Croker," *Gentleman's Magazine*, August 1898, pp. 157–58.
7. Thomas Babington Macaulay, "Samuel Johnson" (1831), *Critical, Historical, and Miscellaneous Essays*, 1860, Volume 2, pp. 368–69.
8. George Birkbeck Hill, "Preface" to *Boswell's Life of Johnson*, 1887, Volume 1, pp. xxii–xxiii.
9. W. E. Henley, "Boswell," *Views and Reviews*, 1890, p. 194.
10. A. V. Dicey, "John Wilson Croker," *Nation*, February 5, 1885, pp. 122–23.

DOUGLAS JERROLD

1. Nathaniel Hawthorne, *The English Note-Books*, April 5, 1856.

2. Hepworth Dixon, *Athenaeum*, December 25, 1858, pp. 830–31.
3. David Masson, *British Novelists and Their Styles*, 1859, pp. 235–37.
4. Charles Dickens, Letter to Blanchard Jerrold (c. 1859), cited in Blanchard Jerrold, *The Life and Remains of Douglas Jerrold*, 1859, pp. 356–57.
5. Harriet Martineau, *Autobiography*, ed. Maria Weston Chapman, 1877, Volume 2, p. 32.
6. Charles Dickens, Letter to Douglas Jerrold (May 3, 1843).
7. James Hannay, "Douglas Jerrold," *Atlantic*, November 1857, pp. 5–7.
8. Edward Copping, "Douglas Jerrold," *New Review*, September 1892, pp. 363–64.
9. G. S. Phillips, "Douglas Jerrold," *North American Review*, October 1859, pp. 431–39.
10. Wilkie Collins, "Douglas Jerrold" (1863), *My Miscellanies*, 1875, pp. 393–96.

RUFUS WILMOT GRISWOLD

1. James Russell Lowell, *A Fable for Critics*, 1848.
2. Charles D. Cleveland, "Rufus Wilmot Griswold," *A Compendium of American Literature*, 1859, p. 690.
3. Edgar Allan Poe, "Rufus W. Griswold" (1842), *Essays and Reviews*, ed. G. R. Thompson, 1984, pp. 553–56.
4. Edwin P. Whipple, "Griswold's *Poets and Poetry of America*," *North American Review*, January 1844, pp. 1–3.
5. Andrew P. Peabody, "American Poetry," *North American Review*, January 1856, pp. 236–37.
6. George E. Woodberry, *Edgar Allan Poe*, 1885, p. 172.
7. Oliver Wendell Holmes, Letter to John Greenleaf Whittier (1891), cited in Samuel T. Pickard, *Life and Letters of John Greenleaf Whittier*, 1895, Volume 2, p. 756.
8. Henry Binney Wallace, "Literary Criticisms," *Literary Criticisms and Other Papers*, 1846, pp. 3–4.
9. John H. Ingram, *Edgar Allan Poe: His Life, Letters and Opinions*, 1880, Volume 2, pp. 242–43.
10. J. S. Redfield, cited in James Cephas Derby, *Fifty Years among Authors, Books and Publishers*, 1884, pp. 587–88.
11. Charles Godfrey Leland, *Memoirs*, 1893, pp. 201–2.
12. George E. Woodberry, "Poe in the South," *Century Magazine*, August 1894, pp. 572–73.

HENRY HALLAM

1. George Ticknor, *Journal* (March 24, 1838), *Life, Letters, and Journals of George Ticknor*, ed. Anna Ticknor, 1876, Volume 2, pp. 144–45.
2. John Lothrop Motley, Letter to His Wife (June 6, 1858), *Correspondence*, ed. George William Curtis, 1889, Volume 1, pp. 251–52.
3. Harriet Martineau, "Henry Hallam" (1859), *Biographical Sketches*, 1869, pp. 84–85.
4. Marguerite, Countess of Blessington, *Conversations of Lord Byron*, 1834.
5. Thomas Babington Macaulay, "Sir James Mackintosh" (1835), *Critical, Historical, and Miscellaneous Essays*, 1860, Volume 3, p. 259.
6. George Gilfillan, "Hazlitt and Hallam," *A Third Gallery of Portraits*, 1854, p. 182.
7. W. Macneile Dixon, "Henry Hallam," *English Prose*, ed. Henry Craik, 1896, Volume 5, pp. 185–87.
8. Robert Southey, "Hallam's *Constitutional History of England*," *Quarterly Review*, January 1828, pp. 259–60.
9. Thomas Babington Macaulay, "Hallam" (1828), *Critical, Historical, and Miscellaneous Essays*, 1860, Volume 1, pp. 435–36.
10. William Smyth, *Lectures on Modern History*, 1840, Note to Lecture 6.

11. Sir George Cornewall Lewis, Letter to E. W. Head (June 2, 1837), *Letters*, ed. Sir Gilbert Frankland Lewis, 1870, p. 80.
12. William Ellery Channing, Letter to Lucy Aikin (April 28, 1839), *Correspondence of William Ellery Channing and Lucy Aikin*, ed. Anna Letitia Le Breton, 1874, p. 338.
13. Francis Bowen, "Hallam's *Introduction to the Literature of Europe*," *North American Review*, January 1843, pp. 47–48.
14. Ralph Waldo Emerson, "Literature," *English Traits*, 1856.
15. Augustine Birrell, "Good Taste," *Scribner's Magazine*, January 1895, p. 119.
16. C. C. Smith, "Hallam as an Historian," *North American Review*, January 1861, pp. 166–77.

WASHINGTON IRVING

1. Fanny Kemble, Letter (April 10, 1833), *Record of a Girlhood*, 1878, p. 572.
2. Charles Dickens, Letter to Washington Irving (1841), cited in Pierre M. Irving, *The Life and Letters of Washington Irving*, 1862–63, Volume 3, pp. 164–65.
3. Oliver Wendell Holmes, *Proceedings of the Massachusetts Historical Society*, December 1859, p. 420.
4. William Makepeace Thackeray, "Nil Nisi Bonum" (1860), *Roundabout Papers*, 1863.
5. S. C. Hall, *Retrospect of a Long Life*, 1883, p. 421.
6. William Hazlitt, "Elia, and Geoffrey Crayon," *The Spirit of the Age*, 1825.
7. Alexander Hill Everett, "Irving's *Life of Columbus*," *North American Review*, January 1829, pp. 113–15.
8. Edgar Allan Poe, "A Chapter on Autography" (1841), *Complete Works*, ed. James A. Harrison, 1902, Volume 15, p. 182.
9. Charles Dickens, Speech at Banquet in His Honour, New York (February 18, 1842).
10. Edgar Allan Poe, "Nathaniel Hawthorne" (1842), *Essays and Reviews*, ed. G. R. Thompson, 1984, pp. 570–71.
11. James Russell Lowell, *A Fable for Critics*, 1848.
12. Mary Russell Mitford, *Recollections of a Literary Life*, 1851, p. 516.
13. Henry Wadsworth Longfellow, *Proceedings of the Massachusetts Historical Society*, December 1859, pp. 393–94.
14. Edward Everett, *Proceedings of the Massachusetts Historical Society*, December 1859, pp. 399–400.
15. William Cullen Bryant, "Washington Irving" (1860), *Prose Writings*, ed. Parke Godwin, 1884, Volume 1, pp. 364–66.
16. Walter Savage Landor, "*On the Widow's Ordeal* by Washington Irving," 1863.
17. Walter Savage Landor, Letter to Rose Graves-Sawle (January 19, 1863).
18. Edward Dowden, "The Poetry of Democracy: Walt Whitman," *Studies in Literature*, 1878, p. 470.
19. Edmund Gosse, "Irving's *Sketch-Book*," *Critic*, March 31, 1883, pp. 140–41.
20. A. G. Sedgwick, "Washington Irving," *Nation*, April 5, 1883, pp. 291–92.
21. Edwin P. Whipple, "American Literature" (1886), *American Literature and Other Papers*, 1887, pp. 42–45.
22. William Dean Howells, "Irving," *My Literary Passions*, 1895.
23. J. H. Millar, "Washington Irving," *English Prose*, ed. Henry Craik, 1896, Volume 5, pp. 233–35.
24. Sir Walter Scott, Letter to Henry Brevoort (April 23, 1813).
25. Washington Irving, "The Author's Apology," *A History of New York*, 1848.

10. C. W. Upham, "Prescott as an Historian," *North American Review*, July 1856, p. 101.
11. George Ticknor, *Life of William Hickling Prescott*, 1864, pp. 217–18.
12. Robert C. Winthrop, *Journal* (November 17, 1880), cited in Robert C. Winthrop, Jr., A *Memoir of Robert C. Winthrop*, 1897, p. 303.
13. John Nichol, *American Literature*, 1882, pp. 147–50.
14. Fred Lewis Pattee, A *History of American Literature*, 1896, pp. 309–10.
15. Henry S. Pancoast, *An Introduction to American Literature*, 1898, pp. 229–30.
16. Barrett Wendell, A *Literary History of America*, 1900, pp. 269–71.
17. H. H. Milman, "Prescott's *History of the Conquest of Mexico*," *Quarterly Review*, December 1843, p. 188.
18. Charles Dickens, Letter to C. C. Felton (January 2, 1844).
19. Washington Irving, Letter to Pierre M. Irving (March 24, 1844), cited in Pierre M. Irving, *The Life and Letters of Washington Irving*, 1863, Volume 3, pp. 143–44.
20. Charles Phillipps, "Prescott's *Conquest of Mexico*," *Edinburgh Review*, April 1845, pp. 434–35.
21. Thomas Babington Macaulay, *Journal* (November 27, 1855), cited in G. Otto Trevelyan, *The Life and Letters of Lord Macaulay*, 1876, Volume 2, p. 323.
22. François Pierre Guillaume Guizot, "Philip II and His Times: Prescott and Motley," *Edinburgh Review*, January 1857, p. 44.
23. Sir William Stirling-Maxwell, "William Hickling Prescott" (1859), *Miscellaneous Essays and Addresses*, 1891, p. 73.
24. Edwin P. Whipple, "Prescott's Histories" (1848), *Essays and Reviews*, 1850, Volume 2, pp. 154–67.
25. Edward Everett Hale, Jr., "William Hickling Prescott," *American Prose*, ed. George Rice Carpenter, 1898, pp. 172–75.

THOMAS BABINGTON MACAULAY

1. Hannah More, Letter to Zachary Macaulay (June 28, 1808), *Letters of Hannah More to Zachary Macaulay*, ed. Arthur Roberts, 1860, pp. 26–27.
2. Henry Crabb Robinson, *Diary*, November 29, 1826.
3. Thomas Carlyle, *Journal* (January 13, 1832), cited in James Anthony Froude, *Thomas Carlyle*, 1882, Volume 2, pp. 186–87.
4. Charles Cavendish Fulke Greville, *Diary*, February 6, 1832.
5. Thomas Moore, *Journal*, October 21, 1840.
6. Henry, Lord Brougham, Letter to Macvey Napier (August 14, 1842), *Selection from the Correspondence of the Late Macvey Napier*, ed. Macvey Napier, 1879, p. 403.
7. Nathaniel Hawthorne, *The English Note-Books*, July 13, 1856.
8. John Lothrop Motley, Letter to His Wife (May 30, 1858), *Correspondence*, ed. George William Curtis, 1889, Volume 1, pp. 236–37.
9. Alfred, Lord Tennyson, Letter to the Duke of Argyll (1860), cited in Hallam Tennyson, *Alfred Lord Tennyson: A Memoir*, 1897, Volume 1, p. 458.
10. Harriet Martineau, *Autobiography*, ed. Maria Weston Chapman, 1877, Volume 1, pp. 261–62.
11. Edgar Allan Poe, "Thomas Babington Macaulay" (1841), *Essays and Reviews*, ed. G. R. Thompson, 1984, pp. 321–24.
12. Ralph Waldo Emerson, "Literature," *English Traits*, 1856.
13. Harriet Martineau, *Autobiography*, ed. Maria Weston Chapman, 1877, Volume 1, pp. 262–64.
14. Augustine Birrell, "Carlyle," *Obiter Dicta*, 1885, pp. 29–32.
15. W. P. Ker, "Thomas Babington Macaulay," *English Prose*, ed. Henry Craik, 1896, Volume 5, pp. 411–18.
16. John Wilson (as "Christopher North"), *Noctes Ambrosianae* (August 1831), 1854.
17. John Wilson Croker, Speech in the House of Commons on the Reform Bill (September 22, 1831), *The Croker Papers*, ed. Louis J. Jennings, 1885, Volume 2, pp. 130–31.
18. James Grant, *Random Recollections of the House of Commons*, 1836, pp. 176–78.
19. H. H. Milman, *Proceedings of the Royal Society of Literature*, 1860–62, Volume 11, pp. xix–xx.
20. Thomas Carlyle, *Journal* (November 1, 1833), cited in James Anthony Froude, *Thomas Carlyle*, 1882, Volume 2, p. 301.
21. Thomas Babington Macaulay, Letter to Macvey Napier (November 26, 1836), *Selection from the Correspondence of the Late Macvey Napier*, ed. Macvey Napier, 1879, pp. 180–81.
22. Henry, Lord Brougham, Letter to Macvey Napier (July 28, 1837), *Selection from the Correspondence of the Late Macvey Napier*, ed. Macvey Napier, 1879, pp. 196–97.
23. Matthew Arnold, "A French Critic on Milton" (1877), *Mixed Essays*, 1879.
24. John Wilson, "*Lays of Ancient Rome*," *Blackwood's Edinburgh Magazine*, December 1842, pp. 805–7, 823–24.
25. John Stuart Mill, "Macaulay's *Lays of Ancient Rome*," *Westminster Review*, February 1843, pp. 105–6.
26. Walter Savage Landor, "To Macaulay," 1846.
27. Edward A. Freeman, "A Review of My Opinions," *Forum*, April 1892, pp. 152–53.
28. Francis, Lord Jeffrey, Letter to Thomas Babington Macaulay (1848), cited in G. Otto Trevelyan, *The Life and Letters of Lord Macaulay*, 1876, Volume 2, pp. 205–6.
29. John Gibson Lockhart, Letter to John Wilson Croker (January 12, 1849), *The Croker Papers*, ed. Louis J. Jennings, 1885, Volume 3, pp. 194–95.
30. Henry Greville, *Diary*, February 7, 1849.
31. Sir Archibald Alison, "Macaulay's *History of England*," *Blackwood's Edinburgh Magazine*, April 1849, pp. 387–90.
32. Maria Edgeworth, Letter to Dr. Holland (April 2, 1849), cited in Helen Zimmern, *Maria Edgeworth*, 1884, pp. 299–300.
33. Leopold von Ranke, *History of England*, 1875, Volume 6, p. 144.
34. Woodrow Wilson, *Mere Literature and Other Essays*, 1896, pp. 167–69.
35. John Wilson Croker, "Mr. Macaulay's *History of England*," *Quarterly Review*, October 1849, pp. 549–53, 629–30.
36. Walter Bagehot, "Mr. Macaulay" (1856), *Collected Works*, ed. Norman St. John-Stevas, 1965, Volume 1, pp. 421–28.
37. Sir Leslie Stephen, "Macaulay," *Hours in a Library* (1874–79), 1904, Volume 3, pp. 237–71.
38. William Ewart Gladstone, "Lord Macaulay," *Quarterly Review*, July 1876, pp. 15–24.
39. A. V. Dicey, "Macaulay and His Critics," *Nation*, May 15, 1902, pp. 388–89.

G. P. R. JAMES

1. John Wilson (as "Christopher North"), *Noctes Ambrosianae* (April 1830), 1854.
2. Thomas De Quincey, "Charlemagne" (1832), *Collected Writings*, ed. David Masson, Volume 5, p. 362.

cited in Julian Hawthorne, *Nathaniel Hawthorne and His Wife*, 1884, Volume 2, p. 241.
58. William Ellery Channing, Letter to Nathaniel Hawthorne (September 3, 1860), cited in Julian Hawthorne, *Nathaniel Hawthorne and His Wife*, 1884, Volume 2, p. 265.
59. James Russell Lowell, "Swinburne's Tragedies" (1866), *Works*, Riverside ed., Volume 2, pp. 125–26.
60. George Parsons Lathrop, A *Study of Hawthorne*, 1876, pp. 260–61.
61. Arthur Sherburne Hardy, "Hawthorne's Italian Romance," *Book Buyer*, November 1889, pp. 427–28.
62. Katharine Lee Bates, *American Literature*, 1897, pp. 314–15.
63. Richard Holt Hutton, "Nathaniel Hawthorne," *Literary Essays*, 1871, pp. 437–58.
64. Sir Leslie Stephen, "Nathaniel Hawthorne" (1875), *Hours in a Library* (1874–79), 1904, Volume 1, pp. 244–70.
65. Henry James, *Hawthorne*, 1879, pp. 106–17.
66. Anthony Trollope, "The Genius of Nathaniel Hawthorne," *North American Review*, September 1879, pp. 204–22.

RICHARD COBDEN

1. Charles Cavendish Fulke Greville, *Diary*, February 8, 1848.
2. Caroline Fox, *Journal* (June 12, 1849), *Memories of Old Friends*, ed. Horace N. Pym, 1882, p. 265.
3. Charles Sumner, Letter to John Bright (April 18, 1865), cited in Edward L. Pierce, *Memoir and Letters of Charles Sumner*, 1893, Volume 4, p. 239.
4. John McGilchrist, *Richard Cobden*, 1865, p. 262.
5. William Cullen Bryant, "Introduction to the American Edition" to *The Political Writings of Richard Cobden*, 1867.
6. Arthur James Balfour, "Morley's *Life of Cobden*," *Nineteenth Century*, January 1882, p. 54.
7. James Cotter Morison, "*The Life of Richard Cobden* by John Morley," *Macmillan's Magazine*, January 1882, p. 213.
8. Richard Gowing, *Richard Cobden*, 1886, pp. 127–28.
9. Sidney Low, "The Decline of Cobdenism," *Nineteenth Century*, August 1896, p. 184.
10. Walter Bagehot, "Mr. Cobden" (1865), *Collected Works*, ed. Norman St. John-Stevas, 1968, Volume 3, pp. 294–97.
11. John Morley, *The Life of Richard Cobden*, 1881.

ELIZABETH GASKELL

1. Walter Savage Landor, "To the Author of *Mary Barton*," 1849.
2. George Eliot, Letter to Mrs. Taylor (February 1, 1853).
3. Charles Kingsley, Letter to Elizabeth Gaskell (July 25, 1853), *Charles Kingsley: His Letters and Memories of His Life*, ed. Fanny E. Kingsley, 1877, pp. 180–81.
4. Elizabeth Barrett Browning, Letter to Mrs. Martin (October 5, 1853).
5. Charles Kingsley, Letter to Elizabeth Gaskell (May 14, 1857), *Charles Kingsley: His Letters and Memories of His Life*, ed. Fanny E. Kingsley, 1877, pp. 269–70.
6. Anne Thackeray Ritchie, "Preface" to *Cranford*, 1891, pp. xvi–xx.
7. Margaret Oliphant, *The Victorian Age of English Literature*, 1892, Volume 1, pp. 326–28.
8. George Saintsbury, A *History of Nineteenth Century Literature*, 1896, p. 335.
9. Clement K. Shorter, *Charlotte Brontë and Her Circle*, 1896, pp. 1, 20.

10. Adolphus William Ward, "Mrs. Gaskell," *English Prose*, ed. Henry Criak, 1896, Volume 5, pp. 523–24.
11. Edmund Gosse, A *Short History of Modern English Literature*, 1897, pp. 355–56.
12. Hugh Walker, *The Age of Tennyson*, 1897, pp. 106–8.
13. Wilbur L. Cross, *The Development of the English Novel*, 1899, pp. 234–36.
14. George Barnett Smith, "Mrs. Gaskell and Her Novels," *Cornhill Magazine*, February 1874, pp. 194–212.
15. William Minto, "Mrs. Gaskell's Novels," *Fortnightly Review*, September 1878, pp. 355–69.
16. Mat Hompes, "Mrs. Gaskell," *Gentleman's Magazine*, August 1895, pp. 133–37.

THOMAS LOVE PEACOCK

1. William Makepeace Thackeray, Letter to Mrs. Brookfield (December 26, 1850).
2. Thomas Babington Macaulay, *Journal* (December 31, 1851), cited in G. Otto Trevelyan, *The Life and Letters of Lord Macaulay*, 1876, Volume 2, pp. 253–54.
3. Sir Mountstuart E. Grant Duff, *Diary* (April 1, 1853), *Notes from a Diary 1851–1872*, 1897, Volume 1, p. 53.
4. Robert Buchanan, "Thomas Love Peacock: A Personal Reminiscence," A *Look round Literature*, 1887, pp. 164–65.
5. Thomas Lovell Beddoes, Letter to Thomas Forbes Kelsall (April 17, 1824).
6. Richard Henry Stoddard, "Thomas Love Peacock," *Under the Evening Lamp*, 1892, pp. 241–42.
7. Richard Garnett, "Thomas Love Peacock" (1891), *Essays of an Ex-Librarian*, 1901, pp. 279–82.
8. Percy Bysshe Shelley, "On *Rhododaphne; or, The Thesalian Spell*," 1818.
9. Percy Bysshe Shelley, *Letter to Maria Gisborne*, 1820, ll. 232–47.
10. Edmund Gosse, "Thomas Love Peacock," *The English Poets*, ed. Thomas Humphry Ward, 1880, Volume 4, pp. 417–19.
11. Algernon Charles Swinburne, "Social Verse," *Forum*, October 1891, p. 180.
12. Agnes Repplier, "Cakes and Ale," *Varia*, 1897, pp. 146–47.
13. Albany Fonblanque, "*Crochet Castle*," *Westminister Review*, July 1831, pp. 208–9, 218.
14. James Davies, "Thomas Love Peacock," *Contemporary Review*, April 1875, pp. 760–62.
15. George Barnett Smith, "Thomas Love Peacock," *Fortnightly Review*, August 1873, pp. 189–206.
16. George Saintsbury, "Peacock" (1886), *Collected Essays and Papers*, 1923, Volume 2, pp. 101–9.

JOHN KEBLE

1. Walter Bagehot, "Hartley Coleridge" (1852), *Collected Works*, ed. Norman St. John-Stevas, 1965, Volume 1, pp. 168–69.
2. William Charles Lake, "Mr. Keble and the *Christian Year*," *Contemporary Review*, July 1866, pp. 325–27.
3. William Ewart Gladstone, "A Chapter of Autobiography" (1868), *Gleanings of Past Years*, 1879, Volume 7, p. 141.
4. Samuel Wilberforce, "Keble's Biography," *Quarterly Review*, April 1869, p. 119.
5. Henry Parry Liddon, "John Keble" (1876), *Clerical Life and Works*, 1895, pp. 335–36.
6. A. P. Stanley, "John Keble," *The English Poets*, ed. Thomas Humphry Ward, 1880, Volume 4, pp. 503–4.
7. Edwin D. Mead, "Arnold of Rugby and the Oxford Movement," *Andover Review*, May 1884, p. 508.
8. R. W. Church, *The Oxford Movement*, 1891, pp. 25–26.

9. G. A. Simcox, *Academy*, March 18, 1893, p. 235.
10. Francis T. Palgrave, *Landscape in Poetry*, 1896, p. 250.
11. George Saintsbury, *A History of Nineteenth Century Literature*, 1896, pp. 363–64.
12. Hugh Walker, *The Age of Tennyson*, 1897, p. 145.
13. Henry Van Dyke, "Aids to the Devout Life," *Outlook*, November 13, 1897, pp. 663–64.
14. Thomas Erskine, Letter to Rachel Erskine (March 11, 1829), *Letters*, ed. William Hanna, 1878, pp. 111–12.
15. Winthrop Macworth Praed, "To Helen: Written in the First Leaf of Keble's *Christian Year*," 1836.
16. John Henry Newman, *Apologia pro Vita Sua*, 1864, Ch. 1.
17. John Campbell Shairp, "Keble," *Studies in Poetry and Philosophy*, 1868, pp. 250–51.
18. C. Kegan Paul, "John Keble" (1869), *Biographical Sketches*, 1883, pp. 42–44.
19. James Anthony Froude, "The Oxford Counter-Reformation" (1881), *Short Studies in Great Subjects*, 1883, Volume 4, pp. 171–74.
20. Henry Morley, *Of English Literature in the Reign of Victoria*, 1881, p. 287.
21. John Tulloch, *Movements of Religious Thought in Britain during the Nineteenth Century*, 1885, p. 66.
22. Walter Lock, *John Keble: A Biography*, 1892, pp. 71–72.
23. A. C. Benson, "The Poetry of Keble," *Essays*, 1896, pp. 185–87.

CATHARINE MARIA SEDGWICK

1. Henry F. Chorley (1839), *Autobiography, Memoir, and Letters*, ed. Henry G. Hewlett, 1873, Volume 1, pp. 279–80.
2. William Cullen Bryant, "Reminiscences of Miss Sedgwick," cited in Mary E. Dewey, *Life and Letters of Catharine M. Sedgwick*, 1871, p. 446.
3. Mary E. Dewey, *Life and Letters of Catharine M. Sedgwick*, 1871, p. 10.
4. Harriet Martineau, *Autobiography*, ed. Maria Weston Chapman, 1877, Volume 1, p. 377.
5. William Cullen Bryant, "Redwood," *North American Review*, April 1825, p. 256.
6. Francis Bowen, "*Merry-Mount, a Romance of the Massachusetts Colony*," *North American Review*, January 1849, p. 205.
7. Fred Lewis Pattee, *A History of American Literature*, 1896, pp. 147–48.
8. Katharine Lee Bates, *American Literature*, 1897, pp. 104–5.
9. W. Hillard, "Clarence," *North American Review*, January 1831, pp. 74–79.
10. Edgar Allan Poe, "Catherine M. Sedgwick," *The Literati of New York City*, 1846.

FITZ-GREENE HALLECK

1. John Jacob Astor, Will, 1848.
2. James Russell Lowell, *A Fable for Critics*, 1848.
3. Oliver Wendell Holmes, "Poem at the Dedication of the Halleck Monument," 1869.
4. William Gilmore Simms, Letter to James Grant Wilson (1869), cited in James Grant Wilson, *The Life and Letters of Fitz-Greene Halleck*, 1869, pp. 544–45.
5. James Grant Wilson, *The Life and Letters of Fitz-Greene Halleck*, 1869, pp. 442–43.
6. Bayard Taylor, "Fitz-Green Halleck," *North American Review*, July 1877, p. 61.
7. John Greenleaf Whittier, "Fitz-Greene Halleck," 1877.
8. Edmund Clarence Stedman, *Poets of America*, 1885, pp. 40–41.
9. Edwin P. Whipple, "American Literature" (1886), *American Literature and Other Papers*, 1887, pp. 51–53.
10. Arthur B. Simonds, *American Song*, 1894, p. 136.
11. James L. Onderdonk, *History of American Verse*, 1901, p. 134.
12. Fitz-Greene Halleck, Letter to His Sister (January 1, 1820), cited in James Grant Wilson, *The Life and Letters of Fitz-Greene Halleck*, 1869, pp. 231–32.
13. William H. Prescott, Letter to Fitz-Greene Halleck (March 15, 1820), cited in James Grant Wilson, *The Life and Letters of Fitz-Greene Halleck*, 1869, p. 239.
14. James Grant Wilson, *The Life and Letters of Fitz-Greene Halleck*, 1869, p. 234.
15. Richard Henry Stoddard, "Fitz-Greene Halleck," *Lippincott's Magazine*, June 1889, pp. 892–93.
16. Edgar Allan Poe, "Fitz-Greene Halleck," *The Literati of New York City*, 1846.
17. William Cullen Bryant, "Fitz-Greene Halleck" (1869), *Prose Writings*, ed. Parke Godwin, 1884, Volume 1, pp. 381–87.

N. P. WILLIS

1. Bayard Taylor, Letter to J. B. Phillips (June 30, 1844), *Life and Letters of Bayard Taylor*, eds. Marie Hansen-Taylor, Horace E. Scudder, 1885, Volume 1, pp. 39–40.
2. Washington Irving, Letter to John Pendleton Kennedy (August 31, 1854), cited in Pierre M. Irving, *The Life and Letters of Washington Irving*, 1862–63, Volume 4, p. 175.
3. Harriet Martineau, *Autobiography*, ed. Maria Weston Chapman, 1877, Volume 1, pp. 384–86.
4. Oliver Wendell Holmes, "Introduction" to *A Moral Antipathy*, 1885.
5. C. C. Felton, "Willis's Writings," *North American Review*, October 1836, p. 407.
6. Edgar Allan Poe, "A Chapter on Autography" (1841), *Collected Works*, ed. James A. Harrison, 1902, Volume 15, p. 190.
7. James Russell Lowell, *A Fable for Critics*, 1848.
8. Thomas Powell, "Nathaniel Parker Willis," *The Living Authors of America*, 1850, pp. 78–80.
9. Henry A. Beers, *Nathaniel Parker Willis*, 1885, pp. 351–52.
10. Edwin P. Whipple, "American Literature" (1886), *American Literature and Other Papers*, 1887, pp. 83–85.
11. M. A. DeWolfe Howe, "Willis, Halleck, and Drake," *American Bookmen*, 1898, pp. 112–13.
12. James L. Onderdonk, *History of American Verse*, 1901, pp. 147–49.
13. Francis Whiting Halsey, "The Pathos of a Master's Fate," *Our Literary Deluge and Some of Its Deeper Waters*, 1902, pp. 102–3.
14. Edgar Allan Poe, "N. P. Willis," *The Literati of New York City*, 1846.

ARTEMUS WARD (CHARLES FARRAR BROWNE)

1. Melville Landon, "Biography of Charles F. Browne," *Artemus Ward: His Works, Complete*, 1875, pp. 22–23.
2. S. S. Cox, "American Humor," *Harper's New Monthly Magazine*, May 1875, pp, 847–48.
3. C. C. Ruthrauff, "Artemus Ward at Cleveland," *Scribner's Monthly*, October 1878, p. 791.
4. John Nichol, *American Literature*, 1882, pp. 417–20.
5. Charles F. Richardson, *American Literature, 1607–1885*, 1887, Volume 1, pp. 523–24.
6. Charles Godfrey Leland, *Memoirs*, 1893, p. 235.
7. William P. Trent, *A History of American Literature, 1607–1865*, 1903, pp. 534–35.

8. E. S. Nadal, "Artemus Ward" (1880), *Essays at Home and Elsewhere*, 1882, pp. 18–30, 40–41.

HENRY, LORD BROUGHAM

1. Sir Samuel Romilly, *Diary* (March 20, 1816), *Memoirs of the Life of Sir Samuel Romilly*, 1840, Volume 3, p. 237.
2. George Ticknor, *Journal* (1819), *Life, Letters, and Journals of George Ticknor*, ed. Anna Ticknor, 1876, Volume 1, p. 266.
3. Sir Walter Scott, Letter to John Gibson Lockhart (March 30, 1820).
4. Leigh Hunt, *Lord Byron and Some of His Contemporaries*, 1828, Volume 1, p. 319, Note.
5. Thomas Carlyle, Letter to John Carlyle (1831), cited in James Anthony Froude, *Thomas Carlyle*, 1882, Volume 1, p. 116.
6. John Wilson (as "Christopher North"), *Noctes Ambrosianae* (November 1832), 1854.
7. George Augustus Sala, "Lord Brougham," *Temple Bar*, June 1868, p. 428.
8. Benjamin Disraeli, Speech in the House of Commons (July 27, 1868).
9. Harriet Martineau, *Autobiography*, ed. Maria Weston Chapman, 1877, Volume 1, pp. 233–36.
10. George Gordon, Lord Byron, *English Bards and Scotch Reviewers*, 1809, ll. 524–25.
11. William Jones, *Biographical Sketches of the Reform Ministers*, 1832, Volume 1, pp. 68–69.
12. Thomas Babington Macaulay, Letter to Macvey Napier (July 20, 1838).
13. Walter Savage Landor, Letter to the Editor of the *Examiner* (August 17, 1843), *Letters Public and Private*, ed. Stephen Wheeler, 1899, pp. 259–61.
14. John Wilson Croker, "Lord Brougham's *Lives of Men of Letters*," *Quarterly Review*, July 1845, p. 62.
15. W. B. O. Peabody, "Brougham's *Lives of Men of Letters and Science*," *North American Review*, October 1845, pp. 383–84, 421.
16. J. H. Millar, "Lord Brougham," *English Prose*, ed. Henry Craik, 1896, Volume 5, pp. 213–15.
17. John Gibson Lockhart, Letter to William Blackwood (October 8, 1831), cited in Margaret Oliphant, *Annals of a Publishing House: William Blackwood and His Sons*, 1897, Volume 1, pp. 250–51.
18. William Forsyth, "The Speeches of Lord Brougham," *Edinburgh Review*, April 1858, p. 463.
19. Lord John Russell, *Recollections and Suggestions 1813–1873*, 1875, pp. 111–13.
20. Justin McCarthy, *A History of Our Own Times*, 1879–80, Ch. 2.
21. William Hazlitt, "Mr. Brougham—Sir F. Burdett," *The Spirit of the Age*, 1825.
22. Walter Bagehot, "Lord Brougham" (1857), *Collected Works*, ed. Norman St. John-Stevas, 1968, Volume 3, pp. 173–93.

H. H. MILMAN

1. A. P. Stanley, Letter to Louisa Stanley (September 28, 1868), cited in Rowland E. Prothero, G. G. Bradley, *The Life and Correspondence of Arthur Penrhyn Stanley*, 1894, Volume 2, p. 365.
2. W. E. H. Lecky, "Preface" to *History of European Morals*, 1869.
3. A. P. Stanley, "The Late Dean of St. Paul's," *Macmillan's Magazine*, January 1869, pp. 182–83.
4. Robert Southey, Letter to Chauncey Hare Townshend (April 12, 1818).

5. W. Loring, "Milman's *Samor*," *North American Review*, June 1819, pp. 26–35.
6. Reginald Heber, "Milman's *Fall of Jerusalem*," *Quarterly Review*, May 1820, p. 225.
7. Felicia Dorothea Hemans, Letter to H. H. Milman (March 7, 1822), cited in Arthur Milman, *Henry Hart Milman: A Biographical Sketch*, 1900, p. 122.
8. George MacDonald, *England's Antiphon*, 1868, p. 312.
9. Lucy Aikin, Letter to William Ellery Channing (February 7, 1841), *Correspondence of William Ellery Channing and Lucy Aikin*, ed. Anna Letitia Le Breton, 1874, p. 380.
10. John Henry Newman, "Milman's View of Christianity" (1841), *Essays Critical and Historical*, 1871, Volume 2, pp. 247–48.
11. James Anthony Froude, Letter to H. H. Milman (1855), cited in Arthur Milman, *Henry Hart Milman: A Biographical Sketch*, 1900, p. 224.
12. William H. Prescott, *History of the Reign of Philip the Second, King of Spain*, 1855, Volume 2, p. 580, Note.
13. Thomas Babington Macaulay, *Journal* (January 1856), cited in G. Otto Trevelyan, *The Life and Letters of Lord Macaulay*, 1876, Volume 2, p. 332.
14. R. W. Church, "Dean Milman's Essays" (1871), *Occasional Papers*, 1897, Volume 1, pp. 156–58.
15. John Tulloch, *Movements of Religious Thought in Britain during the Nineteenth Century*, 1885, pp. 82–85.
16. Frederic Harrison, "Some Great Books of History," *The Meaning of History and Other Historical Pieces*, 1894, pp. 107–8.
17. W. Macneile Dixon, "Henry Hart Milman," *English Prose*, ed. Henry Craik, 1896, Volume 5, pp. 345–47.

SAMUEL LOVER

1. R. H. Horne, "Banim and the Irish Novelists," *A New Spirit of the Age*, 1844, p. 275.
2. N. P. Willis, "Samuel Lover," *Hurry-Graphs*, 1851.
3. Nathaniel Hawthorne, *The English Note-Books*, July 9, 1856.
4. Bayle Bernard, *The Life of Samuel Lover*, 1874, p. 333.
5. Andrew Jones Symington, *Samuel Lover*, 1880, pp. 255–56.
6. S. C. Hall, *Retrospect of a Long Life*, 1883, p. 381.
7. Lester Wallack, *Memories of Fifty Years*, 1889, pp. 187–91.
8. William James Linton, *Threescore and Ten Years*, 1894, p. 174.
9. Fanny Schmid, "The Author of *Rory O'More*," *Century Magazine*, February 1897, p. 583.
10. Hugh Walker, *The Age of Tennyson*, 1897, p. 99.
11. D. J. O'Donoghue, "Samuel Lover," *A Treasury of Irish Poetry in the English Tongue*, eds. Stopford A. Brooke, T. W. Rolleston, 1900, pp. 64–65.
12. James Jeffrey Roche, "Introduction" to *The Collected Writings of Samuel Lover*, 1903, pp. xxiii–xxxi.

WILLIAM CARLETON

1. R. H. Horne, "Banim and the Irish Novelists," *A New Spirit of the Age*, 1844, p. 275.
2. S. C. Hall, *Retrospect of a Long Life*, 1883, p. 385.
3. Margaret Oliphant, *The Victorian Age of English Literature*, 1892, Volume 1, pp. 295–96.
4. Percy Russell, *A Guide to British and American Novels*, 1894, p. 85.
5. Cashel Hoey, "Introduction" to *The Life of William Carleton* by David J. O'Donoghue, 1896, Volume 1, pp. xvii–xx.
6. David J. O'Donoghue, *The Life of William Carleton*, 1896, Volume 2, pp. 350–52.

Volume 9

GEORGE GROTE

ROBERT CHAMBERS

ALICE CARY AND PHOEBE CARY

FREDERICK DENISON MAURICE

1. Roundell Palmer, Earl of Selborne, Letter to William Palmer (1836), *Memorials*, 1896, Volume 1, p. 215.
2. Jane Welsh Carlyle, Letter to John Sterling (February 1, 1837).
3. Thomas Carlyle, Letter to John A. Carlyle (February 1, 1838).
4. Alfred, Lord Tennyson, "To the Rev. F. D. Maurice," 1854.
5. Sir Mountstuart E. Grant Duff, *Diary* (April 22, 1855), *Notes from a Diary 1851–1872*, 1897, Volume 1, p. 78.
6. F. W. Farrar, "Formative Influences," *Forum*, December 1890, pp. 378–79.
7. Elisha Mulford, "Frederick Denison Maurice," *Scribner's Monthly*, September 1872, p. 532.
8. John Stuart Mill, *Autobiography*, 1873, Ch. 5.
9. Sir Leslie Stephen, "Mr. Maurice's Theology," *Fortnightly Review*, May 1874, p. 596.
10. Edward Dowden, "The Transcendental Movement and Literature" (1877), *Studies in Literature*, 1878, pp. 72–73.
11. Richard Holt Hutton, "Frederick Denison Maurice," *Good Words*, 1884, p. 387.
12. Julia Wedgwood, "Frederick Denison Maurice" (1854), *Nineteenth Century Teachers and Other Essays*, 1909, p. 60.
13. John Tulloch, *Movements of Religious Thought in Britain during the Nineteenth Century*, 1885, p. 276.
14. R. W. Church, "Frederick Denison Maurice" (1872), *Occasional Papers*, 1897, Volume 2, pp. 321–26.
15. Charles Kingsley, "Frederick Denison Maurice: In Memoriam," *Macmillan's Magazine*, May 1872, pp. 84–88.

CHARLES LEVER

1. Mary Russell Mitford, Letter to Elizabeth Barrett Browning (September 1848).
2. Elizabeth Barrett Browning, Letter to Mary Russell Mitford (c. July 1849).
3. R. H. Horne, "Banim and the Irish Novelists," *A New Spirit of the Age*, 1844, p. 276.
4. George P. Marsh, *The Origin and History of the English Language*, 1862, p. 567, Note.
5. J. Hain Friswell, "Mr. Charles Lever," *Modern Men of Letters Honestly Criticised*, 1870, p. 179.
6. John S. Hart, A *Manual of English Literature*, 1872, pp. 533–34.
7. N. Robinson, "Charles Lever at Home," *Catholic World*, November 1877, pp. 206–7.
8. J. L. Stewart, "Lever's Military Tales," *Canadian Monthly*, August 1878, pp. 199–201.
9. Justin McCarthy, A *History of Our Own Times*, 1879–80, Ch. 29.
10. W. J. Fitzpatrick, *The Life of Charles Lever*, 1879, Volume 2, pp. 332–35.
11. George Saintsbury, "Two Men of Letters," *Fortnightly Review*, September 1879, pp. 386–87.
12. A. G. Sedgwick, "Charles Lever," *Nation*, November 27, 1879, p. 368.
13. Anthony Trollope, *An Autobiography*, 1883, Ch. 13.
14. W. E. Henley, "Lever," *Views and Reviews*, 1890, pp. 174–76.
15. Andrew Lang, "Charles Lever: His Books, Adventures and Misfortunes," *Essays in Little*, 1891, p. 170.
16. Margaret Oliphant, *The Victorian Age of English Literature*, 1892, Volume 1, pp. 293–94.
17. Alfred H. Miles, "Charles Lever," *The Poets and the Poetry of the Century*, 1894, Volume 10, pp. 309–10.

18. George Saintsbury, A *History of Nineteenth Century Literature*, 1896, pp. 158–59.
19. George Henry Nettleton, *Specimens of the Short Story*, 1901, pp. 112–13.
20. Edgar Allan Poe, "Charles James Lever" (1842), *Essays and Reviews*, ed. G. R. Thompson, 1984, pp. 311–20.

HORACE GREELEY

1. Richard Henry Dana, *Journal* (January 22, 1851), cited in Charles Francis Adams, *Richard Henry Dana: A Biography*, 1890, Volume 1, p. 177.
2. James Parton, *The Life of Horace Greeley* (1855), 1868, p. 4.
3. Horace Greeley, *Recollections of a Busy Life*, 1868, p. 429.
4. Edmund Clarence Stedman, "Horace Greeley," 1872.
5. Thurlow Weed, "Recollections of Horace Greeley," *Galaxy*, March 1873, pp. 381–82.
6. Junius Henri Browne, "Horace Greeley," *Harper's New Monthly Magazine*, April 1873, p. 734.
7. Murat Halstead, "Horace Greeley: A Friendly Estimate of a Great Career," *Cosmopolitan*, February 1890, pp. 460–61.
8. Octavius Brooks Frothingham, *Recollections and Impressions*, 1891, p. 227.
9. David W. Bartlett, "Horace Greeley," *Modern Agitators; or, Pen Portraits of Living American Reformers*, 1854, pp. 315–17.
10. George S. Merriam, *The Life and Times of Samuel Bowles*, 1855, Volume 2, pp. 181–82.
11. Harriet Beecher Stowe, *Men of Our Times*, 1868, p. 310.
12. Joel Benton, "Reminiscences of Horace Greeley," *Cosmopolitan*, July 1887, p. 317.
13. Charles Sotheran, *Horace Greeley and Other Pioneers of American Socialism*, 1892, p. 1.
14. L. D. Ingersoll, *The Life of Horace Greeley*, 1873, pp. 487–93, 505–6.

EDWARD BULWER-LYTTON

1. John Gibson Lockhart, Letter to Sir Walter Scott (November 1828), cited in Andrew Lang, *The Life and Letters of John Gibson Lockhart*, 1897, Volume 2, p. 37.
2. Thomas Babington Macaulay, Letter to Hannah Macaulay (August 5, 1831).
3. Thomas Carlyle, *Journal* (February 13, 1834), cited in James Anthony Froude, *Thomas Carlyle*, 1882, Volume 2, p. 327.
4. N. P. Willis, *Pencillings by the Way*, 1835, Volume 3, pp. 90–93.
5. Matthew Arnold, Letter to His Mother (May 12, 1869).
6. Harriet Martineau, *Autobiography*, ed. Maria Weston Chapman, 1877, Volume 1, pp. 266–67.
7. S. C. Hall, *Retrospect of a Long Life*, 1883, pp. 153–54.
8. John Wilson (as "Christopher North"), *Noctes Ambrosianae* (September 1831), 1854.
9. Henry F. Chorley, "Edward Lytton Bulwer," *The Authors of England*, 1838, pp. 49–50.
10. William Makepeace Thackeray, "Ch-s Y-ll Wpl-sh, Esq. to Sir Edward Lytton Bulwer, Bart.," *Fraser's Magazine*, January 1840, pp. 71–72.
11. Edwin P. Whipple, "Novels and Novelists: Charles Dickens" (1844), *Lectures on Subjects Connected with Literature and Life*, 1850, pp. 55–57.
12. Edgar Allan Poe, *Marginalia*, May 1849.
13. George Gilfillan, "Sir Edward Bulwer Lytton," A *Second Gallery of Literary Portraits*, 1850, pp. 163–64.
14. Ralph Waldo Emerson, "Literature," *English Traits*, 1856.

15. Peter Bayne, "The Modern Novel: Dickens—Bulwer—Thackeray," *Essays in Biography and Criticism*, 1857, p. 388.
16. Connop Thirlwall, Letter (February 27, 1865), *Letters to a Friend*, ed. Arthur Penrhyn Stanley, 1881, p. 19.
17. J. Hain Friswell, "Lord Lytton," *Modern Men of Letters Honestly Criticised*, 1870, pp. 251–52.
18. Sidney Lanier, *The English Novel*, 1883, p. 195.
19. W. D. Howells, *My Literary Passions*, 1895.
20. Edmund Gosse, *A Short History of Modern English Literature*, 1897, p. 329.
21. Walter Frewen Lord, "Lord Lytton's Novels," *Nineteenth Century*, September 1901, pp. 452–53.
22. Sir Walter Scott, Letter to John Gibson Lockhart (November 20, 1828).
23. John Quincy Adams, *Diary*, April 2, 1829.
24. W. Phillips, "Pelham," *North American Review*, April 1829, p. 432.
25. William Godwin, Letter to Edward Bulwer-Lytton (May 13, 1830), cited in C. Kegan Paul, *William Godwin: His Friends and Contemporaries*, 1876, Volume 2, p. 306.
26. G. H. Devereux, "*The Last Days of Pompeii*," *North American Review*, April 1835, pp. 453–56.
27. Matthew Arnold, Letter to Mrs. Forster (April 14, 1835).
28. Mary E. Braddon, "Lord Lytton," *Belgravia*, March 1873, pp. 80–81.
29. T. H. S. Escott, "Bulwer's Last Three Books," *Fraser's Magazine*, June 1874, pp. 766–67.
30. Alfred, Lord Tennyson, "The New Timon and the Poets," 1846.
31. J. M. Bell, "*The New Timon*," *North British Review*, August 1846, pp. 401–3.
32. James Russell Lowell, "*The New Timon*," *North American Review*, April 1847, p. 483.
33. Charlotte Brontë, Letter to W. S. Williams (April 2, 1849).
34. William Spalding, "Sir E. Bulwer Lytton: *King Arthur*," *Edinburgh Review*, July 1849, pp. 210–12.
35. Margaret Oliphant, "Bulwer," *Blackwood's Edinburgh Magazine*, February 1855, pp. 227–33.
36. Justin McCarthy, "Edward Bulwer, Lord Lytton," *Modern Leaders*, 1872, pp. 158–66.
37. Edith Simcox, *Academy*, May 1, 1873, pp. 162–64.

SAMUEL WILBERFORCE

1. John Lothrop Motley, Letter to His Wife (August 20, 1867), *Correspondence*, ed. George William Curtis, 1889, Volume 2, p. 285.
2. Richard William Church, Letter to Asa Gray (July 20, 1873), *Life and Letters of Dean Church*, ed. Mary Church, 1894, pp. 284–85.
3. Thomas Carlyle, Letter to James Anthony Froude (July 29, 1873), cited in James Anthony Froude, *Thomas Carlyle: A History of His Life in London*, 1884, Volume 2, p. 358.
4. William Ewart Gladstone, Speech (December 3, 1873), cited in A. R. Ashwell, Reginald G. Wilberforce, *Life of Samuel Wilberforce, D.D.*, 1883, pp. 549–50.
5. Richard Monckton Milnes, Lord Houghton, "Samuel Wilberforce, Bishop of Oxford and Winchester," *Fortnightly Review*, March 1880, p. 355.
6. G. A. Simcox, "Bishop Wilberforce," *Macmillan's Magazine*, March 1880, p. 403.
7. A. R. Ashwell, "Introduction" to *Life of Samuel Wilberforce, D.D.* by A. R. Ashwell, Reginald G. Wilberforce, 1883, pp. xix–xxiv.
8. Sir G. W. Dasent, "Samuel Wilberforce," *Fortnightly Review*, February 1883, pp. 184–96.

9. James Bryce, "Two Biographies," *Nation*, March 22, 1883, p. 250.
10. George Saintsbury, *A History of Nineteenth Century Literature*, 1896, p. 372.
11. Hugh Walker, *The Age of Tennyson*, 1897, p. 155.

JOHN STUART MILL

1. Thomas Carlyle, Letter to Jane Welsh Carlyle (September 4, 1831).
2. Caroline Fox, *Journal* (April 10, 1840), *Memories of Old Friends*, ed. Horace N. Pym, 1882, pp. 94–96.
3. John Arthur Roebuck, *Autobiography* (c. 1879), *Life and Letters of John Arthur Roebuck*, ed. Robert Eadon Leader, 1897, pp. 38–40.
4. Justin McCarthy, *Reminiscences*, 1900, Volume 1, p. 92.
5. James Martineau, "John Stuart Mill's Philosophy" (1859), *Essays, Reviews and Addresses*, 1891, Volume 3, p. 518.
6. J. Ewing Ritchie, *British Senators; or, Political Sketches, Past and Present*, 1869, pp. 296–301.
7. James Russell Lowell, Letter to Sir Leslie Stephen (April 29, 1873).
8. Henry Sidgwick, "John Stuart Mill," *Academy*, May 15, 1873, p. 193.
9. Walter Bagehot, "The Late Mr. Mill" (1873), *Collected Works*, ed. Norman St. John-Stevas, 1968, Volume 3, pp. 555–59.
10. Edwin Lawrence Godkin, "John Stuart Mill," *Reflections and Comments*, 1895, pp. 76–78.
11. J. H. Millar, "John Stuart Mill," *English Prose*, ed. Henry Craik, 1896, Volume 5, pp. 509–12.
12. George Saintsbury, *A History of Nineteenth Century Literature*, 1896, pp. 347–49.
13. Henry Thomas Buckle, "Mill on Liberty" (1859), *Miscellaneous and Posthumous Works*, ed. Helen Taylor, 1872, Volume 1, pp. 36–37.
14. Simon N. Patten, *The Development of English Thought*, 1899, pp. 337–39.
15. John Stuart Mill, Dedication to *On Liberty*, 1859.
16. Caroline Fox, Letter to E. T. Carne (1859), cited in William L. Courtney, *Life of John Stuart Mill*, 1888, p. 125.
17. Thomas Carlyle, Letter to John Carlyle (November 5, 1873), cited in James Anthony Froude, *Thomas Carlyle: A History of His Life in London*, 1884, Volume 2, p. 358.
18. Edward Everett Hale, "John Stuart Mill," *Old and New*, January 1874, pp. 128–29.
19. B. A. Hinsdale, "John Stuart Mill" (1874), *Schools and Studies*, 1884, pp. 111–12.
20. John Stuart Mill, "General Review of the Remainder of My Life," *Autobiography*, 1873.
21. Frederic Harrison, "John Stuart Mill," *Nineteenth Century*, 1896, pp. 489–508.
22. Sir Leslie Stephen, "Mill on Theology," *The English Utilitarians*, 1900, Volume 3, pp. 433–51.

BRYAN WALLER PROCTER
("BARRY CORNWALL")

1. Charles Sumner, Letter to Goerge S. Hillard (January 23, 1839), cited in Edward L. Pierce, *Memoir and Letters of Charles Sumner*, 1877, Volume 2, p. 44.
2. Peter George Patmore, *My Friends and Acquaintance*, 1854, Volume 3, pp. 86–87.
3. Nathaniel Hawthorne, *The English Note-Books*, June 12, 1854.

4. Bayard Taylor, Letter to Mr. and Mrs. R. H. Stoddard (August 4, 1856), cited in *Life and Letters of Bayard Taylor*, eds. Marie Hansen-Taylor, Horace E. Scudder, 1884, Volume 1, p. 321.
5. Thomas Carlyle, "Edward Irving" (1867), *Reminiscences*, ed. James Anthony Froude, 1881, Volume 1, pp. 233–34.
6. Charles Lamb, "To the Author of Poems, Published under the Name of Barry Cornwall," 1820.
7. William Hazlitt, *Lectures on the Dramatic Literature of the Age of Elizabeth*, 1820.
8. Francis, Lord Jeffrey, "Cornwall's *Marcian Colonna*," *Edinburgh Review*, November 1820, pp. 449–50.
9. George Gordon, Lord Byron, Letter to John Murray (January 4, 1821).
10. Benjamin Robert Haydon, Letter to Mary Russell Mitford (January 12, 1821), *The Life, Letters and Table Talk of Benjamin Robert Haydon*, ed. Richard Henry Stoddard, 1876, pp. 204–5.
11. Thomas Carlyle, Letter to Jane Welsh (June 23, 1824).
12. Charles Lamb, Letter to Leigh Hunt (1825).
13. Walter Savage Landor, "To Barry Cornwall on Reading His *English Songs*," 1836.
14. Edwin P. Whipple, "English Poets of the Nineteenth Century" (1845), *Essays and Reviews*, 1850, Volume 1, pp. 347–48.
15. Henry Wadsworth Longfellow, Letter to Bryan Waller Procter (November 29, 1852).
16. Algernon Charles Swinburne, "In Memory of Barry Cornwall," 1874, Stanzas 2–4.
17. Edmund Clarence Stedman, *Victorian Poets*, 1875, pp. 100–103.
18. G. A. Simcox, "Barry Cornwall," *Fortnightly Review*, May 1877, p. 709.
19. Charles Cowden Clarke, *Recollections of Writers*, 1878, p. 36.
20. Edmund Gosse, "Bryan Waller Procter," *The English Poets*, ed. Thomas Humphry Ward, 1880, Volume 4, pp. 489–90.
21. Edwin P. Whipple, "Barry Cornwall and Some of His Contemporaries," *Recollections of Eminent Men and Other Papers*, 1886, pp. 339–40.
22. George Saintsbury, *A History of Nineteenth Century Literature*, 1896, p. 109.
23. William Carew Hazlitt, *Four Generations of a Literary Family*, 1897, Volume 1, pp. 238–39.

SYDNEY DOBELL

1. Charlotte Brontë, Letter to Sydney Dobell (February 3, 1854).
2. George Gilfillan, "Sydney Yendys," *A Third Gallery of Portraits*, 1854, pp. 130, 144.
3. Alexander Smith, "Sydney Dobell," *Argosy*, 1866, p. 315.
4. Dante Gabriel Rossetti, Letter to James Smetham (1868), cited in *Dante Gabriel Rossetti: His Family Letters*, ed. William Michael Rossetti, 1895, Volume 1, p. 420.
5. Robert Buchanan, "Sydney Dobell and the Spasmodic School" (1879), *A Look round Literature*, 1887, p. 203.
6. Dinah Maria Craik, "Sydney Dobell," *International Review*, May 1879, pp. 485–86.
7. John Nichol, "Sydney Dobell," *The English Poets*, ed. Thomas Humphry Ward, 1880, Volume 4, pp. 615–16.
8. Richard Garnett, "Sydney Dobell," *The Poets and the Poetry of the Century*, ed. Alfred H. Miles, 1892, Volume 5, pp. 213–14.
9. George Saintsbury, *A History of Nineteenth Century Literature*, 1896, p. 306.
10. Hugh Walker, *The Age of Tennyson*, 1897, pp. 247–49.

CHARLES KINGSLEY

1. Elizabeth Barrett Browning, Letter to Mrs. Martin (September 2, 1852).
2. Harriet Beecher Stowe, Letter to C. E. Stowe (November 7, 1856).
3. John Lothrop Motley, Letter to His Wife (May 28, 1858), *Correspondence*, ed. George William Curtis, 1889, Volume 1, p. 232.
4. John Greenleaf Whittier, Letter to Fanny Kingsley (August 30, 1876).
5. Henry James, "Charles Kingsley's *Life and Letters*," *Nation*, January 25, 1877, p. 60.
6. William Cullen Bryant, Letter to Miss J. Dewey (June 2, 1877), cited in Parke Godwin, *A Biography of William Cullen Bryant*, 1883, Volume 2, p. 383.
7. James O. Putnam, "Charles Kingsley" (1877), *Addresses, Speeches, and Miscellanies*, 1880, p. 220.
8. James Martineau, "Alexandria and Her Schools" (1854), *Essays, Philosophical and Theological*, 1868, Volume 2, p. 293.
9. Peter Bayne, "Charles Kingsley," *Essays in Biography and Criticism: Second Series*, 1858, pp. 13–16, 50–51.
10. G. A. Simcox, "The Late Canon Kingsley," *Academy*, January 30, 1875, p. 115.
11. G. A. Simcox, "Charles Kingsley," *Fortnightly Review*, January 1877, p. 31.
12. John Tulloch, *Movements of Religious Thought in Britain during the Nineteenth Century*, 1885, pp. 293–94.
13. Sir Arthur Quiller-Couch, "Henry Kingsley," *Adventures in Criticism*, 1896, pp. 139–40.
14. George Saintsbury, "Charles Kingsley," *English Prose*, ed. Henry Craik, 1896, Volume 5, pp. 647–49.
15. Edmund Gosse, *A Short History of Modern English Literature*, 1897, pp. 371–72.
16. Hugh Walker, *The Age of Tennyson*, 1897, pp. 269–71.
17. Henry Wadsworth Longfellow, *Journal* (April 2, 1852), cited in Samuel Longfellow, *Life of Henry Wadsworth Longfellow*, 1891, Volume 2, p. 233.
18. Frederick Denison Maurice, "Mr. Kingsley and the *Saturday Review*," *Macmillan's Magazine*, December 1859, p. 118.
19. Edmund Clarence Stedman, *Victorian Poets*, 1875, p. 251.
20. W. E. Henley, "Charles Kingsley," *The English Poets*, ed. Thomas Humphry Ward, 1880, Volume 4, pp. 608–9.
21. Moritz Kaufmann, *Charles Kingsley, Christian Socialist and Social Reformer*, 1892, pp. 74–75.
22. Alfred, Lord Tennyson, Letter to Charles Kingsley (1853), cited in Hallam Tennyson, *Alfred Lord Tennyson: A Memoir*, 1897, Volume 1, p. 367.
23. David Masson, *British Novelists and Their Styles*, 1859, pp. 280–81.
24. W. R. Greg, "Kingsley and Carlyle" (1860), *Literary and Social Judgments*, 1873, pp. 138–42.
25. G. A. Simcox, "Charles Kingsley," *Fortnightly Review*, January 1877, pp. 23–24.
26. Frederic Harrison, "Charles Kingsley," *Studies in Early Victorian Literature*, 1895, pp. 176–77.
27. Wilbur L. Cross, *The Development of the English Novel*, 1899, pp. 145–46.
28. Charles William Stubbs, *Charles Kingsley and the Christian Social Movement*, 1899, pp. 182–83.
29. Sir Leslie Stephen, "Charles Kingsley" (1877), *Hours in a Library* (1874–79), 1904, Volume 3, pp. 331–55.
30. Andrew Lang, "Charles Kingsley," *Essays in Little*, 1891, pp. 153–59.

31. William Dean Howells, "Charles Kingsley's *Hypatia*," *Heroines of Fiction*, 1901, pp. 2–10.

HARRIET MARTINEAU

1. Catharine Maria Sedgwick, *Journal* (August 9, 1835), *Life and Letters of Catharine M. Sedgwick*, ed. Mary E. Dewey, 1872, pp. 240–42.
2. William Cullen Bryant, Letter to Frances Bryant (April 27–29, 1836).
3. Elizabeth Barrett Browning, Letter to H. S. Boyd (December 24, 1844).
4. Henry Crabb Robinson, Letter to Miss Fenwick (January 15, 1849).
5. Charlotte Brontë, Letter to W. S. Williams (January 1, 1850).
6. Nathaniel Hawthorne, *The English Note-Books*, August 26, 1854.
7. Matthew Arnold, Letter to G. W. Boyle (March 11, 1877).
8. James Martineau, Letter to Charles Wicksteed (August 5, 1877), cited in James Drummond, *The Life and Letters of James Martineau*, 1902, Volume 1, p. 225.
9. S. C. Hall, *Retrospect of a Long Life*, 1883, pp. 328–29.
10. Lucy Aikin, Letter to William Ellery Channing (October 15, 1832), *Correspondence of William Ellery Channing and Lucy Aikin*, ed. Anna Letitia Le Breton, 1874, p. 148.
11. Leigh Hunt, *Blue-Stocking Revels; or, The Feast of the Violets*, 1837, Canto 2, ll. 149–53.
12. Margaret Oliphant, Letter to William Blackwood (March 8, 1877), *Autobiography and Letters*, ed. Mrs. Harry Coghill, 1899, p. 263.
13. John Morley, "Harriet Martineau" (1877), *Critical Miscellanies*, 1888, Volume 3, pp. 176–77.
14. Mrs. F. Fenwick Miller, *Harriet Martineau*, 1884, pp. 221–24.
15. R. Brimley Johnson, "Harriet Martineau," *English Prose*, ed. Henry Craik, 1896, Volume 5, pp. 461–64.
16. George Eliot, Letter to Mrs. Charles Bray (March 20, 1877).
17. Thomas Wentworth Higginson, "Harriet Martineau's Autobiography," *Nation*, April 19, 1877, p. 237.
18. Edward FitzGerald, Letter to W. F. Pollock (May 24, 1877).
19. William Cullen Bryant, Letter to Miss J. Dewey (June 2, 1877), cited in Parke Godwin, *A Biography of William Cullen Bryant*, 1883, Volume 2, pp. 382–83.
20. W. R. Greg, "Harriet Martineau" (1877), *Miscellaneous Essays*, 1882, pp. 176–88.
21. Margaret Oliphant, "Harriet Martineau," *Blackwood's Edinburgh Magazine*, April 1877, pp. 474–96.

JOHN FORSTER

1. Jane Welsh Carlyle, Letter to John Sterling (January 19, 1842).
2. William Carew Hazlitt, *Four Generations of a Literary Family*, 1897, Volume 2, pp. 130–31.
3. R. R. Madden, *The Literary Life and Correspondence of the Countess of Blessington*, 1855, Volume 2, pp. 396–98.
4. Edward Dowden, "Walter Savage Landor" (1869), *Studies in Literature*, 1878, p. 160.
5. Edward FitzGerald, Letter to W. F. Pollock (March 30, 1873).
6. Andrew Lang, *Academy*, February 21, 1874, p. 190.
7. Samuel R. Gardiner, "Mr. John Forster," *Academy*, February 5, 1876, p. 122.

8. Richard Henry Horne, "John Forster," *Temple Bar*, April 1876, pp. 503–5.
9. Anthony Trollope, *An Autobiography*, 1883, Ch. 5.
10. Margaret Oliphant, *The Victorian Age of English Literature*, 1892, Volume 2, pp. 276–78.
11. John Churton Collins, *Jonathan Swift*, 1893, pp. 9–10.

CAROLINE NORTON

1. Charles Sumner, Letter to George S. Hillard (February 16, 1839), cited in Edward L. Pierce, *Memoir and Letters of Charles Sumner*, 1877, Volume 2, pp. 61–62.
2. Henry Crabb Robinson, Letter to Thomas Robinson (January 31, 1845).
3. Fanny Kemble, *Record of a Girlhood*, 1879, pp. 174–75.
4. S. C. Hall, *Retrospect of a Long Life*, 1883, p. 386.
5. Charles Godfrey Leland, *Memoirs*, 1893, pp. 428–29.
6. John Wilson (as "Christopher North"), *Noctes Ambrosianae* (April 1830), 1854.
7. Leigh Hunt, *Blue-Stocking Revels; or, The Feast of the Violets*, 1837, Canto 2, ll. 178–88.
8. Henry Nelson Coleridge, "Modern English Poetesses," *Quarterly Review*, September 1840, pp. 376–82.
9. Rufus W. Griswold, "Mrs. Norton," *The Poets and Poetry of England in the Nineteenth Century*, 1844, p. 360.
10. R. H. Horne, "Miss E. B. Barrett and Mrs. Norton," *A New Spirit of the Age*, 1844, p. 270.
11. John Gibson Lochart, "The Child of the Islands—by Mrs. Norton," *Quarterly Review*, June 1845, pp. 1–3.
12. Sir Archibald Alison, *History of Europe from 1815 to 1852*, 1852–59, Ch. 5.
13. Edmund Gosse, "The Early Writings of Robert Browning," *Century Magazine*, December 1881, p. 196.
14. Percy Fitzgerald, *The Lives of the Sheridans*, 1886, Volume 2, p. 373.
15. Alfred H. Miles, "Hon. Mrs. Norton," *The Poets and the Poetry of the Century*, ed. Alfred H. Miles, 1892, Volume 8, p. 242.
16. George Saintsbury, *A History of Nineteenth Century Literature*, 1896, p. 315.
17. Hugh Walker, *The Age of Tennyson*, 1897, p. 260.

JOHN LOTHROP MOTLEY

1. Oliver Wendell Holmes, "A Parting Health to J. L. Motley," 1857.
2. John Stuart Mill, Letter to John Lothrop Motley (October 31, 1862).
3. John Richard Green, Letter (June 4, 1877), *Letters*, ed. Sir Leslie Stephen, 1901, pp. 467–68.
4. William Cullen Bryant, "In Memory of John Lothrop Motley," 1877.
5. Otto von Bismarck, cited in Oliver Wendell Holmes, "Memoir of the Hon. John Lothrop Motley, LL.D.," *Proceedings of the Massachusetts Historical Society*, 1878, pp. 410–11.
6. Edwin P. Whipple, "American Literature" (1886), *American Literature and Other Papers*, 1887, pp. 96–97.
7. Edwin P. Whipple, "Motley, the Historian," *Recollections of Eminent Men and Other Papers*, 1886, pp. 202–3.
8. J. Franklin Jameson, *The History of Historical Writing in America*, 1891, pp. 119–20.
9. Katharine Lee Bates, *American Literature*, 1897, p. 246.
10. Edward Everett Hale, Jr., "John Lothrop Motley," *American Prose*, ed. George Rice Carpenter, 1898, pp. 323–25.
11. Henry S. Pancoast, *An Introduction to American Literature*, 1898, pp. 230–33.
12. Barrett Wendell, *A Literary History of America*, 1900, pp. 272–73.

Eliot," *Literary Recollections and Sketches*, 1893, pp. 277–78.
11. Douglas A. Spalding, "Lewes's *Problems of Life and Mind*," *Nature*, May 7, 1874, pp. 1–2.
12. Frederic Harrison, "Mr. Lewes's *Problems of Life and Mind*," *Fortnightly Review*, July 1874, p. 92.
13. Frederick Pollock, *Academy*, May 22, 1875, p. 533.
14. James Sully, *Academy*, April 24, 1880, p. 308.

BAYARD TAYLOR

1. Thomas Bailey Aldrich, "Bayard Taylor," 1878.
2. Sidney Lanier, Letter to Gibson Peacock (December 21, 1878).
3. Moncure D. Conway, *Thomas Carlyle*, 1881, p. 103.
4. Henry Wadsworth Longfellow, Letter to Bayard Taylor (December 25, 1846).
5. Edgar Allan Poe, *Marginalia*, April 1849.
6. John Greenleaf Whittier, "The Last Walk in Autumn," 1856, Stanza 15.
7. Francis H. Underwood, A *Hand-Book of English Literature*, 1872, p. 518.
8. Henry James, "Taylor's *Prophet*," *North American Review*, January 1875, pp. 188–89.
9. Russell H. Conwell, *The Life, Travels, and Literary Career of Bayard Taylor*, 1879, pp. 14–16.
10. John Greenleaf Whittier, "Bayard Taylor," 1879.
11. James Herbert Morse, "The Native Element in American Fiction," *Century Magazine*, July 1883, p. 363.
12. Edwin P. Whipple, "American Literature" (1886), *American Literature and Other Papers*, 1887, pp. 87–88.
13. Charles F. Richardson, *American Literature, 1607–1885*, 1887, Volume 2, pp. 246–48.
14. R. H. Stoddard, "Bayard Taylor," *Lippincott's Magazine*, April 1889, pp. 572–78.
15. Camilla Toulmin Crosland, *Landmarks of a Literary Life*, 1893, pp. 209–10.
16. Henry A. Beers, *Initial Studies in American Letters*, 1895, pp. 177–79.
17. Albert H. Smyth, *Bayard Taylor*, 1896, pp. 273–74.
18. Marie Taylor, "Preface" to *The Poetical Works of Bayard Taylor*, 1902, p. iv.
19. J. V. O'Connor, "Bayard Taylor," *Catholic World*, April 1879, pp. 112–16.
20. Edmund Clarence Stedman, "Bayard Taylor," *Poets of America*, 1885, pp. 398, 409–12, 433–34.

RICHARD HENRY DANA

1. William Cullen Bryant, "Dana's Poems," *North American Review*, January 1828, pp. 239–42.
2. Rufus W. Griswold, "Richard H. Dana," *The Poets and Poetry of America*, 1842, p. 65.
3. Edwin P. Whipple, "Poets and Poetry of America" (1844), *Essays and Reviews*, 1850, Volume 1, pp. 46–52.
4. Edgar Allan Poe, "Fitz-Greene Halleck," *The Literati of New York City*, 1846.
5. James Russell Lowell, A *Fable for Critics*, 1848.
6. S. G. Brown, "Dana's *Poems and Prose Writings*," *North American Review*, January 1851, pp. 134–36.
7. Richard Grant Wilson, "Richard Henry Dana," *Scribner's Montly*, May 1879, pp. 107–10.
8. Henry Wadsworth Longfellow, "The Burial of the Poet: Richard Henry Dana," 1880.
9. John Nichol, *American Literature*, 1882, p. 162.
10. Edwin P. Whipple, "American Literature" (1886), *American Literature and Other Papers*, 1887, pp. 40–41.
11. Walter C. Bronson, A *Short History of American Literature*, 1900, p. 170.

12. James L. Onderdonk, *History of American Verse*, 1901, pp. 123–25.
13. John Greenleaf Whittier, "Preface" to *Songs of Three Centuries*, 1875, p. v.
14. Edmund Gosse, "Richard Henry Dana, Senior," *Academy*, February 15, 1879, p. 144.
15. Richard Henry Stoddard, "Richard Henry Dana," *Harper's New Monthly Magazine*, April 1879, pp. 775–76.
16. W. A. Jones, "The Writings and Literary Character of R. H. Dana," *American Review*, March, 1847, pp. 269–72.

WILLIAM LLOYD GARRISON

1. Frances M. Garrison, Letter to William Lloyd Garrison (June 3, 1823), cited in *William Lloyd Garrison: The Story of His Life Told by His Children*, eds. Wendell Phillips Garrison, Francis Jackson Garrison, 1885, Volume 1, p. 51.
2. Ralph Waldo Emerson, *Journal*, 1845.
3. James Russell Lowell, "To W. L. Garrison," 1848.
4. James Russell Lowell, Letter to C. F. Briggs (March 26, 1848).
5. Harriet Martineau, *Autobiography*, ed. Maria Weston Chapman, 1877, Volume 1, pp. 372–73.
6. John Greenleaf Whittier, "Garrison," 1879.
7. Wendell Phillips Garrison, *William Lloyd Garrison: The Story of His Life Told by His Children*, eds. Wendell Phillips Garrison, Francis Jackson Garrison, 1885, Volume 4, pp. 309–15.
8. Charles Edward Stowe, *Life of Harriet Beecher Stowe*, 1889, pp. 261–62.
9. Fred Lewis Pattee, A *History of American Literature*, 1896, pp. 325–26.
10. Elizabeth Cady Stanton, *Eighty Years and More*, 1898, p. 128.
11. Julia Ward Howe, *Reminiscences, 1819–1899*, 1899, pp. 152–53.
12. Wendell Phillips, "Garrison," *North American Review*, July 1879, pp. 150–52.

CHARLES TENNYSON TURNER

1. Samuel Taylor Coleridge, *Table Talk*, April 18, 1830.
2. A. J. Symington, "Charles (Tennyson) Turner," *International Review*, September 1875, p. 589.
3. Edward FitzGerald, Letter to Charles Eliot Norton (December 15, 1878).
4. Alfred, Lord Tennyson, "Midnight," 1879.
5. James Spedding, "Introductory Essay" (1879) to *Collected Sonnets Old and New* by Charles Tennyson Turner, 1880, p. 28.
6. Alexander H. Japp, "Charles Tennyson Turner," *The Poets and the Poetry of the Century*, ed. Alfred H. Miles, 1892, Volume 4, pp. 47–48.
7. Francis Turner Palgrave, *Landscape in Poetry*, 1896, pp. 277–78.
8. Thomas Bayne, "Charles Tennyson Turner," *Fraser's Magazine*, December 1881, pp. 790–99.

GEORGE ELIOT (MARY ANN EVANS)

1. Nathaniel Hawthorne, *The French and Italian Note-Books*, February 5, 1860.
2. Hallam Tennyson, *Journal* (July 22, 1871), cited in Hallam Tennyson, *Alfred Lord Tennyson: A Memoir*, 1897, Volume 2, p. 107.
3. Justin McCarthy, "'George Eliot' and George Lewes," *Modern Leaders*, 1872, p. 137.
4. Thomas Henry Huxley, Letter to Herbert Spencer (December 27, 1880), cited in Leonard Huxley, *Life and Letters of Thomas Henry Huxley*, 1900, Volume 2, p. 19.

THOMAS CARLYLE

30, 1862), *The Life of Frederick Denison Maurice*, ed. Frederick Maurice, 1884, Volume 2, pp. 404–5.
21. John Stuart Mill, *Autobiography*, 1873, Ch. 5.
22. Edward Dowden, "The Transcendental Movement and Literature" (1877), *Studies in Literature*, 1878, pp. 74–76.
23. Harriet Martineau, *Autobiography*, ed. Maria Weston Chapman, 1877, Volume 1, pp. 291–92.
24. Thomas Henry Huxley, Letter to Lord Stanley (March 9, 1881), cited in Leonard Huxley, *Life and Letters of Thomas Henry Huxley*, 1900, Volume 2, p. 34.
25. Matthew Arnold, Letter to M. Fontanès (March 25, 1881).
26. Walt Whitman, "Death of Thomas Carlyle" (1881), *Prose Works*, ed. Floyd Stovall, 1963, Volume 1, pp. 249–53.
27. Frederic Harrison, "Froude's Life of Carlyle" (1885), *The Choice of Books and Other Literary Pieces*, 1886, pp. 194–99.
28. Edward Caird, "The Genius of Carlyle," *Essays on Literature and Philosophy*, 1892, Volume 1, pp. 264–67.
29. William Roscoe Thayer, "Carlyle" (1895), *Throne-Makers*, 1899, pp. 182–85.
30. Lewis E. Gates, "English Literature of the Nineteenth Century: A Retrospect: II. The Return to Conventional Life," *Critic*, March 1900, pp. 273–75.
31. Alexander H. Everett, "Thomas Carlyle," *North American Review*, October 1835, pp. 459–60.
32. George Eliot, Letter to Martha Jackson (December 16, 1841).
33. Francis Thompson, "*Sartor* Re-read," *Academy*, July 6, 1901, pp. 17–18.
34. John Stuart Mill, "The French Revolution," *London and Westminster Review*, July 1837, pp. 17–18.
35. Lucy Aikin, Letter to William Ellery Channing (April 18, 1838), *Correspondence of William Ellery Channing and Lucy Aikin*, ed. Anna Letitia Le Breton, 1874, p. 309.
36. Edward FitzGerald, Letter to Bernard Barton (April 1838).
37. John Henry Newman, Letter to Mrs. J. Mozley (April 23, 1839).
38. Herman Merivale, "Carlyle on the French Revolution," *Edinburgh Review*, July 1840, pp. 415–16.
39. John Campbell Shairp, "Prose Poets: Thomas Carlyle," *Aspects of Poetry* (1881), 1882, pp. 368–69.
40. George Saintsbury, "Thomas Carlyle," *Corrected Impressions*, 1895.
41. John Gibson Lockhart, Letter to Thomas Carlyle (April 27, 1843), cited in Andrew Lang, *The Life and Letters of John Gibson Lockhart*, 1897, Volume 2, pp. 238–39.
42. Ralph Waldo Emerson, *Dial*, July 1843, pp. 100–101.
43. Arnold Toynbee, *Lectures on the Industrial Revolution in the Eighteenth Century in England*, 1884, pp. 209–11.
44. John Sterling, "Carlyle's Works," *London and Westminster Review*, October 1839, pp. 8–23.
45. Henry David Thoreau, "Thomas Carlyle and His Works" (1847), *Writings*, 1906, Volume 4, pp. 323–33.
46. James Russell Lowell, "Carlyle" (1866), *Works*, Riverside ed., Volume 2, pp. 91–109.
47. Sir Leslie Stephen, "Carlyle's Ethics," *Hours in a Library* (1874–79), 1904, Volume 4, pp. 232–80.

GEORGE BORROW

1. John R. P. Berkeley, "Reminiscences of Borrow in 1854" (1887), cited in William I. Knapp, *Life, Writings, and Correspondence of George Borrow*, 1899, Volume 2, pp. 95–96.
2. Samuel Smiles, *Memoir and Correspondence of the Late John Murray*, 1891, Volume 2, pp. 484–85.
3. Justin McCarthy, A *History of Our Own Times from 1880 to the Diamond Jubilee*, 1897, Ch. 5.
4. A. Egmont Hake, "George Borrow," *Macmillan's Magazine*, November 1881, pp. 56–57.
5. W. E. Henley, "Borrow," *Views and Reviews*, 1890, pp. 133–38.
6. Charles Godfrey Leland, *Memoirs*, 1893, p. 436.
7. Agnes Repplier, "In the Dozy Hours," *In the Dozy Hours and Other Papers*, 1894, pp. 10–11.
8. William I. Knapp, *Life, Writings, and Correspondence of George Borrow*, 1899, Volume 2, pp. 158–60.
9. William A. Dutt, "In Lavengro's Country," *Macmillan's Magazine*, June 1901, p. 148.
10. George Borrow, Letter to John Murray (April 23, 1841), cited in Samuel Smiles, *Memoir and Correspondence of the Late John Murray*, 1891, Volume 2, p. 485.
11. John Gibson Lockhart, "Borrow's Bible in Spain," *Quarterly Review*, December 1842, pp. 169–70.
12. Richard Ford, Letter to John Murray (1842), cited in Samuel Smiles, *Memoir and Correspondence of the Late John Murray*, 1891, Volume 2, pp. 491–92.
13. Richard Ford, "*The Bible in Spain*," *Edinburgh Review*, February 1843, pp. 105–14.
14. Charlotte Brontë, Letter to W. S. Williams (February 4, 1849).
15. Samuel Smiles, *Brief Biographies*, 1860, p. 172.
16. Whitwell Elwin, "Roving Life in England," *Quarterly Review*, April 1857, pp. 472–73.
17. Samuel Smiles, *Brief Biographies*, 1860, p. 158.
18. Wilbur L. Cross, *The Development of the English Novel*, 1899, pp. 211–12.
19. George Saintsbury, "Borrow" (1886), *Collected Essays and Papers*, 1923, Volume 2, pp. 76–81.
20. Augustine Birrell, "George Borrow," *Res Judicatae*, 1892, pp. 115–37.
21. Jane H. Findlater, "George Borrow," *Cornhill Magazine*, November 1899, pp. 596–603.

BENJAMIN DISRAELI

1. N. P. Willis, *Pencillings by the Way*, 1835.
2. Nathaniel Hawthorne, *The English Note-Books*, 1856.
3. L. J. Jennings, "Benjamin Disraeli," *Atlantic*, December 1873, pp. 651–52.
4. Thomas Carlyle, Letter to John Carlyle (January 1, 1875), cited in James Anthony Froude, *Thomas Carlyle: A History of His Life in London*, 1884, Volume 2, p. 369.
5. S. C. Hall, *Retrospect of a Long Life*, 1883, pp. 161–62.
6. Roundell Palmer, Earl of Selborne, *Memorials: Part II*, 1898, Volume 1, pp. 478–79.
7. George Gilfillan, "Benjamin Disraeli," A *Third Gallery of Portraits*, 1854, pp. 410–14.
8. Walter Bagehot, "Mr. Disraeli" (1859), *Collected Works*, ed. Norman St. John-Stevas, 1968, Volume 3, pp. 488–89.
9. George Saintsbury, "Disraeli: A Portrait" (1886), A *Saintsbury Miscellany*, 1947, pp. 177–78.
10. James Anthony Froude, *Lord Beaconsfield*, 1890, pp. 259–60.
11. Frederic Harrison, "Benjamin Disraeli," *Studies in Early Victorian Literature*, 1895, pp. 89–90.
12. Henry Craik, "Lord Beaconsfield," *English Prose*, ed. Henry Craik, 1896, Volume 5, pp. 486–87.
13. James Bryce, "Benjamin Disraeli, Earl of Beaconsfield," *Studies in Contemporary Biography*, 1903, pp. 43–45.
14. Lewis Melville, "Benjamin Disraeli's Novels," *Fortnightly Review*, November 1904, pp. 871–72.
15. James Grant, *The British Senate; or, A Second Series of Random Recollections of the Lords and Commons*, 1838.

5. John Quincy Adams, *Diary*, August 2, 1840.
6. Rufus Dawes, "Boyhood Memories," *Boston Miscellany*, February 1843, p. 60.
7. Henry Crabb Robinson, Letter to Thomas Robinson (April 22, 1848).
8. Arthur Hugh Clough, Letter to Thomas Arnold (July 16, 1848).
9. Maria Mitchell, *Journal* (November 14, 1855), *Life, Letters, and Journals of Maria Mitchell*, ed. Phebe Mitchell Kendall, 1896, pp. 45–47.
10. Walt Whitman, "A Visit, at the Last, to R. W. Emerson" (1881), *Prose Works*, ed. Floyd Stovall, 1963, Volume 1, pp. 278–80.
11. James Martineau, Letter to Alexander Ireland (December 31, 1882), cited in James Drummond, *The Life and Letters of James Martineau*, 1902, Volume 2, pp. 312–13.
12. Orestes Augustus Brownson, "Emerson's *Essays*," *Boston Quarterly Review*, July 1841, p. 292.
13. Caroline Fox, *Journal* (June 8, 1841), *Memories of Old Friends*, ed. Horace N. Pym, 1882, p. 140.
14. Thomas Carlyle, "Preface by the English Editor" to *Essays*, 1841, pp. v–xiii.
15. Edgar Allan Poe, "A Chapter on Autography" (1842), *Complete Works*, ed. James A. Harrison, 1902, Volume 15, p. 260.
16. Henry David Thoreau, *Journal* (1845–47), *Writings*, 1906, Volume 7, pp. 431–33.
17. Thomas Babington Macaulay, *Journal* (January 12, 1850), cited in G. Otto Trevelyan, *The Life and Letters of Lord Macaulay*, 1876, Volume 2, p. 234.
18. Thomas Powell, "Ralph Waldo Emerson," *The Living Authors of America*, 1850, pp. 66–67, 75–77.
19. James Russell Lowell, "Emerson the Lecturer" (1861–68), *Works*, Riverside ed., Volume 1, pp. 349–52.
20. George Ripley, *Journal* (1869), cited in Octavius Brooks Frothingham, *George Ripley*, 1882, pp. 266–68.
21. Walt Whitman, "Emerson's Books (The Shadows of Them)" (1880), *Prose Works*, ed. Floyd Stovall, 1963, Volume 2, pp. 515–18.
22. Coventry Patmore, "Emerson," *Principle in Art*, 1889, pp. 130–31.
23. Henry James, *Nathaniel Hawthorne*, 1879, pp. 82–83.
24. W. L. Courtney, "Ralph Waldo Emerson," *Fortnightly Review*, September 1885, p. 331.
25. Edwin P. Whipple, "American Literature" (1886), *American Literature and Other Papers*, 1887, pp. 59–65.
26. Maurice Maeterlinck, "Emerson," trs. Charlotte Porter, Helen A. Clarke, *Poet-Lore*, 1898, pp. 82–84.
27. George Edward Woodberry, *Ralph Waldo Emerson*, 1907, pp. 186–87.
28. Margaret Fuller, "Emerson's Essays," *New York Daily Tribune*, December 7, 1844.
29. Charlotte Brontë, Letter to W. S. Williams (February 4, 1849).
30. Edward FitzGerald, Letter to John Allen (March 4, 1850).
31. Charles Eliot Norton, "Emerson's *Representative Men*," *North American Review*, April 1850, pp. 520–21.
32. William P. Trent, *A History of American Literature, 1607–1865*, 1903, pp. 333–36.
33. James Russell Lowell, Letter to James B. Thayer (December 24, 1883).
34. C. C. Everett, "The Poems of Emerson," *Andover Review*, March 1887, pp. 239–40.
35. Charles F. Richardson, *American Literature, 1607–1885*, 1887, Volume 2, pp. 169–71.
36. Edmund Gosse, "Has America Produced a Poet?" (1889), *Questions at Issue*, 1893, pp. 86–88.

37. C. P. Cranch, "Emerson's Limitations as a Poet," *Critic*, February 27, 1892, p. 129.
38. George Gilfillan, "Emerson," A *Third Gallery of Portraits*, 1854, pp. 328–36.
39. Matthew Arnold, "Emerson," (1884), *Discourses in America*, 1885, pp. 150–207.
40. Edmund Clarence Stedman, "Ralph Waldo Emerson," *Poets of America*, 1885, pp. 133–79.
41. George Santayana, "Emerson," *Interpretations of Poetry and Religion*, 1900, pp. 217–33.
42. Sir Leslie Stephen, "Emerson," *National Review*, February 1901, pp. 882–98.

WILLIAM HARRISON AINSWORTH

1. Sir Walter Scott, *Journal*, October 17, 1826.
2. R. H. Horne, "William Harrison Ainsworth," A *New Spirit of the Age*, 1844, pp. 314–16.
3. Thomas B. Shaw, *Outlines of English Literature*, 1847.
4. William Bates, "William Harrison Ainsworth," *The Maclise Portrait-Gallery of Illustrious Literary Characters*, 1883, pp. 260–61.
5. S. C. Hall, *Retrospect of a Long Life*, 1883, p. 407.
6. Charles Mackay, *Through the Long Day*, 1887, Volume 1, pp. 240–43.
7. George Augustus Sala, *Life and Adventures*, 1895, Volume 1, pp. 86–87.
8. George Saintsbury, A *History of Nineteenth Century Literature*, 1896, p. 139.
9. W. E. A. Axon, *William Harrison Ainsworth: A Memoir*, 1902, pp. xli–xliii.
10. J. Hain Friswell, "Mr. Harrison Ainsworth," *Modern Men of Letters Honestly Criticised*, 1870, pp. 257–70.
11. Francis Gribble, "Harrison Ainsworth," *Fortnightly Review*, March 1905, pp. 533–42.

HENRY WADSWORTH LONGFELLOW

1. Samuel Kettell, *Specimens of American Poetry*, 1829, Volume 3, p. 238.
2. Charles Sumner, Letter to George Sumner (July 8, 1842), cited in Edward L. Pierce, *Memoir and Letters of Charles Sumner*, 1877, Volume 2, p. 215.
3. James Russell Lowell, "To H. W. L. (On His Birthday, 27th February, 1867)" (1867), cited in Samuel Longfellow, *Life of Henry Wadsworth Longfellow*, 1891, Volume 3, pp. 84–85.
4. Charles Dickens, Letter to Charles Dickens, Jr. (November 30, 1867).
5. Austin Dobson, "H. W. Longfellow: In Memoriam," *Athenaeum*, April 1, 1882, p. 411.
6. Lord Ronald Gower, *My Reminiscences* (1883), 1895, pp. 454–56.
7. Oliver Wendell Holmes, "At the Saturday Club," 1884.
8. William James Stillman, *The Autobiography of a Journalist*, 1901, Volume 1, pp. 233–35.
9. Nathaniel Hawthorne, Letter to Henry Wadsworth Longfellow (December 26, 1839), cited in Samuel Longfellow, *Life of Henry Wadsworth Longfellow*, 1891, Volume 1, p. 349.
10. Edgar Allan Poe, "A Chapter on Autography" (1841), *Complete Works*, ed. James A. Harrison, 1902, Volume 15, pp. 191–92.
11. Edgar Allan Poe, "Henry Wadsworth Longfellow" (1842), *Essays and Reviews*, ed. G. R. Thompson, 1984, pp. 682–83, 690–92.
12. William Cullen Bryant, Letter to Henry Wadsworth Longfellow (January 31, 1846).
13. James Russell Lowell, A *Fable for Critics*, 1848.

33. Grant Allen, "The Net Result," *Charles Darwin*, 1893, pp. 192–201.

ANTHONY TROLLOPE

1. Walter Herries Pollock, "Anthony Trollope," *Harper's New Monthly Magazine*, May 1883, pp. 911–12.
2. Julian Hawthorne, "The Maker of Many Books," *Manhattan*, December 1883, pp. 573–74.
3. Thomas Adolphus Trollope, *What I Remember*, 1888.
4. Nathaniel Hawthorne, Letter to Joseph M. Field (February 11, 1860), cited in Anthony Trollope, *An Autobiography*, 1883, Ch. 8.
5. J. Hain Friswell, "Anthony Trollope," *Modern Men of Letters Honestly Criticised*, 1870, pp. 143–44.
6. Edward FitzGerald, Letter to W. F. Pollock (November 30, 1873).
7. Justin McCarthy, *A History of Our Own Times*, 1879–80, Ch. 67.
8. Richard F. Littledale, *Academy*, October 27, 1883, p. 274.
9. Margaret Oliphant, *The Victorian Age of English Literature*, 1892, Volume 2, pp. 281–87.
10. William Dean Howells, "Valdés, Galdós, Verga, Zola, Trollope, Hardy," *My Literary Passions*, 1895.
11. Frederick Locker-Lampson, *My Confidences*, 1896, pp. 334–35.
12. George Saintsbury, *A History of Nineteenth Century Literature*, 1896, pp. 329–31.
13. H. D. Triall, *Social England*, 1897, Volume 6, p. 517.
14. Wilbur L. Cross, *The Development of the English Novel*, 1899, pp. 223–24.
15. Justin McCarthy, *Reminiscences*, 1899, Volume 1, pp. 374–75.
16. Walter Frewen Lord, "The Novels of Anthony Trollope," *Nineteenth Century*, May 1901, pp. 805–16.
17. James Bryce, "Anthony Trollope," *Studies in Contemporary Biography*, 1903, pp. 123, 130.
18. Unsigned, "Orley Farm," *National Review*, January 1863, pp. 36–40.
19. Anthony Trollope, *An Autobiography*, 1883, Chs. 10, 20.
20. Henry James, "Anthony Trollope," *Century Magazine*, July 1883, pp. 385–95.
21. Frederic Harrison, "Anthony Trollope," *Studies in Early Victorian Literature*, 1895, pp. 183–204.
22. Sir Leslie Stephen, "Anthony Trollope," *National Review*, September 1901, pp. 69–84.

RICHARD HENRY DANA, JR.

1. Thomas Wentworth Higginson, "Adams's Dana," *Nation*, January 15, 1891, p. 53.
2. William Everett, "Two Friends of California," *Overland Monthly*, November 1896, pp. 582–83.
3. Richard Henry Dana, Jr., "Preface" to *Two Years before the Mast*, 1840.
4. Charles Dickens, Speech at the Oxford and Harvard Boat Race, August 30, 1869.
5. Edwin P. Whipple, "American Literature" (1886), *American Literature and Other Papers*, 1887, p. 135.
6. Edward Playfair Anderson, "The Sequel of *Two Years before the Mast*," *Dial*, April 1891, pp. 379–81.
7. W. Clark Russell, "A Claim for American Literature," *North American Review*, February 1892, pp. 138–40.
8. William Everett, "Two Friends of California," *Overland Monthly*, November 1896, p. 582.
9. Edward T. Channing, "*Two Years before the Mast*," *North American Review*, January 1841, pp. 56–75.

DANTE GABRIEL ROSSETTI

1. Ford Madox Brown, *Diary* (October 6, 1854), *Ruskin: Rossetti: Preraphaelitism*, ed. William Michael Rossetti, 1899, p. 19.
2. Robert Browning, Letter to Miss Blagden (February 15, 1862), cited in Mrs. Sutherland Orr, *Life and Letters of Robert Browning*, 1891, Volume 2, p. 375.
3. Philip Bourke Marston, "In Memory of D. G. Rossetti" (1882), *Collected Poems*, 1892, p. 333.
4. Theodore Watts-Dunton, "The Truth about Rossetti," *Nineteenth Century*, March 1883, p. 419.
5. Alfred, Lord Tennyson, Letter (1885), cited in Hallam Tennyson, *Alfred Lord Tennyson: A Memoir*, 1897, Volume 2, pp. 315–16.
6. Gordon Hake, *Memoirs of Eighty Years*, 1892, pp. 220–21.
7. William Holman Hunt, "The Pre-Raphaelite Brotherhood: A Fight for Art: II," *Contemporary Review*, May 1886, pp. 739–40.
8. William James Stillman, *The Autobiography of a Journalist*, 1901, Volume 2, pp. 468–72.
9. Henry Truffry Dunn, *Recollections of Dante Gabriel Rossetti and His Circle*, 1904, pp. 28–29.
10. Leigh Hunt, Letter to Dante Gabriel Rossetti (March 31, 1848), *Dante Gabriel Rossetti: His Family Letters*, ed. William Michael Rossetti, 1895, Volume 1, pp. 122–23.
11. F. W. H. Myers, "Rossetti and the Religion of Beauty," *Cornhill Magazine*, February 1883, pp. 217–18.
12. Harry Quilter, "The Art of Rossetti," *Contemporary Review*, February 1883, pp. 201–3.
13. Coventry Patmore, "Rossetti as a Poet," *Principle in Art*, 1889, pp. 103–5.
14. Hamilton Wright Mabie, "The Poetry of Dante Gabriel Rossetti," *Essays in Literary Interpretation*, 1892, pp. 142–45.
15. William Morris, *Academy*, May 14, 1870, pp. 199–200.
16. Edmund Clarence Stedman, *Victorian Poets*, 1875, pp. 365–66.
17. James Ashcroft Noble, "The Sonnet in England" (1880), *The Sonnet in England and Other Essays*, 1893, pp. 57–58.
18. William Sharp, *Dante Gabriel Rossetti: A Record and a Study*, 1882, pp. 412–14.
19. John Addington Symonds, "Notes on Mr. D. G. Rossetti's New Poems," *Macmillan's Magazine*, February 1882, p. 328.
20. Edward Dowden, "Victorian Literature" (1887), *Transcripts and Studies*, 1888, pp. 228–30.
21. Esther Wood, *Dante Rossetti and the Pre-Raphaelite Movement*, 1894, pp. 301–4.
22. Max Nordau, *Degeneration*, 1895, pp. 92–94.
23. Vida D. Scudder, *The Life of the Spirit in the Modern English Poets*, 1895, pp. 271–74.
24. Arthur Christopher Benson, *Rossetti*, 1904, pp. 78–80.
25. Arthur Symons, "Dante Gabriel Rossetti" (1904), *Figures of Several Centuries*, 1916, pp. 201–6.
26. Cosmo Monkhouse, "Rossetti's Pictures at the Royal Academy," *Academy*, January 6, 1883, p. 15.
27. David Hannay, "The Paintings of Mr. Rossetti," *National Review*, March 1883, p. 133.
28. J. Comyns Carr, "Rossetti's Influence in Art," *English Illustrated Magazine*, October 1883, p. 40.
29. Percy Bate, "Dante Gabriel Rossetti," *The English Pre-Raphaelite Painters*, 1901, pp. 48–51.
30. Algernon Charles Swinburne, "The Poems of Dante Gabriel Rossetti," *Fortnightly Review*, May 1870, pp. 551–57, 577–79.

4. E. H. House, "Anecdotes of Charles Reade," *Atlantic*, October 1887, p. 525.
5. Harriet Prescott Spofford, "Charles Reade," *Atlantic*, August 1864, pp. 137–38, 149.
6. J. Hain Friswell, "Charles Reade," *Modern Men of Letters Honestly Criticised*, 1870, pp. 84–86.
7. A. G. Sedgwick, "Charles Reade," *Nation*, April 17, 1884, pp. 335–36.
8. Richard F. Littledale, "Charles Reade," *Academy*, April 19, 1884, p. 277.
9. Robert Buchanan, "Charles Reade," *Harper's New Monthly Magazine*, September 1884, p. 606.
10. W. L. Courtney, "Charles Reade's Novels," *Fortnightly Review*, October 1884, p. 461.
11. R. R. Bowker, "London as a Literary Centre," *Harper's New Monthly Magazine*, June 1888, p. 3.
12. Margaret Oliphant, *The Victorian Age of English Literature*, 1892, Volume 2, pp. 181–86.
13. William Dean Howells, "Charles Reade," *My Literary Passions*, 1895.
14. Francis Hovey Stoddard, *The Evolution of the English Novel*, 1900, pp. 178–83.
15. E. V. Smith, "Reade's Novels," *North American Review*, April 1856, pp. 370–71, 386–88.
16. Justin McCarthy, "Charles Reade," *Modern Leaders*, 1872, pp. 199–201.
17. Walter Besant, "Charles Reade's Novels," *Gentleman's Magazine*, August 1882, pp. 200–214.
18. Algernon Charles Swinburne, "Charles Reade," *Fortnightly Review*, October 1884, pp. 550–59.

RICHARD MONCKTON MILNES, LORD HOUGHTON

1. Sydney Smith, Letter to Richard Monckton Milnes (April 22, 1842), cited in T. Wemyss Reid, *The Life, Letters, and Friendships of Richard Monckton Milnes, First Lord Houghton*, 1891, Volume 2, pp. 214–15.
2. Thomas Carlyle, Letter to Ralph Waldo Emerson (December 30, 1847).
3. Matthew Arnold, Letter to His Mother (April 1848).
4. John Lothrop Motley, Letter to His Wife (May 28, 1858), *Correspondence*, ed. George William Curtis, 1889, Volume 1, p. 228.
5. Fanny Kemble, Letter to H—— (November 30, 1875), *Further Records*, 1891, pp. 134–35.
6. John Bigelow, "Some Recollections of Lord Houghton," *Harper's New Monthly Magazine*, November 1885, p. 955.
7. T. Wemyss Reid, "Preface" to *The Life, Letters, and Friendships of Richard Monckton Milnes, First Lord Houghton*, 1891, Volume 1, pp. xi–xii.
8. John F. Rolph, *Academy*, January 3, 1891, p. 5.
9. Edward Bulwer-Lytton, "Present State of Poetry" (1838), *Critical and Miscellaneous Writings*, 1841, Volume 3, p. 345.
10. Henry Ware, Jr., "Milnes's Poems," *North American Review*, October 1839, p. 349.
11. George S. Hillard, "Recent English Poetry," *North American Review*, July 1842, p. 218.
12. Sir Archibald Alison, *History of Europe from 1815 to 1852*, 1852–59, Ch. 5.
13. Edmund Clarence Stedman, *Victorian Poets*, 1875, pp. 244–45.
14. Harriet Martineau, *Autobiography*, ed. Maria Weston Chapman, 1877, Volume 1, pp. 259–60.
15. T. H. S. Escott, "Lord Houghton," *Fortnightly Review*, February 1885, pp. 433–35.

16. Richard Henry Stoddard, "Lord Houghton's Poetry," *Critic*, August 22, 1885, pp. 90–91.
17. Edward Peacock, "Richard Monckton Milnes, Lord Houghton," *Dublin Review*, January 1891, p. 34.
18. D. F. Hannigan, "Lord Houghton," *Westminster Review*, February 1891, p. 157.
19. James Bryce, "Reid's Life of Houghton," *Nation*, February 5, 1891, p. 118.
20. H. J. Gibbs, "Lord Houghton," *The Poets and the Poetry of the Century*, ed. Alfred H. Miles, 1892, Volume 4, pp. 242–45.
21. Richard Henry Stoddard, "Richard Monckton Milnes (Lord Houghton)," *Under the Evening Lamp*, 1892, pp. 280–83.
22. George Saintsbury, *A History of Nineteenth Century Literature*, 1896, pp. 301–2.
23. Hugh Walker, *The Age of Tennyson*, 1897, p. 58.
24. R. H. Horne, "R. M. Milnes and H. Coleridge," *A New Spirit of the Age*, 1844, pp. 154–61.

HELEN HUNT JACKSON

1. Emily Dickinson, Letter to Helen Hunt Jackson (March 1885).
2. Alice Wellington Rollins, "Authors at Home," *Critic*, April 25, 1885, p. 193.
3. Susan Coolidge, "H. H." (1885), *Ramona*, 1900, pp. xxviii–xxix.
4. Julia C. R. Dorr, "Emerson's Admiration of 'H. H.,'" *Critic*, August 29, 1885, p. 102.
5. Thomas Wentworth Higginson, "To the Memory of H. H.," *Century Magazine*, May 1886, p. 47.
6. Edith M. Thomas, "To the Memory of Helen Hunt Jackson," *Atlantic*, August 1886, pp. 195–96.
7. Thomas Wentworth Higginson, "Helen Hunt Jackson ('H. H.')," *Short Studies of American Authors*, 1879, pp. 44–50.
8. Charles F. Richardson, *American Literature, 1607–1885*, 1887, Volume 2, pp. 238–39.
9. Fred Lewis Pattee, *A History of American Literature*, 1896, pp. 405–8.
10. Katharine Lee Bates, *American Literature*, 1897, p. 178.
11. Ralph Waldo Emerson, *Journal*, July 23, 1868.
12. Emily Dickinson, Letter to Thomas Wentworth Higginson (November 1871).
13. Edmund Clarence Stedman, *Poets of America*, 1885, p. 445.
14. Edwin P. Whipple, "American Literature" (1886), *American Literature and Other Papers*, 1887, p. 131.
15. Douglas Sladen, "To the Reader," *Younger American Poets*, 1891, pp. xxviii–xxix.
16. G. Barnett Smith, *Academy*, December 20, 1884, p. 408.
17. Charles Dudley Warner, "'H. H.' in Southern California," *Critic*, May 14, 1887, p. 237.
18. Helen Gray Cone, "Woman in American Literature," *Century Magazine*, October 1890, pp. 927–28.
19. Susan Coolidge, "Introduction" to *Ramona*, 1900, pp. v–vi.
20. Louis Swinburne, "Reminiscences of Helen Jackson," *New Princeton Review*, July 1886, pp. 79–82.

SIR HENRY TAYLOR

1. Samuel Taylor Coleridge, Letter to Eliza Nixon (July 9, 1834).
2. Thomas Moore, *Journal*, March 28, 1835.
3. Thomas Carlyle, "Appendix: Southey" (1867), *Reminiscences*, ed. James Anthony Froude, 1881, Volume 2, pp. 312–13.

6. Harriet Beecher Stowe, Letter to George Eliot (March 18, 1876), cited in Charles Edward Stone, *Life of Harriet Beecher Stowe*, 1889, pp. 480–81.
7. Lyman Abbott, *Henry Ward Beecher: A Sketch of His Career*, 1882, p. 190.
8. W. S. Searle, "Beecher's Personality," *North American Review*, May 1887, p. 487.
9. A. Bronson Alcott, *Journal*, November 9, 1856.
10. Theodore Parker, "Henry Ward Beecher," *Atlantic*, May 1858, pp. 865–69.
11. Horace Bushnell, Letter to His Wife (May 11, 1858), cited in Mary A. Cheney, *Life and Letters of Horace Bushnell*, 1880, pp. 413–14.
12. Charles D. Cleveland, *A Compendium of American Literature*, 1859, pp. 679–80.
13. Hugh Reginald Haweis, "Henry Ward Beecher," *Contemporary Review*, February 1872, p. 317.
14. Joseph Parker, "Analyses of His Power, and Reminiscences by Contemporaries," *Henry Ward Beecher: A Sketch of His Career* by Lyman Abbott, 1882, p. 299.
15. Matthew Arnold, Letter to Fanny Arnold (October 28, 1883).
16. Edwin P. Whipple, "American Literature" (1886), *American Literature and Other Papers*, 1887, pp. 133–35.
17. John White Chadwick, "Henry Ward Beecher," *Nation*, March 17, 1887, p. 226.
18. Hugh McCulloch, "Memories of Some Contemporaries," *Scribner's Monthly*, September 1888, p. 281.
19. Walter Lewin, *Academy*, March 30, 1889, p. 216.
20. John Henry Barrows, *Henry Ward Beecher, the Shakespeare of the Pulpit*, 1893, pp. 527–29.
21. Henry A. Beers, *Initial Studies in American Letters*, 1895, p. 182.
22. Charles Noble, *Studies in American Literature*, 1898, p. 341.
23. J. H. Hoppin, "Henry Ward Beecher," *New Englander*, July 1870, pp. 437–40.

DINAH MARIA CRAIK

1. Margaret Oliphant, *Autobiography* (1885), *Autobiography and Letters*, ed. Mrs. Harry Coghill, 1899, p. 38.
2. R. R. Bowker, "London as a Literary Centre," *Harper's New Monthly Magazine*, June 1888, pp. 20–22.
3. Camilla Toulmin Crosland, *Landmarks of a Literary Life*, 1893, pp. 127–28.
4. Mrs. Philip Gilbert Hamerton, *Philip Gilbert Hamerton: An Autobiography and a Memoir*, 1896, pp. 332–33.
5. Robert Nourse, "An Old Book for New Readers," *Dial*, June 1883, pp. 36–37.
6. Frances Martin, "Mrs. Craik," *Athenaeum*, October 22, 1887, p. 539.
7. Alice Wellington Rollins, "The Author of *John Halifax*," *Critic*, October 29, 1887, p. 214.
8. Mildred Rutherford, "Dinah Maria Mulock," *English Authors*, 1890, pp. 585–86.
9. Margaret Oliphant, *The Victorian Age of English Literature*, 1892, Volume 2, pp. 190–91.

RICHARD JEFFERIES

1. J. W. North (c. 1888), cited in Sir Walter Besant, *The Eulogy of Richard Jefferies*, 1893, pp. 356–60.
2. C. E. Dawkins, *Academy*, November 17, 1888, pp. 315–16.
3. W. E. Henley, "Jefferies," *Views and Reviews*, 1890, pp. 179–82.
4. Sir Arthur Quiller-Couch, "The Country as 'Copy,'" *Speaker*, September 30, 1893, p. 358.
5. H. S. Salt, *Richard Jefferies: A Study*, 1894, pp. 103–4.

6. Irving Muntz, "Richard Jefferies as a Descriptive Writer," *Gentleman's Magazine*, November 1894, pp. 515–16.
7. George H. Ellwanger, "Afield with Jefferies," *Idyllists of the Country Side*, 1896, pp. 132–33.
8. George Saintsbury, *A History of Nineteenth Century Literature*, 1896, p. 397.
9. Arthur Symons, "Richard Jefferies," *Studies in Two Literatures*, 1897.
10. Edward Thomas, "Recapitulation," *Richard Jefferies: His Life and Work*, 1909, pp. 317–28.

EMMA LAZARUS

1. Allen Eastman Cross, "To Emma Lazarus," *Critic*, May 14, 1887, p. 245.
2. John Greenleaf Whittier, *American Hebrew*, December 9, 1887, p. 67.
3. John Hay, *American Hebrew*, December 9, 1887, p. 70.
4. Samuel Greenbaum, *American Hebrew*, December 9, 1887, p. 71.
5. Cyrus L. Sulzberger, "Emma Lazarus as a Jew," *American Hebrew*, December 9, 1887, p. 79.
6. Richard Grant White, "Emma Lazarus," *Century Magazine*, February 1888, p. 581.
7. Edmund Clarence Stedman, "The Nature and Elements of Poetry: VIII. The Faculty Divine," *Century Magazine*, October 1892, p. 861.
8. Josephine Lazarus, "Emma Lazarus," *Century Magazine*, October 1888, pp. 875–84.
9. Mary M. Cohen, "Emma Lazarus: Woman; Poet; Patriot," *Poet-Lore*, June 1893, pp. 324–27.

AMOS BRONSON ALCOTT

1. Thomas Carlyle, Letter to Ralph Waldo Emerson (July 19, 1842).
2. Ralph Waldo Emerson, Letter to Thomas Carlyle (October 15, 1842).
3. Henry David Thoreau, Letter to Ralph Waldo Emerson (January 12, 1848).
4. Harriet Prescott Spofford, "Louisa May Alcott," *Chautauquan*, December 1888, p. 160.
5. Rose Hawthorne Lathrop, *Memories of Hawthorne*, 1897, pp. 417–18.
6. Ralph Waldo Emerson, Letter to Margaret Fuller (May 19, 1837).
7. James Russell Lowell, *A Fable for Critics*, 1848.
8. Maria Mitchell, *Journal* (1879), cited in Phebe Mitchell Kendall, *Life, Letters, and Journals of Maria Mitchell*, 1896, p. 246.
9. Edwin P. Whipple, "American Literature" (1886), *American Literature and Other Papers*, 1887, p. 112.
10. Walter Lewin, *Academy*, March 24, 1888, pp. 205–6.
11. E. C. Towne, "A Yankee Pythagoras," *North American Review*, September 1888, pp. 345–46.
12. F. B. Sanborn, *A Bronson Alcott: His Life and Philosophy*, 1893, Volume 2, pp. 514–15.
13. William T. Harris, "Memoir of Bronson Alcott," *A Bronson Alcott: His Life and Philosophy* by F. B. Sanborn, 1893, Volume 2, pp. 618–20.
14. Charles Noble, *Studies in American Literature*, 1898, p. 322.
15. Donald G. Mitchell, *American Lands and Letters: Leather-Stocking to Poe's "Raven,"* 1899, p. 188.
16. Barrett Wendell, *A Literary History of America*, 1900, pp. 329–32.
17. William James Stillman, *The Autobiography of a Journalist*, 1901, Volume 1, pp. 219–21.
18. William P. Trent, *A History of American Literature*, 1903, pp. 312–13.

MATTHEW ARNOLD

1. Thomas Arnold, Letter to William Charles Lake (August 17, 1840), cited in Katharine Lake, *Memorials of William Charles Lake*, 1901, p. 161.
2. Charlotte Brontë, Letter to James Taylor (January 15, 1851).
3. John Tulloch, Letter (1874), cited in Margaret Oliphant, *Memoir of the Life of John Tulloch*, 1889, p. 287.
4. Maria Mitchell, *Journal* (January 9, 1884), *Life, Letters, and Journals of Maria Mitchell*, ed. Phebe Mitchell Kendall, 1896, pp. 195–96.
5. Sir Edwin Arnold, "To Matthew Arnold," *Pall Mall Gazette*, April 15, 1888.
6. George Edward Woodberry, "Matthew Arnold" (1890), *Literary Essays*, 1920, pp. 75–76.
7. A. E. Housman (c. 1891), *Selected Prose*, ed. John Carter, 1961, pp. 196–98.
8. Augustine Birrell, "Matthew Arnold," *Res Judicatae*, 1892, pp. 185–89.
9. Hugh Walker, *Academy*, December 21, 1895, p. 538.
10. W. H. Johnson, "The 'Passing' of Matthew Arnold," *Dial*, November 16, 1899, pp. 352–53.
11. G. K. Chesterton, "Matthew Arnold," *Bookman* (New York), October 1902, pp. 118–20.
12. James Anthony Froude, "Arnold's Poems" (1854), *Essays in Literature and History*, 1906, pp. 4–5.
13. George Eliot, *Westminster Review*, July 1855, pp. 297–98.
14. Andrew Lang, "Matthew Arnold," *Century Magazine*, April 1882, pp. 863–64.
15. Edward Clodd, "Matthew Arnold's Poetry," *Gentleman's Magazine*, March 1886, p. 359.
16. Andrew Lang, "Introductory: Of Modern English Poetry," *Letters on Literature*, 1889, pp. 11–14.
17. W. E. Henley, "Matthew Arnold," *Views and Reviews*, 1890, pp. 83–86.
18. Lionel Johnson, *Academy*, January 10, 1891, pp. 31–32.
19. Edwin P. Whipple, "Matthew Arnold," *North American Review*, May 1884, pp. 439–42.
20. W. E. Henley, "Matthew Arnold," *Views and Reviews*, 1890, pp. 88–91.
21. George Saintsbury, "Matthew Arnold," *Corrected Impressions*, 1895.
22. Frederic Harrison, "Matthew Arnold," *Nineteenth Century*, March 1896, pp. 441–43.
23. J. Llewelyn Davies, "Mr. Arnold's New Religion," *Contemporary Review*, May 1873, pp. 845–46.
24. H. D. Traill, "Neo-Christianity and Mr. Matthew Arnold," *Contemporary Review*, April 1884, pp. 575–76.
25. Richard Holt Hutton, "Newman and Arnold: II. Matthew Arnold," *Contemporary Review*, April 1886, pp. 526–28.
26. Henry Sidgwick, "The Prophet of Culture," *Macmillan's Magazine*, August 1867, pp. 271–80.
27. Algernon Charles Swinburne, "Matthew Arnold's New Poems" (1867), *Essays and Studies*, 1875, pp. 152–83.
28. Sir Leslie Stephen, "Matthew Arnold" (1893), *Studies of a Biographer*, 1899, Volume 2, pp. 76–122.

LOUISA MAY ALCOTT

1. Henry James, *Nation*, October 14, 1875, p. 250.
2. Edwin P. Whipple, "American Literature" (1886), *American Literature and Other Papers*, 1887, p. 126.
3. Walter Lewin, *Academy*, March 24, 1888, p. 206.
4. Lucy C. Lillie, "Louisa May Alcott," *Cosmopolitan*, May 1888, pp. 162–63.
5. Harriet Prescott Spofford, "Louisa May Alcott," *Chautauquan*, December 1888, pp. 161–62.
6. Ednah D. Cheney, "Introduction" to *Louisa May Alcott: Her Life, Letters, and Journals*, 1889, p. iii.
7. John Haberton, "In the Library," *Cosmopolitan*, December 1889, p. 254.
8. Josephine Lazarus, "Louisa May Alcott," *Century Magazine*, May 1891, pp. 59–67.
9. Maria S. Porter, "Recollections of Louisa May Alcott," *New England Magazine*, March 1892, p. 3.
10. Charles Noble, *Studies in American Literature*, 1898, pp. 306–7.
11. Lilian Whiting, "Louisa May Alcott," *Chautauquan*, June 1899, p. 281.
12. Francis Whiting Halsey, *Our Literary Deluge and Some of Its Deeper Waters*, 1902, pp. 124–25.
13. Henry James, "Miss Alcott's Moods," *North American Review*, July 1865, pp. 276–81.
14. Thomas Wentworth Higginson, "Louisa May Alcott," *Short Studies of American Authors* (1879), 1888, pp. 61–67.

ROBERT BROWNING

1. William Charles Macready, *Diary*, December 31, 1835.
2. George Stillman Hillard, *Six Months in Italy*, 1853, p. 114.
3. Nathaniel Hawthorne, *The English Note-Books*, July 13, 1856.
4. Benjamin Jowett, Letter (June 12, 1865), cited in Evelyn Abbott, Lewis Campbell, *The Life and Letters of Benjamin Jowett*, 1897, Volume 1, pp. 400–401.
5. Alfred, Lord Tennyson, Dedication to *Tiresias and Other Poems*, 1885.
6. Thomas Adolphus Trollope, *What I Remember*, 1888.
7. George William Curtis, "Editor's Easy Chair," *Harper's New Monthly Magazine*, March 1890, p. 637.
8. James Fotheringham, *Studies of the Mind and Art of Robert Browning*, 1898, pp. 42–43.
9. Frederic Harrison, "Personal Reminiscences," *George Washington and Other American Addresses*, 1901, p. 207.
10. William James Stillman, *The Autobiography of a Journalist*, 1901, Volume 2, p. 627.
11. Elizabeth Barrett Browning, *Lady Geraldine's Courtship*, 1844, Stanza 41.
12. Walter Savage Landor, "To Robert Browning," 1845.
13. Margaret Fuller, "Browning's Poems" (1846), *Art, Literature, and the Drama*, 1860, p. 209.
14. George Eliot, *Westminster Review*, January 1856, pp. 290–91.
15. John Ruskin, *Modern Painters*, 1856, Pt. 5, Ch. 20.
16. James Thomson, "The Poems of William Blake" (1864), *Biographical and Critical Studies*, 1896, pp. 266–67.
17. Edward FitzGerald, Letter to Alfred, Lord Tennyson (April 1869).
18. Edmund Clarence Stedman, *Victorian Poets*, 1875, pp. 338–41.
19. Algernon Charles Swinburne, *George Chapman: A Critical Essay*, 1875, pp. 15–18.
20. Harriet Martineau, *Autobiography*, ed. Maria Weston Chapman, 1877, Volume 1, pp. 314–15.
21. Justin McCarthy, *A History of Our Own Times*, 1879–80, Ch. 29.
22. William John Alexander, *An Introduction to the Poetry of Robert Browning*, 1889, pp. 2, 210.
23. Andrew Lang, "Introductory: Of Modern English Poetry," *Letters on Literature*, 1889, pp. 8–11.
24. John T. Nettleship, "Robert Browning," *Academy*, December 21, 1889, p. 406.
25. Algernon Charles Swinburne, "A Sequence of Sonnets on

the Death of Robert Browning: I," *Fortnightly Review*, January 1890, p. 1.

26. Aubrey De Vere, "Robert Browning," *Macmillan's Magazine*, February 1890, p. 258.

27. Annie E. Ireland, "Browning's Types of Womanhood," *The Woman's World*, 1890.

28. John Addington Symonds, "A Comparison of Elizabethan with Victorian Poetry," *Essays Speculative and Suggestive*, 1890, Volume 2, p. 246.

29. Barrett Wendell, *English Composition*, 1891, p. 208.

30. Oscar Wilde, *The Critic as Artist*, 1891.

31. Arthur Christopher Benson, "The Poetry of Edmund Gosse" (1894), *Essays*, 1896, p. 298.

32. George Saintsbury, *A History of Nineteenth Century Literature*, 1896, pp. 272–76.

33. Augustine Birrell, "Robert Browning" (1897), *Essays and Addresses*, 1901, pp. 185–94.

34. Thomas Wentworth Higginson, "The Biography of Browning's Fame," *The Boston Browning Society Papers*, 1897, p. 5.

35. Francis Thompson, "Academy Portraits: XXVI. Robert Browning," *Academy*, May 8, 1897, p. 499.

36. Arthur Waugh, *Robert Browning*, 1899, pp. 150–52.

37. W. J. Fox, *Monthly Repository*, November 1835, p. 716.

38. Leigh Hunt, *London Journal*, November 21, 1835, p. 405.

39. John Forster, "Evidences of a New Genius for Dramatic Poetry," *New Monthly Magazine*, March 1836, pp. 289–90.

40. R. H. Horne, "Robert Browning and J. W. Marston," *A New Spirit of the Age*, 1844, pp. 280–82.

41. Thomas Lovell Beddoes, Letter to Thomas Forbes Kelsall (November 13, 1844).

42. Harriet Waters Preston, "Robert and Elizabeth Browning," *Atlantic*, June 1899, p. 814.

43. William Charles Macready, *Diary*, March 19, 1837.

44. Herman Merivale, "Browning's *Strafford*: A Tragedy," *Edinburgh Review*, July 1837, pp. 147–48.

45. Charlotte Porter, "Dramatic Motive in Browning's *Strafford*" (1893), *The Boston Browning Society Papers*, 1897, pp. 190–91.

46. Charles Dickens, Letter to John Forster (November 25, 1842).

47. John Forster, *Examiner*, February 18, 1843, p. 101.

48. Helena Faucit Martin, "On Some of Shakespeare's Female Characters: III. Desdemona," *Blackwood's Edinburgh Magazine*, March 1881, p. 326.

49. Thomas R. Lounsbury, "A Philistine View," *Atlantic*, December 1899, p. 773.

50. Dante Gabriel Rossetti, Letter to William Allingham (November 25, 1855).

51. John Greenleaf Whittier, Letter to Lucy Larcom (1855), cited in Samuel T. Pickard, *Life and Letters of John Greenleaf Whittier*, 1895, Volume 1, p. 370.

52. Margaret Oliphant, "Modern Light Literature—Poetry," *Blackwood's Edinburgh Magazine*, February 1856, p. 137.

53. Andrew Lang, "Adventures among Books," *Scribner's Magazine*, November 1891, p. 652.

54. Dante Gabriel Rossetti, Letter to William Allingham (December 23, 1868).

55. John Morley, "On *The Ring and the Book*," *Fortnightly Review*, March 1869, pp. 341–42.

56. Robert Buchanan, *Athenaeum*, March 20, 1869, p. 399.

57. Gerard Manley Hopkins, Letter to R. W. Dixon (October 12, 1881).

58. Alexandra Orr, *A Handbook to the Works of Robert Browning*, 1885, pp. 75–76.

59. William Dean Howells, "Certain Preferences and Experiences," *My Literary Passions*, 1895.

60. Henry James, "Browning's *Inn Album*," *Nation*, January 20, 1876, p. 49.

61. A. C. Bradley, "Mr. Browning's *Inn Album*," *Macmillan's Magazine*, February 1876, p. 354.

62. Walter Bagehot, "Wordsworth, Tennyson, and Browning; or, Pure, Ornate, and Grotesque Art in English Poetry" (1864), *Collected Works*, ed. Norman St. John-Stevas, 1965, Volume 2, pp. 352–61.

63. Edward Dowden, "Mr. Browning's *Sordello*," *Fraser's Magazine*, October 1867, pp. 518–22.

64. Alfred Austin, "The Poetry of the Period," *Temple Bar*, June 1869, pp. 320–33.

65. Henry James, "Browning in Westminster Abbey," *Speaker*, January 4, 1890, pp. 10–12.

66. George Santayana, "The Poetry of Barbarism: III. Robert Browning," *Interpretations of Poetry and Religion*, 1900, pp. 188–214.

67. G. K. Chesterton, *Robert Browning*, 1903, pp. 177–202.

WILLIAM ALLINGHAM

1. Coventry Patmore, Letter (c. 1850), cited in Derek Patmore, *The Life and Times of Coventry Patmore*, 1949, p. 94.

2. Alfred, Lord Tennyson, Letter to W. E. Gladstone (1865), cited in Hallam Tennyson, *Alfred Lord Tennyson: A Memoir*, 1897, Volume 2, p. 31.

3. Edmund Clarence Stedman, *Victorian Poets*, 1875, pp. 258–59.

4. Cosmo Monkhouse, "Allingham's New Poems," *Academy*, February 3, 1886, pp. 72–73.

5. Hugh Walker, *The Age of Tennyson*, 1897, p. 256.

6. Lionel Johnson, "William Allingham," *A Treasury of Irish Poetry in the English Tongue*, eds. Stopford A. Brooke, T. W. Rolleston, 1900, pp. 364–67.

7. W. B. Yeats, "A Poet We Have Neglected" (1891), *Uncollected Prose*, ed. John P. Frayne, 1970, Volume 1, pp. 209–12.

WILKIE COLLINS

1. Henry Morley, *Journal of a London Playgoer*, October 16, 1858.

2. Margaret Oliphant, "Sensation Novels," *Blackwood's Edinburgh Magazine*, May 1862, p. 566.

3. Alexander Smith, "Novels and Novelists of the Day," *North British Review*, Feburary 1863, pp. 183–85.

4. Henry James, "Miss Braddon," *Nation*, November 9, 1865, p. 593.

5. J. L. Stewart, "Wilkie Collins as a Novelist," *Canadian Monthly and National Review*, November 1878, pp. 586–87.

6. Anthony Trollope, *An Autobiography*, 1883, Ch. 13.

7. Charles L. Reade, Compton Reade, *Charles Reade: A Memoir*, 1887, p. 392.

8. R. R. Bowker, "London as a Literary Centre," *Harper's New Monthly Magazine*, June 1888, pp. 3–4.

9. George Bainton, *The Art of Authorship*, 1890, p. 89.

10. Frank T. Marzials, *Academy*, October 8, 1892, p. 304.

11. Margaret Oliphant, *The Victorian Age of English Literature*, 1892, Volume 2, pp. 186–89.

12. George Meredith, Letter to Samuel Lucas (January 3, 1860).

13. George Meredith, Letter to Samuel Lucas (January 5, 1860).

14. Charles Dickens, Letter to Wilkie Collins (January 7, 1860).

15. Margaret Oliphant, Letter to William Blackwood (1862),

Volume 10

3. Algernon Charles Swinburne, "On the Death of Sir Richard Burton," 1891.
4. Janetta Newton-Robinson, "The *Life of Sir Richard Burton*," *Westminster Review*, November 1893, p. 482.
5. Percy Addleshaw, *Academy*, October 21, 1893, pp. 333–34.

GEORGE BANCROFT

1. James Wynne, "George Bancroft," *Harper's New Monthly Magazine*, June 1862, p. 54.
2. John W. Forney, "George Bancroft," *Anecdotes of Public Men*, 1881, Volume 2, p. 35.
3. B. G. Lovejoy, "Authors at Home: VI. George Bancroft," *Critic*, February 7, 1885, p. 61.
4. Edward Everett, "Bancroft's *History of the United States*," *North American Review*, January 1835, pp. 99, 122.
5. William H. Prescott, "Bancroft's United States" (1841), *Biographical and Critical Miscellanies*, 1845.
6. Edgar Allan Poe, "Fifty Suggestions" (1849), *Essays and Reviews*, ed. G. R. Thompson, 1984, p. 1304.
7. Francis H. Underwood, A *Hand-Book of English Literature*, 1872, p. 201.
8. John Nichol, *American Literature*, 1882, p. 145.
9. Edwin P. Whipple, "American Literature" (1886), *American Literature and Other Papers*, 1887, pp. 91–92.
10. William M. Sloane, "George Bancroft—In Society, in Politics, in Letters," *Century Magazine*, January 1887, pp. 484–85.
11. Fred Lewis Pattee, A *History of American Literature*, 1896, pp. 311–13.
12. M. E. W. Sherwood, *An Epistle to Posterity*, 1897, pp. 124–25.
13. Donald G. Mitchell, *American Lands and Letters: Leather-Stocking to Poe's "Raven,"* 1899, p. 48.
14. Barrett Wendell, A *Literary History of America*, 1900, pp. 271–72.
15. William Cranston Lawton, *Introduction to the Study of American Literature*, 1902, pp. 259–60.
16. William P. Trent, A *History of American Literature*, 1903, pp. 541–44.
17. R. H. Clarke, "Bancroft's *History of the United States*," *Catholic World*, September 1883, pp. 721–24.
18. Thomas Wentworth Higginson, "George Bancroft," *Nation*, January 22, 1891, pp. 66–67.

ALEXANDER WILLIAM KINGLAKE

1. John Lothrop Motley, Letter to His Wife (July 26, 1858), *Correspondence*, ed. George William Curtis, 1889, Volume 1, p. 302.
2. Lady Gregory, "*Eōthen* and the Athenaeum Club," *Blackwood's Edinburgh Magazine*, December 1895, pp. 802–4.
3. Sir Arthur Quiller-Couch, "Alexander William Kinglake" (1891), *Adventures in Criticism*, 1896, pp. 142–46.
4. George Saintsbury, A *History of Nineteenth Century Literature*, 1896, pp. 241–42.
5. Hugh Walker, *The Age of Tennyson*, 1897, pp. 132–33.
6. Eliot Warburton, "*Eōthen*," *Quarterly Review*, December 1844, pp. 56–57.
7. Elizabeth Barrett Browning, Letter to Mrs. Martin (November 16, 1844).
8. Caroline Fox, *Journal* (June 6, 1845), *Memories of Old Friends*, ed. Horace N. Pym, 1882, p. 220.
9. Margaret Oliphant, *The Victorian Age of English Literature*, 1892, Volume 2, pp. 255–56.
10. W. Tuckwell, *A. W. Kinglake: A Biographical and Literary Study*, 1902, pp. 26–32.
11. John Blackwood, Letter to Alexander William Kinglake (October 19, 1862), cited in Mary Blackwood Porter, An-

nals of a Publishing House: William Blackwood and His Sons, 1898, Volume 3, pp. 90–91.
12. Matthew Arnold, "The Literary Influence of Academies" (1864), *Essays in Criticism*, 1865.
13. Justin McCarthy, A *History of Our Own Times*, 1879–80, Ch. 67.
14. George Villiers, Lord Clarendon, "Kinglake's *Invasion of the Crimea*," *Edinburgh Review*, April 1863, pp. 307–11, 352.

JAMES RUSSELL LOWELL

1. Oliver Wendell Holmes, "To James Russell Lowell," 1885.
2. Thomas Bailey Aldrich, "Elmwood," 1891.
3. M. E. W. Sherwood, *An Epistle to Posterity*, 1897, pp. 33–34.
4. William James Stillman, *The Autobiography of a Journalist*, 1901, Volume 1, pp. 243–44.
5. Joseph Story, Letter to William W. Story (February 9, 1841), cited in William W. Story, *Life and Letters of Joseph Story*, 1851, Volume 2, p. 366.
6. Edgar Allan Poe, "A Chapter on Autography" (1841), *Complete Works*, ed. James A. Harrison, 1902, Volume 15, pp. 239–40.
7. George S. Hillard, "Lowell's *Poems*," *North American Review*, April 1841, pp. 454–55.
8. C. C. Felton, "Lowell's *Poems*," *North American Review*, April 1844, pp. 288–89.
9. Elizabeth Barrett Browning, Letter to Robert Browning (December 20, 1845).
10. Margaret Fuller, "American Literature," *Papers on Literature and Art*, 1846.
11. James Russell Lowell, A *Fable for Critics*, 1848.
12. George Eliot, Letter to Barbara Bodichon (June 17, 1871).
13. Francis H. Underwood, A *Hand-Book of English Authors*, 1872, p. 422.
14. Edward FitzGerald, Letter to Elizabeth Cowell (November 13, 1876).
15. Matthew Arnold, Letter to Charles Eliot Norton (October 8, 1884).
16. G. Barnett Smith, "James Russell Lowell," *Nineteenth Century*, June 1885, p. 1008.
17. Edmund Clarence Stedman, *Poets of America*, 1885, pp. 346–48.
18. Charles F. Richardson, *American Literature, 1607–1885*, 1887, Volume 2, pp. 199–200.
19. Harriet Beecher Stowe, Letter to James Russell Lowell (February 16, 1889), *Critic*, February 23, 1889, p. 86.
20. Theodore Roosevelt, *Critic*, February 23, 1889, pp. 86–87.
21. Francis Parkman, *Critic*, February 23, 1889, p. 87.
22. Theodore Watts-Dunton, "James Russell Lowell," *Athenaeum*, August 22, 1891, p. 258.
23. Bret Harte, "A Few Words about Mr. Lowell," *New Review*, September 1891, pp. 197–200.
24. C. T. Winchester, "Lowell as Man of Letters," *Review of Reviews*, October 1891, p. 293.
25. F. W. Farrar, "An English Estimate of Lowell," *Forum*, October 1891, pp. 148–51.
26. George William Curtis, *James Russell Lowell: An Address*, 1893, pp. 61–64.
27. Francis H. Underwood, *The Poet and the Man: Recollections and Appreciations of James Russell Lowell*, 1893, pp. 97–99.
28. Charles Eliot Norton, "James Russell Lowell," *Harper's New Monthly Magazine*, May 1893, p. 851.
29. William Dean Howells, "Certain Preferences and Experiences," *My Literary Passions*, 1895.

HERMAN MELVILLE

ROBERT EDWARD BULWER LYTTON

JOHN GREENLEAF WHITTIER

ALFRED, LORD TENNYSON

New York," *Harper's New Monthly Magazine*, June 1895, p. 65.

31. Willa Cather, "Whitman" (1896), *The Kingdom of Art*, ed. Bernice Slote, 1966, pp. 351–53.

32. Henry Childs Merwin, "Men and Letters," *Atlantic*, May 1897, p. 719.

33. Hallam Tennyson, *Alfred Lord Tennyson: A Memoir*, 1897, Volume 2, p. 424.

34. Jennette Barbour Perry, "Whitmania," *Critic*, February 26, 1898, pp. 137–38.

35. Thomas Wentworth Higginson, "Whitman," *Contemporaries*, 1899, pp. 79–84.

36. J. A. MacCulloch, "Walt Whitman: The Poet of Brotherhood," *Westminster Review*, November 1899, pp. 563–64.

37. William P. Trent, A *History of American Literature*, 1903, pp. 493–94.

38. Ralph Waldo Emerson, Letter to Walt Whitman (July 21, 1855).

39. Charles A. Dana, *New York Tribune*, July 23, 1855, p. 3.

40. Walt Whitman, *Brooklyn Daily Times*, September 29, 1855.

41. Dante Gabriel Rossetti, Letter to William Allingham (April 1856).

42. William Allingham, Letter to Dante Gabriel Rossetti (April 10, 1857).

43. Sidney Lanier, Letter to Bayard Taylor (February 3, 1878).

44. Walter Lewin, *"Leaves of Grass,"* *Murray's Magazine*, September 1887, pp. 327–28.

45. Walt Whitman, "An Old Man's Rejoinder" (1890), *Good-Bye My Fancy*, 1891.

46. C. D. Lanier, "Walt Whitman," *Chautauquan*, June 1902, p. 310.

47. George Saintsbury, *Academy*, October 10, 1874, pp. 398–400.

48. Edmund Clarence Stedman, "Walt Whitman," *Scribner's Monthly*, November 1880, pp. 54–63.

49. Robert Louis Stevenson, "Walt Whitman (1882), *Familiar Studies of Men and Books*, 1882, pp. 104–12.

50. Walter Kennedy, "Walt Whitman," *North American Review*, June 1884, pp. 593–601.

51. Algernon Charles Swinburne, "Whitmania," *Fortnightly Review*, August 1887, pp. 170–76.

52. John Addington Symonds, *Walt Whitman: A Study*, 1893, pp. 67–76.

53. George Santayana, "The Poetry of Barbarism: II. Walt Whitman," *Interpretations of Poetry and Religion*, 1900, pp. 177–87.

EDWARD AUGUSTUS FREEMAN

1. Hannah More, Letter to Edward Augustus Freeman (c. 1832), cited in W. R. W. Stephens, *The Life and Letters of Edward A. Freeman*, 1895, Volume 1, p. 6.

2. Edward A. Freeman, "A Review of My Opinions," *Forum*, April 1892, p. 154.

3. Andrew Lang, "The Month in England," *Cosmopolitan*, October 1895, p. 694.

4. Herbert B. Adams, "Freeman the Scholar and Professor," *Yale Review*, November 1895, pp. 231–32.

5. Justin McCarthy, A *History of Our Own Times from 1880 to the Diamond Jubilee*, 1897, Ch. 14.

6. A. V. Dicey, "Two Historical Essayists: II. Mr. Freeman," *Nation*, December 21, 1871, pp. 403–4.

7. W. F. Allen, "Freeman's *Historical Essays*," *Nation*, April 29, 1880, p. 331.

8. J. H. Round, "Is Mr. Freeman Accurate?," *Antiquary*, June 1886, p. 240.

9. J. S. Cotton, "E. A. Freeman," *Academy*, March 26, 1892, p. 301.

10. Edmund Venables, "Reminiscences of E. A. Freeman," *Fortnightly Review*, May 1892, p. 739.

11. John Fiske, "Edward Augustus Freeman" (1892), A *Century of Science and Other Essays*, 1899, pp. 272–74.

12. Margaret Oliphant, *The Victorian Age of English Literature*, 1892, Volume 2, pp. 254–55.

13. W. R. W. Stephens, *The Life and Letters of Edward A. Freeman*, 1895, Volume 2, pp. 472–73.

14. George Saintsbury, A *History of Nineteenth Century Literature*, 1896, p. 245.

15. G. Gregory Smith, "Edward Freeman," *English Prose*, ed. Henry Craik, 1896, Volume 5, pp. 723–24.

16. Edmund Gosse, A *Short History of Modern English Literature*, 1897, pp. 375–76.

17. Frederic Harrison, "The Historical Method of Professor Freeman," *Nineteenth Century*, November 1898, pp. 791–92.

18. James Bryce, "Edward Freeman," *Studies in Contemporary Biography*, 1903, pp. 281–87.

19. William Clarke, "Edward Augustus Freeman," *New England Magazine*, July 1892, pp. 610–13.

GEORGE WILLIAM CURTIS

1. Mary Abigail Dodge (as "Gail Hamilton"), Letter (November 27, 1865), cited in *Gail Hamilton's Life in Letters*, ed. H. Augusta Dodge, 1901, Volume 1, p. 528.

2. James Russell Lowell, "An Epistle to George William Curtis," 1874.

3. Sherman S. Rogers, "George William Curtis and Civil Service Reform," *Atlantic*, January 1893, pp. 22–23.

4. John White Chadwick, "Recollections of George William Curtis," *Harper's New Monthly Magazine*, February 1893, p. 476.

5. Parke Godwin, "George William Curtis" (1893), *Commemorative Addresses*, 1895, pp. 55–57.

6. Hamilton W. Mabie, "The Speech as Literature," *My Study Fire: Second Series*, 1896, pp. 97–98.

7. George Willis Cooke, "George William Curtis at Concord," *Harper's New Monthly Magazine*, December 1897, p. 149.

8. Henry Wadsworth Longfellow, *Journal* (March 30, 1851), cited in Samuel Longfellow, *Life of Henry Wadsworth Longfellow*, 1891, Volume 2, p. 205.

9. William Dean Howells, "George William Curtis," *North American Review*, July 1868, pp. 115–17.

10. S. S. Conant, "George William Curtis," *Century Magazine*, February 1883, pp. 581–82.

11. Edwin P. Whipple, "American Literature" (1886), *American Literature and Other Papers*, 1887, pp. 88–89.

12. Charles F. Richardson, *American Literature, 1607–1885*, 1887, Volume 1, pp. 381–84.

13. Brander Matthews, "Concerning Certain American Essayists," *Cosmopolitan*, May 1892, pp. 86–87.

14. Walter Lewin, *Academy*, May 7, 1892, p. 441.

15. William Winter, *George William Curtis: A Eulogy*, 1893, pp. 45–46.

16. Edward Cary, *George William Curtis*, 1894, pp. 70–73.

17. Fred Lewis Pattee, A *History of American Literature*, 1896, pp. 237–39.

18. Katharine Lee Bates, *American Literature*, 1897, p. 292.

19. William Cranston Lawton, *Introduction to the Study of American Literature*, 1902, p. 322.

20. Eugene Benson, "New York Journalists: George William Curtis," *Galaxy*, March 1869, pp. 328–30.

Naturalist," *The Foundations of Zoölogy*, 1899, pp. 45–46.

15. John Fiske, "Reminiscences of Huxley" (1901), *Essays Historical and Literary*, 1902, Volume 2, pp. 209–13.
16. J. R. Ainsworth Davis, *Thomas Henry Huxley*, 1907, pp. 252–53.
17. George W. Smalley, "Mr. Huxley," *Scribner's Magazine*, October 1895, pp. 514–24.
18. Sir Leslie Stephen, "Thomas Henry Huxley" (1900), *Studies of a Biographer*, 1902, Volume 3, pp. 193–219.

EUGENE FIELD

1. Hamlin Garland, "Real Conversations: II. A Dialogue between Eugene Field and Hamlin Garland," *McClure's Magazine*, August 1893, p. 195.
2. John D. Barry, "New York Letter," *Literary World*, November 30, 1895, p. 420.
3. Roswell Martin Field, "Eugene Field, a Memory," *The Works of Eugene Field*, 1896, Volume 1, pp. xxii–xxv.
4. Francis Wilson, *The Eugene Field I Knew*, 1898, pp. 1–5.
5. Stanley Waterloo, "Introduction" to *Eugene Field in His Home* by Ida Comstock Below, 1898, pp. xii–xiv.
6. James Whitcomb Riley, "Eugene Field," 1895.
7. Louis J. Block, "Eugene Field," *Dial*, June 1, 1896, pp. 333–34.
8. Katharine Lee Bates, *American Literature*, 1897, p. 204.
9. George W. Cable, "Introduction" to *The Eugene Field Book*, eds. Mary E. Burt, Mary B. Cable, 1898, pp. xiii–xv.
10. Slason Thomson, "By Way of Introduction," *Eugene Field: A Study in Heredity and Contradictions*, 1901, Volume 1, pp. viii–x.
11. William Cranston Lawton, *Introduction to the Study of American Literature*, 1902, p. 331.

HARRIET BEECHER STOWE

1. Joseph H. Twichell, "Authors at Home: XXIII. Mrs. Harriet Beecher Stowe in Hartford," *Critic*, December 18, 1886, p. 302.
2. Elizabeth Stuart Phelps, "Reminiscences of Harriet Beecher Stowe," *McClure's Magazine*, June 1896, p. 6.
3. Annie Fields, *Life and Letters of Harriet Beecher Stowe*, 1898, pp. 306–7.
4. J. W. De Forest, "The Great American Novel," *Nation*, January 9, 1868, p. 28.
5. John Greenleaf Whittier, "A Greeting," 1882.
6. James Herbert Morse, "The Native Element in American Fiction," *Century Magazine*, June 1883, pp. 296–97.
7. Edwin P. Whipple, "American Literature" (1886), *American Literature and Other Papers*, 1887, pp. 122–23.
8. Charles F. Richardson, *American Literature, 1607–1885*, 1887, Volume 2, pp. 410–12.
9. Walter Lewin, *Academy*, March 8, 1890, pp. 162–63.
10. Helen Gray Cone, "Woman in American Literature," *Century Magazine*, October 1890, pp. 925–26.
11. Richard Burton, "Harriet Beecher Stowe," *American Prose*, ed. George Rice Carpenter, 1898, pp. 308–11.
12. Harriet Beecher Stowe, "Preface" to *Uncle Tom's Cabin*, 1852.
13. Henry Wadsworth Longfellow, *Journal* (May 1852), cited in Samuel Longfellow, *Life of Henry Wadsworth Longfellow*, 1891, Volume 2, pp. 237–38.
14. Sir Arthur Helps, "Uncle Tom's Cabin," *Fraser's Magazine*, August 1852, pp. 237–44.
15. S. G. Fisher, "Uncle Tom's Cabin," *North American Review*, October 1853, pp. 466–67.
16. T. Mozley, *Reminiscences Chiefly of Oriel College and the Oxford Movement*, 1882, Volume 2, pp. 395–96.

17. Frances E. Willard, "Harriet Beecher Stowe at Home," *Chautauquan*, February 1888, p. 287.
18. Brander Matthews, "American Fiction Again," *Cosmopolitan*, March 1892, p. 637.
19. William Dean Howells, "Literary Boston as I Knew It" (1895), *Literary Friends and Acquaintance*, 1900, pp. 118–19.
20. James Herbert Morse, "Harriet Beecher Stowe," *Critic*, July 4, 1896, p. 2.
21. Thomas Wentworth Higginson, "Harriet Beecher Stowe," *Nation*, July 9, 1896, p. 25.
22. William Dean Howells, "My Favorite Novelist," *Munsey's Magazine*, April 1897, p. 22.
23. Henry Greville, *Diary*, September 20, 1856.
24. Fanny Kemble, Letter to Henry Greville (c. October 1856), cited in *Leaves from the Diary of Henry Greville*, ed. Viscountess Enfield, 1884, Volume 2, p. 396.
25. George Eliot, *Westminster Review*, October 1856, pp. 571–73.
26. George Sand, *La Presse*, December 17, 1852.
27. Samuel Warren, "Uncle Tom's Cabin," *Blackwood's Edinburgh Magazine*, October 1853, pp. 395–96, 422–23.
28. Julius H. Ward, "Harriet Beecher Stowe," *Forum*, August 1896, pp. 730–34.
29. Gerald Stanley Lee, "Harriet Beecher Stowe," *Critic*, April 24, 1897, pp. 281–83.

COVENTRY PATMORE

1. Nathaniel Hawthorne, *The English Note-Books*, January 3, 1858.
2. Unsigned, "Gold from a Poet's Treasury," *Saturday Review*, November 16, 1895, p. 658.
3. Richard Garnett, "Recollections of Coventry Patmore," *Saturday Review*, December 5, 1896, p. 582.
4. E. C. J., "Coventry Patmore, His Relatives and Friends," *Dial*, January 16, 1901, p. 38.
5. Edmund Gosse, *Coventry Patmore*, 1905, p. 181.
6. Edmund Clarence Stedman, *Victorian Poets*, 1875, pp. 266–67.
7. Louis Garvin, "Coventry Patmore: The Praise of the Odes," *Fortnightly Review*, February 1897, pp. 210–12.
8. Unsigned, *Blackwood's Edinburgh Magazine*, September 1844, pp. 331–42.
9. John Ruskin, Letter to *The Critic* (October 21, 1860), cited in *Memoirs and Correspondence of Coventry Patmore*, ed. Basil Champneys, 1900, Volume 2, pp. 280–82.
10. Unsigned, *Spectator*, October 20, 1860, pp. 1003–4.
11. Unsigned, *Dublin University Magazine*, April 1861, pp. 411–12.
12. Alfred, Lord Tennyson, Letter to Coventry Patmore (October 30, 1854), cited in *Memoirs and Correspondence of Coventry Patmore*, ed. Basil Champneys, 1900, Volume 2, p. 165.
13. Dante Gabriel Rossetti, Letter to William Allingham (January 23, 1855).
14. Henry F. Chorley, *Athenaeum*, January 20, 1856, p. 76.
15. Thomas Carlyle, Letter to Coventry Patmore (July 31, 1856), cited in *Memoirs and Correspondence of Coventry Patmore*, ed. Basil Champneys, 1900, Volume 2, pp. 311–12.
16. Aubrey De Vere, "The Angel in the House," *Edinburgh Review*, January 1858, pp. 66–67.
17. Unsigned, "Coventry Patmore," *Southern Literary Messenger*, June 1859, pp. 416–17.
18. George Brimley, "The Angel in the House" (1856), *Essays*, 1858, pp. 286–87.

5. W. H. Babcock, "The George Movement and Property," *Lippincott's Magazine*, January 1887, p. 133.
6. Edward Gordon Clark, "Henry George's Land Tax," *North American Review*, January 1887, pp. 108–9.
7. Herbert Spencer, "Parliamentary Georgites" (1894), *Various Fragments*, 1897, pp. 123–24.
8. Leo Tolstoy, "Preface to the Russian Edition of Henry George's *Social Problems*," *Tolstoy on Land and Slavery*, 1909, pp. 57–61.
9. Unsigned, "The Forces of Human Progress," *Popular Science Monthly*, February 1881, pp. 553–56.
10. Richard T. Ely, "Recent American Socialism," *Johns Hopkins University Studies in Historical and Political Science*, April 1885, pp. 246–50.

WILLIAM EWART GLADSTONE

1. Arthur Penrhyn Stanley, Letter (June 26, 1828), *Life and Correspondence*, eds. Rowland E. Prothero, G. G. Bradley, 1894, Volume 2, p. 22.
2. Walter Bagehot, "Mr. Gladstone," *National Review*, July 1860, pp. 221–23.
3. John Addington Symonds, "Recollections of Lord Tennyson" (diary entry for December 8, 1865), *Century Magazine*, May 1893, pp. 32–35.
4. Thomas Carlyle, *Journal* (January 23, 1867), cited in James Anthony Froude, *Thomas Carlyle: A History of His Life in London*, 1884, Volume 2, p. 359.
5. Hallam Tennyson, *Journal* (September 8, 1883), *Alfred Lord Tennyson: A Memoir*, 1897, Volume 2, pp. 278–81.
6. Joseph Parker, *A Preacher's Life*, 1899, pp. 289–90.
7. Lord Rosebery, *Appreciations and Addresses*, 1899, pp. 108–9.
8. Scott Holland, "Ruskin and Gladstone," *Letters to M. G. and H. G.* by John Ruskin, 1903, pp. 120–31.
9. Sir Stafford Northcote, Earl of Iddesleigh, Letter (January 1843), *Life, Letters, and Diaries*, ed. Andrew Lang, 1891, p. 43.
10. John Bright, Letter to Charles Sumner (October 10, 1862), cited in Edward L. Pierce, *Memoir and Letters of Charles Sumner*, 1893, Volume 4, pp. 157–58.
11. Alexander William Kinglake, *Invasion of the Crimea*, 1863, Volume 1, pp. 266–67.
12. Benjamin Disraeli, Letter to Lady Bradford (October 3, 1877).
13. W. E. H. Lecky, "Queen Victoria as a Moral Force" (1897), *Historical and Political Essays*, 1908, pp. 286–87.
14. Thomas Babington Macaulay, "Church and State," *Edinburgh Review*, April 1839, pp. 231–34.
15. Oliver Wendell Holmes, *Our Hundred Days in Europe*, 1887, pp. 95–96.
16. W. E. H. Lecky, "Introduction" to *Democracy and Liberty*, 1898, pp. xx–xxx.
17. Sir Edward W. Hamilton, *Mr. Gladstone: A Monograph*, 1898, pp. 1–3.
18. Arthur Hugh Clough, Letter to Charles Eliot Norton (May 17, 1858), *Prose Remains*, 1888, p. 243.
19. Edward A. Freeman, "Mr. Gladstone's *Homer and the Homeric Age*," *National Review*, July 1858, pp. 42–45.
20. Lionel A. Tollemache, *Talks with Mr. Gladstone*, 1898, pp. 12–14.
21. John Morley, *Life of William Ewart Gladstone*, 1903, Volume 3, pp. 543–45.
22. Frank Harrison Hill, "Mr. Gladstone," *Political Portraits*, 1873, pp. 1–21.
23. Edward Dicey, "Mr. Gladstone and Our Empire," *Nineteenth Century*, September 1877, pp. 293–306.

LEWIS CARROLL (C. L. DODGSON)

1. Unsigned, "Rev. C. L. Dodgson," *Nature*, January 20, 1898, p. 280.
2. Stuart Dodgson Collingwood, *The Life and Letters of Lewis Carroll*, 1898, pp. 389–90.
3. Owen Seaman, "Lewis Carroll," cited in Stuart Dodgson Collingwood, *The Life and Letters of Lewis Carroll*, 1898, p. 357.
4. Isa Bowman, *The Story of Lewis Carroll*, 1899, pp. 1–3.
5. Laurence Hutton, *Literary Landmarks of Oxford*, 1903, pp. 77–78.
6. Belle Moses, *Lewis Carroll in Wonderland and at Home: The Story of His Life*, 1910, pp. 287–90.
7. J. B., "Lewis Carroll at Oxford," *Academy*, January 22, 1898, p. 100.
8. J. L. Gilder, "The Creator of Wonderland," *Critic*, February 1899, pp. 135–36.
9. E. G. Johnson, "Lewis Carroll of Wonderland," *Dial*, March 16, 1899, p. 192.
10. Max Beerbohm, "*Alice* Awakened Again," *Saturday Review*, December 22, 1900, p. 791.
11. Carolyn Wells, "Introduction" to *A Nonsense Anthology*, 1903, pp. xxii–xxix.
12. Unsigned, "Children's Books," *Athenaeum*, December 16, 1865, p. 844.
13. Edward Salmon, "Literature for the Little Ones," *Nineteenth Century*, October 1887, pp. 571–72.
14. Unsigned, "Lewis Carroll," *Saturday Review*, January 22, 1898, pp. 102–3.
15. E. S. Leathes, "Lewis Carroll," *Academy*, December 17, 1898, pp. 469–70.
16. Andrew Lang, *Academy*, April 8, 1876, p. 327.
17. Henry Holiday, "The Snark's Significance," *Academy*, January 29, 1898, pp. 128–29.
18. M. H. T., "The Snark's Significance," *Academy*, January 29, 1898, pp. 129–30.
19. E. S. Leathes, "Lewis Carroll," *Academy*, January 22, 1898, pp. 98–99.
20. Lionel A. Tollemache, "Reminiscences of 'Lewis Carroll,'" *Literature*, February 5, 1898, pp. 144–45.
21. Thomas Banks Strong, "Lewis Carroll," *Cornhill Magazine*, March 1898, pp. 303–10.
22. C. M. Aikman, "Lewis Carroll," *Living Age*, February 1899, pp. 427–29.

WILLIAM BLACK

1. Joseph Hatton, "William Black at Home," *Harper's New Monthly Magazine*, December 1882, pp. 15–16.
2. Justin McCarthy, "William Black," *Academy*, December 17, 1898, pp. 481–82.
3. Andrew Lang, "Three New Novels," *Fortnightly Review*, January 1877, pp. 88–93.
4. Justin McCarthy, *A History of Our Own Times*, 1879–80, Ch. 67.
5. Margaret Oliphant, *The Victorian Age of English Literature*, 1892, Volume 2, p. 203.
6. Donald G. Mitchell, *English Lands, Letters and Kings: From Elizabeth to Anne*, 1894, p. 33.
7. Agnes Repplier, "The Novels of William Black," *Critic*, February 1899, pp. 146–48.
8. William Dean Howells, "William Black's Gertrude White," *Heroines of Fiction*, Volume 2, pp. 213–16.
9. William Morton Payne, "William Black," *Editorial Echoes*, 1902, pp. 263–68.

EDWARD BELLAMY

1. William Dean Howells, "Editor's Study," *Harper's New Monthly Magazine*, June 1888, pp. 154–55.

10. Edmund Clarence Stedman, "Charles Dudley Warner," *Appleton's Journal*, June 27, 1874, pp. 803–4.

OSCAR WILDE

1. Thomas F. Plowman, "The Aesthetes: The Story of a Nineteenth-Century Cult," *Pall Mall Magazine*, January 1895, pp. 41–42.
2. Chris Healy, *Confessions of a Journalist*, 1904, pp. 131–38.
3. Wilfrid Scawen Blunt, *My Diaries* (entry for November 16, 1905), 1920, Volume 2, pp. 125–26.
4. Ford Madox Ford, *Ancient Lights and Certain New Reflections*, 1911, pp. 150–53.
5. Katharine Tynan, *Twenty-five Years: Reminiscences*, 1913, pp. 149–50.
6. Ambrose Bierce, "Prattle," *Wasp*, March 31, 1882.
7. W. B. Yeats, "Oscar Wilde's Last Book" (1891), *Uncollected Prose*, ed. John P. Frayne, 1970, Volume 1, pp. 203–4.
8. Arthur Symons, "An Artist in Attitudes: Oscar Wilde" (1901), *Studies in Prose and Verse*, 1904, pp. 124–28.
9. Max Beerbohm, "A Lord of Language," *Vanity Fair*, March 2, 1905, p. 309.
10. J. Comyns Carr, *Some Victorian Poets*, 1908, pp. 213–14.
11. Lord Alfred Douglas, "The Genius of Oscar Wilde," *Academy*, July 11, 1908, p. 35.
12. G. K. Chesterton, "Oscar Wilde" (1909), *A Handful of Authors*, ed. Dorothy Collins, 1953, pp. 143–46.
13. James Joyce, "Oscar Wilde: The Poet of *Salomé*" (1909), *Critical Writings*, eds. Ellsworth Mason, Richard Ellmann, 1959, pp. 203–5.
14. Walter Pater, "A Novel by Mr. Wilde" (1891), *Sketches and Reviews*, 1919, pp. 126–33.
15. Richard Le Gallienne, *Academy*, July 4, 1891, pp. 7–8.
16. Agnes Repplier, "The Best Book of the Year," *North American Review*, January 1892, pp. 97–100.
17. Lord Alfred Douglas, *Spirit Lamp*, May 1893, pp. 21–27.
18. William Archer, "*A Woman of No Importance*" (1893), *The Theatrical "World" of 1893*, 1894, pp. 105–12.
19. George Bernard Shaw, "Two New Plays" (1895), *Works*, 1930–38, Volume 23, pp. 9–11.
20. J. T. Grein, "*The Importance of Being Earnest*" (1901), *Dramatic Criticism*, 1902, Volume 3, pp. 264–66.
21. Max Beerbohm, "A Classic Farce" (1909), *Last Theatres*, ed. Rupert Hart-Davis, 1970, pp. 508–11.
22. E. V. Lucas, *Times Literary Supplement*, February 24, 1905, pp. 64–65.
23. G. Lowes Dickinson, *Independent Review*, April 1905, pp. 375–77.
24. Robert H. Sherard, *Oscar Wilde: The Story of an Unhappy Friendship*, 1905, pp. 183–94.
25. Hugh Walker, "The Birth of a Soul: (Oscar Wilde: The Closing Phase)," *Hibbert Journal*, January 1905, pp. 756–68.
26. Lewis Piaget Shanks, "Oscar Wilde's Place in Literature," *Dial*, April 16, 1910, pp. 261–63.
27. Arthur Ransome, "Afterthought," *Oscar Wilde: A Critical Study*, 1912, pp. 220–34.

ERNEST DOWSON

1. Edgar Jepson, "The Real Ernest Dowson," *Academy*, November 2, 1907, p. 95.
2. Victor Plarr, *Ernest Dowson, 1888–1897: Reminiscences, Unpublished Letters and Marginalia*, 1915, pp. 26–29.
3. Unsigned, "Pale, Tender, and Fragile," *Academy*, April 21, 1900, p. 328.
4. Andrew Lang, "Decadence," *Critic*, August 1900, pp. 171–73.

5. Forrest Reid, "Ernest Dowson," *Monthly Review*, June 1905, pp. 110–13.
6. Unsigned, "'Miserrimus,'" *Saturday Review*, June 17, 1905, p. 808.
7. Arthur Symons, "Ernest Dowson" (1900), *Studies in Prose and Verse* 1904, pp. 268–78.

STEPHEN CRANE

1. Harry Thurston Peck, "Stephen Crane," *Bookman* (New York), May 1895, pp. 229–30.
2. Joseph Conrad, Letter to Stephen Crane (December 1, 1897).
3. Joseph Conrad, Letter to Edward Garnett (December 5, 1897).
4. Unsigned, "Recent Short Stories," *Spectator*, July 23, 1898, pp. 120–21.
5. Edward Garnett, "Mr. Stephen Crane: An Appreciation," *Academy*, December 17, 1898, pp. 483–84.
6. William Dean Howells, "Frank Norris," *North American Review*, December 1902, pp. 770–71.
7. William Dean Howells, "An Appreciation," *Maggie: A Girl of the Streets*, 1896.
8. William Morton Payne, "Recent Fiction," *Dial*, February 1, 1896, p. 80.
9. A. C. McClurg, "The Red Badge of Hysteria," *Dial*, April 16, 1896, pp. 227–28.
10. D. Appleton & Company, "*The Red Badge of Courage*: A Correction," *Dial*, May 1, 1896, p. 263.
11. J. L. Onderdonk, "A Red Badge of Bad English," *Dial*, May 1, 1896, p. 263.
12. Unsigned, "The Rambler," *Book Buyer*, April 1896, pp. 140–41.
13. Charles Dudley Warner, "Editor's Study," *Harper's New Monthly Magazine*, May 1896, p. 962.
14. Unsigned, "*The Red Badge of Courage*," *Spectator*, June 27, 1896, p. 924.
15. Unsigned, "The Latest Fiction," *New York Times*, October 19, 1895, p. 3.
16. Harold Frederic, "Stephen Crane's Triumph," *New York Times*, January 26, 1896, p. 22.
17. H. D. Traill, "The New Realism," *Fortnightly Review*, January 1897, pp. 63–66.
18. Stephen Gwynn, "Novels of American Life," *Edinburgh Review*, April 1898, pp. 411–14.
19. Willa Cather, "When I Knew Stephen Crane," *Library*, June 23, 1900.
20. Hamlin Garland, "Stephen Crane: A Soldier of Fortune," *Saturday Evening Post*, July 28, 1900.
21. H. G. Wells, "Stephen Crane: From an English Standpoint," *North American Review*, August 1900, pp. 233–42.

CHARLOTTE MARY YONGE

1. Mary K. Seeger, "Charlotte Mary Yonge," *Bookman* (New York), May 1901, p. 219.
2. Unsigned, "Charlotte Mary Yonge," *Church Quarterly Review*, January 1904, pp. 350–55.
3. Lucy C. F. Cavendish, "The Secret of Miss Yonge's Influence," *Charlotte Mary Yonge: An Appreciation* by Ethel Romanes, 1908, pp. 197–200.
4. Eleanor Hull, "Introduction" to *The Dove in the Eagle's Nest*, 1908, pp. vii–viii.
5. Hugh Walker, *The Literature of the Victorian Era*, 1910, pp. 748–49.
6. Unsigned, "Ethical and Dogmatic Fiction: Miss Yonge," *National Review*, January 1861, pp. 214–18.
7. Edith Sichel, "Charlotte Yonge as a Chronicler," *Monthly Review*, May 1901, pp. 88–97.

JOHN FISKE

1. Unsigned, "A Scientist's Argument for the Infinite," *Poet-Lore*, April 1899, pp. 309–10.
2. William James, *Atlantic*, August 1901, pp. 283–84.
3. Kendric Charles Babcock, *American Historical Review*, April 1903, pp. 515–16.
4. J. R. G. Hassard, "Myths and Myth-Mongers," *Catholic World*, May 1873, pp. 209–12.
5. Charles Darwin, Letter to John Fiske (December 8, 1874).
6. Josiah Royce, "Introduction" to *Outlines of Cosmic Philosophy*, 1902, pp. xxxv–cxxv.
7. Basil W. Duke, *American Historical Review*, April 1901, p. 600.
8. William Dean Howells, "John Fiske," *Harper's Weekly*, July 20, 1901, p. 732.
9. George L. Beer, "John Fiske," *Critic*, August 1901, p. 118.
10. H. Morse Stephens, "John Fiske as a Popular Historian," *World's Work*, April 1903, pp. 3359–64.

AUBREY DE VERE

1. Walter Savage Landor, "To Aubrey De Vere," 1848.
2. Dante Gabriel Rossetti, Letter to William Allingham (November 22, 1860).
3. I. A. Taylor, "The Recollections of Aubrey De Vere," *Catholic World*, February 1898, p. 621.
4. F. A. Rudd, "Aubrey De Vere," *Catholic World*, October 1866, pp. 74–75.
5. James Ashcroft Noble, *Academy*, January 21, 1888, p. 35.
6. Mackenzie Bell, "Aubrey De Vere," *The Poets and the Poetry of the Century*, ed. Alfred H. Miles, 1892, Volume 4, pp. 415–16.
7. W. Macneile Dixon, "The Poetry of the de Veres," *Quarterly Review*, April 1896, pp. 323–35.
8. Aubrey De Vere, *Recollections*, 1897, p. 355.
9. Alfred H. Miles, "Aubrey De Vere," *The Poets and the Poetry of the Century*, ed. Alfred H. Miles, 1897, Volume 10, pp. 479–80.
10. George Edward Woodberry, "The Poetry of Aubrey De Vere," *Makers of Literature*, 1900, pp. 124–38.

SAMUEL R. GARDINER

1. Unsigned, "Gardiner's History of the Great Civil War.—I," *Nation*, May 12, 1892, pp. 360–61.
2. Margaret Oliphant, *The Victorian Age of English Literature*, 1892, Volume 2, p. 254.
3. George Louis Beer, "Samuel Rawson Gardiner: An Appreciation," *Critic*, June 1901, pp. 546–47.
4. Unsigned, "Dr. S. R. Gardiner," *Athenaeum*, March 1, 1902, p. 272.
5. Unsigned, "The Method of History," *Academy*, March 1, 1902, p. 223.
6. F. Y. Powell, "Two Oxford Historians," *Quarterly Review*, April 1902, p. 551.
7. James Ford Rhodes, "Samuel Rawson Gardiner," *Atlantic*, May 1902, p. 698.
8. W. H. Hutton, "Samuel Rawson Gardiner," *Cornhill Magazine*, December 1903, pp. 788–91.
9. C. H. Firth, "Dr. S. R. Gardiner," *Proceedings of the British Academy*, 1903–04, pp. 298–300.
10. G. P. Gooch, *History and Historians in the Nineteenth Century*, 1913, p. 364.
11. A. V. Dicey, "Gardiner's *History of the Commonwealth*.—I," *Nation*, April 11, 1895, pp. 280–81.

FRANK R. STOCKTON

1. Theodore F. Wolfe, "Where Stockton Wrote His Stories," *Lippincott's Magazine*, September 1899, pp. 370–71.

2. Hamilton W. Mabie, "Frank R. Stockton," *Book Buyer*, June 1902, pp. 355–56.
3. Julie M. Lippman, "To Our 'Merry Chanter,'" *Century Magazine*, July 1902, p. 422.
4. Marian E. Stockton, "A Memorial Sketch," *The Captain's Toll-Gate*, 1903, pp. xxx–xxxii.
5. Clarence Clough Buel, "The Author of 'The Lady, or the Tiger?,'" *Century Magazine*, July 1886, p. 411.
6. Fred Lewis Pattee, *A History of American Literature*, 1896, pp. 445–46.
7. Edwin W. Bowen, "Frank R. Stockton," *Sewanee Review*, October 1903, pp. 476–78.
8. Henry C. Vedder, "Francis Richard Stockton," *American Writers of To-day*, 1895, pp. 290–300.
9. William Dean Howells, "Mr. Stockton and All His Works," *Book Buyer*, February 1900, pp. 19–21.

SAMUEL BUTLER

1. Desmond MacCarthy, "Samuel Butler: An Impression," *Remnants*, 1918, pp. 63–64.
2. George Bernard Shaw, "Preface" to *Major Barbara* (1905), 1906.
3. Hugh Walker, *The Literature of the Victorian Era*, 1910, pp. 813–14.
4. Desmond MacCarthy, "The Author of *Erewhon*," *Quarterly Review*, January 1914, pp. 152–53, 172–73.
5. Gilbert Cannan, *Samuel Butler: A Critical Study*, 1915, pp. 155–59, 193–94.
6. John F. Harris, *Samuel Butler, Author of* Erewhon: *The Man and His Work*, 1916, p. 298.
7. Sidney Colvin, "Some Critical Notices," *Fortnightly Review*, May 1872, pp. 609–10.
8. Frank Jewett Mather, Jr., "Samuel Butler of *Erewhon*," *Nation*, December 29, 1910, pp. 626–67.
9. Grant Allen, *Academy*, May 17, 1879, pp. 426–27.
10. William Barry, "Samuel Butler of *Erewhon*," *Dublin Review*, October 1914, pp. 343–44.
11. George Bernard Shaw, "Mr. Gilbert Cannan on Samuel Butler," *New Statesman*, May 8, 1915, pp. 109–10.
12. E. S. Russell, *Form and Function*, 1916, pp. 335–37.
13. May Sinclair, "The Pan-Psychism of Samuel Butler," *A Defence of Idealism*, 1917, pp. 5–6.
14. Richard Garnett, *Athenaeum*, December 18, 1897, pp. 849–50.
15. F. M. Cornford, "Butler's Translation of the *Odyssey*," *Classical Review*, May 1901, pp. 221–22.
16. William Lyon Phelps, "The Advance of the English Novel: Part IX," *Bookman* (New York), June 1916, pp. 405–6.
17. Walter de la Mare, "Current Literature," *Edinburgh Review*, January 1913, pp. 194–96.
18. Orlo Williams, *The Essay*, 1915, p. 17.
19. J. C. Squire, "Current Literature," *New Statesman*, December 4, 1915, p. 209.
20. W. H. Salter, "Samuel Butler," *Essays on Two Moderns*, 1911, pp. 76–93.
21. George Sampson, "Samuel Butler," *Bookman* (London), August 1915, pp. 129–33.

BRET HARTE

1. M. E. W. Sherwood, *An Epistle to Posterity*, 1897, p. 192.
2. Joaquin Miller, "Good Bye, Bret Harte!," 1902.
3. Mary Stuart Boyd, "Some Letters of Bret Harte," *Harper's New Monthly Magazine*, October 1902, p. 773.
4. Noah Brooks, "Bret Harte," *Scribner's Monthly*, June 1873, p. 161.

5. Edmund Clarence Stedman, *Poets of America*, 1885, pp. 451–52.
6. Edwin P. Whipple, "American Literature" (1886), *American Literature and Other Papers*, 1887, p. 116.
7. Henry A. Beers, *An Outline Sketch of American Literature*, 1887, pp. 263–66.
8. Charles F. Richardson, *American Literature, 1607–1885*, 1887, Volume 2, pp. 423–25.
9. Andrew Lang, "On Vers de Société," *Letters on Literature*, 1889, p. 155.
10. Walter Lewin, "The Abuse of Fiction," *Forum*, August 1889, p. 670.
11. Fred Lewis Pattee, A *History of American Literature*, 1896, pp. 397–99.
12. Charles Warren Stoddard, "Early Recollections of Bret Harte," *Atlantic*, December 1896, pp. 677–78.
13. Mark Twain, "What Paul Bourget Thinks of Us" (1897), *Writings*, 1918, Volume 22, p. 153.
14. Henry S. Pancoast, *An Introduction to American Literature*, 1898, p. 323.
15. Noah Brooks, "Bret Harte in California," *Century Magazine*, July 1899, p. 450.
16. T. Edgar Pemberton, *Bret Harte: A Treatise and a Tribute*, 1900, pp. 199–200.
17. William Dean Howells, "Mr. Bret Harte's Miggles, and Mr. T. B. Aldrich's Marjorie Daw," *Heroines of Fiction*, 1901, Volume 2, pp. 225–28.
18. Noah Brooks, "Bret Harte: A Biographical and Critical Sketch," *Overland Monthly*, September 1902, pp. 206–7.
19. Emily S. Forman, "Bret Harte," *Old and New*, January 1872, pp. 714–17.
20. William Dean Howells, "A Belated Guest," *Literary Friends and Acquaintance*, 1901.
21. G. K. Chesterton, "American Humor and Bret Harte," *Critic*, August 1902, pp. 170–74.

LIONEL JOHNSON

1. Unsigned, "Lionel Johnson," *Academy*, October 11, 1902, pp. 397–98.
2. Unsigned, "Lionel Johnson," *Athenaeum*, October 18, 1902, p. 521.
3. Paul Elmer More, "Two Poets of the Irish Movement" (1903), *Shelburne Essays: First Series*, 1904, pp. 187–88.
4. E. D. A. Morshead, *Academy*, May 11, 1895, p. 395.
5. Unsigned, "Mr. Lionel Johnson's Poems," *Academy*, December 18, 1897, p. 544.
6. W. B. Yeats, "Mr. Lionel Johnson's Poems" (1898), *Uncollected Prose*, eds. John P. Frayne, Colton Johnson, 1976, Volume 2, pp. 89–90.
7. Katherine Brégy, "Lionel Johnson: Poet and Critic," *Catholic World*, July 1906, pp. 479–80.
8. Ezra Pound, "Preface" to *The Poetical Works of Lionel Johnson*, 1915, pp. v–vii.
9. Katharine Tynan, "Lionel Johnson," *Bookman* (London), November 1915, pp. 50–52.
10. Edmund K. Chambers, *Academy*, October 20, 1894, p. 297.
11. Unsigned, *Critic*, March 1895, p. 234.
12. Louise Imogen Guiney, "Of Lionel Johnson: 1867–1902," *Atlantic*, December 1902, pp. 856–62.

FRANK NORRIS

1. Denison Hailey Clift, "The Artist in Frank Norris," *Pacific Monthly*, March 1907, p. 313.
2. William Dallam Armes, "Concerning the Work of the Late Frank Norris," *Sunset Magazine*, December 1902, p. 167.

3. Unsigned, "A Significant Novel," *Outlook*, January 17, 1903, pp. 153–54.
4. Albert Bigelow Paine, "Frank Norris's *The Pit*," *Bookman* (New York), February 1903, pp. 565–67.
5. Denison Hailey Clift, "The Artist in Frank Norris," *Pacific Monthly*, March 1907, pp. 320–21.
6. William Dean Howells, "A Case in Point," *Literature*, March 24, 1899, pp. 241–42.
7. Nancy Huston Banks, "Two Recent Revivals in Realism," *Bookman* (New York), June 1899, p. 357.
8. Unsigned, *Academy*, December 23, 1899, p. 746.
9. A. S. van Westrum, "A Novelist with a Future," *Book Buyer*, May 1901, pp. 326–28.
10. Jack London, "*The Octopus*," *Impressions Quarterly*, June 1901, p. 46.
11. William Dean Howells, "Editor's Easy Chair," *Harper's New Monthly Magazine*, October 1901, pp. 824–25.
12. H. W. Boynton, "Books New and Old," *Atlantic*, May 1902, pp. 708–9.
13. B. O. Flower, "Books of the Day," *Arena*, May 1902, pp. 547–54.
14. Unsigned, "The Romance of Commerce," *Academy*, February 14, 1903, p. 154.
15. William Morton Payne, "Recent Fiction," *Dial*, April 1903, p. 242.
16. Frederic Taber Cooper, "Frank Norris, Realist," *Bookman* (New York), November 1899, pp. 234–38.
17. William Dean Howells, "Frank Norris," *North American Review*, December 1902, pp. 771–78.
18. Hamlin Garland, "The Work of Frank Norris," *Critic*, March 1903, pp. 216–18.
19. Milne B. Levick, "Frank Norris," *Overland Monthly*, June 1905, pp. 504–8.

HERBERT SPENCER

1. Justin McCarthy, *Modern Leaders*, 1872, p. 241.
2. W. J. Linton, *Memories*, 1895, p. 204.
3. Hector Macpherson, *Spencer and Spencerism*, 1900, p. 9.
4. William James, "Herbert Spencer: A Portrait," *Blackwood's Edinburgh Magazine*, January 1904, pp. 101–3.
5. George E. Vincent, "Spencer, the Man," *American Journal of Sociology*, March 1904, pp. 710–11.
6. Josiah Royce, *Herbert Spencer: An Estimate and Review*, 1904, pp. 52–55.
7. James Collier, *Herbert Spencer: An Estimate and Review by Josiah Royce*, 1904, pp. 208–10.
8. J. Arthur Thomson, *Herbert Spencer*, 1906, p. 12.
9. George Eliot, Letter to Sara Hennell (July 10, 1854).
10. John Stuart Mill, *Auguste Comte and Positivism*, 1865.
11. John Fiske, Letter to the Editor, *Nation*, June 5, 1869, p. 434.
12. Theodule Ribot, *English Psychology*, 1874, pp. 124–25.
13. George S. Morris, *British Thought and Thinkers*, 1880, p. 340.
14. Justin McCarthy, A *History of Our Own Times*, 1879–80, Ch. 67.
15. Henry Ward Beecher, "The Herbert Spencer Dinner" (1882), *Lectures and Orations*, ed. Newell Wright Hillis, 1913, pp. 312–17.
16. Grant Allen, "Spencer and Darwin," *Fortnightly Review*, February 1897, p. 262.
17. B. P. Browne, *The Philosophy of Herbert Spencer*, 1874, pp. 280–82.
18. William James, "Herbert Spencer's *Data of Ethics*," *Nation*, September 11, 1879, pp. 178–79.
19. A. M. Fairbairn, "Mr. Herbert Spencer's Philosophy and the Philosophy of Religion," *Contemporary Review*, July 1881, pp. 74–75.

9. F. W. Farrar, *"The Light of the World,"* Longman's Magazine, March 1891, pp. 495–96.
10. E. K. Chambers, *Academy*, April 23, 1892, pp. 391–92.
11. Louise Chandler Moulton, "Three English Poets," *Arena*, June 1892, pp. 50–52.
12. Frank W. Gunsaulus, "After Reading Sir Edwin Arnold's Verses," *Songs of Night and Day*, 1896.
13. Mackenzie Bell, "Sir Edwin Arnold," *The Poets and the Poetry of the Century*, ed. Alfred H. Miles, 1892, Volume 5, pp. 529–34.

SIR LESLIE STEPHEN

1. James Russell Lowell, Letter to Sir Leslie Stephen (May 15, 1876).
2. James Cotter Morison, "Leslie Stephen's *History of English Thought*," *Macmillan's Magazine*, February 1877, pp. 335–36.
3. Augustine Birrell, *"Hours in a Library,"* Essays about Men, Women, and Books, 1894, pp. 191–98.
4. Arthur Symons, "Mr. Leslie Stephen as a Critic," *Saturday Review*, July 23, 1898, pp. 113–14.
5. A. V. Dicey, "Sir Leslie Stephen, K.C.B.," *Nation*, July 17, 1902, pp. 49–50.
6. Edmund Gosse, "Sir Leslie Stephen," *English Illustrated Magazine*, November 1903, pp. 182–84.
7. W. P. Trent, "Leslie Stephen's Agnosticism," *Bookman* (New York), March 1904, pp. 70–71.
8. Frederic Harrison, "Sir Leslie Stephen: In Memoriam," *Cornhill Magazine*, April 1904, pp. 441–43.
9. James Ashcroft Noble, "Living Critics: III.—Leslie Stephen," *Bookman* (New York), January 1896, pp. 399–401.

KATE CHOPIN

1. Unsigned, "Recent Novels," *Nation*, June 9, 1898, p. 447.
2. Unsigned, "The Lounger," *Critic*, August 1899, p. 677.
3. Unsigned, "Kate Chopin," *Hesperian*, October 1904, pp. 383–84.
4. Fred Lewis Pattee, A *History of American Literature since 1870*, 1915, pp. 364–65.
5. Unsigned, "Recent Fiction," *Atlantic*, April 1894, pp. 558–59.
6. Unsigned, *"Bayou Folk,"* Critic, May 5, 1894, pp. 299–300.
7. Unsigned, "Recent Novels," *Nation*, June 28, 1894, p. 488.
8. Maibelle Justice, "Book Reviews," *Godey's Magazine*, April 1895, p. 432.
9. Unsigned, "Kate Chopin's New Book," *Hesperian*, January 1898, pp. 172–73.
10. William Morton Payne, "Recent Fiction," *Dial*, April 1, 1899, p. 75.
11. Frances Porcher, "Kate Chopin's Novel," *St. Louis Mirror*, May 4, 1899, p. 6.

12. Unsigned, "Notes from Bookland," *St. Louis Daily Globe-Democrat*, May 13, 1899, p. 5.
13. C. L. Deyo, *St. Louis Post-Dispatch*, May 20, 1899, p. 4.
14. Unsigned, "Books of the Week," *Outlook*, June 3, 1899, p. 314.
15. Unsigned, "Books of the Week," *Providence Sunday Journal*, June 4, 1899, p. 15.
16. Unsigned, "New Publications," *New Orleans Times-Democrat*, June 18, 1899, p. 15.
17. Unsigned, "Book Reviews," *Public Opinion*, June 22, 1899, p. 794.
18. Unsigned, "Fiction," *Literature*, June 23, 1899, p. 570.
19. Unsigned, "Fresh Literature," *Los Angeles Sunday Times*, June 25, 1899, p. 12.
20. Kate Chopin, "Aims and Autographs of Authors," *Book News Monthly*, July 1899, p. 612.
21. Willa Cather, "Kate Chopin" (1899), *The World and the Parish: Willa Cather's Articles and Reviews 1893–1902*, ed. William M. Curtin, 1970, Volume 2, pp. 697–99.
22. Unsigned, "Recent Novels," *Nation*, August 3, 1899, p. 96.
23. William Schuyler, "Kate Chopin," *Writer*, August 1894, pp. 115–17.
24. Leonidas Rutledge Whipple, "Kate Chopin," *Library of Southern Literature*, eds. Edwin Anderson Alderman, Joel Chandler Harris, 1907, Volume 2, pp. 863–66.
25. Percival Pollard, *Their Day in Court*, 1909, pp. 40–45.

LAFCADIO HEARN

1. Osman Edwards, "Recollections of Lafcadio Hearn," *T.P.'s Weekly*, October 21, 1904, p. 530.
2. K. K. Kawakami, "Yakumo Koizumi: The Interpreter of Japan," *Open Court*, October 1906, p. 631.
3. Harrison Rhodes, "Lafcadio Hearn," *Bookman* (New York), March 1907, p. 74.
4. Unsigned, "An Interpreter of Japan," *Edinburgh Review*, October 1907, pp. 430–31.
5. Warren Barton Blake, "The Problem of Lafcadio Hearn," *Dial*, April 1, 1912, pp. 266–67.
6. Unsigned, *Outlook*, October 16, 1897, pp. 435–36.
7. Paul Elmer More, "Lafcadio Hearn," *Shelburne Essays: Second Series*, 1905, pp. 46–47.
8. Nobushige Amenomori, "Lafcadio Hearn, the Man," *Atlantic*, October 1905, pp. 521–22.
9. George M. Gould, "Lafcadio Hearn: A Study of His Personality and Art," *Putnam's Monthly*, November 1906, p. 164.
10. Ferris Greenslet, "Lafcadio Hearn," *Atlantic*, February 1907, pp. 271–72.
11. Edwin Mims, "The Letters of Lafcadio Hearn," *South Atlantic Quarterly*, April 1911, p. 158.
12. William C. Stewart, "A Note on Lafcadio Hearn," *Contemporary Review*, October 1912, p. 551.
13. Edward Thomas, *Lafcadio Hearn*, 1912, pp. 88–91.
14. Edward Clark Marsh, "Lafcadio Hearn," *Forum*, August 1908, pp. 177–80.

INDEX TO AUTHORS

KINGLAKE, ALEXANDER WILLIAM
  10:5583
KINGSLEY, CHARLES 9:4988
KNOWLES, JAMES SHERIDAN 8:4661
KNOX, JOHN 1:298
KYD, THOMAS 1:394
LAMB, LADY CAROLINE 7:3734
LAMB, CHARLES 7:3933
LAMB, MARY 7:4152
LANDON, LETITIA ELIZABETH 7:4019
LANDOR, WALTER SAVAGE 8:4731
LANGLAND, WILLIAM 1:48
LANIER, SIDNEY 9:5174
LAUD, WILLIAM 3:1437
LAW, WILLIAM 5:2674
LAZARUS, EMMA 9:5445
LECKY, W. E. H. 10:6159
LEE, NATHANIEL 4:1969
L'ESTRANGE, SIR ROGER 4:2072
LEVER, CHARLES 9:4930
LEWES, GEORGE HENRY 9:5054
LEWIS, MATTHEW GREGORY 6:3492
LILLO, GEORGE 5:2381
LOCKE, JOHN 4:2076
LOCKER-LAMPSON, FREDERICK 10:5854
LOCKHART, JOHN GIBSON 8:4453
LODGE, THOMAS 3:1093
LONGFELLOW, HENRY WADSWORTH
  9:5240
LOVELACE, RICHARD 3:1531
LOVER, SAMUEL 8:4863
LOWELL, JAMES RUSSELL 10:5589
LYDGATE, JOHN 1:73
LYLY, JOHN 1:510
MACAULAY, THOMAS BABINGTON
  8:4597
MACKENZIE, HENRY 7:3762
MACKINTOSH, SIR JAMES 7:3824
MACKLIN, CHARLES 6:3227
MACPHERSON, JAMES 6:3175
MALLET, DAVID 5:2753
MALORY, SIR THOMAS 1:186
MALTHUS, THOMAS ROBERT 7:3881
MANDEVILLE, BERNARD 5:2353
MANDEVILLE, SIR JOHN 1:35
MANGAN, JAMES CLARENCE 7:4236
MARLOWE, CHRISTOPHER 1:364
MARRYAT, FREDERICK 7:4166
MARSTON, JOHN 3:1297
MARTINEAU, HARRIET 9:5003
MARVELL, ANDREW 4:1782
MASON, WILLIAM 6:3251
MASSINGER, PHILIP 3:1356
MATHER, COTTON 4:2254

MATURIN, CHARLES ROBERT 7:3624
MAURICE, FREDERICK DENISON 9:4922
MELVILLE, HERMAN 10:5604
MIDDLETON, THOMAS 3:1161
MILL, JAMES 7:4010
MILL, JOHN STUART 9:4980
MILMAN, H. H. 8:4858
MILTON, JOHN 4:1683
MITFORD, MARY RUSSELL 8:4467
MONBODDO, JAMES BURNETT, LORD
  6:3290
MONTAGU, ELIZABETH 6:3299
MONTAGU, LADY MARY WORTLEY
  5:2708
MONTGOMERY, JAMES 8:4437
MOORE, THOMAS 8:4416
MORE, HANNAH 7:3867
MORE, SIR THOMAS 1:230
MORGAN, SYDNEY OWENSON, LADY
  8:4545
MORRIS, WILLIAM 10:5904
MOTLEY, JOHN LOTHROP 9:5019
NAIRNE, CAROLINA OLIPHANT,
  BARONESS 7:4124
NASHE, THOMAS 1:506
NEWCASTLE, MARGARET CAVENDISH,
  DUCHESS OF 4:1647
NEWMAN, JOHN HENRY 9:5551
NEWTON, SIR ISAAC 4:2242
NORRIS, FRANK 10:6123
NORTON, CAROLINE 9:5016
OCCLEVE, THOMAS 1:182
OLDHAM, JOHN 4:1882
OLIPHANT, MARGARET 10:5923
OPIE, AMELIA 8:4434
O'SHAUGHNESSY, ARTHUR 9:5186
OTWAY, THOMAS 4:1886
OVERBURY, SIR THOMAS 1:528
PAINE, THOMAS 6:3379
PALGRAVE, FRANCIS TURNER 10:5919
PARKMAN, FRANCIS 10:5752
PARNELL, THOMAS 4:2164
PARR, SAMUEL 7:3672
PATER, WALTER 10:5810
PATMORE, COVENTRY 10:5890
PEACOCK, THOMAS LOVE 8:4809
PEELE, GEORGE 1:398
PEPYS, SAMUEL 4:2060
PHILIPS, AMBROSE 5:2548
PHILIPS, KATHERINE 3:1552
PIOZZI, HESTER LYNCH 6:3513
POE, EDGAR ALLAN 8:4247
POPE, ALEXANDER 5:2417
PORSON, RICHARD 6:3373

PRAED, WINTHROP MACKWORTH
  7:4034
PRESCOTT, WILLIAM H. 8:4590
PRIESTLEY, JOSEPH 6:3344
PRIOR, MATTHEW 4:2204
PROCTER, BRYAN WALLER ("BARRY
  CORNWALL") 9:4980
PRYNNE, WILLIAM 3:1619
PUTTENHAM, GEORGE 1:497
QUARLES, FRANCIS 3:1424
RADCLIFFE, ANN 7:3605
RALEGH, SIR WALTER 3:1063
RAMSAY, ALLAN 5:2639
RANDOLPH, THOMAS 6:3168
READE, CHARLES 9:5370
REEVE, CLARA 6:3360
REID, THOMAS 6:3168
REYNOLDS, SIR JOSHUA 6:3089
RICARDO, DAVID 7:3619
RICHARDSON, SAMUEL 5:2681
ROBERTSON, WILLIAM 6:3106
ROCHESTER, JOHN WILMOT, EARL OF
  4:1839
ROGERS, SAMUEL 8:4457
ROLLE, RICHARD, OF HAMPOLE 1:34
ROSSETTI, CHRISTINA 10:5797
ROSSETTI, DANTE GABRIEL 9:5313
ROWE, NICHOLAS 4:2157
ROWLEY, WILLIAM 3:1158
RUSKIN, JOHN 10:5979
RYMER, THOMAS 4:2120
SANDYS, GEORGE 3:1418
SAVAGE, RICHARD 5:2405
SCOTT, SIR WALTER 7:3835
SEDGWICK, CATHARINE MARIA 8:4829
SEDLEY, SIR CHARLES 4:2056
SELDEN, JOHN 3:1500
SETTLE, ELKANAH 4:2223
SEWARD, ANNA 6:3392
SHADWELL, THOMAS 4:1965
SHAFTESBURY, ANTHONY ASHLEY
  COOPER, THIRD EARL OF 4:2125
SHAKESPEARE, WILLIAM 2:532
SHELLEY, MARY 8:4396
SHELLEY, PERCY BYSSHE 6:3561
SHENSTONE, WILLIAM 5:2721
SHERIDAN, RICHARD BRINSLEY 6:3421
SHIRLEY, JAMES 3:1559
SIDNEY, SIR PHILIP 1:318
SIMMS, WILLIAM GILMORE 8:4871
SKELTON, JOHN 1:211
SMART, CHRISTOPHER 5:2865
SMITH, ADAM 6:3056
SMITH, CHARLOTTE 6:3352

INDEX TO CRITICS

INDEX TO CRITICS

BARTLETT, DAVID W.
Horace Greeley 9:4938

BASCOM, JOHN
William Collins 5:2665
Mark Akenside 5:2795
William Cowper 6:3316

BASKERVILL, WILLIAM MALONE
Sidney Lanier 9:5178, 5179

BASSE, WILLIAM
William Shakespeare 2:535

BASTARD, THOMAS
Barnabe Barnes 1:525

BATE, PERCY
Dante Gabriel Rossetti 9:5325

BATES, HENRY
Sir Kenelm Digby 3:1556

BATES, KATHARINE LEE
Charles Brockden Brown 6:3400
Philip Freneau 7:3800
Margaret Fuller 8:4361
Nathaniel Hawthorne 8:4777
Catharine Maria Sedgwick 8:4830
William Gilmore Simms 8:4874
Alice and Phoebe Cary 9:4921
John Lothrop Motley 9:5021
William Cullen Bryant 9:5049
Sidney Lanier 9:5180
Helen Hunt Jackson 9:5393
Emily Dickinson 9:5418
Herman Melville 10:5609
George William Curtis 10:5737
Eugene Field 10:5875
Richard Henry Stoddard 10:6154

BATES, WILLIAM
Thomas Campbell 7:4115
William Harrison Ainsworth 9:5233

BATHURST, RICHARD
John Selden 3:1502

BAUDELAIRE, CHARLES
Edgar Allan Poe 8:4262

BAUDOIN, J.
Sir Philip Sidney 1:323

BAXTER, RICHARD
Sir John Davies 3:1144
George Herbert 3:1243
George Wither 3:1570
Abraham Cowley 3:1596
George Villiers, Duke of
　Buckingham 4:1908
Richard Baxter 4:1943

BAXTER, SYLVESTER
Edward Bellamy 10:5967

BAYNE, PETER
John Milton 4:1687, 1695, 1701
Edward Hyde, Earl of Clarendon
　4:1761
Samuel Taylor Coleridge 7:3906
Charlotte Brontë 8:4478
Thomas De Quincey 8:4572
Elizabeth Barrett Browning 8:4634
William Makepeace Thackeray
　8:4707

Charles Dickens 8:4881
Edward Bulwer-Lytton 9:4944
Charles Kingsley 9:4990
Walt Whitman 10:5697

BAYNE, THOMAS
Robert Henryson 1:203
William Dunbar 1:222
Charles Tennyson Turner 9:5078

BAYNE, WILLIAM
James Thomson 5:2538, 2539
Aaron Hill 5:2555
Erasmus Darwin 6:3334

BAYNES, THOMAS SPENCER
William Shakespeare 2:673

BEATTIE, JAMES
Francis Quarles 3:1425
John Milton 4:1698
Thomas Hobbes 4:1807
John Dryden 4:2012
John Locke 4:2078
Joseph Addison 4:2181
Sir Richard Blackmore 4:2263
Daniel Defoe 5:2318
John Arbuthnot 5:2372
Alexander Pope 5:2422
George Berkeley 5:2586
Henry Fielding 5:2599
Allan Ramsay 5:2644
Charles Churchill 5:2734
Edward Young 5:2738
Mark Akenside 5:2794
Thomas Gray 5:2817
Samuel Johnson 6:2994
Edward Gibbon 6:3125
James Boswell 6:3155
Thomas Reid 6:3168
Edmund Burke 6:3269
Hugh Blair 6:3294
Elizabeth Montagu 6:3300
James Beattie 6:3340

BEAUMONT, FRANCIS
Edmund Spenser 1:403, 406
Ben Jonson 3:1326

BEAUMONT, SIR JOHN
Francis Beaumont 3:1039
Ben Jonson 3:1319

BECKER, BERNARD HENRY
Sir John Mandeville 1:37
William Caxton 1:184

BECKET, ANDREW
William Warburton 6:2944

BEDDOES, THOMAS LOVELL
Percy Bysshe Shelley 6:3568
George Gordon, Lord Byron 7:3639
Thomas Campbell 7:4110
Thomas Lovell Beddoes 7:4227
Thomas De Quincey 8:4570
Thomas Love Peacock 8:4810
Robert Browning 9:5500

BEDE, THE VENERABLE
Cædmon 1:7
The Venerable Bede 1:13

BEE, JOHN
Samuel Foote 5:2937

BEECHER, HENRY WARD
Herbert Spencer 10:6142

BEECHER, LYMAN
Timothy Dwight 6:3444

BEECHEY, HENRY WILLIAM
Sir Joshua Reynolds 6:3092

BEECHING, H. C.
George Herbert 3:1249
Richard Crashaw 3:1485
Andrew Marvell 4:1799
John Bunyan 4:1919
Henry Vaughan 4:1984
Thomas Gray 5:2828
John Henry Newman 9:5560
Richard William Church 10:5570

BEER, GEORGE LOUIS
John Fiske 10:6075
Samuel R. Gardiner 10:6082

BEERBOHM, MAX
Lewis Carroll 10:5951
Oscar Wilde 10:6020, 6030

BEERS, HENRY A.
John Milton 4:1694
Cotton Mather 4:2258
James Thomson 5:2539
Jonathan Edwards 5:2652
William Collins 5:2668
Mark Akenside 5:2799
Thomas Chatterton 5:2811
Thomas Warton 6:3078
Horace Walpole 6:3238
William Mason 6:3254
Clara Reeve 6:3361
Thomas Paine 6:3387
Matthew Gregory Lewis 6:3496
Ann Radcliffe 7:3611
Philip Freneau 7:3800
John Wilson 8:4447
William Makepeace Thackeray
　8:4714
Nathaniel Hawthorne 8:4771
N. P. Willis 8:4842
William Gilmore Simms 8:4874
Alice and Phoebe Cary 9:4921
John Lothrop Motley 9:5024
Bayard Taylor 9:5062
Sidney Lanier 9:5178
Henry Ward Beecher 9:5431
William Morris 10:5907
Bret Harte 10:6108

BEHN, APHRA
Edmund Waller 4:1897

BELL, EDWARD
Samuel Rogers 8:4462

BELL, HAROLD IDRIS
Thomas Traherne 4:1764

BELL, J. M.
Edward Bulwer-Lytton 9:4948

BELL, MACKENZIE
Felicia Dorothea Hemans 7:3896
Carolina Oliphant, Baroness Nairne
　7:4125
Aubrey De Vere 10:6078

John Milton 4:1705
Edward Hyde, Earl of Clarendon
4:1752
Nathaniel Lee 4:1971
Sir William Temple 4:1997
John Dryden 4:2031
John Locke 4:2078
George Farquhar 4:2106
Anthony Ashley Cooper, Third Earl
of Shaftesbury 4:2128
Nicholas Rowe 4:2160
Thomas Parnell 4:2166
Joseph Addison 4:2178
Sir John Vanbrugh 4:2235
Samuel Clarke 5:2303
Daniel Defoe 5:2318
John Arbuthnot 5:2372
Alexander Pope 5:2423, 2430,
2434, 2437
Jonathan Swift 5:2481
James Thomson 5:2538
Ambrose Philips 5:2552
Henry St. John, Viscount
Bolingbroke 5:2563
Henry Fielding 5:2599
Colley Cibber 5:2637
Allan Ramsay 5:2644
Samuel Richardson 5:2684
Lady Mary Wortley Montagu
5:2713
William Shenstone 5:2722
Edward Young 5:2743
Mark Akenside 5:2796
James Macpherson 6:3186
Hugh Blair 6:3295

BLAKE, WARREN BARTON
Lafcadio Hearn 10:6211

BLAKE, WILLIAM
Geoffrey Chaucer 1:83
Sir Joshua Reynolds 6:3090, 3091

BLAKEY, ROBERT
John Wilson 8:4443
John Henry Newman 9:5552

BLAKISTON, HERBERT E. D.
Thomas Warton 6:3078

BLANCHARD, LAMAN
Letitia Elizabeth Landon 7:4020

BLENNERHASSETT, SIR ROWLAND
John Henry Newman 9:5553

BLESSINGTON, MARGUERITE,
COUNTESS OF
Percy Bysshe Shelley 6:3564
George Gordon, Lord Byron 7:3634
Thomas Moore 8:4417
Henry Hallam 8:4520

BLOCK, LOUIS J.
Eugene Field 10:5875

BLOOMFIELD, C. J.
Richard Bentley 5:2395
Samuel Parr 7:3675

BLOUNT, EDWARD
John Lyly 1:512

BLOUNT, MRS.
Alexander Pope 5:2418

BLUNT, J. J.
Joseph Butler 5:2577
Samuel Parr 7:3674

BLUNT, JOHN HENRY
William Tyndale 1:253

BLUNT, WILFRED SCAWEN
Edward Robert Bulwer Lytton
10:5628
Oscar Wilde 10:6017

BOADEN, JAMES
David Garrick 6:2955
William Mason 6:3255

BOAS, FREDERICK S.
John Heywood 1:309
Robert Greene 1:362
Thomas Kyd 1:396
George Peele 1:400
John Lyly 1:513
Thomas Sackville, Earl of Dorset
1:522
Nicholas Rowe 4:2161

BOGUE, DAVID
Joseph Priestley 6:3350

BÖHRINGER, FRIEDRICH
John Wyclif 1:41

BOHUN, EDMUND
Roger Ascham 1:289

BOILEAU, NICOLAS
Edmund Spenser 1:409

BOLINGBROKE, HENRY ST. JOHN,
VISCOUNT
Sir Francis Bacon 3:1117
Thomas Hobbes 4:1809
Matthew Prior 4:2205
Alexander Pope 5:2431
William Warburton 6:2941

BOLTON, EDMUND
Henry Howard, Earl of Surrey
1:279
George Gascoigne 1:310
Robert Southwell 1:397
George Puttenham 1:498
Thomas Sackville, Earl of Dorset
1:520
Henry Constable 1:527
Sir Walter Ralegh 3:1068
Samuel Daniel 3:1071
Fulke Greville, Lord Brooke 3:1172
Ben Jonson 3:1318

BOLTON, HENRY CARRINGTON
Joseph Priestley 6:3350

BONAR, JAMES
Joseph Butler 5:2577
Adam Smith 6:3059
Joseph Priestley 6:3350
Dugald Stewart 7:3733
Sir James Mackintosh 7:3829
Thomas Robert Malthus 7:3889
William Cobbett 7:3964

BONNER, MILTON
W. E. Henley 10:6168

BORROW, GEORGE
Daniel Defoe 5:2319
George Borrow 9:5146

BOSWELL, JAMES
George Buchanan 1:314
Robert Burton 3:1367
Izaak Walton 4:1873
John Bunyan 4:1921
Sir William Temple 4:1997
John Locke 4:2083
Gilbert Burnet 4:2140
Sir Isaac Newton 4:2246
Bernard Mandeville 5:2354
John Arbuthnot 5:2371
Jonathan Swift 5:2481
Henry St. John, Viscount
Bolingbroke 5:2560
George Berkeley 5:2586
Henry Fielding 5:2599
Colley Cibber 5:2632, 2634, 2637
Allan Ramsay 5:2639
William Law 5:2677
Samuel Richardson 5:2683, 2684
Charles Churchill 5:2729
Edward Young 5:2738, 2743
David Mallet 5:2755
Laurence Sterne 5:2759, 2765
Mark Akenside 5:2796
Thomas Chatterton 5:2806
Thomas Gray 5:2818
Christopher Smart 5:2866
Philip Dormer Stanhope, Earl of
Chesterfield 5:2873
Oliver Goldsmith 5:2884, 2886,
2889, 2892
David Hume 5:2914, 2915, 2919
Samuel Foote 5:2935
William Warburton 6:2942, 2943,
2946
David Garrick 6:2951
Samuel Johnson 6:2978, 2991,
2995, 2996
Adam Smith 6:3056
Thomas Warton 6:3074
John Wesley 6:3080
Sir Joshua Reynolds 6:3091
William Robertson 6:3108
Edward Gibbon 6:3118
James Boswell 6:3149, 3156
James Macpherson 6:3179
Edmund Burke 6:3257
Hugh Blair 6:3294
Elizabeth Montagu 6:3299, 3302
Joseph Priestley 6:3347
Richard Hurd 6:3366
Junius 6:3481
Anna Laetitia Barbauld 7:3667
Samuel Parr 7:3672

BOURNE, EDWARD GAYLORD
Francis Parkman 10:5757
James Anthony Froude 10:5786

BOURNE, H. R. FOX
Sir Philip Sidney 1:321
Gabriel Harvey 3:1177

BOWEN, EDWIN W.
Frank R. Stockton 10:6089

BOWEN, FRANCIS
Henry Hallam 8:4522
William H. Prescott 8:4592

Benjamin Disraeli 9:5158
Anthony Trollope 9:5287
John Richard Green 9:5362
Richard Monckton Milnes, Lord
  Houghton 9:5387
Edward Augustus Freeman 10:5730

BRYDGES, SIR SAMUEL EGERTON
Thomas Watson 1:357
Thomas Sackville, Earl of Dorset
  1:519
Sir Walter Ralegh 3:1068
William Habington 3:1513
George Wither 3:1570
Margaret Cavendish, Duchess of
  Newcastle 4:1649
William Collins 5:2669
Thomas Warton 6:3073
Sir William Jones 6:3146
Joseph Warton 6:3304, 3305
William Cowper 6:3313
Charlotte Smith 6:3352
Richard Porson 6:3375
Anna Seward 6:3393
Richard Cumberland 6:3411
Jane Austen 6:3447
William Hayley 6:3503
William Gifford 7:3686
George Crabbe 7:3808

BUCHAN, JOHN
Walter Pater 10:5815

BUCHANAN, GEORGE
Roger Ascham 1:289

BUCHANAN, ROBERT
Sir Walter Scott 7:3842
Thomas Moore 8:4423
Thomas Love Peacock 8:4810
Sydney Dobell 9:4985
George Henry Lewes 9:5055
Dante Gabriel Rossetti 9:5329
Charles Reade 9:5372
Robert Browning 9:5503
Herman Melville 10:5607
Walt Whitman 10:5695

BUCKE, CHARLES
Mark Akenside 5:2795

BUCKE, RICHARD MAURICE
Walt Whitman 10:5702

BUCKINGHAM, JOHN SHEFFIELD,
  DUKE OF
John Wilmot, Earl of Rochester
  4:1842
William Congreve 4:2268
Alexander Pope 5:2418

BUCKLAND, ANNA
Sir Philip Sidney 1:325

BUCKLE, HENRY THOMAS
John Knox 1:299
William Chillingworth 3:1436
William Laud 3:1438
Robert Boyle 4:1955
Frances Hutcheson 5:2521
Adam Smith 6:3065
William Robertson 6:3111
Edward Gibbon 6:3129

Thomas Reid 6:3170
Dugald Stewart 7:3733
Henry Thomas Buckle 8:4695
John Stuart Mill 9:4964

BUCKLEY, JAMES M.
Charles Wesley 6:3035

BUCKNILL, JOHN CHARLES
William Shakespeare 2:971

BUEL, CLARENCE CLOUGH
Frank R. Stockton 10:6088

BULKLEY, L.
George Eliot 9:5089

BULLEIN, WILLIAM
John Gower 1:167
John Lydgate 1:174
Alexander Barclay 1:282

BULLEN, A. H.
Robert Greene 1:359
Christopher Marlowe 1:386
George Peele 1:398, 400, 401
Sir Edward Dyer 1:518
Barnabe Barnes 1:525
Thomas Campion 3:1080
Thomas Middleton 3:1163
George Chapman 3:1274
William Browne 3:1414

BULWER, SIR HENRY LYTTON
Sir James Mackintosh 7:3825
William Cobbett 7:3961

BULWER-LYTTON, EDWARD
Jeremy Taylor 3:1581
Sir Thomas Browne 4:1859
Thomas Gray 5:2827
Oliver Goldsmith 5:2887
Lady Caroline Lamb 7:3735
Jeremy Bentham 7:3778
Letitia Elizabeth Landon 7:4019
Robert Southey 7:4088
George Eliot 9:5088
Richard Monckton Milnes, Lord
  Houghton 9:5385

BUNSEN, CHRISTIAN KARL JOSIAS,
  BARON
Thomas Arnold 7:4067

BUNYAN, JOHN
John Bunyan 4:1920

BURGES, SIR JAMES BLAND
Edward Gibbon 5:3120

BURKE, EDMUND
The Venerable Bede 1:14
William Shakespeare 2:840
Sir Francis Bacon 3:1111
Sir Edward Coke 3:1267
Henry St. John, Viscount
  Bolingbroke 5:2562, 2563
Philip Dormer Stanhope, Earl of
  Chesterfield 5:2877
Oliver Goldsmith 5:2891
Adam Smith 6:3060
Sir Joshua Reynolds 6:3090
William Robertson 6:3112
Thomas Paine 6:3386
Junius 6:3484
Fanny Burney 7:4046

BURKE, S. HUBERT
Henry Howard, Earl of Surrey
  1:277

BURNABY, ANDREW
George Berkeley 5:2585

BURNET, GILBERT
Sir Thomas More 1:232
Sir John Cheke 1:286
George Buchanan 1:316
John Foxe 1:356
Edward Hyde, Earl of Clarendon
  4:1751
Thomas Hobbes 4:1808
John Wilmot, Earl of Rochester
  4:1842
George Villiers, Duke of
  Buckingham 4:1908
Robert Boyle 4:1953
George Savile, Marquis of Halifax
  4:1990
Sir Charles Sedley 4:2056
Sir Roger L'Estrange 4:2074
John Evelyn 4:2097
Thomas Sprat 4:2116
Matthew Prior 4:2205

BURNET, THOMAS
Gilbert Burnet 4:2136

BURNEY, CHARLES
John Dryden 4:2025
Samuel Johnson 5:2977
William Wordsworth 8:4302

BURNEY, CHARLOTTE ANN
Thomas Warton 6:3072

BURNEY, FANNY
Alexander Pope 5:2419
Laurence Sterne 5:2767
Christopher Smart 5:2866
Oliver Goldsmith 5:2889
Samuel Johnson 6:2976, 2996
George Colman the Elder 6:3114
Edward Gibbon 6:3119
James Boswell 6:3149
Edmund Burke 6:3257
Elizabeth Montagu 6:3301
James Beattie 6:3337
Richard Hurd 6:3365
Richard Brinsley Sheridan 6:3421
Hester Lynch Piozzi 6:3514
Fanny Burney 7:4044

BURNS, GILBERT
Robert Burns 6:3196

BURNS, ROBERT
John Milton 4:1689
John Dryden 4:2027
James Thomson 5:2538
Allan Ramsay 5:2639
William Falconer 5:2789
Robert Fergusson 5:2907
Robert Burns 6:3191, 3209, 3213
Hugh Blair 6:3293
William Cowper 6:3321
James Beattie 6:3341

BURROUGHS, JOHN
Gilbert White 6:3103

Edward Gibbon 6:3130
Edgar Allan Poe 8:4255
John James Audubon 8:4374
Charles Darwin 9:5272
John Greenleaf Whittier 10:5643
Oliver Wendell Holmes 10:5775

BURTON, JOHN HILL
Thomas of Erceldoune 1:31
John Knox 1:301, 302
Daniel Defoe 5:2317

BURTON, RICHARD
Cædmon 1:9
Thomas Nashe 1:508
Tobias Smollett 5:2844
Charles Dickens 8:4888
James Russell Lowell 10:5595
John Greenleaf Whittier 10:5644
Harriet Beecher Stowe 10:5881

BURTON, ROBERT
Edmund Spenser 1:418

BUSCHIUS, HERMAN
William Tyndale 1:252

BUSHELL, THOMAS
Sir Francis Bacon 3:1107

BUSHNELL, HORACE
Henry Ward Beecher 9:5429

BUTLER, JOSEPH
Thomas Hobbes 4:1808
Joseph Butler 5:2577, 2578

BUTLER, SAMUEL (1612–1680)
Beaumont and Fletcher 3:1047
Ben Jonson 3:1320
George Villiers, Duke of
   Buckingham 4:1907

BUTLER, SAMUEL (1835–1902)
Erasmus Darwin 6:3334

BUTTERWORTH, HEZEKIAH
Anna Seward 6:3393

BYERLEY, J. S.
William Shenstone 5:2722

BYROM, JOHN
Charles Wesley 6:3032
Edward Gibbon 6:3118

BYRON, GEORGE GORDON, LORD
Geoffrey Chaucer 1:62
John Milton 4:1690, 1699
Alexander Pope 5:2424
Jonathan Swift 5:2481
George Berkeley 5:2568
Henry Fielding 5:2600
Samuel Richardson 5:2692
Lady Mary Wortley Montagu
   5:2711
Charles Churchill 5:2728
Laurence Sterne 5:2759
Thomas Gray 5:2826
Philip Dormer Stanhope, Earl of
   Chesterfield 5:2875
Sir William Blackstone 6:2958
Samuel Johnson 6:2984, 2991
Edward Gibbon 6:3119
Robert Burns 6:3196
Horace Walpole 6:3239

William Cowper 6:3324
Henry Kirke White 6:3357
Richard Porson 6:3374
Richard Brinsley Sheridan 6:3422,
   3424
Junius 6:3483
Matthew Gregory Lewis 6:3493,
   3494
William Hayley 6:3502
John Keats 6:3519, 3520
Charles Robert Maturin 7:3625
George Gordon, Lord Byron 7:3645
Samuel Parr 7:3673
Lady Caroline Lamb 7:3735
William Hazlitt 7:3741
George Crabbe 7:3808
Sir James Mackintosh 7:3824
Sir Walter Scott 7:3839, 3843,
   3847
Samuel Taylor Coleridge 7:3893,
   3898, 3908
James Hogg 7:3967
Felicia Dorothea Hemans 7:3982
George Colman the Younger
   7:4006
John Galt 7:4024, 4025
Robert Southey 7:4080, 4081,
   4087, 4088
William Beckford 7:4098
Thomas Campbell 7:4109, 4116
Sydney Smith 7:4129
Isaac D'Israeli 7:4162
Maria Edgeworth 7:4199
William Lisle Bowles 8:4291, 4292
William Wordsworth 8:4302, 4313
Francis, Lord Jeffrey 8:4341
Thomas Moore 8:4417, 4418, 4419
James Montgomery 8:4439
John Wilson 8:4445
Samuel Rogers 8:4458, 4459, 4460
Leigh Hunt 8:4552, 4553
Henry, Lord Brougham 8:4851
Bryan Waller Procter 9:4981

CABLE, GEORGE W.
Eugene Field 10:5876

CAINE, HALL
William Drummond 3:1453
John Milton 4:1704
Laurence Sterne 5:2763
John Keats 6:3529
Samuel Taylor Coleridge 7:3906
Robert Southey 7:4084
Sir Edwin Arnold 10:6188

CAIRD, EDWARD
Thomas Carlyle 9:5118
Benjamin Jowett 10:5749

CAIRD, JOHN
Sir Francis Bacon 3:1115

CALDERWOOD, HENRY
David Hume 5:2923

CALDWELL, JOSHUA W.
James Boswell 6:3154

CALDWELL, WILLIAM
Adam Smith 6:3060

CALLOWAY, MORGAN, JR.
Sidney Lanier 9:5178

CALVERT, GEORGE H.
John Keats 6:3529
Samuel Taylor Coleridge 7:3908

CAMDEN, WILLIAM
Edmund Spenser 1:403, 406
George Puttenham 1:498
Sir Francis Bacon 3:1107

CAMERON, V. LOVETT
Sir Richard Burton 10:5574

CAMPBELL, DR.
David Hume 5:2913

CAMPBELL, DOUGLAS
John Foxe 1:356

CAMPBELL, HELEN
Anne Bradstreet 3:1635, 1636

CAMPBELL, JOHN, LORD
Geoffrey of Monmouth 1:26
Sir Thomas More 1:233, 235
Sir Walter Ralegh 3:1065
Edward Hyde, Earl of Clarendon
   4:1755

CAMPBELL, LEWIS
Benjamin Jowett 10:5747

CAMPBELL, THOMAS
Richard Rolle of Hampole 1:35
William Langland 1:49
Geoffrey Chaucer 1:62
John Gower 1:168
Thomas Occleve 1:182
Sir Thomas Wyatt 1:263
Alexander Barclay 1:282
Sir Philip Sidney 1:320
Robert Greene 1:360
Thomas Kyd 1:395
George Peele 1:401
Thomas Sackville, Earl of Dorset
   1:521
William Warner 1:524
Sir Thomas Overbury 1:529
William Shakespeare 2:574
Beaumont and Fletcher 3:1048
Giles and Phineas Fletcher 3:1088
Nicholas Breton 3:1099
Sir John Davies 3:1145
William Rowley 3:1158
Michael Drayton 3:1186, 1189
John Donne 3:1195, 1197
John Webster 3:1282
John Marston 3:1298
Edward Fairfax 3:1308
Richard Corbett 3:1311
Thomas Randolph 3:1313
Ben Jonson 3:1323
Philip Massinger 3:1357
Thomas Carew 3:1395
Francis Quarles 3:1425
William Drummond 3:1450
Richard Crashaw 3:1465
Thomas Heywood 3:1490
William Habington 3:1511
Joseph Hall 3:1520
James Shirley 3:1560
George Wither 3:1571
Abraham Cowley 3:1597
John Milton 4:1690

Andrew Marvell 4:1784
Thomas Otway 4:1888
Charles Cotton 4:1913
Sir George Etherege 4:1957
Nathaniel Lee 4:1971
Henry Vaughan 4:1976
John Dryden 4:2013
Sir Samuel Garth 4:2172
Matthew Prior 4:2208
John Gay 5:2341
George Lillo 5:2385
Isaac Watts 5:2526
James Thomson 5:2538
Allan Ramsay 5:2644
William Collins 5:2663
William Shenstone 5:2722
Edward Young 5:2746
William Falconer 5:2790
Mark Akenside 5:2795
Thomas Gray 5:2819
Christopher Smart 5:2866
Robert Fergusson 5:2908
Henry Brooke 6:2971
William Whitehead 6:3029
Thomas Warton 6:3073
Sir William Jones 6:3146
Robert Burns 6:3198
William Mason 6:3254, 3255
Joseph Warton 6:3305
William Cowper 6:3322
George Crabbe 7:3806
Sir James Mackintosh 7:3824
Joanna Baillie 8:4366

CANFIELD, DOROTHEA FRANCES
Katherine Philips 3:1554

CANNAN, GILBERT
Samuel Butler 10:6095

CAPGRAVE, JOHN
John Wyclif 1:40

CAREW, THOMAS
John Donne 3:1197
George Sandys 3:1422

CAREY, H. C.
David Ricardo 7:3622

CAREY, HENRY
Henry Carey 5:2402
Ambrose Philips 5:2551

CARGILL, ALEXANDER
Izaak Walton 4:1872, 1873

CARLETON, SIR DUDLEY
Sir Francis Bacon 3:1106

CARLETON, WILLIAM
Henry Fielding 5:2608

CARLYLE, ALEXANDER
Francis Hutcheson 5:2519
James Thomson 5:2531
William Shenstone 5:2722
Tobias Smollett 5:2836
David Hume 5:2915
Benjamin Franklin 6:3038
Adam Smith 6:3058
James Macpherson 6:3180
Hugh Blair 6:3293
John Home 6:3369

CARLYLE, E. IRVING
William Tyndale 1:254

CARLYLE, JANE WELSH
William Makepeace Thackeray
8:4715
Frederick Denison Maurice 9:4923
John Forster 9:5013
George Henry Lewes 9:5055
George Eliot 9:5088
Charles Darwin 9:5275
Alfred, Lord Tennyson 10:5653

CARLYLE, THOMAS
Roger Ascham 1:290
John Knox 1:299, 300
William Shakespeare 2:618
Sir Francis Bacon 3:1109
William Drummond 3:1450
John Milton 4:1691, 1699
Edward Hyde, Earl of Clarendon
4:1752
John Bunyan 4:1922
John Locke 4:2079
Joseph Addison 4:2178
Jonathan Swift 5:2483
Henry Fielding 5:2600
Laurence Sterne 5:2759
Mark Akenside 5:2795
Thomas Chatterton 5:2809
Thomas Gray 5:2819
Tobias Smollett 5:2837
Robert Fergusson 5:2909
David Hume 5:2916, 2917
Henry Home, Lord Kames 6:2967
Samuel Johnson 6:2981, 3007
Benjamin Franklin 6:3040
William Robertson 6:3109
Edward Gibbon 6:3126
James Boswell 6:3157, 3162
Robert Burns 6:3215
Mary Wollstonecraft 6:3279
James Beattie 6:3337
George Gordon, Lord Byron
7:3631, 3639
Dugald Stewart 7:3732
William Hazlitt 7:3739
Jeremy Bentham 7:3779
Sir Walter Scott 7:3850, 3856
Samuel Taylor Coleridge 7:3898
Charles Lamb 7:3935
James Hogg 7:3967
William Godwin 7:3991
William Ellery Channing 7:4060
Robert Southey 7:4083
Thomas Campbell 7:4109
John Sterling 7:4122
Thomas Chalmers 7:4157
Isaac D'Israeli 7:4162
Ebenezer Elliott 7:4210
William Wordsworth 8:4302
Francis, Lord Jeffrey 8:4344
Margaret Fuller 8:4357
James Fenimore Cooper 8:4378
Thomas Moore 8:4425
John Wilson 8:4445
John Gibson Lockhart 8:4453, 4454
Samuel Rogers 8:4458
Sir William Hamilton 8:4501

Leigh Hunt 8:4550, 4553
Thomas De Quincey 8:4568, 4570
Thomas Babington Macaulay
8:4598, 4604
Arthur Hugh Clough 8:4648
Henry David Thoreau 8:4666
William Makepeace Thackeray
8:4706
Walter Savage Landor 8:4733
Henry, Lord Brougham 8:4850
Charles Dickens 8:4878
Frederick Denison Maurice 9:4923
Edward Bulwer-Lytton 9:4940
Samuel Wilberforce 9:4955
John Stuart Mill 9:4959, 4965
Bryan Waller Procter 9:4981, 4982
Thomas Carlyle 9:5110
Benjamin Disraeli 9:5153
Ralph Waldo Emerson 9:5190,
5195
Richard Monckton Milnes, Lord
Houghton 9:5384
Sir Henry Taylor 9:5397
Amos Bronson Alcott 9:5449
Alfred, Lord Tennyson 10:5653,
5666
Coventry Patmore 10:5894
William Ewart Gladstone 10:5937

CARPENTER, FREDERICK IVES
Sir Philip Sidney 1:322
Robert Greene 1:360
George Peele 1:400
Nicholas Breton 3:1100
John Donne 3:1199
John Webster 3:1285, 1287
William Drummond 3:1452
Richard Crashaw 3:1467
Henry Vaughan 4:1978

CARPENTER, GEORGE RICE
John Greenleaf Whittier 10:5642

CARPENTER, NATHANIEL
William Browne 3:1412

CARR, J. COMYNS
Dante Gabriel Rossetti 9:5324
Oscar Wilde 10:6021

CARROLL, LEWIS
William Makepeace Thackeray
8:4706
Alfred, Lord Tennyson 10:5654

CARTER, ELIZABETH
Samuel Richardson 5:2682

CARY, EDWARD
George William Curtis 10:5737

CARY, ELIZABETH LUTHER
William Morris 10:5905

CARY, HENRY FRANCIS
Thomas Gray 5:2819
Sir Walter Scott 7:3839

CASSERLY, D. A.
William Habington 3:1511, 1512

CATHER, WILLA
Walt Whitman 10:5703
Stephen Crane 10:6058
Kate Chopin 10:6206

CAVENDISH, LUCY C. F.
Charlotte Mary Yonge 10:6067

CAWTHORNE, THOMAS
Henry Fielding 5:2606

CAXTON, WILLIAM
Geoffrey Chaucer 1:55, 56
Sir Thomas Malory 1:186
John Skelton 1:211

CAYLEY, ARTHUR
Sir Thomas More 1:233

CECIL, ALGERNON
John Henry Newman 9:5558

CECIL, ROBERT
Sir Walter Ralegh 3:1064

CECIL, WILLIAM (LORD BURGHLEY)
John Knox 1:299

CHADWICK, JOHN WHITE
Henry Ward Beecher 9:5430
Richard William Church 10:5570
George William Curtis 10:5734
Oliver Wendell Holmes 10:5774
Richard Henry Stoddard 10:6152

CHALMERS, ALEXANDER
Charles Cotton 4:1913
Thomas Tickell 5:2390
William Falconer 5:2789
Tobias Smollett 5:2839
William Whitehead 6:3028
Thomas Warton 6:3072
William Mason 6:3252
James Beattie 6:3337

CHALMERS, GEORGE
Allan Ramsay 5:2641

CHALMERS, THOMAS
Dugald Stewart 7:3731

CHAMBERLAIN, NICHOLAS
Sir Francis Bacon 3:1114

CHAMBERS, EDMUND K.
Andrew Marvell 4:1785
Anthony Ashley Cooper, Third Earl
of Shaftesbury 4:2129
Sir Isaac Newton 4:2248
John Gay 5:2343
Christina Rossetti 10:5801
Francis Turner Palgrave 10:5921
Lionel Johnson 10:6121
Sir Edwin Arnold 10:6190

CHAMBERS, ROBERT
John Donne 3:1198

CHAMBERS, WILLIAM
James Hogg 7:3969
Robert Chambers 9:4917

CHANNING, EDWARD T.
Philip Dormer Stanhope, Earl of
Chesterfield 5:2876
Oliver Goldsmith 5:2898
Richard Henry Dana, Jr. 9:5310

CHANNING, WILLIAM ELLERY
John Milton 4:1690, 1705
Sir Richard Steele 4:2297
Mary Russell Mitford 8:4472

Henry Hallam 8:4522
Henry David Thoreau 8:4668
Frances Trollope 8:4701
Nathaniel Hawthorne 8:4776
Herman Melville 10:5605

CHANNING, WILLIAM HENRY
Francis Hutcheson 5:2521
Joseph Butler 5:2577
William Ellery Channing 7:4058

CHAPMAN, EDWARD M.
Robert G. Ingersoll 10:5979

CHAPMAN, GEORGE
Christopher Marlowe 1:364, 365
Sir Francis Bacon 3:1121

CHAPPELL, WILLIAM
Thomas D'Urfey 4:2219

CHARLEMONT, EARL OF
Philip Dormer Stanhope, Earl of
Chesterfield 5:2878
Sir Joshua Reynolds 6:3090
Joseph Warton 6:3305

CHARLES V, KING OF SPAIN
Sir Thomas More 1:231

CHATEAUBRIAND, FRANÇOIS RENÉ,
VICOMTE DE
John Milton 4:1687, 1703
Edward Hyde, Earl of Clarendon
4:1754
Sir William Temple 4:1997
Gilbert Burnet 4:2138
Samuel Richardson 5:2685
Edward Young 5:2740

CHATTERTON, THOMAS
William Collins 5:2663
Thomas Chatterton 5:2801
Oliver Goldsmith 5:2886

CHAUCER, GEOFFREY
John Gower 1:167

CHEETHAM, JAMES
Thomas Paine 6:3385

CHEEVER, GEORGE BARRELL
John Bunyan 4:1928

CHENEY, EDNAH D.
Louisa May Alcott 9:5486

CHENEY, JOHN VANCE
William Cowper 6:3319
William Blake 7:3699
Nathaniel Hawthorne 8:4770

CHESTERFIELD, EARL OF
John Dryden 4:2005

CHESTERFIELD, PHILIP DORMER
STANHOPE, EARL OF
John Arbuthnot 5:2371
Richard Bentley 5:2394
Henry St. John, Viscount
Bolingbroke 5:2559, 2561
George Berkeley 5:2586
Philip Dormer Stanhope, Earl of
Chesterfield 5:2875
Samuel Johnson 5:2994

CHESTERTON, G. K.
William Shakespeare 2:735, 901

Alexander Pope 5:2464
James Boswell 6:3154
George Gordon, Lord Byron 7:3665
James Clarence Mangan 7:4238
Matthew Arnold 9:5457
Robert Browning 9:5520
Alfred, Lord Tennyson 10:5663
Robert Louis Stevenson 10:5836
William Morris 10:5918
Oscar Wilde 10:6023
Bret Harte 10:6114

CHETTLE, HENRY
Robert Greene 1:358
Samuel Daniel 3:1071
Thomas Dekker 3:1227
Ben Jonson 3:1318

CHILD, FRANCIS JAMES
Geoffrey Chaucer 1:67

CHILD, LYDIA MARIA
Elizabeth Barrett Browning 8:4637

CHILDS, GEORGE W.
Anne Bradstreet 3:1635

CHINNOCK, DR. H. S.
George Colman the Younger
7:4006

CHIVERS, THOMAS HOLLEY
Edgar Allan Poe 8:4253

CHOPIN, KATE
Kate Chopin 10:6205

CHORLEY, G. F.
Jane Austen 6:3450
Mary Russell Mitford 8:4474

CHORLEY, HENRY F.
Charles Lamb 7:3941
Felicia Dorothea Hemans 7:3980,
3983
Letitia Elizabeth Landon 7:4023
Robert Southey 7:4079
Thomas Campbell 7:4113
Sydney Smith 7:4130
Thomas Hood 7:4138
Marguerite, Countess of Blessington
7:4218
Anne Brontë 8:4286
Thomas Moore 8:4420
Mary Russell Mitford 8:4468
Charlotte Brontë 8:4482
Sydney Owenson, Lady Morgan
8:4549
Elizabeth Barrett Browning 8:4637
Catharine Maria Sedgwick 8:4829
Edward Bulwer-Lytton 9:4942
Coventry Patmore 10:5894

CHRISTIE, MARY ELIZABETH
Fanny Burney 7:4041

CHURCH, MARY C.
Richard William Church 10:5571

CHURCH, RICHARD WILLIAM
Thomas Sackville, Earl of Dorset
1:520
Lancelot Andrewes 3:1104
Sir Francis Bacon 3:1110, 1121,
1137

Gabriel Harvey 3:1177
Thomas Arnold 7:4070
John Keble 8:4825
H. H. Milman 8:4861
Frederick Denison Maurice 9:4926
Samuel Wilberforce 9:4955
John Henry Newman 9:5551, 5556

CHURCH, SAMUEL HARDEN
John Knox 1:301

CHURCHILL, CHARLES
Ben Jonson 3:1322
Andrew Marvell 4:1783
Edmund Waller 4:1899
John Dryden 4:2010
Alexander Pope 5:2422
Charles Churchill 5:2727
Laurence Sterne 5:2759
Tobias Smollett 5:2836
Samuel Foote 5:2936
William Warburton 6:2947
David Garrick 6:2951
William Whitehead 6:3028
James Macpherson 6:3177
Charles Macklin 6:3228
John Home 6:3370

CHURCHYARD, THOMAS
John Skelton 1:215

CIBBER, COLLEY
Nathaniel Lee 4:1969, 1970
John Dryden 4:2005, 2009
Joseph Addison 4:2184
Jeremy Collier 4:2230
Sir John Vanbrugh 4:2235, 2238
William Congreve 4:2277
John Gay 5:2345
Alexander Pope 5:2435
Henry Fielding 5:2596

CIBBER, THEOPHILUS
John Lydgate 1:174
Sir Thomas Wyatt 1:263
Sir John Harington 1:527
Sir Thomas Overbury 1:529
Thomas Lodge 3:1094
William Drummond 3:1453
Sir John Denham 3:1629
John Milton 4:1698
Sir Charles Sedley 4:2057
Sir Roger L'Estrange 4:2074
George Farquhar 4:2106
Nicholas Rowe 4:2159
George Lillo 5:2382
Thomas Tickell 5:2390
Richard Savage 5:2407
Ambrose Philips 5:2551
Aaron Hill 5:2554
William Mason 6:3254

CLARENDON, EDWARD HYDE, EARL OF
Thomas Carew 3:1395
William Chillingworth 3:1432
John Selden 3:1501
John Hales 3:1523
Edward Hyde, Earl of Clarendon
4:1751
Charles Cotton 4:1912
Sir Roger L'Estrange 4:2073

CLARENDON, GEORGE VILLIERS, LORD
Alexander William Kinglake
10:5587

CLARK, EDWARD GORDON
Henry George 10:5931

CLARK, L. GAYLORD
Noah Webster 7:4073

CLARKE, ADAM
Charles Wesley 6:3033

CLARKE, CHARLES COWDEN
Ben Jonson 3:1323, 1326, 1328
Samuel Butler 4:1836
John Wilmot, Earl of Rochester
4:1844
George Farquhar 4:2108
William Wycherley 4:2152
Sir John Vanbrugh 4:2241
William Congreve 4:2283
Jonathan Swift 5:2502
Tobias Smollett 5:2844
Samuel Foote 5:2936
David Garrick 6:2955
John Keats 6:3518
Thomas Hood 7:4140
Robert Chambers 9:4915
Bryan Waller Procter 9:4983

CLARKE, HELEN F.
Isaac Watts 5:2525

CLARKE, JAMES FREEMAN
William Shakespeare 2:729
Sir Walter Scott 7:3848
William Ellery Channing 7:4059
Margaret Fuller 8:4354

CLARKE, JAMES STAINER
William Falconer 5:2789

CLARKE, MARY COWDEN
Mary Lamb 7:4155
Marguerite, Countess of Blessington
7:4218
Mary Shelley 8:4398
Robert Chambers 9:4915

CLARKE, R. H.
George Bancroft 10:5581

CLARKE, WILLIAM
Samuel Daniel 3:1071
Walt Whitman 10:5701
Edward Augustus Freeman 10:5731

CLAYDEN, P. W.
William Shakespeare 2:965

CLELAND, JOHN
Tobias Smollett 5:2846

CLEMM, MARIA
Edgar Allan Poe 8:4249

CLERK, ARCHIBALD
James Macpherson 6:3184

CLEVELAND, CHARLES D.
Isaac Watts 5:2527
Thomas Campbell 7:4112
Joanna Baillie 8:4368
Rufus Wilmot Griswold 8:4516
Josiah Gilbert Holland 9:5171
Henry Ward Beecher 9:5429

"CLIFFORDIENSIS"
Richard Lovelace 3:1533, 1534

CLIFT, DENISON HAILEY
Frank Norris 10:6123, 6125

CLITHEROW, JAMES
Sir William Blackstone 6:2958

CLIVE, ARTHUR
James Boswell 6:3151
Walt Whitman 10:5697

CLODD, EDWARD
Thomas Hobbes 4:1807
Matthew Arnold 9:5458

CLOUGH, ARTHUR HUGH
Robert Burns 6:3200
Ralph Waldo Emerson 9:5192
Henry Wadsworth Longfellow
9:5251
William Ewart Gladstone 10:5942

CLOUGH, BLANCHE
Arthur Hugh Clough 8:4649

CLYMER, W. B. SHUBRICK
Jane Austen 6:3471
James Fenimore Cooper 8:4381
Walter Savage Landor 8:4738

COBBETT, WILLIAM
Thomas Paine 6:3389

COCKBURN, CATHERINE
Joseph Butler 5:2572

COCKBURN, HENRY, LORD
William Robertson 6:3107
Dugald Stewart 7:3731
Henry Mackenzie 7:3763
Francis, Lord Jeffrey 8:4343
John Wilson 8:4446

CODRINGTON, CHARLES
Sir Samuel Garth 4:2171

COGHILL, ANNIE L.
Margaret Oliphant 10:5925

COHEN, MARY M.
Emma Lazarus 9:5448

COKE, SIR EDWARD
Sir Walter Ralegh 3:1064

COKE, LADY MARY
Laurence Sterne 5:2759

COLE, WILLIAM
Thomas Warton 6:3076

COLERIDGE, DERWENT
Winthrop Mackworth Praed 7:4035
Hartley Coleridge 7:4221

COLERIDGE, HARTLEY
Roger Ascham 1:289
Michael Drayton 3:1187
John Donne 3:1198
Philip Massinger 3:1357
John Ford 3:1387, 1390
John Dryden 4:2014
Thomas Parnell 4:2166
Richard Bentley 5:2400
Charles Churchill 5:2731
Thomas Gray 5:2819

Walter Savage Landor 8:4737
Samuel Butler 10:6096

CONANT, SAMUEL STILLMAN
Sara Coleridge 8:4433
Mary Russell Mitford 8:4472
George William Curtis 10:5735

CONDELL, HENRY
William Shakespeare 2:563

CONDILLAC, ETIENNE BONNOT DE
Sir Francis Bacon 3:1119

CONDORCET, MARIE JEAN ANTOINE
NICOLAS CARITAT, MARQUIS DE
Benjamin Franklin 6:3038

CONE, HELEN GRAY
Margaret Fuller 8:4360
Alice and Phoebe Cary 9:4920
Helen Hunt Jackson 9:5394
Harriet Beecher Stowe 10:5880

CONGREVE, WILLIAM
Ben Jonson 3:1321
John Dryden 4:2005, 2009
Nicholas Rowe 4:2158
Jeremy Collier 4:2229
William Congreve 4:2268, 2276, 2277
Jonathan Swift 5:2489

CONINGTON, JOHN
John Dryden 4:2028
Thomas Tickell 5:2389

CONRAD, JOSEPH
Frederick Marryat 7:4174
James Fenimore Cooper 8:4382
Herman Melville 10:5609
Stephen Crane 10:6047

CONWAY, MONCURE DANIEL
Charles Churchill 5:2729
Thomas Paine 6:3385, 3387
William Blake 7:3712
Sir Walter Scott 7:3845
Felicia Dorothea Hemans 7:3985
John Wilson 8:4446
Henry David Thoreau 8:4666
Bayard Taylor 9:5058
William Barnes 9:5401
Walt Whitman 10:5694

CONWELL, RUSSELL H.
Bayard Taylor 9:5060

CONYBEARE, JOHN JOSIAS
Beowulf 1:1

COOK, WILLIAM
Colley Cibber 5:2637
Samuel Foote 5:2936, 2937
Charles Macklin 6:3230

COOKE, GEORGE WILLIS
George Eliot 9:5094
George William Curtis 10:5734
Francis Parkman 10:5754

COOLIDGE, SUSAN
Helen Hunt Jackson 9:5391, 5395

COOPER, ELIZABETH
Geoffrey Chaucer 1:60

John Skelton 1:213
Alexander Barclay 1:282
Thomas Sackville, Earl of Dorset
1:521
William Warner 1:524
Sir John Harington 1:527
Samuel Daniel 3:1071
Sir John Davies 3:1142
Edward Fairfax 3:1308

COOPER, FREDERIC TABER
Frank Norris 10:6129

COOPER, FREDERICK
Winthrop Mackworth Praed 7:4038

COOPER, THOMPSON
Sir John Cheke 1:286

COOPER, WILLIAM DURRANT
Nicholas Udall 1:288

COPE, WALTER
William Shakespeare 2:773

COPNER, JAMES
Thomas Brown 6:3508

COPPING, EDWARD
Douglas Jerrold 8:4512

CORBETT, RICHARD
Francis Beaumont 3:1040

CORNFORD, F. M.
Samuel Butler 10:6099

CORSON, HIRAM
John Milton 4:1707

COSTE, PIERRE
John Locke 4:2077

COTTERELL, GEORGE
Coventry Patmore 10:5896

COTTLE, JOSEPH
Samuel Taylor Coleridge 7:3896

COTTON, CHARLES
Aphra Behn 4:1936

COTTON, J. S.
Sir Richard Burton 10:5574
Edward Augustus Freeman 10:5728
Benjamin Jowett 10:5747

COURTENAY, JOHN
Samuel Johnson 6:2983

COURTHOPE, WILLIAM JOHN
Cynewulf 1:16
Thomas of Erceldoune 1:32
John Lydgate 1:176
Robert Henryson 1:203
Gavin Douglas 1:207
William Dunbar 1:223
Sir Thomas Wyatt 1:265, 269
Henry Howard, Earl of Surrey
1:279
George Gascoigne 1:311
Christopher Marlowe 1:370
Thomas Kyd 1:396
George Peele 1:400
John Lyly 1:510
Sir Edward Dyer 1:519
Thomas Sackville, Earl of Dorset
1:520

Henry Constable 1:528
Sir Walter Ralegh 3:1069
Samuel Daniel 3:1077
Thomas Lodge 3:1096
John Donne 3:1220
George Chapman 3:1275
Joseph Addison 4:2179
Alexander Pope 5:2432
Lewis Theobald 5:2469
Lady Mary Wortley Montagu
5:2710
Thomas Gray 5:2821
William Warburton 6:2947
Samuel Johnson 6:2992
Thomas Warton 6:3074
Horace Walpole 6:3235
John Keats 6:3547
George Crabbe 7:3820
Sir Walter Scott 7:3847
Edward Robert Bulwer Lytton
10:5627

COURTNEY, W. L.
Roger Bacon 1:30
Ralph Waldo Emerson 9:5199
Charles Reade 9:5373

COURTNEY, W. P.
John Arbuthnot 5:2371

COUSIN, VICTOR
Duns Scotus 1:32

COWLEY, ABRAHAM
Edmund Spenser 1:409, 419
Sir Francis Bacon 3:1118
Sir Henry Wotton 3:1350
Richard Crashaw 3:1464
Katherine Philips 3:1553
Abraham Cowley 3:1594, 1595
Sir William D'Avenant 3:1614
John Evelyn 4:2097

COWPER, J. M.
Sir Thomas More 1:233

COWPER, WILLIAM
Sir Philip Sidney 1:323
Abraham Cowley 3:1595
John Milton 4:1698
John Bunyan 4:1921
John Dryden 4:2012
Joseph Addison 4:2178
Matthew Prior 4:2208
John Dennis 5:2365
Alexander Pope 5:2422, 2437
Jonathan Swift 5:2481
Isaac Watts 5:2526
James Thomson 5:2533
William Collins 5:2662
Charles Churchill 5:2733
Thomas Gray 5:2817
Philip Dormer Stanhope, Earl of
Chesterfield 5:2875
David Hume 5:2917
Samuel Johnson 6:2982, 2998
Benjamin Franklin 6:3042
John Wesley 6:3080
George Colman the Elder 6:3114
Edward Gibbon 6:3120
James Boswell 6:3155
Robert Burns 6:3195

Elizabeth Montagu 6:3301
William Cowper 6:3309
Erasmus Darwin 6:3330
James Beattie 6:3339, 3341
Hannah More 7:3868

Cox, S. S.
  Artemus Ward 8:4846

Coxe, Arthur Cleveland
  Nathaniel Hawthorne 8:4773

Coxe, William
  Philip Dormer Stanhope, Earl of
    Chesterfield 5:2874

Crabbe, George (1754-1832)
  Geoffrey Chaucer 1:87
  George Crabbe 7:3806
  Sir Walter Scott 7:3836

Crabbe, George (1785-1857)
  George Crabbe 7:3806

Cracroft, Bernard
  Sir Francis Bacon 3:1109, 1111

Cradock, Joseph
  Oliver Goldsmith 5:2885
  Richard Hurd 6:3365

Craigie, W. A.
  John Barbour 1:48

Craik, Dinah Maria
  Sydney Dobell 9:4986

Craik, George L.
  William of Malmesbury 1:25
  John Barbour 1:47
  John Lydgate 1:175
  William Dunbar 1:222
  Henry Howard, Earl of Surrey
    1:277, 278
  Richard Hooker 1:502
  William Warner 1:524
  Sir John Harington 1:527
  Giles and Phineas Fletcher 3:1089
  Lancelot Andrewes 3:1102
  John Donne 3:1198
  Richard Corbett 3:1312
  Thomas Randolph 3:1313
  Ben Jonson 3:1327
  William Browne 3:1409
  Richard Crashaw 3:1466
  John Cleveland 3:1539
  Sir John Denham 3:1628
  Thomas Hobbes 4:1808
  Ambrose Philips 5:2552
  Aaron Hill 5:2555
  Erasmus Darwin 6:3331
  Leigh Hunt 8:4556

Craik, Henry
  Sir John Cheke 1:287
  Roger Ascham 1:294
  Joseph Hall 3:1519
  Sir Kenelm Digby 3:1558
  Jeremy Taylor 3:1583
  Edward Hyde, Earl of Clarendon
    4:1756
  Sir William Temple 4:1998
  John Locke 4:2080
  John Evelyn 4:2100
  John Arbuthnot 5:2371, 2373

Jonathan Swift 5:2487
Francis Hutcheson 5:2519
Henry St. John, Viscount
  Bolingbroke 5:2569
Joseph Butler 5:2577
Henry Fielding 5:2603
Allan Ramsay 5:2643
Philip Dormer Stanhope, Earl of
  Chesterfield 5:2879
David Hume 5:2923
Henry Home, Lord Kames 6:2968
Samuel Johnson 6:2990
Thomas Warton 6:3077
John Wesley 6:3086
William Robertson 6:3109
James Boswell 6:3153
James Beattie 6:3340
Dugald Stewart 7:3734
Fanny Burney 7:4043
Isaac D'Israeli 7:4165
Maria Edgeworth 7:4205
George Eliot 9:5087
Benjamin Disraeli 9:5157

Cramer, Frank
  Charles Darwin 9:5274

Cranch, C. P.
  Margaret Fuller 8:4355
  Ralph Waldo Emerson 9:5205

Crane, Stephen
  Harold Frederic 10:5974

Crane, Walter
  William Morris 10:5905

Crashaw, Richard
  Sir Philip Sidney 1:321
  George Herbert 3:1247
  John Ford 3:1390

Crawford, F. Marion
  Richard Brinsley Sheridan 6:4327
  Walter Savage Landor 8:4743

Crawfurd, Oswald
  John Donne 3:1199
  Ben Jonson 3:1324
  Sir John Vanbrugh 4:2237
  William Congreve 4:2274
  John Gay 5:2347
  Colley Cibber 5:2636
  Richard Cumberland 6:3412
  Richard Brinsley Sheridan 6:3426

Creasy, Sir Edward
  Thomas Occleve 1:183

Creighton, Mandell
  Sir John Harington 1:527

Crell, Samuel
  Sir Isaac Newton 4:2243

Croft, Sir Herbert
  Thomas Chatterton 5:2806

Croker, John Wilson
  Jonathan Swift 5:2490
  Lady Mary Wortley Montagu
    5:2713
  James Boswell 6:3157
  Edmund Burke 6:3258
  Joseph Priestley 6:3349

Richard Brinsley Sheridan 6:3425
Junius 6:3483
John Keats 6:3531
Sir James Mackintosh 7:3826
John Galt 7:4025
Fanny Burney 7:4048
Sydney Smith 7:4131
Sydney Owenson, Lady Morgan
  8:4547
Thomas Babington Macaulay
  8:4603, 4609
Henry, Lord Brougham 8:4852
Charles Dickens 8:4888

Cromwell, Henry
  Nicholas Rowe 4:2158

Cromwell, Oliver
  Sir Walter Ralegh 3:1069

Crooks, G. R.
  Joseph Butler 5:2572

Crosland, Camilla Toulmin
  Fanny Burney 7:4047
  Nathaniel Hawthorne 8:4771
  Bayard Taylor 9:5062
  Dinah Maria Craik 9:5433

Cross, Allen Eastman
  Emma Lazarus 9:5445

Cross, Edwin
  Thomas Chatterton 5:2801

Cross, John W.
  George Eliot 9:5081

Cross, Wilbur L.
  Henry Fielding 5:2608
  Samuel Richardson 5:2691
  Laurence Sterne 5:2787
  Tobias Smollett 5:2864
  Jane Austen 6:3477
  Ann Radcliffe 7:3611
  Henry Mackenzie 7:3766
  William Beckford 7:4100
  Emily Brontë 7:4181
  Maria Edgeworth 7:4206
  Charlotte Brontë 8:4484
  Nathaniel Hawthorne 8:4772
  Elizabeth Gaskell 8:4801
  Charles Dickens 8:4888
  Charles Kingsley 9:4995
  George Eliot 9:5088
  George Borrow 9:5148
  Anthony Trollope 9:5286

Crowley, Robert
  William Langland 1:49

Cumberland, Richard
  William Shakespeare 2:592
  Richard Bentley 5:2393
  Oliver Goldsmith 5:2886
  David Garrick 6:2952
  James Boswell 6:3149
  Horace Walpole 6:3235
  Richard Cumberland 6:3412
  Samuel Rogers 8:4459

Cummings, Joseph
  Joseph Butler 5:2574

Cunningham, Allan
  Sir John Vanbrugh 4:2236

Sir Joshua Reynolds 6:3095
Robert Burns 6:3199
William Blake 7:3697
Henry Mackenzie 7:3763
Letitia Elizabeth Landon 7:4021

CURRIE, JAMES
Robert Burns 6:3195, 3210

CURTIS, GEORGE WILLIAM
John Milton 4:1692
Robert Burns 6:3203
Jane Austen 6:3451
Margaret Fuller 8:4356
Elizabeth Barrett Browning 8:4632
Henry David Thoreau 8:4674
William Makepeace Thackeray
8:4707
Nathaniel Hawthorne 8:4767
William Cullen Bryant 9:5051
Charles Darwin 9:5271
Robert Browning 9:5492
James Russell Lowell 10:5594

CURTIS, WILLIAM ELEROY
Thomas Jefferson 7:3683

CUTLER, MANASSEH
Benjamin Franklin 6:3037

DABNEY, J. P.
William Tyndale 1:255

DALL, CAROLINE H.
Margaret Fuller 8:4358

DALLAS, E. S.
Lewis Theobald 5:2469
Richard Porson 6:3376

DALLAWAY, JAMES
Lady Mary Wortley Montagu
5:2711

DANA, CHARLES A.
Walt Whitman 10:5705

DANA, RICHARD HENRY
Charles Brockden Brown 6:3401
Ann Radcliffe 7:3607
Washington Allston 7:4094
Charles Dickens 8:4878
Horace Greeley 9:4936

DANA, RICHARD HENRY, JR.
Richard Henry Dana, Jr. 9:5308

DANIEL, GEORGE
Sir Thomas Overbury 1:529
Michael Drayton 3:1186
John Donne 3:1197
George Herbert 3:1247
Sir Thomas Browne 4:1856
Edmund Waller 4:1898

DANIEL, GEORGE
Charles Lamb 7:3936

DANIEL, SAMUEL
Sir Philip Sidney 1:319
Edmund Spenser 1:406, 418
George Chapman 3:1276

DARMESTETER, MARY
Raphael Holinshed 1:313

DARTMOUTH, WILLIAM LEGGE,
EARL OF
Gilbert Burnet 4:2137

DARWIN, CHARLES
Erasmus Darwin 6:3332
Thomas Robert Malthus 7:3883
Charles Darwin 9:5269, 5275
Thomas Henry Huxley 10:5861
John Fiske 10:6074

DARWIN, FRANCIS
Charles Darwin 9:5273

DASENT, SIR G. W.
Samuel Wilberforce 9:4957

D'AVENANT, WILLIAM
Edmund Spenser 1:409

DAVENPORT, R. A.
Aaron Hill 5:2554
William Falconer 5:2791
William Robertson 6:3109

DAVEY, SAMUEL
Thomas De Quincey 8:4572

DAVIDSON, JAMES
William Gilmore Simms 8:4873

DAVIDSON, JOHN
John Keats 6:3527

DAVIES, J. LLEWELYN
Matthew Arnold 9:5463

DAVIES, JAMES
John Hookham Frere 7:4149
Thomas Love Peacock 8:4815
Edward Robert Bulwer Lytton
10:5627

DAVIES, JOHN, OF HEREFORD
Sir Edward Dyer 1:518
William Shakespeare 2:535
Fulke Greville, Lord Brooke 3:1172
William Browne 3:1411

DAVIES, THOMAS
Ben Jonson 3:1325, 1326
Thomas Otway 4:1891
John Dryden 4:2022
Nahum Tate 4:2144
George Lillo 5:2383
Aaron Hill 5:2556
Colley Cibber 5:2632
Charles Churchill 5:2729, 2733
David Mallet 5:2754
Oliver Goldsmith 5:2894
Samuel Foote 5:2936
Richard Cumberland 6:3410

DAVIS, J. R. AINSWORTH
Thomas Henry Huxley 10:5865

DAVIS, JOHN
Thomas Chatterton 5:2806

DAVYS, SIR JOHN
John Heywood 1:308

DAWES, RUFUS
Ralph Waldo Emerson 9:5191

DAWKINS, C. E.
Richard Jefferies 9:5437

DEARING, SIR EDWARD
William Laud 3:1437

DEFOE, DANIEL
Geoffrey Chaucer 1:60
Daniel Defoe 5:2309, 2317

DE FOREST, J. W.
Harriet Beecher Stowe 10:5878

DEKKER, THOMAS
Thomas Nashe 1:506, 507

DE LA MARE, WALTER
William Shakespeare 2:841, 879,
901, 927, 961, 997
Samuel Butler 10:6100

DELANY, MARY
Tobias Smollett 5:2846
William Mason 6:3254
Fanny Burney 7:4046

DELANY, PATRICK
Jonathan Swift 5:2479

DELILLE, EDWARD
Oliver Wendell Holmes 10:5773

DELPLACE, L.
John Wyclif 1:44

DENHAM, SIR JOHN
Geoffrey Chaucer 1:59
Edmund Spenser 1:404
John Fletcher 3:1041
Abraham Cowley 3:1595
Edmund Waller 4:1898

DENNETT, J. R.
Winthrop Mackworth Praed 7:4037

DENNIS, JOHN (1657-1734)
Edmund Spenser 1:410
William Shakespeare 2:690
Samuel Butler 4:1826
Thomas Otway 4:1887
Sir George Etherege 4:1959
Thomas Shadwell 4:1966
John Dryden 4:2008
William Wycherley 4:2148
Joseph Addison 4:2186
Sir Richard Steele 4:2287, 2295
Alexander Pope 5:2431, 2438
Lewis Theobald 5:2466
William Law 5:2674

DENNIS, JOHN (1825-1911)
William Browne 3:1409
George Sandys 3:1422
Robert Herrick 4:1658
John Milton 4:1693
Nicholas Rowe 4:2161
Thomas Parnell 4:2169
Sir Samuel Garth 4:2174
Sir Richard Steele 4:2293
Bernard Mandeville 5:2356
John Arbuthnot 5:2375
George Lillo 5:2385
Thomas Tickell 5:2391
Aaron Hill 5:2555
Joseph Butler 5:2576
Colley Cibber 5:2636
Allan Ramsay 5:2646
Mark Akenside 5:2799
William Warburton 6:2945
Charles Lamb 7:3943
Robert Southey 7:4092
Thomas Campbell 7:4116

DENT, ARTHUR
John Skelton 1:212

DENTON, W.
  Roger Bacon 1:30
DE QUINCEY, THOMAS
  William Shakespeare 2:615, 960
  Jeremy Taylor 3:1581
  John Milton 4:1691
  Sir Thomas Browne 4:1852
  Nahum Tate 4:2144
  Joseph Addison 4:2186
  Sir Richard Steele 4:2289
  Daniel Defoe 5:2313
  Richard Bentley 5:2394
  Alexander Pope 5:2425
  Jonathan Swift 5:2484
  Henry St. John, Viscount
    Bolingbroke 5:2564
  George Berkeley 5:2585
  William Warburton 6:2947
  Samuel Johnson 6:2999
  Adam Smith 6:3065
  Edward Gibbon 6:3120
  Robert Burns 6:3193
  Edmund Burke 6:3259
  Joseph Priestley 6:3346
  Richard Porson 6:3376
  Junius 6:3485
  John Keats 6:3521
  Percy Bysshe Shelley 6:3564
  David Ricardo 7:3623
  Charles Robert Maturin 7:3625
  Anna Laetitia Barbauld 7:3668
  Samuel Parr 7:3675
  William Hazlitt 7:3746
  Sir James Mackintosh 7:3827
  Hannah More 7:3869
  Thomas Robert Malthus 7:3885
  Samuel Taylor Coleridge 7:3895
  Charles Lamb 7:3938
  William Godwin 7:3999
  Noah Webster 7:4073
  William Wordsworth 8:4299
  John Wilson 8:4444
  Sir William Hamilton 8:4500
  G. P. R. James 8:4625
  Walter Savage Landor 8:4735
  John Clare 8:4758
  Charles Dickens 8:4890
DESCARTES, RENÉ
  Sir Francis Bacon 3:1117
DESHLER, CHARLES D.
  Thomas Warton 6:3075
DE VERE, AUBREY
  The Venerable Bede 1:15
  Edmund Spenser 1:474
  John Milton 4:1702
  Robert Burns 6:3200, 3204
  William Cowper 6:3317
  John Keats 6:3517, 3522
  Hartley Coleridge 7:4221
  William Wordsworth 8:4308
  Sara Coleridge 8:4432
  Sir Henry Taylor 9:5397, 5399
  Robert Browning 9:5497
  John Henry Newman 9:5564
  Alfred, Lord Tennyson 10:5661
  Coventry Patmore 10:5895
  Aubrey De Vere 10:6079

DE VERE, M. SCHELE
  William Langland 1:50
DEVEREUX, G. H.
  Edward Bulwer-Lytton 9:4946
DEWAR, GEORGE A. B.
  William Cowper 6:3320
DEWEY, JOHN
  Herbert Spencer 10:6144
DEWEY, MARY E.
  Catharine Maria Sedgwick 8:4829
DEWEY, ORVILLE
  William Ellery Channing 7:4058
DEYO, C. L.
  Kate Chopin 10:6204
DIBDIN, CHARLES
  George Peele 1:398
  Samuel Daniel 3:1071
  William Camden 3:1084
  Thomas Dekker 3:1227
  John Marston 3:1298
  Ben Jonson 3:1327
  John Ford 3:1388
  Thomas Heywood 3:1490
  John Dryden 4:2023
  Nahum Tate 4:2144
  William Congreve 4:2270
  Colley Cibber 5:2637
  Charles Churchill 5:2729
  Oliver Goldsmith 5:2894
  David Garrick 6:2954
  George Colman the Elder 6:3115
  Charles Macklin 6:3228
DIBDIN, THOMAS FROGNALL
  John Barbour 1:47
  William Caxton 1:185
  Henry Howard, Earl of Surrey
    1:277
  Roger Ascham 1:290
  Raphael Holinshed 1:313
  John Foxe 1:356
  Richard Hakluyt 1:531
  Jeremy Taylor 3:1580
  Edward Hyde, Earl of Clarendon
    4:1754
  Thomas Otway 4:1891
  Sir William Temple 4:1997
  John Evelyn 4:2098
  Daniel Defoe 5:2310
  Isaac Watts 5:2526
DICEY, A. V.
  Edmund Burke 6:3263
  Richard Brinsley Sheridan 6:3431
  Jeremy Bentham 7:3782
  James Mill 7:4013
  John Wilson Croker 8:4508
  Thomas Babington Macaulay
    8:4623
  George Grote 9:4912
  John Richard Green 9:5364
  Edward Augustus Freeman 10:5728
  Samuel R. Gardiner 10:6085
  Sir Leslie Stephen 10:6195
DICEY, EDWARD
  William Ewart Gladstone 10:5946

DICKENS, CHARLES
  Alfred the Great 1:19
  William Shakespeare 2:953
  Thomas Smollett 5:2840
  Thomas Hood 7:4137
  Francis, Lord Jeffrey 8:4340
  John Wilson 8:4444
  Douglas Jerrold 8:4511
  Washington Irving 8:4525, 4527
  Leigh Hunt 8:4556
  William H. Prescott 8:4594
  Henry Thomas Buckle 8:4695
  William Makepeace Thackeray
    8:4706
  Walter Savage Landor 8:4741
  Charles Dickens 8:4893
  William Cullen Bryant 9:5040
  George Eliot 9:5088
  Henry Wadsworth Longfellow
    9:5241
  Richard Henry Dana, Jr. 9:5308
  Henry Ward Beecher 9:5427
  Robert Browning 9:5501
  Wilkie Collins 9:5534, 5535
DICKENS, MAMIE
  Charles Dickens 8:4879
DICKINSON, EMILY
  Nathaniel Hawthorne 8:4769
  George Eliot 9:5081, 5092
  Helen Hunt Jackson 9:5390, 5393
DICKINSON, G. LOWES
  Oscar Wilde 10:6032
DIDEROT, DENIS
  Samuel Richardson 5:2684
  David Garrick 6:2954
DIGBY, SIR KENELM
  Edmund Spenser 1:408
DIGGES, LEONARD
  William Shakespeare 2:563, 566
DILKE, CHARLES WENTWORTH
  Lady Mary Wortley Montagu
    5:2710
  Junius 6:3483
DISRAELI, BENJAMIN
  Lady Caroline Lamb 7:3735
  Letitia Elizabeth Landon 7:4019
  Isaac D'Israeli 7:4163
  Henry, Lord Brougham 8:4850
  William Ewart Gladstone 10:5940
D'ISRAELI, ISAAC
  Caedmon 1:7, 10
  The Venerable Bede 1:14
  Sir John Mandeville 1:37
  William Langland 1:49, 52
  John Gower 1:170
  John Lydgate 1:176
  Thomas Occleve 1:183
  John Skelton 1:219
  Sir Thomas More 1:232
  Sir Thomas Wyatt 1:262, 263
  Sir Thomas Elyot 1:275
  Henry Howard, Earl of Surrey
    1:279
  Alexander Barclay 1:282
  Sir John Cheke 1:286

Roger Ascham 1:290, 294
John Knox 1:301
John Heywood 1:308
George Puttenham 1:498
Richard Hooker 1:502
Thomas Nashe 1:507
Richard Hakluyt 1:531
Sir Walter Ralegh 3:1065
William Camden 3:1085
Sir Francis Bacon 3:1109
Gabriel Harvey 3:1177
Michael Drayton 3:1191
Sir Edward Coke 3:1268
Ben Jonson 3:1323
Sir William D'Avenant 3:1616
William Prynne 3:1620
Edward Hyde, Earl of Clarendon
    4:1755
John Evelyn 4:2099
Sir John Vanbrugh 4:2238
Henry Carey 5:2404
Lewis Theobald 5:2468
William Shenstone 5:2724
Elizabeth Montagu 6:3302

DIX, JOHN
    Thomas Chatterton 5:2807

DIXON, W. MACNEILE
    William Warburton 6:2946
    Edmund Burke 6:3266
    Henry Hallam 8:4520
    Walter Savage Landor 8:4739
    H. H. Milman 8:4863
    George Grote 9:4912
    Francis Turner Palgrave 10:5922
    Aubrey De Vere 10:6079

DIXON, WILLIAM HEPWORTH
    Douglas Jerrold 8:4510
    Sydney Owenson, Lady Morgan
        8:4546

DOBELL, BERTRAM
    Thomas Traherne 4:1764, 1768,
        1772
    James Thomson 9:5339

DOBELL, SYDNEY
    Emily Brontë 7:4180
    Thomas Carlyle 9:5111

DOBSON, AUSTIN
    Robert Herrick 4:1658
    John Dryden 4:2015
    Joseph Addison 4:2182
    Matthew Prior 4:2213
    William Congreve 4:2273
    Sir Richard Steele 4:2300
    John Gay 5:2342
    Alexander Pope 5:2429
    Henry Fielding 5:2598
    Colley Cibber 5:2636
    Samuel Richardson 5:2688, 2692
    Tobias Smollett 5:2847
    Oliver Goldsmith 5:2905
    Horace Walpole 6:3236
    Richard Hurd 6:3366
    Fanny Burney 7:4047
    Thomas Hood 7:4142
    John Hookham Frere 7:4150
    William Lisle Bowles 8:4295

Henry Wadsworth Longfellow
    9:5241
Robert Louis Stevenson 10:5833
Frederick Locker-Lampson 10:5857

DODDS, JAMES MILLER
    Miles Coverdale 1:298
    John Knox 1:300
    John Foxe 1:357
    James Anthony Froude 10:5787

DODGE, MARY ABIGAIL
    George William Curtis 10:5733

DODSLEY, RICHARD
    William Shenstone 5:2724

DOE, CHARLES
    John Bunyan 4:1916

DOLMAN, FREDERICK
    George Gissing 10:6173

DONALDSON, AUGUSTUS B.
    Richard William Church 10:5571

DONNE, JOHN
    John Donne 3:1197
    George Herbert 3:1240
    Sir Henry Wotton 3:1349

DONNE, WILLIAM BODHAM
    John Fletcher 3:1042
    John Gay 5:2346
    Richard Brinsley Sheridan 6:3428

DONNELLY, IGNATIUS
    William Shakespeare 2:733

DORAN, JOHN
    Elkanah Settle 4:2224
    Colley Cibber 5:2632
    Edward Young 5:2745
    Samuel Foote 5:2938
    Charles Macklin 6:3230
    Elizabeth Montagu 6:3300
    John Home 6:3370

DORNER, J. A.
    Duns Scotus 1:33

DORR, JULIA C. R.
    Charles Dickens 8:4893
    Helen Hunt Jackson 9:5391

DOUGHERTY, J. J.
    The Venerable Bede 1:13

DOUGLAS, LORD ALFRED
    Oscar Wilde 10:6022, 6027

DOUGLAS, GAVIN
    Geoffrey Chaucer 1:56

DOUGLAS, SIR GEORGE
    Robert Tannahill 6:3407
    John Galt 7:4030
    John Wilson 8:4448

DOVER, LORD
    Horace Walpole 6:3239

DOWDEN, EDWARD
    Sir Philip Sidney 1:322
    Christopher Marlowe 1:376
    Edmund Spenser 1:471
    Barnabe Barnes 1:525
    William Shakespeare 2:827, 882

Sir Francis Bacon 3:1121
John Donne 3:1199
George Herbert 3:1260
Jeremy Taylor 3:1590
John Milton 4:1688
John Bunyan 4:1931
Henry Vaughan 4:1988
William Falconer 5:2792
Mark Akenside 5:2799
Thomas Gray 5:2822
Robert Burns 6:3208
Edmund Burke 6:3274
Percy Bysshe Shelley 6:3599
George Gordon, Lord Byron 7:3643
Samuel Taylor Coleridge 7:3924
Charles Lamb 7:3942
William Godwin 7:3995
Robert Southey 7:4088
Ebenezer Elliott 7:4214
Hartley Coleridge 7:4222
William Wordsworth 8:4309
Washington Irving 8:4529
Leigh Hunt 8:4559
Thomas De Quincey 8:4574
William Makepeace Thackeray
    8:4710
Walter Savage Landor 8:4740
Frederick Denison Maurice 9:4925
John Forster 9:5014
Thomas Carlyle 9:5115
Dante Gabriel Rossetti 9:5320
Edward FitzGerald 9:5354
Sir Henry Taylor 9:5399
Robert Browning 9:5507
Gerard Manley Hopkins 9:5545
Alfred, Lord Tennyson 10:5680
Walter Pater 10:5821
John Ruskin 10:5982

DOWDEN, JOHN
    Richard Hooker 1:504
    William Laud 3:1438
    Arthur Hugh Clough 8:4652

DOWNES, JOHN
    Thomas Otway 4:1887

DOYLE, SIR FRANCIS HASTINGS
    John Milton 4:1696
    Jane Austen 6:3457
    Arthur Henry Hallam 7:3879
    Sydney Smith 7:4130
    William Barnes 9:5404
    John Henry Newman 9:5552, 5561

DRAKE, JAMES
    William Shakespeare 2:901

DRAKE, NATHAN
    William Dunbar 1:221
    Henry Howard, Earl of Surrey
        1:277
    Thomas, Lord Vaux 1:285
    Sir Philip Sidney 1:321
    Thomas Watson 1:357
    Robert Greene 1:360
    George Peele 1:398
    Richard Hooker 1:501
    John Lyly 1:511
    William Warner 1:524
    George Turberville 1:526
    Sir Thomas Overbury 1:529

ESSEX, EARL OF
　Sir Francis Bacon 3:1106

ETHEREGE, SIR GEORGE
　John Dryden 4:2005, 2026

EVANS, ABEL
　Sir John Vanbrugh 4:2235

EVANS, EDWARD WATERMAN, JR.
　Walter Savage Landor 8:4739

EVANS, HERBERT ARTHUR
　Ben Jonson 3:1324

EVELYN, JOHN
　Sir Francis Bacon 3:1118
　Abraham Cowley 3:1595
　Margaret Cavendish, Duchess of
　　Newcastle 4:1647
　Edward Hyde, Earl of Clarendon
　　4:1754
　John Wilmot, Earl of Rochester
　　4:1840
　Sir Thomas Browne 4:1850
　Robert Boyle 4:1953
　Samuel Pepys 4:2061
　Sir Roger L'Estrange 4:2073
　Richard Bentley 5:2393

EVEREST, CHARLES W.
　Joel Barlow 6:3416
　John Trumbull 7:3772

EVERETT, ALEXANDER HILL
　Adam Smith 6:3064
　Thomas Jefferson 7:3680
　Dugald Stewart 7:3732
　William Ellery Channing 7:4060
　Washington Irving 8:4527
　Thomas Carlyle 9:5119

EVERETT, CHARLES CARROLL
　Elizabeth Barrett Browning 8:4641
　Ralph Waldo Emerson 9:5204

EVERETT, EDWARD
　John Milton 4:1700
　Richard Bentley 5:2395
　Benjamin Franklin 6:3040
　Thomas Jefferson 7:3683
　Washington Irving 8:4528, 4534,
　　4536
　Frances Trollope 8:4703
　George Bancroft 10:5578

EVERETT, WILLIAM
　Richard Henry Dana, Jr. 9:5307,
　　5310

EWALD, ALEXANDER CHARLES
　Sir Walter Ralegh 3:1067
　George Farquhar 4:2108

EYRE-TODD, GEORGE
　Thomas of Erceldoune 1:32
　John Barbour 1:48
　Robert Henryson 1:203
　Gavin Douglas 1:208
　William Dunbar 1:228
　William Drummond 3:1452
　Allan Ramsay 5:2647
　William Falconer 5:2793
　Tobias Smollett 5:2842
　Robert Fergusson 5:2911

F., J.
　Emily Brontë 7:4181

FABIAN, ROBERT
　John Skelton 1:211

FAIRBAIRN, A. M.
　John Henry Newman 9:5556
　Benjamin Jowett 10:5748
　Herbert Spencer 10:6143

FAIRFAX, BRIAN
　George Villiers, Duke of
　　Buckingham 4:1908

FALKLAND, LORD
　George Sandys 3:1422

FANE, FRANCIS
　John Wilmot, Earl of Rochester
　　4:1840

FARNHAM, CHARLES HAIGHT
　Francis Parkman 10:5760

FARQUHAR, GEORGE
　John Dryden 4:2005

FARRAR, ADAM STOREY
　Joseph Butler 5:2573
　Henry Thomas Buckle 8:4697

FARRAR, ELIZA
　Joanna Baillie 8:4363
　Amelia Opie 8:4435

FARRAR, FREDERIC WILLIAM
　Sir Walter Ralegh 3:1066
　Sir Francis Bacon 3:1111
　John Milton 4:1704
　Thomas Arnold 7:4070
　Frederick Denison Maurice 9:4924
　James Russell Lowell 10:5593
　Edward Robert Bulwer Lytton
　　10:5625
　Benjamin Jowett 10:5747
　Sir Edwin Arnold 10:6189

FAWCETT, MILLICENT GARRETT
　Charlotte Brontë 8:4477

FEATLEY, DANIEL
　Giles and Phineas Fletcher 3:1087

FELL, JOHN
　John Locke 4:2076

FELTHAM, OWEN
　Ben Jonson 3:1319　·

FELTON, CORNELIUS CONWAY
　Marguerite, Countess of Blessington
　　7:4219
　Washington Irving 8:4536
　N. P. Willis 8:4841
　William Gilmore Simms 8:4873
　James Russell Lowell 10:5591

FELTON, HENRY
　Sir Walter Ralegh 3:1069
　Edward Hyde, Earl of Clarendon
　　4:1752
　Thomas Sprat 4:2117

FENNOR, WILLIAM
　Thomas Dekker 3:1227

FENTON, ELIJAH
　Alexander Pope 5:2437

FERGUSON, ADAM
　Thomas Reid 6:3169

FERRAR, NICHOLAS
　George Herbert 3:1241

FERRIER, JAMES FREDERICK
　Thomas Reid 6:3170
　James Hogg 7:3968

FIDDES, RICHARD
　Anthony Ashley Cooper, Third Earl
　　of Shaftesbury 4:2126

FIELD, BARRON
　Robert Herrick 4:1655

FIELD, EUGENE
　Izaak Walton 4:1872
　Richard Henry Stoddard 10:6152

FIELD, HENRY M.
　Robert G. Ingersoll 10:5977

FIELD, MAUNSELL B.
　Edgar Allan Poe 8:4251
　James Fenimore Cooper 8:4377
　G. P. R. James 8:4626

FIELD, MICHAEL
　Walter Pater 10:5810

FIELD, ROSWELL MARTIN
　Eugene Field 10:5874

FIELDING, HENRY
　William Shakespeare 2:669
　Aphra Behn 4:1937
　Sir Richard Steele 4:2295
　George Lillo 5:2382
　Alexander Pope 5:2435
　Henry St. John, Viscount
　　Bolingbroke 5:2561
　Henry Fielding 5:2606
　Samuel Richardson 5:2693

FIELDS, ANNIE
　Mary Russell Mitford 8:4471
　John Greenleaf Whittier 10:5634
　Oliver Wendell Holmes 10:5771
　Harriet Beecher Stowe 10:5877

FIELDS, JAMES T.
　William Makepeace Thackeray
　　8:4709, 4717

FILMER, EDWARD
　Jeremy Collier 4:2230

FINDLATER, JANE H.
　George Borrow 9:5150
　George Gissing 10:6177

FINDLAY, J. J.
　Thomas Arnold 7:4069

FINDLAY, JOHN RITCHIE
　Thomas De Quincey 8:4570

FINLAY, JOHN
　Thomas of Erceldoune 1:31

FIRTH, C. H.
　Samuel R. Gardiner 10:6084

FISHER, GEORGE PARK
　John Scotus Erigena 1:17
　Duns Scotus 1:33
　William of Occam 1:34

FRANCE, ANATOLE
William Shakespeare 2:918

FRANCILLON, R. E.
George Eliot 9:5091

FRANCIS, SIR PHILIP
Edmund Burke 6:3269

FRANCIS, WILLIAM
William Caxton 1:184

FRANCK, RICHARD
Izaak Walton 4:1870

FRANKAU, JULIA
Harold Frederic 10:5972

FRANKLIN, BENJAMIN
Cotton Mather 4:2254
Jonathan Edwards 5:2649
Henry Home, Lord Kames 6:2967
Benjamin Franklin 6:3036, 3037, 3048
William Cowper 6:3311
Thomas Paine 6:3379, 3384

FRASER, ALEXANDER CAMPBELL
John Locke 4:2085

FRASER, J.
Thomas Hood 7:4139

FREDERIC, HAROLD
Stephen Crane 10:6054

FREEMAN, EDWARD AUGUSTUS
Joseph Butler 5:2578
Edward Gibbon 6:3130
Thomas Babington Macaulay 8:4607
Thomas Carlyle 9:5113
Edward Augustus Freeman 10:5727
William Ewart Gladstone 10:5942

FREMANTLE, W. H.
John Wyclif 1:44

FRERE, BARTLE
John Hookham Frere 7:4148

FRISWELL, JAMES HAIN
Sir Thomas Overbury 1:529
Philip Massinger 3:1358
George Wither 3:1571
Jeremy Taylor 3:1582
George Grote 9:4910
Charles Lever 9:4931
Edward Bulwer-Lytton 9:4944
William Harrison Ainsworth 9:5235
Anthony Trollope 9:5283
Charles Reade 9:5371
Alfred, Lord Tennyson 10:5659
John Ruskin 10:5981

FROTHINGHAM, OCTAVIUS BROOKS
Thomas Paine 6:3391
Alice and Phoebe Cary 9:4919
Horace Greeley 9:4937

FROUDE, JAMES ANTHONY
John Wyclif 1:42
Sir Thomas More 1:232
William Tyndale 1:255
John Knox 1:301
Richard Hakluyt 1:531

William Shakespeare 2:576
John Milton 4:1693
Henry Thomas Buckle 8:4697
John Keble 8:4828
H. H. Milman 8:4861
John Lothrop Motley 9:5023
Benjamin Disraeli 9:5156
Matthew Arnold 9:5458
John Henry Newman 9:5560, 5562
Alfred, Lord Tennyson 10:5667

FULKE, WILLIAM
Miles Coverdale 1:297

FULLER, MARGARET
Sir Walter Ralegh 3:1068
Edward Lord Herbert 3:1444
Charles Wesley 6:3033
John Wesley 6:3081
Charles Brockden Brown 6:3398
George Crabbe 7:3809
Sir Walter Scott 7:3844
Samuel Taylor Coleridge 7:3900
William Ellery Channing 7:4057, 4061
Thomas Campbell 7:4111
Edgar Allan Poe 8:4256
William Wordsworth 8:4306
James Fenimore Cooper 8:4379
William H. Prescott 8:4591
Elizabeth Barrett Browning 8:4633
Thomas Carlyle 9:5110
Ralph Waldo Emerson 9:5202
Henry Wadsworth Longfellow 9:5255
Sir Henry Taylor 9:5399
Robert Browning 9:5493
James Russell Lowell 10:5591
Alfred, Lord Tennyson 10:5656

FULLER, THOMAS
The Venerable Bede 1:15
Alfred the Great 1:18
William of Malmesbury 1:25
Geoffrey of Monmouth 1:26
Roger Bacon 1:29
Duns Scotus 1:32
William of Occam 1:33
Richard Rolle of Hampole 1:35
John Wyclif 1:41
William Langland 1:49
John Gower 1:167
John Skelton 1:213
Sir Thomas More 1:233, 236
William Tyndale 1:255
Sir Thomas Elyot 1:275
Roger Ascham 1:289
John Foxe 1:356
Robert Southwell 1:396
Edmund Spenser 1:404
Richard Hooker 1:500, 501
Sir Thomas Overbury 1:529
Richard Hakluyt 1:530
William Shakespeare 2:536
John Fletcher 3:1041
Sir Walter Ralegh 3:1064
Samuel Daniel 3:1071, 1074
William Camden 3:1084
Giles and Phineas Fletcher 3:1087
Lancelot Andrewes 3:1101

Sir Francis Bacon 3:1107, 1108
Fulke Greville, Lord Brooke 3:1171
Michael Drayton 3:1184
George Herbert 3:1241
Sir Edward Coke 3:1267
Ben Jonson 3:1317, 1319
Robert Burton 3:1367
George Sandys 3:1419
Francis Quarles 3:1425
William Chillingworth 3:1431
Edward Lord Herbert 3:1443
Joseph Hall 3:1517
John Cleveland 3:1538

FURNESS, W. H.
William Ellery Channing 7:4059

FYFE, J. HAMILTON
Joseph Butler 5:2573

FYVIE, JOHN
George Wither 3:1573

GAIRDNER, JAMES
The Venerable Bede 1:15
Geoffrey of Monmouth 1:27
Sir Thomas More 1:236

GALT, JOHN
Richard Savage 5:2407
David Garrick 6:2955
John Galt 7:4025

GARDINER, SAMUEL R.
Sir Walter Ralegh 3:1066
Sir Francis Bacon 3:1109, 1112, 1117
George Herbert 3:1259
William Chillingworth 3:1437
William Drummond 3:1449
Joseph Hall 3:1518
John Hales 3:1526
William Prynne 3:1621
John Milton 4:1695
Richard Baxter 4:1946
John Forster 9:5015
John Richard Green 9:5362

GARLAND, HAMLIN
Walt Whitman 10:5695
Eugene Field 10:5873
Harold Frederic 10:5973
Stephen Crane 10:6060
Frank Norris 10:6134

GARNETT, EDWARD
Stephen Crane 10:6049
George Gissing 10:6179

GARNETT, JAMES M.
Beowulf 1:2

GARNETT, RICHARD
Beowulf 1:4
Cædmon 1:10
Alfred the Great 1:20
William of Malmesbury 1:26
Geoffrey of Monmouth 1:27
Sir John Mandeville 1:40
John Gower 1:171
William Caxton 1:186
Robert Henryson 1:203
Sir Thomas More 1:237
Sir John Cheke 1:286

Roger Ascham 1:293
William Camden 3:1086
John Milton 4:1707
John Oldham 4:1884
George Villiers, Duke of
Buckingham 4:1909
Charles Cotton 4:1915
John Bunyan 4:1924
Aphra Behn 4:1941
Sir Roger L'Estrange 4:2075
John Locke 4:2084
John Evelyn 4:2101
Thomas Sprat 4:2119
Thomas Rymer 4:2122
Elkanah Settle 4:2225
Jeremy Collier 4:2232
Samuel Taylor Coleridge 7:3905
William Beckford 7:4099
Thomas Hood 7:4143
Emily Brontë 7:4178
Thomas Lovell Beddoes 7:4229
Mary Shelley 8:4414
Sara Coleridge 8:4434
Thomas Love Peacock 8:4811
Sydney Dobell 9:4987
Coventry Patmore 10:5891
Samuel Butler 10:6099

GARNETT, W. J.
William Beckford 7:4100

GARRICK, DAVID
Henry St. John, Viscount
Bolingbroke 5:2561
Charles Churchill 5:2732
Laurence Sterne 5:2759
Oliver Goldsmith 5:2883
Samuel Johnson 6:2994
William Robertson 6:3109
George Colman the Elder 6:3114
Richard Brinsley Sheridan 6:3429

GARRISON, FRANCES M.
William Lloyd Garrison 9:5072

GARRISON, WENDELL PHILLIPS
Frances Trollope 8:4704
William Lloyd Garrison 9:5074

GARRISON, WILLIAM LLOYD
John Greenleaf Whittier 10:5634

GARTH, SIR SAMUEL
John Dryden 4:2009
William Wycherley 4:2148
Sir Richard Blackmore 4:2262
William Congreve 4:2269
John Gay 5:2340

GARVIN, LOUIS
Coventry Patmore 10:5892

GASCOIGNE, GEORGE
Geoffrey Chaucer 1:57

GASKELL, CHARLES MILNES
William Cobbett 7:3963

GASKELL, ELIZABETH
Emily Brontë 7:4178

GASSENDI, PIERRE
Sir Francis Bacon 3:1118

GATES, LEWIS E.
Edgar Allan Poe 8:4279
Francis, Lord Jeffrey 8:4345

Charlotte Brontë 8:4493
Thomas Carlyle 9:5119
John Henry Newman 9:5560
Alfred, Lord Tennyson 10:5690

GAY, JOHN
Edmund Waller 4:1898
Sir Samuel Garth 4:2172
Matthew Prior 4:2207
William Congreve 4:2269
Sir Richard Steele 4:2291
Daniel Defoe 5:2317
John Gay 5:2339, 2344
Alexander Pope 5:2420, 2433
Jonathan Swift 5:2491
Lady Mary Wortley Montagu
5:2708

GEDDES, ALEXANDER
William Tyndale 1:255

GEIKIE, SIR ARCHIBALD
James Macpherson 6:3186
Robert Burns 6:3212
William Cowper 6:3319

GEIKIE, JOHN CUNNINGHAM
William Tyndale 1:253

GEORGE, ANDREW J.
Robert Burns 6:3208

GEORGE, HENRY
Adam Smith 6:3066
Herbert Spencer 10:6143

GERVINUS, G. G.
John Lyly 1:513
William Shakespeare 2:767, 855,
876, 994, 1033
Sir Francis Bacon 3:1111

GIBBINS, H. DE B.
William Langland 1:51

GIBBON, EDWARD
William Caxton 1:184
George Sandys 3:1420
William Chillingworth 3:1435
John Selden 3:1505
Alexander Pope 5:2434
Henry Fielding 5:2607
William Law 5:2674
Samuel Richardson 5:2697
Lady Mary Wortley Montagu
5:2713
David Mallet 5:2755
Philip Dormer Stanhope, Earl of
Chesterfield 5:2877
David Hume 5:2918
William Warburton 5:2943
Thomas Warton 6:3076
William Robertson 6:3108, 3112
Edward Gibbon 6:3119, 3123, 3125
James Boswell 6:3156
Horace Walpole 6:3235
Edmund Burke 6:3258, 3267, 3269
Joseph Priestley 6:3348
Richard Hurd 6:3365
Richard Porson 6:3375
Richard Brinsley Sheridan 6:3431
William Hayley 6:3502

GIBBONS, THOMAS
Isaac Watts 5:2525

GIBBS, H. J.
John Sterling 7:4123
Richard Monckton Milnes, Lord
Houghton 9:5387
Francis Turner Palgrave 10:5920

GIFFEN, ROBERT
Walter Bagehot 9:5029

GIFFORD, WILLIAM
John Lyly 1:511
John Ford 3:1385, 1386
William Drummond 3:1449
John Wolcot ("Peter Pindar")
6:3500
Hester Lynch Piozzi 6:3513
George Crabbe 7:3808
William Wordsworth 8:4302
Mary Russell Mitford 8:4469, 4472

GILCHRIST, ALEXANDER
William Hayley 6:3504

GILCHRIST, ANNE
Mary Lamb 7:4156
Walt Whitman 10:5696

GILCHRIST, OCTAVIUS
John Clare 8:4757

GILDER, J. L.
Lewis Carroll 10:5950

GILDER, JOSEPH B.
Francis Parkman 10:5753
Richard Henry Stoddard 10:6152,
6154

GILDON, CHARLES
Aphra Behn 4:1937

GILES, HENRY
William Shakespeare 2:844
Richard Savage 5:2409
Thomas Chatterton 5:2808
Thomas Hood 7:4146

GILES, J. A.
The Venerable Bede 1:15
Alfred the Great 1:20
William of Malmesbury 1:25
Geoffrey of Monmouth 1:26
Roger Ascham 1:289

GILFILLAN, GEORGE
John Barbour 1:47
John Lydgate 1:175
William Dunbar 1:222
Sir Thomas Wyatt 1:262, 263
Henry Howard, Earl of Surrey
1:278
Robert Southwell 1:396
John Donne 3:1198
George Herbert 3:1243
Francis Quarles 3:1426
Richard Crashaw 3:1464, 1468
Samuel Butler 4:1834
Charles Cotton 4:1914
Thomas Parnell 4:2167
William Collins 5:2665
William Shenstone 5:2725
Charles Churchill 5:2735
Edward Young 5:2740
William Falconer 5:2792

Mark Akenside 5:2798
Tobias Smollett 5:2840
Oliver Goldsmith 5:2892
Thomas Warton 6:3073
Robert Burns 6:3194
James Beattie 6:3337
Henry Kirke White 6:3358
Matthew Gregory Lewis 6:3494
William Gifford 7:3687
George Crabbe 7:3810
Samuel Taylor Coleridge 7:3910
Felicia Dorothea Hemans 7:3987
John Sterling 7:4122
Thomas Hood 7:4143
Thomas Chalmers 7:4159
Edgar Allan Poe 8:4267
Francis, Lord Jeffrey 8:4347
John Wilson 8:4448
Henry Hallam 8:4520
Leigh Hunt 8:4560
Thomas De Quincey 8:4571
Elizabeth Barrett Browning 8:4638
William Makepeace Thackeray
    8:4719
Edward Bulwer-Lytton 9:4943
Sydney Dobell 9:4985
Benjamin Disraeli 9:5155
Ralph Waldo Emerson 9:5205
Henry Wadsworth Longfellow
    9:5245
Alfred, Lord Tennyson 10:5668

GILLIES, R. P.
Sir Walter Scott 7:3846
Thomas De Quincey 8:4569

GILMAN, NICHOLAS P.
Edward Bellamy 10:5968

GILMAN, S.
Thomas Brown 6:3508

GILMORE, J. H.
James Russell Lowell 10:5597

GISSING, GEORGE
Charles Dickens 8:4891

GLADDEN, WASHINGTON
Josiah Gilbert Holland 9:5172

GLADSTONE, WILLIAM EWART
Joseph Butler 5:2582
Philip Dormer Stanhope, Earl of
    Chesterfield 5:2875
Richard Brinsley Sheridan 6:3423
Arthur Henry Hallam 7:3879
Thomas Babington Macaulay
    8:4619
John Keble 8:4824
Samuel Wilberforce 9:4956
Alfred, Lord Tennyson 10:5666

GLENNIE, J. S. S.
Henry Thomas Buckle 8:4695

GODKIN, EDWIN LAURENCE
John Stuart Mill 9:4963
Francis Parkman 10:5752

GODOLPHIN, SIDNEY
George Sandys 3:1422

GODWIN, PARKE
John James Audubon 8:4375
George William Curtis 10:5734

GODWIN, WILLIAM
Geoffrey Chaucer 1:80
Robert Henryson 1:202
Sir Philip Sidney 1:323
Richard Hooker 1:501
William Shakespeare 2:572, 922
John Milton 4:1689, 1698, 1707
Edward Hyde, Earl of Clarendon
    4:1753
John Locke 4:2078
John Dennis 5:2366
Jonathan Swift 5:2489
Samuel Richardson 5:2684
Tobias Smollett 5:2838
Thomas Warton 6:3076
Mary Wollstonecraft 6:3284
Percy Bysshe Shelley 6:3576
William Godwin 7:3996
Mary Shelley 8:4397
Washington Irving 8:4534
Edward Bulwer-Lytton 9:4945

GOETHE, JOHANN WOLFGANG VON
William Shakespeare 2:905
John Milton 4:1703
Oliver Goldsmith 5:2890
James Macpherson 6:3178
Erasmus Darwin 6:3334
George Gordon, Lord Byron
    7:3645, 3647
Thomas Carlyle 9:5112

GOLDSMITH, OLIVER
Sir Philip Sidney 1:328
Michael Drayton 3:1186
Sir John Denham 3:1628
John Milton 4:1705
Sir William Temple 4:1996
John Dryden 4:2010, 2027, 2030
Sir Roger L'Estrange 4:2074
John Locke 4:2077
Anthony Ashley Cooper, Third Earl
    of Shaftesbury 4:2127
Thomas Parnell 4:2169
Sir Samuel Garth 4:2172
Joseph Addison 4:2178
Sir Richard Steele 4:2289
John Gay 5:2340
Thomas Tickell 5:2390
Richard Savage 5:2408
Alexander Pope 5:2419, 2433, 2437
Ambrose Philips 5:2551
Henry St. John, Viscount
    Bolingbroke 5:2560
William Collins 5:2662
William Shenstone 5:2724
Laurence Sterne 5:2765
Thomas Gray 5:2826, 2827
Oliver Goldsmith 5:2889
David Garrick 6:2951
Samuel Johnson 6:2991
Sir Joshua Reynolds 6:3090
Edmund Burke 6:3256
Richard Cumberland 6:3410

GOOCH, G. P.
Samuel R. Gardiner 10:6084

GOOD, JOHN MASON
Junius 6:3488

GOODRICH, CHAUNCEY A.
Noah Webster 7:4073

GOODRICH, SAMUEL GRISWOLD
John Trumbull 7:3772
James Fenimore Cooper 8:4377
Nathaniel Hawthorne 8:4764

GORDON, ALEXANDER
Jeremy Taylor 3:1585
Robert Fergusson 5:2910

GORDON, MARY
Hartley Coleridge 7:4220

GORDON, PRYSE LOCKHART
Richard Porson 6:3375

GORDON, WALTER
James Sheridan Knowles 8:4665

GORRIE, P. DOUGLASS
Charles Wesley 6:3034

GOSSE, EDMUND
John Wyclif 1:46
John Barbour 1:48
William Langland 1:51
John Gower 1:169
John Lydgate 1:176
Thomas Occleve 1:183
William Caxton 1:185
William Dunbar 1:223
Sir Thomas More 1:233
Roger Ascham 1:291
Sir Philip Sidney 1:320
Robert Greene 1:360, 362
Thomas Kyd 1:396
Robert Southwell 1:397
Richard Hooker 1:504
John Lyly 1:512
Thomas Sackville, Earl of Dorset
    1:520
Barnabe Barnes 1:525
Sir Thomas Overbury 1:530
William Shakespeare 2:689
Beaumont and Fletcher 3:1055
Samuel Daniel 3:1073
Thomas Campion 3:1081
William Camden 3:1086
Giles and Phineas Fletcher 3:1091
Thomas Lodge 3:1096
Nicholas Breton 3:1100
Sir Francis Bacon 3:1113, 1115
Sir John Davies 3:1144
William Rowley 3:1160
Thomas Middleton 3:1164
Fulke Greville, Lord Brooke 3:1174
Michael Drayton 3:1188, 1192
John Donne 3:1196, 1199, 1208,
    1216
Thomas Dekker 3:1231
George Herbert 3:1246
George Chapman 3:1274
John Webster 3:1285
Thomas Randolph 3:1314
Ben Jonson 3:1324, 1327
Philip Massinger 3:1363
John Ford 3:1388
Thomas Carew 3:1397
Sir John Suckling 3:1403
William Browne 3:1410

William Drummond 3:1452
Richard Crashaw 3:1476
Thomas Heywood 3:1493
Richard Lovelace 3:1535
Thomas Fuller 3:1549
Katherine Philips 3:1554
George Wither 3:1577
Jeremy Taylor 3:1585
Sir William D'Avenant 3:1614
Sir John Denham 3:1627
Robert Herrick 4:1658, 1660
John Milton 4:1703, 1705
Edward Hyde, Earl of Clarendon
 4:1754
Andrew Marvell 4:1792
John Wilmot, Earl of Rochester
 4:1846
Sir Thomas Browne 4:1855
Izaak Walton 4:1869
John Oldham 4:1884
Thomas Otway 4:1891
Edmund Waller 4:1901
John Bunyan 4:1924
Aphra Behn 4:1939
Robert Boyle 4:1955
Sir George Etherege 4:1962
Nathaniel Lee 4:1971
George Savile, Marquis of Halifax
 4:1991
Sir William Temple 4:1999
John Dryden 4:2018, 2020, 2032
Sir Charles Sedley 4:2058
Samuel Pepys 4:2063
John Locke 4:2080
John Evelyn 4:2100, 2101
George Farquhar 4:2107
Thomas Sprat 4:2118
Gilbert Burnet 4:2141
Thomas Parnell 4:2167
Sir Samuel Garth 4:2173
Joseph Addison 4:2181
Anne Finch, Countess of
 Winchilsea 4:2198
Matthew Prior 4:2210
Thomas D'Urfey 4:2219
Elkanah Settle 4:2225
Jeremy Collier 4:2232
Sir John Vanbrugh 4:2237
William Congreve 4:2275, 2277
Sir Richard Steele 4:2290
Samuel Clarke 5:2305
Bernard Mandeville 5:2357
John Dennis 5:2367
John Arbuthnot 5:2373
George Lillo 5:2385
Thomas Tickell 5:2391
Richard Savage 5:2409
Alexander Pope 5:2429
Jonathan Swift 5:2488, 2489,
 2492
James Thomson 5:2536
Ambrose Philips 5:2552
Joseph Butler 5:2575
Henry Fielding 5:2602, 2604
Colley Cibber 5:2637
Allan Ramsay 5:2643
William Collins 5:2667
William Law 5:2679

Samuel Richardson 5:2689, 2693,
 2696
Lady Mary Wortley Montagu
 5:2713
Charles Churchill 5:2732
Edward Young 5:2746
Laurence Sterne 5:2764
Mark Akenside 5:2798
Thomas Chatterton 5:2810
Thomas Gray 5:2824
Tobias Smollett 5:2842, 2856
Christopher Smart 5:2869
Oliver Goldsmith 5:2889
David Hume 5:2916, 2918
Samuel Foote 5:2938
William Warburton 6:2945
Sir William Blackstone 6:2959
Henry Brooke 6:2971
Benjamin Franklin 6:3045
Sir Joshua Reynolds 6:3093
William Robertson 6:3111
George Colman the Elder 6:3115
Edward Gibbon 6:3131
James Boswell 6:3152
Horace Walpole 6:3236
William Mason 6:3253
Edmund Burke 6:3264
Erasmus Darwin 6:3333
Richard Hurd 6:3367
Richard Brinsley Sheridan 6:3426
Jane Austen 6:3453
Junius 6:3488
Joseph Rodman Drake 6:3511
Percy Bysshe Shelley 6:3573
Henry Mackenzie 7:3765
Sir Walter Scott 7:3849
Fanny Burney 7:4044, 4046
Robert Southey 7:4084
Thomas Campbell 7:4115
Isaac D'Israeli 7:4163
Emily Brontë 7:4183
Thomas Lovell Beddoes 7:4228
Edgar Allan Poe 8:4255
Thomas Moore 8:4422
John Gibson Lockhart 8:4454
Washington Irving 8:4529
Thomas De Quincey 8:4576
William Makepeace Thackeray
 8:4714
Elizabeth Gaskell 8:4800
Thomas Love Peacock 8:4813
Edward Bulwer-Lytton 9:4944
Bryan Waller Procter 9:4983
Charles Kingsley 9:4991
Caroline Norton 9:5019
William Cullen Bryant 9:5048
Richard Henry Dana 9:5069
George Eliot 9:5088
Sidney Lanier 9:5177
Arthur O'Shaughnessy 9:5188
Ralph Waldo Emerson 9:5204
Henry Wadsworth Longfellow
 9:5248
Charles Darwin 9:5274
Richard Henry Horne 9:5370
John Henry Newman 9:5552, 5557
John Greenleaf Whittier 10:5641
Alfred, Lord Tennyson 10:5661

Edward Augustus Freeman 10:5730
Walter Pater 10:5811
Robert Louis Stevenson 10:5833
Coventry Patmore 10:5891
Sir Leslie Stephen 10:6196

GOSSON, STEPHAN
 Sir Philip Sidney 1:318

GOULD, ELIZABETH PETER
 Richard Henry Horne 9:5368

GOULD, GEORGE M.
 Lafcadio Hearn 10:6213

GOULD, ROBERT
 James Shirley 3:1560

GOWER, JOHN
 Geoffrey Chaucer 1:53
 John Gower 1:167

GOWER, LORD RONALD
 Henry Wadsworth Longfellow
 9:5242

GOWING, RICHARD
 Richard Cobden 8:4794

GRAHAM, GEORGE R.
 Edgar Allan Poe 8:4250

GRAHAM, HENRY GREY
 William Robertson 6:3107
 James Boswell 6:3160
 James Macpherson 6:3186
 Robert Burns 6:3208
 James Burnett, Lord Monboddo
 6:3292
 Hugh Blair 6:3294

GRAHAM, P. ANDERSON
 Henry David Thoreau 8:4672

GRAHAM, RICHARD D.
 Emily Brontë 7:4181

GRAHAM, WILLIAM
 Percy Bysshe Shelley 6:3568
 George Gordon, Lord Byron 7:3636

GRANGE, JOHN
 John Skelton 1:211

GRANGER, JAMES
 Ben Jonson 3:1322
 Sir Henry Wotton 3:1350
 Sir John Suckling 3:1401
 Edward Lord Herbert 3:1446
 Katherine Philips 3:1553
 Sir Kenelm Digby 3:1557
 James Shirley 3:1559
 Abraham Cowley 3:1597
 Margaret Cavendish, Duchess of
 Newcastle 4:1649
 Robert Herrick 4:1656
 Edward Hyde, Earl of Clarendon
 4:1752
 Andrew Marvell 4:1783
 Thomas Hobbes 4:1806
 Samuel Butler 4:1828
 John Oldham 4:1883
 Thomas Otway 4:1887
 Edmund Waller 4:1899
 Charles Cotton 4:1912
 Richard Baxter 4:1943

Robert Boyle 4:1953
John Dryden 4:2011
Samuel Pepys 4:2061
Sir Roger L'Estrange 4:2074
John Evelyn 4:2098
Thomas Sprat 4:2117
Sir Isaac Newton 4:2249

GRANT, ANNE
Oliver Goldsmith 5:2889
James Macpherson 6:3175
Mary Wollstonecraft 6:3281
Anna Seward 6:3393
John Wolcot ("Peter Pindar")
6:3499
William Hayley 6:3503
Thomas Brown 6:3506
Charles Robert Maturin 7:3625
Sir Walter Scott 7:3852
Felicia Dorothea Hemans 7:3980
Letitia Elizabeth Landon 7:4021
Thomas Chalmers 7:4156
Maria Edgeworth 7:4200
Sir William Hamilton 8:4500
Sydney Owenson, Lady Morgan
8:4547
Fanny Kemble 10:5743

GRANT, JAMES
William Cobbett 7:3960
Francis, Lord Jeffrey 8:4340
Thomas Babington Macaulay
8:4604
Benjamin Disraeli 9:5158

GRANT DUFF, SIR MOUNTSTUART E.
Thomas Love Peacock 8:4810
Frederick Denison Maurice 9:4924

GRANVILLE, HARRIET, COUNTESS OF
Sydney Smith 7:4129

GRAVES, RICHARD
William Shenstone 5:2721

GRAY, ASA
Sir Francis Bacon 3:1110

GRAY, THOMAS
Geoffrey Chaucer 1:77
John Lydgate 1:174
William Shakespeare 2:570
Joseph Hall 3:1520
John Milton 4:1689, 1698
John Dryden 4:2006, 2010
Anthony Ashley Cooper, Third Earl
of Shaftesbury 4:2127
Thomas Parnell 4:2166
Thomas Tickell 5:2390
Alexander Pope 5:2418
James Thomson 5:2539
Henry Fielding 5:2598
Colley Cibber 5:2637
Lady Mary Wortley Montagu
5:2709, 2713
William Shenstone 5:2722, 2724
Laurence Sterne 5:2759, 2765
Thomas Gray 5:2826
Christopher Smart 5:2866
Samuel Johnson 6:2991
George Colman the Elder 6:3114,
3115

James Boswell 6:3150
Horace Walpole 6:3232
William Mason 6:3252
Joseph Warton 6:3304
Richard Hurd 6:3365

GRAY, WILLIAM
Sir Philip Sidney 1:321

GRAY, ZACHARY
Samuel Butler 4:1828

GREELEY, HORACE
Benjamin Franklin 6:3040
Edgar Allan Poe 8:4251
Margaret Fuller 8:4362
James Fenimore Cooper 8:4377
Horace Greeley 9:4936
Herman Melville 10:5610

GREEN, HENRY
Alexander Barclay 1:282

GREEN, JOHN RICHARD
William of Malmesbury 1:26
William Langland 1:50
Sir Philip Sidney 1:320
John Lyly 1:511
William Shakespeare 2:546
Samuel Daniel 3:1074
Sir Francis Bacon 3:1116
Thomas Hobbes 4:1812
Samuel Butler 4:1829
John Bunyan 4:1923
John Dryden 4:2030
Sir Charles Sedley 4:2056
William Wycherley 4:2153
Joseph Addison 4:2179
Charles Wesley 6:3035
John Wesley 6:3082
Junius 6:3487
John Lothrop Motley 9:5020
John Richard Green 9:5360

GREEN, S. G.
Christopher Smart 5:2867

GREEN, THOMAS
John Milton 4:1696
Edward Young 5:2744
Philip Dormer Stanhope, Earl of
Chesterfield 5:2875
Edmund Burke 6:3268

GREENBAUM, SAMUEL
Emma Lazarus 9:5445

GREENE, GEORGE WASHINGTON
Washington Irving 8:4537
George Grote 9:4910

GREENE, ROBERT
Geoffrey Chaucer 1:69
Christopher Marlowe 1:364
George Peele 1:398
Thomas Nashe 1:507
William Shakespeare 2:535
Thomas Lodge 3:1094

GREENE, SAMUEL A.
Benjamin Franklin 6:3048

GREENSLET, FERRIS
Lafcadio Hearn 10:6214

GREENWELL, DORA
Sir Francis Bacon 3:1116

GREG, W. R.
Thomas Arnold 7:4068
Charles Kingsley 9:4994
Harriet Martineau 9:5007
Benjamin Disraeli 9:5159

GREGORY XI, POPE
John Wyclif 1:40

GREGORY, GEORGE
Thomas Chatterton 5:2806
Tobias Smollett 5:2838

GREGORY, JOHN
Henry Home, Lord Kames 6:2967

GREGORY, LADY
Alexander William Kinglake
10:5583

GREIN, J. T.
Oscar Wilde 10:6029

GREVILLE, CHARLES CAVENDISH
FULKE
Marguerite, Countess of Blessington
7:4218
John Wilson Croker 8:4505
Thomas Babington Macaulay
8:4599
Henry Thomas Buckle 8:4695
Richard Cobden 8:4793

GREVILLE, FULKE (LORD BROOKE)
Sir Philip Sidney 1:319, 323, 336

GREVILLE, HENRY
Thomas Babington Macaulay
8:4607
Benjamin Disraeli 9:5158
Fanny Kemble 10:5742
Harriet Beecher Stowe 10:5883

GRIBBLE, FRANCIS
William Harrison Ainsworth 9:5237

GRIERSON, HERBERT J. C.
Richard Crashaw 3:1468
Thomas Traherne 4:1763

GRIFFIN, EDMUND D.
Henry Mackenzie 7:3763

GRIFFIN, W. HALL
Ben Jonson 3:1326

GRIFFIS, WILLIAM ELLIOT
W. E. H. Lecky 10:6163

GRIMM, FRIEDRICH MELCHIOR
Edward Young 5:2743

GRIMM, HERMAN
Samuel Richardson 5:2686

GRISCOM, JOHN
Thomas Chalmers 7:4158

GRISWOLD, RUFUS W.
Jonathan Edwards 5:2650
Henry Kirke White 6:3357
Charles Brockden Brown 6:3398
Joel Barlow 6:3416
Timothy Dwight 6:3444
John Keats 6:3530
John Trumbull 7:3772
Philip Freneau 7:3799

Letitia Elizabeth Landon 7:4022
Washington Allston 7:4094
Thomas Campbell 7:4111
Ebenezer Elliott 7:4211
Edgar Allan Poe 8:4249
Margaret Fuller 8:4357
Joanna Baillie 8:4367
James Montgomery 8:4440
Leigh Hunt 8:4554
William H. Prescott 8:4591
Nathaniel Hawthorne 8:4766
William Gilmore Simms 8:4872
Alice and Phoebe Cary 9:4919
Caroline Norton 9:5018
William Cullen Bryant 9:5043
Richard Henry Dana 9:5066
Fanny Kemble 10:5743

GROSART, ALEXANDER B.
Sir Philip Sidney 1:327
Robert Southwell 1:397
Thomas Nashe 1:507
Samuel Daniel 3:1074
Nicholas Breton 3:1100
Sir John Davies 3:1145
Gabriel Harvey 3:1181
Thomas Dekker 3:1227
Francis Quarles 3:1428
Richard Crashaw 3:1473
Andrew Marvell 4:1784
Robert Fergusson 5:2911

GROTE, GEORGE
Thomas Hobbes 4:1811
James Mill 7:4011

GRUTER, ISAAC
Sir Francis Bacon 3:1110

GUERNSEY, ALFRED H.
John Wesley 6:3084

GUEST, EDWIN
Cædmon 1:7
Alfred the Great 1:19
William Langland 1:49
Gavin Douglas 1:207
Henry Howard, Earl of Surrey
1:279
John Milton 4:1703

GUILPIN, EVERARD
John Marston 3:1297

GUINEY, LOUISE IMOGEN
Richard Lovelace 3:1532
Izaak Walton 4:1870
Henry Vaughan 4:1979
George Farquhar 4:2112
Sir John Vanbrugh 4:2239
William Hazlitt 7:3744
Gerard Manley Hopkins 9:5547
Francis Turner Palgrave 10:5922
Harold Frederic 10:5973
Lionel Johnson 10:6121

GUIZOT, FRANÇOIS PIERRE GUILLAUME
William Laud 3:1438
Edward Gibbon 6:3127
William H. Prescott 8:4594
John Lothrop Motley 9:5024

GUNSAULUS, FRANK W.
Sir Edwin Arnold 10:6190

GURNEY, J. HAMPDEN
John Wyclif 1:41

GWYNN, STEPHEN
Robert Louis Stevenson 10:5836
Harold Frederic 10:5973
Stephen Crane 10:6057

HABERTON, JOHN
Louisa May Alcott 9:5486

HABINGTON, WILLIAM
George Chapman 3:1270
William Habington 3:1513

HACKET, JOHN
Lancelot Andrewes 3:1102
John Milton 4:1708

HADDEN, J. CUTHBERT
James Hogg 7:3976
Thomas Campbell 7:4115

HAECKEL, ERNST
Thomas Henry Huxley 10:5862

HAGGARD, H. RIDER
Daniel Defoe 5:2320

HAILES, LORD
Thomas of Erceldoune 1:31

HAKE, A. EGMONT
George Borrow 9:5144

HAKE, EDWARD
Thomas Sackville, Earl of Dorset
1:521

HAKE, GORDON
Dante Gabriel Rossetti 9:5314

HALDANE, R. B.
Adam Smith 6:3068

HALE, CHARLES
Henry Thomas Buckle 8:4695

HALE, EDWARD EVERETT
Benjamin Franklin 6:3041

HALE, EDWARD EVERETT, JR.
Jonathan Edwards 5:2653
Benjamin Franklin 6:3041
Margaret Fuller 8:4362
William H. Prescott 8:4596
John Stuart Mill 9:4966
John Lothrop Motley 9:5022

HALE, SARAH JOSEPHA
Alice and Phoebe Cary 9:4920

HALES, JOHN W.
Sir Thomas Malory 1:189
Sir Thomas Wyatt 1:264
George Gascoigne 1:311
Robert Southwell 1:398
William Shakespeare 2:839
Sir John Davies 3:1143
Sir Henry Wotton 3:1351
Joseph Hall 3:1518
John Milton 4:1705
Daniel Defoe 5:2316
Thomas Gray 5:2825
Jane Austen 6:3451
Sir Walter Scott 7:3848

HALIFAX, GEORGE SAVILE,
MARQUIS OF (?)
Gilbert Burnet 4:2136

HALIFAX, SAMUEL
Joseph Butler 5:2572

HALL, HUBERT
Sir Philip Sidney 1:327

HALL, ROBERT
David Hume 5:2919
Sir William Blackstone 6:2960
Edmund Burke 6:3270
Joseph Priestley 6:3347
William Godwin 7:3996

HALL, SAMUEL CARTER
Francis Quarles 3:1425
William Hazlitt 7:3740
Hannah More 7:3871
William Cobbett 7:3962
William Godwin 7:3991
Letitia Elizabeth Landon 7:4021
Robert Southey 7:4079
Thomas Hood 7:4142
Maria Edgeworth 7:4204
Marguerite, Countess of Blessington
7:4219
William Lisle Bowles 8:4292
James Fenimore Cooper 8:4377
Amelia Opie 8:4435
James Montgomery 8:4438
Samuel Rogers 8:4459
Mary Russell Mitford 8:4468
Washington Irving 8:4526
Sydney Owenson, Lady Morgan
8:4546
James Sheridan Knowles 8:4663
John Clare 8:4757
Nathaniel Hawthorne 8:4765
Samuel Lover 8:4864
William Carleton 8:4867
Charles Dickens 8:4889
Edward Bulwer-Lytton 9:4941
Harriet Martineau 9:5004
Caroline Norton 9:5017
Benjamin Disraeli 9:5154
William Harrison Ainsworth 9:5233

HALLAM, ARTHUR HENRY
Alfred, Lord Tennyson 10:5655

HALLAM, HENRY
The Venerable Bede 1:14
Roger Bacon 1:29
John Gower 1:168
John Lydgate 1:174
Gavin Douglas 1:206
John Skelton 1:214
Sir Thomas More 1:233
George Gascoigne 1:310
George Buchanan 1:316
Sir Philip Sidney 1:325, 328
Robert Greene 1:361
Robert Southwell 1:397
George Puttenham 1:498
Richard Hooker 1:501
Thomas Sackville, Earl of Dorset
1:521
William Warner 1:524
John Fletcher 3:1042, 1044
Sir Walter Ralegh 3:1069
Samuel Daniel 3:1072, 1074
Giles and Phineas Fletcher 3:1090

HARVEY, CHRISTOPHER
George Herbert 3:1247

HARVEY, GABRIEL
John Skelton 1:212
Sir John Cheke 1:286
Sir Philip Sidney 1:323
Robert Greene 1:359
Christopher Marlowe 1:371
Edmund Spenser 1:403, 405, 406, 417

HASSALL, ARTHUR
Henry St. John, Viscount
Bolingbroke 5:2565

HASSARD, J. R. G.
John Fiske 10:6074

HASWELL, CHARLES H.
Frances Trollope 8:4704

HATTON, JOSEPH
William Black 10:5962

HAVEN, S. F.
Cotton Mather 4:2258

HAVERS, GEORGE
Sir Francis Bacon 3:1118

HAWEIS, HUGH REGINALD
John Richard Green 9:5360
Henry Ward Beecher 9:5429

HAWES, STEPHEN
John Gower 1:167
John Lydgate 1:173

HAWKINS, SIR JOHN
Thomas D'Urfey 4:2219
John Gay 5:2346
Bernard Mandeville 5:2354
Henry Carey 5:2403
Richard Savage 5:2407
Ambrose Philips 5:2551
Henry Fielding 5:2607
Samuel Richardson 5:2683
Mark Akenside 5:2794
Philip Dormer Stanhope, Earl of
Chesterfield 5:2874
Oliver Goldsmith 5:2883
Samuel Johnson 6:2979

HAWKINS, LAETITIA MATILDA
Horace Walpole 6:3234

HAWKINS, THOMAS
George Peele 1:401

HAWTHORNE, JULIAN
Daniel Defoe 5:2320
Anthony Trollope 9:5283
Herman Melville 10:5611

HAWTHORNE, NATHANIEL
William Shakespeare 2:721
Cotton Mather 4:2255
Samuel Johnson 6:2982
Benjamin Franklin 6:3046
Sir Joshua Reynolds 6:3095
Robert Burns 6:3194
Sir Walter Scott 7:3838
Robert Southey 7:4079
Edgar Allan Poe 8:4259
Margaret Fuller 8:4355

Mary Russell Mitford 8:4468
Douglas Jerrold 8:4510
Leigh Hunt 8:4556
Thomas Babington Macaulay
8:4599
Elizabeth Barrett Browning 8:4629,
4630
William Makepeace Thackeray
8:4717
Nathaniel Hawthorne 8:4764,
4773, 4774, 4776
Samuel Lover 8:4864
Charles Dickens 8:4878
Bryan Waller Procter 9:4981
Harriet Martineau 9:5004
William Cullen Bryant 9:5040
George Eliot 9:5080
Benjamin Disraeli 9:5153
Henry Wadsworth Longfellow
9:5243, 5249
Anthony Trollope 9:5283
Charles Reade 9:5370
Robert Browning 9:5492
Herman Melville 10:5605, 5609
Alfred, Lord Tennyson 10:5654
Coventry Patmore 10:5890

HAWTHORNE, SOPHIA
Nathaniel Hawthorne 8:4774

HAY, JOHN
Emma Lazarus 9:5445

HAYDON, BENJAMIN ROBERT
Samuel Richardson 5:2694
Richard Brinsley Sheridan 6:3425
John Keats 6:3517
William Hazlitt 7:3739
Charles Lamb 7:3937
Francis, Lord Jeffrey 8:4340
Bryan Waller Procter 9:4982

HAYLEY, WILLIAM
Samuel Butler 4:1826
Jonathan Swift 5:2481
William Collins 5:2662
Thomas Chatterton 5:2802
Philip Dormer Stanhope, Earl of
Chesterfield 5:2874
Joseph Warton 6:3305
William Cowper 6:3311
Erasmus Darwin 6:3330

HAYNE, PAUL HAMILTON
William Gilmore Simms 8:4871,
4873
Sidney Lanier 9:5175

HAYWARD, ABRAHAM
Junius 6:3483
Hester Lynch Piozzi 6:3515
Sydney Smith 7:4132
Maria Edgeworth 7:4202
Samuel Rogers 8:4459
William Makepeace Thackeray
8:4715

HAZLITT, WILLIAM
Geoffrey Chaucer 1:89, 90
Sir Philip Sidney 1:338
Christopher Marlowe 1:373
Edmund Spenser 1:405, 440

John Lyly 1:512
Thomas Sackville, Earl of Dorset
1:522
William Shakespeare 2:612, 755,
758, 767, 774, 778, 781, 791,
796, 802, 808, 821, 831, 837,
842, 847, 854, 879, 889, 907,
922, 938, 950, 961, 971, 979,
985, 997, 1000, 1004, 1010
John Fletcher 3:1044
Beaumont and Fletcher 3:1049
Sir Walter Ralegh 3:1068
Thomas Middleton 3:1162
Fulke Greville, Lord Brooke 3:1172
Michael Drayton 3:1186
John Donne 3:1200
Thomas Dekker 3:1231
George Chapman 3:1280
John Webster 3:1282, 1287
John Marston 3:1300
Ben Jonson 3:1330
Philip Massinger 3:1357
John Ford 3:1386
William Browne 3:1412
William Drummond 3:1452
Richard Crashaw 3:1465
Thomas Heywood 3:1491
Jeremy Taylor 3:1580, 1584
Sir William D'Avenant 3:1616
Robert Herrick 4:1657
John Milton 4:1706, 1729
Samuel Butler 4:1833
John Wilmot, Earl of Rochester
4:1844
Sir Thomas Browne 4:1852
Izaak Walton 4:1871
Thomas Otway 4:1889
Sir George Etherege 4:1957
Thomas Shadwell 4:1966
John Dryden 4:2013, 2019
John Locke 4:2082
George Farquhar 4:2106
William Wycherley 4:2150
Joseph Addison 4:2185
Matthew Prior 4:2208
Jeremy Collier 4:2230
Sir John Vanbrugh 4:2236, 2238
William Congreve 4:2271
Sir Richard Steele 4:2293
Daniel Defoe 5:3211
John Gay 5:2341
John Arbuthnot 5:2372
Alexander Pope 5:2451
Jonathan Swift 5:2483
James Thomson 5:2539
Henry St. John, Viscount
Bolingbroke 5:2564
Henry Fielding 5:2600, 2604,
2610
Colley Cibber 5:2635
William Collins 5:2663
Samuel Richardson 5:2694, 2697,
2698
William Shenstone 5:2722
Charles Churchill 5:2733
Edward Young 5:2739
Laurence Sterne 5:2761
Mark Akenside 5:2797

Thomas Chatterton 5:2806, 2807
Thomas Gray 5:2819
Tobias Smollett 5:2840
Oliver Goldsmith 5:2891
David Garrick 6:2955
Samuel Johnson 6:2984
Thomas Warton 6:3075
Sir Joshua Reynolds 6:3092
George Colman the Elder 6:3115
James Boswell 6:3150
Robert Burns 6:3197
Charles Macklin 6:3229
Horace Walpole 6:3238, 3239
Edmund Burke 6:3270
William Cowper 6:3313
Richard Brinsley Sheridan 6:3425
John Keats 6:3520
Percy Bysshe Shelley 6:3563, 3577
Ann Radcliffe 7:3607, 3608
George Gordon, Lord Byron
  7:3637, 3647, 3648, 3649
Anna Laetitia Barbauld 7:3668
William Gifford 7:3688, 3692
Henry Mackenzie 7:3763
Jeremy Bentham 7:3784
George Crabbe 7:3813
Sir James Mackintosh 7:3829
Sir Walter Scott 7:3853
Thomas Robert Malthus 7:3888
Samuel Taylor Coleridge 7:3893,
  3898, 3911
Charles Lamb 7:3935, 3946
William Cobbett 7:3965
William Godwin 7:3993
Fanny Burney 7:4040
Robert Southey 7:4081, 4089
William Beckford 7:4100
Thomas Campbell 7:4110, 4117
Thomas Chalmers 7:4159
William Wordsworth 8:4303, 4312,
  4323
Francis, Lord Jeffrey 8:4346
Joanna Baillie 8:4365
James Fenimore Cooper 8:4378
Thomas Moore 8:4419, 4425
Samuel Rogers 8:4460
Washington Irving 8:4526
Leigh Hunt 8:4550, 4553
James Sheridan Knowles 8:4664
Henry, Lord Brougham 8:4854
Bryan Waller Procter 9:4981

HAZLITT, WILLIAM CAREW
George Gascoigne 1:310
Thomas Carew 3:1396
Robert Herrick 4:1655, 1660
Leigh Hunt 8:4551
Bryan Waller Procter 9:4984
John Forster 9:5013
Richard Henry Horne 9:5369
Frederick Locker-Lampson
  10:5854

HEADLEY, HENRY
William Warner 1:524
Giles and Phineas Fletcher 3:1090
Michael Drayton 3:1189
William Drummond 3:1452
Richard Lovelace 3:1533

HEALY, CHRIS
Oscar Wilde 10:6016

HEARN, LAFCADIO
Herbert Spencer 10:6144

HEARNE, THOMAS
John Wyclif 1:42
Raphael Holinshed 1:313
Robert Burton 3:1367
William Laud 3:1437
John Selden 3:1503
Abraham Cowley 3:1595
William Prynne 3:1619
Thomas Hobbes 4:1806
John Bunyan 4:1916
Richard Baxter 4:1943
John Dryden 4:2005
Gilbert Burnet 4:2136, 2140
Nicholas Rowe 4:2158
Thomas Parnell 4:2165
Joseph Addison 4:2175, 2180
Sir John Vanbrugh 4:2235, 2237
Sir Isaac Newton 4:2243, 2245
Sir Richard Blackmore 4:2263
Sir Richard Steele 4:2287, 2290
Alexander Pope 5:2418
Lewis Theobald 5:2467
William Law 5:2674

HEATH, H. FRANK
William of Malmesbury 1:26
John Gower 1:169
Robert Henryson 1:203

HEATH, RICHARD
John Bunyan 4:1924

HEBER, REGINALD
Jeremy Taylor 3:1584, 1586
John Wesley 6:3083
William Cowper 6:3324
H. H. Milman 8:4860

HEDGE, FREDERICK HENRY
Margaret Fuller 8:4357

HEINE, HEINRICH
William Shakespeare 2:814
William Hazlitt 7:3742
Sir Walter Scott 7:3843

HELPS, SIR ARTHUR
Charles Kingsley 9:4990
Harriet Beecher Stowe 10:5882

HEMANS, FELICIA DOROTHEA
Sir Walter Scott 7:3837
H. H. Milman 8:4860
Sir Henry Taylor 9:5399

HEMINGE, JOHN
William Shakespeare 2:563

HENDERSON, ANDREW
Tobias Smollett 5:2836

HENDERSON, THOMAS F.
Richard Hooker 1:503
William Bradford 3:1529
Robert Burns 6:3212
Robert Chambers 9:4915

HENLEY, WILLIAM ERNEST
Robert Henryson 1:202
Sir Philip Sidney 1:322

William Shakespeare 2:578
Cyril Tourneur 3:1150
Robert Herrick 4:1659
Samuel Butler 4:1830
Izaak Walton 4:1868
William Congreve 4:2275
John Gay 5:2343
Henry Fielding 5:2603
Samuel Richardson 5:2696
John Byrom 5:2719
Tobias Smollett 5:2843
James Boswell 6:3152
Robert Burns 6:3208, 3212
George Gordon, Lord Byron 7:3641
William Hazlitt 7:3745
John Wilson Croker 8:4508
Walter Savage Landor 8:4738
Charles Dickens 8:4886
Robert Chambers 9:4915
Charles Lever 9:4934
Charles Kingsley 9:4993
George Borrow 9:5145
Benjamin Disraeli 9:5168
Henry Wadsworth Longfellow
  9:5248
Richard Jefferies 9:5438
Matthew Arnold 9:5459, 5462
Robert Louis Stevenson 10:5831
Frederick Locker-Lampson 10:5856

HENRY OF HUNTINGDON
Alfred the Great 1:18

HENRY, ROBERT
Giraldus Cambrensis 1:28
John Barbour 1:46

HENRYSON, ROBERT
Geoffrey Chaucer 1:55

HERAUD, JOHN A.
William Lisle Bowles 8:4295

HERBERT, DAVID
Tobias Smollett 5:2846

HERBERT, EDWARD LORD
George Herbert 3:1241

HERBERT, SIR HENRY
James Shirley 3:1559

HERDER, J. G.
Alfred the Great 1:19

HERFORD, BROOKE
John Wyclif 1:43

HERFORD, CHARLES H.
Sir Thomas More 1:233
Miles Coverdale 1:297
John Heywood 1:308
George Gascoigne 1:311
Robert Tannahill 6:3407
Thomas Brown 6:3508
Dugald Stewart 7:3733
Sir James Mackintosh 7:3829
William Cobbett 7:3965
James Hogg 7:3973
Felicia Dorothea Hemans 7:3986
William Godwin 7:3998
George Colman the Younger
  7:4008
John Galt 7:4026

Joanna Baillie 8:4368
Mary Shelley 8:4399
Leigh Hunt 8:4560
Arthur Hugh Clough 8:4656

HERRICK, ROBERT
John Fletcher 3:1041
Sir John Denham 3:1627
Robert Herrick 4:1660

HERRICK, S. E.
John Wyclif 1:46

HERVEY, JOHN, LORD
John Gay 5:2345
Alexander Pope 5:2435
Henry St. John, Viscount
Bolingbroke 5:2559
Philip Dormer Stanhope, Earl of
Chesterfield 5:2874

HEWLETT, HENRY G.
Matthew Prior 4:2209
Winthrop Mackworth Praed 7:4035
Sir Henry Taylor 9:5398

HEYLYN, PETER
Sir Philip Sidney 1:323
Sir Francis Bacon 3:1108
William Laud 3:1437
Joseph Hall 3:1521

HEYWOOD, THOMAS
Thomas Watson 1:357
William Shakespeare 2:1034
Francis Beaumont 3:1039

HICKES, GEORGE
Samuel Pepys 4:2060

HIGGINSON, JOHN
Cotton Mather 4:2257

HIGGINSON, THOMAS WENTWORTH
Charles Brockden Brown 6:3401
Jane Austen 6:3452
Ann Radcliffe 7:3610
Felicia Dorothea Hemans 7:3986
Edgar Allan Poe 8:4253
Margaret Fuller 8:4359
James Fenimore Cooper 8:4381
Henry David Thoreau 8:4670
Nathaniel Hawthorne 8:4769
Alice and Phoebe Cary 9:4919
Harriet Martineau 9:5007
Sidney Lanier 9:5180
Richard Henry Dana, Jr. 9:5307
Helen Hunt Jackson 9:5391, 5392
Edwin P. Whipple 9:5410
Emily Dickinson 9:5413, 5418,
5419
Louisa May Alcott 9:5490
Robert Browning 9:5499
George Bancroft 10:5582
John Greenleaf Whittier 10:5642
Walt Whitman 10:5705
Francis Parkman 10:5752
Oliver Wendell Holmes 10:5771
Harriet Beecher Stowe 10:5883
Charles Dudley Warner 10:6011

HIGGONS, BEVIL
Gilbert Burnet 4:2140

HILDESLEY, BISHOP
Edward Young 5:2738

HILL, AARON
John Dennis 5:2365
Richard Savage 5:2405, 2406
James Thomson 5:2531
Aaron Hill 5:2553
Henry Fielding 5:2606
Samuel Richardson 5:2691
David Mallet 5:2755

HILL, ADAMS SHERMAN
Jonathan Swift 5:2490

HILL, ASTRAEA
Henry Fielding 5:2606

HILL, DAVID J.
William Cullen Bryant 9:5046

HILL, FRANK HARRISON
William Ewart Gladstone 10:5944

HILL, GEORGE BIRKBECK
Samuel Johnson 6:3022
James Boswell 6:3159
John Wilson Croker 8:4508

HILL, JOHN
Hugh Blair 6:3294

HILL, MINERVA
Henry Fielding 5:2606

HILL, THOMAS
Erasmus Darwin 6:3332

HILLARD, GEORGE STILLMAN
John Sterling 7:4121
Hartley Coleridge 7:4220
William H. Prescott 8:4591
Nathaniel Hawthorne 8:4765, 4775
Richard Monckton Milnes, Lord
Houghton 9:5385
Robert Browning 9:5492
James Russell Lowell 10:5590
Fanny Kemble 10:5744

HILLARD, KATE
Thomas Lovell Beddoes 7:4230

HILLARD, W.
Catharine Maria Sedgwick 8:4830

HILLIER, ARTHUR CECIL
John Wilson 8:4448

HINDS, ALLEN B.
John Foxe 1:357

HINES, JOHN A.
John Milton 4:1694

HINSDALE, B. A.
John Stuart Mill 9:4966

HIPPISLEY, J. H.
Sir Philip Sidney 1:321

HIRSCH, EMIL G.
Sir Edwin Arnold 10:6188

HIRST, FRANCIS W.
Adam Smith 6:3068

HITCHMAN, FRANCIS
David Garrick 6:2954

HOADLY, BENJAMIN
Samuel Clarke 5:2303
Daniel Defoe 5:2317

HOARE, H. W.
Thomas Hobbes 4:1820

HOARE, SIR RICHARD COLT
Giraldus Cambrensis 1:28

HOBBES, THOMAS
John Milton 4:1708

HOEY, CASHEL
William Carleton 8:4868

HOGARTH, GEORGE
John Gay 5:2346

HOGARTH, GEORGINA
Charles Dickens 8:4879

HOGG, JAMES
Sir Walter Scott 7:3839
James Hogg 7:3970
John Galt 7:4024
Robert Southey 7:4078, 4087
John Wilson 8:4445
John Gibson Lockhart 8:4453

HOGG, THOMAS JEFFERSON
Percy Bysshe Shelley 6:3566
Robert Southey 7:4079

HOLCROFT, THOMAS
William Godwin 7:3998

HOLIDAY, HENRY
Lewis Carroll 10:5955

HOLLAND, FREDERIC MAY
Roger Bacon 1:29
John Wyclif 1:44
William Langland 1:50

HOLLAND, SIR HENRY
Fanny Burney 7:4039
Sydney Smith 7:4133
Joanna Baillie 8:4363

HOLLAND, HUGH
William Shakespeare 2:563

HOLLAND, LADY
Sydney Smith 7:4129

HOLLAND, SCOTT
William Ewart Gladstone 10:5939

HOLMES, NATHANIEL
William Shakespeare 2:724

HOLMES, OLIVER WENDELL
Robert Burton 3:1376
Jonathan Edwards 5:2651
Robert Burns 6:3202
Rufus Wilmot Griswold 8:4517
Washington Irving 8:4525
Nathaniel Hawthorne 8:4766, 4767
Fitz-Greene Halleck 8:4834
N. P. Willis 8:4841
John Lothrop Motley 9:5020, 5023,
5024
Henry Wadsworth Longfellow
9:5242
Henry Ward Beecher 9:5247
James Russell Lowell 10:5589
John Greenleaf Whittier 10:5634
William Ewart Gladstone 10:5941

HOLROYD, MARIA JOSEPHA
Edward Gibbon 6:3131

HOLT, JOHN
William Shakespeare 2:1003

HOMPES, MAT
Elizabeth Gaskell 8:4808

HONE, J. M.
Gerard Manley Hopkins 9:5547

HONE, PHILIP
William H. Prescott 8:4590
Charles Dickens 8:4878, 4893

HOOD, EDWIN PAXTON
Jeremy Taylor 3:1582, 1584
James Hogg 7:3975
Sydney Smith 7:4133
John Clare 8:4759

HOOD, THOMAS
Samuel Taylor Coleridge 7:3896

HOOK, THEODORE
John Lothrop Motley 9:5023

HOOK, WALTER FARQUHAR
John Wyclif 1:43

HOOKER, RICHARD
Richard Hooker 1:501

HOOLE, JOHN
Samuel Johnson 6:2977

HOPE, ANTHONY
Laurence Sterne 5:2767

HOPE, EVA
William Cowper 6:3323

HOPKINS, GERARD MANLEY
Geoffrey Chaucer 1:65
John Dryden 4:2018
Robert Browning 9:5503
Gerard Manley Hopkins 9:5546
Walt Whitman 10:5698
Robert Louis Stevenson 10:5833

HOPKINS, SAMUEL
Jonathan Edwards 5:2657

HOPPIN, J. H.
Henry Ward Beecher 9:5431

HORNE, GEORGE
Samuel Johnson 6:2981

HORNE, RICHARD HENRY
Roger Bacon 1:29
Geoffrey Chaucer 1:95
Theodore Edward Hook 7:4053
Sydney Smith 7:4131
Thomas Hood 7:4138
Frederick Marryat 7:4169
Hartley Coleridge 7:4221
Mary Shelley 8:4400
Leigh Hunt 8:4555
G. P. R. James 8:4626
Elizabeth Barrett Browning 8:4632
James Sheridan Knowles 8:4662
Frances Trollope 8:4701
Samuel Lover 8:4864
William Carleton 8:4867
Charles Lever 8:4930
John Forster 9:5015
Caroline Norton 9:5018
William Harrison Ainsworth 9:5232

Richard Monckton Milnes, Lord
Houghton 9:5388
Robert Browning 9:5500

HORNER, FRANCIS
Sir Francis Bacon 3:1111
Adam Smith 6:3064
Richard Brinsley Sheridan 6:3422
Dugald Stewart 7:3731
Sir James Mackintosh 7:3824
Thomas Robert Malthus 7:3882
Francis, Lord Jeffrey 8:4339

HORSTMANN, CARL
Richard Rolle of Hampole 1:35

HORTON, ROBERT F.
William Law 5:2677

HOUGHTON, RICHARD MONCKTON
MILNES, LORD
John Keats 6:3529
Walter Savage Landor 8:4735, 4741
Samuel Wilberforce 9:4956

HOUSE, E. H.
Charles Reade 9:5371

HOUSMAN, A. E.
Matthew Arnold 9:5455

HOUSTON, ARTHUR
Thomas Sackville, Earl of Dorset
1:522

HOWE, JULIA WARD
Margaret Fuller 8:4358
Arthur Hugh Clough 8:4649
William Lloyd Garrison 9:5075
Benjamin Disraeli 9:5161

HOWE, M. A. DEWOLFE
N. P. Willis 8:4843

HOWELL, JAMES
John Skelton 1:212

HOWELLS, WILLIAM DEAN
William Shakespeare 2:579
Edward Lord Herbert 3:1447
John Milton 4:1702
Jane Austen 6:3452
Sir Walter Scott 7:3845, 3849
Emily Brontë 7:4182
Washington Irving 8:4531
Thomas De Quincey 8:4575
Henry David Thoreau 8:4674
William Makepeace Thackeray
8:4713
Nathaniel Hawthorne 8:4765
Charles Dickens 8:4886, 4893
Edward Bulwer-Lytton 9:4944
Charles Kingsley 9:5001
George Eliot 9:5089
Henry Wadsworth Longfellow
9:5249
Anthony Trollope 9:5285
Charles Reade 9:5374
Emily Dickinson 9:5415
Robert Browning 9:5504
James Russell Lowell 10:5594
John Greenleaf Whittier 10:5640
Walt Whitman 10:5702
George William Curtis 10:5735

Francis Parkman 10:5753
Oliver Wendell Holmes 10:5775
Harriet Beecher Stowe 10:5882,
5883
William Black 10:5965
Edward Bellamy 10:5967, 5969
Harold Frederic 10:5973
Stephen Crane 10:6049, 6050
John Fiske 10:6075
Frank R. Stockton 10:6091
Bret Harte 10:6111, 6113
Frank Norris 10:6125, 6127, 6131

HOWITT, MARY
Felicia Dorothea Hemans 7:3983
Letitia Elizabeth Landon 7:4019

HOWITT, WILLIAM
John Milton 4:1687

HUBBARD, SARA A.
Gilbert White 6:3102

HUBERT, PHILIP G., JR.
Benjamin Franklin 6:3041

HUCHON, RENÉ LOUIS
Elizabeth Montagu 6:3302, 3303

HUDSON, H. N.
William Shakespeare 2:787

HUDSON, WILLIAM HENRY
Aphra Behn 4:1941
Herbert Spencer 10:6144

HUGHES, HUGH PRICE
John Wesley 6:3086

HUGHES, JABEZ
John Hughes 4:2202

HUGHES, JOHN
Geoffrey Chaucer 1:60
Edmund Spenser 1:425
William Shakespeare 2:937
Robert Boyle 4:1954
Sir William Temple 4:1996
Sir Roger L'Estrange 4:2074
Thomas Sprat 4:2117

HUGHES, THOMAS
Benjamin Franklin 6:3041
Thomas Arnold 7:4069

HUGO, VICTOR
William Shakespeare 2:627, 869,
911
Ben Jonson 3:1323
Nahum Tate 4:2145

HULL, ELEANOR
Charlotte Mary Yonge 10:6068

HUME, DAVID
Alfred the Great 1:19
William of Malmesbury 1:25
John Wyclif 1:42
Sir Thomas More 1:231
John Knox 1:299, 301
William Shakespeare 2:570
Sir Walter Ralegh 3:1065, 1069
William Camden 3:1084
Sir Francis Bacon 3:1108, 1111
Edward Fairfax 3:1308
Ben Jonson 3:1322

Abraham Cowley 3:1595
Sir John Denham 3:1628
John Milton 4:1689, 1706
Edward Hyde, Earl of Clarendon
    4:1752
Thomas Hobbes 4:1806, 1809
John Wilmot, Earl of Rochester
    4:1844
Edmund Waller 4:1899
Sir William Temple 4:1996
John Dryden 4:2010
William Wycherley 4:2149
Thomas Parnell 4:2166
Sir Isaac Newton 4:2246
George Berkeley 5:2586
Laurence Sterne 5:2765
David Hume 5:2923
Benjamin Franklin 6:3042
Adam Smith 6:3060, 3064
William Robertson 6:3110, 3111
Edward Gibbon 6:3124
James Boswell 6:3149
James Macpherson 6:3176, 3178
Richard Hurd 6:3366
John Home 6:3369, 3370

HUMPHRY, OZIAS
Samuel Johnson 6:2976

HUNT, JOHN
Joseph Butler 5:2579
David Hume 5:2920
William Warburton 6:2947

HUNT, LEIGH
Geoffrey Chaucer 1:63, 100, 110
Christopher Marlowe 1:367
Edmund Spenser 1:446, 449
Thomas Sackville, Earl of Dorset
    1:521
William Shakespeare 2:575
Beaumont and Fletcher 3:1049
Sir Francis Bacon 3:1111
Thomas Middleton 3:1162
Thomas Dekker 3:1228
Sir John Suckling 3:1401
Richard Lovelace 3:1532
Katherine Philips 3:1553
Margaret Cavendish, Duchess of
    Newcastle 4:1647
John Milton 4:1691
Andrew Marvell 4:1786
Samuel Butler 4:1827
Thomas Otway 4:1889
Aphra Behn 4:1938
John Dryden 4:2014
Samuel Pepys 4:2062
John Evelyn 4:2098
George Farquhar 4:2107
Nahum Tate 4:2144
William Wycherley 4:2151
Thomas Parnell 4:2166
Sir Samuel Garth 4:2173
Joseph Addison 4:2182
Anne Finch, Countess of
    Winchilsea 4:2198
Sir John Vanbrugh 4:2237
Sir Isaac Newton 4:2247
William Congreve 4:2272
Sir Richard Steele 4:2288

Daniel Defoe 5:2314
Alexander Pope 5:2423
James Thomson 5:2533
Allan Ramsay 5:2639, 2645
William Collins 5:2663
Samuel Richardson 5:2683
Lady Mary Wortley Montagu
    5:2710
William Shenstone 5:2722
Charles Churchill 5:2730
Thomas Gray 5:2827
Tobias Smollett 5:2836
Oliver Goldsmith 5:2901
David Garrick 6:2953
Thomas Warton 6:3075
William Cowper 6:3312
Charlotte Smith 6:3352
Anna Seward 6:3393
Richard Brinsley Sheridan 6:3434
John Wolcot ("Peter Pindar")
    6:3499
John Keats 6:3530, 3535
Percy Bysshe Shelley 6:3565, 3569
Ann Radcliffe 7:3608
George Gordon, Lord Byron
    7:3634, 3637, 3646
Anna Laetitia Barbauld 7:3668
William Gifford 7:3687, 3689
William Hazlitt 7:3739, 3745
Hannah More 7:3870
Samuel Taylor Coleridge 7:3897,
    3900
Charles Lamb 7:3938
George Colman the Younger
    7:4007
Robert Southey 7:4083
Thomas Campbell 7:4109
Thomas Hood 7:4139
Marguerite, Countess of Blessington
    7:4216
William Wordsworth 8:4300, 4306
Thomas Moore 8:4417
Mary Russell Mitford 8:4468
Sydney Owenson, Lady Morgan
    8:4548
G. P. R. James 8:4626
Elizabeth Barrett Browning 8:4630,
    4633
James Sheridan Knowles 8:4662
Walter Savage Landor 8:4732
Henry, Lord Brougham 8:4850
Charles Dickens 8:4880
Harriet Martineau 9:5005
Caroline Norton 9:5017
Thomas Carlyle 9:5111
Dante Gabriel Rossetti 9:5316
Robert Browning 9:5500

HUNT, THEODORE W.
Richard Hooker 1:503

HUNT, THORNTON
Mary Shelley 8:4399
Leigh Hunt 8:4551

HUNT, WILLIAM HOLMAN
Dante Gabriel Rossetti 9:5314

HUNTER, THOMAS
Henry St. John, Viscount
    Bolingbroke 5:2563

HUNTER, W. W.
Sir Edwin Arnold 10:6189

HUNTINGTON, H. A.
George Farquhar 4:2107

HURD, RICHARD
Roger Ascham 1:290
George Buchanan 1:315
Edmund Spenser 1:430
Ben Jonson 3:1325
Abraham Cowley 3:1597
John Locke 4:2078
Gilbert Burnet 4:2140
Joseph Addison 4:2181, 2185
Samuel Clarke 5:2303
William Warburton 6:2943
James Beattie 6:2337

HURDIS, JAMES
John Dryden 4:2012
Sir Samuel Garth 4:2172
Mark Akenside 5:2794

HURST, JOHN FLETCHER
John Knox 1:301

HUSBAND, MARY GILLILAND
George du Maurier 10:5903

HUSK, WILLIAM H.
Henry Carey 5:2404

HUTCHINSON, THOMAS
John Gibson Lockhart 8:4454
Frederick Locker-Lampson 10:5854

HUTCHINSON, WILLIAM G.
Thomas D'Urfey 4:2218

HUTSON, CHARLES WOODWARD
Sir Richard Steele 4:2288

HUTTON, LAURENCE
William Drummond 3:1449
Charles Dickens 8:4888
Lewis Carroll 10:5950

HUTTON, RICHARD HOLT
Samuel Johnson 6:2989
Joanna Baillie 8:4368
Arthur Hugh Clough 8:4651
Nathaniel Hawthorne 8:4777
Frederick Denison Maurice 9:4925
Walter Bagehot 9:5027
Matthew Arnold 9:5464
John Henry Newman 9:5562
Thomas Henry Huxley 10:5863

HUTTON, WILLIAM HOLDEN
Sir Thomas More 1:235, 236
Richard Hooker 1:503
Lancelot Andrewes 3:1103
William Laud 3:1440
Jeremy Taylor 4:1584
Richard Baxter 4:1947
Samuel Johnson 6:2989
Samuel R. Gardiner 10:6084

HUXLEY, THOMAS HENRY
George Berkeley 5:2587
David Hume 5:2922
Joseph Priestley 6:3349
George Eliot 9:5081
Thomas Carlyle 9:5115
Charles Darwin 9:5268, 5271, 5276

HUYSMANS, JORIS-KARL
Edgar Allan Poe 8:4254

IDDLESLEIGH, SIR STAFFORD
NORTHCOTE, EARL OF
William Ewart Gladstone 10:5939

INCHBALD, ELIZABETH
George Lillo 5:2384
Richard Cumberland 6:3412

INGERSOLL, L. D.
Horace Greeley 9:4938

INGERSOLL, ROBERT G.
Thomas Paine 6:3385
Walt Whitman 10:5700

INGLEBY, C. M.
William Shakespeare 2:687

INGRAM, JOHN H.
Rufus Wilmot Griswold 8:4518
Elizabeth Barrett Browning 8:4635
Oliver Wendell Holmes 10:5776

IRELAND, MRS. ALEXANDER
James Anthony Froude 10:5784

IRELAND, ANNIE E.
Robert Browning 9:5497

IRELAND, S. W. H.
Charles Macklin 6:3229

IRELAND, WILLIAM HENRY
Thomas Chatterton 5:2803

IRVING, DAVID
Thomas of Erceldoune 1:31
John Barbour 1:47
Robert Henryson 1:202
William Dunbar 1:221
Alexander Barclay 1:282
George Buchanan 1:316
William Drummond 3:1449
Robert Fergusson 5:2908
Robert Burns 6:3196

IRVING, SIR HENRY
Richard Brinsley Sheridan 6:3427

IRVING, WASHINGTON
Sir John Mandeville 1:36
Sir Philip Sidney 1:323
John Lyly 1:510
William Shakespeare 2:539
Oliver Goldsmith 5:2886
James Boswell 6:3158
Sir Walter Scott 7:3838
Thomas Campbell 7:4111, 4117
John James Audubon 8:4373
Washington Irving 8:4533
William H. Prescott 8:4594
Nathaniel Hawthorne 8:4774
N. P. Willis 8:4840
William Cullen Bryant 9:5041

J., C. C.
Hester Lynch Piozzi 6:3515

J., E. C.
Coventry Patmore 10:5891

JACK, ADOLPHUS ALFRED
Jane Austen 6:3456

JACKSON, THOMAS
Charles Wesley 6:3033

JACOB, GILES
John Dennis 5:2365

JACOX, FRANCIS
Thomas Chalmers 7:4159

JAGO, RICHARD
William Shenstone 5:2722

JAMES I, KING OF SCOTLAND
John Gower 1:167

JAMES I, KING OF ENGLAND
George Buchanan 1:314

JAMES, HENRY
Sir Walter Scott 7:3841
Edgar Allan Poe 8:4260
Henry David Thoreau 8:4670
Nathaniel Hawthorne 8:4784
Charles Kingsley 9:4989
Bayard Taylor 9:5059
George Eliot 9:5082, 5089, 5092
Ralph Waldo Emerson 9:5198
Anthony Trollope 9:5289
Louisa May Alcott 9:5484, 5488
Robert Browning 9:5504, 5514
Wilkie Collins 9:5531
James Russell Lowell 10:5601
Walt Whitman 10:5696
Fanny Kemble 10:5744
Walter Pater 10:5811
Robert Louis Stevenson 10:5837
George du Maurier 10:5903
William Morris 10:5908
George Gissing 10:6172

JAMES, WILLIAM
John Fiske 10:6072
Herbert Spencer 10:6139, 6143,
6149

JAMESON, ANNA BROWNELL
Henry Howard, Earl of Surrey
1:277
Sir Philip Sidney 1:325
John Donne 3:1195
William Drummond 3:1449
William Blake 7:3697
Washington Allston 7:4094

JAMESON, J. FRANKLIN
Washington Irving 8:4533
John Lothrop Motley 9:5021
Francis Parkman 10:5754

JAPP, ALEXANDER HAY
Henry David Thoreau 8:4669
Charles Tennyson Turner 9:5077
Fanny Kemble 10:5744

JEAFFRESON, JOHN CORDY
Sir Samuel Garth 4:2173
Mary Wollstonecraft 6:3289
Clara Reeve 6:3363
Percy Bysshe Shelley 6:3574

JEBB, R. C.
Richard Bentley 5:2400
Richard Porson 6:3377
Alfred, Lord Tennyson 10:5661

JEFFERSON, THOMAS
Henry St. John, Viscount
Bolingbroke 5:2564

Laurence Sterne 5:2767
Benjamin Franklin 6:3038
Edmund Burke 6:3269
Joseph Priestley 6:3345, 3348
Thomas Paine 6:3385

JEFFREY, FRANCIS, LORD
John Ford 3:1385
Samuel Pepys 4:2062
Jonathan Swift 5:2493
Samuel Richardson 5:2685
Lady Mary Wortley Montagu
5:2711
Mark Akenside 5:2795
William Warburton 6:2944
Benjamin Franklin 6:3048, 3050
Sir William Jones 6:3146
Elizabeth Montagu 6:3303
William Cowper 6:3312
James Beattie 6:3341
Joseph Priestley 6:3346
Richard Cumberland 6:3412
Joel Barlow 6:3419
Richard Brinsley Sheridan 6:3426
John Keats 6:3538
Anna Laetitia Barbauld 7:3667
Dugald Stewart 7:3732
George Crabbe 7:3807
Sir James Mackintosh 7:3832
Sir Walter Scott 7:3843, 3846
James Hogg 7:3973
Felicia Dorothea Hemans 7:3983
John Galt 7:4026
Robert Southey 7:4079, 4080,
4085, 4087
Thomas Campbell 7:4116
Maria Edgeworth 7:4200
William Wordsworth 8:4311, 4316
Joanna Baillie 8:4365
Thomas Moore 8:4418, 4424
Amelia Opie 8:4436
James Montgomery 8:4439
John Wilson 8:4445
Samuel Rogers 8:4461
Sir William Hamilton 8:4502
Washington Irving 8:4534, 4535
Thomas Babington Macaulay
8:4607
Charles Dickens 8:4891
Bryan Waller Procter 9:4981
Margaret Oliphant 10:5924

JENKINS, EDWARD
Margaret Cavendish, Duchess of
Newcastle 4:1651

JENKINS, O. L.
Richard Hooker 1:503

JENNINGS, LOUIS J.
John Wilson Croker 8:4506
Benjamin Disraeli 9:5153

JENYNS, SOAME
Samuel Johnson 6:2979

JEPSON, EDGAR
Ernest Dowson 10:6041

JERROLD, DOUGLAS
James Sheridan Knowles 8:4664

JERROLD, WALTER
Samuel Foote 5:2938

JERVAS, CHARLES
Thomas Tickell 5:2388

JESSE, JOHN HENEAGE
Edward Lord Herbert 3:1447

JESSOPP, AUGUSTUS
John Donne 3:1196

JEWETT, SOPHIE
Sidney Lanier 9:5175

JEWSBURY, GERALDINE ENDSOR
Sydney Owenson, Lady Morgan
8:4546, 4548
Wilkie Collins 9:5534

JOHNSON, CHARLES F.
Sir Thomas Malory 1:189
Nathaniel Hawthorne 8:4771

JOHNSON, E. G.
Lewis Carroll 10:5950

JOHNSON, JOHN
William Hayley 6:3503

JOHNSON, LIONEL
Henry Vaughan 4:1986
George Gordon, Lord Byron 7:3644
William Blake 7:3719
James Clarence Mangan 7:4240
William Makepeace Thackeray
8:4711
Matthew Arnold 9:5460
William Allingham 9:5528
William Morris 10:5911
Edward Bellamy 10:5967

JOHNSON, REGINALD BRIMLEY
Sir Joshua Reynolds 6:3094
Hannah More 7:3872
Mary Russell Mitford 8:4471
Leigh Hunt 8:4565, 4566
Thomas De Quincey 8:4576
Harriet Martineau 9:5006

JOHNSON, SAMUEL
Geoffrey Chaucer 1:61, 76
John Gower 1:168
John Skelton 1:213
Roger Ascham 1:289
Edmund Spenser 1:411, 417
William Shakespeare 2:584, 671,
762, 780, 795, 807, 820, 836,
840, 847, 853, 875, 878, 898,
920, 926, 946, 959, 978, 1003
Sir Walter Ralegh 3:1069
Ben Jonson 3:1322
Abraham Cowley 3:1600
Sir John Denham 3:1630
John Milton 4:1686, 1709, 1720
Samuel Butler 4:1830
John Wilmot, Earl of Rochester
4:1848
Sir Thomas Browne 4:1858
Thomas Otway 4:1888
Edmund Waller 4:1901
John Dryden 4:2006, 2024, 2035
Thomas Sprat 4:2119
Thomas Rymer 4:2121
Nicholas Rowe 4:2161
Thomas Parnell 4:2166
Sir Samuel Garth 4:2172

Joseph Addison 4:2180, 2190
John Hughes 4:2203
Matthew Prior 4:2211
Elkanah Settle 4:2224
Jeremy Collier 4:2230
Sir Richard Blackmore 4:2264
William Congreve 4:2270
Sir Richard Steele 4:2288
John Gay 5:2347
John Dennis 5:2365
John Arbuthnot 5:2371, 2375
Thomas Tickell 5:2391
Richard Bentley 5:2399
Richard Savage 5:2410
Alexander Pope 5:2442
Lewis Theobald 5:2467
Jonathan Swift 5:2499
Isaac Watts 5:2528
James Thomson 5:2532
Ambrose Philips 5:2552
William Collins 5:2662, 2668
Samuel Richardson 5:2694
William Shenstone 5:2724
Edward Young 5:2739
David Mallet 5:2757
Mark Akenside 5:2796
Thomas Gray 5:2828
Philip Dormer Stanhope, Earl of
Chesterfield 5:2873
William Warburton 6:2943
Samuel Johnson 6:2976
Sir Joshua Reynolds 6:3090
James Macpherson 6:3175
Junius 6:3484
Hester Lynch Piozzi 6:3513
George Crabbe 7:3807
Hannah More 7:3868

JOHNSON, W. H.
Matthew Arnold 9:5456

JOHNSTON, RICHARD MALCOLM
William Makepeace Thackeray
8:4716

JOHNSTONE, JOHN
Samuel Parr 7:3673

JOLLY, WILLIAM
Robert Burns 6:3204

JONES, ADAM LEROY
Jonathan Edwards 5:2653

JONES, W. A.
Richard Henry Dana 9:5070

JONES, WILLIAM
Henry, Lord Brougham 8:4851

JONSON, BEN
Sir Philip Sidney 1:320
Christopher Marlowe 1:365
Thomas Kyd 1:394
Edmund Spenser 1:403, 406, 408
John Lyly 1:511
Henry Constable 1:527
William Shakespeare 2:535, 564,
566, 875, 999
Francis Beaumont 3:1039, 1040
John Fletcher 3:1043
Sir Walter Ralegh 3:1069
Samuel Daniel 3:1070, 1074

Nicholas Breton 3:1099
Sir Francis Bacon 3:1107
Michael Drayton 3:1184, 1186,
1188
John Donne 3:1197
Thomas Dekker 3:1226
George Chapman 3:1275
John Marston 4:1297
Ben Jonson 3:1316, 1326
William Browne 3:1411
John Selden 3:1503, 1505
Sir Kenelm Digby 3:1556

JORTIN, JOHN
William Warburton 6:2941

JOWETT, BENJAMIN
John Bunyan 4:1920
Richard Baxter 4:1946
Richard Bentley 5:2397
Robert Browning 9:5492

JOYCE, JAMES
James Clarence Mangan 7:4242
Oscar Wilde 10:6023

JOYCE, ROBERT DWYER
Tobias Smollett 5:2846
Oliver Wendell Holmes 10:5771

JUNIUS
Sir William Blackstone 6:2957
Junius 6:3484

JUSSERAND, J. J.
Beowulf 1:3
Richard Rolle of Hampole 1:35
Sir John Mandeville 1:38
John Wyclif 1:44
William Langland 1:51
Sir Thomas Malory 1:187
William Dunbar 1:233
Sir Thomas More 1:234
Sir Philip Sidney 1:325
Robert Greene 1:359
Thomas Nashe 1:508
John Lyly 1:515
William Shakespeare 2:658, 749
John Ford 3:1388
Margaret Cavendish, Duchess of
Newcastle 4:1650
William Blake 7:3699

JUSTICE, MAIBELLE
Kate Chopin 10:6202

K., E.
Edmund Spenser 1:423, 424
Gabriel Harvey 3:1175

K., I.
Aaron Hill 5:2554

KAMES, HENRY HOME, LORD
William Shakespeare 2:571
James Macpherson 6:3178

KAUFMANN, MORITZ
Adam Smith 6:3058
Charles Kingsley 9:4993

KAVANAGH, JULIA
Jane Austen 6:3454

KAWAKAMI, K. K.
Lafcadio Hearn 10:6211

KEATS, JOHN
Edmund Spenser 1:421
William Shakespeare 2:813, 947
George Chapman 3:1277
Katherine Philips 3:1553
John Milton 4:1690, 1699
Thomas Chatterton 5:2803, 2807
Tobias Smollett 5:2840
Robert Burns 6:3193, 3197
John Keats 6:3527
William Hazlitt 7:3741
Charles Lamb 7:3934
William Wordsworth 8:4303
John James Audubon 8:4371
Leigh Hunt 8:4552

KEBBEL, T. E.
Jane Austen 6:3451
George Crabbe 7:3821
James Fenimore Cooper 8:4395
John Wilson Croker 8:4506

KEBLE, JOHN
Richard Hooker 1:502
William Cowper 6:3313
James Montgomery 8:4439

KEDDIE, HENRIETTA
Carolina Oliphant, Baroness Nairne
7:4124

KEENE, H. G.
Sir John Mandeville 1:38

KEIGHTLEY, THOMAS
John Milton 4:1687, 1705
Henry Fielding 5:2601

KEIR, JAMES
Erasmus Darwin 6:3330

KELSALL, THOMAS FORBES
Thomas Lovell Beddoes 7:4227

KELTIE, J. SCOTT
John Richard Green 9:5363

KEMBLE, FANNY
Philip Massinger 3:1359
Jane Austen 6:3449
Lady Caroline Lamb 7:3735
Sir Walter Scott 7:3851
Felicia Dorothea Hemans 7:3983
Theodore Edward Hook 7:4052
William Ellery Channing 7:4057
John Sterling 7:4120
Sydney Smith 7:4130
Samuel Rogers 8:4459
Washington Irving 8:4525
James Sheridan Knowles 8:4664
Charles Dickens 8:4878
Caroline Norton 9:5017
Edward FitzGerald 9:5350
Richard Monckton Milnes, Lord
Houghton 9:5384
Henry Ward Beecher 9:5428
Alfred, Lord Tennyson 10:5653
Harriet Beecher Stowe 10:5883

KENNEDY, W. SLOANE
John Greenleaf Whittier 10:5638

KENNEDY, WALKER
Walt Whitman 10:5717

KENNETT, WHITE
Jonathan Swift 5:2476

KENRICK, WILLIAM
Oliver Goldsmith 5:2886

KENT, ARMINE T.
Leigh Hunt 8:4561

KENT, CHARLES W.
Cynewulf 1:16

KENYON, FREDERIC G.
Elizabeth Barrett Browning 8:4636

KEPPEL, FREDERICK
Sir Joshua Reynolds 6:3096

KER, W. P.
Beowulf 1:3
Ælfric 1:24
Geoffrey Chaucer 1:155
Sir Thomas Malory 1:188
William Tyndale 1:254
John Lyly 1:510
Richard Hakluyt 1:531
Edward Lord Herbert 3:1446
John Dryden 4:2033
Samuel Pepys 4:2063
Thomas Rymer 4:2122
Horace Walpole 6:3237
William Cowper 6:3325
Samuel Taylor Coleridge 7:3903
Thomas Babington Macaulay
8:4603

KERNAHAN, COULSON
Frederick Locker-Lampson 10:5856

KETTELL, SAMUEL
Henry Wadsworth Longfellow
9:5241

KILMER, JOYCE
Gerard Manley Hopkins 9:5546

KILVERT, FRANCIS
Richard Hurd 6:3367

KING, HENRY
John Donne 3:1195
George Sandys 3:1423

KING, RICHARD ASHE
Jonathan Swift 5:2490

KING, WILLIAM
Richard Bentley 5:2398

KINGLAKE, ALEXANDER WILLIAM
William Ewart Gladstone 10:5940

KINGSLEY, CHARLES
George Buchanan 1:315
John Webster 3:1287
Philip Massinger 3:1357
William Cartwright 3:1418
John Milton 4:1692
Henry Brooke 5:2973
Anne Brontë 8:4286
Charlotte Brontë 8:4483
Elizabeth Gaskell 8:4797, 4798
Frederick Denison Maurice 9:4927
Charles Darwin 9:5268

KINGSLEY, J. L.
Noah Webster 7:4074

KIRK, EDWARD (?)
George Gascoigne 1:310

KIRKMAN, JAMES THOMAS
Charles Macklin 6:3229

KIRKPATRICK, JAMES
Michael Drayton 3:1189

KIRKUP, SEYMOUR
William Blake 7:3696

KLEARY, C. F.
George Gissing 10:6175

KLOPSTOCK, MARGARETA MOLLER
Samuel Richardson 5:2683

KNAPP, SAMUEL
John Lydgate 1:174

KNAPP, WILLIAM I.
George Borrow 9:5145

KNAUFFT, ERNEST
George du Maurier 10:5902

KNIGHT, CHARLES
William Caxton 1:184
Robert Greene 1:360
George Peele 1:399
John Lyly 1:511
William Shakespeare 2:994
Thomas Lodge 3:1094
Nahum Tate 4:2145
John Dennis 5:2366
Lewis Theobald 5:2469
William Warburton 6:2947
Samuel Taylor Coleridge 7:3910
Winthrop Mackworth Praed 7:4035
William Makepeace Thackeray
8:4706

KNIGHT, HELEN C.
Hannah More 7:3870
James Montgomery 8:4440

KNIGHT, WILLIAM
David Hume 5:2923
James Burnett, Lord Monboddo
6:3291
Herbert Spencer 10:6144

KNIGHTON, HENRY
John Wyclif 1:45

KNOWLES, JOHN
Mary Wollstonecraft 6:3278

KNOX, JOHN
John Knox 1:300
George Buchanan 1:314

KNOX, VICESIMUS
Isaac Watts 5:2526
Henry Fielding 5:2599
Laurence Sterne 5:2767
Thomas Chatterton 5:2811

KOOPMAN, HARRY LYMAN
John Milton 4:1693

KRAUSE, ERNST
Erasmus Darwin 6:3332

KYD, THOMAS
Christopher Marlowe 1:370

KYNASTON, SIR FRANCIS
Robert Henryson 1:202

LA FARGE, JOHN
John Ruskin 10:5986

LAING, DAVID
Thomas Lodge 3:1094

LAING, MALCOLM
William Drummond 3:1450
Gilbert Burnet 4:2137
James Macpherson 6:3180

LAKE, WILLIAM CHARLES
John Keble 8:4824

LAMARTINE, ALPHONSE DE
John Milton 4:1687, 1700

LAMB, CHARLES
Geoffrey Chaucer 1:62
Sir Philip Sidney 1:320, 323, 325
Christopher Marlowe 1:366
Thomas Kyd 1:395
George Peele 1:401
Edmund Spenser 1:414
Thomas Sackville, Earl of Dorset
   1:522
William Shakespeare 2:860
John Fletcher 3:1043
Fulke Greville, Lord Brooke 3:1172
Thomas Dekker 3:1229
George Chapman 3:1277
John Webster 3:1286
Ben Jonson 3:1325, 1327
Philip Massinger 3:1357
Robert Burton 3:1368
John Ford 3:1388, 1389
Thomas Heywood 3:1490
Thomas Fuller 3:1546
James Shirley 3:1560
George Wither 3:1571
Jeremy Taylor 3:1585
Abraham Cowley 3:1598
Margaret Cavendish, Duchess of
   Newcastle 4:1649
Izaak Walton 4:1870
Charles Cotton 4:1914
John Bunyan 4:1921
Sir William Temple 4:1999
George Farquhar 4:2107
Gilbert Burnet 4:2140
Nahum Tate 4:2144
William Wycherley 4:2150
William Congreve 4:2278
Daniel Defoe 5:2310, 2312
John Dennis 5:2366
Alexander Pope 5:2419
Samuel Richardson 5:2692, 2694
William Cowper 6:3311
Joseph Priestley 6:3348
Richard Brinsley Sheridan 6:3429
Percy Bysshe Shelley 6:3568
William Blake 7:3695
Sir James Mackintosh 7:3824
Hannah More 7:3873
Samuel Taylor Coleridge 7:3895
Charles Lamb 7:3935
William Godwin 7:3999
Robert Southey 7:4085
Mary Lamb 7:4153, 4155
William Wordsworth 8:4302
Leigh Hunt 8:4550

James Sheridan Knowles 8:4663
Walter Savage Landor 8:4740
Bryan Waller Procter 9:4981, 4982

LAMB, JAMES J.
Robert Tannahill 6:3407

LAMB, MARY
Mary Lamb 7:4155

LANCASTER, H. H.
John Ruskin 10:5986

LANDON, LETITIA ELIZABETH
Felicia Dorothea Hemans 7:3981

LANDON, MELVILLE
Artemus Ward 8:4846

LANDOR, WALTER SAVAGE
Geoffrey Chaucer 1:64
John Milton 4:1704
Samuel Butler 4:1829
John Dryden 4:2013
Joseph Addison 4:2177
Daniel Defoe 5:2309
Richard Bentley 5:2394
Edward Young 5:2739, 2740, 2745
Thomas Gray 5:2826
Oliver Goldsmith 5:2886
David Hume 5:2926
John Wesley 6:3083
Edward Gibbon 6:3121
Robert Burns 6:3199
William Mason 6:3253
William Cowper 6:3310
Junius 6:3485
John Keats 6:3522
Percy Bysshe Shelley 6:3565
George Gordon, Lord Byron 7:3640
Felicia Dorothea Hemans 7:3984
Letitia Elizabeth Landon 7:4020
Robert Southey 7:4079, 4081, 4086
Mary Lamb 7:4155
Ebenezer Elliott 7:4213
Marguerite, Countess of Blessington
   7:4217
Margaret Fuller 8:4354
Thomas Moore 8:4421
Mary Russell Mitford 8:4468
Washington Irving 8:4529
Thomas Babington Macaulay
   8:4607
Elizabeth Barrett Browning 8:4637
Walter Savage Landor 8:4734
Elizabeth Gaskell 8:4797
Henry, Lord Brougham 8:4852
Charles Dickens 8:4882
Bryan Waller Procter 9:4982
Robert Browning 9:5493
Alfred, Lord Tennyson 10:5653
Aubrey De Vere 10:6077

LANE-POOLE, STANLEY
Sir Edwin Arnold 10:6187

LANG, ANDREW
Sir John Mandeville 1:38
Gavin Douglas 1:207
Henry Constable 1:528
George Chapman 3:1273
Robert Herrick 4:1658
Izaak Walton 4:1874, 1875

John Bunyan 4:1923
Samuel Pepys 4:2070
Matthew Prior 4:2210
Alexander Pope 5:2429
Henry Fielding 5:2602
Thomas Chatterton 5:2809
John Keats 6:3518
Ann Radcliffe 7:3611
Sydney Smith 7:4133
John Gibson Lockhart 8:4454
Charlotte Brontë 8:4479
Nathaniel Hawthorne 8:4770
Charles Lever 9:4934
Charles Kingsley 9:4999
John Forster 9:5014
Matthew Arnold 9:5458, 5459
Robert Browning 9:5496, 5502
Wilkie Collins 9:5539
Alfred, Lord Tennyson 10:5660
Edward Augustus Freeman 10:5727
Oliver Wendell Holmes 10:5774
Robert Louis Stevenson 10:5833
William Morris 10:5910
Lewis Carroll 10:5954
William Black 10:5963
Ernest Dowson 10:6043
Bret Harte 10:6109

LANG, L. B.
Samuel Richardson 5:2698

LANGBAINE, GERARD
Thomas Kyd 1:395
Beaumont and Fletcher 3:1045
William Rowley 3:1158
Thomas Middleton 3:1161
Thomas Dekker 3:1227
George Chapman 3:1271
John Webster 3:1282
Thomas Randolph 3:1313
Ben Jonson 3:1321
John Ford 3:1385
William Cartwright 3:1416, 1417
George Sandys 3:1420
Thomas Heywood 3:1490
Katherine Philips 3:1553
James Shirley 3:1560
Sir John Denham 3:1627
Margaret Cavendish, Duchess of
   Newcastle 4:1648
John Milton 4:1684
Thomas Otway 4:1887
Charles Cotton 4:1912
Aphra Behn 4:1937
Thomas Shadwell 4:1966
Nathaniel Lee 4:1970
John Dryden 4:2021
Sir Charles Sedley 4:2057
William Wycherley 4:2148
Thomas D'Urfey 4:2218
Elkanah Settle 4:2224

LANGFORD, JOHN ALFRED
Robert Southwell 1:398
John Donne 3:1204

LANGHORNE, JOHN
William Dunbar 1:221

LANGTON, BENNET
Thomas Gray 5:2827

LANGUET, HUBERT
　Sir Edward Dyer 1:518

LANIER, C. D.
　Walt Whitman 10:5707

LANIER, SIDNEY
　John Barbour 1:48
　William Langland 1:50
　Samuel Richardson 5:2687
　Laurence Sterne 5:2765
　Tobias Smollett 5:2842
　Erasmus Darwin 6:3334
　John Keats 6:3530
　Sir Walter Scott 7:3848
　Edward Bulwer-Lytton 9:4944
　Bayard Taylor 9:5058
　George Eliot 9:5081
　Sidney Lanier 9:5175
　Walt Whitman 10:5699, 5706
　William Morris 10:5909

LANSDOWNE, GEORGE GRANVILLE,
　　LORD
　Alexander Pope 5:2429, 2433

LAPLACE, PIERRE SIMON, MARQUIS DE
　Sir Isaac Newton 4:2249

LARCOM, LUCY
　Emily Dickinson 9:5417
　John Greenleaf Whittier 10:5633
　Oliver Wendell Holmes 10:5771

LATHROP, GEORGE PARSONS
　Henry Fielding 5:2602
　Thomas De Quincey 8:4582
　Nathaniel Hawthorne 8:4769, 4776
　George Eliot 9:5083

LATHROP, ROSE HAWTHORNE
　Henry David Thoreau 8:4666
　Amos Bronson Alcott 9:5450

LATROBE, JOHN H. B.
　Edgar Allan Poe 8:4251

LAUD, WILLIAM
　William Laud 3:1437

LAURENCE, FRENCH
　Edmund Burke 6:3258

LAVELEYE, EMILE DE
　Henry George 10:5929

LAW, ALICE
　William Cowper 6:3321
　Henry Kirke White 6:3358

LAWES, HENRY
　John Milton 4:1694

LAWLESS, EMILY
　Maria Edgeworth 7:4206

LAWRENCE, EUGENE
　Gilbert Burnet 4:2138
　Charles Wesley 6:3035
　John Wesley 6:3084
　William Robertson 6:3111

LAWRENCE, FREDERICK
　Colley Cibber 5:2632

LAWTON, WILLIAM CRANSTON
　Sidney Lanier 9:5182
　George Bancroft 10:5580

James Russell Lowell 10:5595
George William Curtis 10:5737
Francis Parkman 10:5757
Eugene Field 10:5876
Charles Dudley Warner 10:6013

LAZARUS, EMMA
　William Morris 10:5906

LAZARUS, JOSEPHINE
　Emma Lazarus 9:5446
　Louisa May Alcott 9:5487

LEAKE, FREDERIC
　John Wyclif 1:46

LEASK, W. KEITH
　James Boswell 6:3160

LEATHES, E. S.
　Lewis Carroll 10:5953, 5955

LE BAS, CHARLES WEBB
　John Wyclif 1:42

LECHLER, GOTTHARD
　John Wyclif 1:43
　William Langland 1:50

LECKY, W. E. H.
　Roger Bacon 1:30
　George Buchanan 1:315
　Richard Hooker 1:502
　Sir Francis Bacon 3:1121
　Jeremy Taylor 3:1582
　John Milton 4:1707
　Thomas Hobbes 4:1811
　John Locke 4:2079
　Anthony Ashley Cooper, Third Earl
　　of Shaftesbury 4:2128
　Gilbert Burnet 4:2138
　Jonathan Swift 5:2485
　Joseph Butler 5:2579
　Jonathan Edwards 5:2656
　Benjamin Franklin 6:3044
　Adam Smith 6:3067
　John Wesley 6:3082
　Mary Wollstonecraft 6:3282
　Thomas Paine 6:3385
　Junius 6:3487
　Henry Thomas Buckle 8:4698
　H. H. Milman 8:4859
　Charles Darwin 9:5274
　William Ewart Gladstone 10:5940,
　　5942

LE CLERC, JEAN
　John Locke 4:2077

LECONTE, JOSEPH
　Charles Darwin 9:5273

LEE, FREDERICK GEORGE
　John Wyclif 1:44
　John Foxe 1:356

LEE, GERALD STANLEY
　Harriet Beecher Stowe 10:5888

LEE, HARRIET
　William Godwin 7:3990

LEE, HENRY
　Fanny Kemble 10:5744

LEE, NATHANIEL
　Nathaniel Lee 4:1970

LEE, SIDNEY
　John Gower 1:169
　Sir Thomas Malory 1:188
　Sir Thomas Wyatt 1:265
　Sir Thomas Elyot 1:275
　Thomas, Lord Vaux 1:285
　Nicholas Udall 1:288
　Raphael Holinshed 1:313
　Thomas Watson 1:358
　Robert Southwell 1:397
　George Puttenham 1:498
　Thomas Sackville, Earl of Dorset
　　1:520
　Henry Constable 1:528
　Sir Thomas Overbury 1:530
　William Shakespeare 2:1010
　Samuel Daniel 3:1074
　Nicholas Breton 3:1100
　Fulke Greville, Lord Brooke 3:1174
　George Sandys 3:1421
　Edward Lord Herbert 3:1445
　Richard Crashaw 3:1467
　Lewis Theobald 5:2469

LEE, VERNON
　John Ford 3:1389

LEE-HAMILTON, EUGENE
　John Milton 4:1696

LEECHMAN, WILLIAM
　Francis Hutcheson 5:2522

LE GALLIENNE, RICHARD
　Michael Drayton 3:1190
　Thomas Carew 3:1399
　Richard Herrick 4:1659
　Arthur Henry Hallam 7:3879
　Sidney Lanier 9:5181
　Arthur O'Shaughnessy 9:5187
　Alfred, Lord Tennyson 10:5655
　John Addington Symonds 10:5765
　Christina Rossetti 10:5801
　Walter Pater 10:5817, 5827
　Oscar Wilde 10:6025

LELAND, CHARLES GODFREY
　Rufus Wilmot Griswold 8:4518
　Artemus Ward 8:4846
　Caroline Norton 9:5017
　George Eliot 9:5082
　George Borrow 9:5145

LELAND, JOHN
　John Gower 1:167
　Edward Lord Herbert 3:1444
　David Hume 5:2919

LE NEVE, PHILIP
　William Drummond 3:1450

LENTON, FRANCIS
　Ben Jonson 3:1318

LESLIE, CHARLES ROBERT
　Sir Walter Scott 7:3837
　Fanny Burney 7:4045
　Sydney Smith 7:4130
　Samuel Rogers 8:4459

LESLIE, T. E. CLIFFE
　Adam Smith 6:3058

LEVICK, MILNE B.
　Frank Norris 10:6135

John Gay 5:2339
Bernard Mandeville 5:2355
John Arbuthnot 5:2372, 2374
Thomas Tickell 5:2390
Richard Bentley 5:2393
Richard Savage 5:2408
Alexander Pope 5:2420
Jonathan Swift 5:2483
William Law 5:2675
Samuel Richardson 5:2694
Mark Akenside 5:2797
Philip Dormer Stanhope, Earl of
   Chesterfield 5:2875
Oliver Goldsmith 5:2893
David Hume 5:2918
David Garrick 6:2953
Samuel Johnson 6:2997, 3001
William Whitehead 6:3028
Edward Gibbon 6:3127
James Boswell 6:3161
James Macpherson 6:3183
Horace Walpole 6:3243
Edmund Burke 6:3259
Hugh Blair 6:3294
William Cowper 6:3322
Richard Porson 6:3376
Richard Brinsley Sheridan 6:3426,
   3431
Jane Austen 6:3449, 3456
Junius 6:3486
Matthew Gregory Lewis 6:3493
Hester Lynch Piozzi 6:3514
Percy Bysshe Shelley 6:3569
George Gordon, Lord Byron
   7:3647, 3652
Samuel Parr 7:3675
William Gifford 7:3686
Jeremy Bentham 7:3779
George Crabbe 7:3808
Sir James Mackintosh 7:3834
Sir Walter Scott 7:3838
Hannah More 7:3868
James Mill 7:4013
Fanny Burney 7:4049
Theodore Edward Hook 7:4054
Robert Southey 7:4090
Thomas Campbell 7:4111
Sydney Smith 7:4129
William Wordsworth 8:4303, 4314
Francis, Lord Jeffrey 8:4340, 4341
Samuel Rogers 8:4458, 4461
John Wilson Croker 8:4507
Henry Hallam 8:4520, 4521
Leigh Hunt 8:4550, 4554
William H. Prescott 8:4594
Thomas Babington Macaulay
   8:4604
Henry Thomas Buckle 8:4696
Thomas Love Peacock 8:4810
Henry, Lord Brougham 8:4851
H. H. Milman 8:4861
Charles Dickens 8:4892
Edward Bulwer-Lytton 9:4940
Thomas Carlyle 9:5113
Ralph Waldo Emerson 9:5195
Alfred, Lord Tennyson 10:5666
William Ewart Gladstone
   10:5941

MacCALL, WILLIAM
   Sir William Hamilton 8:4503

MacCALLUM, M. W.
   William Shakespeare 2:980

M'CARTHY, D. F.
   Richard Crashaw 3:1466

MacCARTHY, DESMOND
   Samuel Butler 10:6093, 6094

McCARTHY, JUSTIN
   Nicholas Rowe 4:2160
   Joseph Addison 4:2177
   Henry, Lord Brougham 8:4854
   Charles Dickens 8:4883
   George Grote 9:4911
   Charles Lever 9:4932
   Edward Bulwer-Lytton 9:4951
   John Stuart Mill 9:4960
   George Henry Lewes 9:5056
   George Eliot 9:5081, 5084
   George Borrow 9:5143
   Charles Darwin 9:5270
   Anthony Trollope 9:5283, 5286
   Charles Reade 9:5375
   Robert Browning 9:5496
   John Henry Newman 9:5552
   Alexander William Kinglake
      10:5587
   Edward Augustus Freeman 10:5727
   James Anthony Froude 10:5786
   Thomas Henry Huxley 10:5862
   William Morris 10:5909
   William Black 10:5963
   Harold Frederic 10:5972
   R. D. Blackmore 10:6006
   Herbert Spencer 10:6138, 6141
   W. E. H. Lecky 10:6162
   George Gissing 10:6179

McCLURG, A. C.
   Stephen Crane 10:6051

M'CORMICK, W. S.
   William Drummond 3:1455
   John Selden 3:1504

McCOSH, JAMES
   Francis Hutcheson 5:2522
   David Hume 5:2922
   James Burnett, Lord Monboddo
      6:3291
   James Beattie 6:3340
   Thomas Brown 6:3507
   Sir James Mackintosh 7:3828
   Thomas Chalmers 7:4160
   Sir William Hamilton 8:4503

McCULLOCH, HUGH
   Henry Ward Beecher 9:5430

MacCULLOCH, J. A.
   Walt Whitman 10:5705

MacCULLOCH, J. R.
   John Locke 4:2085
   David Ricardo 7:3622

MacDIARMID, JOHN
   Sir Thomas More 1:231

MacDONALD, GEORGE
   Henry Howard, Earl of Surrey
      1:279

Sir Philip Sidney 1:321
Robert Southwell 1:398
Sir Walter Ralegh 3:1067
Giles and Phineas Fletcher 3:1091
Sir John Davies 3:1145
Fulke Greville, Lord Brooke 3:1173
John Donne 3:1206
George Herbert 3:1257
William Drummond 3:1450
Richard Crashaw 3:1471
Robert Herrick 4:1657
John Milton 4:1692, 1705
Henry Vaughan 4:1978
Isaac Watts 5:2527
James Thomson 5:2533
John Byrom 5:2718
Charles Wesley 6:3034
H. H. Milman 8:4860

MacDONELL, G. P.
   Sir William Blackstone 6:2961
   Thomas Robert Malthus 7:3884

McDONOUGH, A. R.
   Richard Henry Stoddard 10:6154

McGILCHRIST, JOHN
   Richard Cobden 8:4793

MACHAR, AGNES MAULE
   Robert Burns 6:3204

MACHEN, ARTHUR
   Robert Louis Stevenson 10:5837

MACKAY, AENEAS
   George Buchanan 1:314

MacKAY, ANGUS M.
   Emily Brontë 7:4178, 4195
   Anne Brontë 8:4284
   Charlotte Brontë 8:4480

MACKAY, CHARLES
   Samuel Johnson 6:2995
   Robert Burns 6:3204
   Thomas Jefferson 7:3684
   William Harrison Ainsworth 9:5234

MACKENZIE, HENRY
   William Shakespeare 2:903
   Robert Burns 6:3195
   John Home 6:3369

MACKENZIE, R. SHELTON
   Laurence Sterne 5:2761
   John Gibson Lockhart 8:4454, 4455

MACKINNON, JAMES
   John Wyclif 1:45

MACKINTOSH, SIR JAMES
   Sir Thomas More 1:231, 237
   Thomas Hobbes 4:1817
   John Locke 4:2079, 2081
   Anthony Ashley Cooper, Third Earl
      of Shaftesbury 4:2128
   Nicholas Rowe 4:2160
   Francis Hutcheson 5:2519
   Joseph Butler 5:2579
   Henry Fielding 5:2600
   Jonathan Edwards 5:2650
   Samuel Richardson 5:2685
   Lady Mary Wortley Montagu
      5:2713

MARTIN, FRANCES
Dinah Maria Craik 9:5434

MARTIN, FREDERICK
John Clare 8:4757

MARTIN, HELENA FAUCIT
Robert Browning 9:5502

MARTIN, THEODORE
David Garrick 6:2956

MARTINEAU, HARRIET
Anna Laetitia Barbauld 7:3667
Thomas Robert Malthus 7:3882,
3883
James Hogg 7:3970
Felicia Dorothea Hemans 7:3984
William Godwin 7:3994
James Mill 7:4013
Letitia Elizabeth Landon 7:4020
Thomas Arnold 7:4069
Robert Southey 7:4082
William Beckford 7:4098
Thomas Campbell 7:4109
William Wordsworth 8:4307
Margaret Fuller 8:4355
Joanna Baillie 8:4364
John Wilson 8:4446
John Gibson Lockhart 8:4454
Samuel Rogers 8:4459
Mary Russell Mitford 8:4470, 4473
Charlotte Brontë 8:4477, 4485
Douglas Jerrold 8:4511
Henry Hallam 8:4520
Leigh Hunt 8:4551
Thomas De Quincey 8:4569
Thomas Babington Macaulay
8:4600, 4602
Elizabeth Barrett Browning 8:4635
Frances Trollope 8:4703
William Makepeace Thackeray
8:4709
Walter Savage Landor 8:4734
Catharine Maria Sedgwick 8:4830
N. P. Willis 8:4841
Henry, Lord Brougham 8:4851
Charles Dickens 8:4883
Edward Bulwer-Lytton 9:4941
William Lloyd Garrison 9:5073
Thomas Carlyle 9:5112, 5115
Richard Monckton Milnes, Lord
Houghton 9:5385
Robert Browning 9:5495

MARTINEAU, JAMES
Samuel Clarke 5:2306
Francis Hutcheson 5:2519
Joseph Priestley 6:3349
William Ellery Channing 7:4063
Sir William Hamilton 8:4502
John Stuart Mill 9:4960
Charles Kingsley 9:4989
Harriet Martineau 9:5004
Thomas Carlyle 9:5113
Ralph Waldo Emerson 9:5193

MARVELL, ANDREW
Richard Lovelace 3:1533
John Milton 4:1697, 1708
John Dryden 4:2006

MARX, KARL
Daniel Defoe 5:2320
Thomas Robert Malthus 7:3883

MARZIALS, FRANK T.
Wilkie Collins 9:5533

MASON, GEORGE
Samuel Johnson 6:2983

MASON, ROSALINE ORME
Hester Lynch Piozzi 6:3515

MASON, WILLIAM
David Hume 5:2915

MASSEY, GERALD
Mary Lamb 7:4154

MASSON, DAVID
Sir Thomas Malory 1:187
Sir Philip Sidney 1:324
Giles and Phineas Fletcher 3:1091
Richard Corbett 3:1311
Sir Henry Wotton 3:1351
Thomas Carew 3:1396
Sir John Suckling 3:1401
William Browne 3:1412
Francis Quarles 3:1426
William Laud 3:1438
Edward Lord Herbert 3:1445
William Drummond 3:1449, 1450,
1453
Richard Crashaw 3:1466
William Habington 3:1512
Joseph Hall 3:1521
John Milton 4:1695, 1700
John Bunyan 4:1923
Aphra Behn 4:1938
Daniel Defoe 5:2314
Jonathan Swift 5:2485
Samuel Richardson 5:2701
Laurence Sterne 5:2762
Thomas Chatterton 5:2808
Tobias Smollett 5:2841
Jane Austen 6:3450
John Keats 6:3519
Ann Radcliffe 7:3608
Caroline Oliphant, Baroness Nairne
7:4125
Thomas Hood 7:4139
John Wilson 8:4446
Douglas Jerrold 8:4511
Thomas De Quincey 8:4573
Henry Thomas Buckle 8:4696
William Makepeace Thackeray
8:4724
Charles Dickens 8:4882
Charles Kingsley 9:4993

MASTERMAN, J. HOWARD B.
John Ford 3:1388
Richard Crashaw 3:1467
Richard Lovelace 3:1535
John Cleveland 3:1539
Sir Kenelm Digby 3:1559
James Shirley 3:1562
Jeremy Taylor 3:1585
John Milton 4:1706
Henry Vaughan 4:1978

MASTERS, EDGAR LEE
Robert G. Ingersoll 10:5979

MATHER, COTTON
John Winthrop 3:1461
William Bradford 3:1529
Anne Bradstreet 3:1633

MATHER, FRANK JEWETT, JR.
Samuel Butler 10:6097

MATHEWS, WILLIAM
Sir Francis Bacon 3:1112
Thomas Jefferson 7:3678
Thomas Chalmers 7:4157

MATHIAS, THOMAS JAMES
John Dryden 4:2028
Laurence Sterne 5:2760
Tobias Smollett 5:2838
Sir William Jones 6:3145
James Burnett, Lord Monboddo
6:3290
William Cowper 6:3311
Joseph Priestley 6:3348
Richard Hurd 6:3366
Thomas Paine 6:3379
Matthew Gregory Lewis 6:3494
John Wolcot ("Peter Pindar")
6:3498
Ann Radcliffe 7:3605
Samuel Parr 7:3674
Robert Southey 7:4085

MATTHEW, F. D.
John Wyclif 1:43

MATTHEWS, BRANDER
Daniel Defoe 5:2316
Jonathan Edwards 5:2655
Benjamin Franklin 6:3048
Richard Brinsley Sheridan 6:3429,
3430
Joseph Rodman Drake 6:3512
Sir Walter Scott 7:3850
Charles Lamb 7:3954
Winthrop Mackworth Praed 7:4036
Edgar Allan Poe 8:4258
James Fenimore Cooper 8:4381
Henry David Thoreau 8:4673
William Gilmore Simms 8:4874
James Russell Lowell 10:5596
George William Curtis 10:5736
Frederick Locker-Lampson 10:5855
Harriet Beecher Stowe 10:5882
George du Maurier 10:5902

MAURICE, ARTHUR BARTLETT
R. D. Blackmore 10:6006

MAURICE, FREDERICK DENISON
William of Occam 1:34
Geoffrey Chaucer 1:64
Sir Thomas More 1:232
Richard Hooker 1:502
Sir Francis Bacon 3:1111
John Milton 4:1691
Richard Bentley 5:2396
Alexander Pope 5:2436
Henry St. John, Viscount
Bolingbroke 5:2565
Joseph Butler 5:2573
Jonathan Edwards 5:2654
Edward Gibbon 6:3130
William Cowper 6:3315

PIERCE, FRANKLIN
Nathaniel Hawthorne 8:4764

PILKINGTON, LAETITIA
Samuel Richardson 5:2682

PINERO, ARTHUR WING
Robert Louis Stevenson 10:5835

PINKERTON, JOHN
John Barbour 1:46
John Dryden 4:2027
James Thomson 5:2532
George Colman the Elder 6:3115
Horace Walpole 6:3233

PIOZZI, HESTER LYNCH
Daniel Defoe 5:2318
James Thomson 5:2531
Oliver Goldsmith 5:2883
Samuel Johnson 6:2979
Benjamin Franklin 6:3043
Sir Joshua Reynolds 6:3089
Elizabeth Montagu 6:3299
Fanny Burney 7:4039, 4045
Joanna Baillie 8:4365
Mary Shelley 8:4399

PLANCHÉ, J. R.
Thomas Hood 7:4138

PLARR, VICTOR
Gilbert White 6:3100
Ernest Dowson 10:6042

PLOWMAN, THOMAS F.
Oscar Wilde 10:6015

POE, EDGAR ALLAN
William Shakespeare 2:899
John Milton 4:1695, 1706
Andrew Marvell 4:1786
Daniel Defoe 5:2312
Edward Gibbon 6:3128
Joseph Rodman Drake 6:3510
Percy Bysshe Shelley 6:3570
Samuel Taylor Coleridge 7:3909
William Ellery Channing 7:4061
Robert Southey 7:4089
Washington Allston 7:4094
Thomas Hood 7:4138
Frederick Marryat 7:4169
Edgar Allan Poe 8:4248
Margaret Fuller 8:4357
James Fenimore Cooper 8:4377
Thomas Moore 8:4420
Rufus Wilmot Griswold 8:4516
Washington Irving 8:4527
Thomas Babington Macaulay
8:4601
G. P. R. James 8:4626
Elizabeth Barrett Browning 8:4637
Nathaniel Hawthorne 8:4766, 4772
Catharine Maria Sedgwick 8:4832
Fitz-Greene Halleck 8:4836
N. P. Willis 8:4841, 4844
William Gilmore Simms 8:4875
Charles Dickens 8:4889, 4890
Charles Lever 9:4934
Edward Bulwer-Lytton 9:4943
William Cullen Bryant 9:5051
Bayard Taylor 9:5059
Richard Henry Dana 9:5067

Thomas Carlyle 9:5113
Ralph Waldo Emerson 9:5195
Henry Wadsworth Longfellow
9:5243, 5244
Richard Henry Horne 9:5367
Edwin P. Whipple 9:5408
George Bancroft 10:5578
James Russell Lowell 10:5590, 5596
John Greenleaf Whittier 10:5634
Alfred, Lord Tennyson 10:5658

POLLARD, PERCIVAL
Kate Chopin 10:6209

POLLOCK, FREDERICK
John Milton 4:1693
John Locke 4:2092
George Henry Lewes 9:5057

POLLOCK, W. F.
Jane Austen 6:3467

POLLOCK, WALTER HERRIES
Anthony Trollope 9:5282

POLWHELE, JOHN
George Herbert 3:1247

POMFRET, LADY HENRIETTA
Lady Mary Wortley Montagu
5:2713

POND, JAMES BURTON
Sir Edwin Arnold 10:6186

POOLE, R. L.
John Scotus Erigena 1:18
Roger Bacon 1:30
Duns Scotus 1:33
William of Occam 1:34

POOLE, REGINALD STUART
Amelia B. Edwards 10:5740

POOR, HENRY V.
Adam Smith 6:3066

POPE, ALEXANDER
Geoffrey Chaucer 1:60
John Gower 1:168
John Skelton 1:213
Henry Howard, Earl of Surrey
1:277
Sir Philip Sidney 1:321
Edmund Spenser 1:416, 421
William Shakespeare 2:582, 666
Sir Francis Bacon 3:1108, 1111
George Chapman 3:1276
Sir John Suckling 3:1401
Francis Quarles 3:1425
Richard Crashaw 3:1465
George Wither 3:1570
Abraham Cowley 3:1595, 1596
Sir William D'Avenant 3:1612,
1616
Sir John Denham 3:1628
John Milton 4:1689, 1698
Samuel Butler 4:1827
John Oldham 4:1883
Thomas Otway 4:1887
Edmund Waller 4:1898
George Villiers, Duke of
Buckingham 4:1908
Aphra Behn 4:1937

Thomas Shadwell 4:1966
Sir William Temple 4:1996
John Dryden 4:2006, 2009, 2010,
2018, 2027
Sir Charles Sedley 4:2057
George Farquhar 4:2106
Thomas Sprat 4:2117
Thomas Rymer 4:2121
Nahum Tate 4:2143
William Wycherley 4:2148, 2149
Nicholas Rowe 4:2158, 2159
Thomas Parnell 4:2165
Sir Samuel Garth 4:2171
Joseph Addison 4:2176, 2183
John Hughes 4:2202
Matthew Prior 4:2205, 2208
Thomas D'Urfey 4:2218
Sir John Vanbrugh 4:2235
Sir Isaac Newton 4:2244, 2245
Sir Richard Blackmore 4:2262,
2263
William Congreve 4:2268
Daniel Defoe 5:2309
John Gay 5:2339, 2345
John Dennis 5:2364, 2365, 2368
John Arbuthnot 5:2370, 2374
Thomas Tickell 5:2389
Richard Bentley 5:2393, 2399
Richard Savage 5:2406
Alexander Pope 5:2417, 2418,
2433, 2434, 2440
Lewis Theobald 5:2467, 2469
Jonathan Swift 5:2477, 2480, 2489,
2491
Ambrose Philips 5:2549, 2550,
2551
Aaron Hill 5:2553, 2554
Henry St. John, Viscount
Bolingbroke 5:2559, 2560
George Berkeley 5:2585
Colley Cibber 5:2632, 2633
Lady Mary Wortley Montagu
5:2708, 2712
William Warburton 6:2946

PORCHER, FRANCES
Kate Chopin 10:6203

PORSON, RICHARD
Edward Gibbon 6:3126

PORTER, CHARLOTTE
Robert Browning 9:5501

PORTER, JANE
Thomas Chatterton 5:2807

PORTER, MARIA S.
Louisa May Alcott 9:5487

PORTER, NOAH
Sir Philip Sidney 1:329
Joseph Butler 5:2573
Nathaniel Hawthorne 8:4768
George Eliot 9:5088
Thomas Henry Huxley 10:5862

PORTER, WILLIAM T. (?)
Herman Melville 10:5606

PORTEUS, BEILBY
James Beattie 6:3338
Thomas Paine 6:3385

POSNETT, HUTCHESON MACAULAY
John Milton 4:1693

POTTER, JOHN
Colley Cibber 5:2636

POULTON, EDWARD B.
Thomas Henry Huxley 10:5864

POUND, EZRA
Lionel Johnson 10:6119

POWELL, E. P.
Benjamin Franklin 6:3045
Thomas Paine 6:3386

POWELL, F. Y.
Samuel R. Gardiner 10:6083

POWELL, THOMAS
Henry Vaughan 4:1974

POWELL, THOMAS
Edgar Allan Poe 8:4250
Margaret Fuller 8:4357
James Fenimore Cooper 8:4383
N. P. Willis 8:4842
Ralph Waldo Emerson 9:5196
Henry Wadsworth Longfellow
9:5245
Alfred, Lord Tennyson 10:5658

POWER, MISS
Marguerite, Countess of Blessington
7:4217

POWERS, HORATIO N.
William Cullen Bryant 9:5045

PRAED, WINTHROP MACKWORTH
John Keble 8:4827

PRESCOTT, WILLIAM H.
Charles Brockden Brown 6:3397
Ann Radcliffe 7:3608
George Gordon, Lord Byron 7:3640
Sir Walter Scott 7:3848
Maria Edgeworth 7:4201
Joanna Baillie 8:4366
John Gibson Lockhart 8:4454
Washington Irving 8:4536
Fitz-Greene Halleck 8:4836
H. H. Milman 8:4861
John Lothrop Motley 9:5023
William Cullen Bryant 9:5042
George Bancroft 10:5578

PRESTON, HARRIET WATERS
Robert Browning 9:5501
Margaret Oliphant 10:5926

PRESTON, MARGARET J.
John Keats 6:3531

PRESTON, MARY
William Shakespeare 2:762

PRÉVOST, ABBÉ
Samuel Richardson 5:2693

PRICE, WARWICK JAMES
Emily Dickinson 9:5419

PRIDEAUX, HUMPHREY
John Locke 4:2076

PRIESTLEY, JOSEPH
David Hume 5:2917

Joseph Priestley 6:3345
Thomas Paine 6:3386

PRIOR, SIR JAMES
James Boswell 6:3158

PRIOR, MATTHEW
Edmund Spenser 1:410, 419
Samuel Butler 4:1826
Matthew Prior 4:2205
Richard Bentley 5:2392

PROCTER, BRYAN WALLER
Charlotte Brontë 8:4485
Elizabeth Barrett Browning 8:4637
Nathaniel Hawthorne 8:4773

PRYME, ABRAHAM DE LA
Sir Isaac Newton 4:2242

PRYNNE, WILLIAM
Christopher Marlowe 1:365

PUFENDORF, SAMUEL
Sir Francis Bacon 3:1118

PURNEY, THOMAS
William Shakespeare 2:570

PURVES, JAMES
Sir Thomas Overbury 1:529

PUSHKIN, ALEXANDER
Laurence Sterne 5:2761

PUTNAM, JAMES O.
Charles Kingsley 9:4989

PUTTENHAM, GEORGE
William Langland 1:49
Geoffrey Chaucer 1:58
John Gower 1:167
John Lydgate 1:174
John Skelton 1:212
Sir Thomas Wyatt 1:263
Thomas, Lord Vaux 1:285
John Heywood 1:308
George Gascoigne 1:310
Sir Edward Dyer 1:518

PYE, HENRY JAMES
Thomas Warton 6:3074

PYM, JOHN
Sir Walter Ralegh 3:1064

PYNCHON, THOMAS RUGGLES
Joseph Butler 5:2576

QUARLES, FRANCIS
Giles and Phineas Fletcher 3:1087,
1088

QUEENSBURY, CATHERINE HYDE,
DUCHESS OF
John Gay 5:2339, 2344

QUILLER-COUCH, SIR ARTHUR T.
William Shakespeare 2:1034
Samuel Daniel 3:1074
William Browne 3:1410
John Milton 4:1705
Laurence Sterne 5:2763
Sir Walter Scott 7:3839
Charles Kingsley 9:4991
Richard Jefferies 9:5439
Alexander William Kinglake
10:5584

QUILLINAN, EDWARD
Arthur Hugh Clough 8:4649

QUILTER, HARRY
Dante Gabriel Rossetti 9:5316

QUINCY, EDMUND
Anna Laetitia Barbauld 7:3669

QUINCY, JOSIAH
William Ellery Channing 7:4059

QUINT, ALONZO H.
Cotton Mather 4:2256

RACKET, MRS.
Alexander Pope 5:2435

RADFORD, G. H.
William Shakespeare 2:778

RAE, W. FRASER
William Cowper 6:3318
Richard Brinsley Sheridan 6:3423
Junius 6:3483
George Crabbe 7:3811
Thomas Campbell 7:4116

RAGSDALE, JOHN
William Collins 5:2662

RALEGH, SIR WALTER
George Gascoigne 1:310
Sir Philip Sidney 1:331
Edmund Spenser 1:417
Sir Walter Ralegh 3:1064

RALEIGH, WALTER
Geoffrey Chaucer 1:164
Sir Thomas Malory 1:188
Sir Philip Sidney 1:345
Ben Jonson 3:1324
John Milton 4:1694
John Bunyan 4:1918
Aphra Behn 4:1940
Thomas Sprat 4:2118
Jonathan Swift 5:2493
Samuel Richardson 5:2697
Laurence Sterne 5:2766
Tobias Smollett 5:2858
Henry Brooke 6:2973
Samuel Johnson 6:2997
Robert Burns 6:3208
Horace Walpole 6:3238
Jane Austen 6:3475
Matthew Gregory Lewis 6:3495
Percy Bysshe Shelley 6:3574
Ann Radcliffe 7:3618
Charles Robert Maturin 7:3626
Henry Mackenzie 7:3766
William Cobbett 7:3965
William Godwin 7:3995
Fanny Burney 7:4043
William Beckford 7:4099
Robert Louis Stevenson 10:5835

RAMSAY, ALLAN
Matthew Prior 4:2207
Alexander Pope 5:2434

RAMSAY, CHEVALIER
Sir Isaac Newton 4:2244, 2245
Alexander Pope 5:2421

RAMSAY, H.
Ben Jonson 3:1319

RAMSAY, PHILIP A.
Robert Tannahill 6:3408

RANDOLPH, SARAH N.
Thomas Jefferson 7:3678

RANKE, LEOPOLD VON
Alfred the Great 1:20
Sir Francis Bacon 3:1115
Sir Edward Coke 3:1270
Edward Hyde, Earl of Clarendon
4:1757
Thomas Hobbes 4:1813
Thomas Babington Macaulay
8:4608

RANSOME, ARTHUR
Oscar Wilde 10:6039

RAUSCHENBUSCH-CLOUGH, EMMA
Mary Wollstonecraft 6:3280, 3283

RAVENSCROFT, EDWARD
William Shakespeare 2:875

RAWLEY, WILLIAM
Sir Francis Bacon 3:1122

RAWNSLEY, H. D.
Hartley Coleridge 7:4222
John Ruskin 10:5981

RAYNER, B. L.
Thomas Jefferson 7:3680

READ, W. B.
Thomas Paine 6:3382

READE, CHARLES
Charles Reade 9:5370

READE, CHARLES L.
George Eliot 9:5085
Wilkie Collins 9:5532

READE, COMPTON
George Eliot 9:5085
Wilkie Collins 9:5532

REDDING, CYRUS
John Wolcot ("Peter Pindar")
6:3499
William Beckford 7:4105
Thomas Campbell 7:4113
Sydney Owenson, Lady Morgan
8:4548
Leigh Hunt 8:4556

REDFIELD, J. S.
Rufus Wilmot Griswold 8:4518

REED, HENRY
John Milton 4:1705
Izaak Walton 4:1871

REES, THOMAS
Theodore Edward Hook 7:4054

REEVE, CLARA
Clara Reeve 6:3362

REICHEL, H. R.
Sir Thomas More 1:235, 236, 250

REID, FORREST
Ernest Dowson 10:6043

REID, STUART J.
Sydney Smith 7:4133
R. D. Blackmore 10:6005

REID, T. WEMYSS
Emily Brontë 7:4180
Charlotte Brontë 8:4489
Richard Monckton Milnes, Lord
Houghton 9:5384

REID, THOMAS
Joseph Butler 5:2578
David Hume 5:2919
Henry Home, Lord Kames 6:2967

REPPLIER, AGNES
Thomas Carew 3:1398
William Habington 3:1514
Robert Herrick 4:1655
Sir Charles Sedley 4:2058
Samuel Richardson 5:2689
William Cowper 6:3325
Fanny Burney 7:4046
Thomas Lovell Beddoes 7:4228
Mary Russell Mitford 8:4469
Elizabeth Barrett Browning 8:4635
Thomas Love Peacock 8:4814
George Borrow 9:5145
Edward FitzGerald 9:5354
William Black 10:5964
Oscar Wilde 10:6026

RESOLUTION OF CONGRESS
Thomas Paine 6:3380

REYNOLDS, HENRY
Edmund Spenser 1:418

REYNOLDS, JOHN
George Herbert 3:1243

REYNOLDS, JOHN HAMILTON
John Keats 6:3533

REYNOLDS, SIR JOSHUA
Samuel Johnson 6:2981

REYNOLDS, MYRA
Anne Finch, Countess of
Winchilsea 4:2200
James Thomson 5:2545
William Whitehead 6:3029
Thomas Warton 6:3074

RHODES, HARRISON
Lafcadio Hearn 10:6211

RHODES, JAMES FORD
Samuel R. Gardiner 10:6083

RHYS, ERNEST
Thomas Dekker 3:1227
Robert Herrick 4:1658
Thomas Chatterton 5:2804
Robert Burns 6:3207
Walt Whitman 10:5695

RHYS, JOHN
Sir Thomas Malory 1:188

RIBOT, THEODULE
Herbert Spencer 10:6140

RICARDO, DAVID
Adam Smith 6:3064

RICE, GEORGE EDWARD
Edmund Waller 4:1900

RICHARDS, C. A. L.
John Arbuthnot 5:2379
Richard William Church 10:5569
Benjamin Jowett 10:5748

RICHARDSON, CHARLES F.
John Winthrop 3:1460
William Bradford 3:1529
Roger Williams 4:1879
Cotton Mather 4:2257
Jonathan Edwards 5:2655
Benjamin Franklin 6:3051
Thomas Paine 6:3386
Joseph Rodman Drake 6:3511
Philip Freneau 7:3799
William Ellery Channing 7:4062
Margaret Fuller 8:4359
Henry David Thoreau 8:4671
Artemus Ward 8:4846
William Gilmore Simms 8:4874
William Cullen Bryant 9:5048
Bayard Taylor 9:5061
Josiah Gilbert Holland 9:5173
Sidney Lanier 9:5177
Ralph Waldo Emerson 9:5204
Helen Hunt Jackson 9:5393
Edwin P. Whipple 9:5409
James Russell Lowell 10:5592
Herman Melville 10:5607
John Greenleaf Whittier 10:5647
Walt Whitman 10:5699
George William Curtis 10:5736
Oliver Wendell Holmes 10:5779
Harriet Beecher Stowe 10:5879
Charles Dudley Warner 10:6012
Bret Harte 10:6109
Richard Henry Stoddard 10:6154

RICHARDSON, JONATHAN
John Milton 4:1685

RICHARDSON, SAMUEL
John Locke 4:2083
Nahum Tate 4:2143
Jonathan Swift 5:2478
Aaron Hill 5:2554
Henry Fielding 5:2598, 2606
Samuel Richardson 5:2682
Samuel Johnson 6:2992

RICHE, BARNABE (?)
Robert Greene 1:359

RICHMOND, JOHN
Thomas Chatterton 5:2814

RICKMAN, THOMAS CLIO
Thomas Paine 6:3387

RIDDELL, HENRY SCOTT
James Hogg 7:3969

RIDDELL, MARIA
Robert Burns 6:3191

RIETHMÜLLER, CHRISTOPHER JAMES
Thomas Jefferson 7:3681

RIGBY, ELIZABETH
Charlotte Brontë 8:4485

RILEY, JAMES WHITCOMB
Robert Burns 6:3206
Henry Wadsworth Longfellow
9:5249
Eugene Field 10:5874

RIMBAULT, EDWARD F.
Sir Thomas Overbury 1:529
Thomas D'Urfey 4:2217

ROSE, J. HOLLAND
Jeremy Bentham 7:3783

ROSEBERY, LORD
Robert Louis Stevenson 10:5834
William Ewart Gladstone 10:5938

ROSS, JOHN MERRY
Thomas of Erceldoune 1:31
John Barbour 1:48
Gavin Douglas 1:207

ROSSETTI, CHRISTINA
John Keats 6:3518
John Henry Newman 9:5552

ROSSETTI, DANTE GABRIEL
Thomas Chatterton 5:2804
Robert Burns 6:3194
John Keats 6:3518
Percy Bysshe Shelley 6:3572
William Blake 7:3697
George Crabbe 7:3810
Samuel Taylor Coleridge 7:3902
Emily Brontë 7:4180
Leigh Hunt 8:4551
Elizabeth Barrett Browning 8:4637
Sydney Dobell 9:4985
Robert Browning 9:5502
Edward Robert Bulwer Lytton
10:5625
Walt Whitman 10:5706
Coventry Patmore 10:5894
Aubrey De Vere 10:6077

ROSSETTI, LUCY MADOX
Mary Shelley 8:4410

ROSSETTI, WILLIAM MICHAEL
William Langland 1:50
Abraham Cowley 3:1597
Robert Herrick 4:1657
John Milton 4:1693
Samuel Butler 4:1830
John Dryden 4:2016
James Thomson 5:2534
Thomas Gray 5:2817
Oliver Goldsmith 5:2893
William Cowper 5:3317
John Keats 6:3526
George Gordon, Lord Byron 7:3641
Sir Walter Scott 7:3845
Felicia Dorothea Hemans 7:3985
Thomas Campbell 7:4114
Thomas Hood 7:4141
Thomas Moore 8:4421
Henry Wadsworth Longfellow
9:5246
Walt Whitman 10:5696, 5697
Christina Rossetti 10:5798, 5801

ROUND, J. H.
Edward Augustus Freeman 10:5728

ROUSSEAU, JEAN JACQUES
Daniel Defoe 5:2317
Samuel Richardson 5:2684

ROWE, NICHOLAS
William Shakespeare 2:536

ROWLANDSON, JAMES
Henry Vaughan 4:1974

ROWLEY, WILLIAM
John Webster 3:1286

ROWTON, FREDERIC
Letitia Elizabeth Landon 7:4022
Amelia Opie 8:4437
Elizabeth Barrett Browning 8:4634
Fanny Kemble 10:5743

ROYCE, JOSIAH
John Locke 4:2083
David Hume 5:2933
George Gordon, Lord Byron 7:3645
John Fiske 10:6074
Herbert Spencer 10:6139

ROYDON, MATTHEW
Sir Philip Sidney 1:334

RUDD, F. A.
Aubrey De Vere 10:6078

RUFFHEAD, OWEN
Edward Young 5:2738

RUSH, BENJAMIN
Benjamin Franklin 6:3036

RUSKIN, JOHN
Geoffrey Chaucer 1:65, 114
Sir Philip Sidney 1:327
Edmund Spenser 1:414, 423
Sir Francis Bacon 3:1109
George Herbert 3:1245
Samuel Johnson 6:2989
Sir Joshua Reynolds 6:3096
John Keats 6:3522, 3530
Sir Walter Scott 7:3852
Robert Southey 7:4078
Charles Dickens 8:4881
Robert Browning 9:5494
Alfred, Lord Tennyson 10:5658
Walt Whitman 10:5697
Coventry Patmore 10:5893
John Ruskin 10:5980

RUSSELL, ADDISON PEALE
Samuel Foote 5:2936

RUSSELL, CHARLES E.
Thomas Chatterton 5:2805

RUSSELL, E. S.
Samuel Butler 10:6098

RUSSELL, LORD JOHN
Edmund Burke 6:3261
Henry, Lord Brougham 8:4854

RUSSELL, PERCY
William Carleton 8:4867

RUSSELL, TOM
Richard Savage 5:2414

RUSSELL, WILLIAM CLARK
Ambrose Philips 5:2549
Frederick Marryat 7:4172
Emily Brontë 7:4180
Richard Henry Dana, Jr. 9:5309
Herman Melville 10:5607

RUTHERFORD, MILDRED
Dinah Maria Craik 9:5435

RUTHRAUFF, C. C.
Artemus Ward 8:4846

RYMER, THOMAS
Edmund Spenser 1:419
Thomas Sackville, Earl of Dorset
1:521

William Shakespeare 2:889, 927
Sir William D'Avenant 3:1615
John Milton 4:1697
John Wilmot, Earl of Rochester
4:1843
Edmund Waller 4:1898

S., I. M.
William Shakespeare 2:565

SACKVILLE-WEST, REGINALD W.
Thomas Sackville 1:519

SAINTE-BEUVE, C. A.
Philip Dormer Stanhope, Earl of
Chesterfield 5:2878
Benjamin Franklin 6:3129
Edward Gibbon 6:3129

SAINTSBURY, GEORGE
Beowulf 1:4
Richard Rolle of Hampole 1:35
Sir John Mandeville 1:38
William Langland 1:51
Geoffrey Chaucer 1:67
William Caxton 1:185
Sir Thomas Malory 1:189
Gavin Douglas 1:208
Sir Thomas More 1:235, 236
Sir Thomas Wyatt 1:264, 266
Sir Thomas Elyot 1:276
Henry Howard, Earl of Surrey
1:279
Alexander Barclay 1:283
Nicholas Udall 1:288
Roger Ascham 1:291, 292
John Heywood 1:309
George Gascoigne 1:311, 312
George Buchanan 1:316
Sir Philip Sidney 1:323, 328, 330
Thomas Watson 1:358
Robert Greene 1:359, 361
Christopher Marlowe 1:369
Thomas Kyd 1:395
George Peele 1:399
George Puttenham 1:499
Richard Hooker 1:504
Thomas Nashe 1:508
John Lyly 1:513
Sir Edward Dyer 1:519
Thomas Sackville, Earl of Dorset
1:521
William Warner 1:524
Barnabe Barnes 1:525
George Turberville 1:526
Henry Constable 1:528
William Shakespeare 2:637, 652,
1010, 1013
Beaumont and Fletcher 3:1052
Sir Walter Ralegh 3:1070
Samuel Daniel 3:1073
Thomas Campion 3:1081
Thomas Lodge 3:1095
Nicholas Breton 3:1100
Sir Francis Bacon 3:1114, 1117
Sir John Davies 3:1144
Cyril Tourneur 3:1150
Thomas Middleton 3:1164
Fulke Greville, Lord Brooke 3:1174
Gabriel Harvey 3:1178
Michael Drayton 3:1187

SHARP, WILLIAM
Ebenezer Elliott 7:4214
Hartley Coleridge 7:4222
Thomas De Quincey 8:4574
Elizabeth Barrett Browning 8:4635
Dante Gabriel Rossetti 9:5320
James Thomson 9:5337
Richard Henry Horne 9:5368
John Addington Symonds 10:5763
Walter Pater 10:5817
William Morris 10:5911
W. E. H. Lecky 10:6164

SHARPE, JOHN
William of Malmesbury 1:25

SHAW, CUTHBERT
David Mallet 5:2755
Tobias Smollett 5:2836
Samuel Johnson 6:2976

SHAW, GEORGE BERNARD
Christopher Marlowe 1:392
William Shakespeare 2:636
John Bunyan 4:1924
William Morris 10:5905
Oscar Wilde 10:6029
Samuel Butler 10:6094, 6098

SHAW, PETER
Robert Boyle 4:1954

SHAW, THOMAS B.
John Webster 3:1283
Lewis Theobald 5:2468
William Collins 5:2664
Samuel Taylor Coleridge 7:3906
William Beckford 7:4099
Frederick Marryat 7:4170
G. P. R. James 8:4626
William Harrison Ainsworth 9:5233

SHEFFIELD, EARL OF
Edward Gibbon 6:3133

SHEFFIELD, JOHN, LORD
Edward Gibbon 6:3131

SHELLEY, MARY
Mary Wollstonecraft 6:3278
Percy Bysshe Shelley 6:3563, 3578
Mary Shelley 8:4397

SHELLEY, PERCY BYSSHE
Sir Philip Sidney 1:320
William Shakespeare 2:947
John Milton 4:1690, 1699
Mary Wollstonecraft 6:3279
John Keats 6:3517, 3528, 3529, 3540
George Gordon, Lord Byron 7:3638
Samuel Taylor Coleridge 7:3899
William Godwin 7:3991, 3993
William Wordsworth 8:4303
Mary Shelley 8:4401
Leigh Hunt 8:4549
Thomas Love Peacock 8:4812, 4813

SHELLEY, SIR TIMOTHY
Mary Shelley 8:4397

SHELTON, F. W.
James Boswell 6:3150

SHENSTONE, WILLIAM
James Thomson 5:2531
Samuel Johnson 6:2993

SHEPHERD, HENRY E.
John Evelyn 4:2099
Richard Bentley 5:2397
Sidney Lanier 9:5182

SHEPPARD, SAMUEL
John Webster 3:1282

SHERARD, ROBERT H.
Oscar Wilde 10:6032

SHERIDAN, RICHARD BRINSLEY
Richard Savage 5:2407
David Garrick 6:2956
Richard Cumberland 6:3410
Richard Brinsley Sheridan 6:3422

SHERWIN, W. T.
Thomas Paine 6:3381

SHERWOOD, M. E. W.
Margaret Fuller 8:4356
William H. Prescott 8:4590
William Makepeace Thackeray 8:4719
George Bancroft 10:5580
James Russell Lowell 10:5590
Bret Harte 10:6107

SHIRLEY, JAMES
John Fletcher 3:1041
Beaumont and Fletcher 3:1045
John Ford 3:1390

SHIRLEY, JOHN
Geoffrey Chaucer 1:55

SHORTER, CLEMENT K.
Emily Brontë 7:4181, 4183
Anne Brontë 8:4284
Charlotte Brontë 8:4477
Elizabeth Gaskell 8:4799

SHUCKBURGH, E. S.
Fanny Burney 7:4049

SICHEL, EDITH
Charlotte Mary Yonge 10:6069

SICHEL, WALTER
John Evelyn 4:2101
Sir Richard Steele 4:2294
Daniel Defoe 5:2317
John Arbuthnot 5:2373

SIDGWICK, HENRY
Thomas Hobbes 3:1823
Samuel Clarke 5:2304
Bernard Mandeville 5:2356
Adam Smith 6:3067
Jeremy Bentham 7:3795
John Stuart Mill 9:4961
Matthew Arnold 9:5465

SIDNEY, SIR PHILIP
Geoffrey Chaucer 1:57
Henry Howard, Earl of Surrey 1:277
Edmund Spenser 1:416
Thomas Sackville, Earl of Dorset 1:521

SIGMOND, GEORGE GABRIEL
Richard Brinsley Sheridan 6:3435

SIGOURNEY, LYDIA HOWARD HUNTLEY
Felicia Dorothea Hemans 7:3982
Maria Edgeworth 8:4200

SILLARD, P. A.
James Boswell 6:3153
John Wilson Croker 8:4507

SIMCOX, EDITH
Edward Bulwer-Lytton 9:4953

SIMCOX, GEORGE AUGUSTUS
George Herbert 3:1245
George Sandys 3:1420
Richard Crashaw 3:1467
Henry Vaughan 4:1978
Henry Thomas Buckle 8:4697
John Keble 8:4825
Samuel Wilberforce 9:4956
Bryan Waller Procter 9:4983
Charles Kingsley 9:4990, 4994
William Cullen Bryant 9:5045
James Thomson 9:5338

SIMMS, WILLIAM GILMORE
James Fenimore Cooper 8:4384
Fitz-Greene Halleck 8:4834
William Gilmore Simms 8:4871

SIMON, T. COLLYNS
George Berkeley 5:2590

SIMONDS, ARTHUR B.
Fitz-Greene Halleck 8:4835
Alice and Phoebe Cary 9:4921

SIMONDS, WILLIAM EDWARD
Laurence Sterne 5:2764
William Beckford 7:4100

SIMPKINSON, C. H.
William Laud 3:1439

SINCLAIR, MAY
Samuel Butler 10:6099

SINGLETON, ROY
Sir William Blackstone 6:2960

SKEAT, WALTER W.
William Langland 1:50, 53
Thomas Chatterton 5:2809

SKELTON, JOHN (C. 1460-1529)
Geoffrey Chaucer 1:68
John Lydgate 1:174

SKELTON, JOHN (1831-1897)
John Knox 1:300
Charlotte Brontë 8:4488
Benjamin Disraeli 9:5160
William Morris 10:5906

SLADEN, DOUGLAS B. W.
Adam Smith 6:3067
Sidney Lanier 9:5177
Helen Hunt Jackson 9:5394

SLATER, GERTRUDE
Margaret Oliphant 10:5927

SLOANE, WILLIAM M.
George Bancroft 10:5579

SMALLEY, GEORGE W.
John Henry Newman 9:5556
Benjamin Jowett 10:5747
James Anthony Froude 10:5787
Thomas Henry Huxley 10:5865

SMART, CHRISTOPHER
William Shakespeare 2:925
Henry Fielding 5:2598

SMEATON, OLIPHANT
Allan Ramsay 5:2643
Tobias Smollett 5:2860

SMELLIE, WILLIAM
Adam Smith 6:3056

SMETHAM, JAMES
Sir Joshua Reynolds 6:3096
William Blake 7:3697

SMILES, SAMUEL
Thomas Arnold 7:4069
George Borrow 9:5143, 5147

SMITH, ADAM
Thomas Hobbes 4:1809
Bernard Mandeville 5:2359
Alexander Pope 5:2435
Francis Hutcheson 5:2519
Thomas Gray 5:2827
David Hume 5:2914
Samuel Johnson 6:2994
Adam Smith 6:3064
Edward Gibbon 6:3125

SMITH, ALEXANDER
William Dunbar 1:222
Sir Francis Bacon 3:1115
John Bunyan 4:1917
James Boswell 6:3158
Ebenezer Elliott 7:4213
Nathaniel Hawthorne 8:4767
Charles Dickens 8:4882
Sydney Dobell 9:4985
Wilkie Collins 9:5531

SMITH, C. C.
Isaac D'Israeli 7:4163
Henry Hallam 8:4522

SMITH, E. V.
Charles Reade 9:5374

SMITH, EDWARD
William Cobbett 7:3962

SMITH, FREDERICK M.
Henry David Thoreau 8:4691

SMITH, G. GREGORY
John Richard Green 9:5364
Edward Augustus Freeman 10:5730

SMITH, GEORGE BARNETT
William Tyndale 1:253
Sir John Suckling 3:1405
James Shirley 3:1562
Robert Herrick 4:1657
Edmund Waller 4:1901
Matthew Prior 4:2209
Samuel Richardson 5:2686
Tobias Smollett 5:2853
Charles Brockden Brown 6:3399
Richard Cumberland 6:3411
Jane Austen 6:3452
Lady Caroline Lamb 7:3736
Winthrop Mackworth Praed 7:4036
John Hookham Frere 7:4150
Emily Brontë 7:4184
Elizabeth Gaskell 8:4801
Thomas Love Peacock 8:4815
William Carleton 8:4869
Helen Hunt Jackson 9:5394

James Russell Lowell 10:5591
Frederick Locker-Lampson 10:5855
R. D. Blackmore 10:6007

SMITH, SIR GEORGE MURRAY
Charlotte Brontë 8:4481
Leigh Hunt 8:4552

SMITH, GOLDWIN
Andrew Marvell 4:1787
Jane Austen 6:3470
William Hayley 6:3504
Maria Edgeworth 7:4204
Mary Russell Mitford 8:4470

SMITH, HENRY JUSTIN
William Blake 7:3725

SMITH, HORACE
Thomas Campbell 7:4111

SMITH, JAMES
George Colman the Younger
7:4007

SMITH, SYDNEY
Horace Walpole 6:3239
Hugh Blair 6:3294
Thomas Brown 6:3507
George Gordon, Lord Byron 7:3631
Samuel Parr 7:3674
Dugald Stewart 7:3731, 3732
Sir James Mackintosh 7:3824
Sir Walter Scott 7:3852
Hannah More 7:3873
Thomas Robert Malthus 7:3882
John Galt 7:4025
William Ellery Channing 7:4061
Maria Edgeworth 7:4200
William Wordsworth 8:4303
Samuel Rogers 8:4458
George Grote 9:4909
Richard Monckton Milnes, Lord
Houghton 9:5384
Fanny Kemble 10:5743

SMITH, WILLIAM
Robert Southey 7:4087

SMITHES, SIR THOMAS
Sir Philip Sidney 1:320

SMOLLETT, TOBIAS
Sir Samuel Garth 4:2172
Henry Fielding 5:2596
Lady Mary Wortley Montagu
5:2713
Charles Churchill 5:2732
Philip Dormer Stanhope, Earl of
Chesterfield 5:2875
David Hume 5:2914
Samuel Johnson 6:2975

SMYTH, ALBERT H.
Bayard Taylor 9:5062

SMYTH, JAMES MOORE
John Arbuthnot 5:2372

SMYTH, WILLIAM
Richard Hakluyt 1:531
Gilbert Burnet 4:2137
Sir William Blackstone 6:2959
William Robertson 6:3112
Horace Walpole 6:3235

John Home 6:3370
Thomas Paine 6:3385
Sir James Mackintosh 7:3826
Henry Hallam 8:4521

SNEATH, E. HERSHEY
Sir John Davies 3:1147

SNELL, F. J.
John Gower 1:170
Charles Wesley 6:3036
John Wesley 6:3083

SNELLING, W. J.
William Cullen Bryant 9:5041

SNIDER, DENTON J.
William Shakespeare 2:796, 849

SOAMES, HENRY
Ælfric 1:24

SOMERSET, FRANCES THYNNE
HERTFORD, DUCHESS OF
Henry Fielding 5:2598
Lady Mary Wortley Montagu
5:2709

SOMERVILLE, WILLIAM
Alexander Pope 5:2436
Allan Ramsay 5:2640

SOMMERS, THOMAS
Robert Fergusson 5:2908

SOTHERAN, CHARLES
Horace Greeley 9:4938

SOUTHERN, H.
Sir Thomas Urquhart 3:1541

SOUTHERNE, THOMAS
Aphra Behn 4:1937

SOUTHEY, CHARLES CUTHBERT
Robert Southey 7:4078

SOUTHEY, ROBERT
John Skelton 1:214
Sir Philip Sidney 1:320, 321
Thomas Sackville, Earl of Dorset
1:520
Samuel Daniel 3:1072
Michael Drayton 3:1186
John Donne 3:1197
Robert Herrick 4:1657
John Milton 4:1690, 1695, 1696
Edward Hyde, Earl of Clarendon
4:1754
Roger Williams 4:1878
John Bunyan 4:1921
John Evelyn 4:2101
Gilbert Burnet 4:2140
Cotton Mather 4:2257
Sir Richard Blackmore 4:2264
Isaac Watts 5:2527
Joseph Butler 5:2571
Henry Fielding 5:2600
William Law 5:2675
John Byrom 5:2718
Charles Churchill 5:2728
Thomas Chatterton 5:2803, 2806
Christopher Smart 5:2866
Philip Dormer Stanhope, Earl of
Chesterfield 5:2878

William Warburton 6:2942
John Wesley 6:3083
William Robertson 6:3112
William Mason 6:3252
Edmund Burke 6:3258
Mary Wollstonecraft 6:3278
William Cowper 6:3322
Joseph Priestley 6:3345
Henry Kirke White 6:3356
Timothy Dwight 6:3443
William Hayley 6:3503, 3504
George Gordon, Lord Byron
7:3638, 3646
Anna Laetitia Barbauld 7:3670
Hannah More 7:3868
Thomas Robert Malthus 7:3882
Charles Lamb 7:3937, 3940
William Godwin 7:3996
Robert Southey 7:4087
Washington Allston 7:4094
John Hookham Frere 7:4148
Isaac D'Israeli 7:4162
Hartley Coleridge 7:4220
William Lisle Bowles 8:4293
William Wordsworth 8:4297, 4302,
4313
James Montgomery 8:4439
Charlotte Brontë 8:4476
Henry Hallam 8:4521
Thomas De Quincey 8:4568
Walter Savage Landor 8:4732, 4740
John Clare 8:4760
H. H. Milman 8:4859
Sir Henry Taylor 9:5397

SOUTHWORTH, GEORGE C. S.
George Gascoigne 1:311

SPALDING, DOUGLAS A.
George Henry Lewes 9:5056

SPALDING, JOHN LANCASTER
John Greenleaf Whittier 10:5636

SPALDING, WILLIAM
John Barbour 1:47
Lancelot Andrewes 3:1102
Francis Hutcheson 5:2521
Mark Akenside 5:2797
Edward Bulwer-Lytton 9:4949

SPARKS, JARED
Benjamin Franklin 6:3039, 3043
Noah Webster 7:4074

SPEDDING, JAMES
William Shakespeare 2:727
Sir Walter Ralegh 3:1066
Sir Francis Bacon 3:1109, 1117
Hartley Coleridge 7:4221
Charles Dickens 8:4892
Charles Tennyson Turner 9:5077

SPEGHT, THOMAS
Geoffrey Chaucer 1:71

SPENCE, J. (?)
John Donne 3:1200

SPENCE, JOSEPH
Edmund Spenser 1:411
Isaac Newton 4:2244
Alexander Pope 5:2433

SPENCER, HERBERT
Henry George 10:5931

SPENDER, A. EDMUND
William Cowper 6:3321

SPENSER, EDMUND
Geoffrey Chaucer 1:57, 58, 59
Sir Philip Sidney 1:318, 331
Thomas Watson 1:357
Thomas Sackville, Earl of Dorset
1:520
Sir Walter Ralegh 3:1067, 1068
Samuel Daniel 3:1071
William Camden 3:1084
Gabriel Harvey 3:1176

SPINGARN, JOEL ELIAS
Roger Ascham 1:291
Sir Philip Sidney 1:350

SPOFFORD, HARRIET PRESCOTT
Charles Reade 9:5371
Amos Bronson Alcott 9:5450
Louisa May Alcott 9:5486
John Greenleaf Whittier 10:5643

SPOTTISWOOD, JOHN
Thomas of Erceldoune 1:31
George Buchanan 1:315

SPRAT, THOMAS
Sir Francis Bacon 3:1108, 1118
Abraham Cowley 3:1599

SQUIRE, J. C.
Samuel Butler 10:6100

STAËL, MADAME DE
Henry Fielding 5:2607
Edward Young 5:2739

STAFFORD, ANTHONY
Sir Philip Sidney 1:319

STANLEY, ARTHUR PENRHYN
Richard Hooker 1:500
Lancelot Andrewes 3:1103
Ben Jonson 3:1318
Richard Baxter 4:1946
Charles Wesley 6:3035
John Wesley 6:3085
Hugh Blair 6:3294
Thomas Arnold 7:4068
John Keble 8:4825
H. H. Milman 8:4858, 4859
William Ewart Gladstone 10:5936

STANLEY, HIRAM M.
Jane Austen 6:3476

STANLEY, THOMAS
Sir John Suckling 3:1399

STANTON, ELIZABETH CADY
William Lloyd Garrison 9:5075

STAPFER, PAUL
Sir Philip Sidney 1:329
Thomas Sackville, Earl of Dorset
1:522
William Shakespeare 2:702

STATHAM, F. REGINALD
Arthur Hugh Clough 8:4655

STEBBING, WILLIAM
Sir Walter Ralegh 3:1069
Tobias Smollett 5:2842

STEDMAN, EDMUND CLARENCE
Sir Philip Sidney 1:329
William Shakespeare 2:1005
John Milton 4:1702
Joseph Rodman Drake 6:3510
John Trumbull 7:3773
Thomas Hood 7:4141
Edgar Allan Poe 8:4269
Arthur Hugh Clough 8:4653
Walter Savage Landor 8:4742
Nathaniel Hawthorne 8:4769
Fitz-Greene Halleck 8:4835
Horace Greeley 9:4937
Bryan Waller Procter 9:4983
Charles Kingsley 9:4992
William Cullen Bryant 9:5040,
5047
Bayard Taylor 9:5063
George Eliot 9:5083
Josiah Gilbert Holland 9:5173
Sidney Lanier 9:5176, 5178
Arthur O'Shaughnessy 9:5187
Ralph Waldo Emerson 9:5213
Dante Gabriel Rossetti 9:5319
James Thomson 9:5338
Richard Henry Horne 9:5368
Richard Monckton Milnes, Lord
Houghton 9:5385
Helen Hunt Jackson 9:5393
Sir Henry Taylor 9:5398
Emma Lazarus 9:5446
Robert Browning 9:5495
William Allingham 9:5527
James Russell Lowell 10:5592
Edward Robert Bulwer Lytton
10:5626
John Greenleaf Whittier 10:5638
Alfred, Lord Tennyson 10:5666
Walt Whitman 10:5695, 5710
Oliver Wendell Holmes 10:5772
Coventry Patmore 10:5891
Francis Turner Palgrave 10:5920
Charles Dudley Warner 10:6013
Bret Harte 10:6108
Richard Henry Stoddard 10:6153
Sir Edwin Arnold 10:6188

STEELE, MARY DAVIES
John Evelyn 4:2103

STEELE, SIR RICHARD
Sir John Mandeville 1:36
Edmund Spenser 1:421
William Shakespeare 2:826, 839
Sir George Etherege 4:1959
William Wycherley 4:2148
Sir Samuel Garth 4:2171
John Hughes 4:2202
Thomas D'Urfey 4:2218
William Congreve 4:2278
Sir Richard Steele 4:2291, 2295
John Dennis 5:2368

STEEVENS, GEORGE
Samuel Johnson 6:2978

STENDHAL
Sir Walter Scott 7:3847

STEPHEN, SIR JAMES
Richard Baxter 4:1945

James Hogg 7:3972
Thomas Campbell 7:4116
Ebenezer Elliott 7:4214
Hartley Coleridge 7:4222
Thomas Lovell Beddoes 7:4229
John Clare 8:4759
Thomas Love Peacock 8:4811
Fitz-Greene Halleck 8:4836
Bayard Taylor 9:5061
Richard Henry Dana 9:5070
Edward FitzGerald 9:5350
Richard Monckton Milnes, Lord
  Houghton 9:5386, 5388
Herman Melville 10:5608
John Greenleaf Whittier 10:5636,
  5637
Oliver Wendell Holmes 10:5776
Sir Edwin Arnold 10:6189

STOKES, FREDERICK A.
Sir John Suckling 3:1403

STOPES, CHARLOTTE CARMICHAEL
William Shakespeare 2:758

STOROJENKO, NICHOLAS
Robert Greene 1:361

STORY, ALFRED T.
William Blake 7:3722

STORY, JOSEPH
Sir William Jones 6:3145
Robert Southey 7:4079
Washington Irving 8:4535
James Russell Lowell 10:5590

STORY, WILLIAM WETMORE
Sir Walter Scott 7:3853

STOWE, CHARLES EDWARD
William Lloyd Garrison 9:5074

STOWE, HARRIET BEECHER
Jonathan Edwards 5:2651
Horace Greeley 9:4938
Charles Kingsley 9:4988
George Eliot 9:5091
Henry Ward Beecher 9:5428
James Russell Lowell 10:5592
Harriet Beecher Stowe 10:5881

STRACHEY, JOHN ST. LOE
John Gay 5:2342
Herman Melville 10:5608

STRACHEY, LYTTON
William Shakespeare 2:646
Samuel Johnson 6:3001

STRAHAN, ANDREW
William Robertson 6:3110

STREET, G. S.
George Villiers, Duke of
  Buckingham 4:1910
Robert Boyle 4:1955
Sir George Etherege 4:1958
Horace Walpole 6:3241
Richard Brinsley Sheridan 6:3440

STRONG, AUGUSTUS HOPKINS
John Milton 4:1703

STRONG, THOMAS BANKS
Lewis Carroll 10:5958

STRYPE, JOHN
John Foxe 1:356

STUART, LADY LOUISA
George Lillo 5:2385
Henry Fielding 5:2597
Lady Mary Wortley Montagu
  5:2713
Horace Walpole 6:3234

STUBBE, HENRY
Sir Francis Bacon 3:1110

STUBBES, PHILIP
John Foxe 1:355

STUBBS, CHARLES WILLIAM
Charles Kingsley 9:4995

STUBBS, WILLIAM
John Wyclif 1:43

SUCKLING, ALFRED
Sir John Suckling 3:1403

SUCKLING, SIR JOHN
Ben Jonson 3:1316
Thomas Carew 3:1395
Sir John Suckling 3:1399
John Hales 3:1522
Sir William D'Avenant 3:1610,
  1612

SULLIVAN, MARGARET F.
Sir Walter Ralegh 3:1066

SULLY, JAMES
George Henry Lewes 9:5057

SULZBERGER, CYRUS L.
Emma Lazarus 9:5445

SUMNER, CHARLES
William Ellery Channing 7:4061
Washington Allston 7:4094
Thomas De Quincey 8:4568
William H. Prescott 8:4590
Nathaniel Hawthorne 8:4767
Richard Cobden 8:4793
Bryan Waller Procter 9:4980
Caroline Norton 9:5016
Thomas Carlyle 9:5110
Ralph Waldo Emerson 9:5191
Henry Wadsworth Longfellow
  9:5241

SURREY, HENRY HOWARD, EARL OF
Sir Thomas Wyatt 1:261

SWEAT, MARGARET
Anne Brontë 8:4286

SWIFT, DEANE
Jonathan Swift 5:2479

SWIFT, JONATHAN
Sir Thomas More 1:231
John Milton 4:1697
John Bunyan 4:1921
Robert Boyle 4:1953
John Dryden 4:2009, 2027, 2031
Gilbert Burnet 4:2139
Nahum Tate 4:2143
Joseph Addison 4:2175
John Hughes 4:2202
Sir John Vanbrugh 4:2237
Sir Isaac Newton 4:2245

William Congreve 4:2268, 2279
Sir Richard Steele 4:2289
Daniel Defoe 5:2308
John Gay 5:2338, 2339
John Arbuthnot 5:2370
Richard Bentley 5:2393, 2399
Alexander Pope 5:2418, 2421, 2433
Jonathan Swift 5:2477, 2495
Ambrose Philips 5:2549
Henry St. John, Viscount
  Bolingbroke 5:2558
George Berkeley 5:2584, 2585
Edward Young 5:2737

SWIGGETT, GLEN LEVIN
Sidney Lanier 9:5182

SWINBURNE, ALGERNON CHARLES
Geoffrey Chaucer 1:65, 134
Sir Philip Sidney 1:352
Christopher Marlowe 1:380
George Peele 1:399
William Shakespeare 2:577, 871
Francis Beaumont 3:1040
Beaumont and Fletcher 3:1052,
  1059
Thomas Lodge 3:1095
Cyril Tourneur 3:1153
William Rowley 3:1160
Thomas Middleton 3:1163
Thomas Dekker 3:1226, 1231
George Chapman 3:1273
John Webster 3:1284, 1286, 1288
John Marston 3:1303
Thomas Randolph 3:1314
Ben Jonson 3:1324, 1332
John Ford 3:1390
Sir John Suckling 3:1403
Thomas Heywood 3:1491, 1495
James Shirley 3:1561, 1565
Robert Herrick 4:1670
John Wilmot, Earl of Rochester
  4:1846
Aphra Behn 4:1940
William Congreve 4:2273
William Collins 5:2672
Lady Mary Wortley Montagu
  5:2710
Robert Burns 6:3208
John Keats 6:3545
Percy Bysshe Shelley 6:3573, 3587
George Gordon, Lord Byron 7:3657
William Blake 7:3710
Samuel Taylor Coleridge 7:3919
Charles Lamb 7:3944, 3945
Emily Brontë 7:4189
Edgar Allan Poe 8:4254
Anne Brontë 8:4286
Charlotte Brontë 8:4483
John Wilson Croker 8:4506
Arthur Hugh Clough 8:4653
William Makepeace Thackeray
  8:4711
Walter Savage Landor 8:4736, 4737
Thomas Love Peacock 8:4813
Charles Dickens 8:4883, 4903
Bryan Waller Procter 9:4983
Dante Gabriel Rossetti 9:5325
James Thomson 9:5337

Edward FitzGerald 9:5352
Charles Reade 9:5379
Sir Henry Taylor 9:5397
Matthew Arnold 9:5470
Robert Browning 9:5495, 5496
Wilkie Collins 9:5536
Sir Richard Burton 10:5575
Alfred, Lord Tennyson 10:5667
Walt Whitman 10:5720
Benjamin Jowett 10:5746
Christina Rossetti 10:5798
Coventry Patmore 10:5898
William Morris 10:5912

SWINBURNE, LOUIS
Helen Hunt Jackson 9:5395

SYDENHAM, THOMAS
John Locke 4:2076

SYLVESTER, JOSHUA
Edmund Spenser 1:406

SYMINGTON, ANDREW JAMES
Samuel Lover 8:4864
Charles Tennyson Turner 9:5077

SYMONDS, EMILY MORSE
Richard Cumberland 6:3411

SYMONDS, JOHN ADDINGTON
Nicholas Udall 1:288
John Heywood 1:308
Sir Philip Sidney 1:320
Robert Greene 1:359, 361
Christopher Marlowe 1:384
George Peele 1:401
Thomas Nashe 1:508
John Lyly 1:512
William Shakespeare 2:577, 1012
John Webster 3:1284, 1287
John Milton 4:1706
Samuel Richardson 5:2694
John Keats 6:3526, 3531
Percy Bysshe Shelley 6:3572
George Gordon, Lord Byron 7:3647
Dante Gabriel Rossetti 9:5320
James Thomson 9:5337
Edward FitzGerald 9:5353
Robert Browning 9:5497
Walt Whitman 10:5723
Benjamin Jowett 10:5746
Walter Pater 10:5816, 5817
Robert Louis Stevenson 10:5836
William Ewart Gladstone 10:5937

SYMONS, ARTHUR
John Donne 3:1199
Philip Massinger 3:1359
Thomas Lovell Beddoes 7:4234
Leigh Hunt 8:4563
Thomas De Quincey 8:4577
John Clare 8:4760
Dante Gabriel Rossetti 9:5323
Richard Jefferies 9:5440
Walter Pater 10:5818
Robert Louis Stevenson 10:5846
Coventry Patmore 10:5895, 5896
William Morris 10:5915
Oscar Wilde 10:6019
Ernest Dowson 10:6043
W. E. Henley 10:6166
Sir Leslie Stephen 10:6195

T., M. H.
Lewis Carroll 10:5955

TAINE, HIPPOLYTE
Beowulf 1:2
Cædmon 1:8
Alfred the Great 1:20
Sir John Mandeville 1:37
William Langland 1:52
Geoffrey Chaucer 1:120
John Gower 1:168
John Lydgate 1:175
John Skelton 1:215
William Tyndale 1:255
Henry Howard, Earl of Surrey
    1:278
Sir Philip Sidney 1:325, 327
Robert Greene 1:360
Christopher Marlowe 1:368
Richard Hooker 1:502
John Lyly 1:510
John Donne 3:1198
Robert Burton 3:1369
Sir John Suckling 3:1401
Edward Lord Herbert 3:1445
Abraham Cowley 3:1596
Sir John Denham 3:1629
John Milton 4:1692, 1700
Thomas Hobbes 4:1819
Samuel Butler 4:1829
John Wilmot, Earl of Rochester
    4:1845
Thomas Otway 4:1890
Edmund Waller 4:1901
Sir William Temple 4:1998
John Dryden 4:2015
Sir Charles Sedley 4:2057
John Locke 4:2079
William Wycherley 4:2153
Joseph Addison 4:2179
Matthew Prior 4:2209
Samuel Clarke 5:2304
Daniel Defoe 5:2315
John Gay 5:2347
Alexander Pope 5:2428
Jonathan Swift 5:2494
Henry Fielding 5:2617
Samuel Richardson 5:2686
Lady Mary Wortley Montagu
    5:2711
Edward Young 5:2740
Laurence Sterne 5:2775
Tobias Smollett 5:2852
Oliver Goldsmith 5:2891
Samuel Johnson 6:2986
John Wesley 6:3082
James Macpherson 6:3184
Robert Burns 6:3202
William Cowper 6:3315
James Beattie 6:3338
Richard Brinsley Sheridan 6:3436
Percy Bysshe Shelley 6:3572
Alfred, Lord Tennyson 10:5659

TALBOT, CATHERINE
Joseph Butler 5:2571
Colley Cibber 5:2633
Samuel Richardson 5:2682
Edward Young 5:2743

TALBOT, GEORGE
William Habington 3:1513

TALFOURD, THOMAS NOON
Jeremy Taylor 3:1581
John Dennis 5:2366
Henry Fielding 5:2601
Colley Cibber 5:2638
Laurence Sterne 5:2761
Tobias Smollett 5:2844
Henry Brooke 6:2972
Ann Radcliffe 7:3608, 3613
Charles Robert Maturin 7:3627
William Hazlitt 7:3740
Henry Mackenzie 7:3768
Mary Lamb 7:4154

TALLENTYRE, S. G.
Lady Mary Wortley Montagu
    5:2715
Philip Dormer Stanhope, Earl of
    Chesterfield 5:2880

TARBOX, I. N.
Jonathan Edwards 5:2652

TARVER, J. C.
William Cowper 6:3321

TATE, NAHUM
William Shakespeare 2:568, 945
John Oldham 4:1883
Aphra Behn 4:1936
Sir Roger L'Estrange 4:2073

TATHAM, FREDERICK
William Blake 7:3696

TAYLOR, BAYARD
William Makepeace Thackeray
    8:4709
Fitz-Greene Halleck 8:4834
N. P. Willis 8:4840
Bryan Waller Procter 9:4981
George Eliot 9:5092
John Greenleaf Whittier 10:5633
Alfred, Lord Tennyson 10:5663

TAYLOR, E. R.
Henry George 10:5929

TAYLOR, HANNIS
Sir Thomas More 1:234

TAYLOR, HELEN
Henry Thomas Buckle 8:4697

TAYLOR, SIR HENRY
Robert Southey 7:4091
Thomas Campbell 7:4118
William Wordsworth 8:4305
Samuel Rogers 8:4462

TAYLOR, I. A.
Aubrey De Vere 10:6077

TAYLOR, ISAAC
Thomas Chalmers 7:4157, 4160

TAYLOR, JOHN
Junius 6:3482

TAYLOR, MARIE
Bayard Taylor 9:5062

TAYLOR, THOMAS
William Cowper 6:3314

TAYLOR, TOM
Fanny Burney 7:4045

TAYLOR, W. C.
Isaac D'Israeli 7:4163

TAYLOR, WILLIAM M.
John Knox 1:300
Hugh Blair 6:3295
Thomas Chalmers 7:4157

TEDDER, H. R.
Geoffrey of Monmouth 1:27
Miles Coverdale 1:297

TEIGNMOUTH, LORD
Sir William Jones 6:3145

TEMPLE, SIR WILLIAM
Sir Philip Sidney 1:321
Edmund Spenser 1:419
William Shakespeare 2:749
Edmund Waller 4:1898
Richard Bentley 5:2398
Jonathan Swift 5:2476

TEMPLE, WILLIAM
Thomas Gray 5:2817

TENISON, THOMAS
Sir Francis Bacon 3:1118

TENNEMANN, WILLIAM GOTTLIEB
William of Occam 1:34
Joseph Priestley 6:3348

TENNYSON, ALFRED, LORD
Alfred the Great 1:19
William Caxton 1:185
John Milton 4:1692
Sir Walter Scott 7:3851
Arthur Henry Hallam 7:3878
John Wilson 8:4445
Thomas Babington Macaulay
8:4600
Frederick Denison Maurice 9:4923
Edward Bulwer-Lytton 9:4947
Charles Kingsley 9:4993
Charles Tennyson Turner 9:5077
Dante Gabriel Rossetti 9:5314
Edward FitzGerald 9:5349
Robert Browning 9:5492
William Allingham 9:5527
Coventry Patmore 10:5894

TENNYSON, HALLAM
William Shakespeare 2:580
John Keats 6:3527
George Crabbe 7:3812
Hartley Coleridge 7:4221
Edgar Allan Poe 8:4254
George Eliot 9:5080
Walt Whitman 10:5703
William Ewart Gladstone 10:5937

TEXTE, JOSEPH
George Lillo 5:2386
Samuel Richardson 5:2689
Laurence Sterne 5:2764

THACKERAY, WILLIAM MAKEPEACE
Joseph Addison 4:2196
Matthew Prior 4:2208
William Congreve 4:2282
Sir Richard Steele 4:2299
John Gay 5:2341
Alexander Pope 5:2426

Jonathan Swift 5:2484
Henry Fielding 5:2615
Samuel Richardson 5:2683, 2694
Laurence Sterne 5:2761
Tobias Smollett 5:2840
Oliver Goldsmith 5:2888
John Wesley 6:3081
Horace Walpole 6:3240
Sir Walter Scott 7:3838
Robert Southey 7:4083
Thomas Hood 7:4138, 4139
Charlotte Brontë 8:4483
Washington Irving 8:4525
Thomas Love Peacock 8:4810
Charles Dickens 8:4892, 4893
Edward Bulwer-Lytton 9:4942
Wilkie Collins 9:5534

THANET, OCTAVE
Horace Walpole 6:3240

THAXTER, CELIA
Charlotte Brontë 8:4478

THAYER, HARVEY WATERMAN
Matthew Prior 4:2211

THAYER, W. S.
John Greenleaf Whittier 10:5636

THAYER, WILLIAM ROSCOE
William Cullen Bryant 9:5053
Thomas Carlyle 9:5118

THEOBALD, LEWIS
William Shakespeare 2:667, 696
Alexander Pope 5:2433

THIRLWALL, CONNOP
William Cowper 6:3322
George Grote 9:4910
Edward Bulwer-Lytton 9:4944
George Eliot 9:5090
James Anthony Froude 10:5784

THOMAS OF ERCELDOUNE
Thomas of Erceldoune 1:31

THOMAS, EDITH M.
Elizabeth Barrett Browning 8:4636
Helen Hunt Jackson 9:5391

THOMAS, EDWARD
Richard Jefferies 9:5441
Lafcadio Hearn 10:6214

THOMAS, W. MOY
Richard Savage 5:2408
Lady Mary Wortley Montagu
5:2714

THOMPSON, E. MAUNDE
William Camden 3:1084

THOMPSON, FRANCIS
Richard Crashaw 3:1468, 1482
Robert Burns 6:3208
Samuel Taylor Coleridge 7:3905
Edgar Allan Poe 8:4259
Thomas Carlyle 9:5121
Robert Browning 9:5499
W. E. Henley 10:6170

THOMPSON, JOHN R.
Edgar Allan Poe 8:4252

THOMPSON, RICHARD W.
Thomas Jefferson 7:3679

THOMPSON, SIDNEY R.
Robert Southey 7:4086

THOMPSON, T. P.
Sydney Owenson, Lady Morgan
8:4548

THOMSON, DR. ANTHONY TODD
Letitia Elizabeth Landon 7:4020

THOMSON, CLARA LINKLATER
Aaron Hill 5:2555
Henry Fielding 5:2627
Samuel Richardson 5:2706
Henry Mackenzie 7:3766

THOMSON, J. ARTHUR
Herbert Spencer 10:6139

THOMSON, JAMES (1700-1748)
Sir Philip Sidney 1:321
John Milton 4:1689
Nicholas Rowe 4:2159
Sir Isaac Newton 4:2250
James Thomson 5:2529

THOMSON, JAMES (1834-1882)
Jonathan Swift 5:2485
William Blake 7:3705
Elizabeth Barrett Browning 8:4630,
4635
Robert Browning 9:5494

THOMSON, KATHERINE
Sir Thomas Wyatt 1:262
Sir Walter Ralegh 3:1067
John Gay 5:2346
Colley Cibber 5:2632
Elizabeth Montagu 6:3301
James Beattie 6:3337
Fanny Burney 7:4047

THOMSON, SLASON
Eugene Field 10:5876

THOMSON, THOMAS
Robert Boyle 4:1954

THOREAU, HENRY DAVID
Geoffrey Chaucer 1:107
Francis Quarles 3:1425
Thomas Carlyle 9:5128
Ralph Waldo Emerson 9:5195
Amos Bronson Alcott 9:5449
Walt Whitman 10:5696

THORNBURY, GEORGE WALTER
Ben Jonson 3:1317
William Blake 7:3697

THORPE, BENJAMIN
Beowulf 1:1
Ælfric 1:24

THORPE, THOMAS
William Shakespeare 2:1012

TICKELL, THOMAS
Joseph Addison 4:2176, 2182
Thomas Tickell 5:2388
Ambrose Philips 5:2550

TICKNOR, GEORGE
Sir Philip Sidney 1:323
George Gordon, Lord Byron 7:3631
Thomas Jefferson 7:3678

John Keble 8:4828
H. H. Milman 8:4862
Frederick Denison Maurice 9:4926
Charles Kingsley 9:4990
George Eliot 9:5085
Matthew Arnold 9:5454

TULLOCH, W. W.
Allan Ramsay 5:2645

TURK, MILTON HAIGHT
Alfred the Great 1:20

TURNBULL, ROBERT
Thomas Chalmers 7:4157

TURNBULL, WILLIAM B.
Richard Crashaw 3:1466

TURNER, SHARON
The Venerable Bede 1:14
John Lydgate 1:174
Sir Thomas More 1:231

TUSSER, THOMAS
Nicholas Udall 1:288

TUTIN, J. R.
Richard Crashaw 3:1467

TWAIN, MARK
William Shakespeare 2:737
Jonathan Edwards 5:2654
Sir Walter Scott 7:3841
William Godwin 7:3994
James Fenimore Cooper 8:4391
Robert G. Ingersoll 10:5977
Bret Harte 10:6110

TWICHELL, JOSEPH HOPKINS
John Winthrop 3:1460
Harriet Beecher Stowe 10:5877
Charles Dudley Warner 10:6012,
6013

TYERMAN, LUKE
John Wesley 6:3085

TYERS, THOMAS
Samuel Johnson 6:2978

TYLER, MOSES COIT
Anne Bradstreet 3:1643
Roger Williams 4:1879
Cotton Mather 4:2256
Jonathan Edwards 5:2660
Benjamin Franklin 6:3048
Joel Barlow 6:3418
Timothy Dwight 6:3445
Thomas Jefferson 7:3684
John Trumbull 7:3774
Philip Freneau 7:3800

TYLER, ROYALL
William Shakespeare 2:573
Thomas Paine 6:3380

TYLOR, E. B.
Thomas Henry Huxley 10:5836

TYNAN, KATHARINE
Oscar Wilde 10:6018
Lionel Johnson 10:6120

TYNDALE, WILLIAM
Sir Thomas More 1:232
William Tyndale 1:254

TYNDALL, JOHN
Charles Darwin 9:5269

TYRWHITT, THOMAS
Thomas Chatterton 5:2805

TYTLER, PATRICK FRASER
John Barbour 1:47
Gavin Douglas 1:206
George Buchanan 1:314

ÜBERWEG, FRIEDRICH
Duns Scotus 1:33
Richard Hooker 1:502
Sir John Davies 3:1145
Sir Isaac Newton 4:2248
Samuel Clarke 5:2304
Bernard Mandeville 5:2355
Jonathan Edwards 5:2651
David Hume 5:2921

ULRICI, HERMANN
Nicholas Udall 1:288
Robert Greene 1:361
George Peele 1:400
John Lyly 1:510
Ben Jonson 3:1323

UNDERHILL, GEORGE F.
Robert Greene 1:360
Sir Walter Ralegh 3:1069

UNDERHILL, JOHN
John Gay 5:2350

UNDERWOOD, FRANCIS H.
Roger Ascham 1:290
William Ellery Channing 7:4062
John James Audubon 8:4374
William Gilmore Simms 8:4873
Alice and Phoebe Cary 9:4920
William Cullen Bryant 9:5051
Bayard Taylor 9:5059
Josiah Gilbert Holland 9:5172
Edwin P. Whipple 9:5408
George Bancroft 10:5579
James Russell Lowell 10:5591, 5594
John Greenleaf Whittier 10:5638
Francis Parkman 10:5753
Oliver Wendell Holmes 10:5778

UPHAM, C. W.
William H. Prescott 8:4592

UPSON, ANSON J.
Fanny Kemble 10:5743

USK, THOMAS
Geoffrey Chaucer 1:53

VANDAM, ALBERT D.
George du Maurier 10:5902

VAN DYKE, HENRY
John Milton 4:1707
John Keble 8:4827

VAN WESTRUM, A. S.
Frank Norris 10:6126

VAUGHAN, HENRY
George Herbert 3:1243
William Cartwright 3:1417
Sir William D'Avenant 3:1615
Henry Vaughan 4:1976

VAUGHAN, ROBERT
John Wyclif 1:41
John Locke 4:2079

VAUGHAN, ROBERT ALFRED
William Law 5:2675

VAUGHAN, WILLIAM
Christopher Marlowe 1:365

VEDDER, HENRY C.
Francis Parkman 10:5755
Frank R. Stockton 10:6090
Richard Henry Stoddard 10:6157

VEITCH, JOHN
Robert Fergusson 5:2909
James Macpherson 6:3185
James Hogg 7:3971, 3972

VENABLES, EDMUND
Edward Augustus Freeman 10:5729

VENABLES, GEORGE STOVIN
William Cobbett 7:3961

VERPLANCK, GULIAN CROMMELIN
Charles Brockden Brown 6:3397
Washington Irving 8:4534

VICTOR, ORVILLE J.
Alice and Phoebe Cary 9:4920

VICTORIA, QUEEN OF ENGLAND
Charlotte Brontë 8:4483
Alfred, Lord Tennyson 10:5655

VINCENT, GEORGE E.
Herbert Spencer 10:6139

VINCENT, LEON H.
John Keats 6:3552

VIVIAN, PERCIVAL
Thomas Campion 3:1082

VOLTAIRE, FRANÇOIS MARIE
AROUET DE
William Shakespeare 2:826, 859,
897
Sir Francis Bacon 3:1126
John Milton 4:1698, 1717
Thomas Hobbes 4:1810
John Locke 4:2077, 2082, 2085
William Wycherley 4:2149
Joseph Addison 4:2184
Sir John Vanbrugh 4:2235
Sir Isaac Newton 4:2246
William Congreve 4:2269
Alexander Pope 5:2421
Jonathan Swift 5:2480
James Thomson 5:2530
Henry St. John, Viscount
Bolingbroke 5:2558
Samuel Richardson 5:2694
Lady Mary Wortley Montagu
5:2708
Edward Young 5:2743

W., M.
Richard Lovelace 3:1537

WACKERBARTH, A. DIEDRICH
Beowulf 1:1

WADDINGTON, SAMUEL
Arthur Hugh Clough 8:4653

WAGNER, JOHN ALFRED
Richard Lovelace 3:1532

WAITE, ARTHUR EDWARD
Richard Lovelace 3:1532

William Shakespeare 2:751, 823
Beaumont and Fletcher 3:1051
Cyril Tourneur 3:1150
William Rowley 3:1159
Thomas Middleton 3:1162
Fulke Greville, Lord Brooke
    3:1173
Thomas Dekker 3:1228, 1229
George Chapman 3:1279, 1281
John Webster 3:1283, 1286, 1287
John Marston 3:1300
Ben Jonson 3:1318, 1326, 1327
Sir Henry Wotton 3:1351
John Ford 3:1388, 1390
William Cartwright 3:1418
Thomas Heywood 3:1494
Abraham Cowley 3:1599
Sir William D'Avenant 3:1613
William Prynne 3:1620
Sir John Denham 3:1627
Margaret Cavendish, Duchess of
    Newcastle 4:1649
John Milton 4:1695, 1703
John Oldham 4:1884
Thomas Otway 4:1890
Aphra Behn 4:1938
Sir George Etherege 4:1958
Thomas Shadwell 4:1966
Nathaniel Lee 4:1972
John Dryden 4:2020, 2022, 2023,
    2024, 2025, 2026
Sir Charles Sedley 4:2058
George Farquhar 4:2111
Nahum Tate 4:2145
William Wycherley 4:2153
Nicholas Rowe 4:2162
John Hughes 4:2204
Thomas D'Urfey 4:2219
Elkanah Settle 4:2225
Jeremy Collier 4:2231
Sir John Vanbrugh 4:2239
William Congreve 4:2272, 2276,
    2277, 2278
Sir Richard Steele 4:2295
John Dennis 5:2366
Ambrose Philips 5:2552
Aaron Hill 5:2555
Colley Cibber 5:2636
Lady Mary Wortley Montagu
    5:2714
Elizabeth Gaskell 8:4800
Charles Dickens 8:4884

WARD, JOHN
    William Shakespeare 2:535

WARD, JULIUS H.
    Edwin P. Whipple 9:5409
    Francis Parkman 10:5755
    Harriet Beecher Stowe 10:5886

WARD, MARY A.
    Sir Philip Sidney 1:327
    Sir Edward Dyer 1:518
    Sir John Davies 3:1144
    Emily Brontë 7:4196
    Anne Brontë 8:4288

WARD, NATHANIEL
    Anne Bradstreet 3:1633

WARD, THOMAS HUMPHRY
    Thomas Watson 1:358
    Sir Francis Bacon 3:1121
    William Drummond 3:1451
    Abraham Cowley 3:1607
    Christopher Smart 5:2867
    William Whitehead 6:3029
    Thomas Warton 6:3074
    Arthur Hugh Clough 8:4659

WARD, WILFRID
    Thomas Henry Huxley 10:5859

WARD, WILLIAM C.
    William Wycherley 4:2156
    Sir John Vanbrugh 4:2239
    Samuel Richardson 5:2698

WARD, WILLIAM HAYES
    Sidney Lanier 9:5176

WARE, HENRY, JR.
    Robert Southey 7:4088
    Richard Monckton Milnes, Lord
        Houghton 9:5385

WARE, WILLIAM
    Washington Allston 7:4096

WARNER, CHARLES DUDLEY
    Washington Irving 8:4539
    Helen Hunt Jackson 9:5394
    Stephen Crane 10:6052

WARRE, F. CORNISH
    Robert Herrick 4:1677
    Leigh Hunt 8:4558

WARREN, F. M.
    John Lyly 1:512
    Thomas Lodge 3:1096

WARREN, SAMUEL
    Harriet Beecher Stowe 10:5885

WARTON, JOSEPH
    Geoffrey Chaucer 1:62
    William Shakespeare 2:947
    Nicholas Rowe 4:2160
    Joseph Addison 4:2184
    John Gay 5:2340
    Alexander Pope 5:2421
    Jonathan Swift 5:2493
    James Thomson 5:2532
    Henry Fielding 5:2596
    David Mallet 5:2755
    Mark Akenside 5:2794
    William Warburton 6:2946

WARTON, THOMAS
    Richard Rolle of Hampole 1:35
    John Barbour 1:46
    William Langland 1:49
    Geoffrey Chaucer 1:79
    John Gower 1:167, 168
    John Lydgate 1:174
    Thomas Occleve 1:182
    John Skelton 1:216
    William Dunbar 1:221
    Sir Thomas Wyatt 1:263, 266
    Henry Howard, Earl of Surrey
        1:277
    Alexander Barclay 1:282
    Thomas, Lord Vaux 1:285

John Heywood 1:308, 309
George Gascoigne 1:310
Christopher Marlowe 1:372
Edmund Spenser 1:436
Thomas Sackville, Earl of Dorset
    1:522
Sir John Harington 1:527
George Chapman 3:1276
John Marston 3:1298
Joseph Hall 3:1520, 1521
John Milton 4:1694, 1696
Joseph Addison 4:2178
William Collins 5:2662
Thomas Chatterton 5:2805
Thomas Gray 5:2818
Oliver Goldsmith 5:2883
Thomas Warton 6:3076
Elizabeth Montagu 6:3301

WASHBURN, EMELYN W.
    Thomas Occleve 1:183
    Richard Hooker 1:503
    Sir Francis Bacon 3:1115

WASHINGTON, GEORGE
    Benjamin Franklin 6:3037
    Thomas Paine 6:3384

WASSON, DAVID ATWOOD
    John Greenleaf Whittier 10:5644

WATERLOO, STANLEY
    Eugene Field 10:5874

WATKINS, CHARLES
    Sir William Blackstone 6:2960

WATKINS, JOHN
    Richard Brinsley Sheridan 6:3428
    Ebenezer Elliott 7:4211

WATSON, ELKANAH
    Benjamin Franklin 6:3037
    Thomas Paine 6:3384

WATSON, FOSTER
    Sir Henry Wotton 3:1354

WATSON, H. B. MARRIOTT
    W. E. Henley 10:6166, 6167

WATSON, J. L.
    Carolina Oliphant, Baroness Nairne
        7:4124

WATSON, JOHN SELBY
    William Warburton 6:2945
    Richard Porson 6:3377

WATSON, RICHARD
    John Wesley 6:3083

WATSON, ROBERT SPENCE
    Cædmon 1:8

WATSON, ROSAMUND MARRIOTT
    W. E. Henley 10:6167

WATSON, WILLIAM
    John Ford 3:1389
    John Milton 4:1694
    Samuel Taylor Coleridge 7:3908,
        3909
    Charles Lamb 7:3940
    William Wordsworth 8:4309
    Leigh Hunt 8:4557

James Russell Lowell 10:5603
Alfred, Lord Tennyson 10:5668
John Addington Symonds 10:5765

WATTERSON, HENRY
Thomas Jefferson 7:3679

WATTS, ISAAC
Isaac Watts 5:2526

WATTS-DUNTON, THEODORE
Thomas Chatterton 5:2809
Dante Gabriel Rossetti 9:5314
James Russell Lowell 10:5592
Christina Rossetti 10:5798

WAUGH, ARTHUR
Robert Browning 9:5500
George Gissing 10:6179

WEBB, DANIEL
Richard Hooker 1:501

WEBBE, WILLIAM
William Langland 1:49
Geoffrey Chaucer 1:58
John Gower 1:167
John Lydgate 1:174
John Skelton 1:211
George Gascoigne 1:310
Edmund Spenser 1:415
John Lyly 1:511
Gabriel Harvey 3:1176

WEBER, ALFRED
John Scotus Erigena 1:17
Roger Bacon 1:30

WEBSTER, DANIEL
Thomas Jefferson 7:3683

WEBSTER, JOHN
George Chapman 3:1271
John Webster 3:1285

WEBSTER, NOAH
Samuel Johnson 6:2995
Noah Webster 7:4074

WEBSTER, WENTWORTH
George Herbert 3:1246

WEDDERBURN, ALEXANDER
David Mallet 5:2753

WEDGWOOD, JULIA
William Law 5:2678
John Wesley 6:3081
Frederick Denison Maurice 9:4925

WEDMORE, F.
George du Maurier 10:5901

WEED, THURLOW
Junius 6:3483
Horace Greeley 9:4937

WEEVER, JOHN
William Shakespeare 2:563, 888
Thomas Middleton 3:1161
Michael Drayton 3:1185
John Marston 3:1297

WELLS, BENJAMIN W
Charles Dudley Warner 10:6012

WELLS, CAROLYN
Lewis Carroll 10:5951

WELLS, H. G.
William Morris 10:5912
Stephen Crane 10:6062
George Gissing 10:6173, 6178

WELSFORD, HENRY
Sir William Jones 6:3146

WELSH, ALFRED H.
Sir John Mandeville 1:37
Thomas Sackville, Earl of Dorset 1:522
John Donne 3:1198
Mark Akenside 5:2796
Henry David Thoreau 8:4671
Nathaniel Hawthorne 8:4770
George Eliot 9:5090

WELSH, DAVID
Thomas Brown 6:3506

WELWOOD, JAMES
Nicholas Rowe 4:2159

WENDELL, BARRETT
Jonathan Edwards 5:2652
Benjamin Franklin 6:3045
Charles Brockden Brown 6:3405
Joel Barlow 6:3419
Joseph Rodman Drake 6:3512
John Trumbull 7:3774
Philip Freneau 7:3801
William Godwin 7:3997
Edgar Allan Poe 8:4260
James Fenimore Cooper 8:4384
Washington Irving 8:4542
William H. Prescott 8:4593
Henry David Thoreau 8:4674
Nathaniel Hawthorne 8:4771
John Lothrop Motley 9:5022
William Cullen Bryant 9:5050
Amos Bronson Alcott 9:5452
Robert Browning 9:5497
George Bancroft 10:5580
John Greenleaf Whittier 10:5640
Walt Whitman 10:5702
Francis Parkman 10:5756

WESLEY, CHARLES
Charles Wesley 6:3032

WESLEY, JOHN
William Law 5:2677
John Byrom 5:2718
Laurence Sterne 5:2767
Henry Brooke 6:2972
Charles Wesley 6:3032
John Wesley 6:3079

WESLEY, SAMUEL
Edmund Spenser 1:410
John Wesley 6:3079

WEST, KENYON
Nahum Tate 4:2145
Nicholas Rowe 4:2161

WESTCOTT, BROOKE FOSS
William Tyndale 1:255

WHALLEY, PETER
Ben Jonson 3:1317
Joseph Hall 3:1520

WHARTON, THOMAS
Thomas Gray 5:2827

WHATELY, RICHARD
Joseph Butler 5:2572
Jane Austen 6:3462

WHEATON, HENRY
Beowulf 1:1

WHETSTONE, GEORGE
George Gascoigne 1:310

WHIBLEY, CHARLES
Sir Thomas Urquhart 3:1543
Robert Burns 6:3213
Edgar Allan Poe 8:4276
William Makepeace Thackeray 8:4715

WHIPPLE, EDWIN P.
Sir Philip Sidney 1:324
Thomas Sackville, Earl of Dorset 1:520
William Warner 1:524
John Fletcher 3:1043, 1044
Beaumont and Fletcher 3:1051
Sir Walter Ralegh 3:1070
Samuel Daniel 3:1072
Sir John Davies 3:1143
John Donne 3:1196, 1198
John Webster 3:1283
John Marston 3:1299
Ben Jonson 3:1317, 1323, 1326
Philip Massinger 3:1358
Thomas Heywood 3:1491
Joseph Hall 3:1521
Izaak Walton 4:1873
John Bunyan 4:1916
Sir Charles Sedley 4:2057
Henry Fielding 5:2605
Benjamin Franklin 6:3046
Thomas Paine 6:3382
Charles Brockden Brown 6:3399
Joel Barlow 6:3417
Timothy Dwight 6:3445
Joseph Rodman Drake 6:3511
John Keats 6:3521
Percy Bysshe Shelley 6:3580
Thomas Jefferson 7:3682
William Gifford 7:3686
John Trumbull 7:3773
Philip Freneau 7:3799
Sir James Mackintosh 7:3827
William Ellery Channing 7:4062
Robert Southey 7:4082
Washington Allston 7:4095
Thomas Campbell 7:4111
Sydney Smith 7:4131
Emily Brontë 7:4179
Ebenezer Elliott 7:4211
Anne Brontë 8:4286
Francis, Lord Jeffrey 8:4342
Thomas Moore 8:4421
Charlotte Brontë 8:4483
Sir William Hamilton 8:4502
Rufus Wilmot Griswold 8:4517
Washington Irving 8:4531
Leigh Hunt 8:4555
William H. Prescott 8:4594
G. P. R. James 8:4626
Elizabeth Barrett Browning 8:4632
Henry David Thoreau 8:4671

William Makepeace Thackeray
8:4716
Fitz-Greene Halleck 8:4835
N. P. Willis 8:4843
Charles Dickens 8:4880, 4885
Edward Bulwer-Lytton 9:4943
Bryan Waller Procter 9:4982, 4984
John Lothrop Motley 9:5020, 5021
William Cullen Bryant 9:5044,
5047
Bayard Taylor 9:5060
Richard Henry Dana 9:5067, 5068
Ralph Waldo Emerson 9:5200
Henry Wadsworth Longfellow
9:5253
Richard Henry Dana, Jr. 9:5308
Helen Hunt Jackson 9:5393
Henry Ward Beecher 9:5430
Amos Bronson Alcott 9:5450
Matthew Arnold 9:5461
Louisa May Alcott 9:5484
George Bancroft 10:5579
Herman Melville 10:5607
John Greenleaf Whittier 10:5635
Alfred, Lord Tennyson 10:5658
Walt Whitman 10:5699
George William Curtis 10:5735
Francis Parkman 10:5753
Oliver Wendell Holmes 10:5772,
5775
Harriet Beecher Stowe 10:5879
Charles Dudley Warner 10:6012
Bret Harte 10:6108
Richard Henry Stoddard 10:6153

WHIPPLE, LEONIDAS RUTLEDGE
Kate Chopin 10:6207

WHISTLER, JAMES MCNEILL
John Ruskin 10:5981

WHISTON, WILLIAM
Samuel Clarke 5:2305

WHITAKER, JOHN
John Knox 1:299
George Buchanan 1:314

WHITAKER, THOMAS D.
William Warburton 6:2948
Richard Hurd 6:3367

WHITE, ANDREW D.
Sir Walter Scott 7:3848

WHITE, CAROLINE LOUISA
Ælfric 1:25

WHITE, GILBERT
William Collins 5:2662

WHITE, GREENOUGH
Cynewulf 1:16
John Wyclif 1:44
John Gower 1:169
Arthur Hugh Clough 8:4656

WHITE, HENRY KIRKE
Sir Philip Sidney 1:325
John Donne 3:1197
Thomas Warton 6:3075
Robert Southey 7:4085
Thomas Moore 8:4418

WHITE, RICHARD GRANT
John Lyly 1:513
William Shakespeare 2:755
Lewis Theobald 5:2469
William Warburton 6:2947
Charles Dickens 8:4889
Benjamin Disraeli 9:5160
Edwin P. Whipple 9:5408
Emma Lazarus 9:5446

WHITE, SALLY JOY
Amelia B. Edwards 10:5741

WHITEFIELD, GEORGE
Jonathan Edwards 5:2647
William Law 5:2677
Laurence Sterne 5:2767
John Wesley 6:3079

WHITEFOOT, JOHN
Sir Thomas Browne 4:1851

WHITEHEAD, CHARLES
Frederick Marryat 7:4170

WHITEHEAD, JOHN
Charles Wesley 6:3033
John Wesley 6:3087

WHITEHEAD, WILLIAM
William Whitehead 6:3028

WHITING, LILIAN
Elizabeth Barrett Browning 8:4636
Louisa May Alcott 9:5488

WHITMAN, SARAH HELEN
Edgar Allan Poe 8:4251

WHITMAN, WALT
William Shakespeare 2:578, 815
Robert Burns 6:3225
Edgar Allan Poe 8:4254
William Cullen Bryant 9:5040,
5046
Thomas Carlyle 9:5116
Ralph Waldo Emerson 9:5192,
5198
Henry Wadsworth Longfellow
9:5247
John Greenleaf Whittier 10:5637
Alfred, Lord Tennyson 10:5660
Walt Whitman 10:5706, 5707

WHITMORE, W. H.
Winthrop Mackworth Praed 7:4035

WHITNEY, ERNEST
Joel Barlow 6:3417

WHITNEY, HENRY
William Cullen Bryant 9:5040

WHITTIER, JOHN GREENLEAF
Izaak Walton 4:1871
John Bunyan 4:1919
Richard Baxter 4:1947
Robert Burns 6:3200
William Ellery Channing 7:4058,
4059
Ebenezer Elliott 7:4212
Fitz-Greene Halleck 8:4835
Alice and Phoebe Cary 9:4919
Charles Kingsley 9:4988
William Cullen Bryant 9:5043

Bayard Taylor 9:5059, 5060, 5069
William Lloyd Garrison 9:5073
Josiah Gilbert Holland 9:5172
Edwin P. Whipple 9:5409
Henry Ward Beecher 9:5427
Emma Lazarus 9:5445
Robert Browning 9:5502
James Russell Lowell 10:5597
Oliver Wendell Holmes 10:5770,
5771
Harriet Beecher Stowe 10:5878

WHYTE, WALTER
James Hogg 7:3972
Walter Savage Landor 8:4741

WILBERFORCE, SAMUEL
John Keble 8:4824
Charles Darwin 9:5275
John Henry Newman 9:5559

WILBERFORCE, WILLIAM
Thomas Paine 6:3386
Sir Walter Scott 7:3852

WILDE, OSCAR
William Shakespeare 2:900, 1013
Robert Browning 9:5497
Walter Pater 10:5818
William Morris 10:5906

WILKES, JOHN
Charles Churchill 5:2728

WILKIN, SIMON
Sir Thomas Browne 4:1857

WILKINSON, WILLIAM CLEAVER
George Eliot 9:5083

WILLARD, FRANCES E.
Harriet Beecher Stowe 10:5882

WILLARD, S.
Timothy Dwight 6:3443

WILLCOX, LOUISE COLLIER
Thomas Traherne 4:1780

WILLIAM OF MALMESBURY
The Venerable Bede 1:14
John Scotus Erigena 1:17

WILLIAM OF NEWBURY
Geoffrey of Monmouth 1:26

WILLIAMS, ALFRED M.
Carolina Oliphant, Baroness Nairne
7:4126
Emily Brontë 7:4193

WILLIAMS, EDWARD
Jeremy Taylor 3:1579

WILLIAMS, GILLY
Horace Walpole 6:3238

WILLIAMS, JANE
Aphra Behn 4:1938
Charlotte Smith 6:3353

WILLIAMS, ORLO
Samuel Butler 10:6100

WILLIS, N. P.
Mary Lamb 7:4153
Marguerite, Countess of Blessington
7:4216

WOODBRIDGE, ELISABETH
Ben Jonson 3:1344

WOODBRIDGE, JOHN
Anne Bradstreet 3:1636

WOODFALL, WILLIAM
John Wesley 6:3080

WOODHOUSELEE, ALEXANDER FRASER
TYTLER, LORD
Giles and Phineas Fletcher 3:1089
Allan Ramsay 5:2641
Tobias Smollett 5:2838
Henry Home, Lord Kames 6:2968
James Burnett, Lord Monboddo
6:3291
Hugh Blair 6:3295

WOOLF, VIRGINIA
George Gissing 10:6177

WOOLL, JOHN
Joseph Warton 6:3305

WOOLSEY, SARAH CHAUNCEY
Fanny Burney 7:4048

WORDE, WINKYN DE
Sir John Mandeville 1:36

WORDSWORTH, CHARLES
Lancelot Andrewes 3:1103

WORDSWORTH, CHRISTOPHER
John Foxe 1:356

WORDSWORTH, DOROTHY
Robert Burns 6:3192
Sir Walter Scott 7:3836
Samuel Taylor Coleridge 7:3893
William Wordsworth 8:4297

WORDSWORTH, WILLIAM
Alfred the Great 1:19
John Wyclif 1:41
Geoffrey Chaucer 1:62
John Skelton 1:214
Edmund Spenser 1:405, 412, 421
Francis Beaumont 3:1039
William Laud 3:1438
John Milton 4:1686, 1689, 1704
Izaak Walton 4:1873
Charles Cotton 4:1913
John Dryden 4:2012
Anne Finch, Countess of
Winchilsea 4:2197
Alexander Pope 5:2423
James Thomson 5:2533, 2538
William Collins 5:2663
Thomas Chatterton 5:2803
Thomas Gray 5:2818, 2819
James Macpherson 6:3182, 3183
Robert Burns 6:3193, 3197
Horace Walpole 6:3234
Charlotte Smith 6:3352
John Keats 6:3516
Sir Walter Scott 7:3837, 3840
Samuel Taylor Coleridge 7:3893
Charles Lamb 7:3936
James Hogg 7:3968
Felicia Dorothea Hemans 7:3981
Robert Southey 7:4078
Hartley Coleridge 7:4220

William Wordsworth 8:4310, 4315
Sara Coleridge 8:4431

WORSFOLD, W. BASIL
Joseph Addison 4:2186

WOTTON, SIR HENRY
William Shakespeare 2:853
Sir Francis Bacon 3:1116
John Donne 3:1195
John Milton 4:1694

WOTTON, WILLIAM
John Evelyn 4:2098

WRAXALL, SIR NATHANIEL
Henry Fielding 5:2600
Elizabeth Montagu 6:3300
Richard Brinsley Sheridan 6:3424

WRIGHT, J. C.
Nahum Tate 4:2145
William Whitehead 6:3029

WRIGHT, J. M. F.
Sir Isaac Newton 4:2249

WRIGHT, THOMAS
Cædmon 1:7
Ælfric 1:24
William of Malmesbury 1:25
Geoffrey of Monmouth 1:27
Giraldus Cambrensis 1:28
William Langland 1:52
William Dunbar 1:222
William Cowper 6:3311
Edward FitzGerald 9:5354

WRIGHT, WILLIAM
Charlotte Brontë 8:4477

WYATT, SIR THOMAS
Geoffrey Chaucer 1:56

WYCHERLEY, WILLIAM
Sir Richard Steele 4:2290
Alexander Pope 5:2430

WYLIE, LAURA JOHNSON
Sir Philip Sidney 1:329
Samuel Taylor Coleridge 7:3911

WYNNE, JAMES
George Bancroft 10:5577

YATES, EDMUND
Wilkie Collins 9:5542

YEATS, W. B.
Edmund Spenser 1:495
William Shakespeare 2:644
Percy Bysshe Shelley 6:3603
William Blake 7:3715, 3724
James Clarence Mangan 7:4238
William Allingham 9:5528
William Morris 10:5916
Oscar Wilde 10:6018
Lionel Johnson 10:6119

YEOWELL, JAMES
Sir Thomas Wyatt 1:262

YONGE, CHARLES DUKE
Horace Walpole 6:3240

YONGE, CHARLOTTE MARY
Hannah More 7:3868

YOUNG, ARTHUR
Edward Gibbon 6:3132

YOUNG, CHARLES MAYNE
William Wordsworth 8:4299

YOUNG, EDWARD
William Shakespeare 2:571
Ben Jonson 3:1322
John Dryden 4:2010
Joseph Addison 4:2175, 2183, 2188
William Congreve 4:2268
Thomas Tickell 5:2388
Alexander Pope 5:2422
Jonathan Swift 5:2491
James Thomson 5:2529
Ambrose Philips 5:2549
Edward Young 5:2743

YOUNG, F. E. BRETT
Gerard Manley Hopkins 9:5546

YOUNG, GEORGE
Winthrop Mackworth Praed 7:4036

YULE, H.
Sir John Mandeville 1:37

ZANGWILL, ISRAEL
George du Maurier 10:5902

ZIMMERN, HELEN
Maria Edgeworth 7:4207

ZOUCH, THOMAS
Sir Philip Sidney 1:323
Richard Hakluyt 1:530
Izaak Walton 4:1870

UNSIGNED
William Shakespeare 2:1031
Thomas Lodge 3:1094
Sir John Davies 3:1142
Michael Drayton 3:1185
George Herbert 3:1244
John Marston 3:1298
Robert Burton 3:1369
Richard Crashaw 3:1465
John Selden 3:1505
James Shirley 3:1561
Anne Bradstreet 3:1634, 1636
Robert Herrick 4:1660
Thomas Traherne 4:1765, 1766
John Wilmot, Earl of Rochester
4:1844
John Oldham 4:1882
Thomas Otway 4:1887
Thomas Shadwell 4:1966
John Dryden 4:2005
John Evelyn 4:2104
Gilbert Burnet 4:2141
Henry Carey 5:2402
James Thomson 5:2537
Joseph Butler 5:2571
Colley Cibber 5:2634
Jonathan Edwards 5:2648
Lady Mary Wortley Montagu
5:2715
Edward Young 5:2744
William Falconer 5:2788
Philip Dormer Stanhope, Earl of
Chesterfield 5:2877
Mary Wollstonecraft 6:3279